The Real World

FIFTH EDITION

The Real World

An Introduction to Sociology

FIFTH EDITION

Kerry Ferris | Jill Stein

W.W. NORTON
NEW YORK · LONDON

W. W. Norton & Company has been independent since its founding in 1923, when William Warder Norton and Mary D. Herter Norton first published lectures delivered at the People's Institute, the adult education division of New York City's Cooper Union. The firm soon expanded its program beyond the Institute, publishing books by celebrated academics from America and abroad. By midcentury, the two major pillars of Norton's publishing program—trade books and college texts—were firmly established. In the 1950s, the Norton family transferred control of the company to its employees, and today—with a staff of four hundred and a comparable number of trade, college, and professional titles published each year—W. W. Norton & Company stands as the largest and oldest publishing house owned wholly by its employees.

Editor: Sasha Levitt
Project Editor: Rachel Mayer
Editorial Assistant: Mary Williams
Manuscript Editor: Jackie Estrada
Managing Editor, College: Marian Johnson
Managing Editor, College Digital Media: Kim Yi
Production Manager: Eric Pier-Hocking
Media Editor: Eileen Connell
Media Project Editor: Danielle Belfiore
Media Editorial Assistant: Grace Tuttle
Marketing Manager, Sociology: Julia Hall
Design Director: Rubina Yeh
Photo Editor: Ted Szczepanski
Permissions Manager: Megan Jackson
Permissions Clearer: Bethany Salminen
Composition: Jouve
Illustrations: Alex Eben Meyer
Manufacturing: Transcontinental Interglobe, Inc.

Permission to use copyrighted material begins on C-1.

ISBN: 978-0-393-26430-2

W. W. Norton & Company, Inc., 500 Fifth Avenue, New York, NY 10110-0017

wwnorton.com

W. W. Norton & Company Ltd., 15 Carlisle Street London W1D 3BS

4 5 6 7 8 9 0

About the Authors

KERRY FERRIS is Associate Professor of Sociology at Northern Illinois University. She uses ethnographic methods and a symbolic interactionist approach to study celebrity as a system of social power. Her past studies have included analyses of fan-celebrity relations, celebrity sightings, celebrity stalking, red-carpet celebrity interviews, and the work lives of professional celebrity impersonators. Her current project examines small-market television newscasters in the American Midwest and their experiences of celebrity on a local level. Her work has been published in *Symbolic Interaction, Journal of Contemporary Ethnography, The Journal of Popular Culture,* and *Text & Performance Quarterly.* She is the co-author, with Scott R. Harris, of *Stargazing: Celebrity, Fame, and Social Interaction.*

JILL STEIN is Professor of Sociology at Santa Barbara City College, which was recently named the top community college in the United States by the Aspen Institute. She teaches Introduction to Sociology in both face-to-face and online formats every semester. In addition, she is involved in many student-success initiatives at the local and state levels. Her research examines narrative processes in twelve-step programs, the role of popular culture in higher learning, and group culture among professional rock musicians. Her work has been published in *Symbolic Interaction, Youth & Society,* and *TRAILS* (Teaching Resources and Innovations Library).

Contents

PREFACE xxiii

CHAPTER 2: Studying Social Life: Sociological Research Methods 38

PART II: Framing Social Life 67

CHAPTER 3: Culture 70

CHAPTER 5: Separate and Together: Life in Groups 120

CHAPTER 6: Deviance 148

PART III: Understanding Inequality 175

CHAPTER 7: Social Class: The Structure of Inequality 178

CHAPTER 8: Race and Ethnicity as Lived Experience 212

CHAPTER 9: Constructing Gender and Sexuality 240

CHAPTER 11: The Economy and Work 314

CHAPTER 13: Leisure and Media 372

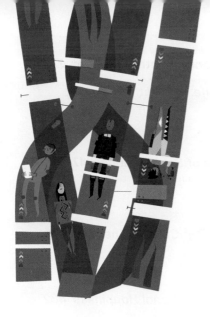

PART V: Envisioning the Future and Creating Social Change 429

CHAPTER 15: Populations, Cities, and the Environment 432

CHAPTER 16: Social Change 464

Preface

Welcome to the new fifth edition of *The Real World: An Introduction to Sociology*. We hope you will appreciate what is new not only in the textbook's fresh look and updated materials, but also what is new in the innovative ways it goes about teaching sociology. That's exactly what we set out to do when we first embarked on the original project of writing this textbook, and it's what we continue to do here in the fifth edition.

At the beginning, we'd had years of experience in college and university classrooms, teaching Introductory Sociology to thousands of students from all backgrounds and walks of life; we had discovered a lot about what works and what doesn't when it comes to making sociology exciting and effective. As seasoned instructors, we had developed an approach to teaching and learning that reflected our passion for the subject and our concern with best practices in pedagogy. But we were having trouble finding a textbook that encompassed all the elements we had identified and that made such a difference in our own experience. We were tired of seeing the same old formulas found in almost every textbook. And we figured we were not alone. Other students and instructors were probably equally frustrated with repetitive formats, stodgy styles, and seemingly irrelevant or overly predictable materials. That is a great misfortune, for sociology, at its best, is a discipline that holds great value and is both intellectually stimulating and personally resonant. While the impetus to write this textbook began as a way of answering our own needs, our goal became to create a textbook of even greater benefit to others who might also be looking for something new.

We are gratified by the response *The Real World* has received from instructors and students alike, so we are preserving many of the features that have made the textbook a success. At the same time, we have done more than just simply revise the textbook. In this edition, you will find significant new content and added features that will further enhance the teaching and learning process, and keep us as close to the cutting edge as possible. Many of the original elements we developed for students and instructors appear again in these pages. As a foundation, we have maintained a writing style that we hope is accessible and interesting as well as scholarly. One of the core pedagogical strengths of this textbook is its focus on everyday life, the media, technology, and pop culture. We know that the combination of these themes is inherently appealing to students, and that it relates to their lives. And since both new generation and more experienced sociology instructors might also be looking for something different, another of this book's strengths is an integrated emphasis on critical thinking and analytic skills. Rather than merely presenting or reviewing major concepts in sociology, which can often seem dry and remote, we seek to make the abstract more concrete through real-world examples and hands-on applications.

In this text we take a fresh and accessible theoretical approach appropriate to our contemporary world. While we emphasize the interactionist perspective, we cover a range of theoretical thought, including postmodernism. We also build innovative methodological exercises into each chapter, giving students the opportunity to put into practice what they are learning. We present material that is familiar and relevant to students in a way that allows them to make profound analytic connections between their individual lives and the structure of their society. We provide instructors with ways to reenergize their teaching, and we give even general education students a reason to be fascinated by and engrossed in their sociology courses. We do this by staying in touch with our students and the rapidly changing real world, and by bringing our insight, experience, and intellectual rigor to bear on a new way of teaching introductory sociology.

Whether you are a student or an instructor, you have probably seen a lot of textbooks. As authors, we have thought very carefully about how to write this textbook so as to make it more meaningful and effective for you. We think it is important to point out some newly added and unique features of this textbook and to tell you why they are included and what we hope you will get out of them.

Part Introductions

The sixteen chapters in this text are grouped into five parts, and each part opens with its own introductory essay. Each part introduction highlights a piece of original sociological research that encompasses the major themes that group the chapters together. The in-depth discussion of the featured book shows what the real work of academic sociologists consists of and reveals how sociological research frequently unites topics covered in separate chapters in introductory textbooks.

Opening Vignettes

Each chapter begins with an opening vignette that gives students an idea about the topics or themes they will encounter in the chapter. The vignettes are drawn from current events and everyday life, the media, arts, and popular culture. They are designed to grab your attention and stimulate your curiosity to learn more by reading the chapter that follows.

How to Read This Chapter

After the vignette, you will find a section that provides you with some goals and strategies that we believe will be useful in reading that particular chapter. We know from our experience in teaching Introductory Sociology that it is often worthwhile to let students know what to expect in advance so that they can better make their way through the material. Not all chapters require the same approach; we want to bring to your attention what we think is the best approach to each one, so you can keep that in mind while reading.

Theory in Everyday Life

Although we provide thorough coverage in Chapter 1, we find that students often benefit from additional help with understanding the mechanics of social theory and how to apply it to various real-world phenomena. These boxes in every chapter break down the major theoretical approaches and illustrate how each perspective might be used to analyze a particular real-world case study. This serves as a simple, practical model for students to then make their own applications and analyses.

Bolded In-Text Terms

As a student of sociology, you will be learning many new concepts and terms. Throughout each chapter, you will see a number of words or phrases in bold type. You may already recognize some of these from their more common vernacular use. But it is important to pay special attention to the way that they are used sociologically. For this reason you will find definitions in the margins of each page, where you can refer to them as you read. You should consider these bolded words and phrases your conceptual "tools" for doing sociology. As you progress through the chapters in this textbook, you will be collecting the contents of a toolkit that you can use to better understand yourself and the world around you. The bolded terms can also be found in the Glossary at the back of the book.

Relevance Boxes

In each chapter you will find Relevance Boxes with three different themes: "On the Job," "In Relationships," and "In the Future." Relevance Boxes allow students to see the practical implications and personal value of sociology in their lives. "On the Job" explores the ways different people use sociological training or insights in a variety of work settings. "In Relationships" looks at how sociology can help us to better understand our friendships, intimate partnerships, and family relations. "In the Future" provides a glimpse into emerging trends in a rapidly changing society, and what students might expect to encounter on the horizon. We include these boxes to show how taking this course could bear fruit in your life (and in the lives of others) beyond just fulfilling your college requirements.

Data Workshops

Data Workshops are designed to give students the opportunity to gain hands-on experience in the practice of sociology while they are learning. We think this is one of the most fun parts of being a sociologist. Each chapter features two Data Workshops, one on "Analyzing Everyday Life" and one on "Analyzing Media and Pop Culture." Students will use one of the research methods covered in Chapter 2 to deal with actual data from the real world—whether it's data they collect themselves or raw data provided from another source. The Data Workshops lead students through the process of analyzing data using the related conceptual tools they have just acquired in the chapter. For the Fifth Edition, we've reconceived these workshops to make them richer and more assignable. New "Prep-Pair-Share" and "Do-It-Yourself" completion options make this popular feature even easier for instructors to use as in-class activities or to assign as homework. Each Data Workshop is also included in the Interactive Instructor's Guide (IIG), so they're easy to assign whether an instructor teaches online or in the classroom.

Global Perspective Boxes

While this textbook focuses primarily on contemporary American society, we believe that in this time of increasing globalization, it is also important to look at other societies around the world. Each chapter includes a "Global Perspective" box that highlights some of the differences and similarities between the United States and other cultures. This feature will help students develop the ability to see comparative and analogous patterns across cultures, which is one of the key functions of a sociological perspective.

Images and Graphics

We think that it is crucial to include not only written information but also images and graphics in the textbook. This kind of presentation is increasingly common and students are likely to encounter complex information in graphical form in many of their textbooks. We want to help students gain in visual literacy as they are exposed to a variety of materials and learn in different ways. We also know that students share our interest in media, technology, and popular culture, and we want to show the connections between real life and sociological thinking. For these reasons, you will find many kinds of images and graphics in each chapter. These are not just decorations; they are an integral part of the text, so please study these as carefully as you would the rest of the printed page.

Closing Comments

Each chapter ends with closing comments that wrap up the discussion and give some final thoughts about the important themes that have been covered. This gives us a chance not so much to summarize or reiterate but to reflect, in a slightly different way, on what we have discussed, as well as to point to the future. We hope that the closing comments will give you something to think about, or even talk about with others, long after you've finished reading the chapter.

End-of-Chapter Materials

The end of each chapter contains additional materials that will enhance the learning process. The fifth edition features "Everything You Need to Know About ____" review apparatus at the end of each chapter, which includes checklists, review questions, prompts about the Everyday Sociology blog, and infographics. They are designed to be easy to read and understand quickly, condensing the most important information from the chapter into two pages.

In our experience, the most important thing for students to take away from an introductory sociology class is a sociological perspective—not just a storehouse of facts, which will inevitably fade over time. Sociology promises a new way of looking at and thinking about the social world, which can serve students in good stead no matter what they find themselves doing in the future. We hope that this textbook delivers on that promise, making introductory sociology an intellectually stimulating and personally relevant enterprise for professors and students, in the classroom as well as outside it.

Resources

InQuizitive

This adaptive learning tool personalizes quiz questions for each student in an engaging, game-like environment to help them master the core sociological concepts presented in every chapter of *The Real World*. Used as a pre-lecture tool, InQuizitive helps students come to class better prepared to apply the sociological concepts from the reading.

The Real World ebook "Same great book, a fraction of the price"

The Norton Ebook Reader provides students and instructors with an enhanced reading experience at a fraction of the cost of the print textbook. The Norton Ebook Reader works on all computers and mobile devices and includes intuitive highlighting, note-taking, and bookmarking features.

Everyday Sociology blog everydaysociologyblog.com

Designed for a general audience, this exciting and unique online forum encourages visitors to actively explore sociology's relevance to pop culture, media, and everyday life. Moderated by Karen Sternheimer (University of Southern California), the blog features postings on topical subjects, video interviews with well-known sociologists, as well as contributions from special guests during the academic year. Contributors include Janis A. Prince (University of South Florida), Sally Raskoff (Los Angeles Valley College), Teresa Gonzales (University of California at Berkeley), and Peter Kaufman (SUNY New Paltz).

Sociology in Practice DVDs

These four DVDs, including a new *Sociology in Practice: Thinking about Race and Ethnicity* DVD, contain over twelve hours of video clips drawn from documentaries by independent filmmakers. The DVDs are ideal for initiating classroom discussion and encouraging students to apply sociological concepts to popular and real-world issues. The clips are also offered in streaming versions in the Coursepack. Each streamed clip is accompanied by a quiz, exercise, or activity.

Instructor's Website wwnorton.com/instructors

The Instructor's Website features instructional content for use in lecture and distance education:

* FREE, customizable coursepacks for Blackboard, Canvas, Moodle, and D2L

* Lecture PowerPoint slides with bulleted classroom lecture notes in the notes field

* All the art from the book in PowerPoint and JPEG formats, sized for classroom display

* Test Bank in ExamView, PDF, and RTF formats

Coursepack

The Coursepack for the Fifth Edition of *The Real World* offers a variety of activities and assessment and review materials for instructors who use Blackboard and other learning management systems. The Coursepack includes an optional ebook and many exclusive features:

* All the interactive, concept-based activities and assessments included in the very popular 4e Coursepack

* A "Writing about Sociology" section that includes practice activities and assessments

* Improved chapter-review quizzes

* *Sociology in Practice* DVD activities that include multiple-choice assessments that connect each clip to key sociological concepts (select clips only)

* Gradable activities based on the *Society Pages* podcasts, "graphic sociology" posts, and other media-rich content

* Thirty-four streaming clips from our new *Sociology in Practice: Thinking about Race and Ethnicity* DVD as well as all the other clips from the *Sociology in Practice* DVD series

* Key term flashcards and matching quizzes

Test Bank

Written to conform to Bloom's taxonomy, the revised test bank for *The Real World,* Fifth Edition, includes 50–60 multiple-choice and 10–15 essay questions per chapter. In addition to Bloom's, each question is tagged with difficulty level and metadata that places it in the context of the chapter, making it easy to construct tests.

Norton Sociology, Your Way

With the *Norton Mix: Sociology* (www.wwnorton.com/web/socmix), instructors can create the perfect book for their course by mixing and matching chapters from *The Real World* and Norton's other introductory sociology texts and adding their own collection of readings from a database of more than 200 selections. Also, as with previous editions, these paperbacks can be packaged for free with *The Real World*: Elijah Anderson's *The Cosmopolitan Canopy, More than Just Race* by William Julius Wilson, and any volume from *The Society Pages* series edited by Douglas Hartmann and Chris Uggen. For only $10 more, instructors can choose to package *The Contexts Reader*, 2e; *The Everyday Sociology Reader*; or Garth Massey's *Readings for Sociology*, 7e with *The Real World*.

Acknowledgments

The authors would like to thank the many people who helped make this textbook possible. To everyone at W. W. Norton, we believe you are absolutely the best publishers in the business and that we are fortunate to get to work with you. Thank you, Roby Harrington, for signing us. Our deep appreciation goes out to Steve Dunn for believing in us and playing such a critical role in shaping the original vision of this project. Thank you for showing us we could do this and for your substantial support throughout. We would like to acknowledge Melea Seward for her efforts during the early drafts of the book. Her innovative approach and enthusiasm were much appreciated. We owe much gratitude to Karl Bakeman for his tremendous talent, work, and dedication on our behalf. His vision and leadership has been an inspiration, and a central reason for the success of this book. We feel so lucky to be a part of your team. With this new edition, we welcomed a new and equally gifted editor, Sasha Levitt, who brought phenomenally great ideas, energy, and enthusiasm to the project. We appreciate how much you invested in joining us in this work. This edition is all the better because of your exceptional generosity, creativity, and determination.

We have many others to thank as well. We are especially grateful to our project editor Rachel Mayer; production manager Eric Pier-Hocking; and editorial assistant Mary Williams for managing the countless details involved in creating this book. Copyeditor Jackie Estrada and proofreader Barbara Necol did a marvelous job suggesting improvements to the manuscript that have contributed in important ways to the book's final form. Danielle Nilva and Ted Szczepanski showed wonderful creativity in the photo research that they did for *The Real World*. Media editor Eileen Connell and digital media assistant Grace Tuttle developed the best textbook support materials in sociology. Associate Design Director Hope Miller Goodell, illustrator Alex Eben Meyer, and the designers at Faceout Studio deserve special thanks for creating the beautiful design and art for the book. And we are very appreciative of the exceptional Norton "travelers"; it is through their efforts that this book has gotten out into the world.

In the course of our creating the fifth edition, many instructors offered advice and comments on particular chapters, or in some cases, large sections of the text. We are deeply indebted to them.

Brooke Bain, California State University, Fullerton
Chris Baker, Walters State Community College
Leslie Baker-Kimmons, Chicago State University
Marissa Bañuelos, California State University, Fullerton

Thomas Barry, Central Oregon Community College
Elson Boles, Saginaw Valley State University
Mike Bossick, Central Piedmont Community College
Sergio Bouda, California State University, Fullerton
Jeneve Brooks, Troy University
Nina Brown, Community College of Baltimore County
Laura Colmenero-Chilberg, Black Hills State University
Molly Cueto, Lone Star College-Kingwood
Gayle D'Andrea, J Sargeant Reynolds Community College
Sophia Demasi, Montgomery County Community College
Gianna Durso-Finley, Mercer County Community College
Marilyn Espitia, San Diego Miramar College
Catherine Felton, Central Piedmont Community College
Janie Filoteo, Lone Star College-Tomball
John Gannon, College of Southern Nevada-Charleston
Tiffany Gause, Saddleback College
Jan Gordon, Surry Community College
Melissa Gosdin, Albany State University
Edward Gott, Northeast Wisconsin Technical College
Matt Gregory, University of Massachusetts Boston
Tara Hefferan, Central Michigan University
Anthony Hickey, Western Carolina University
David Hilton, Mississippi Gulf Coast Community College
Christopher Huggins, University of Kentucky
Danielle James, Community College of Baltimore County
Leigh Keever, Chattahoochee Technical College
Thomas LaPorte, Chattahoochee Technical College
Andrew Lash, Valencia College
Jon Loessin, Wharton County Junior College
Crystal Lupo, Auburn University
Lori Maida, Westchester County Community College
Kenneth Mentor, University of North Carolina-Pembroke
Barret Michalec, University of Delaware
Susan Miller, Palomar College
Tina Mougouris, San Jacinto College-Central
Ken Muir, Appalachian State University
Layana Navarre-Jackson, University of Iowa
Christina Partin, University of South Florida
Michael Perez, California State University, Fullerton
Carla Pfeffer, University of South Carolina
Robert Pullen, Troy University
Aaryn Purvis, Pearl River Community College
Carter Rakovski, California State University, Fullerton
Julie Reid, University of Southern Mississippi
Tamatha Renae Esguerra, California State University,
    Fullerton
Michael Rutz, John Tyler Community College

Emery Smith, Umpqua Community College
Mindy Stombler, Georgia State University
Adrienne Trier-Bieniek, Valencia College
Linda Vang, Fresno City College
James Williams, John Tyler Community College
Terri Winnick, Ohio State University-Mansfield
Amy Wong, San Diego State University
Jennifer Woodruff, Heartland Community College
Susan Wurtzburg, University of Hawaii-Manoa
Sharon Wiederstein, Blinn College
Matt Wray, Temple University

We would also like to thank the research assistants who worked with us on this project: Laurica Brown, Nathaniel Burke, Whitney Bush, Kate Grimaldi, Lauren Gunther, Mary Ingram, Ja'Nean Palacios, and Karl Thulin. Very special thanks to Neil Dryden, and also to Natasha Chen Christiansen, whose thoughtful contributions to multiple editions of the text have proven invaluable.

We wish to especially thank Al Ferris for his wise and generous counsel in helping us to establish our corporate identity and at every juncture along the way. Thanks to Kevin Ebenhoch for his friendly and efficient services. We would like to thank our families and friends whose encouragement and support helped to sustain us through the length of this project and beyond. It is also with great pleasure that we thank our spouses Greg Wennerdahl and David Unger, respectively—you appeared in our lives just as we were completing the first edition, and your continued presence through this process has been a source of strength and joy. We are happy to have shared these many editions with you. To Marissa Unger, an impressive reader and writer herself, thanks for being such a positive model of your generation for us. And to our newest reader, Eliot Julian Ferris-Wennerdahl (E.J.): may you always approach life's challenges with wonder, hope, and a sense of endless possibility.

We are grateful to colleagues who have served as mentors in our intellectual development and as inspiration to a life of writing. And finally, we offer our thanks to all of the students we have had the privilege to work with over the years. Getting to share the sociological imagination with you makes it all worthwhile.

Kerry Ferris
Jill Stein

Changes in the 5th Edition

Part 1: Thinking Sociologically and Doing Sociology: The Part 1 opener now includes a brief bio of sociologist Victor Rios.

Chapter 1 (Sociology and the Real World): An updated opener about reality television looks at the History Channel's *Pawn Stars*, E!'s *Keeping Up with the Kardashians*, and Fox's *Hell's Kitchen*. The second Data Workshop, "Theories of Celebrity Gossip," now discusses how TMZ broke the news about former L.A. Clippers' owner Donald Sterling's racist remarks. TMZ speaks to a larger trend where the line between entertainment and news is increasingly blurred.

Chapter 2 (Studying Social Life: Sociological Research Methods): The entire overview of research methods has been substantially reworked for clarity. Students are encouraged to apply these methods like a recipe when conducting hands-on research for the Data Workshops in every chapter. The first Data Workshop has been reconceived as an exercise in participant observation and retitled "Watching People Talk." *Focus groups* is a new key term. The second Data Workshop has been reworked as a richer experiment in survey research. The section on existing sources has been reworked and now introduces *unobtrusive methods* as a new key term. In the section on research ethics, the authors use Rik Scarce's participant observation study of an animal rights group as a new example of the risks involved in research.

Chapter 3 (Culture): The chapter opener on the heavy metal band Acrassicauda has been updated. *Moral holiday* has been added as a new key term. A new "In Relationships" box, titled "Individual Values vs. University Culture," asks students to consider what it means for their college to have its own culture and value system. The discussion of countercultures has been streamlined. Miley Cyrus and her controversial performance at the Video Music Awards is used as an example in the section on culture wars. The second Data Workshop, now titled "How the Image Shapes the Need," has been rewritten to feature more up-to-date examples. A new "On the Job" box, titled "The Sharing Economy and Unlikely Cultural Ambassadors" explores the rising popularity of services like Airbnb and Couchsurfing.

Chapter 4 (Socialization, Interaction, and the Self): A new chapter opener examines the phenomenon of "selfies" and how we shape our presentation of self on Facebook and other social media. In the section on social isolation, there is a new discussion of Genie, a feral child who suffered from severe neglect and social isolation. The "Psychoanalytic Theory: Sigmund Freud" section now includes a discussion of Freud's *Civilization and Its Discontents*. Daniel Murphy, a major league baseball player who was criticized for missing Opening Day to be with his wife during the birth of his son, is used as a new example in the section on multiple roles and role conflict. The "Television as an Agent of Socialization" Data Workshop now uses *Modern Family* and the show's portrayal of women as a new example of how to do a content analysis of a TV show. The "New Interactional Contexts" section has been updated with discussions of Sherry Turkle's new book *Alone Together* (2014) as well as danah boyd's new book *It's Complicated* (2014).

Chapter 5 (Separate and Together: Life in Groups): The chapter opener on the tragic FAMU marching band hazing incident has been updated now that the marching band's suspension has been lifted. The "Who's in Your Feed?" Data Workshop has been updated to include a more up-to-date discussion of the current state of social media and expanded to be a richer assignment for students. The new "In Relationships" box ("Social Networking: You're Not the Customer— You're the Product") explores privacy concerns related to the rise of social media, using Facebook and OkCupid as examples of companies that have mined users' data for research purposes. The Penn State sex abuse scandal involving Jerry Sandusky is used as a new example of the dangers of groupthink. The experiences of AA members are used to demonstrate the three forms of conformity, in the section on social influence. The "Global Perspective" box has been revised to consider the more recent case of Don Spirit. The "Responding to Bureaucratic Constraints" section examines policies implemented by Google in an effort to hire and retain more female employees. The discussion of Burning Man now refers to Matt Wray's research.

Chapter 6 (Deviance): A new chapter opener uses marijuana, and our views regarding marijuana use, to illustrate how cultural values, including what we consider to be deviant, change over time. A new "Global Perspective" box ("Crime, Fear, and Compassion: U.S. vs. Scandinavian Prisons") examines the use of "open prisons" in Scandinavia. The section on conflict theory references the recent controversy over voter ID laws. The authors have added a discussion of Claude Steele's work on stereotype threat and Jennifer Lee and Min Zhou's research on stereotype promise. A new "In Relationships" box ("Masculinity and Disability in Murderball") explores how murderball, a high-intensity competitive sport played by paraplegic athletes, gives players an outlet for reasserting their masculinity. The "Norm-Breaking on Television" Data Workshop now includes *The Black List, Orange Is the New Black*, and *Family Guy* as examples of shows that deal with deviance. The "The Foreground of Deviance: The Emotional Attraction of Doing Bad Deeds" section now includes a reference to Elliot Rodger, the mass shooter

who killed seven people in Isla Vista, California. Data on cyberbullying have been updated. The data in the section on "Crime and Punishment" on violent crime and property crime rates have been updated.

Chapter 7 (Social Classes: The Structure of Inequality): The "Case of South Africa" section has been updated with a discussion of the enduring income gap between whites and blacks. Within the section on social class, a brand new section introduces the concept of intersectionality, drawing on Karyn Lacy's research on black middle-class suburbanites to illustrate how our experiences of race, class, and gender are intertwined. The discussion of occupational prestige has been updated. The Data Workshop titled "Everyday Class Consciousness" has been expanded. In the "Socioeconomic Status and Life Changes" section, data on educational attainment, access to health care, median income, college enrollment, government aid, and poverty rate have been updated. The "In Relationships" box now refers to dating sites like The League and BlackPeopleMeet. A new "On the Job" box, titled "Get a Job! Minimum Wage or Living Wage?" considers who works at minimum-wage jobs and how working full time at these jobs is often not enough to keep people and their families out of poverty. The "Social Welfare and Welfare Reform" section references new research by the Pew Research Center on public opinion about government responsibility to help the poor. Data in the section on the digital divide have been updated. Data on homelessness have been updated. In the Data Workshop, data on student loans and credit card debt have been updated.

Chapter 8 (Race and Ethnicity as Lived Experience): The chapter opener has been updated with more current data on the proportion of Americans who identify as mixed race and also highlights the plan by the Census Bureau to revise the racial categories for 2020 to better match the way Americans conceive of their own racial identities. An entirely new section, titled "White Privilege and Color-Blind Racism," introduces readers to the concept of white privilege and presents an alternative to color-blind racism: race consciousness. Another new section explores the issues surrounding cultural appropriation, using examples from pop culture and the world of sports to problematize the tendency of members of the dominant group to adopt cultural elements of more marginalized groups. The controversy surrounding Rachel Dolezal is highlighted. The authors cite more current polls asking people whether they believe race relations have improved or worsened since Obama was elected president. In the section on passing, the authors now include coverage of Jeffrey McCune's 2014 ethnographic study of a Chicago nightclub that caters to gay black men. The "In Relationships" box highlights the results of a 2014 Pew poll on approval of mixed-race relationships. In the "Race, Ethnicity, and Life Chances" section, data on interracial dating and marriage, marriage and birth rates by race, life expectancy, median income by race, and occupational segregation have been updated. A new chart looks at intermarriage rates by race. Data in the section on criminal justice have been updated and the section mentions the 2015 shooting in a black church in Charleston, South Carolina. A new "On the Job" box (titled "Diversity Training: Does It Work?") looks at research into the effectiveness of various diversity training programs. The "Analyzing Media and Pop Culture" Data Workshop has been retitled "The Politics and Poetics of Racial Identity" and now features Richard Blanco's poem "One Today," which he read at Barack Obama's second inauguration.

Chapter 9 (Constructing Gender and Sexuality): This chapter has been completely reorganized and reconceived to address sexuality and gender in tandem rather than separately. The introductory section on gender has been expanded and *gender expression, cisgender,* and *gender nonconforming* have been added as key terms. The section titled "Sexuality and Sexual Orientation" has been moved earlier in the chapter. The section on socialization now explores how socialization perpetuates both gender conformity and supports heteronormativity. The section on the media as an agent of socialization now discusses new shows *Transparent* and *I Am Cait.* A new section titled "Inequalities of Sex, Gender, and Sexuality" explores how both our gender and sexuality have become the basis for hierarchies of inequality; *sexism, transphobia, heterosexism,* and *cisgenderism* have been added as key terms in this section. The authors highlight Anita Sarkeesian as an example of someone who experienced both institutional and individual sexism. The new "Gendered Language and 'Microaggressions'" section explores how the vocabulary associated with sex, gender, and sexuality can be a confusing minefield; *microaggression* is a new key term. The reorganized "Sociological Theories of Gender Inequality" section, which now comes later in the chapter, breaks out functionalist theory, interactionism, and conflict theory more clearly. A new "In Relationships" box titled "Rape Culture and Campus Social Life" tackles the issue of campus sexual assault, introducing students to the idea of "rape culture" and analyzing different aspects of campus life that promote a culture that normalizes sexual violence against women. Data on marriage and divorce rates by gender, the gender gap in life expectancy, educational attainment by gender, labor force participation rates by gender, the gender pay gap, and occupational sex segregation have been updated. The section on gender and sexuality in the military discusses the repeal of Don't Ask, Don't Tell and includes updated data on sexual assault. The section on the criminal justice system now considers the experiences of LGBTQ persons and includes data on anti-gay and anti-transgender hate crimes. The reconceived "Political and Social Movements" section has combined the discussions of women's movements, men's movements, and the LGBTQ rights movement into one cohesive section; the section on LGBTQ rights includes a discussion of the legalization of same-sex marriage in the United States.

Chapter 10 (Social Institutions: Politics, Education, and Religion): The section on voting has been updated with voter turnout data for the 2014 midterm elections. The discussion of voter ID laws has also been updated. There is a new discussion of political campaigns funded by billionaires, and a new figure looks at the top spenders on lobbying. The "Real and Fake News" Data Workshop has been reworked and now asks students to watch an episode of *Last Week Tonight with John Oliver* or *The Nightly Show with Larry Wilmore.* The completely updated and expanded "Social Media and Politics" section looks at how Americans are getting their political and campaign news online, highlighting studies Facebook has conducted on voter behavior. The authors also discuss Barack Obama's savvy use of social media, specifically how he released key points from his 2015 State of the Union address directly to social media. The "Patriotism and Protest" section now includes a discussion of the Black Lives Matter movement. Data in the section on education and inequality on graduation rates, lifetime earnings, and unemployment have been updated. The education-focused "In the Future" box has been updated with a discussion of schools that have adopted flipped classroom models. In the section on the future of education, the authors highlight the growing achievement gap between students from high and low socioeconomic backgrounds. The section on No Child Left Behind now includes a discussion of the Common Core and Race to the Top. The section on charter schools now mentions school vouchers. The discussion of homeschooling has been updated with more current data and expanded to consider the phenomenon of "unschooling." Dual-enrollment programs are now examined. The authors have expanded the discussion of community colleges, highlighting Obama's federal initiative to make community college free. The section on online learning includes updated data and a new discussion of MOOCs. A new "On the Job" box titled "For-Profit Colleges: At What Cost?" looks critically at how for-profit schools stack up to traditional public or private nonprofits on indicators like completion rate and future employment. The "Global Perspective" box on religion has also been updated with a discussion of the growing power of ISIS in the Middle East. A new map in the section on religion shows the second-largest religious tradition in each state. The reconceived "In Relationships" box ("Can a Relationship with God Improve Your GPA?") discusses a recent study that found that spiritual growth has positive effects on traditional college outcomes, including academic performance.

Chapter 11 (The Economy and Work): A new section titled "Agricultural Work" looks at how new technologies such as crop rotation and mass production, and the "agribusiness system," have transformed agricultural work. Data on telecommuting have been updated. A new "In Relationships" box ("The Value of Break Time") looks at research into the "communities of coping" that workers form during coffee breaks. The "In The Future" box has been retitled "A College Degree: What's It Worth?" and has been updated with new data from the Pew Research Center. Data on union membership have been updated. The section on corporate America now includes a discussion of corporate social responsibility and explores the role that corporations played in striking down the Religious Freedom Restoration Act. The section also mentions Dan Price, the CEO of Gravity Payments, who made headlines when he raised the company's minimum yearly salary to $70,000. Data on transnational corporations and outsourcing have been updated. The updated examination of internships in the "On the Job" box now problematizes internships and the exploitation of student workers. Data on volunteerism and nonprofits have been updated.

Chapter 12 (Life at Home: Families and Relationships): This chapter has been significantly reorganized. A new section on feminist and queer theoretical perspectives examines the interplay of gender and sexuality in families and society. The "Selecting Mates" section examines the growing proportion of mixed-race unions in the United States. The reorganized "Relationship Trends" section has been expanded and now looks at unmarried life in the United States, including trends in cohabitation; solo parenting; blended families; and childfree living. In the "Breaking Up" section, data on marriage, divorce, and remarriage have been updated. Data on Social Security, elderly poverty, and the living arrangements of the older population have been updated. The list of films in the "Family Troubles in Film" Data Workshop has been updated. A new "In the Future" box, titled "Trends in Baby Making: Back to the Future?" looks at advancements in assisted reproductive technology and asks students to consider what these developments mean for the future of the family.

Chapter 13 (Leisure and Media): The opening section has been reworked to more clearly differentiate recreation and leisure. A new "In the Future" box, titled "The Return of Free-Range Kids?" considers the rise of helicopter parents and the new trend toward free-range parenting. Data on Americans' amount of leisure time and time spent watching TV have been updated. The "On the Job" box on professional musicians now refers to Malcolm Gladwell's research into "outliers." Net neutrality is discussed in the section on the structure of media industries. A new section on alternative voices looks at how bloggers and podcasters are able to circumvent the constraints of traditional media. The section on power shifts considers the growing importance of companies that provide access to entertainment and media. Tom Brady and "Deflategate" are highlighted in the section on "Leisure and Relationships." The section on hangouts now considers apps like Meetup and Foursquare. Data on tourism have been updated.

Chapter 14 (The Sociology of Medicine, Health, and Illness): The authors have added a discussion of the measles outbreak that started at Disneyland in early 2015. The "Student Health Issues Survey" Data Workshop has been reconceived and now asks students to conduct a small-scale interview study. In the section on epidemiology, the authors now look at the West African Ebola outbreak and how traditional burial practices contributed to the rapid spread of the disease. Data on HIV/AIDS have been updated. A new "In Relationships" box, titled "Better Relationships through Chemistry," explores Big Pharma's use of direct-to-consumer drug marketing. The section on doctor-patient relations has been expanded and now looks at recent research into the geographic influences on medical interaction. The "Global Perspective" box on Anne Fadiman's book has been updated. The list of TV shows in the "Medicine on Television" Data Workshop has been updated. The section on health care reform has been updated in light of the Affordable Care Act. Data on the use of complementary and alternative medicine have been updated. The section on end-of-life care now highlights Brittany Maynard and her fight to die with dignity after being diagnosed with terminal brain cancer at the age of twenty-nine.

Chapter 15 (Populations, Cities, and the Environment): Data in the section on global fertility rates, mortality rates, life expectancy, and migration have been updated. A new world map looks at global life expectancy. Data on population growth rates and hunger have been updated. Data on urbanization, including urban density, have been updated. A new map of the United States looks at the urban population of each state. The list of films in the "Imagining the Cities of Tomorrow" Data Workshop has been updated. The discussion of Kitty Genovese has been updated to reflect recent research into the circumstances surrounding her murder. The section on the environment has been reorganized and updated. A new "Global Perspective" box explores the issue of water scarcity across the globe.

Chapter 16 (Social Change): In the section on collective behavior, the authors compare and contrast a street party in Isla Vista, California, and the protest rallies in Baltimore in order to illustrate how collective behavior can develop into riots. The hit TV show *Empire* is used as an example of how TV can inspire fashion trends. Crowdfunding sites like Indiegogo and Kickstarter are considered in the section on mobilizing resources. The authors point to the American Border Patrol as an example of a regressive social movement. This section also highlights Dylann Roof, the mass shooter who was inspired by the work of the Council of Conservative Citizens. The discussion of Bhutan in the "Global Perspective" box has been updated.

The Real World

FIFTH EDITION

PART I
Thinking Sociologically and Doing Sociology

Pepper went to Yale when the school had just begun to admit female students, and some campus buildings didn't even have women's restrooms yet. She was soon documenting the sexual revolution as it took shape on campus. Her academic work spilled over into the popular media, when she began writing a sex advice column for *Glamour* magazine. Since then she has become a go-to authority on everything sex, love, and relationships.

Victor was a gang member who dropped out of school when he was fourteen and learned to steal cars, landing him in juvenile detention. If it had not been for the intervention of one extraordinarily dedicated high school teacher who held onto her high expectations for him, Victor's life story might not have turned out so well. He went on to earn a doctorate in ethnic studies, examining the street life he had once known.

Jody was a cheerleader and beauty queen who dated the high school football captain in her small midwestern town; she dreamed of living on a farm. In college, she stumbled into a women's studies class that changed everything, leading her into the field of criminology. Her research uses photojournalism and focuses on crime and women, here and abroad. Jody married a man from Sri Lanka and founded a philanthropic organization there after the tsunami hit in 2004.

What do these people have in common? They are all prominent American sociology professors. You may not have heard of them (yet), but they have each made an exceptional impact on their profession.

Pepper Schwartz, a sociology professor at the University of Washington, is a leading researcher on sex and intimate relationships. Her work has resonated widely with the public; she is often cited in the press and makes frequent appearances across a variety of media outlets. Victor Rios has become a sought-after author and speaker whose sometimes autobiographical research on race, law enforcement, and social control also led him to found a program for at-risk youth in Santa Barbara, where he is a professor at the University of

California. Jody Miller's work on gender and violence led her to South Asia to study the commercial sex trade; she continues her humanitarian work from her office at Rutgers University in New Jersey.

Each sociologist has a unique story about how he or she ended up in sociology and built a career in academia. It was not obvious from the beginning that any of them would be academic superstars; they each faced a different set of obstacles to success but were somehow motivated to keep on. Perhaps it was because they had been deeply touched by something happening in the real world, something that was also relevant to their own lives. It inspired in them a passion for pursuing a question, an issue, or a cause that was meaningful to them. Each of them has made important connections between their personal lives and their professional careers. In turn, their work extends beyond academia, making a collective contribution to the lives of individuals and even to society as a whole.

Their paths to sociology were very different, and they have each taught and researched different topics. Despite these differences, they share a way of looking at the world. Sociologists have a unique viewpoint called the "sociological

Pepper Schwartz

Victor Rios

Jody Miller

perspective." In fact, we hope that you will acquire your own version of the sociological perspective over the course of this term. Then you will share something in common with these and other sociology professors, including your own.

Schwartz, Rios, and Miller also hold in common their commitment to sociological theories and concepts. This means that their ideas—and the questions they ask and answer—are guided by the established traditions of sociological thought. They may build on those traditions or criticize them, but every sociologist engages in a theoretical dialogue that links centuries and generations. You will become part of this dialogue as you learn more about sociological theory.

Finally, Schwartz, Rios, Miller, and others like them, conduct their research using specific sociological methods. Whether quantitative or qualitative, these means of gathering and analyzing data are distinctive to sociology, and every sociologist develops research projects using the methods best suited to the questions she wants to answer.

Each sociologist's personal journey affects his professional legacy, and knowing something about an author's life helps students understand the author's work. A person's values, experiences, and family context all shape her interests and objectives—and this is as true of eminent sociologists as it will be for you.

In this first part, we will introduce you to the discipline of sociology and its theoretical traditions (Chapter 1) and to the work of sociology and its research methodologies (Chapter 2). This section is your opportunity to get to know sociology—its perspectives, theories, and research practices.

Perhaps someday your intellectual autobiography will be added to those of Schwartz, Rios, and Miller—and your story will start by opening this book.

CHAPTER 1

Sociology and the Real World

The Gold & Silver Pawn Shop is a family-owned business located less than two miles off the Las Vegas strip. Open twenty-four hours a day, it attracts a wide variety of customers who come to buy and sell an even wider array of items, both common and rare. Richard "The Old Man" Harrison and his son Rick opened the business together in 1989. Through their doors come everything from antique coins to a Samurai sword, a Super Bowl ring, or a never-before-seen photo of Jimi Hendrix. The challenge is figuring out whether something's authentic or fake and then negotiating what price to pay. Sometimes experts are called to weigh in on the value of an item. But the real fun is watching the Harrisons haggle with customers—and each other—over good deals and bad.

A blond Brit rants and raves, haranguing aspiring chefs until they break down in tears. Fear of Chef Gordon Ramsey's famous temper causes brawls among the cooks. The winner of the competition has the opportunity to be head chef in a high-end restaurant; yet to win, the contestants are put through a rigorous hazing process in which losing teams have to clean kitchens, hand-wash the winning team's laundry, or prep all the ingredients for the next challenge. The competitors are allowed to vent in a confession booth, but this does not seem to give pause to Ramsey, who bullies, humiliates, and even physically abuses the contestants on a regular basis.

Three sisters, whose names all start with the letter *K*, alternately squabble and cooperate with each other and members of their large blended family, including a brother, mother, stepparent, half-sisters, stepbrothers, and assorted significant others. Their privileged lives are on continual display, and they have become famous mainly for being famous. Their family dramas, rife with both glamorous and embarrassing moments, are chronicled in excruciating detail. With her music mogul husband on her arm, Kim attends galas, fashion shows, and awards ceremonies with fellow members of the glitterati. Meanwhile, sisters Khloe and Kourtney jet set around the globe, opening up boutiques in cities like New York and Miami. The sisters shop constantly and take countless selfies while millions of fans follow them on Instagram.

Is any of this real? Yes—kind of. It's "reality television." Specifically the History Channel's *Pawn Stars*, Fox's *Hell's Kitchen,* and E!'s *Keeping Up with the Kardashians*. And there's a lot more where those came from. In the fall 2015 lineup, there were literally hundreds of reality shows on the major networks and cable stations, with an unknown number of programs undoubtedly in the works. *Duck Dynasty, The Voice, Million Dollar Listing,* and *16 and Pregnant* were just a few of the more popular shows, as well as the show that started it all in 1992, MTV's *The Real World*, which filmed its thirtieth season in 2015.

Some of the shows claim to follow real people through their everyday lives or on the job, while others impose bizarre conditions on participants, subject them to stylized competitions and gross-out stunts, or make their dreams come true. Millions tune in every week to see real people eat bugs, get fired, suffer romantic rejection, reveal their poor parenting, get branded as fat or ugly, cry over their misfortunes, or get voted out of the house or off the island—mortifying themselves on camera for the possibility of success, money, or fame.

Why are we so interested in these people? Because people are interesting! Because we are people, too. No matter how different we are from the folks on reality TV, we are part of the same society, and for that reason we are curious about how they live. We compare their lives with ours, wonder how common or unusual they or we are, and marvel that we are all part of the same, real world. We, too, may want to win competitions, date an attractive guy or girl, find a high-profile job, feel pretty or handsome, be part of an exclusive group, or have a lovely home and family. We may even want to get on a reality show ourselves.

HOW TO READ THIS CHAPTER

You are embarking on a fascinating journey as you learn to see, think, and analyze yourself and the world around you from a sociological perspective. The tools presented here will help you build a foundation for new knowledge and insights into social life.

We will also share the story of the historical and intellectual development of the discipline of sociology. We want to show you how the ideas that shape sociology are linked and introduce you to the interesting men and women who came up with those ideas. Too often, theorists seem to be talking heads, icons of social analysis who experience neither life-altering calamities nor shifting professional fortunes. We want to overcome that perception. We believe that our individual experiences and historical contexts shape our thoughts and the professional worlds we choose to join. This is as true for Karl Marx as it is for Kerry Ferris, as true for Jane Addams as it is for Jill Stein—it's true for all of us; your own experiences and cultural and historical contexts will shape your ideas and work. In fact, someday, someone may write a chapter about you!

As authors and teachers, we encourage you to develop some basic study techniques that will assist you in your success as a new student to sociology (and perhaps beyond). You may want to highlight portions of the text or take notes while you read. Mark passages you don't understand, or keep a list of questions about any aspect of the chapter. Don't hesitate to discuss those questions with your instructor or fellow students; those dialogues can be one of the most gratifying parts of the learning process. Finally, we recommend that you attend class regularly—whether you're in a face-to-face classroom or online—as there is really no substitute for the shared experience of learning sociology with others.

We are excited to join you on this journey of discovery. Though you may know a lot about social life already, we hope to introduce you to even more—about yourself and the world around you—and to provide valuable tools for the future. We wouldn't want you to miss a thing. So here is where we start.

Practical vs. Scientific Knowledge

You already possess many of the skills of an astute analyst of social life, but you take your knowledge for granted because you gained it as an everyday actor. In this course, you will build a new identity: social analyst. These are two very different ways of experiencing the same social world.

The everyday actor approaches his social world with what is referred to as "reciped," or practical, knowledge (Schutz 1962), which allows him to get along in his everyday life. However, practical knowledge is not necessarily as coherent, clear, and consistent as it could be. For example, you are probably very skilled at using a cell phone. It brings you into daily contact with friends and family, puts you in touch with the pizza delivery guy, and allows you to register for classes and find out your grades at the end of the term. But you probably can't explain how it works in a technical way; you know only how it works for you in a practical, everyday way. This is the important feature of the everyday actor's knowledge: it is practical, not scientific.

To acquire knowledge about the social world that is systematic, comprehensive, coherent, clear, and consistent, you'll need to take a different approach. The social analyst has to "place in question everything that seems unquestionable" to the everyday actor (Schutz 1962, p. 96). In other words, the social analyst takes the perspective of a stranger in the social world; she tries to verify what the everyday actor might just accept as truth. For instance, people tend to believe that women are more talkative than men. This might seem so evident, in fact, as not to be worth investigating. The social analyst, however, *would* investigate, and deliver a more complex conclusion than you might think.

There are strengths and weaknesses in both approaches: the analyst sees with clarity what the actor glosses over, but the actor understands implicitly what the analyst labors to grasp. Once you've learned more about the theories and methods that come next, you'll be able to combine the virtues of both analyst and actor. The result will be a more profound and comprehensive understanding of the social world in which we all live.

What Is Sociology?

Even among those working in the field, there is some debate about defining **sociology**. A look at the term's Latin and Greek roots, *socius* and *logos*, suggests that sociology means the study of **society**, which is a good place to start. A slightly more elaborate definition might be the systematic or scientific study of human society and social behavior. This could include almost any level within the structure of society, from large-scale institutions and mass culture to small groups and relationships between individuals.

Another definition comes from Howard Becker (1986), who suggests that sociology can best be understood as the study of people "doing things together." This version reminds us that neither society nor the individual exists in isolation and that humans are essentially social beings. Not only is our survival contingent on the fact that we live in various groups (families, neighborhoods, dorms), but our sense of self derives from our membership in society. In turn, the accumulated activities that people do together create the patterns and structures we call society.

> **SOCIOLOGY** the systematic or scientific study of human society and social behavior, from large-scale institutions and mass culture to small groups and individual interactions
>
> **SOCIETY** a group of people who shape their lives in aggregated and patterned ways that distinguish their group from others

So sociologists want to understand how humans affect society, as well as how society affects humans.

One way to better understand sociology is to contrast it with other **social sciences**, disciplines that examine the human or social world, much as the natural sciences examine the natural or physical world. These include anthropology, psychology, economics, political science, and sometimes history, geography, and communication studies. Each has its own particular focus on the social world. In some ways, sociology's territory overlaps with other social sciences, even while maintaining its own approach.

Like history, sociology compares the past and the present in order to understand both; unlike history, sociology is more likely to focus on contemporary society. Sociology is interested in societies at all levels of development, while anthropology is more likely to concentrate on traditional or small, indigenous cultures. Sociology looks at a range of social institutions, unlike economics or political science, which each focus on a single institution. Like geography, sociology considers the relationship of people to places, though geography is more concerned with the places themselves. And like communication studies, sociology examines human communication—at both the social and the interpersonal levels, rather than one or the other. Finally, sociology looks at the individual in relationship to external social forces, whereas psychology specializes in internal states of mind. As you can begin to see, sociology covers a huge intellectual territory, making it exceptional among the social sciences in taking a comprehensive, integrative approach to understanding human life (Figure 1.1).

The Sociological Perspective

How do sociologists go about understanding human life in society? The first step is to develop what we call the **sociological perspective**, which is also referred to as taking a sociological approach or thinking sociologically. In any case, it means looking at the world in a unique way and seeing it in a whole new light. You may be naturally inclined to think sociologically, but, for many, the following practices are helpful.

Beginner's Mind

One technique for gaining a sociological perspective comes from Bernard McGrane (1994), who promotes a shift in thinking borrowed from the Zen Buddhist tradition. McGrane suggests that we practice what is called **beginner's mind**— the opposite of expert's mind, which is so filled with facts,

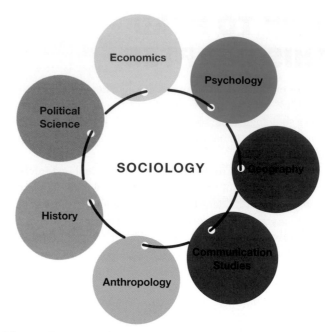

Figure 1.1   Sociology and the Social Sciences

Sociology overlaps with other social sciences, but much of the territory it covers is unique.

projections, assumptions, opinions, and explanations that it can't learn anything new. If we would like to better understand the world around us, we must unlearn what we already know. Beginner's mind approaches the world without knowing in advance what it will find; it is open and receptive to experience.

Perhaps our greatest obstacle to making new discoveries is our habitual ways of thinking. "Discovery," McGrane says, "is not the seeing of a new thing—but rather a new way of seeing things" (1994, p. 3). One way to achieve this kind of awareness is to practice being present in the moment. We are all too often preoccupied with thoughts and feelings that prevent us from fully participating in reality. If we can find some inner stillness and stop our normal mental chatter, then McGrane says there is a possibility for true learning to occur. It is in this quiet space that a personal "paradigm shift" (a new model for understanding self and society) can take place.

DATA WORKSHOP
Analyzing Everyday Life

Doing Nothing

Bernard McGrane suggests that we actually "do" sociology, rather than just study it. His book *The Un-TV and the 10 MPH Car* (1994) features exercises designed to help students experience the mundane, routine, and everyday level of society in a new way. This Data Workshop is an adaptation of one of his experiments. You will be practicing beginner's mind, one of the ways to gain a sociological perspective, or to think like a sociologist.

Step 1: Conducting the Experiment
This exercise requires that you go stand in a relatively busy public space (a mall, street corner, park, or campus quad) and literally do nothing for ten minutes. That means just standing there and being unoccupied. Don't wait for someone, take a break, sightsee, or otherwise engage in a normal kind of activity. Also don't daydream or think about the past or the future; don't entertain yourself with plans or internal dialogues. Don't whistle, hum, fidget, look in your bag, play with your phone, take notes, or do anything else that might distract you from just being there and doing nothing. Do, however, observe the reactions of others to you, and pay attention to your own thoughts and feelings during these ten minutes.

Step 2: Taking Notes about the Experience
Immediately after conducting the experiment, write some informal notes about what happened or did not happen. These notes can be loosely structured (with sentence fragments or bullet points, if you wish), and they should be casual and written in the first person. Discuss the experience and its meaning to you in as much detail as possible. Include a description of other people's reactions as well as your own thoughts and feelings before, during, and after the experiment.

This exercise may seem deceptively simple at first, but the subtle change from "doing something" to "doing nothing" makes everything different. It helps turn the ordinary world into a strange place. It makes you more aware of your own sense of self (or lack thereof) and how identity is constructed through interaction. You may find it a challenge to put aside the mental and physical activities that you normally engage in to pass the time. And you may feel uncomfortable standing in a public place when other people can't quite figure out who you are and what you're doing. Finally, you will no longer be able to take for granted how the meaning of a situation is being defined or interpreted. Divested of your role as an everyday actor, you'll learn how the most mundane activities (like just standing around) can become major objects of sociological inquiry.

There are two options for completing this Data Workshop:

PREP-PAIR-SHARE Complete the exercise and bring your written notes to class. Partner with another student and take turns presenting your findings. Discuss the ways in which your experiences were similar or different. What

Doing Nothing How does standing in a crowded place and doing nothing change how you experience the ordinary world?

was it like to "do" sociology? Did you see things in a new way? What was the most interesting part about conducting the experiment?

DO-IT-YOURSELF Complete the exercise and write a two- to three-page essay based on the main concepts and prompts from this Data Workshop. Describe your experience and the results of your research. How did the experiment help you learn to think more like a sociologist? You may want to include snippets of your informal written notes to illustrate your points. Attach the informal notes to your finished essay.

Culture Shock

Peter Berger (1963) describes what kind of person becomes a sociologist: someone with a passionate interest in the world of human affairs, someone who is intense, curious, and daring in the pursuit of knowledge. "People who like to avoid shocking discoveries . . . should stay away from sociology," he warns (p. 24). The sociologist cares about the issues of ultimate importance to humanity, as well as the most mundane occurrences of everyday existence.

Another way to gain a sociological perspective is to attempt to create in ourselves a sense of **culture shock**. Anthropologists use the term to describe the experience of visiting an "exotic"

CULTURE SHOCK a sense of disorientation that occurs when entering a radically new social or cultural environment

IN RELATIONSHIPS
It's Official: Men Talk More than Women

The practice of sociology may look pretty simple or natural at the outset. It doesn't seem to require much special training to figure out other people and to know something about how the world works. All it takes is membership in society and some life experience to count yourself an expert on the topic. Look at how successful you are already, just to have arrived at the point of being a college student. So what more can sociology deliver?

The practice of sociology may also seem to be about just a bunch of common sense. But this is true only part of the time. Some of what you learn may indeed seem familiar and may confirm some of the conclusions you've made about it. Drawing on the personal knowledge you have accumulated in life will be a valuable asset as a starting place, but it can also be a stumbling block to deeper understanding. There are times that the things that "everyone knows" turn out not to be true, or at least not as simple as we might have thought.

Take, for instance, the widely held belief that women talk more than men. Experience seems to confirm that this is true, obviously! Women are chatty, and a lot of men, if not the strong silent type, definitely have trouble getting a word in edgewise. And women have a hard time getting men to talk when they want them to; sometimes, to get a man to tell you what he's thinking, you have to drag it out of him. While you may recognize this description of the different genders, and may be able to relate with your own anecdote of such an encounter (or perhaps many such encounters), your casual assumptions about who talks most may need some revising. Numerous sociological studies that analyze conversational dynamics show that, despite stereotypes to the contrary, it's actually men who are slightly more talkative (Leaper and Ayres 2007). How could that be?

Actually, there are some nuances. It's true that researchers have found that men are more talkative overall, but especially in certain contexts. Men are more talkative with their wives and with strangers. Women are more talkative with their children and with college classmates. With close friends and families, men and women are equally talkative. Studies have also showed other, perhaps more easily predictable, gender differences, such as that men use speech that is more assertive (they want to persuade others), while women use speech that is more affiliative (they are more focused on connecting with others). These findings even seem to defy what had been considered a biological fact, that the female brain is wired to be more verbal. But because who talks more varies by situation, the evidence seems to point to language and conversational differences as influenced more by social than biological forces. So despite how it might feel from your own personal experience, sociology has debunked a common myth about women and men, requiring that we rethink simplistic gender stereotypes.

This is why doing sociology is in some regards a radical undertaking. It requires of us a willingness to suspend our own preconceptions, assumptions, and beliefs about the way things are. As sociologists, we need to learn to question everything, especially our own taken-for-granted notions about others and ourselves. Once these notions have been set aside, even temporarily, we gain a fresh perspective with which to uncover and discover aspects of social life we hadn't noticed before. We are then able to reinterpret our previous understanding of the world, perhaps challenging, or possibly confirming, what we thought we already knew.

Kanye West takes the microphone away from Taylor Swift to make a speech at the MTV Video Music Awards.

foreign culture. The first encounters with the local natives and their way of life can seem so strange to us that they produce a kind of disorientation and doubt about our ability to make sense of things. Putting all judgment aside for the moment, this state of mind can be very useful. For it is at this point, when we so completely lack an understanding of our surroundings, that we are truly able to perceive what is right in front of our eyes.

As sociologists, we try to create this effect without necessarily displacing ourselves geographically: we become curious and eager visitors to our own lives. We often find that what is familiar to us, if viewed from an outsider's perspective, is just as exotic as some foreign culture, only we've forgotten this is true because it's our own and we know it so well. To better understand this state of mind, you might imagine what it would be like to return home from a desert island.

Consider the real-life case of Roger Lextrait, who worked for eight years as the caretaker of Palmyra, a small, remote island in the South Pacific. During that time, Lextrait had limited radio contact with Honolulu and Tahiti and lived mostly in the company of his three dogs. He arrived with a boat full of canned food, 500 pounds of flour, 30 gallons of olive oil, and plenty of red wine. His provisions lasted for two years; after that, he managed to live off the land. He fished, hunted, sang, and played guitar to try to keep loneliness and boredom at bay. In 1992, when Lextrait moved to Palmyra, the Internet only transmitted text, no images, and was used only by people in technology and higher education. By 2000, technology had changed exponentially, and more than 350 million people were using the Internet (users now number in the billions). When Lextrait finally reentered civilization, he experienced immense culture shock. "I had no idea that the cellular phone existed. I was so lost," he said. "I came back with different eyes— I was a different person" (Maslin Nir 2010). You don't have to live on a deserted island to experience culture shock. Perhaps it's something you've also experienced, but didn't know what to call, if you've traveled or moved away to attend college.

The Sociological Imagination

One of the classic statements about the sociological perspective comes from C. Wright Mills (1916–1962), who describes a quality of mind that all great social analysts seem to possess: the **sociological imagination**. By this, he means the ability to understand "the intersection between biography and history," or the interplay of self and the world; this is sociology's task and its "promise" (Mills 1959).

We normally think of our own problems as being a private matter of character, chance, or circumstance, and we overlook the fact that these may be caused in part by, or at least occur within, a specific cultural and historical context. For example, if you can't find a job, you may feel that it's because you don't have the right skills, educational background, or experience. But it may also be the result of problems in the larger economy such as outsourcing, downsizing, restrictive policies, changing technologies, or migration patterns. In other words, your individual unemployment may be part of a larger social and historical phenomenon.

Most of the time, we use psychological rather than sociological arguments to explain the way things are. For instance, if someone is carrying a lot of credit card debt, psychological reasoning might focus on the person's lack of self-control or inability to delay gratification. Sociological reasoning, however, might focus on the impact of cultural norms that promote a lifestyle beyond most people's means, or on economic changes that require more Americans to rely on credit cards because their wages have not kept up with inflation.

The sociological imagination searches for the link between micro and macro levels of analysis. We must look for how larger social forces, such as race, class, gender, religion, economics, or politics, are involved in creating the context of a person's life. Mills's characterization of sociology as the intersection between biography and history reminds us that the process works in both directions: while larger social forces influence individual lives, individual lives can affect society as well.

One of the most important benefits of using the sociological imagination is access to a world beyond our own immediate sphere, where we can discover radically different ways of experiencing life and interpreting reality. It can help us appreciate alternative viewpoints and understand how they may have come about. This, in turn, helps us to better understand how we developed our own values, beliefs, and attitudes.

SOCIOLOGICAL IMAGINATION a quality of the mind that allows us to understand the relationship between our individual circumstances and larger social forces

Sociology asks us to see our familiar world in a new way, and doing so means we may need to abandon, or at least reevaluate, our opinions about that world and our place in it. It is tempting to believe that our opinions are widely held, that our worldview is the best or, at least, most common. Taking a sociological perspective forces us to see fallacies in our way of thinking. Because other individuals are different from us—belonging to different social groups, participating in different social institutions, living in different cities or countries, listening to different songs, watching different TV programs, engaging in different religious practices— they may look at the world very differently than we do. But a sociological perspective also allows us to see the other side of this equation: in cases where we assume that others are different from us, we may be surprised to find that their approach to their everyday world is quite similar to ours.

C. Wright Mills

Sociology continues to be a popular major at colleges and universities in the United States and in countries such as Canada, the United Kingdom, and Australia. According to the American Sociological Association (ASA), over a half million bachelor of arts degrees in sociology were awarded in the United States between 1990 and 2012 (National Center for Education Statistics 2012). Clearly, there are many reasons students are enthusiastic about the subject. What may be less clear is how to turn this passion into a paycheck. Students considering majoring in the subject often ask, "What can I do with a degree in sociology?" Their parents may be asking the same question.

Students interested in academic careers can pursue graduate degrees and become professors and researchers—real practicing sociologists. But the vast majority of sociology majors will not necessarily become sociologists with a capital *S*. Their studies have prepared them to be valuable, accomplished participants in a variety of fields, including law

and government, business administration, social welfare, public health, education, counseling and human resources, advertising and marketing, public relations and the media, and nonprofit organizations. A major in sociology, in other words, can lead almost anywhere. And while the roster of former sociology majors contains names both well known and unsung, from President Ronald Reagan and civil rights leader Martin Luther King Jr. to the public defender giving legal aid to low-income clients and the health-care professional bringing wellness programs into large corporations, we will focus here on three important Americans you may not have associated with sociology.

The first individual may be the least likely to be identified as a sociology major, since his career was centered in the arts. Saul Bellow (1915–2005) was one of the most acclaimed American novelists of the twentieth century; his books include *Seize the Day*, *Herzog*, and *Humboldt's Gift*. He won numerous literary awards, including the National Book Award (three times), the Pulitzer Prize, and the Nobel Prize for Literature. He was also a successful playwright and journalist and taught at several universities. Bellow was born in Montreal to Jewish parents, Russian émigrés who later settled in the slums of Chicago while he was still a child. He began his undergraduate studies in English at the University of Chicago but left within two years

Saul Bellow

Michelle Obama

Kal Penn

Levels of Analysis: Micro- and Macrosociology

Consider a photographer with state-of-the-art equipment. She can view her subject through either a zoom lens or a wide-angle lens. Through the zoom lens, she sees intricate details about the subject's appearance; through the wide-angle lens, she gets the "big picture" and a sense of the broader context in which the subject is located. Both views are valuable in

understanding the subject, and both result in photographs of the same thing.

Sociological perspectives are like the photographer's lenses, allowing us different ways of looking at a common subject (Newman 2000). Sociologists can take a microsociological (zoom lens) perspective, a macrosociological (wide-angle lens) perspective, or any number of perspectives located on the continuum between the two (Figure 1.2).

Microsociology concentrates on the interactions between individuals and the ways in which those interactions construct the larger patterns, processes, and institutions of society. As the word indicates ("micro" means small), microsociology looks at the smallest building blocks of society in order to understand its large-scale structure. A classic

MICROSOCIOLOGY the level of analysis that studies face-to-face and small-group interactions in order to understand how they affect the larger patterns and structures of society

after being told by the department chair that no Jew could really grasp English literature. He then enrolled at Northwestern University, graduating in 1937 with honors in sociology. Literary critics have noted that Bellow's background in sociology, as well as his own personal history, may have influenced both the style and subject of his work. Many of the great themes of American social life appear in his novels: culture, power, wealth and poverty, war, religion, urban life, gender relations, and, above all, the social contract that keeps us together in the face of forces that threaten to tear us apart.

Our next profile is of Michelle Robinson Obama (b. 1964), the first African American First Lady of the United States. Michelle Obama has become one of the most recognizable and widely admired sociology majors in the world, using her role as First Lady to fight childhood obesity, help working mothers and military families, and encourage public service. Born and raised in working-class Chicago, she can trace her ancestry to slaves on both sides of her family tree. Her father worked for the city's water department but saw both of his children graduate from Princeton University and go on to successful professional careers. After obtaining her BA in sociology—her senior thesis dealt with alienation experienced by African American students in an Ivy League institution—she earned her law degree at Harvard, worked at a prestigious law firm in Chicago, and then served in the mayor's office. In addition to law and politics, her choice of majors was a critical stepping stone on her way to success.

Our last sociology major is Kalpen Modi (b. 1977), who has served as an associate director with the White House Office of Public Engagement (OPE) on and off since 2009. This may come as a surprise to those who know him as the actor Kal Penn, most famous for his role as the wisecracking, easygoing stoner Kumar in the *Harold and Kumar* film series or as Kevin on *How I Met Your Mother*. Joining the OPE meant that Penn had to temporarily leave acting to become the liaison to young Americans, the arts, and Asian American and Pacific Islander communities. As much as Penn wants success as an actor, he has also been critical of the racial and ethnic stereotypes often associated with playing a person of South Asian descent. At one point, he nearly turned down a recurring role as a terrorist on the TV drama *24* because he didn't want to reinforce the negative "connection between media images and people's thought processes" (Yuan 2007). While it might be easy to make similar claims against *Harold and Kumar Go to White Castle*, one of his co-stars defended the film by arguing that it "approached the level of sociology, albeit scatological, sexually obsessed sociology," as "it probed questions of ethnic identity, conformism and family expectations versus personal satisfaction" (Garvin 2008, p. M1). Penn's career change reflects his deep commitment to sociological ideals and a desire to use his influence to help build more positive media portrayals of minorities.

Regardless of whether you go any further in this discipline—or if you end up working in politics, the arts, or public service—the most important thing to take away from an introductory sociology class is a sociological perspective. Sociology promises a new way of looking at, thinking about, and taking action in the world around us, all of which will serve you well no matter where you find yourself in the future.

example of research that takes a micro approach is Pam Fishman's article "Interaction: The Work Women Do" (1978). Like many scholars who had observed the feminist movements of the 1960s and '70s, Fishman was concerned with issues of power and domination in male-female relationships: Are men more powerful than women in our society? If so, how is this power created and maintained in everyday interactions? In her research, Fishman recorded and analyzed heterosexual couples' everyday conversations in their homes. She found some real differences in the conversational strategies of men and women, and some surprising results about who talked most.

One such conversation took place in the kitchen, where a woman was having a difficult time getting her partner to join her in a discussion about the history of education. He frequently interrupted, changed the subject, failed to respond for long stretches, and even flipped on the garbage disposal while she was speaking. She persevered, trying to gain control of the conversation. Fishman recorded many more conversations between couples and identified a variety of patterns. One of her findings was that women ask nearly three times as many questions as men do. While other researchers have proposed that women's psychological insecurities are the reason for this finding, Fishman noted that women are in fact following a firmly held rule of conversational structure: when the speaker cannot guarantee that she or he will get a response, she or he is more likely to ask a question. Questions provoke answers, which makes them a useful conversational tool for

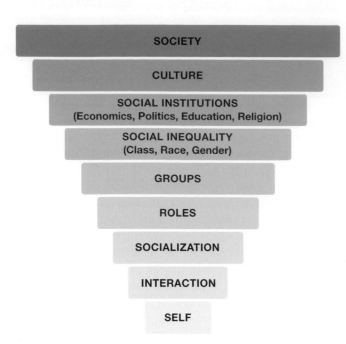

Figure 1.2 The Macro-Micro Continuum

Sociology covers a wide range of topics at different levels of analysis.

those who may have less power in interpersonal relationships and in society at large. And women are more likely to be in this position than men. Thus, in her micro-level analysis of conversation, Fishman was able to see how macro-level ("macro" means large) phenomena such as gender and power are manifested in everyday interactions.

Macrosociology approaches the study of society from the opposite direction, by looking at large-scale social structure to determine how it affects the lives of groups and individuals. If we

MACROSOCIOLOGY the level of analysis that studies large-scale social structures in order to determine how they affect the lives of groups and individuals

want to stick to the topic of gender inequality, we can find plenty of examples of research projects that take a macro approach; many deal with the workplace. Despite the gains made in recent years, the U.S. labor market is still predominantly sex segregated—that is, men and women are concentrated in different occupations. For example, in 2014, 99 percent of auto mechanics were male, whereas 94 percent of secretaries and administrative assistants were female (U.S. Bureau of Labor Statistics 2015c). This feature of social structure, some argue, has a direct effect on the bottom line for individual workers, male and female. Our social institutions, from religion to the family and education, also play a part in sending women and men on different career trajectories, which often results in them earning differing paychecks.

A related example comes from the work of Christine Williams. She found that while women in male-dominated fields experience limits on their advancement, dubbed the "glass ceiling" effect, men in female-dominated occupations experience unusually rapid rates of upward mobility—the "glass escalator" (Williams 1995). Here, then, we see a macro approach to the topic of gender and power: large-scale features of social structure (patterns of occupational sex segregation) create the constraints within which individuals and groups (women and men in the workplace) experience successes or failures in their everyday lives.

As you can see, these two perspectives make different assumptions about how society works: the micro perspective assumes that society's larger structures are shaped through individual interactions, while the macro perspective assumes that society's larger structures shape those individual interactions. It is useful to think of these perspectives as being on a continuum with each other; while some sociologists adhere to radically micro or exclusively macro perspectives, most are somewhere in between. The next part of this chapter explores some specific theoretical traditions within sociology and shows you where each falls along this continuum.

Levels of Analysis These two views of the New York Public Library represent different levels of analysis in sociology. Microsociology zooms in to focus on individuals, their interactions, and groups in order to understand their contribution to larger social structures. In contrast, macrosociology pulls back to examine large-scale social processes and their effects on individuals and groups.

IN THE FUTURE
C. Wright Mills and the Sociological Imagination

The "sociological imagination" is a term that seemingly every sociology student encounters. It was first introduced by C. Wright Mills in his 1959 book by the same name, and over time it has become an enduring cornerstone of the discipline. It captures the spirit of inquiry, the quality of mind, and the guiding principles that all sociologists should embrace. Mills was sometimes critical of sociology as a discipline, so he offered himself as a "public intellectual," one who could speak beyond the confines of academia and address some of the most pressing social issues of the time. Mills was convinced that sociology had something to offer everyone, not just academics.

Mills highlighted the distinction between "personal troubles" and "public issues" as "an essential tool of the sociological imagination and a feature of all classic work in social science" (Mills 1959, p. 8). He explained that almost any feature of an individual's daily life can be better understood if this distinction is applied to it. Unemployment, war, marriage, and housing are all experienced as personal troubles, but to be fully understood, they must also be seen as manifestations of long-standing institutions and larger social structures. As Mills pointed out, "In so far as an economy is so arranged that slumps occur, the problem of unemployment becomes incapable of personal solution" (Mills 1959, p. 10). This lesson was driven home again during the Great Recession, which began in 2007. A series of major banks had created securities that bundled a large number of mortgages made to so-called sub-prime borrowers. When many of these mortgages went into default, it led to an economic chain reaction that culminated in unemployment levels higher than any seen since the Great Depression of the 1930s. For the many millions of people thrown out of work, unemployment was experienced as a personal trouble, but one that could be understood only as a public issue.

In even more fundamental ways, Mills believed that people are shaped by the connections between "the patterns of their own lives and the course of world history" (Mills 1959, p. 4). These connections could influence the most personal features of someone's life, shaping the very kind of people "they are becoming" (p. 4). In her book *Unbearable Weight* (1995), Susan Bordo describes how anorexia came to be recognized as a national mental health problem. In 1973, psychiatrists still considered anorexia quite rare, so why is there so much awareness about eating disorders now? Anorexia and bulimia are experienced in intensely personal ways, and eating disorders are usually explained in purely psychological terms. But Bordo, thinking about them sociologically, argues that cultural factors help create eating disorders. Contemporary culture's obsession with bodies that are "slim, tight, and young" (p. 140) shapes individual psychologies. Eating disorders, then, are symptoms of a troubled culture as well as a troubled individual. This is not to deny that personal and psychological factors aren't important, but it is a reminder that social and cultural factors create the environment that makes it possible to experience problems like eating disorders in the first place.

Today you may be a student in an introductory sociology class; this year, more than 25,000 students will receive bachelor's degrees in sociology. Whether or not you end up majoring in sociology, C. Wright Mills wanted everyone to develop and sharpen a sociological imagination. In fact, that is the goal we share in writing this textbook. How might the sociological imagination be useful to you in the future?

Personal Troubles and Public Issues High foreclosure rates in the wake of the recent recession are both a personal trouble and a public issue.

Glass Escalators Christine Williams's study of the occupational status of men in female-dominated industries such as teaching is a good example of macrosociology.

Sociology's Family Tree

Great thinkers have been trying to understand the world and our place in it since the beginning of time. Some have done this by developing **theories**: abstract propositions about how things are as well as how they should be. Sometimes we also refer to theories as "approaches," "schools of thought," "**paradigms**," or "perspectives." Social theories, then, are guiding principles or abstract models that attempt to explain and predict the social world.

As we embark on the discussion of theory, it may be useful to think of sociology as having a "family tree" made up of real people who were living in a particular time and place and who were related along various intertwining lines to other members of the same larger family tree. First, we will examine sociology's early historical roots. Then, as we follow the growth of the discipline, we will identify its major branches and trace the relationships among their offshoots and the other "limbs" that make up the entire family tree. Finally, we will examine some of the newest theoretical approaches and members of the family tree (page 19), and consider the possible future of sociological theory.

THEORIES abstract propositions that explain the social world and make predictions about the future

PARADIGMS a set of assumptions, theories, and perspectives that make up a way of understanding social reality

POSITIVISM the theory that sense perceptions are the only valid source of knowledge

Sociology's Roots

The earliest Western social theorists focused on establishing society as an appropriate object of scientific scrutiny, which was itself a revolutionary concept. None of these early theorists were themselves sociologists (since the discipline didn't yet exist) but rather people from a variety of backgrounds—philosophers, theologians, economists, historians, journalists—who were trying to look at society in a new way. In doing so, they laid the groundwork not only for the discipline as a whole but also for the different schools of thought that are still shaping sociology today.

AUGUSTE COMTE (1798–1857) was the first to provide a program for the scientific study of society, or a "social physics," as he labeled it. Comte, a French scientist, developed a theory of the progress of human thinking from its early theological and metaphysical stages toward a final "positive," or scientific, stage. **Positivism** seeks to identify laws that describe the behavior of a particular reality, such as the laws of mathematics and physics, in which people gain knowledge of the world directly through their senses. Having grown up in the aftermath of the French Revolution and its lingering political instability, Comte felt that society needed positivist guidance toward both social progress and social order. After studying at an elite science and technology college, where he was introduced to the newly discovered scientific method, he began to imagine a way of applying the methodology to social affairs. His ideas, featured in *Introduction to Positive Philosophy* (1842), became the foundation of a scientific discipline that would describe the laws of social phenomena and help control social life; he called it "sociology."

Although Comte is remembered today mainly for coining the term, he played a significant role in the development of sociology as a discipline. His efforts to distinguish appropriate methods and topics for sociologists provided the kernel of a discipline. Other social thinkers advanced his work: Harriet Martineau and Herbert Spencer in England and Émile Durkheim in France.

HARRIET MARTINEAU (1802–1876) was born in England to progressive parents who made sure their daughter was well educated. She became a journalist and political

Auguste Comte

Harriet Martineau

economist, proclaiming views that were radical for her time: endorsing labor unions, the abolition of slavery, and women's suffrage. Though Martineau never married, she preferred to be addressed as "Mrs."—not because she wished for a husband (indeed, she strongly rejected marriage, seeing it as a tool for the subjugation of women) but because she recognized that the title conveyed respect and status in her culture. She felt that respect was denied to her as a single woman.

In 1835, "Mrs." Martineau traveled to the United States to judge the new democracy on its own terms rather than by European standards. But she was disappointed: by condoning slavery and denying full citizenship rights to women and blacks, the American experiment was, in her eyes, flawed and hypocritical. She wrote two books describing her observations, *Society in America* (1837) and *Retrospect of Western Travel* (1838), both critical of American leadership and culture. By holding the United States to its own publicly stated democratic standards, rather than seeing the country from an ethnocentric British perspective, she was a precursor to the naturalistic sociologists who would establish the discipline in America. In 1853, Martineau made perhaps her most important contribution to sociology: she translated Comte's *Introduction to Positive Philosophy* into English, thus making his ideas accessible in England and America.

HERBERT SPENCER (1820–1903) was primarily responsible for the establishment of sociology in Britain and America. Although Spencer did not receive academic training, he grew up in a highly individualistic family and was encouraged to think and learn on his own. His interests leaned heavily toward physical science, and, instead of attending college, Spencer chose to become a railway engineer. When railway work dried up, he turned to journalism and eventually worked for a major periodical in London. There he became acquainted with leading English academics and began to publish his own thoughts in book form.

In 1862, Spencer drew up a list of what he called "first principles" (in a book by that name), and near the top of the list was the notion of evolution driven by natural selection. Charles Darwin is the best-known proponent of the theory, but the idea of evolution was in wide circulation before Darwin made it famous. Spencer proposed that societies, like biological organisms, evolve through time by adapting to changing conditions, with less successful adaptations falling by the wayside. He coined the phrase "survival of the fittest," and his social philosophy is sometimes known as **social Darwinism**. In the late 1800s, Spencer's work, including *The Study of Sociology* (1873) and *The Principles of Sociology* (1897), was virtually synonymous with sociology in the English-speaking world. The scope and volume of his writing served to announce sociology as a serious discipline and laid the groundwork for the next generation of theorists, whose observations of large-scale social change would bring a new viewpoint to social theory.

Herbert Spencer

Macrosociological Theory

Theorists in late-nineteenth-century Europe were living during extraordinary times. They were attempting to explain social order, social change, and social inequality while the world around them changed as a result of the Industrial Revolution. At the same time, they were witnessing political upheaval and the birth of democracy brought about by the French and American Revolutions. These were changes on the grandest of scale in the macro order of society. Frequently referred to as classical sociology, the theories that arose during this period reflect the broad subject matter of a sweeping era.

Structural Functionalism

Structural functionalism, or functionalist theory, was the dominant theoretical perspective within sociology well into the mid-twentieth century. New (or neo-) functionalists continue to apply their own vision of the theory to study a wide variety of social phenomena today.

FOUNDER AND KEY CONTRIBUTIONS Émile Durkheim (1858–1917) is the central figure in functionalist theory. He was born into a close-knit and deeply religious Jewish family who instilled in him a strong sense of morality (not just as an abstract concept but as a concrete influence on social relations) and a strong work ethic. After witnessing the ravages of the Franco-Prussian War (1870–71), he hoped that applied science could stabilize and revitalize France in the aftermath of its devastating defeat. He did not believe that traditional, abstract moral philosophy was effective in increasing understanding and bringing about social change, so he turned instead to the concrete science of sociology as represented in Comte's work.

In his first major study, *The Division of Labor in Society* (1893), Durkheim stated that social bonds were present in all types of societies but that different types of societies created

Émile Durkheim

different types of bonds. He suggested that the **mechanical solidarity** experienced by people in a simple agricultural society bound them together on the basis of shared traditions, beliefs, and experiences. In industrial societies, where factory work was becoming increasingly specialized, **organic solidarity** prevailed: people's bonds were based on the tasks they performed, interdependence, and individual rights. Both types of solidarity have interpersonal bonds—just with different qualities.

Durkheim believed that even the most individualistic actions have sociological explanations and set out to establish a scientific methodology for studying these actions. He chose for his case study the most individualistic of actions, suicide, and used statistical data to show that suicides were related to social factors such as religious affiliation, marital status, and employment. Explaining a particular suicide by focusing exclusively on the victim's psychological makeup neglected the impact of social bonds. According to Durkheim in his now-classic study *Suicide* (1897), even the darkest depression has its roots in an individual's connections to the social world, or rather his lack of connection. Durkheim theorized that suicide is one result of **anomie**, a sense of disconnection brought about by the changing conditions of modern life. The more firmly anchored a person is to family, religion, and the workplace, the less anomie he is likely to experience.

In his final major study, *The Elementary Forms of Religious Life* (1912), Durkheim suggested that religion is a powerful source of social **solidarity**, or unity, because it reinforced collective bonds and shared moral values. He believed that society could be understood through examining the most basic forms of religion. Durkheim's study of the indigenous peoples of Australia led him to a universal definition of religion: though religious traditions might differ, any form of religion is unified in its definition of what is considered to be **sacred** and **profane**. Every person who follows a particular set of beliefs and practices will "unite into one single moral community" (Durkheim 1912/1995, p. 44).

Durkheim also noted that rituals or ceremonies that brought people together into communities were created and practiced to enhance the feeling of emotional unity that reaffirmed solidarity and social order. When people gathered for religious events, their individual acts, taken together, created a feeling of being swept up in something larger than themselves. It made them feel as if they had entered a "special world inhabited by exceptionally intense forces that invade and transform" them (Durkheim 1912/1995, p. 220). Durkheim referred to this as **collective effervescence**. This

sense of participants being transported by a shared wave of energy can happen during a Catholic Mass, for instance, as much as it can by attending a live concert or sporting event at a sold-out arena.

A distinction between the sacred and the profane, and the creation of and participation in shared ritual activity, creates a **collective conscience** (or collective consciousness) that contains the morality, the cosmology, and the beliefs "common to the group" (p. 379). The shared beliefs and values that make up the collective conscience of the group are what make social solidarity possible, but they must be frequently renewed through the ritual, by which a group "revitalizes the sense it has of itself and its unity" (p. 379). Durkheim believed that this process happens in all societies, whether united through a common religious tradition or through shared secular beliefs and practices.

Durkheim's attempt to establish sociology as an important, independent academic discipline was enormously successful. He not only made significant contributions to the existing literature but also demonstrated the effectiveness of using scientific, **empirical** methods to study "social reality," essentially validating Comte's proposal from half a century earlier. Durkheim became the first professor of social science in France, at the University of Bordeaux in 1887, and later won a similar appointment at the Sorbonne in Paris, the very heart of French academic life. Today, Durkheim's eminence in the social sciences is as strong as ever, and his ideas are still applied and extended by contemporary theorists.

MECHANICAL SOLIDARITY the type of social bonds present in premodern, agrarian societies, in which shared traditions and beliefs created a sense of social cohesion

ORGANIC SOLIDARITY the type of social bonds present in modern societies, based on difference, interdependence, and individual rights

ANOMIE "normlessness"; term used to describe the alienation and loss of purpose that result from weaker social bonds and an increased pace of change

SOLIDARITY the degree of integration or unity within a particular society; the extent to which individuals feel connected to other members of their group

SACRED the holy, divine, or supernatural

PROFANE the ordinary, mundane, or everyday

COLLECTIVE EFFERVESCENCE an intense energy in shared events where people feel swept up in something larger than themselves

COLLECTIVE CONSCIENCE the shared morals and beliefs that are common to a group and that foster social solidarity

EMPIRICAL based on scientific experimentation or observation

ORIGINAL PRINCIPLES The origins of structural functionalism can be traced back to the roots of sociology. Auguste Comte proposed that society itself could and should be studied. Herbert Spencer added the idea that societies are living organisms that grow and evolve, just like other species on the planet. As the discipline of biology might study the physical organism of the human body, the discipline of sociology could study social organisms in the world of human development. Durkheim integrated and advanced these insights into a comprehensive theory for understanding the nature of society.

There are two main principles of functionalism. First, society is conceived as a stable, ordered system made up of interrelated parts, or **structures**. Second, each structure has a function that contributes to the continued stability or equilibrium of the unified whole. Structures are identified as social institutions such as the family, the educational system, politics, the economy, and religion. They meet society's needs by performing different functions, and every function is necessary to maintain social order and stability. Any disorganization or **dysfunction** in a structure leads to change and a new equilibrium; if one structure is transformed, the others must also adjust. For example, if families fail to discipline children, then schools, churches, and the courts must pick up the slack.

It may seem contradictory that a theory concerned with order and stability would emerge in a discipline that arose in a period of rapid social change. But it is important to remember that change had previously occurred much more slowly and that one response to rapid social change is to try to understand what had come before—stability, order, and equilibrium.

OFFSHOOTS Structural functionalism was the dominant theoretical perspective in Europe for much of the early twentieth century. It was exported and updated by American functionalists, who increased its popularity and helped spread its reach well into the 1960s. For example, Talcott Parsons (1902–1979) elaborated on the theory and applied it to modern society, specifying some of the functions that social structures might fulfill in contemporary life. A healthy society must provide a means for people to adapt to their environment; for example, families, schools, and religious institutions work together to socialize children. A functional society includes opportunities for success—for example, promoting education to help its members pursue and realize their goals. For society to survive, there must be social cohesion; for example, shared religious and moral values.

Another modern American functionalist, Robert Merton (1910–2003), delineated the theory even further, identifying manifest and latent functions for different social structures. **Manifest functions** are the obvious, intended functions of a social structure, while **latent functions** are the less obvious, perhaps unintended functions. For example, the manifest functions of education are to prepare future members of society by teaching them how to read and write and by instructing them on society's system of norms, values, and laws. However, education has a latent function as well, which is to keep kids busy and out of trouble eight hours a day, five days a week, for twelve years (or longer). Do not doubt that this is also an important contribution to social order!

Functionalism's influence waned in the late twentieth century but did not die out. A "neofunctionalist" movement, begun in the 1980s and '90s, attempted to reconstruct functionalist theories so that they remain relevant in a rapidly changing world. Theorists such as Neil Smelser and Jeffrey Alexander have attempted to modify functionalist theory to better incorporate problems such as racial and ethnic identity in a diverse society (Alexander 1988; Alexander and Smelser 1998; Smelser 1985).

ADVANTAGES AND CRITIQUES One of the great advantages of functionalism is its inclusion of all social institutions. Functionalism attempts to provide a universal social theory, a way of explaining society in one comprehensive model. Part of functionalism's appeal may also lie in its ability to bring order to a potentially disorderly world. Were it not for some of the volcanic social upheavals of recent history—the civil rights, antiwar, and women's liberation movements are not easily explained using this model—functionalist theory might still reign supreme in American sociology. Functionalism, generally preoccupied with stability, takes the position that only dysfunction can create social change. This conservative bias is part of a larger problem with the theory: functionalism provides little insight into social processes because its model of society is static rather than dynamic. Its focus on the macro level also means that functionalism has less interest in explaining independent human action; there is no apparent approach to the lives of individuals except as part of social institutions.

Functionalism's explanations of social inequality are especially unsatisfying: if poverty, racism, and sexism exist, they must serve a function for society; they must be necessary and inevitable. This view is problematic for many. Sociologist

Talcott Parsons

Robert Merton

Herbert Gans, in a critical essay (1971), reviewed the functions of poverty for society. The poor, for example, do our "dirty work," filling the menial, low-wage jobs that are necessary to keep society running smoothly but that others refuse to do. The poor provide a market for used and off-price goods and keep thrift stores and social welfare agencies in business. They have symbolic value as well, allowing those higher in the social hierarchy to feel compassion toward the "deserving" poor and to feel threatened by the "undeserving" poor, who are often seen as dangerous social deviants. Ultimately, the circular reasoning that characterizes functionalist thought turns out to be its biggest problem: the mere persistence of an institution should not be seen as an adequate explanation for its existence.

Conflict Theory

Conflict theory is the second major school of thought in sociology. Like structural functionalism, it's a macro-level approach to understanding social life that dates to mid-nineteenth-century Europe. As conflict theory developed, however, its emphasis on **social inequality** as the basic characteristic of society helped answer some of the critiques of structural functionalism.

FOUNDER AND KEY CONTRIBUTIONS The work of Karl Marx (1818–1883), a German social philosopher, cultural commentator, and political activist, was the inspiration for conflict theory, so the terms "conflict theory" and "Marxism" are sometimes used interchangeably in the social sciences. Marx's ideas have become more well known to the world as the basis for communism, the political system adopted by numerous countries (such as China, North Korea, and Cuba) that have often been viewed as enemies of democracy and the United States. This association has led many to a narrow belief that Marx was nothing more than a misguided agitator who helped cause more than a century of political turmoil. It is important to separate Marx himself from the current, political application of communism and to consider the possibility that he might not have supported the ways political leaders used his ideas decades later. Sociologists have found that Marx's theory continues to provide a powerful tool for understanding social phenomena. The idea that conflict between social groups is central to the workings of society and serves as the engine of social change is one of the most vital perspectives in sociology today.

Marx grew up in a modernizing, industrializing yet politically and religiously conservative monarchy; this, plus the fact that his was a restless, argumentative personality, accounts in great part for his social theory. Marx studied law and philosophy in Bonn and Berlin, receiving a PhD in 1841. His personal ties with radicals effectively barred him from entering academia, so he turned to journalism, writing stories that often antagonized government censors and officials.

Karl Marx

For most of his life, Marx led an economically fragile existence. He managed to maintain a tenuous middle-class lifestyle, but only with financial support from his close friend and chief intellectual collaborator Friedrich Engels, who studied the conditions of the English working class. Marx's own circumstances may have sparked his interest in social inequality, or the uneven and often unfair distribution of resources (in this case, wealth) in society, but he never experienced firsthand the particular burdens and difficulties of the working class.

The Industrial Revolution was a time of rapid social change, when large numbers of people were moving from an agricultural life in rural areas to manufacturing jobs in urban areas. Technological advances and a wage-based economy promised an age of prosperity and abundance, but they created new kinds of poverty, crime, and disease. Marx believed that most of those problems were a result of capitalism, the emerging economic system based on the private for-profit operation of industry. He proposed a radical alternative to the inherent inequalities of this system in the *Manifesto of the Communist Party* (1848), perhaps his most famous book.

In industrial society, the forces of capitalism were creating distinct social and economic classes, exacerbating the disparities between the wealthy and the poor. Marx felt that this would inevitably lead to class struggle between those who owned the **means of production** (anything that could create more wealth: money, property, factories, other types of businesses) and those who worked for them. He argued that the most important factor in social life was a person's relationship to the means of production; in other words, whether someone was a worker, and thus a member of the **proletariat**, or an owner, and thus a member of the **bourgeoisie**. Everything of value in society resulted from human labor, which was the proletariat's

CONFLICT THEORY a paradigm that sees social conflict as the basis of society and social change and that emphasizes a materialist view of society, a critical view of the status quo, and a dynamic model of historical change

SOCIAL INEQUALITY the unequal distribution of wealth, power, or prestige among members of a society

MEANS OF PRODUCTION anything that can create wealth: money, property, factories, and other types of businesses, and the infrastructure necessary to run them

PROLETARIAT workers; those who have no means of production of their own and so are reduced to selling their labor power in order to live

BOURGEOISIE owners; the class of modern capitalists who own the means of production and employ wage laborers

most valuable asset. Yet, they suffered from what Marx called **alienation** because they were unable to directly benefit from the fruits of their own labor. Workers were paid wages, but it was the factory owners who grew rich as a result of their toil.

The powerful few in the bourgeoisie were not only wealthy but also enjoyed social privilege and power. They were able to protect their interests, preserve their positions, and pass along their advantages to their heirs. The proletariat were often so absorbed in making a living that they were less apt to protest the conditions that led to their oppression. But eventually, Marx believed, the oppression would become unbearable, and the proletariat would rise up against the bourgeoisie, abolishing capitalism for good. He envisioned in its place a classless society—socialism—in which each person contributed to and benefited from the public good. Freed from oppressive conditions, individuals would then be able to pursue higher interests such as art and education and eventually live in a more egalitarian, utopian society. But in order to achieve such a state, the oppressed must first recognize how the current system worked against them.

In 1849, Marx withdrew from political activity in order to concentrate on writing *Das Kapital* (edited by Engels and published in 1890). The multivolume work provided a thorough exposition of his program for social change, which later became the foundation of political systems such as communism and socialism. Marx intended it to be his main contribution to sociology, but developments in the social sciences have placed more emphasis on his earlier writings. Because Marx held such radical ideas, his ideas were not immediately embraced by sociologists in general. It was not until the 1960s when conflict theory became a dominant perspective that Marx was truly received as a giant of sociology.

ORIGINAL PRINCIPLES Conflict theory proposes that conflict and tension are basic facts of social life and suggests that people have disagreements over goals and values and are involved in struggles over both resources and power. The theory thus focuses on the processes of dominance, competition, upheaval, and social change.

Conflict theory takes a materialist view of society (focused on labor practices and economic reality) and extends it to other social inequalities. Marx maintained that economic productivity is related to other processes in society, including political and intellectual life. The wealthy and powerful bourgeoisie control major social institutions, reinforcing the class structure so that the state, education, religion, and even the family are organized to represent their interests. Conflict theory takes a critical stance toward existing social arrangements and attempts to expose their inner workings.

Because the **ideology**, or belief system, that permeates society arises from the values of the ruling class, beliefs that seem to be widely held are actually a kind of justification that help rationalize and explain the status quo. Most people readily accept the prevailing ideology, despite its failure to represent the reality of their lives. Marx referred to this acceptance as **false consciousness**, a denial of the truth that allows for the perpetuation of the inequalities inherent in the class structure. For example, he is often quoted as saying, "Religion is the opiate of the masses." This is not a criticism of religion so much as a criticism of the use of religion to create false consciousness in the working class. Encouraged in their piety, the proletariat focus on the happiness promised in the afterlife rather than on deprivations suffered in this world. Indeed, heaven is seen as a reward for patiently suffering those deprivations. How does this serve the interests of the ruling class? By keeping the working class from demanding better conditions in this life.

Conflict theory sees the transformation of society over time as inevitable. Marx argued that the only way to change the status quo is for the masses to attain **class consciousness**, or revolutionary consciousness. This can happen only when people recognize how society works and challenge those in power. He believed that social change would occur when there was enough tension and conflict. Marx proposed a **dialectical model** of historical or social change, whereby two extreme positions would eventually necessitate some kind of compromise: the resulting "middle ground" would mean that society had actually moved forward. Any existing social arrangement, called the **thesis**, would inevitably generate its opposite, or **antithesis**, and the contradictions and conflicts between the two would lead to an altogether new social arrangement, or **synthesis**.

OFFSHOOTS Marx's work has been reinterpreted and applied in various ways, and conflict theory has evolved within the greater intellectual community. Despite Marx's single-minded focus on economic exploitation and transformation, his ideas have helped inspire theorists interested in all forms of power and inequality.

ALIENATION the sense of dissatisfaction the modern worker feels as a result of producing goods that are owned and controlled by someone else

IDEOLOGY a system of beliefs, attitudes, and values that directs a society and reproduces the status quo of the bourgeoisie

FALSE CONSCIOUSNESS a denial of the truth on the part of the oppressed when they fail to recognize that the interests of the ruling class are embedded in the dominant ideology

CLASS CONSCIOUSNESS the recognition of social inequality on the part of the oppressed, leading to revolutionary action

DIALECTICAL MODEL Karl Marx's model of historical change, whereby two extreme positions come into conflict and create some new outcome

THESIS the existing social arrangements in a dialectical model

ANTITHESIS the opposition to the existing arrangements in a dialectical model

SYNTHESIS the new social system created out of the conflict between thesis and antithesis in a dialectical model

The Frankfurt School Critical theorist Theodore Adorno with his colleagues in Frankfurt.

the postmodernists, who were considered the cutting edge of social theory in the 1980s and '90s (Habermas 1984, 1987).

Other modern perspectives have taken conflict theory's insights on economic inequality and adapted them to the study of contemporary inequalities of race, gender, and sexuality (Crenshaw et al. 1996; Matsuda et al. 1993). Beginning with the pioneering work of W.E.B. DuBois, sociology started to focus on inequalities of race and ethnicity, inspiring important studies about the causes and consequences of prejudice and discrimination and helping propel momentous social changes resulting from the civil rights movement of the 1960s.

Feminist theory developed alongside the twentieth-century women's rights movement. By applying assumptions about gender inequality to various social institutions—the family, education, the economy, or the media—feminist theory allows for a new way of understanding those institutions and the changing role of gender in contemporary society. Theorists such as Judith Butler (1999), bell hooks (2003), and Catharine MacKinnon (2005) link gender with inequality in other social hierarchies—race and ethnicity, class, and sexual orientation—and argue that gender and power are inextricably intertwined in our society.

The gay and lesbian rights movement that gained momentum in the 1970s and '80s inspired a new set of theoretical and conceptual tools for social scientists: **queer theory**. Queer theory proposes that categories of sexuality—homo, hetero, bi, trans—should be viewed as "social constructs" (Seidman

CRITICAL THEORY a contemporary form of conflict theory that criticizes many different systems and ideologies of domination and oppression

FEMINIST THEORY a theoretical approach that looks at gender inequities in society and the way that gender structures the social world

QUEER THEORY social theory about gender and sexual identity; emphasizes the importance of difference and rejects ideas of innate identities or restrictive categories

One of the most widely adopted forms of modern Marxism is called **critical theory** (also sometimes referred to as the Frankfurt School or neo-Marxism). From the 1930s to the 1960s, critical theory was arguably at the cutting edge of social theory. Critical theorists were among the first to see the importance of mass communications and popular culture as powerful ideological tools in capitalist societies. They coined the term "culture industries" to refer to these increasingly important social institutions, which came to dominate and permeate social life (Adorno and Horkheimer 1979). They also criticized the growing consumerism associated with the spread of capitalism, believing that this could ultimately lead to a decline in personal freedom and the decay of democracy (Marcuse 1964/1991). Critical theory influenced several generations of radical thinkers throughout Europe and the United States, inspiring the cultural studies movement and

bell hooks Feminist theorists such as bell hooks consider the intersection of gender and race.

2003). It asserts that no sexual category is fundamentally deviant or normal; we create such definitions, so we can change them as well. Indeed, some theorists, such as Marjorie Garber (1997), argue that strict categories themselves are no longer relevant and that more fluid notions of identity should replace conventional dichotomies such as gay/straight.

ADVANTAGES AND CRITIQUES One of Karl Marx's great contributions to the social sciences is the principle of **praxis**, or practical action: intellectuals should act on what they believe. Marx wished not only to describe the world but also to change it. Indeed, Marxist ideas have been important in achieving change through many twentieth-century social movements, including civil rights, antiwar, women's rights, gay rights, animal rights, environmentalism, and multiculturalism. If these groups had not protested the status quo, we might never have addressed some of the century's social problems. Conflict theory is useful in understanding not only macro-level social issues (such as systematic discrimination against minority groups) but also micro-level personal interactions (such as those between bosses and employees).

Conflict theory stands in sharp contrast to structural functionalism. Conflict theory argues that a social arrangement's existence does not mean that it's beneficial; it may merely represent the interests of those in power. The theory challenges the status quo and emphasizes the need for social upheaval. In focusing on tension and conflict, however, conflict theory can often ignore those parts of society that are truly orderly, stable, and enduring. Although society certainly has its share of disagreements, there are also shared values and common beliefs that hold it together. Conflict theory can be criticized for overlooking these less-controversial dimensions of social reality.

PRAXIS the application of theory to practical action in an effort to improve aspects of society

RATIONALIZATION the application of economic logic to human activity; the use of formal rules and regulations in order to maximize efficiency without consideration of subjective or individual concerns

BUREAUCRACIES secondary groups designed to perform tasks efficiently, characterized by specialization, technical competence, hierarchy, written rules, impersonality, and formal written communication

IRON CAGE Max Weber's pessimistic description of modern life, in which we are caught in bureaucratic structures that control our lives through rigid rules and rationalization

Weberian Theory

Max Weber (1864–1920) was another important European macrosociological theorist during the Industrial Revolution. His work forms another large branch of sociology's family tree, and his ideas continue to inspire in their current application, yet he is not always included among the three *major* branches of the discipline. Weberian theory is not a minor branch of sociology, nor is it considered merely an offshoot of one or the other major branches of the tree. It draws from a background shared by the other macro theorists but forms its own independent limb.

Max Weber

Weber grew up in the German city of Berlin. His father was a successful entrepreneur and member of a traditional and authoritarian aristocracy. Both his parents were Protestants and descendants of victims of religious persecution. Weber, though not religious himself, exhibited the relentless work ethic held in high regard by devout Protestants. Although he was sickly and withdrawn as a young man, work served as a way for him to rebel against his father and the leisure classes in general. He studied law and history and worked as a lawyer while establishing his credentials for a university teaching position.

While pursuing his studies, Weber remained at home and financially dependent on his father, a situation he came to resent. Eventually he broke away, marrying his second cousin in 1893 and beginning a career teaching economics at the University of Freiburg and later the University of Heidelberg. Weber rapidly established himself as a prominent member of the German intellectual scene. He might have continued in this manner had it not been for a disastrous visit from his parents in 1897, during which Weber fought bitterly with his father and threw him out of the house. When his father died a month later, Weber suffered a nervous breakdown that left him unable to work for several years. The strain of these events and years of incessant labor had apparently caught up with him. He eventually recovered and resumed his intense scholarship, but the breakdown left Weber disillusioned with the strict academic regimen.

Weber subsequently expressed a pessimistic view of social forces, such as the work ethic, that shaped modern life. Like other social theorists of his time, Weber was interested in the shift from a more traditional society to a modern industrial one. Perhaps his most overriding concern was with the process of **rationalization**, or the application of economic logic to all spheres of human activity. In *Economy and Society* (1921), Weber proposed that modern industrialized societies were characterized by efficient, goal-oriented, rule-governed **bureaucracies**. He believed that individual behavior was increasingly driven by such bureaucratic goals, which had become more important motivational factors than traditions, values, or emotions. Weber's classic sociological discussion of the origins of the capitalist system, *The Protestant Ethic and the Spirit of Capitalism* (1904), concluded with the image of people trapped by their industrious way of life in what he called an **iron cage** of bureaucratic rules. He believed that contemporary life was filled with **disenchantment** (similar to Durkheim's concept of anomie and Marx's of alienation) as the inevitable result of the dehumanizing features of the bureaucracies that dominated the modern social landscape.

Weber provided invaluable insights into the nature of society that continue to inspire sociologists today. For instance, George Ritzer has applied Weber's theories of bureaucracy and rationality to the fast-food industry and has warned about "McDonaldization" creeping into many other aspects of contemporary life. The key concepts we have touched on here will be expanded as we apply Weberian theory to a variety of topics in upcoming chapters of the text. In addition to making some of the most important contributions to theory within the discipline, Weber was also influential in improving research methods by suggesting that researchers avoid imposing their own opinions on their scientific analysis; we'll examine these ideas more closely in Chapter 2.

Weber's work served as a bridge between early social theory, which focused primarily on the macro level of society, and subsequent theories that focused more intently on the micro level. He was interested in how individual motivation led to certain social actions, and how those actions helped shape society as a whole. Unlike Marx and Durkheim, Weber was cautious about attributing any reality to social institutions or forces independent of individual action and meaningful thought. He invoked the German term *verstehen* ("empathic understanding") to describe how a social scientist should study human action: with a kind of scientific empathy for actors' experiences, intentions, and actions. In this way, Weber helped lay the groundwork for the third grand theory in sociology.

Microsociological Theory

As the twentieth century dawned and the careers of the macro theorists such as Durkheim, Marx, and Weber matured, political, cultural, and academic power began to shift from Europe. As manifested by the waves of emigrants leaving the Old World for the New, America was seen as the land of opportunity, both material and intellectual. So it was in the twentieth century, and increasingly in the United States, that the discipline of sociology continued to develop and the ideas of its third major school of thought began to coalesce.

Symbolic Interactionism

Sociology's third grand theory, **symbolic interactionism** (or interactionist theory), proved its greatest influence through much of the 1900s. It is America's unique contribution to the discipline and an answer to many of the criticisms of other paradigms. Symbolic interactionism helps us explain both our individual personalities and the ways in which we are all linked together; it allows us to understand the processes by which social order and social change are constructed. As a theoretical perspective, it is vital, versatile, and still evolving.

FOUNDER AND KEY CONTRIBUTIONS Symbolic interactionism is derived largely from the teachings of George Herbert Mead (1863–1931). But there were many others involved in the development of this particular school of thought, and it is worthwhile to examine the social context in which they lived and worked.

At the start of the twentieth century, sociology was still something of an import from the European intellectual scene, and American practitioners had just begun developing their own ideas regarding the nature and workings of society. The University of Chicago of the 1920s provided a stimulating intellectual setting for a handful of academics who built on each other's work and advanced what became known as the first new major branch within the discipline. Since there were so few social theorists in the country, the head of the department, Albion Small, a philosopher by training, recruited professors from various eastern colleges who had often studied other disciplines such as theology and psychology. The fledgling sociology department grew to include such influential members as Robert Park, W. I. Thomas, Charles Horton Cooley, and later Mead and Herbert Blumer. This group, the theories they developed together, and the way they went about studying the social world are frequently referred to (either individually or collectively) as the **Chicago School** of sociology.

Chicago was in many ways a frontier city in the early twentieth century. Rapidly transformed by industrialization, immigration, and ethnic diversity, Chicago became a unique laboratory in which to practice a new type of sociology that differed both theoretically and methodologically from the European models. Instead of doing comparative and historical work like the macro theorists before them, the members of the Chicago School went out into the city to conduct interviews and collect observational data. Their studies were particularly inspired by Max Weber's concept of *verstehen* as the proper attitude to adopt in the field. Their focus was on the micro level of everyday interactions (such as race relations in

George Herbert Mead

DISENCHANTMENT the rationalization of modern society

VERSTEHEN "empathic understanding"; Weber's term to describe good social research, which tries to understand the meanings that individuals attach to various aspects of social reality

SYMBOLIC INTERACTIONISM a paradigm that sees interaction and meaning as central to society and assumes that meanings are not inherent but are created through interaction

CHICAGO SCHOOL a type of sociology practiced at the University of Chicago in the 1920s and 1930s that centered on urban settings and field research methods

GLOBAL PERSPECTIVE
Eurocentrism and Sociological Theory

You might get the impression from this chapter that the major sociological theorists were all either European or American. In fact, some ideas central to sociological theory were proposed in Asia, Africa, and the Middle East centuries before Marx, Weber, and Durkheim were even born, but we give these Western thinkers all the credit. Why?

Both the social world and social theory are often **Eurocentric**: they tend to privilege Europe and the West over other cultures. This means that hierarchies of global power, in which superpowers such as the United States and former colonial rulers such as Britain and France dominate, are replicated in academic disciplines like sociology. Scholars who work against inequality and exploitation should note this distressing irony.

EUROCENTRIC the tendency to favor European or Western histories, cultures, and values over those of non-Western societies

One influential non-Western thinker was Ibn Khaldun (1332–1406), an Arab Muslim philosopher and politician who lived in fourteenth-century North Africa. His coining of the term *as sabiyah*, or "social cohesion," precedes Durkheim's work on the same subject by more than 500 years, and his argument that larger social and historical forces shape individual lives predates Mills's insight about sociology as "the intersection of biography and history" by almost 600 years! Yet Khaldun is rarely credited for proposing sociology as a discipline—*ilm alumran*, he called it, or "the science of civilization." This honor is reserved for French scholar Auguste Comte, working centuries later in the West.

Also overlooked in conventional histories of sociology are Indian scholar Benoy Sarkar (1887–1949), Filipino activist and poet José Rizal (1861–1896), and Japanese folklorist Kunio Yanagita (1875–1962)—all of whom applied sociological insights to the problems of their nations. Sarkar explored India's religious divisions, Rizal analyzed the Philippines' fight for independence from Spain, and Yanagita used qualitative methods to explore Japan's culture and its long-standing isolationism. They have received virtually no notice for their achievements outside their own countries (Alatas and Sinha 2001).

Filipino sociologist Clarence Batan (2004) argues that Western theorists like Marx, Weber, and Durkheim may inspire non-Western scholars but that their theories arose in response to specific social problems that were particular to Western societies. Non-Western societies face different issues, including the legacy of colonialism imposed by the Western countries from which those classical sociological theories sprang. Batan calls for sociologists in non-Western countries to respond to the needs of their societies by developing new theoretical frameworks that take postcolonial realities into account. Batan himself, along with other contemporary non-Western sociologists, works toward this goal every day in his research and teaching. Shouldn't your sociology professors do the same?

Ibn Khaldun

urban neighborhoods) as the building blocks of larger social phenomena (such as racial inequality).

The new school of thought was strongly influenced by a philosophical perspective called **pragmatism**, developed largely by William James and John Dewey, which was gaining acceptance among American social theorists in the early 1900s. James was a Harvard professor whose interests spanned art, medicine, law, education, theology, philosophy, and psychology;

PRAGMATISM a perspective that assumes organisms (including humans) make practical adaptations to their environments; humans do this through cognition, interpretation, and interaction

he also traveled extensively and was acquainted with some of the most important scholars of the time. To James, pragmatism meant seeking the truth of an idea by evaluating its usefulness in everyday life; in other words, if it works, it's true! He thought that living in the world involved making practical adaptations to whatever we encountered; if those adaptations made our lives run more smoothly, then the ideas behind them must be both useful and true. James's ideas inspired educational psychologist and philosopher John Dewey, who also grappled with pragmatism's main questions: How do we adapt to our environments? How do we acquire the knowledge that allows us to act in our everyday lives? Unlike the social Darwinists, pragmatists implied that the process of adaptation is essentially immediate and that it involves conscious thought. George Herbert Mead would be the one who eventually pulled these ideas (and others, too) together into a theory meant to address questions about the relationship between thought and action, the individual and society.

Mead came from a progressive family and grew up in the Midwest and Northeast during the late 1800s, where his father, a professor of theology at Oberlin College, died when George was a teenager, and his widowed mother eventually became president of Mount Holyoke College. Mead attended college at Oberlin and Harvard, and did his graduate studies in psychology at the universities of Leipzig and Berlin in Germany. Before he became a full-time professor of psychology at the University of Michigan and later the University of Chicago, Mead waited tables and did railroad surveying and construction work. He was also a tutor to William James's family in Cambridge, Massachusetts; since his later theories were influenced by James, we can only wonder exactly who was tutoring whom in this arrangement! Mead's background and training uniquely positioned him to bridge the gap between sociology and psychology and to address the links between the individual and society.

Mead proposed that both human development and the meanings we assign to everyday objects and events are fundamentally social processes; they require the interaction of multiple individuals. And what is crucial to the development of self and society is language, the means by which we communicate with one another. For Mead, there is no mind without language, and language itself is a product of social interactions (1934, pp. 191–92). According to Mead, the most important human behaviors consist of linguistic "gestures," such as words and facial expressions. People develop the ability to engage in conversation using these gestures; further, both society and individual selves are constructed through this kind of symbolic communication. Mead argued that we use language to "name ourselves, think about ourselves, talk to ourselves, and feel proud or ashamed of ourselves" and that "we can act toward ourselves in all the ways we can act toward others" (Hewitt 2000, p. 10). He was curious about how the mind develops but did not believe that it develops separately from its social environment. For Mead, then, society and self are created through communicative acts such as speech and gestures; the individual personality is shaped by society, and vice versa.

Herbert Blumer (1900–1987), a graduate student and later a professor at the University of Chicago, was closely associated with Mead and was largely credited with continuing Mead's life's work. While completing his master's degree, Blumer played football for the University of Missouri Tigers, and during the 1920s and 1930s he maintained dual careers as a sociology professor and a professional football player for the former Chicago Cardinals. On Mondays, he would often come to class wrapped in bandages after a tough Sunday

Herbert Blumer

W.E.B. DuBois

game. What he did off the gridiron, however, was of critical importance to the discipline. Blumer appealed for researchers to get "down and dirty" with the dynamics of social life. He also published a clear and compelling series of works based on Mead's fundamental ideas. After Mead's death in 1931, Blumer gave Mead's theory the name it now goes by: symbolic interactionism. Thus, Mead and Blumer became the somewhat-unwitting founders of a much larger theoretical perspective. Blumer's long career at the University of Chicago and later at the University of California, Berkeley, ensured the training of many future scholars and secured the inclusion of symbolic interactionism as one of the major schools of thought within the discipline.

Despite its geographical location in a city full of real-world inequality (or perhaps because of it), the Chicago School of sociology had very few women or people of color among its membership. Take W.E.B. DuBois and Jane Addams, for example: these two scholars were neither students nor faculty members at the University of Chicago, although both are often associated with Chicago School perspectives, values, and methods. Both led the way for other minorities and women to become influential scholars in the discipline of sociology.

William Edward Burghardt (W.E.B.) DuBois (1868–1963) was a notable pioneer in the study of race relations as a professor of sociology at Atlanta University and one of the most influential African American leaders of his time. After becoming the first African American to earn a PhD from Harvard University, DuBois did groundbreaking research on the history of the slave trade, post–Civil War reconstruction, the problems of urban ghetto life, and the nature of black American society. DuBois was so brilliant and prolific that it is often said that all subsequent studies of race and racial inequality in America depend to some degree on his work. Throughout his life, DuBois was involved in various forms of social activism. He was an indispensable forerunner in the civil rights movement; among his many civic and political achievements, DuBois was a founding member, in 1909, of the National Association for the Advancement of Colored People (NAACP), an organization committed to the cause of ending racism and injustice.

Jane Addams

Erving Goffman

Because of his anti-racist, anti-poverty, and anti-war activism, DuBois was targeted by FBI Director J. Edgar Hoover and Senator Joseph McCarthy as a communist. However, he did not become a member of the Communist Party until he was 93 years old, and then only did so as a form of political protest against the persecution of its members by the U.S. government. Eventually, DuBois became disillusioned by the persistent injustices of American society and emigrated to Ghana, where he died at 95, one year before the historic Civil Rights Act of 1964 was signed into law.

Jane Addams (1860–1935) was another pioneer in the field of sociology whose numerous accomplishments range from the halls of academia to the forefront of social activism. Though she never officially joined the faculty because she feared it would curtail her political activism, Addams did teach extension courses at the University of Chicago and was among a handful of women teaching in American universities at the time. Though not a mother herself, Addams believed that women have a special kind of responsibility toward solving social problems because they are trained to care for others. She was one of the first proponents of applied sociology—addressing the most pressing problems of her day through hands-on work with the people and places that were the subject of her research. This practical approach is perhaps best demonstrated by Hull House, the Chicago community center she established in 1889 to offer shelter, medical care, legal advice, training, and education to new immigrants, single mothers, and the poor. As a result of her commitment to delivering support and services where they were most needed, Addams is often considered the founder of what is now a separate field outside the discipline: social work. Addams also helped found two important organizations that continue to fight for freedom and equality today: the American Civil Liberties Union (ACLU) and, along with W.E.B. DuBois, the NAACP. She served as the president of the Women's International League for Peace and Freedom and in 1931 became the first American woman to receive the Nobel Peace Prize.

DRAMATURGY an approach pioneered by Erving Goffman in which social life is analyzed in terms of its similarities to theatrical performance

ORIGINAL PRINCIPLES For symbolic interactionists, society is produced and reproduced through our interactions with each other by means of language and our interpretations of that language. Symbolic interactionism sees face-to-face interaction as the building block of everything else in society, because it is through interaction that we create a meaningful social reality.

Here are the three basic tenets of symbolic interactionism, as laid out by Blumer (1969, p. 2). First, *we act toward things on the basis of their meanings*. For example, a tree can provide a shady place to rest, or it can be an obstacle to building a road or home; each of these meanings suggests a different set of actions. This is as true for physical objects like trees as it is for people (like mothers or cops), institutions (church or school), beliefs (honesty or equality), or any social activity. Second, *meanings are not inherent; rather, they are negotiated through interaction with others*. That is, whether the tree is an obstacle or an oasis is not an intrinsic quality of the tree itself but rather something that people must figure out among themselves. The same tree can mean one thing to one person and something else to another. And third, *meanings can change or be modified through interaction*. For example, the contractor who sees the tree as an obstacle might be persuaded to spare it by the neighbor who appreciates its shade. Now the tree means the same thing to both of them: it is something to protect and build around rather than to condemn and bulldoze.

Symbolic interactionism proposes that social facts exist only because we create and re-create them through our interactions; this gives the theory wide explanatory power and a versatility that allows it to address any sociological issue. Although symbolic interactionism is focused on how self and society develop through interaction with others, it is useful in explaining and analyzing a wide variety of specific social issues, from inequalities of race and gender to the group dynamics of families or co-workers.

OFFSHOOTS Symbolic interactionism opened the door for innovative sociologists who focused on social acts (such as face-to-face interaction) rather than social facts (such as vast bureaucratic institutions). They were able to extend the field in a variety of ways, allowing new perspectives to come under the umbrella of symbolic interactionism.

Erving Goffman (1922–1982) furthered symbolic interactionist conceptions of the self in a seemingly radical way, indicating that the self is essentially "on loan" to us from society; it is created through interaction with others and hence ever-changing within various social contexts. For example, you may want to make a different kind of impression on a first date than you do on a job interview or when you face an opponent in a game of poker. Goffman used the theatrical metaphor of **dramaturgy** to describe the ways in which we engage in a strategic presentation of ourselves to others. In this way, he elaborated on Mead's ideas in a specific fashion, utilizing a wide range of data to help support his arguments.

Harold Garfinkel, the founder of **ethnomethodology** (the study of "folk methods," or everyday analysis of interaction), maintains that as members of society we must acquire the necessary knowledge and skills to act practically in our everyday lives (Garfinkel 1967). He argues that much of this knowledge remains in the background, "seen but unnoticed," and that we assume that others have the same knowledge we do when we interact with them. These assumptions allow us to make meaning out of even seemingly troublesome or ambiguous events; but such shared understandings can also be quite precarious, and there is a good deal of work required to sustain them, even as we are unaware that we are doing so.

Conversation analysis, pioneered by sociologists at the University of California, Los Angeles, is also related to symbolic interactionism. It is based on the ethnomethodological idea that as everyday actors we are constantly analyzing and giving meaning to our social world (Schegloff 1986, 1999; Clayman 2002). Conversation analysts are convinced that the best place to look for the social processes of meaning-production is in naturally occurring conversation and that the best way to get at the meanings an everyday actor gives to the things others say and do is to look closely at how he responds. Conversation analysts therefore use highly technical methods to scrutinize each conversational turn closely, operating on the assumption that any larger social phenomenon is constructed step-by-step through interaction.

ADVANTAGES AND CRITIQUES As society changes, so must the discipline that studies it, and symbolic interactionism has invigorated sociology in ways that are linked to the past and looking toward the future. The founding of symbolic interactionism provided a new and different way of looking at the world. It is "the only perspective that assumes an active, expressive model of the human actor and that treats the individual and the social at the same level of analysis" (O'Brien and Kollock 1997, p. 39). Therein lies much of its power and its appeal.

As a new school of thought focusing on the micro level of society, symbolic interactionism was not always met with immediate approval by the academy. Over time, symbolic interactionism has been integrated relatively seamlessly into sociology, and its fundamental precepts have become widely accepted. During the second half of the twentieth century, the scope of symbolic interactionism widened, its topics multiplied, and its theoretical linkages became more varied. In fact, there was some concern that symbolic interactionism was expanding so much that it risked erupting into something else entirely (Fine 1993). One of symbolic interactionism's most enduring contributions is in the area of research methods. Practices such as ethnography and conversation analysis are data-rich, technically complex, and empirically well grounded (Katz 1997; Schegloff 1999), giving us new insights into perennial questions about social life.

As a relative newcomer to the field of social theory, symbolic interactionism was dubbed "the loyal opposition" (Mullins 1973) by those who saw it solely as a reaction or as merely a supplement to the more dominant macrosociological theories that preceded it. Gary Fine sums up the critiques in this way: symbolic interactionism is "apolitical (and hence, supportive of the status quo), unscientific (hence, little more than tenured journalism), hostile to the classical questions of macrosociology (hence, limited to social psychology), and astructural (hence, fundamentally nonsociological)" (1993, p. 65). Critiques argue that the scope of symbolic interactionism is limited, that it cannot address the most important sociological issues, and that its authority is restricted to the study of face-to-face interaction.

Each of these critiques has been answered over the years. Ultimately, some critics have seen the usefulness of an interactionist perspective and have even begun incorporating it into more macro work. Even in the hotly contested micro-versus-macro debate, a kind of détente has been established, recognizing that all levels of analysis are necessary for sociological understanding and that interactionist theories and methods are critical for a full picture of social life.

> **ETHNOMETHODOLOGY** the study of "folk methods" and background knowledge that sustains a shared sense of reality in everyday interactions
>
> **CONVERSATION ANALYSIS** a sociological approach that looks at how we create meaning in naturally occurring conversation, often by taping conversations and examining their transcripts

DATA WORKSHOP
Analyzing Media and Pop Culture

Theories of Celebrity Gossip

TMZ, which debuted in 2005, has become one of the most popular celebrity gossip sites in the world. It is consistently among the top 100 websites (of any kind) in the United States, with upward of 25 million unique visitors a month. TMZ provides users with up-to-the-minute pop culture news, publishing hundreds of posts each day exposing the real and rumored doings of celebrities. It has become the go-to site any time a celebrity gets arrested, dies, goes to rehab, cheats, or behaves badly in some other way.

TMZ is part of a new breed of celebrity gossip outlets, including PerezHilton, Gawker, and PopSugar, that have radically transformed the way that celebrities and other public figures are covered in the media. They're providing more coverage than ever, and at greater speed. Stories that used to take at least a week to appear in printed gossip magazines such as *People* or *Us* can now be posted online nearly instantaneously. TMZ was the first outlet to

Celebrity Gossip TMZ was the first outlet to break the news of Michael Jackson's death in 2009.

break the news of Michael Jackson's death in 2009, beating the mainstream media by one hour. Readers can also jump in and respond in real time.

It's not just the volume or speed of delivery that's different; celebrity gossip sites are changing the substance of the coverage as well. Traditionally, print magazines or mainstream television programs such as *Entertainment Tonight* or *E! News* provided mostly flattering coverage of celebrities. They were unwilling to report too many negative stories because they relied on the goodwill of celebrities to gain access into their lives. To be sure, there is no shortage of promotional puff pieces and lightweight fare without much bite. More recently, however, gossip sites such as TMZ have been taking a harsher, more critical stance toward their subjects. Gossip sites are also using the kind of investigative journalism that was formerly reserved for politicians and business executives, and they are investigating a wider range of celebrities. TMZ now regularly includes athletes among the celebrities they cover, spinning off TMZ Sports as a dedicated space for sports-related gossip.

In 2014, TMZ got the scoop on an important sports story involving racially inflammatory remarks made by billionaire Donald Sterling, then owner of the Los Angeles Clippers basketball team. Sterling was recorded in a phone conversation berating his personal assistant (and purported girlfriend) V. Stiviano for having posted pictures on Instagram of herself with former L.A. Lakers star Magic Johnson, and asking her not to broadcast that she is associating with black people. Within hours the story was picked up by every major news organization. The public backlash was fierce and swift, as players and fans threatened to sit out games. The National Basketball Association (NBA) fined Sterling $2.5 million and issued him a lifetime ban. He was later forced to sell the team. Whatever your opinion of tabloid news, and many people

regard it as just mean, stupid, or shallow, you don't have to enjoy celebrity gossip to see its sociological relevance.

For this Data Workshop, we'd like you to immerse yourself in the celebrity gossip site of your choice. Pick three stories to work with. Scrutinize the pictures, read the headlines and text carefully, and review the reader comments. Then consider how you might answer the following questions according to each of sociology's three major schools of thought:

1. Structural Functionalism
What is the function (or functions) of celebrity gossip for society? What purpose(s) does it serve, and how does it help society maintain stability and order? Discuss how notions of the sacred and profane are characterized. Are there manifest and latent functions of celebrity gossip? And are there any dysfunctions in it?

2. Conflict Theory
What forms of inequality are revealed in celebrity gossip? In particular, what does it have to say about class, race, gender, sexuality, or other inequalities? Whose interests are being served and who gets exploited? Who suffers and who benefits from celebrity gossip?

3. Symbolic Interactionism
What does celebrity gossip mean to society as a whole? What does it mean to individual members of society? Can gossip have different meanings for different individuals or groups of individuals? How do those meanings get constructed in interaction? And how does celebrity gossip shape and influence our everyday lives?

There are two options for completing this Data Workshop:

PREP-PAIR-SHARE Print out your three stories and bring them to class. Consider how each of the three sets of questions might be applied. Jot down your thoughts and make note of particular images and text. Get together in groups of two or three, and talk about your findings. How does each sociological theory fit with your examples? What new insights were provided by each perspective?

DO-IT-YOURSELF Select the material you will analyze, and answer each of the three sets of questions in a three-page essay. Discuss the main principles of the three theoretical perspectives and explain how each can be applied. You will want to include specific examples from your chosen stories to illustrate your points. Did the theories overlap at all, or did they contradict each other? Was there any one theory you felt did a better or worse job of explaining celebrity gossip? Attach printouts of the stories to your paper.

New Theoretical Approaches

Because the three major schools of thought and their offshoots all have weaknesses as well as strengths, they will probably never fully explain the totality of social phenomena, even when taken together. And because society itself is always changing, there are always new phenomena to explain. So new perspectives will, and indeed must, continue to arise. In this section, we will consider two more contemporary approaches: postmodernism and midrange theory. Both grew out of the deep groundwork established by the other major schools of thought within sociology, as well as by looking beyond the confines of the discipline for inspiration. Each is a response to conditions both in the fast-changing social world around us and within the ongoing intellectual dialogues taking place among those continuing to study our times and selves.

Postmodern Theory

In the late twentieth century, some social thinkers looked at the proliferation of theories and data and began to question whether we could ever know society or ourselves with any certainty. What is truth, and who has the right to claim it? Or, for that matter, what is reality, and how can it be known? In an era of increasing doubt and cynicism, has meaning become meaningless? **Postmodernism**, a theory that encompasses a wide range of areas—from art and architecture, music and film, to communications and technology—addresses these and other questions.

The postmodern perspective developed primarily out of the French intellectual scene in the second half of the twentieth century and is still associated with three of its most important proponents. It's probably worth noting that postmodernists themselves don't really like that label, but nonetheless Jacques Derrida (1930–2004), Jean Baudrillard (1929–2007), and Michel Foucault (1926–1984) are the major figures most often included in the group.

In order to understand postmodernism, we first need to juxtapose it with **modernism**, the movement against which it reacted. Modernism is both a historical period and an ideological stance that began with the eighteenth-century Enlightenment, or Age of Reason. Modernist thought values scientific knowledge, a linear (or timeline-like) view of history, and a belief in the universality of human nature. In postmodernism, on the other hand, there are no absolutes—no claims to truth, reason, right, order, or stability. Everything is therefore relative—fragmented, temporary, and contingent. Postmodernists believe that certainty is illusory and prefer to play with the possibilities created by fluidity, complexity, multidimensionality, and even nonsense. They propose that there are no universal human truths from which we can interpret the meaning of existence. On one hand, postmodernism can be celebrated as a liberating influence that rescues us from the stifling effects of rationality and tradition. On the other hand, it can be condemned as a detrimental influence that imprisons us in a world of relativity, nihilism, and chaos.

Postmodernists are also critical of what they call "grand narratives," overarching stories and theories that justify dominant beliefs and give a (false) sense of order and coherence to the world. Postmodernists are interested in **deconstruction**, or taking apart and examining these stories and theories. For example, they claim that "factual" accounts of history are no more accurate than those that might be found in fiction. They prefer the notion of mini-narratives, or small-scale stories, that describe individual or group practices rather than narratives that attempt to be universal or global. These mini-narratives can then be combined in a variety of ways, creating a collage of meaning.

One way of understanding what postmodernism looks like is to examine how it has crept into our popular culture. Hip-hop is an example of a postmodern art form. It is a hybrid that borrows from other established genres, from rhythm and blues

POSTMODERNISM a paradigm that suggests that social reality is diverse, pluralistic, and constantly in flux

MODERNISM a paradigm that places trust in the power of science and technology to create progress, solve problems, and improve life

DECONSTRUCTION a type of critical postmodern analysis that involves taking apart or disassembling old ways of thinking

Jacques Derrida, Michel Foucault, and Jean Baudrillard

to rock and reggae. Hip-hop also takes samples from existing songs, mixes these with new musical tracks, and overlays it all with rap lyrics, resulting in a unique new sound. Mash-ups are another postmodern twist in music. Take for instance the *Grey Album* by DJ Danger Mouse, which uses tracks from the Beatles' classic *White Album* and combines them with Jay-Z's *Black Album* to create something wholly new yet borrowed.

Many resist the postmodern position against essential meaning or truth; the rise in religious fundamentalism may be a reaction to the postmodern view, an expression of the desire to return to absolute truths and steadfast traditions. Sociologists are quick to criticize postmodernism for discarding the scientific method and the knowledge they believe it has generated. Social leaders with a conservative agenda have been suspicious of the postmodern impulse to dismiss moral standards. While it is clear that many people criticize postmodernism, a much larger number are probably oblivious to it, which in itself may be more damning than any other response.

Although it is not a widely practiced perspective, postmodernism *has* nevertheless gained supporters. Those who challenge the status quo, whether in the arts, politics, or the academy, find attractive postmodernism's ability to embrace a multiplicity of powerful and promising alternatives. At the very least, postmodernism allows us to question scientific ideals about clarity and coherence, revealing inherent shortcomings and weaknesses in our current arguments and providing a way toward a deeper, more nuanced understanding of social life. As one of the most contemporary of the theoretical perspectives, postmodernism corresponds to the Information Age and feels natural and intuitive for many students whose lives are immersed in this world. By focusing on individuals and small-scale activities in which change happens on a local, limited basis, postmodernism offers an alternative to such cultural trends as consumerism and globalization. However unwelcome the theory might be to some critics, it is likely that the postmodern shifts we have seen in society (in music and films, for example) will continue.

Midrange Theory

The second new theoretical approach is **midrange theory**. It shares some views with postmodernism, especially in its preference for mini-narratives over sweeping statements or "grand theories" made by the classical social theorists—a period dominated by what Robert Merton calls "total sociological systems" (1996, p. 46), which provided an overarching, comprehensive explanation of society as a whole.

MIDRANGE THEORY an approach that integrates empiricism and grand theory

Merton feared that an uncritical reverence for classical theory and an excessive attachment to tradition could impede the flow of new ideas and was just as likely to hold sociology back as to advance it. Because classical theories sought to develop large-scale theoretical systems that applied to the most macro level of society, they were often extremely difficult to test or research in any practical way. As one critic lamented, too "many sociological products can—effectively and unfortunately—be considered both bad science and bad literature" (Boudon 1991, p. 522).

To counter this tendency, Merton proposed that sociologists focus more on "theories of the middle range." Midrange (or middle range) theory is not a theory of something in particular, but rather a *style* of theorizing. It is an attempt not so much to make the elusive macro-micro link, but to strike a balance somewhere between those polarities, shifting both the sights and the process of doing sociology. Work in this vein concentrates on incorporating research questions and empirical data into smaller-scale theories that eventually build into a more comprehensive body of sociological theory. Midrange theories are those "that lie between the minor but necessary working hypotheses that evolve in abundance during day-to-day research and the all-inclusive systematic efforts to develop a unified theory that will explain" the whole social world (Merton 1996, p. 41).

Since the 1990s and 2000s, a host of sociologists have taken up the call to midrange theory, from Sharon Hays's study of the contradictions within modern motherhood (1996) to Dalton Conley's work on racial identity (2000) and his examination of what constitutes leisure in the digital age (2009). Midrange theory connects specific research projects that generate empirical data with larger-scale theories about social structure. It aims to build knowledge cumulatively while offering a way to make sociology more effective as a science rather than just a way of thinking. With more sociologists appreciating such a stance, midrange theory is helping to push the discipline forward into the sociology of the future.

CLOSING COMMENTS

We hope that this chapter has given you a thorough and compelling introduction to the study of sociology and that perhaps you, too, will find it an appealing pursuit. Many of you will have already started a sociological journey, although likely a casual or personal one . . . until now. The popularity of reality TV speaks to our fascination with the everyday lives of other people, whether *Hoarders* or *Ice Road Truckers* or *The Real Housewives of* _____ (fill in the blank). As students of sociology, we are interested in everyday life because we are excited to understand more about how its patterns and processes create our larger social reality. As we become better social analysts, using strategies to set aside any blinding preconceptions or distracting conclusions, we can become better acquainted with some of the fundamental tools that can

Table 1.1 Theory in Everyday Life

Perspective	Approach to Society	Case Study: College Admissions in the United States
Structural Functionalism	Assumes that society is a unified whole that functions because of the contributions of its separate structures.	Those who are admitted are worthy and well qualified, while those who are not admitted do not deserve to be. There are other places in society for them besides the university.
Conflict Theory	Sees social conflict as the basis of society and social change and emphasizes a materialist view of society, a critical view of the status quo, and a dynamic model of historical change.	Admissions decisions may be made on the basis of criteria other than grades and scores. For example, some applicants may get in because their fathers are major university donors, while others may get in because of their talents in sports or music. Some may be denied admission based on criteria like race, gender, or sexuality.
Symbolic Interactionism	Asserts that interaction and meaning are central to society and assumes that meanings are not inherent but are created through interaction.	University admissions processes are all about self-presentation and meaning-making in interaction. How does an applicant present himself or herself to impress the admissions committee? How does the admissions committee develop an understanding of the kind of applicant it's looking for? How do applicants interpret their acceptances and rejections?
Postmodernism	Suggests that social reality is diverse, pluralistic, and constantly in flux.	An acceptance doesn't mean you're smart, and a rejection doesn't mean you're stupid; be careful of any "facts" you may be presented with, as they are illusory and contingent.

turn our natural curiosity into scientific inquiry. A sociological perspective allows us to grasp the connection between our individual experiences and the forces and structures of society. As Bernard McGrane says, "Sociology is both dangerous and liberating" (1994, p. 10), as much because of what we can learn about ourselves as because of what we can learn about the world around us.

As a discipline, sociology possesses some of the qualities of the society it seeks to understand: it is broad, complex, and ever-changing. This can make mastering sociology a rather unwieldy business, as much for the students and teachers who grapple with it in the classroom as for the experts out working in the field. We want you to become familiar with the members of sociology's family tree from its varied historical roots to the tips of its offshoots that might one day become important future branches. Because we have no

single acknowledged universal sociological theory that satisfactorily explains all social phenomena (despite claims otherwise by some theorists), new theories can be developed all the time. Social theory tries to explain what is happening in, to, and around us. For any and every possible new, different, or important phenomenon—from the most mundane personal experience to questions of ultimate global significance—sociologists will attempt to explain it, understand it, analyze it, and predict its future. By looking at the development of the discipline, we are reminded that the contemporary grows out of the classical, and that older theories inspire and provoke newer ones. Theorists past and present remain engaged in a continual and evolving dialogue through their ideas and their work, and until such time as society is completely explained, the branches of sociology's family tree will continue to grow in remarkable ways.

Everything You Need to Know about Sociology

> **"Sociology is the systematic or scientific study of human society and social behavior, from large-scale institutions and mass culture to small groups and individual interactions."**

THEORIES OF SOCIOLOGY

* **Structural functionalism:** the assumption that society is a unified whole that functions because of the contributions of its separate structures

* **Conflict theory:** the belief that social conflict is the basis of society and social change that emphasizes a materialist view of society, a critical view of the status quo, and a dynamic model of historical change

* **Weberian theory:** the application of economic logic to human activity that uses formal rules and regulations in order to maximize efficiency without consideration of subjective or individual concerns

* **Symbolic interactionism:** approach that sees interaction and meaning as central to society and assumes that meanings are not inherent but are created through interaction

* **Postmodern theory:** approach that suggests that social reality is diverse, pluralistic, and constantly in flux

* **Midrange theory:** an approach that integrates empiricism and grand theory

REVIEW

1. What does it mean to possess a sociological imagination? Think of your favorite food. What historical events had to happen and what institutions have to function in order for this food to be available? What sort of meanings does it have?

2. How does the level of analysis you adopt affect your assumptions about how society works? Could Pam Fishman have done her research on gender and power in conversations from a macro perspective? Perhaps with a survey? Could Christine Williams have done her research on gender and power in occupations from a micro perspective? Perhaps with interviews? How might this change their conclusions?

3. Symbolic interactionism argues that meanings are not inherent in things themselves but are socially derived and negotiated through interaction with others. Think of some recent fashion trend. Can you describe this trend in terms of what it means to those who embrace it? What sorts of interactions produce and maintain this meaning?

Key Works in Sociology

Year	Work
1837	Harriet Martineau, *Society in America*
1838	Auguste Comte, *Cours de Philosophie Positive*
1848	Karl Marx & Friedrich Engels, *Communist Manifesto*
1867	Karl Marx, *Das Kapital*
1893	Émile Durkheim, *The Division of Labor in Society*
1897	Émile Durkheim, *Suicide*
1902	Charles Cooley, *Human Nature and the Social Order*
1903	W. E. B. DuBois, *The Souls of Black Folk*
1904	Max Weber, *The Protestant Ethic and the Spirit of Capitalism*
1912	Émile Durkheim, *The Elementary Forms of the Religious Life*
1921	Max Weber, *Economy and Society*
1934	George Herbert Mead, *Mind, Self, and Society*
1937	Talcott Parsons, *The Structure of Social Action*
1949	Robert Merton, *Social Theory and Social Structure*
1956	C. Wright Mills, *The Power Elite*
1959	C. Wright Mills, *The Sociological Imagination*
1959	Erving Goffman, *The Presentation of Self in Everyday Life*
1966	Peter Berger & Thomas Luckmann, *The Social Construction of Reality*
1981	bell hooks, *Ain't I a Woman?*
1984	Pierre Bourdieu, *Distinction*
1989	Catharine MacKinnon, *Toward a Feminist Theory of the State*

EXPLORE

The Rationality of Irrationality

George Ritzer applied Max Weber's theories of bureaucracy and rationality to the fast-food industry. Visit the Everyday Sociology Blog to learn how Weber's theories adapt to everyday life.

http://wwnPag.es/trw401

CHAPTER 2

Studying Social Life: Sociological Research Methods

Humorist Dave Barry, the Pulitzer Prize–winning columnist and author, has written many entertaining articles as a reporter and social commentator. Some of his thoughts on college, however, seem particularly appropriate for this chapter. In one of his most popular essays, Barry advises students not to choose a major that involves "known facts" and "right answers" but rather a subject in which "nobody really understands what anybody else is talking about, and which involves virtually no actual facts" (Barry 1987, p. 203). For example, sociology:

For sheer lack of intelligibility, sociology is far and away the number-one subject. I sat through hundreds of hours of sociology courses, and read gobs of sociology writing, and I never once heard or read a coherent statement. This is because sociologists want to be considered scientists, so they spend most of their time translating simple, obvious observations into scientific-sounding code. If you plan to major in sociology, you'll have to learn to do the same thing. For example, suppose you have observed that children cry when they fall down. You should write: "Methodological observation of the sociometrical behavior tendencies of prematurated isolates indicates that a causal relationship exists between groundward tropism and lachrimatory, or 'crying' behavior forms." If you can keep this up for fifty or sixty pages, you will get a large government grant.

Although Barry exaggerates a bit, if there weren't some truth to what he is saying, his joke would be meaningless. While sociologists draw much of their inspiration from the natural (or "hard") sciences (such as chemistry and biology) and try to study society in a scientific way, many people still think of sociology as "unscientific" or a "soft" science. In response, some sociologists may try too hard to sound scientific and incorporate complicated terminology in their writing.

It is possible, of course, to conduct research and write about it in a clear, straightforward, and even elegant way, as the best sociologists have demonstrated. Contrary to Barry's humorous claims, sociology can be both scientific and comprehensible. So let's turn now to a discussion of how sociologists conduct their research, which includes the methods of gathering information and conveying that information to others. For the record, Dave Barry went to Haverford College near Philadelphia, where he majored in English.

HOW TO READ THIS CHAPTER

In Chapter 1 we introduced you to a set of tools that will help you develop a sociological imagination and apply particular theoretical perspectives to the social world. In this chapter you will acquire methodological tools that will help you to further understand social life. The tools will also help you in the Data Workshops throughout the book, which are designed to give you the experience of conducting the same type of research that professional sociologists do. For this reason, we recommend that you look at this chapter as a sort of "how-to" guide: read through all the "directions" first, recognizing that you will soon be putting these methods into practice. Then remember that you have this chapter as a resource for future reference. These methods are your tools for real-world research—it's important that you understand them, but even more important that you get a chance to use them.

An Overview of Research Methods

While theories make hypothetical claims, methods produce data that will support, disprove, or modify those claims. Sociologists who do **quantitative research** work with numerical data; that is, they translate the social world into numbers that can then be manipulated mathematically. Any type of social statistic is an example of quantitative data: you may have read in the newspaper, for instance, that in 2013 some 38 percent of male drivers involved in fatal motor vehicle crashes had a blood alcohol content at or above 0.08 percent, compared with 20 percent of female drivers (Insurance Institute for Highway Safety 2014). Quantitative methodologies distill large amounts of information into numbers that are more easily communicated to others, often in the form of rates and percentages or charts and graphs.

Sociologists who do **qualitative research** work with non-numerical data such as texts, written field notes, interview transcripts, videos, or photographs. Rather than condensing lived experience into numbers, qualitative researchers try to describe the cases they study in great detail. They may engage in participant observation, in which they enter the social world they wish to study, or they may do in-depth interviews; analyze transcripts of conversations; glean data from historical books, letters, or diaries; or even use social networking sites or text messages as sources of data for their investigations. Sociologist Gary Fine, for example, has observed a variety of different social worlds, including those of professional restaurant chefs (1996), members of high school debate teams (2001), and meteorologists who predict the weather (2010). Fine was able to discover important sociological insights through immersion in each of the social worlds he studied.

Sociological Methods Take Many Forms They can be quantitative, but they can also include interviews and participant observation.

Qualitative researchers like Fine find patterns in their data by using interpretive rather than statistical analysis.

The Scientific Approach

The **scientific method** is the standard procedure for acquiring and verifying empirical (concrete, scientific) knowledge. The scientific method provides researchers with a series of basic steps to follow; over the years, sociologists have updated and modified this model so that it better fits the study of human behaviors. While not every sociologist adheres to each of the steps in order, the scientific method provides a general plan for conducting research in a systematic way (see Figure 2.1).

QUANTITATIVE RESEARCH research that translates the social world into numbers that can be treated mathematically; this type of research often tries to find cause-and-effect relationships

QUALITATIVE RESEARCH research that works with non numerical data such as texts, field notes, interview transcripts, photographs, and tape recordings; this type of research more often tries to understand how people make sense of their world

SCIENTIFIC METHOD a procedure for acquiring knowledge that emphasizes collecting concrete data through observation and experimentation

LITERATURE REVIEW a thorough search through previously published studies relevant to a particular topic

1. In the first step, the researcher identifies a problem or asks a general question, like "Does violent TV lead to violent behavior?" and begins to think about a specific research plan designed to answer that question.

2. Before proceeding, however, a researcher usually does a **literature review** to become thoroughly familiar with all other research done previously on a given topic. Doing so will prevent a researcher from duplicating work that has already been done and may also provide the background upon which to conduct new research.

Violence on Television In his famous 1965 study, Albert Bandura supported his hypothesis—watching violence on TV causes children to act violently in real life—by observing children who had watched a video of an adult beating a doll behaving similarly toward the doll afterward.

HYPOTHESIS a theoretical statement explaining the relationship between two or more phenomena

VARIABLES two or more phenomena that a researcher believes are related; these will be examined in the experiment

OPERATIONAL DEFINITION a clear and precise definition of a variable that facilitates its measurement

CORRELATION a relationship between variables in which they change together, and may or may not be causal

CAUSATION a relationship between variables in which a change in one directly produces a change in the other

INTERVENING VARIABLE a third variable, sometimes overlooked, that explains the relationship between two other variables

SPURIOUS CORRELATION the appearance of causation produced by an intervening variable

3. Next, the researcher forms a **hypothesis**, a theoretical statement that she thinks will explain the relationship between two phenomena, which are known as **variables**. In the hypothesis "Watching violence on TV causes children to act violently in real life," the two variables are "watching violence on TV" and "acting violently." In short, the researcher is saying one variable has a causal connection to the other. The researcher can use the hypothesis to predict possible outcomes: "If watching violence on TV causes children to act violently in real life, then exposing five-year-olds to violent TV shows will make them more likely to hit the inflatable clown doll placed in the room with them." The researcher must clearly give an **operational definition** to the variables so that she can observe and measure them accurately. For example, there is a wide range of violence on television and in real life. Does "violence" include words as well as actions, a slap as well as murder?

4. In this step, the researcher chooses a research design or method to use to conduct her study. A classic example is to perform an experiment meant to isolate variables in order to best examine their relationship to one another. Sociologists use a range of methods and sometimes combine one or more methods. These will be discussed in greater depth later in the chapter.

5. The researcher then collects the data. In this case, the researcher would conduct the experiment by first exposing kids to TV violence, then observing their behavior toward the clown doll. Data might be collected by using video equipment as well as by taking notes.

6. Next, the researcher must analyze the data, evaluating the accuracy or inaccuracy of the hypothesis in predicting the outcome. In the real-life experiment this example is based on, the children were more likely to hit the clown doll themselves if they saw the TV actors being rewarded for their violent behavior; if the actors were punished for their behavior, the children were less likely to hit the doll (Bandura 1965).

7. Finally, the researcher then disseminates the findings of the experiment in the scientific community (often through presentations at professional meetings, through publications, or in the classroom) as well as among the general public, thus completing the last step in the research process.

One limit of the scientific method is that it can't always distinguish between **correlation** and **causation**. If two variables change in conjunction with each other, or if a change in one seems to lead to a change in the other, they are correlated. Even if they are correlated, though, the change in one variable may not be caused by the change in the other variable. Instead, there may be some **intervening variable** that causes the changes in both. The classic example is the correlation between ice cream sales and rates of violent crime. As ice cream sales increase, so do rates of violent crime like murder and rape. Does ice cream consumption cause people to act violently? Or do violent actions cause people to buy ice cream? Turns out, it's neither—this is what is known as a **spurious correlation**. Both ice cream sales and violent crime rates are influenced by a third variable: weather. As the temperature climbs, so do people's rates of ice cream purchase and the likelihood that they'll be involved in a violent crime (probably because they are outside for more hours of the day and hence available to each other in a way that makes violent crime possible). Knowing that correlation does not equal causation is important, as it can help us all be more critical consumers of scientific findings.

We are constantly gathering data in order to understand what is true. Philosopher of science Thomas Kuhn, in fact, argued that truth is relative and dependent on the paradigm

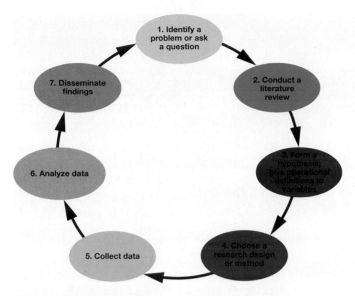

Figure 2.1 Steps of the Scientific Method

through which one sees the world (1962/1970). Paradigms are broad theoretical models about how things work in the social and natural worlds. For example, humans believed for centuries that the universe revolved around the earth. It's easy to understand why. The available data, after all, seemed to support such a theory: we don't feel the earth moving beneath us, and it appears from our vantage point that the stars, sun, and moon rise and set on our horizon. This earth-centered, or geocentric, view of the universe was the basis for all scientific theory until 1543, when the Polish astronomer Nicolaus Copernicus proposed that the earth revolved around the sun (Armitage 1951). Using mathematical methods, Copernicus arrived at a new theory, heliocentrism, in which the earth rotates around the sun and on its own axis—thereby accounting for the twenty-four-hour days as well as the four seasons of the year. This caused what Kuhn called a **paradigm shift**, a major break from the assumptions made by the previous model. Paradigm shifts occur when new data force new ways of looking at the world. And methods are what generate data.

Which Method to Use?

Since each sociological method has specific benefits and limitations, each is more appropriate for certain types of research. Thus, when a researcher begins a project, one of her most important decisions is which methods to use. Suppose, for example, a sociologist is interested in studying Woodstock, one of the major musical and cultural milestones of the 1960s. Although there are many ways to approach this event, our sociologist wants to study the attendees' experiences. What was it really like to be at Woodstock? What did it mean to those who were there? What are their interpretations of this iconic moment in hippie culture?

During the event itself, the ideal method for studying the festivalgoers at Woodstock might have been to assemble a team of researchers trained in participant observation; that is, they would actually be in the thick of things, observing and participating at the same time. They could gather firsthand data on the music, clothes, dancing, drugs, "free love," and so forth. However, the opportunity to be a participant observer of that particular cultural phenomenon has long since passed. What are some other options?

Interviews are a possibility. The researcher could ask Woodstock attendees to recount their experiences. But how would she recruit them? Woodstock-goers live all over the world now, and it might be difficult (and expensive) to track down enough of them to make an interview study feasible. Another problem with interviewing this group: the three-day event happened more than forty years ago. How would the passage of time affect their memories? How much detail could they actually remember about the experience after so long?

How about a survey? The researcher could certainly send a questionnaire through the mail or administer it online, and this method would be much less expensive than face-to-face interviews. But here she runs into the same problem as with an interview study: how does she find all these folks? A standard tactic for recruiting survey participants involves placing an ad in a local newspaper. But an ad in the *New York Times*, for example, or even a community website like Craigslist would draw only a limited number of Woodstock alumni. Also, some attendees might want to put that part of their lives behind them;

PARADIGM SHIFT a major change in basic assumptions of a particular scientific discipline

others who receive the questionnaire in the mail might send it straight into the trash. Finally, the researcher might encounter the problem of impostors—people who say they were at Woodstock but were really nowhere near it.

What about using existing sources? Plenty has been written about Woodstock over the years. Many firsthand accounts have been published, and there is an abundance of film and photography as well. Our researcher could use these materials to analyze the concert from the perspectives of the participants. These accounts would necessarily be selective, focusing only on particular aspects of the Woodstock experience.

Is it possible to conduct an experiment that replicates the original Woodstock? Some would say that Woodstock 1999 was such an experiment and that it failed miserably, with fires, violence, arrests, and acres of mud. However, systematic scientific experiments are different from blatant attempts to cash in on the Woodstock mystique. While the unique conditions of the 1969 gathering cannot be re-created in a lab setting, it is possible to identify some of the defining features of the Woodstock experience and to explore those experimentally. Over a three-day period, tens of thousands of strangers came together in a mass gathering, mostly devoid of any official presence (no cops, fences, roads, ticket booths, or porta-potties) and had an almost entirely peaceful experience. How did this

What Was It Really Like at Woodstock? You could use many different methodologies to investigate this question, including ethnography, interviews, surveys, existing sources, or experiments.

happen? Altruism, cooperation, and trust between strangers are some of the measurable group qualities that seem to have been present. An experimenter might be able to create laboratory environments in which subjects participate in activities that highlight one or more of these qualities—even without the mud, music, and drugs that were part of the original Woodstock experience.

No matter what methodological choice our researcher makes, she will sacrifice some types of information in order to acquire others, and she will trade in one set of advantages and disadvantages for another. Her choices will be guided not only by what she wants to accomplish sociologically but also by the methods she is a competent practitioner of, the time in which she wants to complete the project, the resources available from any funding agencies, and her access to cooperative, qualified people, both as respondents and as research assistants.

The rest of this chapter will discuss five methods in detail: ethnography/participant observation, interviews, surveys, existing sources, and experiments. We will see how various sociologists have used these methods to conduct research on the general topic of "family dynamics."

Ethnography/Participant Observation

 Ethnography is one of the most commonly used research methods in the social sciences. Also referred to as ethnographic research, it is a qualitative method that allows for the study of a wide variety of people and places. A key feature of this method is fieldwork; research takes place in naturally occurring social environments out in the real world, where the researcher can study firsthand the day-to-day lives of the people there. Ethnographic research is conducted through **participant observation**, so the terms are often used interchangeably. With this method the researcher must become a participant in the group or setting being studied as well as an observer of it. This method often entails deep immersion

ETHNOGRAPHY a naturalistic method based on studying people in their own environment in order to understand the meanings they attribute to their activities; also, the written work that results from the study

PARTICIPANT OBSERVATION a methodology associated with ethnography whereby the researcher both observes and becomes a member in a social setting

into a field site, sometimes lasting over a period of months or even years, so that the researcher can develop a member's eye view and come to know the social world from the inside out. Ethnography, which literally means "writing [from the Greek *graphos*] culture [*ethnos*]," is also the term used for the product of participant observation research; it is a written report of the results of the study, often presented in book form.

The first order of business in participant observation research is to gain entry or **access** to the chosen field site or setting. Certain groups may be more or less difficult to approach, as you can imagine, and there may be some places where no outsider is allowed to go. Still, sociologists have been able to study an astounding number of different and varied social worlds. Once access has been negotiated, it is also important for researchers to establish good **rapport** with their subjects. Researchers may differ in their levels of involvement with a group or in their closeness to certain members. But it is often the case that trust and acceptance are necessary before research can begin in earnest.

Data are collected primarily through writing detailed **field notes** every day to document what happened. Some researchers may also take photos or videos in the course of their fieldwork, but honing their own observational skills is most critical. Field notes describe the scene or setting, as well as the activities and interactions of the researcher and the group members, in as much detail as possible; they become the basis of the data analysis the researcher does later on. Some researchers do a form of participant observation called **autoethnography**, where they produce richly detailed accounts of their own thoughts, feelings, and experiences in the field as a focal point of their study (Ellis 1997).

Sometimes, researchers take brief, sketchy notes in the field, writing key words or short quotations in small notebooks, on cocktail napkins, or in text messages. These jottings can help jog their memories when they sit down to write at the end of the day and elaborate on the details. Sometimes, however, it is not possible to write while in the field and researchers must rely on "head notes"—memory alone.

Anthropologist Clifford Geertz (1973), well known for his work on Indonesian culture and society, coined the term **thick description** to convey the qualities of well-written field notes. It takes more than mere photographic detail to make field notes "thick"; sensitivity to the context and to interactional details such as facial expressions and tone of voice enrich what might otherwise be just a list of events. Thick description involves exploring all the possible meanings of a phenomenon (for example, a blinking eye) within a particular cultural setting. A good ethnography is not only systematic and holistic, it should also allow the reader to understand what the world is like from another's perspective.

One example of participant observation research is Kathryn Edin and Maria Kefalas's study of poor moms, in their ethnography *Promises I Can Keep: Why Poor Women Put Motherhood before Marriage* (2005). Edin and Kefalas wanted to examine a group that faces harsh judgments from the mainstream: urban single moms. For years, policymakers and mainstream Americans have focused on single motherhood as a source of a variety of social problems. Edin and Kefalas wanted to see the issue from the perspective and lives of the women being stigmatized in order to uncover the realities of single motherhood. Their goal was to give poor single mothers the ability to personally answer the question that wealthier Americans ask of them: Why don't they get married? And why have babies if they have to struggle so hard to support them? Because Edin and Kefalas knew they needed to access a group that was notorious for being hard to study, their participant observation required full immersion in the community. Edin moved her entire family to East Camden, New Jersey, where they lived for two and a half years while she did her research. In order to become more integrated into the community, she joined the local church,

ACCESS the process by which an ethnographer gains entry to a field setting

RAPPORT a positive relationship often characterized by mutual trust or sympathy

FIELD NOTES detailed notes taken by an ethnographer describing her activities and interactions, which later become the basis of the analysis

AUTOETHNOGRAPHY a form of participant observation where the feelings and actions of the researcher become a focal point of the ethnographic study

THICK DESCRIPTION the presentation of detailed data on interactions and meaning within a cultural context, from the perspective of its members

volunteered at after-school and summer programs, ate at local restaurants, shopped at local stores, taught Sunday school, and went to community events. Kefalas volunteered at the local GED tutoring program for teen mothers.

Edin and Kefalas were able to study 162 mothers with an even distribution among black, white, and Puerto Rican and an average age of twenty-five. All of them were single parents who earned less than $16,000 a year. What Edin and Kefalas discovered was that motherhood, from the perspective of many of the women they met, was a stabilizing agent in their lives. Rather than disrupting their path to success, many of the moms viewed their babies as the only positive factor in their lives. Numerous stories detailed the troubled directions the women's lives were heading before they had their children. The conclusions Edin and Kefalas were able to draw from their ethnographic research were contrary to widespread opinion about the consequences of single motherhood: for many women in poverty, the (perceived) low cost of early child-rearing and the high value and worth of mothering are enough to combat the difficulties of single motherhood.

Ethnographic researchers must pay attention to how their own social statuses—including gender, age, race, and parenthood—shape the kind of access they can have, and hence the kind of knowledge they can obtain as part of their research. The fact that Edin and Kefalas were women and mothers themselves played a role in their ability to create rapport and gain access as they lived and worked in East

REFLEXIVITY how the identity and activities of the researcher influence what is going on in the field setting

GROUNDED THEORY an inductive method of generating theory from data by creating categories in which to place data and then looking for relationships among categories

REPLICABILITY research that can be repeated, and thus verified, by other researchers later

VALIDITY the accuracy of a question or measurement tool; the degree to which a researcher is measuring what he thinks he is measuring

REPRESENTATIVENESS the degree to which a particular studied group is similar to, or represents, any part of the larger society

BIAS an opinion held by the researcher that might affect the research or analysis

Camden. Participant-observers must also consider that their own presence probably affects the interactions and relationships in the group they are observing, an idea known as **reflexivity**. A researcher's personal feelings about the members of a group also come into play. Ethnographers may feel respect, contempt, curiosity, boredom, and other emotions during their time in the field, and these feelings may influence their observations. It is true that other kinds of researchers also have to take their feelings into account. But because ethnographers have such close personal ties to the people they study, the issue of reflexivity is especially important to them.

Like Edin and Kefalas, most ethnographers are "overt" about their research roles; that is, they are open about their sociological intentions. Overt research is generally preferred, because it eliminates the potential ethical problems of deceit. Sometimes, however, circumstances dictate that researchers take a "covert" role and observe members without letting them know that they are doing research. One researcher who kept his identity secret is Richard Mitchell, who studied militant survivalist groups for many years (2001). In order to be a participant observer in such groups, Mitchell sometimes had to present himself as an eager apostle, a true believer in the survivalists' paranoid, racist ideologies. Often, this meant being surrounded by men who were heavily armed and deeply suspicious of outsiders (Mitchell and Charmaz 1996). However, he also felt that the value of the research was worth the risk, that it was more important than his own personal peril and the ethical objections of those who disapprove of covert research because it provided insight into a secretive group whose actions could pose a danger to the larger society.

Ethnographers look for patterns and themes that are revealed in their field notes. In other words, they use an inductive approach: they start by immersing themselves in their field notes and fitting the data into categories, such as "episodes of conflict" or "common vocabulary shared by members." Identifying relationships among these categories then allows ethnographers to build theoretical propositions, a form of analysis known as **grounded theory** (Glaser and Strauss 1967).

Advantages and Disadvantages

ADVANTAGES

1. Ethnographic research excels at telling richly detailed stories that contribute to our understanding of social life. It offers a means of studying groups whose stories might not otherwise have been told (Katz 1997). These include deviant groups such as fight clubs (Jackson-Jacobs 2004) as well as exceptional groups such as elite college athletes (Adler and Adler 1991).

2. Ethnographic research can challenge our taken-for-granted notions about groups we thought we knew. For instance, from Edin and Kefalas's work on single mothers, we learn that these women aren't the irresponsible, unstable individuals we may have thought they were. They desire and seek out the best for their children, just like mothers in other groups and communities.

3. The detailed nature of ethnographic research can help reshape the stereotypes we hold about others and on which social policy is often based. A study like Edin and Kefalas's can have policy consequences because it sheds light on the motivations and needs of single urban mothers, as well as giving us a clear picture of the resources available to them.

4. Much of the pioneering methodological innovation of the last half-century has come from ethnography, especially on the issue of reflexivity and researcher roles in the field.

Richard Mitchell's *Dancing at Armageddon* In order to learn about militant groups' ideologies, Richard Mitchell had to conceal his identity and use covert methods.

DISADVANTAGES

1. Ethnographic research suffers from a lack of **replicability**, the ability of another researcher to repeat or replicate the study. Repeating a study in order to test the **validity** of its results is an important element of the scientific method, but because of the unique combinations of people, timing, setting, and researcher role, no one can ever undertake the same study twice.

2. A major critique has to do with an ethnography's degree of **representativeness**—whether a particular study can apply to anything larger. What is the value of studying relatively small groups of people if one cannot then say that these groups represent parts of the society at large? Though Edin and Kefalas's work focused on East Camden, their conclusions are supposed to apply to single mothers in any number of other cities as well.

3. Participant observers must also be wary of personal **bias**. There is always a possibility that prejudice or favor can slip into the research process. Not all researchers are transparent about their own agendas. We need to keep in mind how a researcher's own values and opinions might affect his research and analysis.

DATA WORKSHOP
Analyzing Everyday Life

Watching People Talk

Participant observation research requires a keen eye and ear, and field notes must faithfully capture the details of what is seen and heard. While writing field notes may sound fairly easy (don't we all know how to describe the things we've observed?), it's actually one of the most grueling forms of data collection in the social sciences. Why? Because thick description is a much more demanding task than the casual description you're used to providing in everyday conversation. It requires a rigorous consciousness of what is going on around you while it is happening and a strenuous effort to recall those goings-on after leaving the field and returning to your computer to type them up.

This Data Workshop gives you an opportunity to practice doing ethnographic research (make sure you have read and reviewed that section of the chapter). Specifically, it is an exercise in writing field notes

using what Clifford Geertz calls thick description. To make things a little easier, you'll focus on listening first and then on watching. The verbal and the visual are separated so that you can concentrate on one kind of description at a time. In your future ethnographic work, you'll be writing field notes that describe both verbal and nonverbal behavior at once.

* *Field Observations:* First, for five to ten minutes, listen to (eavesdrop on) a conversation whose participants you can't see. They might be sitting behind you on a bus or at a nearby table in a restaurant—you're close enough to hear them but positioned so that you can't see them. Then, for five to ten minutes, observe a conversation you can't hear—one taking place, for example, on the other side of the campus quad. Even though you can't hear what's being said, you can see the interaction as it takes place.

* *Written Descriptions:* Write an extremely detailed description of each conversation. Describe the participants and the setting, and include your ideas about what you think is going on and what you think you know about the participants. Try to describe everything you heard or saw to support any conclusions you draw. For each of the five- to ten-minute observation periods, you should aim to take two or more double-spaced pages of field notes.

There are two options for completing this Data Workshop:

PREP-PAIR-SHARE Choose a partner and exchange your field notes. As you read through your partner's descriptions, mark with a star (*) the passages where you can see and hear clearly the things your partner describes. Circle the passages that contain evaluative words (like "angry" or "sweet") or summaries of action or conversation rather than detailed description (like "They argued about who would pay the bill"). And place a question mark next to the passages where you are left feeling like you would like to know more. Your partner will do this with your descriptions as well, and you can discuss your responses to each other's work. Finally, as a class, use your discussions to develop a group consensus about what constitutes good descriptive detail. This is the kind of detail ethnographers strive to produce in their field notes every day.

DO-IT-YOURSELF Write a two- to three-page essay discussing your field work experience. What was it like to do participant observation research? Did you find listening or watching more or less difficult, and why? How did your data differ with each of the observations? Provide examples of thick description from your field notes, and make sure to attach your field notes to your paper.

Interviews

You've probably seen countless interviewers, microphone in hand, clamoring to ask their questions at the crime scene, after the big game, or on the red carpet. Sociologists also use **interviews**—face-to-face, information-seeking conversations—to gather qualitative data directly from research subjects, or **respondents**. When sociologists conduct interviews, they try to do so systematically and with a more scientific approach than is used for the kind of interviews you might typically see on TV or read in the news. Sometimes, interviews are the only method used in a research project, but sociologists may also combine interviews with other methods, such as participant observation or analysis of existing sources. Closely related to interviews are surveys, which we will consider in the next section. Both methods are concerned with asking people questions, usually very specific groups of people as well as particular kinds of questions. Interviews, however, are always conducted by the researcher, whereas surveys may be taken independently by the respondent.

When using interviews to collect data about a particular question or project, sociologists must first identify a **target population**, or group that is the focus of their study. If it is a large group, for instance all parents with children under eighteen years of age, it might be impossible to study each and every one of them. Researchers, then, must select a **sample**, or a smaller group that is representative of the larger group. The sample will be used to make generalizations that can apply to the larger target population. The number of possible respondents in a sample depends on the type of study, the nature of the questions, and the amount of time and staff available. In most research studies, interviews can be administered to only a limited number of people, so the scope of such projects is usually smaller than for other methods, such as surveys. While most interviews are conducted one on one, some researchers will organize a **focus group**, in which a number of participants (perhaps five to ten) will be interviewed at the same time, also allowing for group members to interact with each other. This

may be one means of increasing the sample size of a study. Researchers must also get **informed consent** from those who will be participating in the study; in other words, respondents must know what they are getting into and explicitly agree to participate. This is particularly important because most interviews are audio or video recorded.

Arlie Hochschild used interviews to conduct her landmark study on parents in two-career families, *The Second Shift* (Hochschild and Machung 1989). In this book, Hochschild looks at how couples handle the pressures of working at a job and then coming home to what she calls "the second shift"—doing housework and taking care of children. Hochschild, who was herself in a two-career family, wanted to find out how couples were dealing with changing family roles in light of the fact that more women had entered the workforce. Were women able to juggle all their responsibilities, and to what extent were men helping their wives in running the household? Hochschild and her assistants interviewed fifty couples in two-career marriages and forty-five other people who were also a part of the respondents' domestic arrangements, such as babysitters, day-care providers, and teachers. From this sample of households that Hochschild studied, we can now extrapolate to a much larger population; her findings should also be applicable to similar couples elsewhere.

When conducting an interview, how do you know what to ask? Composing good questions is one of the most difficult parts of interviewing. Most interviewers use many different questions, covering a range of issues related to the project. Questions may be closed- or open-ended. A **closed-ended question** imposes a limit on the possible response: for example, "Are you for or against couples living together before they

The Second Shift In her groundbreaking book, Arlie Hochschild interviewed working women and their partners to learn about the time binds that they face as they balance work, family, and running a household.

INTERVIEWS person-to-person conversations for the purpose of gathering information by means of questions posed to respondents

RESPONDENT a participant in a study from whom the researcher seeks to gather information

TARGET POPULATION the entire group about which a researcher would like to be able to generalize

SAMPLE the members of the target population who will actually be studied

FOCUS GROUP a process for interviewing a number of participants together, it also allows for interaction among group members

INFORMED CONSENT a safeguard through which the researcher makes sure that respondents are freely participating and understand the nature of the research

CLOSED-ENDED QUESTION a question asked of a respondent that imposes a limit on the possible responses

are married?" An **open-ended question**, on the other hand, allows for a wide variety of responses: "What do you think about couples living together before they are married?"

Researchers must be careful to avoid biased or **leading questions**, those that predispose a respondent to answer in a certain way. Overly complex questions are a problem, as are **double-barreled questions**, those that involve too many issues at one time. It is also important to be aware of any ambiguous or inflammatory language that might confuse or spark an emotional reaction on the part of the respondent. Asking a single parent how difficult her life is will elicit data about the difficulties, but not about the joys, of parenthood. More neutral language, such as "Tell me about the pluses and minuses of single parenthood" is preferable. In some studies, researchers will solicit the entire **life history** of a respondent, a chronological account of the story of his life from childhood to the present or of some portion of it.

Once the interviews have been conducted, they are usually transcribed so that researchers can analyze them in textual form; they can sort through the material looking for patterns of similarities and differences among the answers. Some researchers may use computer applications designed to help analyze such data; others do it "by hand." For her analysis, Hochschild categorized the types of household chores done by men and women and quantified the amount of time spent daily and weekly on those chores. She then categorized couples as "traditional," "transitional," or "egalitarian," depending on how they divided up household labor.

Advantages and Disadvantages

ADVANTAGES

1. Interviews allow respondents to speak in their own words; they can reveal their own thoughts, feelings, and beliefs, internal states that would not necessarily be accessible by any other means. In so many other instances, it is the researcher who tells the story. A book like *The Second Shift*, which features direct quotations from interview transcripts, provides the reader with an authentic and intimate portrait of the lives of married couples. Hochschild was able to get at the different subjective experiences of the women and men in her study and to see how each of them perceived the reality of his or her situation.

2. Interviews may help the researcher dispel certain preconceptions and discover issues that might have otherwise been overlooked. For example, before Hochschild began her project, many other studies had already been conducted on families with two working parents, but few seemed to examine in depth the real-life dilemma of the two-career family that Hochschild herself was experiencing.

DISADVANTAGES

1. Interview respondents are not always forthcoming or truthful. They may be selective about what they say in order to present themselves in the most favorable light. Sometimes they are difficult to talk to, and at other times they may try too hard to be helpful. Although an adept interviewer will be able to encourage meaningful responses, she can never take at face value what any respondent might say. To counteract this problem, Hochschild observed a few of the families she had interviewed. She saw that what these couples said about themselves in interviews was sometimes at odds with how they acted at home.

2. Another problem is representativeness: whether the conclusions of interview research can be applied to larger groups. Because face-to-face interviewing is time consuming, interviews are rarely used with large numbers of people. Can findings from a small sample be generalized to a larger population? In regard to Hochschild's research, can we say that interviews with fifty couples, although carefully selected by the researcher, give a true picture of the lives of all two-career families? Hochschild answered this question by comparing selected information about her couples with data from a huge national survey.

OPEN-ENDED QUESTION a question asked of a respondent that allows the answer to take whatever form the respondent chooses

LEADING QUESTIONS questions that predispose a respondent to answer in a certain way

DOUBLE-BARRELED QUESTIONS questions that attempt to get at multiple issues at once, and so tend to receive incomplete or confusing answers

LIFE HISTORY an approach to interviewing that asks for a chronological account of the respondent's entire life, or some portion of it

SURVEYS research method based on questionnaires that are administered to a sample of respondents selected from a target population

Surveys

 How many times have you filled out a survey? Probably more times than you realize. If you responded to the last U.S. government census, if you have ever been solicited by a polling agency to give your opinion about a public issue, or if you have ever been asked to evaluate your college classes and instructors at the end of a semester, you were part of somebody's survey research.

Surveys are questionnaires that are administered to a sample of respondents selected from a target population. One of the earliest sociologists to use informal surveys was Karl Marx. In the 1880s, Marx sent questionnaires to more than 25,000 French workers in an effort to determine the extent to which they were exploited by employers. Although we don't know how many surveys were returned to him or what the

IN THE FUTURE
Action Research

In addition to the other methods discussed in this chapter, **action research** is a growing trend in social science methodology. Action research combines social science research with community problem solving and social change, in a way that calls into question some of sociology's closely held beliefs about ethics, bias, and the role of the researcher.

While action research is not exactly new, it has been gaining popularity recently, across the social sciences as well as in practice-oriented disciplines such as nursing, public health, education, urban planning, and management. Pioneers in action research tended to come from the areas of inequality studies such as feminist research, critical race studies, and poverty and community development research, and there is a clear historical link to the ethnographers of the Chicago School, with their community and reform-oriented approaches (Emerson 2002; Marullo 1999).

ACTION RESEARCH
a type of research aimed at creating social change, in which the researcher works closely with members of a community who participate in the research process and collaborate toward the goal of social change

Action researchers are more likely than traditional researchers to be invested in social change and community improvement goals. They see their research skills as problem-solving tools, and they view those whom others might call "research subjects" as active, collaborative, equal participants in the project. In other words, action researchers do research *with* people, not *on* people, and see their work as part of a "scholarship of engagement" (Rajaram 2007, p. 139), rather than one of erudite distance.

An award-winning example of action research is the work of Chicago's Community Organizing and Family Issues group (COFI). Their project "Why Isn't Johnny in Preschool?" sought to answer this question, particularly among families in low-income, racially diverse neighborhoods, where kids are less likely to be enrolled in early childhood education programs. They sent community members, trained in sociological interview methods, out into their neighborhoods to talk with more than 5,000 other parents about the barriers to preschool enrollment. Their findings included family concerns about cost, transportation, and confusing paperwork and bureaucracies, among other obstacles. These findings were used to design outreach and public awareness campaigns that promoted the importance of preschool attendance and provided information packets that helped families find solutions to some of the problems identified in the research. Preschool attendance increased in the targeted neighborhoods as a result (COFI 2009), and COFI received the Leo P. Chall Award for its work "successfully link[ing] research with social action, thereby strengthening

individual responses were, the project clearly influenced his writing, which focused heavily on workers' rights.

Today, many universities have research centers devoted to conducting survey research. One such center is the National Marriage Project at Rutgers University in New Jersey, where sociologists have been engaged in ongoing studies on the health of marriage and family in America, issuing a series of reports on what they call "The State of Our Unions" over the past several years. Researchers have surveyed young adults in their twenties about a range of topics, including their attitudes toward dating, cohabitation, marriage, and parenthood.

Survey research tends to be macro and quantitative in nature: it looks at large-scale social patterns and employs statistics and other mathematical means of analysis. Social scientists who use surveys must follow specific procedures in order to produce valid results. They need a good questionnaire and wise sample selection. Most surveys are composed of closed-ended questions, or those for which all possible answers are provided. Answers may be as simple as a "yes" or "no," or more complex. A common type of questionnaire is based on the **Likert scale**, a format in which respondents can choose along a continuum—from "strongly agree" to "strongly disagree," for example. Some questionnaires also offer such options as "don't know" or "doesn't apply." Surveys may include open-ended questions, or those to which the respondents provide their own answers. These are often formatted as write-in questions and can provide researchers with more qualitative data.

LIKERT SCALE a way of formatting a survey questionnaire so that the respondent can choose an answer along a continuum

NEGATIVE QUESTIONS survey questions that ask respondents what they don't think instead of what they do

Both questions and possible (given) answers on a survey must be written in such a way as to avoid confusion or ambiguity. While this is also true for interviews, it is even more important for surveys because the researcher is not generally present to clarify any misunderstandings. Common

community organizations and influencing public policy" (Sociological Initiatives Foundation 2010).

As citizens become research collaborators and sociologists become research activists, there will inevitably be some tension between research goals and practical goals.

Head Start A teacher works with the children of migrant and seasonal workers in Illinois.

Addressing real-world problems means that methodologies must be tailored to the constraints of the actual situation, rather than adhere to the ideal-type models required by the discipline. All participants must be allowed to be part of the decision-making process, and all must be provided equal access to information, data, and findings (which even the most open-minded traditional researchers may balk at). Ethical considerations differ from those of traditional research as well: action research is designed to bring about change and is "aligned with values" (Riel 2010), so claims of objectivity are out of the question.

These differences make action research controversial among more traditional social scientists, but this method is gaining popularity among students. Action research provides both graduate and undergraduate students with the opportunity to be of service in their communities, while also fulfilling academic requirements, and many students prefer this active approach to social change over a research project that takes place entirely in a library or lab. More high schools and colleges are making community service projects part of their graduation requirements, and even more will likely do so in the near future. Action research itself is fundamentally future oriented due to its focus on social change and community improvement, and it provides a way to make a positive impact while also advancing social science research. Does it get any better than that?

pitfalls are leading questions; **negative questions**, which ask respondents what they don't think instead of what they do; and double-barreled questions. Bias can also be a problem if questions or answers are worded in a slanted fashion.

The format of a questionnaire is also important. Something as simple as the order in which the items are presented can influence responses. Mentioning an issue like divorce or infidelity in earlier questions can mean that respondents are thinking about it when they answer later questions, and as a result, their answers might be different than they would otherwise have been. Questionnaires should be clear and easy to follow. Once a questionnaire is constructed, it is a good idea to have a small group pretest it to help eliminate flaws and make sure it is clear and comprehensible. A preliminary small-scale **pilot study** can help to work out any issues with the survey design before administering it to a larger group.

Another important element in survey research is sampling techniques. As with interviews, the researcher must identify the specific target population she wishes to study: for example, "all married couples with children living at home" or "all young adults between the ages of twenty and twenty-nine."

By using correct sampling techniques, researchers can survey a smaller number of respondents and then make accurate inferences about the larger population. In quantitative research, social scientists use **probability sampling**, in which the sample group mathematically reflects the characteristics of the larger target population. Researchers might generate a **simple random sample**, where each member of the larger target population has an equal chance of being

PILOT STUDY a small-scale study carried out to test the feasibility of a larger one

PROBABILITY SAMPLING a procedure that results in a sample group that reflects the characteristics of members in the target population

SIMPLE RANDOM SAMPLE a particular type of probability sample in which every member of the population has an equal chance of being selected

REPRESENTATIVE SAMPLE
a sample taken so that findings from members of the sample group can be generalized to the larger population; also referred to as a stratified sample

RESPONSE RATE the number or percentage of surveys completed by respondents and returned to researchers

RELIABILITY the consistency of a question or measurement tool; the degree to which the same questions will produce similar answers

included in the sample based on random selection. In other cases, a more advanced type of sampling is used. For example, in the National Marriage Project study, researchers surveyed a statistically **representative sample** of 1,003 young adults. Here they would have used more sophisticated manipulating or weighting techniques, ensuring that the proportion of certain variables such as race, class, gender, or age in the sample group is more accurately representative of the larger population.

An increasing number of survey researchers have turned to utilizing the Internet rather than conducting research person-to-person or by mail (Best and Krueger 2004; Sue and Ritter 2007). The Internet has opened up new possibilities for reaching respondents as more and more people have Internet access. While online surveys promise a certain amount of ease and cost effectiveness, they also present researchers with significant challenges, especially in terms of scientific sampling.

In order for a survey to be considered valid, there must be a sufficiently high **response rate**. It is sometimes difficult to get enough individuals to participate in a survey. Even if only half of a sample group actually returned the completed surveys, that would be considered a very good result. General claims can be made about a larger population from a survey with a response rate of only 20 or 30 percent. Once the surveys are returned, the researchers begin the process of tabulating and analyzing the data. Responses are usually coded or turned into numerical figures so that they can be more easily analyzed on a computer. Researchers often want to understand the relationship between certain variables; for instance, what is the effect of infidelity on divorce? There are many computer applications, such as SPSS (Statistical Package for the Social Sciences), that can help researchers perform complicated calculations and reach conclusions about relationships. This is where advanced statistical skills become an important part of social analysis.

Advantages and Disadvantages

ADVANTAGES

1. Survey research is one of the best methods for gathering original data on a population that is too large to study by other means, such as by direct observation or interviewing. Surveys can be widely distributed, reaching a large number of people. Researchers can then generalize their findings to an even larger population.

2. Survey research is also relatively quick and economical and can provide a vast amount of data. Online surveys now promise a way to gain access to even greater numbers of people at even lower cost.

3. In general, survey research is comparatively strong on **reliability**. This means that we can be sure that the same kind of data are collected each time the same question is asked.

4. In survey research, there is less concern about interviewer or observer bias entering into the research process. Respondents may feel more comfortable giving candid answers to sensitive questions because they answer the questions in private and are usually assured of the anonymity of their responses.

DISADVANTAGES

1. Survey research generally lacks qualitative data that might better capture the social reality the researcher wishes to examine. Because most survey questions don't allow the respondent to qualify his answer, they don't allow for a full range of expression and may not accurately reflect the true meaning of the respondent's thoughts. For example, asking a respondent to choose one reason from a list of reasons for divorce might not provide a full explanation for the failure of that person's marriage. The reasons may have been both financial and emotional, but the survey may not provide the respondent with the ability to convey this. Adding write-in questions is one way to minimize this disadvantage.

2. In general, since not all respondents are honest in self-reports, survey research is comparatively weak on validity. For example, a respondent may be ashamed about his divorce and may not want to reveal the true reasons behind it to a stranger on a questionnaire.

3. Often, there are problems with the sampling process, especially when respondents self-select to participate, that make generalizability more difficult. Gathering data online only exacerbates this problem. For instance, if a survey seeking to know the incidence of domestic violence in the population is administered only to the members of a domestic violence support group, then the incidence of domestic violence will be 100 percent—misrepresenting the true rate of incidence in the larger population.

4. It's possible that survey research will be used to make a claim or support a point of view rather than for pure scientific discovery; for example, a manufacturer of SUVs may report that 90 percent of all American families surveyed wish they had a larger car. We will consider this limitation later, in the section on nonacademic uses of research methods.

DATA WORKSHOP
Analyzing Media and Pop Culture

Media Usage Patterns

Recent studies have shown that the average American spends around eleven hours a day using some type of electronic media—computers, tablets, TV, radio, smartphones, and so on (Nielsen 2014). That's almost half a day, or nearly two-thirds of our waking hours each day. For many people this means that they rarely unplug. But there is more to the picture than just the total number of hours Americans spend using media. What other kinds of questions might we be interested in asking about this increasingly important aspect of our lives?

For example, we might ask people what kind of media they are using. How much time is spent with each of these, as well as when and where? How much money do individuals spend on media-related equipment or activities? How much do people multitask, using more than one device at a time? Do different groups prefer different types of media? How do factors like age, education, gender, or income influence media usage? What else do people do while using media—do they work, eat, clean, talk, drive, exercise, study, or even sleep? Now come up with more of your own questions!

In this Data Workshop, you will be conducting your own survey research about media usage in everyday life. Consult the relevant section of this chapter for a review of this method. Your task is twofold. First, you will get some practice designing a study and constructing and administering a survey questionnaire. Second, you will get the chance to do a preliminary analysis of the data you collect and possibly discover something for yourself about the patterns of media usage among those who participate in your pilot study.

Because there are a variety of ways of doing such a project, you should choose how you would like to customize your research. Since this is only a preliminary effort at survey research, the project will have to be somewhat limited. Nonetheless, try to follow these basic steps in order to make your research process as scientific as possible:

1. Decide what aspects of media usage you want to study.

2. Select a sample from the target population you wish to study (student athletes, seniors, people with a college degree, and so on).

3. Write and format your survey questionnaire.

4. Administer the questionnaire to the individuals in your sample.

5. Analyze the data collected in the survey, and present your findings.

There are two options for completing this Data Workshop:

PREP-PAIR-SHARE Working in small groups of three to four students, begin designing a survey project by discussing Steps 1 and 2. Then collaborate on Step 3. If time allows, play the role of a pilot group and test the questionnaire by filling out the survey as outlined in Step 4. Then consider Step 5, looking for any patterns that may have emerged from the data. Finally, discuss as a group what needs to be changed or what else needs to be accomplished to complete an actual survey.

DO-IT-YOURSELF Design your own survey research project, completing all of the above steps. Choose at least five to eight people to be included in your sample. After administering the questionnaire, write a three- to four-page essay discussing the research process and your preliminary findings. What was the most challenging part of doing survey research? What insights did you gain about media usage from the participants in your study? What would you change if you intended to do a larger study in the future? Remember to attach the survey questionnaire to your paper.

Existing Sources

Nearly all sociologists use **existing sources** when they approach a particular research question. As the term implies, an almost unlimited amount of data already exists out there in the world that can be useful to sociologists for their studies. With other methods, researchers have to generate their own data firsthand from field notes, interviews, or surveys. With existing (or secondary) sources, researchers may discover a treasure trove of data in unexpected places or hidden in plain view, ready for the taking. This material can include everything from archival or historical records such as marriage licenses or building permits to various forms of media such as books, magazines, TV shows, or websites. While all these materials may have been created for

EXISTING SOURCES materials that have been produced for some other reason but that can be used as data for social research

another purpose, they can constitute valuable data to be used in social research. Existing sources are considered **unobtrusive measures** because they don't require that the researcher intrude upon or disturb the people in a social context or setting they are studying.

Sociologists take different approaches to working with existing sources. For instance, social demographers study the size, composition, growth, and distribution of human populations. The statistical information used in such research is generally produced by other social scientists, or by government agencies such as public health departments. In fact, the U.S. Census Bureau makes a massive amount of its data freely available to the public on its website, census.gov. Other sociologists do what could be called "social archaeology." They dig through and examine the social environment in order to understand the people in it. For instance the average American throws away over two pounds of garbage a day. What might we learn by looking through someone's trash?

Some sociologists do what is called **comparative historical research**, which seeks to understand relationships between elements of society in various regions and time periods. These researchers are able to go back in time and analyze cultural artifacts such as literature, paintings, newspapers, and photographs (Bauer and Gaskell 2000). As an example, Alice Miller consulted various existing sources for her book *For Your Own Good: Hidden Cruelty in Child-Rearing and the Roots of Violence* (1990) to investigate the childhood experiences of several notorious historical figures, including Adolf Hitler. She examined child-rearing manuals that were popular at the time, as well as family records such as diaries and letters. These documents showed that prevailing social norms endorsed physical punishment as a means of raising good, obedient children. But were there unintended consequences of such parenting practices for children and society alike? Miller found that Hitler was the product of a fairly traditional child-rearing, with traditional gender-role socialization and disciplinary practices. Her findings force us to acknowledge that seemingly "normal" child-rearing practices have the potential to create someone like Hitler—that it is not always the exceptions but the rules themselves that can make a monster. Miller's use of existing sources allowed her to gain insight into not only the development of an individual personality but also the structure of an entire society and the role that society played in creating one of the twentieth century's most malevolent individuals.

Alice Miller's *For Your Own Good* By analyzing historical sources and child-rearing guides, Miller argued that some of the methods used to raise children that are accepted as normal and ordinary can create seriously aberrant individuals as well as regular folks.

Content analysis is another widely used approach to working with existing sources. Researchers look for recurrent themes or count the number of times that specific variables—such as particular words or visual elements—appear in a text, image, or media message. They then analyze the variables and relationships among them. For example, content analysis has shown that the roles women typically play on television are of lower status than men's, with women more likely to be portrayed as housewives, mothers, secretaries, and nurses, while men are doctors, judges, celebrities, and athletes in addition to being husbands and fathers (Kolbe and Langefeld 1993). Despite some recent improvements in the depiction of women in the media, this pattern has persisted. If we look at the top-rated network sitcoms of 2013, which included *The Big Bang Theory, Modern Family, Two Broke Girls, Two and a Half Men,* and *How I Met Your Mother*, we see that the majority of men were highly accomplished professionals while the women were unemployed or struggling. This contradicts the reality of unemployment in the United States; in 2013, 7.6 percent of men in the workforce were unemployed compared to 7.1 percent of women (U.S. Bureau of Labor Statistics 2015d).

After obtaining their data, researchers must decide which analytic tools will be best suited to their research questions. The analysis of existing sources can be qualitative or quantitative in nature. Sometimes new data sets can challenge old findings. For instance, in 2006, *Newsweek* magazine revisited a controversial article written twenty years earlier, "The Marriage Crunch," which reported that college-educated women over the age of forty had less than a 3 percent chance of getting married. After reviewing new census data, *Newsweek* had to revise that number to more than 40 percent (McGinn 2006). You can count this book's two authors as among those women who would marry in their forties.

Advantages and Disadvantages

ADVANTAGES

1. Researchers are able to work with information they could not possibly obtain on their own. The U.S. Census Bureau, for example, collects information about the entire national population (family size, education, income, occupational status, and residential patterns), something an individual researcher has neither the time nor funds to do. In addition, the analysis of existing data can be a convenient way for sociologists to pool their resources; one researcher can take data collected by another and use it for his own project, increasing what can be learned from the same set of data.

2. Using sources such as newspapers, political speeches, and cultural artifacts, sociologists are able to learn about many social worlds, in different time periods, that they would never be able to enter themselves; for example, preserved letters and diaries from the early 1800s have allowed researchers to analyze the experiences of wives and mothers on the American frontier (Peavy and Smith 1998).

3. Researchers can use the same data to replicate projects that have been conducted before, which is a good way to test findings for reliability or to see changes across time.

DISADVANTAGES

1. Researchers drawing on existing sources often seek to answer questions that the original authors did not have in mind. If you were interested in the sex lives of those frontier women in the early 1800s, for example, you would be unlikely to find any clear references in their letters or diaries.

2. Similarly, content analysis, although it can describe the messages inherent in the media, does not illuminate how such messages are interpreted. So we can say that women's roles on television have lower status than men's, but additional research would be required to identify the effects of these images on viewers.

Experimental Methods

 Unlike participant observation, interviews, surveys, or existing sources, **experiments** actually closely resemble the scientific method with which we began this chapter. You might associate experiments with laboratory scientists in white coats, but experimental research methods are also used by social scientists, some of whom are interested in such issues as group power dynamics, racial discrimination, and gender socialization. Experiments take place not only in laboratory settings but also in corporate boardrooms and even on street corners.

When sociologists conduct experiments, they start with two basic goals. First, they strive to develop precise tools with which to observe, record, and measure their data. Second, they attempt to control for all possible variables except the one under investigation: they regulate everything except the variable they're interested in so that they can draw clearer conclusions about what caused that variable to change (if it did).

For instance, a classic social experiment might be set up like this: A researcher who is interested in divorce wants to investigate whether marriage counseling actually helps couples stay together. He would recruit couples for the experiment and then randomly assign them into two different groups, making sure that members of each group were similar in terms of age, income, education, and religion as well as length of time married. One group, the **experimental group**, would receive marriage counseling, while the other, the **control group**, would not. In this experiment, marriage counseling is the **independent variable**; it is the factor that is predicted to cause change in the experimental group. The **dependent variable** (or factor that is changed by the independent variable) is the likelihood of staying married or getting divorced. In such an experiment, the researcher could compare the two groups and then make conclusions about whether receiving marriage counseling leads to more couples staying married, leads to more couples getting divorced, or has no impact at all.

Another area in which sociological experiments have been conducted is gender-role socialization in families. Research has shown that a child's earliest exposure to what it means to be a boy or girl comes from parents and other caregivers. Boy and girl infants are treated differently by

EXPERIMENTS formal tests of specific variables and effects, performed in a setting where all aspects of the situation can be controlled

EXPERIMENTAL GROUP the members of a test group who receive the experimental treatment

CONTROL GROUP the members of a test group who are allowed to continue without intervention so that they can be compared with the experimental group

INDEPENDENT VARIABLE the factor that is predicted to cause change

DEPENDENT VARIABLE the factor that is changed (or not) by the independent variable

Gender Role Socialization Starts in Infancy In Barrie Thorne's experiment, she asked adults to play with babies dressed in either blue or pink. Thorne found that people treated the baby differently depending on whether they thought it was a girl or a boy.

adults—from the way they're dressed to the toys they're given to play with—and are expected to act differently (Thorne 1993). In one experiment, adult subjects were asked to play with a small baby, who was dressed in either pink or blue. The subjects assumed the gender of the infant by the color of its clothes and acted accordingly. When they thought it was a boy (in blue), they handled the baby less gently and talked in a louder voice, saying things like, "Aren't you a big, strong boy?" When they thought it was a girl (in pink), they held the baby closer to themselves and spoke more softly: "What a sweet little girl!" In both cases, it was actually the same baby; only the color of the clothing was changed. From this experiment, we can see how gender influences the way that we perceive and interact with others from a very early age.

Sociologists may also use quasi-experimental methods when they study ethnic and gender discrimination in housing, employment, or policing (McIntyre et al. 1980; Brief et al. 1995; Charles 2001). In such studies, individuals who were similar in all respects except for ethnicity or gender were asked to interview for the same jobs, apply for the same mortgage loans, or engage in some other activity. As in the pink-and-blue baby experiment, people who had exactly the same qualifications were treated differently based on their race and gender, with whites and men given better jobs or mortgage rates, and women and minorities given inferior jobs or rates, or none at all. Through such studies, researchers are able to observe behaviors that may indicate discrimination or unequal treatment.

On the whole, data analysis for experimental sociology tends to be quantitative rather than qualitative because the main goal of an experiment is to isolate a variable and explore the degree to which that variable affects a particular social situation (Smith 1990). The quantitative techniques for analyzing data range from straightforward statistical analyses to complex mathematical modeling.

Advantages and Disadvantages

ADVANTAGES

1. Experiments give sociologists a way to manipulate and control the social environment they seek to understand. Experiments can be designed so that there is a minimal amount of outside interference. Researchers can also select participants who have exactly the characteristics they want to explore, such as the babies and adults in the gender-role socialization experiment.

2. Experimental methods are especially appropriate for researchers who are developing theories about the way the social world operates. A researcher can construct a model of the social situation she is interested in and watch as it unfolds before her, without any of the unpredictable intrusions of the real world. For instance, if she wants to study what makes bystanders want to intervene, this might be easier to measure in a laboratory setting than among strangers on a busy public street.

3. Much like physics experiments, highly controlled sociological experiments can theoretically be repeated—they have replicability—so that findings can be tested more than once. An experiment such as the pink-and-blue baby study could easily be performed again and again to gauge historical and cultural changes in gender socialization.

DISADVANTAGES

1. Experiments are applicable only to certain types of research that can be constructed and measured in a controlled setting. Laboratories are by design artificial

IN RELATIONSHIPS
Social Networking Sites as Sources of Data

While sociologists interested in studying interpersonal relationships use a wide variety of archival materials, the Internet has created whole new ways of conducting research. Letters, journals, and diaries have always been a rich source of data, but ones that have usually been unavailable until many years after they were produced. On the other hand, social networking sites like Twitter, YouTube, and Facebook create a treasure trove of data that can be accessed unobtrusively in real time. Given that Facebook is one of the most-visited sites on the Internet and is full of sociologically fascinating phenomena, it's not surprising to find that numerous researchers are using Facebook as a source of data to study such issues as relationships, identity, self-esteem, and popularity.

One of the earliest and most ambitious projects using social networking sites was conducted by Nicholas Christakis and Jason Kaufman of Harvard and Andreas Wimmer of UCLA. Their data consisted of all the publicly available Facebook profiles of an entire class at an anonymous East Coast university from their freshman to senior years. The researchers were interested in examining the relationship "between patterns of social affiliation and aesthetic proclivities" (Kaufman 2008). In other words, they were looking at the relationship between the number and type of friends someone had and the kind of books, music, and movies the person liked.

The researchers found that online social networks looked a lot like social networks established through traditional, real-life, face-to-face contact. People's networks on Facebook tended to exhibit "homophily"; that is, people tend to be Facebook friends with other people like them, especially in terms of race and gender. In some ways, this isn't surprising. Increasingly, an individual's online profile is an extension of her everyday life. What might be more surprising, however, is the way in which social networks can spread influence. Researchers now have the data to show how such seemingly individual things as a person's taste in clothes, level of happiness, and even body size are influenced by social networks (Christakis and Fowler 2009). For researchers, Facebook is

Mining Social Media As more people of varying ages, races, and backgrounds use social media, researchers can analyze these networks as a major part of real life.

especially exciting because it offers a data set rich enough to test ideas that up to now have only been theorized about. As Christakis points out, concepts about how social networks function were "first described by Simmel 100 years ago. . . . He just theorize[d] about it 100 years ago, but he didn't have the data. Now we can engage that data" (Rosenbloom 2007).

But social networking sites do more than just provide researchers with new data to answer old questions; they also connect friends and family in new ways. Young people use the "relationship status" feature of Facebook as the new standard for evaluating dating; they aren't really a couple until they change their status to "in a relationship." And Facebook has also changed the ways that families interact. The extended family, which is often now separated geographically, is more easily reunited online. Facebook was originally created for college students, but it now attracts their parents, and even their grandparents, all logging on to stay in touch. And be aware that with our interconnected web of relationships, if your friend's friend's friend on Facebook has quit smoking or gained weight, it can influence the likelihood that you will do the same.

---

environments. We take a leap in claiming that the same results found in the lab will also occur in the real world.

2. Achieving distance from the messy realities of the social world is also the major weakness with sociological experiments. Although experiments can be useful for the development of theory and for explaining the impact of isolated variables, they are generally not very effective for describing more complex processes and interactions. By definition, experiments seek to eliminate

elements that will have an unforeseen effect, and that's just not the way the real world works.

Issues in Sociological Research

As sociologists, we don't conduct our research in a cultural vacuum. In our professional as well as personal lives, all our actions have consequences, and we must be aware of how the things we do affect others. For this reason, any introduction to sociological methods is incomplete without a discussion of three topics: the nonacademic uses of sociological research; values, objectivity, and reactivity in the research process; and the importance of ethics in conducting social research.

Nonacademic Uses of Research Methods

The research methods discussed in this chapter are frequently applied outside the field of sociology. The U.S. Census Bureau, for example, has been taking a survey of the total population once every ten years since 1790. The census attempts to reach every person residing in the country and makes reports available on a wide range of social, demographic, and economic features. Many government decisions, from where to build a new school or hospital to where to install a new stoplight, are made using demographic data from the census and other major surveys.

Sociological research methods are also used by private organizations, such as political campaign offices and news agencies. You are probably familiar with polls (another form of survey research) conducted by organizations like Gallup, Zogby, and Roper. And you have certainly seen the results of election polls, which indicate the candidates or issues voters are likely to support. Polls, however, do not just reflect public opinion; they can also be used to shape it. Not all of them are conducted under strict scientific protocols. Whenever you hear poll results, try to learn who commissioned the poll and determine whether they are promoting (or opposing) any particular agenda.

Businesses and corporations have turned to sociological research in order to better understand the human dynamics within their companies. Some ethnographers, for instance, have studied organizational culture and reported their findings to executives. Edgar Schein (1997, 2010) is often referred to as an industrial ethnographer because he conducts fieldwork in business settings in order to help management identify and deal with dilemmas in the workplace, such as how to motivate workers. Many of the experimental "games" developed by sociological researchers can be put to use in the business world to build teams, train employees, or even conduct job interviews. During a corporate retreat, for example, employees might be asked to participate in an obstacle or ropes course, in which they have to work together in order to succeed. By observing the strategies participants use, an employer might learn how task-oriented networks are formed, how leaders are chosen, or how cooperation emerges under pressure. Similarly, experimental games that require subjects to budget imaginary money or communicate an idea in a round of charades may offer insight into how social groups operate or may identify the most effective communicators from a pool of applicants. These experiments clearly benefit the corporation; do they help workers as well?

Market research is perhaps the most common of all nonacademic uses of sociological methods. In order to be successful, most companies will engage in some sort of study of the marketplace, either through their own internal sales and marketing departments or by hiring an outside consultant. The efforts of all these companies to understand the buying public have created a multibillion-dollar marketing and advertising industry. If you've ever filled out a product warranty card after making a purchase, clicked "yes" on a pop-up dialog box from a website, allowed "cookies" onto your browser, or cast a vote for your favorite contestants on *Dancing with the Stars*, then someone has gathered data about your tastes and habits. It is important to note, however, that not all market studies, in fact probably very few, meet the rigorous standards that are otherwise applied to "scientific" research. Remember, too, that the bottom line for any company that uses market research is the desire to sell you their products or services. Just how well do these marketers know you already?

Values, Objectivity, and Reactivity

It's important to recognize that scientific research is done by human beings, not robots. Humans have flaws, prejudices, and blind spots, and all these things can affect the way they conduct research.

VALUES Like biological or physical scientists, most sociologists believe that they should not allow their personal beliefs to influence their research. The classic sociological statement on neutrality comes from Max Weber (1925/1946), who, in his essay "Science as a Vocation," coined the phrase **value-free sociology** to convey the idea that in doing research sociologists need to separate facts from their own individual values. Although most sociologists have agreed with this ideal, some have challenged the notion of value-free sociology. For instance, some Marxist researchers believe it is appropriate to combine social research and social action or praxis. For them, the study of society is intimately linked to a commitment to actively solve social problems. Likewise, action research seeks not only to understand but to change the social world. On the other hand, some symbolic interactionists, like David Matza (1969), believe that the very intention of changing the world prohibits a researcher from truly understanding that world. The question of whether sociologists should engage only in **basic research**, which is justified as the search for knowledge for its own sake, or rather engage in **applied research**,

---

VALUE-FREE SOCIOLOGY an ideal whereby researchers identify facts without allowing their own personal beliefs or biases to interfere

BASIC RESEARCH the search for knowledge without an agenda or practical goal in mind

APPLIED RESEARCH gathering knowledge that can be used to create social change

ON THE JOB
Commercial Ethnography

Recently, advertisers have become interested in the complex relationships between people and products and are looking to ethnographic methods to help them understand these relationships. Companies are hiring commercial ethnographers to learn how ordinary citizens bathe, dress, make breakfast, drive to work, do laundry, or flip hamburgers on their backyard grill—all in order to understand how consumers relate to various products. While Nissan Motors was developing the Infiniti line, for example, the company used ethnographic market research to help them understand the differences between Japanese and American perceptions of luxury. That's right—they drove around with people and talked to them about their cars! Nissan found that to Americans, high-end goods are more valuable if their lavish features are visible. This is in contrast to the Japanese concept of luxury, which values simplicity and hidden charm. Understanding these differences allowed Nissan to successfully redesign the Infiniti line to be more attractive to American buyers; other automakers realized the benefits of ethnographic market research and followed in Nissan's footsteps (Osborne 2002).

Some commercial ethnographers, known as "cool hunters," search for the newest, hippest trends in popular culture. Look-Look, a Hollywood trend-forecasting firm, recruited "youth correspondents" and amateur photographers in cities around the world as part of its "living research" strategy. Founded by Dee Dee Gordon and Sharon Lee, Look-Look counted on these correspondents to provide information on the latest trends in music, fashion, technology, and hip activities and hangouts. Says Gordon, "We look for kids who are ahead of the pack, because they'll influence what all the other kids do" (PBS 2001). Look-Look is somewhat secretive about its client list, which has included Universal Pictures, Disney Films, and Skyy Vodka. Other market research firms report that companies such as Xerox, Colgate-Palmolive, Kraft Foods, Duracell, Playtex, Honda, Pioneer Stereo, and Anheuser-Busch have all utilized qualitative market research to direct their production, distribution, and

marketing strategies. Sociology students who become proficient in ethnographic methods may well be the hottest new hires in the field of commercial ethnography.

Cool Hunter Loic Bizel, a French "cool hunter" in Japan, picks up a pair of hand-painted sneakers in Tokyo's Harajuku shopping district. His job is to observe and report on the fast-changing street fads of Japan.

which requires putting into action what is learned, continues to be debated within the discipline.

Despite the safeguards built into research methodologies, there are still opportunities for bias, or personal preferences, to subtly influence how the work is done. Bias can infiltrate every part of the research process—from identifying a project to selecting a sample, from the wording of questions to the analysis and write-up of the data. Earl Babbie (2002)

claims that research biases have come into play in the area of U.S. racial relations, and he documents several historical cases to illustrate the point. In 1896, the Supreme Court established the doctrine of "separate but equal" as a means of "guaranteeing equal protection" for African Americans while still allowing racial segregation. Although no research was directly cited, it is widely believed that the ruling was influenced by the work of William Graham Sumner, a leading

OBJECTIVITY impartiality, the ability to allow the facts to speak for themselves

social scientist at the time. Sumner believed that the customs of a society were relatively impervious to outside influence and that therefore the legal system should not be used to enforce social change. The saying "You can't legislate morality" is a reflection of such thinking. So instead of allowing blacks the same rights and access to resources, the Court continued to uphold segregation.

The doctrine of "separate but equal" persisted until it was finally overturned in 1954 in the landmark civil rights case *Brown v. Board of Education of Topeka, Kansas*, which outlawed racial segregation in schools. This time, the Supreme Court justices based their unanimous decision on several other, more contemporary sociological and psychological studies (Blaunstein and Zangrando 1970). Apparently, the Court was now of the belief that morality *could* be legislated.

A decade later, controversy erupted again when in 1966 a noted sociologist, James Coleman, published his findings about a national study on race and education. Coleman claimed that the academic performance of African American students attending integrated schools was no better than that of those attending segregated schools; that such things

Little Rock Nine Students try to prevent Elizabeth Eckford from getting to Little Rock's Central High School after a federal court ordered the school to desegregate.

as libraries, laboratories, or expenditures per student had less influence on academic performance than neighborhoods or family. While some criticized Coleman on methodological grounds, others were more concerned that his findings might be used to support a return to segregation. This has not happened, but neither has complete integration. We still need to work toward creating an educational system that serves all students well, and social research will continue to be part of that process. Most social scientists, and the American public in general, support civil rights and racial equality. These beliefs inspire research at the same time that research inspires continued social change. Even though we aim for value-free sociology, there are some topics on which it is hard to remain neutral.

OBJECTIVITY The notion of **objectivity**, or impartiality, plays a fundamental role in scientific practice. As far back as Auguste Comte, sociologists have maintained that they could study society rationally and objectively. If a researcher is rational and objective, then he should be able to observe reality, distinguish actual facts from mental concepts, and separate truth from feeling or opinion. This ideal may be desirable and reasonable, but can "facts" really speak for themselves? And if so, can we discover those facts without somehow involving ourselves in them?

Some "facts" that sociologists once took to be objective reality have since been invalidated. Racist, sexist, and ethnocentric perspectives long dominated the field and passed for "truth." For many years, scientific reality consisted only of the experience of white European males, and the realities of women, ethnic minorities, and others outside the mainstream were categorically ignored or dismissed.

For example, until recently, heart problems in women were likely to go undiagnosed, which meant that women were more likely than men to die from heart attacks. Why? Because medical research on heart attacks used mostly male subjects and so had not discovered that women's symptoms are different from men's (Rabin 2008). It is easy now, through hindsight, to see that our "knowledge" was severely distorted. We must, therefore, be willing to recognize that what currently passes for fact may some day be challenged.

Another obstacle to achieving objectivity is our subjective nature as human beings. Our own experience of the world, and therefore sense of reality, is inevitably personal and idiosyncratic. Although we recognize our innate subjectivity, we still long for and actively pursue what we call absolute truth. But some social scientists question this ideal; they propose that subjectivity is not only unavoidable, it may be preferable when it comes to the study of human beings. This is especially true of sociologists who do autoethnography, in which they themselves—and their own thoughts, feelings, and experiences—are the focus of their study (Ellis 1997). Furthermore, some postmodern thinkers have gone so far as to reject the notion that there is any objective reality out there in the first place. Their arguments parallel certain trends in the physical sciences as well, where developments such as chaos theory and fuzzy logic suggest the need to reconsider the assumption of an orderly universe.

REACTIVITY In addition to maintaining their objectivity, social scientists must be concerned with **reactivity**, the ways that people and events respond to being studied. One classic example of reactivity comes from studies that were conducted from 1927 to 1932 at the Hawthorne plant of Western Electric in Chicago. Elton Mayo (1949), a Harvard business school professor, sought to examine the effect of varying work conditions on motivation and productivity in the factory. When he changed certain conditions—such as lighting levels, rest breaks, and even rates of pay—he found that each change resulted in a rise in productivity both in the individual worker and in the group. What was more surprising, however, was that returning to the original conditions also resulted in a rise in productivity. Mayo concluded, then, that the variables he had manipulated were not the causes of productivity; rather, *it was the effect of being studied*, or what is now referred to as the **Hawthorne effect**. In other words, the workers had responded to the researchers' taking interest in their performance, and it was this attention that had caused the improvement.

Researchers must always be aware that their subjects, whether in an experiment or in a natural observation, are active and intelligent participants. The subjects may be able to sense what the researchers are trying to understand or prove and in effect "give them what they want" by responding to even the unspoken goals of the research. Our presence as researchers always has some effect on those we study, whether noticeable to us or not.

Research Ethics

Doing research that involves other human beings means that we must address moral issues (questions about right and wrong conduct) as we make decisions that will affect them. For this reason, various academic disciplines have developed ethical guidelines—professional standards for honest and honorable dealings with others—meant to help direct the decision making of such researchers. When we use other people as means to an end, we must protect them as ends in themselves.

It's easy to understand the risks of participating in, say, a pharmaceutical drug trial or a study of the effects of radiation treatment on certain types of cancers. The risks of participating in social research are different and more subtle. It is often the case, for example, that social researchers don't fully explain the details of their research project to the participating subjects. Sometimes this is necessary; survey respondents, for example, must be able to answer questions without interference from the researcher and the potential for bias. Also, ethnographic field-workers operate on various levels of secrecy or **deception**; even when an ethnographer has openly declared herself a researcher, it is often impossible for her to remind every person she speaks with that she is a scientific observer as well as a participant. And if she engages in "covert" research and deliberately presents an inauthentic self to the group, that makes all her interactions inauthentic as well. This can affect the field-worker's ability to discover the members' real, grounded meanings. What, then, has she really been able to learn about the setting and its members?

Codes of ethics in the social sciences do not provide strict rules for researchers to abide by in these cases; rather, they set out principles to guide the researcher's decision making. Secrecy and deceit are thus never strictly prohibited; instead, researchers are cautioned to acquire the informed consent of their subjects and to conduct themselves in a way that protects the subjects from harm.

What other kinds of harm can come to participants? They're not likely to get diseases, and there is usually little physical risk in sitting down to complete a survey questionnaire! But harm *can* result, mostly as a result of the breaching of **confidentiality**. Research subjects are entitled to "rights of biographical anonymity": researchers are required to protect their privacy. This protection is essential to gathering valid data, especially when dealing with controversial topics or vulnerable populations. Respondents must be guaranteed that no one will be able to identify them from reading the research findings. But while most researchers take steps to disguise the identities of individuals and locations, it is sometimes difficult to keep others from uncovering them. For example, in two

> **REACTIVITY** the tendency of people and events to react to the process of being studied
>
> **HAWTHORNE EFFECT** a specific example of reactivity, in which the desired effect is the result not of the independent variable but of the research itself
>
> **DECEPTION** the extent to which the participants in a research project are unaware of the project or its goals
>
> **CONFIDENTIALITY** the assurance that no one other than the researcher will know the identity of a respondent

"Middletown" Although Robert S. Lynd and Helen Merrell Lynd used the pseudonym "Middletown" in their classic studies of stagnation and change in modern American culture, it was long ago revealed that Middletown is actually Muncie, Indiana.

The origins of contemporary research ethics can be traced back to the Nuremberg military tribunals of the late 1940s, in which a group of Nazi doctors were tried for the horrific "experiments" they had performed during World War II. These experiments involved the torture and death of thousands of concentration camp inmates. Of the twenty-three Nazi doctors tried at Nuremberg, sixteen were convicted of war crimes. Besides a kind of justice for the deaths of so many, the other enduring result of the trials was the Nuremberg Code, a set of moral and ethical guidelines for performing research on human beings. According to these guidelines, developed by two doctors, Andrew Ivy and Leo Alexander, scientists must accept certain responsibilities: to perform only research that can "yield fruitful results for the good of society, unprocurable by other methods"; to protect their human subjects from "all unnecessary physical and mental suffering and injury"; and to perform research only on subjects who give their informed, noncoerced consent.

In the United States, there was strong support for the Nuremberg Code. But at the same time that the code was being developed, the U.S. government was involved in its own medical atrocity, though it would not be revealed to the public until decades later: the Tuskegee Syphilis Study. In 1932, the U.S. Public Health Service began a forty-year-long study of "untreated syphilis in the male negro": 399 African American men from Tuskegee, an impoverished region of Alabama,

who were infected with syphilis were left untreated so that doctors could observe the natural progression of the disease. The symptoms include painful sores, hair loss, sterility, blindness, paralysis, and insanity, and almost always lead to death. The disease can be transmitted by men to their sexual partners, and infected women can pass it on to their infants. By 1947, penicillin was widely accepted as the preferred treatment for syphilis, but government doctors decided to leave the Tuskegee men untreated to avoid interfering with the study's results.

While these doctors had not intentionally inflicted the disease on the subjects, neither had they offered a cure when it became available. The full story of the Tuskegee experiment was not revealed until 1972, and it was not until 1997 that President Bill Clinton issued an official apology from the U.S. government to the victims and their families. Clearly, Americans were as guilty of violating moral and ethical codes as Germans had been at a similar time in history.

What is important to take away from this lesson is the need for all scientific research to adhere to ethical standards—this includes the social as well as medical sciences. In either case, researchers must consider the potential harm that they can cause to human subjects. You may not think of sociologists as dealing with life-and-death issues; yet, as researchers, we often find ourselves in positions where certain kinds of studies can't be undertaken because of concerns for the well-being of the potential subjects.

The Nuremberg Code In the wake of the Nuremberg Military Tribunals after World War II, science organizations adopted a set of guidelines to regulate researchers' ethical conduct. Whether in biology, psychiatry, or sociology, researchers must consider the potential harm they can cause to research participants.

classic sociological studies the pseudonym "Middletown" was used to evoke the notion of an "average" American city and to conceal that city's real name and location (Lynd and Lynd 1929/1959, 1937). In spite of this intention, it was long ago revealed to be Muncie, Indiana—and since the town featured in the Middletown studies was widely viewed as an example of the shallowness and triviality of modern American culture, this was not such a good thing for Muncie's reputation!

Sometimes worse than having others recognize a place or person is having subjects themselves find out what was written about them. Carolyn Ellis (1995, 2007) had an unsettling experience when she returned to the small mid-Atlantic fishing village in which she had spent years living and doing fieldwork. In the time she had been gone, she had published a book about the village, and excerpts had made their way back to the villagers, who were upset with the way that Ellis had depicted them. These villagers, who had considered Ellis to be their friend, felt deeply betrayed; they felt that she had abused their hospitality and misrepresented them as uncouth, uneducated hicks. Despite her protests that she was simply doing her job as a sociologist, many villagers refused to speak with her again, and she was shut out of a social world of which she had once been an integral part.

Researchers may undertake other kinds of risks in doing their work that can put them in personal peril as well. Ethnographer Rik Scarce found himself at risk of a prison term when members of the animal rights group that Scarce was studying were suspected of breaking into a research lab at Scarce's university. A subpoena was issued requiring him to testify in the case. If he did, it would incriminate the activists whose trust he had gained over months of fieldwork; if he didn't, he would doom himself to a jail sentence. Scarce felt a strong moral obligation to protect the confidentiality of his subjects and refused to testify against them in court. He spent four months in jail for contempt of court and ended up writing a book about his own experiences in the criminal justice system (Scarce 2005).

In order to encourage the protection of research subjects, each academic discipline has adopted its own **code of ethics** to provide guidelines for researchers. The American Sociological Association Code of Ethics, for example, sets out recommendations for how to avoid bias, adhere to professional standards, and protect respondents from harm. In addition, universities where research is conducted have a body known as an **institutional review board**, or IRB, a group of scholars who meet regularly to review the research proposals of their colleagues. If an IRB has reservations about the safety of the participants in a given research project, it may require changes to the protocol or may even stop the project from going forward. In extreme cases, funding may be revoked if the participants are being put at undue risk; entire university power structures have been undermined as a result of pervasive research ethics problems.

The power invested in IRBs is seen as controversial by some. The boards are often made up entirely of scholars in medicine, biology, chemistry, and physics; social scientists have questioned these scholars' ability to make judgments about social research. Because IRBs have the power to shut down research projects, perhaps they should be discipline-specific, with biologists judging biologists, psychologists judging psychologists, and sociologists judging sociologists.

CODE OF ETHICS ethical guidelines for researchers to consult as they design a project

INSTITUTIONAL REVIEW BOARD a group of scholars within a university who meet regularly to review and approve the research proposals of their colleagues and make recommendations for how to protect human subjects

CLOSING COMMENTS

In this chapter, you have learned the different methods used by sociologists to investigate the social world. Each method has its strengths and limitations, and each can be fruitfully applied to a variety of research questions. In fact, this is exactly what you will be doing.

Each chapter from this point on will feature two Data Workshops in which you will be asked to apply one of the methods from this chapter to an actual sociological research project. You will get a chance to practice doing the work of sociological research by actually gathering and analyzing your own data. You may find yourself referring back to this chapter to remind yourself of the specific mechanics of one or another of the research methods. This is exactly what you should be doing; it's okay if two months from now you don't remember all the details. Just because you're moving on to Chapter 3, don't forget that Chapter 2 can continue to be useful to you throughout the term—and maybe even beyond that.

Everything You Need to Know about Sociological Research Methods

❝ Research methods are strategies that produce data to support, disprove, or modify theoretical claims. ❞

THE SCIENTIFIC METHOD

1. Identify a problem or ask a question

2. Conduct a literature review

3. Form a hypothesis; give operational definitions to variables

4. Choose research design or method

5. Collect data

6. Analyze data

7. Disseminate findings

REVIEW

1. Try to write a survey or interview question that asks about a respondent's political affiliation without being biased or using language that might spark an emotional response.

2. Imagine that your teacher asks you to do a simple random sample of your class. How would you select your sample so that you could be sure each member had an equal chance of being included?

3. Researchers are now using social networking websites like Facebook and Twitter to gather a wide variety of data. If researchers read your profile (or those of your friends or family), do you think they would have a valid understanding of who you (or they) are? Is there a weakness of research that relies on existing sources?

Sociological Research Methods

Method	Advantages	Disadvantages
Ethnography	Study groups that are often overlooked by other methods Challenge our taken-for-granted notions about groups we thought we knew Reshape the stereotypes we hold about others	Lack of replicability Lack of representativeness Respondents are not always forthcoming or truthful
Interviews	Allow respondents to speak in their own words Dispel certain preconceptions Discover issues that might have otherwise been overlooked	Lack of representativeness
Surveys	Gather original data on a population that is too large to study by other means Relatively quick and economical and can provide a vast amount of data Comparatively strong on reliability Less concern about research bias	Lacks qualitative data that might better capture the social reality Not all respondents are honest in self-reports Problems with the sampling process can make generalizability difficult
Existing Sources	Work with information researchers could not possibly obtain for themselves	Answers to questions that the original authors did not have in mind are not available Does not illuminate how original sources were interpreted
Experiments	Manipulate and control the social environment researchers to minimize outside interference High replicability	Applicable only to certain types of research that can be constructed and measured in a controlled setting Not very effective for describing more complex processes and interactions

EXPLORE

A Random Invitation: The American Community Survey

The ACS is a survey conducted by the U.S. Census Bureau each year to learn more about the American population. The survey not only provides data on population changes but also provides annual data on marital status, housing, education, and income. Visit the Everyday Sociology Blog to find out if the American Community Survey really paints an accurate picture of the American population.

http://wwnPag.es/trw402

PART II
Framing
Social Life

How does culture shape our social worlds? How are our personal identities produced by our cultural contexts and social interactions? How does participation in group life shape both individual experience and social structure? How are what is normal and what is deviant defined, and what are the consequences for people who are labeled accordingly? Part II of this text addresses these questions in the next four chapters on culture (Chapter 3), the self and interaction (Chapter 4), groups (Chapter 5), and deviance (Chapter 6). The ability to examine, describe, analyze, and explain the points of intersection between the individual world and the social world is sociology's special contribution to the larger scholarly endeavor. Within the next four chapters, you will encounter many works by sociologists that illustrate the links between the individual and society. Leila Rupp and Verta Taylor's book *Drag Queens at the 801 Cabaret* (2003) is perfect for highlighting these themes.

Drag Queens at the 801 Cabaret is an ethnographic portrait of a Key West, Florida, drag club, where gay male performers don sexy dresses, lavish wigs, and theatrical makeup and sing and dance for a diverse audience: tourists and locals, men and women, gays and straights. Rupp and Taylor get to know the "801 girls" and their friends, family, and audience members, and the authors even try out their own sort of drag. (That's right—women dressed as men dressed as women!)

Rupp and Taylor recognize that the particular culture of the 801 Cabaret is nestled within multiple contemporary American subcultures. For example, Key West is an island subculture that offers a year-round, touristy, carnivalesque atmosphere as part of its charm. It "remains a flamboyant mix of cultures. . . . [I]t shelters not only vibrant Cuban and Bahamian enclaves, but also artistic, hippie, and gay communities. . . . The city [says journalist Charles Kuralt] is 'full of dreamers, drifters, and dropouts, spongers and idlers and barflies, writers and fishermen, islanders from the Caribbean and gays from the big cities, painters and pensioners, treasure hunters, real estate speculators, smugglers, runaways, old Conchs and young lovers . . . all elaborately tolerant of one another'" (Rupp and Taylor 2003, pp. 50–51). For the 801 girls, this means that the subcultures associated with both gay masculinity and drag performance are supported and sustained on the island in ways they might not be on the mainland. Because of the island's unique mix of subcultures, one of the performers asserts that "Key West is the true home of accepted diversity" (p. 55).

In Key West's culture, many kinds of people feel free to be themselves. But what does that really mean? For the drag queens at the 801 Cabaret, their performances are about putting on a different identity than the one they present in their everyday lives. These are men with flashy female alter-egos: Kevin becomes "Kylie"; Roger becomes "Inga"; Dean becomes "Milla." And their process of becoming is elaborate and grueling:

Sociologists Verta Taylor and Leila Rupp The authors getting into drag themselves.

Some of the girls shave all over their bodies, some their faces, chests, legs, and arms, some just their faces. . . . They powder their faces, necks, and chests, using a thick base to hide their beards. . . . Eyeliner, eye shadow, mascara, false eyelashes, lip liner, and lipstick are painstakingly applied. (pp. 12–13)

So far, this doesn't sound all that different than the rituals many women perform every morning in front of the mirror. After the makeup, however, things get a little more intricate, as the "girls" tuck their penises and testicles between their legs, using a gaff [a special panty], or several, to make sure everything stays out of sight . . . panty hose, sometimes several layers . . . corsets and waist cinchers . . . they all, of course, wear bras . . . [filled with] water balloons (the tied end makes an amazingly realistic nipple), half a Nerf football, lentil beans in a pair of nylons, foam or silicone prostheses. (pp. 20–21)

All this work to look like women—and that's not taking into account the exhausting work of acting the part, onstage and off. While drag queens do not seek to convince their audiences that they are "real" women, they do move, speak, sing, and dance in stereotypically feminine style as part of their performances. And that's the insight that drag queens provide about our own identities: it's *all* performance! Our male and female selves are the products of interactional accomplishments, and "real" women do many of the same things that drag queens do in order to express femininity.

Because the drag queens perform different identities onstage and off, the 801 Cabaret calls into question some of our most important and taken-for-granted boundaries between social groups: males and females, and gays and straights. In fact, drag queens are living examples of the intersections between these groups. One of the performers says:

Last night—though this happens almost every night—[this woman] goes, "I'm straight, I'm a woman, I'm not a lesbian, but you're so beautiful, I find you so attractive" . . . [and] a straight guy, has been straight for like fifty years or something like that . . . goes, "You know, I've been straight all my life, and I know you're a man, but you're so beautiful. . . . I can't keep my eyes off you." (p. 201)

Drag queens and drag shows allow others to cross between groups, to see what life might be like in a world in which gender boundaries are fluid and homosexuality is normal:

As one of the few ways that straight people encounter gay culture—where, in fact, straight people live for an hour or two in an environment where gay is normal and straight is other—drag shows . . . play an important role for the gay/lesbian movement. Precisely because drag shows are entertaining, they attract people who might never otherwise be exposed to gay politics. As one female audience member put it, they "take something difficult and make it light." (pp. 207–8)

Finally, drag shows also challenge our notions about what is normal and what is deviant; performers embrace what would otherwise be considered a stigmatized identity and turn it into something to be proud of. Drag queens can be seen as voluntary outsiders, unconcerned about fitting into

Performing Gender Drag queens and "real" women perform femininity in similar ways.

mainstream society. Rupp and Taylor make the argument that drag is a form of social protest—against a society in which gender and sexual orientation are crammed into limiting, two-category systems; in which identities are seen as immutable; and in which certain forms of cultural expression are marginalized. Their analysis of the social world of one Key West drag club offers sociological insights into the lives of the individual performers who work against social stigma and limitations to provide new ways of looking at culture, self, and society.

Drag Queens on Stage How do drag queens use entertainment and performance to undermine gender stereotypes?

CHAPTER 3

Culture

Heavy metal music has long been associated with young, white, alienated, angry, blue collar men in America. With extremely loud, pounding music accompanied by lyrics dealing with the themes of death, sex, and alienation, heavy metal has many critics among mainstream conservative Americans. Acrassicauda (the word is Arabic for "black scorpion") is an Iraqi heavy metal band that represents both a clash and a connection between American and Iraqi culture. Heavy metal music became popular in Iraq in the early 1990s, as middle-class Iraqi teenagers discovered bands like Metallica, Slayer, and the Scorpions through black market CDs. The themes of anger, death, rebellion, and violence were all too familiar for Iraqi teens.

In 2001, four Iraqi musicians formed the band Acrassicauda, which gained fame through the 2007 documentary *Heavy Metal in Baghdad* (VBS.tv 2007). During Saddam Hussein's regime, the band was able to perform but was forced to write a song glorifying Hussein with lyrics like "Following our leader Saddam Hussein, we'll make them fall, we'll drive them insane!" They were also subject to restrictions on the heavy metal custom of headbanging because of the dance's similarity to a Jewish prayer ritual called *davening*. After Hussein was overthrown, the group's lyrics became increasingly political and reflected on the horrors of a country torn apart by war. In *Vice*, a youth culture magazine, writer Gideon Yago asserted that Acrassicauda's version of metal was intensified through the terror and violence that Iraqis had to encounter on a daily basis (Moore 2004).

Because any gathering of people in Iraq becomes a target for terrorists, Acrassicauda was able to play only six live concerts in a span of five years. Islamic militants equated heavy metal music with Satan worshipping, much like Christian conservatives in the United States did. However, in the United States, opponents attempted to use legislation to rid the culture of heavy metal. In Iraq, the perception of heavy metal as Satan worshipping was exacerbated by the American origins of the music. Acrassicauda received death threats that read, "You are Americanized, playing Western music. You either quit or you will be dead." These death threats escalated to the point where the members of Acrassicauda feared for their lives.

Acrassicauda did not quit playing but instead used strategies like having random band practices rather than playing at regular times. They would hold concerts while mortar shells dropped around the venues. At the same time, they realized the danger of continuing to live in Iraq while spreading their message through heavy metal.

After watching the band's story in *Heavy Metal in Baghdad*, Alex Skolnick, from the metal band Testament, met the band and helped them record an EP, *Only the Dead See the End of the War*. The EP gathered more publicity for the group, and *Vice* magazine set up a PayPal account for donations to help members of Acrassicauda emigrate to the United States. Metal fans throughout the world donated a total of $40,000, the United States granted the band refugee status, and now Acrassicauda is living and performing in the United States. Another crowd-funding platform, Kickstarter, was used to provide support for the band's first full-length album, *Gilgamesh*, which was finally released in 2015.

It's interesting how an alienated U.S. subculture like heavy metal can come to represent mainstream Western culture to militant Islamic fundamentalists. It's also enlightening to see how music enjoyed by disenfranchised, rebellious American youth can be attractive to those living in the real-life horrors of a war-torn nation. The study of culture provides an endless number of fascinating possibilities for understanding ourselves and others.

HOW TO READ
THIS CHAPTER

Culture is one of the fundamental elements of social life and thus a very important topic in sociology. Many of the concepts presented here will come up again in almost every subsequent chapter. You will need to keep these concepts in mind as you learn about other substantive areas. You will also want to think about how culture is relevant to the things you already know from your own life experience. Try to come up with some of your own examples as you read along. The subject of culture is probably inherently interesting to most people. But although culture is familiar to all of us, you should be seeing it in a new and different way by the time you finish this chapter.

What Is Culture?

Culture encompasses practically all of human civilization and touches on almost every aspect of social life. It is so much a part of the world around us that we may not recognize the extent to which it shapes and defines who we are. In the broadest sense, we can say that **culture** is the entire way of life of a group of people. It can include everything from language and gestures to style of dress and standards of beauty, from customs and rituals to tools and artifacts, from music and child-rearing practices to the proper way for customers to line up in a grocery store. It forms basic beliefs and assumptions about the world and the way things work, and it defines the moral parameters of what is right and wrong, good and bad.

Although culture varies from group to group, all societies develop some form of culture. It is the human equivalent of instinct in animals: although we humans do have some basic instincts, culture actually accounts for our great success as a species. We are totally dependent on it to deal with the demands of life in society. As culture develops, it is shared among members of a group, handed down from generation to generation, and passed along from one group or individual to another.

Although culture may seem to us to be "second nature," it is actually learned, rather than innate. Because we learn it so slowly and incrementally, we are often unaware of the process. For instance, few of us would be conscious of having *learned* all the slang words we currently use or the distance we typically maintain from someone while talking with him. We may not remember exactly when we first felt patriotic or how we formed our opinions about people from the upper class. We all carry culture inside ourselves; it becomes ingrained and internalized into our way of thinking and acting. Culture guides the way we make sense of the world around us and the way we make decisions about what to do and how to do it. We can talk about the culture of a given country, state, or community, of people belonging to an ethnic or religious group, or of those working in the same profession. We can even say that sports enthusiasts, schoolmates, or a clique of friends share in a common culture. We'll discuss some of these cultural variations later in the chapter.

How Has Culture Been Studied?

People study culture in a variety of ways. Theologians and philosophers, for example, might debate the morals and values of an ideal culture. Art, literature, and film scholars focus on certain aspects of culture—novels, films, paintings, plays—as expressive, symbolic activities. Cultural anthropologists often investigate societies outside the United States, traveling around the world engaging in empirical fieldwork, while archaeologists study the cultures of the past, digging for artifacts that document the historical realities of peoples long dead.

In contrast, sociologists usually focus on culture closer to home, often in the same societies to which they belong. They do this by using the different theories discussed in Chapter 1—functionalism, conflict theory, symbolic interactionism, and postmodernism—as well as the research methods discussed in Chapter 2. At the same time, however, sociologists may also engage in the process of "othering" by studying the unusual, extraordinary, or deviant in cultural groups. In so doing, they may fail to consider some aspects of the culture that is right in front of them. This is where the sociology of everyday life offers certain benefits. By studying the mundane as well as the exceptional, we can learn about culture in all of its interesting permutations. We can learn not only about the differences between cultural groups—"us" and "them"—but also about the similarities.

> **CULTURE** the entire way of life of a group of people (including both material and symbolic elements) that acts as a lens through which one views the world and that is passed from one generation to the next

Ethnocentrism and Cultural Relativism

Culture acts as a lens through which we view the world. That lens, however, can either elucidate or obscure what we are looking at. Often, we can't clearly see our own culture, precisely because we are so familiar with it. Yet, when exposed to another culture, through travel, television, or other means, we can readily see what is different or seemingly "exotic." Rarely does our perspective allow us to recognize the strangeness in our own culture.

One of the best examples of the challenges in observing culture is presented in a famous article by Horace Miner called "Body Ritual among the Nacirema" (1956). The article focuses on the beliefs and practices of this North American people concerning the care of their bodies. Miner observes that their fundamental belief appears to be that the human body is ugly

"Body Ritual among the Nacirema" Horace Miner reminds us how easy it is to overlook aspects of our own culture, precisely because it seems so normal to us.

and is susceptible to decay and disease and that the only way to counter these conditions is to engage in elaborate ceremonies and rituals. All members of the Nacirema culture conform to a greater or lesser degree to these practices and then pass them along to their children. One passage describes the household shrine where many of the body rituals take place:

> While each family has at least one shrine, the rituals associated with it are not family ceremonies but are private and secret. . . . The focal point of the shrine is a box or chest which is built into a wall. In this chest are kept the many charms and magical potions without which no native believes he could live. . . . Beneath the charm-box is a small font. Each day every member of the family, in succession, enters the shrine room, bows his head before the charm-box, mingles different sorts of holy water in the font, and proceeds with a brief rite of ablution. (p. 504)

The Nacirema regularly visit medicine men, "holy-mouth men,"

ETHNOCENTRISM the principle of using one's own culture as a means or standard by which to evaluate another group or individual, leading to the view that cultures other than one's own are abnormal or inferior

CULTURAL RELATIVISM the principle of understanding other cultures on their own terms, rather than judging or evaluating according to one's own culture

and other specialized practitioners from whom they procure magical potions:

> The Nacirema have an almost pathological horror of and fascination with the mouth, the condition of which is believed to have a supernatural influence on all social relationships. Were it not for the rituals of the mouth, they believe that their teeth would fall out, their gums bleed, their jaws shrink, their friends desert them, and their lovers reject them. The daily body ritual performed by everyone includes a mouth-rite. It was reported to me that the ritual consists of inserting a small bundle of hog hairs into the mouth, along with certain magical powders, and then moving the bundle in a highly formalized series of gestures.

Do the Nacirema seem like a strange group of people, or are they somehow familiar? Miner writes as though he were an anthropologist studying some exotic tribe of primitive people. In actuality, the passages above describe the bathroom and personal health-care habits of the average American. (Note that "Nacirema" is "American" spelled backward.) He doesn't embellish or make up anything; he merely approaches the topic as if he knows nothing about its meaning. So the "charm-box" is the standard medicine cabinet, the "holy water" font is a sink, the medicine men and "holy-mouth men" are doctors and dentists, and the exotic "mouth-rite" is the practice of brushing teeth.

One of the reasons that Miner's article has become so popular is that it demonstrates how easy it is to fail to see our own culture, precisely because we take it for granted. The article reminds students who are becoming social analysts how useful culture shock is in helping to see even what is most familiar as bizarre or strange. Throughout this chapter, keep in mind that your powers of observation must be applied to looking at both "them" and "us."

Another, related problem arises when trying to understand cultures other than our own. Generally, we think of our own culture as being the "normal" one, a belief known as **ethnocentrism**. We don't realize that culture is something learned and that there is nothing inherently better about ours. Ethnocentrism means that we use our own culture as a kind of measuring stick with which to judge other individuals or societies; anyone outside our group seems "off-center" or abnormal.

As sociologists, we want to have as clear a view of any society as possible; this requires that we suspend, at least temporarily, our ethnocentrism. There are several ways to do this. In Chapter 1, we learned about the beginner's mind, culture shock, and the sociological imagination—all ways to see the world anew. We can add to that list **cultural relativism**, which means seeing each different culture as simply that—different. Not better or worse, not right or wrong, but on its own terms. Doing so helps us place different values, beliefs, norms, and practices within their own cultural context. By practicing cultural relativism, or being culturally sensitive, we begin to see others more clearly, and without judgment, and therefore

IN THE FUTURE
Otaku Culture and the Globalization of Niche Interests

If you are not an *otaku*, you probably don't know what *otaku* is. If you are an *otaku*, you may not want others to know what *otaku* is, since *otaku* culture has often been misunderstood by those on the outside. So, what is *otaku*?

Otaku is a Japanese word used to describe devoted fans, usually of manga, anime, or video games. *Otaku* are extremely knowledgeable about whatever it is they are fans of—and while that kind of obsessive interest is sometimes looked down upon by others who don't share it, *otaku* themselves see this intense knowledge as a badge of honor. They view themselves as dedicated rather than obsessed, connoisseurs rather than fanatics, and superior to other hobbyists who aren't as erudite about the object of their enthusiasm. In fact, *otaku* may now be certified as experts in Japan by taking a rigorous, nationally recognized exam (McNicol 2006).

Organizing and displaying their belongings is a central part of *otaku* culture—many *otaku* have special rooms in their homes for their museum-like collections of action figures, paintings, or comic books. Photographs of *otaku* in their "*otaku* spaces" (Galbraith 2012) illuminate the connection among fantasy worlds, material commodities, and virtual communities that *otaku* culture uniquely embodies.

Once confined entirely to Japan (and to small neighborhood clubs even there), the Internet has made *otaku* culture accessible to people all over the world. Indeed, fans of just about everything now depend on social media to connect them with one another, and to allow them to share their fascinations with others who appreciate what it means to be truly dedicated. *Otaku* who in the past might have been viewed with suspicion because of their intense involvement in what others considered a fringe pastime can now validate their commitments by interacting with others who share their interests, whether they are down the street or a world away.

Closely related to its reliance on social media, *otaku* culture is also characterized by its global reach. Indeed, what is distinctive about *otaku* culture is the uncommon direction in which it has traveled. Instead of the United States or another Western culture spreading eastward, *otaku* culture is an example of the East influencing the West: *otaku* represents the globalization and transnationalization of what had previously been Japan-specific.

This is one of the ways that *otaku*, to quote the science fiction writer William Gibson, "live in the future" (Gibson 2001). "There is something post-national about it, extra-geographic," Gibson goes on to say, meaning that in *otaku* culture, citizenship matters less than shared interests, nationality less than knowledge, and location less than expertise. Your identity is defined by what you're into, by where your passions lie, and by what "geeks you out."

And here lies the paradox of *otaku* culture: *otaku* are both extraordinarily detached and extraordinarily connected (LaMarre 2004). They are detached from the local, connected to the global; detached from broad knowledge, connected to hyperfocused data; detached from conventional interactions, connected via mediated relationships. Is this paradox of detachment and connection a "harbinger for the future" (Hayase 2010)? Will we all be *otaku* someday?

East to West The Internet helped spread *otaku* culture from Japan to the rest of the world.

Material Culture and the Architecture of Santa Barbara Local leaders have preserved the city's history and resisted the pressures of encroaching urban development by insisting on maintaining the look of "old California."

to appreciate their way of life. We can discover viewpoints and interpretations of reality different from our own. Cultural relativism becomes all the more important in our increasingly diverse society.

Components of Culture

Since culture is such a broad concept, it is more easily grasped if we break it down into its constituent parts. Sociologists conceive of culture as consisting of two major categories: material culture and symbolic culture.

Material Culture

Material culture is any physical object to which we give social meaning: art and artifacts, tools and utensils, machines and weapons, clothing and furniture, buildings and toys—the list is immense. Any physical thing that people create, use, or appreciate might be considered material culture.

Examining material culture can tell us a great deal about a particular group or society. Just look around you, whether in your dorm room, a library, a coffeehouse, or a park—there should be many items that you can identify as belonging to material culture. Start with your own clothes and accessories and then extend your observations to your surroundings—the room, building, landscaping, street, neighborhood, community, and further outward. For instance, the designer label on a woman's purse might convey that she follows the current fashion trends, or the athletic logo on a man's T-shirt might tell us that

MATERIAL CULTURE the objects associated with a cultural group, such as tools, machines, utensils, buildings, and artwork; any physical object to which we give social meaning

he is into skateboarding. Likewise, the carpeting, light fixtures, furniture, and artwork in a building can tell us something about the people who live or work there. And the sports arenas, modes of transportation, historical monuments, and city dumps reveal the characteristics of a community. Perhaps the proliferation of drive-thru fast-food restaurants in practically every corner of the United States says something about American tastes and lifestyle: we spend more time on the road, cook fewer meals at home, and prefer the ease and predictability of knowing what we'll get each time we pull up to our favorite chain. If you were visiting another country, you might see some very different items of material culture.

Studying the significance of material culture is like going on an archeological dig, but learning about the present rather than the distant past. Let's take as an example a sociological "dig" in Santa Barbara, California, where one of the authors of this book lives. Local leaders there have been active in preserving the image of the city, particularly in its downtown historical area. The original mission, *presidio* (military post), courthouse, and other landmarks built by early Spanish settlers are all still intact. Although the town has grown up around these buildings, zoning regulations require that new construction fit with the distinctive Mediterranean architecture of the "red tile roof" district. The size and design are restricted, as are the use of signs, lighting, paint, and landscaping. Thus, the newly built grocery store with its textured stucco walls, tile murals, and arched porticos may be difficult to distinguish from the century-old post office a few blocks away. By studying its material culture, we can see how Santa Barbara manages to preserve its history and heritage and successfully resist the pressures of encroaching urban development. The distinctive "old California" look and feel of the city is perhaps its greatest charm, something that appeals to locals and a steady flock of tourists alike.

Symbolic Culture

Nonmaterial or **symbolic culture** reflects the ideas and beliefs of a group of people. It can be something as specific as a certain rule or custom, such as driving on the right side of the road in the United States and on the left side in the United Kingdom. It can also be a broad social system, such as democracy, or a large-scale social pattern, such as marriage. Because symbolic culture is so important to social life, let's look further at some of its main components.

COMMUNICATION: SIGNS, GESTURES, AND LANGUAGE One of the most important functions of symbolic culture is to allow us to communicate—through signs, gestures, and language. These form the basis of social interaction and are the foundation of culture.

Signs (or symbols) such as a traffic signal, price tag, notes on sheet music, or product logo are something designed to meaningfully represent something else. They all convey information. Numbers and letters are the most common signs, but you are probably familiar with other graphic symbols indicating, for instance, which is the men's or women's bathroom, where the elevator is going, how to eject a DVD from the disk drive, or in what lane you should be driving.

While we can easily take for granted the meaning of most symbols, others we may have to learn when we first encounter them. Take emojis, for instance, those cute (or devious) little expressions that we can add to our text messages and social media posts. Some symbols may be nearly universal, while others may be particular to a given culture. It may take some interpretive work to understand what a sign means if you are unfamiliar with the context in which it is displayed.

Gestures are signs made with the body—clapping, nodding, smiling, or any number of facial expressions. Sometimes, these acts are referred to as "body language" or "nonverbal communication," since they don't require any words. Gestures can be as subtle as a knowing glance or as obvious as a raised fist. Most of the time, we can assume that other people will get what we are trying to say with our gestures. But, while gestures might seem natural and universal, just a matter of common sense, few of them besides those that

SYMBOLIC CULTURE the ideas associated with a cultural group, including ways of thinking (beliefs, values, and assumptions) and ways of behaving (norms, interactions, and communication)

SIGNS symbols that stand for or convey an idea

GESTURES the ways in which people use their bodies to communicate without words; actions that have symbolic meaning

Gestures and Body Language If you travel to a foreign culture, pay special attention to how others interpret your body language. Common friendly gestures in one culture can be offensive or confusing in another.

LANGUAGE a system of communication using vocal sounds, gestures, or written symbols; the basis of symbolic culture and the primary means through which we communicate with one another and perpetuate our culture

SAPIR-WHORF HYPOTHESIS the idea that language structures thought and that ways of looking at the world are embedded in language

represent basic emotions are innate; most have to be learned. For instance, the "thumbs up" sign, which is associated with praise or approval in the United States, might be interpreted as an obscene or insulting gesture in parts of Asia or South America. Every culture has its own way of expressing praise and insulting others. So before leaving for a country whose culture is unfamiliar, it might be worth finding out whether shaking hands and waving good-bye are appropriate ways to communicate.

Language, probably the most significant component of culture, is what has allowed us to fully develop and express ourselves as human beings, and it is what distinguishes us from all other species on the planet. Although language varies from culture to culture, it is a human universal and present in all societies. It is one of the most complex, fluid, and creative symbol systems: letters or pictograms are combined to form words, and words combined to form sentences, in an almost infinite number of possible ways.

Language is the basis of symbolic culture and the primary means through which we communicate with one another. It allows us to convey complicated abstract concepts and to pass along a culture from one generation to the next. Language helps us to conceive of the past and to plan for the future; to categorize the people, places, and things around us; and to

share our perspectives on reality. In this way, the cumulative experience of a group of people—their culture—can be contained in and presented through language.

Language is so important that many have argued that it shapes not only our communication but our perception—the way that we see things—as well. In the 1930s, two anthropologists, Edward Sapir and Benjamin Lee Whorf, conducted research on the impact of language on the mind. In working with the Hopi tribe in the American Southwest, the anthropologists claimed to have discovered that the Hopi had no words to distinguish the past, present, or future and that, therefore, they did not "see" or experience time in the same way as those whose language provided such words. The result of this research was the development of what is known as the **Sapir-Whorf hypothesis** (sometimes referred to as the *principle of linguistic relativity*). Their hypothesis broke from traditional understandings about language by asserting that language actually structures thought, that perception not only suggests the need for words with which to express what is perceived but also that the words themselves help create those same perceptions (Sapir 1949; Whorf 1956).

The studies by Sapir and Whorf were not published until the 1950s, when they were met with competing linguistic theories. In particular, the idea that Eskimos (or Inuits, as they are now called) had many more words for snow than people of Western cultures was sharply challenged, as was the notion that the Hopi had no words for future or past tense (Martin 1986; Pullum 1991). Although there is still some disagreement about how strongly language influences thought (Edgerton 1992), the ideas behind the Sapir-Whorf hypothesis continue

Mean Girls and the Cafeteria Classification System A scene from the film *Mean Girls* illustrates the different classification schemes that are used to identify and categorize the world around us.

to influence numerous social thinkers. Language does play a significant role in how people construct a sense of reality and how they categorize the people, places, and things around them. For instance, the work of sociologist Eviatar Zerubavel (2003) looks at how different groups (such as Jews and Arabs, or Serbs and Croats) use language to construct an understanding of their heritage—through what he calls "social memory." In a country like the United States, where there are approximately 50 million foreign-born people who speak well over 100 different languages, there are bound to be differences in perceptual realities as a result.

Does the Sapir-Whorf hypothesis hold true for your world? Let's take an example closer to home. Perhaps you have seen the 2004 movie *Mean Girls*, loosely based on a pop sociology book by Rosalind Wiseman, *Queen Bees and Wannabes*, about the culture of high school girls (2002). Both book and film present a social map of the cafeteria and school grounds, identifying where different groups of students—the "jocks," "cheerleaders," "goths," "preppies," "skaters," "nerds," "hackysack kids," "easy girls," and "partiers"—hang out. The book also includes the "populars" (referred to in the movie as the "plastics") and the popular "wannabes."

You were probably aware of similar categories for distinguishing groups at your school. Do such classification systems influence the way you see other people? Do they lead you to identify people by type and place them into those categories? If no such labels existed (or if your school had different labels), would you still perceive your former classmates the same way? Probably not. These kinds of questions highlight how important language is to the meanings we give to our everyday world.

Values, Norms, and Sanctions

Values and norms are symbolic culture in thought and action. When we know the values of a particular group and see how individuals are controlled by its social norms, then we can appreciate their beliefs and ideals and find the evidence of these throughout their everyday lives.

VALUES Values are the set of shared beliefs that a group of people consider to be worthwhile or desirable in life—what is good or bad, right or wrong, beautiful or ugly. They articulate the essence of everything that a cultural group cherishes in its society. For instance, most Americans value the equality and individual freedoms of democracy. Structural functionalists, such as Durkheim, stress the strength of shared values and their role in regulating the behavior of society's members. However, there is not always widespread agreement about which values should represent a society, and values may change or new values may emerge over time. For example, workers' loyalty to their company was once much more important than it is now. In today's economy, workers realize that they may be "downsized" in times of financial trouble or that they may change careers over the course of their lifetime and hence feel less obligation to an employer.

NORMS Norms are the rules and guidelines regarding what kinds of behavior are acceptable; they develop directly out of a culture's value system. Whether legal regulations or just social expectations, norms are largely agreed upon by most members of a group. Some norms are formal, which means they are officially codified and explicitly stated. These include **laws** such as those making it illegal to speed in a school zone or drink before you turn twenty-one. Other formal norms include the rules for playing basketball or the requirements for membership in your college's honor society, the rights secured by the Amendments to the U.S. Constitution, and the behavioral prescriptions conveyed in the Ten Commandments. Despite the relative authority of formal norms, they are not always followed.

Other norms are informal, meaning that they are implicit and unspoken. For instance, when we wait in line to buy tickets for a movie, we expect that no one will cut in front of us. Informal norms are so much a part of our assumptions about life that they are embedded in our consciousness; they cover almost every aspect of our social lives, from what we say and do to even how we think and feel. Though we might have difficulty listing all the norms that are a part of everyday life, most of us have learned them quite well. They are simply "the way things are done." Often, it is only when norms are violated (as when someone cuts in line) that we recognize they exist.

Norms can be broken down further into three types. **Folkways** are the ordinary conventions of everyday life about what is acceptable or proper and are not always strictly enforced. Folkways are the customary ways that people do things, and they ensure for smooth and orderly social interactions. Examples are standards of dress and rules of etiquette: in most places, wearing flip-flops with a business suit and eating with your fingers from the buffet line is just not done! When people do not conform to folkways, they are thought of as peculiar or eccentric but not necessarily dangerous. **Mores** are norms that carry a greater moral significance and are more closely related to the core values of a cultural group. Unlike folkways, mores are norms to which practically everyone is expected to conform. Breaches are treated

VALUES ideas about what is right or wrong, good or bad, desirable or worthy in a particular group; they express what the group cherishes and honors

NORMS rules or guidelines regarding what kinds of behavior are acceptable and appropriate within a particular culture; these typically emanate from the group's values

LAWS types of norms that are formally codified to provide an explicit statement about what is permissible or forbidden, legal or illegal in a given society

FOLKWAY a loosely enforced norm involving common customs, practices, or procedures that ensure smooth social interaction and acceptance

MORES norms that carry great moral significance, are closely related to the core values of a cultural group, and often involve severe repercussions for violators

TABOO a norm ingrained so deeply that even thinking about violating it evokes strong feelings of disgust, horror, or revulsion

MORAL HOLIDAY a specified time period during which some norm violations are allowed

SANCTIONS positive or negative reactions to the ways that people follow or disobey norms, including rewards for conformity and punishments for violations

SOCIAL CONTROL the formal and informal mechanisms used to elicit conformity to values and norms and thus promote social cohesion

seriously and in some cases can bring severe repercussions. Such mores as the prohibition of theft, rape, and murder are also formalized, so that there is not only public condemnation for such acts but also strict laws against them. **Taboos**, actually a type of mores, are the most powerful of all norms. We sometimes use the word in a casual way to indicate, say, a forbidden subject. But as a sociological term it holds even greater meaning. Taboos are extremely serious. Sociologists say that our sense of what is taboo is so deeply ingrained that the very thought of committing a taboo act, such as cannibalism or incest, evokes strong feelings of disgust or horror.

Norms are specific to a culture, time period, and situation. What is a folkway to one group might be a more to another. For instance, public nudity is acceptable in many cultures, whereas it is not only frowned upon in American culture but also illegal in most instances. At the same time, Americans do permit nudity in such situations as strip clubs and nudist resorts, allowing for a kind of **moral holiday** from the strictures of imposed norms. At certain times, such as Mardi Gras and spring break, mild norm violations are tolerated. Certain places may also lend themselves to the suspension of norms—think Las Vegas (and the slogan "What happens in Vegas, stays in Vegas").

Similarly, what would be considered murder on the city streets might be regarded as valor on the battlefield. And we are probably all aware of how the folkways around proper etiquette and attire can vary greatly from one generation to the next; fifty years ago, girls were just starting to wear jeans to school, for example. Now they come to school in all sorts of casual attire, including pajama bottoms and slippers.

SANCTIONS **Sanctions** are a means of enforcing norms. They include rewards for conformity and punishments for violations. *Positive sanctions* express approval and may come in the form of a handshake, a smile, praise, or perhaps an award. *Negative sanctions* express disapproval and may come in the form of a frown, harsh words, or perhaps a fine or incarceration.

From a functionalist perspective, we can see how sanctions help to establish **social control**, ensuring that people behave to some degree in acceptable ways and thus promoting social cohesion. There are many forms of authority in our culture—from the government and police to school administrators, work supervisors, and even parents. Each has a certain amount of power that they can exercise to get others to follow their rules. So when someone is caught violating a norm, there is usually some prescribed sanction that will then be administered, serving as a deterrent to that behavior.

But equally important in maintaining social order is the process of socialization by which people internalize norms. For instance, in 1983, the U.S. Department of Transportation pioneered the slogan "Friends don't let friends drive drunk"; a few years later, the term "designated driver" was introduced into the popular lexicon. Over the years, these slogans have helped change the way we think about our personal responsibility for others, with nearly 80 percent of Americans now claiming that they have taken action to prevent someone from driving while intoxicated. What began as an external statement of social mores quickly became our own personal sense of morality. We are often unaware of the extent to which our own conscience keeps us from violating social norms in the first place. If we have internalized norms, then outside sanctions are no longer needed to make us do the right thing. Social control, then, frequently looks like self-control and is taught through the socialization process by family, peers, the media, and religious organizations, among others.

Norms Are Specific to a Situation, Culture, and Time Period For example, at Mardi Gras or during spring break trips, mild norm violations are tolerated.

DATA WORKSHOP

Analyzing Everyday Life

Seeing Culture in Religious Services

Some people argue that religions are like cultures unto themselves. This is easiest to see in the case of radical splinter groups such as the FLDS (a fundamentalist Mormon sect whose members practice polygamy and tend to live in isolated rural compounds) or the white supremacist World Church of the Creator (whose leader, Matt Hale, is currently in prison for conspiring to kill a federal judge). But even your friendly neighborhood congregation has its own particular character that might seem odd, at first, to an outsider.

This Data Workshop will challenge you to suspend ethnocentrism and practice cultural relativism as you delve into the material and symbolic culture of a particular religious group. You will be doing participant observation research at a religious service and writing field notes that will become your data for discussion and analysis. Refer back to Chapter 2 if you need a refresher on ethnography/participant observation as a research method.

Step 1: Observing Services
Select a house of worship—church, synagogue, temple, mosque, or other place of worship—and attend a service there. It may be of a faith you belong to already, or one that is unfamiliar. Sometimes it can be more difficult to "see" culture in a familiar setting than in one that is very different for you. Any choice is fine as long as it is open to the public. You may want to call the offices first, to find out if there are any dress codes or other requirements you should know about before attending. Remember, when you visit your chosen house of worship, you must behave in a respectful manner. Once there, your task will be to closely observe your surroundings and all that takes place (and in which you might also participate).

Step 2: Writing Field Notes
Since it is probably not appropriate for you to jot down notes during the services, you should make an effort to write your field notes as soon as you can afterward so you can preserve as many details as possible from the experience. Your field notes should comprise two to three (or more) pages and include descriptions of both material and symbolic culture. Consider some of the material culture that you might find in the setting, such as the

Religious Cultures Every religion has a culture, and every congregation has its own particular way of expressing it. Christians, Hindus, and Muslims at worship services.

architecture, furniture, any decorations, clothing worn by various participants, and the other physical objects, such as books, scrolls, musical instruments, statues, paintings, vessels, and collection plates. You will also want to consider the elements of symbolic culture featured in the services. Pay close attention to the people there and what they do—their roles, activities, and interactions. Notice how the services are structured, and any customs, practices, or rituals that participants engage in.

Step 3: Identifying Culture

Read through your field notes and reflect on your experience. Then consider the following questions:

* What aspects of material culture did you notice at the house of worship? How were things arranged in the space? Can you identify the function or purpose of various items of material culture? Were any objects used as part of the service?

* What did you notice about language? Was there a "text" or "script" for the services? What sources were used (sacred books, hymnals, photocopied programs)? What messages were uttered (and by whom, and when)? Was music played or sung?

* Who was present for the services—clergy, congregants, and others? Were there adults and children, men and women? What different types of roles did people take on in the ceremony—leaders, helpers, participants?

* When did participants stand, sit or kneel, speak, read, pray, sing, meditate, or take part in other activities? Was everybody deeply involved at all times, or were some people on the margins? How did participants behave toward each other (and you)?

* According to Émile Durkheim (1912/1995), every religion has a set of practices that are designed to connect the holy and the worldly in some way. Think about the meaning of different rituals you observed: taking communion, for example, or simply praying or singing in a specially designated space. In what ways were the rituals an expression of the collective conscience or beliefs of the group? How do rituals help create a sense of collective effervescence and belonging among congregants?

* What did you observe that seemed especially unfamiliar to you? What did you observe that seemed the most familiar, even if it was in an unfamiliar setting? What insights were you able to gain by suspending ethnocentrism and practicing cultural relativism?

There are two options for completing this Data Workshop:

PREP-PAIR-SHARE Do the fieldwork outlined in Steps 1 and 2, and bring your field notes with you to class to refer to. In groups of two or three, discuss your experiences and work together to answer the questions in Step 3. Take this opportunity to learn more about culture and different religious traditions.

DO-IT-YOURSELF Write a three- to four-page essay analyzing your field experiences and taking into consideration the questions in Step 3. Make sure to refer to your field notes in the essay and include them as an attachment to your paper.

Variations in Culture

We know there are differences between cultures, but there can also be variations within cultures. For instance, sociologists who have tried to identify the core values that make up American society (Robin Williams 1965; Bellah et al. 1985) have found that while there do seem to be certain beliefs that most Americans share, such as freedom and democracy, there are also inconsistencies between such beliefs as individualism (in which we do what is best for ourselves) and humanitarianism (in which we do what is best for others), and between equality and group superiority. New values such as self-fulfillment and environmentalism could also be added to the list, having gained popularity in recent years.

It is even difficult to speak of an "American culture." "Cultural diversity" and "multiculturalism" have both become buzzwords in the past few decades, precisely because people are aware of the increasing variety of cultural groups within American society. **Multiculturalism** generally describes a policy that involves honoring the diverse racial, ethnic, national, and linguistic backgrounds of various individuals and groups. In the following chapters, we will explore some of these differences in greater depth.

Dominant Culture

Although "culture" is a term we usually apply to an entire group of people, what we find in reality is that there are often many subgroups within a larger culture, each with its own particular makeup. These subgroups, however, are not all equal. Some, by virtue of size, wealth, or historical happenstance, are able to lay claim to greater power and influence in society than others. The values, norms, and practices of the most powerful groups are referred to as the mainstream or **dominant culture**, while others are seen as "alternative" or minority views. The power of the dominant culture may mean that other ways of seeing and doing things are relegated to second-class status—in this way, dominant culture can produce cultural **hegemony**, or dominance (Gramsci 1985, 1988).

Let's take popular music as an example. Commercial radio stations often have very limited playlists. No matter what the genre (country, pop, hip-hop, metal), the songs played are determined by station and record company business interests, not your artistic preferences. Truly new artists and alternative sounds are more likely to be heard on public, college, or satellite radio stations or online. Even music streaming services like Pandora or Spotify must deliver audiences to advertisers, which may make it harder to resist the pressure to "mainstream." The dominant status of commercial radio (even online) and the corporate interests of the music industry dictate that musicians outside the mainstream will never be as big as Lady Gaga or Justin Bieber.

Subcultures and Countercultures

If sociologists focus only on the dominant culture in American society, we risk overlooking the inequalities that structure our society—as well as the influences that even small cultural groups outside the mainstream can exert. The United States is filled with thousands of different cultural groups, any of which could be called a **subculture**—a culture within a culture. A subculture is a particular social group that has a distinctive way of life, including its own set of values and norms, practices, and beliefs, but that exists harmoniously within the larger mainstream culture. A subculture can be based on ethnicity, age, interests, or anything else that draws individuals together. Any of the following groups could be considered subcultures within American society: Korean Americans, senior citizens, snowboarders, White Sox fans, greyhound owners, firefighters, Trekkers.

A **counterculture**, another kind of subgroup, differs from a subculture in that its norms and values are often incompatible with or in direct opposition to the mainstream (Zellner 1995). Some countercultures are political or activist groups attempting to bring about social change; others resist mainstream values by living outside society or practicing an alternative lifestyle. In the 1960s, hippies, antiwar protesters, feminists, and others on the so-called political left were collectively known as "the counterculture." But radicals come in many stripes. Any group that opposes the dominant culture—whether they are eco-terrorists, computer hackers, or modern-day polygamists—can be considered a counterculture.

In the mid-1990s, American countercultures of the far right gained prominence with the revelation that the main perpetrator of the April 1995 bombing of the Alfred R. Murrah Federal Building in Oklahoma City, Timothy McVeigh, had ties to "militia" or "patriot" groups. And he wasn't the only American with such ties. In 1996, the Southern Poverty Law Center counted 858 active groups in the United States belonging to the "militia movement" (the number was at 1,096 in 2013 [Southern Poverty Law Center 2014]). Members of this movement, who trace their heritage to the Minutemen of the American Revolution (an elite fighting force, the first to arrive at a battle), see themselves as the last line of defense for the liberties outlined in the U.S. Constitution. They believe, moreover, that the federal government has become the enemy of those liberties. They hold that gun control, environmental protection laws, and other legislation violate individual

MULTICULTURALISM a policy that values diverse racial, ethnic, national, and linguistic backgrounds and so encourages the retention of cultural differences within the larger society

DOMINANT CULTURE the values, norms, and practices of the group within society that is most powerful (in terms of wealth, prestige, status, influence, etc.)

HEGEMONY term developed by Antonio Gramsci to describe the cultural aspects of social control, whereby the ideas of the dominant group are accepted by all

SUBCULTURE a group within society that is differentiated by its distinctive values, norms, and lifestyle

COUNTERCULTURE a group within society that openly rejects or actively opposes society's values and norms

Culture Wars Often Play Out in the Media George Stephanopoulos (second from left) spends every Sunday morning interviewing politicians on *This Week with George Stephanopoulos*. On Saturday nights, comic actors on *Saturday Night Live* satirize politicians, media pundits, and other participants in the latest cultural clash.

Let's talk about sex on campus.

Both Dr. Ferris's and Dr. Stein's schools (public, state-funded institutions) provide on-campus sexual health services for students, including a wide range of contraceptive choices, STI (sexually transmitted infection) testing and treatment, and pregnancy testing. Does your college health services center offer these services too?

Many colleges and universities do not offer students the full range of sexual health-care services, and some offer none at all. For example, Gonzaga University in Spokane, Washington, offers no contraceptive benefits to students but does cover STIs. While only a small percentage of Catholic universities in the United States have offered any kind of contraception to students there has been some pushback at campuses such as Fordham, especially since the passage of the Affordable Care Act, which mandated coverage (Catholics for a Free Choice 2002; Edwards-Levy 2012). It's harder to generalize about non-Catholic religious schools—some do, some don't. Brigham Young University in Salt Lake City and Texas Christian University in Fort Worth, for example, do offer contraception to students, while Liberty University in Virginia and Eastern Nazarene College in Massachusetts don't appear to offer any birth control services. Schools without religious affiliations are more likely to offer contraceptive services if they have a student health center, but these are not found on all campuses.

Universities have their own cultures that include traditions, customs, beliefs, and values, just like any other cultural group. Some universities borrow their cultural values from the larger organizations (such as religious groups) that sponsor them; even unaffiliated universities have statements of their institutional values on their websites.

What does it mean for you that your college may be guided by a set of institutional policies that prohibit dispensing contraception to students? It means that some of your most personal, private, individual choices have already been made for you (or at least made more complicated for you) by your school.

It's possible that your individual values coincide with your college's culture when it comes to issues like this. But if your university's institutional values and your individual values are different, you may find yourself in a situation where the university has some unanticipated control over your everyday life and personal relationships. Schools can mandate who your roommate can be (and whether you can room with someone you know, or someone of the same or opposite sex); they can make and enforce rules about your academic and athletic activities; they can decide what kind of medical care you can get on campus. They can even influence your sex life.

University Culture Like other cultural groups, universities have traditions, customs, beliefs, and values, which can affect students' everyday lives.

and states' rights, and they are inspired by events like the FBI's 1993 siege of the Branch Davidian compound in Waco, Texas (resulting in eighty-two deaths), to call for armed grassroots organization. According to the FBI, such "sovereign citizens," as they are sometimes called, are among the greatest threat to law enforcement in the United States (Dickson 2014).

Culture Wars

Although a countercultural group can pose a threat to the larger society, conflict does not always come from the extreme margins of society; it can also emerge from within the mainstream. Culture in any diverse society is characterized by points of tension and division. There is not always uniform agreement about which values and norms ought to be upheld. The term **culture wars** is often used to describe the clashes that arise as a result of conflicting viewpoints (Bloom 1987; Garber 1998). These clashes are frequently played out in the media, where social commentators and pundits debate the issues. Culture wars are mainly waged over values and morality and the solutions to social problems, with liberals and conservatives fighting to define culture in the United States (Hunter 1991, 2006).

To some degree, the rise of the ultraconservative Tea Party movement in the past decade was a response to contentious political and social issues. Tea Partyers favor small government and have called for drastic cuts in taxes and social welfare funding, among other things. Popular culture and its influence on young people is another site of frequent debate. Miley Cyrus caused an uproar over her sexually suggestive "twerking" during a televised performance at the MTV Video Music Awards. We could add many more examples to the list of battleground issues, including family values, gay rights, bio-medical ethics, gun violence, and school prayer. Culture wars are bound to continue as we confront the difficult realities that are a part of living in a multicultural, democratic society.

Ideal vs. Real Culture

Some norms and values are more aspired to than actually practiced. It is useful to draw a distinction between **ideal culture**, the norms and values that members of a society believe should be observed in principle, and **real culture**, the patterns of behavior that actually exist. Whether it is an organization that falls short of its own mission statement or a person who says one thing and does another (a self-described vegetarian, for example, who sometimes enjoys a Big Mac), what people believe in and what they do may be two different things.

An enduring example of the difference between ideal and real cultures is the United States itself. For a nation that has enshrined in its founding documents the notion that "all men are created equal," it continues to have trouble realizing full equality for all its citizens. From slavery to Western expansion, from the oppression of women and discrimination against ethnic minorities to the battle for same-sex marriage rights, we are still a nation that believes in equality but doesn't always deliver it.

CULTURE WARS clashes within mainstream society over the values and norms that should be upheld

IDEAL CULTURE the norms, values, and patterns of behavior that members of a society believe should be observed in principle

REAL CULTURE the norms, values, and patterns of behavior that actually exist within a society (which may or may not correspond to the society's ideals)

DATA WORKSHOP
Analyzing Media and Pop Culture

How the Image Shapes the Need

 Yet another photo of Kim Kardashian in sky-high Louboutins is splashed across the tabloids. This time she's at a service station, pumping her own gas into a white-hot Ferrari 458 Italia. Most of us cannot afford such status symbols, but it doesn't stop us from wondering what it would be like to wear designer shoes or drive an exotic sports car. In fact, advertisers want to sell us just those kind of fantasies, effectively cashing in on two of our most basic human needs in contemporary

Popular Magazines What kinds of lifestyles are these magazines trying to sell to consumers?

society—clothing and transportation. For most people, clothes and cars have become something of a necessity of modern life, even if we don't actually need these things to survive. For many reasons we need to get dressed and we need to get around somehow, but our desire for clothing and transportation is not determined by instinct alone. So how does culture, in particular through the media, influence the ways in which we satisfy those needs?

For this Data Workshop, you will be using existing sources—specifically, popular magazines in print or online—to discover how culture gives meaning to items considered necessary for modern living. You will be doing content analysis to arrive at your conclusions. Refer back to Chapter 2 for a review of this research method.

Pick your necessity—clothes or cars. Now go to your local bookstore or newsstand, or go online, and identify a magazine dedicated to that necessity. For example, you could choose a magazine such as *Lucky*, *InStyle*, *Essence*, or *Vogue* for women's clothing, or *GQ Details*, *Esquire*, or *Maxim* for men's clothing. For cars, you could choose *Car and Driver*, *Road and Track*, or *Motor Trend*. Immerse yourself in the content of the magazine, looking over the headlines, articles, photo spreads, and advertisements. Then consider the following questions. Support your answers with data in the form of clippings, photocopies, or screenshots of images and text taken from the print magazines or their websites.

* How is the modern necessity of [clothing or cars] presented in the magazine? Can you find any themes, patterns, or topics that seem predominant in the magazine?

* Describe one example of material culture (physical objects) and one example of symbolic culture (language, norms) that best represents the magazine's approach to [clothing or cars].

* What values or beliefs about [clothing or cars] are reflected in the magazine? What kind of messages are embedded in the images and text in articles and advertisements?

* How does the magazine suggest that we satisfy our needs for [clothing or cars]? How much of the magazine's content is about satisfying just the bare minimum of our need for [clothing or cars]?

* Who is the magazine's intended audience? How are you addressed as the reader? How does the magazine affect you and your desires for [clothing or cars]? Do you find yourself wanting the [clothing or cars] pictured?

* Who benefits when you act on your desires by purchasing the products featured in the magazine?

* Finally, which force is more important in shaping human behavior when it comes to modern necessities—instinct or culture?

There are two options for completing this Data Workshop:

PREP-PAIR-SHARE Collect your data from the magazine and jot down some preliminary notes based on your answers to the questions provided. Bring your examples to class and present them to a partner who has chosen the same topic (cars or clothing). Compare and contrast your answers and develop them further together.

DO-IT-YOURSELF Write a three- to four-page essay based on your answers to the questions provided. In addition, discuss your experience of doing content analysis of existing sources for research. Provide your examples of data (in print or digital format) as an attachment to the paper.

Cultural Change

Cultures usually change slowly and incrementally, although change can also happen in rapid and dramatic ways. We saw rapid change as a result of the social movements of the 1960s, and we may be seeing it again, albeit for different reasons, as we move through the early decades of the 2000s. Change is usually thought of as "progress"—we move from what seem to be outmoded ways of doing things to more innovative practices. Earlier in the chapter, we saw how variations in culture, whether they resulted from multiculturalism, countercultures, or culture wars, could all lead to growth and change in the larger society. Now we look at several other important processes that can also contribute to cultural change.

Technological Change

One of the most significant influences on any society is its material culture. And most changes in material culture tend to be technological. We usually equate **technology** with "hi-tech" electronic or digital devices. But technology can be anything from a hammer to the space shuttle, from

ON THE JOB
The Sharing Economy and Unlikely Cultural Ambassadors

In 1949 Bob Luitweiler founded Servas International "to build understanding, tolerance, and world peace." Instead of trying to change the behavior of world leaders, or the way that governments worked, Luitweiler's goal was to convince ordinary people to do one simple thing: visit each other. Servas International was the first modern hospitality exchange program. People all over the world signed up to be "hosts," volunteering to open their homes, free of charge, to travelers from all over the globe. During these relatively short visits, hosts would "share with travelers their daily lives, their concerns about social and economic issues, and their commitment to promoting peace through friendship and cultural exchange." The hope was that both the hosts and the guests would be able to learn more about the other's culture.

Almost seventy years later, however, it was the emergence of the "sharing economy" that really allowed hospitality exchange to take off. The sharing economy, sometimes called the "peer to peer" economy, refers to a new business model made possible by the spread of the Internet and mobile devices. It was always possible to try to rent out a spare bedroom, car, or power tool lying around in the garage, but for almost everyone it was far more trouble than it was worth. The Internet changed all that by allowing far more information to be collected and shared, solving the trust problem that kept networks like Servas small and relatively exclusive. Following the model pioneered by companies like eBay, sharing economy websites allow users to rate each other and thereby build a reputation for trustworthiness:

> Reputation is a requirement of the sharing economy. For Airbnb hosts and Uber and Lyft drivers, positive ratings are paramount to their success. It might seem crazy to stay at a stranger's house, but on Airbnb host reviews facilitate trust among strangers. (Schlegel 2014)

The results of these technological innovations have been staggering. Airbnb, founded in 2008 to allow people to rent out their homes and apartments on a short-term basis, now boasts that it has had more than 20 million guests book a stay through their website, which lists rentals in 190 countries and more than 30,000 cities.

While Airbnb likes to brag that its rental listings include more than 600 castles, their rivals at Couchsurfing.com have taken a different approach to the sharing economy. Their website tells the story of how their CEO surfed a Dumpster that a University of Texas professor had "converted and refinished as part of a sustainable micro-housing project." Rather than letting people rent out their living spaces, Couchsurfing allows travelers to connect with people who are willing to let them crash on the "couch" for free. The Couchsurfing mission statement emphasizes the way this mode of travel can promote social change: "We envision a world made better by travel and travel made richer by connection," and hope that when couchsurfers "share their lives with" their hosts, the resulting friendships will help generate "cultural exchange and mutual respect." Though the organization has had a somewhat tumultuous history, they claim 7 million members in more than 100,000 cities worldwide.

However much Airbnb and Couchsurfing differ in their business models, both agree that one of the advantages of traveling this way is that it can turn everyday people into unlikely but effective cultural ambassadors. A search of Airbnb's website shows scores of people describing themselves as the "unofficial ambassador" for their communities. When people "list their couch" on Couchsurfing's website they're inviting strangers into their homes and taking on the role of tour guide as well as host. You can even simply set your couch's status to "Not Right Now (but I can hang out)" if you aren't able to host guests but still "want to be available as a city resource for travelers." Although some remain cynical about the motives of traveling Couchsurfers, seeing them as more interested in traveling cheaply than in creating connections, it's hard to deny that cultural exchange is really happening thanks to these and other similar organizations.

Cultural Exchange When people use sites like Airbnb, which started operations in Cuba in April 2015, they often get more than just a place to sleep.

TECHNOLOGY material artifacts and the knowledge and techniques required to use them

CULTURAL DIFFUSION the dissemination of material and symbolic culture (tools and technology, beliefs and behavior) from one group to another

CULTURAL LEVELING the process by which cultures that were once unique and distinct become increasingly similar

graffiti to a search engine algorithm to hypertext markup language (HTML), as well as the "know-how" it takes to use it.

New technology often provides the basis and structure through which culture is disseminated to members of a social group. For instance, we are currently living in the Digital Age or Information Age, a revolutionary time in history spurred by the invention of the microchip. This technology has already produced radical changes in society, much as the steam engine did during the Industrial Revolution of the eighteenth and nineteenth centuries.

Shoppers at a Gap Store in Tokyo, Japan As global capitalism and large multinational corporations become more dominant, we increasingly see the same companies, brands, and products around the world. Is this cultural leveling good or bad?

One of the most prominent features of this Information Age is the spread of mass and social media. It was not until the 1950s that television became a regular part of daily life in the United States, and only in the 1990s that the Internet became commonplace. Most of us now would have trouble remembering life before these technological advancements; that's how much we rely on them and take them for granted. This digital revolution is shaping our culture—and the rest of the world's—at an increasingly rapid pace.

Cultural Diffusion and Cultural Leveling

Cultural change can also occur when different groups share their material and nonmaterial culture with each other, a process called **cultural diffusion**. Since each culture has its own tools, beliefs, and practices, exposure to another culture may mean that certain aspects of it will then be appropriated. For example, as McDonald's-style restaurants set up shop in cultures where fast food had previously been unknown, it wasn't only hamburgers that got relocated—other aspects of fast-food culture came along as well. According to Eric Schlosser (2002), Japanese diners during the 1980s doubled their consumption of fast-food meals—and their rates of obesity. Their risks of heart disease and stroke have also increased. While there is no direct proof of cause and effect here, it is clear that a single cultural product cannot be exported without carrying a raft of cultural consequences with it.

Cultural diffusion usually occurs in the direction from more developed to less developed nations. In particular, "Western" culture has spread rapidly to the rest of the world—driven by capitalism and globalization and aided by new forms of transportation and communication that allow for ever-faster exchanges.

Cultural leveling occurs when cultures that were once distinct become increasingly similar to one another. If you travel, you may have already seen this phenomenon in towns across the United States and countries around the world. The Walmarts on the interstates, for instance, have driven independent mom-and-pop stores from Main Streets all over the country. Many people bemoan this development and the consequent loss of uniqueness and diversity it represents. As cultures begin to blend, new mixes emerge. This can result in an interesting hybrid—for example, of East and West—but it can also mean a blander, more diluted culture of sameness. While Western culture is a dominant force in this process, cultural diffusion and cultural leveling do not have to occur in a one-way direction. Other societies have also had an influence on culture in the United States. For instance, Japanese anime was for many years a fringe interest in the United States, usually associated with computer geeks and other outsiders; now Disney has teamed up with Hayao Miyazaki, Japan's leading anime filmmaker, to sell his movies (such as *Spirited Away*,

GLOBAL PERSPECTIVE
The Twitter Revolution: Social Media and Social Change

On June 20, 2009, while attending a protest over the disputed presidential election in Iran, Nedā Āghā-Soltān was shot and killed. While this sort of tragedy is all too common at political protests around the world, this death was different because it was caught on video. Within minutes of her death, the heartbreaking video had been uploaded to Facebook and YouTube, where it quickly went viral. Although the protests were ultimately unsuccessful in their attempt to challenge the election results, Nedā Āghā-Soltān's death has remained a powerful rallying point for the Iranian opposition—in Iran and around the world.

The use of social media during the protests in Iran, as well as similar uprisings in Moldova, led some commentators to call it the "Twitter revolution," in recognition of the growing role that social media played in the protests (Musgrove 2009). The next few years saw even more prominent protests in Tunisia, Egypt, Libya, Yemen, Bahrain, and Syria that seemed to be facilitated by social media use. Although they were originally used exclusively for entertainment, social media sites like Twitter, Facebook, YouTube, and Flickr are playing an increasingly prominent role in social protests all around the world, both as organizing tools and a way to document events as they happen. In many countries where the government exercises control over traditional media outlets, social media provides protesters with a way to coordinate their activities and let the rest of the world know what is happening.

Arab Spring Anti-government protesters turned to the street and to social media.

Philip Howard, a sociologist and director of the Project on Information Technology and Political Islam, studied the effect that social media like Twitter had on the revolutions in Tunisia and Egypt. He concluded that "social media played a central role in shaping political debates" during the Arab Spring. Although this conclusion is hotly contested by some, Howard and his fellow researchers looked at patterns of activity on Twitter, concluding that not only did the volume of tweets from Egypt increase almost tenfold during their protests but that "spike(s) in online revolutionary conversations often preceded major events on the ground." The report went on to conclude that the relatively young and tech-savvy populations in Tunisia and Egypt, combined with the justified distrust many had for the media, made social media a powerful tool for protesters. The researchers also found that more than 30 percent of the tweets with hash tags connected to the protests were from female tweeters, suggesting that social media sites may enable much greater female participation in social movements than might have otherwise been possible.

Not everyone believes that social media were instrumental in these protests. Some argue that widely connected social networks spread confusion as much as they coordinate action. Others believe that the sort of weak social ties created online are incapable of supporting anything as difficult as a revolution. Despite these objections, social media have their defenders, who point out that although "the Arab world has long had democratic activists," before the social media–rich Arab Spring they had never "toppled a dictator" (Howard 2011). As Howard pointed out, revolutionaries "were not inspired by Facebook; they were inspired by the real tragedies documented on Facebook."

However, almost everyone agrees that there is a dark side to the use of social media. In the days following the failed protests in Iran (a non-Arab country), the government showed it could also use social media to rally its own supporters and as a source of incriminating evidence when arresting protesters. Some reports have even suggested that Iranian officials monitor the social media activity of Iranians abroad and use the information to crack down on their families.

From the start, the Internet has been used in unexpected and unintended ways, toward both harmful and helpful ends. How will the Internet be used in the future? Keep your eye on the global news to find out.

Cultural Imperialism

Other countries around the world are becoming inundated with America's TV programs, movies, music, satellite radio, newspapers, magazines, and web content. You can watch MTV in India and *Jackass 3D* in Uzbekistan, surf the Internet in Vietnam, or listen to Rihanna in Morocco. Many view this increased access to information and entertainment as good news for the spread of freedom and democracy. But the media are necessarily a reflection of the culture in which they are produced. So not only are we selling entertainment, we are also implicitly promoting certain Western ideas. And it can become a problem when the images and ideas found in the media conflict with the traditional norms and values of other countries.

The proliferation of Western media amounts to what some social critics call **cultural imperialism** (Schiller 1995). These critics conceive of media as a kind of invading force that enters a country and takes it over—much like an army, but with film, television, music, soft drinks, and running shoes instead of guns. Historically, imperialism involved the conquering of other nations by monarchies for their own glory and enrichment. The British Empire, for example, was once able to use its military might to occupy and control a third of the world's total land area. But now it is possible to cross a border and to occupy a territory culturally, without setting foot on foreign soil. Because they command so many economic resources, Western media companies are powerful enough to create a form of cultural domination wherever their products go.

Of the countries that consider the messages in Western media dangerous, some forbid or restrict the flow of

Lady Gaga Lands in Dubai Some social critics maintain that the spread of Western media, such as pop music by Lady Gaga, amounts to cultural imperialism.

CULTURAL IMPERIALISM
the imposition of one culture's beliefs and practices on another culture through media and consumer products rather than by military force

Howl's Moving Castle, and *Ponyo*) to a mainstream American audience. Still, the United States, the dominant producer of global media, remains the primary exporter of cultural content throughout the world.

Table 3.1 Theory in Everyday Life

Perspective	Approach to Culture	Case Study: Religion
Structural Functionalism	Values and norms are widely shared and agreed upon; they contribute to social stability by reinforcing common bonds and constraining individual behavior.	Religion is an important social institution that functions as the basis for the morals and ethics that followers embrace and that are applied to both society and the individual, thus promoting social order.
Conflict Theory	Values and norms are part of the dominant culture and tend to represent and protect the interests of the most powerful groups in society.	Religion serves to control the masses by creating rules for behavior; sanctions against violators may not be equally or fairly applied. Culture wars reflect tensions among groups over which values and norms will dominate.
Symbolic Interactionism	Values and norms are social constructions that may vary over time and in different contexts; meaning is created, maintained, and changed through ongoing social interaction.	Religion consists of beliefs and rituals that are part of the interaction among followers. Reciting the Lord's Prayer, bowing toward Mecca, and keeping a kosher home are meaningful displays of different religious values and norms. Leaders may play a role in creating social change.

information, others impose various kinds of censorship, and still others try to promote their own cultural productions. Iran, for example, officially censors all non-Islamic media content on television, radio, film, and the Internet (though many Iranians use hidden satellite dishes to plug into illegal Western programming). In the long run, it may be very difficult to prevent cultural imperialism from spreading.

American Culture in Perspective

Because American culture is highly visible worldwide, the country's moral and political values have equally high visibility. That means when reruns of *Friends* or *Grey's Anatomy* air in places like Egypt or Malaysia or Lebanon, American values on the topics of sex, gender, work, and family are being transmitted as well. When such military ventures as Operation Enduring Freedom (in Afghanistan) or Operation Iraqi Freedom are undertaken, part of their mission involves exporting the political values associated with democracy, capitalism, and even Christianity. Well, you may say, *Friends* is funny, and *Grey's* is a great way to kill time, and democracy is a good thing—so what's the problem here?

In some parts of the world, the premise of these shows would be unthinkable in real life: in many traditional cultures, both women and men live with their parents until they marry, sometimes to partners chosen for them by their families. A show in which young men and women live on their own, with almost no family involvement, dating and sleeping with people to whom they are not married, presents values that are distasteful in these cultures. American values, or at least the perceptions of them shaped by Hollywood and pop-culture exports, can breed negative feelings toward the United States. The value placed on individualism, sexual freedom, and material satisfaction in American life can antagonize cultures that place a higher value on familial involvement and moral and social restraint, and may result in anti-American sentiment.

Politics can generate the same anti-American feelings. For example, the United States has recently been involved in attempts to stem the development of nuclear weapons in developing countries like Iran and Pakistan while still maintaining its own nuclear arsenal at home. Other nations may question why American politicians think they should be able to withhold from other countries privileges the United States itself enjoys, such as developing a nuclear weapons program. Much of the resentment against the United States abroad emerges as a result of this type of phenomenon—America's perceived failure to live up to its own political values and ideals or to apply them fairly to others.

Putting American culture in perspective means recognizing that because it is pervasive, it may also be viewed with suspicion and even contempt when the values it expresses clash with those of other cultures. But the nature of anti-Americanism is complex—it's not merely a failure by other nations to understand "good" television shows or accept "superior" political systems. There are meaningful cultural differences between Americans and others, and we should keep those differences in mind as we read about or travel to other cultures. Indeed, there are cultural differences of similar magnitude within the United States as well. The question of the meaning of American culture in a larger global context is a complicated one.

CLOSING COMMENTS

In this chapter, we have seen how seemingly simple elements of material culture (cars and comic books) and symbolic culture (norms and values) create complex links between the individual and society, as well as between different societies around the globe. American culture in particular, sociologists often argue, is hegemonic (dominant), in that certain interests (such as creating a global market for American products) prevail, while others (such as encouraging local development and self-determination) are subordinated. Within the United States, this can mean that the cultural norms, values, beliefs, and practices of certain subcultures—such as minority ethnic or religious groups—are devalued. Elsewhere, it can mean that the United States is accused of cultural imperialism by nations whose values and practices are different from its own.

Whose cultural values and practices are "better" or "right"? The sociological perspective avoids these evaluative terms when examining culture, choosing instead to take a relativistic approach. In other words, different cultures should (in most cases) be evaluated not according to outside standards but according to their own sets of values and norms. But we should always recognize that this commitment to cultural relativism is a value in itself—which makes cultural relativism neither right nor wrong but rather a proper subject for intellectual examination.

Everything You Need to Know about Culture

Culture is the entire way of life of a group of people, including both material and symbolic elements, that acts as a lens through which one views the world and is passed from one generation to the next. "

COMPONENTS OF CULTURE

* **Material culture:** any physical object to which we give social meaning

* **Signs:** symbols that stand for or convey ideas

* **Gestures:** the ways people use their bodies to communicate without words

* **Language:** a system of communication using vocal sounds, gestures, or written symbols; the primary means through which we communicate with each other and perpetuate our culture

* **Values:** shared beliefs that a group of people consider to be worthwhile or desirable; they articulate everything that a cultural group cherishes and honors

* **Norms:** rules or guidelines regarding what kinds of behavior are acceptable and appropriate

* **Sanctions:** positive or negative reactions to the ways people follow or disobey norms

REVIEW

1. List five pieces of material culture you have with you right now, and explain what these pieces indicate about the tastes, habits, and lifestyles supported by your cultural group.

2. When was the last time you violated a folkway? How were you sanctioned? What sorts of sanctions do we impose on those who go against our accepted mores?

3. Make a list of ways in which the media—including advertisements—reach you each day. How many of these media messages represent mainstream Western ideals? What kinds of media messages do not conform to these norms?

Seeing Red

What does the color red mean in different cultures?

Passion
1,2,3,4,6

Success
4,5,9

Marriage
3,5

Strength
2

Power
6

Happiness
5

Repels Evil
2

Love
1,6

Good Luck
5,6,8

Erotic
1,3

Excitement
1

Courage
1,6

Anger
1,2,6,8

Danger
1,9

Energy
3

Heat
1,3,6,7

Beauty
6

Desire
1

Radicalism
1,6

Number Key

1 - Western/American	**6** - Eastern European
2 - Japanese	**7** - Muslim
3 - Hindu	**8** - African
4 - Native American	**9** - South American
5 - Chinese	

SOURCE: Information from McCandless et al. 2009

EXPLORE

Breaching Age Norms on Television

Norm breaching tells us a lot about the unwritten rules of social life. When everyday norms are violated, people often get very uncomfortable. Visit the Everyday Sociology Blog to find out what a hidden camera show can tell us about how society deals with people who break norms.

http://wwnPag.es/trw403

CHAPTER 4

Socialization, Interaction, and the Self

What do you look like? Well, it really depends on the situation. Sometimes, we don't have complete control over how we present ourselves. If you work at a place with a dress code or uniform, you don't get to choose what you wear. If you are visiting your grandparents, you might dress more conservatively than you would if you were going to a party with your friends. Other times, how you look is a reflection of what you are doing. If you are lounging around your house reading, you will look drastically different than you would for a job interview. These are all facets of who you are, grounded in the real activities of your

everyday life—school, work, hobbies, relationships. Online, though, reality doesn't have to limit you to such mundane identities. Online, you can look however you want.

We are constantly asked to attach our image to various platforms. If you take a look at your driver's license, passport, or student ID card, you probably have a picture that you had no control over (and may even hide from other people). If your best friend inputted a picture of you on her phone so that she can see who is texting or calling her, she may have chosen a picture that you don't find particularly flattering. However, if you are involved in social media such as Facebook, Twitter, or Instagram, you can carefully craft your image by controlling what you wear, who you are with, the angle you are viewed from, what your hair looks like, and what expression is on your face—all through your profile picture.

More often than not, the pictures used on Facebook, Twitter, and Instagram are "selfies" taken with cell phones. Through technology, we are able to capture our identity without the photographer as intermediary. For some, the ability to photograph ourselves allows for a freedom of expression that wouldn't exist if we were being observed by another person. And the selfies we choose to represent ourselves can reveal more than just what we look like.

Look at your own profile picture. Are you pictured with another person (that's an "ussie")? Are you doing an activity? Do you have a prop? Are you smiling? Are you frowning? Are you making a silly face? Do you look like you do in everyday life, or are you dressed up for a function? Are you in costume? Are you photographed from above or below? What's the background? Is your profile picture even a photograph of yourself? Is it instead your kid, your kitty, or the camellias in your front yard?

Choosing a profile picture is one of many ways we express ourselves in social interaction. Because our online identities are often removed from the context of our everyday lives, we can express anything we want about who we are (or think we are, or wish to be).

HOW TO READ THIS CHAPTER

In this chapter, you will learn how the self is connected to all social phenomena (such as gender, race, and the media) and how interaction constructs them all. You will be acquiring some new analytic tools, including the concepts of socialization and impression management, which will be referenced again in the chapters to come. In addition, you will be introduced to a new way of looking at the self—indeed, a new way of looking at *your* self—that emphasizes the role of the social in creating the individual. And you will be reminded of the reverse: as your society makes you who you are, you have a role (in fact, many roles) to play in shaping your society.

What Is Human Nature?

"That's just human nature" is a phrase often used to explain everything from violence and jealousy to love and altruism. But what is human nature, really? What is the thing about us that is unique and irreducible, that we all have in common and that separates us from other creatures? From a sociologist's perspective, it is culture and society that make us human. These things that we have created also make us who we are. We have to learn the meanings we give to food, housing, sex, and everything else, and society is the teacher.

You would be a very different person if you had been born in fourteenth-century Japan, in an Aztec peasant family, or in the Norwegian royal court. You would have learned a different language, a different set of everyday skills, and a different set of meanings about how the world works. Also, your sense of who you are would be radically different in each case because of the particular social structures and interactions you would encounter. If you were a member of an Aztec peasant family, for example, you would expect to be married to someone of your parents' choosing in your early teens (McCaa 1994). Girls were considered old maids if they were still single at age fifteen and might have ended up as prostitutes or concubines if they did not find a husband by this tender age.

The Nature vs. Nurture Debate

If it is culture and society that make us human, what role does our genetic makeup play? Aren't we *born* with certain instincts? These are questions posed in what is often called the **nature vs. nurture debate**. Those taking the nature side—often sociobiologists, some psychologists, and others in the natural sciences—argue that behavioral traits can be explained by genetics. Those taking the nurture side—sociologists and others in the social sciences—argue that human behavior is learned and shaped through social interaction. Which of these arguments is right?

Both are right. You don't have to look far to see that genetics, or nature, plays a role in who we are. For example, research shows that high levels of testosterone contribute to stereotypically masculine traits such as aggressiveness and competitiveness (Van Goozen et al. 1994). However, it is also true that facing a competitive challenge (such as a baseball game) causes testosterone levels to rise (Booth et al. 1989). So is it the hormone that makes us competitive, or is it competition that stimulates hormone production? An additional example involves a study of moral and social development in people with brain injuries. Steven W. Anderson and colleagues (1999) studied patients whose prefrontal cortex had been damaged. Those who had received the injury as infants struggled with moral and social reasoning, finding it difficult or impossible to puzzle out questions like "Is it acceptable for a man to steal the drug needed to save his wife's life if he can't afford to pay for it?" People who received the same injury as adults, however, were able to deal with such issues. Anderson and his research team hypothesized that there is a crucial period in brain development when people acquire the capacity for moral reasoning. In other words, nature provides a biological window through which social and moral development occurs.

The point is, there is a complex relationship between nature and nurture. Either one alone is insufficient to explain what makes us human. Certainly, heredity gives us a basic potential, but it is primarily our social environment that determines whether we will realize or fall short of that potential or develop new ones. We are subject to social influences from the moment we are born (and even before), and these influences only increase over the years. In part because the influence of social contact happens so gradually and to some extent unconsciously, we don't really notice what or how we are learning.

> **NATURE VS. NURTURE DEBATE** the ongoing discussion of the respective roles of genetics and socialization in determining individual behaviors and traits
>
> **SOCIALIZATION** the process of learning and internalizing the values, beliefs, and norms of our social group, by which we become functioning members of society

The Process of Socialization

We often speak of "socializing" with our friends, yet the idea of "socializing" is only part of what sociologists mean by **socialization**. Socialization is a twofold process. It includes the process by which a society, culture, or group teaches individuals to become functioning members, and the process by which individuals learn and internalize the values and norms of the group. Socialization thus works on both an individual and a social level: we learn our society's way of life and make it our own. Socialization accomplishes two main goals. First, it teaches members the skills necessary to satisfy basic human needs and to defend themselves against danger, thus ensuring

IN THE FUTURE
Genetics and Sociology

Sociologists have long been interested in resolving the nature vs. nurture debate and just how much each side contributes to human behavior, or even determines it. In the 1990s, dramatic new possibilities for gathering scientific data were made available as a result of discoveries in the emerging field of genetics. In 2003, the Human Genome Project was completed, which identified all the genes constituting human DNA. At the same time that geneticists had hoped that knowledge of the genes would reveal all the answers to human behavior, they were finding that the social environment could actually change genes. Thus geneticists became interested in some of the same questions that a small but influential offshoot of sociologists had also been studying.

Sociobiology became a controversial topic within sociology in 1975 with the publication of Edward O. Wilson's *Sociobiology: The New Synthesis*. Many sociologists criticized the book, seeing it as an example of genetic determinism, as Wilson came down squarely on the nature side of the debate when he proposed that genes play a far greater role in human behavior than social or cultural factors. Wilson continued to develop these ideas in his 1978 work *On Human Nature*, in which he argued "that the evidence is strong that a substantial fraction of human behavioral variation is based on genetic difference" (p. 43).

SOCIOBIOLOGY a branch of science that uses biological and evolutionary explanations for social behavior

Other sociologists who followed Wilson's argument that genes play a larger role in human behavior caused further controversy as they stood in opposition to long-held and widely embraced sociological models of the self. In 1994, Richard Herrnstein and Charles Murray published *The Bell Curve: Intelligence and Class Structure in American Life*, in which they argued, among other things, that there are measurable differences in intelligence between races. In 2005, Larry Summers, then president of Harvard University, gave a speech in which he suggested that one of the reasons there were so few women teaching science and engineering at elite universities was because of genetic differences between the sexes. Despite widespread criticism, psychologist Steven Pinker publicly defended Summers's remarks. Pinker argued that if there was greater innate variability in men's mathematical abilities, then "there would be a slightly higher proportion of men at the high end of the scale," which would lead to an overrepresentation of men in elite positions (Pinker 2005).

These debates made any discussion of genes and behavior frustrating. For example, there was an enormous amount of evidence that intelligence was not simply inheritable and that it certainly didn't vary by race. Likewise, the "evidence" that Pinker cited, showing that men and women have natural differences in their mathematical ability, is suspect. While studies in the United States, and some other countries, show men with a greater variability in mathematical ability, studies in Lithuania, Germany, the Netherlands, Slovenia, and

---

that society itself will continue to exist. Second, socialization teaches individuals the norms, values, and beliefs associated with their culture and provides ways to ensure that members adhere to their shared way of life.

Social Isolation

We can appreciate how important socialization is when we see what happens to people who are deprived of social contact. When infants are born, they exhibit almost none of the learned behaviors that characterize human beings. Even their instincts for food or shelter or self-preservation are barely recognizable and almost impossible for them to act on alone. Babies do have innate capacities but can fully develop as human beings only through contact

FERAL CHILDREN in myths and rare real-world cases, children who have had little human contact and may have lived in social isolation from a young age

with others. There are several startling cases that demonstrate this (Newton 2004).

Perhaps you have heard myths about **feral children**, or children who have grown up in the wild. Supposedly, there are real cases of children being raised by wolves, as well as works of fiction such as *Tarzan of the Apes* and *The Jungle Book*. Such stories present images of primitive humans who have survived outside of society and who are both heathen and uncivilized yet pure and uncorrupt, who lack in social graces but possess the keenest of instincts. Legend has it that as far back as the thirteenth century, experiments were conducted by German emperor Frederick II to see whether humans could return to their natural and perfect state as depicted in the biblical Garden of Eden. Without human contact, the children who were used in these cruel experiments did not reveal any divine truths to the experimenters—they simply perished (Van Cleve 1972).

Although scientific ethics would never allow such experiments today, there are unfortunately some real-life instances

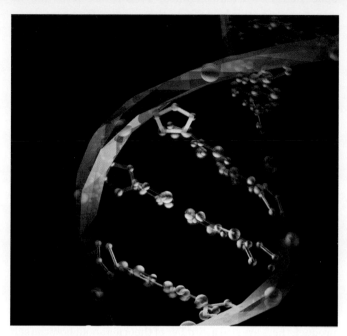

Nature vs. Nurture What parts of your life are affected by your genes? by your society?

gene, the mass media rushed to report, often in oversimplified ways, new research on the relationship between genetics and behavior.

A new generation of sociologists is trying to unite genetics and sociology in more interesting ways, beyond a simple opposition between nature and nurture. The term "sociobiology" is even falling out of favor, as researchers like University of North Carolina sociologist Guang Guo have taken to calling their work "genetically informed sociology" instead. These trailblazers caution us to remember that genetics are conditioned by social experience, and that there may be no simple cause-and-effect equation between genes and behavior. With the human genome containing 25,000 individual genes, it should not be surprising that behaviors do not spring from a single gene. Instead, "genes 'hunt in packs,' meaning that behaviors likely reflect networks of genes that work together" (Shanahan, Bauldry, and Freeman 2010, p. 36). Moreover, these genes do not work independently of social or cultural factors; rather, they work with them. Today there is increasing evidence "pointing to the importance of social factors in regulating genetic action" (Shanahan, Bauldry, and Freeman 2010, p. 37). For example, some researchers now suggest that social or environmental context can significantly alter the way a gene expresses itself. This theory, often referred to as *gene-by-environment interaction,* or $G \times E$, would require sociology and genetics to work together to understand where behaviors come from. In the future, this should give all of us a great deal more insight into the nature vs. nurture debate.

Denmark failed to produce the same results (Feingold 1992). For sociologists, this suggested that something much more complicated was going on. Despite these challenges, Pinker seemed to feed a popular desire to find genes that "controlled" behaviors. From the "gay" gene to the "promiscuity" involving children who have lived in extreme social isolation. Though rare, these cases give social scientists the chance to study the effects of social isolation and to better understand the relationship between human development and socialization (Davis 1940; Davis and Moore 1947).

One well-known modern case involves a child named Genie (a pseudonym), who was discovered by child welfare services in 1970 (Rymer 1994). At the time she was thirteen years old and had been living with her family in Arcadia, California, where she had been severely neglected and abused. The authorities were shocked to find that the young girl had not developed like a normal child. Since infancy, Genie's father had kept her locked in a small room, where she was often tied to a potty chair or crib, and she was deprived of practically all human interaction. She had not been exposed to language much and therefore had not learned to speak. Because her movements had been restricted, and she was also malnourished, Genie lacked in physical development. She was afraid of strangers and devoid of any social skills. She exhibited some animal-like qualities; she clawed and sniffed and spat frequently.

Genie was taken into custody and placed in the care of a team of scientists who were given an unprecedented opportunity to both study and treat her case. Would it be possible to reverse the effects of extreme social isolation? Could Genie learn language and how to talk? Could she be socialized and learn to interact with others? Or would it be too late for her to develop normally? The team commenced at once to study the process of socialization and language acquisition, exposing Genie to caring people and a whole new world. At first she made rapid progress with both sign language and nonverbal communication. She was also learning to vocalize, quickly adding new words to her vocabulary. She was gaining some social skills and forming relationships with the researchers, all of which made them optimistic about Genie's prognosis for recovery.

The team began to splinter as they disagreed about Genie's care. Over the next few years, she moved between

Mowgli, the "Man Cub" Fictional accounts of feral children such as Mowgli, the hero of the animated Disney film *The Jungle Book*, are quite different from real socially isolated children who struggle to learn language and interact with others.

several homes and her progress faltered. At one point she went back to live with her mother (her father had committed suicide when Genie was discovered), who was unable to properly care for her. The research project was in trouble. Despite collecting mounds of data on Genie, the scientists had failed to follow research protocols, and parts of the study were improperly conducted and poorly documented. Funding to support further research was withdrawn, and all testing and scientific observation ended. Genie was placed in a series of foster homes, where she suffered further abuse and lost much of her capacity for speech. Genie's case was effectively closed in 1978, and we know little about her current status. There is still debate over the ethics of such research on humans.

Unfortunately, Genie was not the last child to be raised in social isolation. Real-life cases occasionally emerge, such as the 2008 case of Elizabeth Fritzl in Austria, who was held captive for twenty-four years in her father's basement, along with four of her children. Each case confirms that the effects of extreme social isolation are devastating and tragic. It is only through contact with others that people develop the qualities we consider natural and normal in a human being.

The socialization process begins in infancy and is especially productive once a child begins to understand and use language (Ochs 1986). But socialization is not complete at that point. It is a lifelong process that continues to shape us through experiences such as school, work, marriage, and parenthood, as we will see in the next few sections.

SELF the individual's conscious, reflexive experience of a personal identity separate and distinct from others

Theories of the Self

Having a sense of one's self is perhaps the most fundamental of all human experiences. When seventeenth-century philosopher René Descartes exclaimed, "I think, therefore I am," he was expressing this basic fact—that we possess a consciousness about ourselves. More recently, some have examined whether higher mammals or primates might also have this same self-consciousness; while that has yet to be determined, we do know that consciousness is at the core of humanness.

The **self** is our experience of a distinct, real, personal identity that is separate and different from all other people. We can be "proud of ourselves," "lose control of ourselves," or want to "change ourselves," suggesting that we have the ability to think about ourselves as if we were more than one being and to see ourselves from the vantage point of an observer. Our thoughts and feelings emanate both *from* and *toward* ourselves; this is, in effect, how we come to "know" ourselves.

But just where does this sense of a self come from? How do we arrive at self-knowledge? When sociologists address these questions, they look at both the individual and society to find the answer. They believe that the self is created and modified through social interaction over the course of a lifetime. But while sociologists agree that the self is largely a social product, there are still a number of theories about how the self develops, as we will see.

Psychoanalytic Theory: Sigmund Freud

The psychoanalytic perspective on the self, which is usually associated with Sigmund Freud, emphasizes childhood and sexual development as indelible influences on an individual's identity, and in turn how society is upheld through the transformation of human instincts. While Freud's ideas have generated a great deal of controversy, they remain compelling for sociologists.

Perhaps Freud's greatest contribution to understanding the self is his idea of the unconscious mind, as featured in *The Interpretation of Dreams* (1900/1955). Freud believed that the conscious level of awareness is but the tip of the iceberg and that just below the surface is a far greater area of the mind, the subconscious and the unconscious. He proposed that this unconscious energy is the source of conscious thoughts and behavior. For example, the unconscious urge to slay one's rivals may manifest itself in a conscious decision to work harder at the office in order to outshine a competitive co-worker.

According to Freud, the mind consists of three interrelated systems: the id, the ego, and the superego. The **id**, which is composed of biological drives, is the source of instinctive, psychic energy. Its main goal is to achieve pleasure and to avoid pain in all situations, which makes the id a selfish and unrealistic part of the mind. For example, despite all your hard work, sometimes

Dreams and the Subconscious In his book *The Interpretation of Dreams*, psychoanalyst Sigmund Freud outlined three psychological systems—the id, the ego, and the superego—that regulate subconscious drives and help keep an individual mentally balanced.

mental or emotional function, yet they all work together to keep the individual in a more or less healthy state of balance.

Freud (1905) also proposed that between infancy and adulthood, the personality passes through four distinct **psychosexual stages of development**. Each stage is associated with a different erogenous zone. Freud's theory emerged from his therapy work with adult patients who were asked to try to recall earlier periods from their lives. According to the theory, a child passes through the first three stages of development between the ages of one and five. Most people have little or no memory whatsoever of this period. Yet, according to psychoanalytic theory, it sets the stage for the rest of one's adult life. The last stage of development begins around the age of twelve, but few people successfully complete this final transition to maturity. In some cases, the transitions through the first three stages are not completely successful either, so that people may find themselves stuck, or "fixated," at an earlier stage. Perhaps you've known someone who is considered to have an "oral fixation"—this person, thought to be partially stuck in the first stage of development, might smoke, overeat, or be verbally aggressive. Someone who is "anal retentive"—a neatnik, tightwad, or control freak—is thought to be partially stuck in the second stage. These kinds of personality traits, rooted in early childhood (according to Freud), appear as "hang-ups" in the adult.

Another of Freud's important contributions to sociology is found in his later work *Civilization and Its Discontents* (1930/2010). In it he extended his thesis to show how the psychological makeup of the individual helps to create social order, or civilization, while at the same time being constrained by society's structures and demands, causing the person to become discontent. Again Freud focused on the subconscious drives or instincts of the individual. He referred to two main impulses: "Eros," the libido or life instinct, and "Thanatos," which is aggression or the death instinct. To live successfully in human community, we must find socially acceptable ways of channeling these instincts. We cannot simply act out on our sexual or aggressive impulses without harming ourselves and others and threatening the larger collective. The raw and primitive drives of the individual must be managed somehow. When instincts are repressed or turned inward they become the conscience and a source of guilt and neuroses. When instincts are sublimated or turned outward, they are positively transformed. There are many constructive ways of expressing sexual energy,

that competitive co-worker is the one who gets the raise—not exactly what the pleasure-seeking, power-hungry id desired. The **ego**, by contrast, is the part that deals with the real world. It operates on the basis of reason and helps to mediate and integrate the demands of both the id and the superego. So the ego is the part of the self that says, "Okay, this time the other guy won, but if I keep trying, I'm bound to get that raise eventually."

The **superego** is composed of two components: the conscience and the ego-ideal. The conscience serves to keep us from engaging in socially undesirable behavior, and the ego-ideal upholds our vision of who we believe we should ideally be. The superego develops as a result of parental guidance, particularly in the form of the rewards and punishments we receive as children. It inhibits the urges of the id and encourages the ego to find morally acceptable forms of behavior. So the superego helps suppress the urge to kill your competitor and keeps you working toward getting that raise in socially acceptable ways. Each of these systems serves a different

LOOKING-GLASS SELF the notion that the self develops through our perception of others' evaluations and appraisals of us

PREPARATORY STAGE the first stage in Mead's theory of the development of self wherein children mimic or imitate others

PLAY STAGE the second stage in Mead's theory of the development of self wherein children pretend to play the role of the particular or significant other

redirecting it toward creative pursuits that produce the great works of culture, commerce, or scientific discoveries. Likewise, aggressive instincts can find appropriate outlets in competitive sports, politics, and other competitions, or can be felt vicariously through forms of entertainment like video games or amusement park rides. To live in a civilized society means agreeing to norms and sanctions that infringe on personal freedom but serve to protect the well-being of the group. Civilization demands that we give up some satisfaction of acting on instinct to gain the lesser happiness but greater security of living within the bounds of society.

Other sociologists have extended Freud's work in this area, focusing especially on gender identity—seeing oneself as feminine or masculine. Nancy Chodorow, a feminist and psychoanalytic sociologist, has written widely on human behavior and internal psychic structures and how patterns of gendered parenting and early childhood development can lead to the reproduction of traditional gender roles in society (1978, 1994).

The Looking-Glass Self: Charles Cooley

Around the same time Freud was developing his theories (early 1900s), other social theorists interested in the self were working on the other side of the Atlantic. Charles Cooley, an early member of the Chicago School of sociology, devised a simple but elegant way to conceptualize how individuals gain a sense of self. His idea is captured in the following short poem, which summarizes a profound and complex process.

> *Each to each a looking-glass,*
> *Reflects the other that doth pass.*

Cooley (1909) referred to this concept as the **looking-glass self**. He believed that we all act like mirrors to each other, reflecting back to one another an image of ourselves. We do this in three steps.

1. *We imagine how we look to others*—not just in a physical sense, but in how we present ourselves. For example, we may imagine that others find us friendly, funny, or hardworking. The idea we have of ourselves is particularly important in regard to significant others. Whether they are parents, bosses, friends, or partners, we care about how we look to these people.

2. *We imagine other people's judgment of us.* We try to picture others' reactions and to interpret what they must

be feeling. What is their opinion of me? Do they think I am smart enough? Lazy? Boring? Too tall? Not talkative enough?

3. *We experience some kind of feeling about ourselves based on our perception of other people's judgments.* If we imagine, for instance, that they think of us as competent, we may feel pride; conversely, if we think they consider us inadequate, we may feel shame or embarrassment. The important point here is that we respond to the judgments that we *believe* others make about us, without really knowing for sure what they think. And we're not always right. We may draw wildly unrealistic conclusions. But according to Cooley, it is these perceptions, not reality, that determine the feelings we ultimately have about ourselves.

The social looking glass—the way we see ourselves reflected back from others—together with the feelings we develop as a result of what we imagine they see in us, forms our concept of self. For Cooley, there could be no sense of self without society, for there is no individual self without a corresponding "other" to provide us with our looking-glass self-image.

The suggestion that we are dependent on what others think of us—or rather what we think they think—for our own self-concept might seem appalling: are we really that hung up on what other people think? But while some of us may be influenced to a greater or lesser degree, *all* of us come to know ourselves through relationships, either real or imagined, with others.

Mind, Self, and Society: George Herbert Mead

Another member of the Chicago School, George Herbert Mead, expanded on Cooley's ideas about the development of the self and laid the essential groundwork that became the theory of symbolic interactionism. Mead also believed that the self is created through social interaction. He believed that this process starts in childhood—that children begin to develop a sense of self at about the same time that they began to learn language. The acquisition of language skills coincides with the growth of mental capacities, including the ability to think of ourselves as separate and distinct and to see ourselves in relationship to others (Mead 1934).

According to Mead, the development of the self unfolds in several stages as we move through childhood. First is the **preparatory stage**. Children under the age of three lack a completely developed sense of self, and so they have difficulty distinguishing themselves from others. Such children begin the development process by simply imitating or mimicking others around them (making faces, playing patty-cake) without fully understanding the meaning of their behavior. After age three, children enter the **play stage** of development

The Particular Other According to Mead, children begin to develop a sense of self by imitating others and playing roles.

when they start to pretend or play at being "mommy," "firefighter," "princess," or "doctor." This is referred to as taking the role of the **particular or significant other**. As children learn the behavior associated with being a mother or doctor, they internalize the expectations of those particular others and begin to gain new perspectives in addition to their own. Such play also serves the purpose of anticipatory socialization for the real-life roles a child might play in the future.

In the final or **game stage** of development, children's self-awareness increases through a process Mead described using the example of games. By the early school years, children begin to take part in organized games. Each child must follow the rules of the game, which means that he or she must simultaneously take into account the roles of all the other players. Mead calls this overview the perspective of the **generalized other**. Thus, children begin to understand the set of standards common to a social group—their playmates—and to see themselves from others' viewpoints. By taking the perspective of the generalized other, children are able to see themselves as objects. They gradually learn to internalize the expectations

of the generalized other for themselves and to evaluate their own behavior. This is the beginning of understanding the attitudes and expectations of society as a whole.

Mead also recognized the dialectical or **dual nature of the self**—that is, the self as both subject and object. What we refer to as "I" is the subject component—the experience of a spontaneous, active, and creative part of ourselves, somewhat less socialized. What we refer to as "me" is the object component—the experience of a norm-abiding, conforming part of ourselves, more socialized and therefore reliant on others. The two components are inseparable and are united to form a single self in each of us. It is this process of recognizing the dual nature of the self, taking the role of the particular other, and seeing the perspective of the generalized other that Mead suggests leads to the development of the self.

PARTICULAR OR SIGNIFICANT OTHER the perspectives and expectations of a particular role that a child learns and internalizes

GAME STAGE the third stage in Mead's theory of the development of self wherein children play organized games and take on the perspective of the generalized other

GENERALIZED OTHER the perspectives and expectations of a network of others (or of society in general) that a child learns and then takes into account when shaping his or her own behavior

DUAL NATURE OF THE SELF the idea that we experience the self as both subject and object, the "I" and the "me"

THOMAS THEOREM classic formulation of the way individuals determine reality, whereby "if people define situations as real, they are real in their consequences"

Dramaturgy: Erving Goffman

Erving Goffman is another among the group of symbolic interactionists who saw micro-level, face-to-face interaction as the building block of every other aspect of society. Goffman believed that all meaning, as well as our individual selves, is constructed through interaction. Many of his key ideas are expressed in *The Presentation of Self in Everyday Life* (1956).

To understand Goffman's work, we first need to briefly consider another of the early Chicago School sociologists, W. I. Thomas. What is now called the **Thomas theorem** states that "if people define situations as real, they are real in their consequences" (Thomas and Thomas 1928, p. 572). In other words, because we encounter ambiguous situations every day, many meanings are possible. The way we define each situation, then, becomes its reality.

For example, suppose you're walking down the street and you witness a woman slapping a man in public. What are the possible meanings of that situation? It could be a fight or spousal abuse; it could be a joke or a friendly greeting, depending on how hard the slap is; it could be that he has just passed out and she is hoping to revive him; or the participants could be actors shooting a scene from a film. Each of these definitions leads to a different set of potential consequences—you might intervene, call the police, stand by and laugh, ignore them,

DEFINITION OF THE SITUATION
an agreement with others about "what is going on" in a given circumstance; this consensus allows us to coordinate our actions with others and realize goals

EXPRESSIONS OF BEHAVIOR
small actions such as an eye roll or head nod that serve as an interactional tool to help project our definition of the situation to others

EXPRESSIONS GIVEN
expressions that are intentional and usually verbal, such as utterances

EXPRESSIONS GIVEN OFF
observable expressions that can be either intended or unintended and are usually nonverbal

IMPRESSION MANAGEMENT
the effort to control the impressions we make on others so that they form a desired view of us and the situation; the use of self-presentation and performance tactics

summon paramedics, or ask for an autograph, depending on which meaning you act upon. Each **definition of the situation** lends itself to a different approach, and the consequences are real.

Goffman looked at how we define situations interactionally—not just cognitively within our own heads, but in interaction with others. Think about it: How do you get your definition of the situation across to others? If you think a classroom lecture is boring, you may look over at your best friend and roll your eyes . . . she nods, indicating that she knows what you mean. The eye roll and the nod are **expressions of behavior**, tools we use to project our definitions of the situation to others.

What Goffman calls **expressions given** are typically verbal and intended—most of our speech falls into this category. Almost all of what we say, we *mean* to say, at least at that moment. Only in situations of extreme emotional response—such as fear, pain, or ecstasy—might we

make unintended utterances. **Expressions given off**, like the eye roll and the nod, are typically nonverbal but observable in various ways and may be intended or unintended. Things like facial expressions, mannerisms, body language, and styles of dress are important indicators to others about the definition of the situation.

IMPRESSION MANAGEMENT Reading meaning in others' expressions of behavior requires a bit of caution. We know that people may deliberately say things to hide what they really feel, so we tend to think we get more real insight from expressions given off because we believe them to be unintended. But expressions given off can be manipulated as well. In a sense, Goffman was saying that it's not just what you say but how you say it that creates meaning. And he was a cynic, although he believed that everyday actors can be sincere. Goffman saw social life as a sort of con game, in which we work at controlling the impressions others have of us. He called this process **impression management**. Like actors on a stage, we play our parts and use all our communicative resources (verbal and nonverbal) to present a particular impression to others. We say and do what we think is necessary to communicate who we are and what we think, and we refrain from saying and doing things that might damage the impression we want others to have of us.

It is this focus on the performance strategies of impression management that has led scholars to refer to Goffman's central ideas as **dramaturgy**—and the theatrical allusion is entirely intended. As in the theater, we use certain tools to

Table 4.1 Theory in Everyday Life

Perspective	Approach to Self and Interaction	Case Study: Identity in Childhood
Psychoanalysis	Freud's theory of the unconscious mind as composed of an interrelated system (id, ego, superego) that underlies human behavior; personality develops through psychosexual stages.	Parents instill a conscience (superego) in children through rules that govern their instinctual behavior (id) until children mature and are self-governing (ego).
Looking-Glass Self	Cooley's theory of the self concept as derived from how we imagine others see us, and the feelings about our selves based on the perceived judgments of others.	Parents and significant others serve as a reflection to children, who develop a sense of self based on their appraisals, real or imagined.
Mind, Self, and Society	Mead's theory of the self that develops through three stages (preparatory, play, and game); in role taking the particular or generalized other, we learn to see ourselves as others do.	Children gain a sense of self through imitation, play, and games, in which they learn various roles and take on the perspectives of others.
Dramaturgy	Goffman's theory of the presentation of self; we are like actors on a stage whose performance strategies aid in impression management.	Children learn the arts of impression management and may present a different self to their parents than to other children or to teachers.

Dramaturgy Playing the role of Daenerys Targaryen in the HBO series *Game of Thrones*, actress Emilia Clarke is barely recognizable from her everyday self. While most of us don't go to such lengths to get into character, we, too, use makeup, costumes, and props for the purpose of impression management.

aid in our impression management. The **front**, for example, is the setting that helps establish a particular meaning (like a classroom for teaching or a bar for drinking). The specific social setting, or **region** (which includes the location, scenery, décor, and props), provides more elements that help establish the boundaries of the interactional context. You might carry a briefcase into a bar, but it's probably not a good idea to carry a bottle of beer into the classroom.

The front makes a big difference in how we perceive and interact with the people we encounter there. Students and professors recognize one another and know how to interact when on campus or in the classroom. But in other venues, we are out of context, and this can confuse us. We seldom think of our professors as people who have off-campus lives—it's hard to see them as people who dine out, see movies, or buy underwear (for that matter, professors rarely think of their students this way either!). So when we encounter one another in unfamiliar regions, we often don't know how to behave because the old classroom scripts don't work.

Our **personal front**—appearance, manner, and style of dress (or "costume"), as well as gender, race, and age—helps establish the definition of the situation as well. For example, Dr. Ferris is told quite often that she "doesn't look like a professor." This illustrates how we use elements of personal front to make judgments about people: if our images of professors involve gruff, grizzled, older men in unfashionable clothes, then someone who is younger, friendlier, and female and who wears edgy, hipper styles must work harder at convincing others that she is in fact a professor. Similarly, when a student happens to see Dr. Ferris at a restaurant, movie theater, or department store, the student's response is almost always the same: "what are you doing here?"

In addition, there are places known as back regions, or **backstage**, where we prepare (or rehearse) for our performances. And then there are front regions, or **frontstage**, where we play a particular role and perform for an "audience" of others. We behave differently—and present different selves—frontstage than we do backstage; your professor behaved differently this morning while he showered, shaved, dressed, and made breakfast for his kids than he is behaving now, lecturing and answering questions in his sociology class. For Goffman, the key to understanding these nuances in impression management is to recognize that we present different selves in different situations, and the responses of others to those selves continually shape and mold our definitions of situation *and* self. Thus we can say that the self is a **social construction** (Berger and Luckmann 1966). The self is something that is created or invented in interaction with others who also participate in agreeing to the reality or meaning of that self as it is being presented in the situation.

We also make claims about who we are in our interactions. These claims can be either accepted or contradicted by others, which can make things either easier or harder for our self-image. Most of the time, others support the selves we project. For example, when your professor starts lecturing and you begin to take notes, you are supporting the version of self that he is presenting: he is "doing professor," and in response, you are "doing student." Another way that we support the selves that people present is to allow them to save face—to prevent them from realizing that they've done something embarrassing. Goffman calls this **cooling the mark out**, a phrase borrowed from con games, but it can be used as a tool of civility and tact as well. When the professor mixes up two related concepts in a lecture, for example, you let it pass because you know what she really meant to say. Or, even worse, you overlook the spinach between your professor's teeth until it can be called to his attention privately!

There are also situations in which the selves we project are contested or even destroyed. For example, if you raised your

DRAMATURGY an approach pioneered by Erving Goffman in which social life is analyzed in terms of its similarities to theatrical performance

FRONT in the dramaturgical perspective, the setting or scene of performances that helps establish the definition of the situation

REGION the context in which the performance takes place, including location, decor, and props

PERSONAL FRONT the performance tactics we use to present ourselves to others, including appearance, costume, and manner

BACKSTAGE the places in which we rehearse and prepare for our performances

FRONTSTAGE the places in which we deliver our performances to an audience of others

SOCIAL CONSTRUCTION the process by which a concept or practice is created and maintained by participants who collectively agree that it exists

COOLING THE MARK OUT behaviors that help others to save face or avoid embarrassment, often referred to as civility or tact

hand in a 200-person lecture hall and told the professor that he had spinach between his teeth, you would be undermining the self he is trying to present. His identity as an expert, an authority figure, and a senior mentor would be publicly damaged once you called attention to his dental gaffe (unless he was able to deflect the situation gracefully). In Goffman's view, then, the presentation of self and impression management are about power as well as about self. If you embarrass your professor in front of an auditorium full of students, he no longer possesses quite as much power as he did a few moments before.

Goffman's view of our interactions can be disturbing to some people, for it suggests that we are always acting, that we are never being honest about who we really are. But Goffman would challenge this interpretation of his work. Yes, some people deliberately deceive others in their presentation of self, but we must all present *some* type of self in social situations. Why wouldn't those selves be presented sincerely? As Goffman-inspired sociologist Josh Meyrowitz says, "While a dishonest judge may pretend to be an honest judge, even an honest judge must play the role of 'honest judge'" (1985, p. 30).

DATA WORKSHOP
Analyzing Everyday Life

Impression Management in Action

They say that you never get to make a first impression twice, that people can size us up in a matter of seconds and quickly jump to conclusions about who we are. How well do you know yourself and the impressions you make on others? This exercise is designed to help make your own impression management work visible—and to help you see how integral it is to your everyday life. For this Data Workshop you will be doing participant observation research with yourself as the subject. Research that involves observing one's own behavior is known as autoethnography. Refer to Chapter 2 for a review of this method.

Your task will be to observe yourself as you participate in two different social situations. Afterward, you will do a comparative analysis of your presentation of self in each setting. As you examine the most minute details of yourself in interactions, you will probably discover that you perform somewhat different versions of yourself in the two situations. "Doing student," for instance, might be very different from "doing boyfriend." Let's see.

Step 1: Observation
Choose two different situations that you will encounter this week in your everyday life, and commit to observing yourself for thirty minutes as you participate in each. For example, you may observe yourself at work, at a family birthday celebration, at lunch with friends, in your math class, riding on the bus or train, or watching an athletic match. The two situations you choose don't need to be extraordinary in any way; in fact, the more mundane, the better. But they should be markedly different from one another.

Step 2: Field notes
In an autoethnography, your own actions, thoughts, and feelings are the focus of study. Write some informal field notes about your experience so that you can refer to them when you discuss your findings. Your notes can be casual in tone and loose in format, but, as always, it's a good idea to write them as soon as possible after your time in the field. That way you capture more of the details you'll want to remember. Aim for at least one (or more!) full page of notes for each of the two situations.

Step 3: Analysis
After observing yourself in the two situations, read through your field notes and consider the following questions:

* What type of "front" do you encounter when you enter each situation? What role do you play and who is your "audience"?

* How does the "region" or setting (location, scenery, and props) affect your presentation of self there?

* Can you identify "backstage" and "frontstage" regions for each situation? Which of your activities are preparation and which are performance?

* What type of "personal front" (appearance, manner, dress) do you bring to each situation?

* How are your facial expressions, body language, and so forth ("expressions given off") different in each situation?

* What kinds of things do you say ("expressions given") in each situation?

* How convincing are you at managing the impression you want to make on others in each of the two situations?

* Who are you in each situation? Do you present a slightly different version of yourself in each? Why?

A final Goffman-inspired question to ask is this: does engaging in impression management mean that we have no basic, unchanging self? If we bring different selves to different situations, what does that say about the idea of a "true self"? This issue is an important one, and we hope you use your Data Workshop findings to pursue it in greater depth.

There are two options for completing the Data Workshop:

PREP-PAIR-SHARE Carry out your observations and bring your field notes to class with you. Partner with another student and discuss your experiences. Work together on developing your analysis by responding to the Data Workshop questions. Use this as a way to learn more about yourself and others.

DO-IT-YOURSELF For Step 1, use ethnographic methods of data gathering. Create written field notes to record your actions, interactions, and thoughts during each thirty-minute observation period. Be as detailed as possible. Then write a three- to four-page essay applying Goffman's dramaturgical analysis to your own experiences, in response to the questions in Step 3. Refer to your field notes in the essay, and include them as an attachment to your paper.

Agents of Socialization

Since our sense of self is shaped by social interaction, we should now turn our attention to the socializing forces that have the most significant impact on our lives. These forces, called **agents of socialization**, provide structured situations in which socialization takes place. While there are a variety of such influences in American society, notably religion, as well as our political and economic systems, we will focus here on what may be the four most predominant agents of socialization: the family, schools, peers, and the media.

The Family

The family is the single most significant agent of socialization in all societies. It's easy to see why. The family is the original group to which we belong. It is where early emotional and social bonds are created, where language is learned, and where we first begin to internalize the norms and values of our society. Most of our primary socialization, which teaches us to become mature, responsible members of society, takes place within the family. It is not surprising, then, that the family has perhaps the longest-lasting influence on the individual.

Much research has focused on the role of mothers in child-rearing practices (Goode 1982), although attention has also turned to the significance of fathers, as well as siblings and other relatives. For example, Scott Coltrane's book *Family Man* (1997) looks at historical changes in the roles of men as active parents and how men feel about their involvement in their children's lives. The family has such a powerful impact on us partly because as young children we have limited

> **AGENTS OF SOCIALIZATION** social groups, institutions, and individuals (especially the family, schools, peers, and the mass media) that provide structured situations in which socialization takes place

Family Has the Longest-Lasting Influence The family is the original group to which each person belongs, and it is the most important agent of socialization.

outside contact (until we start day care or school) and therefore few if any other influences. The family is our world.

The family is also *in* the world. Where a family is located, both geographically and socially—its ethnic, class, religious, educational, and political background—will affect family members (Lareau 2003). For example, one of the most important lessons we learn in families is about gender roles: we see what moms and dads, sisters and brothers are expected to do (like mow the lawn or fold the laundry) and convert these observations into general rules about gender in society (Chodorow 1978).

Socialization differs from family to family because each family has its own particular set of values and beliefs. A single family can also change over time. As years pass, children may not be raised in the same way as their older siblings, for the simple reason that parents have no experience with babies when their first child is born but plenty of experience by the time the youngest comes along. Nor are all aspects of socialization deliberate; some in fact are quite unintentional (as when a father's violent temper or a mother's depression is passed down to the next generation).

Schools

Many people remember their school years with fondness, dread, or perhaps relief that they're over! No wonder school makes such a great subject for bad dreams and movie scripts. Public elementary and secondary schools were first established in the United States in the 1800s. While attendance was uneven at first, education advocates believed that schooling played a critical role in maintaining a democracy (though blacks and women still lacked the right to vote) and in shaping future generations of citizens. Over the years, schools have gradually taken on greater responsibilities than merely teaching a prescribed curriculum. Schools now provide physical education, meals, discipline, and child care, all formerly the provinces of other social institutions.

HIDDEN CURRICULUM values or behaviors that students learn indirectly over the course of their schooling

When children begin attending school (including preschool and day care), it may be their first significant experience away from home. School helps them to become less dependent on the family, providing a bridge to other social groups. In school, children learn that they will be judged on their behavior and on academic performance. They learn not only formal subjects but also a **hidden curriculum** (Jackson 1968), a set of behavioral traits such as punctuality, neatness, discipline, hard work, competition, and obedience. The socialization children receive from teachers, staff members, and other students occurs simultaneously and overlaps with what they learn in the family.

Recently, there has been increasing scrutiny regarding the role of teachers, especially in public schools. Because teachers are such potent role models for students, parents are concerned about the moral standing of those who are in charge of teaching their children, as well as their training and competence. There is increasing pressure for schools to take on even more responsibilities, including dealing with issues that used to be taught at home or in church—such as sex, violence, drugs and alcohol, and general morality and citizenship.

Peers

Peer groups are groups of people who are about the same age and have similar social characteristics. Peers may be friends at school or from the neighborhood, members of a sports team, or cabin mates at summer camp. As children get older, peers often become more important than parents as agents of socialization. As the influence of peers increases, the influence of parents decreases. While the family still has the most long-lasting influence on an individual, it is peers who have the most intense and immediate effect on each other.

By adolescence, young people spend more time with their peers than with their parents or anyone else (Larson and Richards 1991). Membership in a peer group provides young people with a way of exercising independence from, and possibly reacting against, adult control. Young people tend to form peer subcultures that are almost entirely centered on their own interests, such as video gaming or disc golf or garage bands, with distinct values and norms related to those interests.

The need to "fit in" with a peer group may seem overwhelming to some young people. Some will do almost anything to belong—even betray their own values: Bradley and Wildman (2002) found that peer pressure was a predictor of adolescent participation in risky behaviors such as dangerous driving, unsafe sex, and drug and alcohol use. Peer groups, while providing important and enjoyable social bonds, can also be the source of painful self-doubt, ridicule, or rejection for many young people.

The Media

The media's role as one of the most significant sources of socialization is a somewhat recent phenomenon. Television began infiltrating American homes in the 1950s, and usage of the Internet has become widespread only in the past two decades. Yet, for many of us, it would be almost impossible to imagine life without the media—whether print, broadcast, or digital. This huge explosion, the dawning of the Information Age, is something we already take for granted, but we don't always see the ways in which it is changing our lives.

Many sociologists question whether the media may have even usurped some of the functions of the family in teaching basic norms and values and giving advice on common problems. As an example, take the people of Fiji, a South Pacific island that lacked widespread access to television until 1995. A group of Harvard Medical School researchers took this

Fashion for Whom? Most women do not look like this model, yet her body type is held up as the ideal in magazines and other forms of media.

unique opportunity to study the effects of television on the local population. Specifically, they were interested in the ways in which Western programs influenced eating habits and body image among adolescent girls in a culture that "traditionally supported robust appetites and body shapes" (A. Becker et al. 2002).

Through surveys and interviews with the young women (the mean age was around seventeen) in 1995, just months after television was introduced, and again in 1998, the researchers ascertained that Western television was in fact affecting body image and corresponding behaviors among the Fijian girls. In those three years, the percentage of subjects whose survey responses indicated an eating disorder jumped from 12 to 29, and the percentage who reported self-induced vomiting as a form of weight control rose from none to 11. Dieting and dissatisfaction with weight were prevalent—and 83 percent of the girls who were interviewed reported that they felt television "had specifically influenced their friends and/or themselves to feel differently about or change their body shape or weight" (A. Becker et al. 2002).

The women of Fiji only recently encountered TV and other forms of modern media. How do we measure the cumulative effect of the ubiquitous exposure to the media that pervade

American society, day in and day out? Whose messages are we listening to, and what are we being told about ourselves and each other? On average, Americans watch between two and seven hours of television per day and spend more hours listening to music, reading, watching movies, playing video games, surfing the web, or using social media. By the time young people graduate from high school, they will have spent far more time with the media than in the classroom. While some worry that this means kids are lost in a fantasy world, Hodge and Tripp (1986) have argued that watching TV actually helps kids learn to distinguish between reality and fantasy, an important developmental milestone. In addition to their ability to entertain, the media also have great potential to inform and educate. It is clear that we internalize many of the values, beliefs, and norms presented in the media and that their powerful influence in our lives only stands to increase as we proceed deeper into the Information Age.

DATA WORKSHOP
Analyzing Media and Pop Culture

Television as an Agent of Socialization

Television is a powerful and surreptitious agent of socialization. It is everywhere, and we devour thousands of hours of it—so it seems important to ask what kinds of messages we are getting about ourselves and our society from all that viewing. How does TV socialize us? You're going to help answer that question.

For this Data Workshop you will be using existing sources and doing a content analysis of a particular TV program. See the section on existing sources in Chapter 2 for a review of this research method. Choose one of the most popular TV series currently on the air—at the time of this writing, your choices might include *NCIS*, *The Big Bang Theory*, or *Orange Is the New Black*. Choose a regular drama or comedy series rather than a news program, talk show, game show, or reality show. Make sure that the show takes place in contemporary times (rather than in the past or in some fantasy world), since your aim will be to analyze how the show depicts modern society and affects today's viewer.

Now choose some aspect of social status and individual identity that you want to focus on, such as gender (how women or men are portrayed), race/ethnicity (how a particular ethnic group, such as African Americans or

Latinos, is portrayed), sexuality (heterosexuals, gay men, or lesbians), or class (poor people, wealthy people, or the middle class). For instance, you might look at the depiction of women in *New Girl* or men in *The Big Bang Theory*, the role of Latinos in *CSI* or African Americans in *How to Get Away with Murder*, or the portrayal of gays in *Brooklyn Nine-Nine* or the wealthy in *Revenge*.

Watch an episode of your chosen program in its entirety. You will want to record the program or look for an episode on DVD, Netflix, Hulu, or another online source so that you can review certain scenes or bits of dialogue several times if you need to. It is important to take some notes as you watch, paying attention to the program's content with reference to your particular topic choice.

To give you an example of how to do this workshop, we use depictions of women (in brackets below) as our topic and the program *Modern Family*. You should substitute your own TV program and choice of topic for each of the following questions:

* In this episode of the program, how many [women] characters are there? How does the number of [women] characters compare with the number of other characters? Are the [women's] roles major characters or minor characters? How can you tell?

* What types of roles do the [women] characters have? What are their activities, attitudes, and interactions like on the show? What kinds of things do they do and say that tell you who they are and what they are like?

* Are the portrayals of [women] positive or negative? Humorous or serious? One-dimensional or multidimensional? How can you tell?

* What image(s) of [women] does this program portray? In other words, what messages do the words, pictures, plot lines, and characters convey to viewers about [women] in general?

In the case of *Modern Family*, there are some interesting portrayals of women to analyze. There are two adult women as part of the main cast ensemble: Claire Dunphy and Gloria Pritchett. The women are related to each other through Jay Pritchett, who is Claire's father and Gloria's husband (it's a second marriage for both). Claire and Gloria are both stay-at-home moms; Gloria appears to be just a sexy, gold-digging "trophy wife" but is also portrayed as having a depth of wisdom and strength that results from her experiences in a tough neighborhood of her Colombian hometown. Claire is a "daddy's girl" who is initially jealous of Gloria and who searches for meaningful work as her children grow older (she eventually gets a job at her father's company). These women relate to each other,

as well as the men in their lives, in ways that provided powerful messages about gender roles and femininity to both female and male viewers.

Now that you have examined the roles and portrayals, let's consider the effects on society:

* How does the content of this program contribute to our socialization process? What do we learn about [women] in society from watching the program? After finishing your analysis, what do you think about TV's powers of socialization?

There are two options for completing this Data Workshop:

PREP-PAIR-SHARE Watch your chosen episode of TV and bring your notes with you to class. Partner with another student and present your findings. Work together on responding to the Data Workshop questions. Listen for any differences or variations in each other's insights.

DO-IT-YOURSELF Write a three- to four-page essay in response to the Data Workshop questions, including a content analysis of your chosen TV program. Make sure to refer to specific segments of the episode that help to support your discussion of TV as an agent of socialization. Attach your notes on the program to your paper.

Adult Socialization

Being an "adult" somehow signifies that we've learned well enough how to conduct ourselves as autonomous members of society. But adults are by no means completely socialized. Life is continually presenting us with new situations and new roles with unfamiliar norms and values. We are constantly learning and adjusting to new conditions over the life course and thereby participating in secondary socialization.

For example, your college training will teach you a great deal about the behaviors that will be expected of you in your chosen profession, such as responsibility and punctuality. But after graduating and obtaining a job, you will likely find further, unanticipated expectations. At the very least, you will be socialized to the local culture of a specific workplace, where new rules and customs (like "Always be closing!" in a real estate office) are observed. As your career unfolds, such episodes of socialization will recur as you take on different responsibilities or switch jobs.

Other examples of altered life circumstances include marrying, becoming divorced or widowed, raising a family, moving to a new community, losing a job, or retiring—all of which require modifying attitudes and behaviors. For example, being divorced or widowed after many years of marriage means jumping into a dating pool that may look quite different from the last time you were in it—"safe sex," "splitting the check,"

Desocialization Total Institutions such as the military and cults put new members through a process of resocialization by controlling most aspects of their lives and stripping them of old identities to create new ones. On the left, officers lead new recruits through drills at boot camp; followers of Sun Myung Moon's Unification Church, "Moonies", get married en masse.

and other new norms may be hard for older daters to assimilate. Adult socialization often requires the replacement of previously learned norms and values with different ones, what is known as **resocialization**. Facing a serious illness or growing old also often involves intensive resocialization. In order to cope with a new view of what their aging body will permit them to do, people must discard previous behaviors in favor of others (not working out every day, for example).

Another dramatic example of resocialization is found in **total institutions** (Goffman 1961), such as prisons, cults, and mental hospitals, and, in some cases, even boarding schools, nursing homes, monasteries, and the military.

In total institutions, residents are severed from their previous relations with society, and their former identities are systematically stripped away and reformed. There may be different ends toward which total institutions are geared, such as creating good soldiers, punishing criminals, or managing mental illness, but the process of resocialization is similar: all previous identities are suppressed, and an entirely new, disciplined self is created.

Relatively few adults experience resocialization to the degree of the total institution. All, however, continue to learn and synthesize norms and values throughout their lives as they move into different roles and social settings that present them once again with the challenges and opportunities of continued socialization.

Statuses and Roles

While agents of socialization play an important role in developing our individual identities, so does the larger scaffolding of society. This happens as we take on (or have imposed upon us) different statuses and roles.

A **status** is a position in a social hierarchy that comes with a set of expectations. Sometimes these positions are formalized: "professor," "president," or even "parent." Parental obligations, for example, are written into laws that prohibit the neglect and abuse of children. Other statuses are more informal: you may be the "class clown," for instance, or the "conscience" of your group of friends. The contours of these informal statuses are less explicit but still widely recognizable. We all occupy a number of statuses, as we hold positions in multiple social hierarchies at once. Some statuses change over the course of a lifetime (e.g., marital or parental status), while others usually do not (e.g., gender).

RESOCIALIZATION the process of replacing previously learned norms and values with new ones as a part of a transition in life

TOTAL INSTITUTIONS institutions in which individuals are cut off from the rest of society so that they can be controlled and regulated for the purpose of systematically stripping away previous roles and identities in order to create new ones

STATUS a position in a social hierarchy that carries a particular set of expectations

IN RELATIONSHIPS
Sister Pauline Quinn and Training Dogs in Prison

Can adopting a puppy change your fundamental sense of self for the better? According to Sister Pauline Quinn, a Dominican nun, it can when the puppies are adopted by prison inmates who train them to become service or therapy dogs. Sister Pauline knew something firsthand about life in a total institution, and not just the convent. Born Kathy Quinn, she was once a chronic runaway because of a dysfunctional family life and was eventually institutionalized for lack of another place for her to go. For several years afterward, she was homeless, staying in abandoned buildings and trying to avoid getting picked up by the police as a vagrant. Kathy Quinn could well have died on the streets of Los Angeles, but instead her life was turned around when she found Joni, a German shepherd.

Quinn felt that the dog was the beginning of the process of resocialization that helped return her to being a functioning member of society. It was the first time she had a true friend, one whose unconditional love was restoring her badly damaged self-esteem. Her time in institutions had left her "depersonalized," stripped of any positive identity with which to tackle the demands of life on the "outside." The bond that forms between a human and a dog provides positive feedback and a loving relationship that can influence one's sense of self. The work that Quinn did in training Joni transformed not only the dog but the person as well, eventually leading her to a happier and more productive life devoted to helping others.

Quinn was particularly drawn to the plight of women prisoners and believed that they, too, could find similar benefits through contact with dogs. She knew that life in prison could be extremely depersonalizing, especially for women, and that rehabilitation, if it was offered at all, was too often unsuccessful, returning convicts to the streets without having rebuilt their identities and their lives. In 1981, with the assistance of Dr. Leo Bustad, a professor of veterinary science at the University of Washington, she approached the Washington State Correctional Center for Women and proposed that inmates volunteer to train puppies adopted from local shelters and rescue organizations to become service and therapy dogs. The result was the Prison Pet Partnership Program.

The women selected to participate in the program get more than just dogs to train; they get the opportunity for substantial resocialization, which helps them to develop new, positive identities and learn valuable social skills that can translate to the outside world. The labor-intensive process of training a dog is perfectly suited to the needs and abilities of inmates, who have a great surplus of time and a desperate need to find constructive ways to occupy it. The rigors of dog training, which place an emphasis on achieving discipline and

Can a Dog Transform an Inmate's Life? Sister Pauline Quinn has brought dog training programs to prisons across the country. Inmates reap many benefits when they train service and therapy dogs.

obedience through repetition and positive reinforcement, is a lesson not lost on the trainers. During the months of training, the animals even sleep with the inmates, providing added psychological benefits. Prisons report significant improvements in morale and behavior once dog-training programs are in place. Allowing prisoners access to the dogs' unconditional love and giving the prisoners a chance to contribute to society in a meaningful way increase the likelihood that the prisoners will reenter mainstream society successfully.

The original program, in the Washington penal system, has placed more than 700 dogs as service or therapy dogs. Prisons in at least nineteen states have established similar dog-training programs, and military prisons have begun comparable programs to train service dogs for disabled veterans. A service animal can cost as much as $10,000 to train, so these prison programs make a difference in placing more dogs with the people who need them. Just as important here, each relationship with a dog transforms the life of the inmate, who gets another chance at developing a more positive sense of self in the process.

There are different kinds of statuses. An **ascribed status** is one we are born with that is unlikely to change (such as our gender or race). An **embodied status** is located in our physical selves (such as beauty or disability). Finally, an **achieved status** is one we have earned through our own efforts (such as an occupation, hobby, or skill) or that has been acquired in some other way (such as a criminal identity, mental illness, or drug addiction). All statuses influence how others see and respond to us. However, some ascribed, embodied, or achieved statuses take on the power of what sociologists call a **master status**—a status that seems to override all others in our identities.

Master statuses carry with them expectations that may blind people to other facets of our personalities. People quickly make assumptions about what women, Asians, doctors, or alcoholics are like and may judge us according to those expectations rather than our actual attributes. This kind of judgment, often referred to as **stereotyping**, is looked upon as negative or destructive. However, it is important to realize that we all use these expectations in our everyday lives; stereotyping, as problematic as it is, is all but unavoidable.

A **role** is the set of behaviors expected from a particular status position. Sociologists such as Erving Goffman (1956) and Ralph Turner (1978) deliberately use the theatrical analogy to describe how roles provide a kind of script, outlining what we are expected to say and do as a result of our position in the social structure. Professors, then, are expected to be responsible teachers and researchers. Employment contracts and faculty handbooks may specify the role even further: professors must hold a certain number of office hours per week, for example, and must obtain permission from the university in order to skip classes or take a leave of absence. Class clowns don't sign a contract, nor are they issued a handbook, but they have role expectations nonetheless: they are expected to turn a classroom event into a joke whenever possible and to sacrifice their own success in order to provide laughs for others.

Multiple Roles and Role Conflict

In setting out general expectations for behavior, roles help shape our actions in ways that may come to define us to ourselves and others. For example, we often describe ourselves according to personality traits: "I am a responsible person," "a nurturer," "competitive," or "always cheerful." These traits are often the same as the role expectations attached to our various statuses as professionals, parents, athletes, or friends. If a person can play a number of different roles well, it can enhance her sense of self, but it is not always easy to juggle the varying demands and expectations associated with multiple roles. Sometimes problems arise in our everyday lives because of our roles.

The story of professional baseball player Daniel Murphy illustrates some of these problems. In 2014, Murphy and his wife, Tori, were expecting a baby whose due date coincided with the beginning of the baseball season. Murphy ended up taking three days off for the birth of baby Noah and missed both the Mets' season opener and an away-game against the Washington Nationals (the Mets lost both games). As a result of taking three days of paternity leave, Murphy became the focus of an unexpected controversy as several high-profile sportscasters criticized him for missing work to be with his family. This highlights what is known as **role conflict**, a situation in which two or more roles have contradictory expectations. His occupational role as professional athlete required actions that were seemingly incompatible with his familial role as husband and father. Murphy's situation may have caused him to experience **role strain** as well, which occurs when there are contradictory expectations within one single role a person plays. It is easy to see how Murphy fulfilled some of the traditional gender role expectations for men: Major League All-Star, he is a hardworking guy with a good batting average and a successful athletic career. But he is also a devoted family man, and he wanted to be home to provide hands-on care and support for his wife and their newborn son. Murphy chose his family over baseball. As he said in an interview, "My wife and I discussed it and we felt the best thing for our family was for me to try to stay" for a few days after the baby's birth (Rubin 2014). If Murphy were to be traded to another team in the future, he may experience a process known as **role exit**, when a person leaves behind a role he once occupied. After the paternity leave controversy, Murphy was invited to the White House as a speaker at President Obama's 2014 Working Family Summit.

You may not become a professional athlete with a new baby arriving on Opening Day, but it is certain that you will find yourself in situations where there are competing demands between multiple roles or within a single role you play. How will you resolve those tensions?

Statuses and roles help shape our identities by providing guidelines (sometimes formal, sometimes informal) for our

ASCRIBED STATUS a status that is inborn; usually difficult or impossible to change

EMBODIED STATUS a status generated by physical characteristics

ACHIEVED STATUS a status earned through individual effort or imposed by others

MASTER STATUS a status that is always relevant and affects all other statuses we possess

STEREOTYPING judging others based on preconceived generalizations about groups or categories of people

ROLE the set of behaviors expected of someone because of his or her status

ROLE CONFLICT experienced when we occupy two or more roles with contradictory expectations

ROLE STRAIN experienced when there are contradictory expectations within one role

ROLE EXIT the process of leaving a role that we will no longer occupy

Daniel Murphy Sportscaster Boomer Esiason suggested that Daniel Murphy's wife Tori schedule a caesarean section to delivery their baby before the start of the baseball season rather than have Murphy miss Opening Day.

own behavior and by providing the patterns that others use to interact with us. They are part of the construction of our social selves.

Emotions and Personality

As the Murphys' experience demonstrates, role conflicts can be very emotional events. Our emotions are intensely personal responses to the unique situations of our lives. We react with happiness, anger, fear, or sorrow to our own experiences, as well as things that happen to others, even fictionalized events in books, movies, or video games. Individuals sometimes react very differently—what makes one person laugh may make another cry. It would seem, then, that our emotions are the one thing about our lives that aren't dictated by society, that can't be explained with reference to sociological concepts or theories.

Well, our emotions aren't fully determined by society, but they are indeed social. We respond individually, but there also are social patterns in our emotional responses. For example, some emotional responses differ according to the culture—even an emotion as personal as grief, as noted in the Global Perspective box on the next page.

ROLE-TAKING EMOTIONS emotions such as sympathy, embarrassment, or shame that require that we assume the perspective of another person or group and respond accordingly

FEELING RULES norms regarding the expression and display of emotions; expectations about the acceptable or desirable feelings in a given situation

EMOTION WORK (EMOTIONAL LABOR) the process of evoking, suppressing, or otherwise managing feelings to create a publicly observable display of emotion

COPRESENCE face-to-face interaction or being in the presence of others

The Social Construction of Emotions

Sometimes our interaction with others affects our emotional responses: we may yell angrily at a political rally along with everyone else, realizing only later that we don't really feel that strongly about the issue at all; we may stifle our tears in front of the coach but shed them freely after the game. **Role-taking emotions**, such as sympathy, embarrassment, and shame, require that we be able to see things from someone else's point of view. When a friend is injured in an accident, you know she is feeling pain, so you feel sympathy for her. **Feeling rules** (Hochschild 1975) are socially constructed norms regarding the appropriate feelings and displays of emotion. We are aware of the pressure to conform to feeling rules even when they are unspoken or we don't agree with them (for example, "Boys don't cry," "No laughing at funerals"). Emotions are thus sociological phenomena, and our individual reactions are influenced (if not determined) by our social and cultural surroundings.

Finally, emotions can also be influenced by social institutions, such as workplaces or religious groups. Arlie Hochschild's (1983) study of flight attendants revealed that when airlines required their employees to be cheerful on the job, the employees' authentic emotions were displaced (they weren't necessarily always cheerful). Flight attendants were required to manage their own feelings as a requirement of their job—what Hochschild calls **emotion work**—maintaining a bright, perky, happy demeanor in-flight, no matter what they actually felt. Because of the structural pressures of emotion work, they became alienated from their own real feelings.

New Interactional Contexts

As we learned in earlier chapters, sociological theories and approaches can change over time—indeed, they must. As the society around them changes, sociologists can't always hold on to their tried-and-true ways of looking at the world. New and innovative approaches take the place of traditional paradigms.

Most sociological perspectives on interaction, for example, focus on interactions that occur in **copresence**—that is, when individuals are in one another's face-to-face, physical company. More and more, however, we find ourselves in situations outside physical copresence, aided by rapidly developing technologies.

Businesspeople can hold video conferences with colleagues in other cities. The lovelorn can seek relationship advice and find prospective mates online. Students can text their friends at faraway colleges and carry on real-time conversations using Skype or Facetime. Doctors on the mainland can perform remote robotic surgery on shipboard patients in the middle of the ocean. Do conventional theories have the

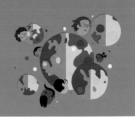

When it comes to emotions, grief seems one of the strongest. No matter what we believe about the afterlife (or lack thereof), we mourn the passing of our loved ones. In many different societies, the cultural practices surrounding grief and mourning are directed toward giving the deceased a proper send-off and comforting those left behind. But you might be surprised at what other cultures consider comforting in times of grief!

For example, Maoris (the native people of New Zealand) believe that death is not final until all funeral rites are complete—which takes an entire year. Though the body is buried after three days, the relatives and friends of the deceased speak of and to her as if she were alive until the year of mourning is complete.

The Roma (often incorrectly referred to as "Gypsies") mourn in particularly intense and public ways: both men and women refuse to wash, shave, or comb their hair, neglect to eat for three days, and absorb themselves totally in the process of mourning, sometimes to the point of harming themselves. In addition to this passionate grieving, Roma mourners provide the dead with clothes, money, and other useful objects for their journey to the afterlife. In contrast to Western societies, where black is the prevailing color of grief, Roma mourners traditionally wear white clothes, and the favored color for funeral decorations is red.

Red is also the color of grief for the Ashanti of Ghana, who wear red clothing, smear red clay on their arms and foreheads, and wear headbands festooned with red peppers. Proper Ashanti expressions of grief are distinguished by gender: women must wail, and men must fire guns into the air. In fact, the amount of gunpowder used in a funeral is considered a mark of the grieving family's status in the community.

When mourning their dead, many cultures, including the Irish, hold "wakes": long-lasting, heavily attended parties honoring and celebrating the lives of the dead. At a wake, while tears may fall, there is also likely to be singing, dancing, drinking, laughing, and all manner of seemingly celebratory emotional outbursts. So despite the fact that all cultures mourn and all individuals feel grief, we can express those emotions in different ways depending on the society of which we are a part.

How Different Cultures Grieve Maori warriors row a coffin to their burial ground (top), mourning Roma women weep over a coffin (center), and Ashanti women practice a traditional funeral dance (bottom).

ON THE JOB
The Wages of Emotion Work

According to executives at Nordstrom department stores, keeping the customer happy is what it's all about. Nordstrom, along with a host of other stores, takes a great interest in developing a corporate culture based on customer service (Zemke and Schaaf 1990; Spector and McCarthy 1996). After all, loyal, satisfied customers are the key to profit making. Nordstrom has become so successful at customer service that it ranks as the national standard. The secret to the company's success lies partly in what Hochschild (1983) calls "the commercialization of feeling," or emotion work.

Nordstrom became a leader in this area through a variety of training techniques. By holding staff meetings and workshops, managers coached employees in customer service. Using videotapes and role-playing scenarios, workers learned how to act out various emotions convincingly. But their acting techniques went beyond such displays as smiling and showing friendliness. Salespeople were also supposed to take an in-depth interest in their customers by keeping a "client book" with detailed information about customers' likes and dislikes, favorite brands, style preferences, color choices, and anything else that might help salespeople to

better anticipate their clients' needs. Some Nordstrom managers even required their salespeople to perform extra duties while off the clock, like writing thank-you notes to customers and delivering items to their homes.

While these practices were good for Nordstrom's bottom line, the consequences for the workers themselves were a different story. The work of producing emotions takes its toll. Though displays of feeling are actually "sold" to the customer as a kind of commodity, the worker is not necessarily compensated. What was once a private resource has now become a company asset, a new source of labor—emotional labor. But because it is impossible for anyone to be that upbeat all the time, workers must find ways to display or evoke the required emotions. They may do so through surface acting, displaying the emotion by wearing a smile, for example. In contrast, a very dedicated employee may do deep acting by trying to actually feel the emotion that he or she must display. There are consequences for faking or conjuring emotional responses: workers may experience "emotional exhaustion and burnout" (Grandey 2003) or become estranged from their real feelings (as did Hochschild's flight attendants)—a situation that Marx would refer to as alienation.

Despite a number of employee protests—and a 1991 class-action suit involving off-the-clock work—many of the problems relating to emotion work remain unresolved (Nogaki 1993). Employees at Nordstrom and elsewhere are still trying to figure out how to preserve some sense of authenticity while making the necessary emotional adjustments to perform their job. The risk remains that employees may become burned out, cynical, or numb from the demands of their occupational roles.

Many of you will be dealing with these same issues in your careers. How will you factor in the cost to yourself of emotional labor? Do you think employees should be compensated financially for emotion work, or do you consider it part of being a good employee? What other kind of compensation—extra days off, more frequent breaks—might be appropriate, especially for salespeople?

Emotion Work In many sales and service jobs, employees must engage in surface or deep acting to display the emotions that their jobs require.

explanatory power to encompass these new ways of interacting? And since interaction is vital to the development of the self, how do these new ways of interacting create new types of social identities?

Researchers like Josh Meyrowitz (1985), Marc Smith and Peter Kollock (1998), Steve Jones (1997), Philip Howard (Jones and Howard 2003), and Barry Wellman (2004)

were among the pioneers in the sociology of technologically mediated interaction. They looked at how we began interacting with each other in virtual space and via electronic media—and how we interacted with the machines themselves. Today, people like Sherry Turkle, who directs the Initiative on Technology and the Self at the Massachusetts Institute of Technology (MIT), study different ways that technology and identity intersect—through our use of computers, robots, technologically sophisticated toys, and so on (1997, 2005). Turkle's book *Alone Together* (2011) focuses on the problems of the social media age. Online interactions allow us to contain and reduce risks—not risk to life and limb, necessarily, but risk to self. When we interact online, we can control when, where, and how we communicate. This means that, if we want, we can keep others at arm's length, which further allows us to perform a self that may or may not correspond to who we are in real life. We have become less willing to take risks in terms of forging intimate bonds online, and while we may have lots of connections (friends, fans, followers), we experience less depth in our relationships with them.

danah boyd is slightly less gloomy about technology. She finds that Internet users—especially teens—seek private spaces in which to conduct their personal relationships, and view online environments like Facebook, Instagram, and Twitter as places that can offer such privacy. They invite only their close friends into their electronic circles and then use those virtual spaces as getaways from the pressures of parents, teachers, and other adults. This is contrary to the ways that adults use social media—grownups tweet and post to expand their social circles and spread the word about their accomplishments, while teens do so only for the chosen few. The differences in generational cohorts' perspectives on online interaction are conveyed by the title of boyd's book: *It's Complicated* (2014).

These and other researchers seek answers to the following question: who will we become as we increasingly interact with and through digital technologies? Their work is helping sociology enter the age of interactive media and giving us new ways of looking at interactions and identities.

Mediating Interaction Using new technologies like webcams, we can interact with each other outside of physical copresence. How will these new technologies affect our interactions and identities?

Postmodern theorists claim that the role of technology in interaction is one of the primary features of postmodern life. They believe that in the Information Age, social thinkers must arrive at new ways to explain the development of the self in light of the digital media that inundate our social world (Holstein and Gubrium 2000). We are now exposed to more sources and multiple points of view that may shape our sense of self and socialize us in different ways than ever before (Gottschalk 1993). Kenneth Gergen (1991) coined the term the **saturated self** to refer to this phenomenon and claims that the postmodern individual tends to have a "pastiche personality," one that "borrow[s] bits and pieces of identity from whatever sources are available" (p. 150). What this means is that the self is being constructed in new ways that were unforeseen by early symbolic interactionists, who could not have imagined that interaction would one day include so many possible influences from both the real world and the world of virtual reality.

CLOSING COMMENTS

By now you may be wondering, are we all just prisoners of socialization? How much freedom do we really have if we are all shaped and influenced to such an extent by others and by society? Are our ideas of ourselves as individuals—unique and independent—just a sorry illusion?

It is true that the process of socialization can be rather homogenizing. And it tends to be conservative, pushing people toward some sort of lowest common denominator, toward the mainstream. But still, not everybody ends up the same. In fact, no two people are ever really alike. Despite all the social forces at play in creating the individual, the process by which we gain a sense of self, or become socialized members of society, is never wholly finished.

We are not just passive recipients of all the influences around us. We are active participants. We possess what is called **agency**, meaning that we are spontaneous, intelligent, and creative. We exercise free will. Symbolic interactionism tells us that we are always doing the work of interpreting, defining, making sense of, and responding to our social environment. That gives us a great deal of personal power in every social situation. The process is not unilateral; rather, it is reciprocal and multidirectional. Remember that you are shaping society as much as it is shaping you.

SATURATED SELF a postmodern idea that the self is now developed by multiple influences chosen from a wide range of media sources

AGENCY the ability of the individual to act freely and independently

Everything You Need to Know about Socialization

> " Socialization is the process of learning and internalizing the values, beliefs, and norms of our social groups, by which we become functioning members of society. "

AGENTS OF SOCIALIZATION

* **Family:** the original group to which people belong, where early emotional and social bonds are created, language is learned, and where we first begin to internalize the norms and values of society

* **School:** helps people become less dependent on their family and provides a bridge to other social groups

* **Peers:** provide young people with a way of exercising independence from, and possibly reacting against, adult control

* **Mass media:** entertains, informs, educates, and is responsible for the internalization of many values, beliefs, and norms of society

REVIEW

1. Think about a social issue about which you hold a very different opinion than your grandparents or people their age, such as drug legalization, sexual mores, or even fashion. How might this difference of opinion be the result of different socialization?

2. According to Erving Goffman, we all engage in impression management to control what others think of us. Choose one interaction, and list every aspect of the personal front you use to manage the impression you create.

3. Describe yourself in terms of your statuses and roles. Which are master statuses? Which roles are less important? Which statuses have changed over the course of your lifetime? Which roles do you anticipate occupying in the future?

Presentation of Self in the Age of Social Media

More privacy and reputation management on social networking sites

Untagged Photos
37%

Deleted Comments
44%

Unfriended Someone
63%

Regretted Posted Content
11% of social media users have posted content they regret.
11%

Regretted Posted Content
Males on social media sites such as Facebook or Twitter are almost twice as likely as females to express regret for posting content (15% vs. 8%).
15%
8%

% of Social Networking Site Users Who Have Taken These Steps on Their Profiles

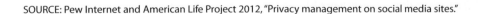

SOURCE: Pew Internet and American Life Project 2012, "Privacy management on social media sites."

EXPLORE

Harry's Law, Girls, and the Media Marketplace

Does popular entertainment provide an accurate representation of society? What does learning about society through television tell us? Visit the Everyday Sociology Blog to explore these questions through the lens of HBO's show *Girls.*

http://wwnPag.es/trw404

CHAPTER 5

Separate and Together: Life in Groups

I f you're a college student and a musician, we hope you're *not* familiar with these terms and their definitions: "hot seat" (being beaten with drum sticks, mallets, and straps while covered with a blanket in the back of the band bus) and "crossing over" (being kicked and hit by your bandmates as you run down the aisle of the bus). It might seem like being subjected to these brutal attacks would mean that it is time to quit the band. In reality, this ritual is how your bandmates might let you know that they want you to stay—and even advance in the band leadership hierarchy. But on November 19, 2011, this ritual went horribly wrong on the Florida

A&M University (FAMU) "Marching 100" band bus. Drum major Robert Champion suffered such severe injuries at the hands of his bandmates that he died at a hospital later that night. His family, friends, fellow musicians, and university community were grief-stricken, of course. But his death also touched off a national controversy over "hazing" that has yet to subside.

The hazing process is meant to test newcomers and transform them into group members; if you can endure the abuse, you can be part of the group. Although hazing is usually associated with college fraternities, it has been known to occur in high school and college clubs, athletic teams, sororities, marching bands, and even church groups, as well as in police and fire departments and the military. Although hazing is against the law in almost every state and is usually prohibited by group charters, it is still a popular—though risky—way of initiating new members. Every year, it results in at least one death and countless injuries. All told, there have been over 100 hazing deaths among U.S. college students since 1970. Experts estimate that alcohol plays a major role in around 80 percent of these incidents (Nuwer 1999, 2004, 2014).

The FAMU hazing has left a tragic legacy. Twelve of Champion's bandmates were charged with manslaughter in his death and four were ultimately convicted and sentenced to prison. The band itself was suspended for nearly two years, the band director was fired, and the FAMU president resigned in the wake of the incident. In addition, Champion's parents filed a wrongful death lawsuit against the university.

In response to all these allegations, some of Champion's bandmates have protested that he and other students volunteered to be hazed that night because they wanted to be able to move into leadership roles in the band. This fact highlights a key question in all hazing cases: who is responsible when the consequences of hazing include illegality, injury, or even death—the host group or the individual who submits to hazing?

The relationship between the individual and the group is a complex one. We sometimes do things in groups, both good and bad, that we might never do as individuals. Exploring group dynamics from a sociological perspective can help us understand and even eliminate problems like hazing and maximize the benefits of group life as well.

HOW TO READ THIS CHAPTER

This chapter explores some of the different ways we organize our lives in groups. Here you will gain some of the analytic tools you can use to understand the specific groups we'll be investigating in later chapters. Concepts such as peer pressure, teamwork, bureaucratization, and anomie can be fruitfully applied to analyses of families, work and volunteer organizations, political groups, and religious communities. Consider this chapter an introduction to group dynamics in general—a springboard from which to begin our sociological analysis of particular types of groups. As you read, think about the groups you belong to and how they affect your values and behavior. What is your influence on such groups? Have you ever "gone along" with group rules but later wished you hadn't?

What Is a Group?

We often use the term *group* to refer to any collection of two or more people who have something in common, whether it's their appearance, culture, occupation, or just a physical proximity. When sociologists speak of a **group** or social group, however, they mean a collection of people who not only share some attribute but also identify with one another and have ongoing social relations—like a family, a *Star Trek* fan club, a soccer team, a sorority, or the guys you play poker with every month.

A **crowd**, such as the throngs of sightseers at a tourist attraction or people who gather to watch a fire, would not usually be considered a group in the sociological sense. While crowd members do interact (Goffman 1971), they don't necessarily have a sense of common identity, and they rarely assemble again once they disperse. Collections of people such as crowds, audiences, and queues are known as **aggregates**—people who happen to find themselves together in a particular physical location. People in aggregates don't form lasting social relations, but people in groups do. Similarly, people belonging in the same **category**—everyone eighteen years of age or all owners of Chevy trucks, for example—don't regularly interact with one another or have any common sense of connection other than their status in the category.

Primary and Secondary Groups

Groups in which we are intimately associated with the other members, such as families and close friends, are known as **primary groups**. Primary groups typically involve more face-to-face interaction, greater cooperation, and deeper feelings of belonging. Members often associate with each other for no other reason than to spend time together.

Charles Horton Cooley (1909) introduced the term *primary* for this type of group because such groups have the most profound effects on us as individuals. Primary groups provide most of our emotional satisfaction through interaction with other members, are responsible for much of our socialization, and remain central to our identities throughout our lives. We measure who we are, and perhaps how we've changed, by the way we interact with primary group members. To Cooley (as we saw in Chapter 4), primary groups represent the most important "looking glasses" in the formation of our social selves—they constitute our "significant others."

Larger, less intimate groups are known as **secondary groups**: these include co-workers, college classes, athletic organizations, labor unions, and political parties. Interaction here is more formal and impersonal. Secondary groups are usually organized around a specific activity or the accomplishment of a task. Membership is often temporary and does not usually carry the same potential for emotional satisfaction that primary group membership does. Nonetheless, a great deal of what we do involves secondary groups.

Because secondary groups can include larger numbers of people and be geographically diffuse, membership can be almost completely anonymous. At the same time, however, secondary group membership often generates primary group ties as well. Close personal relationships can begin with the more impersonal ties of secondary groups (the friends you make at work, for example) and are sometimes a direct outgrowth of our attempts to counteract the depersonalizing nature of secondary groups. For this reason, it is sometimes difficult to classify a particular group. Your soccer team may indeed be goal oriented, but you've probably also developed personal ties to at least some of your teammates. So, is your team a primary or secondary group? It features elements of both, proving that real life can be even more complex than the models sociologists devise to explain it.

There are other ways that seemingly insignificant relationships with near strangers can have a powerful and positive impact on our own lives. Many social researchers are interested in examining the ways in which people make up for the

GROUP a collection of people who share some attribute, identify with one another, and interact with each other

CROWD a temporary gathering of people in a public place; members might interact but do not identify with each other and will not remain in contact

AGGREGATES collections of people who share a physical location but do not have lasting social relations

CATEGORY people who share one or more attributes but who lack a sense of common identity or belonging

PRIMARY GROUPS the people who are most important to our sense of self; members' relationships are typically characterized by face-to-face interaction, high levels of cooperation, and intense feelings of belonging

SECONDARY GROUPS groups that are larger and less intimate than primary groups; members' relationships are usually organized around a specific goal and are often temporary

Primary Groups Are Typically Families or Close Friends Deborah Daniels (front left, in pink) opened her home to four generations of her family after Hurricane Katrina destroyed their New Orleans homes in 2005.

loss of intimate contact that is commonly shared among those who belong to primary groups. Melinda Blau and Karen Fingerman (2009) have identified what they call "consequential strangers"—people we might not think of as mattering much to our sense of happiness or well-being but who nonetheless play an important role in our otherwise fragmented postmodern lives. These people are not total strangers but are more likely to be acquaintances from the places we work, shop, play, or conduct business—from the local barista at the coffeehouse or our favorite manicurist to the checkout clerk at the grocery store or that guy at the gym. These are people who become familiar and essential parts of our everyday lives. These people serve as social anchors, just as our close friends or family members do. Blau and Fingerman suggest that we need a new framework or perspective with which to look at the people in our world and perhaps to expand the number and range, as well as the value we ascribe to them, when we include them in our larger social circle. It seems that we need both primary and secondary relationships, as well as those along the continuum between the two.

> **SOCIAL NETWORK** the web of direct and indirect ties connecting an individual to other people who may also affect the individual
>
> **SOCIAL TIES** connections between individuals

Social Networks

You and your family, your friends, peers, colleagues, teachers, and co-workers constitute a **social network**. Sociologists who study networks call the connections between individuals **social ties**. Social ties can be direct, such as the tie between you and your friend, or indirect, such as the tie between you and your friend's cousin whom you've never met.

To understand how a social network works, think of yourself at the center with lines connecting you to all your friends, family, peers, and so on. These lines represent direct ties. Now think about all the family, friends, and peers who belong to each of *these* people. The lines connecting you to this second group must pass through the people in your first network; this second set of lines represent indirect ties. Indirect ties can include business transactions—flows of goods, services, materials, or monies—between organizations or nations. They can even represent the flow of ideas. For instance, when you read ancient Greek philosophy, you become part of a network that spans centuries of writing, thinking, and educating.

You've probably already heard about the principle of "six degrees of separation," which suggests that everyone in the world is connected to everyone else within six steps: "If you know 100 people, and each of them knows 100 more, then you have 10,000 friends of friends. Take that a step further to three degrees and you are connected to 1 million people. At six degrees, the number increases to 9 billion" (Schofield 2004). This means, theoretically, that you're connected to every human on the planet. It might be the case that somebody you know knows someone who knows somebody else who knows the president of the United States or a yak herdsman in the Himalayas; in other words, you might be separated from either of these others by just four degrees.

Sociologists who study networks are concerned not only with how networks are constructed but also how influence moves along a network, and thus which persons or organizations have more influence than others within the network. In his book *Six Degrees: The Science of a Connected Age* (2003), sociologist Duncan Watts examined not only the connections individuals have to one another but also how those connections shape our actions. He found, for example, that we may change our minds about whom to vote for if enough of our friends are voting for the other candidate. Social networks can help us understand everything from the spread of fads and fashions to the way people hear about job openings to how sexually transmitted diseases are spread among various segments of the population.

WINNERS, LOSERS, AND INFLUENCE How does the flow of influence work at the level of an international organization? We could take the World Trade Organization (WTO) as an example. Comprising 161 member nations, the WTO monitors the trade rules among countries and resolves international disputes over trade. While all member nations are part of the network, they hold different positions of power within it. We might hypothesize that nations that win the most disputes have the most influence within the network. But Joseph Conti (2003, 2005) finds that while the United States, one of the most powerful members of the

WTO, is involved in the vast majority of disputes, it usually loses. The question that remains for the network theorist is whether "winning" or "losing" is an effective way to measure influence. What Conti concludes is that America's *centrality*, a network analysis term that means an actor with the most ties in a given network, is what gives it powerful influence and not the actual outcomes of the disputes.

JOBS, GENDER, AND NETWORKS How does the flow of influence work at the level of interactions between individuals? Sociologists look at how personal ties, both direct and indirect, can influence a person's life.

In the pathbreaking work "The Strength of Weak Ties" (1973), Mark Granovetter measured how a person's distant relatives and acquaintances, attached to different social networks, pass along information about job opportunities. An individual with high socioeconomic status, or SES (taking into account income, education, and occupation), for example, usually has relatives and acquaintances with similarly high SES. Because those relatives and acquaintances belong to different social networks, all with high SES, the job seeker now has indirect connections with a vast array of high-SES contacts who can provide job leads. In other words, if your father, mother, and sister are all actors, you would likely "inherit" a network of acting contacts. The implications of Granovetter's findings are that people tend to form homogeneous social networks—to have direct ties to those who are like themselves, whether through race, class background, national origin, or religion. Further, individuals with low SES are likely to form direct ties to others with low SES and thus indirect ties as well. Information about job opportunities is less likely to travel along those networks.

More recent findings about the strength of weak ties, from Matt Hoffman and Lisa Torres (2002), indicate that women who are part of networks that include more men than women are more likely to hear about good job leads. But if their networks include more women than men, then those same women are less likely to hear about quality jobs. The number of men or women within a man's network doesn't seem to matter; men are just as likely to get quality information about job opportunities from both men and women in their social networks. Hoffman and Torres offer two rationales to explain their findings. First, women are simply less likely than men to hear about job leads. Second, women who do hear about job leads are more likely to pass along that information to men; they may feel threatened by the idea of more women in their places of employment and fear loss of their own jobs. So our networks work for us, but they may also work against us.

SEXUAL HEALTH AND NETWORKS Nicholas Christakis and James Fowler (2009) provide another example of how transmission happens between individuals belonging to similar social networks. They explain two principles: first, all social networks have a *connection*, and second, there is *contagion*, which refers to what flows through social ties. While we may have complete control over whom we are connected to directly, we exert little control over our indirect connections. Contagion not only influences an individual's health but can spread everything from obesity to smoking and substance abuse. For example, sexually transmitted diseases are more likely among people who have had four or more partners in the past year. In particular, whites who have many partners tend to have sex with other whites who have many partners, and whites who have few partners tend to have sex with whites who have few partners. STDs, then, are kept in "core" groups of active white partners and are found less often in less active groups. This spread of STDs can be seen as a literal consequence of the *contagion* principle of social networks.

When we think of someone as being "well connected," we imagine that they not only have lots of close friends but might also have relationships and acquaintances in a large and diverse social circle. As the old adage goes, it's not *what* you know, it's *who* you know. And who they know, and who *they* know—and now you have a social network.

Separate from Groups: Anomie or Virtual Membership?

According to Durkheim, all the social groups with which we are connected (families, peers, co-workers, and so on) have this particular feature: the norms of the group place certain limits on our individual actions. For example, you may have wanted to backpack through Europe after you graduated from high school, but your parents demanded that you stay home, work, and save money for college. Durkheim argues that we need these limits—otherwise, we would want many things we could never have, and the lengths to which we would go in search of our unattainable desires would be boundless. Think about it: if you were always searching for but never getting the things you wanted, you would be very unhappy and over time might even become suicidal. Durkheim (1893/1964) called such a state of normlessness **anomie** and believed that group membership keeps us from feeling it. So group membership not only anchors us to the social world—it's what keeps us alive.

Durkheim was worried that in our increasingly fragmented modern society, anomie would become more and more common. Other scholars share Durkheim's position, noting that Americans today are less likely than ever to belong to the types of civic organizations and community groups that can combat anomie and keep us connected to one another. Harvard professor Robert Putnam, in his book *Bowling Alone: The Collapse and Revival of American Community* (2000), argues that we no longer practice the type of "civic engagement" that builds democratic community and keeps anomie at

ANOMIE "normlessness"; term used to describe the alienation and loss of purpose that result from weaker social bonds and an increased pace of change

You may know this person (in fact, you may be this person): the one who has 500, or 1,300, or 2,100, or even more Facebook friends. "How is this possible?" you wonder; can she really "know" all those people? Is she just a "friend collector"? If someone really does "know" that many thousands of people, what are the qualities of those connections? How many of those friends are known intimately and personally, "IRL" (in real life)? And what does this mean for the future of our social bonds?

The debate over the effects of social media on social life is intense. Some argue that Internet technologies make us lonely, replacing our face-to-face bonds with a set of "broader but shallower" online connections that don't really do the trick (Marche 2012). This argument also includes the criticism that we are more disconnected from our communities as a result of our immersion in online worlds: we are not as committed to civic life, local politics, or public service as we should be or once were. This is an extension of Robert Putnam's (2000) view on the effects of television and other technologies on our social engagement. Even scholars who once saw promise in the rise of Internet communication systems, such as MIT's Sherry Turkle (2011), now worry that we have come to prioritize technologies over relationships.

There is another side to this issue, of course. The Pew Research Center study of the Internet and American Life (Hampton et al. 2011) produced a set of findings that contradict the anxieties of the authors we've cited. According to the Pew study, users of social media may actually be more connected with others than nonusers. Facebook users were found to have more close relationships and more social support and to be more trusting of others and more politically engaged than users of other social media and nonusers. In addition, sociologists Eric Klinenberg (2012a) and Claude Fischer (2011) make the case that, despite a rise in social media use and an increase in single-person households, Americans are no more or less lonely or detached from one another than they have ever been.

So what will the future hold with regard to technology and our relationships with one another? To answer that, we might actually want to look to the past. Remember Émile Durkheim's concerns about anomie and modern life? Durkheim was worried that the technological and cultural changes that accompanied the Industrial Revolution would cause people to become more disconnected from one another and that this disconnection would be detrimental both to individuals (who might be more likely to commit suicide as a result) and for society (which would lack necessary cohesion and solidarity). Over 100 years later, authors like Stephen Marche and Sherry Turkle express the same concerns about the changes associated with the Digital Revolution. It seems that rapid changes in technology and society, no matter what they look like or when they occur, arouse similar anxieties. When it comes to relationships and group ties, the future may not look as different as we think it will . . .

Social Networks Do websites like Facebook facilitate relationships and civic engagement? Or do they undermine our "real world" connections?

VIRTUAL COMMUNITIES
social groups whose interactions are mediated through information technologies, particularly the Internet

bay: fewer people bowl in leagues than ever before, and people are less likely to participate in organizations like the League of Women Voters, PTA, or Kiwanis or engage in regular activities like monthly bridge games or Sunday picnics. He even offers statistics on how many angry drivers "flip the bird" at other drivers every year—all part of his argument about our disintegrating collective bonds.

Putnam's critics argue that he longs for the "good old days" that will never be again (and perhaps never were). It may be true that we don't belong to bridge clubs anymore, but we have a new set of resources to help us connect with others and avoid anomie. In the decade since Putnam's influential work first appeared, there has been an explosion of

The Good Old Days? In *Bowling Alone*, Robert Putnam argues that the decline of group activities, such as bingo nights or league bowling, represents a decline in civic engagement. However, technologies such as the Internet and social networking sites have allowed large numbers of people to gather, connect, and avoid anomie.

new communications technology. Some social thinkers were concerned that the Internet would only serve to exacerbate our condition of isolation and separation from one another, as individuals became further distanced from face-to-face contact and more immersed in living online. Yet, the Internet has made it possible for people who might not otherwise have met to come together—albeit in cyberspace—and to belong to a variety of online groups. From participants involved in massively multiplayer online role-playing games (MMORPGs), such as World of Warcraft or Second Life, to support groups who "meet" regularly to deal with personal issues or medical conditions, to fans of different authors, bands, artists, or filmmakers swapping comments, technology offers us new opportunities to connect by making us members of **virtual communities**.

If both types of groups, the ones based on face-to-face contact and those that facilitate online interaction, can each serve as social anchors, then is one necessarily better for us (and for society) than the other?

DATA WORKSHOP
Analyzing Media and Pop Culture

"Who's in Your Feed?"

Did you know that almost 75 percent of all adults who go online use some kind of social networking site? That Facebook has almost 1.5 billion

users on mobile devices, that 500 million tweets are sent on Twitter every day, or that more than 20 billion photos have been uploaded to Instagram? And then there's also the tens (or hundreds) of millions of things that are happening right now on LinkedIn, Pinterest, and Snapchat. The statistics for social media usage are astounding. And there's a good likelihood you're adding to those numbers with each status update, selfie, or pin.

The skyrocketing popularity of social networking sites has social scientists scrambling to keep up with studying what this rapidly evolving technology means not only for our personal identity and everyday lives but also for our relationships with others and the nature of social interaction in groups. The very idea of what constitutes a group has changed, and sociologists have had to broaden their definition of the term to include what people are doing in online or virtual communities. If people gather together to share interests, offer advice, provide support, or exchange ideas but never meet in person, are they still a group?

In sociological terms, we can see how social networking can help us make the most of our primary and secondary group connections. It is easier than ever to stay in touch with the important people in our lives (even if they are not in close physical proximity) and reconnect with old acquaintances. Social networking has brought people together who might not have otherwise been able to find each other in the past, when it was not possible to search for others based on their common interests, backgrounds, and demographic details. Now you can find that long-lost friend from fifth grade, meet new people who are into the same things as you, or keep tabs on someone you already see on a daily basis. So, who's in your feed?

For this Data Workshop you will be conducting interviews to find out how people use social networking in their everyday lives and its role in shaping individual and group identity online. You'll begin to see how group life is created, maintained, and changed online by group members who might share many things in common—especially other people. Your task will be to construct a set of interview questions and to gather responses from subjects you recruit to take part in your pilot study. Then you can make some preliminary analyses based on your findings. Refer to the section on interviews in Chapter 2 for a review of this research method.

There are several choices to make in the way you structure your research project. Because this is such a small-scale study, you do not need to take a scientific sample, but you should include members of the target population you want to study—for example, college students or lacrosse players. Because there are many social networking sites that people use, you will also need to choose whether to focus on just one, such as Facebook, or to make your questions apply more broadly to multiple sites. You'll need to customize your interview questions accordingly. Here are some questions to get you started. You may choose some or all of these, modify them as needed, put them in a different order, or add some questions of your own.

* What social networking sites do you use? When, where, and how often?

* How do you decide to whom to send friend/connection/follower requests?

* How do you decide from whom to accept friend/connection/follower requests?

* How many people do you feel comfortable having on your friends/connections/followers list?

* How many of the people in your social network do you know in real life?

* Are there people in your life with whom you refuse to interact on social media?

* Are your networks public or for approved friends/connections/followers only?

* When you look at your list of friends/connections/followers, how much diversity is there in terms of race, ethnicity, gender, class, age, sexuality, geographic location, or other factors?

* What do you like to do most on social networking sites?

* How often do you post something to social networking sites?

* Does your friends/connections/followers list affect what you decide to post online?

* What kinds of groups have you joined online? Why?

* Does social networking help you feel more connected to others? Why or why not?

* What other functions does social networking play in your life?

There are two options for completing this Data Workshop:

PREP-PAIR-SHARE Construct your interview questions and obtain some initial responses from yourself and one or two others. Jot down some notes about your preliminary findings. Bring your questionnaire to class and interview a partner. Discuss your answers and what else you might like to know about social networking. Listen for any differences in others' insights.

DO-IT-YOURSELF Conduct a small pilot study on social networking. Prepare a questionnaire and interview three to five respondents. Ask permission if you would like to record their answers. Write a three- to four-page essay discussing your experience and preliminary findings. What more would you like to know about social networking?

Group Dynamics

Sociologists have always been interested in how groups form, change, disintegrate, achieve great goals, or commit horrendous wrongs. Add all these phenomena together, and they constitute **group dynamics**. How do groups affect an individual's sense of self? What forces bind members to a group? How do groups influence their members? When do groups excel at the tasks they undertake? What are the qualities of group leaders? When are groups destructive to the individual? How can relations between groups be improved? We will attempt to answer some of these questions in the next sections.

Dyads, Triads, and More

The size of a group affects how it operates and the types of individual relationships that can occur within it (Figure 5.1). A **dyad**, the smallest possible social group, consists of only two members—a romantic couple, two best friends, or two siblings, for example (Simmel 1950). Although relationships in a dyad are usually intense, dyads are also fundamentally unstable, because if one person wants out of the group, it's over. A **triad** is slightly more stable because the addition of a third person means that conflicts between two members can be refereed by the third. As additional people are added to a group, it may no longer be possible for everyone to know or

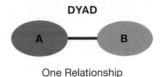

DYAD

One Relationship

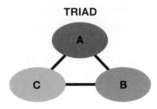

TRIAD

Three Relationships

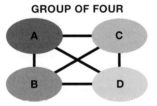

GROUP OF FOUR

Six Relationships

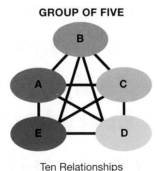

GROUP OF FIVE

Ten Relationships

Figure 5.1 The Effects of Group Size on Relationships

Smaller groups feature fewer and more intimate personal ties; larger groups feature more relationships, but they are also likely to be more impersonal.

interact with everyone else personally (think of all the residents of a large apartment building), and so policies may have to be established to help with communication and resolve conflicts. The features of dyads and triads point out an important axiom of group dynamics in general: the smaller a group is, the more likely it is to be based on personal ties; larger groups are more likely to be based on rules and regulations (as we'll see later when we examine bureaucracies).

In-Groups and Out-Groups

An **in-group** is a group a member identifies with and feels loyalty toward. Members usually feel a certain distinctness from or even hostility toward other groups, known as **out-groups**. Most of us are associated with a number of in- and out-groups, stemming from our ethnic, familial, professional, athletic, and educational backgrounds, for example. Group loyalty and cohesion intensify when differences are strongly defined between the "us" of an in-group and the "them" of an out-group; we may also feel a sense of superiority toward those who are excluded from our in-group. School sports rivalries make clear in-group and out-group distinctions, as evident in this popular slogan seen on T-shirts and bumper stickers all over Los Angeles: "My favorite teams are UCLA and whoever's playing USC!"

As we might expect, in-group membership can be a source of prejudice and discrimination based on class, race, gender, sexual orientation, religion, or political opinion. The differences attributed to an out-group often become exaggerated, if not entirely fabricated to begin with: "All Irishmen are drunks" or "All Mexicans are lazy," for example. Robert Merton (1968) noted how the same qualities or behaviors that are viewed positively when they are "ours" are viewed negatively when they are "theirs": the out-group is "lazy," whereas the in-group is "laid-back"; they are "snobbish," we are "classy"; they are "zealots," we are "devout." At their worst, in-group/out-group dynamics create the backdrop for such social tragedies as slavery and genocide.

GROUP DYNAMICS the patterns of interaction between groups and individuals

DYAD a two-person social group

TRIAD a three-person social group

IN-GROUP a group that one identifies with and feels loyalty toward

OUT-GROUPS groups toward which an individual feels opposition, rivalry, or hostility

REFERENCE GROUP a group that provides a standard of comparison against which we evaluate ourselves

Reference Groups

Our perception of a group and what it takes to be a bona fide member can be crucial to our sense of self. When a group provides standards by which a person evaluates his own personal attributes, it is known as a **reference**

Social networking sites have come a long way since the early days of the Internet. Today Facebook, Twitter, LinkedIn, Tumblr, Pinterest, and Instagram are all in the top twenty-five most visited sites by Internet users in the United States. In 2014, Facebook alone boasted more than 850 million daily users.

The rise of social networking has been so rapid that social scientists can barely keep pace with studying what this new technology means, but it has become clear that when social networks become *online* social networks they also become big business. "When something online is free, you're not the customer, you're the product." This aphorism seems to have been independently coined by a number of different people, and it expresses one of the most significant features of social networking websites. Online, social networks exist because businesses like Facebook facilitate them. For everyone who participates, the rewards and benefits are obvious—staying in touch with faraway friends and family, sharing photos of cute babies and kittens, organizing for political change. But are there risks as well?

In June 2014 researchers at Facebook and Cornell University published a paper arguing that "emotional states can be transferred to others via emotional contagion, leading people to experience the same emotions without their awareness," and this can happen through exposure to emotionally charged posts on Facebook (Kramer, Guillory, and Hancock 2014). The researchers wondered if "exposure to emotional content led people to post content that was consistent with the exposure." Does seeing happy posts lead to more happy posts, and seeing sad posts lead to more downbeat ones?

To test this hypothesis, Facebook performed an experiment on almost 700,000 users. Every time someone logs into Facebook, the site displays a newsfeed of posts by people in their network; however, rather than simply displaying every post, Facebook uses an algorithm to pick a smaller subset of material. For one week in 2012 Facebook tweaked this algorithm so hundreds of thousands of unwitting users saw posts that were either slightly more positive, or slightly more negative, than usual. Researchers then analyzed the emotional content of the posts created by their test subjects and determined that the users who saw happier content wrote posts with more positive words, while users who saw more depressing content created posts with more negative words.

An uproar followed the publication of these findings. Not only did Facebook experiment on people without their knowledge or permission, they did so in a way that caused emotional harm. Facebook was almost universally condemned, and the lead investigator of the study issued a public apology.

group. A common reference group is one's family. We often try to "live up to" the standards of our parents, siblings, and extended family members and compare ourselves to them. If we don't see ourselves as having the same desirable qualities, we may adopt a negative self-image. We make such comparisons often, evaluating whether and how we measure up to others who provide a model or benchmark for us. We might ask ourselves: Am I maintaining a higher or lower grade point average than other students in my class? Am I faster or slower than other runners on the track team, or about the same? A reference group may also be one to which we aspire to belong but of which we are not yet members; we saw one example at the beginning of this chapter—the musicians who wanted to belong to the marching band so much that they were willing to risk their own health, safety, and lives, as well as those of others.

DATA WORKSHOP
Analyzing Everyday Life

The Twenty Statements Test: Who Am I?

The Twenty Statements Test, or TST, is a well-known and widely used instrument to measure self-concept. The TST was originally developed in the 1950s by social psychologist Manfred Kuhn as a way of determining the degree to which we base our

However, not everyone thought Facebook was in the wrong. Their most prominent defender was Christian Rudder, the co-founder of dating/social networking website OkCupid. In the aftermath of Facebook's experiment he posted a blog entry on OkCupid titled "We Experiment on Human Beings!" Rudder is unapologetic about OkCupid's practices and doesn't think anyone should be upset at Facebook either: "We noticed recently that people didn't like it when Facebook 'experimented' with their newsfeed. . . . Guess what, everybody: If you use the Internet, you're the subject of hundreds of experiments at any given time, on every site. That's how websites work." Although he detailed a number of "experiments," the one that got the most attention was based on OkCupid's "match percentage." OkCupid asks users a number of questions and then matches people who answered in complementary ways. For this experiment they took people who were only a 30 percent match and told them they were a 90 percent match. They found that when people were told they were a better match, the odds of them carrying on a conversation online did in fact increase, but some were shocked that a site dedicated to helping people find love would resort to this sort of deception.

Facebook apologized for the way it handled the publication of the experiment, while OkCupid seemed positively proud of theirs, but neither organization said anything to indicate that they would stop doing such experiments. Online social networks are an increasingly important part of people's lives, but the consequences of giving so much power over our personal lives to a for-profit business are still not well understood. What does it mean to live in a world where a corporation has a profit motive to meddle in our social networks?

Social Networks Are Big Business For one week in 2012, Facebook conducted an experiment on users of the social networking site to determine whether emotional states can be transferred.

self-concepts on our membership in different groups (Kuhn and McPartland 1954). Group affiliation proved to be a significant and prevalent quality that defined Americans of the 1950s and 1960s. In the following decades, the TST was adopted by other researchers because of its ease of use and ability to provide direct first-hand data from respondents. Despite some methodological critiques, the TST has been used to examine the self-concept of members of various ethnic, gender, and generational groups, as well as to make cross-cultural comparisons (Carpenter and Meade-Pruitt 2008).

In some of the earliest and most influential work using the TST, Louis Zurcher (1977) studied the changing self-images of Americans in the 1970s and 1980s. Zurcher found that this later group of respondents were more likely to base their self-concept on individual traits and independent action rather than on group membership. These results represented a major shift in how people defined themselves, and perhaps in society as a whole. While you might think this trend toward greater uniqueness and independence seems unremarkable and largely preferable, not all social scientists would agree. Zurcher and his colleague Ralph Turner (1976) became concerned about this shift away from group identification and toward a more radically individualistic sense of self. Why were they so concerned? We might also ask, what are people like now? Have things continued to change since the 1980s? What can the TST tell us about contemporary society and ourselves today?

For this Data Workshop, you will be using the Twenty Statements Test to examine how self-concept is defined within a particular group of respondents. The TST is a questionnaire that elicits open-ended responses; it can be treated as a quasi-survey research method. Return to the section in Chapter 2 for a review of survey research. We have provided a format for the questionnaire below. Start by completing Steps 1 and 2 and taking this simple test yourself. Then we will find out more about what your responses mean—for you and for society, in Step 3.

Step 1: The Twenty Statements Test (TST)
In the spaces provided below, write down twenty different responses to the question "Who am I?" Don't worry about evaluating the logic or importance of your responses—just write the statements quickly and in whatever order they occur to you. Leave the "Response Mode" spaces blank for the moment; they will be used for scoring after you have completed the statements. Give yourself five minutes to complete this task.

Statements	Response Mode
1. I am _____.	_____
2. I am _____.	_____
3. I am _____.	_____
4. I am _____.	_____
5. I am _____.	_____
6. I am _____.	_____
7. I am _____.	_____
8. I am _____.	_____
9. I am _____.	_____
10. I am _____.	_____
11. I am _____.	_____
12. I am _____.	_____
13. I am _____.	_____
14. I am _____.	_____
15. I am _____.	_____
16. I am _____.	_____
17. I am _____.	_____
18. I am _____.	_____
19. I am _____.	_____
20. I am _____.	_____

TOTALS: A-Mode: _____ **B-Mode:** _____

C-Mode: _____ **D-Mode:** _____

Step 2: Scoring
Now it's time to score your responses according to the four categories listed below. Evaluate, to the best of your ability, which responses fall into the A-mode, B-mode, C-mode, and D-mode categories.

A-mode responses are physical characteristics of the type that might be found on your driver's license: "I am a blonde"; "I am short"; "I am a Wisconsin resident"; "I am strong"; "I am tired."

B-mode responses describe socially defined roles and statuses usually associated with group membership of some sort: "I am a college student"; "I am a Catholic"; "I am an African American"; "I am a quarterback"; "I am a daughter"; "I am a sales clerk."

C-mode responses reflect personal traits, styles of behavior, or emotional states: "I am a happy person"; "I am a country music fan"; "I am competitive"; "I am laid-back"; "I am a fashionable dresser."

D-mode responses are more general than specific; they may express an abstract or existential quality: "I am me"; "I am part of the universe"; "I am a human being"; "I am alive."

You may have some difficulty deciding how to categorize some of your responses—for example, where does "I am an American" go? Is it an A-mode, because it is where I live as a physical location, or is it a B-mode, because it is my nationality and the country with which I identify? Or where does "I am lazy" go? Is it an A-mode, because it describes my current physical state, or is it a C-mode, because it is one of my habitual character traits? Use your best judgment for scoring each statement. Now count the number of each type of response and provide the totals for each mode at the bottom.

So, which category got the most responses?

We predict that although some of you may have given more B-mode responses, the predominant mode among those taking the test will be C-mode. Often, respondents have a combination of these two modes. People with more B-mode responses base their self-concept on group membership and institutional roles, whereas people with more C-mode responses see themselves as more independent and define themselves according to their individual actions and emotions rather than their connections to others. It is likely that there are few (if any) people whose responses fall predominantly in the A or D mode. Those with more A-mode responses may feel that they have a "skin deep" self-concept, based more on their appearance to others than on their internal qualities. Those with more D-mode responses are harder to categorize and may feel uncertain about the source of their sense of self.

Step 3: Analysis

Does the shift from a predominantly B-mode society to a predominantly C-mode society still hold today? And if so, what are we to make of it? The primary characteristics of the B-mode, or "institutional," self are a willingness to adhere to group standards and accept group obligations as well as an orientation toward the future and a sense that the individual is linked to others (Turner 1976). The primary characteristics of the C-mode, or "impulsive," self are the pursuit of individual satisfaction, an orientation toward the present, and a sense that the individual should not be linked to others and that group obligations inhibit individual expression. Zurcher and Turner worried that a society full of self-interested (and even selfish), impulsive individuals might no longer care about the common good and would only work to satisfy their own needs.

What do you think are the consequences for a society overwhelmingly populated by one type of mode or the other? How would schools, families, workplaces, sports teams, governments, and charitable organizations and other groups function if almost everyone fell into the B-mode or C-mode category? Are these two orientations mutually exclusive, or can you combine the best parts of both? What can you do to optimize the qualities of each mode for yourself and for the groups you belong to?

There are two options for completing this Data Workshop:

PREP-PAIR-SHARE Take the TST yourself (Step 1), and score it (Step 2). Get ready to discuss the results with others by jotting down some initial thoughts about your results. Bring your completed questionnaire and notes to class, and discuss them with two or more students in small groups. How many "institutional" or "impulsive" selves are part of your discussion group? Compare your responses and work together on analyzing the group's findings (Step 3).

DO-IT-YOURSELF Conduct a pilot study using the TST. Find a small sample population of three to five other people and administer the test to each of them. Collect, compare, and analyze the responses from your group. Present and analyze your findings in a three-page essay. Make sure to refer to your TST data in the essay; as long as you've preserved the confidentiality of respondents, include the completed questionnaires as an attachment to your paper.

Group Cohesion

A basic concept in the study of group dynamics is **group cohesion**, the sense of solidarity or team spirit that members feel toward their group. Put another way, group cohesion is the force that binds members together. A group is said to be more cohesive when individuals feel strongly tied to membership, so it is likely that a group of fraternity brothers is more cohesive than a random group of classmates. The life of a group depends on at least a minimum level of cohesion. If members begin to lose their strong sense of commitment, the group will gradually disintegrate (Friedkin 2004).

Cohesion is enhanced in a number of ways. It tends to rely

GROUP COHESION the sense of solidarity or loyalty that individuals feel toward a group to which they belong

Group Cohesion Why might fraternity brothers feel more group cohesion than a large group of students attending a lecture?

heavily on interpersonal factors such as shared values and shared demographic traits like race, age, gender, or class (Cota et al. 1995). We can see this kind of cohesion, for example, in a clique of junior high school girls or members of a church congregation. Cohesion also tends to rely on an attraction to the group as a whole or to certain individuals as exemplars of the group. Cohesion may be enhanced when members are able to cooperate and work together in achieving goals (Thye and Lawler 2002). This might help explain cohesion among fans of the Green Bay Packers or members of a local Elks lodge.

GROUPTHINK Whereas a high degree of cohesion might seem desirable, it can also lead to the kind of poor decision making seen in hazing cases. In a process Irving Janus (1971, 1982) called **groupthink**, highly cohesive groups may demand absolute conformity and punish those who threaten to undermine the consensus. Although groupthink does help maintain solidarity, it can also short-circuit the decision-making process, letting a desire for unanimity prevail over critical reasoning. When this happens, groups may begin to feel invulnerable and morally superior (White 1989). Members who would otherwise wish to dissent may instead cave in to peer pressure and go along with the group.

The problem of groupthink can be found in insular groups such as fraternities or private clubs and even reach into the highest level of industry or government, sometimes with disastrous results. For instance, there are those who believe that the explosion of the space shuttle *Challenger* in 1986 may have been a result of NASA scientists' failing to take seriously those who suspected weaknesses in the shuttle's launch design (Vaughan 1996). In the instance of the U.S. military, groupthink may have been to blame for the failure of the CIA and the White House to accurately assess the state of Saddam Hussein's programs for weapons of mass destruction; the perceived existence of such weapons was a primary rationale for waging the Iraq War in 2003. A report by the Senate Intelligence Committee claimed that a groupthink dynamic caused those involved to lose objectivity and to embellish or exaggerate findings that justified the U.S. invasion (Ehrenreich 2004; Isikoff 2004). More recently, groupthink was invoked as the reason for the cover-up of child sexual abuse involving Penn State assistant football coach Jerry Sandusky. Rumors, complaints, and dissent were systematically quashed by the university leadership in an effort to retain group solidarity and uphold the reputation of the award-winning Nittany Lions football program. Those in power seemed more concerned with protecting their public image than with ensuring the safety of young children (Cohen and DeBenedet 2012).

GROUPTHINK in very cohesive groups, the tendency to enforce a high degree of conformity among members, creating a demand for unanimous agreement

SOCIAL INFLUENCE exerting group control over others' decisions

Social Influence (Peer Pressure)

While you may not have any personal experience with groupthink, you are certain to find the next set of sociological concepts all too familiar. When individuals are part of groups, they are necessarily influenced by other members. Sociologists refer to this as **social influence**, or peer pressure. Knowing how social influence works can help you when you need to convince others to act in a certain way (like agreeing on a specific restaurant or movie). In turn, it can also help you recognize when others are trying to influence you (to drink too much or drive too fast, for example).

The idea of social influence is not new: the Greek philosopher Aristotle considered persuasion in his *Rhetoric*. But the more modern studies on social influence date back to World War II, when social scientists were trying to help in the war effort by using motivational films to boost morale among servicemen. Since then, the study of social influence has become an expanding part of the field devoted to discovering the principles that determine our beliefs, create our attitudes, and move us to action (Friedkin and Cook 1990; Cialdini and Trost 1998; Friedkin and Granovetter 1998). Recent research on social influence has revealed that everything from our performance in school (Altermatt and Pomerantz 2005) to the likelihood that we will commit rape (Bohner et al. 2006) can be subject to the influence of others. We will focus here on how social influence functions in everyday situations.

Almost all members of society are susceptible to what is either real or imagined social pressure to conform. In general, we conform because we want to gain acceptance and approval (positive sanctions) and avoid rejection and disapproval (negative sanctions). We follow *prescriptions,* doing the things we're supposed to do, as well as *proscriptions,* avoiding the things we're not supposed to do.

Social psychologists have determined that social influence produces one of three kinds of conformity: compliance, identification, or internalization (Kelman 1958). *Compliance,* the mildest kind of conformity, means going along with something because you expect to gain rewards or avoid punishments. When people comply, however, they don't actually change their own ideas or beliefs. Take, for example, someone who is court ordered to attend Alcoholics Anonymous meetings because of a drunk driving offense. This person might comply in order to avoid a jail sentence or hefty fine, but he might not be persuaded to join AA once the required visits are done. *Identification,* a somewhat stronger kind of conformity, is induced by a person's desire to establish or maintain a relationship with a person or group. It's possible that the person required to attend AA might actually begin to identify with other members. A person who identifies with a group conforms to their wishes and follows their behavior. This is especially true when there is a strong attraction to the group. So perhaps the person who was first ordered to attend AA decides to keep going to meetings, stay sober, and become a member of the group himself.

Internalization, the strongest kind of conformity and most long-lasting, occurs when an individual adopts the beliefs of a leader or group as his own. When internalization occurs, there is no separation between beliefs and behavior; people believe in what they are doing and feel that it is morally right. Members of Alcoholics Anonymous practice the principles of the 12-step program, making it an integral part of their identity and way of life.

Experiments in Conformity

Three rather famous social psychological studies were conducted in the 1950s, '60s, and '70s with the related goal of trying to understand more about the dynamics of social pressure and, in particular, about group conformity and obedience to authority.

THE ASCH EXPERIMENT The first of these experiments was a study on compliance conducted in 1951 by Solomon Asch (1958), who gathered groups of seven or eight students to participate in what he called an experiment on visual perception. In fact, only one of the students in each group was a real research subject; the others knew ahead of time how they were supposed to act. During the experiment, the participants were asked to look at a set of three straight lines and to match the length of a fourth line to one of the other three (see Figure 5.2). In each case, the real research subjects would be the last to give an answer. At first, all participants gave the same correct answer. After a few rounds, however, the experimenter's confederates began to give the same consistently wrong answer. They were completely unanimous in perceiving the line lengths incorrectly. How would the real subjects react when it came to their turn?

Most subjects felt considerable pressure to comply with the rest of the group. A third (33 percent) were "yielders" who gave in at least half the time to what they knew were the

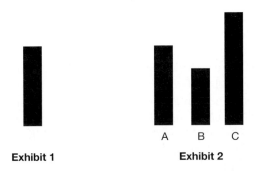

Exhibit 1   **Exhibit 2**

Figure 5.2 **Which Line in Exhibit 2 Matches Exhibit 1?**

Solomon Asch's studies showed that some people will go against the evidence of their own senses if others around them seem to have different perceptions.

wrong answers. Another 40 percent yielded less frequently but still gave some wrong answers. Only 25 percent were "independents," refusing to give in to the majority. In a debriefing period after the experiment, some subjects reported that they had assumed the rest of the participants were right and they were wrong. Other subjects knew they were not wrong but did not want to appear different from the rest of the group. Almost all of them were greatly distressed by the discrepancy between their own perceptions and those of the other participants. Clearly, it can be difficult to resist peer pressure and to maintain independence in a group situation. What would you have done?

THE MILGRAM EXPERIMENT Stanley Milgram's experience as a graduate student of Solomon Asch's led him to work further on conformity. His first experiments were conducted in 1961, just after the trial of Nazi war criminal Adolf Eichmann had begun in Israel. Many of those who were prosecuted in the years after World War II offered the defense that they were "only following orders." But it was not just soldiers who sent millions of innocents to concentration camps—ordinary citizens turned in their neighbors. Milgram wanted to know whether something particular about the German national psyche led so many to act as accomplices to the mass executions, why they complied with authority figures even when orders conflicted with their own consciences. While we usually think that following orders is a good thing, in the case of the Holocaust, it amounted to a "crime of obedience."

The Milgram experiment (1963, 1974) used a laboratory setting to test the lengths to which ordinary people would follow orders from a legitimate authority figure. The experiment included three roles: the "experimenter" (a scientist in a white lab coat), a "teacher," and a "learner." The teachers were the only real research subjects in the experiment: although the teachers were led to believe otherwise, the learners were actually confederates of the experimenters. When roles were assigned at the outset of the experiment, the research subjects were always picked to play the teacher, despite a seemingly random assignment of roles.

The stated goal of the experiment was to measure the effect of punishment on memory and learning. The teacher was instructed to read aloud a set of word pairs for the learner to memorize. The teacher would then repeat the first word in the pair and, for each incorrect answer, administer a shock of increasing voltage to the learner. The teacher watched while the experimenter strapped the learner to a chair and applied electrodes to his arms. The teacher was then directed to an adjoining room where he could communicate with, but not see, the learner. This room contained a machine with a series of levers indicating the increasing levels of voltage that would be administered for each successive incorrect answer. (In actuality, the machine was not connected to the learner, and he received no shocks.)

GLOBAL PERSPECTIVE
Group vs. Individual Norms: Honor Killings

In American culture, when reports of family members murdering each other emerge, the reasons generally include abuse, crimes of passion, or monetary gain. The murder of Kathleen Savio by her ex-husband Drew Peterson in 2004 is among the most notorious cases of murder within a family. Her death was ruled an accident until 2007, when the case grabbed headlines as Peterson's fourth wife, Stacy, vanished without a trace. Stacy had also been Drew's alibi on the night that Savio went missing. This led law enforcement to re-open the case into Savio's death and eventually led to Peterson being convicted of murder and sentenced to thirty-eight years in prison.

In 2014, Don Spirit murdered his daughter and all six of her children. Sarah Spirit and her children had moved in with her father not long before the murder. After shooting his daughter and then all six of his grandchildren—the youngest of whom was only three months old—Spirit called 911, informed them of what he had done, and then shot himself as law enforcement arrived. Although no definite motive can be established, the family had a long history of abuse and neglect.

While "murders involving family members killing other family members are not terribly rare," the reaction to such tragedies is especially harsh, judging murderers like Peterson and Spirit as dishonorable traitors to their families, men who were more concerned with their own personal gain than their loyalty to family (Berman 2014). But what if the reason for a murder of a family member is to uphold the reputation of the family as a whole? **Honor killing** is the murder of a family member based on the belief that the victim is bringing dishonor to the family or the community. In an honor killing, which is primarily seen in Middle Eastern and South Asian cultures, the victim of the murder is usually a woman in the family who has not lived up to the moral codes set by the religion or community. Reasons for honor killings may include refusing to enter into an arranged marriage, being a rape victim, being immodest in dress or behavior, or having sex outside marriage.

HONOR KILLING the murder of a family member—usually female—who is believed to have brought dishonor to her family

In 2000, the United Nations estimated that as many as 5,000 women a year are murdered in honor killings, though there is no reliable or definitive accounting, and these crimes are rarely classified or prosecuted as such. Researchers believe the numbers may be far greater, and they point to an increase in incidents between 1989 and 2009 (Chesler 2010). The methods of killing range from shooting the victim to setting her on fire or stoning her to death. In each case, the person who commits the murder is seen as the norm enforcer and not the norm violator, as he is doing it in order to seek vindication and to right the wrong committed by the wife, daughter, or sister. In this cultural context, the murdered woman is viewed as someone who deserved to die for betraying and dishonoring her family.

Richard Wilkinson (2005) maintains that in countries with less access to basic resources, health care, and human capital, there is a correlating lack of social power and equality for women. Gender inequality is exacerbated in places where there are fewer social resources, making honor killings more likely. Clashes occur when the cultural practice of honor killing is brought to Western countries like France, Canada, and the United States, where a woman's sexual freedom may face informal sanctions but is widely accepted as the norm.

In October 2009, in a suburb of Phoenix, Arizona, twenty-year-old Noor al-Maleki was run over by a Jeep driven by her father, Faleh al-Maleki, formerly from Iraq, because he feared she was becoming too Westernized. Banned from wearing jeans, social networking on the Internet, and interacting with boys, Noor had sought to live life as an American. Growing up in the United States since the age of four, Noor was immersed in American cultural norms. Defying her father's rules, Noor refused an arranged marriage at age seventeen and moved into her boyfriend's parents' home in 2009. In 2011, Faleh al-Maleki was convicted of second-degree murder for killing his daughter.

The cultural norm promoting strong family values that causes such disgust toward Scott Peterson or Don Spirit is the same norm behind honor killings. However, in honor killings, the family is seen as more important than each family member; therefore, an individual member should suffer severe punishment for bringing shame to the family. While al-Maleki's actions toward his daughter seem to most Americans' individualist notions of justice as a betrayal of the family, they are justified in his cultural understandings of family honor.

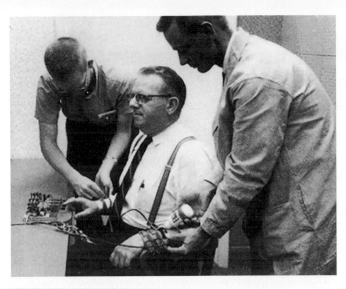

The Milgram Experiment How did Stanley Milgram test participants' obedience to authority? Do you think he would get the same results today?

psychologically healthy and stable were recruited to participate in a two-week mock prison simulation. Role assignment as prisoner or guard was based on a coin toss. Guards were given batons, khaki clothing, and mirrored sunglasses and were told they could not physically harm the prisoners but could otherwise create feelings of boredom, fear, or powerlessness. Prisoners were "arrested" and taken to a mock "jail" set up in the basement of a university building, where they were strip-searched, dressed in smocks and stocking caps (to simulate shaven heads), and assigned identity numbers. A research assistant played the role of warden, while Zimbardo himself was the superintendent.

The students quickly inhabited their roles, but soon exceeded the experimenters' expectations, resulting in an abusive and potentially dangerous situation. Rioting began by the second day; the guards quelled it harshly, harassing the prisoners and depriving them of food, sleep, and basic sanitation. Several guards became increasingly sadistic as the experiment went on, degrading and punishing any prisoner

The experiment began. As the teacher amplified the voltage for each incorrect answer, the learner responded in increasingly vocal ways. In reality, the teacher was hearing a prerecorded tape that included exclamations, banging on the wall, complaints by the learner about a heart condition, and finally, silence. Many subjects grew uncomfortable at around 135 volts, often pausing and expressing a desire to check on the learner or discontinue the experiment. At that point, the experimenter would give a succession of orders, prodding the teacher to continue. After being assured that they would not be held responsible, most subjects continued, many reaching the maximum of 450 volts.

Milgram and his colleagues were stunned by the results. They had predicted that only a few of the subjects would be willing to inflict the maximum voltage. In the first set of experiments, 65 percent of the participants administered the maximum voltage, though many were very uncomfortable doing so and all paused at some point. Only one participant refused outright to administer even low-voltage shocks. Milgram's results highlight the dynamics of conformity revealed in the Asch experiment. A subject will often rely on the expertise of an individual or group, in this case the experimenter, when faced with a difficult decision. We also see how thoroughly socialized most people are to obey authority and carry out orders, especially when they no longer consider themselves responsible for their actions. Clearly, few people have the personal resources to resist authority, even when it goes against their consciences.

THE STANFORD PRISON EXPERIMENT The Stanford Prison Experiment, conducted by Milgram's high school classmate Philip Zimbardo (1971), also examined the power of authority. Twenty-four undergraduates deemed

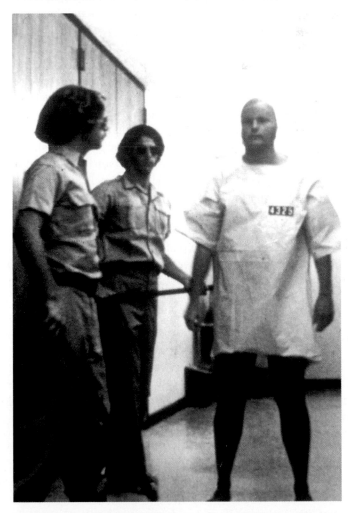

The Stanford Prison Experiment Why do you think the students in Zimbardo's experiment inhabited their roles so completely? What does it reveal about group behavior?

who challenged their authority, and several prisoners showed signs of psychological trauma. After only six days, Zimbardo was compelled to shut down the experiment after a graduate student researcher (whom he later married) became appalled by the conditions.

The Stanford Prison Experiment provided another example of the way situational dynamics, rather than individuals' personal attributes, can determine behavior.

MILGRAM REVISITED Some researchers have claimed that the Asch experiment was a "child of its time"—that students in the 1950s were more obedient in their roles, and the culture placed greater emphasis on the value of conformity (Perrin and Spencer 1980, 1981). Researchers in recent decades who have replicated the Asch experiment have in fact seen significantly lower rates of compliance, suggesting that the historical and cultural context in which the experiment was conducted had an effect on how subjects performed (Bond and Sussex 1996). This conclusion echoes some of Ralph Turner's findings about the institutional or impulsive self, discussed in an earlier Data Workshop; namely, he found that patterns of behavior can change over time and that separate generations may respond differently to social pressures.

The power of the group continues to interest sociologists, psychologists, and others who want to understand what drives our powerful impulse to comply (Cialdini 1998). Both the Milgram and Stanford Prison experiments would be considered unethical by today's professional standards. Although each of the experiments revealed important truths about obedience to authority, some of the participants involved suffered real, and in some cases long-lasting, psychological pain beyond what is considered an acceptable threshold of minimal harm.

Yet the experiments remain relevant because real-life examples of crimes of obedience continue to occur—whether in the case of the prison guards at Abu Ghraib or in a serial telephone hoax perpetrated on fast-food workers in which a caller posing as a police officer instructed assistant managers to abuse fellow workers (Wolfson 2005).

Nearly half a century elapsed before researchers at Santa Clara University found a means of replicating the Milgram experiment that would pass the Institutional Review Board process for research on human subjects. After a careful screening process, Jerry Burger (2009) conducted a modified version of the famous experiment that protected the well-being of the participants while still providing a valid comparison to the original. Contrary to expectations, obedience rates were only slightly lower in Burger's replication than they had been in Milgram's lab more than forty-five years earlier.

Although we might like to imagine ourselves as being more able to resist the same forces of conformity that trip up research participants who consistently cave in to social pressure, it's likely that if we found ourselves in situations similar to those created in the laboratory, we'd go along and obey authority too.

Working Together: Teams and Leadership

What does it mean to make a "group effort"? Sometimes we can accomplish things together that we could not do alone. But such outcomes are far from guaranteed. Whether group efforts result in synergy or inefficiency may depend on a number of factors, including the makeup of its members and the relationship between leaders and followers.

Teamwork

Are two heads better than one? Or do too many cooks spoil the broth? Early research on groups (Homans 1951) typically assumed that it was always more productive to work in a team rather than alone. However, researchers soon recognized that both the nature of the task and the characteristics of the group have a lot to do with the comparative advantage or disadvantage of working in a group (Goodacre 1953). When we measure productivity, groups almost always outperform single individuals. Things get a bit more complicated, however, when groups are compared with the same number of people working by themselves.

In one of the earliest attempts to systematically study group productivity, experimental social psychologist Ivan Steiner (1972) compared the potential productivity of a group (what they should be able to do) with the group's actual productivity (what they in fact got done). According to Steiner, actual group productivity can never equal potential productivity because there will always be losses in the team process. Two major sources of inefficiency in particular come with the group process, and both get worse as group size increases. One source is organization: coordinating activities and delegating

Firefighters Mourn Fellow Team Members Nineteen members of the Granite Mountain Hotshots, an elite crew of wildland firefighters in Prescott, Arizona, perished in the 2013 Yarnell Fire despite following safety and survival protocols. Erratic weather and a gap in radio communications were cited as contributing factors.

ON THE JOB
Teamwork and the Tour de France

The Tour de France is the world's premiere competitive cycling event. It is a race that lasts more than three weeks, covers more than 2,000 miles, and traverses the European Alps. Each summer, it draws a television audience of millions worldwide, many of whom never ride their own bikes and do not pay attention to any other bicycle racing events at any other time of year. It has also seen more than its share of controversy: seven-time Tour winner Lance Armstrong was stripped of his medals and banned from competitive cycling for life after admitting to "doping," or using banned substances to improve his athletic performance. Other recent winners, including American Floyd Landis and Spain's Alberto Contador, have also been stripped of their wins and been banned for doping; in fact, in the more than 110-year history of the Tour de France, the race has been fraught with doping scandals. Early riders used alcohol, ether, and strychnine to improve their stamina and speed.

Since 2010, the winners of the Tour have been verifiably drug-free. But they still cannot say that their victories were achieved without assistance. In fact, no one wins the Tour de France on his own. Winning riders are supported by teams of eight other premier athletes who must coordinate complex teamwork relations to prevail over the other twenty or so teams in competition. As with so many other areas of social life, individual success is buoyed by the work of many. No one can become president of the United States, win an Oscar, reach the summit of Mt. Everest, open a restaurant, meet their sales quota, or earn a bachelor's degree without relying on others—groups as well as individuals—to support his or her efforts. So, although the winner of the Tour is listed individually, he didn't do it alone.

Each team member has a particular specialty, and each stage of the race requires a different strategy. Sprinters may be needed to make a "breakaway" early in the race; "super-climbers" are necessary in the mountainous regions; and sometimes the entire team has to protect the team leader, "blocking" and "drafting" in order to save energy. Teamwork is required to organize bathroom and food breaks, as the race stops for no man. Extremely consistent riders (*rouleurs*) are prized, as are those who ride with aggressiveness and bravery (*combativité*). When the individual winner crosses the finish line on the Champs-Elysées in Paris, it is the sacrifices of his altruistic teammates that have made his win possible.

Which position will you find yourself in when you enter the workplace? Will you be the team leader whose individual successes depend on the contributions of others? Or will you be the team member whose special skills support the achievements of the group? It is likely that you will find yourself in both situations over the course of your working life. So remember, when you don the *maillot jaune* (the yellow jersey worn by the Tour de France leader), in most cases it takes a team effort to get you to the winner's circle.

Group Effort Italian cyclist Vincenzo Nibali, in the yellow jersey, completed the Tour de France with the support of his teammates.

---

tasks. For example, if four friends are going to help you move to a new apartment, some time will be lost while you figure out who should pack what, how the furniture will be arranged in the truck, where the boxes should go in the new apartment, and so forth.

Another source of inefficiency is the phenomenon known as **social loafing**, which means that as more individuals are added to a task, each one takes it a little easier (Karau and Williams 1993). Furthermore, as more people become involved, the harder it is to discern individual effort. If it is impossible for any single person to receive credit or blame, motivation usually suffers. Have you ever asked too many people to help you move to a new apartment? If so, chances are that a few did most of the work, some showed up late and helped out a bit, and others did very little but had a good time talking and eating pizza. Having too many "helpers" may contribute to social loafing.

SOCIAL LOAFING the phenomenon in which as more individuals are added to a task, each individual contributes a little less; a source of inefficiency when working in teams

Solutions to the problem of social loafing include recognizing individual effort and finding ways to make a task more interesting or personally rewarding. But such solutions are not always possible. It might be difficult, for instance, to make "moving day" more rewarding. Another solution, however, is suggested by **social identity theory**. Having a social identity, as opposed to a personal one, involves thinking and feeling like a representative of a group (Turner and Killian 1987); you have a real desire to belong to, not simply keep company with, the group. According to this model, the most efficient teams are characterized by the greatest shared social identity among their members; such social identity increases motivation and places the needs of the group above purely personal concerns.

Power, Authority, and Style

Effective group leaders possess a variety of qualities, some of which are particular to the kind of group they lead. The leader of a therapeutic support group, for example, needs the proper credentials as well as experience and compassion for his patients. The captain of a sports team must display expertise at her game as well as the ability to inspire her teammates. An office manager must be well organized and good at dealing with different kinds of people. A police commander must be in good physical shape, skilled in law enforcement tactics, and quick-thinking in a crisis.

One thing almost all leaders have in common, though, is **power**—the ability to control the actions of others. Whether it is **coercive power** (backed by the threat of force) or merely **influential power** (supported by persuasion), leadership involves getting people to do things they may or may not want to do. For example, a football coach might wield both coercive and influential power over his players. Although the athletes would definitely want to win games, they might not want to run their training drills every day. During a workout, team members might respond to either the threat of being kicked off the team or the encouragement from the coach. Power, in whatever form it takes, is both a privilege and a requirement of leadership.

Because leadership requires the exercise of power, most formal organizations have institutionalized it in some officially recognized form of **authority**. Max Weber (1913/1962) identified three types of authority that may be found in social organizations. **Traditional authority**, based in custom, birthright, or divine right, is usually associated with monarchies and dynasties. Kings and queens inherit the throne, not only through lineage but also by divine appointment, meaning by higher authority. Their personal qualities don't really matter, and they can't be replaced by legal proceedings. **Legal-rational authority**, on the other hand, is based in laws and rules, not in the lineage of any individual leader. Modern presidencies and parliaments are built on this kind of authority. The third type, **charismatic authority**, is based in the remarkable personal qualities of the leader. Neither rules nor traditions are necessary for the establishment of a charismatic leader—indeed, the leader can be a revolutionary, breaking rules and defying traditions. This is perhaps the only place we will ever find Jesus Christ and Adolf Hitler in the same category—by all accounts both were extremely charismatic leaders.

The three types of authority are not necessarily mutually exclusive; they can coexist within the same leader. Bill Clinton and Ronald Reagan were appealing and charismatic leaders within the context of the legal-rational authority of the presidency; the Kennedy family is considered an American political dynasty of sorts, following a tradition of leadership within the structure of electoral politics. The late King Hussein of Jordan was revered for his extraordinary charisma and statesmanship despite his traumatic ascent to the throne: as a teenager, he witnessed his grandfather's assassination and, as his heir, was crowned less than a year later. For people like Bill Clinton (a legal-rational ruler) and King Hussein (a traditional ruler), their charisma was not necessarily the root of their authority, but it did play a part in their ability to rule.

In addition to different types of power and authority, group leaders may exhibit different personal leadership styles as well. Some are more **instrumental**—that is, they are task or goal oriented—while others are more **expressive**, or concerned with maintaining harmony within the group (Parsons and Bales 1955). An instrumental leader is less concerned with people's feelings than with getting the job done, whereas an expressive leader conveys interest in group members' emotions as well as their achievements. We often consider leadership styles through the lens of gender, expecting men to be more instrumental and women to be more expressive. In fact, we sometimes feel surprised or upset when these gendered expectations aren't met: a male leader with a more expressive style (like California governor Jerry Brown, once nicknamed "Moonbeam" for his emotive, touchy-feely style) is sometimes seen as weak, while a female leader with a more instrumental style (such as former First Lady, senator, and U.S. secretary of state

SOCIAL IDENTITY THEORY a theory of group formation and maintenance that stresses the need of individual members to feel a sense of belonging

POWER the ability to control the actions of others

COERCIVE POWER power that is backed by the threat of force

INFLUENTIAL POWER power that is supported by persuasion

AUTHORITY the legitimate right to wield power

TRADITIONAL AUTHORITY authority based in custom, birthright, or divine right

LEGAL-RATIONAL AUTHORITY authority based in laws, rules, and procedures, not in the heredity or personality of any individual leader

CHARISMATIC AUTHORITY authority based in the perception of remarkable personal qualities in a leader

INSTRUMENTAL LEADERSHIP leadership that is task or goal oriented

EXPRESSIVE LEADERSHIP leadership concerned with maintaining emotional and relational harmony within the group

Qualities of Leadership Nelson Mandela, pictured here with the South African rugby team, the Springboks, is an example of a leader with both legal-rational and charismatic authority. Mandela used his charismatic leadership to unite post-apartheid South Africa through rugby, culminating in a narrow victory in the 1995 Rugby World Cup final.

Hillary Clinton, whose ambition and drive have earned her criticism throughout her political career) is sometimes seen as pushy.

Bureaucracy

Examples of **bureaucracy**, a specific type of secondary group, are everywhere in your life—your university, employer, Internet service provider, fast-food restaurant, and even church are likely to be organized bureaucratically. Bureaucracies are designed to perform tasks efficiently, and they approach their tasks, whatever they are, with calculations designed deliberately to meet their goals.

Bureaucracies have certain organizational traits that help them operate efficiently. Max Weber (1921/1968) identified these characteristics as follows:

1. Specialization: All members of a bureaucracy are assigned specialized roles and tasks.

2. Technical competence: All members are expressly trained and qualified for their specific roles within the organization.

3. Hierarchy: Bureaucracies always feature the supervision of subordinates by higher-ranking managers and bosses.

4. Rules and regulations: These are meant to make all operations as predictable as possible.

> **BUREAUCRACY** a type of secondary group designed to perform tasks efficiently, characterized by specialization, technical competence, hierarchy, written rules, impersonality, and formal written communication

5. Impersonality: In a bureaucracy, rules come before people; no individual receives special treatment.

6. Formal written communication: Documents such as memos (or e-mails) are the heart of the organization and the most effective way to communicate.

You can see these traits in action at your own college or university. Take specialization and technical competence, for instance. Virtually none of your professors could teach another's classes: your sociology professor would likely be completely useless in a chemistry lab, a math classroom, or even an English seminar. The groundskeepers,

Bureaucracies Are Everywhere Bureaucratic regulations are supposed to make organizations run smoothly; however, bureaucracy can also be impersonal, inflexible, and hyperrational.

campus police officers, soccer coaches, and librarians are all specially qualified to do their own jobs and no one else's. In addition, there are layers of hierarchy at a university, from the trustees and president to the vice chancellors, provosts, deans, and department chairs. Professors are, in some ways, at the bottom of the academic hierarchy (except for you, the students)! And every other campus unit (athletics, residence life, food service, facilities maintenance) has its own hierarchy as well.

RATIONALIZATION the application of economic logic to human activity; the use of formal rules and regulations in order to maximize efficiency without consideration of subjective or individual concerns

MCDONALDIZATION George Ritzer's term describing the spread of bureaucratic rationalization and the accompanying increases in efficiency and dehumanization

Regulations keep a university running smoothly—or at least that's what they are meant to do. Undoubtedly, though, you have run up against a regulation that kept you from doing something you really wanted to do—add a class after a deadline, move into a campus apartment. This is where the feature of impersonality also comes into play: the rules of the bureaucracy trumped your individual needs, no matter how deserving you thought you were. This is especially true at larger universities; at small schools, special treatment is still sometimes possible. But big bureaucracies often treat you "like a number"—and in fact, you *are* a number to your college; your student ID number is the first thing you are issued on arrival.

The McDonaldization of Society

Weber's model of bureaucracy seems cold and heartless, alienating and impersonal, rule-bound, inflexible, and undemocratic. Indeed, many bureaucracies *are* like this. They are highly efficient secondary groups that operate on the principle of **rationalization**, where the focus is on logical procedures, rules and regulations are paramount, and an individual's unique personal qualities are unimportant. Worse yet, some of the hyperrationalized features of successful bureaucracies are trickling down into other areas of our everyday lives.

Sociologist George Ritzer (1993, 1996, 2013) called this trickle-down rationalization process **McDonaldization**. We touch-tone our way through telephone calls at work, never speaking to a real person; at lunch, we construct our own salads at the salad bar and bus our own tables afterward; at the bank, we no longer interact with human tellers but rather drive through the ATM on the way home, where we microwave our dinners and watch increasingly predictable sitcoms or movie sequels on TV. Ritzer is critical of the dehumanizing aspects of McDonaldization and hopes that increased awareness of the process will help us avoid the "iron cage" of bureaucracy—a term coined by Weber to illustrate the way bureaucracies can trap individuals.

Sociologist Robin Leidner delved further into the McDonaldization phenomenon in her book *Fast Food, Fast Talk* (1993). Through fieldwork in actual McDonald's franchises, Leidner developed a model for understanding the

McDonaldization In her ethnography book *Fast Food, Fast Talk*, Robin Leidner studied how the routinization of services and physical atmosphere at McDonald's restaurants standardized the types of interactions occurring there.

increasing routinization of service industries, in this case the ubiquitous fast-food restaurant. In particular, she looks at how standardized "scripts" for interaction help shape customers' experiences. The physical atmosphere of a McDonald's is not conducive to hanging out (unlike, say, a café); customers don't expect to sit down and be waited on. Rather, they respond to expectations that they will enter, order food from a predetermined menu and pay for it, eat quickly, deposit trash in the receptacles, and then leave. Leidner exposes these processes of routinization by looking at what happens when breakdowns occur in these expectations.

For example, Leidner noted that McDonald's trains workers to refer to customers as "guests," reinforcing the obligation to serve them respectfully even if that respect is not reciprocated. Leidner observed that if customers were angry or uncooperative, workers tried even harder to serve them swiftly so that they would leave faster and have less time to make trouble in the restaurant. Workers developed a mind-set that allowed them to handle problem customers in a way that minimized trouble and facilitated the workers' routinized job.

Responding to Bureaucratic Constraints

Not everything about bureaucracies is bad. In fact, in contemporary, postindustrial society, just about everything you need or want is created, produced, distributed, and serviced by a bureaucracy. The water in the tap, the lights, the streets, the car and its insurance, the food on the table, the table itself, the clothes on your back, and the movies, songs, and books you enjoy—all are the products of bureaucratic organizations. As problematic as they are, we can't live without them. So how can we benefit from our contact with bureaucracies without being controlled by them?

For one thing, even the most overrationalized, McDonaldized bureaucracy is populated by people who are capable of forming primary group relationships as well, who might celebrate birthdays, throw parties, and go out for drinks after work. Indeed, interpersonal interactions help humanize bureaucracies. Further, in forward-thinking organizations, new management strategies meant to address alienation and disenchantment are being implemented. Yes, bureaucracies still seek to be as efficient and predictable as possible in their daily operations. But some, such as Apple, Toyota, and Google, are trying to play up their human side as well—becoming "enlightened" bureaucracies by being inclusive, sharing responsibility, and providing opportunities for all to advance.

In fact, businesses like Google have come to believe that corporate success and employee well-being are complementary. Larry Page and Sergey Brin founded Google with the idea that analyzing information could lead to a better search engine, and as their company grew, they also embraced the idea that data analysis could create a better, happier workplace. For example, they found that they weren't hiring enough women, and those they hired were quitting significantly faster than men. When they crunched the numbers, Google's human resources department—or, as they call it, People Operations—found that women who turned down job offers had disproportionately been interviewed by men, a problem that was easily solved (Miller 2012). When they looked at who exactly was quitting, they found that "women who had recently given birth were leaving at twice Google's average departure rate," a problem they addressed by increasing maternity leave from three months to five (Manjoo 2013).

For the past few decades, businesses have spent an increasing amount of time and money on employee training and development, with over $46 billion devoted to just team-building games and exercises alone (Browning 2014). Many large businesses are also involved in organizing employee retreats to teach managers how to understand individual strengths and weaknesses, support individual skills and talents, and encourage cooperation, trust, and leadership. Some, such as Fidelity Financial, have adopted the Japanese management technique called *kaizen*, in which lower-level workers are encouraged to suggest innovative ways to improve the organization, and upper-level managers are required to actually put these ideas into practice, rewarding individual creativity and benefiting the company at the same time (Pollack 1999; Hakim 2001). Make no mistake—corporations are not sacrificing the bottom line for the good of the individual. They're still looking for ways to improve productivity and cut costs. But often they are finding that the needs of the individual and those of the organization are not mutually exclusive.

BURNING MAN In the barren Black Rock Desert of Nevada, some people actively seek out an escape from their bureaucratically regimented life, at least for one week every summer, at a festival called Burning Man (Sonner 2002; Chen 2004). The festival, begun in 1990 on a beach near San Francisco with just twenty participants, drew more than 65,000 people in 2014. Burning Man is hard to describe for those who have never attended. It is a freewheeling experiment in temporary community, where there are no rules except to protect the well-being of participants ("burners") and where everyone gathers together to celebrate various forms of self-expression and self-reliance not normally encountered in everyday life.

Burning Man attracts a wide variety of individuals from different backgrounds (though it may be difficult to tell beneath the body paint, mud, or costumes that many wear). Unlike in many places in the real world, participants are encouraged to interact with each other; there are no strangers at "the Burn." Each year is characterized by a different theme—"American Dream" in 2008, "Rites of Passage" in 2011, "Caravansary" in 2014—and participants are invited to contribute in some meaningful way to its realization, most often artistically. Matt Wray (2011), a sociologist who's also a burner, explains that "fire, art, dust, and bodies collide and collude to make bizarre and unforgettable transformations" as thousands of people step outside their normal lives and interact in new ways.

Much of what is appealing about Burning Man is that it challenges many of the norms and values of mainstream society, especially those associated with conformity, bureaucracy,

Burning Man Finale Each year thousands of "burners" gather in the Black Rock Desert to celebrate the rejection of such values as conformity, bureaucracy, and capitalism.

and capitalism. Black Rock resembles a city when the thousands of participants converge, but one composed of tents and RVs gathered into neighborhoods with names like "Tic Toc Town" and "Capitalist Pig Camp" (Doherty 2000, 2004). The

Table 5.1 Theory in Everyday Life

Perspective	Approach to Groups	Case Study: Fraternities
Structural Functionalism	Life in groups helps to regulate and give meaning to individual experience, contributing to social cohesion and stability.	Affiliation groups like fraternities help create social cohesion in the context of a larger, possibly alienating, university system by bringing young men with shared values together.
Conflict Theory	Group membership is often the basis for the distrbution of rewards, privileges, and opportunities in our society. An individual may be treated preferentially or prejudicially based on his or her group membership.	In-group and out-group dynamics can contribute to stereotyping and conflict as fraternity brothers develop an "us vs. them" perspective regarding other frats and non-Greeks.
Symbolic Interactionism	Group norms, values, and dynamics are generated situationally, in interaction with other members.	The pressure to conform to group culture (as in the cases of peer pressure and groupthink) can lead individuals to do things they might never do alone, and can have negative consequences, as in the case of fraternity hazing and binge drinking. It can also lead to positive actions, such as when fraternity members volunteer or raise money for charity.

city has its own informal economy as well. Once an admission fee is paid, money is no longer used. Participants must bring enough supplies to support themselves or use alternate forms of currency, such as barter, trade, gifts, or services. Corporate sponsorship is strictly avoided, and logos of any kind are banned.

Despite its stated ideals, there is not total freedom at Burning Man. Over the years, various government and local law-enforcement agencies have imposed some restrictions on the event such as bans on fireworks, guns, and dogs. However, most conflict is handled by the Black Rock City Rangers, who "are volunteers trained in dispute resolution techniques that help diffuse conflict and manage disruptive behavior before it escalates" (Gomez 2013).

On the last night of the festival, the giant wooden structure known as the Burning Man is lit on fire, and the celebrants discover their own personal epiphanies as they watch it burn. When the festival is over, participants are committed to leaving no trace behind. One burner called the festival "authentic life," with the other days of the year "a tasteless mirage, a pacific struggle against the backwardness of Middle America—consumer culture, bad politics, *Fear Factor,* and

fear thy neighbor" (Babiak 2004). So while Burning Man participants don't abandon permanently the web of contemporary bureaucracies that shapes their lives, they gain some relief by ditching it all once a year, if just for a few days.

CLOSING COMMENTS

Groups make our lives possible by providing the necessities of our existence—food, clothes, cars, homes, and all the other things we use on a daily basis. Groups make our lives enjoyable by providing us with companionship and recreation—from our friends and families to the entertainment conglomerates that produce our favorite music and films. Groups also make our lives problematic. Bureaucracies can squelch our individuality, major manufacturers can create social and environmental problems, and some organizations can engender conflict and prejudice among groups. We are at our best in groups, and our worst. We can do great things together, and horrible things. Sociology helps us understand group life at both extremes and everywhere in between.

Group Effort Members of the U.S. women's soccer team celebrate after clinching the FIFA Women's World Cup in July 2015.

Everything You Need to Know about Groups

> " A group is a collection of people who share some attribute, identify with one another, and interact with each other. "

TYPES OF GROUPS

* **Primary groups:** people who are most important to our sense of self; characterized by face-to-face interaction, high levels of cooperation, and intense feelings of belonging

* **Secondary groups:** groups that are larger and less intimate than primary groups; relationships are organized around a specific goal

* **Dyads:** the smallest possible group, consisting of only two members

* **Triads:** a slightly more stable small group consisting of three people; the third member can referee conflicts that arise between the other two

* **In-groups:** groups that members identify with and feel loyalty toward

* **Out-groups:** any group that an individual feels opposition, rivalry, or hostility toward

* **Reference group:** group that provides a standard of comparison against which we evaluate ourselves

REVIEW

1. Which groups serve as your reference groups? Are you a member of all your reference groups? How do these reference groups affect your self-image?

2. The text identifies three types of conformity: compliance, identification, and internalization. Describe some moments when you've exhibited each type of conformity.

3. Theorist George Ritzer believes that McDonaldization, the spread of the organizational principles of bureaucracies to all areas of life, is a growing concern. Thinking about Weber's six characteristics of bureaucracies, can you identify areas of your life that have been McDonaldized?

Strong or Weak?

The kinds of people you know can determine your next job. "Ties" or contacts become a key method to network and reach a higher status.

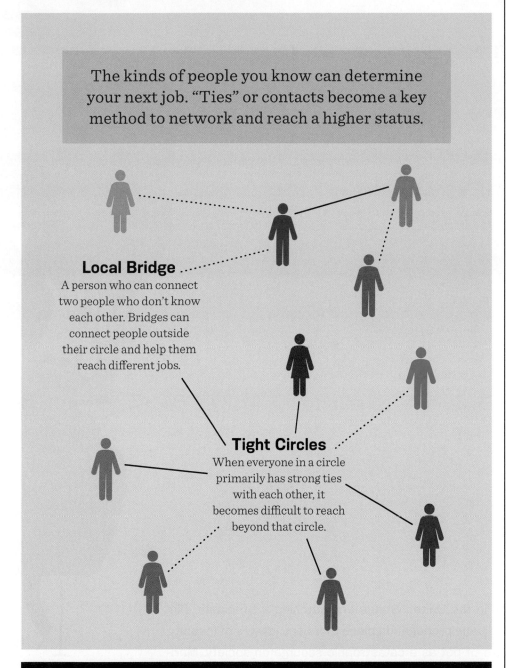

Local Bridge
A person who can connect two people who don't know each other. Bridges can connect people outside their circle and help them reach different jobs.

Tight Circles
When everyone in a circle primarily has strong ties with each other, it becomes difficult to reach beyond that circle.

——— **STRONG TIES** are people you are close with, such as relatives, good friends, and mentors.

·········· **WEAK TIES** are acquaintances.

SOURCE: Granovetter 1973

EXPLORE

It Takes a Village . . . to Create Binge Drinkers

What group of people do you think has the biggest influence over teens' drinking habits? The answer might not be what you think. Visit the Everyday Sociology Blog to discover how social groups can influence teen drinking.

http://wwnPag.es/trw405

CHAPTER 6

Deviance

Flashback: It's 1937, and students in the United States are watching a scholastic film called *Reefer Madness,* an anti-marijuana propaganda piece that uses images of insanity, rape, and murder to paint a picture of pot as a catastrophic scourge on society. Marijuana was associated with criminals, reprobates, jazz musicians, and (gasp!) ethnic minorities and was presented to schoolchildren as the cause of immediate social and moral chaos.

Flashforward: It's 2012, and author David Maraniss releases a new biography of President Barack Obama. Maraniss reveals in great detail what Obama had already admitted to in his earlier autobiography: that, as a young man, he had smoked pot. Maraniss's book tells the story of Obama's membership in the "Choom Gang" while a student at Hawaii's private Punahou High School. This was a group of young men dedicated to "chooming" (getting high) together, and it

appears that Obama smoked often and with great relish. A few months after Mara-niss's biography is published, Obama is re-elected to a second term as president.

Along with cultural values, definitions of deviance change over time, and we can sometimes observe them as they swing back and forth, from one extreme to the other, over the course of history. In the case of our culture's values and beliefs about marijuana, they were mainstream to begin with. George Washington and Thomas Jefferson both grew hemp (*Cannabis sativa*, the same botanical classifi-cation as marijuana) on their farms in the American colonies. Hemp was used to make fabric, rope, and paper, including the paper on which Jefferson drafted the Declaration of Independence.

Over time, hemp as an industrial crop began to have more and more competition—from other agricultural products, such as cotton and timber, and from other chem-ical and industrial processes that had the backing of powerful industries and individuals. In the 1920s and 1930s, William Randolph Hearst, along with others in hemp-competitive industries, exerted pressure on government officials to make hemp's intoxicating by-product, marijuana, illegal. A propaganda campaign against marijuana was led by Hearst's media outlets, promoting it as a dangerous threat to America's youth, public health, and national security. By 1937, every state had outlawed the use of marijuana as an intoxicant, and cannabis farming had been effectively eliminated by the passage of the prohibitively high Marijuana Tax Act.

Flashforward: It's 2015, and twenty-three states have decriminalized marijuana use and possession to varying degrees, including allowing the medical use of mari-juana for chemotherapy and AIDS patients. Three states—Alaska, Colorado, and Washington—have decriminalized recreational pot use as well, making it possible for individuals to purchase, carry, and use small amounts of marijuana for nonmed-ical reasons. Other states are considering similar laws.

What was once mainstream became defined as deviant; what is now seen as deviant may some day be normal and acceptable. Why? Because values change over time. The current surge in environmentalism, for example, is part of the change in views about *Cannabis sativa*: legal hemp farming would allow the production of tree-free paper products, which would please many people who are worried about the depletion of environmental resources.

How is it possible that there could be such different reactions to the same humble plant? Changing values lead to changing laws and changing practices in everyday life. It seems like we should be able to agree on whether marijuana pro-duction and use are deviant. But as we shall see, nothing is inherently deviant—rather, it is the cultural, historical, and situational context that makes it so.

HOW TO READ THIS CHAPTER

Have you ever driven faster than the posted speed limit? Have you ever gotten caught picking your nose in public? Did you have your first taste of beer, wine, or hard liquor before you reached the legal drinking age? Did you pierce something (your lip, eyebrow, or belly button) that your grandmother wouldn't have wanted you to pierce? If you work in an office, did you ever take home a pen, pencil, or packet of Post-it notes?

If you answered yes to any of these questions, you are the embodiment of what we seek to understand in this chapter: you are deviant. Remember this as you read the chapter.

Defining Deviance

Deviance is a behavior, trait, or belief that departs from a norm and generates a negative reaction in a particular group. The norms and the group reactions are necessary for a behavior or characteristic to be defined as deviant (Goode 1997). The importance of norms becomes clear when we remember that what is deviant in one culture might be normal in another (see Chapter 3); even within the same culture, what was deviant a century ago—like marijuana use—might be perfectly acceptable now (and vice versa). The importance of group reactions is clear when we look at the varied reactions that norm violations generate: some violations are seen as only mildly deviant (like chewing with your mouth open), while others are so strongly taboo that they are almost unthinkable (like cannibalism).

Deviant behavior must be sufficiently serious or unusual to spark a negative sanction or punishment. For example, if you were having dinner with friends and used the wrong fork for your salad, you would be violating a minor norm but your friends probably wouldn't react in a negative fashion; they might not even notice. On the other hand, if you ate an entire steak dinner—meat, mashed potatoes, and salad—with your hands, your friends probably *would* react. They might criticize your behavior strongly ("That's totally disgusting!") and even refuse to eat with you again. This latter example, then, would be considered deviant behavior among your group of friends—and among most groups in American society.

Because definitions of deviance are constructed from cultural, historical, and situational norms, sociologists are interested in a number of topics under the rubric of deviance. First, how are norms and rules created, and how do certain norms and rules become especially important? Second, who is subject to the rules, and how is rule breaking identified? Third, what types of sanctions (punishments or rewards) are dispensed to society's violators? Fourth, how do people who break the rules see themselves, and how do others see them?

And finally, how have sociologists attempted to explain rule making, rule breaking, and responses to rule breaking?

Deviance across Cultures

It is important to remember that when sociologists use the term "deviant," they are making a social judgment, never a moral one. If a particular behavior is considered deviant, this means that it violates the values and norms of a *particular* group, not that it is inherently wrong or that other groups will make the same judgment.

Much of the literature on deviance focuses on crime, but not only do different cultures define strikingly different behaviors as criminal, they also differ in how those crimes are punished. Most serious crime in the United States today is punished by imprisonment. This method of punishment was rare until the nineteenth century, however, as maintaining a prison requires considerable resources. Buildings must be constructed and maintained, guards and other staff must be paid, and prisoners must be fed and clothed. For groups without these resources, incarceration is not a possibility, even assuming it would be a desirable option. Instead, there are a whole host of other techniques of punishment.

For example, the Amish, a religious community whose members do without modern devices like electricity, cars, and telephones, practice *meidung*, which means shunning those who violate the strict norms of the group (Kephart 2000). A biblical rule instructs them "not to associate with any one who bears the name of brother if he is guilty

> **DEVIANCE** a behavior, trait, belief, or other characteristic that violates a norm and causes a negative reaction

of immorality or greed, or is an idolater, reviler, drunkard, or robber—not even to eat with such a one" (1 Corinthians 5:11). In other words, the Amish believe they should not associate with rule breakers even when they come from within their own family. No one does business with, eats with, or even talks to the guilty party. The shunning is temporary, however: after a short period, the violator is expected to publicly apologize and make amends and is then welcomed back into the community.

A much more permanent method of punishment is total banishment from the community. For many Native American people, the social group was so important that banishment was considered a fate worse than death (Champagne 1994). It was one of a variety of practices used to maintain social control (along with shaming songs, contests, and challenges of strength) and something of a rarity because it completely severed ties between the group and the individual. Banishment has a long history of use in all parts of the world, from British prisoners being "transported" to Australia to Russian dissidents being exiled to Siberia, and has been one of the most cost-effective methods of punishment ever discovered.

Just as methods of punishment vary between societies and groups, they also change over time. In Colonial America, for example, corporal punishment was the rule for the majority of crimes (Walker 1997). These days, the phrase "corporal punishment" may conjure up images of elementary school teachers spanking students, probably because spanking was the last vestige of what was once a vast repertoire of techniques. Thieves, pickpockets, and others who would today be considered petty criminals were flogged, had their ears cropped, had their noses slit, had their fingers or hands cut off, or were branded. These punishments were designed not only to deliver pain but also to mark the offender. As such, the particular punishment was often designed to fit the crime. A pickpocket might have a hand cut off; a forger might have an "F" branded on his forehead. Brands were also used to mark African American slaves as property during the 1800s.

Body Modification

Branding has long since died out as a method of punishment, but in a perfect illustration of the mutability of deviance, it has made something of a comeback as a form of body decoration (Parker 1998). What used to be an involuntary mark of shame has been reclaimed as a voluntary mark of pride. Small branding irons of stainless steel are heated with a blowtorch until white hot and are held on the skin for a second or two.

Branding Spencer Evans displays his fraternity Omega Psi Phi's brand on his chest. Branding of one's Greek letter organization by black men has a history dating back to the 1900s to symbolize unity and commitment among members.

Some who undergo the procedure burn incense to cover the smell of their own flesh burning. Many African American fraternities have a long tradition of branding, usually in the shape of one of the fraternity's Greek letters. The practice has received a public boost as several popular athletes have prominently displayed their fraternity brands. Basketball legend Michael Jordan sports such a brand, as does the Detroit Lions' Christopher Owens. Branding is spreading to other subcultures, where it is just another extension of tattoos, Mohawks, and body piercings as an outward manifestation of youthful rebellion, or an expression of personal aesthetic or group identification.

When it comes to body modification, what Americans might label deviant might be identified as desirable or normal in other cultures and vice versa. Among the Suri of southwest Ethiopia, progressively larger plates are inserted into the lower lip so that it gradually becomes enlarged. The Padaung women of Burma stretch their necks with brass rings. Young girls begin by encircling their necks with just a few rings, then add more as they grow; by the time of maturity, their necks are considerably elongated. Breast augmentation surgery is commonplace in the United States, while butt augmentation is popular in Brazil.

Body modification does not always need to be dramatic. In reality, there are a great number of subtle methods of body modification practiced by most Americans that may not seem so obvious if we concentrate on nose rings and biker tattoos. First of all, there have always been body modifications for the middle and upper classes. Corsets, worn by women through the ages until the early twentieth century, are an obvious example. Stomachs were flattened with "stays," long strips of some rigid material like whalebone. A tightly laced corset could achieve a dramatically narrow waistline, but often at a serious cost to the wearer's health. Women sometimes even had ribs removed in order to accommodate them.

These days, we have a rich array of techniques to bring our bodies into line with contemporary standards. Injections of Botox, a strain of the deadly toxin botulism, work by freezing facial nerves, thus reducing fine lines and wrinkles on the forehead that are otherwise caused by normal facial expressions. The hair salon is another great unacknowledged center for body modification. If you get a perm, you are breaking the disulfide bonds in your hair and reshaping them to straighten them or make them curly. Even a simple haircut is a type of body modification—luckily, for those of us who have gotten bad haircuts, they're temporary! Some body modifications seem so "normal" that we practice them as routines without considering how they may seem deviant elsewhere. Other cultures may view Americans' obsession with hair removal—shaving, plucking, tweezing, and waxing—as bizarre. As you can see, whether it's wearing a corset, branding yourself, or shaving your legs, the boundaries between beauty and deviance are fluid across time and place.

One Culture's Deviant Behavior Might Be Desirable or Normal in Another Padaung women use brass rings to stretch their necks, a Suri woman uses plates to modify her lip, an American man has split and pierced his tongue, and J. R. Smith sports extensive body tattoos.

Theories of Deviance

In this section, we will learn how three sociological paradigms discussed in Chapter 1—functionalism, conflict theory, and symbolic interactionism—can be applied to deviance. We will also learn about other, related theories that have been developed specifically to explain particular aspects of deviance.

Functionalism

As you may recall, adherents of functionalism argue that each element of social structure helps maintain the stability of society. What, then, is the function of deviance for society? Émile Durkheim came up with a couple of functions. First, deviance can help a society clarify its moral boundaries. We are reminded about our shared notions of what is right when we have to address wrongdoings of various sorts. In 2005, Terri Schiavo, a hospital patient in St. Petersburg, Florida, received national attention when a legal battle was fought over her life. Schiavo had been in a persistent vegetative state since 1990 and kept alive through a gastric feeding tube. Her husband, Michael, petitioned the courts in 1998 to end life support; he thought it was the right thing to do and was what Terri would have wanted. Her parents, Mary and Robert Schindler, took legal action against Michael's decision—they thought it was wrong. While most people might have had a vague idea of how they felt about artificially prolonging life, the Schiavo case forced them to think concretely about how such choices affect actual people. After a seven-year process, the courts sided with Michael Schiavo, and on March 18, 2005, his wife's feeding tube was removed. She died thirteen days later.

Another function of deviance is to promote social cohesion (one of functionalism's valued ideals); people can be brought together as a community in the face of crime or other violations. For example, while the country was divided over the decision in the Schiavo case, an opinion poll by ABC News on March 21, 2005, reported that 70 percent of Americans believed that Michael Schiavo had the authority to make decisions on behalf of his wife and that the case should not have been a federal matter. In the same poll, 63 percent maintained that the federal government was involved solely for political advantage. Whatever they believed about prolonging life, the majority of Americans thus agreed that the choice was best made by family and not the government.

INNOVATORS individuals who accept society's approved goals but not society's approved means to achieve them

RITUALISTS individuals who have given up hope of achieving society's approved goals but still operate according to society's approved means

RETREATISTS individuals who renounce society's approved goals and means entirely and live outside conventional norms altogether

REBELS individuals who reject society's approved goals and means and instead create and work toward their own (sometimes revolutionary) goals using new means

STRUCTURAL STRAIN THEORY Sociologist Robert Merton (1938/1976) provides a bridge between functionalist and conflict theories of deviance. Like Durkheim, Merton acknowledges that some deviance is inevitable in society. But like conflict theorists, he argues that an individual's position in the social structure will affect his experience of deviance and conformity. Social inequality can create situations in which people experience tension (or strain) between the goals society says they should be working toward (like financial success) and the means they have available to meet those goals (not everyone is able to work hard at a legitimate job). The rewards of conformity, therefore, are available only to those who can pursue approved goals through approved means. Any other combination of means and goals is deviant in one way or another (see Figure 6.1). **Innovators**, for example, might seek financial success via unconventional means (such as drug dealing or embezzlement). **Ritualists** go through the conventional motions while abandoning all hope of success, and **retreatists** (like dropouts or hermits) renounce the culture's goals and means entirely and live outside conventional norms altogether. At the far end of the continuum, **rebels** reject the cultural definitions of success and the normative means of achieving it and advocate radical alternatives to the existing social order.

For example, consider the characters in the 2008 film *The Dark Knight*, an action movie that documents Batman's clean-up of Gotham City. The goal is to combat the corruption that has overcome Gotham through multiple lucrative criminal mobs. In the movie, conformity is represented by District Attorney Harvey Dent, who is attempting to fight crime

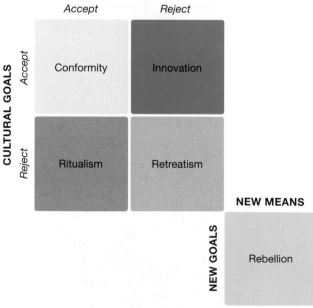

Figure 6.1   Merton's Typology of Deviance

Different orientations toward society's goals and differential access to the means to achieve those goals combine to create different categories of deviance.

Rebel with a Cause In the 2008 film *The Dark Knight*, Batman is an innovator who fights crime unconventionally, Harvey Dent is a ritualist who conforms to established parameters, and the Joker is a rebel intent on bringing about the downfall of Gotham.

through the approved means of the law. Dent, along with Police Lieutenant James Gordon and Assistant D.A. Rachel Dawes, enact a tough campaign to convict all mob bosses through the testimony of their accountant. Batman is an innovator who fights crimes using cunning, high-tech weaponry, and unconventional means that ignore legal process. As always, traditional bureaucrats like Police Commissioner Loeb and the Gotham mayor are ritualists who operate within the parameters that they have been given with little hope of quelling the crime wave. The corrupt Officer Ramirez is a retreatist who actually helps out the mob rather than attempt to fight it. Finally, the Joker, whose portrayal by Heath Ledger won him a posthumous Academy Award, embodies the true spirit of the rebel. Rather than attempting to fight crime, the Joker causes mayhem for both law enforcers and the mob bosses with the ultimate goal of bringing about the downfall of all of Gotham. While the mob bosses stand to gain financially from their crime sprees, the Joker's sadistic goal is to see the entire city descend into chaos and anarchy.

Conflict Theory

Conflict theorists, who study inequalities of wealth and power, note that inequalities are present in our definitions of deviance as well. In other words, conflict theorists believe that rules are applied unequally and that punishments for rule violators are unequally distributed: those at the top are subject to different rules and sanctions than those nearer the bottom, and the behaviors of less powerful groups and individuals are more likely to be criminalized than the behaviors of the powerful. Norms, rules, and laws are used to regulate the behavior of individuals and groups. This process, known as **social control**, can be either informal, as in the exercise of control

through customs, norms, and expectations, or formal, as in the exercise of control through laws or other official regulations. Both formal social control and informal social control can be exercised unequally in a hierarchical society, and this is what conflict theory is concerned with when it comes to the topic of deviance.

As recently as 2003, more than a dozen U.S. states still imposed heterosexuality on their citizens through anti-sodomy laws, which prohibited any sexual acts that did not lead to procreation. While in theory anti-sodomy laws could include acts like masturbation and heterosexual oral sex, in practice these laws were generally imposed against same-sex partners. Before a Supreme Court ruling invalidated all state anti-sodomy laws in *Lawrence v. Texas* (2003), sexual acts done in the privacy of your own home could be penalized with fines and jail time in states such as Florida, Idaho, and Michigan. From a conflict theorist perspective, anti-sodomy laws were a way for the heterosexual majority to exercise control over same-sex minorities.

As another example, in 2006, Rochester, New York, had the highest murder rate per capita in the entire state, including New York City. The mayor, Robert Duffy, proposed a new law that would require all young people age sixteen and under living within city limits to be off the streets from 11:00 PM to 6:00 AM during the summer break from school. Because statistics have shown that more crime occurs during the summer among youth living in the city, Duffy believed that the curfew would reduce violence. The curfew demonstrates not only ageism, in that control is wielded by adults over relatively powerless youth, but also classism, as the curfew applies only to kids who live in the city, leaving wealthier teens in the suburbs free to do what they like.

> **SOCIAL CONTROL**
> the formal and informal mechanisms used to elicit conformity to values and norms and thus promote social cohesion

Social Control The HBO series *The Wire* was set in Baltimore and focused on topics such as drug dealing, government corruption, and failed school systems. How might a conflict theorist analyze this scene?

DIFFERENTIAL ASSOCIATION THEORY Edwin Sutherland's hypothesis that we learn to be deviant through our associations with deviant peers

LABELING THEORY Howard Becker's idea that deviance is a consequence of external judgments, or labels, that modify the individual's self-concept and change the way others respond to the labeled person

The recent and ongoing controversy over voter identification laws reveals how policies that some would argue are neutral really do affect some groups differently than others. As of summer 2015, twelve states had a photo identification requirement for voters, meaning that voters must show a photo ID in order to cast a vote. While supporters of such laws argue that they help stem voter fraud, opponents say that voter fraud is almost nonexistent. They argue that voter ID requirements are really meant to keep various groups—ethnic and racial minorities, immigrants, the elderly, and the poor, all of whom tend to vote Democrat—away from the voting booth. These groups don't always have IDs and may have trouble getting them, especially if there is a fee involved. Unfortunately, there is a good deal of evidence to support the conflict theorists' argument that rules are applied unequally in our hierarchical society.

Symbolic Interactionism

While conflict theorists and functionalists focus on inequalities and the social functions of deviance, interactionists consider the way that interpersonal relationships and everyday interactions shape definitions of deviance.

DIFFERENTIAL ASSOCIATION THEORY One such approach is Edwin Sutherland's **differential association theory** (Sutherland 1939; Sutherland et al. 1992), which asserts that we learn to be deviant through our interactions with others who break the rules. This is the theory of deviance that your parents subscribed to when you were a teenager: don't hang out with the bad kids! Simple peer pressure by those you associate with can lead to deviant behavior. For instance, an athlete who uses steroids to help build strength might also influence his teammate to start "doping" even though this practice is banned in most sports. Have you ever been influenced by others to do something deviant that you would have never tried on your own?

This theory of deviance seems at first glance to be pretty sensible—interacting often with those who break the rules would seem to socialize an individual into their rule-breaking culture. But, as it turns out, not all who hang out with deviants become deviant themselves, and plenty of people who engage in deviant acts have never consorted with other rule breakers. Also, in cases where deviance is not the result of a willful act (mental illness, for example), a learning theory such as this one is not a useful explanation. While differential association theory seeks to explain "why they do it," it cannot fully explain every case of deviant behavior—nor can any theory of deviance.

LABELING THEORY Howard Becker's **labeling theory** (1963) proposes that deviance is not inherent in any act, belief, or condition; instead, it is determined by the social context. A man who kills an intruder who is attacking his child may be labeled a hero, while a man who kills a cashier in the process of robbing a store may be labeled a villain. Even though the act of homicide is the same, the way the person who did it is treated differs greatly depending on the label.

Labeling theory recognizes that labels will vary depending on the culture, time period, and situation. David Rosenhan's study "On Being Sane in Insane Places" (1973) provides a striking demonstration of the power of labeling and the importance of context. Rosenhan and seven other researchers gained admission to psychiatric hospitals as patients. Other than falsifying their names and occupations, the eight subjects gave honest answers to all but one of the questions in the entrance examination. They all complained of hearing voices, a symptom often linked to schizophrenia. Nevertheless, the subjects felt certain that once they were hospitalized, they would be quickly exposed as "pseudo-patients," not really mentally ill.

In fact, the opposite turned out to be true. Once admitted, the pseudo-patients turned immediately to the task of getting themselves discharged—and failed miserably. Although they behaved as normally and pleasantly as possible, doctors and nurses continued to treat them as mentally ill patients in need of treatment. No amount of explanation on the part of the pseudo-patients could convince the hospital staff of their sanity (though, in an interesting twist, it was usually obvious to the other patients). When they were finally discharged (after one to seven weeks!), it was not because the staff had finally seen through the deception; they were all released with their schizophrenia "in remission." As Rosenhan concluded,

"Once labeled schizophrenic, the pseudo-patient was stuck with that label" (1973, p. 253). The effects of this "sticky" deviant label on actual patients can follow them through their lives, even after they leave the hospital.

Labeling theory is also concerned with how individuals think of themselves once a deviant label has been applied. Recall Cooley's concept of the "looking-glass self": how we perceive ourselves depends in part on how others see us, so if others react to us as deviant, we are likely to internalize that label (even if we object to it). Applying deviant labels can also lead to further deviance, as a person moves from **primary deviance** (the thing that gets her labeled in the first place) to **secondary deviance** (a deviant identity or career) (Lemert 1951).

If you watched VH1's *Celebrity Rehab with Dr. Drew*, you've seen examples of both types of deviance. In the show, washed-up celebrities who suffered from addiction checked themselves into a fancy rehab center, and viewers followed the ups and downs of their treatment over the course of each season. Their drug use, which is illegal, was an example of primary deviance,

PRIMARY DEVIANCE in labeling theory, the initial act or attitude that causes one to be labeled deviant

SECONDARY DEVIANCE in labeling theory, the subsequent deviant identity or career that develops as a result of being labeled deviant

Labeling Theory VH1's reality show *Celebrity Rehab with Dr. Drew* centered on celebrities struggling with addiction and showed how their illness influenced their identity and how others perceived them.

and their recognition that they were addicts was an example of secondary deviance.

Although deviant labels are sticky and hard to shake, it is sometimes possible for an individual to turn what could have been a negative identity into a positive one. John Kitsuse (1980) calls this **tertiary deviance**, which occurs when the person labeled deviant rejects the notion of deviance entirely and attempts to redefine her "deviant" attributes or behavior as normal. Some members of the *Celebrity Rehab* cast demonstrated this level of deviance as well. Every once in a while, one of the celebrities would decide that he was no longer interested in undergoing rehab, often arguing that there was really nothing wrong with his drug use and that he should be able to indulge in it as he saw fit. This argument— "sure, I'm an addict, but there shouldn't be anything wrong with that"—is an attempt to recast that identity as acceptable difference rather than deviance.

Some of the most exciting, but also disturbing, research on labeling theory has focused on **self-fulfilling prophecy**, a term coined by Robert Merton in his 1948 article of the same name. Merton's concept was derived from the so-called Thomas theorem, formulated by sociologist W. I. Thomas in 1928, which held that "if men define situations as real, they are real in their consequences." From this theorem, Merton developed his notion of the self-fulfilling prophecy, which is basically a prediction that causes itself to come true merely by being stated. He offered the example of a bank in the Depression-era 1930s that collapsed through "a rumor of insolvency," when enough investors became convinced that the bank was out of money (1948, p. 194).

Merton argued that the self-fulfilling prophecy can be used to explain some racial and ethnic issues in the United States, and subsequent research has borne him out. For example, Elijah Anderson's *Streetwise* (1990) details how the police and community perceive black male inner-city teenagers as a criminal element, with the result that they are more likely to be arrested than other teenagers, and citizens are also more likely to report black males for crimes. This cloud of suspicion that surrounds black urban teens requires them to defend their innocence in situations that other teens can negotiate with little or no difficulty. Young black males are also more likely to be incarcerated, which only feeds the public image of criminality. The racial discrimination and profiling by police and the community thus lead to a negative cycle that is difficult to break.

Stereotypes are often part of self-fulfilling prophecies. Claude Steele's research (1997) on **stereotype threat** shows that when students worry that their own poor academic

TERTIARY DEVIANCE redefining the stigma associated with a deviant label as a positive phenomenon

SELF-FULFILLING PROPHECY an inaccurate statement or belief that, by altering the situation, becomes accurate; a prediction that causes itself to come true

STEREOTYPE THREAT a kind of self-fulfilling prophecy in which the fear of performing poorly— and confirming stereotypes about their social groups—causes students to perform poorly.

Table 6.1   Theory in Everyday Life

Perspective	Approach to Deviance	Case Study: Plagiarism
Structural Functionalism	Deviance clarifies moral boundaries and promotes social cohesion.	Punishing those who plagiarize separates those who should be in college from those who aren't responsible enough.
Structural Strain Theory	An individual's position in society determines whether she has the means to achieve her goals or must otherwise turn to deviance.	A student's attitude about plagiarizing depends on whether she has the means to write the paper.
Conflict Theory	Definitions and rules of deviance are applied unequally based on power.	Students with fewer resources are punished harshly and have fewer options afterward; students with more money or connections can either transfer to another school or rely on their parents for help.
Symbolic Interactionism	The definition of deviance is relative and depends on the culture, time period, and situation.	Plagiarism may be labeled as deviant in the United States but not in Russia or India.
Differential Association Theory	Deviance is learned through interactions with others who break the rules.	Students learn to cheat because they hang out with other students who plagiarize.
Labeling Theory	Deviance is determined by the reactions of others; applying deviant labels to an individual may lead her to further deviance.	A student who is caught plagiarizing may come to believe she is unable to write without cheating.

performance could unintentionally confirm a negative stereotype of their social group, they actually perform poorly, thus confirming that stereotype. Stereotype threat has been measured in high-achieving African American students as well as highly ranked female math students (Spencer, Steele, and Quinn, 1999). And because both stereotypes and self-fulfilling prophecies are not always negative, Jennifer Lee and Min Zhou (2014) found that Asian American students can actually benefit from both. In the case of **stereotype promise**, Asian American students are more likely to be placed in Advanced Placement (AP) classes, receive high grades, and be treated well by teachers because others assume that they are high achievers. In both cases, the stereotypes become real as people (teachers, students, others) act based on them—even in cases where students are trying to avoid this very problem.

Labels alone are not 100 percent deterministic, and prophecies are not always self-fulfilling. But in our society, deviant labels can override other aspects of individual identity and exert powerful effects on self-image, treatment by others, and even social and institutional policies.

Stigma and Deviant Identity

In ancient Greece, criminals and slaves were branded with hot irons, making a mark called a **stigma**, from the Greek word for tattoo. The stigma was meant to serve as an outward indication that there was something shameful about the bearer, and to this day we continue to use the term to signify some disgrace or failing. Although we no longer live in a society where we are forced to wear our rule violations branded onto our bodies, stigmatized identities still carry serious social consequences.

Stigma, a central concept in the sociology of deviance, was analyzed and elaborated by Erving Goffman in his book of the same name (1962). Once an individual has been labeled as deviant, he is stigmatized and acquires what Goffman calls a "spoiled identity." There are three main types of stigma: physical (including physical or mental impairments), moral (signs of a flawed character), and tribal (membership in a discredited or oppressed group). Almost any departure from the norm can have a stigmatizing effect, including a physical disability, a past battle with alcohol or mental illness, time served in jail, or sexual transgressions. Goffman recognizes that what may once have been a stigmatized identity may change over time or may vary according to culture or social context. Being black or Jewish is a stigma only if one lives in a racist or anti-Semitic society. In a community entirely populated by African Americans, it is white people who may be stigmatized; an all-Jewish enclave may see non-Jews as outside the norm. Goffman is careful to note that not all stigmatized identities are just or deserved—only that they are specific to the norms and prejudices of a particular group, time period, or context.

Goffman was particularly interested in the effects of stigmatization on individual identity and interactions with others. At the macro level, society does not treat the stigmatized very well; if you suffer from serious depression, for example, you may find that your health insurance does not cover your treatment. At the micro level, you may also find that your friends don't fully understand your depression-related problems. In fact, you may find yourself working to keep others from finding out that you are depressed or receiving treatment for depression precisely in order to avoid such situations. Having a stigmatized identity—of any sort—makes navigating the social world difficult.

Passing

How can stigmatized individuals negotiate the perils of everyday interaction? One strategy analyzed by Goffman is called **passing**, or concealing stigmatizing information. The allusion to racial passing is entirely intended—Goffman meant to call to mind the experiences of light-skinned African Americans who, for more than 300 years and particularly

Imitation of Life In this 1959 film, Juanita Moore (right) plays a widow whose daughter, played by Susan Kohner (left), tries to pass as white and shuns her mother.

STEREOTYPE PROMISE a kind of self-fulfilling prophecy in which positive stereotypes, such as the "model minority" label applied to Asian Americans, lead to positive performance outcomes for Asian Americans.

STIGMA Erving Goffman's term for any physical or social attribute that devalues a person or group's identity and that may exclude those who are devalued from normal social interaction

PASSING presenting yourself as a member of a different group than the stigmatized group you belong to

in the decades before the civil rights movement of the 1960s, sought access to the privileges of whiteness (and relief from discrimination) by concealing their racial heritage and passing as white. The case of racial passing is instructive in developing an understanding of all types of passing—such as the passing a depressed person might engage in to hide his condition. There are reasons why members of other stigmatized groups might also use passing in order to conceal their deviant identities in certain social contexts.

In-Group Orientation

Not everyone can pass, though, because not all stigma is concealable. While it may be possible to conceal your status as an ex-convict or survivor of rape, it is more difficult to conceal extreme shortness or obesity. And while some people cannot pass, others refuse to do so as a matter of principle. These people don't believe that their identities should be seen as deviant, and they certainly don't believe that they should have to change or conceal those identities just to make "normals" feel more comfortable. They have what Goffman calls an **in-group orientation**—they reject the standards that mark them as deviant and may even actively propose new standards in which their special identities are well within the

normal range. For example, such groups as PFLAG (Parents, Families, and Friends of Lesbians and Gays), NAD (National Association of the Deaf), and NAAFA (the National Association to Advance Fat Acceptance) have allowed members of stigmatized groups to feel greater self-esteem and to unite in fighting against prejudice and discrimination. Activism might also take a more individual form of merely being "out," open, and unapologetic about one's identity. This in itself can be difficult and exhausting (as passing is); however, those with an in-group orientation see it as a powerful way to address society's changing definitions of deviance.

Deviance Avowal and Voluntary Outsiders

Under most circumstances, people reject the deviant label and what it seems to imply about their personal identity. However, there are some who *choose* to be called a deviant. Those who belong to a particular subculture, for example—whether outlaw biker, rock musician, or eco-warrior—may celebrate their membership in a deviant group. Howard Becker (1963) referred to such individuals as **outsiders**, people living in one way or another outside mainstream society. They may pass among "normals," continuing to work and participate in everyday life. Or their deviant identity may have become a master status, thus preventing them from interacting along conventional lines; when this happens, a person's deviance may be thought to reveal his underlying nature. For instance, members of the punk subculture, easily identified by their distinctive look, are generally assumed to be loud troublemakers, whatever their individual personality traits may be.

Some potential deviants may actually initiate the labeling process against themselves or provoke others to do so, a condition Ralph Turner (1972) calls **deviance avowal**. Turner suggests that it may be useful to conceive of deviance as a role rather than as an isolated behavior that violates a single norm. And in some cases, it may be beneficial for an individual to identify with the deviant role. In the Alcoholics Anonymous program, for example, the first step in recovery is for a member to admit that she is an alcoholic. Since total abstinence from drinking is the goal, only those who believe they have a drinking problem and who willingly accept the label of alcoholic can take the suggested steps toward recovery.

Deviance avowal can also help a person avoid the pressures of having to adopt certain conventional norms, or what Turner calls the "neutralization of commitment." For instance, a recovering alcoholic might resist taking a typical nine-to-five job, claiming that the stress of corporate work had always made him drink before. Another recovering alcoholic who refuses to attend family gatherings might offer as an excuse that she can't be around family because they drink at every occasion. In such ways, people become voluntary outsiders, finding it preferable to be a deviant in spite of the prevailing norms of mainstream society.

United Against Prejudice Through events like the Million Pound March, groups like the National Association to Advance Fat Acceptance embrace an in-group orientation and reject the standards that mark them as deviant.

DATA WORKSHOP
Analyzing Everyday Life

AA's Pioneer Women

Alcoholics Anonymous offers an interesting case where members choose to embrace a deviant identity as a positive aspect of themselves, one that is critical to their success in the program. Research by Melvin Pollner and Jill Stein (1996, 2001) has focused on the role of narrative storytelling as a key feature of reconstructing the alcoholic's sense of self and turning a stigmatized identity into a valued asset in the process of recovery. The basic text of the 12-step program is laid out in the book *Alcoholics Anonymous* (1939/2001), often referred to by members as the "Big Book." Its first 164 pages have remained virtually the same since it was first published in 1939; it is now in its fourth edition. The book also includes dozens of personal stories written by AA members themselves. These chapters always begin with the "Pioneers of A.A.," but in each subsequent edition some new (and more modern) stories have been added, while others have been dropped. That such a large part of the Big Book is devoted to the personal stories of members shows their importance. They are intended to help newcomers to the program identify with and relate to the lives of other recovering alcoholics and to follow their examples.

In this Data Workshop, you will examine the story of "Marty M."—one of AA's pioneers and one of the first women to join the program, way back in 1939, when the book was just being written. Her story is the fourth that appears (but not until the second and subsequent editions) and is called "Women Suffer Too." The title refers to a widely held notion at the time that only men could be alcoholics. The idea of a woman alcoholic was almost unthinkable. Marty M. defied the conventions of her day in many ways. She was a divorcee, entrepreneur, world traveler, and later, philanthropist. But first and foremost, she was a sober drunk. Marty M.'s story follows the classic narrative structure of all AA stories: what we used to be like, what happened, and what we are like now. It is told from the perspective of a sober alcoholic looking back on her life and understanding that through the process of deviance avowal (by accepting her alcoholism) she was able to transform a negative past into a positive life.

For this Data Workshop you will be examining an existing source and doing a content analysis of the story "Women Suffer Too." Refer to Chapter 2 for a review of this research method. The text of the story can be found in the Big Book (pages 222–229) and accessed online at various websites, including http://www.aa.org/assets/en_US/en_bigbook_personalstories_partI.pdf.

Read the story in its entirety, keeping in mind how the study of life histories or oral histories can reveal important features of societal norms and everyday life. Remember that Marty M. lived in a particular time period and social context. Pay close attention to how the story describes both deviant behavior and the process of deviance avowal, and consider the following questions:

* Identify the instances of deviance described in the author's story. Why were these behaviors considered deviant?

* In what ways was she in denial about her condition early on? How did she actively try to disavow the deviant label?

* At what point did she begin the process of deviance avowal? How did admitting that she was an alcoholic affect her self-concept?

* In what ways did deviance avowal allow her to see her past in a different light? How did her deviant identity finally become a positive part of her life?

* How have our perceptions about alcoholics and alcoholism changed since the pioneer days of AA?

There are two options for completing this Data Workshop:

PREP-PAIR-SHARE Prepare some written notes based on your answers to the questions that you can refer to during in-class discussions. Share your reactions and conclusions with other students in small groups. Listen for any differences in each other's insights.

DO-IT-YOURSELF Write a three- to four-page essay answering the questions. Include your own reactions to the story. Make sure to refer to specific passages from the story that help to support your analysis.

What is "murderball"? Well, technically it's wheelchair rugby played by quadriplegics in specially modified chairs. But as described by a member of the USA Paralympic team, it's basically "kill the man with the ball." This incredibly rough-and-tumble game, chronicled in the eponymous 2005 documentary, has a set of adapted rules that make it look a bit like full-tackle basketball. The rugby wheelchairs are dented and dinged, bearing the scars of violent play that often sees players dumped upside-down onto the gym floor, unable to right themselves without assistance. Except for the wheelchairs, murderball is on a par with any other high-level competitive sport.

The filmmakers follow the team to practices, games, and autograph signings and watch them field questions on press junkets and during motivational speeches. The athletes are buff, the training is grueling, the fans are loud, and the machismo is unescapable. These guys (Team USA is all male, though the sport does have female players) drink as much beer, have as many tattoos, and talk as much trash as other elite athletes. Indeed, they may engage in the performance of heteromasculinity more strenuously and more openly than athletes who are not disabled (Barounis 2013). A good portion of the film is given over to the team members' conversations about sex, with each of them asserting that they are completely functional, sexually, and that they really like women. Girlfriends and female groupies appear in the film by way of underscoring this point, and when the men are amongst themselves there is much talk of "woodies," "jerking off," and other references to their fully operational phalluses.

Murderball emphasizes the importance to these men of their sexual and romantic relationships with women, but these are not the only significant relationships in their lives. Their bonds with their teammates feature a distinctive combination of empathy and competitiveness. Their family relationships are important because of the role they played (and still play) in each man's rehabilitation from his injuries. The coach of the rival Canadian team (also quadriplegic) talks about what a tough disciplinarian he is with his children. And

Wheelchair rugby, also known as murderball, gives the quadriplegic players the opportunity to assert their masculinity in a society where being disabled means being deviant.

their patriotic relationship to their nation is significant, as they represent the United States in international competition.

All of these relationships are conducted under the shadow of disability. Being a quadriplegic means being deviant in a society that privileges able bodies, and so these men work hard to show how ordinary they are in the relationship department. In that way, they seem to be trying to conform to norms of heterosexuality and expectations for becoming husbands and fathers. Indeed, they present their injuries as the result of notably manly activities (for example, drunken fights, motorcycle stunt accidents, etc.)—so in some way, quadriplegia confirms their masculinity rather than challenging it. As a result, they seem to put very little energy into "normalizing" their bodies. Those who wear prostheses do so only occasionally, and only when unavoidable. They spend almost no camera time talking about wanting to walk or wishing they could use their arms or hands again the way they used to before their injuries. By framing their relationships (especially sexual relationships with women) and their athlete status as meeting and even exceeding normative standards of masculinity, they seek to make the question of their bodies' deviance moot.

Studying Deviance

When studying deviance, sociologists have often focused on the most obvious forms of deviant behavior—crime, mental illness, and sexual deviance. This "nuts and sluts" approach (Liazos 1972) usually focuses on the deviance of the poor and powerless, while accepting the values and norms of the powerful in an unacknowledged way. Social scientists tended to apply definitions of deviance uncritically in their research and failed to question the ways in which the definitions themselves may have perpetuated inequalities and untruths.

David Matza (1969), a sociologist at the University of California, Berkeley, set out to remedy this situation. He urged social scientists to set aside their preconceived notions in order to understand deviant phenomena on their own terms—a perspective he called "naturalism." Leila Rupp and Verta Taylor, for example, spent three years with a dozen drag queens in order to gain perspective for their research in *Drag Queens at the 801 Cabaret* (2003)—at one point, they even performed onstage (see Part II's introduction to read more). Matza's fundamental admonition to those studying deviance is that they must appreciate the diversity and complexity of a particular social world—the world of street gangs, drug addicts, strippers, fight clubs, outlaw bikers, homeless people, or the severly disfigured. If such a world is approached as a simple social pathology that needs correcting, the researcher will never fully understand it. A sociological perspective requires that we seek insight without applying judgment—a difficult task indeed.

The Foreground of Deviance: The Emotional Attraction of Doing Bad Deeds

Most sociological perspectives on deviance focus on aspects of a person's background that would influence him to act in deviant ways. This is the case with both functionalist and conflict perspectives. For example, many sociological studies of crime make the case that youth with limited access to education may be more likely to turn to dealing drugs or theft. Labeling theory also suggests that a person's social location is a crucial determinant: it shapes how others see the person, as well as his or her own self-view, and these perceptions can lead a person from primary to secondary deviance and into a deviant career. One of the main problems with such theories, however, is that they can't explain why some people with backgrounds that should incline them to deviance never actually violate any rules, while others with no defining background factors do become deviant.

Approaches that focus exclusively on background factors neglect one very important element: the deviant's own in-the-moment experience of committing a deviant act, what sociologist Jack Katz refers to as the "foreground" of deviance. In *The Seductions of Crime* (1988), Katz looks at how emotionally seductive crime can be, how shoplifting or even committing murder might produce a particular kind of rush that becomes the very reason for carrying out the act. For example, what shoplifters often seek is not the DVD or perfume itself as much as the "sneaky thrill" of stealing it. Initially drawn to stealing by the thought of just how easy it might be, the shoplifter tests her ability to be secretly deviant—in public—while appearing to be perfectly normal. This perspective explains why the vast majority of shoplifters are not from underprivileged backgrounds but are people who could easily afford the stolen items. How else might we explain why a wealthy and famous actress such as Lindsay Lohan would try to steal a necklace from a jewelry store?

Similarly, muggers' and robbers' actions reveal that they get more satisfaction from their crimes than from the things they steal. They are excited by the sense of superiority they gain by setting up and playing tricks on their victims. In fact, they can come to feel morally superior, thinking that their victims deserve their fate because they are less observant and savvy. Even murderous rages can be seen as seductive ways to overcome an overwhelming sense of humiliation. A victim of adultery, for example, may kill instead of simply ending the relationship because murder, or "righteous slaughter," feels like the most appropriate response. In a real-life example from 2014, twenty-two-year-old gunman Elliott Rodger killed seven people (including himself) and wounded thirteen in Isla Vista, California. He left behind a video manifesto explaining that he was angry after being romantically rejected by women. In effect, he was seduced by the possibility of becoming a powerful avenger rather than remaining a wounded and impotent victim.

Katz's foreground model of deviance deepens our appreciation for the complexity of deviant behavior and reminds us that social actors are not mere products of their environment but active participants in creating meaningful experiences for themselves, even if harmful to others.

Deviance in a New Interactional Context: Cyberbullying

Although parents and schools have been worried about cyberbullying ever since children and teenagers started using the Internet, the phenomenon moved to the forefront of national consciousness after the suicide of thirteen-year-old Megan Meier in October 2006. Megan had received an online message from a boy named Josh, who said he lived nearby but that his family didn't have a phone. During the next several

IN THE FUTURE
Porn Studies and Changing Definitions of Deviance

Meet Dr. Chauntelle Tibbals.

She holds a PhD in sociology from the University of Texas at Austin, and she has published her research in some of the highest-ranking academic journals in her field. Over the course of her career, she has earned a visiting scholar position at the University of Southern California, provided authoritative commentary in major media outlets like CNN, and spoken in prestigious venues such as the Stanford University School of Law. She maintains a popular blog and produces regular podcasts on issues related to her research. So, what is this distinguished scholar's area of expertise?

Porn.

That's right. Dr. Chauntelle (as she's often called on the Internet) is a sociologist who specializes in the study of pornography and the adult entertainment industry. Only a few years ago, a career like hers would have been unimaginable. The topics she addresses range widely and include condom use in adult content (Tibbals 2012), the increase and then decline in breast augmentation among women adult performers (Tibbals 2010), and an ethnographic perspective on women's work behind the scenes in the porn industry (Tibbals 2013). While she is a feminist who takes a social justice perspective in her work, her research does not assume a negative perspective on the adult film industry.

Past studies have tended to concentrate on whether and how pornography is harmful to individuals (women, men, and children) and society (Attwood 2011), and the larger culture still seems committed to this view of pornographic media as dangerous and corrupting. Policy perspectives on sexuality tend to reflect this outlook. Indeed, in 2012, a tenured sociology professor was disciplined by Appalachian State University for showing a documentary about the pornography industry in her classroom (she had borrowed it from the school's own library!). But new research reflects a "paradigm shift" in social and cultural studies' view of pornography (Attwood 2011).

Porn itself is more readily available than ever before due to technological advances such as the Internet and mobile phones—no longer does one have to hide one's stash of magazines under the proverbial mattress! Porn is also more influential in the wider media world, with mainstream media borrowing the "styles, gestures and aesthetics" of the genre (Attwood 2011, p. 15). Our culture itself is becoming

Dr. Chauntelle Tibbals Her new book, *Exposure* (2015), explores sex, society, and adult entertainment.

more sexualized (Attwood 2009), and pornographic metaphors have crept into other areas of social life. People throw around terms like "food porn," "travel porn," or "car porn" to talk about media representations of alluring but out-of-reach victuals, vacations, and vehicles. Phrases like "money shot" and "fluffing" (which Dr. Chauntelle says is actually a myth) are moving into common parlance, and almost all of us have heard someone laughingly imitate '70s porn soundtracks: "bow-chicka-wow-wow." What used to be "obscene" is now "on-scene"—meaning that it is increasingly present in ordinary public discourse (Williams 2004).

As public responses to pornography change, so do those of social science researchers. For example, whereas scholars were once almost universally critical of porn as a media genre that objectifies women and contributes to sexual violence, people like Dr. Chauntelle are now addressing previously overlooked and under-researched topics and issues such as cybersex (Waskul 2004; Valkyrie 2011), women's porn consumption (McCleary and Tewksbury 2010), and the "pornification" of other media (Paasonen et al. 2007). This paradigm-shifting pornography research will likely make its way into public debates in the future, which means that society will have to expand its sense of what is "normal" to include things that have in the past been framed as dangerous and deviant . . . and legislate accordingly. Are we ready for that?

weeks, they sent messages back and forth and seemed to have become close very quickly. Then, without warning, Josh started taunting and abusing her. Megan was devastated and hung herself in her closet. Several weeks later, the Meiers learned that "Josh" was not a real person and that the online account had been created by neighborhood mom Lori Drew, in order to get back at Megan for snubbing her daughter. Megan was a victim of **cyberbullying**, the use of electronic and social media to tease, harass, threaten, or humiliate someone. In 2014, 35 percent of all young people said they had been the victim of cyberbullying (Patchin and Hinduja 2014).

Although cyberbullying is still less common than its off-line equivalent, in several ways it's more frightening. Like every phenomenon created by the Information Revolution, cyberbullying (sometimes called "electronic aggression") is faster and connects more people than off-line activity. Traditional bullying usually happens at school, while cyberbullying can happen anytime and in the privacy of your own home. Likewise, the effects are longer lasting. One of the most

common forms of cyberbullying is spreading rumors about someone. Traditional bullying relied on word of mouth or the proverbial graffiti on the bathroom wall to do this. But word

> **CYBERBULLYING** the use of electronic media (web pages, social networking sites, e-mail, Twitter, cell phones) to tease, harass, threaten, or humiliate someone

of mouth is limited, and only so many people can read nasty comments scrawled on the stall in the bathroom before the janitor washes it off. Online, there is almost no limit to how many people might see a nasty comment, even if it is later taken down.

So far, most research has focused on cyberbullying that is perpetrated by someone who knows the victim in real life, but there have always been Internet bullies (or "trolls") who seek to abuse people they've never met or have only encountered online. For example, after Megan Meier's suicide, a blog was created called "Megan Had It Coming" that contained posts from a cast of characters who purported to know Megan, all expressing a distinct lack of remorse. Later it was established that the entire blog was really the work of a thirty-two-year-old computer programmer from Seattle with no connection to anyone involved in the case but who had a history of humiliating others online and expressed pride at his achievements in this regard. Indeed, "trolls" seem to enjoy their abusive activities and often continue under different usernames even after they have been blocked by service providers or website administrators. As more and more of people's lives play out online, cyberbullying will only become more common.

Cyberbullying Tina Meier holds two pictures of her daughter Megan, who committed suicide after receiving cruel online messages.

DATA WORKSHOP
Analyzing Media and Pop Culture

Norm Breaking on Television

It's clear that deviance is a fascinating subject not only for sociologists but for millions of television viewers as well. That's why we've seen a proliferation of shows in recent years that feature people breaking almost every kind of social norm imaginable, from folkways to taboos. We might expect to see deviance covered in a talk show or newsmagazine program, but it's a staple of many other genres. We see it in reality TV shows like *Teen Mom*, which focuses on how high schoolers deal with pregnancy and parenthood, and *Mafia Wives*, which portrays women whose husbands may be criminals with mob connections. But it's not just reality TV shows that feature deviance. Dramas such as *NCIS* or *The Black List*, comedies such as *Unbreakable Kimmy Schmidt* or *Mom*, hybrids such as *Transparent* or *Orange Is the New Black*, and even animated shows such as *The Simpsons* or *Family Guy* all deal with various elements of the pathological or dysfunctional. And there are many more such shows that we could add to the list.

Why is there so much deviance on television? Are these shows merely entertainment, or is something more going on here? When we watch them, do we feel morally superior or get some kind of vicarious thrill? Does exposure to so much deviance help reinforce our social norms or serve to erode them?

For this Data Workshop you will be using existing sources and doing a content analysis of an episode from a particular TV show. Return to Chapter 2 for a review of this research method. Choose a contemporary TV show that is available for multiple viewings, either by recording it or accessing it online or on DVD. As you watch the episode, take some notes about the content and try to document all the ways in which deviant behavior is portrayed on the show. Then consider the following:

* Who is the intended audience for this program? Why did you choose it?

* What kind of deviance is featured? Give specific examples of situations, scenes, dialogue, or characters, and explain why they are examples of deviance.

* Is the deviance celebrated or condemned?

* How does it make you feel to watch the program?

* What effect do you think the show has on other viewers?

Orange Is the New Black, which follows the lives of female inmates at the fictional Litchfield Penitentiary, is one of many shows currently on air that features deviance.

* Do you think the program supports or challenges prevailing social norms?

There are two options for completing this Data Workshop:

PREP-PAIR-SHARE Watch your chosen episode and bring some written notes to class that you can refer to in small-group discussions. Compare and contrast the analyses of the different programs in your group. What are the similarities and differences among programs?

DO-IT-YOURSELF View your chosen TV program, taking some informal notes about the episode. Write a three- to four-page essay answering the questions and reflecting on your own experience conducting this content analysis. What do you think these shows tell us about contemporary American society and our attitudes toward deviance? Attach your notes to the paper, and include a citation for the episode you viewed.

Crime and Punishment

Crime is a particular type of deviance: it is the violation of a norm that has been codified into law, for which you could be arrested and imprisoned. Official state-backed sanctions, such as laws, exert more power over the individual than do nonlegal norms. For example, if you risked arrest for gossiping about your roommate, you might think twice about doing it. "Might," however, is the key word here, for the risk of arrest and jail time does not always deter people from breaking laws. In fact, ordinary people break laws every day without really thinking about it (speeding, underage drinking, stealing those pens and pencils from the office). As we saw earlier, being bad can feel good, and even murder can feel righteous at the time, depending on the circumstances (Katz 1988).

In the United States, crime is officially measured by the **Uniform Crime Report (UCR)**, the FBI's tabulation of every crime reported by more than 18,000 law enforcement agencies around the country. In particular, the UCR is used to track the "crime index," or the eight offenses considered especially reprehensible in our society (see Figure 6.2). Murder, rape, aggravated assault, and robbery are categorized as **violent crime**. Burglary (theft inside the home), larceny (of personal property), motor vehicle theft, and arson are considered **property crime**. Even though the UCR has been shown to be a flawed system (participation by agencies is voluntary, and the FBI rarely audits it for accuracy), it is useful in helping track trends in overall crime as well as particular patterns; it also records the number of arrests made compared with the number of crimes committed, which is the most traditional measure of police effectiveness.

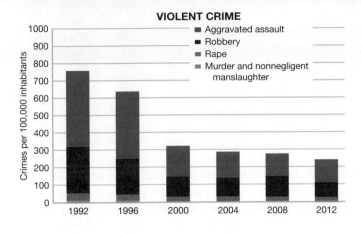

Figure 6.2 Crime in the United States, 1992–2012

SOURCE: Federal Bureau of Investigation 2014a.

Through the UCR, criminologists are able to make comparisons in crime rates using such variables as year and region. One notable finding is that rates of violent crime declined significantly in the last decade of the twentieth century. The year 1991 saw the highest homicide rates in U.S. history, at 9.8 per 100,000 persons or 24,700 murders. Between 1991 and 2000, there was a dramatic drop in homicide rates, and the number continued to decline to 4.5 per 100,000 persons, or 14,196 murders, in 2013 (Federal Bureau of Investigation 2014a). Other findings include the observation that murder rates peak in the months of July and August. Perhaps related to summer heat and humidity, they are also higher in the Southern states. Financial hardship may influence murder rates, as Southern states also have the lowest median family incomes. Other patterns identifiable in UCR data: murder is committed most frequently by a friend or relative of the victim and seldom by a stranger; robbery occurs most frequently in urban areas among youth.

Other trends are visible in the UCR as well. Property crimes occur more frequently than violent crimes. The most common crime is larceny, with burglary and motor vehicle theft trailing far behind. Although there has also been a decline in rates of property crime in the last decade, it is not as extreme as the drop in violent crime.

Crime and Demographics

When criminologists look at quantitative crime data, which provide information on who is more likely to commit or be a victim of crime, they may learn more about the cause of crime. We should, however, question the assumptions and biases of the data. For example, Robert Merton's theory of the self-fulfilling prophecy prompts us to ask, if society has a tendency to cast certain categories of people as criminal types, will this assumption ensure that they will indeed be labeled and treated like criminals? This has certainly

seemed to be true in cases like the high-profile 2014 killing of unarmed black teenager Michael Brown by Ferguson, Missouri, police officer Darren Wilson. And, as David Matza warned, will our preconceived notions about a category of people influence our interpretations of numerical data? In this section, we look at the relationship between crime and demographics such as class, age, gender, and race and examine alternate explanations for what may seem like clear numerical fact.

CLASS Statistics consistently tell us that crime rates are higher in poor urban areas than in wealthier suburbs, but these higher crime rates may not actually be the result of increased criminal behavior. Rather, police tend to concentrate their efforts in urban areas, which they assume are more prone to crime, and thus make more arrests there. It appears that social class is more directly related to how citizens are officially treated by the police, courts, and prisons than to which individuals are likely to commit crime. And even if we do accept these statistics as an accurate representation of crime rates, such theorists as Robert Sampson and William Julius Wilson (2005) argue that the same factors that cause an area to become economically and socially disadvantaged also encourage criminal activity. Lack of jobs, lack of after-school child care, and lack of good schools, for example, are all factors that can lead to economic strain and criminal activity.

CRIME a violation of a norm that has been codified into law

UNIFORM CRIME REPORT (UCR) an official measure of crime in the United States, produced by the FBI's official tabulation of every crime reported by more than 18,000 law enforcement agencies

VIOLENT CRIME crimes in which violence is either the objective or the means to an end, including murder, rape, aggravated assault, and robbery

PROPERTY CRIME crimes that do not involve violence, including burglary, larceny-theft, motor vehicle theft, and arson

ON THE JOB
Is "Cash Register Honesty" Good Enough?

While we might like to think that most employees wouldn't take money from the cash register or merchandise from the showroom floor, walk away with a laptop computer, drive away with the company car, or filter sales receipts to their own bank account, employee theft is still a major problem. According to a 2010 survey by the Association of Certified Fraud Examiners (2012), the typical business is estimated to lose about 5 percent of its annual revenues to employee fraud. This translates to a median loss of $140,000 per year per organization. Others estimate that employee theft is involved in up to one-third of all U.S. corporate bankruptcies (Russakoff and Goodman 2011). The U.S. Chamber of Commerce reports that 75 percent of all employees steal once, and that half of those individuals will steal repeatedly (Jones 2012). Michael Cunningham (2010), a professor of psychology at the University of Louisville and a consultant to the security industry, warns that only one in every three potential employees will be completely trustworthy. Of the other two, one may be tempted to steal given the opportunity, while the other will be more or less constantly looking for a chance to get away with taking company property.

Although we may consider ourselves the trustworthy ones, we may not recognize that our own behavior could still be contributing to the tens of billions of dollars lost each year. How? Well, have you ever taken home paper clips, Post-it notes, a pen, or a pad of paper from the office? Made personal copies on the office copier? Used your work computer to surf the web, download music or movies, play video games, or send an e-mail to a friend? Eaten or drunk company products? How about taking a little more time than you're supposed to on your lunch break or leaving work a little early?

It's called pilfering, and it happens on the job tens of thousands of times a day. And it all adds up. Most companies consider these kinds of losses as just another factor in the cost of doing business. But how is it that so many people think nothing of these small infractions in spite of prevailing social norms that discourage stealing and while otherwise being upstanding or even exemplary employees?

You could say that these people are practicing "cash register honesty." That is, they draw the line at actually stealing money (or its equivalent) out of the till but don't hesitate to make off with other odds and ends that might have a less easily calculable value. They might be appalled at the suggestion that they are less than honest, especially since everyone else seems to take something (if only Internet or texting time) now and then. But is this kind of honesty really enough? And is it more closely related to "real" white-collar crimes like fraud and embezzlement than we would like to think? What kind of honesty do you practice in the workplace?

On the other end of the social class spectrum, **white collar crime** has been defined by sociologist Edwin Sutherland as "a crime committed by a person of respectability and high social status in the course of his occupation." White collar crime can include fraud, embezzlement, or insider trading. Most white collar criminals come from a relatively privileged background (Shover and Wright 2001), and it is no coincidence that white collar crime is policed and punished less strenuously than street crime.

WHITE COLLAR CRIME crime committed by a high-status individual in the course of his occupation

AGE The younger the population, the more likely its members are to commit crimes. Criminologists have shown that this relationship between age and crime has remained stable since 1935, with the peak age for arrests being nineteen. In the United States, fifteen- to nineteen-year-olds make up about 7 percent of the population yet account for 15 percent of criminal arrests. On the other end of the spectrum, people sixty-five and older make up more than 13 percent of the population and account for less than 1 percent of arrests (U.S. Bureau of the Census 2013a; Federal Bureau of Investigation 2014c). We call this trend aging out of crime. Here, too, however, we must be careful about what we read into official statistics. Since our stereotypical image of a criminal is youthful, it may be that the public and police are more likely to accuse and arrest young people and less likely to target seniors. In addition, youth may commit more visible crimes (like robbery or assault), while older people may commit crimes that are more difficult to detect, like embezzlement or fraud.

GENDER Males are more likely to commit crime. In fact, males constitute 88 percent of all arrests for aggravated assault, robbery, rape, murder, and nonnegligent manslaughter. Earlier researchers hypothesized that the gender difference in crime rates was based on physical, emotional, and psychological differences between men and women. The logic was that women were too weak, passive, or unintelligent to commit crime. This argument has been replaced by a focus on the social and economic roles of women. Starting in the 1970s, criminologists found that lower crime rates among women could be explained by their lower status in the power hierarchy. Conflict theorists such as James Messerschmidt (1993) argued that once women start gaining power in the labor market through education and income, crime rates among women will rise to more closely match those among men. This hypothesis has been largely supported by recent trends. Between 2003 and 2012, male arrest rates decreased by 18 percent, while female arrest rates decreased by only 5 percent (Federal Bureau of Investigation 2014d). So while at first glance it may seem logical to argue that women's crime rates are lower because of genetics, on closer examination, we see that social structure plays an important role.

RACE The relationship between race and crime is a controversial one. According to the UCR, African Americans make up 12 percent of the U.S. population but account for 28 percent of all arrests. Once again, sociologists caution against making a link between biology and criminal activity. Instead, they maintain that the relationship can be explained by Merton's self-fulfilling prophecy and by class variables. For example, we could hypothesize that African Americans are exposed to higher rates of crime because more of them live in lower-class neighborhoods—and that here, it is class that matters more than race.

Finally, it is important to recognize that none of these variables—class, age, gender, race—affect crime rates in isolation; they work together to shape the experiences of individuals as well as the larger society. Nikki Jones's (2012) ethnographic study of inner-city African American girls in Philadelphia shows how all of these variables contribute to young women's experiences with violence in their everyday lives. For example, the girls in Jones's study find themselves caught in a bind as they attempt to navigate community standards of both respectability and practicality. In order to be perceived as "respectable," they must adhere to expectations, be "good girls," and avoid violence, while also meeting feminine and race-based appearance norms (such as slender bodies and light complexions). On the other hand, the practical realities of life in what are often risky neighborhoods mean these girls must be ready at any time to look and act tough and be willing to fight to defend themselves and others. Thus, their race, class, gender, and age put them in a situation where they must navigate the competing demands of respectability and toughness, balancing their good girl image while always being prepared for the realities of crime and violence.

Deterrence and Punishment

The question of **deterrence** is part of an ongoing debate about our criminal laws. Theorists who maintain that offenders carefully calculate the cost and benefits of each crime argue that punishment has a deterrent effect—that if the punishment seems too severe, people won't commit the crime. That's the logic behind California's controversial "three strikes" law: the punishment for three felonies is an automatic life sentence. While deterrence theory seems practical enough, it is important to note that in matters of sociology, seldom is there such a direct and causal link between two factors—in this case, the cost of punishment versus the benefit of the crime.

Other justifications for punishment include **retribution**—the notion that society has the right to "get even"—and **incapacitation**, the notion that criminals should be confined or even executed to protect society from further injury. Some argue, though, that society should focus not on punishment but on **rehabilitation**: the prison system should try to reform the criminal so that once released, he will not return to a life of crime. Each approach to punishment invokes different ideas about who the criminal is and what his relationship is to the larger society: Is he someone who can plan ahead and curb his illegal behavior so as not to face a possible negative outcome? Is she someone who can work toward personal transformation? Is he someone who must be punished quid pro quo? Or should she just be removed from society permanently?

In the United States, the local, state, and federal government bureaucracies responsible for making laws together with the police, courts, and prison systems make up the **criminal justice system**—a system that, like any other social institution, reflects the society in which it operates. This means that while the American criminal justice system provides important benefits, such as social control and even employment for its workers, it also replicates some of the inequalities of power in our society. The research of Victor Rios, whom we introduced in the Part I opener, focuses on this issue. Rios, a professor of sociology at the University of California, Santa Barbara, went from gang member to PhD partly because a teacher intervened and put him in touch with a mentoring program at a local university. Otherwise, Rios believes, he would have become another victim of the "youth control complex," his term for the way a variety of institutions, including law enforcement, the judicial system, and public schools, work together to "criminalize, stigmatize, and punish" working-class youth. Rios believes that the educational system has embraced a self-defeating strategy by adopting the attitudes and tactics of law enforcement, even as law enforcement and the judicial system have turned to more draconian measures. Increasingly, our society attempts to control gang violence and drug use with brute

DETERRENCE an approach to punishment that relies on the threat of harsh penalties to discourage people from committing crimes

RETRIBUTION an approach to punishment that emphasizes retaliation or revenge for the crime as the appropriate goal

INCAPACITATION an approach to punishment that seeks to protect society from criminals by imprisoning or executing them

REHABILITATION an approach to punishment that attempts to reform criminals as part of their penalty

CRIMINAL JUSTICE SYSTEM a collection of social institutions, such as legislatures, police, courts, and prisons, that create and enforce laws

In the United States, we tend to think of prisons as places where criminals receive punishment for their crimes and where they are kept to protect the rest of society from their unavoidable recidivism. This means that prisons are usually imposing, windowless buildings, walled off with high fences, barbed wire, and armed guards. They are infamously over-crowded and often violent, and prisoners are in need of medical, mental health, and rehabilitative care that they receive little of. American prisons are placed either in the middle of nowhere (rural and less inhabited areas) or in the middle of impoverished and depopulated urban areas (so as to remain largely invisible to those who live in more privileged circumstances). Visiting a prison is something we only consider doing if we have an incarcerated relative to see or we want to rack up some volunteer hours. We certainly wouldn't consider touring prisons as vacation spots, nor would we want to stay long at any vacation spot that was itself too near a prison. We react to prisons and prisoners with fear and revulsion and institutionalize those emotions in the way we situate, construct, operate, and populate our penitentiaries.

This is not always the case in other parts of the world. In Scandinavia (Sweden, Denmark, and Norway) and neighboring Nordic countries like Finland and Iceland in particular, many of the penal complexes are what criminologists call "open" prisons. Organized more like boarding schools than detention centers, open prisons operate on a model very different than that used in the United States. Instead of focusing on retribution and incapacitation, Scandinavia's open prisons provide prisoners with an opportunity to rehabilitate themselves and re-enter society as reformed, contributing members.

For example, Helsinki's Suomenlinna Island prison is not walled off from the surrounding town, which is located in a scenic archipelago that caters to tourists, arts patrons, and picnickers. Prisoners live in dormitory-like accommodations and hold jobs in the town's maintenance and tourism departments, doing upkeep on the facilities for wages that run from $6 to $10 per hour. They wear their own clothes, cook their own meals, and have televisions and sound systems in their rooms. They can visit with their families in Helsinki, and they have supportive rather than adversarial relationships with the guards. Once released, they have a recidivism rate that is less than half that of U.S. prisoners.

Places like Sweden, Denmark, Finland, and Norway are of course smaller than the United States and somewhat more demographically homogeneous. However, Scandinavian prison populations are *proportionally* much smaller

Open Prisons Norway's Halden Prison uses education, job training, and therapy to help rehabilitate inmates. The Norwegian Correctional Service makes all inmates a "reintegration guarantee," helping them find homes and jobs once they are released.

than U.S. prison populations (U.S. rates are ten times those of Scandinavian countries) and much more representative of the larger society in terms of racial and ethnic diversity. And as noted earlier, after serving their debt to society, Scandinavian ex-cons are far less likely to re-offend.

How do they do it?

Pundits will, of course, argue about which Scandinavian strategy is the key to such successful prisoner rehabilitation. But throughout the Nordic countries, criminal justice policy is governed by research rather than politics. Legislators do not make decisions about how to house, treat, or control prison populations; instead, social scientists do. Criminological research on what does and doesn't work forms the basis for decision making, and professionals in the criminal justice field are the ones who make those decisions. This is in stark contrast to the United States, in which "tough on crime" politics, fear-mongering media, and private corporate interests have created an overcrowded, violent, expensive, and ineffective prison system. If we were to approach criminal offenders with compassion rather than fear, would the results be different?

force, but this sort of indiscriminate policing often creates the very crime it is designed to eliminate as "enhanced policing, surveillance, and punitive treatment of youth of color" help to create a "school-to-prison pipeline" (Rios 2009, p. 151).

In another example of the dysfunctions of the criminal justice system, in 2003 seventeen inmates on Illinois's death row were found to be innocent of the crimes for which they had been sentenced to die. Some cases involved errors made by overworked or underqualified defense attorneys. Further, more than two-thirds of the inmates were African American, many of them convicted by all-white juries (Ryan 2003). As a result, then-governor George Ryan became convinced that **capital punishment** was unfairly and even wrongly applied in some cases, and he suspended the death penalty altogether (it was officially abolished in 2011). When inequities and errors such as these exist in the criminal justice system, we must question the true meaning of the word "justice" in our society.

"Positive" Deviance?

Are there instances in which a rule violation is actually a principled act that should generate a positive rather than negative reaction? The next two examples are cases of what we might call **positive deviance**. Both individuals broke laws; in hindsight, they are now considered heroes.

The first example is the simple act of civil disobedience performed by Rosa Parks on December 1, 1955, in Montgomery, Alabama, an act often considered pivotal in launching the civil rights movement. In those days, a Montgomery city ordinance required buses to be segregated: whites sat in front and blacks in the back. Rosa Parks defied the law by refusing to give up her front seat to a white man and move to the back. Her arrest galvanized the black community and triggered a bus boycott and subsequent protests that eventually ended segregation in the South.

It is worth recognizing that Parks was not an accidental symbol; she was an experienced activist. In her one small, courageous act of defiance, she served as a catalyst that eventually helped advance the fight against racial discrimination all across America. More than forty years after the day she took her seat on the bus, Parks was awarded the Presidential Medal of Freedom in 1996. When she died in 2005, it was front-page news. Her funeral was attended by luminaries of all types and races: mayors, members of Congress, presidents, CEOs, clergy, celebrities, and as many others as could fit into the packed church and spill outside its doors.

The second example is the story of three soldiers who put a stop to a massacre during the Vietnam War. On March 16, 1968, the men of Charlie Company, a U.S. battalion under the command of Lieutenant William Calley, stormed into the village of My Lai in South Vietnam on a "search and destroy" mission and opened fire on its civilian inhabitants. The boys and men of the village had gone to tend the fields, leaving only unarmed women, children, and the elderly. Hundreds were killed on that terrible day, in direct violation of military law. Although the soldiers should have ceased fire when they saw that the enemy (members of the Viet Cong) was not present, they obeyed the commands of their leaders and continued ravaging the village. Calley was later convicted in a court martial; his men, claiming that they were only "following orders," were not held responsible.

The massacre would have continued unchecked had it not been for three other American soldiers—Hugh Thompson, Lawrence Colburn, and Glenn Andreotta—who flew their helicopter into the middle of the carnage at My Lai, against the orders of their superiors, and called for backup help to airlift dozens of survivors to safety. They then turned their guns on their fellow Americans, threatening to shoot if they tried to harm any more villagers. For years, the army tried to cover up the three men's heroism in order to keep the whole ugly truth of My Lai a secret. But finally, in 1998, the men were recognized for their bravery and heroism with medals and citations—for having had the courage and skill to perform a perilous rescue and the moral conviction necessary to defy authority.

CAPITAL PUNISHMENT the death penalty

POSITIVE DEVIANCE actions considered deviant within a given context but are later reinterpreted as appropriate or even heroic

CLOSING COMMENTS

The sociological study of crime and deviance raises complicated issues of morality and ethics. When we study sensitive topics like rape and alcoholism or vulnerable populations like juvenile delinquents and the mentally ill, we have a responsibility as scholars to recognize the effects our attention may have on the people we study. As David Matza noted, we must try to eschew moral judgments in our work, no matter how difficult that may be. And as our professional code of ethics demonstrates, we must protect the people we study from any negative outcomes. Groups lodged under the rubric of deviance can be disempowered by this label, and policy decisions made on the basis of social science research may further injure an already marginal group. On the other hand, a sociological perspective on deviance and crime provides for the possibility that groups previously labeled and marginalized may someday receive assistance and legitimacy from the larger society as well. The sociological perspective is a powerful tool.

Everything You Need to Know about Deviance

> " Deviance is a behavior, trait, or belief that departs from the norm and generates a negative reaction in a particular group. "

THEORIES OF DEVIANCE

* **Functionalism:** deviance reminds us of our shared notions of wrong and right and promotes social cohesion

* **Structural strain:** social inequality creates tension between society's goals and the means an individual has to achieve those goals

* **Conflict:** both society's rules and the punishments for breaking those rules are applied unequally

* **Differential association:** we learn to be deviant through interactions with people who break rules

* **Labeling:** deviance is determined by the social context

REVIEW

1. There are many ways to be mildly deviant without breaking any laws. How do we sanction minor deviant acts?

2. Have you ever known someone to reject the "deviant" label and turn his or her negative identity into a positive one? What was the deviant identity? What term describes this sort of deviance? Do you know anyone who has embraced a stigmatized role through deviance avowal? How might these strategies be useful to individuals?

3. The United States has the dubious distinction of leading every other nation in both the largest total number and largest percentage of incarcerated citizens. Why do you think America has more prisoners than any other country?

Who Goes to Prison in the USA?

Prison Population (by Race and Hispanic Origin), 2013

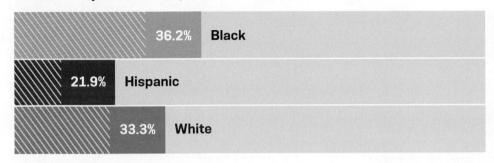

36.2% Black

21.9% Hispanic

33.3% White

Total U.S. Population (by Race and Hispanic Origin), 2013

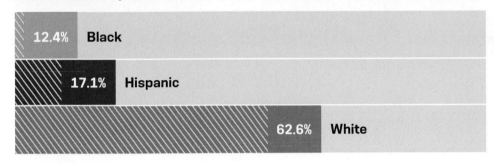

12.4% Black

17.1% Hispanic

62.6% White

Prison Population (by Gender), 2013

7% Female

93% Male

Total U.S. Population (by Gender), 2013

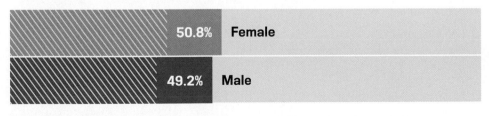

50.8% Female

49.2% Male

SOURCES: Bureau of Justice Statistics 2014c, "Prisoners in 2013"; U.S. Census Bureau 2014, "Population Estimates: National Characteristics 2013f"

EXPLORE

Women, Gaming, and Violence

Women in the online gaming community are subject to intense scrutiny, and women in the games themselves are portrayed in stereotypical ways. Visit the Everyday Sociology Blog to find out what happens when a woman wants to study images of women in the gaming world.

http://wwnPag.es/trw406

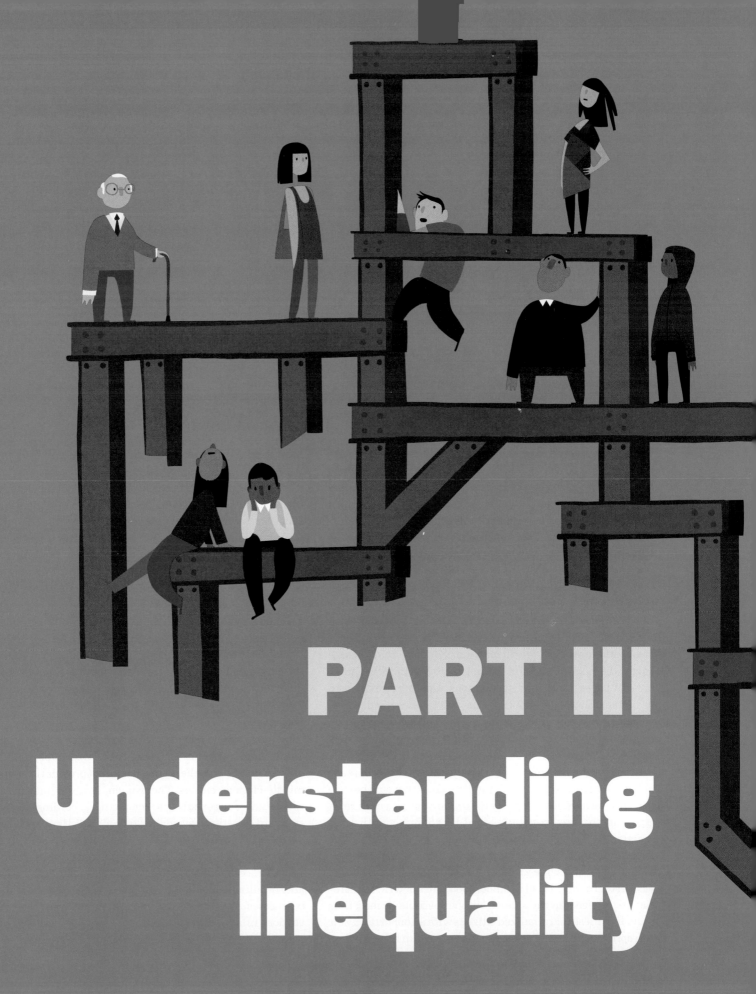

PART III
Understanding Inequality

All societies have systems for grouping, ranking, and categorizing people, and within any social structure, some people occupy superior positions and others hold inferior positions. While such distinctions may appear to be natural, emanating from real differences among people, they are actually social constructions. Society has created and given meaning to such concepts as class, race, and gender, and consequently, those concepts have taken on great social significance. The social analyst's job is to understand how these categories are established in the first place, how they are maintained or changed, and the ways they affect society and the lives of individuals.

For instance, sociologist Mitchell Duneier's book *Sidewalk* (Duneier and Carter 1999) tells the story of a marginalized group of New York City street vendors whose lives and social identities are much more complex than the casual passerby might imagine. The story considers the convergence of class (Chapter 7), race (Chapter 8), and gender (Chapter 9) in the social structure of the city and its inhabitants' everyday interactions. In many ways, *Sidewalk* brings together the themes of these next three chapters.

Duneier studied men and women who live on the streets of New York's Greenwich Village, selling used goods—mostly books and magazines—to passersby. Duneier befriended the vendors and became part of their curbside culture for five years, during which he conducted his ethnographic research. By examining the intersecting lives of people who frequent the Village, Duneier shows what social inequality looks and feels like and what it means to those who live with it every day. On Sixth Avenue, the class differences between the vendors and their customers are obvious. The vendors live from day to day in a cash-based, informal economy; they are poor and often "unhoused"; most are African American males; some are educated, others are not; and all have stories of how they became part of the sidewalk culture. The passersby, on the other hand, are of all ages, races, and occupations, and they are likely to be both employed and housed. They are often well educated; some are wealthy. Interactions between these vendors and customers cut across boundaries of class, race, and sometimes gender—all interrelated forms of social inequality.

A key insight in Duneier's work is that the street vendors are not necessarily what they seem at first glance. It would be easy to characterize these people as lacking any social aspirations, given that so many are homeless and don't fit into conventional social roles. Though they might offend some by their appearance, few are drug addicts, alcoholics, or criminals—and they are pursuing the same kinds of goals as those of many of the passersby. In this liberal neighborhood, sales of written material are allowed on the streets without permits or fees, thus providing these marginalized citizens with an opportunity for entrepreneurial activity and a chance to earn an honest living.

Most vendors say they are trying "to live 'better' lives within the framework of their own and society's weaknesses." Most work hard to construct a sense of decency and reputability in their dealings with customers. Although some of them violate social norms, in most ways the vendors adhere to a code of conduct that minimizes any negative impact they might have on the surrounding community.

Many vendors develop friendly, ongoing relations with regular buyers despite their different positions in social status hierarchies. Sometimes, however, the chasm between the vendors and their customers is difficult to bridge. For example, the male vendors in Duneier's study regularly engaged in flirtatious banter with female passersby. Their efforts at engaging the women in interactions brought a fleeting sense of entitlement and power to men who otherwise have few resources. Typically, the vendors were ignored or rebuffed by the women. When asked why this was the case, one of the vendors said, "She wants room and board, clothing, makeup, hairdos, fabulous dinners, and rent" (Duneier and Carter 1999, p. 196). In other words, because he is poor, he cannot provide these upper-middle-class amenities. The women, however, may perceive this behavior as sexual harassment and, accordingly, may use standard streetwise avoidance techniques. Here, social class becomes the great divide in everyday gender relations.

Some people oppose the street vendors' presence in the neighborhood, and the vendors are frequently the target of anti-peddling campaigns by the mayor's office, police, and local businesses. Yet Duneier believes that expelling these street vendors in an effort to "improve" the neighborhood would actually be counterproductive. Without the unconventional

form of employment that street vending provides to these otherwise destitute people, there would likely be more crime, panhandling, and deviance. Moreover, as law-abiding citizens with a strong desire to conform to social norms, the vendors often serve as mentors to other homeless people, easing them back into mainstream society. Duneier contends that street vendors are an asset to the area and that they contribute to the vibrancy and health of the Village.

While the study is focused on New York's Sixth Avenue vendors, it provides insights into the structure of difference and social inequality in the United States, showing that interactionist perspectives can also be relevant to the study of class, race, and gender, which are more often examined through macrosociological theories. What we come to learn is that the world of sidewalk vending is highly complex and organized, with its own rules and social order.

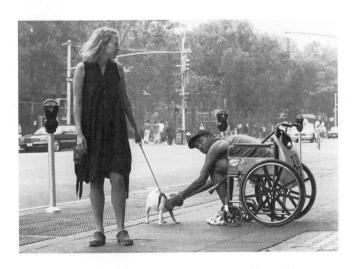

CHAPTER 7

Social Class: The Structure of Inequality

The photographs on page 183 show average families from six countries—the United States, Iceland, Mali, Bhutan, Thailand, and Kuwait. They are each pictured outside the family home, with all their worldly goods displayed around them. These pictures, from Peter Menzel's book *Material World: A Global Family Portrait* (1995), clearly illustrate some of the most striking inequalities of wealth and power that exist among societies worldwide. How do these drastically different realities arise?

Compare, for example, the U.S. and Thai families, the Skeens and the Kuenkaews. What are the differences between these families as evidenced by their possessions? The two Skeen children have their own bedrooms; the two Kuenkaew children sleep on one bed covered in mosquito netting. The Kuenkaews own two water buffaloes, several chickens, and a family dog; their home is surrounded by banana, coconut, mango, and other fruit trees. In contrast, the Skeens have a pet dog and several stuffed deer heads hanging on the wall, trophies of Mr. Skeen's favorite pastime, hunting. The Skeens have three radios, three stereos, five telephones, two televisions, a VCR, a computer, and three vehicles; the Kuenkaews own one radio, one black-and-white television, a recently purchased handheld video game that the children and parents enjoy playing, and their most valued possession, a motor scooter.

Similar comparisons may be made between the Natoma family in Mali, the Namgay family in Bhutan, the Thoroddsen family in Iceland, and the Abdulla family in Kuwait. The younger Mrs. Natoma carries water from the village well in a bucket balanced on her head; the Abdullas have a private indoor swimming pool. The Thoroddsens enjoy weekend trips to the hot springs in their town; the Namgays own little and live near a Buddhist monastery where monks chant daily for peace.

These photographs reveal stark contrasts between the world's wealthiest citizens in places like the United States and Kuwait and its poorest people in countries like Mali and Bhutan. These families represent vastly different lifestyles and life chances resulting from very different economic and social conditions. Imagine yourself in their place. What are the real meanings of terms like "rich" and "poor," and how do sociologists define and apply them? These family photos provide a place to start.

Family Portraits Clockwise from the top left: the Skeens (Pearland, Texas), the Thoroddsens (Hafnarfjordur, Iceland), the Abdullas (Kuwait City, Kuwait), the Natomas (Kouakourou, Mali), the Kuenkaews (Ban Muang Wa, Thailand), and the Namgays (Shingkhey, Bhutan).

HOW TO READ THIS CHAPTER

In this chapter, we will examine the phenomenon of stratification that occurs in all human societies, our own included. Despite rhetorical claims about equality of opportunity for all, America is a profoundly hierarchical society, with the benefits and rewards of living here unequally distributed among its people. A sociological perspective on stratification will increase your understanding in several important ways. First, it will help you recognize inequities in places you may have overlooked, such as your own town, neighborhood, or school, and in the media. Second, it will help you consider how social divisions and hierarchies of privilege and disadvantage appear across many of our institutions; access to health care, the justice system, employment, and housing are all governed by structures of inequality. Third, it should enable you to identify your own place in these social arrangements and to see how some of your own life chances have been shaped by your position (or your family's position) in certain hierarchies. Finally, a knowledge of stratification may help you play a role in changing systems of inequality. Look for ways that you can alleviate some of the problems that social inequality causes—if you can have an impact, even a small one, then this chapter will not have been in vain!

Social Stratification and Social Inequality

Social stratification in one form or another is present in all societies. This means that members of a given society are categorized and divided into groups, which are then placed in a social hierarchy. Members may be grouped according to their gender, race, class, age, or other characteristics, depending on whatever criteria are important to that society. Some groups will be ranked higher in the social strata (levels), while others will fall into the lower ranks. The higher-level groups enjoy more access to the rewards and resources within that society, leaving lower-level groups with less.

This unequal distribution of wealth, power, and prestige results in what is called **social inequality**. We find several different systems of stratification operating in the United States, where it is not hard to demonstrate that being wealthy, white, or male typically confers a higher status (and all that goes along with it) on a person than does being poor, nonwhite, or female. Because social inequality affects

SOCIAL STRATIFICATION the division of society into groups arranged in a social hierarchy

SOCIAL INEQUALITY the unequal distribution of wealth, power, or prestige among members of a society

SLAVERY the most extreme form of social stratification, based on the legal ownership of people

a person's life experience so profoundly, it is worthwhile to examine how stratification works.

There are four basic principles of social stratification. First, it is a characteristic of a society, rather than a reflection of individual differences. For instance, if we say that in Japan men rank higher in the social hierarchy than women, this doesn't mean that a particular woman, such as actress/singer Ryoko Hirosue, couldn't attain a higher status than a particular man; it means only that in Japan as a whole, men rank higher. Second, social stratification persists over generations. In Great Britain, a child inherits not only physical characteristics such as race but also other indicators of class standing, such as regional accent. It is because of this principle of stratification that wealthy families remain wealthy from one generation to the next.

Third, while all societies stratify their members, different societies use different criteria for ranking them. For instance, the criterion in industrialized nations is material wealth (social class), but in hunter-gatherer societies, such as the Khoisan Bushmen of southern Africa, it is gender. Fourth, social stratification is maintained through beliefs that are widely shared by members of society. In the United States, it is still common to think that people are poor not only because of the existing class structure but also because they have somehow failed to "pull themselves up by their bootstraps."

Systems of Stratification

In order to better understand social stratification, it is useful to examine various historical periods and to make global comparisons across cultures. So here we look at three major systems of stratification: slavery, caste, and social class.

Slavery

Slavery, the most extreme system of social stratification, relegates people to the status of property, mainly for the purpose of providing labor for the slave owner. Slaves can thus be bought and sold like any other commodity. They aren't paid for their labor and in fact are forced to work under mental or physical threat. Occupying the lowest rank in the social hierarchy, slaves have none of the rights common to free members of the same societies in which they live.

Slavery has been practiced since the earliest times (the Bible features stories of the Israelites as slaves) and has continued for millennia in South America, Europe, and the United States. Sometimes the race, nationality, or religion of the slave owners was the same as the slaves', as was the case in ancient Greece and Rome. Historically, a person could become enslaved in one of several ways. One way was through debt; a person who couldn't repay what he owed might be taken into slavery by his creditor. Another way was through warfare: groups of vanquished soldiers might become slaves to the victors, and the women and children of the losing side could also be taken into slavery. A person who was caught committing a

Modern-Day Slavery In 2014, Pope Francis, along with representatives of the world's religions, signed a statement with the goal of eradicating modern slavery and trafficking before 2020.

crime could become a slave as a kind of punishment and as a means of compensating the victim. And some slaves were captured and kidnapped, as was the case of the transatlantic slave trade from Africa to the Americas.

Slavery as an economic system was profitable for the slave owner. In most systems of slavery, people were slaves for life, doing work in agriculture, construction, mining, or domestic service, and sometimes in the military, industry, or commerce. Their children would become slaves too, thus making the owner a greater profit. In some systems, however, slavery was temporary, and some slaves could buy their own freedom.

Slavery is now prohibited by every nation in the world, as stated in the Universal Declaration of Human Rights. Not only is it illegal, it is considered immoral as well. Nevertheless, the shocking fact is that slavery continues to exist today in such places as India, South Asia, West Africa, and many other countries around the world in the form of child soldiers, serfdom, forced and bonded laborers, human trafficking, and sex slaves.

America and the Western world are not exempt from these same shocking practices either, where people are held as agricultural, domestic, and sex slaves. And Americans may also play an indirect role in supporting slavery elsewhere in the world by means of our material appetites and the type of labor utilized in certain countries to satisfy our varied consumer demands (Bales and Soodalter 2009). Using a somewhat broader definition of slavery that includes all of the above plus other conditions such as forced marriage, debt bondage, and the sale or exploitation of children, researchers at the Walk Free Foundation (2014) believe there are an estimated 35 million people trapped in some form of modern slavery. That is more enslaved people in terms of total numbers (not proportion) than at any other time in human history (Bales 2000).

Caste

Caste represents another type of social stratification found in various parts of the world. The traditional **caste system** is based on heredity, whereby whole groups of people are born into a certain strata. Castes may be differentiated along religious, economic, or political lines, as well as by skin color or other physical characteristics. The caste system creates a highly stratified society where there is little or no chance of a person changing her position within the hierarchy, no matter what she may achieve individually. Members must marry within their own group, and their caste ranking is passed on to their children. In general, members of higher-ranking castes tend to be more prosperous, whereas members of lower-ranking castes tend to have fewer material resources, live in abject poverty, and suffer discrimination.

India is the country most closely associated with the caste system, based there in the Hindu (majority) religion. The caste system ranks individuals into one of five categories: *Brahman* (scholars and priests), *ksatriya* or *chhetri* (rulers and warriors), *vaisya* (merchants and traders), *sudra* (farmers, artisans, and laborers), and *the untouchables* (social outcasts). The caste system is a reflection of what Hindus call *karma*, the complex moral law of cause and effect that governs the universe (Cohen 2001). According to this belief, membership in a particular caste is seen as a well-deserved reward or punishment for virtuous or sinful behavior in a past life. Caste is thus considered a spiritual rather than material status, but it still results in real-world inequalities. Caste-related segregation and discrimination were prohibited in 1949 by India's constitution, but they are still prevalent. Resistance to social change remains, and thus far the social ramifications of the caste system have not been completely dismantled.

> **CASTE SYSTEM** a form of social stratification in which status is determined by one's family history and background and cannot be changed
>
> **APARTHEID** the system of segregation of racial and ethnic groups that was legal in South Africa between 1948 and 1991

THE CASE OF SOUTH AFRICA An interesting example of the caste system was the **apartheid** system, a legal separation of racial and ethnic groups that was enforced between 1948 and 1991 in South Africa. The term itself literally means "apartness" in Afrikaans and Dutch. The consequence of apartheid was to create great disparity among those in the different strata of society.

South Africans were legally classified into four main racial groups: white (English and Dutch heritage), Indian (from India), "colored" (mixed race), and black. Blacks formed a large majority, at 60 percent of the population. These groups were geographically and socially separated from one another. Blacks were forcibly removed from almost 80 percent of the country, which was reserved for the three minority groups, and were relocated to independent "homelands" similar to the Indian reservations in the United States. They could not enter other parts of the country without a pass—usually in order to work as "guest laborers" in white areas. Ironically, African Americans visiting South Africa were given "honorary white" status and could move freely within white and nonwhite areas.

Social services for whites and nonwhites were separate as well: schools, hospitals, buses, trains, parks, beaches, libraries, theaters, public restrooms, and even graveyards were segregated. Indians and "coloreds" were also discriminated against, though they usually led slightly more privileged lives than blacks. Despite claims of "separate but equal," the standard of living among whites far exceeded that of any other group.

In South Africa under the apartheid system, whites held all the political, economic, and social power, despite being a numerical minority. It was not long before civil unrest and resistance to the system began developing within South Africa and among the international community. Blacks and even some whites began to organize wage strikes and demonstrations, and sanctions were imposed by Western nations. The plights of high-profile anti-apartheid leaders such as Steve Biko and Nelson Mandela became known worldwide. Pressure on the white government continued to grow, until the country was in an almost constant state of emergency. In 1991, apartheid as a legal institution was finally abolished. Its legacy, however, has been much more difficult to dismantle.

It has been over twenty years since democratic elections in which all South African citizens could participate were first held in 1994. And still change is happening very slowly. Although nonwhites now share the same rights and privileges as whites, social inequality and discrimination between the races have decreased little (Nattras and Seekings 2001; Seekings and Nattras 2005). South Africa remains a country with one of the most unequal distributions of income in the world. Though black incomes and employment rates have improved, a large income gap remains, with the rich, and especially the already rich whites, getting richer (Boyle 2009). On average, whites are still paid six times more than blacks (Laing 2012). The wealthiest 10 percent of the population earn nearly 60 percent of the nation's total income; this upper economic strata is almost exclusively composed of whites, a group that makes up just under 9 percent of South Africa's population (Chiles 2012). There are other measures of wealth inequality that persist as well. Whites still own around 70 percent of the land in South Africa, despite promises to redistribute 30 percent of that to blacks (Atauhene 2011). The restoration of land seized during apartheid is only slowly being accomplished and at a price to those making claims. Similar inequalities between whites and other races in South Africa are present in education, health care, and the criminal justice system. In some ways, new patterns of class stratification are replacing rather than erasing old patterns of racial stratification.

SOCIAL CLASS a system of stratification based on access to such resources as wealth, property, power, and prestige

SOCIOECONOMIC STATUS (SES) a measure of an individual's place within a social class system; often used interchangeably with "class"

INTERSECTIONALITY a concept that identifies how different categories of inequality (race, class, gender, etc.) intersect to shape the lives of individuals and groups

Social Class

Social class, a system of stratification practiced primarily in capitalist societies, ranks groups of people according to their wealth, property, power, and prestige. It is also referred to by sociologists as **socioeconomic status (SES)** to keep in mind the social as well as economic basis of this system of stratification. The social class system is much less rigid than the caste system. Although children tend to "inherit" the social class of their parents, during the course of a lifetime they can move up or down levels in the strata. Strictly speaking, social class is not based on race, ethnicity, gender, or age, although, as we will see, there is often an overlap between class and other variables.

INTERSECTIONALITY It is important to recognize that while social statistics often address issues of inequality one variable at a time, social actors don't. In other words, we experience our lives not just as "middle-class" or "working-class" or "upper-class" people, but as women and men; blacks, whites, Latinos, and Asians; college or high school graduates; Christians, Jews, or Muslims; spouses or singles; and so on. Our lived experience is one of **intersectionality**, a concept that acknowledges that multiple dimensions of status and inequality intersect to shape who we are and how we live. Our life chances are influenced by our class *and* our race *and* our gender *and* our religion *and* our age (*and* multiple other categories) all together, not one at a time.

An example of this can be seen in the ethnographic research of sociologist Karyn R. Lacy (2007), who studied black middle-class suburbanites in the Washington, DC, region. As Lacy's findings show, social status is more complex than just a "middle-class" salary might indicate: Her respondents' identities were shaped by their income, occupation (in mostly white-dominated professions), residential status (as suburban homeowners), and race. In fact, many reported being frustrated as they tried to convince others (such as store employees, real-estate agents, and bankers) that they were among the middle class in the first place; their race obscured their class in the eyes of whites and made it difficult for whites to see them as "belonging" in certain neighborhoods or business establishments at all. This is an example of how, in the reality of everyday life, race and class are experienced as inseparable; their effects on our experiences are intertwined, even as we attempt to unravel them in different chapters in sociology textbooks. Keep this concept of intersectionality in mind as you read on about class and then again in subsequent chapters when we address other forms of social inequality.

Sociologists are not always in agreement about what determines class standing or where the boundaries are between different social classes. We will consider some of these disagreements after first taking a look at the United States and its class system.

Social Classes in the United States

It is difficult to draw exact lines between the social classes in the United States; in fact, it may be useful to imagine them as occurring along a continuum rather than being strictly divided. The most commonly identified categories are upper class, middle class, and lower class. If we want to make even finer distinctions, the middle class can be divided into the upper-middle, middle, and working (or lower-middle) class (Wright et al. 1982; Gilbert 2014). You probably have some idea of which class you belong to, even if you don't know the exact definition for each category. Interestingly, most Americans claim that they belong somewhere in the middle class even when their life experiences and backgrounds would suggest otherwise. While keeping in mind that the borders between the classes can be blurry, let's examine a typical model of the different social classes (Figure 7.1).

The Upper Class

The **upper class** makes up just 1 percent of the U.S. population, and its total net worth is greater than that of the entire other 99 percent (Beeghley 2008). The upper class consists of elites who have gained membership in various ways. Some, like the Rockefellers and Carnegies, come into "old money" through family fortunes; others, like Mark Zuckerberg or Lady Gaga, generate "new money" through individual achievements. Members of this class make around $2 million per year (and sometimes far more than that) and are often highly educated and influential. They tend to attend private schools and prestigious universities and display a distinctive lifestyle; some seek positions of power in government or philanthropy. The upper class is largely self-sustaining, with most members remaining stable and few new ones able to gain membership in its ranks.

The Upper-Middle Class

The **upper-middle class** comprises about 14 percent of the population. This group tends to be well educated (with college or postgraduate degrees) and highly skilled. Members work primarily in executive, managerial, and professional jobs.

UPPER CLASS an elite and largely self-sustaining group who possess most of the country's wealth; they constitute about 1 percent of the U.S. population

UPPER-MIDDLE CLASS social class consisting of mostly highly educated professionals and managers who have considerable financial stability; they constitute about 14 percent of the U.S. population

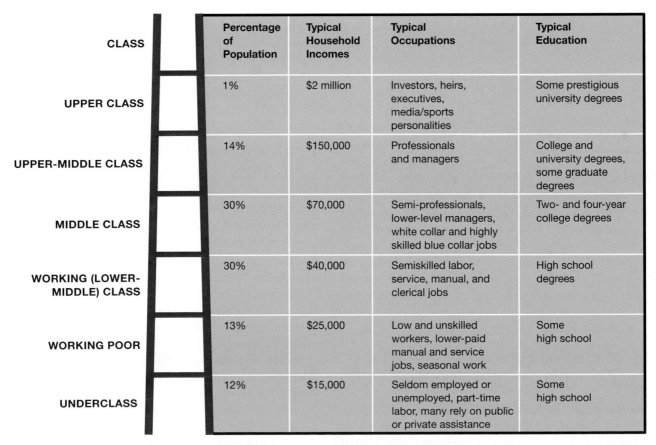

CLASS	Percentage of Population	Typical Household Incomes	Typical Occupations	Typical Education
UPPER CLASS	1%	$2 million	Investors, heirs, executives, media/sports personalities	Some prestigious university degrees
UPPER-MIDDLE CLASS	14%	$150,000	Professionals and managers	College and university degrees, some graduate degrees
MIDDLE CLASS	30%	$70,000	Semi-professionals, lower-level managers, white collar and highly skilled blue collar jobs	Two- and four-year college degrees
WORKING (LOWER-MIDDLE) CLASS	30%	$40,000	Semiskilled labor, service, manual, and clerical jobs	High school degrees
WORKING POOR	13%	$25,000	Low and unskilled workers, lower-paid manual and service jobs, seasonal work	Some high school
UNDERCLASS	12%	$15,000	Seldom employed or unemployed, part-time labor, many rely on public or private assistance	Some high school

Figure 7.1 **The U.S. Social Class Ladder**

SOURCE: Gilbert 2014.

MIDDLE CLASS social class composed primarily of white collar workers with a broad range of education and incomes; they constitute about 30 percent of the U.S. population

WHITE COLLAR a description characterizing lower-level professional and management workers and some highly skilled laborers in technical jobs

WORKING CLASS or **LOWER-MIDDLE CLASS** social class consisting of mostly blue collar or service industry workers who are less likely to have a college degree; they constitute about 30 percent of the U.S. population

BLUE COLLAR a description characterizing skilled and semi-skilled workers who perform manual labor or work in service or clerical jobs

WORKING POOR poorly educated manual and service workers who may work full-time but remain near or below the poverty line; they constitute about 13 percent of the U.S. population

UNDERCLASS the poorest group, comprising the homeless and chronically unemployed who may depend on public or private assistance; they constitute about 12 percent of the U.S. population

They may enjoy modest support from investments but generally depend on income from salaried work, making around $150,000 per year. As a result, the upper-middle class is most likely to feel some financial stability. They usually own their homes and may especially value activities like travel and higher education.

The Middle Class

The **middle class** makes up about 30 percent of the population, though some social analysts believe that the middle class is shrinking as a result of a variety of phenomena, including economic recession and the housing market crash, along with high unemployment, corporate downsizing, and outsourcing of work to foreign countries. Many people who would have once been considered middle class may have moved down to the lower-middle class, while some others have moved up to the upper-middle class. The middle class comprises primarily **white collar** workers, skilled laborers in technical and lower-management jobs, small entrepreneurs, and others earning around $70,000 per year. Most members have a high school education and a two- or four-year college degree. While members of the middle class have traditionally been homeowners (a sign of having achieved the American Dream), this trend changed during the recent recession and the associated banking and mortgage crises. Along with issues like the cost of housing, and given other debts carried by many Americans, not all middle-class people can afford their own homes anymore.

The Working (Lower-Middle) Class

The **working class**, or **lower-middle class**, makes up about 30 percent of the population. Members typically have a high school education and generally work in manual labor, or **blue collar**, jobs, as well as in the service industry (retail, restaurant, tourism, etc.)—jobs that are often more routine, where

employees have little control in the workplace. Members of the working class typically earn around $40,000 per year. A small portion, especially those who belong to a union, may earn above-average incomes for this class. Working-class people typically have a low net worth and live in rental housing or in a modest home they have inherited or long saved for.

The Working Poor and Underclass

The **working poor** constitute approximately 13 percent of the population. Members are generally not well educated; most have not completed high school and experience lower levels of literacy than the other classes. They may also lack other work skills valuable in the job market. Typical occupations include unskilled, temporary, and seasonal jobs—including minimum-wage jobs, housekeeping, day labor, and migrant agricultural work. The average income is around $25,000. This group suffers from higher rates of unemployment and underemployment, with some members receiving social welfare subsidies.

In addition, another 12 percent of the population, the **underclass**, could be categorized as truly disadvantaged. These Americans live in poverty conditions and typically earn $15,000 or less per year. As such, they may have chronic difficulty getting enough money to support their basic needs. They may hold few steady jobs and depend on public benefits or charity to survive. They are often found in inner cities, where they live in substandard housing or are homeless; their numbers are increasing in the suburbs as well. They are part of a group that is considered officially impoverished by federal government standards. A separate section later in this chapter will be devoted to discussing poverty.

Problematic Categories

Because SES is based on a collection of complex variables (including income, wealth, and education, as well as power or prestige), it is difficult to say exactly where, for example, middle class ends and upper class begins. In addition, individuals may embody a variety of characteristics that make precise SES classification difficult. Someone may be highly educated, for example, but make money cleaning houses while working on her novel. Also, as we learned during the recent financial crisis, people of all social classes, including the very wealthy, can find themselves unable to pay their mortgages when real estate "bubbles" burst.

So how would we categorize a person such as the late Sam Walton, founder of Walmart? He was the product of a struggling "Okie" family, a farm boy and state college graduate who became a billionaire businessman. Walton did not come from a background of privilege; he neither attended an elite university nor worked in a prestigious occupation. He was called "America's shopkeeper," and despite amassing a huge fortune, Walton remained close to his rural roots. What sociologists

Status Inconsistencies Sam Walton, the "Okie" billionaire, and Mother Teresa, the Catholic nun who was revered around the world but had no personal wealth, are two examples that complicate SES classifications.

would say is that Walton is an example of **status inconsistency**, or stark contrasts between the levels of the various statuses he occupied. Another example is Mother Teresa, a Catholic nun who ministered to the poor, sick, and dying in Calcutta, India. As a member of the clergy, she held some occupational prestige, but her religious order took vows of poverty, and she had virtually no personal wealth. Yet Mother Teresa was regularly ranked as among the most admired people of the twentieth century. She garnered numerous honors, including the Nobel Peace Prize, but she was most concerned with how to parlay whatever power she gained into helping the world's most needy.

Of course, not all examples are quite this dramatic, but status inconsistencies are especially prevalent in the United States because of our "open" class system. Class mobility (which will be discussed in more detail later) is more easily attainable here than in many other countries, so we are more likely to see people with a mixture of different statuses. While we seem to be able to recognize class distinctions implicitly, there are no systematic ways of delineating each category. Still, sociologists have made an effort to understand and define class, and we turn now to the theories that result from those efforts.

Theories of Social Class

In this section, we will look at social stratification from the perspectives of each of the major schools of thought within sociology. We start with classical conflict and Weberian theories and structural functionalism, and then consider postmodern and symbolic interactionist theories. Each perspective offers different ideas about what determines social class, with the macro theorists focusing on larger-scale social structures and the postmodern and micro theorists focusing more on meaning, interpretation, and interactions in everyday life.

Conflict Theory

Karl Marx formed his social theories at a time when monumental changes were occurring in the stratification systems that characterized nineteenth-century Europe. The **feudal system**, which consisted of a hierarchy of privileged nobles who were responsible for and served by a lower stratum of serfs (forced laborers), was breaking down. Cities were growing larger as more people moved from rural areas to take part in the new forms of industry that were emerging there. With these changes, what had traditionally determined a person's social standing (whether they were born a noble or a serf) was no longer as relevant. Marx was concerned about a new kind of social inequality that he saw emerging—between the capitalists (bourgeoisie), who owned the means of production, and the workers (proletariat), who owned only their own labor.

STATUS INCONSISTENCY a situation in which an individual has differing levels of status in terms of wealth, power, prestige, or other elements of socioeconomic status

FEUDAL SYSTEM a system of social stratification based on a hereditary nobility who were responsible for and served by a lower stratum of forced laborers called serfs

Marx argued that economic relationships were quickly becoming the only social relationships that mattered: the impersonal forces of the market were creating a new, rigid system of social stratification in which capitalists had every economic advantage and workers had none. He believed that

Although stratification systems in other countries may appear different from those in the United States, they share many features. For one thing, most such systems result in patterns of inequality.

Brazil

Race is a powerful influence on social stratification in Brazil, where the situation is even more complex than in the United States. By any standards, Brazil is a remarkably diverse nation. The early settlers to the area were mainly European, and with their arrival the number of native inhabitants declined sharply as a result of violence and disease, although they remained a factor in the local population. Through the mid-1800s, slaves from Africa were imported, and in the twentieth century, a new wave of immigrants arrived from Asia and the Middle East.

For much of Brazilian history, the European whites enjoyed a privileged status. However, as people from different races married and raised children, new racial categories emerged. Sociologist Gilberto Freyre claimed in 1970 that this new mixture of races and cultures was a unique strength that led to something like a "racial democracy." Although the idea was appealing, it was subsequently challenged by

Polite Racism As different ethnic groups in Brazil intermarried and had children, new racial categories emerged. Many have argued that this has led to a new "racial democracy"; however, critics say stratification still exists. They refer to it as "polite racism."

WEALTH a measure of net worth that includes income, property, and other assets

PRESTIGE the social honor people are given because of their membership in well-regarded social groups

the classes would remain divided and social inequality would grow; that wealth and privilege would be concentrated among a small group of capitalists and that workers would continue to be exploited. Contemporary conflict theorists continue to understand social class in a similar way. Erik Olin Wright (1997), for example, describes an animated film he made as a student in which the pawns on a chessboard attempt to overthrow the aristocracy (kings, queens, knights, and bishops) but realize that the "rules of the game" doom them to relive the same unequal roles—a metaphor for the way social structure shapes and sustains inequality.

Weberian Theory

Max Weber noted that owning the means of production was not the only way of achieving upper-class status; a person

could also accumulate **wealth** consisting of income and property. As a contemporary example, Microsoft and Facebook are both publicly traded companies on the stock market, which means that they are owned by thousands of individual shareholders who benefit when the company turns a profit. But the people who started those companies have amassed far greater fortunes. In 2014, Microsoft co-founder Bill Gates (worth $78.5 billion) was ranked the #1 richest person in the world, while Facebook co-founder Mark Zuckerberg (worth $33.4 billion) was ranked #11 in the United States and #16 in the world (Forbes 2014, 2015). Weber suggested that power (the ability to impose one's will on others) should be considered as part of the equation when measuring a person's class standing. Although they may not own their corporations, executives can exert influence over the marketplace, consumers, and the work lives of their employees. And they can use their wealth to support various causes and campaigns.

Weber believed that another important element in social class has to do with **prestige**, the social honor granted to people because of their membership in certain groups. A person's

other social scientists, who argued that Brazil was still highly stratified by race, if only in a less obvious way (Telles 2004). Intermarriage may have eliminated clearly defined racial groups, but skin color still largely defines an individual's place in society, with light-skinned Brazilians enjoying privileges of wealth and power denied to their dark-skinned counterparts. Contemporary critics have referred to this inequality as *racismo cordial*, or "polite racism."

Iran

The basis for social stratification in Iran has undergone radical changes since the Islamic Revolution in 1979, which transformed the country from a constitutional monarchy to a theocracy. Before the revolution, political and economic power was concentrated in the upper class, made up of landowners, industrialists, and business executives; the middle class consisted of entrepreneurs, small-business owners, merchants, and members of the civil service. Economic mobility was an option largely for those with secular values and a Western education—that is, those who had gone to college in the United States or Europe and who believed in the separation of church and state. After the revolution, however, religion became a primary influence on stratification.

Many members of the civil service who were not Muslim or who held Western university degrees were forced into exile; those who remained were required to attend special classes on Islamic law in order to keep their positions. Strict observance of Islamic law and custom has become a prerequisite for maintaining one's social position, and many of the new political elites are religious leaders.

Sweden

Sweden has deliberately attempted to craft a system that lessens social inequality, a policy made somewhat easier, perhaps, by the country's relative homogeneity of race, ethnicity, and religion. Sweden provides its citizens with a far greater number of social services than the United States does: the government guarantees its citizens a high level of access to health care, education, child and elderly care, unemployment benefits, and public facilities like libraries and parks. In order to furnish such programs, taxes are high, with a top taxation rate of 60 percent for the wealthiest Swedes. Although the Swedish system certainly has its problems (high taxation rates among them), there are demonstrated benefits, including increased life expectancy and literacy, and decreased infant mortality, homelessness, poverty, and crime.

occupation is a common source of prestige: in a typical ranking, you might find physicians near the top and janitors near the bottom. Take note that athletes rank higher than sociologists in Table 7.1. People's relative prestige can affect not only their wealth or power but also how they are perceived in social situations. Wealth by itself can also be a source of prestige, though not always. In some social circles, especially those that are more traditional or have a history of aristocracy, a distinction is made between "old money" and "new money." In the United States it is more prestigious to come from a family heritage of wealth than to have recently made a fortune.

For Weber, wealth, power, and prestige are interrelated because they often come together, but it is also possible to convert one to the other. Paris Hilton, for example, a socialite from a wealthy, hotel-owning family, turned that aspect of her status into a certain type of contemporary prestige—celebrity. Still, it is important to distinguish these three elements: property and wealth can be inherited or earned, power usually comes from occupying certain roles within organizations, and prestige is based on a person's social identity and is bestowed by others.

Structural Functionalism

Functionalism emphasizes social order and solidarity based on commonly shared values about what is good and worthwhile. The system of stratification that has emerged over time, though not egalitarian, is still functional for society in a number of ways. Because there are a variety of roles to perform for the maintenance and good of the whole, there must be incentives to ensure that individuals will occupy those roles that are most necessary or important. Kingsley Davis and Wilbert Moore (1945) discuss some of the principles of stratification that result in a system of rewards that are unequally distributed among various roles. The assumption is that some roles are more desirable than others and may require greater talent or training. In addition, certain roles may be more critical than others to the functioning of society, as well as difficult to fill, so there must be a mechanism for attracting and securing the best individuals to those positions. This would mean that there is widespread consensus about which positions are most important—either in terms of their special

Table 7.1 The Relative Social Prestige of Selected Occupations in the United States

White Collar Occupations	Prestige Score	Blue Collar Occupations
Physician	86	
Lawyer	75	
Professor	74	
Architect	73	
Dentist	72	
Member of the Clergy	69	
Pharmacist	68	
Registered Nurse	66	
	65	Athlete
Electrical Engineer	64	
Veterinarian	62	
Airplane Pilot	61	
Sociologist	61	
	60	Police Officer
Actor	58	
	53	Firefighter
Social Worker	52	
	51	Electrician
	46	Secretary
	40	Farmer
	36	Child-Care Worker
	36	Hairdresser
	31	Auto-body Repairperson
Cashier	29	
	28	Waiter/Waitress
	22	Janitor

SOURCE: National Opinion Research Center 2015.

an important role in providing highly prized services to other members of society. Think of the steps it takes to become a doctor. A person must have an extensive education and graduate training and must complete a long and intensive internship before being certified to practice medicine. This individual also devotes a great deal of her personal resources of time and money to this process. It is further assumed that there are only so many people who might have the talent and determination to become doctors, and so it follows that there must be incentives or rewards for them to enter the field of medicine.

The functionalist perspective helps explain the existing system of social stratification and its persistence, but it still leaves us with questions about the structured inequalities that it continues to reproduce. Is it really functional for social rewards (such as wealth, power, and prestige) to be so unequally divided among members of society? And while we might agree that doctors are very important to society, are they more so than teachers and carpenters? Our heroes of pop culture (famous actors, athletes, musicians) can rise to the highest ranks while our everyday heroes (day-care providers,

Social Reproduction Paris Hilton is heiress to the Hilton Hotel & Resort chain. How did Hilton's family influence her career path?

qualifications or the potential scarcity of qualified individuals to occupy those positions—and that society accepts the need to bestow rewards upon people who are considered of greater importance.

Take, for instance, the role of a physician, which has the highest ranking of occupational prestige in American society (National Opinion Research Center 2015). Doctors play

firefighters, mechanics) may struggle to make a living. Whose values are structuring the system and, after closer scrutiny, is it clear that compensating stockbrokers more than bricklayers is really functional to society as a whole? Despite these questions, Americans largely agree with functionalist principles of social class. We will revisit some of these questions in later sections of the chapter.

Postmodernism

Sociologist Pierre Bourdieu (1973, 1984) studied French schools to examine a phenomenon referred to as **social reproduction**, which means that social class is passed down from one generation to the next and thus remains relatively stable. According to Bourdieu, this happens as a result of each generation's acquisition of what he called **cultural capital**: children inherit tastes, habits, and expectations from their parents, and this cultural capital either helps or hinders them as they become adults. For example, having highly educated parents who can help with homework and enforce useful study habits makes it more likely a child will succeed in school. Just the parents' expectation that their children will earn similar credentials can be a powerful incentive. Since better-educated parents tend to come from the middle and upper classes, their children will also have better chances to attain that same status.

According to Bourdieu, cultural capital also shapes the perceptions that others form about a person. For instance, in job interviews, the candidates who can best impress a potential employer with their social skills may be chosen over other workers who may be equally qualified but less adept socially. Since cultural capital has such profound effects, people often try to acquire it—to "better" themselves. They may take adult education classes, attend lectures and concerts, join a tennis club, or travel to Europe—all in an attempt to improve their cultural capital. Often, however, the effects of early childhood are too powerful to overcome. It can be difficult for someone who grew up in a less privileged environment to project a different class background; their accent, for example, may give them away ("He talks like a hillbilly," "She just sounds too 'street'"). There is evidence to suggest that social mobility in the United States remains stagnant; Americans today are no more or less likely to climb the social class ladder than children born more than fifty years ago (Chetty et al. 2014). Around half of all children will wind up with the same SES as their parents, despite efforts to climb the social class ladder (Krueger 2002, 2012).

Symbolic Interactionism

If macrosociologists believe that there is little an individual can do to change systems of structured inequality, interactionists believe that all social structures—including systems of inequality—are constructed from the building blocks of everyday interaction. For instance, sociologist David Sudnow (1972) argues that we make split-second judgments about who people are and which social status they occupy based on appearance. We take action based on what we observe "at a glance." Along the same lines, Aaron Cicourel (1972) suggests that we make inferences about the status of others when we encounter them in different social situations. For example, you may assume that the passengers sitting in the first-class cabin of an airplane are wealthier than those in coach, whether or not this is true. Maybe one of those first-class passengers is a "starving student" whose seat was upgraded because coach was overbooked—by thrifty millionaires. "Wealthy," "poor," and "middle class" are statuses that, rather than existing in and of themselves, are continuously being negotiated in interaction.

Erving Goffman (1956) noted that we "read" different aspects of identity by interpreting the behavior of others and that we become accustomed to others "reading" our behavior in the same way. This means that our clothing, our speech, our gestures, the cars we drive, the homes we live in, the people we hang out with, and the things we do on vacation are all part of our presentation of self and provide information that others

SOCIAL REPRODUCTION the tendency of social classes to remain relatively stable as class status is passed down from one generation to the next

CULTURAL CAPITAL the tastes, habits, expectations, skills, knowledge, and other cultural assets that help us gain advantages in society

Everyday Class Consciousness Clothes, cars, homes, and vacation plans are all indicators of socioeconomic status. What impression does this living room give of who might live here?

IN RELATIONSHIPS
Socioeconomic Status and Mate Selection

You say you don't judge a book by its cover? You say it's the person who matters, and not the social categories he or she belongs to? We may believe these things, but sociological studies strongly suggest that we don't act on them. When it comes to dating, courtship, and marriage ("mate selection" activities, as defined by social scientists), we tend to make homogamous choices. **Homogamy** ("like marries like") means that we choose romantic partners based on our similarities in background and group membership. Despite the old adage that "opposites attract," decades of sociological research show that we make choices based on similarities in race, ethnicity, religion, class, education, age—even height and levels of physical attractiveness (Kalmijn 1998). Homogamy based on socioeconomic status is especially clear: we tend to marry those who share the same economic and educational backgrounds. This holds true even if we practice **heterogamy** (marrying someone who is different from us) in other areas, such as race or religion. Why is class-based homogamy so prevalent?

As it turns out, we have relatively few opportunities to meet people of different socioeconomic backgrounds during the course of our everyday lives. At home, at school, on the job, at the coffee shop or gym, we are likely to be surrounded by those who are like us, classwise. Homogamy is more strictly enforced in upper-class families than in other social classes. Those who enjoy the privileges of wealth often want to make sure those privileges continue into the next generation and may monitor their children's activities by sending them to prestigious schools and posh summer camps so that they don't get the opportunity to meet anyone but other privileged kids. This helps ensure that wealth and power remain consolidated within a relatively small community. If you spend all your free time at the country club pool instead of getting a summer job at Starbucks or McDonald's, your opportunities to meet the hoi polloi are limited.

If we focus only on those in the public eye, it is easy to see how limits on opportunity result in marriages between affluent and powerful families. This happens in political families. For example, Julie Nixon, daughter of a former U.S. president, married David Eisenhower, grandson of another former president. Kerry Kennedy, daughter of former attorney general Robert Kennedy, married (and later divorced) Andrew Cuomo, son of former New York governor Mario Cuomo. After the divorce, Andrew ascended to the N. Y. governor's mansion as well and found love again with Food Network star Sandra Lee. And it happens among celebrities, whether movie stars Brad Pitt and Angelina Jolie, singers Beyoncé Knowles and Jay-Z, or NFL quarterback Tom Brady and supermodel

HOMOGAMY the tendency to choose romantic partners who are similar to us in terms of class, race, education, religion, and other social group membership

HETEROGAMY choosing romantic partners who are dissimilar to us in terms of class, race, education, religion, and other social group membership

EVERYDAY CLASS CONSCIOUSNESS awareness of one's own social status and that of others

use to make judgments about our SES. In turn, we look for these same clues in the behavior of others. This type of **everyday class consciousness**, or awareness of our own and others' social status, is important for us to understand but difficult to identify empirically.

As a humorous answer to this dilemma, University of Pennsylvania English professor Paul Fussell (1983) created the "living room scale," which lists items that we may find in someone's living room and attaches point values to them. For example, if you have a copy of the *New York Review of Books* on your coffee table, add five points. A copy of *Popular Mechanics*? Subtract five. A working fireplace? Add four. A wall unit with built-in television and stereo?

Subtract four. Add three points for each black-and-white family photograph in a sterling silver frame; subtract three points for any work of art depicting cowboys. When we total the final score, higher numbers indicate higher SES, and vice versa.

While Fussell's living room scale may seem like a joke, we really do make snap judgments about the status of others based on just this sort of information. (Here it should be noted that in Dr. Stein's living room, the fireplace and TV wall unit are side by side, while Dr. Ferris's living room features a silver-framed black-and-white photograph of her father as a child—dressed like a cowboy, on horseback! As we've said before, real life sometimes defies easy categorization.) The Data Workshop on the next page will help you see how swiftly and automatically you employ class categories in your interactions with others.

Gisele Bündchen. All practiced a form of status homogamy by partnering with people from the same social circles—other famous and wealthy celebrities. Whether they met on the set, at the yacht club, or at an awards show, they met in a status-restricted setting to which not everyone is eligible for entry.

Questions have arisen recently about how Internet technologies may facilitate—or impede—our tendency toward homogamy. Popular dating websites such as OkCupid, Match.com, Zoosk, and others allow people who occupy vastly different social circles to meet online—and perhaps fall in love. In this way, it would seem that Internet dating has the potential to inhibit our off-line predilection for people who belong to the same social groups as we do. On the other hand, Internet dating can also assist us in choosing people who are like us, in that certain sites cater to particular social groups: J Date (for Jewish singles), The League (for Ivy Leaguers), Black-PeopleMeet (for black singles), and even TrekDating.com (for *Star Trek* fans). As these and other such sites specifically select for social group membership, they may actually strengthen homogamous effects in online mate selection processes.

Vast differences in class standing between marital partners are usually the stuff of fairy tales and fantasy. The "Cinderella story," in which a low-status woman is romantically "rescued" by a high-status man, is familiar to us all—yet we likely have seen it happen only in storybooks and movie theaters. *Pretty Woman*, in which Julia Roberts plays a prostitute who is romanced by Richard Gere's wealthy businessman, is a perfect

Jay-Z and Beyoncé Knowles "Like marries like."

example of this type of heterogamous fantasy, as is *Maid in Manhattan*, in which Jennifer Lopez plays a hotel housekeeper who is wooed by Ralph Fiennes's character, a rich political candidate. The only touch of sociological reality in these tales is the portrayal of women's **hypergamy** and men's **hypogamy**; that is, when class boundaries are crossed, women usually marry up while men marry down. Take a look at the role of SES in your own mate selection activities: are you homogamous or heterogamous?

> **HYPERGAMY** marrying "up" in the social class hierarchy
>
> **HYPOGAMY** marrying "down" in the social class hierarchy

While we have considered the theories of macrosociologists and symbolic interactionists separately here, there are actually some intersections between interaction and structure. Our identities as "working-class" or "privileged" individuals may be structured by preexisting categories, yet those identities are also performed every day in our interactions with others. The structural perspective and the interactionist perspective are not mutually exclusive when it comes to a discussion of class: they are complementary. Status inequality is structured, categorical, and external; it is also interactionally created and sustained. Structure shapes interaction, and interaction generates structure.

Contemporary sociologists have conducted studies that make this connection clear. For example, Geoffrey Hunt and Saundra Satterlee (1986), who studied drinking habits in village pubs, found that pub interactions tended to reinforce class divisions in the larger society: the village men chose drinking and billiards companions based on the class divisions already in place outside the pub.

All the information that we gather at a glance is used to make evaluations of others' wealth, income, occupation, education, and other categories that indicate status and prestige. In some ways, it doesn't matter whether we're right—especially in anonymous public places like airports. You should be aware, however, that you do use these cues to evaluate the status of others in split seconds and that you act on those evaluations every day. Maybe you chose to stand on the bus or on the subway rather than sit next to someone who didn't look quite "right"—whatever that means to you. Often, we end up falling back on stereotypes that may lead us to false conclusions about a person's status or character. When it comes to everyday class consciousness, appearances are sometimes deceiving, but they are always consequential.

Table 7.2 Theory in Everyday Life

Perspective	Approach to Social Inequality	Case Study: Poverty
Structural Functionalism	Social inequality is a necessary part of society. Different reward structures are necessary as an incentive for the best qualified people to occupy the most important positions. Even poverty has functions that help maintain social order.	The functions of poverty for society include the facts that the poor take otherwise undesirable jobs and housing, purchase discount and secondhand goods, and provide work for thousands, including social service caseworkers and others who work with the poor.
Conflict Theory	Social inequality creates intergroup conflict—poor and rich groups have different interests and may find themselves at odds as they attempt to secure and protect these interests.	Social welfare programs that assist the poor are funded by tax dollars, which some wealthy citizens may be reluctant to provide because taxes reduce their net income. This can create conflict between rich and poor groups in society.
Symbolic Interactionism	Social inequality is part of our presentation of self. We develop everyday class consciousness as a way to distinguish the status of others.	Poor and wealthy persons have differential access to the "props" used to project particular versions of self. In particular, professional clothing such as business suits can be too expensive for poor individuals to purchase, which can put them at a disadvantage in job interviews, where a professional image is necessary. Organizations like Dress for Success provide professional clothing for those who can't afford it, leveling the playing field a bit in terms of impression management.

DATA WORKSHOP
Analyzing Everyday Life

Everyday Class Consciousness

When we are out in public places, we can quickly gather bits of information about other people in the social environment. These "data" are useful in forming judgments and evaluations about them. Even the smallest presentational details can tell us something about who they are. So, how do you know what social class other people belong to? How do you feel about the fact that others will also be trying to figure out *your* class status? Do the assessments we make about others (and that they make about us) influence our thoughts, attitudes, and behavior? What are the consequences of everyday class consciousness?

In this Data Workshop you will be conducting participant observation research to understand more about how we size up other people in terms of their socioeconomic status. Return to the section in Chapter 2 for a refresher on ethnography/participant observation

research methods. First, choose a location to be the field site for your study; it should be a busy public place with a variety of passersby. You will want to be both a participant and an observer in the setting. So, for example, you could pretend to be waiting for someone at the airport, sitting in the food court at the mall, or standing in line at the post office. Next, you'll want to make some discreet but in-depth observations about a small number of people in the setting. One way to take a simple sample of the population is to select every seventh or tenth person who walks by you. Spend several long moments looking closely at him or her. Ask yourself quickly: what class status do you think this person holds? Don't think too long at this point; just register your guess. Continue this process as you observe another three or four people. Now it is time to write some ethnographic field notes, preferably while you're still in the field, or as soon as possible afterward. You'll want your notes to provide as many details as you can remember about the people you selected.

Consider the following questions as you analyze your data. What kinds of things did you observe about others that helped inform your evaluation of their class status—height, weight, race, age, gender, hairstyle, tattoos, piercings, watch or other jewelry, or makeup? Perhaps their style of dress, the colors, fabrics, or logos on a T-shirt, hat, purse, sunglasses, or shoes caught your attention? Did you notice anything else, such as the person's posture, voice, or mannerisms? If you observed someone on the street, did you see the car he or she was driving? What was its make, age, and condition? Did you notice other status clues in any accessories the person had—a laptop or smartphone, a baby stroller or shopping bags? How did the setting itself (mall, post office, airport) influence your assumptions about their social class standing?

There are two options for completing this Data Workshop:

PREP-PAIR-SHARE Conduct your participant observation research according to the instructions. Prepare some ethnographic field notes that you can refer to in class. Get together with one or more of your fellow students and share your experiences. Note similarities and differences in the criteria used by each group member to determine the social class of the people they observed.

DO-IT-YOURSELF Conduct your research in a public place and write a three- to four-page essay describing your observations of four to five people from the field site. Answer the questions in the preceding section, and make specific reference to your field notes as the data to support your analysis (remember to attach the field notes to your paper). What are the consequences of everyday class consciousness? How does it affect your perceptions, attitudes, and behavior?

Socioeconomic Status and Life Chances

Belonging to a certain social class brings such profound consequences that it's possible to make general predictions about a person's life chances in regard to education, work, crime, family, and health just by knowing his SES. The following discussion may help you appreciate the respective privileges and hardships associated with different levels of the social hierarchy.

Family

Sociologists know that people are likely to marry or have long-term relationships with persons whose social and cultural backgrounds are similar to their own—not because they are looking for such similarities, but simply because they have more access to people like themselves. When you develop ties to classmates, fellow workers, neighbors, and members of clubs, these people may share your cultural background as well as your social class. It is from such groups that marriage and domestic partners most often come.

Social class also plays a role in the age at which people marry: the average age of first marriage for women with high school diplomas is twenty-five, while for women with graduate degrees it is thirty. The age at which people start a family and the number of children they have are also related to educational attainment. In 2011, 66 percent of new mothers had at least some college education, while 34 percent had a high school diploma or less. While 48 percent of new mothers without a high school diploma were younger than twenty-five, only 3 percent of new mothers with a bachelor's degree were younger than twenty-five. Less educated women have a higher average number of births throughout their lifetime than more educated women. On average, women without a high school diploma have 2.5 children, whereas women with a bachelor's degree have about 1.7 children (Livingston and Cohn 2013).

Health

Those at the bottom of the social class ladder are the least likely to obtain adequate nutrition, shelter, clothing, and health care and are thus more prone to illness. Often they cannot afford to see a doctor, fill a prescription, or go to a hospital. Instead of preventing an illness from becoming worse, they must wait until a health crisis occurs, and then they have no option but expensive emergency room care. Health-care reforms, such as those provided by the Affordable Care Act of 2010, are meant to help change that pattern.

Sociologists have found that people who occupy a higher SES are more likely to have access to health care resources. In one study of Americans, researchers found that regardless of age, race, or gender, people with more education were more likely to have health insurance: only 55 percent of those with high school diplomas had access to health insurance, relative to 69 percent with bachelor's degrees and 73 percent with advanced degrees (Baum, Ma, and Payea 2013). Another study found that not only do people of higher SES feel healthier, they in fact live longer—almost five years longer than people of low SES (Singh and Siahpush 2006).

One factor that contributes to disparities in health is exercise. As education and income increase, so does the likelihood of a person engaging in some exercise, as reported in 2014 by the CDC's National Center for Health Statistics (2014c). For instance, in 2012 nearly 61 percent of respondents living below the poverty level did not meet guidelines for physical activity (aerobic or strength training exercise), compared with only 36 percent of those living at four times above the poverty level (Centers for Disease Control & Prevention [CDC] 2013b). Only 24 percent of respondents living below the poverty level reported engaging in physical activity regularly, compared with 43 percent of those living at the higher income level (CDC 2013b). Education may have something to do with these contrasts, as more knowledge about the health benefits of exercise may lead to more active participation. But we can also see exercise as rather a luxury for those in higher social classes, who are not struggling with the day-to-day efforts to survive that characterize the lives of the poor.

Education

How children perform in school determines whether and where they go to college, what professions they enter, and how much they are paid. And generally, those with more education make more money. According to a 2014 report by the U.S. Department of Labor, the median annual income for those with advanced professional (medical and law) degrees was $89,128, followed by doctoral degrees at $84,396, master's degrees at $69,108, bachelor's degrees at $57,616, and high school diplomas at $33,852 (U.S. Bureau of Labor Statistics 2014b). On the surface, these earnings may seem fair. After all, shouldn't people with more education make more money? However, as sociologists, we must probe further and ask some fundamental questions; for example, who has access to education, and how good is that education?

One of the main goals of education is to make sure students get a chance to succeed both in school and in life. But to meet this goal, schools would have to serve all students equally, and they aren't always able to do so. Schools with low-income students often receive fewer resources, have greater difficulty in attracting qualified teachers, and experience less support from parents (Fischer and Kmec 2004). A student's social class background will also influence her attitude toward education. The higher the family's SES, the higher the student's expectations for educational achievement. Students from higher social classes are expected to complete more years of school and are more likely to attend college than those from lower social classes (Berends 1995; Goyette and Xie 1999; Bozick et al. 2010). It's not surprising to find that 81 percent of children from high-income families are enrolled in college, whereas 65 percent of those from middle-income and 51 percent from lower-income families are enrolled in college (see Figure 7.2).

According to a U.S. Census Bureau report (2015a), approximately 88 percent of adults aged twenty-five and over had a high school diploma, 59 percent had at least some college, 32 percent had a bachelor's degree, and 12 percent had advanced degrees. Although educational attainment is at an all-time high in the United States, a high school education doesn't mean what it once did. College and advanced degrees are becoming more important. If the trends continue, fewer and fewer jobs will be available to those without college degrees, and of those jobs, fewer will support middle-class lifestyles. Yet, not all students are equally prepared for or able to afford a college education, which creates a risk that children from lower socioeconomic backgrounds will slip farther down the social class ladder.

Work and Income

In the past couple of decades, we have seen a widening income gap between those at the top, middle, and bottom of the scale (see Figure 7.3). According to a report in 2014, upper-income families were seven times more wealthy than middle-income families, and more than 70 times more wealthy than lower-income ones (Pew Research Center 2014a). Income is the product of work, and members of different social classes, with unequal educational opportunities, tend to work in different types of jobs.

At the bottom of the scale, members of the lower class generally experience difficulties in the job market and may endure periods of unemployment or underemployment (working in a job that doesn't pay enough to support a person's needs, is

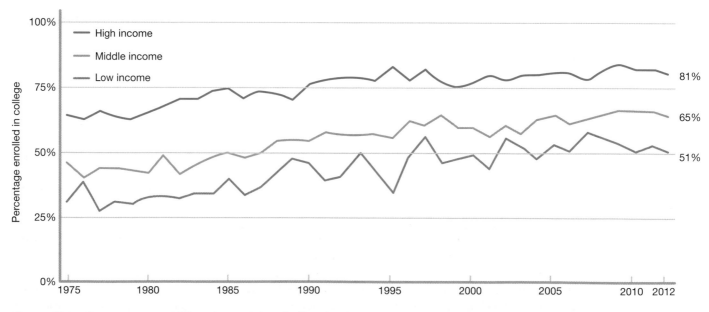

Figure 7.2   Percentage of High School Grads Enrolled in Two- or Four-Year College, by Income Level, 1975–2012

SOURCE: DeSilver 2014.

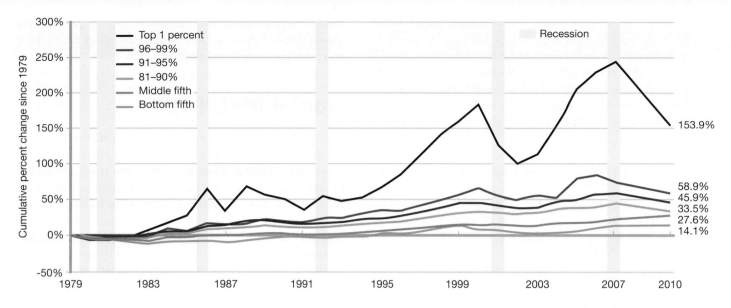

Figure 7.3 Change in Average Real Annual Household Income, by Income Group, 1979–2010

SOURCE: Gould 2014.

seasonal or temporary, or doesn't make full use of their skills). Among the lower class are people receiving a variety of forms of government aid. In 2014, some 3.5 million were receiving Temporary Assistance for Needy Families (Office of Family Assistance 2015) and in 2015, 46.4 million were receiving help from the Supplemental Nutrition Assistance Program, or food stamps (U.S. Department of Agriculture 2015).

Members of the working (lower-middle) class work for wages in a variety of blue collar jobs. They can generally earn a dependable income through skilled or semiskilled occupations, but they may also experience periods of unemployment tied to fluctuations in the economy, layoffs, and plant closings. For example, in 2008 alone, the United States lost more than 600,000 jobs as a result of factory shutdowns and other problems associated with the economic downturn (Garr 2008).

While factory work and other types of skilled labor were once enough to support a middle-class lifestyle, most middle-class jobs today are found in the service, information, and technology sectors. Most households here require two incomes to maintain a comfortable lifestyle, and many middle-class jobs require some sort of college degree.

Those in the upper-middle class tend to work in executive and professional fields. Some members are business owners; a small portion own large farms or ranches. Others, known as the "creative class" (Florida 2002)—architects, writers, scientists, artists, professors, and engineers—tend to cluster in "creative" cities, such as Austin, San Francisco, and Seattle.

Through exceptional success in any profession or art, or sometimes through inheritance, one can join the upper class. In the United States, the upper class is influential in politics, business, and culture, largely because of its economic privilege: in our highly stratified society, the top 1 percent consistently controlled more than 33 percent of the national wealth in the 2000s (Wolff 2004; Kennickell 2009). That trend

accelerated, and by 2011 the top 1 percent had gained control of 40 percent of the country's wealth (Stiglitz 2011).

As a result of the recent recession, workers—most often in lower-middle and lower-class occupations—increasingly find themselves engaging in what is termed "precarious labor" (Kalleberg 2009). Precarious labor is work that is uncertain, unpredictable, and unprotected, such as contract labor, temporary work, or part-time work. Economic fluctuations often affect these workers first, placing them at greater risk of layoffs because of downsizing and outsourcing. Corporations seeking to cut costs have resorted to a variety of strategies. Some have restructured their workforce and made do with leaner payrolls, while others have relocated their operations overseas in countries where labor costs are lower. Both manufacturing and service jobs are subject to downsizing and outsourcing, meaning that blue collar and white collar workers—and even some higher-ranking executives—are now vulnerable. Their jobs, and class status, may be more precarious than ever before.

Criminal Justice

In general, people of lower SES are more likely to encounter the criminal justice system, whether as a perpetrator or victim of a crime, than those of higher SES. But the statistics are not as straightforward as they might seem. One influential study (Blau and Blau 1982) showed that while poverty is associated with higher rates of violent crime, variables such as dense population and anomie (a sense of alienation or lack of social connections) have an even greater impact on crime rates.

People in lower classes are often more visible, less powerful, and thus more likely to be apprehended and labeled as criminals than those from higher social classes. There are also differences in how crimes are prosecuted. White collar criminals are less likely to be arrested, prosecuted, or convicted than ordinary "street" criminals (Schwellenbach 2008). White collar criminals (such as Enron heads Jeffrey Skilling and the late Kenneth Lay, and Bernie Madoff, whose Ponzi scheme bilked wealthy clients of billions of dollars) can also afford the best legal representation and hence enjoy distinct advantages in the courtroom. If white collar criminals are convicted, their sentences are likely to be lighter. Still, while Enron's Kenneth Lay avoided prison time by dying of a massive heart attack several months before his October 2006 sentencing date, Jeffrey Skilling was sentenced to twenty-four years in prison, and Madoff received 150 years for his crimes. Perhaps their punishments will serve as a deterrent for other high-status criminals.

Studies have claimed that 90 percent of inmates on death row could not afford to hire a lawyer when they were tried (Lane and Tabak 1991) and that the quality of representation, rather than the actual facts presented in a trial, determines whether someone is sentenced to death (ACLU 2003). Studies have also shown that race and SES influence whether the death penalty is sought. Prosecutors are more likely to seek the death penalty if the killer is black or if the victim was white, while those who are able to hire legal counsel are less likely to be sentenced to death. Therefore, the intersection of race and SES can dramatically affect the outcome of criminal sentencing (Phillips 2009).

Lower-class people are also more likely to be the victims of violent crime. Statistics consistently show that poor people are more than one and a half times as likely to be victims of violent crime than those in higher social class brackets (Levinson 2002). At the same time, people with lower SES are also more likely to feel at risk of harassment by police. As both education and income decreased, respondents reported feeling more threatened by police; as education and income increased, they felt less threatened (Levinson 2002).

Social class affects more than just our financial or material state—it is intricately woven into the fabric of our lives. You may once have concluded that differences in people's education, work, family, or health were simply a matter of individual preference or effort, or that each individual is responsible for her own circumstances. While this may be true to some extent, research shows that social class background has a profound impact on one's life chances, leading those with different statuses into very different life courses. This means that we can't take for granted whatever advantages or disadvantages we might experience but should acknowledge how hierarchies of inequality have helped create our particular social realities.

SOCIAL MOBILITY the movement of individuals or groups within the hierarchical system of social classes

CLOSED SYSTEM a social system with very little opportunity to move from one class to another

OPEN SYSTEM a social system with ample opportunities to move from one class to another

INTERGENERATIONAL MOBILITY movement between social classes that occurs from one generation to the next

INTRAGENERATIONAL MOBILITY the movement between social classes that occurs during the course of an individual's lifetime

HORIZONTAL SOCIAL MOBILITY the movement of individuals or groups within a particular social class, most often a result of changing occupations

Social Mobility

How do people move from one social class to another? In other words, how do they achieve social mobility? Sociologists use the concept of **social mobility** to measure movement within the stratification system of a particular society, whether it's a small town, a state, or a nation. In some societies, social mobility is highly restricted by formal or informal rules. India's caste system is an example of what sociologists refer to as a **closed system**: there is very little opportunity for social mobility among classes. The United States, where social mobility is possible, is perceived to be an **open system**. It was not always so, however. In the period before the Civil War, slavery was widespread, keeping African Americans from climbing the social class ladder.

The movement of people among social classes can happen in three ways: through intergenerational mobility, intragenerational mobility, or structural mobility. **Intergenerational mobility** refers to the movement that occurs from one generation to the next, when a child eventually moves into a different social class from that of her parents. Americans have always placed great faith in the idea of economic mobility. Research shows that Baby Boomers (the generation of children born immediately after World War II) have, for the most part, achieved upward intergenerational mobility: on the whole, they amassed more wealth during the course of their lives and consequently moved up the social class ladder.

Since then, however, mobility seems to have stalled and in the last fifty years it has not gotten any easier to climb the social class ladder, despite progressive social policy changes that were intended to help more people. An individual's overall standing in terms of income distribution still closely tracks that of her parents. Some social scientists claim that there are fewer opportunities for advancement than before (Krueger 2002, 2012). While the majority of Americans exceed their parents' income and wealth, the amount of their upward movement may not lift them to a higher position on the social class ladder (Mazumder 2012; Pew Research Center 2012d). Perhaps more distressing is the finding that people born near the bottom tend to stay near the bottom. Conversely, there are many mechanisms in place, such as tax laws and social policies, that allow those at the top of the ladder to protect their assets and pass them down to the next generation, making it more difficult for the middle and lower classes to improve their positions (Chetty et al. 2014).

Intragenerational mobility refers to the movement that occurs during the course of an individual's lifetime. In other words, it is the measure between the social class a person is born into and the social class status she achieves during her lifetime. Intragenerational mobility can be measured in two directions. **Horizontal social mobility**, which is fairly common, refers to the changing of jobs within a social class: a therapist who shifts careers so that he can teach college experiences horizontal mobility. **Vertical social mobility** is movement up or down the social ladder, and thus is often called upward or downward mobility. If this same therapist marries a president of a large corporation, he might experience upward mobility. On the other hand, if he or his wife becomes unemployed, he might experience downward mobility. People are far more likely to experience horizontal than vertical social mobility.

Although we usually think of social mobility as the result of individual effort (or lack thereof), other factors can contribute to a change in one's social class. **Structural mobility** occurs when large numbers of people move up or down the social ladder because of structural changes in society as a whole, particularly when the economy is affected by large-scale events. For instance, during the Great Depression of the early 1930s, precipitated by the stock market crash of 1929, huge numbers of upper- and middle-class people suddenly found themselves among the poor. Conversely, during the dot-com boom of the late 1990s, developing and investing in new technologies made many people into overnight millionaires. Both of these extreme periods eventually leveled out. Still, many people in the Depression era remained in their new class, never able to climb up the social ladder again. We have yet to see if the Great Recession of 2008 will have a similar long-term effect.

Poverty

Social mobility is most difficult—and most essential—for those who live at the bottom of the socioeconomic ladder. In this section, we look at what it means to experience poverty in the United States.

Poverty can be defined in relative or absolute terms. **Relative deprivation** is a comparative measure, whereby people are considered impoverished if their standard of living is lower than that of other members of society—for example, a retail clerk who works part-time for minimum wage might be considered among the working poor compared with a neurosurgeon whose salary places her comfortably in the upper-middle class. Many communities are characterized by such dual realities. **Absolute deprivation**, on the other hand, is a measure whereby people are unable to meet minimal standards for food, shelter, clothing, and health care. In the African country of Burundi, for example, 53 percent of children under the age of five experience chronic malnutrition, and in some poor provinces the number jumps to over 90 percent (UNICEF 2010). In Swaziland, more than 26 percent of adults are living with HIV/AIDS. Poverty has resulted in a lack of access to health care, exacerbating the HIV epidemic and making this country among the lowest in terms of life expectancy, averaging less than fifty years (Central Intelligence Agency 2014i). Hunger, malnutrition, and the inability to afford medications are some of the basic indicators of absolute poverty.

In the United States, the federal poverty line—an absolute measure, calculated annually—indicates the total annual income below which a family would be impoverished. These figures are derived from either the poverty thresholds established by the Census Bureau or the guidelines determined by the Department of Health and Human Services. In 2015, the poverty threshold was $24,250 for a family of four, $20,990 for a family of three, $15,930 for a family of two, and $11,770 for an individual (Federal Register 2015). In fact, families making much more than these amounts, although not officially qualifying as below the poverty line, might still be unable to afford some basic necessities.

How many people fall below the poverty line? The numbers are startling, given that we usually think of the United States as a wealthy nation. In 2013, 14.5 percent of the population, or 45.3 million people, were considered to be living in poverty, a slight decrease in both percentage and numbers from the previous year (U.S. Census Bureau 2014g). During the past forty years, the percentage of people living in poverty has fluctuated in the low teens, but it has never dipped below 10 percent. In fact, the number has occasionally risen to more than 15 percent, as it did in 2009 and 2011, while in the late 1950s it rose to as high as 22 percent (see Figure 7.4).

Contrary to popular myth, most people living in poverty are not unemployed; this is why they are often categorized as among the working poor. The annual earnings of a full-time worker making $7.25 an hour (the prevailing federal minimum wage since 2009) still put him below the poverty line if he is trying to support a family. In fact, at no time in its nearly eighty-year history has the federal minimum wage been sufficient for a worker to exist above the poverty line with a dependent, such as a child, unemployed spouse, or family member. According to researchers, more than 80 percent of low-income minimum-wage workers, even if they are working full-time, are not earning enough to guarantee a decent standard of living, and many cannot afford some of the basic necessities (Wicks-Lim and Thompson 2010).

The poverty line has often been criticized because of the way it is uniformly applied without regard to regional or other differences. For instance, a family living in Washington, DC, might need twice or three times as much income as a family in Des Moines, Iowa, for expenses like rent, transportation, health insurance, and child care (exceptions are made for Alaska and Hawaii, both states with extremely high costs of living). In addition, some families may be eligible for some

VERTICAL SOCIAL MOBILITY the movement between different class statuses, often called either upward mobility or downward mobility

STRUCTURAL MOBILITY changes in the social status of large numbers of people as a result of structural changes in society

RELATIVE DEPRIVATION a relative measure of poverty based on the standard of living in a particular society

ABSOLUTE DEPRIVATION an objective measure of poverty, defined by the inability to meet minimal standards for food, shelter, clothing, or health care

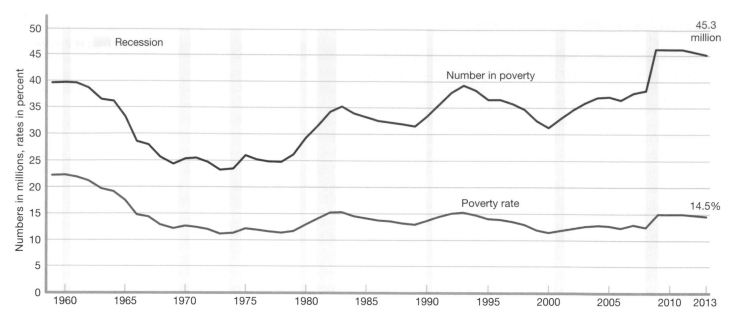

Figure 7.4 Number in Poverty and Poverty Rate, 1959–2013

SOURCE: U.S. Census Bureau 2014g.

form of government assistance, such as food stamps (SNAP) or the earned income tax credit (EITC), which makes a difference in the total amount of their household money. Many working families thus live close to the edge and struggle to make ends meet but are not included as part of the official poverty statistics (Waldron et al. 2004; Sherman 2012).

Poverty is also more prominent among certain population groups (Figure 7.5). For instance, poverty rates are higher among blacks (27.2 percent) and Hispanics (23.5 percent) than Asians (10.5 percent) or whites (9.6 percent) (U.S. Census Bureau 2014g). They are higher for the elderly, disabled, and those who are foreign born, as well as for women, children, and single-parent households. By geographic region, poverty is highest in the South, though there are concentrations of people living in poverty in every region of the country, in inner cities, in rural areas, and also in suburbs (Plumer 2013).

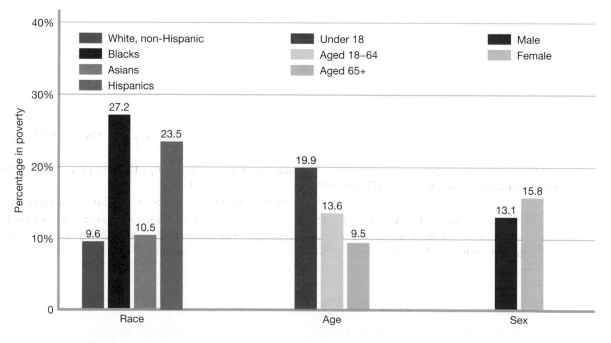

Figure 7.5 Poverty in the United States by Selected Characteristics, 2013

SOURCE: U.S. Census Bureau 2014g.

Social Welfare and Welfare Reform

Some of the most heated debates about the nature of poverty involve how or even whether society should help those who are impoverished. Some argue that government assistance lifts people out of poverty and helps them become self-supporting; others say that it just fosters a dependence on aid and causes further problems.

The idea behind the current American welfare state, which consists of such programs as Social Security, unemployment insurance, and Temporary Assistance for Needy Families (TANF), was first proposed by President Franklin D. Roosevelt during the Great Depression. These programs, collectively called the New Deal, were a response to a national crisis and were meant to serve as a safety net for citizens, helping them in times of adversity or old age, poverty, or joblessness. The 1960s ushered in a new War on Poverty. A second wave of programs, such as Medicaid and Head Start, intended to solve a variety of social and economic problems, was proposed by President John F. Kennedy and instituted by President Lyndon B. Johnson as part of his Great Society program in 1964.

The welfare system attempted to be fair by providing uniform, standard benefits to all the nation's needy without regard to their personal circumstances and with no time limit. Social Security and Medicaid lifted seniors out of poverty, and programs like Head Start and Upward Bound offered educational support for poor children. Food stamps improved nutrition for those with limited incomes, and job-training programs helped the poor gain marketable skills. By 1970, the poverty rate had declined from 22.2 percent to 12.6 percent (Califano 1999), the fastest it has ever dropped.

In the 1980s, political opinion turned against social welfare programs despite their successes. Critics claimed that these programs were responsible for creating a permanent underclass of people living off government checks—some receiving benefits they didn't deserve—and essentially discouraging them from seeking work. Much of the rhetoric surrounding welfare programs stems from concerns about federal spending. People commonly assume that welfare constitutes a large portion of the federal budget, when in fact welfare and unemployment together represented just over 13 percent of government spending in 2011, or $324 billion (Figure 7.6). Compare that with Social Security (about 21 percent of spending, or $608 billion) or defense and the war on terror (about 20 percent of spending, or $626 billion). But given these misconceptions, it makes sense that welfare abuse and reform have received so much press, both in past decades and now.

In response to criticism of welfare programs, reforms arrived in the 1990s. Under President Bill Clinton, the Personal Responsibility and Work Opportunity Reconciliation Act was passed into law in 1996. Often referred to as the Welfare Reform Act, it ended the concept of "entitlements" by requiring recipients to find work within two years of

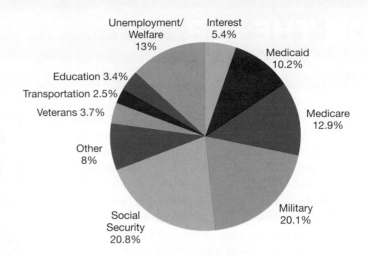

Figure 7.6 Federal Spending, 2011

SOURCE: U.S. Government Printing Office 2011.

receiving assistance and imposing a limit of five years as the total amount of time in which families could receive assistance. The act also decentralized the federal system of public assistance, allowing individual states to design their own programs, some of which would deny or reduce certain benefits and impose their own criteria for eligibility. The rationale was to encourage people on welfare to take responsibility for working themselves out of poverty. In 2003, Congress approved changes to the act, requiring an even larger percentage of recipients to take jobs and work longer hours.

While welfare reform has been an economic success in terms of reducing the number of people on welfare, there is still a great deal to be learned about its success or failure in transforming the lives of the poor. Evidence suggests that moving from welfare to work does not increase income levels—in other words, federal assistance is merely replaced with an equally low-paying job, which has the effect of keeping families beneath the poverty line once they're off welfare. The reasons for this—the increased costs of child care, health insurance, and transportation—make it difficult for former welfare recipients to succeed outside the system (Hays 2003).

Studies have sought to evaluate the consequences of welfare policy changes. One of the largest, "Welfare, Children, and Families: A Three-City Study," is a longitudinal study (one that follows the children of welfare over time) done in Boston, Chicago, and San Antonio. A team of researchers from three universities, including sociologists, anthropologists, psychologists, and economists, using methods as diverse as survey research, interviews, and in-depth ethnographies, sought to discover whether welfare reform was really helping to eradicate poverty and what kind of an impact welfare reform had on the lives of struggling families. The study found that for families leaving welfare, their income rose only incrementally (less than 20 percent), and the impact on the lives of children (school achievement, mental health, etc.) was also only mildly positive (Hao and Cherlin 2004; Slack et al. 2006). So getting

ON THE JOB
Get a Job! Minimum Wage or Living Wage?

There are many misconceptions about people living in poverty, and one is that they're in such conditions because they're unwilling to work. What many fail to realize is that working, even full time at forty or more hours per week, may not be enough to lift people and their families out of poverty. So telling someone to just go get a job (assuming work is available) may be short-sighted. While unemployment and underemployment are both issues in themselves, full-time employment in a minimum-wage job can also be problematic.

Who are minimum-wage workers? While the common perception is that they are predominately teenagers or other young people working part-time, the average minimum-wage worker is thirty-five years old, female, white, and working full-time. More than 80 percent of minimum-wage workers are older than twenty, and 33 percent are over forty (Cooper and Essrow 2013). They work largely in service industries such as hospitality and retail and are particularly concentrated in the fast-food sector.

First passed into law as part of the New Deal in the years following the Great Depression, the federal minimum wage—the lowest hourly amount an employer is required to pay workers—is considered a fundamental measure to protect workers from exploitation. Yet at no time in its more than eighty-year history has the minimum wage been sufficient for a full-time worker with a dependent (such as a child, unemployed spouse, or relative for whom they provide care) to earn above the federally defined poverty line. Since 2009, the federal minimum wage has been set at $7.25 per hour. At that rate, a full-time minimum-wage worker earns approximately $1,256 per month before taxes. Despite increases over the years, the minimum wage has not kept pace with inflation. There are other problems as well. Even when adjusted for inflation, the minimum wage is worth 10 percent less than it was in 2004, and over 30 percent less than in the late 1960s, making it increasingly difficult to survive on minimum wage.

In response, there is a growing movement to establish a "living wage" instead of a minimum wage. Whereas the minimum wage is defined as pay sufficient for basic survival, a living wage is defined as the minimum income necessary for a decent standard of living. Most consider it the minimum income necessary to obtain not only food, clothing, and shelter, but also utilities, transportation, health care, education, and savings for retirement. A living wage, then, might vary depending on the community and its cost of living, but it can run from 50 to 150 percent higher than a minimum wage.

Fight for 15 Fast-food workers in Los Angeles protest for higher wages, calling for a living wage of $15.00 per hour.

More than 125 U.S. municipalities have already passed some form of living wage ordinance since the first one was instated in Baltimore in 1994 (Neumark 2004; NELP 2011), including such major cities as Seattle, St. Louis, Philadelphia, and Miami. Activists in dozens more cities across the country, both large and small, have launched similar living wage campaigns. Among some of the most high profile are living wage movements in Los Angeles and New York City, both places with millions of low-wage workers and high costs of living (Kirkham and Hsu 2014).

In the wake of more cities passing local minimum wage ordinances, some of America's biggest retail firms have also followed suit. Walmart, the nation's largest private employer, raised wages for its lowest paid workers to $9.00 per hour in 2015 and over $10.00 per hour in 2016. This was seen as something of a victory, although activists were pushing for a starting rate of $15.00 per hour, a figure that is closer to a living wage. Other retailers had little choice but to do likewise, with the parent company of T.J. Maxx and Marshalls boosting their rates accordingly (Gustafson 2015).

Debates about raising the federal minimum wage have persisted over many decades. It is a complex issue that brings up many questions about whether higher wages will also lead businesses to increase consumer prices, lay off workers, or relocate to where labor is less expensive. More important, will raising the minimum wage or establishing a living wage help reduce poverty in America and provide millions more working people with a decent standard of living? Your future, or that of someone you know, is likely at stake.

off welfare does bring positive results, but often those results aren't strong enough to serve as much of an incentive. It is likely that new policy recommendations will emerge in the future as a result of such research.

Support for a government social safety net to help the poor has long been split, often along political lines. In 2012, a majority of 59 percent said that it is the government's responsibility to care for those who cannot care for themselves; though this was down from 63 percent in 2009 and 69 percent in 2007 (Pew Research Center 2012f). In 2014, Americans were again divided about the social safety net; 48 percent said government aid to the poor does more harm than good, while 47 percent said it does more good than harm. Just 43 percent of Americans agreed that the government should do more to help needy people, even if it means going deeper in debt, a decline from 48 percent in 2009 and 54 percent in 2007 (Pew Research Center 2012g, 2014b).

Americans also remain conflicted in their opinions about people living in poverty. Overall, 50 percent said that circumstances beyond one's control are more often to blame if a person is impoverished, while 39 percent said that an individual's lack of effort is more often to blame. A sizable majority believes that people living in poverty do work but that they are unable to earn enough money; far fewer believe that they do not work. Still, 32 percent of Americans contend that hard work in itself is no guarantee of success (Pew Research Center 2014b).

The "Culture of Poverty" and Its Critics

Some argue that what keeps people impoverished is not public policy but rather the result of entrenched cultural attitudes. Oscar Lewis (1959) first promoted the idea of a **culture of poverty** after he studied poor Hispanics in Mexico and the United States. Lewis suggested that the poor, because they were excluded from the mainstream, developed a way of life that was qualitatively different from that of middle-class groups that allowed them to cope with the dire circumstance of poverty. This way of life includes attitudes of resignation and fatalism, which lead them to accept their fate rather than trying to improve their lot. It also emphasizes immediate gratification, making it difficult for impoverished people to plan or save for the future or to join trade unions or community groups that might help them improve their situation. Once such a culture is formed, Lewis argued, it takes on a life of its own and is passed on from parents to children, leaving them ill-equipped to change.

The culture of poverty theory was later adopted by other social scientists (Banfield 1970) and applied to Americans living in poverty, particularly those in inner cities. Not surprisingly, though, the theory has been met with considerable controversy, in part because it suggests that there is little point in trying to eradicate poverty because it's more a problem of culture (attitudes, lifestyle, and behavior) than of economics. By focusing on individual character and personality, the theory tends to blame the victims of poverty for their own misfortunes while overlooking the force of their social conditions.

The tendency to see victims of social injustice as deserving of their fates is explained by what social psychologists call the **just-world hypothesis**. According to this argument, we have a strong need to believe that the world is orderly, predictable, and fair in order to achieve our goals in life. When we encounter situations that contradict this belief, we either act quickly to restore justice and order or persuade ourselves that no injustice has occurred. This can result in assuming that victims have "asked for it" or deserve whatever has befallen them. This attitude is continually reinforced through the morality tales that are a ubiquitous part of our news and entertainment, which tell us that good is rewarded and evil punished (say, in a news story about a homeless man who returns a lost wallet full of cash to its owner, who then shares the money with him).

The just-world hypothesis, developed by Melvin Lerner (1965, 1980), was tested through a series of experiments that documented how people can convince themselves that others deserve what they get. In these experiments, cash prizes were randomly distributed to students completing the exact same tasks in the exact same way. Observers, however, judged the cash recipients as the more deserving, harder workers. Other researchers (Rubin and Peplau 1975) have found that people with strong beliefs in a just world tend to "feel less of a need to engage in activities to change society or to alleviate the plight of social victims." In the face of poverty, many simply become apathetic. It is important to be aware of our own tendencies to follow such thinking, so that we might avoid becoming blind to others' misfortunes.

> **CULTURE OF POVERTY** entrenched attitudes that can develop among poor communities and lead the poor to accept their fate rather than attempt to improve their lot
>
> **JUST-WORLD HYPOTHESIS** argues that people have a deep need to see the world as orderly, predictable, and fair, which creates a tendency to view victims of social injustice as deserving of their fates

Another problem with the culture of poverty theory is that it lacks a certain sociological imagination. It fails to take into account the structural factors that shape culture and are part of the preexisting problem in which impoverished individuals find themselves. Dalton Conley (2002) argues that to solve the problem of poverty, we must examine wealth as well. A social system that allows extremes of both wealth and poverty (as ours does) reveals structural reasons why poverty persists, such as laws that protect the inheritances of the wealthy but provide few breaks for working families. Research like Conley's helps us understand that there are alternative explanations for why people are poor and even suggests that extreme wealth ought to be conceptualized as a social problem similar to that of extreme poverty. This idea resonated with the Occupy Movement that emerged during the recent recession. Activists questioned the health of an economic system in which just 1 percent of the population has amassed so much of the nation's wealth and power.

The Invisibility of Poverty

Although we are used to seeing televised images of abject poverty from overseas—crying children with bloated bellies and spindly limbs in Asia, Africa, or Latin America—we rarely see similar images from the United States. While it may be true that few Americans are as impoverished as people living in Zimbabwe, Haiti, or Honduras, some 45.3 million Americans lived below the poverty line in 2013 (U.S. Census Bureau 2014g). That's more than 14 percent of the population of the wealthiest nation in the world. How can such large numbers of people remain all but hidden to their fellow Americans? What makes poverty invisible? Consider some of these factors.

RESIDENTIAL SEGREGATION One factor is **residential segregation**—the geographical isolation of the impoverished from the rest of the city (or in the case of rural areas, from any neighbors at all). Such segregation often occurs along racial as well as socioeconomic lines, further exacerbating class divisions (Massey and Denton 1993). In the phrase "wrong side of the tracks," used to describe poverty-stricken neighborhoods, there is usually a racial connotation as well, since railroad tracks traditionally served as boundaries that kept black neighborhoods separated from white ones in the nineteenth century (Ananat 2005).

> **RESIDENTIAL SEGREGATION**
> the geographical separation of the poor from the rest of an area's population
>
> **DISENFRANCHISEMENT**
> the removal of the rights of citizenship through economic, political, or legal means

Residential segregation is accomplished most notably through public housing projects, which are typically high-density apartment complexes in urban areas, funded and managed by the Department of Housing and Urban Development (HUD). Living in these apartment complexes, many of which are in low-income, high-crime neighborhoods and are poorly maintained, can be dangerous as well as unpleasant.

Residential segregation is also exacerbated by the practice of "redlining," in which banks and mortgage lenders identify high-risk areas (usually low-income or minority neighborhoods) and either refuse mortgages to applicants from those neighborhoods or offer loans at prohibitively high rates. Redlining keeps low-income people from acquiring assets (such as real estate) that might allow them to rise out of poverty and move to a more affluent neighborhood. Though redlining is technically illegal, there is evidence that it is still practiced today in banking, insurance, and other industries, disproportionately affecting the poor and minorities (Wilson 2009). In one instance, a major mortgage company, MidAmerica Bank, settled a redlining case in Chicago by agreeing to open more branches in low-income and minority neighborhoods and to include those community's consumers in their advertising campaigns, which had previously targeted only buyers at higher income levels.

POLITICAL DISENFRANCHISEMENT People living in poverty may also remain invisible to the larger society because of their lack of political power. **Disenfranchisement** is a correlate of poverty: the impoverished are less likely to vote or otherwise participate in political life (Kerbo and Gonzalez 2003). When everyday life is a struggle to make ends meet, it is difficult to muster the extra energy necessary to work for political change. The impoverished may also feel that the system has not served them; if the government ignores their interests, why bother to become involved? Because of their lack of involvement, the impoverished lack political clout and the resources to make their plight a high-profile political priority. Politicians at the local and national levels have little motivation to address their needs, because as a constituency the impoverished wield less power than such groups as senior citizens, "soccer moms," and small-business owners. When the impoverished do organize politically, even their successes may not be well known. One group, Mothers of East Los Angeles (whose motto includes the phrase "not economically rich, but culturally wealthy"), has been successfully protecting its neighborhood from environmental degradation and exploitation for decades. The group has rebuffed plans to build a prison, toxic waste plants, and an oil pipeline near homes and schools in its community. But have you ever heard of it?

High-profile occasions, such as political conventions and major sporting events, put a media spotlight on city streets. In the summer of 2000, for example, on the eve of the Republican National Convention, the city of Philadelphia denied a permit to a group of welfare rights protesters who wanted to demonstrate against government poverty policies. The hope was that in denying the permit, the group would not make

Residential Segregation High-density housing projects isolate the poor from the rest of the city.

an appearance on streets already crawling with politicians, demonstrators, journalists, and photographers. But the protesters marched anyway—with a police escort—and were able to make their voices heard despite the lack of official permission to do so.

THE DIGITAL DIVIDE In a postindustrial economy, most people will have to demonstrate a certain level of computer proficiency in order to secure a job. One way or another, the majority of jobs in contemporary society involve computers, so it's likely you'll have to know how to use certain programs to do your work, whatever it may be. Because you are attending college, you'll probably be lucky enough to acquire some of these skills in the course of your education. But not everyone has the same opportunities, and many Americans lack the basic computer literacy, experience, and access necessary to compete in a job market that increasingly demands such skills. This inequality in access to and use of digital technology is known as the **digital divide**.

The hierarchies of inequality in the larger society—such as socioeconomic status, race, age, and educational attainment—all shape one's access to technology (Glaser 2007). For example, while 87 percent of all adults in the United States use the Internet regularly, there are differences in access among various demographic groups. In 2014 there were lower Internet usage rates among Hispanics (83 percent), households with an income under $30,000 (77 percent), those with a high school education or less (76 percent), and seniors (57 percent) (Pew Research Center 2014d). With the rise in popularity and availability of smartphones, more underrepresented groups are gaining Internet access. Still, some researchers expect the digital divides between the "haves" and the "have-nots" to continue and even expand into the next decades (Pew Research Center 2013).

These disparities mirror the contours of other sorts of social inequality, especially because technology requires resources—funds to purchase devices and the means to get online. Those higher up the social class ladder have more of these resources than the working poor or underclass. The digital divide is really about the benefits of having technological competence and access, especially as it relates to the additional opportunities and advantages it brings. Most important, the digital divide matters in the areas of education and the job market. Too many are still getting left behind.

HOMELESSNESS In certain situations, the people who are most impoverished are deliberately removed from public view. Police are sometimes ordered to scour the streets, rousting the homeless and herding them out of sight, as they did in 1988 in New York City's Tompkins Square Park (an infamous riot ensued).

Mostly, though, the homeless remain invisible. We don't know exactly how many homeless live in the United States. The Census Bureau focuses its population counts on households, so the homeless living in long-term shelters may get counted, but not those on the streets. One recent estimate is that at least 2.5 to 3.5 million people (approximately 1 percent of the U.S. population) will experience homelessness at least once during a given year, with an additional 7.4 million people living doubled up with others out of economic necessity (National Law Center on Homelessness and Poverty 2015). The recent recession left many people unemployed and their finances drained, creating a surge in homelessness that included many who were formerly among the middle classes. "Nationally, homelessness has now reached crisis proportions not seen since the Great Depression," said Maria Foscarinis, executive director of the National Law Center on Homelessness and Poverty (Goodman 2010).

Each year, the city of New York attempts to measure the number of homeless men and women. Volunteers comb the streets in the overnight hours, making note of all those they find sleeping on park benches or in building stairwells. They do not, however, enter abandoned buildings or subway tunnels, where many of New York's homeless seek shelter. The 2014 count of the homeless population found a 44 percent increase in people living on the city's streets versus 2009 (3,357 in 2014 compared with 2,328 in 2009), along with another 60,352 living in shelters (Saul 2014; Coalition for the Homeless 2015). Although this is sometimes a difficult population to locate and there may be questions about the accuracy of reports, such counts help the city estimate its needs for homeless services in the coming year.

> **DIGITAL DIVIDE** the unequal access to computer and Internet technology, both globally and within the United States

Counting the Homeless Volunteers speak with a homeless man on a subway for the all-night Homeless Outreach Population Estimate (HOPE). The goal is to obtain an estimate of individuals living on the street in New York City in order to help the government provide better services for the homeless population.

The homeless also remain invisible to most of us because of our own feelings of discomfort and guilt. John Coleman, a former college president and business executive, discovered this when he lived in poverty, if only temporarily, on the streets of Manhattan. Coleman went "undercover" as a homeless man for ten days and found that the minute he shed his privileged identity, people looked at him differently—or not at all. During his days on the streets, Coleman passed by and made eye contact with his accountant, his landlord, and a co-worker—each looked right through him, without recognition. But he was not invisible to everyone. Police officers often shook him awake to get him moving from whatever meager shelter he had found for the night. A waiter at a diner took one look at him and forced him to pay up front for his 99-cent breakfast special. Other homeless men, though, showed him kindness and generosity (Coleman 1983).

To whom are the homeless (and others living in poverty) most visible? Those who work with them: caseworkers, social service providers, government bureaucrats, volunteers and charity workers, clergy, cops, business owners (including those who may not want to deal with them, as well as those who may exploit them). And now, they are more visible to you.

With a sociological perspective, you can now see the effects of social stratification everywhere you turn. And when you recognize the multiple, complex causes of poverty—such as limited educational and job opportunities, stagnating wages, economic downturns, racism, mental illness, and substance abuse—it will no longer be as simple to consider each individual responsible for his or her own plight. Finally, the sociological perspective will give you the ability to imagine possible solutions to the problems associated with poverty—solutions that focus on large-scale social changes as well as individual actions, including your own. Don't let poverty remain invisible.

Inequality and the Ideology of the American Dream

Ask almost anyone about the American Dream and they are likely to mention some of the following: owning your own home; having a good marriage and great kids; finding a good job that you enjoy; being able to afford nice vacations; having a big-screen TV, nice clothes, or season tickets to your team's home games. For most Americans, the dream also means that all people, no matter how humble their beginnings, can succeed in whatever they set out to do if they work hard enough. In other words, a poor boy or girl could grow up to become president of the United States, an astronaut, a professional basketball player, a captain of industry, or a movie star.

One problem with the American Dream, however, is that it doesn't always match reality. It's more of an ideology: a belief system that explains and justifies some sort of social arrangement, in this case America's social class hierarchy. The ideology of the American Dream legitimizes stratification by reinforcing the idea that everyone has the same chance to get ahead and that success or failure depends on the person (Hochschild 1996). Inequality is presented as a system of incentives and rewards for achievement. If we can credit anyone who does succeed, then logically we must also blame anyone who fails. The well-socialized American buys into this belief system, without recognizing its structural flaws. We are caught in what Marx would call "false consciousness," the inability to see the ways in which we may be oppressed.

Nevertheless, it's not easy to dismiss the idea of the American Dream, especially when there are so many high-profile examples. Take, for instance, Oprah Winfrey. Born in Mississippi in 1954, Winfrey endured a childhood of abject poverty. In 2014, *Forbes* magazine listed her as number 217 of the 400 richest Americans, a ranking she has climbed to over a period of years, with a likewise impressive personal wealth of $3 billion. In 2010, *Forbes* honored her as the world's most powerful celebrity (of 100), based on a composite that included earnings ($165 million that year) and dominance across various media. In that same year, Oprah Winfrey launched her own independent cable network—the Oprah Winfrey Network, or OWN. The accolades and awards span many categories. Not only is she extremely successful as a media mogul and personality, but she is also widely praised for her philanthropic efforts and is

The American Dream Oprah Winfrey's meteoric rise from a childhood of poverty to her position as one of the most powerful celebrities in America is often cited as a prime example of the American Dream. How does Oprah's success represent the exception rather than the rule?

Nikita and Parissah, both eighteen, and Jack, nineteen, are college students. They anticipate being in debt by the time they graduate, although they do not foresee getting the kinds of good-paying jobs their education should secure. Twenty-two-year-old Kate is a teacher, and twenty-nine-year-old Chayanne a university employee; they are both college students as well, trying to work and at the same time finish up their degrees. For Chayanne, things are tough; each day is a battle. Kate accepts that she will never do better than her parents. Elena, twenty-five, studied sociology, something she says was great for her brain but that has not so far led to a full-time job. Blanca, a lawyer, and Peter, a medical sales rep, are both thirty years old and refer to themselves as overeducated. Yet it took years before either could find gainful employment in their fields. Saeed, twenty-nine, quit high school and went to work at a grocery store while his college-bound friends ended up with what he calls lousy jobs anyway.

What do all these young people have in common? They are members of what's often called the Millennial generation, or alternately Generation Y—Americans under thirty-five years old, born roughly between the early 1980s and 2000. Lately they've been called other things as well, the least heartening of which might be "Generation Screwed." They are unlike other contemporary generations before them. The Millennials are entering the world of work and finance at a particularly challenging time that looks much less favorable to their generation. Their predominantly Baby Boomer (and some Gen-X) parents started out as adults under very different, and much better, economic conditions. The current economic conditions were not created by the Millennials themselves, but it is what they are inheriting. To what extent the American economy may be recovering is still being determined, but the hurt from a prolonged downturn has inflicted significant, long-term wounds. The economy has undergone profound and lasting changes that are threatening the future prospects of this large group of approximately 80 million. They are at risk of losing in pursuit of an American Dream that their parents

and grandparents before them could reasonably believe in, if not outright presume, for themselves.

So in just what ways are the Millennials screwed compared to previous generations? The widest wealth gap in history divides the young from the old. The net worth of households headed by sixty-five-year-olds rose more than 40 percent in the last twenty-five years; conversely, the net worth of younger households fell almost 70 percent (Kotkin 2012). The Millennials suffered disproportionately during the recent recession and beyond. In 2013, the unemployment rate for people under twenty-five years of age was twice as high as the national average (Shierholz, Sabadish, and Finio 2013). And many older people who would have been retiring could not afford to leave the workforce, compounding problems of a tight job market. While a higher level of educational attainment usually translates to a higher income, the Millennials have seen their income drop by 11 percent in the past decade. Does a college education that continues to rise in cost actually pay off when more than 40 percent of recent graduates are working at jobs that don't require a college degree? And what about the debt that Millennials are carrying, from student loans as well as credit cards?

All this leaves many young people wondering and worrying about their prospects for the future. Will they be the first generation that ends up being downwardly mobile from their parents? A majority of Millennials already say that they do not expect to do as well as their parents financially. And it's affecting some major life decisions and delaying their entry into adulthood. One-quarter of people between eighteen and thirty-four have moved back in with their parents, and almost one-third have put off marriage or starting a family. The idea of homeownership, so central to the American Dream, may also be out of reach. The Millennials are growing up at a time that does not favor their collective success. When the aspirations of an entire generation are thwarted, it hurts not just them, but the whole country. What will be the larger repercussions of a "Generation Screwed"?

---

admired as a symbol of what can be achieved in pursuit of the American Dream. The problem is, we tend to think of her as representing the rule rather than the exception. For most Americans, the rags-to-riches upward mobility she has achieved is very unrealistic.

Though popular opinion and rhetoric espouse the American Dream ideology or that the United States is a **meritocracy** (a system in which rewards are distributed based on merit),

sociologists find contrary evidence. In fact, no matter how hard they work or if they seek a good education, most people will make little movement at all. And the degree of mobility they do achieve can depend on their ethnicity, class status, or gender rather than merit. For example, whites are more likely to experience upward mobility than

MERITOCRACY a system in which rewards are distributed based on merit

persons of color (Davis 1995; Mazumder 2012), and married women are more likely to experience upward mobility than nonmarried women (Li and Singelmann 1998). Immigrant persons of color are the most likely to experience downward social mobility (McCall 2001). It is also harder for those who start at the bottom of the class ladder to rise up the ranks (DeParle 2012).

A poll of college-age Millennials between the ages of eighteen and twenty-four conducted in 2012 defined the American Dream as "If you work hard, you will get ahead." Survey results were split; 40 percent of young Millennials believe the American Dream still exists, while 45 percent believe it "once held true, but not anymore"; and another 10 percent said it has never existed (Jones, Cox, and Banchoff 2012). The numbers shift when broken down by such background factors as income, education, and race of the respondent (Bailey 2010). People with annual household incomes above $75,000 were more likely to believe in the dream (57 percent) than those making less than $25,000 per year (46 percent). More college graduates (58 percent) believe in the American Dream than those with just a high school education (48 percent). More non-whites believe in it (57 percent) than whites (48 percent).

Although the American Dream tends to promote consumerism as a way to achieve "the good life," the fact is that chasing after it has left us feeling less secure and satisfied—not to mention less wealthy—than previous generations (De Graaf et al. 2002). Some pundits suggest that we have lost focus on the original meaning of the American Dream, that our increasing obsession with the idea of "more (or newer or bigger) is better" is leading to more debt, less free time, and greater discontent. Americans now carry twice as much credit card debt than they did in 1990 (Walker 2004). In 2009, the average credit card debt hit a high of $5,719; by 2014, credit card holders had lowered their average balance owed to $5,234 (Veiga 2014). An Ohio State University study reported that Americans have less free time and feel more rushed than they did thirty years ago (Sayer and Mattingly 2006).

A countervailing trend in American life, however, sometimes referred to as the **simplicity movement**, rejects rampant consumerism and seeks to reverse some of its consequences for the individual, for society, and for the planet. This movement, a backlash against the traditional American Dream, encourages people to "downshift" by working less, earning less, and spending less in order to put their lifestyles in sync with their (nonmaterialistic) values (Schor 1999). What does this mean in practice? Growing your own vegetables, perhaps, or riding your bike to work, wearing second-hand clothes, and spending more time with friends and family and less time commuting, shopping, or watching TV.

One of the most radical extensions of this philosophy

SIMPLICITY MOVEMENT
a loosely knit movement that opposes consumerism and encourages people to work less, earn less, and spend less, in accordance with nonmaterialistic values

is embraced by "freegans"—a term that merges "free" with "vegan" (a person who eats no animal products). Freegans are people who avoid consumerism and who engage in strategies to support themselves without participating in a conventional economic system. This can mean scavenging for usable food, clothing, and other goods, sometimes called "urban foraging" or "dumpster diving," along with sharing housing and transportation with others in order to work less and minimize their impact on the planet.

DATA WORKSHOP
Analyzing Media and Pop Culture

Advertising and the American Dream

We are surrounded by advertising, which aims not only to give us information about products but also to create and stimulate a buying public with demands for an ever-increasing array of goods and services. Advertising shapes our consciousness and tells us what to dream and how to pursue those dreams. It provides us with a concept of the good life and tells us that it's available to everyone. Advertising equates shopping and acquisition with emotional fulfillment, freedom, fun, happiness, security, and self-satisfaction.

And the sales pitch seems to be working. Like no other generation, today's eighteen- to thirty-four-year-olds have grown up in a consumer culture with all its varied enticements, but they are having a harder time reaching financial stability in adulthood than did their parents. Many young people are finding themselves caught in a difficult job market, with too few positions and too little pay, at the same time they are carrying larger student loans and mounting credit card debt. The credit card industry has garnered many critics who claim that it is designed to keep people in debt. Some reforms to the industry and a declining number of credit card holders during post-recession years have made a dent in the student debt crisis. Yet many young people still embrace easy credit only to discover that late-payment fees and high interest rates can keep them from paying down their balances.

In 2013, more than two-thirds of all college graduates left school with student loan debt; the average amount owed rose to $28,400 (TICAS 2014). On top of that, more than one-third of all college students also use credit cards (Sallie Mae 2013). While some students may be spending on luxuries like fancy clothes, expensive meals, and high-tech toys that they really can't afford, many young people are using credit cards for basic household needs and expenses, such as prescription medications and car repairs. And the appeal to spend more is always there, urging you to buy your way into the American Dream, and perhaps leading you further into debt. So let's examine where some of this pressure to spend comes from—advertising.

In this Data Workshop, you will analyze some advertisements in terms of the ideology of the American Dream. This entails the use of existing sources and doing a content analysis to look for patterns of meaning within and across the ads. See the section on existing sources in Chapter 2 for a review of this research method.

To start your research, find three or four ads from magazines, newspapers, websites, or other sources. These should be "print" ads rather than video clips. Look for ads that are of interest to your particular age, gender, or other demographic group. In particular, try to identify ads that are selling the idea of the American Dream of wealth, success, or living the "good life." Examine both the visual (images and layout) and textual (words) elements of the advertisements.

For each of the ads, consider the following questions:

* What product or service is being advertised?

* For whom is the advertisement intended?

* Does the ad "work"? Would you like to buy the product or service? Why or why not?

* In addition to a product or service, what else are the advertisers trying to "sell"?

* What are the explicit (obvious) and implicit (subtle) messages conveyed in the ad?

* How do these messages make you feel? Do they play on your emotions, desires, or sense of self-worth? If so, in what ways?

Once you have examined all the ads, consider these more general questions:

* What were the similarities or differences between the ads you chose with regard to their underlying ideology?

* How do the ads represent a particular lifestyle that you should aspire to? How does that influence your buying habits?

* What types of ads have a strong effect on you? Why?

* What kinds of pressures do you feel to keep up with the material possessions of your friends, neighbors, or co-workers?

* Why do you think we are lured into shopping and acquiring material possessions?

There are two options for completing this Data Workshop:

PREP-PAIR-SHARE Select three ads and bring them with you to class (either the physical ads from a magazine or newspaper, photocopies, or screen shots of online ads). Reflect on the questions as they apply to one or more of your ads, and be ready to discuss your answers with other students, in pairs or small groups. Compare and contrast each other's contributions.

DO-IT-YOURSELF Write a three- to four-page essay discussing your general thoughts on advertising, consumption, and the American Dream. Include an analysis of the specific ads you chose, answering the sets of questions. Make sure to attach the ads to your paper.

CLOSING COMMENTS

Social stratification is all about power. Stratification systems, like SES, allocate different types of social power, such as wealth, political influence, and occupational prestige, and do so in fundamentally unequal ways. These inequalities are part of both the larger social structure and our everyday interactions. In the following chapters, we will examine other systems of stratification—namely, race and ethnicity, and gender and sexuality. While we separate these topics for organizational purposes, they are not experienced as separate in our everyday lives. We are women or men, working class or upper class, black or white, gay or straight simultaneously. Our experiences of these social categories are intertwined. We will continue to examine intersectionality ahead, and the complex relationship between our positions in the social structure and the varying social forces that shape our lives.

Everything You Need to Know about Social Stratification

> **"Social stratification is present in all societies. People are categorized and divided into groups, including gender, race, class, and age, which are then placed in a social hierarchy."**

THEORIES OF SOCIAL CLASS

* **Conflict:** social classes are highly stratified and continue to grow further apart

* **Weberian:** wealth, power, and prestige are interrelated, but one can also be converted into another

* **Structural functionalism:** stratification is necessary for society to function

* **Postmodernism:** social class is passed down from one generation to the next through cultural capital

* **Symbolic interactionism:** we judge people's social class constantly during everyday interactions

REVIEW

1. Think about your own class status. Is it consistent across the criteria that make up socioeconomic status (income, wealth, education, occupation, and power)? Or are you an example of status inconsistency?

2. According to Pierre Bourdieu, the cultural tools we inherit from our parents can be very important in trying to gain economic assets. What sort of cultural capital did you inherit? Has it ever helped you materially? Have you ever done something to acquire more cultural capital?

3. Erving Goffman says we "read" other people through social interaction to get a sense of their class status. What sort of clues can tell you about a person's social class within thirty seconds of meeting that person?

How Rich Are You?

The average undergraduate sociology major earns

around **$35,000** in an entry level job. That salary makes you the **48,656,639th** richest person on Earth

by income. In **1 hour** you would earn **$18.23**.

The average worker in Zimbabwe earns only **$0.53**

in the same time. If you earn **$35,000** in your first job after

college, it would take the average worker in Ghana

218 years to earn the same amount. It'll only take you

2 minutes to earn enough for a refreshing can

of soda. The average Indonesian worker has to work for

approximately **2 hours** to buy a can of soda.

SOURCE: Poke 2013

EXPLORE

Food: What's Class Got to Do with It?

Income and obesity are related: Poorer people have limited access to and less money to spend on fresh produce and high-quality brands. Visit the Everyday Sociology Blog to find out what happens when a sociologist from the middle-class in Culver City tries to shop for food in the low-income city of Compton.

http://wwnPag.es/trw407

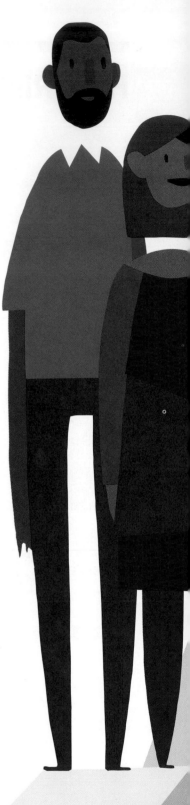

CHAPTER 8

Race and Ethnicity as Lived Experience

Despite past scandals, Tiger Woods is often hailed as the person who opened up the field of professional golf to African Americans. But Woods doesn't describe himself as black: he's "Cablinasian," a term he coined to describe his multiracial background (which includes Caucasian, black, American Indian, and Asian American ancestries). In 2002, Halle Berry became the first African American ever to win the Academy Award for Best Actress. As she tearfully accepted the statuette on stage, the camera cut to her mother sitting in the audience, beaming with pride at her daughter's accomplishment—and unmistakably white. Former *Daily Show* correspondent and *Newsroom* actress Olivia Munn is of Chinese, German, and Irish

descent. And *Parks and Recreation*'s light-skinned, straight-haired Rashida Jones is black, Russian-Jewish, Irish, Portuguese, and Cherokee. "In the next 50 years," Jones says, "people will start looking more and more like me" (Melnick 2011).

She's right. Despite America's record of racial discrimination and segregation, there have always been multiracial people in its history, beginning with the European settlers who mixed with Native Americans and black slaves alike (Clinton and Gillespie 1997; Brooks 2002). More and more, we are recognizing and celebrating our multiracial heritage.

The U.S. Census Bureau conducts a comprehensive nationwide survey of the American people every ten years. In the 2000 Census, Americans were given the opportunity for the first time to check multiple boxes to identify their race, thus creating sixty-three different racial categories. Approximately 7 million people, or 2.4 percent of the population, took advantage of the new option. Ten years later, the 2010 Census reported that approximately 9 million Americans, or 2.9 percent of the population, identified themselves as belonging to more than one racial category, a 32 percent increase from 2000 (U.S. Census Bureau 2012g). The Census Bureau is considering revising the categories for the next count in 2020 to better match the way Americans conceive of their own racial identities.

By all estimates the number of people identifying themselves as multiracial will only continue to grow: by 2050, demographers project that as many as one in five Americans could claim a multiracial identity (Lee and Bean 2010). As the United States is a nation of immigrants (some involuntary), it is only logical that the separate lineages of the American population would eventually meld. We might, therefore, wonder: will race continue to be as important in the future as it has been in the past? In this chapter, we will examine the sociological understandings of race, which will provide us with the insights we need to answer this question.

HOW TO READ THIS CHAPTER

Our goal in this chapter is for you to acquire a fundamental understanding of race and ethnicity as socially constructed categories. While each is based on traits we may see as biological, such as skin color or facial features, the meanings attached to race and ethnicity are created, maintained, and modified over time through social processes in which we all take part.

When a society categorizes people based on their race and ethnicity (and all societies do), it creates a system of stratification that leads to inequality. Society's resources—wealth, power, privilege, opportunity—are distributed according to these categories, thereby perpetuating inequalities that are all too familiar here in the United States. We also hope you will come to understand the importance of race and ethnicity in forming individual identity. Our racial and ethnic identities have profound effects on our sense of self, and our bonds to other people may be based on shared identities—or may transcend those categories entirely.

Defining Race and Ethnicity

"Race" and "ethnicity" are words we use so often in everyday speech that we might not think we need a definition of either. But people tend to use the words interchangeably, as if they mean essentially the same thing. There is, however, a significant difference between commonsense notions of race and ethnicity and what social scientists have to say about them.

The idea of different races as belonging to distinguishable categories has existed for hundreds of years. In the nineteenth century, biologists came up with a schema that grouped humans into three races: Negroid, Mongoloid, and Caucasoid (corresponding roughly to black, Asian, and white). It was believed that each race was characterized by its own biological makeup, separate and distinct from the others. Modern scientists, however, possess advanced tools for examining race in a much more sophisticated way. What they have found, ironically, is that there are no "pure" races—that the lines among races are blurry rather than fixed. A person who looks white will inevitably have biological material from other races, as will someone who looks black.

There is also no such thing as a "superior" race, as race itself is not the reason that different groups might display positive or negative characteristics (such as intelligence, athleticism, or artistic ability). Furthermore, there is greater genetic diversity *within* racial populations than between them. So within the Asian population, members differ more from each other (Koreans from Chinese, for example) than they do from whites. From a biological standpoint, the difference between someone with type O blood and someone with type A blood is much more significant than the differences between a dark-skinned and a light-skinned person. And yet blood types are not used in our society as a way of distinguishing groups for any reason other than medical treatment.

New genetic testing technologies seem to hold out the prospect of accurately identifying biological differences among racial groups. Some "ancestry testing" services purport to be able to identify clients' genetic and geographic origins down to the region, village, or tribe. However precise or imprecise such conclusions may be, they overlook the fact that all humans, whatever racial categories they seem to inhabit, are

What Is Race? Actress Rashida Jones (left) is the daughter of black producer Quincy Jones and white actress and model Peggy Lipton. Twins Kian and Remee, with their parents Remi Horder and Kylee Hodgson, were born within a minute of each other with different skin colors.

RACE a socially defined category based on real or perceived biological differences between groups of people

ETHNICITY a socially defined category based on a common language, religion, nationality, history, or some other cultural factor

99.9 percent genetically identical. And of that remaining 0.1 percent of our genetic material, only 15 percent of its variation occurs between geographically distinct groups. In other words, there's not enough "wiggle room" in the human genome for race to be a genetic trait (*Harvard Magazine* 2008).

Sociologists, then, have come to understand **race** as a social category, based on real or perceived biological differences between groups of people. Race is more meaningful to us on a social level than it is on a biological level (Montagu 1998). Actress Rashida Jones may "look white" to many, but in some Southern states in 1925, she could just as easily have been considered black or Native American. Does knowing Jones's racial background now make you think of her in a different way?

Ethnicity is another social category that is applied to a group with a shared ancestry or cultural heritage. The Amish, for instance, are a distinct ethnic group in American society, linked by a common heritage that includes language, religion, and history; the Amish people, with few exceptions, are also white. The Jewish people, on the other hand, contrary to what the Nazis and other white supremacists may believe, are an ethnic group but not a race. The stereotypical image is challenged when we see a blond, blue-eyed Jew from Scandinavia or a black Ethiopian Jew.

As an example of the social construction of race and ethnicity, let's look at the evidence documenting the historical changes in the boundaries of the category "white." In the early 1900s, native-born Americans, who were frequently Protestant, did not consider recent Irish, Italian, or Jewish immigrants to be white and restricted where these groups could live and work (Ignatiev 1996; Brodkin 1999). Such housing discrimination forced new immigrants to cluster in urban neighborhoods or "ghettos." After World War II, however, as the second generation of Irish, Italian, and Jewish immigrants reached adulthood, the importance of ethnic identity declined and skin color became the main way to differentiate between who was white and who was not. Today, the question is whether people of Middle Eastern descent are white. In the post–9/11 climate, Arabs and Muslims have been identified as racially and ethnically distinct in significant and even harmful ways. While these groups possess a range of skin colors and facial features, it may be their symbolic labeling in these difficult times that makes them "nonwhite."

"Ethnic Options": Symbolic and Situational Ethnicity

How do we display our racial and ethnic group membership? We may do so in a number of ways: through dress; language; food; religious practices; preferences in music, art, or literature; even the projects we find interesting and the topics we pursue at school. Sometimes these practices make our group

Mulberry Street at the Turn of the Century In the early 1900s, Irish, Italian, and Jewish immigrants were not considered "whites." Because of residential segregation, new immigrants poured into densely populated neighborhoods like this one on New York's Lower East Side, where they had little choice but to live in squalid tenements and work in sweatshops.

With the appearance of websites such as Ancestry.com and television shows like NBC's *Who Do You Think You Are?*, many of us have become increasingly interested in genealogy. The process of tracing family roots can help us answer important questions about both our ancestors and ourselves. Many amateur genealogists find that their research is not just a journey through family history, but a voyage of self-discovery as well. And in some cases, "journey" and "voyage" are not just figures of speech.

As global travel becomes easier, faster, and more affordable, a phenomenon called "heritage tourism" has been on the rise. Heritage tourism is related to the idea of the pilgrimage—a journey to a geographical location of significance to one's religion. One type of traditional pilgrimage is the *hajj*, an excursion to Mecca in Saudi Arabia, which is required of all Muslims once in their lifetime. Catholics may travel to the Vatican or to other important sites such as the grotto and sanctuary at Lourdes in France or the Cathedral of Santiago de Compostela in Spain. But heritage tourism is less about religion and more about the cultural legacies of different racial and ethnic groups. Members of racial and ethnic groups who now live outside the countries of their ancestors (such as African Americans or Irish Americans) are sometimes attracted by the possibility of traveling to the "old country," and tourism ministries worldwide market their countries and cultures as must-see places for members of the diaspora—displaced peoples who may have emigrated generations ago. Here are a few examples of heritage tourism campaigns from around the world:

Ireland

The U.S. Census reports that approximately 11 percent of the American population—or more than 33 million people—claimed Irish heritage in 2013 (U.S. Census Bureau 2015d). That's a lot of potential tourists (over seven times the population of Ireland itself), and the official Irish tourist bureau caters specifically to those who wish to investigate their Irish ancestry. The tourism industry in Ireland encourages people of Irish descent to take tours that trace their family's heritage. The tourism office, in association with the Irish Genealogical Project, entices travelers to visit Irish Family History Foundation Centres around the country and promises "a personal and emotional journey . . . of discovery" as travelers discover the roots of their family trees.

Israel

For many contemporary Jews, their Jewish identity is as much ethnic as it is religious, and the existence of a Jewish state may have an impact on their travel plans. For example, Israel's Ministry of Tourism encourages American Jewish families to consider traveling to Israel for their children's Bar or Bat Mitzvah celebrations. Ceremonies can be held at any of a number of well-known historical locations, such as the Western Wall or Masada, and Bar or Bat Mitzvah visitors may also tour the important religious, cultural, and political sites of Jerusalem as part of their holiday. Taglit-Birthright targets a slightly older group (eighteen- to twenty-six-year-olds) offering free ten-day educational trips to Israel to learn about the history and people of the Jewish state. Parents and politicians alike hope that vacations such as these will strengthen young people's connection to their Jewish heritage and begin a process of attachment to Israel itself that may ultimately lead to "making *aliyah*," or moving there permanently.

Ghana

Because of the historical brutalities of slavery, it is often difficult for African Americans to pinpoint their cities or countries of ancestral origin, but since most African slaves were taken from West Africa, some countries in that region have begun exploring the touristic implications of slavery's tragic legacy. Ghanaian tourism officials, for example, want the far-flung "diasporan" descendants of American, European, and Caribbean slaves to think of Africa as home and to consider making a pilgrimage to the land of their ancestors. They offer tours that focus on slave-trade sites, such as the forts in which newly enslaved Africans were imprisoned before being shipped to the New World (which most visitors find both deeply moving and disturbing). But they also entertain visitors and educate them about Ghanaian culture and customs with colorful festivals, dancing, and feasting. Ghanaian officials hope that some visitors will choose to make Ghana their permanent home, offering special visas for diasporans to make it easy to travel to and from the homeland.

Symbolic Ethnicity Irish Americans and Mexican Americans often embrace ethnic identity on special occasions like St. Patrick's Day and Cinco de Mayo.

membership obvious to others; sometimes they don't. White ethnics like Irish Americans and Italian Americans, for example, can actually choose when and how they display their ethnic group membership to others.

One way group membership is displayed is through **symbolic ethnicity**, enactments of ethnic identity that occur only on special occasions. For example, most Irish Americans have been so fully assimilated for multiple generations that their Irish ancestry may not matter much to them on a daily basis. But on St. Patrick's Day (especially in cities like Boston and New York), displays of Irish identity can be pretty overwhelming! Parades, hats, "Kiss me, I'm Irish" buttons, green clothing, green beer (and in Chicago, a green river!), corned beef and cabbage—all are elements of symbolic ethnicity. Similar ethnic displays occur on such holidays as Passover, Cinco de Mayo, and Nouruz.

Another way we can show group membership is through **situational ethnicity**, when we deliberately assert our ethnicity in some situations while downplaying it in others. Situational ethnicity involves a kind of cost-benefit analysis that symbolic ethnicity does not: we need to appraise each situation to determine whether or not it favors our ethnicity. For example, Dr. Ferris's Lebanese ancestry never mattered much, outside her own family, when she lived in Southern California. In fact, it was often something she felt she should downplay, given a political climate in which people of Arabic background were sometimes viewed with suspicion. But when she moved to Peoria, Illinois, she discovered that this small city had a relatively large population of Lebanese descent and that the mayor, a city councilman, the state senator, the congressman, local business, arts, and religious leaders, and prominent families were all Lebanese.

SYMBOLIC ETHNICITY an ethnic identity that is only relevant on specific occasions and does not significantly affect everyday life

SITUATIONAL ETHNICITY an ethnic identity that can be either displayed or concealed depending on its usefulness in a given situation

This suddenly made Dr. Ferris's ethnicity a valuable asset in a way that it had never been before. She received a good deal of social support and made new friends based on shared revelations of ethnic group membership. In the case of situational ethnicity, we see how larger social forces can govern the identities we choose—if we have a choice.

Neither situational nor symbolic ethnicity is available to those who are visibly nonmainstream, whatever that may look like in a given society. In the United States, this generally means that nonwhites find themselves in fewer situations where they have a choice about whether to display their group membership (although this may eventually change as we become a "majority minority" nation). As sociologist Mary Waters explains, "The social and political consequences of being Asian or Hispanic or black are not, for the most part, symbolic, nor are they voluntary. They are real, unavoidable, and sometimes hurtful" (1990, p. 156).

DATA WORKSHOP
Analyzing Everyday Life

Displaying Ethnicity

Choose a setting where you can watch people "doing" ethnicity, either situational or symbolic. You should be able to find multiple places, occasions, or other opportunities to conduct this kind of research. For instance, you can go to a St. Patrick's Day parade, if your city hosts one, or attend an ethnic festival of some sort (such as St. Anthony's Feast Day in Boston's Italian North End or Los

Angeles's annual African Marketplace). Or just visit one of your city's ethnic neighborhoods: stroll through an Italian market in South Philadelphia, or shop the streets of Chicago's Ukrainian Village, Greektown, or Pilsen (a Mexican American neighborhood). You could check out the windmills and eat pastry in Solvang, a small city in central California founded by Danish teachers. If you think your town is too tiny to have any ethnic diversity, think again: even minuscule Postville, Iowa (population 2,200), includes a large Hasidic Jewish population, with significant clusters of Mexican, Guatemalan, Ukrainian, Nigerian, Bosnian, and Czech immigrants. You may even find an appropriate setting on your college campus or at one of your own family gatherings.

For this Data Workshop you will be doing participant observation in order to produce a short ethnographic study. Return to Chapter 2 for a review of this research method. Once you have chosen a setting, notice your surroundings. Join in the activities around you while at the same time carefully observing how the other participants display their ethnic membership. As part of your observation, you will be writing field notes. Consider the following:

* What are participants wearing: traditional ethnic costumes, contemporary T-shirts, other symbols displaying their ethnic identity?

* What kind of music is being played, and what types of foods or crafts are available?

* Are different languages being spoken? If so, by whom and in what situations?

* What are the differences in the activities of adults and children, men and women, members and visitors?

* Listen for snatches of conversation in which members explain such traditions as buying a goldfish on the first day of spring (Iranian), wrapping and tying a tamale (Mexican), or wearing the claddagh ring (Irish).

* Can you identify any other elements relating to ethnicity in the setting, such as architecture, decor, art, or other items of material culture?

Finally, ask yourself these questions about your own ethnic identity:

* Do you have the option to display your ethnicity in some situations and withhold it in others? Why or why not?

* How do you decide whether/when/how to display your ethnicity? What kind of cost-benefit analysis do you use?

* What role do ethnic and racial stereotypes, or stereotypes based on nationality, play in the process of displaying ethnicity?

* How do you think ethnic displays are received by others?

There are two options for completing this Data Workshop:

PREP-PAIR-SHARE Prepare written notes about your fieldwork that you can refer to in class. Discuss your experience with two or more students in a small group. Compare and contrast your fieldwork findings with those of your group members. Listen as each person describes his or her own ethnic displays. As a group, can you come up with an overarching statement (or set of statements) about situational and/or symbolic ethnicity that helps explain what you learned?

DO-IT-YOURSELF Prepare written notes about your fieldwork. Consider all the questions and prompts provided, and write a three-page paper describing your observations and experience, and applying the concepts of situational and symbolic ethnicity in your analysis. Remember to attach your field notes to the paper.

What Is a Minority?

A *minority* is commonly thought of as a group that's smaller in numbers than the dominant group. Thus, most Americans would say that in the United States, whites are a majority while African Americans, Asians, Hispanics/Latinos, and Native Americans are minorities, because whites outnumber each of these other groups. Figure 8.1 shows the breakdown of various racial and ethnic groups and their percentage of the U.S. population. But numbers don't tell the whole story. In South Africa, for instance, blacks dramatically outnumber whites by a ratio of seven to one, yet before the 1994 election of President Nelson Mandela, whites controlled the country while blacks occupied the lowest status in that society. California provides us with a different kind of example. In 2013, non-Hispanic whites made up less than 40 percent of the state's population, whereas other ethnic groups (Hispanics, African Americans, Asian Americans, Native Americans) when added together constituted a majority of 60 percent (U.S. Census Bureau 2015e). California, then, is technically a "majority minority" state: whites are less than half the population but still remain the dominant group in terms of power, resources, and representation in social institutions (Hawaii, Texas, and New Mexico are also "majority minority" states, as is the District of Columbia). Hispanics/Latinos continue to be underrepresented in the University of California system (as both students and faculty) as well as in

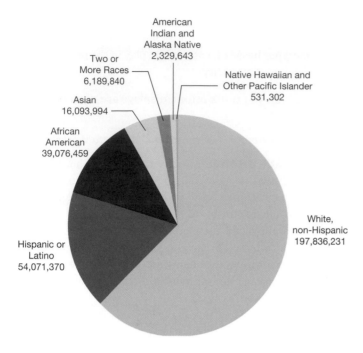

American
Indian and
Alaska Native
2,329,643

Two or
More Races
6,189,840

Asian
16,093,994

African
American
39,076,459

Hispanic or
Latino
54,071,370

Native Hawaiian and
Other Pacific Islander
531,302

White,
non-Hispanic
197,836,231

Figure 8.1 Racial and Ethnic Populations in the United States, 2013

SOURCE: U.S. Census Bureau 2014b.

the state government and as business owners, but overrepresented in prisons, in poverty counts, and as victims of violent crimes.

As sociologists, then, we must recognize that minority status is not just about numbers—it's about social inequalities. Sociologists define a **minority group** as people who are recognized as belonging to a social category (here either a racial or ethnic group) and who suffer from unequal treatment as a result of that status. A minority group is denied the access to power and resources generally accorded to others in the dominant groups. Members of a minority group are likely to perceive themselves as targets of collective discrimination (Wirth 1945).

Membership in a minority group may serve as a kind of "master status," overriding any other status, such as gender or age. Members may be subjected to racist beliefs about the group as a whole and thus suffer from a range of social disadvantages.

Unequal and unfair treatment, as well as lack of access to power and resources, typically generates a strong sense of common identity and solidarity among members of minority groups. Perhaps because of this sense of identification, minorities also tend to practice high rates of in-group marriage (endogamy), although the percentage of mixed-race couples in the United States continues to grow.

Racism in Its Many Forms

In order for social inequality to persist, the unequal treatment that minority groups suffer must be supported by the dominant groups. **Racism**, an ideology or set of beliefs about the claimed superiority of one racial or ethnic group over another, provides this support; it is used to justify unequal social arrangements between the dominant and minority groups. Racist beliefs are often rooted in the assumption that differences among groups are innate, or biologically based. They can also arise from a negative view of a group's cultural characteristics. In both cases, racism presumes that one group is better than another.

Prejudice and Discrimination

Prejudice and discrimination are closely related to racism, and though the terms are often used interchangeably, there are important distinctions between them. **Prejudice**, literally a "prejudgment," is an inflexible attitude (usually negative, although it can work in the reverse) about a particular group of people and is rooted in generalizations or stereotypes. Examples of prejudice include opinions like "All Irish are drunks" or "All Mexicans are lazy." Prejudice often, though not always, leads to **discrimination**: an action or behavior that results in the unequal treatment of individuals because of their membership in a certain racial or ethnic group. A person might be said to suffer discrimination if she is turned down for a job promotion or a home loan because she's black or Hispanic.

It is possible, though unlikely, that a person can be prejudiced and still not discriminate against others. For example, a teacher can believe that Asian American students are better at math and science, yet deliberately not let this belief influence his grading of Asian American students. Conversely, a person may not be prejudiced at all but still unknowingly participate in discrimination. Members of the dominant group, still whites in America, may enjoy certain benefits and advantages denied to minority group members. Whites may believe in equality but not act in such a way as to challenge the injustices perpetuated by our systems of stratification.

And prejudice and discrimination don't always flow from the dominant group toward minorities. The 2008 film *Gran Torino* features Clint Eastwood as a crotchety old white man with prejudices against his Italian barber, Irish construction workers, black street kids, and Asian neighbors. But in an

MINORITY GROUP social group that is systematically denied the same access to power and resources available to society's dominant groups though they are not necessarily fewer in number than the dominant groups

RACISM a set of beliefs about the claimed superiority of one racial or ethnic group; used to justify inequality and often rooted in the assumption that differences among groups are genetic

PREJUDICE an idea about the characteristics of a group that is applied to all members of that group and is unlikely to change regardless of the evidence against it

DISCRIMINATION unequal treatment of individuals based on their membership in a social group; usually motivated by prejudice

Gran Torino Both Clint Eastwood's white character and his Hmong neighbors draw conclusions about each other based on race.

interesting turn of storytelling, the prejudice goes both ways; for example, while Eastwood's character complains about the Hmong families moving into his neighborhood, his Hmong neighbors wish that he would move out of the neighborhood like all the other white people. And even given this mutual dislike based on ethnic backgrounds, Eastwood's character comes to know and love his Hmong neighbors, protecting them with a tremendous act of self-sacrifice.

Discrimination can also take different forms. **Individual discrimination** occurs when one person treats others unfairly because of their race or ethnicity. A racist teacher might discriminate against a Hispanic student by assigning him a lower grade than he deserves. **Institutional discrimination**, in contrast, is usually more systematic and widespread and occurs when institutions (such as governments, schools, or banks) practice discriminatory policies that affect whole groups of individuals.

A rather startling example of institutional discrimination comes from Ira Katznelson (2005) in his book *When Affirmative Action Was White: An Untold History of Racial Inequality in Twentieth Century America*. We usually associate affirmative action with the advances of the civil rights movement of the 1960s and with benefiting blacks and other minorities. Katznelson, however, examines one instance of special government policies benefiting whites. In 1944, Congress passed the G.I. Bill of Rights, which provided funding for college or vocational education and home loans to returning World War II veterans. While this should have supported black and white veterans alike, in practice blacks were largely impeded from taking advantage of the new benefits, while whites more easily climbed into the rapidly expanding American middle class. Typically, loans were granted only to those

buying homes in all-white neighborhoods. And blacks were effectively barred from buying homes in those neighborhoods, either through legal restrictions or from hostile actions on the part of loan officers, real-estate agents, and homeowners who were prejudiced against having blacks live next door. To make matters worse, loans were even denied to blacks who wished to buy homes in black neighborhoods; these were seen as risky investments. Later affirmative action programs for other groups were actually modeled after those of the postwar era that had benefited whites and, ironically, created an even greater economic disparity between racial groups.

Another example comes from Lawrence Otis Graham (1996), a Princeton- and Harvard-trained African American lawyer who investigated firsthand institutionalized racism in the upper-crust world of the East Coast elite. He found that, for example, he was not able to join a particular Connecticut country club as a member; however, he was welcome to serve in the capacity of busboy to the club's all-white membership and waitstaff. This shocked Graham; he believed his Ivy League credentials would open any door but discovered that in a racially stratified society, a black man with privileged socioeconomic status is still a black man in the end. Sadly, little has changed in a generation. Graham (2014) recently wrote of his teenage son's experience of being called the "N-word" from a moving car as he walked to class at a prestigious East Coast boarding school.

INDIVIDUAL DISCRIMINATION discrimination carried out by one person against another

INSTITUTIONAL DISCRIMINATION discrimination carried out systematically by institutions (political, economic, educational, and others) that affect all members of a group who come into contact with it

Some students have difficulty recognizing just how persistent and pervasive racism is in contemporary American society, while others experience it on a daily basis. We hear claims that it has been erased. But although there have been tremendous strides, especially in the wake of the civil rights movement, racism is not yet a thing of the past. There is still deep skepticism among minorities that negative racial attitudes are changing in America (Bobo, Kluegel, and Smith 1997; Bobo and Smith 1998). A survey conducted by NBC News in 2014 found that only 20 percent of Americans believed race relations had gotten better since the 2008 election of President Barack Obama, while 38 percent said they had gotten worse (NBC 2014). A 2013 Gallup poll revealed that 39 percent of whites and 49 percent of blacks believed that race relations will always be a problem in the United States (Gallup 2015).

White Privilege and Color-Blind Racism

The concept of **privilege** is gaining greater currency while still garnering much debate. There are various mechanisms of privilege. In a stratified society one may have privilege based on class, race, gender, sexuality, or other factors. The idea of the privileges of race dates back to early sociology and the work of W. E. B. DuBois (1903). More recently, Peggy McIntosh (1988) reintroduced the idea in a well-known article about "unpacking the invisible knapsack" of white privilege. In the past few decades, the idea has made its way into the various branches of academia and more widely into the national conversation. "White privilege" is the idea that one group (whites) in a society enjoys certain unearned advantages not available to others (nonwhites) and that group members (whites) are largely unaware of the unequal benefits they possess. Privilege can include a wide range of advantages that are experienced within our large social institutions as well as in our small everyday interactions.

Because privilege is often invisible to the privileged, it can blind them to the challenges faced by members of nonprivileged groups. Whites may claim, for example, that race no longer matters, and that we live in a "color-blind" society. After all, we elected a black president, so racism must be a thing of the past, right? The notion of colorblindness sounds good (judging people by the "content of their character" rather than by the color of their skin), but it is also problematic because it implies that race should be both invisible and inconsequential. And that just isn't true.

Race does matter, and racism does still exist. Racism today is neither as blatant as it once was—blacks and whites don't use separate bathrooms or drinking fountains—nor is it only a black-and-white issue. But it has taken other, more subtle forms, such as the high concentration of liquor stores in predominantly black urban areas or the high concentration of Latino immigrants in low-wage jobs. Claims of colorblindness make these more subtle forms of racism difficult to acknowledge and, therefore, difficult to address productively. According to social scientists like Eduardo Bonilla-Silva (2009; 2013), colorblindness is just a new form of racism.

Color-blind racism is hard to combat. But there is an alternative: **race consciousness**, or an awareness of the importance of race in our everyday lives and in our dealings with social institutions. A race-conscious approach recognizes that despite the civil rights gains of the last hundred years, race is still a powerful factor in shaping our everyday lives. If we are to have a truly egalitarian society, we must recognize the historical record of racism and the social conditions that perpetuate contemporary inequalities

Cultural Appropriation

Another, not always subtle, form of racism has been identified as the practice of **cultural appropriation**. Cultural appropriation is when members of the dominant group adopt, co-opt, or otherwise take cultural elements from a marginalized group and use them for their own advantage. Cultural elements can include art, music, dance, dress, language, religious rituals, and other forms of expression that originate in a particular group. We see this borrowing (or some would say stealing) of cultural elements in a range of contexts, from costumes for Halloween or for college theme parties, to the carefully crafted images and musical stylings of singers like Katy Perry and Iggy Azalea.

Let's look at some of the many instances of using the cultural symbols of various Native American peoples. Recent fashion runway trends have included suede and fringe, moccasins and turquoise jewelry. Add to that some championship sports teams like the MLB's Cleveland Indians or the NFL's Washington Redskins, both of which continue to use their derogatory names (and mascots) despite widespread objections. Critics contend that it is a problem when specific items or practices with sacred value (such as a headdress or a sweat lodge) are used without awareness of their significance or in a disrespectful way. Furthermore, cultural appropriation most often benefits the dominant group, which takes an oppressed group's cultural symbols and turn them into a commodity for profit. This kind of pillaging is postmodern cultural imperialism.

PRIVILEGE unearned advantage accorded to members of dominant social groups (males, whites, heterosexuals, the physically able, etc.)

COLOR-BLIND RACISM an ideology that removes race as an explanation for any form of unequal treatment

RACE CONSCIOUSNESS an ideology that acknowledges race as a powerful social construct that shapes our individual and social experiences

CULTURAL APPROPRIATION the adoption of cultural elements belonging to an oppressed group by members of the dominant group, without permission and often for the dominant group's gain

Cultural Appropriation For her performance of "Unconditionally" at the American Music Awards, Katy Perry donned a geisha-inspired costume that sparked controversy over her appropriation of Japanese culture.

Rachel Dolezal The former leader of the Spokane, Washington, branch of the NAACP identifies as black despite being born to two white parents.

Sometimes cultural appropriation is just insensitive. It can hurt the members of an aggrieved group, who may feel wronged, insulted, and offended. At the same time, it can have broader effects and serve to perpetuate negative stereotypes, exacerbate interracial relations, and further entrench social inequalities.

It is not always clear when the use of cultural elements by an outsider constitutes cultural appropriation and when it is cultural appreciation, and this ambiguity has been a source of debate. A case in point is the story of Rachel Dolezal, a white woman who identified as black and went to great lengths to embody that chosen identity. A civil rights activist, leader of a local chapter of the NAACP, and professor of Africana studies, Dolezal presented herself as black for many years until her parents revealed in 2015 that their daughter was white like them. Suddenly, Dolezal was the center of controversy and the subject of much impassioned dialogue about race and racial identity. Some characterized what Dolezal did as "passing," although in the opposite way it usually works. Others sympathized with her deep identification and desire to immerse herself in black culture (Michael 2015). Others questioned why she hadn't just been honest about her racial background, remaining an ally to the black community and to the cause of justice. Still many more felt deeply incensed by Dolezal's deception and by her claims to have experienced, as a black woman, racial oppression. She was widely rebuked and accused of cultural appropriation—and worse.

With increasing awareness of the issues of cultural appropriation, some of the most blatant incidents are being addressed. But it is not altogether easy to avoid some use of cultural elements that belong to other groups, and sometimes that usage is meant as an homage. What can you do? First, become aware. Educate yourself about the cultural traditions of a group you admire or emulate so you will have some idea about how to approach that group with sensitivity and respect. Let them define what is appropriate and inappropriate for outsiders. Give proper credit for attribution if you use elements of their culture. Lastly, work toward authentic cultural exchange, which must be based on greater social equality.

Theoretical Approaches to Understanding Race

Sociologists reject the notion that race has an objective or scientific meaning and instead seek to understand why race continues to play such a critical role in society. They have produced a number of theories about the connections between race, discrimination, and social inequality.

Functionalist Approaches

For example, functionalist theory has provided a useful lens for analyzing how certain ethnic groups, mainly European immigrants (such as the Irish and Italians) arriving in the early 1900s, eventually became assimilated into the larger society. Functionalism, however, has proven less successful in explaining the persistence of racial divisions and why other races and ethnicities, such as African Americans and Hispanics, have continued to maintain their distinct identities alongside the white majority culture today.

Perhaps what functionalism can best offer is an explanation of how prejudice and discrimination develop, by focusing on social solidarity and group cohesion. Groups have a tendency toward ethnocentrism, or the belief that one's own culture and way of life are right and normal. Functionalists contend that positive feelings about one's group are strong ties that bind people together. At the same time, however, this cohesiveness can lead members to see others, especially those of other races or ethnicities, in an unfavorable light. According

Table 8.1 Theory in Everyday Life

Perspective	Approach to Race and Ethnicity	Case Study: Racial Inequality
Structural Functionalism	Racial and ethnic differences are a necessary part of society. Even racial inequality has functions that help maintain social order.	The functions of racial inequality and conflict for society could include the creation of social cohesion within both the dominant and minority groups.
Conflict Theory	Racial and ethnic differences create intergroup conflict; minority and majority groups have different interests and may find themselves at odds as they attempt to secure and protect their interests.	Some members of majority groups (whites and men in particular) object to affirmative action programs that assist underrepresented groups. This can create conflict among racial groups in society.
Symbolic Interactionism	Race and ethnicity are part of our identity as displayed through our presentation of self.	Some individuals (white ethnics and light-skinned nonwhites in particular) have the option to conceal their race or ethnicity in situations where it might be advantageous to do so. This may allow them as individuals to escape the effects of racial inequality but does not erase it from society at large.

to functionalists, these cultural differences and the lack of integration into the larger society on the part of minorities tend to feed fear and hostility.

Conflict Approaches

Conflict theory focuses on the struggle for power and control. Classic Marxist analyses of race, developed by sociologists in the 1960s, looked for the source of racism in capitalist hierarchies. Edna Bonacich (1980), for instance, argued that racism is partly driven by economic competition and the struggle over scarce resources. A "split labor market," in which one group of workers (usually defined by race, ethnicity, or gender) is routinely paid less than those in other groups, keeps wages low for racial and ethnic minorities, compounding the effects of racism with those of poverty. William Julius Wilson (1980) posited that openly racist government policies and individual racist attitudes were the driving forces behind the creation of a black underclass but that the underclass is now perpetuated by economic factors, not racial ones. While this link between race and class is useful and important, it doesn't provide a satisfactory explanation for all forms of racial and ethnic stratification.

In recent years, conflict theorists have developed new approaches to understanding race. In his book *Racial Fault Lines: The Historical Origins of White Supremacy in California* (2008), for example, Tomas Almaguer looks at the history of race relations in California during the late nineteenth century. He describes a racial hierarchy that placed whites at the top, followed by Mexicans, blacks, Asians, and Native Americans at the bottom. Rather than focusing exclusively on class, he examines how white supremacist ideology became institutionalized. Racist beliefs became a part of political and

economic life during that period. Ideas like "manifest destiny" (the belief that the United States had a mission to expand its territories) helped justify the taking of lands, and the notion that Native Americans were "uncivilized heathens" helped justify killing them. Sociologists also argue that race isn't just a secondary phenomenon that results from the class system: it permeates both lived experience and larger-scale activity, such as the economy and the government (Omi and Winant 1994).

Still others have sought to understand the meaning of race from the individual's point of view and have begun to analyze the ways that race, class, and gender inequalities intersect. For instance, writers like Patricia Hill Collins (2006), bell hooks (1990), and Gloria Anzaldúa (1987) argue that race must be explained in the terms in which it is experienced, not as overarching general theories. Though some of these writers have been sharply critical of the symbolic interactionist tradition, which they believe does not take into account macro social forces that shape the realities of stratification, they share with interactionism a conviction that race, like all other aspects of social life, is created symbolically in everyday interactions. It is this idea to which we now turn.

The Social Construction of Race

Sociologists understand race as a social rather than a biological category. Students often find this idea confusing, because the everyday understanding of race in the United States is that it is based on skin color, which is an inherited physical trait. Sociologists who study race, however, point out that there is no physical trait that will always accurately identify what race someone belongs to. As Michael Omi and Howard Winant point out in *Racial Formation in the United States* (1994), "although the concept of race invokes biologically based human characteristics," which particular features are chosen to make racial distinctions "is always and necessarily a social and historical process" (p. 55). Indeed, although Americans talk about skin color as the principal physical marker of racial identity, some scholars argue that hair is a more important factor (Banks 2000). Even though they are expressed in terms of physical traits, the definitions of different racial groups are "at best imprecise and at worst completely arbitrary" (Omi and Winant 1994, p. 55). The definition of race is not stable but rather changes over time as racial categories are contested and developed.

This is not to say that race is unimportant. Omi and Winant show how racial groups are created socially and historically by arguing that "race can be understood as a fundamental dimension of social organization and cultural meaning in the U.S." (p. viii). Real, physical bodies still matter to this process, but it is the meaning attributed to these bodies that determines what racial categories will exist, who will belong in them, and what they will mean.

For example, the late sociologist Stuart Hall was born in Jamaica but immigrated to England as a young man, where he became one of the founding figures in the development of cultural studies. He explained the social construction of race by recounting a conversation he had with his young son, who was the product of a mixed marriage. Hall describes a moment when his "son, who was two and a half, was learning the colors." Hall explained to him, "'You're Black.' And he said, 'No. I'm brown'" (2006, p. 222). Hall's son was thinking in purely physical terms. If race really were biological, he would have been correct, but as Hall explains, he has the "wrong referent," because he was not "talking about your paintbox" (p. 222). Hall understands that it is not skin color that created racial categories. If that were true, his son would belong to a different race than he. Race is not a preexisting biological category; it is a social one that is framed in terms of biological features.

Another aspect of the social construction of race is that we "read" others through myriad cues, and we in turn make ourselves readable to others by our own self-presentations. Our identity is constructed in the negotiation between what we project and what others recognize. Even master statuses such as race, gender, and age are negotiated in this way. So how *do* we project our racial or ethnic identities and read the racial or ethnic identities of others? We might think immediately of stereotypes like hip-hoppers with baggy pants, skateboard dudes, sorority girls, "welfare moms," and so on. But in fact there are more subtle ways in which we project and receive our racial and ethnic identities. The interactional accomplishment of race is often easiest to see in the most unusual situations.

PASSING Racial **passing**, or living as if one is a member of a different racial category, has a long history in the United States. Both during and after slavery, some light-skinned African Americans attempted to live as whites in order to avoid the dire consequences of being black in a racist society. And people of different racial and ethnic backgrounds still pass, intentionally or unintentionally, every day in the United States. Passing involves manufacturing or maintaining a new identity that is more beneficial than one's real identity. W. E. B. DuBois, a pioneer in the study of race, devised the concept of **double-consciousness**, which seems relevant to a discussion of passing. DuBois asked whether one could be black and at the same time claim one's rights as an American. Given the history of oppression and enslavement of African Americans, DuBois was not the only person to wonder whether this was possible. There are many social forces that disenfranchise and exclude minorities, and the phenomenon of passing suggests that in some places and times, it has been more advantageous to appear white if at all possible.

One hundred years later, a different kind of passing is gaining attention in the black community. Black masculinity makes demands on black men that include a public persona of heterosexuality. For black men who have sex with other men, this often creates a pressure to "pass," or live an apparently hetero lifestyle in which sexual relations with men happen only "on the down low" or "DL." Jeffrey McCune's (2014) ethnographic study of a Chicago nightclub catering to gay black men reveals the ways in which race shapes the performance of both gender and sexuality for men on the DL. "The Gate" played hip-hop music, infamous for its hypermasculine, heteronormative, and sometimes homophobic lyrics, but that didn't stop the clientele from turning the Gate into a space where their same-sex desires could be comfortably expressed. In their everyday lives, these men did the interactional work necessary to keep their sexuality private and their conventionally masculine and heterosexual images intact. But on Friday nights at the Gate, McCune observes that they could enjoy the coexistence of their multiple identities. Dancing to hip-hop music with other black men allowed them to both reinforce and accept dominant definitions of race, gender, and sexuality while also resisting and subverting them.

PASSING presenting yourself as a member of a different group than the stigmatized group you belong to

DOUBLE-CONSCIOUSNESS
W.E.B. DuBois's term for the divided identity experienced by blacks in the United States

EMBODIED (AND DISEMBODIED) IDENTITIES Are we heading toward a future when race will matter less and less? In a digital age does race disappear when more and more interactions take place exclusively online? When we're interacting online, we may not always be able to see what others look like. In many online spaces, such as in e-mail, chat functions, or text messaging, we may not have any of the kind of physical cues that can tell us something about the other person. We may only have their written words to decipher and maybe just a small, inscrutable thumbnail photo of them in

IN RELATIONSHIPS

From the Lovings to Kimye: Interracial Dating and Marriage

Though it is now rather commonplace, at one point in history forty-one out of the fifty American states prohibited **miscegenation**—the romantic, sexual, or marital relationships between people of different races. In 1958, for example, Mildred and Richard Loving, an African American woman and a white man, married and settled in their native state of Virginia. In July of that year, they were arrested for violating the state's "Act to Preserve Racial Purity" and convicted. The judge sentenced them to a year in prison but suspended the sentence on the condition that the couple leave the state. The Lovings moved to Washington, DC, where in 1967 the Supreme Court overturned all such laws, ruling that the state of Virginia had denied the Lovings their constitutional rights. While the Loving decision technically cleared the way for interracial marriages nationwide, states were slow to change their laws. It took until 2000 for the state of Alabama to finally overturn the last anti-miscegenation statute left in the nation.

Just because it's legal doesn't always make it easy. People who date interracially may still face stigma and discrimination at a social and personal level. They may have to deal with in-group pressures from family, peers, and others to date (and especially marry) someone of their own race. Partnering with someone outside of one's group may be perceived as being disloyal and can elicit strong sanctions from other members. Stereotypes about members of different racial and ethnic groups are also slow to disappear. People may hold on to racist and sexist notions about the attributes (or deficits) of men and women

MISCEGENATION
romantic, sexual, or marital relationships between people of different races

Mildred and Richard Loving Their interracial marriage was illegal in 1958.

from different ethnic backgrounds, and their suitability as romantic partners. We see these tensions played out in popular culture, in films, on TV shows, and in our own everyday lives. But real change is happening.

As diversity has rapidly increased in the United States, so has the rise in multiracial marriages. Young adults have more relationships with more people from diverse backgrounds, and they are more favorable to forming a romantic partnership with someone from another racial or ethnic group. Spurred in part by a rise in immigration to the United States,

a corner of the posts, which makes it all the more difficult to ascertain their racial or ethnic background. This has been touted as one of the more democratizing traits of the Internet—that it can transcend, even obliterate, the real-world physical traits associated with categories like race, gender, or age, that normally define us. It is just such aspects of **embodied identity** (the way we are perceived in the physical world), that have historically been used as the basis for discrimination. These same ways of knowing about others through embodied characteristics are not necessarily available to those interacting online.

EMBODIED IDENTITY those elements of identity that are generated through others' perceptions of our physical traits

While the Internet has the potential to minimize race and other visible traits, that's not always desirable. It depends on the context. Sometimes we go online and want to display our racial identity, but that's not always an easy thing to do, especially when all we have are words. For instance, in online communities that are *based* on racial identity, race must still be "done" interactionally (in this case, textually), as sociologist Byron Burkhalter (1999) found in his study of an Internet community based on African American culture. To sound authentically African American online, for instance, you have to include what Burkhalter calls "racially relevant" content and language—for example, "sister" to refer to other African American women. Responses also help establish racial identity: it's not just what you say, but how others receive it.

multiracial marriages went from only 0.4 percent in 1960 to 8.4 percent in 2010; the rate climbs to 15 percent among newlyweds, who have had perhaps the most diverse dating pool of any generation (Rainer and Rainer 2011). These figures do not yet reflect same-sex partners or unmarried cohabiters, groups that would certainly add to the trend toward a greater number of interracial relationships in the future.

Rates for mixed-race relationships vary among various demographic groups, and at the intersections of race, gender, and age. The data point to a marked rise in the number of interracial relationships across all the major ethnic and racial groups in the United States. Increases have been greater among Asians, Hispanics, and Native Indians/Alaskan Natives. Whites and blacks have lagged behind somewhat, but they are also marrying other races more often. The data are somewhat complex. For instance, if we also consider the variable of gender, Asian women marry outside their race far more often than Asian men do, while African American women marry far less often outside their race than African American men do (Frey 2014).

Since the time of the Loving case, society's attitudes about mixed-race relationships have radically changed and are now overwhelmingly positive. There are, however, variations in the rates of approval among different groups (Pew Research Center 2014e). More Millennials (50 percent) say this trend is good for society than Gen Xers (38 percent) or Baby Boomers (33 percent) do. Among Millennials, whites (49 percent) and nonwhites (50 percent) are equally likely to view this as a positive trend. In contrast, disapproval rates are highest among older adults (21 percent) and lowest among all younger adults (7 percent).

Interracial Couples on TV The popular TV show *Scandal* is centered on the interracial romance between Olivia Pope, played by Kerry Washington, and fictional president Fitzgerald Grant.

Stigma, prejudice, and restrictive racial stereotypes, as well as entrenched negative beliefs on the part of some people, all remain persistent challenges to creating a more widely accepting, multicultural, and multiracial society. Nonetheless, the growing number of interracial marriages, while still relatively small, is an indication of significant social change. One researcher said that this trend "reflects an important shift toward blurring a long-held color line in the United States" (Frey 2014).

How do you feel about interracial relationships? There's some likelihood that you or someone you know is already in one. Or, just look around—there are more interracial couples now than ever.

In some discussions, the African American identity of participants is accepted, but in other cases, that status is contested, in what Burkhalter calls "identity challenges." Identity challenges are usually accusations that one is not "really" black or not black enough, or that one is a "Tom" (a derogatory reference to a servile slave from Harriet Beecher Stowe's 1852 novel *Uncle Tom's Cabin*) or a racist. These challenges are usually made when postings reveal opinions that don't fit into a certain set of socially approved boundaries, such as opinions about the use of "proper" English versus slang.

Burkhalter argues that race is not irrefutably identifiable even in face-to-face interactions and that we must establish it interactionally both on- and off-line. We can't always tell by looking what race someone belongs to and how that person might define his own racial identity. We may make mistakes of attribution. An example can be seen in racial "micro-aggressions," the small-scale racial slights, insults, and misperceptions that play out in everyday interactions between people. Questions like, "What are you?" or "Where are you really from?" show the persistence of racial stereotypes and their power in shaping how we see and perceive each other. Stereotypes can come into play in either arena but in different directions: in face-to-face interaction, seeing racial characteristics leads to stereotyping; online, applying stereotypical templates leads to assumptions about race. The Internet is thus not a place where all the problematic distinctions disappear—they just manifest themselves in different ways.

Race, Ethnicity, and Life Chances

A law professor decides that it is time to buy a house. After careful research into neighborhoods and land values, she picks one. With her excellent credit history and prestigious job, she easily obtains a mortgage over the phone. When the mortgage forms arrive in the mail, she sees to her surprise that the phone representative has identified her race as "white." Smiling, she checks another box, "African American," and mails back the form. Suddenly, everything changes. The lending bank wants a bigger down payment and a higher interest rate. When she threatens to sue, the bank backs down. She learns that the bank's motivation is falling property values in the proposed neighborhood. She doesn't understand this; those property values were completely stable when she was researching the area. Then she realizes that *she* is the reason for the plummeting values.

As Patricia Williams's (1997) experience illustrates, membership in socially constructed categories of race and ethnicity can often carry a high price. We now look at other ways this price might be paid, in the areas of family, health, education, work, and criminal justice.

Family

Race, ethnicity, and their correlates (such as SES) shape family life in a variety of ways. Data from the U.S. Census Bureau (2014a) showed that in 2014, of the white population

over fifteen years of age, 53.2 percent were married, 10.4 percent divorced, 5.8 percent widowed, and 28.8 percent never married. Of the African American population over age fifteen, 31.9 percent were married, 10.8 percent divorced, 5.8 percent widowed, and 47.3 percent never married. The Hispanic population reported 44.6 percent over age fifteen married, 8.0 percent divorced, 3.2 percent widowed, and 40.5 percent never married. Thus, African Americans are more likely than whites and Hispanics to never marry or to be divorced.

Kathryn Edin (2000) argues that low-income women of all ethnicities see marriage as having few benefits. They feel that the men they are likely to encounter as possible husbands will not offer the advantages (financial stability, respectability, trust) that make the rewards of marriage worth the risks. This doesn't mean, of course, that most low-income women don't love their male companions; it only means that they believe a legal bond would not substantially improve their lot in life.

In 2013, the birth rates for American teenage mothers (ages fifteen to nineteen) varied significantly by race. The birth rate for white teenage moms was 19 per 1,000 births, while the birth rate for African Americans was 39 per 1,000; for Hispanics it was 42 per 1,000 (Martin et al. 2015). Social thinkers such as Angela Y. Davis argue that African American teenage girls in particular see fewer opportunities for education and work, and choose motherhood instead (2001). Davis believes that social policies aimed at punishing teenage mothers of color will be ineffective; only by attacking the racism inherent in the educational system and the workforce will these teens be at less risk of becoming mothers.

Health

Health is an area in which we find widespread disparity among racial and ethnic groups. Health-care consumers must rely on insurance benefits provided through their employer or buy individual policies in order to meet their medical needs. This has meant that many Americans cannot afford basic health-care coverage. In 2013, 9.8 percent of whites were without health insurance, along with 14.5 percent of Asian Americans, 15.9 percent of blacks, and 24.3 percent of Hispanics (Figure 8.3). The Affordable Health Care Act of 2010 was designed to address such inequities by providing something like universal health-care coverage, but the law has remained an area of contention.

Disparities in access to health care can adversely affect members of a racial group. This may help explain the life expectancy rates for men and women of different races. White male children born in 2013 can expect to live to be 76.7 years old, while white females can expect to live to age 81.4. However, African American males' life expectancy is only 72.3 years, and African American females' is 78.4. Hispanic males' life expectancy, on the other hand, is 79.1 years, and Hispanic females' is 83.8 (Centers for Disease Control and Prevention 2014b). Minorities are also often disproportionately exposed

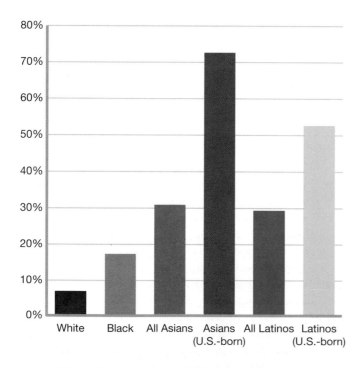

Figure 8.2   Intermarriage Rates by Race

SOURCE: Lee and Bean 2012.

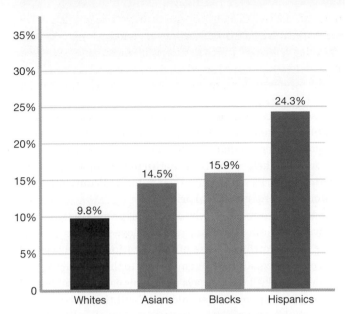

Figure 8.3 Americans without Health Insurance by Race/Ethnicity, 2013

SOURCE: U.S. Census Bureau 2014g.

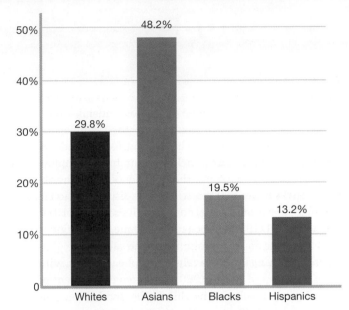

Figure 8.4 U.S. Bachelor's Degree Holders by Race/Ethnicity, 2014

SOURCE: U.S. Census Bureau 2014e.

to other factors that affect lifespan, such as dangers in the workplace, toxins in the environment, or personal behaviors such as lack of exercise and poor diet. While life expectancy statistics are only crude indicators of general health, they do reveal continuing race-based discrepancies, including the ongoing mystery of why Hispanics live longer, a question researchers are still trying to answer.

Education

One of America's cultural myths is that everyone has equal access to education, the key to a secure, well-paying job. However, by looking at those who actually receive degrees, we can see that the playing field is not that level. According to the U.S. Census Bureau (2014e), in 2014 88.1 percent of white students age eighteen and over earned a high school diploma, while 85.0 percent of African American students and 68.1 percent of Hispanic students did so. The reasons for dropping out of high school are complex, but the highest rates are associated with those from economically disadvantaged and non–English-speaking backgrounds.

In higher education, the numbers are similar. In 2014, 48.2 percent of Asian Americans over the age of eighteen, 29.8 percent of whites, 19.5 percent of blacks, and 13.2 percent of Hispanics earned bachelor's degrees (Figure 8.4). Further, 18.8 percent of Asian Americans, 10.6 percent of whites, 6.5 percent of African Americans, and 3.8 percent of Hispanics age eighteen and over earned advanced degrees (master's, professional degrees, and doctorates) (U.S. Census Bureau 2014e). Thus, Asian Americans and whites enjoy more success overall in the U.S. educational system than African Americans and Hispanics do. The reasons for the disparity are again complex, involving both economic and cultural factors. Earning an education is extremely important in American society. Not only does it translate to greater success in the workforce, it also confers social status and cultural capital that can prove valuable in other arenas.

Work and Income

In 2014, African Americans made up 11.4 percent and Hispanics 16.1 percent of the total workforce (U.S. Bureau of Labor Statistics 2015c). If jobs were truly given to people regardless of racial or ethnic identity, we would expect to see these same distributions across occupations. However, that is not the case. For example, in 2014, African Americans constituted 8.8 percent and Hispanics 8.7 percent of all management, professional, and related occupations (U.S. Bureau of Labor Statistics 2015c). That means that these positions, which usually require advanced degrees, are primarily held by whites.

In contrast, persons of color carry the burden of some of society's most difficult jobs. In 2014, 35.9 percent of all nursing, psychiatric, and home health aides and 30.8 percent of all postal clerks were black, while Hispanics were more likely to be employed in farming (43 percent of total) and as maids and house cleaners (43.8 percent of total) (U.S. Bureau of Labor Statistics 2015c). Except for nursing, these jobs are more likely to be semiskilled or unskilled. Thus, people of color, who are less likely to achieve high levels of education, are more likely to swell the bottom rungs of the job market. Interestingly enough, some lower-level jobs have shifted from African Americans to Hispanics over time. For instance, in 1983, African Americans accounted for 42.4 percent and Hispanics for 11.8 percent of all private household cleaners; by 2014, blacks

Many workplaces—academic and nonacademic—offer programs of "diversity training" to their employees. These programs, often just a few hours long, focus on education and consciousness-raising, helping nonminority employers and coworkers understand the experiences of minority colleagues, in the hopes that this will reduce discrimination in the workplace and lead to greater opportunities for minorities (such as women; LGBT persons; racial, ethnic, and religious minorities; and the disabled) to compete and succeed.

Diversity training is a relatively recent phenomenon, with its origins attributed to the 1968 classroom experiment of Iowa third-grade teacher Jane Elliot. She divided her students into a "superior" group (those with blue eyes) and an "inferior" group (those with brown eyes), and then watched while the blue-eyed group became more confident and condescending and began getting better grades, while the brown-eyed group became meeker and more fearful and began to see their grades decline. The effects were so striking that word of the exercise spread, and Elliot eventually became the "foremother" of modern diversity training, traveling to schools and workplaces around the country and the world replicating the "blue eyes–brown eyes" exercise to increase sensitivity to the powerful effects of prejudice and discrimination.

From these humble beginnings, diversity training has grown into a major industry, using a variety of strategies to increase cultural awareness, promote inclusion, and improve teamwork across different groups of people in workplaces. Such training shows moderate levels of effectiveness, and a 2006 study published in the *American Sociological Review* shows that different strategies have different types of effects:

> Efforts to moderate managerial bias through diversity training and diversity evaluations are least effective at increasing the share of white women, black women, and black men in management. Efforts to attack social isolation through mentoring and networking show modest effects. Efforts to establish responsibility for diversity lead to the broadest increases in managerial diversity. (Kalev, Dobbin, and Kelly 2006, p. 589)

This study suggests that merely increasing awareness, knowledge, and sensitivity to workplace inequality does little to remedy it, whereas strengthening social networks for minority employees does seem to help. But it is making someone (or multiple someones) responsible for actually increasing employee diversity that has the greatest impact. If no one person or unit is held responsible for hiring, promoting, and supporting minority employees, then doing so is unlikely to be treated as an organizational priority.

Of course, there are those who argue that promoting workplace diversity through training and employee-support programs is not a worthwhile use of organizational resources. Everyone has an equal chance of making it to the top, they say, and women, blacks, Latinos, gays and lesbians, the disabled, and other minority workers should just "pull themselves up by their own bootstraps." The debate over whether historically disadvantaged groups should receive any kind of special attention has been with us for decades and will continue to rumble as long as inequality exists in our society. But think about it this way: if you were the CEO, president, or director of an organization, wouldn't you want to make sure you were doing everything you could to benefit from the skills and talents of everyone working for you? And that you weren't overlooking the skills and talents of potential employees for baseless reasons like their gender, race, sexual orientation, or . . . eye color? Diversity training can help us see things a little differently, and that is usually a worthwhile exercise.

Diversity Training In 2015, tech giant Google announced a $150 million plan to get more women and minorities into technology.

accounted for only 16.8 percent. A similar shift may be seen with other low-wage jobs. This means that persons of color increasingly compete with each other for such jobs.

In 2013, the median income for whites was $58,270, for Hispanics $40,963, and for African Americans $34,598. Asian Americans had the highest median income at $67,065 (DeNavas-Walt and Proctor 2014). The median incomes of Asian Americans and whites thus place them in the middle class, while those of blacks and Hispanics place them in the lower-middle (working) class. African Americans and Hispanics are more disproportionately represented than whites in the income brackets between $0 and $49,999, while whites are more disproportionately represented in income brackets above $50,000. In 2013, 9.6 percent of whites lived below the poverty line, compared with 27.2 percent of African Americans and 23.5 percent of Hispanics (DeNavas-Walt and Proctor 2014). These numbers make it easy to see how race and class intersect to influence life outcomes.

Hate Crimes After a racially charged mass shooting in a black church in Charleston, South Carolina, that claimed nine lives, protesters called for the removal of the Confederate flag from the state capitol grounds.

Criminal Justice

Although the majority of the U.S. population is white—about 64 percent, as opposed to about 12 percent black and 11 percent Hispanic—we don't find these same proportions in the prison population. Of all state and federal male prisoners in 2012, 37 percent were African American, while 46 percent were white and 15 percent Hispanic (Minton 2013). Why are larger proportions of African American and Hispanic men in prison?

Some laws that don't seem race based still create racially differentiated outcomes (Table 8.2). For example, federal law until 2007 handed out tougher sentences to crack users (who are more likely to be black) than to users of powdered cocaine (who are more likely to be white or Hispanic). If you possessed a small amount of crack (for personal use), you'd get the same

stringent sentence you would receive if you possessed a huge amount of cocaine (enough for hundreds of uses). While this discrepancy was remedied in 2007, it left more than 17,000 people convicted of crack possession awaiting official reductions in their sentences—more than 15,000 of whom are black (U.S. Sentencing Commission 2010). Unemployment rates are higher among minority groups, as are dropout rates, and these may affect incarceration rates. There is also some evidence that there are connections between declining marriage rates and incarceration (Pettit and Western 2004).

It is also clear that African Americans are far more likely than whites to be murdered: in 2013, while both whites and blacks accounted for approximately 45 and 51 percent of murder victims nationwide, respectively, these percentages don't at all reflect the racial distribution of the U.S. population as a whole (Federal Bureau of Investigation 2014f). Finally, nearly half of the reported hate crimes in 2013 were attributed to racial discrimination (48.5 percent), with 66.4 percent targeting blacks (Federal Bureau of Investigation 2014g).

Intersectionality

As you might have already concluded, race and ethnicity do not shape our life chances in isolation from other social statuses and aspects of identity. Sociologist France Winddance Twine (2011b) demonstrates this in her ethnographic study of white women who have families with black men. As the intimate partners of black men, these women effectively lose some of their whiteness—especially in the eyes of their white working-class friends and family—and become "honorary blacks." This loss of whiteness is a form of punishment exacted by their ethnicity- and class-based communities, but it is not meted out equally to white men who marry black women. Twine's work identifies the intersection of class,

Table 8.2 Federal Cocaine Offenders by Race/Ethnicity, 2010

Race/Ethnicity	Powder Percent	Crack Percent
White	16.7	7.3
Black	26.7	78.6
Hispanic	54.9	13.0
Other	1.6	1.1

SOURCE: U.S. Sentencing Commission 2011.

race, and gender by showing the ways in which "interracial intimacy and the racism that accompanies it is a gendered experience" (p. 30).

An additional social status, motherhood, is also part of the intersectionality in Twine's study. White mothers of interracial children may not possess the racial literacy to raise those children in a world that will almost certainly see and treat them as black. From cooking and hair care to preparation for experiencing racism, these mothers—because they are women and because they are white—must calibrate their parenting practices in order to address race and racism in ways that their own mothers did not. In Twine's work, race, class, gender, and parenthood combine to shape the lived experiences of individuals and families.

DATA WORKSHOP
Analyzing Media and Pop Culture

The Politics and Poetics of Racial Identity

Racial identity is expressed through a variety of elements in symbolic culture; its many messages are captured in words and images, performed in the arts, and portrayed through the media. Racial identity is established and shaped by our face-to-face and online interactions, and sometimes it is expressed through the collective action of the many fighting for social change. Read the following poem; it is one expression that is, in turns, personal and public.

One sun rose on us today, kindled over our shores,
peeking over the Smokies, greeting the faces
of the Great Lakes, spreading a simple truth
across the Great Plains, then charging across the Rockies.
One light, waking up rooftops, under each one, a story
told by our silent gestures moving behind windows.

My face, your face, millions of faces in morning's mirrors,
each one yawning to life, crescendoing into our day:
pencil-yellow school buses, the rhythm of traffic lights,
fruit stands: apples, limes, and oranges arrayed like rainbows
begging our praise. Silver trucks heavy with oil or paper—
bricks or milk, teeming over highways alongside us,
on our way to clean tables, read ledgers, or save lives—
to teach geometry, or ring-up groceries as my mother did
for twenty years, so I could write this poem.

All of us as vital as the one light we move through,
the same light on blackboards with lessons for the day:

equations to solve, history to question, or atoms imagined,
the "I have a dream" we keep dreaming,
or the impossible vocabulary of sorrow that won't explain
the empty desks of twenty children marked absent
today, and forever. Many prayers, but one light
breathing color into stained glass windows,
life into the faces of bronze statues, warmth
onto the steps of our museums and park benches
as mothers watch children slide into the day.

From Richard Blanco's poem "One Today," read at the inauguration of President Obama, January 21, 2013.

Barack Obama, the forty-fourth president of the United States, was the first black man to be elected to the office (twice), in 2008 and 2012. Issues of race featured prominently in his presidential campaigns and terms in office. For his second inauguration, Obama selected poet Richard Blanco to read the poem Blanco had written for the occasion, titled "One Today." The poem was discussed, analyzed, scrutinized, and evaluated by pundits and ordinary citizens alike for months afterward. Blanco was the youngest poet ever to read at a presidential inauguration; he was also the first Latino, and the first openly gay, poet to compose verse for a president. Does Blanco's racial identity matter for your understanding of the poem? Does Obama's? Does yours?

This Data Workshop asks you to do a content analysis of an existing source such as a poem, speech, song, or performance piece that deals with racial and ethnic identity. Return to Chapter 2 for a refresher on this research method. Whatever you choose, the primary focus of your analysis will be the words. Keep in mind that if you want to use a speech, song, or performance from a video clip, you will need to provide a transcript of the portion you want to work with. Even a short excerpt from a longer piece is often enough, so limiting the amount of text you have to transcribe will make it easier for you to manage. There are many places to look for material across a variety of media:

* You can search for a poem from a well-known writer such as Langston Hughes, Maya Angelou, Lorna Dee Cervantes, or Victoria Chang, or from your favorite poet. There are many books, journals, and websites devoted to poets belonging to various racial and ethnic groups. You could also use a poem performed by one of the many spoken word artists featured on HBO's *Def Poetry Jam*.

* Many speeches are available in a variety of formats. You can look for the text of a speech from a civil rights activist such as Dr. Martin Luther King Jr., Cesar Chavez, Al Sharpton, or Janet Murguia, or

from a political leader such as former L.A. mayor Antonio Villaraigosa or current U.S. Senator Cory Booker of New Jersey.

* You could browse the Library of Congress and its American Memory website, dedicated to preserving all types of material about the American experience. Visit the library's StoryCorps website, an ambitious, ongoing project that aims to collect the oral histories of people from all walks of life. Listen to one of its many stories on the theme of identity. You can even contribute to the project by recording your own story as well.

* You can choose the lyrics from one of your favorite songs; there are many songs that deal with issues of racial and ethnic identity. Among the long list of examples is the Academy Award–winning song "Glory" by John Legend and Common.

* You can also take an excerpt of a performance by stand-up comedians such as Indian American Aziz Ansari, Korean American Margaret Cho, African Americans Hannibal Burress or Mo'Nique, the Chicano comedy troupe Culture Clash, or the Middle Eastern comics in Axis of Evil.

* Finally, you can choose to write an original poem, speech, song lyric, or comedy routine about your own racial or ethnic experience.

Once you have found your chosen text, consider the following prompts:

* What is the overall message of the text, its major themes or patterns? Take note of the usage and frequency of specific words, phrases, terms, or other descriptive language, as well as their meaning. Consider the significance of tone, humor, sarcasm, or hyperbole, if any. How do these narrative elements contribute to the larger message of the text?

* How is the race or ethnicity of the writer, speaker, or performer established within the text?

* Who is the intended audience for the text? What kind of reaction is the text trying to elicit?

* What is the importance of the historical and social context in which the text was created? Are there references to people, events, or social problems?

* How does the text tackle issues such as racial and ethnic identity; racism, prejudice and discrimination; social inequalities; and intergroup relations?

* Does the text deal with intersectionality, where race or ethnicity is also linked to class, gender, sexuality, age, or other forms of inequality?

* In what ways is the text both an individual story and the story of a larger group?

* Why did you choose the text? What about it is interesting or meaningful to you? What did it make you think or feel?

There are two options for completing this Data Workshop:

PREP-PAIR-SHARE With a transcript of the text to refer to, do a preliminary content analysis, making note of your responses to the prompts provided. Form a small group with one or more classmates, and take turns reading your texts together. Discuss your own findings, and listen to how others in the group interpreted your text. What are the similarities or differences in your individual interpretations? Can you come to an agreement about the meaning of the text? Finally, were there any common themes that emerged across everyone's selected texts?

DO-IT-YOURSELF Choose a poem, speech, song, or performance piece and do a content analysis of the text. Write a three-page essay, responding to the prompts. Make sure to incorporate the relevant sociological concepts in your discussion. Attach a copy of the text to your paper.

Intergroup Relations: Conflict or Cooperation

The relationships among racial and ethnic groups in a society can take different forms. In some instances, groups may be tolerant and respectful of one another, while in other cases there is unending hostility. In this section, we will examine five basic patterns of intergroup relationships, from the most violent to the most tolerant. Keep in mind that some ethnic groups, such as Native Americans, may suffer several different patterns of hardship over a period of time.

Genocide

The first pattern represents the worst possible outcome between a dominant and a subordinate group. Not only has **genocide**—the deliberate and systematic extermination of a racial, ethnic, national, or cultural group—taken place in the past, it continues today in certain parts of the globe.

GENOCIDE the deliberate and systematic extermination of a racial, ethnic, national, or cultural group

Survivors of Genocide Holocaust survivor Ehud Valter displays the card documenting his transfer between the Auschwitz and Buchenwald concentration camps. Annie Karakaian, 101, survived the mass killings of Armenians in 1915 in what was then the Ottoman Empire.

POPULATION TRANSFER the forcible removal of a group of people from the territory they have occupied

The twentieth century witnessed numerous incidents of genocide. From 1915 to 1923, during and after World War I, the Turkish government massacred 1.5 million Armenians in what is often referred to as the "forgotten genocide." Nazi Germany under Adolf Hitler's rule killed two-thirds of the Jews of Europe. Few paid attention to the Armenian tragedy, and many refused to believe the initial reports of Hitler's death camps as well (Hitler himself recognized this, and is alleged to have asked, "Who remembers the Armenians?" when he embarked on his own genocidal project). In the latter half of the century, such events became all too common. From the atrocities of Darfur to Slobodan Milošević's ethnic cleansing in the Balkans and the Hutu slaughter of Tutsi in Rwanda, genocide has become a familiar feature of the modern landscape.

It is also possible to consider the violence perpetuated by the early Americans against the Native American tribes who occupied North America as a form of genocide. While Native Americans died from diseases introduced by the settlers, they were also systematically killed by the European colonists. In the few hundred years that it took for the United States to be settled from coast to coast, the Native American population was almost completely wiped out. Estimates for the total number killed range anywhere from 15 million up to 100 million (Stannard 1993; Cook 1998).

Population Transfer

The treatment of Native Americans leads us to the next pattern of group relations—**population transfer**, or the forcible removal of a group of people from the territory they have occupied. In the early nineteenth century, Native Americans who had not perished in battles with U.S. soldiers were forced by the U.S. government to move onto Indian reservations (also referred to as tribal lands or American Indian nations) west of the Mississippi River. They were often moved far away from the lands where they had lived for generations (mostly Southern states), as these were desirable territories that the whites wished to acquire for themselves. Between 1838 and 1839, in one of the most well-known examples, the state of Georgia and the federal government forcibly marched 17,000 Cherokees westward over 800 miles, a grueling journey known as the Trail of Tears. Along the way, more than 4,000 people died of hunger, exposure, or disease.

The separate territories established for the Native Americans are an example of a kind of partitioning that we can see happening today in Israel between the Israelis and Palestinians in the West Bank and Gaza Strip. There, the Israeli government restricts the movement of Palestinians and has even built miles of barriers designed to wall them in and keep them separate from the Israeli population. Sometimes, population transfer takes a more indirect form. For instance, it is possible to make life so miserable in a region that a group of people

IN THE FUTURE
The Majority-Minority Generation

What is race going to look like in the future? In fictional and film renditions of the future, there are various depictions of race. In the very first *Star Trek* series in 1966, all races were equally represented in the future. This is a trend that remained through all the *Star Trek* franchises, with racially diverse casts staffing the U.S.S. *Enterprise* in the future. However, it is interesting to note that most of the central characters in the *Star Trek* franchise seem to be white. In Joss Whedon's *Firefly*, even though China and the United States have fused together to inhabit different planets in 2510, the cast is primarily white. *Blade Runner*'s dystopic future Los Angeles appears otherwise ethnically diverse, but almost devoid of blacks. In J. D. Robb's *In Death* series, which takes place in New York City in the late 2050s, whites are in the minority and most of the city is mixed race.

But we don't need science fiction to tell us what the racial future of the United States will be. In 2012, the U.S. Census reported that Latino, African American, Asian, and mixed-race births made up the majority of births for the first time. In the twelve-month period ending in July 2011, Latino, African American, Asian American, and mixed-race babies made up 50.4 percent of all live births (U.S. Census Bureau 2012i). This historical moment made for some odd headlines, as anyone who is in those racial categories is defined as a "minority." How can minorities be the majority? How will the rising number of nonwhites in America affect the future of our society? What will a future "majority-minority" nation be like?

The census defines "majority" members as non-Hispanic, single-race whites and projects that by 2042 we will become a country where that demographic is outnumbered by non-whites. However, it doesn't mean that whites will become a minority group. As mentioned already in this chapter, a minority group consists of people who are recognized as belonging to a social category and who suffer from unequal treatment as a result of that status. Therefore, it is possible to be in the numerical majority and still have minority status with regard to power and opportunity, as well as to be in the numerical minority and still hold majority status with regard to power and opportunity. For example, Texas and California are already "majority-minority" states, and although there are fewer whites than nonwhites, whites are still dominant.

But the change is visible in other areas of social life: already, more and more advertising features nonwhite actors, as a way of reaching out to a growing nonwhite customer base. Being multiracial is becoming more common and more accepted, and college-aged Americans, in particular, are used to seeing racially ambiguous faces. Indeed, the forty-fourth president of the United States, Barack Obama, had one white parent and one black parent. So, even though we have not reached a state of racial equality in the United States, the possibility for social change as our demographics change seems hopeful.

Should we change the language of racial relations? Are the words "majority" and "minority" too confusing now that racial demographics have changed? At this moment in history, race is still a difficult and controversial topic for many people. But perhaps, as the babies born in 2012 grow up, racial difference will cease to be the basis of discrimination and conflict, and race relations will become easier in a majority-minority nation.

Multiracial Families An increasing number of families are mixed race, like the Greenwoods of Toms River, New Jersey.

will choose to leave "voluntarily." This was the case with early Mormons, whose religious persecution in the East and Midwest between 1846 and 1869 drove 70,000 to cross the country (taking what is called the Mormon Pioneer Trail) and settle in the Great Salt Lake Valley region of Utah.

Internal Colonialism and Segregation

The term "colonialism" refers to a policy whereby a stronger nation takes control of a weaker nation (the "colony") in order to extend the stronger nation's territory or to exploit the colony's resources for the stronger nation's own enrichment. The British Empire, which once included such distant countries as India, Burma (now Myanmar), the West Indies, South Africa, and Australia, as well as America before its independence, is an example of colonialism.

Internal colonialism describes the exploitation of a minority group within the dominant group's own borders. Internal colonialism often takes the form of economic exploitation and includes some sort of physical **segregation** of groups by race or ethnicity. For example, in the U.S. South up to the 1960s, not only did blacks live in separate neighborhoods, but they also were restricted to "coloreds"-only sections of buses, parks, restaurants, and even drinking fountains. If members of the minority group live close by yet in their own part of town (for instance, on the "other side of the tracks"), they are separate, and hence unequal, but still near enough to serve as workers for the dominant group. Segregation was not just confined to the South; it permeated other areas of society. Separation by races could be found in divisions serving in the U.S. military and among teams playing in professional sports like baseball, football, and basketball. Efforts to desegregate American society accelerated through the civil rights movement.

INTERNAL COLONIALISM the economic and political subjugation of the minority group by the dominant group within a nation

SEGREGATION the physical and legal separation of groups by race or ethnicity

ASSIMILATION a pattern of relations between ethnic or racial groups in which the minority group is absorbed into the mainstream or dominant group, making society more homogenous

RACIAL ASSIMILATION the process by which racial minority groups are absorbed into the dominant group through intermarriage

CULTURAL ASSIMILATION the process by which racial or ethnic groups are absorbed into the dominant group by adopting the dominant group's culture

PLURALISM a cultural pattern of intergroup relations that encourages racial and ethnic variation and acceptance within a society

Assimilation

With **assimilation**, a minority group is absorbed into the dominant group; this process is the central idea behind America's "melting pot." On the surface, assimilation seems like a reasonable solution to the potential conflicts among different groups. If everyone belongs to the same group, if the society is largely homogenous, then conflict will decrease.

During much of the twentieth century, immigrants to the United States were eager to adopt an American way of life, become citizens, learn English, and lose any trace of their "foreign-ness." The Irish, Italians, and Eastern Europeans were all once considered "ethnics" but were eventually assimilated into the larger category of white Americans. Today, they are practically unrecognizable as distinct ethnic groups, unless they choose to emphasize characteristics that would so distinguish them. It is likely that this process will continue with the newer wave of immigrants; for instance, some census-type forms no longer distinguish Hispanic or Middle Eastern as separate categories from white.

But although there is something to be gained by assimilation—namely, membership in the dominant population—there is also something to be sacrificed. Minority group members may lose their previous ethnic or racial identity, either through **racial assimilation**, having children with the dominant group until the different races are completely mixed, or through **cultural assimilation**, in which members learn the cultural practices of the dominant group. In some cases, both types of assimilation take place at the same time.

In addition, the process of assimilation is not always entered into voluntarily. Sometimes, members of a minority group may be forced to acquire new behaviors and are forbidden to practice their own religion or speak their own language, until these are all but forgotten. For some, assimilation results in the tragic loss of a distinctive racial or ethnic identity. This is true for many Native Americans, for instance, who in just a few generations have lost the ability to speak their tribal languages or have forgotten cultural practices of their not-so-distant ancestors.

Pluralism

Pluralism not only permits racial and ethnic variation within one society, it actually encourages people to embrace diversity as a positive feature of a society. The traditional image of the melting pot is exchanged with a "salad bowl" in which all the different ingredients maintain their distinct qualities, even as they are tossed together. In the last few decades, the United States has seen more and more groups celebrating their racial or ethnic roots, developing a strong common consciousness, and expressing pride in their unique identity.

At the core of pluralism, also referred to as *multiculturalism*, is tolerance of racial and ethnic differences. An example of successful multiculturalism is Canada. This country's population is diverse, composed of not only two official linguistic groups (English and French) but also ethnic and racial

Jackie Robinson is most often cited as the first athlete to break the "color barrier" in professional sports when he made his debut in major league baseball in 1947.

minorities that include European, Chinese, and Indian immigrants as well as members of "First Nations," or Canadian native peoples. The Canadian government is committed to the ideals of multiculturalism, with a great deal of funding directed to programs aimed at improving race relations and encouraging multicultural harmony. As a sign of that commitment, the 1988 Canadian Multiculturalism Act declared that the role of government is to bring about "equal access for all Canadians in the economic, social, cultural, and political realms" (Mitchell 1993).

The United States is still moving toward becoming a more multicultural and egalitarian society, although in recent years there has been a backlash against the idea of pluralism. Some critics blame the educational system for allowing what they consider marginal academic areas, such as ethnic studies, women's studies, gay and lesbian studies, and the like, to be featured alongside the classic curriculum. Others question the need for bilingual education and English as a second language (ESL) programs, despite research showing benefits to nonnative speakers (Krashen 1996). And groups such as U.S. English and English First advocate for legislation making English the national language and setting limits on the use of other languages. Nevertheless, since the future seems sure to bring an ever-greater racial and ethnic mix to the country, Americans may yet be able to incorporate multiculturalism into our sense of national identity.

CLOSING COMMENTS

Constructing categories of race and ethnicity seems inevitably to lead to stratification and inequality and to such destructive social processes as stereotyping, segregation, prejudice, and discrimination. Are there any positive consequences, either for society or for individuals? As it turns out, there are.

Racial and ethnic categories help create a sense of identity for members of these groups, which can lead to feelings of unity and solidarity—a sense of belonging to something that is larger than oneself, of cultural connection, and of shared history. We see this in action during ethnic festivals and holidays. When we share our own group unity with others in this way, we contribute to the diversity of our community and society. The more we understand and appreciate the diverse population of our nation, the less likely we may be to contribute to the destructive consequences of racial and ethnic categorization.

The important sociological insight here is that since categories of race and ethnicity are socially constructed, their meanings are socially constructed as well. Historically, we have constructed meanings that favor some and exploit and oppress others. Is it possible to construct meanings for racial and ethnic categories that value and celebrate them all? Over time, and with your newly acquired sociological insights, we hope you will be part of that transformation.

Everything You Need to Know about Race and Ethnicity

> " Race is a social category based on real or perceived biological differences among groups of people. Ethnicity is a social category based on a group's shared ancestry or cultural heritage. "

THEORIES OF RACE AND ETHNICITY

* **Structural functionalism:** groups have a tendency toward ethnocentrism, which binds people together but also makes them act unfavorably toward those outside the group

* **Conflict theory:** majority groups use racism and ethnocentrism to protect their interests

* **Symbolic interactionism:** race and ethnicity are created symbolically in everyday interactions

REVIEW

1. How do you identify yourself in terms of race or ethnicity? Are there special occasions or situations in which you are more likely to display your ethnicity or race? Do you identify with more than one racial or ethnic group or know anyone who does? What does this tell you about the origin of these categories?

2. Affirmative action in college admissions is one of the most controversial topics in America today. Why would a college want to consider race or ethnicity when making admissions decisions? What factors do you think admissions boards should consider?

3. Although the Supreme Court ruled against antimiscegenation laws in 1967, homogamy, or assortive mating, is reinforced by social conventions. Would you date someone of a different race? Does your answer change depending on which racial or ethnic group you're thinking about?

U.S. Population by Race in 2060

Percent of total population | ■ 2013 ■ 2060

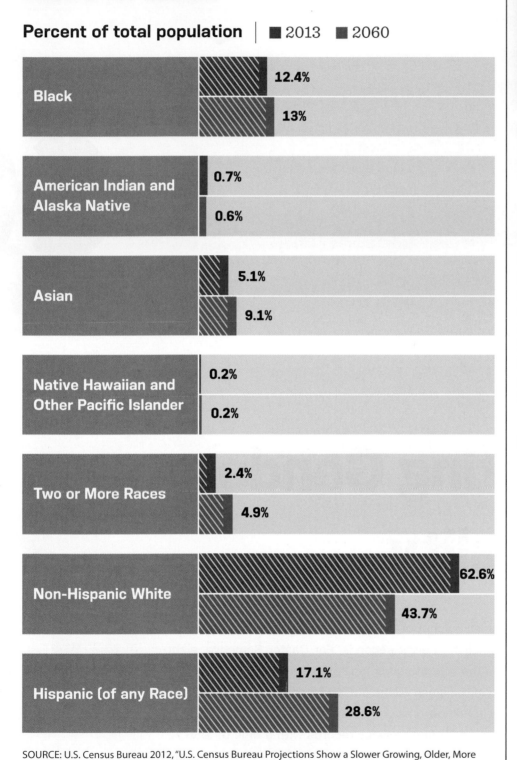

Black	12.4%
	13%
American Indian and Alaska Native	0.7%
	0.6%
Asian	5.1%
	9.1%
Native Hawaiian and Other Pacific Islander	0.2%
	0.2%
Two or More Races	2.4%
	4.9%
Non-Hispanic White	62.6%
	43.7%
Hispanic (of any Race)	17.1%
	28.6%

SOURCE: U.S. Census Bureau 2012, "U.S. Census Bureau Projections Show a Slower Growing, Older, More Diverse Nation a Half Century from Now"

EXPLORE

What's Funny about Racism?

Have you seen a comedic skit in which people pretend to be someone of another race? Such skits can be found on popular TV shows like *Saturday Night Live* but also in everyday life, like high schools. Visit the Everyday Sociology Blog to read about the problematic idea that racism is a viable form of entertainment.

http://wwnPag.es/trw408

CHAPTER 9

Constructing Gender and Sexuality

Eight seconds is an infinitesimally small amount of time to most people. In fact, there are very few tasks that you can accomplish in eight seconds. For Caster Semenya, eight seconds was enough time to cause the world to question her identity for an entire year.

Semenya was born in 1991 and raised in the small village of Ga-Masehlong in South Africa. She lived her life as female without any question until her outstanding performance at the 2009 African Junior Championships, where she broke previous records with a time of 1:56.72 in the 800-meter race. One month later, she broke the world record at the 2009 World Championships, drawing the attention of the International Association of Athletics Federations (IAAF)

because her race time beat her performance in a 2008 competition by eight seconds. Eight seconds was all it took for Semenya to be cast into the world spotlight by the fall of 2009.

Female athletes frequently have to face the stigma of not being seen as feminine because of the physicality required to be a superior athlete. The low body-fat percentages and accentuated musculatures that result from intensive sports training may even cause women to stop having menstrual periods. As our notions of gender are strongly linked to the body, female athletes often find themselves in the difficult position of defending themselves against the sanctions associated with being perceived as "masculine." In fact, sex-determination testing has been a recurring theme for female athletes since the 1968 Olympics, when many Soviet female athletes were accused of being male. Sex-determination testing is generally performed by a team of physicians, including gynecologists and endocrinologists. Critics claim that these tests are humiliating, inaccurate, and insensitive.

In 2009, the IAAF required Semenya to undergo sex-determination testing to confirm eligibility to compete as a woman after her unprecedented eight-second improvement in the 800-meter race. In the media storm that followed, the public at large speculated that Semenya had no uterus, or that she possessed undescended testicles that produced extra testosterone, enhancing her performance. Bloggers, tabloids, and talk shows all made Semenya a household name around the world. It seemed like everyone had a diagnosis for Caster Semenya, and few of them involved her being a "normal" female. In the eleven months that it took the IAAF to complete the testing, Semenya was banned from competing. If the testing revealed that she was not biologically female, her gold medals would be taken from her and she would relinquish her title as world champion in the 800-meter.

On July 6, 2010, the IAAF publicly announced that Semenya could keep her title and medals and that she was eligible to compete in future races as a woman. The results of the sex-determination test were never officially released to the public. She won the first 800-meter race that she was allowed to compete in after the IAAF made its decision, and won silver in the 800-meter race at the 2012 London Olympics (after carrying the South African flag in the opening ceremonies). Since then, Semenya has suffered a couple of disappointing seasons. She was also the subject of a new round of celebrity gossip about a purported romance with fellow runner Violet Raseboya, which Semenya denied. In 2015, Semenya resumed training—and winning—at North-West University, near Johannesburg, where she studies sports science.

Should any female athlete have to face the public humiliation that Semenya did? Does sex or gender even still matter in athletic competition? It will be fascinating to see how future cases of sex-determination testing will be handled after the trauma that Semenya had to endure for almost an entire year. Eight seconds changed Semenya's life and raised our awareness of how important and complicated issues of sex and gender are for society.

HOW TO READ THIS CHAPTER

We often think of gender and sexuality as part of our biological inheritance, unchanging and unchangeable. We hope that after reading this chapter you will understand the ways in which our gender and sexual identities are about *what we do* in addition to being about *who we are*. Gender and sexuality may be based in physiology, but their meanings are constructed in social contexts. As you read, pay attention to the processes involved in constructing the meanings of genders and sexualities, as well as to the real consequences of gender and sexual inequality. As you become aware of these problems, perhaps you'll begin to think about solutions as well.

Sex and Gender

Although people often use the terms "sex" and "gender" interchangeably, sociologists differentiate between the two: most view "sex" as biological but "gender" as social or cultural. Even though a person is usually the same sex and gender, this is not always the case, as we will see. Our gender identity and gender expression may differ from the sex we are assigned at birth. This raises the question of which set of attributes is most consequential to our everyday lives.

Sex

Sex refers to an individual's membership in one of two categories—male or female. The distinctions between male and female are based on such biological factors as chromosomes, hormones, and reproductive organs, all of which make up the primary sex characteristics. Males and females also possess different secondary sex characteristics, such as facial and body hair and musculature (Table 9.1).

Most people assume that everyone is either male or female. However, about 17 babies in 1,000 are born **intersex**, having a variant chromosomal makeup and mixed or indeterminate male and female sex characteristics (Fausto-Sterling 2000). While most cases of intersex are detected at birth, some do not appear until puberty or adulthood. When a baby is born intersex, nature hasn't clearly indicated whether the infant is male or female. In modern Western society, the prospect of an ambiguously sexed person seems so threatening and unacceptable that most parents seek out surgical and other procedures to quickly remedy the situation (in most cases, female is the most viable and expedient choice). More recently, the rights of intersex people have come into focus; many adults maintain they should have the freedom to choose for themselves whether to take medical measures or remain as they are.

Gender

Gender refers to the physical, behavioral, and personality traits that a group considers to be normal, natural, right, and good for its male and female members. In other words, gender reflects our notions about what is appropriately "masculine" or "feminine." Some societies, for example, expect men to be more aggressive and competitive and women to be more emotional and nurturing. We often think of such characteristics

SEX an individual's membership in one of two categories—male or female—based on biological factors

INTERSEX term used to describe a person whose chromosomes or sex characteristics are neither exclusively male nor exclusively female

GENDER the physical, behavioral, and personality traits that a group considers normal for its male and female members

Table 9.1 Human Sex Characteristics

	Females	Males
Chromosomes	XX	XY
Dominant Hormone	Estrogen	Testosterone
Primary Sex Characteristics	Reproductive organs: vagina, cervix, uterus, ovaries, fallopian tubes, other glands	Reproductive organs: penis, testicles, scrotum, prostate, other glands
Secondary Sex Characteristics	Shorter than males; larger breasts; wider hips than shoulders; less facial hair; more subcutaneous fat; fat deposits around buttocks, thighs, and hips; smoother skin texture	Abdominal, chest, body, and facial hair; larger hands and feet; broader shoulders and chest; heavier skull and bone structure; greater muscle mass and strength; Adam's apple and deeper voice; fat deposits around abdominals and waist; coarser skin texture

GLOBAL PERSPECTIVE
Different Societies, Different Genders

In modern Western societies, we don't have a voice in what our gender will be. Someone looks us over at birth (or even before) and declares, "It's a boy!" or "It's a girl!" Even though some infants are born with indeterminate genitals, they are almost always assigned to one gender or the other as soon as possible, even if surgery is required. We have no words for someone who identifies as neither male nor female, nor do we find such an identity acceptable. But consider two societies that do acknowledge a "third gender."

Berdaches or "Two-Spirit" People

When nineteenth-century explorers and missionaries wrote about the native tribes they encountered in America, they also described individuals within those tribes who were neither male nor female but somehow both. These people—called "berdaches" by non-natives and "two-spirit" by natives—were usually biological males who dressed as women and took on types of work we think of as feminine, such as cooking and domestic labor. They could also be biological females who took on traditionally male pursuits, such as hunting, trapping, and warfare. Male two-spirits have been documented in nearly 150 Native American cultures, and female two-spirits in almost half that number. Some researchers believe that people who became two-spirits were assigned to such a role from a very young age, if not from birth, for reasons of "demographic necessity" (Trexler 2002). In the northern reaches of what is now Canada, for example, couples who had given birth to all girls may have decided that their next child would be raised as a boy (and therefore a hunter who could provide food for the family)—no matter what. In more southern regions, a family who needed a female child may have deliberately raised a boy as a girl; male two-spirits were valued for their height and strength.

Research on two-spirits seems contradictory. Some believe that, based on the records of the early Europeans, they were looked down on by their own tribes. Others point out that some two-spirits were respected and played important roles in the religious life of their communities. What we do know is that two-spirits were acknowledged as a third gender. Native creation myths include such references as "When the spirit people made men and women, they also made berdaches" (Roscoe 2000, p. 4)—allowing this group a recognized place in the order of things.

Hijras

The *hijras* of South Asia are a modern example of third-gender individuals. Like berdaches, hijras are recognized by their society as an acceptable variation on gender—neither male nor female but something else entirely. They are usually biological males who have all or part of their genitals removed, and most become hijras voluntarily in their teens or twenties. They dress and live as females and are referred to as daughter, sister, grandmother, or aunt.

GENDER IDENTITY an individual's self-definition or sense of gender

CISGENDER term used when gender identity and/or expression aligns with the sex assigned at birth

TRANSGENDER term used when gender identity and/or expression is different from the sex assigned at birth

GENDER EXPRESSION an individual's behavioral manifestations of gender

as biologically determined or "natural," but no society leaves it completely up to nature to dictate the behavior of its male and female members. While we tend to feel that our gender is a deeply personal part of who we are, we also learn to interpret and enact gender in ways that are culturally and historically specific.

Our deeply held sense of ourselves as male, female, or some other gender is called our **gender identity**. Our gender identity may or may not correspond with the sex we have been assigned at birth. When our sex and gender identity match up (e.g., female sex, female gender identity), we are **cisgender**—the prefix *cis* means "same," indicating that our sex and gender correspond. We use the term **transgender** (or noncisgender) to describe someone whose gender identity does not align with their sex assigned at birth.

Separate from our gender identity is our **gender expression**, or our external manifestations of gender, which include "masculine" or "feminine" clothing, grooming, behavior, body language, gestures, and even names. Transgender persons ("trans" persons for short) may or may not undergo medical or surgical procedures as part of a transition during which they change their gender expression to align with their gender identity rather than with the sex they were assigned at birth.

"Two-Spirit" People Berdaches (left), a term used by anthropologists and sociologists but considered insulting by many Native Americans, provide an example of a third gender that is neither male nor female. Hijras (right) occupy a similar place in the society of India. It is considered good luck to have a hijra at a wedding or at the birth of a male child.

Like berdaches, hijras take part in the religious life of their people; they are specifically mentioned (and thus validated) in the epic Hindu texts as having been recognized by the deity Rama. Today, the presence of hijras at weddings and at the births of male children is thought to be auspicious. In 2012, the third gender option was officially added to Pakistan's national identity cards (Frayer 2012).

The two-spirit and hijra may sound similar to cross-dressers or transgender persons in Western society, but the analogy isn't entirely appropriate. A two-spirit or hijra is always referred to by that term, not "he" or "she," whereas in the United States we still struggle with terminology and fret over how to fit trans people into existing male or female pigeonholes. Keep in mind that characteristics we think of as definitive, such as sex, gender, and sexuality, may be viewed differently in other cultures and time periods, which means that it should be possible to view them differently here and now.

It is important to remember that transgender identity is not dependent upon medical procedures.

Trans individuals are just one group of **gender-nonconforming** persons in contemporary society; others include those with multiple genders (bigender, trigender, pangender), those with no gender (nongender), and those whose gender fluctuates over time (genderfluid). Recognizing that this type of gender nonconformity exists is sometimes difficult for people who are used to thinking of sex and gender as **binary** classifications: We assume that there are two, and only two, categories for sex (male/female) and for gender (masculine/feminine), and that our membership in one or the other category is permanent and unchanging. However, it has become clear to sociologists that not everyone experiences sex, gender, or sexuality in unambiguous ways.

Essentialist and Constructionist Approaches

Depending on their field of study, sociologists look at gender from different perspectives. **Essentialists** see gender as immutable and biological, and as an unambiguous, two-category system. According to this view, you're either male or female from birth to death, and you have no other option. Chromosomes,

GENDER NONCONFORMING term used when gender identity and/or expression differs from societal expectations about gender roles

BINARY a system of classification with only two distinct and opposite categories

ESSENTIALISTS those who believe gender roles have a genetic or biological origin and therefore cannot be changed

CONSTRUCTIONISTS those who believe that notions of gender are socially determined, such that a dichotomous binary system is just one possibility among many

SEXUALITY the character or quality of being sexual

SEXUAL ORIENTATION or **IDENTITY** the inclination to feel sexual desire toward people of a particular gender or toward both genders

HETEROSEXUALITY sexual attraction toward members of the other gender

HOMOSEXUALITY sexual attraction toward members of one's own gender

BISEXUALITY sexual attraction toward members of both genders

ASEXUALITY the lack of sexual attraction of any kind; no interest in or desire for sex

hormones, and genitalia determine your identity—the way you see yourself, the way you interact with others, and the activities you engage in every day. Culture plays no role. Because it is a dispreferred perspective in sociology, essentialism is generally found outside the discipline in such fields as medicine, theology, and biology, and within sociology in the subfield of sociobiology. Some sociobiologists reduce male-female categorization to the biological function of procreation.

Most mainstream sociologists, however, use a **constructionist** approach to gender: they see gender as a social construction and acknowledge the possibility that binary male-female categories aren't the only way to classify individuals. Nor are the systems of gender inequality that result from these labels necessary or natural. Constructionists believe that the meaning of masculinity and femininity may differ drastically in different societies and historical periods. We'll use a variety of sociological perspectives in this inquiry but will find ourselves returning again and again to constructionism as a helpful way to comprehend both the phenomenon of gender inequality and the theories that attempt to explain it.

Sexuality and Sexual Orientation

What is **sexuality**? And what is it doing in a sociology textbook? The term "sexuality" is used in a variety of ways; for example, it is used to describe sexual behavior, desires, and fantasies (the things people actually do as well as the things they think or dream about doing). It is also used to describe **sexual orientation or identity**, which is the inclination to

feel sexual desire toward and engage in sexual behavior with persons of a particular gender.

Our society recognizes a number of sexual orientations, and they are each related to our two-category or binary gender system. **Heterosexuality**, or sexual desire for the other gender, is the normative and dominant category, which may be why the slang term for it is "straight." Most people identify themselves as heterosexual, and there are privileges attached to membership in this category. **Homosexuality**, or sexual desire for the same gender, is a minority category; the National Survey of Sexual Health and Behavior found that about 4 percent of adults self-identify as gay or lesbian (Reece et al. 2010). As with other minority statuses, there are a variety of difficulties and disadvantages attached to membership in this category. **Bisexuality**—sexual attraction to both genders—is also a minority category, with about 3 percent of men and 4 percent of women identifying as bisexual (Reece et al. 2010). **Asexuality** involves the lack of sexual attraction of any kind. Asexual people are basically nonsexual and are a very small minority group, with only about 1 percent of adults identifying as asexual (Bogaert 2004). There have been various claims and controversy about the exact percentage of adults who identify with each category of sexual orientation. Another recent study found somewhat different numbers; 96.6 identified as heterosexual, 1.6 percent gay or lesbian, 0.7 percent bisexual, and the remaining 1.1 percent identified as "something else," "I don't know the answer," or refused to provide an answer (CDC 2014d).

Still, even these categories are limiting. As early as the 1940s, the pioneering sex researcher Alfred Kinsey suggested that human sexuality is far more diverse than commonly assumed. His own studies led him to believe that people are not exclusively heterosexual or homosexual but can fall along a wide spectrum (Kinsey et al. 1948/1998; Kinsey and Gebhard 1953/1998). Kinsey and others who have followed him have suggested that we can best understand sexual orientation not through binary categories (gay versus straight) but rather as a fluid continuum that can change over the course of a person's lifetime (Figure 9.1).

"Queering the Binary"

For most of the twentieth century, "queer" was a pejorative term applied mainly to gay men (before that, it was used

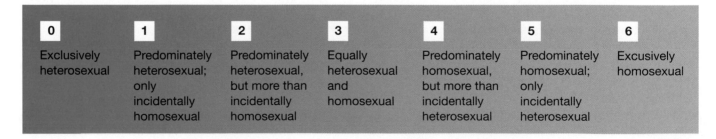

0	1	2	3	4	5	6
Exclusively heterosexual	Predominately heterosexual; only incidentally homosexual	Predominately heterosexual, but more than incidentally homosexual	Equally heterosexual and homosexual	Predominately homosexual, but more than incidentally heterosexual	Predominately homosexual; only incidentally heterosexual	Excusively homosexual

Figure 9.1 **The Kinsey Scale of Sexuality**

to mean "odd" or "peculiar" in a nonsexual way). But in the 1990s, with the emergence of "queer theory," the term underwent a remarkable transformation as both activists and academics began using it in a very different way. The term is now used to describe anything that challenges prevailing binary notions of sex, gender, and sexuality (and is sometimes used to describe nonconformity in other areas as well). "Queer" encompasses a wider range of gender and sexual diversity than terms like "gay" and "trans" and implies a questioning of society's traditional gender and sexual arrangements. It has come to be represented by a "Q" appended to the acronym "LGBT" to make it more inclusive, as in **LGBTQ**. In academia, **queer theory** rejects the idea of a single gay, lesbian, bisexual, heterosexual, or transgender identity, emphasizing instead the importance of difference (Butler 1993). It asserts that being queer is about "possibilities, gaps, overlaps, dissonances, and resonances" (Sedgwick 1993, p. 8) and suggests that any kind of categorization is outmoded and limiting.

Socialization, Gender, and Sexuality

Gender role socialization—the subtle, pervasive process of learning what constitutes masculinity and femininity—begins early and continues throughout our lives. It is accomplished primarily by the four major agents of socialization: families, schools, peers, and the media, though other social institutions, such as religion, may also play a part in the process. In addition to perpetuating binary notions of gender and gender conformity, the process of socialization also tends to support **heteronormativity** (the assumption that heterosexuality is the only acceptable orientation).

Families

Families are usually the primary source of socialization. Indeed, Kara Smith (2005) argues that gender role socialization begins even before birth. Because the sex of the fetus can now be determined in utero, families may begin relating to the new baby as either a girl or a boy far in advance of the baby's arrival. Smith's research demonstrates how knowing the baby's sex affects how the mother talks to her fetus—the choice of words as well as tone of voice. Once babies are born, female and male clothes, rooms, and toys will differ, as will the stories the children are told.

Most telling, however, is the way in which significant others—parents, siblings, extended family, and caregivers—interact with the baby. Through **social learning**, the process of learning behaviors and meanings through social interaction, babies respond to and internalize the expectations of others around them. For example, a baby girl who is treated gently may observe the roughhousing of baby boys with alarm. Sometimes there is a conscious effort to instill certain behaviors in children—such as by reprimanding a young boy for crying. At other times, social learning happens in a more subtle way, as the baby learns through observation, imitation, and play. Children rather quickly begin to exhibit gender-stereotyped behaviors. By the age of two, they are aware of their own and others' gender, and by age three, they begin to identify specific traits associated with each gender.

Gender pervades every aspect of family life. It may be implicit in the chores or privileges girls and boys are given (washing the dishes versus mowing the lawn), the way they are disciplined or punished, where they go or don't go, or what they are encouraged or forbidden to do. Lessons such as "that's not very ladylike" and "big boys don't cry" are echoed in children's literature, in toys made specifically for girls or boys, and in the games they play. And as we grow up, we are always watching our other family members, using them as role models for our own beliefs and behaviors. In adulthood, our families may still influence what kind of career or mate we choose, how we run our household, and how we raise our own children.

How families are formed matters for the socialization process as well. To the extent that laws have historically ratified only heterosexual marriages, we have learned that heterosexuality and biological parenting are the "normal" or "natural" ways to form a family. Of course, these assumptions overlook the many other ways real families are formed.

Schools

Differences in the educational experiences of girls and boys also begin to appear early, both in the classroom and on the playground. Early on, girls and boys are frequently put in same-sex groups and assigned gender-stereotyped tasks, such as playing with dolls or playing with trucks. Same-sex groups also form on the playground, with girls and boys engaging in different kinds of social and athletic activities (Thorne 1993). By the fifth grade, gender norms are firmly established, as can be seen in the segregation that takes place even in co-ed schools.

One of the key areas of difference is in the way that teachers, both women and men, typically interact with students. Whether or not they realize it, teachers tend to favor boys in several ways. Boys receive more attention and instructional time and are more likely to be called on in class. And boys are posed with more challenging questions or tasks and are given more praise for the quality of their work. Boys are also, however, more likely to make teachers angry by misbehaving

LGBTQ lesbian, gay, bisexual, transgender, and queer (sometimes "A" is added to include "allies")

QUEER THEORY social theory about gender and sexual identity; emphasizes the importance of difference and rejects ideas of innate identities or restrictive categories

GENDER ROLE SOCIALIZATION the lifelong process of learning to be masculine or feminine, primarily through agents of socialization

HETERONORMATIVITY the belief that heterosexuality is and should be the norm

SOCIAL LEARNING the process of learning behaviors and meanings through social interaction

IN RELATIONSHIPS
Rape Culture and Campus Social Life

The ongoing epidemic of campus sexual assaults has gotten a lot of press lately, as has the concept of **rape culture**, or an environment in which sexual violence against women is normalized and perpetuated through cultural norms and values. While rape culture is not unique to college campuses, there are some features of campus life that make distinctive contributions to campus rape culture. You may find yourself reexamining your own social life if you, even unwittingly, participate in some of the activities that contribute to campus rape culture.

An Indiana University study found that some aspects of campus life that don't appear to be directly related to sexual assaults can actually contribute to campus rape culture (Armstrong, Hamilton, and Sweeney 2006). For example, a widely held notion about college life is that students are supposed to party. So, before freshmen even set foot on campus, they may feel a certain amount of pressure to participate in the party scene. This can be especially true at larger universities or on commuter campuses, where it is harder to make friends or meet possible romantic partners in classrooms or living situations. Concerns about social status—whether one is popular, attractive, or well regarded by others—are also something that college students traditionally wrestle with, and this may mean that students will do (or refrain from doing) whatever it takes in order to be included in group life.

College policies can contribute to rape culture as well, and many universities have notoriously bad records when it comes to investigating and responding to campus sexual assault. A 2013 case at James Madison University in Virginia involved sentencing three offenders to "expulsion after graduation," meaning that the men were allowed to remain on campus (two for one year, one for two years) to complete their degrees but were then banned from JMU post-commencement. Is this even punishment at all? Knowing that little may be done to bring a campus rapist to justice can mean that survivors don't feel comfortable reporting assaults to campus authorities.

Many campuses now have policies that restrict alcohol use, which makes on-campus locales unattractive settings for those big parties everyone is supposed to enjoy attending. This pushes the party scene off campus, often into privately owned fraternity houses, giving frat brothers more control over how

RAPE CULTURE a set of beliefs, norms, and values that normalizes sexual violence against women

Fraternity Row Many colleges don't allow students to drink alcohol on campus, pushing the party scene off campus, often to fraternity houses.

parties are organized, who attends, how alcohol is served, and what happens if something goes wrong. This can be a recipe for disaster, including alcohol poisoning, injury, and death, as well as sexual assault. And it means that the fraternities, rather than the universities, are held responsible.

Finally, and usually without meaning to, those in charge of student services and campus life often participate in the larger culture of "victim blaming" in their attempts to prevent sexual assault. Women are advised repeatedly on how to avoid being raped (don't go to parties alone, don't get intoxicated, don't accept drinks or rides home from people you don't know, etc.), implying that if a woman is assaulted, it is because she failed to follow these instructions. Meanwhile, there has been far less focus on educating men in rape prevention—skills that can help them challenge other men who engage in risky or violent behaviors and that may allow them to intervene in situations to protect the health and safety of women.

This is where you can make a difference. Support efforts to provide comprehensive prevention education and to change campus culture for the better. Urge your school to offer sufficient on-campus activities to support a vibrant student social life, so that alcohol-drenched off-campus parties aren't the only option—and then participate in these activities yourselves. Work to create a sense of solidarity among women and between women and men, so that all feel some responsibility for each other's welfare. Healthier relationships and a healthier campus community are within your reach.

Heteronormativity in Schools Coy Mathis, a transgender girl, had to sue for the right to use the girls' bathroom at her elementary school in Colorado.

and therefore to receive some form of punishment more often (Smith 1999).

Despite boys' favorable treatment, girls in elementary school tend to earn higher grades. But their academic achievements are often discounted. In fact, the media often paint this gender discrepancy as a crisis for boys. When they do perform well, girls are typically credited for hard work rather than intellectual ability. They are encouraged to focus on social skills or appearance rather than brain power. By the time they reach middle or junior high school, girls begin to slip behind and to lose their sense of academic self-esteem. These troubles are compounded in adolescent girls, who begin to feel uneasy about competing with boys, embarrassed by their own success, or uncomfortable engaging in male-dominated subjects like math or science.

Gender role socialization in schools can take other forms as well. Textbooks often still contain sexist language and gender stereotypes. Women and minorities are underrepresented, both as subjects and as authors (Robson 2001). In the social structure of the school itself, women tend to be concentrated at the lower levels, as teachers and aides, while men tend to occupy upper-management and administrative positions. In such ways, schooling as a whole reinforces gender stereotypes.

For LGBTQ students, school is often a place where they learn (or relearn) the lesson that they will only be accepted if they hide their true identities. Heteronormativity pervades school life, from canonical texts showing traditional families, to an emphasis on heterosexual dating (prom and homecoming queens and their kings), to the binary division of restrooms in school buildings.

Peers

In Western societies, peer groups are an increasingly important agent of socialization. By the age of three, children develop a preference for same-sex playmates, a tendency that increases markedly as childhood progresses. Children in preschool are three times more likely to play with same-sex playmates—eleven times more likely in kindergarten—and it is not until well after puberty that this pattern changes even a little (Maccoby and Jacklin 1987). While some have argued that such gender segregation is the *result* of inherent differences between men and women, there is evidence to support the notion that same-sex peer groups can help *create* gendered behavior. Researchers have found, for example, that when children play with same-sex peers, their activities are more likely to be gender typed (girls have pretend tea parties, for example) than when boys and girls play together (Fabes, Martin, and Hanish 2003). In addition, children (especially boys) are punished (mocked) by their peers for crossing over these gendered borders (Thorne 1993).

C. J. Pascoe's ethnography of high school boys, *Dude, You're a Fag*, shows just how powerful peer groups can be in enforcing gender roles and the assumptions about sexuality that underlie them. Not only do boys police each other's performance of masculinity by criticizing non-normative (and, in their minds, effeminate) behavior, dress, and other practices, they "lay claim to masculine identities by lobbing homophobic epithets at one another" (Pascoe 2007, p. 5). Calling someone a "fag" inflates the offender's own sense of masculinity, while demonstrating to others the consequences of deviating from masculine norms.

The need to impress others and to feel popular with peers increases in the teenage years. Boys tend to gain prestige through athletic ability, a well-developed sense of humor, or taking risks and defying norms. Girls tend to gain prestige through social position and physical attractiveness. It's easy to imagine what kinds of behaviors result from such peer pressure and the consequences of falling short in any way. In the extreme, it can lead to bullying, rebellious behavior, or eating disorders. Similar pressures in regard to dating and mating continue through the early adult years as well, enforcing heteronormativity and privileging cisgender identities by ostracizing transgressors or worse.

The Media

From a variety of media sources, such as movies, comic books, or popular music, we learn "how to behave, how to be accepted, what to value, and what is normal" as well as "how gender fits into society" (Barner 1999). When it comes to television, there is no question that "sex-role behavior is portrayed in highly

LGBTQ on TV In 2015, Jeffrey Tambor won a Golden Globe for his portrayal of an older transgender woman in Netflix's original series *Transparent*. At the 2015 ESPY Awards, Caitlyn Jenner was honored with the Arthur Ashe Courage Award.

stereotypic fashion in virtually every aspect" of the programming (McGhee and Frueh 1980). Boys and girls learn that certain activities and attitudes are more appropriate for one gender than for the other. Girls should be beautiful, caring, sensitive, and reserved, while boys should be assertive, strong, and analytic. This starts at a particularly young age: "by the time a child reaches kindergarten, she will 'know' more television characters than real people" (Barner 1999). In addition to TV, magazines like *Seventeen* and *Teen Vogue* are aimed mostly at adolescents. Some have even speculated that increases in anorexia and bulimia among teenage girls can be linked to the images of women they see in the media (Kilbourne 1999). Teenage girls may consider actresses and models the standard of beauty to aspire to, even though such women "often are far below the normal weight recommendations" (Schiller et al. 1998).

The case of video games presents some contradictions regarding media and gender role socialization. What was once thought of as a male bastion is becoming increasingly more gender balanced (perhaps precipitating conflicts like those experienced by Anita Sarkeesian and other women). The stereotype of a video game enthusiast used to be a male player who preferred first-person-shooter games like *Call of Duty*, *Halo*, and *Bioshock*. While males still make up some 60 percent of video game players, some interesting changes are happening to the market. Females are beginning to represent a greater portion of game players, particularly when it comes to online games played on computers (as opposed to video games played on consoles). And the games they are interested in most are multiplayer games such as *World of Warcraft* and the top-selling *The Sims* series, both of which focus on building relationships. An even greater number of females play arcade-style, or what are referred to as casual, games, where they represent 74 percent of all players. Gaming is no longer dominated by males, but the games that boys and girls choose to play may still be guided by gender differences.

Before the 1960s, sexual diversity was altogether absent from television. When it did appear, it was usually treated in a negative manner: in the 1967 CBS documentary *The Homosexuals*, one psychiatrist claims that "the fact that somebody's homosexual . . . automatically rules out the possibility that he will remain happy for long." In recent years, however, increasing levels of tolerance toward LGBTQ people have been reflected in increasingly positive representations of gays, lesbians, and trans persons on television, although these gains have not been without controversy. In 1997, the ABC sitcom *Ellen* introduced the first lesbian lead character in a prime-time series; two years later, the NBC sitcom *Will & Grace* featured two gay male characters. Other shows followed, while cable networks also developed LGBTQ-themed shows, such as *Queer as Folk, Queer Eye for the Straight Guy*, and *The L Word*. In 2013, transgender actress LaVerne Cox was cast as a transgender inmate in Netflix's prison drama *Orange Is the New Black* (which not incidentally featured a bisexual lead character, as well), and in 2014 Jeffrey Tambor starred as Maura Pfefferman, a retired professor who comes out as transgender late in life, in *Transparent*. In 2015, Caitlyn Jenner starred in an eight-part documentary series titled *I Am Cait* about her transition to living life as a transgender woman.

Just because LGBTQ persons are included on television, however, doesn't mean that they have achieved equal status. Clearly, there is not the same kind of acceptance of same-sex relations as of heterosexual relations, as evidenced by how romantic couples are treated on TV. Until 2000, there had never been a gay male kiss on a network program (although there had been two lesbian kisses). As recently as 2014, the sports world was scandalized when Michael Sam, the first openly gay player drafted by the NFL, celebrated joining the St. Louis Rams by kissing his boyfriend on camera. Trans characters are still often presented as villains, victims, or sex workers rather than in more ordinary and more positive roles. Some social scientists argue that the more personal contact between members of different social groups, the less prejudice and discrimination may occur between them (Pettigrew and Tropp 2011). If the media provide people with their only exposure to gays and lesbians, then it is all the more important that their portrayals represent those communities in realistic ways.

For many centuries of human history, children have learned how to act appropriately from family, peers, and school. As the influence of the media becomes more pervasive in our society, we can see how it may compete with or even contradict the influence of other agents of socialization. At the same time, the media also serve to socialize families, peers, and educators, giving them an even more overarching power in society.

DATA WORKSHOP
Analyzing Media and Pop Culture

The Fashion Police: Gender and the Rules of Beauty

 Gender role socialization starts with a baby wrapped in pink or blue and continues to permeate every stage in our lives from there. Messages about what it means to be a girl or a boy are everywhere. We are told over and over, and in a million subtle ways, what is appropriate or desirable for each sex. Ideas about masculinity and femininity are played out innumerable times across an expanding media landscape. Gender norms reflect our ideals about beauty, style, fitness, and physical or sexual attractiveness, and examples of these ideals are on constant display—on our TVs and touch screens, in the grocery store, and at the bus stop. We can't avoid them.

This Data Workshop asks you to closely examine the covers of men's and women's magazines to discover what they have to say about gender and the rules of beauty. You will be using existing sources and doing a content analysis of the magazine covers. Refer to the section on existing sources in Chapter 2 for a review of this research method.

Choose one magazine that focuses on either women's fashion or fitness and one magazine that focuses on either men's fashion or fitness. Here are some suggestions:

- For women's fashion: *Vogue, Elle, Essence, Glamour, Latina, InStyle*

- For women's fitness: *Health, Shape*, or *Women's Health*, or a sports-related magazine such as *Outside, Yoga, Golf Digest*, or *Runner's World* that features a female cover model

- For men's fashion: *Details, Esquire, GQ, Maxim, Krave*

- For men's fitness: *Men's Health, Men's Fitness*, or *Men's Journal*, or a sports-related magazine such as *Outside, Yoga, Golf Digest*, or *Runner's World* that features a male cover model

Locate a recent issue of each of the two magazines you've chosen; you can find hard copies at a bookstore, library, or newsstand, or you can access a digital issue online. Keep in mind that you'll need a physical printout (or digital file) of the cover to work with, so make a tearsheet or photocopy of it, or take a screen shot or digital photo that you can refer to and share. Once you've got your two magazine covers, you're ready to do a content analysis.

Immerse yourself in all the visual elements and text on each cover. Look at the general display and layout, the specific photos, and any other kinds of graphics. Scrutinize the headlines and which words were used. All of this becomes your data. As you examine the covers more closely, consider this set of questions:

* How are the cover models presented? Describe their body type. Does it reflect the ideals for masculine and feminine beauty? How are they posing? What does their posture, facial expressions, gestures, or other physical attributes convey?

* How are the cover models styled? Describe their clothing, hair, makeup, and accessories. Are the cover models engaged in any activities? What do their actions (or inaction) tell us about who they are?

* What is the background or scene of the magazine cover? Does it appear to be taken in a studio, or is it a location shot of some kind? What does the background convey?

* What colors are used for the magazine cover? Look at the background, the title or masthead, and any kind of text or added graphics. What, if any, are the other visual aspects of the cover?

* What words and phrases appear on the cover? Which words are bold, italicized, in capital letters, in larger or smaller font sizes, and why? What is the overall tone? What are the explicit and implicit messages embedded in the words?

* As a whole, what are the major themes and patterns that emerge from the cover? Do these themes support or challenge gender norms and the rules of beauty? Besides gender, do other factors of intersectionality—race, class, age, or sexual orientation—seem to affect the message?

* Compare and contrast the women's and the men's magazines. What are the similarities and differences between the two covers, and how do you explain them? How do you think such magazines influence how we see ourselves and others?

There are two options for completing this Data Workshop:

PREP-PAIR-SHARE Examine the content of the two magazine covers, and take some preliminary notes based on your answers to the Data Workshop questions. Bring copies of the magazine covers to class and pair with a partner to discuss them. What kinds of similarities and differences did you find in your data? Work together to further develop each of your analyses.

DO-IT-YOURSELF Do a content analysis of your two magazine covers, and write a three-page essay based on your answers to the Data Workshop questions. Support your analysis with specific examples from your data. Make sure to attach copies of the magazine covers (in print or digital format) to your paper.

Inequalities of Sex, Gender, and Sexuality

As with other aspects of our identities, gender and sexuality have become the basis for hierarchies of inequality, and hence for prejudice and discrimination as well. What is important to remember is that privileges, opportunities, and resources in an unequal society are distributed based on category membership.

PATRIARCHY literally meaning "rule of the father"; a male-dominated society

SEXISM the belief that one sex, usually male, is superior to the other

HOMOPHOBIA fear of or discrimination toward gay, lesbian, and bisexual people

TRANSPHOBIA fear of or discrimination toward transgender or other gender-nonconforming people

HETEROSEXISM belief in the superiority of heterosexuality and heterosexuals

CISGENDERISM belief in the superiority of cisgender persons and identities

Gender inequality can be found in all past and present societies. It invariably takes the form of **patriarchy**, or male domination. There is little evidence that a matriarchal (female-dominated) society has ever existed, although some societies have been more pro-feminine than others. The Vanatinai, for example, are a small society in New Guinea in which women share equal access to positions of prestige, power, and control over the means of production (Lepowsky 1993).

From the patriarchal point of view, gender inequality can be traced back to biological differences in early societies, when activities like hunting and warfare were more essential to the livelihood of human groups. Women could not participate as effectively as men in these activities because of their lesser physical strength and because of the demands of bearing and nursing children. Therefore, a division of labor arose, with women handling activities within the secured, "home" territory. Men delivered the scarcest and most prized resources to the group, such as game from hunting or territory from warfare, and thus became powerful by controlling the distribution of these resources.

But this account of the origins of gender inequality does not explain its persistence in contemporary societies. Physical strength is no longer required in the vast majority of jobs. Nor are large numbers of children required for the continuation of society, and women are not necessarily restricted in their activities because of the demands of caring for them. Still, **sexism**—the belief that one sex, usually male, is superior to the other—persists to some degree in all contemporary cultures. Women experience both institutional and individual discrimination in a wide variety of forms.

A striking recent example of both forms of sexism involved feminist media critic Anita Sarkeesian. In 2012, Sarkeesian began producing a series of videos critiquing a form of institutional sexism, the stereotyping of female characters in video games (like the "damsel in distress" who must be rescued by a male character). The videos triggered an angry backlash from individual, anonymous, and presumably male gamers, who sent Sarkeesian death and rape threats and even developed a video game in which an image of Sarkeesian was used as a target for bloody assaults. All this was an attempt to silence her criticism of sexism in gaming. While Sarkeesian's case is especially high profile it is not, unfortunately, unusual. From unequal pay to sexual assault, patriarchy systematically devalues women and their contributions to society. This hurts all of us, men and women alike.

Inequality can also be based on sexual orientation, gender expression, and gender identity. **Homophobia** (fear of those who are not heterosexual) and **transphobia** (fear of those who don't conform to society's gender expectations) form the basis for discrimination against gays, lesbians, and bisexuals, as well as trans and gender-nonconforming persons. Some have pointed out that homophobia and transphobia are not true "phobias," like agoraphobia or claustrophobia, which are psychological phenomena. Rather, they are prejudices, like racism or sexism, which are cultural norms that are learned and transmitted socially. Some find the terms homophobia and transphobia problematic because they suggest that the problems faced by LGBTQ persons are the result of a few maladjusted individuals rather than the product of deeply institutionalized cultural values and norms (Kitzinger 1987). Indeed, some have suggested that "**heterosexism**" or "**cisgenderism**" would be more useful terms in that they are analogous to sexism and racism and describe an ideological system that stigmatizes any nonheterosexual or noncisgender identities or behaviors (Herek 1990; Rothblum 1996).

The discrimination faced by LGBTQ persons ranges from subtle social exclusion to violent assaults and is one of the reasons that gays, lesbians, and trans persons sometimes hide their true identities from family, friends, or coworkers. "**Coming out**," or revealing one's identity, can feel unsafe in a homophobic and transphobic society.

Gendered Language and "Microaggressions"

Some sociologists argue that language shapes culture, while others say the opposite. In any case, by looking at our language, we can see how certain words reflect cultural values and norms, particularly sexism, heterosexism, and cisgenderism. We often use such language without thinking, and this form of (unintended) discrimination is called a **microaggression** (Sue 2010). Microaggression can be experienced as insulting and demeaning by those whom it targets and excludes.

For instance, the English language has long assumed that the default category for all human experience is male. We have traditionally used the generic "he," referred to the human race as "mankind," and noted that "all men are created equal." If something is man-made, it is made by humans, not just male humans. But clearly, not everyone experiences the world from a male perspective, and using this kind of language can make some women feel excluded and demeaned.

Not everyone experiences the world from a heterosexual perspective, either, but in most societies heterosexuality is assumed and is part of the structure of society in ways that we may not even notice. For example, some people use the terms "gay" or "queer" to describe things they don't like, implying that being gay or queer is a bad thing. Even less obvious: assumptions of heterosexuality on the part of others, such as the new acquaintance who asks a woman what her husband does, or the well-meaning auntie who buys her cute nephew a T-shirt that says "Ladies' Man." Small acts such as these reinforce heterosexist assumptions and can make gays, lesbians, and bisexuals feel invisible and invalidated.

Trans persons also experience microaggressions, often when, intentionally or unintentionally, they are "misgendered" by others. While it can be accidental (calling a trans woman "sir" on the phone, for example), it is sometimes deliberate, as when an unsupportive family member refuses to use the trans person's preferred name or gender pronoun.

The vocabulary associated with sex, gender, and sexuality may seem to be a confusing minefield for those who are unfamiliar with it. Preferred terms may change faster within LGBTQ communities than outside of them, leaving open the possibility for individuals to give and take offense. Various LGBTQ organizations post glossaries on the Internet to help guide speakers, writers, and others who seek accurate language. Check out the websites of GLAAD (a media advocacy organization) or HRC (Human Rights Campaign) for examples of such glossaries. In addition, when interacting with LGBTQ persons, it is important to respect them and their preferences. As tempting as it might be to slap a label on someone when we first encounter them, the right thing to do is to allow others to self-identify and to then affirm that self-identification by using the person's chosen name and preferred pronoun (he or she, or a neutral pronoun like they).

Sociological Theories of Gender Inequality

Each of the three main sociological paradigms has explained gender inequality in different ways; in addition, there is a theoretical perspective devoted entirely to the questions surrounding gender and gender inequality in society. We will take a brief look at each in this section.

Functionalism

Functionalists generally believe that there are still social roles better suited to one gender than the other, and societies are more stable when norms are fulfilled by the appropriate sex. In particular, functionalists emphasize how "female" roles may work in tandem with "male" roles within the family. Talcott Parsons, for example, identified two complementary roles (Parsons and Bales 1955). One is an **instrumental role**: being task oriented, a "breadwinner," and an authority figure. The other is an **expressive role**: providing emotional support and nurturing. The expressive role is crucial not only to the care of children but also for stabilizing the personality of the instrumental partner against the stresses of the competitive world. In this view, since women are considered better suited to the expressive role and men to the instrumental role, gender segregation serves to uphold the traditional family and its social functions.

Expressive and instrumental roles may be complementary, but the social rewards for filling them are far from equal. The functionalist view does not explain very well why gender relations are characterized by such inequality. While the work of raising children and maintaining a household is intensive and difficult, there is a tendency to dismiss it as being unskilled and instinctive, which results in the devaluation of traditionally feminine work. Those who support a patriarchal society argue that this is again because resources provided by men in

COMING OUT to openly declare one's true identity to those who might not be aware of it; short for "coming out of the closet," a phrase used to describe how gays and lesbians have felt compelled to keep their sexual orientation secret

MICROAGGRESSION everyday uses of ordinary language that may send denigrating messages to members of certain social groups

INSTRUMENTAL ROLE the position of the family member who provides material support; often an authority figure

EXPRESSIVE ROLE the position of the family member who provides emotional support and nurturing

The Function of Gender Inequality In the 1950s, Talcott Parsons argued that gendered role expectations upheld the traditional family. Male "breadwinners" fulfilled an instrumental role by being task oriented and authoritative, while female "homemakers" embodied an expressive role by providing emotional support. *The Adventures of Ozzie and Harriet* featured the era's prototypical family.

their instrumental roles are ultimately more valuable. This value, however, is being questioned in light of evidence indicating that juvenile delinquency and crime rates are higher when there is no adult supervision in the home and that expressive roles are thus important. The functionalist view also fails to acknowledge that families are often sources of social instability, with violence and abuse in families all too common.

Conflict Theory

Conflict theorists take a different approach. According to this perspective, men have historically had access to most of society's material resources and privileges, and consequently they generally seek to maintain their dominant status. Thus, conflict theorists see gender inequality in much the same way as they see race and class inequality—as manifestations of exploitation.

Some conflict theorists argue that gender inequality is just a derivative of class inequality and that it therefore originates with private property. This theory was introduced by Friedrich Engels in 1884. Engels noted that capitalists (the owners of property) benefited from maintaining patriarchal families, with women in the private sphere and men in the public workplace, in at least two ways. Women do the work of reproducing the labor force (on which the capitalists depend) without receiving any direct compensation, and they serve as an inexpensive "reserve army" of labor when the need arises. Engels suggested that if private property were abolished, the material inequalities producing social classes would disappear, and there would no longer be powerful interests forcing women into domestic roles.

Conflict theorists point out that whether or not gender inequality is a product of class conflict, all men benefit from it in the short term. Zillah Eisenstein (1979) notes that men stand to lose a good deal if gender segregation disappears: they would have to do more unpaid work, or pay to have their homes kept up and children cared for; they would have to find jobs in a larger and more competitive market; and they would lose some power and prestige if they were no longer the most viable breadwinners.

Interactionism

While conflict theorists and functionalists focus on gender from a macrosociological perspective, interactionists emphasize how gender is socially constructed and maintained in our everyday lives. According to interactionists, gender is so important to our social selves that we can barely interact with anyone without first determining that person's gender identity. We need to categorize, and we need to be categorizable as well. For some people, this is no easy matter. For example, gender-nonconforming people such as transgender or nongendered individuals may not fit easily into society's preexisting categories, and hence may experience difficulty in their interactions with others who expect them to do so.

UCLA's Harold Garfinkel (1967/1984) was one of the first sociologists to focus on the interactional work involved in expressing gender identity in a world of binary categories. He conducted intensive interviews with "Agnes," a trans woman born with male genitalia and raised as a boy, who was undergoing sex-reassignment treatment at the UCLA medical center. While Agnes had always known that she was a "120 percent natural normal woman," it was only when she was seventeen that she began to learn how to "do being female"—to look, behave, and talk like a woman. Agnes got a job and a roommate—even a boyfriend—and set about learning what would be expected of her as a woman. She carefully adopted her female roommate's style of dress, makeup, and body language; she listened to what her female friends said and how they spoke. She learned how to maintain "proper" deference (it was a different era) to her male boss at work, and she listened to her boyfriend and his female family members as they expressed their expectations for her as a future wife and mother. Unlike other women, though, Agnes had to take extra precautions, such as avoiding sexual intercourse with

Table 9.2 Theory in Everyday Life

Perspective	Approach to Gender Inequality	Case Study: Male- and Female-Dominated Occupations
Functionalism	Sex determines which roles men and women are best suited to; it is more appropriate for men to play instrumental roles and for women to play expressive roles.	Women are naturally more nurturing and thus make better nurses and teachers of young children; men are naturally more logical and thus make better lawyers and computer programmers.
Conflict Theory	Because of the traditional division of labor in families, males have had more access to resources and privileges and have sought to maintain their dominance.	Male-dominated occupations generally hold more prestige and are better paid; women may encounter difficulties entering male-dominated occupations, whereas men may more easily succeed in female-dominated occupations.
Symbolic Interactionism	Gender is learned through the process of socialization; gender inequalities are reproduced through interactions with family, peers, schools, and the media.	Girls and boys are socialized differently and may be encouraged to seek out gender-appropriate training, college majors, and career goals, leading them to enter male- and female-dominated occupations.

her boyfriend (not too unusual in the early 1960s), wearing skirts and other clothing that would disguise her male anatomy, and avoiding activities (such as swimming at the beach) that would make her differences obvious until after she had completed her surgical transition.

"Passing" as a female was a good deal of work for Agnes, and she constantly dealt with the fear that her secret would be discovered. But even Garfinkel, who knew her secret already, found her enactment of femininity quite convincing. Indeed, he was utterly charmed by her. Even though you may think you have nothing in common with Agnes or other transgender people, you actually enact gender in much the same way Agnes did.

Feminist Theory

Feminist theory has developed in the last thirty years in a way that has revolutionized society and the social sciences. Related to both conflict theory (in its focus on inequality) and interactionist theory (in its focus on the lived experiences of women and men), feminist theory flourished alongside the women's movement dedicated to securing the same rights and freedoms for both women and men in society. It developed into a way of looking at the world that focuses on enhancing scholarly understanding of gender inequities in society. By applying assumptions about gender inequality to various social institutions—the family, education, the economy, or media—feminist theory allows for a new way of understanding those institutions and the changing role of gender in contemporary society. Feminist theory and methods contribute to "writing women back in" to scholarship in history, literature, art, and the social and natural sciences, areas in which the lives and contributions of women have

traditionally been minimized or overlooked entirely. Theorists such as Judith Butler (1999), bell hooks (2003), and Catharine MacKinnon (2005) link gender inequality with inequality in other social hierarchies—race and ethnicity, class, and sexual orientation—and argue that gender and power are inextricably intertwined in our society.

Gender, Sexuality, and Life Chances

If two infants, one girl and one boy, are born at the same time in the same location from parents of similar racial and socioeconomic background, sociologists can predict answers to questions like the following: Who is more likely to live longer, attend college, or go to prison? Who might make a good living or live in poverty? Who is more likely to be married, divorced, or widowed, be a single parent or the victim of a violent crime, or join the military?

In this section, we will analyze how gender affects our lives. We will look specifically at how expectations regarding gender and sexuality shape our experiences with family, health, education, work and income, the military, and criminal justice. For instance, women traditionally are caretakers of their families and more likely than men to go to college. Men make more money than women and are more likely to head religious institutions. These conditions are the result of values and norms that encourage certain behaviors in women and men.

It is important to remember the concept of intersectionality—that gender and sexuality are intertwined with other factors, such as race and class. Therefore, it is difficult to separate out the effects of gender on categories like marriage, education, and work. Single women with children are probably more likely to live in poverty, less likely to have a college education, and more likely to work in service-sector jobs. However, a person is not automatically poor or destined to be divorced because she is female. The categories all work together to construct the complexity of a person's life.

Families

When it comes to family, men are more likely than women to report never having been married (35 percent of men compared to 29 percent of women), perhaps reflecting the stronger societal pressure for women to marry at some point in their lives. Men are also slightly more likely than women to report being married, 54 percent of men compared to 51 percent of women. About 9 percent of women are widowed (only 2.5 percent of men are), and 11 percent of women (9 percent of men) are currently divorced (U.S. Census Bureau 2015g). Some of these differences may be accounted for by the longer lifespans of women.

Divorce seems to be much more difficult for women with children than for men. Women are more likely to retain the primary caregiving role after divorce and to suffer financially because of it. In 2011, about five of every six (or 81.7 percent of) custodial parents were mothers. A little more than 43 percent of all custodial parents received the full amount of child support due, and more than 30 percent received none. In 2011, about 29 percent of all custodial parents and their children had incomes below the poverty level, a rate almost twice as high as the total population. The poverty rate of custodial mothers (31.8 percent) was almost double the poverty rate of custodial fathers (16.2 percent) (Grall 2013).

The legacy of a woman's traditional role as caretaker of her family can be seen in a variety of statistical data. First, women are more likely than men to be single parents. Women headed 67 percent of households of those who never married, 78 percent of those who were separated, and 72 percent of those who were divorced (Grall 2013).

And while women are contributing to household income by working outside the home, they are finding that they are still responsible for being the family's primary caretaker. In the workplace, this creates problems. Time taken out of work in order to care for sick children is seen as nonproductive time, and women who do take such time off may face discrimination (Wharton and Blair-Loy 2002). And most women, when they leave work, still face household chores at home—the second shift.

Up until recently LGBTQ individuals couldn't legally marry at all. When surveyed, 56 percent of gay men, and 58 percent of lesbians said they would like to get married someday (Desilver 2013). By 2013 more than 71,000 same-sex couples had been issued marriage licenses in the United States; researchers believe that number is likely higher, as not all states track such records the same way (Desilver 2013). With

the Supreme Court decision in 2015 granting same-sex couples the right to marry, the number of such unions is likely to increase.

Health

Of the almost 320 million Americans, more than half are female. Why are there more women? One reason is that women live longer; females born in 2013 are expected to live for an average of 81.2 years, whereas males are expected to live 76.4 years (Centers for Disease Control and Prevention 2015b). The longer men live, the closer their life expectancy comes to that of women, but the overall average is depressed because young men are at greater risk of accidental death. Research by the Centers for Disease Control and Prevention shows that men ages twenty to twenty-four are almost three times as likely to die as a result of accidents, four times as likely to commit suicide, and six times more likely to be murdered (Centers for Disease Control and Prevention 2014a).

These days, however, more women are engaged in stress-related behavior—such as working outside the home, smoking, and drinking—so the gap may be closing. While the five-year difference in life expectancy for children born in 2013 is significant, this gender gap is still the lowest it's been in fifty years. And while life expectancy has increased for all Americans, predicted lifespans for American women rose by 2.7 years over the last twenty-five years, compared to 4.6 years for men. Some of the change can be attributed to men taking more care with their health, but at the same time women have increased risk factors for disease. For example, in the past several decades the rate of new lung cancer cases has decreased 28 percent for men, while it has increased 98 percent for women (NIH 2014). Such trends have led researchers to call smoking "the great equalizer" (Perls and Fretts 1998).

While both women and men suffer from heart disease and cancer in fairly equal numbers, other health disorders are gender related. One example is depression, which women are almost twice as likely to suffer from as men (Kessler 2003; Burton 2012). Historically, the medical profession has diagnosed women far more than men with depression, "hysteria," and other mental conditions. Thus, women have been denied equal rights and equitable working conditions and pay if they were thought, as a category, to be mentally unfit. This issue, however, is controversial. Some maintain that the larger percentage of depressed women may be a result of reporting rather than the actual numbers of cases. In other words, women may be more likely to report such symptoms, whereas men may ignore them or may feel a greater sense of stigma in reporting them (Byrne 1981; Martin et al. 2013).

Systematic data about the life expectancy of LGBTQ individuals isn't available yet, but early research suggests that being gay might have implications for health as well, but only if you live in less tolerant areas. One study found that "living in communities with high levels of anti-gay prejudice" was associated with a "life expectancy difference of roughly 12 years" (Hatzenbuehler et al. 2014). Some of this decrease in life expectancy can be connected to issues like suicide and homicide that may also result from prejudice. But researchers also report that "psychosocial stressors are strongly linked to cardiovascular risk, and this kind of stress may represent an indirect pathway through which prejudice contributes to mortality" (Hatzenbuehler et al. 2014). Additionally, LGBTQ adults are less likely to have health insurance and less likely to have a personal doctor (Gates 2014).

Education

In fall 2014, 21.0 million students headed off to colleges in the United States, and about 12 million of them were female (National Center for Education Statistics 2015). In fact, since 1980, women have increasingly outnumbered men in college, especially in the traditional eighteen-to-twenty-two age group (U.S. Bureau of Labor Statistics 2011b). Starting in the mid-1990s women made up the majority of college graduates, and in 2012 they earned 57 percent of bachelor's degrees. By 2000 more women than men were earning master's degrees, and in 2009 women earned the majority of PhDs as well (Kena 2014). However, men are more likely to earn more money per degree granted. In fact, men out-earn women at every level of education, from incomplete high school to advanced degrees. These wage discrepancies make gender inequality very difficult to ignore. Women with four-year and professional degrees earn significantly less than their male counterparts.

The picture is more complicated when examining educational attainment among LGBTQ individuals. Census data show that people in same-sex couples who live together are significantly more likely to have college degrees than people in opposite-sex couples, 46 percent compared to 33 percent (Kurtzleben 2013). However, when researchers survey all self-identified LGBTQ individuals they find that "Americans with lower levels of education are more likely than their higher educated counterparts to identify as LGBT" (Gates 2012).

For many queer youth, the most difficult period in dealing with their sexual and gender identities in a transphobic and homophobic culture occurs during their adolescent years. Research shows that LGBTQ youth are up to four times more likely to attempt suicide (Ryan et al. 2009). The 2009 National School Climate Survey (Kosciw et al. 2010) showed that nearly nine out of ten LGBTQ students experienced harassment in school. Almost 85 percent of LGBTQ students reported being verbally harassed, while 40.1 percent reported being physically harassed, and 18.8 reported physical assault in the past year because of their sexual orientation.

Bullying has recently come to public attention as a problem for youth of all sexual orientations. Those schools that enact anti-bullying policies have not only lower instances of harassment but also higher rates of staff intervention in such instances—an important factor specifically for transgender youth who face even higher rates of harassment and abuse in school than their lesbian, gay, and bisexual peers. A supportive peer environment can also help LGBTQ students to be open about their sexual orientation and/or gender identity. School programs can heighten all students' awareness of stigma and its consequences (Rabow, Stein, and Conley 1999), and clubs such as Gay-Straight Alliances can enhance feelings of belonging, healthy development, and positive well-being.

Work and Income

In whatever aspect of work we analyze—the rates of participation in the labor force, the kinds of jobs, the levels of pay, the balance between work and family—gender inequality is highly visible. For example, in 2013, 69.7 percent of men were in the labor force, but only 57.2 percent of women, though women's participation rates have been increasing over time (U.S. Bureau of Labor Statistics 2014d). Interestingly men and women have historically had relatively similar rates of unemployment; in 2014 about as many men (6.3 percent) were unemployed as women (6.1 percent). But because traditional family dynamics still endure, women are more likely than men to be found outside the labor force altogether (U.S. Census Bureau 2012h).

Marriage seems to have opposite effects on women and men's participation rates. Single women are more likely to work than married women, while married men are more likely to work than single men. In 2013, 63.0 percent of single women (as opposed to 58.9 percent of married women) worked, while 74.2 percent of married men (compared with nearly 66.9 percent of single men) did (U.S. Bureau of Labor Statistics 2014d). This discrepancy could possibly be explained by the assumption that men are heads of households, and single women are considered responsible for their own finances.

Since 1970, the number of mothers in the labor force has been on the rise. Only 53 percent of single mothers and 40.8 percent of married mothers in 1970 participated in the labor force. In 2013, this rose to 75.4 percent for unmarried mothers and 68.1 percent for married mothers (U.S. Bureau of Labor Statistics 2014d).

Many jobs are gendered; they traditionally have been and continue to be performed by women or men. As Table 9.3 shows, nurses, kindergarten teachers, dental hygienists, secretaries, paralegals, and housekeepers are female-dominated professions, whereas airplane pilots, auto mechanics, firefighters, carpenters, and the clergy are male-dominated professions. In 2014, 97 percent of all teachers of young children and 94 percent of secretaries were women. Only 1.4 percent of all automotive mechanics and less than 6 percent of all firefighters were women. Gendered jobs have far-reaching

In 1995, law enforcement raided a factory in El Monte, a suburb on the eastern side of Los Angeles, because the people working in the factory were, effectively, slaves. It is not a word that is often used in a contemporary context, but seventy-two men and women were living there, prevented from leaving by armed guards and razor-wire fences. The "workers" were recruited under false pretenses in Thailand, then smuggled into the United States and told that if they tried to leave the factory they would be abused and deported. The vast majority of them were women, who were seen as more vulnerable and easier to control than men. Some of the women were cowed by their captors' earlier descriptions of U.S. police, so much so that they refused to unlock the door when the factory was finally raided by law enforcement (Watanabe 2008). Some of the victims had been there more than four years at that point.

The incident was widely considered the first case of slavery in the United States since the Civil War, but since then others have come to light. This has led to a dramatic increase in the awareness of human trafficking around the world. In 2000, the United Nations organized a convention to fight transnational organized crime and drafted the *Protocol to Prevent, Suppress and Punish Trafficking in Persons, Especially Women and Children*. This was the first time that there was an internationally recognized definition of human trafficking: "the recruitment, transportation, transfer, harboring or receipt of persons, by means of the threat or use of force or other forms of coercion, of abduction, of fraud, of deception, of the abuse of power or of a position of vulnerability . . . for the purpose of exploitation." In other words, modern-day slavery not only exists but is perhaps a problem of greater proportion than we might expect.

Human trafficking takes many forms, and while labor trafficking is a significant problem, victims who are trafficked into the sex industry often garner more attention, because this crime seems even more heinous. As with all illegal activities, it is difficult to get accurate numbers on sex trafficking, with estimates ranging from 600,000 to more than 2.5 million people being trafficked worldwide each year. In the 1990s, some organizations were claiming "that there were 4 million sex workers in Thailand," which "would have meant that 24 percent of the female population . . . between the age of ten and thirty-nine was engaged in commercial sex work" (Feingold 2010, p. 51). One of the more rigorous studies that used sampling methods to survey sex workers in Cambodia arrived at an estimate of 20,829 total sex workers in the country, with about 2,488 of

Modern-Day Slavery Victims of human trafficking line up at a massage parlor in Houston, Texas.

those being trafficked, a considerably lower number than usually mentioned by the media (Steinfatt et al. 2002).

In 1999, the U.S. State Department estimated that "50,000 slaves were pouring into the United States every year" and that many of them were forced into prostitution (Markon 2007). That estimate was later reduced to a lower number of cases, closer to 15,000. Between the years 2000 and 2007, only 1,362 victims of trafficking were actually identified by the federal government. And in 2012, the United Nations estimated that there were 2.4 million victims of human trafficking across the globe and that some 80 percent of them were being exploited as sexual slaves. High or low, the numbers are shocking. Michelle Bachelet, president of Chile and former head of the U.N. agency on women's rights and gender equality, called sex trafficking "one of the fastest growing" and most lucrative crimes in the world (Lederer 2012). And according to the United Nations, only 1 in 100 victims is ever rescued (Lederer 2012).

The trafficking of girls and women as sex slaves remains an emotional issue, regardless of the arguments about the accuracy of the numbers. It is still something that is hard to imagine existing in modern-day form, in the United States or elsewhere in the world. Because it is a crime that is so difficult to combat, future efforts to stop trafficking must involve raising awareness of the issue, identifying and resolving the problems that make people vulnerable to trafficking (such as extreme poverty and sexism), and coordinating international law enforcement efforts. Sociological insight is necessary for all of these things to occur.

Table 9.3 Selected Occupations by Gender, 2014

Occupation	Percent Women
Preschool and kindergarten teachers	97.2
Secretaries and administrative assistants	94.2
Dental hygienists	97.1
Registered nurses	90.0
Maids and housekeepers	88.6
Paralegals and legal assistants	87.3
Librarians	84.8
Waiters and waitresses	71.8
Psychologists	71.9
Customer service representative	64.6
Medical scientists	52.5
Retail salespersons	49.8
News reporters and correspondents	43.9
Physicians and surgeons	36.7
Lawyers	32.9
Chief executives	26.3
Computer programmers	21.4
Clergy	18.6
Aircraft pilots and flight engineers	7.2
Firefighters	5.7
Carpenters	1.7
Automotive service technicians and mechanics	1.4

SOURCE: Bureau of Labor Statistics 2015c.

consequences. For example, physicians often earn four or more times as much as nurses. So when women constitute 90 percent of all nurses but only 37 percent of all physicians and surgeons, the monetary stakes are striking.

Why are some jobs considered best performed by women and others by men? Why are women vastly underrepresented as pilots and auto mechanics and men nearly absent as nurses, secretaries, and child-care workers? Socially constructed categories of occupations are extremely resilient. Despite advances in workplace technologies that would enable both women and men to perform similarly in jobs, men still vastly outnumber women in certain professions, especially those with high salaries and prestige. It is also interesting to note that jobs that are traditionally female are consistently undervalued and underpaid. "Pink-collar" jobs—nurses, secretaries, librarians—are considered less desirable in a patriarchal society (England 1992).

Income levels and poverty rates also show inequality between women and men. In 2013, men earned an average of $50,033, while the average for women was $39,157 (U.S. Census Bureau 2014g). The earnings ratio (sometimes called the earnings gap) has improved since the 1960s and 1970s; however, the 2013 earnings ratio of 78:100 still translates to 78 cents earned by women for each dollar earned by men (Figure 9.2).

In 2013, the median income for married-couple households was $76,509. For male-headed households with no wife present, the median income was $50,625—dramatically higher than the $35,154 for female-headed households with no husband present. The median household income for women living alone was $26,425, while for single men it was $36,876. Finally, women are more likely to live in poverty than men. This situation, often referred to as the **feminization of poverty**, results from a combination of social forces, including the gendered gap in wages, the higher proportion of single women taking on the financial responsibility of children, and increasing costs of child care. Of the 45.3 million Americans living below the poverty line in 2013, females constituted the largest group, whether living alone or in female-headed households (U.S. Census Bureau 2014g).

In states that do not have laws prohibiting it, employers can still discriminate against LGBTQ persons in hiring and pay. Between 15 and 43 percent of LGBTQ workers report that they have experienced some form of job discrimination based on their gender or sexual identity (Burns and Krehely 2011). Given the number of LGBTQ workers compared to, say, the number of women workers, this means that the rate of LGBTQ discrimination is several times higher—a concerning statistic. The Employment Non-Discrimination Act (ENDA) places both sexual orientation and gender identity in a protected class along with race and gender, but it has consistently failed to pass both Houses of Congress to make it to the president's desk. As of the end of 2015 it still languishes in a congressional committee, awaiting action.

FEMINIZATION OF POVERTY
the economic trend showing that women are more likely than men to live in poverty, caused in part by the gendered gap in wages, the higher proportion of single mothers compared to single fathers, and the increasing costs of child care

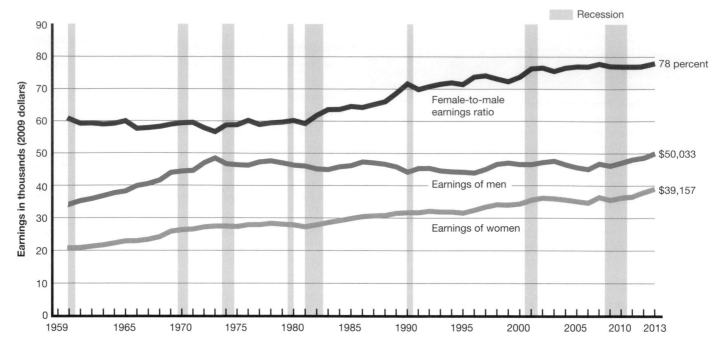

Figure 9.2. Female-to-Male Earnings Ratio, 1960–2013

SOURCE: U.S. Census Bureau 2014g.

DATA WORKSHOP
Analyzing Everyday Life

The Second Shift: Gender Norms and Household Labor

Q+A Gender roles have changed a great deal in recent decades, giving men and women a much larger range of options than before. Still we continue to conform to many traditional gender norms, both in the workplace and at home. When it comes to couples and families, it is easy to see the extent to which expectations for men and women differ. Sociologist Arlie Hochschild has conducted extensive studies of two-parent households and the division of labor for the many tasks of domestic life (Hochschild and Machung 1989). She coined the term the **second shift** to refer to the unpaid work—cooking, cleaning, laundry, child care, home repair, yard work—that must be done at home after the day's paid labor, the first shift, is complete.

With the typical couple today, both men and women work outside the home, and for most households it takes two incomes to pay the bills and raise a family. If both people are already working a first shift, then whose responsibility is it to take on all the other tasks waiting at home? It's probably not surprising that Hochschild found that women do most of the second shift—but not always. Perhaps you have noticed this second shift work in your own home or family.

You'll notice that some tasks must be done every day, or even several times each day—like cooking meals, for example. Other tasks, like laundry, are done less often but on a regular basis. Still others are irregular or seasonal like raking leaves or unstopping a clogged drain. Some tasks are focused on people, like helping kids with homework, whereas others, like cleaning out the gutters, are focused on objects. Studies show that men tend to participate in more instrumental tasks, such as car repair and yard work, while women tend to engage in more expressive tasks, such as mediating arguments and calming upset children. And then there are all the seemingly endless tasks that revolve around the family's daily needs, and who is doing that? Most often, it's women; this is how they rack up an extra month of housework a year (that's a month of twenty-four-hour days)!

For this Data Workshop, you will investigate the second shift by interviewing one working parent in a two-person couple who share a household with one or more children. Return to the section on interviews in Chapter 2 for a review of Hochschild and this research method.

Construct a set of interview questions to ask a working parent about how he or she juggles family and work. These can include some closed-ended as well as open-ended questions. One of the easiest ways to start an interview like this is to just ask the person to describe everything she or he does in a typical day, perhaps using the previous day as an example. This can be done in chronological order. Try to identify all the types of work that your respondent does in a typical day, including paid work, unpaid work, interaction work, emotion work, and so on. Be aware you may need to prompt your respondent if you suspect the person has overlooked some part of his or her day or if you need more details.

You'll also want to ask some other questions about how tasks are divided among members of the household (spouse/partner, children, others). Who does what and why? Ask your interviewee to describe both his or her own tasks and also what his or her partner does. You might also try to determine how completing these tasks (or not completing them) affects the respondent's relationships with other members of the household. Feel free to develop some additional questions of your own.

Once your questionnaire is ready, identify an interviewee who is a member of the target population, and ask for the person's consent to participate in your pilot study. Ask your respondent to be candid and to answer your questions as fully as possible. Be prepared to take detailed notes and/or record your interview. Either way you'll need to produce a rough transcription of the responses to review and analyze.

After completing the interview, refer to your written notes or transcripts and do some further analysis. Reflect on the data and ask yourself the following questions:

* Does there appear to be a gendered division of labor in the home? How are the tasks divided? Who does most of the daily work and why?

* Did your interview confirm that women do more of the second shift, or was your respondent an exception to the rule?

* Is it inevitable that one person in a couple always does more work than the other? What effects might these inequities have on marriages and live-in relationships? Can you think of a better solution to sharing household labor?

* What might you have learned if you could have interviewed the other partner as well?

* Although a single interview is not a scientific sample, do you think your findings could still apply to a larger population?

There are two options for completing this Data Workshop:

PREP-PAIR-SHARE Conduct the interview and bring your questionnaire and notes and/or transcripts to class.

Pair up with a partner, present your preliminary findings, and compare and contrast what you learned from the experience. Try to further develop your analyses together.

DO-IT-YOURSELF Conduct the interview and make some preliminary notes and/or transcripts. Write a three-page essay analyzing your data. Make sure to use specific quotations from your respondent to support your analysis. Include a copy of your interview questionnaire and your notes/transcripts as attachments to your paper.

THE MILITARY The military provides a particular case study when it comes to issues of work and gender. The huge institution that is the military is composed mostly of men. Until recently, women were restricted to noncombat units (though the reality of war meant they often found themselves in the midst of combat situations). In 2011, only 14.5 percent of enlisted personnel were female. Of the reserves, only 17 percent were women. In 2008, Lieutenant General Ann E. Dunwoody became the first woman promoted to the rank of four-star general in the U.S. armed forces. Beginning in 2012, U.S. armed forces began implementing plans to include women in all units, including those previously closed to them.

The LGBTQ rights movement won a large victory in 2010 with the repeal of Don't Ask, Don't Tell (DADT). Signed into law in 1993, DADT arose amidst existing military policies that required the discharge of gay military service members. DADT was an attempt to curb those discharges by requiring that military administration not "ask" about a service member's sexual orientation and that service members not "tell" about it, either. Initially offering promise that gay service members would be allowed to serve, DADT brought about an environment of secrecy in which gay service members had to keep silent—or lie—about their personal lives, as well as accept or even engage in anti-gay activities and discourse, or face discharge. This environment spurred "witch hunts" that brought about the involuntary discharge of more than 14,000 service members. The repeal of DADT did not come quickly or easily, but President Obama signed the bill into law in 2010, allowing gay service members to serve openly without recrimination or threat of discharge.

SECOND SHIFT the unpaid housework and child care often expected of women after they complete their day's paid labor

Rape and sexual assault are increasingly acknowledged as a serious problem in the military, and women are far more likely than men to report gender harassment. Laura Miller (1997) makes the distinction that gender harassment, rather than being sexual in nature, instead is used to enforce traditional gender norms, such as aggression in males and nurturing in

ON THE JOB
The Mancession

February of 2009 saw a milestone in U.S. economic history. For the first time ever, the federal government reported that women made up the majority of the American workforce. The number of women who worked climbed dramatically through the second half of the twentieth century, while the number of men in the workforce declined. In 1950, only 34 percent of women worked, compared to 86 percent of men. By the 1990s, the proportion of men in the workforce had declined to 76 percent, while women's labor force participation had skyrocketed to 58 percent. These changes were largely seen as positive developments. The men who left the workforce were mostly those who wanted to, while new career paths opened up for women (Toossi 2006, p. 25). These trends, however, took on a different meaning in the most recent economic downturn. The recession that hit the United States from 2007 to 2009 was called the "mancession" or "he-cession" by some because of the way it hurt male workers.

Economic recessions have long affected men and women differently, but until the recession of 1981–1982, it was usually women whose unemployment rate rose higher. Starting in the 1980s, this changed. While "unemployment rates by gender were approximately equal during economic expansions," they were "significantly higher for men than women during recessions" (Perry 2010, p. 5). The first "male-based recession" of 1981–1982 was "followed by subsequent male-based

recessions in 1990–1991 and 2001" (Perry 2010, p. 5). However, while the recession of 2007–2009 followed the pattern of these previous economic crises, it did so on an unprecedented scale. During this recession, 7.5 million jobs vanished and "men accounted for 5.4 million, or 71 percent" of them (Kochhar 2011, p. 1). The male unemployment rate went from around 5 percent to 10.5 percent, while the female rate increased from 4.8 percent to 8 percent. This change, from the male unemployment rate being marginally higher than the female rate to the male rate being 2.5 percent higher, "set a new all-time historical record for the greatest male-female jobless gap" since the Labor Department started keeping such statistics (Perry 2010, p. 2). It is estimated that in addition to changes in the economy, both the declining birth rate and declining marriage rate account for over 37 percent of the decline in male employment.

Although a difference of 2.5 percent may not seem like much, this difference represented "huge, historically unprecedented disparities in jobless rates"; "never before in American history has a recession had such a disproportionate effect on one gender" (Perry 2010, p. 5). What remains unclear is the effect that this will have in the long run. Since the economy began its recovery in mid-2009, this trend has sharply reversed, leading some to call the recovery a "he-covery," as the male unemployment rate fell sharply, while the female rate increased slightly. The gap between men and

females, as well as to punish violations of these norms. Interestingly, the men in Miller's study were more likely to report being harassed by their drill sergeants, while women were more likely to be harassed by their fellow trainees.

The Sexual Assault Prevention and Response Office was formed in 2004 by the Department of Defense to coordinate the military's response to sexual assault. Their report to the White House showed that in 2013 more than 5,000 sexual assaults were reported by active duty members of the military (Cooper 2014). This report was criticized by some because, unlike previous annual reports, it did not attempt to measure how many sexual assaults went unreported. Reports of sexual assault increased more than 350 percent from 2004 to 2014. The Pentagon has long acknowledged that the number of officially reported cases of sexual harassment in the military may represent only a fraction of the total number of victims. Counterintuitively, military leaders argue that the recent dramatic

increase in reports of sexual assault is good news. Because sexual assault and sexual harassment so often went unreported in the past, "increased reporting signals not only growing trust of command and confidence in the response system, but serves as the gateway to provide more victims with support and to hold a greater number of offenders appropriately accountable" (U.S. Department of Defense 2014). Despite the progress made, the military can still be an inhospitable place for female and gay service members.

Criminal Justice

The experience of men and women differs with regard to almost every social institution, and the criminal justice system is no exception. The social construction of masculinity as aggressive, dominant, and physical corresponds to statistics on gender and crime. Men are more likely to die violent deaths

A He-covery? Job-seekers attended the Big East Career Fair in 2013.

women's unemployment, which hit its peak in 2010, has leveled off in recent years, with a difference of 0.2 percent in 2014 (U.S. Bureau of Labor Statistics 2015d).

The implications of the "mancession," however, are profound. Men lost jobs so much more quickly because the industries hit hardest by the recession were male dominated, especially construction and manufacturing, while the industries least affected, like health care and education, have long been female preserves. These changes are almost certainly permanent. Manufacturing jobs have been declining for years, and "of the thirty professions projected to add the most jobs over the next decade, women dominate twenty, including nursing, accounting, home health assistance, child care and food preparation" (Rosin 2012, p. 124). Some speculate that this will lead to a dramatic shift in gender roles, as the work-home dichotomy that long structured masculinity and femininity is deconstructed.

Yet not all men's nonemployment can be accounted for as a result of unavailability of work. More men are becoming stay-at-home fathers, as a result of changes to both men's and women's participation in the labor force. While these fathers account for a very small percentage of the nonemployed stay-at-home parents (3 percent are men, 97 percent are women), such changes have the potential to challenge entrenched gendered beliefs, reduce gender differences in parenting, and provide increased support for women's participation in paid labor (Chesley 2011). Some, such as Hannah Rosin in her provocatively titled book *The End of Men: And the Rise of Women*, see this as the beginning of a female renaissance. Still others think that it will simply lead to a shift in the jobs that are primarily female, as men move into professions that used to be dominated by women. Regardless of what the future holds, the "mancession" has shown not only that the very nature of the U.S. economy is changing but that as it changes, all of society will shift with it.

and to be victims of assault. Women are slightly more likely to be victims of personal theft and much more likely to be victims of rape. Also, women are far more likely to be victimized by their intimate partners (spouses or current or former boyfriends). Between 1994 and 2010, 80 percent of spousal abuse victims were female (Catalano 2012).

In analyzing arrest rates for 2012, we find that men are overwhelmingly represented in nearly all categories, including murder, rape, sex offenses, theft, assault, and drug charges. In only one category do women and girls outnumber men and boys: prostitution. In 2013, there were 24,438 arrests of women for prostitution and 11,124 arrests of men for the same charge (Federal Bureau of Investigation 2014d). It is important for us as sociologists to recognize this discrepancy as an example of how crime is influenced by the social construction of gender. Because males are perceived as being more likely to be involved in violent and property crime, they are generally kept under more scrutiny by the police than females are. Of the more than 2.2 million people in state and federal prisons and local jails, the vast majority (around 90 percent) are men (U.S. Bureau of Justice Statistics 2014a).

The experiences of LGBTQ persons are distinctive both as victims and as offenders. Bias-motivated attacks on the basis of sexual orientation are the second-highest category of hate crimes tracked by the federal government. More individuals are assaulted because of their sexual orientation than any other category except race. In 2013 federal records show 1,402 anti-gay hate crimes and 30 anti-transgender attacks (Federal Bureau of Investigation 2014g). While it is difficult to find crime statistics that record the sexual orientation and/or gender identity of the offender, it is important to recognize that LGBTQ persons do experience arrest, trial, conviction, and imprisonment. Once in prison, LGBTQ inmates are vulnerable to sexual victimization at up to thirteen times the level of risk for the average inmate (Sexton, Jenness, and Sumner 2009).

Intersectionality

Once again, the issue of intersectionality is important to keep in mind when we discuss gender and life chances: gender rarely shapes individual experience in isolation but is instead linked to other social statuses in the effects it has on our lives. The intersection of gender with class, race, ethnicity, and immigration status is visible in Miliann Kang's (2010) study of the work of Asian immigrant women (mostly from Korea) in nail salons. Kang argues that the femininity that is central to the beauty rituals performed in salons is also racialized. For example, the expectations our society has for *Asian* women are different from the expectations for their *non-Asian* female clientele. Because the quality of "subservience," for instance, is often seen as "natural" in Asian women, customers may feel that they can make more demands upon their manicurists than they would with other service providers. Indeed, Kang observed manicurists providing "massage, elder-care, counseling for teens, community outreach [and] therapy for stressed-out clients" (p. 240) in addition to the salon services for which they were ostensibly being paid.

When customers and workers meet over the manicure table, they are not just coming together as women who share gendered experiences. Indeed, they may not share experiences at all, given their different class, race, ethnic, and sexual identities. For example, you might think of manicures as a kind of girly indulgence—an activity that, while not strictly a necessity, is an important part of a woman's beauty regimen. But not all participants see their manicures the same way. One of Kang's respondents, an African American customer, talks about the meaning of her manicure by referencing race rather than gender: "Black people on a whole have not been the ones who get pampered. There was a time when only white people could do this" (p. 165). For her, manicures are a symbol of progress (for black people, at least) in the arena of racial justice. In addition, male clients are often viewed with suspicion because, as one manicurist says, they come "just to hold a woman's hand" (Kang, 2010, p. 88). Kang's work shows us how race and gender, along with other social statuses like class and sexual orientation, intersect at the nail salon (and in other settings as well).

By analyzing such visible indicators as labor participation rates, income levels, arrest rates, and experiences related to the family, work, education, and the military, we can easily see the real consequences of gender inequality: women and men experience life differently. So what can we say about the life outcomes of our two infants? The female is more likely to live longer. Though they are both likely to marry, she is

Salons and Status Class, race, and gender intersect at the salon. For some women, manicures represent a hard-won indulgence; for the female salon workers, their immigrant status is often linked to an expectation of subservience.

more likely to be divorced or widowed. If she doesn't drop out in response to anti-LGBTQ harassment or exclusion, she is more likely to graduate from high school and to attend college. However, if the male also attends college, he is more likely to graduate. If they earn the same degree, he will probably earn more money. Each has a good chance of ending up in certain professions over others (the military for him, nursing for her). He is more likely to die a violent death, while she is more likely to experience rape or some other crime perpetrated by someone with whom she's intimate. If either is LGBTQ, that person is at higher risk of bias-motivated attacks as well. While their gender and sexual categories surely do not guarantee these experiences, we as sociologists can safely make such predictions in the aggregate.

Political and Social Movements

Because most societies, throughout most of human history, have been patriarchal and heteronormative, women and LGBTQ people have often struggled to attain and preserve their most basic human and civil rights. In the recent history of the United States, there have been several important political and social movements intended to improve the status of these groups.

Women's Movements

Feminism is the belief in the social, political, and economic equality of the sexes *and* the social movements organized around that belief. Thus, feminism is both a theoretical perspective (as discussed earlier in this chapter) and a social movement. It is important to keep in mind that feminist concepts and goals are not static but are always focused on bringing about greater gender equality in a particular time and

FEMINISM belief in the social, political, and economic equality of the sexes; also the social movements organized around that belief

place. Rebecca West, an early-twentieth-century feminist, put it this way in 1913: "I myself have never been able to find out precisely what feminism is. I only know that people call me a feminist whenever I express sentiments that differentiate me from a doormat or a prostitute" (Shiach 1999).

FIRST WAVE In the United States, the history of the women's movement can be divided into three historical waves. The **first wave** began with a convention held in Seneca Falls, New York, in 1848, organized by Elizabeth Cady Stanton and Lucretia Mott. The convention, numbering about 300 people, issued a Declaration of Sentiments stating generally that "all men and women are created equal" and demanded specifically that women be given the right to vote. Stanton believed that in a democracy the right to vote is the fundamental right on which all others depend. Not surprisingly, then, the campaign to win the vote, known as the **suffrage movement**, became the cause most identified with the first wave of the women's movement, even though that goal would not be achieved until 1920. Neither Stanton nor Mott nor the well-known suffragist Susan B. Anthony would live to see victory. Of the 100 women and men who signed the Declaration of Sentiments, only one, a young worker named Charlotte Woodward, lived to cast a ballot.

SECOND WAVE Just as the first wave of feminism is most closely associated with the right to vote, the **second wave**, which took place during the 1960s and 1970s, is associated with equal access to education and employment. The publication of Betty Friedan's *The Feminine Mystique* in 1963, the establishment of the National Organization for Women (NOW) in 1966, and the emergence of women's consciousness-raising groups were key events in second-wave feminism. In those decades, young activists felt that the women's movement had lost its momentum after the vote was won and that other issues needed to be addressed. In the opening pages of *The Feminine Mystique*, Friedan spoke of "the problem that had no name," a problem that "lay buried, unspoken, for many years in the minds of American women" (p. 55): the sense of limitation and dissatisfaction that many women felt with their lives.

During one of the most prosperous periods in American history, Friedan was discovering that countless women were unhappy with the traditional roles they had been assigned, that the "mystique of feminine fulfillment" was no longer so fulfilling (1963/2001, p. 18). Women were restricted from pursuing activities outside these traditional roles, whether by cultural norms or by actual laws that barred them from schools, workplaces, and professional organizations. Women who tried to breach these barriers were seen as "unfeminine." Some were even told, as former North Carolina senator Elizabeth Dole was when she entered Harvard Law School in 1962, that they were taking an opportunity away from a more deserving man.

The second wave of the women's movement pushed for and achieved such reforms as equal opportunity laws, legislation against sexual harassment and marital rape, and a general increase in public awareness about gender discrimination in our society. Some of the public, however, reacted with hostility to women's demands for legal and cultural "liberation," and there continues to be a certain amount of backlash against feminist causes as a result.

THIRD WAVE Beginning in the 1980s and 1990s, the **third wave** of feminism focused primarily on diversity. These feminists criticize the first two waves for concentrating on "women" as one category (mainly white and middle class) and marginalizing the concerns of women of color, lesbians, and working-class women. Third-wave feminists are more focused on intersectionality. And they have become more concerned with ideas about personal identity and freedom from limiting categories. Third-wave feminism is also concerned with globalization and the rights of women in all countries along with environmental and animal rights. The movement includes many if not most college students—even if you don't call yourself a feminist, you likely believe in feminist values, such as equality, diversity, and global interconnectedness. You are the third wave, and you will help make a difference.

FIRST WAVE the earliest period of feminist activism, from the mid-nineteenth century until American women won the right to vote in 1920

SUFFRAGE MOVEMENT the movement organized around gaining voting rights for women

SECOND WAVE the period of feminist activism during the 1960s and 1970s, often associated with the issues of women's equal access to employment and education

THIRD WAVE the most recent period of feminist activism, focusing on issues of diversity, globalization, and the variety of identities women can possess

The Problem That Had No Name In *The Feminine Mystique*, Betty Friedan (center) articulated a sense of limitation and dissatisfaction that many women felt with their lives.

Men's Movements

The women's movement, especially the second and third waves, has asked us to rethink gender roles and the place of women in society, and men have responded in a variety of ways. Some have countered feminists' arguments, some have agreed with and supported feminism, and some have taken positions somewhere in between. And just as feminism called existing definitions of womanhood into question, so too did it ask us to reexamine what it means to be a man.

In the mid-1970s, the notion of **men's liberation** (or the need to free men from oppressive gender roles) became more widespread. Influential studies pointed to evidence that men suffer from greater stress, poorer health, and a shorter life expectancy and argued that these resulted from pressures to achieve success combined with men's inability to express themselves and their emotions (Farrell 1975; Goldberg 1976). American men had become confused about what it means to be a "real man" (Kimmel 1987). They were facing new discomfort and anxiety about their masculinity. These ideas became fairly popular, largely among middle-class, white, heterosexual men, and some sought counseling or formed discussion groups about "the male role" (Segal 1990). Men were coming together and organizing in an attempt to address their own concerns, and what was called a "crisis of masculinity" (Bly 1990; Connell 1995; Faludi 1999).

As the men's movement grew, it also splintered into two primary factions. The **men's rights movement** (which also includes the fathers' rights movement) argues that because of feminism, men are actually discriminated against and even oppressed both in the legal arena and in everyday life. These men (and some women too) suggest that feminism has created a new kind of sexism by privileging women, or by attempting to erase differences altogether. The **pro-feminist men's movement**, on the other hand, is based in the belief that men should support feminism in the interest of fairness to women and because men's lives are also constrained by gender and sexism—and are enriched by feminist social change. Pro-feminist men suggest that the idea that men are superior is a burden and that, in the long term, men will be happier if society becomes less sexist. They argue that men need to share more of the responsibilities of child care, contest economic disparities and violence against women, and generally respect and value

women's lives. However much society has changed because of these movements, serious questions remain about men's and women's roles and the future of their relations with each other.

LGBTQ Movements

In 1968, police raided a gay bar in New York City called the Stonewall Inn. At the time, patrons of gay bars were frequently singled out for harassment from the police, and the pent-up resentment and frustration this caused erupted into a week of violence following the raid. While this was not the first time gay citizens had been harassed by law enforcement, nor was it the first time gay citizens had protested the harassment, Stonewall was a watershed moment, jump-starting a larger, more visible LGBTQ liberation movement. The Stonewall riots ushered in a new era of campaigning for civil rights for gays, lesbians, bisexuals, and trans individuals.

Dana Rosenfeld (2003), who studies LGBTQ identity, asserts that there are two distinct cohorts among members: those who lived before the gay liberation movement of the 1960s and 1970s and those who lived during and after it. The earlier generation would have felt discredited if their sexual orientation had become public knowledge, whereas the later generation believed that making their identity public was celebrating an essential aspect of the self that should not be denied. This was both a personal and political struggle to advance acceptance and equal rights. There were many LGBTQ rights groups that emerged after Stonewall, and they continue to fight for progressive change on many fronts, from AIDS research to anti–hate-crime legislation. When successful, such social movements can change society and make a difference in the individual lives of many.

For the last several decades, the battle for marriage equality has grown into one of the most visible—and controversial—issues for the LGBTQ rights movements, and for the nation as a whole. Some of the first victories for LGBTQ families came from the passage of legal statutes in some parts of the country that granted same-sex couples certain rights as "domestic partners" and greater privileges and protections through civil unions. In 2004, the first states in the nation began legalizing **same-sex marriages**; at the same time, other states began banning it.

There were many legal (and moral) challenges from both sides. Opponents of same-sex marriage have put forth a number of arguments against it. Some have used the rhetoric of "protecting marriage" or "protecting family," implying that same-sex marriage would harm or destroy those institutions. This largely ignores prolific research that shows that the psychological and physical well-being of children benefit from being raised by two parents whose union is legally recognized by social institutions. Others have argued that marriage has

MEN'S LIBERATION a movement that originated in the 1970s to discuss the challenges of masculinity

MEN'S RIGHTS MOVEMENT an offshoot of male liberationism whose members believe that feminism promotes discrimination against men

PRO-FEMINIST MEN'S MOVEMENT an offshoot of male liberationism whose members support feminism and believe that sexism harms both men and women

SAME-SEX MARRIAGE federally recognized marriage between members of the same sex; made legal in the United States in 2015

deep religious meaning; many religions do not support or condone same-sex relations, and many clergy refuse to officiate such marriages.

Proponents of same-sex marriage emphasize that marriage is a state-sanctioned right. There are many benefits that legal marriages convey upon spouses that do not apply to those in domestic partnerships and civil unions. As federally recognized, marriages offer "portability" across all fifty states; if you're married in one state, you're married in all states. This has financial ramifications for families, as many couples depend on Social Security, veterans' benefits, or disability benefits; it also allows a spouse to inherit those benefits upon his or her partner's passing. Many federal agencies, such as the IRS and the Social Security Administration, base eligibility on state of residence (Halloran 2013).

In 2015, the Supreme Court made a landmark decision in *Obergefell v. Hodges* that legalized same-sex marriage across the United States. The Court upheld the notion that the right to marry is guaranteed by the Fourteenth Amendment, and that same-sex couples should be accorded equal protection under the Constitution. Before that ruling, same-sex marriage was legal in thirty-seven states and the District of Columbia and banned in thirteen states. The United States joined twenty-one other national governments in legally recognizing same-sex marriages.

Public opinion, as well as laws governing same-sex marriage have changed rapidly. In 2001, 57 percent of Americans opposed same-sex marriage and 35 percent were in favor. In a dramatic switch, 57 percent of Americans were in favor and 39 percent opposed. Attitudes differed among demographic groups, with young Americans showing the highest approval rates, and white evangelicals and black Protestants showing the lowest levels of support (Pew Research Center 2015b).

It is important to note that amid these debates, generalizations run rampant. Opponents to gay marriage are largely portrayed as members of religious institutions and the conservative right, but there are many institutions and members within those groups that support same-sex marriage. Conversely, there are many within the LGBTQ community who do not support same-sex marriage, as it is viewed as assimilationist and as an acceptance of heteronormative structures, such as binary gender roles and monogamy, rather than a critique of them. Lisa Duggan (2003) and Cathy Cohen (2005) contend that arguing for same-sex marriage creates "hierarchies of worthiness," in that benefits are afforded to the most "socially acceptable" within the LGBTQ community—those who most closely mimic heterosexual unions.

As we can see, the same-sex marriage debate is a political, social, civil rights, moral, and religious issue. Now that same-sex marriage is legally recognized nationwide, gay families will be afforded the same legal standing as heterosexual families.

Marriage Equality In June 2015, the Supreme Court legalized gay marriage in *Obergefell v. Hodges,* guaranteeing married same-sex couples the same rights as married opposite-sex couples.

LGBTQ rights issues are still plentiful in other areas: sexual minorities and gender-nonconforming persons face discrimination in housing, education, employment, and health care, as well as everyday microaggressions, harassment, and violence, but awareness of these problems is increasing. Hate crimes based on sexual or gender identity are punishable under federal law, and a growing minority of states and territories (including Puerto Rico and Washington, D.C.) outlaw discrimination based on sexual orientation, gender identity, or gender expression. In his 2015 State of the Union address, Barack Obama became the first president to explicitly condemn discrimination against transgender persons. But while legal discrimination against LGBTQ persons may slowly be ending, other forms of prejudice can be harder to overcome.

CLOSING COMMENTS

Sex, gender, sexual orientation, and trans identities are status categories that structure social inequality and shape individual identities. They are different but interrelated, and we all experience their overlap in our everyday lives: we categorize ourselves and others and make assumptions about one another based on these perceived categories. A sociological perspective allows us to see the cultural and environmental influences on what may be considered biologically based identities and lets us identify and critique the stratification systems that have resulted from these influences. Most important, a sociological perspective allows us to see how destructive sexism is for men and women and how crippling homophobia and transphobia can be for the straight, cisgender majority as well as the queer minority. Stereotypes are socially constructed; therefore, they can be socially deconstructed and socially reconstructed as well.

Everything You Need to Know about Gender and Sexuality

> "Sociologists differentiate *sex* as biological and *gender* as social. *Sex* refers to two biologically distinct categories: male or female. *Gender* refers to physical and behavioral traits that society considers "normal" for men and women."

THEORIES OF GENDER AND SEXUALITY

* **Functionalism:** men and women should remain in traditional social roles to keep society stable

* **Conflict theory:** men have control over most of society's resources and privileges and will continue to maintain their dominant status through the exploitation of women

* **Symbolic interactionism:** gender is socially constructed and maintained in our everyday lives

REVIEW

1. Consider the ways you were socialized by your family. In what ways was your socialization gendered? What toys did you play with as a child? What extracurricular activities were you encouraged to pursue? What household chores did you perform?

2. Our society upholds expectations about which gender more appropriately fills the instrumental and the expressive roles. In your family, were the nurturing and emotional support primarily provided by women? How do these gendered expectations reinforce the traditional family structure? How do they perpetuate gender inequality?

3. The second shift refers to the housework that must be done after the day's paid labor is complete; women do a disproportionate amount of this work. Why do you think this is? What types of tasks does our society expect women to do? How do the tasks expected of men differ?

Number of Women on Corporate Boards of Directors

By Country

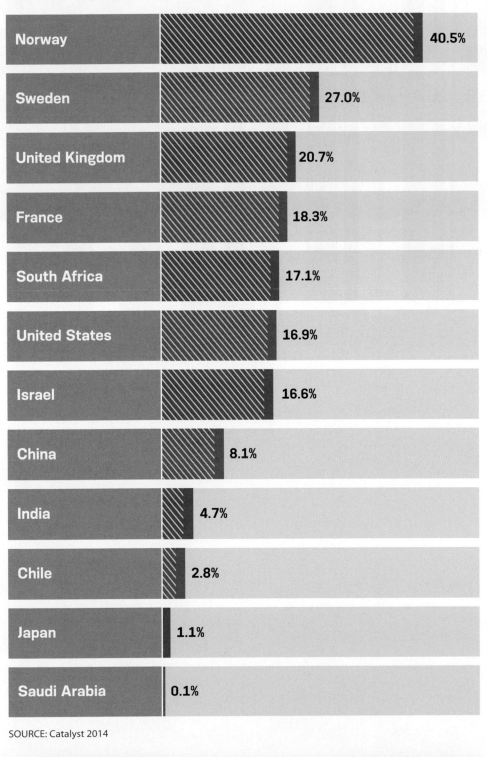

Country	Percentage
Norway	40.5%
Sweden	27.0%
United Kingdom	20.7%
France	18.3%
South Africa	17.1%
United States	16.9%
Israel	16.6%
China	8.1%
India	4.7%
Chile	2.8%
Japan	1.1%
Saudi Arabia	0.1%

SOURCE: Catalyst 2014

EXPLORE

Gender and Sports: Forty Years of Title IX

Title IX, passed in 1972, is an amendment to the Civil Rights Act banning gender discrimination in school sports. Even though it is now over forty years old and many female athletes have benefited from it, there are still significant challenges in getting equal funding, facilities, and support. Visit the Everyday Sociology Blog to read more about a sociologist's analysis of the effects of Title IX.

http://wwnPag.es/trw409

PART IV
Social Institutions and the Micro-Macro Link

Our everyday lives take place within the contexts of many overlapping and interdependent social institutions. A social institution is a collection of patterned social practices that are repeated continuously and regularly over time and supported by social norms. Politics, education, religion, the economy, the family, the media, and health care are all social institutions, and you have contact with many of these (and others) on a daily basis. The macro-level patterns and structures of social institutions shape your own micro-level individual experiences; at the same time, it's important to remember that social institutions are created, maintained, and changed by individual actions and interaction.

In the next four chapters, we will look at specific social institutions, including politics, education, and religion (Chapter 10), the economy (Chapter 11), the family (Chapter 12), the media (Chapter 13), and the health-care system (Chapter 14), and their role in structuring your everyday life. You will be introduced to a variety of sociological research that focuses on how these social institutions and others work; here, we highlight a sociological researcher whose work integrates many of them. In his book *Heat Wave: A Social Autopsy of Disaster in Chicago* (2002), Eric Klinenberg examines the circumstances surrounding Chicago's catastrophic heat wave in 1995, which killed more than 700 people. Klinenberg analyzes the week-long heat wave as more than a meteorological phenomenon. People died, he argues, because of a combination of disturbing demographic trends and dangerous institutional policies present at all times in all major urban areas.

For one week in mid-July of 1995, the city of Chicago suffered the worst heat wave in its history: temperatures exceeded 100 degrees for four days in a row, and heat indices (the "real feel" air temperature) hit a high of 126 degrees. Historic buildings baked like ovens, but fear of crime left many people feeling trapped inside their apartments. Children passed out in overheated school buses. City residents blasted their air conditioning (if they had it), mobbed the tiny beaches of Lake Michigan, and broke open fire hydrants to stay cool. As a result, power outages peppered the area and water pressure dropped dangerously. Roads buckled, train tracks warped, and people suffered from heat-related illnesses in large numbers. The city's 911 emergency system overloaded, and some callers waited two hours for ambulances to arrive; more than twenty hospitals closed their emergency rooms, overwhelmed with patients. The death toll mounted, with the elderly and the poor especially vulnerable. In this single week, 739 Chicagoans died as a result of the heat. According to Klinenberg, the individual "isolation, deprivation, and vulnerability" that led to these deaths resulted from a variety of institutional structures, including poverty, racial segregation, family dislocation, and city politics. These institutional arrangements must be examined and changed in order to avoid future tragedies.

Many of those who died during the heat wave were elderly people who lived alone: sick or fragile, their mobility compromised, their neighborhoods changing around them, their families far away or neglectful, and their social networks dissolving. In many cases, the elderly victims of the heat wave were so isolated that no one ever claimed their bodies

(Klinenberg 2002, p. 15). The story of Pauline Jankowitz, eighty-five, who (happily) survived the heat wave, illustrates these demographic trends (Klinenberg 2002, pp. 50–54). Pauline lived alone on the third floor of an apartment building with no elevator. She suffered from incontinence and walked with a crutch. She recognized her vulnerability and left her apartment only once every two months. Her two children lived in other states and rarely visited, so a volunteer from a charitable organization did Pauline's weekly grocery shopping. However, Pauline no longer had any connections with her immigrant neighbors and spent most of her time in her apartment listening to radio talk shows. Pauline's isolation is hardly unique. Her circumstances illustrate the ways that the geographic mobility of the contemporary family, the changing populations of urban neighborhoods, the financial limitations of retirement incomes, and the lack of supportive social services all contribute to situations in which elderly individuals may live, face crises, and die alone.

Klinenberg argues that race and class inequality also contributed to the death toll in the Chicago heat wave. He shows that the death tolls were highest in the city's "black belt," a group of predominantly African American neighborhoods on the south and west sides of the city. (These neighborhoods also have relatively high levels of poverty and crime and relatively large populations of elderly residents.) Social ties in these neighborhoods are hard to maintain: poverty contributes to residential transiency, so neighbors may not get to know one another before they must move to housing elsewhere. Gang activity and crime make residents afraid to walk down the street or sit on their own front porches. And although some of the neighborhoods in question have powerful religious organizations in their midst, even the most proactive church needs significant financial resources to reach out to its members—and such resources may be hard to come by

in poor neighborhoods. So a person's risk of heat-related death during July of 1995 was partly place-based. In Chicago, as in most major cities, place, race, and class are closely connected.

In July 1995, Chicago's government services also failed in a number of ways when the city's residents needed them most. However, Klinenberg argues that the city's bureaucracies were no more ill-prepared to deal with catastrophe during that week than during any other. Long-term, macrolevel changes in city politics mean that both the political will and the material resources to provide assistance to the poor were fatally absent. For example, overextended paramedics and firefighters had no centralized office with which to register their observations or complaints. As a result, many problems went unheeded by the city until emergency services were too swamped to provide timely assistance. There was little coordination among the local, state, and federal agencies that dealt with social welfare and emergency services. Finally, Klinenberg indicts city officials for "governing by public relations" (p. 143)—that is, for using the media to deflect attention from the city's problems, including minimizing both the scope of the heat wave and the city's accountability.

Klinenberg's "social autopsy" reveals the failure of social institutions on a massive scale—and the disturbing prospect that this disaster could happen again, anywhere, if we do not take steps to change flawed social systems. Structural and institutional arrangements—including city government, health-care providers, families, schools, religious organizations, and the media—must change in order to avoid individual tragedies. But individual actions help bring about institutional change, and *Heat Wave* reveals important ways in which all our fates intertwine, as they are shaped by the social institutions we encounter every day. How can we better manage this interdependence, for the good of all?

CHAPTER 10

Social Institutions: Politics, Education, and Religion

You probably know the Pledge of Allegiance by heart and said it countless times in elementary and high school, but you may not have thought much about its words or why you were required to say them.

I pledge allegiance to the Flag
of the United States of America,
and to the Republic for which it stands:
one Nation, under God, indivisible,
with Liberty and Justice for all.

For decades, reciting the pledge was just a routine part of being a student in the United States. How could it possibly be controversial? A lot of people think it is. As you will see, the Pledge of Allegiance brings together questions about three important social institutions in American life: politics, education, and religion.

The Pledge of Allegiance was originally written in 1892 and did not contain the phrase "under God"; that was added in 1954, when President Eisenhower signed a bill making the change official. The added words generated no controversy at the time. The president declared that their addition would affirm "the dedication of our nation and our people to the Almighty," and Senator Joseph McCarthy said "it was a clear indication that the United States was committed to ending the threat of 'godless' Communism" (Brinkley-Rogers 2002).

Since as early as 1943, the Supreme Court has ruled that children cannot be forced to recite the pledge. In 1943, the issue revolved around the patriotic nature of the pledge. However, in 2002 the issue became its religious nature. Judge Alfred Goodwin of the Ninth Circuit Court of Appeals ruled that reciting the pledge in public schools "places students in the untenable position of choosing between participating in an exercise with religious content or protesting," an especially damaging scenario because "the coercive effect of the policy here is particularly pronounced in the school setting, given the age and impressionability of school-children" (Weinstein 2003). After all, how many second-graders would be willing to stand out from their peers in so dramatic a fashion?

California physician Dr. Michael Newdow is a long-standing activist committed to preserving the separation of church and state. When his daughter's second-grade class began reciting the Pledge of Allegiance, Newdow became disturbed because it contained the phrase "one Nation, *under God*." Newdow filed a lawsuit, and in February 2003 the Ninth Circuit Court held the pledge to be in violation of the Constitution because the reference to God violated the separation of church and state.

Many civic and political leaders—liberals as well as conservatives—denounced the decision. The Senate passed a resolution condemning it, and the attorney general announced that the Justice Department would "spare no effort to preserve the rights of all our citizens to pledge allegiance to the American flag" (Weinstein 2003). Almost universally, lawmakers came out in defense of the pledge, agreeing with Judge Ferdinand Fernandez, who in his dissenting opinion argued that the phrase "under God" had "no tendency to establish a religion in this country or to suppress anyone's exercise, or non-exercise, of religion, except in the fevered eye of persons who most fervently would like to drive all tincture of religion out of the public life of our polity" (Egelko 2002). Ultimately, the case went all the way to the Supreme Court, which overturned the lower court's ruling on a technicality but did not address whether the language in the pledge violates the First Amendment.

Although there is a great deal of disagreement over what should be done in this case, all the participants agree, even if only implicitly, that social institutions play an important role in the lives of Americans. For example, if school starts at 8:00 a.m. and ends at 3:00 p.m., this structures the life of an entire household. It dictates what time children should go to bed and get up in the morning; when breakfast and dinner are prepared, served, and eaten; and what types of arrangements must be made for transportation, after-school activities, and child care. In turn, a school exists only because of the actions of the teachers, students, parents, and administrators who are part of the surrounding community.

Social institutions represent a bit of a sociological paradox. They function at the macro level to shape our everyday interactions, but at the micro level those same everyday interactions construct social institutions. Because they are at the center of both micro- and macrosociology, social institutions give us the opportunity to examine the connection between interaction and structure, between the individual and society. In this chapter, we will focus on the social institutions of politics, education, and religion as places where the micro and the macro come together, and we will show how the intersections among social institutions shape everyday life.

HOW TO READ THIS CHAPTER

We have devoted entire chapters to other **social institutions** such as health care, work, and family, but here we have grouped politics, education, and religion together for a reason. These institutions intersect in distinctive and often unexamined ways in our everyday lives—the daily recitation of the Pledge of Allegiance is just one example. Local and national controversies over school vouchers and sex education are other examples of the ways in which political, educational, and religious concerns overlap. Every day we make decisions or engage in debates that address moral values, political practicalities, and educational expectations all bundled together.

When you read this chapter, we want you to be able to see the relationships among these three social institutions as well as make the connection between micro- and macrosociology. This is a key opportunity to use the sociological theories and methods you have learned in previous chapters to find the intersections between individual experience and social structure, and the overlaps among various social institutions in everyday life. After reading this chapter, you should have a deeper understanding of how social institutions shape your individual experience and how you as an individual contribute to shaping those institutions.

What Is Politics?

Politics has concerned social thinkers since at least the time of the philosophers in ancient Greece. The word "politics" comes from the Greek *politikos*, meaning "of or relating to citizens." As a sociological term, **politics** pertains especially to the methods and tactics of managing a political entity, such as a nation or state, as well as the administration and control of its internal and external affairs. But it can also mean the attitudes and activities of groups and individuals. To understand the relationship between citizens and their particular political environment, we must first look at the variety of political systems and study the American system of democracy. Then we will examine elections and voting, lobbies and special interest groups, and the role of the media in the political process.

Political Systems: Government

Government is the formal, organized agency that exercises power and control in modern society. Governments are vested with the power and authority to make laws and enforce them. Max Weber defined **power** as the ability to get others to do one's bidding. When sociologists talk about **authority**, they are referring to the legitimate, noncoercive exercise of power. Throughout the world and throughout history, governments have taken a variety of forms. When evaluating types of governance as sociologists, we ask certain questions about the relationship between leaders and followers: who has power and who does not, what kind of power is exerted, and how far does that power extend?

SOCIAL INSTITUTIONS systems and structures within society that shape the activities of groups and individuals

POLITICS methods and tactics intended to influence government policy, policy-related attitudes, and activities

GOVERNMENT the formal, organized agency that exercises power and control in modern society, especially through the creation and enforcement of laws

POWER the ability to impose one's will on others

AUTHORITY the legitimate right to wield power

AUTHORITARIANISM system of government by and for a small number of elites that does not include representation of ordinary citizens

TOTAL POWER AND AUTHORITY Authoritarianism is a political system that denies ordinary citizens representation by and control over their own government. Thus, citizens have no say in who rules them, what laws are made, or how those laws are enforced. Generally, political power is concentrated in the hands of a few elites who control military and economic resources. A *dictatorship* is one form of authoritarianism. In most instances, a dictator does not gain power by being elected or through succession but seizes power and becomes an absolute ruler. Dictators may gain control

Dictators Try to Control All Aspects of Citizens' Lives Leaders such as Kim Jong Un of North Korea, Augusto Pinochet of Chile, and Charles Taylor of Liberia are among the world's most notorious dictators.

through a military coup, as occurred when General Augusto Pinochet came to power in Chile in 1973. In other cases, leaders may be legally elected or appointed (often with coercion) but then become dictators once in power, abolishing any constitutional limits on their authority—such as President Charles Taylor of Liberia. In 2012, Taylor was sentenced by the war crimes tribunal in The Hague to fifty years in prison for crimes against humanity. Dictators are most often individuals but can also be associated with political parties or groups, such as the Taliban in Afghanistan.

Totalitarianism is the most extreme and modern version of authoritarianism. The government seeks to control every aspect, public and private, of citizens' lives. Unlike older forms of authoritarianism, a totalitarian government can utilize all the contrivances of surveillance technology, systems of mass communication, and modern weapons to control its citizens (Arendt 1958). Totalitarian governments are usually headed by a dictator, whether a ruler or a single political party. Through propaganda, totalitarian regimes can further control the population by disseminating ideology aimed at shaping their thoughts, values, and attitudes. An example of a modern totalitarian ruler is Kim Jong Un of North Korea, who succeeded his father, the notorious Kim Jong Il, in 2011. Under the Kims, North Korea has maintained one of the worst human rights records in the world, restricting the basic freedoms of its people. The country also has a stagnant, internationally isolated economy, which is further drained by its nuclear arms program.

MONARCHY a government ruled by a king or queen, with succession of rulers kept within the family

DEMOCRACY a political system in which all citizens have the right to participate

MONARCHIES AND THE STATE Monarchies are governments ruled by a king or queen. In a **monarchy**, sovereignty is vested in a successive line of rulers, usually within a family, such as the Tudors of England, the Ming Dynasty of China, and the Romanovs of Russia. Nobility is handed down through family lines and can include numerous family members who hold royal titles. Monarchs are not popularly elected and are not usually accountable to the general citizenry, and some may rule by "divine right," the claim that they are leaders chosen by God.

Monarchies can be divided into two categories: absolute and constitutional. Absolute monarchs typically have complete authority over their subjects, much like a dictator. Constitutional monarchs are royal figures whose powers are defined by a political charter and limited by a parliament or other governing body. Most monarchies were weakened, overthrown, or otherwise made obsolete during the many social revolutions of the eighteenth, nineteenth, and twentieth centuries, such as the French Revolution (1789) and the Russian Revolution (1917). In contemporary times, some Asian and European nations, such as Japan, Thailand, Great Britain, and Sweden, still enjoy their royal families as national figureheads and celebrities, though their kings, queens, princes, and princesses don't have any real power in these constitutional monarchies. There are, however, a few remaining modern examples of more absolute monarchies in the world, among them Saudi Arabia and Brunei.

CITIZENS AND DEMOCRACY Democracy originated in ancient Greece and represented a radical new political system. In a **democracy**, citizens share in directing the activities of their government rather than being ruled by an autocratic individual or authoritarian group. The idea is that educated citizens should participate in the election of officials who then represent their interests in law making, law enforcement, resource allocation, and international affairs. Democracy is not only a political system but also a philosophy that emphasizes the right and capacity of individuals, acting either directly or through representatives, to control through majority rule the institutions that govern them. Democracy is

Table 10.1 Theory in Everyday Life

Perspective	Approach to Social Institutions	Case Study: Understanding Political Power in America
Structural Functionalism	Social institutions such as politics, education, and religion provide critical functions for the needs of society and help maintain order and unity.	The theory of pluralism suggests that in a democracy, power is held in a variety of hands; each group is assumed to have equal access to power and can thus serve as a system of checks and balances.
Conflict Theory	Social institutions such as politics, education, and religion represent the interests of those in power and thus create and maintain inequalities in society.	The theory of the power elite suggests that power in the United States is concentrated in the hands of a small group of decision makers and that the masses have little power in the democratic process.
Symbolic Interactionism	Social institution such as politics, education, and religion are created through individual participation; they give meaning to and are part of the everyday experience of members.	The theory of the social construction of presidential candidates suggests that the messages we receive from the media help shape our perceptions and influence public opinion and voting behavior.

associated with the values of basic human rights, civil liberties, freedom, and equality.

Democracy may seem like the ideal system of government, but remember that not all citizens are equally represented even by a democratic government. In many democratic nations, women, ethnic or racial minorities, members of certain religions, and immigrants have been excluded from citizenship or from equal participation in the political process. In the United States, women did not have the right to vote until 1920. And while the Fifteenth Amendment to the U.S. Constitution technically gave adult males of all races voting rights in 1870, barriers such as poll taxes, literacy tests, and "grandfather clauses" kept African Americans from exercising those rights for almost 100 years, until the 1965 Voting Rights Act was passed. Native Americans were legally excluded from voting in federal elections until 1924, and residents of the District of Columbia were not allowed to vote in presidential elections until 1961. As you can see, even the world's leading democracy has not always seen all citizens as equal.

The American Political System

When American colonists rebelled against British authority in 1776, they created the first modern democracy. American democracy, however, is much more complicated than "rule by the people." In the following sections, we focus on voting, theories about who governs, the power of interest groups, and the influence of the media on the political system.

VOTING IN THE UNITED STATES The American political system prides itself on being a democracy, a government that confers power to the people. In this form of government,

power is formally exercised through the election process, which provides each person with a vote. Sociologists have long been interested in the social factors—such as age, education, religion, or ethnic background—that influence whether and how individuals vote.

By the end of the twentieth century, many had become concerned about a steady, decades-long decline in American voter turnout. For example, in the 1960 presidential election, 64 percent of the electorate cast ballots, but by 1996, that number had fallen to below 50 percent for the first time since 1924.

Voter turnout began improving in the 2004 presidential election, but it is important to consider how voter turnout has been measured. Prior to the 2004 election, the voter turnout rate was typically calculated by dividing the total number of votes by the "voting-age population"—*everyone* aged eighteen and older residing in the United States. This figure included people who were ineligible to vote—mainly noncitizens and felons—and excluded eligible overseas voters. Since the 2004 election, voting rates have been based on the "voting-eligible population," which changes the overall voting picture and challenges the notion of decline in voter turnout. In 2004, voter turnout was 55 percent for the "voting-age population" and 60 percent for the "voting-eligible population." And among eligible voters under age twenty-five, turnout rose by almost 6 percent over the 2000 election, with some 10.5 million of them going to the polls.

Voter turnout improved again in the presidential election of 2008, in which Barack Obama, the first African American president, was elected. An estimated 62 percent of the voting-eligible population, or 131 million Americans, cast their ballots. That represents an increase of 1.5 percentage points over 2004 but falls short of the record turnout of 64 percent in 1960. Among young voters ages eighteen

Oath of Office Joined by his wife, Michelle, Barack Obama takes the oath of office to inaugurate his second term as president of the United States. He placed his hand on two Bibles—one owned by Martin Luther King Jr. and one owned by Abraham Lincoln.

to twenty-nine, the 2008 election represented the second highest turnout in history, with approximately 22 million to 24 million, or 52 percent to 53 percent of eligible voters, casting their ballots. The record youth voter turnout belongs to the 1972 election, the first year that eighteen-year-olds had the right to vote. In 2012, 58.2 percent of all eligible voters turned out to reelect Barack Obama (McDonald 2013). Voter turnout in midterm elections is typically lower than in presidential elections, especially among younger voters (DeSilver 2014). In the 2014 midterms, voter participation in the United States hit its lowest mark in seventy years, with just 35.9 percent of eligible voters turning up at the polls (McDonald 2014).

Even with these fluctuations, voter participation rates are much lower in the United States than in some comparable democratic nations. Why? A number of social factors affect the likelihood that someone will or will not vote. Age, race, gender, sexual orientation, religion, geographic location, social class, and education are all demographic variables that influence voter participation, as well as how people vote. For example, Minnesota had the highest voter turnout of any state in the 2012 presidential election—almost 75 percent of its citizens voted—whereas only 44 percent of the eligible voters from Hawaii turned out (McDonald 2013). What explains this difference? Turnout may be affected by factors ranging from the number of items on the ballot to the weather. Senior citizens are much more likely to vote than young adults—compare a 70 percent

DISENFRANCHISED stripped of voting rights, either temporarily or permanently

reported turnout for those over age fifty-five with a 41 percent reported turnout among eighteen- to twenty-four-year-olds (U.S. Census Bureau 2012h). But the top reasons people gave for not voting in 2012 were that they were too busy, had a scheduling conflict, or were simply uninterested (U.S. Census Bureau 2012d).

In some instances, however, people do not vote because they are **disenfranchised**—barred from voting. All states except Maine and Vermont disenfranchise convicted felons while they are incarcerated. Thirty-five states disenfranchise felons on parole, thirty do so for felons on probation, and eleven others permanently disenfranchise some or all felons who have completed their sentences (Uggen et al. 2012). Human rights groups have long protested this policy, arguing that it is not a legitimate function of the penal system. In addition, individuals may be mistakenly identified as former felons and improperly stricken from the rolls, which occurred in Florida in the 2000 presidential election (Hull 2002; Uggen and Manza 2002). Consequently, many eligible voters were turned away from the polls.

Another obstacle to potential voters lies with registration, which must be done well in advance of an election. In the United States, even individuals with the legal right to vote cannot do so unless they are registered. Recent legislation, such as the 2000 Motor-Voter Act, allows voters to register when renewing a driver's license, and a few states offer online voter registration, making registration easier. Another problem for many working Americans is that elections are held on a Tuesday rather than a weekend or a national holiday (something done in other democratic countries). Finally, thirty states require voters to present identification in order to vote in federal, state, and local elections, with fifteen states requiring photo identification. Studies indicate that turnout declines when IDs are required (de Alth 2009). Because more than 21 million Americans lack proper photo identification, voter participation is affected, with minorities, the elderly, and low-income Americans disproportionately affected (ACLU 2011).

Even when voters do appear at the polls, there may be other troubles. During the 2000 presidential election, irregularities in ballots and vote counts in Florida delayed the state's ability to declare a winner for several weeks. In some of Florida's poor and minority districts, faulty voting equipment, poorly trained poll workers, and scarce resources kept almost 200,000 votes from being counted—votes that were likely predominantly Democratic. The National Association for the Advancement of Colored People (NAACP) brought a voting discrimination suit against the state of Florida that was settled with a donation to the organization's efforts toward voter education and mobilization. Much media attention has focused on the invisible disenfranchisement of poor and minority voters, and some states have enacted more progressive laws to deal with these problems by providing greater access to the disabled, making absentee balloting easier, or keeping the polls open longer. This election controversy is an example of how structural issues (unequal state voting resources) can affect individual experience (the ability to make one's vote count) and how those individual experiences in turn affect the larger society (electing George W. Bush in 2000 rather than Al Gore).

Who Rules America?

Ideally, in a democracy, elected officials represent the interests of the people in doing the business of government. But how much do we really know about what legislators do or how government business is conducted? What about the interests of other groups besides "the people"? To what extent do other groups influence how government is run? Who has the most power in directing the course of the nation? The president and Congress? Judges? Big business and the military? What happens behind the scenes? Who really rules America? Sociologists have devised two answers to the question of who rules America—the *pluralist* theory of power and the idea of a *power elite*.

PLURALISM According to the **pluralist model**, power is held by a variety of organizations and institutions (such as corporations, political parties, professional organizations, and ethnic and religious groups), each with its own resources and interests. Each organization is assumed to have equal access to the power structure, and a system of checks and balances in the form of laws, policies, and the courts keeps any one group from having too much power over the others (Dahl 1961).

THE POWER ELITE Conflict theorists, on the other hand, argue that power is held by a small but extremely influential group of individuals who form an elite social class. C. Wright Mills (1956, 1970) was one of the first to propose a theory of the **power elite**, a relatively small number of influential individuals who occupy the top positions within the major economic, political, and military institutions of the country. This insular and self-perpetuating group controls much of the key decision-making processes in the United States. Members of the power elite have the full power and weight of their respective institutions at their disposal. Their close association allows them to collaborate in ways that best serve their particular interests, which may not coincide with those of the people. Thus, their actions have tremendous implications for the rest of the population. For instance, military leaders may persuade the president to declare war, senators may pass legislation that cuts billions of dollars from social welfare programs, and corporate executives may post record gains for stockholders or downsize companies and lay off thousands of workers.

PLURALIST MODEL a system of political power in which a wide variety of individuals and groups have equal access to resources and the mechanisms of power

POWER ELITE a relatively small group of people in the top ranks of economic, political, and military institutions who make many of the important decisions in American society

Power Elites Many of the most powerful men in the United States spend two weeks of every summer in a campground north of San Francisco called Bohemian Grove. Founded as a place for the nation's leaders to gather and escape from outside concerns like business, politics, and power, the Men's Club's members include every Republican president since 1923, many CEOs, and other prominent businessmen. In this photo, Ronald Reagan and Richard Nixon sit on either side of Harvey Hancock (standing).

G. William Domhoff has studied the power elite extensively, looking at how the economic, political, and military institutions overlap and form a network of influence (1983, 1987, 1990, 2002, 2013). The power elite not only know each other personally and professionally, but they also recognize their status as part of the ultimate "members only" club. Many of them were born into powerful families who still control huge U.S. corporations. Many of the power elite attended the same prep schools and Ivy League colleges. They may live in the same neighborhoods or belong to the same country clubs. They may go to the same churches or give to the same charities. More important, they often serve on each other's boards of directors and do business directly with other members. One related study identified only 5,778 individuals in these elite positions, meaning that less than 0.0026 percent of the entire U.S. population are among the power elite (Dye 2002). These individuals are overwhelmingly white males. Although a few powerful women and ethnic or racial minorities also hold elite positions, diversity among corporate leaders has been declining since its peak in 2007–2011 (Zweigenhaft and Domhoff 2014).

What are the implications of this class dominance theory of power? For one, it debunks the original American rags-to-riches mythology that says anyone who works hard can get to the top. If power is concentrated in such a small fraction of a percentage of the population, chances are that the average person will never wield any real power, regardless of his or her work ethic or life choices. Furthermore, the United States continues to be controlled by white upper-class men. Finally, those who have the power to create social change by economic, political, or military reforms may choose to do so only when it is to their own advantage. So who runs America after all?

INTEREST GROUPS The American political system is organized so that individuals, groups, and organizations can contribute to candidates' campaigns. **Special interest groups** (sometimes called advocacy groups) play an important role in the political process. These are organizations formed expressly to raise and spend money in order to influence elected officials and public opinion. Special interest groups can include corporate organizations, lobbies, political action committees (PACs), and 527 groups (named after the corresponding IRS code). Many 527s run by special interest groups raise unlimited amounts of "soft money," which can be used for various types of advocacy, if not directly for candidates. Special interest groups' contributions to candidates and causes can reach into the hundreds of millions of dollars.

SPECIAL INTEREST GROUPS
organizations that raise and spend money to influence elected officials and/or public opinion

POLITICAL ACTION COMMITTEES (PACS)
organizations that raise money to support the interests of a select group or organization

The average citizen may have little idea of the influence of wealthy donor organizations in the political process. There is almost always a positive correlation between a candidate's campaign spending and his or her success: money wins elections. During the 2008 election, for instance, in 93 percent of House of Representatives races and 94 percent of Senate races, the candidate who spent the most money won. In the 2012 presidential race, Barack Obama raised more than $715 million to Mitt Romney's $446 million. As in the presidential race, incumbents (those already occupying the electoral seat) are usually in the best position to raise money because of their high-profile position; incumbency, therefore, is one of the most important advantages a candidate can have because it tends to lead to fund-raising success and victory at the polls. It is also an advantage to have your campaign backed by a billionaire (like the Koch brothers or George Soros). In the 2014 midterm elections, some 85 percent of congressional candidates funded by billionaires won their seats (Boerma 2014). Billionaires backed candidates on both sides of the aisle, thus assuring they would win the race regardless of the outcome of the election.

A political action committees (PAC) is a type of tax-exempt 527 group that was designed to raise money to campaign for or against candidates, ballot measures, or other legislation. A PAC typically supports the interests or agenda of a select group or organization. For instance, BAMPAC, or the Black America Political Action Committee, represents the special interests of African Americans, while AAPAC, the Arab American PAC, lobbies for political interests of Arab Americans. NOW PAC, the National Organization for Women PAC, advocates feminist issues. Some of the biggest PACs are

Table 10.2   Top 10 Spenders on Lobbying, 1998–2015

Lobbying Client	Total
U.S. Chamber of Commerce	$1,160,065,680
American Medical Association	$326,122,500
National Association of Realtors	$321,195,913
General Electric	$318,050,000
American Hospital Association	$280,630,905
Pharmaceutical Research & Manufacturers of America	$272,551,420
Blue Cross/Blue Shield	$254,276,770
AARP	$243,202,064
Northrop Grumman	$222,532,213
Exxon Mobil	$211,632,742

SOURCE: Center for Responsive Politics 2015.

connected to trades, such as the National Education Association or the Carpenters & Joiners Union. The National Football League is represented by the "Gridiron PAC," and Major League Baseball has its own PAC as well. Even the interests of extraterrestrials are represented through X-PPAC, the Extraterrestrial Phenomena PAC.

As a result of a 2010 Supreme Court ruling, corporate funding of independent, campaign-related expenditures is no longer prohibited. In fact, the *Citizens United v. Federal Election Committee* decision allowed unlimited spending by corporations, unions, and other noncampaign entities, calling it a First Amendment right. This opened the door to a new kind of PAC—the "Super PAC," which can accept these unlimited contributions and use the monies to do things like produce and air issue-based ads, as long as they do not coordinate with the candidate or the candidate's political party. What this has meant in practice is that political candidates can benefit from the unlimited spending of a Super PAC without being in violation of the campaign finance laws that still apply to their own party organizations. Following the inception of *Citizens United,* research has shown that Super PACs are being funded primarily by a small group of ultra-wealthy contributors. In fact, since *Citizens United,* 60 percent of the money spent by Super PACs was funded by only 195 wealthy donors and their spouses, accounting for $600 million in federal election spending. Contributions in Senate elections have more than doubled with "dark money," or spending by donors who remain hidden, playing a significant role in funding (Vanderwalken and Perty 2014).

In the 2012 presidential election cycle, the top two Super PACs spent almost $250 million in support of Republican candidate Mitt Romney and against President Barack Obama and other Democratic candidates and issues, while the third biggest Super PAC spent more than $60 million to oppose Romney's candidacy (Center for Responsive Politics 2013). These amounts are astronomically higher than they might have been

The Power of Special Interests Members of the National Rifle Association, a special interest group that lobbies for gun rights, gather in Tennessee for the 114th annual meeting.

had *Citizens United* not removed the limits on corporate donations by calling them "free speech." Though it has been difficult to make definitive conclusions about the relationships between special interest groups and legislators, the staggering amounts of money these groups generate cannot be ignored. As sociologists, we seek to uncover the mechanisms of influence in our political system. Monitoring the actions of top donors, PACs, Super PACs, and other special interest groups provides insight into how our political system works.

The Media and the Political Process

THE MEDIA AS THE FOURTH ESTATE

In addition to the executive, legislative, and judicial branches of government, the media play a key role in the political process. This has been true since the founding of the country and has taken on even more significant proportions in the Information Age. Often referred to as the **Fourth Estate** of government, the media render checks and balances on power much like the three government branches. Although the media can also serve to entertain, they were originally intended to inform and educate the populace and to serve as a watchdog on government. In fact, the framers of the U.S. Constitution probably envisioned the watchdog role as the media's primary function.

> **FOURTH ESTATE** the media, which are considered like a fourth branch of government (after the executive, legislative, and judiciary) and thus serve as another of the checks and balances on power

After all, they believed that a free press was essential to the health of the new democracy. Thus, the First Amendment guarantees freedom of expression and freedom of the press (along with other rights).

Still, it's hard to imagine that the country's founders could have envisioned what "the press" would become. To them, it literally meant printing presses. There were no broadcast media or digital media back then—no mass media as we know them. So contemporary lawmakers have had to interpret the Constitution in light of modern concerns and developments. They must try to balance the rights of a free press while protecting the country from abuses of power by the media or by the individuals who own the media. And we must all consider the media's tremendous potential to sway and manipulate our thoughts and feelings and to influence the political process.

The media have always played a role in American politics, informing the public about the important issues of the day. But their role has increased dramatically during the past fifty years, coinciding with the spread of television in the 1950s and '60s and the Internet in the 1990s and 2000s. Many of the social movements and landmark political events of the past several decades have unfolded before us on the TV or computer screen. It's unlikely that the civil rights movement, the Vietnam War, Watergate, the impeachment of President Clinton, the attacks of 9/11, the tragedy of Hurricane Katrina, the Boston Marathon bombings, or the Supreme Court's 2015 ruling on same-sex marriage would have emerged, developed, and resolved in quite the way they did without the media bringing those issues and images into our living rooms. And for a little while, Americans talked about race, sexual orientation, war, terrorism, poverty, and gun violence. Social media added to the immediacy and shared nature of the conversation. The media can make momentous events a part of the national dialogue and involve voters, citizens, and even global attention, influencing public opinion and promoting political activism and change.

The Media's Role in the Political Process The power of media to bring political news from across the nation has transformed the political process. For example, the Boston Marathon bombings, the attacks on September 11, 2001, and the disaster surrounding Hurricane Katrina would not have had such widespread impact without the media.

MEDIA INFLUENCE ON POLITICS Some of the most significant changes in the political process have occurred in the realm of campaigns and elections. Political actors have adapted to a media-saturated society, and their strategies for success must include great media savvy (Dutta and Fraser 2008, Skarzynska 2004). Any group or individual wishing to influence voters must court the media, either by attempting to gain coverage of a particular issue or candidate or by directly buying space or time through advertisements. Fundraising—gathering money to spend on media exposure—has become the first order of political business (Gainous and Wagner 2011, Ulbrich 2004).

At one time, the voting public was informed of the issues through local political party representatives, town hall meetings, church groups, speeches made by politicians or activists out on the stump, or exhaustive coverage in newspapers or on radio. Nowadays, media coverage of politics is more likely to emphasize human interest stories, personalities, high-profile spectacles, and planned events—and less likely to explain the background and implications of issues and policy debates (Kellner 2005, Thompson 2012). And not all news programs offer strictly objective reporting. We hear a lot about politics through pundits, media personalities who offer political commentary (and their own opinions) along with the news. Sean Hannity, Rachel Maddow, Bill Maher, Glenn Beck, Matt Taibbi, Andrew Sullivan, Melissa Harris-Perry, Arianna Huffington, and Matt Drudge are just a few of the many pundits found on either side of the aisle and across media platforms.

The public is also influenced by **opinion leaders**, high-profile people who interpret political information for us (Katz and Lazarsfeld 1955). Instead of getting information about the issues directly, we allow our views to be shaped by these opinion leaders whom we trust to tell us what to believe. Someone like Oprah Winfrey, for instance, can influence not only what we read but also our political values. Even within your group of friends, there may be someone who, while not as famous as Oprah, is more politically savvy than the rest of the group and can communicate information to you in ways that may influence your opinions.

One of the first and most dramatic examples of the media's impact on politics occurred during the presidential campaign of 1960. The debates between John F. Kennedy, the Democrat, and Richard Nixon, the Republican, were the first to be broadcast live on television. Kennedy, the younger candidate, recognized the power of television and understood the importance of presenting a "telegenic" image. He allowed media handlers to advise him on makeup, hairstyle, clothes, and the appropriate demeanor for the TV cameras. Conversely, Nixon refused to make any special preparation for the event. As a seasoned politician, he planned to rely on his command of the issues and his considerable debating skills.

Those who watched the debates on television saw dramatic differences between the two candidates. Kennedy looked fresh, young, and energetic; Nixon looked sweaty, old, and tired. Those who listened to the debates on the radio, as previous generations had for years, judged the two candidates not by looks or mannerisms but by the content of their speech. When polled after the debates, audiences who watched on TV thought that Kennedy won the debate; audiences who listened on radio thought Nixon was the winner. As history shows, Kennedy won the election and helped to change the relationship between the media and political campaigns. Although Kennedy's performance during the debate was only one factor in the election, it was significant. Other presidential candidates became so nervous about the effects of televised debates that none agreed to participate in them until 1976.

STYLE OVER SUBSTANCE? Another feature of modern politics is "soundbites"—those short audio or visual snippets taken from press releases, press conferences, photo opportunities, or sometimes protests. In our postmodern era, the news has been condensed into just a few seconds' worth of information. What politicians say to the press is often scripted by "spin doctors" who manipulate rhetoric to give it a positive appearance designed to be catchy and compelling while not necessarily delivering much substance; many people form their views of candidates from these processed bits of information. It is no wonder that celebrity politicians are becoming more common and popular. After all, who knows better how to use the media, how to stand before the cameras and speak in interviews, than those who have been professionally trained as actors? President Ronald Reagan, formerly a Hollywood actor and commercial spokesperson, is perhaps the greatest example of this. He knew how to hit his marks and deliver his lines. He was even called "The Great Communicator" despite his inability to speak extemporaneously.

OPINION LEADERS high-profile individuals whose interpretation of events influences the public

Any form of celebrity seems to make an individual more visible and popular. Others have followed in Reagan's path, including basketball star Bill Bradley, astronaut John Glenn, and comedian Al Franken, who became senators; wrestler Jesse Ventura and actor Arnold Schwarzenegger, who both became governors; singer Sonny Bono, who became a congressman; and actor Clint Eastwood, who became a mayor.

Sarah Palin provides another example; she was a politician who became a kind of celebrity. As the Republican vice presidential candidate in the 2008 election, the former Alaska governor gained notoriety and became a high-profile political figure. Critics claimed that she was a case in point of what some call "style over substance." Her image as a Washington outsider and folksy hockey mom was carefully promoted; she was coached and groomed for public appearances. Critics cited her lack of knowledge and experience, but it was her personal life, or at least the part of it that was portrayed in the media, that people were relating to. She has continued to be popular among supporters, even after losing the election

Celebrity Politics How do politicians such as Sarah Palin carefully craft their image to appear more relatable to the public?

and leaving her governorship. Since then she has authored two best-selling books, served as a regular contributor to Fox News, starred in two reality TV series, and established her own online news channel. The media have helped make Sarah Palin a galvanizing and controversial political figure.

Does the increased focus on a politician's style and personality, rather than platform and policies, mean that we are getting less substance in what we consume? This Data Workshop may help you answer this question.

SIMULACRUM an image or media representation that does not reflect reality in any meaningful way but is treated as real

DATA WORKSHOP
Analyzing Media and Pop Culture

Real and Fake News

The media have a longstanding relationship with the political process and the American people. A free press is meant to inform the public about important matters facing the nation. As the formats for media continue to change, so has the delivery of news. Postmodern sociologist Jean Baudrillard claimed that "the image has come to replace the real" (1981/1994). By this, he meant that we have lost the ability to distinguish between what is real and what is fake, especially where media representations are involved, and that we have also come to accept the fake as sufficient—thereby no longer needing the real. He called this new artificially

constructed "reality" the **simulacrum**, or a simulation that becomes as good as the original. Some would warn that we need to be more aware of how this plays out in the political arena, even beyond its role in style over substance.

A key example of Baudrillard's simulacrum can be found in the growing popularity of "fake news." Journalism and political satire share a long history, and the number of outlets for this kind of mix has recently exploded. The list includes TV shows like *The Daily Show*, *Last Week Tonight with John Oliver*, *The Nightly Show with Larry Wilmore*, and *Saturday Night Live*'s "Weekend Update" segment, as well as online sites like *The Onion News Network* and the *HuffPostShow*.

Fake news TV shows so closely resemble real news TV shows that it is often hard to tell which is which. Fake news TV shows get their humor from parodying or satirizing real news, so they often mirror the mainstream press in covering certain topics and events. The same material is fodder for both. But fake news, of course, is not held to the same journalistic standards that apply to reporting the real news. Fake newscasters readily mimic their network anchor counterparts, and the shows are made with the same production values viewers have come to expect on the broadcast dial. All of this is making it more and more difficult to tell the difference between the simulation and the real thing.

The Daily Show set the bar for fake news on TV, spawning many copycats and spinoffs. The show has won multiple awards and distinctions and has consistently been ranked among the most popular shows of any kind for the eighteen to thirty-four age group (Gross 2010). Although Jon Stewart only played at being a journalist on air, he often looked like—and even functioned like—the real thing. A poll taken during the 2008 election cycle revealed that more than 40 percent of young people between eighteen and twenty-nine cited Stewart and *The Daily Show* and Stephen Colbert of *The Colbert Report* as their primary sources of political news (Pew Research Center 2008). By the time he retired from *The Daily Show* in 2015, Stewart had been dubbed "the most trusted name in fake news" or the "Walter Cronkite" of fake news (Page 2015). As Baurdrillard might say, the fake [newscaster] had come to replace the real [one].

Today you can see many more sources for the dissemination of fake news. Although the primary intent of fake news is to be funny and entertaining, it doesn't preclude taking on serious subjects and disseminating messages with a viewpoint and the potential to influence audiences. As fake news has become more popular and more widespread, what does that mean for real news and its role in educating and informing the people? It seems that fake news has become an important and enduring voice in humor and in American political culture.

This Data Workshop asks you to analyze the phenomenon of fake news, its real popularity, and its possible influence on young people and politics. Choose your fake news show—*The Daily Show, Last Week Tonight with John Oliver*, or *The Nightly Show with Larry Wilmore*. Select a recent episode of the show, and make sure it is available for multiple viewings. You will be gathering data from an existing source and doing a content analysis of the episode. Refer to the section in Chapter 2 for a review of this research method.

As you watch the episode, consider the following points (you may want to take informal notes while viewing and add more of your own comments and observations afterward):

* In what ways does the show resemble a traditional network news program? Examine the format of the show, the cast and correspondents, the regular program segments (news reporting, interviews), the structure of the stage set, the design of the graphics, and other aspects of the production.

* Make a list of the topics that are covered on the show. Compare the stories presented on the fake news show with stories presented in the real news during the same time period. How much of the news is completely fake, and how much is actually about real-world events?

* A fake news show, even when it covers real issues, is not held to the same journalistic standards as traditional news outlets. How does an audience member know what to believe about the truth of any particular statement or story?

* Despite being satirical, fake news shows also provide serious commentary about important issues in American life. What are some of the underlying messages of the humorous material on the show?

* Are you among the audience members who get political news from fake news shows? To what extent do you believe these shows might influence people's political ideas? Do you think that they increase young people's awareness of issues, or are they a confounding distraction?

* If we consider what postmodernists say about the increasing power of the image or simulacrum in our everyday lives, how can we tell the difference between what is real and what is fake?

Fake News on TV *Last Week Tonight with John Oliver* and *The Nightly Show with Larry Wilmore* blur the lines between real and fake news.

There are two options for completing this Data Workshop:

PREP-PAIR-SHARE Choose a recent episode of *The Daily Show, Last Week Tonight with John Oliver,* or *The Nightly Show with Larry Wilmore* and take notes while watching. Be ready with some preliminary answers to the Data Workshop questions. Pair up with one or more classmates and discuss your findings in small groups. Were your thoughts about fake news shared by others?

DO-IT-YOURSELF Choose a recent episode of *The Daily Show, Last Week Tonight with John Oliver,* or *The Nightly Show with Larry Wilmore* and take notes while watching. Write a three-page paper answering the Data Workshop questions and analyzing the role of journalism—real and fake—in the American political process.

SOCIAL MEDIA AND POLITICS As much as the media changed the political process in the twentieth century, it seems likely that new forms of media will transform it all the more. The power of social media goes beyond simply providing information; it also allows for interaction, networking, and user-generated content.

An increasing number of Americans are getting their political and campaign news online, and social networking sites play an important part in the story. In the 2012 presidential election, 47 percent of Americans used the Internet as their main source of campaign news, surpassing newspapers (27 percent) and radio (20 percent), but still trailing behind television (67 percent). Among young people ages eighteen to twenty-nine, 54 percent used the Internet as their primary source of campaign news, compared to 43 percent of thirty- to forty-nine-year-olds, 28 percent of fifty- to sixty-four-year-olds, and only 14 percent of people ages sixty-five and older (see Table 10.3).

As smartphone usage has increased over the last few years, cell phones and social media platforms like Facebook and Twitter have played an increasingly prominent role in the dissemination of voter information (Smith 2014). In 2014, 28 percent of registered voters received election news via cell phone and 16 percent followed political figures on social media. These "mobile election" news consumers are also more active than other voters. They are more likely to encourage others to support a particular candidate (58 percent) and to attend campaign events (11 percent). Forty-one percent of these users follow political figures so that they can find out about political news before others do, and more than 35 percent follow leaders on social media because they enjoy feeling personally connected to politicians.

Can spending time on social media affect your voting behavior? Ask Facebook. In every national election since 2008, the social networking site has featured an "I'm voting" or "I'm a voter" button that is meant to encourage its users to vote. But that's not all it does. The tool (known as the "voter megaphone") was designed as one part of larger, ongoing experiments by the company to see how it could affect voter behavior (Sifry 2014). One study examined how information within newsfeeds affects interest in voting. Three months prior to the 2012 election, Facebook increased the amount of hard news stories in the feeds of 1.9 million users. Researchers found that shifting the newsfeed—which users were not informed about—raised civic engagement and increased voter turnout. While this may seem like a good thing, many people were alarmed when they learned that Facebook had manipulated user accounts in an effort to influence the public. Facebook officials claim that they will no longer engage in voter research on the site, but that they will make the voter megaphone button available in future elections, with the hope that some positive social pressure from friends will increase participation at the polls.

Politicians are interested in leveraging the power of social media to get their message out to hundreds of millions of users.

Table 10.3   For Young People, Internet Rivals TV as Campaign News Source

Top Sources for Campaign News	18–29 (%)	30–49 (%)	50–64 (%)	65+ (%)
Television	64	68	83	86
Internet	54	43	28	14
Newspaper	14	17	27	41
Radio	17	20	18	12
Magazine	1	4	2	5
Other	7	2	2	2
Don't know	6	5	2	1

SOURCE: Pew Research Center for the People & the Press 2012a.

Barack Obama was the first U.S. president to fully understand and embrace social media. In 2015, he released key points from his State of the Union address directly to social media in advance of the event. Among the issues he touched upon, his speech included a proposal to make community college free for all Americans. Almost immediately it spawned the hashtag campaign #FreeCommunityCollege, while a video clip was also posted to the White House Facebook page. This represented a change in strategy from previous administrations that relied heavily on the broadcast media to get their message out. Some were critical of the president for going directly to the people through social media; this approach allowed him to deliver a message that was unfiltered by the established channels of media outlets (Cutter 2015).

Clearly, the media play an important role in informing and educating the voting public. Despite our "free press," however, we must also be aware of how the media can be used to further the purposes of powerful interest groups and individuals. The democratic system stands to suffer if only those with the most money or celebrity can influence public opinion by buying their way into the hearts and minds of Americans.

Patriotism and Protest

Even though freedom of speech is a legal right in the United States, when we criticize some policy or some action of the government, we may, ironically, be called unpatriotic by those who support it. This is especially true in times of war or national crisis, when many citizens believe we should pull together as a country and present a united front to the world. During the 1960s, for example, at the height of U.S. involvement in Vietnam, many Americans considered anti-war protesters "un-American" because of their vocal criticism of American intervention in Southeast Asia. After September 11, 2001, those who questioned the competence of U.S. intelligence agencies (such as journalists, elected representatives, and survivors of those killed in the attacks) were effectively silenced until more than a year later, when Congress impaneled a commission to investigate intelligence agencies' preparation for and response to the attacks. The commission's report confirmed problems within the intelligence community that contributed to the inability to foresee and forestall the attacks—corroborating the criticisms of "unpatriotic" protesters.

Numerous protests occurred during the course of the Iraq War, attracting both proponents and critics. Protests at the 2004 Democratic and Republican national conventions in Boston and New York City were notable for their size, their creativity, and the intense response they provoked from law enforcement. Both protesters and police used the Internet and mobile phones to coordinate their actions, and in one demonstration, 5,000 bicyclists clogged the streets of Manhattan for a protest ride. Using a different strategy, peace activist Cindy Sheehan, whose son was killed in Iraq, set up camp outside George W. Bush's Texas ranch in August 2005, vowing to stay there until the president came outside and spoke with her. He never did, and in July 2006 Sheehan purchased several acres of land near the Bush ranch to create a more permanent memorial to her son.

In 2010, the Museum of Contemporary Art (MOCA) commissioned noted street artist Blu to paint a mural on the outside wall of their Geffen building in downtown Los Angeles. Before the painting could be viewed by the public, MOCA's director ordered it to be whitewashed. The museum had been unaware that Blu's mural would feature powerful anti-war symbolism in the form of coffins draped in dollar bills. While some, including the artist, called MOCA's action censorship, others were equally upset about the insensitivity of displaying the art so close to the Veteran's Administration Building and a nearby Japanese American war memorial (Vankin 2010).

Wide-scale protest can also take aim at other institutions that are part of the American power structure. In 2011, the Occupy Movement spread from New York City's Zuccotti Park all over the country and the world, protesting social, economic, and political inequality. Carrying signs saying "We Are the 99%," Occupy protesters expressed their opposition to a system that allows a small minority (the "1%") to hold a majority of the wealth and power while ordinary middle-class citizens suffered unemployment, foreclosure, and disempowerment during the Great Recession.

In 2013, the Black Lives Matter movement emerged after George Zimmerman, a neighborhood watch volunteer, was acquitted in the case of the shooting death of black teenager Trayvon Martin. Protests grew in 2014 in the wake of several incidents where unarmed black men, including Michael Brown in Ferguson, Missouri, and Eric Garner in New York City, were killed by police officers. In each case, a grand jury decided not to indict the officers involved. Protesters claim that these are not isolated incidents, but rather they point to a long and ongoing history of inequities in policing in minority communities, racial profiling, and excessive use of force by law enforcement. Black Lives Matter supporters organized hundreds of protests across the country, with large turnouts in cities such as St. Louis, New York, Washington, D.C., Oakland, Detroit, Miami, and Columbus. The scope of the protests against law enforcement and the judicial system broadened beyond initial demands to end police brutality, the mass incarceration of black men, and the militarization of police. Black Lives Matter symbols and slogans entered into popular culture: the hoodie worn by Trayvon Martin when he was shot to death, and "I Can't Breathe"—Eric Garner's last words before he was killed in a chokehold. These symbols and slogans serve as an expression of solidarity and support, a reminder about larger issues concerning civil rights and social inequality that have yet to be resolved.

Is it unpatriotic to criticize your government in times of national crisis or to call for change to an unfair legal system? Those who do so argue that such criticism is the most patriotic

Hands Up, Don't Shoot The Black Lives Matter movement was formed in response to the acquittal of George Zimmerman in the shooting death of unarmed black teenager Trayvon Martin in 2012.

act of all: that blind acceptance of government is not the same as patriotism and that citizens should make every effort to correct society's flaws. Those on the opposite side may say, "My country, right or wrong" and believe that the decisions of our elected leaders and the actions of those who carry out our laws are beyond reproach. Regardless of your views, keep in mind that those who criticize government policies are doing exactly what our democratic system calls for and protects. Dissent and its tolerance are crucial elements of an open society, and you have a constitutionally protected right to oppose, criticize, and protest.

Politics: The Micro-Macro Link

Political institutions and their products (such as laws or bureaucratic systems) shape our everyday lives. A law such as Title VII of the Civil Rights Act of 1964 ensures your right to apply for and hold a job without being discriminated against because of race, gender, or religion. No matter who you are or what kind of work you do, you are protected by this law. And even if you have never experienced discrimination in the workplace, this law is probably one of the reasons why.

Huge government bureaucracies like the Department of Education shape your everyday life as well. Even if you attend a private university, you had to submit a FAFSA (Free Application for Federal Student Aid) in order to determine your eligibility for any type of financial aid—federal and state grants and loans and aid programs administered by your campus. All these student aid sources require the FAFSA, and your ability

to attend the college of your choice may therefore depend on the decisions made by this government bureaucracy.

In addition to seeing how political institutions shape our everyday lives, it is important to remember that we have built these institutions ourselves, through our participation in the democratic process. When we vote, sign petitions, or participate in demonstrations, we bring our individual influence to bear on the larger social structure—even if, ultimately, the cause or candidate we support doesn't prevail. So remember, micro-macro connections are made every day as you participate with others in political processes and live in a culture shaped by its political institutions.

Democratic processes require a free press and an educated polity; to make decisions and cast votes, you must have the tools to gather information and comprehend the issues your vote will influence. This is only one of the many links between political and educational institutions in our society. As we move into the segment of this chapter that deals with education, try to think of all the ways that politics and education are connected—and remember to look for micro-macro connections as you learn about educational institutions as well.

What Is Education?

Most modern political systems recognize the importance of universal education. The framers of the U.S. Constitution realized that an informed public was essential to the survival of democracy. Education, therefore, was seen as critical to the founding of the new republic. In the United States, public education has traditionally been under state and local control, although the federal government began playing a larger role in the latter half of the twentieth century. However, private schools and religious schools are also involved in education. About 9 percent of K–12 students attend private schools (either religious or secular), 88 percent attend public schools, and 3 percent are homeschooled (U.S. Department of Education 2013).

Education is the central means by which a society transmits its knowledge, values, and expectations to its members. The general goal of education is to give students the necessary understanding for effective social functioning. Education often includes the transmission of information, principles and values, the regulation of personal character, and discipline of the mind. Education can be either formal or informal and can occur in a variety of settings, although we commonly think of it as tied to school systems.

A Brief History of Modern Education

Formal, institutionalized, secular education in Western civilization began in ancient Greece around the eighth century B.C.E., when students studied philosophy, mathematics, music, and gymnastics. Higher education was carried out by philosophers before the rise of schools as an institution. In the Middle Ages, the church was the main educator, with schools in monasteries and cathedrals, and until about 1200 C.E., the schools focused mainly on training students to be priests. During the thirteenth century, lay education emerged. It consisted of apprentice training for a small group of the common people or education in chivalry for the more privileged. During the Middle Ages, universities offered courses in three subjects—law, theology, and medicine—and these courses were available only to the most privileged members of society: royals, aristocrats, and those from families with ties to the monarchy and the church.

While systems of education have evolved a great deal since the Middle Ages, the roots of what we would recognize as modern mass education can be traced back to the idealism of the European Enlightenment of the eighteenth and nineteenth centuries. During this period, the value of education greatly increased. The leading thinkers of the day, such as Voltaire, Locke, and Franklin, emphasized knowledge—reason, logic, and science—over religious tradition. They were convinced that the well-being and future of modern society depended on enlightened self-knowledge, which could be achieved only through learning.

Education in the United States grew rapidly during this same period. The founders' belief that it is the government's responsibility to provide basic education to all its citizens—and that fulfilling this obligation is beneficial for both society and the individual—helped create the U.S. public education system. Schooling came to be seen as a necessity rather than a luxury and became legally mandatory for all children age sixteen and younger; Massachusetts was the first state to enact such a law, in 1852. As larger proportions of the population began attending schools, curricula became more varied and included both academic and vocational education to prepare students for a diversifying set of future occupations (not just farming or housewifery). By 1929, elementary, junior high, and high schools had spread to every state and territory in the nation, including Alaska, and opportunities for higher

EDUCATION the process by which a society transmits its knowledge, values, and expectations to its members so they can function effectively

The Rise of Mass Education Beginning in the nineteenth century, schooling began to be considered a necessity for preparing children to enter modern industrial occupations.

education also expanded, especially in the land-grant colleges of the western United States.

Higher education is now available to everyone in the United States. Before 1900, less than 2 percent of Americans finished high school, and even fewer went on to college. In 2012, the high school graduation rate topped 80 percent for the first time in U.S. history, with a record high number of high school students earning diplomas (Stetser 2014). High school dropout rates are also at a record low, with only 7 percent of students dropping out of high school in 2013. The increase in high school graduation rates is marked by a significant decrease in dropouts among black and Hispanic students, whose dropout rate has decreased to 8 percent and 14 percent, respectively (U.S. Census Bureau 2014b). There are variations according to state and school district: Nevada had the lowest high school graduation rate of 63 percent, and Iowa had the highest, at 89 percent (Stetser 2014). Different racial and ethnic groups have varying graduation rates: in 2011–2012, 88 percent of Asian/Pacific Islander students, 86 percent of white students, 69 percent of black students, and 73 percent of Hispanic students graduated high school on time (Stetser 2014).

Education and the Reproduction of Society

Schooling serves a number of important functions in our society. The transmission of knowledge is a clear function of education, but in addition, we learn to follow society's rules and to respect authority, and we are socialized to develop other qualities that will eventually make us efficient and obedient workers. In school, we also learn our places in the larger society—practices such as **tracking**, in which students are identified as "gifted" or are placed into remedial or vocational education, teach us about success and achievement and our chances for both. When placed in a lower ability or remedial track, for instance, students lose access to courses such as calculus and Advanced Placement (AP) classes (Useem 1990), which effectively locks them out of certain colleges, certain majors, and even certain future careers, all by the time they're sixteen.

TRACKING the placement of students in educational "tracks," or programs of study (e.g., college prep, remedial), that determine the types of classes they take

HIDDEN CURRICULUM values or behaviors that students learn indirectly over the course of their schooling

EDUCATION AND INEQUALITY While we firmly believe, as a society, that education is the key to achievement and success, it is also true that educational institutions can replicate systems of inequality. Educational achievements do improve our life chances; U.S. Census data consistently indicate that those with higher educational attainment also have higher median incomes. In 2010, the average lifetime earnings for someone with an advanced degree totaled around $3 million, compared with $2.3 million for those with a bachelor's degree, or $1.3 million for those with only a high school diploma (Carnevale, Rose, and Cheah 2011). Moreover, unemployment rates are directly correlated with educational attainment: in 2014 those with a high school degree experienced an unemployment rate of 6.0 percent, those with a bachelor's degree a rate of 3.5 percent, and those with a master's degree a rate of 2.8 percent (U.S. Bureau of Labor Statistics 2014b).

It is also worth noting some of the complexity of gender inequality in higher education, as we find that among young adults ages twenty-five to twenty-nine, there is a growing gap between the percentage of women (37 percent) and men (30 percent) with bachelor's degrees or higher (U.S. Department of Education 2014b). Although more women than men earn bachelor's degrees, on the job market they make considerably less than their male counterparts. In 2013, the median weekly earnings of women with bachelor's degrees or higher was $1,043 compared to $1,395 for men, or 75 percent of what men make (U.S. Bureau of Labor Statistics 2014c). Likewise, college accessibility remains unequal: only 10 percent of people from low-income backgrounds, compared to half of people from high-income families, obtain bachelor's degrees (Bailey and Dynarski 2014). So education benefits everyone, but it does not benefit everyone equally, and inequality in educational benefits mirrors inequality in the larger society.

How do these patterns manifest themselves? What do these educational inequalities look and feel like for students in the classroom? Female students may notice, for instance, that their teachers pay more attention to male students, and they may learn to think that boys are smarter than girls. Caucasian or Asian students may notice that there are fewer African American and Hispanic students in the gifted classroom than in the remedial classroom, and they may learn to think that whites and Asians are smarter than blacks and Hispanics. Children without disabilities may see disabled kids left out of activities or sent to the special education center and learn to think that these students are less worthy than nondisabled kids. These micro-inequities are common in American classrooms.

They are experienced by individuals but are the result of structural forces external to those individuals. In other words, micro-inequities result from macro-level inequalities in the larger educational and social systems. And these micro-inequities teach us as much as our more explicit lessons in math, literature, or history. Acquiring a sociological perspective on educational institutions and processes will help you "unlearn" these lessons and understand that educational attainment is often as much about social stratification as it is about individual ability.

THE HIDDEN CURRICULUM Sociologists have long been interested in the **hidden curriculum**, the lessons that students learn indirectly but that are an implicit part of their

Hidden Curriculum Bowles and Gintis argue that schools train students to be ideal workers by promoting a curriculum of "rules, routines, and regulations."

socialization in the school environment (Jackson 1968). Many sociologists have analyzed the hidden curriculum to explain the nonacademic roles filled by mass education.

One such role is the training of future workers, which was examined by Bowles and Gintis (1977) in their study *Schooling in Capitalist America*. They argue that schools train a labor force with the appropriate skills, personalities, and attitudes for a corporate economy. Although the official curriculum is supposed to promote personal improvement and social mobility, the hidden curriculum of "rules, routines, and regulations" actually produces a submissive and obedient workforce that is prepared to take orders and perform repetitive tasks. According to this analysis, schools look a lot like factories. Students have no control over their curriculum, must obey instructions, and gain little intrinsic satisfaction from their schoolwork. Because students learn these norms and values in school, they are willing to accept similar conditions when they become workers.

A similar analysis can explain how the hidden curriculum reinforces and reproduces conditions of social inequality by presenting and reinforcing an image of what is considered "normal," "right," or "good." While the official curriculum has come a long way toward recognizing the racial, ethnic, and gender diversity of the nation, there are still major gaps and exclusions (FitzGerald 1980; Thornton 2003). Schools cannot always rectify these oversights because the hidden curriculum can work through much more subtle mechanisms as well. How the curriculum is presented and the way the school is organized can be powerful messengers of the hidden curriculum. For instance, even schools that attempt to implement multicultural education may undermine their own efforts if the staff and administration do not mirror the lessons they teach. If teachers and administrators are mostly white, mostly heterosexual, or mostly male (or mostly female, as is the case in lower grades), they may belie the very lessons they try to teach—what students hear and what they see just don't add up. When schools attempt to alter only what

is taught and not the way it is taught, they may change the curriculum, but they won't affect what students are learning (Christakis 1995, Falconer and Byrnes 2003).

Classic Studies of Education

Sociologists and other researchers have studied education from a variety of perspectives. In this section, we review three classic studies of education, each offering a different approach and distinctive insights into its significance, both as a social institution and in the lives of individuals.

A SYMBOLIC INTERACTIONIST STUDY The first study looks at education from the symbolic interactionist perspective, which maintains that the social world is constructed through the interactions of individuals. Robert Rosenthal, a Harvard psychologist, and Leonore Jacobson, an elementary school principal, worked together on *Pygmalion in the Classroom: Teacher Expectation and Pupils' Intellectual Development* (1968). The researchers began the experiment by administering a basic IQ test to students in the first through sixth grades, although they told teachers the test was designed to predict which students would "bloom" academically in the next year. They then randomly selected an experimental group of students and falsely told their teachers that these students were predicted to develop rapidly in the coming school year. At the end of the year, the researchers administered the same IQ test and found that students in the experimental group had increased their IQ scores by a significantly greater margin than their peers in the control group. The researchers concluded that the teachers' attitudes about their students unintentionally influenced the students' academic performance. In other words, when teachers expected students to succeed, the students indeed tended to improve (and it was assumed that the opposite would be true as well).

IN THE FUTURE
Educational Trends: "Flipping the Classroom"

One of the enduring complaints about public educational institutions in the United States is that such systems of mass education cannot always meet the unique needs of individual students. For example, students with physical or learning disabilities, students with less preparation or less help at home, older and returning students, students whose learning pace or style is different—these and other types of students are not always well served by the one-size-fits-all methods of teaching and learning that are an entrenched part of traditional educational institutions. As schools feel more pressure to standardize education and boost student performance, they may look for new ways to meet those needs. This is where one innovative individual and his not-for-profit Khan Academy offer real change to business as usual in education.

Salman Khan, a Harvard MBA and former hedge-fund analyst, started by tutoring his cousins who were having problems with their math homework. As word spread to family members around the world who couldn't make it to in-person sessions, he started videotaping his lessons and posting them on YouTube. Once online, the tutoring sessions went viral and were soon being used by students and educators across the globe. Originally funded by small donations from family and friends, the Khan Academy is now funded by the Bill & Melinda Gates Foundation, Google, and other major foundations. Now it's Khan's full-time job to create lesson plans and produce, star in (as the voice of the teacher), and post videos on his Khan Academy website. He has a skilled and growing staff helping him do these things.

The academy provides free open-access online education to any student, anytime, anywhere in the world, in about sixty languages. Khan breaks down tough lessons into smaller bits and teaches them in a clear, concise, and easy-to-understand way. One concept, idea, or equation—graphing derivatives, for example, or the Cuban Missile Crisis, or photosynthesis—in about ten minutes; that's it. His videos cover a variety of disciplines—math and science, art history, American government, economics, history, and even test prep for exams such as the SAT. The lessons range from elementary school to college-level material and include a system for mapping students' progress toward mastery in various areas.

Unlike an ordinary classroom, where a teacher doesn't have time to go over a concept repeatedly, students can watch the videos as often as they like in order to competently grasp a concept. The Khan approach allows students to master concepts before moving forward (rather than being swept along in grade-level groups whether they get it or not). Khan's approach is called "flipping the classroom," a kind of inversion of traditional teaching methods. Instead of starting with an in-class lecture and then sending students home to work on questions, readings, and exercises on their own, Khan advocates doing problem-solving activities together, in class, with the "lectures" delivered online, for students to watch as their "homework."

Over the past several years, the idea of the flipped classroom has garnered a lot of attention among educators in a broad range of institutions. Both the increase in technology

---

The results of *Pygmalion in the Classroom* have been critiqued by other researchers, on both theoretical and methodological grounds, especially because the researchers used standardized IQ tests and small subject samples (Baker and Crist 1971). Nonetheless, this study and others support the proposition that teacher expectations affect students' behavior and achievement in measurable ways. Some studies indicate that student labeling is often arbitrary and biased, with the result that teachers—whether consciously or unconsciously—may be reinforcing existing class, ethnic, ability, and gender inequalities (Fairbanks 1992; Sadker and Sadker 1995). This also means that changes in classroom interaction could lead to an improvement in academic performance among students from underprivileged backgrounds.

A CONFLICT STUDY The next study, which also looks at inequalities in schools, is consistent with a conflict perspective, which sees society as a system characterized by inequality and competition. Jonathan Kozol's *Savage Inequalities* (1991) is an ethnographic study of public schools in cities across the country, including Washington, D.C., Chicago, and San Antonio. Kozol, a former teacher, contends that because schools are funded by local property taxes, children in poor neighborhoods are trapped in poor schools, which reinforces inequality. He documents the significant differences among America's schools: "the highest spending districts have twice as many art, music, and foreign language teachers . . . 75 percent more physical education teachers . . . 50 percent more nurses, school librarians, guidance counselors, and psychologists . . . and 60 percent more personnel in school administration than the low-spending districts" (Kozol 1991, p. 167).

When Kozol interviewed the parents and students in wealthy school districts, he discovered that many of them believe educational inequalities are a thing of the past,

usage, particularly online videos, and the prevalence of poor learning outcomes have shaped the growth of the "flipped classroom" method (Knewton 2015). The idea of the flipped classroom has gained traction in a variety of classroom settings. Recently, a high school near Detroit became the first school in the United States to completely switch over to flipped classrooms and has since inspired many other schools to try out the teaching model (Rosenberg 2013). Before formally adopting flipped classrooms, Clintondale High School conducted an experiment to test their effectiveness by having one teacher hold two classes—a "flipped" class and a traditionally taught class—and see how students responded. After twenty weeks, they studied the results and found that while there was no change in achievement within the traditional classroom setting, students within the flipped classroom setting performed at higher rates and were less likely to fail. After completely flipping all its classrooms, Clintondale High School significantly lowered its dropout rate—from about 30 percent to under 10 percent—and increased its graduation rate to over 90 percent despite having once been considered one of the lowest-achieving schools in Michigan.

However, the growth in flipped classrooms has not been without its critiques. One such criticism stems from the disparity in technology access among students (Acedo 2013). With an already wide achievement gap between low-income students and economically advantaged students, critics have pointed out the significant consequences of adopting flipped teaching methods when not all students have equal access to technology and the Internet. Many teachers worry about the consequences of moving teaching onto computers and out of the classroom, as doing so not only requires students to watch the lectures on their own but also can affect students' achievement differently depending on their learning styles. While some students may excel in learning online, others might need in-person instruction from a teacher to be able to grasp new content and ideas. What will the future of education look like in the United States? The Khan Academy and the flipped classroom may provide a preview.

Flipping the Script Schools across the country, including this middle school in Massachusetts, are flipping their classrooms by focusing class time on problem-solving activities.

"something dating maybe back to slavery or maybe to the era of official segregation" but not to anything "recent or contemporary or ongoing" (Kozol 1991, p. 179). In stark contrast to this view, Kozol describes underfunded schools he visited—the hundreds of classrooms without teachers in Chicago, the thousands of children without classrooms in schools throughout New Jersey. His overall impression was that these urban schools were, by and large, extraordinarily unhappy places. How, he asks, could the children in these schools have an equal chance at success? A structural functionalist might respond that schools are not intended to provide equal chances.

A STRUCTURAL FUNCTIONALIST STUDY According to the structural functionalist perspective, educational inequality is merely preparation for occupational inequalities later in life. (Remember, functionalists believe that every social phenomenon has a role to play in keeping society at equilibrium.) In the third study, *The Credential Society*, sociologist Randall Collins (1979) argues that class inequalities are reproduced in educational settings and that there is very little schools can do to increase learning. Although many people assume that better teachers, better facilities, and better funding can increase test scores, he points out that when class background factors are held constant, none of these other factors seems to have any effect.

Collins believes that reproducing the existing class structure is the true function of education. Schools, for example, provide the credentials to ensure that the children of the middle class will continue to receive middle-class jobs. To protect their own job security, members of lucrative occupations, such as accountants, lawyers, and financial analysts, have set up a complicated credential system (education) to keep the number of job applicants down and to ensure that there is a large population forced to work at unpleasant jobs for low wages. Collins makes the radical recommendation that we consider "abolishing compulsory school requirements and making formal credential requirements for employment illegal" (Collins 1979, p. 198). This would make it illegal for employers to ask how much education a job applicant has, much as it is currently illegal to ask about race or gender.

The Present and Future of Education

During the past several decades, many educators, parents, and legislators have come to believe that America's educational system is in crisis, that public schools are failing to provide adequate training for students. Critics list a variety of problems, including low rates of literacy and poor standardized test scores, lack of sufficient funding and crumbling infrastructure, low pay for teachers, overcrowded classrooms, and high rates of crime on campus.

In 1983, the National Commission on Excellence in Education released a report on the state of American public schools. *A Nation at Risk* concluded, in apocalyptic terms, that the American educational system was in a crisis so serious that "if an unfriendly foreign power" had created it, "we might well have viewed it as an act of war." Largely on the basis of declining standardized test scores, the report argued that the United States was "committing an act of unthinking, unilateral educational disarmament." Not all the commission's conclusions have been affirmed, but three decades later, numerous studies point to ongoing problems in education and the persistence of an "achievement gap" between students from different demographic groups.

Much of the research surrounding America's failing public education system points toward a connection between poverty and academic underachievement. A recent study showed that nearly half of all public school students within the United States live in poverty, marking an increase in the growing rates of poverty within the public education system (Sparks 2013). With only about half of students from high-poverty high schools going on to attend college, poverty remains one of the biggest predictors of academic achievement and educational attainment (Sparks and Adams 2013). Concerns about the decline in American educational standards and competitiveness have elicited a variety of responses on the part of parents, communities, the government, and other agencies. A number of educational trends are already in place and may play an important role in shaping the future of American education.

NO CHILD LEFT BEHIND AND THE COMMON CORE
Some efforts have been aimed at trying to address problems at the K–12 level. One such tactic was the "No Child Left Behind"

CHARTER SCHOOLS public schools run by private entities to give parents greater control over their children's education

(NCLB) act, which Congress passed in 2002. According to this policy, each state was responsible for testing every student in its public education system at specific grade intervals to determine levels of success. Low-performing schools were identified with "school report cards" and were required to improve both student and teacher performance. Parents also had the option of removing their children from consistently low-performing schools and placing them in other schools within the district.

In theory, No Child Left Behind seemed to promote equal education, but in practice it has had mixed results, and many constituencies were left frustrated by the law. NCLB relied on standardized test scores (in reading comprehension, writing, and math) even though researchers have long known that standardized test scores are ambiguous predictors of success for female students and students of color (Epps 2001) and do not directly measure teacher or school performance at all. Though test scores have marginally increased since NCLB, the achievement gap among students still persists within all states. There have been little data to show that students from low-income families have benefited from No Child Left Behind at the same level as more economically advantaged students (Blank 2011). Amid growing dissatisfaction with No Child Left Behind, legislation has been aimed at fixing its most unworkable requirements, while President Obama has proposed dismantling the law and replacing it with a new blueprint for change.

The Common Core State Standards were developed in 2009 with the intention to remedy America's stagnant academic achievement levels. Currently, forty-three states have voluntarily adopted the Common Core as a way to standardize and improve test scores while better preparing students for college. Unlike No Child Left Behind, the Common Core is a state-led rather than federal initiative, and state adoption of standards is voluntary, although President Obama did create a grant incentive program, Race to the Top, for states who adopt the standards (Common Core State Standards Initiative 2015). Because the Common Core is still being rolled out within public schools, it remains unclear how the program will affect the trajectory of public education; however, many concerns remain regarding the ability of any one-size-fits-all attempt to reform America's education system. Whether states retain NCLB or choose the Common Core, debates about course content, standards, testing and accountability continue.

CHARTER SCHOOLS AND SCHOOL VOUCHERS
Charter schools are public schools, but they are run by private entities, such as a parents' group or an educational corporation. Also, they operate with relative freedom from many of the bureaucratic regulations that apply to traditional public schools. Charter schools represent a compromise position between public and private schools and provide a way for parents to exercise control over their students' educational experiences without completely abandoning the

public school system. By 2013, forty states and the District of Columbia had established charter school programs, and more than 6,000 charter schools were serving a total of more than 2 million students (Keaton 2014; U.S. Department of Education 2014a). State laws regarding charter schools govern sponsorship, number of schools, regulatory waivers, degree of fiscal or legal autonomy, and performance expectations.

The "charter" establishing such schools is a contract detailing the school's mission, program, goals, students served, methods of assessment, and ways to measure success. Charter schools are designed to support educational innovation; some have special emphases like arts or science; others offer special services like health clinics or community-based internships for students. A high school in St. Louis called the Construction Careers Center instructs students in the skills needed to work in the building trades while also teaching the traditional high school curriculum. In Madison, Wisconsin, educators started Nuestro Mundo Community School, a Spanish immersion program. By fifth grade, all the students are equally fluent in Spanish and English. The Madison school district created the school to help close the gap between the test scores of Hispanic students and their non-Hispanic peers.

Ideally, charter schools can make changes and implement decisions faster than ordinary public schools because of their freedom from district governance. They can monitor their successes (and failures) more closely and are more responsive to the needs of students, parents, and communities. In reality, charter schools face many challenges. They are difficult and sometimes expensive to launch and run. Though charter schools are publicly funded, they are exempt from certain state and local regulatory requirements and, as such, have become somewhat controversial among public school advocates. Because charter schools are free from certain regulations, they have the freedom to operate independently and on private sponsorship. Still, many of them struggle to raise funds. This can potentially create disparities in public education and exclude certain student populations (National Center for the Study of Privatization in Education 2015).

There are also questions about whether charter schools are any better than ordinary public schools. They have met with only mixed success. A report on charter school students in California found great variation in how well the schools and their students performed (RAND Education 2003). Although achievement varies by school and by subject matter, charter school students generally have comparable or slightly lower test scores than those in conventional schools. These schools did not necessarily serve more minority students. Nonetheless, charter schools continue to be popular, and more will probably open in the coming years, looking to benefit from both the experience of earlier charter schools and the findings of social scientific research.

First proposed in the 1990s, **school vouchers** allow parents in neighborhoods where the public schools are inadequate to send their children to the private school of their choice.

In other words, taxpayers receive a voucher for some of the money that a public school would have received to educate their child, and they apply that money to private school tuition. Most school-voucher programs fund 75 percent to 90 percent of the cost of a private school, with parents making up the rest.

Despite the growing use of school vouchers, there has been little evidence to indicate that vouchers increase academic achievement (Usher and Kober 2011). Proponents of school vouchers argue that they give parents more choice and control over their children's education and pressure public schools to improve or risk the loss of their voucher-eligible student body. Opponents argue that vouchers do not improve public education but do the opposite: they drain funds from vulnerable public schools and cause them to deteriorate further. Opponents also say that if parents use vouchers for parochial schools, public monies are funding religious education, thus threatening the separation of church and state. While the Supreme Court has ruled the voucher system to be constitutional and numerous experimental voucher programs are already in place, the privatization of public education remains controversial in any form.

HOMESCHOOLING AND UNSCHOOLING Homeschooling or home-based education is the education of school-aged children under their parents' supervision outside a regular school campus. Many parents homeschool their children not only to control their academic education but also to limit their exposure to the socializing effects of peer culture in public schools. Some homeschooled children enroll in regular schools part-time or share instruction with other families, but most of their education takes place at home. While many families homeschool their children for their entire K–12 years, many others try it for only a short time.

Homeschooling in the United States has been growing steadily since the 1980s, with current growth rates of 5–12 percent a year. In 2012, an estimated 1.8 million students in the United States were homeschooled, accounting for approximately 3 percent of the school-age population. Homeschools account for about the same percentage of students as either charter schools or private schools in the United States (U.S. Department of Education 2013X).

Clearly, homeschooling is a significant phenomenon in education, but how is it working? One of the largest studies of homeschooling arrived at rather startling results. The academic achievement of homeschooled students, on average, was significantly above that of public school students (Ray 1997, 2008, 2013). In addition, homeschooled students did well even if their parents were not certified teachers and the

SCHOOL VOUCHERS payments from the government to parents whose children attend failing public schools; the money helps parents pay private school tuition

HOMESCHOOLING the education of children by their parents, at home

Homeschooling The Wilson family in Myrtle Point, Oregon, study together at the kitchen table as part of their homeschooling program.

state did not highly regulate homeschooling. One advantage of homeschooling seems to be the flexibility in customizing curriculum and pedagogy to the needs of each child. Yet, questions remain about the possible academic and social disadvantages to students removed from typical school environments.

More recently, the **unschooling** movement has gained popularity. Although it is similar to homeschooling in that parents oversee their child's learning, unschooling is an alternative to traditional education and homeschooling alike. As its name suggests, unschooling rejects the standard curriculum that is typically taught to students, as well as conventional teaching methods and classroom environments. Unschooling, as a philosophy, advocates student-centered learning by encouraging students to learn through their own freely chosen activities, interests, and real-world experiences. Parents offer support, guidance, and resources, but children initiate their own direction and exploration of subject matter. A parent may give instruction when asked, and so facilitate lessons, but the point of departure is always the child's innate curiosity and desire to learn. This approach makes lessons more meaningful to the students and honors their particular aptitudes and learning styles. Students become lifelong learners and gain useful life skills.

Although their numbers are still relatively small, adults who were unschooled report high levels of satisfaction in their later careers. Many proponents of unschooling denounce

UNSCHOOLING a homeschooling alternative that rejects the standard curriculum in favor of student-driven types of learning

EARLY COLLEGE HIGH SCHOOLS institutions in which students earn a high school diploma and two years of credit toward a bachelor's degree

the traditional model of formal education, which they say is not conducive to learning or future success. Some critics believe that unschooling is too radical an approach and worry about isolation and children who lack social skills and self-motivation. Homeschooling and unschooling are educational trends that continue to grow, as they offer an attractive alternative to the shortcomings of traditional education.

EARLY COLLEGE HIGH SCHOOLS AND DUAL ENROLL-MENT PROGRAMS **Early college high schools** are new institutions that blend high school and college into a coherent educational program in which students earn both a high school diploma and two years of college credit toward a bachelor's degree. In addition to local efforts to create these schools, the Bill & Melinda Gates Foundation, in partnership with the Carnegie Corporation of New York, the Ford Foundation, and the W. K. Kellogg Foundation, has contributed over $120 million to launch early college high schools. Since 2002, more than 240 early college high schools in twenty-eight states have served over 75,000 students. The goal of these programs is to serve students who might otherwise face greater obstacles making the transition from high school to higher education. In an effort to address the achievement gap in public education, early college high schools aim to serve low-income students and minorities, with 75 percent of early college students identifying as Latino or African American (Early College Design Services 2013).

Each early college high school is a collaborative endeavor between a public school district and an accredited higher education partner. In Phoenix, Arizona, high school students can join the Gateway High School program and simultaneously get a high school diploma and an associate's degree from

Gateway Community College. Antioch University in Seattle, Washington, offers a similar program for Native American youth, who have the highest college dropout rate and the lowest graduation rate of any ethnic group in the United States. These new high schools aim to engage students by offering them challenging academic work while simultaneously providing the necessary guidance and support structures. Early college high schools are small (with no more than 75–100 students per grade) and thus can provide the benefits of a close community, an intimate learning environment, and personalized academic attention. Compared to other high schools, early college high schools boast a higher rate of graduation while also addressing the issue of dropouts. A recent study showed that 81 percent of early college students go on to attend college compared to only 72 percent of students attending other schools (Berger et al. 2014).

Dual enrollment programs allow high school students to gain college credit for the courses they take through a concurrent enrollment agreement with a local college. Through this exchange, dual enrollment students take classes, often at a local community college, and simultaneously earn high school and college credit for their work. While AP classes provide high-achieving students the opportunity to earn college credits, dual enrollment allows many more high school students the opportunity to take college-level courses. By providing high school students with the opportunity to get a head start on college work, dual enrollment programs can help ease the transition to college and allow students to "try on" or rehearse college attendance (Karp 2012). It has also been shown that dual enrollment programs can increase postsecondary academic achievement while also decreasing the amount of time students take to obtain their degree (Allen and Dadgar 2012).

For many students, the path to postsecondary education is difficult. Large, impersonal middle and high school programs, limited financial resources, and the daunting processes of applying to and entering higher education may hinder academic achievement. By changing the structure of the high school and compressing the number of years required for an undergraduate degree, early college high schools and dual enrollment programs are having a significant impact on high school students, who are demonstrating high levels of attendance, improved promotion rates, and success in college-level courses.

COMMUNITY COLLEGES You know what a community college is—you may even attend one right now. A **community college** is a two-year school that provides general education classes for students who want to save money while preparing to transfer to a four-year university, right? While this definition of a community college is technically true, community colleges have become much more than just a springboard to a four-year degree. They provide vocational and technical training for people planning practical careers, retrain "downsized" workers seeking new career paths, offer enrichment classes for retirees, and currently provide opportunities of all sorts. In 1901, six students enrolled at the first "junior college" in Joliet, Illinois; just over 100 years later, there are 1,123 community colleges across the country (American Association of Community Colleges 2015). In 2013, approximately 5.3 million students were enrolled in two-year community colleges, making up about 27 percent of all students enrolled in college in the United States (U.S. Census Bureau 2014h). Another 5 million or more community college students take various noncredit courses, such as English as a Second Language or job force training (American Association of Community Colleges 2015).

The contemporary community college typically offers more than just basic general education and college preparatory courses. In fact, the California Community College system, the largest in the nation, offers classes in more than 175 fields (California Community College Chancellor's Office 2015). Honors programs, study abroad options, intercollegiate sports, music programs, on-campus residence halls, and internships can now be part of the two-year experience. Community colleges help students prepare for careers that give back to the community—two of the most in-demand programs of study are administration of justice and health sciences, with 80 percent of firefighters, police officers, and EMTs and more than half of all new nurses and health-care workers trained at community colleges (American Association of Community Colleges 2011).

Community colleges have gained recognition for playing a critical role in preparing the country's workforce. In an effort to serve more people in need of training, many states are now offering programs in which students enrolled in community college can earn a bachelor's degree on campus, rather than transferring to a four-year university. Community college baccalaureate programs allow students to still earn a bachelor's degree while avoiding the high costs and barriers to access that surround four-year university admission. In 2014, twenty-one states already offered such programs, with more states planning to follow (Koseff 2014).

In 2015, President Obama announced a federal initiative to make community college attendance free for students. Inspired by the success of Tennessee and Chicago's tuition-free community college programs, this new initiative could affect up to 9 million students by increasing community college accessibility (Parsons 2015). With increasing tuition costs at four-year universities, the passage of a free community college initiative could help propel many students who would not otherwise be able to afford tuition to pursue higher education. While much of this is good news, community colleges also struggle with such issues as declining public funding sources and the changing needs of a growing, diverse

DUAL ENROLLMENT programs that allow high school students to simultaneously enroll in college classes, earning credit for both high school and college degrees

COMMUNITY COLLEGE two-year institution that provides students with general education and facilitates transfer to a four-year university

ON THE JOB
For-Profit Colleges: At What Cost?

Perhaps you watched the Super Bowl in 2015, when the game was played at the University of Phoenix Stadium in Glendale, Arizona. The corporation that runs the University of Phoenix paid over $150 million for the naming rights to the municipal stadium. The University of Phoenix is one of the most successful for-profit colleges in the country, part of an industry that has experienced explosive growth in the last decade. Perhaps you know someone who is among the millions of students who attend for-profit colleges each year. Or perhaps you've seen one of those TV commercials that for profits colleges run, the kind that show successful graduates giving testimonials about their great new careers in the aerospace industry and how they owe it all to the education they received at ITT Tech—and how you can do it too!

Among the reasons for the growth in popularity of for-profit colleges is their open enrollment policies and flexibility in scheduling. Many offer night and weekend classes as well as fully online degree and certificate programs, often with a special focus on job-related curriculum and training. For-profits are especially interested in serving nontraditional students, including minorities, low-income, and first-generation students, along with veterans and adult learners. Many students are seeking to acquire specific skills or training they hope will make them more successful in a competitive job market. So why not choose a for-profit school?

Historically, most colleges and universities in the United States have been not-for-profit institutions. The expansion of the University of Phoenix—along with other for-profits such as ITT

Technical Institute, DeVry University, and "off-shore" schools like Ross Schools of Medicine—is somewhat new. These colleges are run more like businesses than traditional schools. Many are subsidiaries of larger corporations, and all are expected to make money for investors and shareholders. The proliferation of for-profits has been a boon to students; they now enroll about 13 percent of all college students in the United States. At the same time, there has been growing concern and criticism from lawmakers, educators, and even President Obama about the role of for-profits in the recent student-loan debt crisis, and whether the schools are really delivering the kind of success that they promise.

For-profit colleges compare less favorably to traditional two- and four-year colleges on a number of key indicators. One issue is cost. According to the College Board annual report, the average cost of tuition and fees in 2014 was $15,230 at for-profit institutions, compared to $3,347 at two-year public nonprofit schools and $9,139 at the four-year level; only private nonprofits cost more at $31,231 per year (College Board 2015). Another issue is how students bear those costs. The majority of students take out loans to pay for college: 62 percent of students at public schools, 70 percent at private schools, and 90 percent at for-profit schools. While for-profits enroll about 13 percent of all college students, they account for about 33 percent of all student loans. The majority of those loans come through federal aid programs or are secured through government agencies. Nearly 90 percent of graduates of for-profits had student loans, with the average debt among those who borrowed reaching nearly $40,000 (Snider 2014).

---

student body. Despite these hurdles, though, community colleges continue to provide a wealth of opportunities.

ONLINE LEARNING Online education (also called distance learning) is not really a new concept—"correspondence courses" have been available for hundreds of years and served as a way for people in remote locations (like farmers and their families) or people who were homebound or physically disabled to benefit from the same educational opportunities available to others. In previous eras, distance learning courses relied on the postal service and more recently on audiotapes

> **ONLINE EDUCATION** any educational course or program in which the teacher and the student meet via the Internet, rather than meeting physically in a classroom

and videos to help students learn independently. With the advent of the Internet and real-time electronic communication, distance learning was transformed forever. Universities and private businesses use these technologies to offer courses to anyone with an Internet connection. Certificates and degrees of all kinds are within the reach of students who, because of time, geography, or other constraints, cannot come to campus.

According to a frequently cited report by the Online Learning Consortium (2013) on the state of online learning, in 2012 more than 6.7 million, or 32 percent of all college students, were taking at least one class online, an increase of more than a half million students over the previous year. Online enrollments have been growing steadily even while overall higher education enrollment has been declining.

The quality of education at for-profit college programs also varies greatly, with some providing much better outcomes for students than others. Completion rates are another issue. Only 33 percent of students who attend for-profit schools actually graduate, compared to 55 percent of students at public nonprofits and 65 percent at private nonprofits. Graduates of for-profit institutions may also struggle to have their degrees taken seriously. While for-profit colleges boast many student success stories, these all too often fail to materialize. They are accused of making inflated promises, and in some cases even falsifying reports about their student job placement rates. Graduates of for-profit schools are less likely to secure employment in their fields of choice, and many have to settle for jobs that don't even require the higher education they invested in. And this happens at just the time when student loan repayments come due. A higher percentage of graduates of for-profits are in default within the first three years than graduates from public and private nonprofit schools.

In the face of these growing problems, the for-profit industry has recently come under investigation by state and federal agencies. In 2014, the U.S. Department of Education led a crackdown on abuses at Corinthian Colleges, including violations of state laws and predatory lending practices (the corporate college shut down all operations in 2015). Congress is considering new regulations on how federal loans are used, and the White House has proposed debt-relief measures to help students who were duped into spending more on education than they can afford to repay (Kirkham 2015). While this has the potential to change the for-profit college industry in the future, many students are suffering in the meantime. They're still looking for work and carrying unmanageable debt loads that won't go away, even if they declare bankruptcy. Student activists have begun to organize around these issues and to work with other groups in protest of "business as usual" among for-profit colleges.

Certificate of Debt Only about a third of students who attend for-profit colleges like the University of Phoenix and DeVry University actually graduate, and those who do often carry significant student loan debt.

In an effort to increase access to higher education learning, many institutions have begun offering free online courses, or massive open online courses (MOOCs), to anyone wanting to take a course, from anywhere in the world. Stanford, Yale, Harvard, and Princeton, along with the university systems in Texas, Pennsylvania, and Michigan, are among the list of elite schools that have paired up with online organizations to bring an exclusive education within the reach of the public (Lewin 2012). Three of the largest providers are Coursera, Udacity, and edX. Coursera offers nearly 200 courses in eighteen subjects, including math, computer science, business, and the social sciences and humanities, partnering with thirty-three of the top universities.

The popularity of MOOCs is demonstrated by the many millions of learners who have enrolled in their courses. A typical MOOC attracts about 20,000 students, but retention rates are much lower than for traditional courses. Researchers report that completion rates can reach 40 percent but are often less than 13 percent (Parr 2013). While in principle a MOOC is free of cost, if students want to receive official verification or degree credit for their work, they may have to pay additional fees. Still, the availability of such courses has the potential to affect learners across the globe. By providing universal and open access to online courses from some of the world's top universities, MOOCs are revolutionizing the scope of distance learning and increasing who can obtain a quality education.

While technological advances make it increasingly easy to produce and offer online courses, as with any application of technology to education there are both pros and cons. Like the

RELIGION any institutionalized system of shared beliefs and rituals that identify a relationship between the sacred and the profane

BELIEF a proposition or idea held on the basis of faith

RITUAL a practice based on religious beliefs

SACRED the holy, divine, or supernatural

PROFANE the ordinary, mundane, or everyday

old-fashioned correspondence courses, online technologies provide educational access for those who might otherwise not be able to pursue a degree. However, distance learning is not a good fit for all students, and attrition rates from online courses are notoriously high. Online classes often lack the personal touch and dynamic interaction of standard classroom instruction. For this reason, students may feel that there is something important (if intangible) missing from their educational experience. Since you will probably experience both traditional and online learning in your college career, ultimately you'll be the judge.

Education: The Micro-Macro Link

As societies change, so do educational institutions, and so does the individual's experience of education. For example, a big part of being a student today is knowing how to use digital technology. The typical student today does a good amount of work online, whether it's reading an e-book, accessing course materials from a teacher's website, or watching videos as homework. Digital technology is so integrated into the teaching and learning process that many students now take it for granted. This is one of the many ways that macro-level change (in this case, the development of technology) affects your everyday life through your participation in the social institution of education. What you learn about the world in school on an everyday basis—as well as how you learn it—is shaped by larger social forces.

Education is not the only social institution concerned with teaching members of society important information, values, and norms. Religion is another social institution from which we learn a great deal about being members of society. Even if we rebel against our religious upbringing or have no religious affiliation, our lives are touched in important ways by religion because it is a dominant social institution in the United States. As you read the following section, think about the intersection of the micro and the macro in the study of religion and about the intersection of religion with other social institutions, including politics and education.

What Is Religion?

No doubt we each have our own definition of religion based on personal experience. But a sociological definition must be broad enough to encompass all kinds of religious experiences.

For sociologists, **religion** includes any institutionalized system of shared **beliefs** (propositions and ideas held on the basis of faith) and **rituals** (practices based on those beliefs) that identify a relationship between the **sacred** (holy, divine, or supernatural) and the **profane** (ordinary, mundane, or everyday). Those who study religion recognize that there are different types of religious groups: denominations (major subgroups of larger religions, such as Protestantism within Christianity or Shia within Islam), sects (smaller subgroups, such as the Amish or Mennonites), and cults (usually very small, intense, close-knit groups focused on individual leaders—like David Koresh and the Branch Davidians—or specific issues like the UFO cult Heaven's Gate). Sociologists do not evaluate the truth of any system of beliefs; they study the ways that religions shape and are shaped by cultural institutions and processes, as well as the ways that religions influence and are influenced by the behavior of individuals.

Theoretical Approaches to Religion

STRUCTURAL FUNCTIONALISM For members of any religion, beliefs and rituals serve a number of functions. First, religion shapes everyday behavior by providing morals, values, rules, and norms for its participants. From the Judeo-Christian commandment "Thou shalt not kill" to the Buddhist commitment to reconcile strife to the Qur'anic requirement to eschew alcohol and impure foods, religious rules govern both the largest and smallest events and actions of followers' daily lives. Religious practices usually include some type of penance or rehabilitation for those who break the rules: Catholics can confess their sins to a priest and be assigned prayer or good works to redeem themselves; Muslims spend the month of Ramadan fasting during daylight hours to purify their bodies and souls; Yom Kippur is the Jewish Day of Atonement and also involves fasting, as well as appeals for wrongs to be forgiven.

Another function of religion is to give meaning to our lives. Religious beliefs can help us understand just about everything we encounter because every religion has a system of beliefs that explains such fundamental questions as, How did we get here? What is our purpose in life? Why do bad things happen to good people? All religious traditions address these questions, helping their followers explain the inexplicable, making the terrible more tolerable, and assuring believers that there is a larger plan. Finally, religion provides the opportunity to come together with others—to share in group activity and identity, form cohesive social organizations, and be part of a congregation of like-minded others.

CONFLICT THEORY These are the (mostly unifying) functions of religion for individuals and for society, but there

Religion and Social Justice Óscar Romero, the late archbishop of El Salvador, who was beatified by Pope Francis in 2015 (left), and Lech Walesa (right, speaking into a bullhorn) of Poland both led movements against repressive political regimes.

are also ways in which religion can promote inequality, conflict, and change. From a conflict perspective, the doctrines of the three major **monotheistic** religions—religions that worship one divine figure (Judaism, Christianity, and Islam)—are quite sexist. Orthodox Judaism mandates the separation of men and women in worship and in everyday life; Catholicism and many Protestant sects prohibit women from becoming priests or pastors; traditional, observant Muslim women must keep their bodies completely covered at all times. There are very few nonsexist religions, and those with strongly nonsexist values and practices (such as Wicca) are usually marginalized. Some religions have anti-LGBTQ or racist doctrines as well: some Protestant sects refuse to ordain gay clergy, and until 1978 the Church of Jesus Christ of Latter Day Saints (LDS, or Mormons) believed that people with dark skin were cursed by God and forbade African Americans from marrying in the temple.

Religious organizations have also been agents of social justice and political change. For example, religion has been closely linked to movements for African American rights. The movement for the abolition of slavery was entwined with Christian reformers like the Methodists and Baptists. The civil rights movement in the twentieth century began in Southern Protestant churches and was led by a team of Christian ministers, including the Reverend Martin Luther King Jr. In Africa and Latin America, **liberation theology** has been instrumental in fighting exploitation, oppression, and poverty. Archbishop Óscar Romero of El Salvador used this distinctive combination of Marxism and Christianity to argue against the country's repressive military dictatorship. Though Romero was assassinated while saying Mass in 1980, his legacy lives on in human rights movements all over the world. The Polish labor movement Solidarność, led by Catholic shipyard workers in Gdańsk and supported by the late Pope John Paul II, was the

crucible for democratic change in the Eastern bloc in the 1980s. Communist regimes throughout Eastern Europe had restricted religious freedom and labor union organizing for decades; Solidarność helped break down both of those barriers.

From a conflict perspective, then, religion is complex: it can subjugate and oppress at the same time it can liberate. This may help explain Americans' seemingly contradictory approach to religion. While quasi-religious principles are at the core of many of our closely held national ideologies, many Americans also believe that religion should be kept separate from our collective political life.

SYMBOLIC INTERACTIONISM

Symbolic interactionist approaches to religion focus on how religious meaning is constructed in interaction and how religion is incorporated into the everyday life of individuals and groups. With its focus on interaction and interpretation, this approach is appropriate for examining religious symbolism, religious communication, and religious practices. For example, one might think that being female in a conservative religion would be oppressive and difficult to tolerate (see the previous section on sexism in religion). But interactionist studies show that it is possible to refashion the meaning of religious proclamations about gender in ways that benefit religious women's sense of value and personal power. Orit Avishai's 2008 study of Orthodox Jewish women, for example, shows that they are anything but "doormats"—rather, they are able to construct meaningful ways of "doing religion" that preserve their sense of personal agency and self-determination within the value system of their faith.

MONOTHEISTIC a term describing religions that worship a single divine figure

LIBERATION THEOLOGY a movement within the Catholic Church to understand Christianity from the perspective of the poor and oppressed, with a focus on fighting injustice

RELIGIOSITY the regular practice of religious beliefs, often measured in terms of frequency of attendance at worship services and the importance of religious beliefs to an individual

EXTRINSIC RELIGIOSITY a person's public display of commitment to a religious faith

INTRINSIC RELIGIOSITY a person's inner religious life or personal relationship to the divine

FUNDAMENTALISM the practice of emphasizing literal interpretation of texts and a "return" to a time of greater religious purity; represented by the most conservative group within any religion

Similar studies of religious women (Bartkowski and Read 2003; Gallagher 2004; Mahmood 2004) have identified related trends among Muslims and Christians: despite religious doctrines that appear to prescribe docility, women are able to construct agency, empowerment, and resistance in their everyday interactions by framing their roles as individual choices, their work as central to family and community, and their obedience as a way of triumphing over social and personal problems.

Recent studies have found that 58 percent of Americans say religion is very important to them and that on average, 37 percent of Americans say they go to religious services at least once a week (Pew Research Center 2012c; Lipka 2013). These numbers are somewhat misleading, however, because there are big differences in religious affiliation and participation across demographic groups. Gender, age, race, geographic region, political party, and education are all variables that influence religiosity. For example, more than one-fifth of the total U.S. public (22.8 percent), and more than a third of Millennials are religiously unaffiliated, the highest percentages ever reported. Whites are more likely to identify as religiously unaffiliated than both blacks and Hispanics (Pew Research Center 2015a).

Religion in America

How religious is the American public? That depends on the measures used (Hill and Wood 1999). Sociologists usually define **religiosity** as the consistent and regular practice of religious beliefs, and they gauge religiosity in terms of frequency of attendance at worship services and the importance of religious beliefs to an individual. Researchers have identified two broad categories of religiosity: extrinsic and intrinsic (Allport and Ross 1967). **Extrinsic religiosity** refers to a person's public display of commitment, such as attendance at religious services or other related functions. **Intrinsic religiosity** refers to a person's inner religious life or personal relationship to the divine.

Religious Trends

There is a moderate level of religious diversity in the United States compared to other countries in the world (Pew Research Center 2014c). The United States is largely Christian (divided into different sects), but Buddhism, Islam, Judaism, and other religions are also practiced by a portion of the population (see Figure 10.1). A slim majority of 56 percent of Americans maintain the same religious affiliation throughout their lifetimes, but there have been shifts in religious preferences in the past few decades (Pew Forum on Religion and Public Life 2011). One of those trends is toward fundamentalism, which is not a religion in itself but a traditionalist approach that can be applied to any religion. Another trend is away from organized churches toward an "unchurched" spirituality that borrows elements from many traditions but is affiliated with none.

FUNDAMENTALISM Fundamentalist approaches to religious belief and practice are on the rise both worldwide and in the United States. **Fundamentalism** is a way of

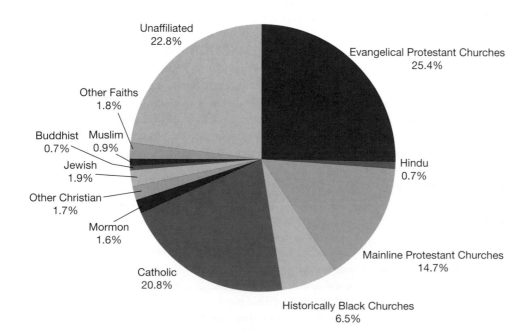

Figure 10.1 Religious Composition of the United States, 2014

- Unaffiliated 22.8%
- Evangelical Protestant Churches 25.4%
- Other Faiths 1.8%
- Buddhist 0.7%
- Muslim 0.9%
- Jewish 1.9%
- Other Christian 1.7%
- Mormon 1.6%
- Catholic 20.8%
- Hindu 0.7%
- Mainline Protestant Churches 14.7%
- Historically Black Churches 6.5%

SOURCE: Pew Research Center 2015a.

The history of religious conflict is extensive and convoluted, having been around for as long as humans have worshipped gods. No faith is exempt, and religion has played a significant role in conflicts from the ancient Israelites and Canaanites around 1200 B.C.E. to al-Qaeda's destruction of New York City's World Trade Center in 2001 to Sri Lanka's civil war between the Hindu Tamil Tigers and the Buddhist Sinhalese, which lasted more than twenty-five years before finally ending in 2009.

Mark Juergensmeyer's book *Terror in the Mind of God* (2003) analyzes the history and meaning of religious violence in general and terrorism in particular. He notes that groups using terror have historically had diverse agendas and motivations, but only within the past thirty years has religion come to play a prominent role in terrorist violence. A recent study confirms this trend. The number of countries with high or very high levels of social hostilities involving religion reached a peak in 2012. Of the 198 countries studied, some 33 percent had high or very high levels of religion-related terrorist violence; these countries represent 74 percent of the world's population. Christians and Muslims, who combined make up more than half of the world's population, faced harassment in the largest number of countries. The harassment of Jews also reached a seven-year high in 2013 (Pew Research Center 2015b).

Juergensmeyer's work uses many examples to illustrate the cross-cultural similarities of religious violence. Within the Christian tradition, Juergensmeyer discusses the Irish Republican Army (IRA) in Northern Ireland and the killing of doctors who perform abortions in the United States. Within Judaism, he examines the case of Baruch Goldstein, who killed twenty-eight Muslims in 1994 when he opened fire in the Ibrahim Mosque in the Cave of the Patriarchs, a shrine holy to both Jews and Muslims. Juergensmeyer also investigated Islamic terrorism, such as the first attempt to bomb the World Trade Center in 1993 and the activities of the Palestinian group Hamas, which pioneered the use of suicide bombings in the Middle East. Sikh terrorists were responsible for the assassination of Indira Gandhi by her bodyguard in India in 1984, and a Buddhist Japanese cult, Aum Shinrikyo, launched the notorious Sarin nerve gas attack on the Tokyo subway in 1995.

More recently, an Islamic splinter group that was once tied to al-Qaeda has waged widespread terror campaigns designed to establish religious rule and outlaw the spread of Western ideas in the Middle East. ISIS or ISIL (Islamic State in Iraq and Syria/Levant), a terrorist group that controls parts of Syria and Iraq and is present in other territories in the Middle East, has asserted its authority to establish an Islamic state and to expand its reach through armed warfare. The group has gained notoriety for using social media as a means of recruitment and to spread its propaganda. The release of videos showing mass executions and beheadings of "infidels," foreign soldiers, aid workers, and journalists has been widely condemned by Muslims and by governments and international organizations worldwide. Sadly, terror in the name of religion persists, and we suspect that you will be able to add new incidents to the list of recent religious violence.

Juergensmeyer argues that the common thread linking religious violence in such disparate traditions and far-flung corners of the world is a reliance on a particular kind of religious perspective. "The social tensions of this moment of history . . . cry out for absolute solutions," he says, and in a world that seems increasingly beyond individual control, religious violence offers a way to reassert some kind of power.

The list of wars, conflicts, and terrorist acts inspired or justified by religion is tragically long, extending throughout history and reaching across continents. Religious conflict is not a thing of the past, nor is your country (or your religion, whatever it may be) untouched by it.

Je Suis Charlie In January 2015, two brothers with ties to al-Qaeda opened fire in the offices of *Charlie Hebdo*, a satirical weekly newspaper based in Paris, killing eleven people and injuring eleven more.

understanding and interpreting sacred texts that can be part of any denomination or sect. Fundamentalist Christianity, for example, centers on a strict, sometimes literal, interpretation of the Bible and advocates a return to the historic founding principles of Christianity, arguing that modern approaches to Christianity are corrupt and inauthentic. Other religions have fundamentalist strains as well. Orthodox Judaism, for example, promotes a literal reading of the Torah and other Jewish spiritual and legal tracts. Fundamentalist Islam parallels Jewish and Christian fundamentalisms in that it also requires strict, literal, and traditional interpretations of the Qur'an and other sacred texts. Fundamentalist approaches to all three of these major religions gained popularity in response to the complex social changes of the 1960s and 1970s in the United States and around the world (Patterson 2004) because fundamentalism provides a return to tradition and to simple, unambiguous values and ideologies. Declaring one's loyalty to a traditional religious group that promises certainty in the face of change may be comforting to individuals—but it has broader social and political consequences as well.

EVANGELICAL a term describing conservative Christians who emphasize converting others to their faith

UNCHURCHED a term describing those who consider themselves spiritual but not religious and who often adopt aspects of various religious traditions

Between 1990 and 2001, the number of Americans who described themselves as "Fundamentalist Christians" tripled, and the number describing themselves as "evangelical Christians" (a variant of fundamentalist groups) more than quadrupled (Kosmin, Mayer, and Keysar 2001). The Institute for the Study of American Evangelicals estimates that 30 percent or more of the U.S. population, or roughly

The Rise of Fundamentalism Members of the New Birth Baptist Church in Atlanta, Georgia, come together in prayer. A megachurch with upward of 25,000 members, New Birth Baptist Church reflects the growth of evangelicalism in the United States.

100 million Americans, could be called evangelicals, though they occupy many different denominations (Eskridge 2012). Fundamentalists who take an **evangelical** approach attempt to convert individuals to their way of worshipping. Evangelicals see their conversion work as a service to others—an attempt to save souls—and have adapted many modern technologies (including television and social media) to their cause. With the growth of the evangelical movement, their beliefs have also spilled over into other areas of social life. For example, evangelical Protestants are less likely to see the separation of church and state as a good thing; they may believe religion plays too little role in politics rather than too much (Pew Research Center 2012e).

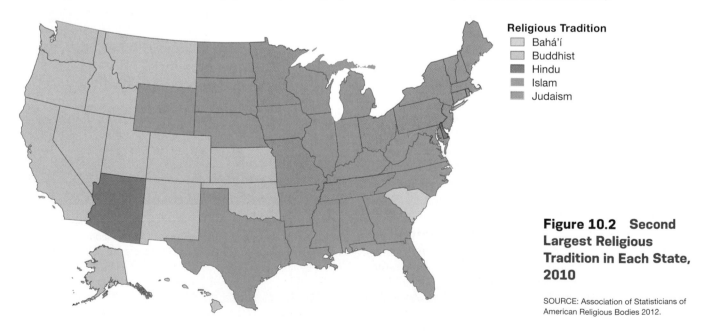

Religious Tradition
- Bahá'í
- Buddhist
- Hindu
- Islam
- Judaism

Figure 10.2 Second Largest Religious Tradition in Each State, 2010

SOURCE: Association of Statisticians of American Religious Bodies 2012.

UNCHURCHED SPIRITUALITY About 23 percent of Americans claim no religious affiliation (Pew Research Center 2015c)—interestingly, this group is more likely to be younger and to live in western states such as California, Colorado, Nevada, and New Mexico (Kosmin, Mayer, and Keysar 2001). Having no religious affiliation, however, does not necessarily mean that a person is an "unbeliever." In fact, less than 2 percent describe themselves as atheists, and agnostics are another 2 percent. As yet another indicator of our paradoxical attitudes about religion, Americans are increasingly seeking guidance and fulfillment through nontraditional means, with many labeling themselves "spiritual but not religious." This trend involves new definitions of belief and practice, often expressed privately and individually rather than in organized group settings.

As noted earlier, some organized religions still include elements of sexism, racial prejudice, homophobia, anti-Semitism, and conformity that turn people off, and so spiritual seekers may utilize a kind of "cafeteria" strategy, choosing elements from various traditions and weaving them together into something unique. This type of **unchurched** spirituality (Fuller 2002), frowned upon by some religious organizations, is becoming increasingly popular, as spiritual seekers mix bits of astrology, alternative healing, twelve-step programs, and even witchcraft with elements of more traditional doctrines.

DATA WORKSHOP
Analyzing Everyday Life

Measures of Religiosity

The term "religiosity" refers to the extent of a person's commitment to a religion. From what the majority of Americans report to pollsters, we can conclude that they are significantly more religious than people of other industrialized nations. Almost 60 percent of Americans say that religion is important to them, while just 21 percent of Europeans say the same. Are Americans really that much more religious? It's not always an easy thing to measure. Some researchers suspect, however, that these varying results may be caused by the discrepancy between what people say and what they actually do (Vedantam 2010; Holifield 2015). Sociologists debate about how studies are conducted and whether respondents give accurate accounts. One widely used instrument is the Santa Clara Strength of Religious Faith

Questionnaire (Plante and Boccaccini 1997). Since its development, the questionnaire has been applied to many populations across a variety of people, places, and times. Now it is your turn to ask the questions and learn more about the role of religion in everyday life by conducting your own small-scale study.

This Data Workshop asks you to examine the religiosity of a sample group of research participants. You will be designing a questionnaire, conducting interviews, and then analyzing the responses you get. Review the section on interviews in Chapter 2 to help you prepare.

Begin by choosing a population you wish to study. This could be other college students, family members, co-workers, or some other group; remember to ask for their consent to participate. You'll want to gather some basic demographic background from each respondent. Consider such variables as race and ethnicity, class, national background, gender, and/or age of your sample. Researchers have documented variations of religiosity across different social groups. There are many possibilities for comparing and contrasting within or across categories. Because this is only a pilot study, the number of people you can interview will necessarily be small. You'll probably have to draw from what is referred to as a "convenience sample" of respondents, rather than using a more scientific random sample. How many people you include in your sample may also depend on how many questions you'd like to ask each respondent.

For this study you will be conducting one-on-one interviews. You will need to record your interviewees' answers, either by taking notes or by digital means. Your questionnaire is likely to have both closed- and open-ended questions. The kinds of questions you ask may also help determine the number of questions to include. Closed-ended questions typically have yes or no answers, which can be quickly noted, but you can also ask your respondents to elaborate. Your questionnaire may also include some open-ended questions, which respondents can answer in a variety of ways. Whatever kinds of questions you include, you'll need to consider the total length of the interview and just how much talk you can easily transcribe.

To help you with the design of your questionnaire, you can start by choosing from the following list of questions (adapted from Lewis et al. 2001). You may want to modify the order or wording of the questions, or delete some. And definitely try adding some questions of your own. Questions about religious affiliation, membership, and attendance at services can tell you something about an individual's level of commitment, but there are many other ways to measure religiosity, both extrinsic and intrinsic. You can create questions that measure people's concrete practice of religion and their abstract sense of what religion means to them. Once you've finalized the questions, you're ready to conduct the interviews.

* Are you affiliated with any religion?

* Are you affiliated with any particular sect or denomination?

* Do you belong to a church, synagogue, temple, or other place of worship?

* How often do you attend religious services?

* Do you participate in other church-related activities?

* How often do you read or study sacred texts or scripture?

* How often do you pray or meditate or engage in some other religious practice?

* How important is your relationship with God [or another religious figure]?

* To what extent is your religious faith important to you?

* To what extent do you consider your religious faith to be an important part of who you are as a person?

* Do you look to your faith as a source of comfort?

* Do you look to your faith as a source of inspiration?

* Do you look to your faith as providing meaning, direction, or purpose in your life?

* Does your faith affect your relationships with other people?

* Does your faith influence your decisions in regard to family, friends, work, school, or other aspects of your life?

* How has your commitment to your religion changed over time?

After gathering data through interviews, you'll want to begin to analyze your findings. Sift through your notes or transcripts and compile the answers to various questions. See what kinds of patterns you can find—similarities, differences, comparisons, and contradictions. What do you think these data reveal about the role of religion in your subjects' lives?

There are two options for completing this Data Workshop:

PREP-PAIR-SHARE Design a questionnaire and conduct interviews with a small sample from your population (perhaps three or four people). Look over their answers, make notes about any preliminary results, and bring them with you to class. Get together with one or two other students and discuss your findings. Look for similarities and differences in both your own findings and those of your discussion group members. See if you can identify any patterns that emerge from the data gathered by the entire group.

DO-IT-YOURSELF Design a questionnaire and conduct interviews with a small group of respondents from your sample (perhaps six or seven people). Write a two- to three-page essay describing the interview research process and analyzing your findings, attaching any notes or transcripts to your paper. How do your findings confirm or refute any hypotheses you might have had before beginning the study? What does your data suggest about the role of religion in society?

A Secular Society?

The separation of church and state is a time-honored (and controversial) American principle, established by the founders to preserve freedom of religion—one of the main reasons Europeans came to North America. As important and central as this principle is to American politics, we haven't always been able to maintain it in practice. Consider the dollar bill with the motto "In God We Trust." Witness the 2003 controversy over displaying the Ten Commandments in public buildings in Alabama, or President George W. Bush's allocation of federal monies to "faith-based" charitable organizations. Even the school-voucher debate centers on this issue: should public education funds be used to send children to private schools, many of which are religious? And, of course,

Separation of Church and State? This portrait of Jesus hung in the main hallway of Bridgeport High School, a public school in Bridgeport, West Virginia, for more than three decades. In 2006, the American Civil Liberties Union filed a lawsuit to have the portrait removed.

specifically Christian values and practices shape the everyday life of all Americans—Christian or not. Whether we are a **secular** society, one that separates church and state, is a complicated issue.

In both government and private industry, schedules are organized around Christian holidays with little or no attention paid to religious holidays of other groups. Schools, banks, and government agencies are all closed on Christmas Day, even though this holiday is not observed by more than 15 percent of Americans. Your university's system of vacation periods is likely organized around both Christmas and Easter—important Christian holidays. Universities rarely give days off for Yom Kippur or Passover, two very important Jewish holidays. This means that Jewish students and staff who observe these holidays must go through the hassle of making special arrangements to compensate for classes or meetings missed. They may have to use valuable vacation or sick time or even forfeit credit for exams given on that day. Eid al Fitr, the last day of the Muslim holy month of Ramadan, calls for a variety of special celebrations that schools and employers rarely recognize; those who wish to observe this holiday must make their own arrangements as well.

RELIGION IN THE WHITE HOUSE The only official eligibility requirements for the job of U.S. president are that the person be thirty-five years old, a natural-born U.S. citizen, and a resident in the United States for at least fourteen years. There is no requirement that the president be a man, though all of them have been, or a Christian, but all of them have been. It seems that an unspoken requirement for the presidency includes being a man of Christian faith, with Protestant Christianity being preferred. The only Catholic to hold the office, John F. Kennedy, endured a storm of controversy during his 1960 campaign, when critics feared that America would be ruled by the Pope if Kennedy was elected.

More recently, Republican Mitt Romney's Mormonism simmered beneath the surface of the 2012 presidential campaign. While many Americans are either ignorant about or uncomfortable with the LDS faith and its historic associations with things like polygamy and racism, Romney's advisors managed to minimize Mormonism as an issue while focusing on moral and social issues that appealed to his largely Christian Republican base. Meanwhile, in 2012, 17 percent of Americans continued to believe that President Barack Obama was a Muslim, a rumor that may have derived from his middle name, Hussein, despite his clear affiliation as a Christian (Pew Forum on Religion and Public Life 2012b). About half of adults thought he was Christian, while more than 30 percent said they didn't know his religion. The view that Obama is Muslim was more widespread among his political opponents than it was among supporters (Pew Forum on Religion and Public Life 2012b).

Given the United States' explicit constitutional commitment to the separation of church and state, it seems we shouldn't be concerned about a president's religious affiliation (or lack thereof). But it matters. The administration of George W. Bush was particularly notable for the controversy it stirred over the influence of religion on the leader of the free world. President Bush was famously quoted by former aide David Frum as saying that "I had a drinking problem . . . [and] there is only one reason I am in the Oval Office and not in a bar. I found faith. I found God" (Goodstein 2004). Bush managed, to some degree, to placate opponents concerned with the separation between church and state. His public comments on the subject were consistently conciliatory and inclusive. In his first press conference after winning reelection in 2004, Bush was asked by a reporter, "What do you say to those who are concerned about the role of a faith they do not share in public life and in your policies?" (Noah 2004). The president answered:

> I will be your president regardless of your faith, and I don't expect you to agree with me necessarily on religion. As a matter of fact, no president should ever try to impose religion on our society. A great—the great—tradition of America is one where people can worship the way they want to worship. And if they choose not to worship, they're just as patriotic as your neighbor. That is an essential part of why we are a great nation. (Noah 2004)

Bush was one of many presidents who were advised by the unofficial White House chaplain, the Reverend Billy Graham.

Religion and the White House President Barack Obama prays alongside churchgoers during a Sunday morning service at the Harvest Cathedral Chapel in Macon, Georgia.

IN RELATIONSHIPS

Can a Relationship with God Improve Your GPA?

Sociologists don't usually address questions like "Is there a God?" as these are not questions to which empirical, scientific methods can be applied. It is impossible to prove that God exists (at least by the rules of science)—and it is equally impossible to prove that God doesn't exist. Social scientists can't prove or deny God's existence, but they are interested in studying the important role that religion and spirituality play in our everyday lives. In fact, sociologists have been addressing that question since the discipline first began.

From a sociological perspective, religion serves many functions. It is the basis for community and it permeates many of our social institutions. It is woven into the social fabric and our personal lives. In many cultures, religious participation is a requirement of group membership (Caughey 1984, 1999). On an individual level, members may be expected to demonstrate their belief by engaging in a personal relationship with God (or gods, saints, or spirits). Members are encouraged to work on that relationship through a variety of practices. Prayer and meditation are central to many faiths, and an important means of communicating with a higher power. In many ways a relationship with God resembles our face-to-face interactions in the real world. Many believe that they can talk with and listen to God and that a close relationship brings many of the same kinds of comfort and support that we get from family and friends (Sharp 2010).

Much contemporary research examines religiosity, or the rates at which people engage in religious and spiritual beliefs and practices. Recently, there has been growing concern about the declining rates of religiosity among young people attending college. It raises many questions about what happens over the course of a student's academic life. Does college pose a threat to one's religious or spiritual beliefs, or can it serve to deepen them? Does higher education interfere with a relationship to a higher power or actually make it stronger?

While young Americans as a group are becoming increasingly secular, some researchers have found that there is a renewed engagement with religion and spirituality among undergraduate college students across the United States.

College students today can be almost evenly divided into three groups according to their worldviews, with 32 percent identifying as religious, 32 percent identifying as spiritual, and another 28 percent identifying as secular (Kosman and Keysar 2013). Although some religious behavior (such as attendance at religious services) declines during college, overall spirituality among students increases significantly. Such spiritual growth seems to benefit students in many ways.

A major nationwide longitudinal study on spirituality in higher education was recently completed by researchers at UCLA (Astin et al. 2010). They collected data from more than 14,500 undergraduates attending 136 colleges and universities. Among the measures they developed were five qualities of spirituality: equanimity (the capacity to maintain a sense of calm centeredness), spiritual quest (the active search for answers to life's big questions), ethic caring (a sense of care or compassion for others), charitable involvement (a lifestyle that includes service to others), and an ecumenical worldview (a global perspective that transcends egocentrism and ethnocentrism).

The researchers found that spiritual growth has a positive effect on traditional college outcomes such as academic performance, psychological well-being, leadership skills, and satisfaction with college. Study abroad programs, interdisciplinary coursework, service learning, and other forms of civic engagement contribute to spiritual growth by exposing students to new and diverse people, cultures, and ideas. Students also grow in global awareness and caring and are more committed to social justice. Students who are also actively engaged in some form of "inner work," such as self-reflection, contemplation, prayer, or meditation, show the greatest growth in spirituality. Inner work helps facilitate intellectual self-confidence and psychological well-being, and it is even shown to have a positive effect on students' grade point averages.

Spirituality is an important part of many students' lives, and it can also enhance their college experience in many ways. So yes, a relationship with God—if it leads you to spiritual growth—really can improve your GPA.

Graham advised every president from Dwight D. Eisenhower up through George W. Bush on matters of state and personal spirituality. With a man of the cloth as such a high-profile presidential adviser, and with Christianity as an unstated requirement for holding presidential office, are we really a secular society? Are church and state truly separate? Is every person equally free to practice his or her faith in American society?

Religion: The Micro-Macro Link

Religion is a source of conflict and misunderstanding but also a wellspring of comfort and meaning for many. Whether you are Catholic or Methodist, Jewish, Muslim or Buddhist, a Mormon or Wiccan or Scientologist, you share common experiences with others in the practice of your religion, no matter how different your belief systems and rituals may be. A sense of meaning, a set of rules and guidelines by which to live your life, a way of explaining the world around you, a feeling of belonging and group identity—sociologists recognize these patterns across religious traditions.

Religion is yet another social institution that helps us see the link between macro-level social structure and micro-level everyday experience. Religious beliefs, practices, and prejudices can inflame global conflicts and resolve them and can shape national political life in observable and unexamined ways. At the same time, religion is integral in the everyday lives of many Americans who find comfort and kinship in their religious beliefs and practices. "In God We Trust" is the motto for both our nation and many of its people, no matter what their faith.

CLOSING COMMENTS

All three of the social institutions examined in this chapter—politics, education, and religion—are part of the structure of our society, and they are linked in a variety of ways. For example, state and federal policy decisions about school vouchers affect individual students and neighborhood public schools, and they benefit parochial schools and the religious institutions that run them. Politics, education, religion, and other social institutions influence your everyday life in ways you may not have realized. We hope you have gained greater awareness of how these social institutions shape your life as a member of society—and how you can influence them as well. Your vote changes the political landscape; your role as a student influences the culture of your college and university; your membership in a religious congregation affects the lives of fellow worshippers. Institutions affect individuals, but individuals can influence institutions as well—this is the essence of the sociological imagination and the macro-micro link.

Everything You Need to Know about Social Institutions

> **"** Social institutions such as school, religion, and government organize our group life and constrain our everyday lives. By studying them, we can examine connections between the individual and society. **"**

THEORIES OF SOCIAL INSTITUTIONS

* **Structural functionalism:** social institutions provide critical functions and help to maintain order

* **Conflict theory:** social institutions represent the interests of those in power and thus create and maintain inequalities

* **Symbolic interactionism:** social institutions are created through individual participation

REVIEW

1. Were you eligible to vote in the last election? If so, did you? If you didn't vote, why not? The voting rates for voting-eligible U.S. citizens ages eighteen to twenty-four are much lower than those for senior citizens; why do you think that is?

2. Much of this chapter's discussion of education focuses on elementary and high schools. Do you think the same theories apply to college classrooms? Have you experienced a hidden curriculum since you left high school?

3. There is some debate over how to measure religiosity: Should it be based on how spiritual you feel or on how often you attend religious services? Which way do you think is more valid? Why? Can you think of a better way than either of these?

Voter turnout in the 2012 Election by Educational Level

■ **Total Citizen Population**　　■ **Reported Voters**

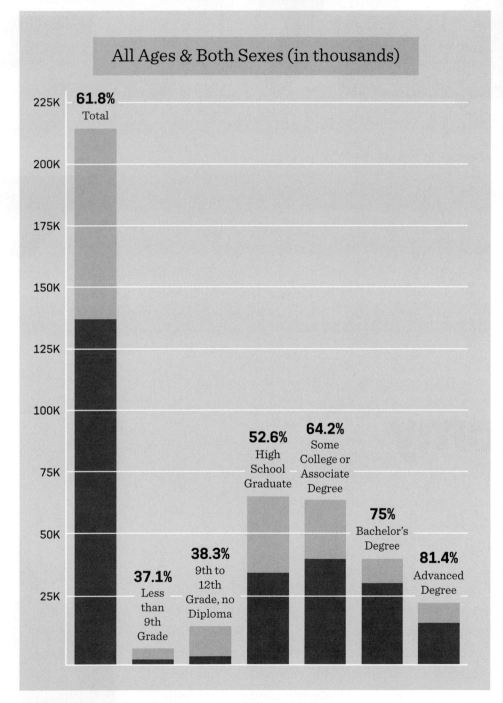

All Ages & Both Sexes (in thousands)

61.8%
Total

52.6%
High School Graduate

64.2%
Some College or Associate Degree

75%
Bachelor's Degree

81.4%
Advanced Degree

37.1%
Less than 9th Grade

38.3%
9th to 12th Grade, no Diploma

225K
200K
175K
150K
125K
100K
75K
50K
25K

SOURCE: U.S. Census Bureau 2012, "Voting and Registration in the Election of November 2012 — Detailed Tables"

EXPLORE

Happy Interdependence Day!

The idea of interdependence is that everyone and everything is connected. Your personal successes and failures may also be the result of social systems like education and politics. Visit the Everyday Sociology Blog to read more on how interdependence can change society.

http://wwnPag.es/trw410

CHAPTER 11

The Economy and Work

The history of one family's jobs and occupations can provide some sociological insight into the development of work and the economy over time. For example, Dr. Ferris's great-grandfathers included a military man in Missouri, a tailor in Texas, and a stonemason and a butcher, both in a tiny mountain village in Lebanon. Despite their geographical and cultural distance from one another, they all were involved in occupations that have existed since ancient times and were still common in the late nineteenth century. Their various jobs represent much of the range of possible jobs in agricultural societies. Some people were skilled craftsmen, some were soldiers, and most others farmed. While women sometimes

helped with the farming or other types of work, their primary task was homemaking and child-rearing.

Moving up a generation in the family tree, you can see that in the first half of the twentieth century, Ferris's grandparents were involved in military and service work, with some industrial labor experience as well. One grandfather emigrated from Lebanon to Massachusetts, where he worked in the local brass foundry. This kind of hard physical labor in a stiflingly hot factory was the norm during the industrial era. While he worked at the foundry, his wife secretly worked at a local laundry, hiding her earnings from him. These secret earnings later helped them afford to take a step up in the occupational hierarchy: they bought a restaurant and ran it successfully. Ferris's other grandfather was an army doctor who was stationed all over the United States and the world. His wife followed, making a home with the children wherever they were stationed. She served as a hostess and provided crucial support for her husband's career, which was customary in the early twentieth century.

By the time Ferris's parents started working in the second half of the twentieth century, her mother was part of a new generation of women who were far more likely than their own mothers to pursue a college education and a career outside the home, even while raising children. Both of Ferris's parents earned advanced degrees (mom an MA and dad a JD); as a writer and an attorney, respectively, they both engaged in service- and knowledge-based work. These areas experienced tremendous growth as the country moved into a postindustrial Information Age economy. Dr. Ferris, as a professor with a PhD, is also a knowledge worker—still just three generations away from great-grandparents without formal educations. Because of historical changes in gendered career expectations, she has enjoyed opportunities her grandmothers and great-grandmothers could never have imagined. And as we move further into the twenty-first century, developments in the economic and occupational landscape are likely to create a world in which Dr. Ferris's son, E. J., may hold a job that has not even been invented yet—perhaps in an entirely new, currently unimagined field.

Your own occupational family tree probably holds similar insights into the development of both world and U.S. economic systems over time. And this is no accident—as different as our families and their experiences may be, the patterns and trends in the kinds of work our relatives did can be a rich topic for sociological analysis. Our individual occupational choices are always made within the context of larger economic and social structures, both local and global. In this chapter, we will examine those structures and the experiences of individuals within them.

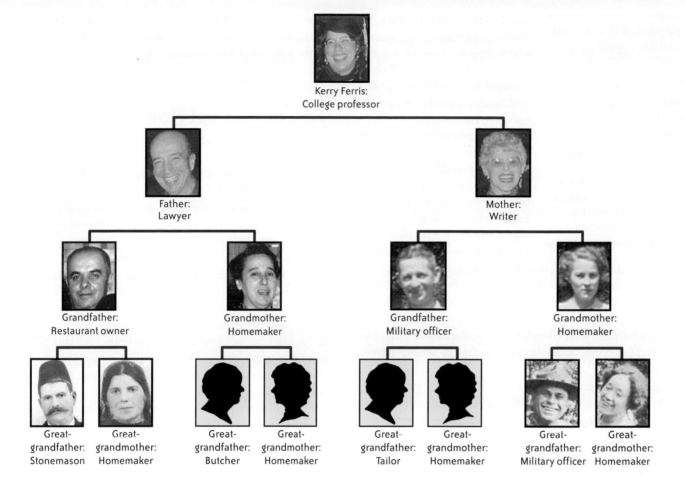

Kerry Ferris:
College professor

Father:
Lawyer

Mother:
Writer

Grandfather:
Restaurant owner

Grandmother:
Homemaker

Grandfather:
Military officer

Grandmother:
Homemaker

Great-
grandfather:
Stonemason

Great-
grandmother:
Homemaker

Great-
grandfather:
Butcher

Great-
grandmother:
Homemaker

Great-
grandfather:
Tailor

Great-
grandmother:
Homemaker

Great-
grandfather:
Military officer

Great-
grandmother:
Homemaker

HOW TO READ THIS CHAPTER

After reading this chapter, you should understand why work is a classic topic of sociological inquiry: it is a fulcrum point between the micro and the macro and a link between the individual and the social. You will see the connection between the everyday conditions of your life on the job and the larger structural changes related to history, technology, and the economic system in which you work. We want you to become familiar with the classic and more recent sociological studies in this area and how they have shaped our ways of thinking about the social world of economy and work. You will know something about the past and perhaps have more insight about the future and your place in it.

An economy deals not only with money but also with the production, distribution, and consumption of goods and services within a society. In this chapter, we look at issues regarding the economy, focusing specifically on work, because the economy shapes the types of work available as well as our patterns of working.

Historical and Economic Changes

We start with the history of U.S. economies, paying special attention to the agricultural, industrial, and postindustrial periods—and how new technologies have changed the nature of work in each of these periods.

The Agricultural Revolution

Perhaps the earliest form of economy in North America was found in pre-sixteenth-century Native American societies. An estimated 2 million to 10 million indigenous people inhabited the continent prior to colonization by Europeans. Some were hunting-and-gathering societies, which had to be highly mobile, relocating for food and weather conditions. The division of labor revolved around survival, with the men hunting animals or foraging for plant sources of food. The women, children, and elderly cooked, sewed, and did other tasks at the campsite. Some were horticultural societies based on the domestication of animals, farming, and generating a surplus of resources. They had more permanent settlements and a greater diversification of labor because different types of workers, such as farmers, craftspeople, and traders, were all necessary to the economy.

The **Agricultural Revolution** continued some of the social and economic trends that began with horticultural societies. Better farming and ranching techniques allowed larger groups to thrive and remain in one location for longer periods of time. The Agricultural Revolution lasted for many centuries, but in the eighteenth century, food production was greatly increased by new innovations in farming and animal husbandry. Among those developments were the invention of new types of plows and mechanized seed spreaders, new techniques of crop rotation and irrigation, and advancements in the selective breeding of livestock.

The agricultural economy that flourished in the early United States encouraged a stratified labor force. For large plantation owners to accumulate wealth from cotton or sugarcane crops, they depended on cheap, plentiful labor. The division of labor fell largely along race, gender, and class lines (Amott and Matthaei 1996). In the pre–Civil War era, many of the plantations of the South that were owned by whites were farmed by black slaves brought from Africa (Davis 2001). Poor

Slaves at Work in the Field The Southern agricultural economy depended on slave labor to grow cotton and tobacco.

white people sometimes owned small farms or worked as tenant farmers or sharecroppers. White men were usually owners of land and small businesses, while white women were usually household managers.

The Industrial Revolution

The **Industrial Revolution** was a time of rapid technological, social, and economic change that almost completely transformed life in modern times—a radical break from the past, disrupting social patterns that had been relatively stable for centuries. When we discuss the Industrial Revolution in this section, we will look at the technological innovations of the era and how they changed American society and culture, the economy, and the lives of workers.

The Industrial Revolution began in England with the invention of the steam engine in 1769, which was first used to power machinery, starting with the manufacture of textiles. By the end of the eighteenth century, steam-powered factories had spread to the United States and other nations (Hughes and Cain 1994). With more mechanized machinery such as the cotton gin, the American economy moved from manual labor to machine manufacturing. Even farming would change with the introduction of mechanical plows and reapers. The nineteenth century brought steam-powered ships and railways, the internal combustion engine, electrical power generation, and new tools and appliances. By the end of the 1800s, the modern corporation had emerged—a business that could manage a range of activities across geographic regions. A successful corporation not only manufactured products but also managed all aspects of marketing and distribution.

With the shift to a manufacturing economy, vast numbers of people migrated into cities from rural areas in search of work. There was a great influx of immigrants, primarily from Europe, who provided a steady source of cheap, easily exploitable labor. By 1910, more than 13 million people living in the United States were foreign born (Gibson and Lennon 2001). Densely populated neighborhoods sprang up to accommodate the masses, housing was often substandard, and many families lived in poverty. Employment in manufacturing meant that people no longer worked in or around their homes as artisans or craftsmen, as many had in the past, but that they went off into the industrial districts of large cities to work in factories. Wage labor replaced the household subsistence model of the agricultural society.

The industrial economy increased stratification of the workforce along class, race, and gender lines (Amott and Matthaei 1996). Wealthy white families owned the means of production, such as factories, energy sources, or land, and the financial institutions that supported the accumulation of wealth; the men were in the workplace, while the women ran the household. A middle class of educated, skilled workers emerged, often in managerial professions. Working-class white men now earned a "family wage" at the factory, while

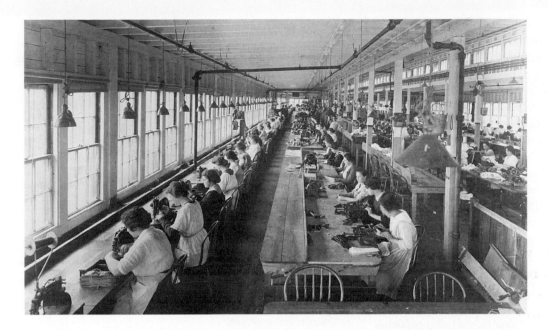

Women Working in a Shoe Factory Many factory jobs that were reserved for women paid meager wages and required working under dangerous conditions.

women worked without pay in the home. But for families that needed more than one income, women and even children joined the workforce. Poor women, immigrant women, and women of color increasingly performed domestic labor in white women's households (Amott and Matthaei 1996). But they also worked at factory jobs that were reserved for women, such as millwork and sewing in textile factories, for meager wages and under dangerous conditions.

The industrial economy revolved around the mass production of goods, aided by use of the assembly line in the manufacturing process, in which parts were added to a product in sequential order. The moving assembly line is attributed to Henry Ford, who in 1913 used it to manufacture automobiles in Detroit, Michigan. With assembly-line production, the process of manufacturing became not only more mechanized but also more routine driven. In contrast to the artisan mode, in which one worker or a team of workers would produce an item in its entirety from start to finish, on an assembly line each worker would do one or two specific tasks over and over again. Many workers disliked the assembly line because they never had the satisfaction of seeing the finished product, and they were also frustrated with the unsafe, exhausting working conditions.

The Industrial Revolution changed not only working conditions but also the lives of workers. The United States and most other industrializing nations experienced great population booms not only because of immigration but also because of discoveries in science and medicine that led to increased life expectancy and decreased infant mortality. Also, many more people had access to dependable food and water sources and some form of health care. Laws giving some protections to workers, such as child labor reforms, also emerged as an important aspect of the overall health of working populations. Although many factory workers were unskilled, the American workforce of the early twentieth century was becoming better trained and more educated than that of any previous generation.

The growing population of the United States became a market for the mass-produced goods it was manufacturing. Because industrial workers no longer worked on farms and in the home producing their own food and clothes, they had to purchase those items with the wages they earned for their labor. They also had to buy services, such as health care and child care, from other providers. Other changes in everyday life were also part of the Industrial Revolution: Americans were introduced to new forms of communication with the invention of the Morse telegraph in 1837 and the telephone in 1876, and they traveled more easily across the country with the completion of the transcontinental railroad in 1869.

The Information Revolution

The **Information Revolution** is the most recent of the historical and technological changes that have led to new economic and working conditions in the United States and around the world. Also referred to as the Digital Revolution, Digital Age, or Postindustrial Age, it is expected to bring about as dramatic a transformation of society as the revolutions that preceded it (Castells 2000). We may not recognize how truly radical this change is, partly because we are at the edge of a revolution that will continue to evolve over our lifetimes.

The Information Revolution began in the 1970s with the development of the microchip or microprocessor used in computers and other electronic devices. The capacity and speed of microprocessors have continued to increase according to Moore's

INFORMATION REVOLUTION the recent social revolution made possible by the development of the microchip in the 1970s, which brought about vast improvements in the ability to manage information

Law (doubling every eighteen months to two years). When computers were coupled with the introduction of the Internet in the early 1990s and became more affordable, they were soon widely used. Other technologies associated with the Information Revolution include computer networking and all types of digital media, satellite and cable broadcasting, and telecommunications. These technologies have become a ubiquitous part of everyday life in the twenty-first century.

The Information Revolution brought a profound shift from an economy based on the production of goods to one based on the production of knowledge and services (Castells 2000). Of course, the United States is still involved in agriculture and manufacturing, but these are shrinking parts of our economy. As American companies compete on the global market, they may find it more profitable to move production overseas to exploit cheaper materials and labor in developing countries. According to the Department of Labor, the U.S. economy currently consists of ten "supersectors" (or areas in which people work) that fall under two broad categories: goods-producing industries and service-providing industries (U.S. Bureau of Labor Statistics 2015e). Fully two-thirds of the supersectors deal in knowledge or service work.

Supersectors of the U.S. Economy:

Construction

Education and Health Services

Financial Activities

Information

Leisure and Hospitality

Manufacturing

Natural Resources and Mining

Other Services

Professional and Business Services

Trade, Transportation, and Utilities

Knowledge work is done by anyone who works primarily with information or who develops and uses knowledge in the workplace (Drucker 1959, 2003). For such workers, information and knowledge are both the raw material and the product of their labor. Knowledge workers produce with their heads rather than with their hands. They create value in the economy through their ideas, judgments, analyses, designs, and innovations. Some examples of knowledge work include advertising, engineering,

KNOWLEDGE WORK work that primarily deals with information; producing value in the economy through ideas, judgments, analyses, designs, or innovations

SERVICE WORK work that involves providing a service to businesses or individual clients, customers, or consumers rather than manufacturing goods

Knowledge Workers The Information Revolution has shifted the economy away from manufacturing toward jobs that produce knowledge and provide services. Knowledge workers, like these employees at Google, create value through their ideas, judgments, and analyses.

marketing, product development, research, science, urban planning, and web design. Microsoft, a major software development company, further broadens this category to include anyone who works with the flow of information within businesses.

The service sector, or service industry, has also experienced tremendous growth in the postindustrial economy and employs a large number of American workers. **Service work** is done by anyone who provides a service to businesses or individual clients. Services may entail the distribution or sale of goods from producer to consumer (wholesaling and retailing), transformation of goods in the process of delivering them (the restaurant business), or no goods at all (massage therapy). All service work has a focus on serving and interacting with people. Service work can be found in such industries as banking, consulting, education, entertainment, health care, insurance, investment, legal services, leisure, news media, restaurants (including fast food), retailing, tourism, and transportation.

Some service work pays well, particularly at the management and executive levels, and in certain fields, such as banking, entertainment, and law; but much service sector employment is unstable, part-time or temporary, low paying, and often without such benefits as health care or retirement. Women, persons of color, and the poor are likely to be found in the service sector, thus perpetuating a lower-class status among those holding such positions (Amott and Matthaei 1996). Finally, unemployment rates for service sector workers remain higher than for knowledge workers (U.S. Bureau of Labor Statistics 2015b).

During the last recession, all sectors of the contemporary global economy experienced slowdown, but some were hit harder than others. The United States saw some of its highest unemployment rates since the Great Depression—close to 10 percent overall, with much higher rates in certain regions and industries. States like California and Nevada, previously the sites of seemingly nonstop growth, topped the unemployment numbers along with more traditional "rust-belt" states like Michigan and Illinois, as well as in the South in places like Georgia and North Carolina (U.S. Bureau of Labor Statistics 2012b). This was the result of a crash in the real estate and finance sectors, in addition to a drop in the construction and manufacturing trades. The recession also affected groups of workers accustomed to seeing themselves as immune to layoffs; older workers, the college educated, men, and whites saw higher rates of unemployment compared with other groups (Anderson 2009).

The postindustrial economy presents a very different social reality from the economy in other periods in history. The Information Revolution has changed almost every aspect of our lives and has become a part of many of our social institutions, including the economy and work. And with those changes have come new vulnerabilities, as the recent recession has demonstrated. In the next sections, we look at current world economic systems and the features of work in industrial and postindustrial settings.

DATA WORKSHOP
Analyzing Media and Pop Culture

The World of Work and Workers as Seen on TV

 FBI agent, judge, nurse, salesperson, newscaster, football coach, city council member, firefighter, private investigator, district attorney,

forensics expert, restaurant server, police officer, interior designer, school principal, military officer—these are just some of the jobs of characters you'd find on television's most popular dramas and sitcoms. As one of the most powerful sources of socialization in the lives of young people, television may contribute to our attitudes and ideas about the working world. Some jobs are totally absent from the TV landscape, some are shown as merely the butt of jokes, and others are made to seem impossibly hip, glamorous, and exciting. How real is any of it? Do the jobs on TV accurately reflect those jobs in real life? How do TV jobs compare with those of your family, friends, or acquaintances? What kinds of work-related issues do characters on television experience compared to those of real people in those same types of jobs or industries? What are the underlying messages of the depictions of work and workers on TV?

Sociologists who are interested in the media often ask such questions when comparing media content to the real world. This Data Workshop asks you to look at how fictionalized TV dramas and sitcoms portray jobs and the realities of working life. Your instructor might want you to do both of the exercises, or just one of the two. For either exercise you will be using existing sources and doing a content analysis of what you find. Refer to Chapter 2 for a refresher on this research method.

Exercise One: Working Conditions and TV Jobs
Examine the modern workplace as depicted on a current TV drama or sitcom. You'll want to take notes as you view one episode of the program, and you may need multiple viewings to collect your data. Look at the way characters perform their jobs in the show. Often workers are shown socializing or engaging in other kinds of personal activities while on the job. How much real work gets done?

Working in Prime Time How do television shows like *The Good Wife* (left) and *Silicon Valley* (right) represent working life?

And when characters are actually working, what aspects of that work are featured during the program? Often we see only the most unusual or glamorous aspects of work while the day-to-day routine or behind-the-scenes aspects rarely appear. Another dimension is how characters relate to their jobs and to their co-workers. Are they happy and fulfilled by the work they do? Do they complain about work, or experience other kinds of troubles with their jobs? How are power and resistance exercised in the workplace? Discuss your findings and assess the extent to which you believe the programs accurately reflect these professions in real life.

Exercise Two: Making a Living on TV

Examine the modern worker as depicted on a current TV drama or sitcom. View an episode of your chosen program and do a content analysis. Take written notes and describe as many of the details as possible about the character's work and lifestyle to answer the following prompts. What kinds of lessons do we learn about work and money from a TV show? We rarely get much information about how characters have gotten their jobs or what kind of training or experience got them to their positions. We also know very little about how hard they work or what they get paid. TV characters often seem to live extravagant lifestyles with little relationship between actual salaries and what they can afford to buy. Provide examples from the show and discuss the characters' standard of living. Could real people working comparable jobs afford the same lifestyle that the television characters seem to enjoy? Finally, how do television characters influence our own career goals and aspirations?

There are two options for completing this Data Workshop:

PREP-PAIR-SHARE Complete one or both of the exercises provided and follow the instructions as outlined. Bring your notes to class and get together with one or two students to discuss. (Your instructor may organize groups according to which exercises were completed.) Compare your findings with those of other members of the group. What conclusions do you share?

DO-IT-YOURSELF Choose one of the exercises provided (or your instructor may assign a specific exercise) and follow the instructions as outlined. Write a three- to four-page essay analyzing your findings. Make sure to attach your notes to the paper.

World Economic Systems

Capitalism, socialism, and communism are political-economic systems found around the world, often in overlapping forms. Each system can be conceived of in an idealized form, but in the real world most nations feature a mix of elements drawn from different systems.

Capitalism

Capitalism is an economic system based on the laws of free market competition, privatization of the means of production, and production for profit. In capitalism's purest form, values for goods and services are derived solely by the market relationship between supply and demand, and the resources necessary for production of goods and services are all privately owned. Owners, or capitalists, must employ workers to make products and perform services to generate a profit. Workers sell their labor to owners for a wage. The difference between the cost of production of a product or service and its price is profit to which the owner is entitled.

Capitalism tends to encourage class stratification. Because owners make profits, they can accumulate wealth. Workers are not in a structural position to get ahead financially. The ideologies of the free market, private property, and profit-seeking motives that define capitalism also shape institutions other than the economy. In capitalist nations, we see increasing privatization of such basic human services as water and transportation systems, health care, housing, and education. Thus, hospitals, public schools, prisons, and even government health and welfare agencies are increasingly taken over by private for-profit firms.

Under capitalism, workers must sell their labor to capitalists for a wage. They are encouraged to be productive and efficient or they will suffer reduced wages, decreased social welfare services such as health insurance and retirement, downsizing, and layoffs. Until recently, under the capitalist system in the United States, disgruntled workers could withhold their labor by striking. Now, under a transnational capitalist system, firms experiencing strikes may decide to move their operations overseas to countries where few workers have the right to strike.

A capitalist economy encourages efficiency through technological innovation, expansion of markets, and reduction of production costs. Thus, owners, in their efforts to seek efficiency, often seek to replace workers with new technologies, reduce social welfare spending, and cut labor costs. Therefore, workers are responsible for maintaining their own competitiveness. They must seek an education and/or skills to compete for jobs and maintain their competency over their working lifetimes. However, firms must also increase their competitiveness. They may move production operations to overseas sites where they can take advantage of deregulated environments and cheap labor costs.

Socialism

Socialism is an economic system based on collective ownership of the means of production, collective distribution of goods and services, and government regulation of the economy. Under socialism, there are no private for-profit transactions. In its purest form, socialism seeks to meet the basic needs of all citizens rather than encouraging profits for some individuals over others.

In a socialist system, the government rather than individuals owns—or at least regulates the ownership of—all businesses, farms, and factories, and profits are redistributed to the collective citizenry. This system encourages a collectivist work ethic with individuals theoretically working for the common good of all citizens. Citizens have access to such resources as health care, food, housing, and other social services to meet their basic needs. Unlike with capitalism, these services are an entitlement of all people, not just those who can afford them.

In socialism, a central and usually highly bureaucratic government regulates all aspects of the economy—ownership of resources and means of production, regulation of lending policies, interest rates, and currency values—as well as setting labor policies regarding such issues as parental leave, retirement, and the right to strike. Such intense regulation of the economy should reduce class inequalities and extreme poverty. In **communism**, the most extreme form of socialism, the government owns everything and all citizens work for the government and are considered equal, with no class distinctions. Socialism and communism, like capitalism, are theoretical or ideal types. Thus, no nations are purely socialist or communist. Even communist countries like Cuba or China are increasingly incorporating capitalist ideologies into their regimes.

Under socialism, workers are not at risk of extreme poverty and class division as they might be within a capitalist society. They are not as vulnerable as capitalist workers to being replaced by new technological innovations or the transnational movement of capital. However, they also do not enjoy the same consumption patterns that capitalist economies encourage. Socialism cannot provide capitalism's middle-class luxuries. Though class division is reduced, it is still present. Many socialist nations have political elites who enjoy a higher class of living than workers, and urban workers often benefit from having closer access to resources than rural workers. Further, reduction of class inequalities does not guarantee a reduction in other types of inequalities, such as racism, sexism, and ageism.

The Political Economy of the United States

To understand the political economy of various nations, think of capitalism and socialism as opposite ends of a continuum with nations placed along its span as being more capitalist or more socialist. The United States would undoubtedly lie closer to the capitalist side than Sweden would, but even U.S. capitalism is not a pure form.

While the United States is a capitalist nation, it also has socialist elements. Although capitalist businesses are privately owned, many benefit from government subsidies—grants, tax incentives, and special contracts. This is often referred to as "corporate welfare." In pure capitalism, such support would not exist. Government intervenes in the economy in other ways as well. Agencies such as the Federal Reserve Board often manipulate interest rates to stimulate the economy and control inflation. The Emergency Economic Stabilization Act of 2008 (also referred to as the "bailout bill") funneled more than $700 billion in government funds into banks, insurance companies, and other struggling private corporations in order to prop up the U.S. economy. Such government interventions constitute forms of socialism.

If the United States were purely capitalist, such institutions as education and health care would all be privately owned. However, most schools and many universities are publicly owned and operated. Even private universities usually get government subsidies. Health care is a trickier example, as much change is taking place in this arena. Medicare and Medicaid are long-standing federal programs that provide subsidized health care for the elderly and the poor. The Affordable Care Act of 2010, which rolled out in 2013–2014, ushered in more federally mandated health care coverage for millions of Americans. But many individuals and their employers still buy health insurance from for-profit insurers, and hospitals are often run for profit as well.

The government also spends millions of dollars annually for other general assistance or public aid programs for low-income families, including the Supplemental Nutrition Assistance Program (or SNAP—previously known as food stamps) and Temporary Assistance to Needy Families (TANF), often referred to as "entitlements." Thus, public services are available to meet some of the basic needs of the poor, elderly, and disabled; current and former armed forces personnel; and expectant mothers, infants, and children. Even our Social Security system, though partially funded through payroll taxes, is a public system providing retirement, survivorship, and disability benefits to eligible Americans. Debates continue about whether these populations' needs are satisfactorily met and whether it's the government's responsibility

CAPITALISM an economic system based on the laws of free market competition, privatization of the means of production, and production for profit

SOCIALISM an economic system based on the collective ownership of the means of production, collective distribution of goods and services, and government regulation of the economy

COMMUNISM a system of government that eliminates private property; it is the most extreme form of socialism, because all citizens work for the government and there are no class distinctions

to provide these services. Conservative politicians who periodically accuse their rivals of "socialist" tendencies may need to be reminded that things they enjoy every day—like streetlights and highway maintenance, police protection and firefighters, libraries and public schools—are all part of a system of centrally funded and regulated services they likely would not want to do without.

In theory, capitalism and socialism are opposites. In reality, there is no pure form of either capitalism or socialism; rather, nations typically have some features of both economic systems. Each system represents a different political ideology and economic reality for the people and workers in its economy. Economic systems evolve and change over time, and with them, the institution of work.

On the Nature of Work

Historical and technological changes leading to the Agricultural, Industrial, and Information revolutions fundamentally changed societies across several centuries. Societies have also adopted economic systems—capitalist, socialist, or a combination of both—that influence the types of work available, as well as our patterns of working.

Agricultural Work

As humans shifted from hunting-and-gathering communities, the ways in which we provisioned for ourselves began to change into what we now term agricultural work. Because there are no written works from this time period, the theories for this change are still debated. Agricultural work involves farming in small groups, families, or communities to grow the food and materials necessary to sustain oneself. During this period of labor, agricultural work meant that instead of buying flour at a store, you would sow, maintain, grow, and harvest wheat, and mill your own flour to then cook with in your home. This was in addition to weaving fabrics and caring for livestock. Anthropologists have contended that this shift from hunting and gathering to agricultural work increased the amount of labor individuals had to perform daily, which led to divisions of labor as well as to, eventually, slave labor in order to maintain larger and larger farms.

While agricultural work continues to be a large part of the U.S. and global labor market today, it looks significantly different as a result of industrial and postindustrial changes. For example, farmers now utilize technologies such as crop rotation, irrigation, mass production, and transportation. These elements are part of what is termed the "agribusiness" system, a marriage of agriculture and business, which refers to an integrated and interdependent system that includes the actual labor of farming as well as developing and selling farm equipment, food processing, marketing, and sales. Agricultural work, which was once a family or small community endeavor, is becoming less and less common as large agribusiness corporations such

The New Look of Agricultural Work A tomato breeder at Monsanto, a large agribusiness corporation, surveys his plants.

as Dow, DuPont, and Monsanto are able to push smaller farms out of the market. Agricultural work is also becoming increasingly stratified, with numerous hierarchical positions ranging from contract field-workers to farm executives (Holmes 2011).

Industrial Work

The spread of industrialism in the eighteenth and nineteenth centuries created "work" in the modern sense. Before the Industrial Revolution, most of the population engaged in agriculture, and the production of goods was organized around the household or small craft shops. In the industrial world, progress meant making machines that could produce more goods, more efficiently. Industrialization ushered in dramatic changes in how people worked.

The theories of Karl Marx are most often associated with the spread of industrialization, the capitalist economies that it produced, and the workers who toiled in its factories. His ideas provide a classic analysis of industrial work then and now. Much of what Marx asserted about class conflict and the circumstances of his time can apply with slight modification to capitalists and workers in the current industrial workplace.

According to Marx, the powerful have always exploited workers. As he asserted in *The Communist Manifesto*, "oppressor and oppressed stood in constant opposition to one another" in a perpetual struggle for economic resources, as all history "is the history of class struggles" (Marx 2001, p. 245). Economic exploitation is still present in a modern industrial economy, which allows for the accumulation of what is called "surplus value." The proletariat, or workers, in an industrial economy possess only one thing of economic value, and that is their time, which they sell to capitalists who own the means of production. Workers are paid for their time and labor, but their wages do not represent the full profit from the sale of the goods they produce. The sale of the goods not only covers the workers' wages and the expenses of running the factory but also generates additional revenue or surplus value, which then belongs to the owner.

Marx believed that workers in capitalist societies experienced alienation in many ways as a result of that system. Workers are alienated, Marx argued, because they are paid for their labor but do not own the things they produce. Unlike the farmers and craft workers of prior eras, industrial workers feel no sense of personal satisfaction in producing goods that are owned and controlled by someone else. Workers are also alienated from the process of work and their own creative activity. In traditional, precapitalist societies, many found joy and fulfillment in the process of production. But the worker under capitalism cannot feel that kind of satisfaction, and instead work is merely a means of making a living. The worker is alienated from other people, "the alienation of man from man," as Marx called it. Instead of cooperating, workers are forced to compete for scarce jobs and resources, turning other workers into rivals rather than partners. Workers are also alienated from the owners, as they recognize work as "an activity that is under the domination, oppression, and yoke of another man" (Marx 2001, p. 92).

Lastly, workers are alienated from what Marx referred to as "human essence." He believed that work should not be an unhappy burden taken up only out of the need to preserve physical existence. Instead, it is in our nature to seek out "work, vital activity, and productive life" (Marx 2001, p. 90). In his view, the essence of what it means to be human is to engage in free conscious activity, but capitalism degrades human labor to a mere means of survival. Marx acknowledged that all species must work to satisfy immediate physical needs, but only human beings "fashion things according to the laws of beauty" and find satisfaction in their work (p. 90). However, in a capitalist economy, this capacity is largely lost, as workers are alienated from their own human qualities.

Marx was describing work in the industrial era of the nineteenth century, but his analyses can apply to today's industrial workers as well. While some industrial firms may allow workers greater autonomy, dignity, and a personal stake in the process and goods they produce, many workers still toil in the same conditions of exploitation, alienation, and class struggle that Marx thought needed to change.

Postindustrial Work

Social theorists of the Industrial Age, like Karl Marx and his contemporaries, were unable to predict how technological innovation would transform work and the economy in the twentieth century and beyond. They could not foresee the transition to a postindustrial, service-oriented economy. Nor could they foresee the advent of easily available consumer credit, which has meant that workers can buy things they can't currently afford, materially improving their everyday lives without the hassle of starting a class revolution (even if it means they may never pay off their debts).

SERVICE WORK Service work, as the dominant form of employment in the postindustrial economy, often involves direct contact with clients, customers, patients, or students by those rendering the service, whether they are waiters, cashiers, nurses, doctors, teachers, or receptionists. In service work, situations arise when the worker's concerns, standards, and expectations conflict with those of clients. For example, an emergency for a client may be routine for a worker, as when your TV cable service goes out during a Green Bay Packers game and the customer service representative just keeps telling you they're working on it! As another example, you have a toothache, but the dentist doesn't have an open appointment until tomorrow. It's not the dentist who has to give you the bad news but the receptionist who must try to convince you to wait until then.

At the same time, service workers are subject to the scrutiny and critique of a manager or supervisor, so in addition to the potential clash between workers and clients, there are also issues of autonomy and control over their work. This can create distinctive tensions in service work interactions, and power relationships both subtle and more obvious are clearly present in this type of work.

One case study provides a classic—and highly personal—analysis of service work. Barbara Ehrenreich explored some of the issues of power and work in her book *Nickel and Dimed: On (Not) Getting By in America* (2001). As research for the book, Ehrenreich took minimum-wage service jobs in three different cities—as a waitress in Florida, a hotel maid in Maine, and a Walmart employee in Minnesota—and experienced the difficulties of trying to make ends meet and maintain her self-respect in low-wage service positions.

Ehrenreich found that service workers in these types of jobs are likely to be exploited in a number of ways. First, the low wages, lack of benefits, and grueling hours make it difficult to pay even the most basic bills. She discovered this herself

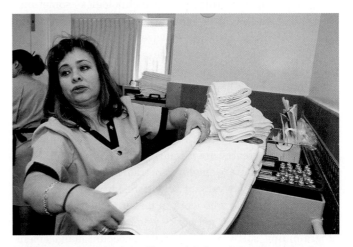

Nickel and Dimed Barbara Ehrenreich found that many service workers barely scrape by working long hours for minimum wage and no benefits. Because many service workers live paycheck to paycheck, they often have trouble asserting their rights or taking time off for illnesses because of fear of losing their jobs.

1) FROM PRODUCT LABOR
2) FROM FELLOW WORKERS   4) FROM OWN PRODUCTIVE
3) FROM HUMAN NATURE   ACTIVITY

when she couldn't scrape up enough money for a deposit on an apartment and ended up living in a sleazy hotel and getting her dinner from the local charity's food pantry. Her co-workers lived in flophouses, in their cars, or in small apartments crowded with family, friends, and strangers, and one ate nothing but a small bag of Doritos every day for lunch. They were fired for asserting their rights or for getting ill or injured, and they developed chronic health problems because of the stress and poor conditions under which they labored. And yet, they couldn't stop—they were all reliant on the next paycheck to get by (or not get by, as Ehrenreich argues), and so they had to endure abuse, exploitation, and all sorts of risks for the tenuous security of serving, scrubbing, and selling.

TELECOMMUNTING working from home while staying connected to the office through communications technology

You encounter these people every day—when you eat at a restaurant, shop at a "big box" retailer, or stay at a hotel—and you may even be one such person yourself. Ehrenreich argues that there's no way to "make it" under these circumstances, and her experiences illustrate this argument with chilling clarity.

Inequalities of power in service work have many sources—gender, race, age, and immigration status—and those with greater power (clients, managers) may take advantage without even realizing it. Ehrenreich reminds us that even in "respectable" forms of service work, exploitation is common. What about jobs that are illegal—such as prostitution or the work of undocumented farm laborers? These workers lack the legal protections that even Walmart employees or chain restaurant waitstaff have access to, and they may be subject to prosecution and punishment merely for doing their jobs.

KNOWLEDGE WORK In the twenty-first century knowledge or information work is increasingly common while manual labor is increasingly rare (Tapscott 1997). The massive changes wrought by information technologies—sometimes referred to as the "new economy"—have transformed the nature of work again in ways that are not yet fully understood (Kellner 2001). While many of these technologies purport to increase productivity and save time, the average worker is also working more hours in a week than her predecessor in the pre–Information Age workplace.

The majority of the workforce in the United States now holds jobs that involve working with information, and most new jobs being created are primarily within this sector. Many knowledge workers are employed in traditional fields as teachers, accountants, lawyers, or scientists, but knowledge work also includes people who work in newer areas such as wireless communications, network systems analysis, computer programming, software development, account management, information security, and database administration.

Another important feature of the Information Age workplace is greatly diminished importance of place. This phenomenon has been called the "death of distance" (Caincross 1995).

Work that can be done on a computer can be done from any location, as networking technologies make workers' location almost irrelevant to their ability to get the work done and to work with others (Poster 2002).

A look at telecommuting reveals more about the nature of knowledge work. More and more workers are doing telework or **telecommuting**. About 10 percent of American workers (excluding the self-employed and volunteers) telecommute at least part-time (U.S. Census Bureau 2012a). They stay at home rather than commute to the office, and they are connected to their workplace through communications technology.

Supporters claim that telecommuting has many benefits for the worker, the business, and society at large. Employees get flexible work schedules. Traffic delays, parking problems, and time wasted commuting don't exist for the telecommuter. Businesses get increased productivity and fewer sick days when they allow employees to telecommute. Although many employers worry that allowing employees to work from home would reduce accountability, some believe that the opposite is true. In traditional office environments, the only measure of employee value is the number of hours present in the office, regardless of what gets done, whereas telecommuters must demonstrate their accomplishments more concretely. According to studies, telecommuting decreases workplace distractions and boosts worker productivity; telecommuters often work longer hours and are more efficient than their in-office peers and co-workers (Wisenberg Brin 2013).

Telecommuting has also made it easier for a wider range of employees to participate in the workforce; this helps many groups, including single parents, seniors, or workers with disabilities, stay employed full-time (Tugend 2014). While telecommuting is on the rise, it has not been universally embraced. In an interesting reversal to this trend, Internet giant Yahoo restricted telecommuting in 2013 and asked many employees to return to the office. Best Buy followed suit, making it seem as if telecommuting was losing favor among big employers. Still, research suggests that telecommuting will continue to grow. If managed effectively, it has the potential to yield happier and more productive employees (O'Leary 2013).

As technology develops, debates remain about the positive and negative aspects of physically and geographically separating workers from one another. Some suggest that new technologies will actually increase the need for face-to-face contact and tightly knit workplaces. For example, workers who write code for computer software can do so anywhere they have a computer and instantly send the results to those who will package and market the software, but software companies are still the most geographically concentrated of any industry. Microsoft, the world's largest software company, refers to its home office in Redmond, Washington, as "the campus" and has gone to great lengths to make it an appealing place for employees precisely because the company still wants them at the same location in order to foster greater creativity and group cohesion. Other tech firms are concentrated

IN RELATIONSHIPS
The Value of Break Time

f the model employee is someone who is supposed to be singularly focused on his or her job, it might seem like a contradiction to say that taking breaks or socializing with others at work is actually a sign of a healthy work environment. According to recent research, however, coffee breaks should not be considered a waste of time or productivity; instead, they have important social as well as financial value for organizations (Stroeback 2013). Other studies have confirmed that the social bonds that are formed when sharing coffee breaks help create a positive group climate, which, in turn, has the potential to increase productivity within the organization (Waber et al. 2010). The proverbial coffee break is a subject that sociologists take very seriously.

Let's face it, work can be stressful. Whether you work in an office, in retail, or on a factory floor, the workplace is fraught with difficulties and demands. Coffee breaks are an important social practice within workplace culture, as they provide a crucial coping mechanism for workers. The kind of casual, informal encounters that take place during breaks in the workday are essential in promoting the professional and personal well-being of employees. This is especially true of difficult or stressful jobs. One study found that job stress was relieved by forming "communities of coping" during coffee breaks with co-workers.

Collegial relations are created during coffee breaks because "when having a coffee break, employees talk about themselves, their lives, and each other with symbols and stories not necessarily related to work relationships or organizational membership" (Stroeback 2013, p. 383). These communities provide a space for social interaction with fellow employees, allowing them to share both professional opinions and personal frustrations with their work. Co-workers thus nurture a shared sense of investment in their jobs and in one another as a community.

This is not the first time that a sociologist has essentially endorsed goofing off with your co-workers. Play can be understood as resistance or opposition to work, but it is also an integral part of making work more enjoyable and, in the long run, more productive. Paradoxically, we find that play emerges in even the most harsh and strenuous work environments, demonstrated by Donald Roy in his classic study of "banana time," a short break in the day where workers use play to subvert the monotony of factory work (Roy 1959). If work is seen as unpleasant and painful, then workers must find ways to make it more tolerable. Roy, quoting social theorist Henri de Man, relates that even in a factory system, it was "psychologically impossible to deprive any kind of work of all its positive emotional elements . . . the instinct for play and the creative impulse" (Roy 1959, p. 160).

Play, then, helps workers reclaim and assert their identity when the workplace seems otherwise devoid of positive meaning. Informal interactions with co-workers while on the job are not just distractions from the workload at hand. Instead, these shared breaks turn out to be crucial to job satisfaction. And that's good for the employee and the company alike.

Banana Time Studies show that the "communities of coping" that workers form during coffee breaks reduce stress and promote a positive group climate.

The Postindustrial Office? To attract the best knowledge workers and to motivate them to work long hours, information and technology companies like Google and Microsoft go to great lengths to make the workplace appealing.

in areas such as California's "Silicon Valley" or Playa Vista ("Silicon South"). In the Information Age, more and more work requires the creative manipulation of knowledge, and for this workers need to brainstorm and share ideas in more interactive ways than technology currently allows. The tech industry suggests that even when work can be done anywhere, there will still be a real need to bring people together, at least some of the time.

The rise of new technologies may roll back many of the original effects of the Industrial Revolution. Manufacturing made it necessary for many people to work at the same location, causing the growth of cities and the decline of rural and small-town populations. However, with new technologies that let people work from anywhere, perhaps telecommuting will cause cities to shrink again as more people will be able to live without reference to the company that employs them. Small towns are now offering an attractive alternative to outsourcing. High-tech jobs are beginning to relocate to rural areas, where companies are finding it cheaper to do business and more attractive for their employees (Pinto 2005). It's possible that information technology may one day reunite the worlds of work and home that the Industrial Revolution tore asunder.

Resistance Strategies: How Workers Cope

Individuals and groups cope with their working conditions in a variety of ways called **resistance strategies**. These are tactics that let workers take back a degree of control over the conditions of their labor and feel that they have some sense of autonomy

even in the face of dehumanizing, alienating constraints imposed by the terms and demands of their employment.

Individual resistance can range from the fairly benign, such as using work time to surf the web, to the truly dangerous, such as sabotaging the assembly line. More often, individual resistance may be simply personalizing the workspace with photos or daydreaming on the job as a type of escape. Collective forms of resistance that seek solutions to shared workplace problems include union organizing and membership, strikes, walkouts, and work stoppages.

This discussion begins with an examination of individual resistance strategies within service work. We bring Max Weber's theory on bureaucracy into the present to see how workers today are coping with the constraints of those organizations. Last, we look at collective resistance strategies—union organization, both past and present.

Individual Resistance: Handling Bureaucracy

Bureaucratic organizations are found in almost every sector of the economy. In Weber's theory of bureaucracies, he highlighted the rational, impersonal, and coldly efficient nature of this form of social organization (refer to Chapter 5 for a review). Workers in highly bureaucratic organizations often feel the lack of autonomy in their everyday work lives. Autonomy is the ability to direct one's individual destiny—to have the power to control the conditions of one's labor—and this is generally lacking for people who work in highly structured, rule-bound, and depersonalized environments. Their daily tasks are structured by external forces; for example, the pace of the assembly line is decided for them and they cannot slow it down or speed it up if they need to take a break or want to finish work early.

In many corporate settings, employees at all levels are under various types of surveillance: electronic key cards monitor their comings and goings, cameras record their activities, computer transactions are screened, and phone calls are recorded. In retail sales, workers' interactions with customers are often scripted, so that even what they say to others is outside their control. Not only is there a lack of autonomy, but there is also a lack of individuality in these workplaces. Workers are treated more like robots than people. Unlike a robot, however, human workers can resist and undermine the bureaucratic constraints that limit their autonomy in the workplace—and they do so in a wide variety of ways.

Robin Leidner's study *Fast Food, Fast Talk* (1993) provides an in-depth look at individual resistance strategies in the workplace. The study focused on McDonald's employees and the routinized nature of their interactions with customers. Under the golden arches, every contact between the counter staff and the hungry consumer is strictly scripted, seemingly with no room for improvisation or creativity. Or is there?

McDonald's workers are trained to interact with customers using "The Six Steps": greeting, taking orders, assembling food, presenting it, receiving payment, and thanking them for their business. As monotonous as these steps are, workers don't necessarily resent routinization—it helps them do their jobs effectively. And some workers, like this woman, improvise on the steps, personalizing them in tiny but still noticeable ways:

> Just do the Six Steps, but do it in your own way. It's not like you have to say "Hi, welcome to McDonald's." You can say, "Hi, how are you doing?" or "Good morning," "Good afternoon," "Good evening," things like that. (p. 138)

Leidner observed that there were limits within which workers could

> use the script as a starting point and inject [their] own personality into the interactions. Thus, some window

Fast Food, Fast Talk In her study of restaurant employees, Robin Leidner looks at the ways that workers subvert the scripts that McDonald's requires them to follow when interacting with customers.

> workers joked or chatted with customers and tried to make the exchanges enjoyable for both parties. This stance implied an assertion of equality with customers and a refusal to suppress the self completely. (p. 190)

Leidner proposes that submitting to scripted interactions all day long suppresses the real self and that this sort of tightly controlled work environment can actually be damaging to the individual.

One of the functions of McDonald's service script is to regulate the power relationship between customer and worker: customers' demands can be delivered with all types of attitude, but workers must always serve customers with a smile. The script constrains workers' responses. If they have rude or even abusive customers, they must still stick to the script:

> You have to take their crap. [Laughs.] I'm not the type of person to say, "OK, have it your way." I mean, I have to admit, I'm tempted to backtalk a lot. That gets me in a lot of trouble. So I mean, when a customer's rude to me I just have to walk away and say, "Could you take this order please, before I say something I'm not supposed to say?" (p. 133)

If they do pervert the script or talk back to a rude customer, workers may be inviting a reprimand from their supervisor. But they are also engaging in resistance, asserting their own identities in the face of the depersonalizing routine. They are being active rather than passive, controlling the interaction rather than being controlled by it. They are asserting their own autonomy on the job, and it is apparently worth the risk.

It is difficult to think of a form of employment that would allow us to avoid bureaucratic constraints altogether. What types of resistance strategies have you used to regain a bit of independence and power in the workplace?

Collective Resistance: Unions

Although individual resistance strategies may provide a small measure of autonomy for some workers, they don't fundamentally change the working conditions or make permanent improvements to the terms of employment for all workers. That is why workers sometimes seek more lasting solutions to their problems by organizing to instigate collective resistance strategies. They do so by forming unions.

A **union** benefits workers in various ways and serves to counterbalance the power of employers. A labor union is an association of workers who come together to improve their economic status and working

> **UNION** an association of workers who bargain collectively for increased wages and benefits and better working conditions

IN THE FUTURE
A College Degree: What's It Worth?

Young Americans are told that a college degree is the best way to prepare for the job market. However, as far back as the 1970s, sociologists like Randall Collins have wondered whether college is always a sound investment. The usual argument in favor of higher education, even as it has become increasingly expensive, is that students are "investing in themselves." But this "investment" theory makes sense only if education is producing graduates who have skills and knowledge they can turn into higher wages. In *The Credential Society*, Collins argued that "job skills of all sorts are actually acquired in the work situation rather than in a formal training institution," while college only provides a credential (1979, p. 193). That credential can be enormously valuable, of course, but it's subject to inflation. As more and more people attend college, jobs that used to require high school diplomas start wanting bachelor's degrees, and so on. If Collins is correct, or even partially correct, sooner or later school will become a bad investment. Are we there yet? Experts disagree.

Many experts stand by higher education as a sound investment from which graduates reap good returns. Mary Daly, a senior vice president and researcher at the Federal Reserve Bank, says there is strong evidence that a college degree still gives people an "earnings advantage" (Bengali and Daly 2014). Research shows that the benefits of college in terms of higher earnings far outweigh the costs of obtaining a degree. Despite rising tuition costs and soaring student loan debt, college graduates still tend to receive about a 15 percent return rate on both bachelor's and associate's degrees (Abel and Dietz 2014). According to the Pew Research Center, a college degree is worth more than ever as the earnings gap between those with a college education and those without continues to widen. While high school graduates earn about $28,000 a year, college graduates with a bachelor's degree earn over $45,000 a year on average, making for an approximate $650,000 difference in earnings over a lifetime (Pew Research Center 2012a).

While supporters see these figures as zingers, there are some cracks in the consensus. The most obvious disclaimer when "investing" in a four-year college is the one attached to any investment: past returns are no guarantee of future returns. College was a terrific investment in the past, but will that still be true for those applying for admission today? Of course, a lot depends on just how much a particular college costs. For many students, it makes sense to attend a more affordable college, where it still takes about nine years after graduation to get to the breakeven point. For those students

New College Graduates Is the cost of a college degree still a smart investment?

paying higher tuition costs (say, at a private college), it may take closer to seventeen years to break even. Those figures presume that a student finishes a BA in four years. There's also the question of your college major. Students graduating in some fields, such as engineering or nursing, earn more than those majoring in psychology or art history. But any college degree, either two-year or four-year and regardless of major, still outearns a high school diploma. Such differences continue to accrue over a lifetime, making college look like a wise investment.

Still, there are some pretty high-profile dissenters. Nobel Prize–winning economist James Heckman believes the value of college depends on the student: "Even with these high prices, you're still finding a high return for individuals who are bright and motivated," but for those who aren't "college ready," then the answer is no, it's not worth it" (McArdle 2012). Another skeptic is Peter Capelli (2015), a professor of management at the University of Pennsylvania's Wharton School. He notes that many college graduates end up in jobs for which they don't need a degree and that some students would be better off financially by not going to college at all.

One of the most visible challenges to the idea that everyone should go to college comes from PayPal co-founder Peter Thiel. In 2011 he created the Thiel Fellowship, which pays twenty young people $100,000 for two years to pursue their ideas and business plans outside of school. With such notable college dropouts as Bill Gates or Mark Zuckerberg to point to, college might actually stand in the way of success for some people. Undoubtedly, though, such cases are the rare exception, making a college degree a pretty safe bet.

conditions. The two main types of unions are craft unions, in which all the members are skilled in a certain craft (e.g., the International Brotherhood of Carpenters and Joiners), and industrial unions, in which all the members work in the same industry regardless of their particular skill (e.g., the Service Employees International Union). Some unions are local with small memberships; others are large national organizations representing millions of workers.

When disagreements arise between management and employees, unionized workers may threaten to or actually stage a temporary walkout, work stoppage, or strike to express their grievance and force corporate managers and owners to negotiate. Often the striking workers will try to discourage the public from patronizing the businesses implicated in the labor dispute and try to prevent other, outside replacement workers (sometimes called "scab labor") from taking their jobs while they are out on strike. Union negotiations with employers about the terms of employment and working conditions are coordinated through collective bargaining, in which contract decisions between management and union representatives must be mutually agreed upon rather than imposed unilaterally.

Unions have a long history in the United States. At various times, they have existed on the margins of society and been vigorously opposed by capitalists and other free-market supporters. Unions in the nineteenth and early twentieth centuries were brutally suppressed by capitalists, and union organizers were frequently arrested and jailed. Often they were charged with conspiracy because attempts to form unions were illegal for much of U.S. history. The Typographical Union (representing print typesetters), which formed in 1852, is usually considered the "first durable national organization of workers" in the United States. By 1881, a number of smaller labor groups banded together to form the American Federation of Labor (AFL), eventually becoming the AFL-CIO (by adding the groups in the Congress of Industrial Organizations), still recognized as a powerful union today.

Unions of this era fought for a variety of workplace reforms. During the 1912 textile mill strikes in Lawrence, Massachusetts, the workers' slogan was "bread and roses," emphasizing their desire for something more than wages sufficient to survive. Unions also led campaigns to end child labor, to establish an eight-hour workday and a five-day workweek, and to increase workplace safety. For this reason, unions are still sometimes referred to as "the people who brought you the weekend." We now take for granted much of what the early unions won to improve the lives of American workers. It is not surprising that many were willing to fight for unionization even in the face of extreme opposition.

In 2014, approximately 14.6 million American workers belonged to a union organization (U.S. Bureau of Labor Statistics 2015f). However, union membership has been in steep decline since its peak in the 1950s. In 1955, approximately 35 percent of the labor force was unionized; by 2014, only 11 percent of the workforce belonged to a union (U.S. Bureau of Labor Statistics 2015f). With a shift in the U.S. economy from manufacturing to the service sector, the only unions to grow since the early 1970s have been public sector employees' unions. Compared to private sector workers, public sector workers are five times more likely to be a part of a union, with workers in education and training most likely to hold union membership (U.S. Bureau of Labor Statistics 2015f).

At the same time that unions were growing in strength and numbers, challenges came from industry and government. Beginning with the Taft-Hartley Act of 1947, laws have been established that limit the power of unions and the activities of members. Some twenty-four states have passed "right-to-work" laws that prohibit workplaces from making union membership a requirement of all employees. As long as the economy was growing rapidly, and wages and benefits continued to rise, the perceived need for unions waned. However, when the economy faltered in the 1970s, American corporations found it was cheaper to move production

Lawrence, Massachusetts, 1912 During the textile mill strike, workers demanded "bread and roses," eloquently capturing their desire for something more than just the wages needed to survive.

overseas to countries whose working conditions were practically unregulated. Industries that leave the United States, referred to as "runaway shops," have been especially prevalent in manufacturing, where firms take advantage of cheap labor and lax environmental laws in other countries. More recently, an increasing number of service sector jobs have been moved overseas. As a result, many unions have largely changed focus from fighting for better wages and working conditions to keeping jobs in this country.

The number of labor actions has also been on the decline. In the 1950s, an average of 352 major strikes occurred each year; by 2014, that number had fallen to just eleven, marking the second-lowest annual total of work stoppages in the United States since 1947 (U.S. Bureau of Labor Statistics 2015i). Many strategies have been used by major U.S. corporations to successfully block union efforts across a variety of work disputes. Although strikes may occur less often now than in the past (and they are not always resolved in the workers' favor), there are still cases to show for their effectiveness in winning battles between unions and employers.

A strike at the ports of Los Angeles and Long Beach, California, is illustrative. In November 2012, a small number of striking clerical workers effectively shut down the nation's busiest shipping complex right as cargoes of holiday goods were headed for port. Unlike in other industries, union loyalty remains strong in shipping. At fewer than 800, the number of striking office and clerical workers was relatively small, but as a unit of the larger International Longshore and Warehouse Union (with close to 60,000 members), no dockworkers or truckers would cross the picket line, thereby crippling trade through the port terminals. At issue were not working conditions or wages; rather, the clerical workers' grievance was over job security—not just for current employees but for those in the future. The workers contended that their employers wanted to transfer higher-paying union jobs to other states or outsource them to other countries where lower-paid workers would be plentiful. The strike disrupted deliveries valued in the billions of dollars a day and brought to a standstill some 600,000 additional workers. The cost of the strike threatened not only the ports but also the fragile U.S. economy. It was settled after eight days with new contracts promising no outsourcing of union jobs (Lopez, White, and Pfiefer 2012).

Just a few years later, another labor dispute between West Coast dockworkers and their employers erupted. Again it brought import and export cargo shipments to a standstill, severely affecting agricultural trade in particular. With workers dissatisfied with the curtailing of union negotiation, ports on the West Coast faced severe delays in offloading and shipping, leaving freight ships stuck at the docks and unable to unload. After a nine-month standoff, the International Longshore and Warehouse Union, which represented the dockworkers, signed a five-year agreement with the employer organization, the Pacific Maritime Association, and settled long-standing issues regarding wages and benefits (Weise and Woodyard 2015). Whether such collective resistance strategies become more or less prevalent in the future remains to be seen.

The Conscience of Corporate America

From a Weberian perspective, we can see that large bureaucracies laden with rules and procedures can deprive employees of a sense of autonomy, individuality, and control. From a Marxist perspective, we can see how large capitalist corporations sometimes exploit their workers and cause alienation and that their power hierarchies often exclude women and minorities. These criticisms are true in the aggregate. Money, power, and influence converge in corporate America, and with these forms of power come opportunities for greed, exploitation, and abuse. But not all corporations are bad actors, and sometimes we see major corporate players transcend self-interest and act with great altruism.

Unfortunately, negative stories about corporate America are not scarce, whether it concerns oil and energy firms, pharmaceutical companies, health insurance providers, or the world of high finance. Cases of corporate malfeasance continue to occur as they have throughout the history of capitalism. Some involve illegal activities, while others are characterized by unethical, if not criminal, behaviors. There can be devastating and deadly consequences when corporations privilege profit making above any costs or damage done to individuals, society, or the planet.

The financial crisis that hit the country in 2007–2008 was precipitated in part by financial scandals involving major Wall Street players such as Lehman Brothers, Merrill Lynch, Morgan Stanley, and Goldman Sachs. After a slew of financial deceptions, security frauds, bankruptcies, bank failures, bailouts, and mortgage foreclosures, the U.S. economy suffered a deep and lengthy recession whose effects have continued to be far-reaching. Despite the economic toll on the country and criminal actions on the part of some corporate officers, many of those top executives escaped legal prosecution or paying for the enormous losses they caused. As news about corporate wrongdoing of all kinds continues to surface, it is leading to more widespread criticism and mistrust of corporate motives and practices.

Of course, not all corporations are evil (or at least not always evil) and in recent years a growing number of organizations are taking it upon themselves to become good corporate citizens. In an effort to bolster their reputations, and perhaps avoid outside intervention, corporations are adopting new forms of self-regulation and taking proactive measures to integrate social and ethical concerns into their business models. Corporate social responsibility, or CSR (also called corporate conscience or citizenship), is a relatively new movement, but one that is spreading. At best, this shift is leading more corporations to take steps toward making a more positive impact

Gravity Payments Dan Price, CEO of Gravity Payments, a credit card processing company based in Seattle, took a $930,000 pay cut in order to raise the minimum yearly salary for all employees to $70,000.

on society and the world. Corporations engage in good citizenship in a number of ways; some are focused on environmental issues or workers' rights, others on a range of social programs and philanthropic giving. A recent example is illustrative.

In March 2015 Indiana Governor Mike Pence signed the Religious Freedom Restoration Act. The Indiana law differed from most legislation covering religious freedoms in two ways. First, it applied to the religious feelings of businesses and corporations, rather than simply protecting individuals. Second it applied "regardless of whether the state or any other governmental entity is a party to the proceeding." In other words, most legal analysts agreed that it would allow businesses to deny service to gays and lesbians (or almost any other group). Not surprisingly, the law was met with swift rebuke from many constituencies.

Facing widespread protests, Indiana quickly revised the law so that it could not be used as a defense for discrimination on the basis of sexual orientation or gender identity. Everyone from actor George Takei to the alternative rock band Wilco got involved in these protests, but a great deal of the credit for the decisive change has to go to corporate America. Salesforce.com declared a boycott on the state and announced they would cancel any business trips that would require employees to travel to Indiana. Tim Cook, the openly gay CEO of Apple, wrote a widely distributed op-ed piece for *The Washington Post* criticizing the law both because "discrimination, in all its forms, is bad for business" and because it existed only to "rationalize injustice" (Cook 2015). By the time the law was amended, the list of corporations that had publicly come out against it included PayPal, Gap, Nike, Angie's List, Anthem, Walmart, and Levi Strauss.

It's important to remember, though, that there is no federal law prohibiting discrimination based on sexual orientation or gender identity. In Indiana, like the majority of states, it is still perfectly legal to discriminate on the basis of sexual orientation except where cities have passed local laws. In contrast,

89 percent of Fortune 500 companies now specifically ban discrimination on the basis of sexual orientation. Whether it's based on altruism or just good for business, big corporations are suddenly part of the national conversation about discrimination in a way they never have been before. Nowadays it seems like good citizenship and good business can go hand in hand.

The Economics of Globalization

Globalization describes the cultural and economic changes that have occurred as a result of dramatically increased international trade and exchange in the late twentieth and early twenty-first centuries. Although there has always been some global economic trade—East Asia's ancient spice and silk trade routes and the sixteenth-century English and Dutch shipping empires are early examples—the effects of globalization have become more highly visible since the 1970s. Globalization has been fostered through the development of international economic institutions; innovations in technology; the movement of money, information, and people; and infrastructure that supports such expansion. Today, it is possible to view the world as having one global economy, with huge corporations whose production processes span national borders, international regulatory bodies such as the World Trade Organization (WTO), financial bodies such as the International Monetary Fund (IMF), and transnational trade agreements such as the North American Free Trade Agreement (NAFTA) redefining economic relationships between and among nations.

> **GLOBALIZATION** the cultural and economic changes resulting from dramatically increased international trade and exchange in the late twentieth and early twenty-first centuries

Supporters of globalization believe that "free trade" can lead to more efficient allocation of resources, lower prices, more employment, and higher output, with all countries involved in the trade benefiting. Critics believe that free trade promotes a self-interested corporate agenda and that powerful and autonomous multinational corporations can exploit workers and increasingly shape the politics of nation-states. And the recent global recession, marked by financial crises in the United States, Europe, and China, shows us that all world economies are connected, for better or for worse.

International Trade

To explain economic globalization, social scientists have used the terms "shallow integration" and "deep integration" (Dicken 1998). Shallow integration refers to the flow of goods and services that characterized international trade until several decades ago. In a shallow integration model, a national company would arrange with a foreign company to either import or export products exclusively within that single nation's economy. For example, thirty years ago, a Japanese car would have been made almost entirely in Japan, and a pair of American jeans would have been made in the United States. Thus, Japan would export cars to the United States, which would import Japanese cars. And the United States would export jeans to Japan, which would import American jeans. To protect their interests, nations would impose taxes on imports, sometimes making those imports more expensive to buy than similar products made at home.

Deep integration refers to the global flow of goods and services in today's economy. While companies still make arrangements with other companies for imports and exports, their relationships are far more complex. Most significantly, companies are no longer national; they are multinational, with major decision making, production, and/or distribution branches of a particular company spread all over the world. When we look at the labels on our clothing, the global nature of their origin is often concealed. The label may say "Made in . . . ," but the raw materials or other parts may have originated somewhere else.

When nations make laws to protect national economic interests, they must often do so with a host of other nations in mind. NAFTA is an excellent example of this complex web of global relationships. Many major apparel companies, such as Nike and the Gap, have marketing and design headquarters in the United States, but many of their garment factories are in Mexico, another country in NAFTA. Under NAFTA, American companies can avoid paying taxes when they export raw materials to Mexico and then import the finished products. These global trade agreements often benefit private industry much more than they do nations.

Transnational Corporations

Transnational corporations (TNCs) are another part of the global economy. These firms purposefully transcend national borders so that their products can be manufactured, distributed, marketed, and sold from many bases all over the world. We may think of companies like Coca-Cola or General Electric as quintessentially American, but they are more accurately understood as global or transnational corporations. What is distinctive about today's TNCs is the way they shape the global economy. In the past fifty years, they have experienced unprecedented growth in both numbers of firms and amount of economic impact.

The UN's 2014 list of "The World's Top 100 Non-Financial TNCs" assigns firms a "transnationality index" by assessing the ratios between foreign employment and total employment, foreign investments and total investments, and foreign sales and total sales (United Nations Conference on Trade and Development 2014). Among the top twenty-five "transnational"

SWEATSHOP a workplace where workers are subject to extreme exploitation, including below-standard wages, long hours, and poor working conditions that may pose health or safety hazards

Coca-Cola and the Global Economy An employee oversees production at a new Coca-Cola plant in Indonesia. While Coca-Cola is headquartered in Atlanta, Georgia, the company has plants that span the globe.

firms are five U.S. companies: General Electric (1), ExxonMobil (4), Chevron (9), Apple (19), and Johnson & Johnson (25). The petroleum industry is the most transnational, followed by electronics and pharmaceuticals. All of these firms make products that are marketed strongly as "American" brands, yet they are clearly global organizations.

TNCs exert tremendous influence in the global economy. They can be found among the top global economies, ranked by either gross domestic product (GDP) or total sales. Firms such as Walmart, Royal Dutch Shell, and ExxonMobil actually rank higher than the nations of Denmark, Thailand, and Chile (see Table 11.1). As corporations grow, new TNCs have been added to the list. When we consider that firms have the economic weight of nations, we can understand just how much political clout TNCs wield in terms of global governance. For instance, an American TNC can exercise powerful influence by donating huge amounts of money to lobbyists and political campaigns. Further, in international regulatory bodies, such as the WTO, TNCs are often able to influence trade law at a global level.

Another manifestation of the ever-increasing economic power of TNCs is competition in the global market. Because TNCs can take advantage of cheap pools of labor by either relocating their own factories or outsourcing the work, nations compete with each other for these contracts by undercutting their citizens' wages and offering incentives, such as tax-free zones. Scholars, politicians, activists, and commentators have called this the "race to the bottom." These kinds of policies hurt the local populations, often depriving workers of decent wages and the potential benefits, such as schools and hospitals, that would have been derived from taxes.

Global Sweatshop Labor

One way the race to the bottom hurts workers in their own countries is by creating an environment where sweatshop labor can exist. A **sweatshop** is a workplace where

Table 11.1 Ranking the World's Economies

Rank 2011	Company/Country	GDP/Revenues (billions)	Rank 2011	Company/Country	GDP/Revenues (billions)
1	United States	$16,800	26	Norway	$513
2	China, including Hong Kong SAR	$9,514	27	Belgium	$509
3	Japan	$4,902	**28**	**Walmart**	$476
4	Germany	$3,635	**29**	**Royal Dutch Shell**	$460
5	France	$2,735	**30**	**Sinopec (China Petroleum & Chemical)**	$457
6	United Kingdom	$2,521	31	Venezuela	$438
7	South Asia	$2,355	**32**	**China National Petroleum**	$432
8	Brazil	$2,246	33	Austria	$416
9	Russian Federation	$2,097	**34**	**Exxon Mobil**	$408
10	Italy	$2,071	**35**	**BP (British Petroleum)**	$396
11	India	$1,877	36	Thailand	$387
12	Canada	$1,827	37	Colombia	$378
13	Australia	$1,561	38	Iran, Islamic Rep.	$369
14	Spain	$1,358	39	South Africa	$351
15	Korea, Rep.	$1,305	**40**	**State Grid (China)**	$333
16	Mexico	$1,261	41	Denmark	$331
17	Indonesia	$868	42	Malaysia	$312
18	Turkey	$820	43	Singapore	$298
19	Netherlands	$800	44	Israel	$291
20	Saudi Arabia	$745	45	Chile	$277
21	Switzerland	$650	**46**	**Volkswagen**	$262
22	Argentina	$610	**47**	**Toyota**	$257
23	Sweden	$559	**48**	**Glencore**	$233
24	Nigeria	$522	**49**	**Total Oil**	$228
25	Poland	$518	**50**	**Chevron**	$220

SOURCES: Mehta 2014; World Bank 2014.

workers are subjected to extreme exploitation, including below-standard wages, long hours, and poor working conditions that may pose health or safety hazards. Sweatshop workers are often intimidated with threats of physical discipline and are prevented from forming unions or other workers' rights groups. Historically, sweatshops originated during the Industrial Revolution as a system where middlemen earned profits from the difference between what they received for delivering on a contract and the amount they paid to the workers who produced the contracted goods. The profit was said to be "sweated" from the workers, because they received minimal wages and worked excessive hours under unsanitary and dangerous conditions.

Sweatshops, however, are not a thing of the past. Unfortunately, there are many in the world today making large numbers of the goods that we unknowingly consume. Though perhaps more prevalent overseas, sweatshops exist in the United States as well. The General Accounting Office (GAO) defines a sweatshop as "an employer that violates more than one federal or state labor law governing minimum wage and overtime, child labor, industrial homework, occupational safety and health, workers compensation, or industrial regulation" (Ross 1997, p. 12). Such cases are not isolated. In 2001 the Department of Labor estimated that there were more than 7,000 sweatshops in U.S. cities such as New York, New Orleans, Chicago, Philadelphia, and El Paso. In 2012 an undercover investigation of ten garment contractors in the fashion district of Los Angeles found widespread labor violations and workers operating under sweatshop conditions (U.S. Department of Labor 2012). More than thirty different retailers, including Forever 21 and Urban Outfitters, had garments being produced by contractors in violation. According to the investigation, garment workers were being paid less than both the federal and California minimum wages and were not being paid overtime, amounting to over $300,000 recovered in unpaid wages. It might be shocking to imagine that such abuse and exploitation of workers still occur in the United States.

American companies may also manufacture goods overseas using foreign sweatshop labor. Nike, the Gap, and clothing lines associated with Mary-Kate and Ashley Olsen, Jay-Z, and Sean "Puff Daddy" Combs have all been charged with using sweatshop labor in Southeast Asia, Central America, and elsewhere and have been pressured to reform their practices. Factory fires in 2012 killed 289 garment workers in Pakistan and 117 in Bangladesh, and in April 2013, over 1,000 garment workers in Bangladesh were killed when their factory building collapsed. In the first two cases, workers were trapped in buildings without proper emergency exits, where clothing was made for American companies such as Walmart, J. C. Penney, and Kohl's (Ahmed 2012). In the last case, the deadliest garment-industry accident in history, the building was made of shoddy materials and constructed on unstable ground and thus could not withstand the vibrations of machinery within (Associated Press 2013).

Many universities have also been in the practice of purchasing their logo apparel from clothing manufacturers that use sweatshop labor. In 1999, students at the University of Michigan, University of North Carolina, University of Wisconsin–Madison, Duke University, and Georgetown University staged sit-ins to pressure their respective administrators into agreeing to fully disclose factory conditions and wages paid to workers who produce university apparel (Greenhouse 1999). Similar campaigns were launched at Seattle Community College in 2004 and systemwide at the University of California in 2005 to change university purchasing policy to allow for preferences for union-made and verifiably sweatshop-free products. By 2015, more than 180 colleges and universities had joined the Worker Rights Consortium and pledged to uphold the Fair Labor Association workplace code of conduct when it comes to choosing manufacturers for their apparel. We encourage you to do your own research on whether sweatshop products have reached the student store on your campus or wherever you shop for clothing—and whether such items are in your own closet already.

Blood, Sweat, and Tears (Left) Activists lead a demonstration in protest of working conditions at a factory in Bangladesh used by H&M. (Right) People crowd outside the ruins of Rana Plaza, an eight-story garment factory that collapsed in April 2013, killing more than 1,000 workers.

DATA WORKSHOP
Analyzing Everyday Life

Are Your Clothes Part of the Global Commodity Chain?

You probably own and consume a large number of products that originated in far-away countries, including your car, clothing, or shoes. These items have traveled widely during the process from production to consumption. Food, pharmaceuticals, and electronics are other examples of globally made products. Social scientists call such international movements of goods "global commodity chains" (Gereffi and Korzeniewicz 1994; Dunaway 2014).

Global commodity chains are networks of corporations, product designers and engineers, manufacturing firms, distribution channels (such as ocean freightliners, railroads, and trucking firms), and consumer outlets (such as Walmart). Global commodity chains start with a product design and brand name and end with the consumer making a purchase. But between start and finish is often a complex global process involving many different people, in many different nations, all contributing to the final product.

The manufacturing of goods, from garments to electronics to automobiles, used to happen primarily in the United States and other Western nations; today's manufacturing centers are located primarily in poorer nations, such as the Philippines, China, Indonesia, and many Latin American countries. American corporations such as Nike, the Gap, and Levi-Strauss have closed all their U.S. manufacturing plants and hired contractors and subcontractors from East Asia and Latin America to make their products at substantially lower prices. Now these companies focus large amounts of financial resources on "branding" their products (Klein 2000). Branding is the process, usually accomplished through advertising, by which companies gain consumers' attention and loyalty. Much of the money you pay for some products goes toward financing these branding campaigns, while a much smaller sum pays the workers who actually make the products.

In this Data Workshop you will be using existing sources in your research and analysis. Return to the section in Chapter 2 for a review of this method. The following three exercises will help you better understand where the things that you buy come from and the continuing disparity between product values and workers' wages. Document what you find in written notes. (You can also take photos of the items.)

Exercise One: The Global Closet

Pick out five to ten items of clothing from your closet. Now check the labels. Where were your clothes made? Make a list of the nations represented in your closet. How many nations are in East Asia or Latin America or other parts of the globe? Is there a difference between where an item is made and where it is assembled? Does the label indicate where the fabric originated?

Exercise Two: Once "Made in the U.S.A."

Ask your parents, aunts or uncles, or grandparents if you can look at the labels of their older clothes. Or go to a thrift store or secondhand store and look for older or vintage clothes there. Again pick out five to ten items of clothing. How many of those items were made in the United States? How many were made elsewhere? What does this tell you about the globalization of the garment manufacturing industry over the past several decades?

Exercise Three: Are Your Favorite Brands "Sweat Free"?

Choose one or more of your favorite brands of clothing, shoes, or other fashion accessories. What is your brand's stance on sweatshop labor? Do workers who make your favorite products earn a living wage? You can check many corporations' ethics regarding labor conditions by doing a simple search on the Internet. Or visit the website of one of the following pro-labor organizations to see how your brands score:

* Institute for Global Labour and Human Rights: www.globallabourrights.org

* CorpWatch: www.corpwatch.org

* Global Exchange: www.globalexchange.org

There are two options for completing this Data Workshop:

PREP-PAIR-SHARE Complete the exercises provided, following the instructions as outlined. Bring your notes to class to discuss with other students in pairs or small groups. Your instructor may organize groups so that all members have done the same exercise or all members have done a different exercise. Compare your findings as a group. Did you find similar or different results?

DO-IT-YOURSELF Complete the exercises provided and follow the instructions as outlined. Write a three- to four-page essay analyzing your findings. Attach any written notes or other documentation to your paper.

Many people are familiar with the concept of sweatshops, where cheap labor is exploited to make clothing and goods for people in industrialized nations. While people easily understand how labor can be exploited for the production of material goods, a more difficult concept to grasp is how labor can be exploited in the market for virtual goods. Rather than working long hours under inhumane conditions for little pay in order to produce luxury items such as Nikes and Ray-Bans, "gold farmers" are exploited in order to create the ultimate luxury product—status in an online computer game.

Some of the most popular forms of video games are massively multiplayer online role-playing games (MMOR-PGs) such as *World of Warcraft* (WoW), *Ultima Online*, and *Everquest*. WoW is the most popular of these games, with approximately 10 million subscribers, or about 35 percent of the market; it earned over $1 billion in revenues in 2013 (Tassi 2014). As with many MMORPGs, players make an initial investment to purchase the software for the game, and they are also charged a monthly subscription fee in order to play. In *WoW*, players use a character avatar through which they explore the virtual world, complete quests, and interact with other players or nonplayer characters (NPCs). Quests are assignments given by an NPC that usually involve killing a monster, gathering resources, or finding a difficult-to-locate object. Successful quests are rewarded with in-game money and experience points that a character can use to buy new skills and equipment. Because of the interactive nature of *WoW*, advancing in the game isn't just a matter of personal achievement but also a matter of reputation and status in the community.

"Gold farms" profit from the importance of advancement in an MMORPG. According to estimates, around 100,000 people in China are employed as gold farmers, making $120 to $250 (U.S.) per month playing *WoW* for twelve- to eighteen-hour shifts (Vincent 2011). These Chinese gold farmers carry out in-game actions so that they can earn virtual money to buy equipment, skills, and status. These virtual assets are sold to real (recreational) players for real-world money, creating a unique intersection of virtual and real-world economies. Literally, a player can spend real-world money to buy status and reputation in an online game. Since many of the beginning levels of *WoW* involve spending long hours doing repetitive and dull virtual tasks, the idea of being able to bypass this tedium to start at more advanced levels appeals to many players. Creating characters requires time and effort that players who use the services of gold farmers are unable or unwilling to devote to the game.

Many of the criticisms of manufacturing sweatshops can be applied to the gold-farming phenomenon. Gold farmers labor for the benefit of middle-class gamers in industrialized nations. Ge Jin (2006), a PhD student at the University of California, San Diego, has documented working conditions in gold-farming "sweatshops," where he filmed workers crowded into an airport hangar, bleary eyed, chain smoking, and sleeping two to a single mat on the floor. Are bad jobs better than

Outsourcing

The U.S. economy is increasingly affected by globalization, and as a result, American companies have sought out new business models to reduce costs and remain competitive. One increasingly popular approach is outsourcing or offshoring. **Outsourcing** involves "contracting out" or transferring to another country the labor that a company might otherwise have employed its own staff to perform. Typically, a company's decision to outsource is made for financial reasons and is usually achieved by transferring employment to locations where the cost of labor is much cheaper. In the 1990s, when this trend was just beginning, U.S. firms employed 7 million workers in other countries (O'Reilly 1992). With technological advances, over the past couple of decades more businesses have been able to increase their foreign employment pools significantly. Foreign employment by U.S. multinational companies grew to 11 million workers in 2010 (U.S. Department of Commerce 2012).

The economic benefits of outsourcing are gained by businesses, but the drawbacks are felt by the people who make up the American labor pool. Figures vary regarding the number of jobs that have been lost as the practice of outsourcing has continued to grow. While offshoring is practiced by numerous U.S. businesses, they are often reluctant to fully disclose details. Companies like General Electric, Caterpillar, Microsoft, and Walmart employ close to one-fifth of all American workers. Yet during the 2000s, companies like these shrank their domestic workforces by 2.9 million while

OUTSOURCING "contracting out" or transferring to another country the labor that a company might otherwise have employed its own staff to perform; typically done for financial reasons

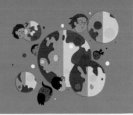

Chinese Gold Farmers How has the popularity of online games such as *World of Warcraft* led to the rise of new types of sweatshops?

pay to buy them. The sum of $200 can buy 500 pieces of online gold in *WoW*, which would take an estimated 100 hours of playing to earn.

The gaming world is up in arms about the gold-farming phenomenon. While some gamers find that the opportunity to buy gold augments their playing experience, other gamers hold that buying from gold farmers confers an unfair advantage to those with expendable income. Purists argue that MMORPGs should be free of the corruption of the real world and that escapism is not possible with people buying status and reputation. Players who use the services of gold farmers affect the virtual economy by driving up the prices of the rarest items. Traditional players then become resentful, as these price increases require them to work longer for items that players with real-world cash can purchase with little effort.

Strategies for retaliation against players identified as gold farmers include verbal harassment inside the game. Rather than taking out their frustrations on the gold farm brokers who benefit from the process, some players will follow suspected gold farmers within the game and bombard them with racist comments. Gold farming then becomes a matter not just of class and economics, but also of race and racism.

Are gold farms good or bad? Should the virtual world be free of the corruption of the real world? Are gamers just too invested in their games? These are all questions to ask when pondering the intersections of the virtual world and real world that collide in the gold-farming sweatshops.

no jobs? Though most people in developed nations would view $3 a day as extremely low pay, in impoverished communities "$1 or $2 a day can be a life-transforming wage" (Kristof and WuDunn 2000). While there are those who argue that playing a computer game takes less of a physical toll than subsistence farming or factory work, it is evident that there is an imbalance between the amount of money that workers are paid to produce these virtual resources and the prices that gamers

increasing their rosters of foreign employees by 2.4 million (U.S. Department of Commerce 2012). Data show that outsourcing to China between 2001 and 2013 cost the United States 3.2 million jobs, almost two-thirds of which were in manufacturing (Scott and Kimball 2014).

A variety of jobs are suitable for outsourcing. Manufacturing jobs were some of the first to go, but an increasing number of service jobs have followed in the last couple of decades. Among them are office and clerical staff, purchasing, finance, and human resources workers. Offshoring is also happening in other service areas requiring highly skilled workers. Jobs in information technology–producing industries, such as data entry, communication services, communication equipment, and computer hardware, software, and services, are some of the main jobs involved in outsourcing. In a recent five-year period, Oracle, a business hardware and software giant, hired

twice as many workers abroad as in the United States (Wessel 2011). Over the last decade, Cisco Systems, another tech firm, increased its portion of foreign workers from 26 percent to 46 percent of all company employees.

Although countries in Southeast Asia, such as the Philippines, and those in Eastern Europe are key sites for information technology offshoring, India has become the primary location for this practice because of the shared English language and cheap employment. It makes sense to employ workers abroad if, for instance, a company can hire a computer engineer in India for $10,000 a year compared with one who does the same work but costs $60,000 to $90,000 in the United States. By 2013, information technology export revenue from the United States to India had grown into a $65 billion business (India Brand Equity Foundation 2015). China has become the second largest outsourcing provider to the

A Surrogate Baby Boom India has become a key site for outsourcing the womb. Young women serve as surrogates for infertile American couples who wish to have their own biological children at a fraction of the cost of an American surrogate.

Sociologist France Winddance Twine (2011a) has researched the growing trend in outsourcing the womb. For the past several decades, infertile couples who wish to have biological children have been hiring women to serve as surrogates. These woman are impregnated in vitro with the egg and sperm of a couple who are unable to conceive on their own. Although this practice is legal in the United States, it has been outlawed in other Western countries. In recent years, there has been a surrogate baby boom in places such as India. Outsourcing has occurred in this market for the same reasons as in other industries: there is an available workforce overseas where the costs are much cheaper than in the United States. A burgeoning number of agencies in India specialize in surrogacy. Prospective American parents who use these services can more easily fulfill their desire for a biological baby and at a fifth of what it would cost at home. The arrangement also benefits the surrogate in India who might earn as much in nine months carrying a baby to term as she would for ten years of labor as a maid. While there are concerns about this practice and the exploitation of young, poor women in places like India, it is also an opportunity for them to afford a home for their families, something that would otherwise be out of reach. If we can now outsource pregnancy, what other jobs might be next?

United States, with service contracts totaling $23 billion in 2011 (Zheng 2012).

When we think about outsourcing, we may picture a foreign worker assembling an American model automobile, or we may remember the foreign accent of someone we spoke with at a help desk or call center who provided us with tech support or customer service. Although outsourcing is still most common in areas such as manufacturing and information services, it has spread into new and what might seem like far less likely types of employment.

Different Ways of Working

There are alternative ways of working, not all of which fit into typical categories of work. First we look at professional socialization, the process by which new members learn and internalize the norms and values of their group, examining case studies of workers in three unusual fields. Then we examine the contingent workforce—those who work in positions

Table 11.2 Theory in Everyday Life

Perspective	Approach to Work and the Economy	Case Study: Outsourcing of Work
Functionalism	Different types of work (high prestige and pay to low prestige and pay) are necessary to the economy and have functions that help maintain social order.	Outsourcing is necessary to keep both national and global economies stable in the current market.
Conflict Theory	A stratified labor market creates intergroup conflict—wealthier capitalists may exploit less-powerful workers.	Outsourcing exploits poor and developing nations and laid-off local workers, all while enriching corporations.
Symbolic Interactionism	Work is central to our self-concept. We are intensely identified with our work, both by ourselves and by others.	Workers whose jobs are outsourced may come to see themselves as worthless and expendable because it seems that others see them that way too.

that are temporary or freelance or who work as independent contractors. Finally, we take a look at nonprofit corporations—private organizations whose missions go beyond the bottom line—and volunteerism, the work of people who seek no compensation for their investment of time and energy.

Professional Socialization in Unusual Fields

Every new job requires some sort of training for the prospective employee. Anyone in a new position confronts an unfamiliar set of expectations and workplace norms that must be learned so the new person can fit into the environment. This process, called professional socialization, involves learning not only the social role but also the various details about how to do the job. Several sociological studies have explored the process of professional socialization, focusing on medical students (Fox 1957; Becker et al. 1961; Haas and Shaffir 1977, 1982), teachers (Lortie 1968), clergy (Kleinman 1984), nurses (Stimson 1967), social workers (Loseke and Cahill 1986), and lawyers (Granfield 1992).

Spencer Cahill's study of students preparing to become funeral directors focused on the practical skills developed by mortuary science students and the "emotional labor" (see Hochschild 1983) involved in this occupation. Most social interaction within the mortuary science program revolved around death; as a result, students learned how to engage in the practice of "normalizing talk." "Mortuary science education requires students to adopt an occupational rhetoric and esoteric language that communicate professional authority and a calm composure towards matters that most of the lay public finds emotionally upsetting" (Cahill 1999, p. 106). In addition, students were required to control their own emotional responses to the work. "Some students told me that they found 'cases' of young children emotionally disturbing. . . . Yet, these students reportedly did 'get used to it,' 'keep it down,' and deal with emotionally distressing 'cases'" (pp. 108–109). Cahill found that successful mortuary science students were those who could best deal with the emotional component of the work.

Loren Bourassa and Blake Ashforth studied how inexperienced newcomers are socialized into the work life onboard an Alaskan fishing boat. The occupation of a fisherman differs greatly from other occupations because it requires no previous experience or even a high school education; physical strength and stamina are the primary prerequisites. Work on a fishing boat pays well for a relatively short amount of time, and this often lures a large number of workers. However, their romantic notions about life on a fishing boat are quickly dispelled. "New workers were indoctrinated collectively by their more experienced co-workers and underwent a process of divestiture. . . . Specifically, newcomers were called 'new guys,' rather than by name, were subjected to constant taunts and verbal abuse, were constantly made to perform the least desirable jobs and

Deadliest Catch New workers on an Alaskan fishing boat undergo intense socialization, often enduring verbal abuse and performing the least desirable tasks onboard.

other odd tasks, were required to obey incessant and often arbitrary instructions, and were routinely denied the privileges given to more experienced members" (Bourassa and Ashforth 1998, p. 181).

This intense socialization proved effective, as newcomers worked hard and came to understand the culture of the fishing boat workplace. "It became a badge of honor to survive the initiation phase" (Bourassa and Ashforth 1998, p. 189). Yet, the fleeting moment of self-satisfaction and positive feelings gave way to the continuous physical demands. Even the promise of economic rewards failed to sustain them. "The money was generally held in bank accounts until the completion of a contract. Workers could not use their money or even hold their paycheck in their hands. Thus, onboard the ship, money remained an abstract and distant notion" (Bourassa and Ashforth 1998, p. 189).

Jacqueline Lewis (1998) examined the socialization of exotic dancers and what goes into learning their job. "For exotic dancers, achieving job competence involves getting accustomed to working in a sex-related occupation and the practice of taking their clothes off in public for money" (Lewis 1998, p. 1). On-the-job socialization was essential for the women who entered this line of work: "Similar to the socialization experiences of individuals in other occupations, novice dancers learn through interaction and observation while on the job. . . . Since there is no formal certification structure, peers play an important role in this transformation process" (p. 5). Lewis found that several women felt the socialization process "inadequately prepared them for some of the realities of the life of an exotic dancer" (p. 12)—mainly the negative impact it would have on their private lives and the difficulties

Someone mentions an internship, and you think . . . what? Bored college students making coffee for the boss? Beleaguered production assistants on a film set? Monica Lewinsky in the White House? Whatever your impression, the fact is internships are an increasingly important part of the college experience. According to studies, on average about 38 percent of the class of 2012 interned at some point during their undergraduate careers. At worst, the hapless intern may get really good at adding toner to the copier and not much else, or conversely, the employer may engage in exploitative practices in which student interns are overworked and quite often unpaid. At best, however, an internship can benefit both the intern and the company and may be useful in the long run for everyone involved.

Depending on where you're enrolled, you may be able to arrange an internship through your college or university and receive academic credit, or you may have to set up a nonacademic internship that leaves out the school altogether. Organizations of all kinds—corporate, public, nonprofit, and others—look for college students to fill some of their employment needs. Of course, there's always the possibility that the work you're assigned as an intern will be mind-numbing or pointless, or that you'll have to work long hours, and oftentimes forgo a paycheck! In 2013, about 52 percent of internships were paid and 48 percent unpaid (National Association of Colleges and Employers 2013b). There is a difference, however, in who gets what kinds of positions. Typically men and students from higher-income backgrounds are more likely to obtain paid internships than are women and lower-income students (Gardner 2011).

Many might ask, why bother with an internship? For starters, an internship may help you decide what you want to be—or don't want to be—when you graduate. After interning in a state's attorney's office, you may decide that being a lawyer isn't everything you thought it would be and you'd like to work with crime victims in a social service capacity instead. Even if you are sure about your future career path, you may want to consider branching out in the internships you apply for. You'll gain diverse skills and experience and be exposed to careers you might like just as much. Most Americans don't remain in the same job for their entire working lives, so keeping your options open during college isn't such a bad idea. Even if you decide you'd prefer not to work for that corporation or in that field, the contacts you develop may help you find another position. These are people who are already established in the profession, and a good reference is always valuable when you're in the job market.

An internship on your résumé is also likely to make you a more attractive job candidate. Even if your experience doesn't deal directly with the job you're applying for, having completed an internship demonstrates to potential employers your ability to work hard and manage your time. Here, too, the benefits of a paid internship go beyond just receiving a paycheck. According to the results from a survey on the graduating class of 2013 by the National Association of Colleges and Employers, approximately 63 percent of students who worked in paid internships during college received at least one job offer. The results were less auspicious for those who worked in unpaid internships. Only 37 percent of students in unpaid internships received a job offer, which is only 1 percent higher than for students with no internship experience at all (National Association of Colleges and Employers 2013a). In addition, many organizations turn first to their own interns when hiring. In 2012, employers made full-time job offers to 56 percent of their interns (National Association of Colleges and Employers 2013a). The entire internship can, in some respects, be viewed as an extended job interview.

Internships work out well for employers too—some say too well. At the very least, they're getting cheap (and often free) labor. Critics have raised questions about the value of unpaid internships, further intensifying debates regarding the exploitation of student workers (Perlin 2011, 2012). Recently, unpaid internships made headline news after unpaid interns sued several high-profile companies, including NBC Universal, Fox Searchlight, Sony, and Condé Nast. The lawsuits claimed that the companies violated the two requirements for unpaid workers, as set by the U.S. Department of Labor: interns must be assigned different work than paid employees and must receive training in an educational environment.

Enlightened organizations are mindful of the many other benefits they reap when employing interns, paid and unpaid. They are often rewarded with a highly educated or highly trained workforce. Taking on young workers can also help a company stay connected to younger and more diverse student populations and may provide them with some new perspectives and ideas. Organizations also realize that providing internships can create goodwill—from the students who intern with them, from the universities through which the internships are organized, and even from the general public.

of having long-term heterosexual relationships with men outside the industry.

The Contingent Workforce

Traditionally, most Americans have hoped to find a job they would keep their whole lives, one that would provide forty-hour workweeks along with vacations and health and retirement benefits. Increasingly, this sort of job is becoming rare. A growing percentage of Americans have less steady work arrangements that could be defined as work that does not involve explicit or implicit contracts for long-term employment. These workers are referred to as the **contingent workforce**. It is made up of four categories: independent contractors, on-call workers, temporary workers, and contract company workers—sometimes called "temps" or "freelancers."

During the past couple of decades, contingent work has become an alternative to long-term, full-time employment and has grown three times faster than traditional jobs. If we count the self-employed in this group, the total contingent workforce in 2012 numbered almost 44 million, or 31 percent of all workers. The U.S. Department of Labor projects that by 2020 there will be almost 65 million contingent workers, constituting approximately 40 percent of the total workforce (U.S. Bureau of Labor Statistics 2012a).

Many see this situation as a potential disaster, as inferior jobs are created by corporations seeking to slash overhead, especially those costs associated with health benefits, which are almost never available to contingent workers. Employers have a number of financial and legal responsibilities to their regular workers—overtime pay, health insurance, Social Security, disability, and workers' compensation benefits—that don't apply to temps or independent contractors. Many fear businesses will increasingly turn to alternative employment arrangements solely to cut costs to the distinct disadvantage of their employees.

The case histories of two giant firms show the potential for the exploitation of contingent workers. Sometimes, businesses will classify workers as "independent contractors" even though they do the same work in the same place as regular workers. In an infamous example in the late 1990s, Microsoft was forced to pay $97 million to settle a lawsuit alleging it had wrongly classified a group of employees as independent contractors, making them ineligible for benefits. These workers had been hired as freelancers to work on specific projects, but "the workers were fully integrated into Microsoft's workforce, working under nearly identical circumstances as Microsoft's regular employees . . . the same core hours at the same location and the same supervisors as regular employees" (Muhl 2002).

A different, though equally exploitative, tactic was used by the contractors hired to clean Walmart stores. In 2003, federal agents arrested 245 undocumented workers in sixty different Walmart stores around the country. The workers came from eighteen nations, but very few of them actually worked for Walmart. Instead, they were employed by independent

The Just-in-Time Professor The postsecondary academic workforce has experienced a profound shift away from full-time tenured or tenure-track faculty to part-time adjunct instructors. Adjunct instructors now represent half of all higher-education faculty, up from 20 percent in 1970.

contractors hired by Walmart to do its nightly cleaning (Bartels 2003). Although companies are not responsible for the actions of subcontractors they hire, they can be held responsible if it is proven they knew something illegal was going on. This is especially important when the jobs that are offered to undocumented workers are exploitative or abusive. When contractors hire employees who work seven days a week and receive no overtime pay or benefits, then those contractors are in violation of overtime, Social Security, and workers' compensation laws. Furthermore, it is much harder for legitimate contractors to win bids for contracts when their competition can offer lower prices by illegally underpaying their workers.

It is not surprising to discover a lack of job satisfaction among temporary workers, mainly clerical and manufacturing workers and on-call workers, such as construction workers, nurses, adjunct instructors, and truck drivers (Dickson and Lorenz 2009). Many temporary workers hope they will be able to use their temp job as a springboard to a permanent one, but often this does not happen. However, the flexibility and freedom of alternative work arrangements appeal to a substantial number of workers, such as students, parents with children at home, and retirees. Though the increase in nontraditional employment has many potential negative effects, there is a great deal of diversity in the characteristics of contingent workers, some of whom may experience more or less satisfaction with their work arrangements. While there is clearly a downside to being a temp or independent contractor,

CONTINGENT WORKFORCE those who work in positions that are temporary or freelance or who work as independent contractors

INDEPENDENT (OR THIRD) SECTOR the part of the economy composed of nonprofit organizations; their workers are mission driven, rather than profit driven, and such organizations direct surplus funds to the causes they support

research indicates that there can also be great satisfaction among these freelance workers.

Of the four categories tracked by the Bureau of Labor Statistics, independent contractors make up the largest group—almost two-thirds of the total. In contrast to the traditional worker, the occupational profile of the independent contractor is skewed toward several high-skilled fields, including writers and artists, insurance and real estate agents, construction trade employees, and other technical and computer-related professions. They tend to be better paid than the average worker and prefer their employment situation for the flexibility and freedom it offers (Fishman 2011). However, even in this category, a significant minority of workers, especially women, make less money and are less satisfied with their situation. Some also suffer from alienation, disenchantment, and burnout.

The Third Sector and Volunteerism

Not all corporations seek a profit, nor do all workers get paid a wage for their labor. Numerous organizations engage in social welfare, social justice, or environmental services. Typically, these are churches, schools, hospitals, philanthropic foundations, art institutions, scientific research centers, and a multitude of other organizations, both permanent and temporary. They are private, rather than government, organizations and are devoted to serving the general welfare, not their own financial interests. They are nonprofit organizations, designed to run as cost-effectively as possible and to direct any gains or earnings, above basic operating expenses, back into the causes they support. Together, these organizations and the workers who staff them constitute what social scientists call the **Independent (or Third) Sector** of the economy.

The Third Sector represents one of the most distinctive and commendable features of our society. In 2012, more than 1.4 million nonprofit organizations were registered with the Internal Revenue Service and accorded tax privileges. This represents an increase of over 8 percent in the previous decade. Nonprofits contributed an estimated $887 million to the U.S. economy in 2012, which amounted to more than 5 percent of the nation's gross domestic product (Pettijohn 2014).

The Third Sector helps society in a number of ways. First, these organizations play a significant part in the American system of pluralism, operating alongside the first two sectors of government and business while helping to strengthen and make them work better. Although we think of nonprofits, business, and government as separate, they are really interconnected through their impact on public policy. Second, nonprofit organizations deliver a wide range of vital services to millions of people in almost every social category. Last, they are a humanizing force in American society, allowing an important avenue of expression for altruism.

While most nonprofits have some paid employees, they also rely on volunteers to deliver their services to the public. Volunteerism reflects a profound and important American value—that citizens in a democracy have a personal responsibility to serve those in need. The U.S. Bureau of Labor Statistics (2015h) reported that in 2014, an estimated 62.8 million Americans, or more than 25 percent of the total population, engaged in some form of volunteer work. Volunteers each spent a median of fifty hours on volunteer activities during the given year. Women tend to volunteer in larger numbers: more than 28 percent of all U.S. women, compared to 22 percent of men, volunteered in 2014. Volunteers are represented fairly evenly from all age groups, though persons thirty-five to forty-four years old were the most likely to volunteer. Volunteer rates were lowest among those in their early twenties. Volunteers come from every socioeconomic level, but members of the middle and upper-middle classes are most likely to volunteer, as are those with a higher level of educational attainment. All races and ethnicities are represented as well. The estimated total value of donated hours in 2013 was more than $173 billion (Corporation for National & Community Service 2014).

The Third Sector A Williams College student volunteers at a local high school, where she tutors English language learners.

People engage in volunteer work for many reasons—for social justice, social change, religious values, work experience, and participation in clubs and social groups, and even out of boredom. Not only does volunteering satisfy our most altruistic ideals; it can also be a way to enhance our careers, strengthen our relationships, and even let us live out fantasies or dreams that are not part of our normal, everyday lives. And in so doing, volunteers help create a different world for themselves and others. There are many ways of working—some conventional, some alternative. Not all workers have jobs in traditional fields; not all workers have permanent or full-time jobs; and not all workers do it for a paycheck.

CLOSING COMMENTS

You may never have imagined that work was such a big part of life. You might have had a job of some kind, but now you probably have a better idea of just how important work is on both a collective and an individual level. Work is so important that sociologists have devoted much of their own work to studying it. We can be fairly certain that work will remain a major reality in the human experience into the distant future. We hope that you have gained some insight into the structure and meaning of work in your own lives and the lives of others in society.

Everything You Need to Know about the Economy and Work

> **"** Work is a fulcrum point between the micro and the macro and a link between the individual and the social.**"**

THEORIES OF THE ECONOMY AND WORK

* **Structural functionalism:** different types of work, even ones with low prestige and pay, are necessary to the economy and help maintain social order

* **Conflict theory:** a stratified labor market creates intergroup conflict in which wealthier capitalists may exploit less-powerful workers

* **Symbolic interactionism:** we are intensely identified with our work, both by ourselves and by others

REVIEW

1. Think about the jobs you would like to get after you finish college. Do any of them involve directly participating in the production of physical goods?

2. Thinking of the United States as a capitalist nation with some socialist elements, are there any ways you directly benefit from government intervention in the economy?

3. Marx described four ways that modern wage labor is alienating. Do you think these apply to you and to the job you have or would like to have? If you have a job, would you choose to keep it even if you became independently wealthy?

Who Works at Minimum Wage?

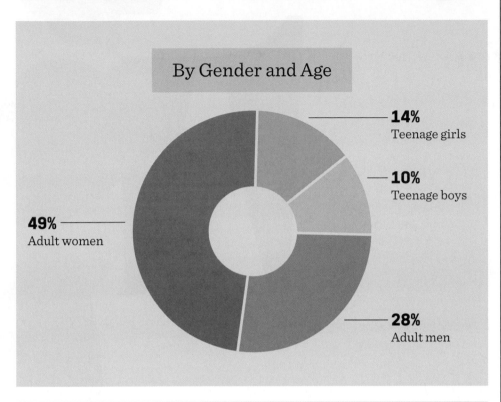

By Gender and Age

14%
Teenage girls

10%
Teenage boys

49%
Adult women

28%
Adult men

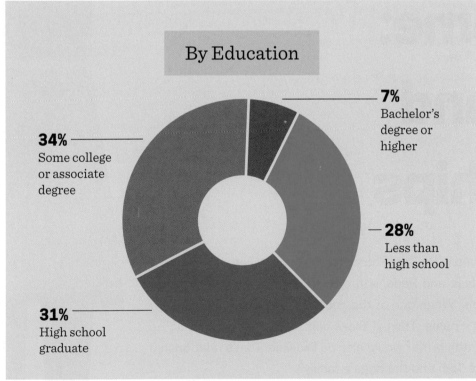

By Education

7%
Bachelor's degree or higher

34%
Some college or associate degree

28%
Less than high school

31%
High school graduate

SOURCE: Kurtz 2013

EXPLORE

In Defense of Face Time

In the age of digital communication, why bother to meet with someone face-to-face? Meetings allow us to see expressions and hear tones of voice—important social cues to someone's feelings and intent. Visit the Everyday Sociology Blog to read more about a sociology professor's thoughts on the benefits of meeting with students in person.

http://wwnPag.es/trw411

CHAPTER 12

Life at Home: Families and Relationships

Tom, a single doctor in his sixties, lived in the same home for thirty years with three much-loved dogs: two boxers named Blaze and Pepe, and a Boston terrier named Brownie. They were his devoted companions. When one of the dogs died, Tom would get a new dog of the same breed and keep the dog's name. Thus, if Blaze died, the new boxer would be named Blaze; if Brownie died, the new Boston terrier would also be Brownie. Tom's relationship with his dogs went on for thirty years. Are Tom and the dogs a family?

Stacie and Eric met in graduate school and married the year they received their degrees. Their job hunts, however, led them in different directions: Stacie took a job with an international

policy agency in Washington, D.C., and Eric went to work for a major corporation in Miami. Living in their respective cities, they spent lots of time Skyping and lots of money on weekend plane tickets. After about five years, Stacie became pregnant, and the baby is due in a few months. Are Stacie and Eric a family?

Jeannie and Elena also met in graduate school—almost twenty years ago. They are both professors in Minneapolis, Kansas, and together they bought and fixed up an old house. They have wanted to formalize their commitment to one another, but they could not do so for many years because of a ban on same-sex marriage in Kansas. Nevertheless, they adopted a little boy named Conor, who is now in his teens. Are Jeannie, Elena, and Conor a family?

For some of you, the answers may come easily, but others may find yourselves wondering—are these groups really families? Tom loves Brownie, Blaze, and Pepe, but can you really be a family if most of your members aren't human? And is Tom's replacement policy similar to or different from the practice of remarrying when a spouse dies? What about Stacie and Eric? They're married and are having a biological child, which seems to make them easily definable as a family. Yet they don't live under the same roof or even in the same state. What does that make them? Even Tom and the dogs live together. And so do Jeannie and Elena, who own their home together. And they're raising their son Conor together, even though they couldn't jointly adopt him like a married heterosexual couple could. Instead, Elena had to adopt him on her own first, with Jeannie becoming his second parent later. With same-sex marriage now legal across the United States they are thinking about tying the knot. Do these complications mean that they aren't a real family?

It all depends on how you define family. If emotional bonds and mutual support are the only criteria, then all of these groups are families. But if a marital bond is required, then only Stacie and Eric are a family. If other legal ties are included, then Elena, Jeannie, and Conor can be a family too. If you have to be heterosexual, then Jeannie and Elena are out, and we really don't know about Tom, do we? If the longevity of the relationships is the key, then Tom and the dogs win over both of these other potential families. But if you have to be human and irreplaceable, then all those Brownies, Blazes, and Pepes don't qualify. And if a shared residence must be part of the equation, then Tom and the dogs are in and so are Jeannie and Elena, but Stacie and Eric are out. In *Counted Out*, Brian Powell and his co-authors (2010) note that, while public opinion in the United States is rapidly changing, the archetypal image of family continues to be the married heterosexual couple with children.

So how do you define family?

HOW TO READ THIS CHAPTER

In this chapter, we examine society's most basic social group—the family. Yet, what makes a family is subject to debate. Sociology doesn't define a family by who its members are but by what they do, how they relate to one another, and what their relationship is to the larger society. We'll look at the dynamic diversity of family forms in the contemporary United States, the functions of family for society, the hierarchies of inequality that shape family life, the work that gets done by and in families, the kinds of troubles families experience, and the political and cultural controversies that affect families. You will learn that when it comes to family life, change is the only constant.

What Is the Family?

The U.S. Census Bureau defines "family" as two or more individuals related by blood, **marriage**, or **adoption** living in the same household. This definition is a starting point, but it's too limited to encompass even the family arrangements described in the opening vignette. Contemporary sociologists use the word **family** to mean a social group whose members are bound by some type of tie—legal, biological, emotional, or a combination of all three. They may or may not share a household, but family members are interdependent and have a sense of mutual responsibility for one another's care. We don't define family by specific types of people (parents or children) or specific types of ties (marriage or biology) because we believe the definition should be broad enough to encompass a variety of forms. However, this very variety is the source of controversy both within and outside academia. Regardless of the definition, most people recognize family as an integral social institution found in every society.

The family as an institution has always changed in response to its social, cultural, political, and economic milieu. Before the Industrial Revolution, "family" tended to mean **extended family**—a large group of **kin**, or relatives, which could include grandparents, uncles, aunts, and cousins living in one household. After the Industrial Revolution, this configuration was largely superseded by the **nuclear family**—a heterosexual couple, usually married, living in their own household and raising children. Along the way, the family moved from a more public social institution to a private one, as many functions formerly associated with the family were transferred to other institutions. For example, work and production moved from the family to the factory, education moved from the family to the school, and government took over a variety of social welfare and support services formerly taken care of by the extended family.

Subsequent waves of social change, such as the women's liberation movement and the move toward individual independence and self-fulfillment, have begun to erode the dominance of the married, heterosexual nuclear family, as increased divorce rates, working mothers, single parents, same-sex marriage, LGBTQ families, and other alternative family arrangements become more common. Many sociologists speak of the sociology not of *the* family but rather of *families*. "Family situations in contemporary society are so varied and diverse that it simply makes no sociological sense to speak of a single ideal-type model of 'the family' at all" (Bernardes 1985, p. 209).

Even though a two-heterosexual-married-parent household with a stay-at-home mother, a breadwinning father, and their two biological children is no longer the norm, this type of family remains the model by which new forms of family are judged. However, there are exceptions, as common-sense definitions of family reflect the changes occurring in the larger society at any given moment. Children seem to be important in our customary definitions of family: one study found that unmarried couples, both gay and heterosexual, are more likely to be considered a family if children are present (Powell et al. 2010). And in an earlier study, Powell (2003) found that unrelated roommates who are not romantically involved are significantly more likely to be considered family by those over the age of sixty-five.

As you will see as you read this chapter, what constitutes the model or hypothetical family may be very different from how families define themselves "on the ground."

Sociological Perspectives on Families

Among the sociological perspectives on the family, structural functionalists view it as a cultural universal and try to identify its functions for society. Conflict theorists argue that there are inherent inequalities both within and between families. Symbolic interactionists focus on the family as the product of interactional processes, while feminist and queer theoretical perspectives question male dominance and heteronormativity as yardsticks for determining what is "normal" when it comes to family. Each of these theories offers useful insights into our understanding of family units.

MARRIAGE a formally recognized bond between two spouses, establishing contractual rights and obligations between them

ADOPTION the legal process of acquiring parental responsibilities for a child other than one's biological offspring

FAMILY a social group whose members are bound by legal, biological, or emotional ties, or a combination of all three

EXTENDED FAMILY a large group of relatives, usually including at least three generations living either in one household or in close proximity

KIN relatives or relations, usually those related by common descent

NUCLEAR FAMILY a heterosexual couple with one or more children living in a single household

In P. D. Eastman's children's book *Are You My Mother?* a newly hatched bird wanders about asking everyone—and everything—she encounters, "Are you my mother?" Sadly for the newborn, neither the construction crane, nor the cow, nor the cat is the parent she is searching for. On the last page of the book, however, the tiny bird is serendipitously returned to her nest and reunited with a maternal-looking chickadee.

When reading something like *Are You My Mother?* most people in the Western world would assume that the word "mother" means "female parent." However, in the Hawaiian language, *makuahine* means both "mother" and "aunt" and refers to any female relative in the generation of that person's parents; *makuakane* is the equivalent term for men (Stanton 1995; Schwimmer 2001). In Hawaiian, then, "Are you my mother?" could just as easily mean "Are you my father's brother's wife?" In China, though, kinship terms are very precise. There are particular terms for a "father's brother's wife" that vary depending on whether the wife is married to the older brother or a younger one (Levi-Strauss 1949/1969)!

FICTIVE KIN close relations with people we consider "like family" but who are not related to us by blood or marriage

One reason we name our kin is to delineate the relationships and obligations we share. In some cases, we use the term **fictive kin** to refer to people who are not related to us through blood or through marriage. Such kin are created through closely knit friendships to the family. You may have a family friend you call Auntie So-and-So. In other societies, fictive kin may be culturally prescribed. In Jordan, it is perfectly normal for adult strangers to address one another with the Arabic equivalents of brother/sister, maternal aunt/uncle, and paternal aunt/uncle. In addition, an older Jordanian woman may affectionately refer to a child (of either gender) as "mother" (Farghal and Shakir 1994).

Sometimes fictive kinship ties are formalized through ceremony, as when a female in India ties a sacred thread around the wrist of an unrelated close male friend to indicate that she considers him a brother. In Latin America, godparents (*compadrazgo*, a word that can be translated as "co-parent" rather than "godparent") are considered permanent members of their godchildren's family. Not surprisingly, the Spanish words for "daughter" and "son" are very close to the words for "goddaughter" and "godson" (Davila 1971; van den Berghe 1979).

Examining kinship terms is one way to understand the diversity of families and how kin fulfill their social roles. As you can see, aunts, elder brothers, godparents, and family friends can all be important family members.

Structural Functionalism

In *Suicide*, Émile Durkheim (1897/1951) argued that the Industrial Revolution and the division of labor had undermined the older social institutions that formerly regulated society, leaving some people suffering from anomie, or normlessness, that sometimes resulted in suicide. He found that marriage and family, at least for men, decreased the chances of suicide because they provide the structure and regulation that Durkheim believed people require to be happy. Durkheim hypothesized that men who were married and had children were less likely to kill themselves because of their obligations to their families, while single men had less to tether them to this mortal coil, and hence would be more likely to succumb to suicidal impulses.

The structural functionalists who followed Durkheim argued that society's survival requires institutions that can serve its essential functions: economic production, the socialization of children, instrumental and emotional support, and sexual control. Although the family is no longer directly involved in economic production, it performs the functions that allow production to happen. Talcott Parsons (1955) argued that "the modern nuclear family was especially complementary to the requirements of an industrial economy" because it freed individuals from onerous obligations to extended family members and made possible the geographic and social mobility demanded by the modern economy (Mann et al. 1997). In the most basic sense, the family is responsible for the reproduction of society as it produces and socializes children who will in turn become future workers and produce and socialize more new members of society. This is what Parsons referred to as "pattern maintenance," whereby the values and norms of a society are passed on to the next generation. Family also, ideally, brings emotional support for its members by providing us with significant others such as spouses, parents, and siblings, and regulates sexuality by helping define with whom we can and cannot mate (in most societies, our brothers, sisters, or parents). These patterns, according to functionalists, help society run smoothly and maintain stability and order, and family as a social institution contributes to social order as a result.

Conflict Theory

Conflict theorists recognize that the family produces and socializes children to function efficiently in a capitalist economy, but they see this function as problematic. The nuclear family, a relatively recent historical invention, acts as the primary economic unit in modern capitalist society, and since conflict theorists see capitalism as oppressive, they claim that this form of family contributes to that oppression—and is often understood as an oppressive institution in itself. Conflict theorists believe that society revolves around conflict over scarce resources and that conflict within the family is also about the competition for resources: time, energy, and the leisure to pursue more interesting recreational activities.

In this analysis, the family can allow exploitation through a sexual rather than a class-based division of labor. Conflict perspectives overlap with feminist perspectives on the family, as feminists assume that the family is a gendered social institution and that men and women experience family differently. In patriarchal societies, men wield greater power than women, both within and outside the family, and women's contribution to family and society (such as household labor, child rearing, and other traditionally female work) is devalued and unpaid or underpaid (Thorne 1992). Considering men to be "heads of household" and providing them with legal rights that women don't have (which in some countries include the right to inherit, or to seek a divorce) means that families themselves are places in which women are discriminated against.

Gender is not the only system of stratification that shapes our experience in families. Age and ability may be the basis for inequality, conflict, and even violence within families, and will be discussed in more detail later in the chapter.

Symbolic Interactionism

As Jim Holstein and Jay Gubrium point out in their book *What Is Family* (1990), the *family* does not exist, only *families*. These symbolic interactionists consider it more effective to look at how family relations are created and maintained in interaction than how they are structured. Even though the legal bond of marriage has the same technical meaning for every couple, individual marriages may have very different expectations and rules for behavior. One couple may require sexual monogamy within their marriage, while their neighbors may not; one couple may pool their finances while their neighbors may keep separate bank accounts. This approach conceives of family as a fluid, adaptable set of concepts and practices that people use "for constructing the meaning of social bonds" (Holstein and Gubrium 1995), a set of vocabularies to describe particular relationships.

Consider the number of relatives, defined by blood or marriage, most people have who play no meaningful role in their lives, who "aren't really family." When we describe people in terms of family, we are making claims about the "rights, obligations, and sentiments" that exist within their relationships (Gubrium and Buckholdt 1982). Consequently, we are constantly evaluating and reevaluating the attitudes and behaviors of those around us, assigning family status to new people and dismissing others from our circle of meaningful family relations. In *All Our Kin*, an ethnography of kinship relations in an urban African American community, Carol Stack (1974) found this dynamic at work in the way people talked about family—including this woman, who explained,

> Most people kin to me are in this neighborhood . . . but I got people in the South, in Chicago, and in Ohio too. I couldn't tell most of their names and most of them aren't really kinfolk to me. . . . Take my father, he's no father to me. I ain't got but one daddy and that's Jason. The one who raised me. My kids' daddies, that's something else, all their daddies' people really take to them—they always doing things and making a fuss about them. We help each other out and that's what kinfolks are all about. (p. 45)

A symbolic interactionist might say that "family members do not merely passively conform to others' expectations" but rather "actively and creatively construct and modify their roles through interactions" (Dupuis and Smale 2000, p. 311)—that is, the people who help each other out, who care for each other, and who express that care are family, whether or not they are legally or biologically related. Sociologist Philip Cohen (2014) has coined the term "personal family" to describe some of these relationships.

Feminist and Queer Theory

Feminist and queer theoretical perspectives on family address what other sociological perspectives overlook: the interplay of gender and sexuality in family and society. Feminist theorists question male dominance, both within and outside families. Why, for example, when heterosexual partners share a home, do we refer to the male partner as the "head of household"? This simple and often taken-for-granted designation bestows upon men the power to make decisions, control financial and other resources, and expect domestic labor and emotional support from the women in their families. This is just one of many elements of family and social structure that tend to privilege men and exploit women, and assumptions like this about gender in families affect us all. That includes the authors of this textbook. When Dr. Ferris married her husband, she did not take his last name, but they did want to share joint access to each other's bank accounts. She arranged with her bank to add her husband's name to her account, giving them both the authority to sign checks. When the next month's bank statement arrived, it was addressed to her husband alone! Dr. Ferris's name had been removed from her own financial life once she acquired a male "head of household." As you might imagine, the bank president got an earful about this error.

Queer theorists further critique traditional perspectives on family by resisting heteronormativity as well as sexism in their analyses. The male head of household example works here, too. If men are assumed to be "heads" of families, who, then, heads nonheterosexual families? How would gay or lesbian couples determine who is the "head"? What about single women—who heads their households? Neither masculinity nor heterosexuality should be a requirement for individuals to have power and autonomy within families (or outside them). Feminist and queer theories help us see that more diverse and egalitarian family structures are possible (Oswald et al. 2005).

Mate Selection

You may think that you are attracted to certain people because of their unique individual characteristics or something intangible called "chemistry." In reality, however, Cupid's arrow is largely aimed by society. Two time-tested concepts in social science—homogamy and propinquity—tell us a lot about how the mate-selection process works. **Homogamy** literally means "like marries like": we tend to choose mates who are similar to us in class, race, ethnicity, age, religion, education, and even levels of attractiveness. Indeed, some groups encourage and even enforce this practice by requiring that their members choose mates from within the group (**endogamy**) and punishing them if they choose mates from outside the group (**exogamy**). You can certainly find examples of people whose romantic relationships cross group and category lines—interracial or interreligious couples, or "May/December" romances—but these relationships are often viewed with disapproval by others in the couples' social circles. There are considerable social pressures to adhere to homogamy.

Propinquity refers to geographical proximity: we tend to choose people who live nearby. This is logical; we are likely to

---

HOMOGAMY the tendency to choose romantic partners who are similar to us in terms of class, race, religion, education, or other social group membership

ENDOGAMY marriage to someone within one's social group

EXOGAMY marriage to someone from a different social group

PROPINQUITY the tendency to partner with people who live close by

---

Table 12.1 Theory in Everyday Life

Perspective	Approach to Family	Case Study: Marriage
Structural Functionalism	Family performs necessary functions, such as the socialization of children, that help society run smoothly and maintain social order.	Marriage regulates sexuality and forms the basis for family, with all its other functions.
Conflict Theory	Family is a site of various forms of stratification and can produce and reproduce inequalities based on these statuses.	Marriage as a civil right was not extended to all same-sex couples in the United States until 2015. Nontraditional families are still marginalized in many ways, while the nuclear family remains the standard.
Symbolic Interactionism	Family is a social construction; it is created, changed, and maintained in interaction.	Marriage is not made solely by completing a legal contract but is also constructed through the accretion of everyday interactions between partners over the years.

find possible mates among the people in our neighborhood, at work, or at school. The Internet makes courtship and romance possible across much greater geographical distances, as we can now meet and converse with people in all parts of the world, so our pool of potential mates moves beyond local bounds. But this technology, while it can weaken the effects of propinquity, can also intensify the effects of homogamy by bringing together people with very specific interests and identities. Examples include online dating services such as Christian Mingle for Christian singles; OurTime.com for people over age fifty; and Athletic Passions for people into fitness and sports. Online dating giant eHarmony hosts special subsites for black, Hispanic, Asian, and Jewish daters who wish to meet people like themselves. There's even a service for rural daters called Farmersonly.com!

Courtship, romance, and intimacy are all influenced by the larger culture—and are also historically specific. As an example of how family forms and definitions change over time, marriage between people of different racial, ethnic, or national backgrounds was actually prohibited for most of U.S. history. From the time of slavery through the 1960s, mixed-race relationships were considered criminal and were also punished outside the law. Fears of interracial relationships led to the lynching of African American men and the creation of **antimiscegenation** laws in several states that prohibited the mixing of racial groups through marriage, cohabitation, or sexual interaction (Messerschmidt 1998). The most significant of these laws fell after the 1967 Supreme Court declared that Virginia's law banning marriage between persons of different races was unconstitutional under the Fourteenth Amendment (*Loving v. Virginia* 1967).

While once uncommon, mixed-race unions are increasing. In 1960, only 0.4 percent of all couples were interracial, increasing to 2.2 percent by 1992 (U.S. Census Bureau 1994), 7.4 percent in 2000, and 9.5 percent in 2010 (U.S. Census Bureau 2012g). Mixed-race couples still face discrimination; in their analysis of a white supremacist Internet chatroom, Glaser, Dixit, and Green (2002) found that respondents were far more threatened by interracial marriage than by persons of color moving into white neighborhoods or competing for jobs.

In addition, same-sex marriage has been one of the most high-profile issues of the past decade. The United States was deeply divided over the issue, with some states passing bans on same-sex marriage and others making it legal. In 2015, the Supreme Court ruled that such bans were unconstitutional, effectively allowing gays and lesbians to marry nationwide. Of course, not all gay and lesbian partners will want to marry. And some queer couples were already able to marry without any changes in the law—a cisgender woman and her transgender male partner, for example (Pfeffer 2012). Finally, neither LGBTQ nor heterosexual persons need legal marriage to form romantic relationships or establish families. So the notion that marriage is the basis for family—as well as the traditional

Kimye and Mixed-Race Unions While once uncommon, mixed-race unions have increased from only 0.4 percent of all couples in 1960 to nearly 10 percent in 2010.

definitions of marriage and family—are called into question by modern family trends.

Monogamy, or marrying only one individual at a time, is still considered the only legal form of marriage in modern Western culture. **Polygamy**, or having multiple spouses, may be practiced among some subcultures around the world but is not widely acknowledged as a legitimate form of marriage. The more commonly known form of polygamy is **polygyny**, in which a man is married to multiple wives. **Polyandry**, in which a woman has multiple husbands, has been documented in Tibet but is the rarer form of polygamy. **Polyamory** is a type of multiple-person partnership in which each individual, regardless of gender or sexual orientation, is in a relationship with each of the other individuals belonging to the group.

While we experience courtship at an individual, interactional level, it will always be shaped by macro-structural forces in the larger society, such as racial, ethnic, or religious prejudices and gendered role expectations. But courtship changes as other aspects of the surrounding culture change. As our society becomes less racist, sexist, and heterosexist, romantic options will expand as well. The development of intimate romantic relationships is not something "natural"; it is socially constructed to *appear* natural.

ANTIMISCEGENATION the prohibition of interracial marriage, cohabitation, or sexual interaction

MONOGAMY the practice of marrying (or being in a relationship with) one person at a time

POLYGAMY a system of marriage that allows people to have more than one spouse at a time

POLYGYNY a system of marriage that allows men to have multiple wives

POLYANDRY a system of marriage that allows women to have multiple husbands

POLYAMORY a system of multiple-person partnership

Relationship Trends

"There's this pervasive idea in America that puts marriage and family at the center of everyone's lives," says Bella M. DePaulo, visiting professor of psychology at the University of California, Santa Barbara, "when in fact it's becoming less and less so" (personal communication 2003). Many people live outside such arrangements. In fact, the average American now spends the majority of his or her life unmarried because people live longer, delay marriage, or choose a single lifestyle (Kreider and Fields 2002).

Unmarried Life

The term "single" often implies a young heterosexual adult who is actively seeking a partner for a relationship or marriage. But singles also include people of any sexual orientation who live together or are in a relationship without opting to get married, people living alone who are in long-distance relationships, people living in communes, widows and widowers, minors in group homes, and some clergy members as well as those who are single as a result of divorce or who simply choose not to have a partner.

Married couples were the dominant model through the 1950s, but their numbers have slipped from nearly 80 percent of households in 1960 to 48 percent in 2014 (U.S. Census Bureau 2014j). Married couples with children—the traditional model of family—totaled less than 20 percent of households in 2014, and that number is projected to drop. The remaining households are single parents, cohabiting partners, or others. A stunning 28 percent of all households in 2014 consisted of people who lived alone, and unmarried people have been the majority in the United States since 2005 (U.S. Census Bureau 2014k).

Some unmarried couples live together before or instead of being married. Demographers call this **cohabitation**. Between 1960 and 2010, the number of unmarried cohabiting couples in the United States increased significantly. More than 8 million people are living with an unmarried partner, including both same-sex and different-sex couples (U.S. Census Bureau 2013c; U.S. Census Bureau 2014a). In addition, marriage is no longer the prerequisite for childbearing. In 2013, nearly 41 percent of all births were to unmarried couples, 58 percent of which were to cohabitating couples (Curtin, Ventura, and Martinez 2014). One-quarter of all first births are to cohabiting parents (National Center for Health Statistics 2012). Forty percent of opposite-sex cohabiting couples have children, while about 14 percent of same-sex male cohabiting couples and 26 percent of same-sex female cohabiting couples have children (Krivickas and Lofquist 2011; U.S. Census Bureau 2012f). Most couples that choose to cohabit rather than marry are twenty-five to thirty-four years of age. A possible reason may be the growing economic independence of individuals today, resulting in less financial motivation for marriage as a legal contract. Also, changing attitudes about religion have made sexual relationships outside marriage more socially acceptable.

Because marriage has for so long been seen as the normative basis for families and households, unmarried people can sometimes feel as if the world is organized specifically to exclude them. Indeed, single people are usually charged more for auto and health insurance than married people; some tax breaks are only available to married couples, and even hotel rooms and vacation packages are usually advertised with "double occupancy" rates. Single people routinely grumble about relatives who ask when they are going to "settle down and get married." Since those who live alone are more likely to be older women (Klinenberg 2012b, p. 5), they may experience multiple forms of discrimination at once.

But as the number of people who live alone increase, so does their potential power to change a society in which they are no longer a minority. Among the growing movement of activists promoting the rights of unmarried people in the United States is the nonprofit group Unmarried Equality. They engage in research, education, and advocacy for unmarried and single adults of all types and are concerned about discrimination that is built into the American social system, especially at an economic and political level but also in terms of culture and values. One of their efforts is to increase recognition of unmarrieds and singles as a constituency of voters, workers, taxpayers, and consumers worthy of equal rights and protection.

As an increasing number of people choose to remain or become single, cohabit with others, or choose something else altogether, they are creating alternative models to organize their lives. Some join an **intentional community**, an inclusive term for a variety of groups who form communal living arrangements that include cohousing, communes, monasteries and ashrams, farming collectives, student co-ops, and urban housing cooperatives. Though small in both size and number, intentional communities are attractive to people for a variety of reasons.

Members of an intentional community have chosen to live together with a common purpose, working cooperatively to create a lifestyle that reflects their shared core values. They may live on rural land, in a suburban home, or in an urban neighborhood, and they may share a single residence or live in a cluster of dwellings. Although quite diverse in philosophy and lifestyle, each of these groups places a high priority on fostering a sense of community—a feeling of belonging and mutual support that is increasingly hard to find in mainstream Western society (Kozeny 1995).

COHABITATION living together as a romantic couple without being married

INTENTIONAL COMMUNITY a group of people living together pursuing a common goal

---

Single and Solo Parenting

Although some people become single parents through divorce or death, others choose to go solo and have children without the support of a committed partner—through adoption, artificial insemination, or surrogacy. Attitudes about solo mothers vary greatly and often depend on the mother's age, education level, occupation, income, and support network of friends and extended family members. Women with more of these resources, including solo celebrity moms like Sandra Bullock, Charlize Theron, and Sheryl Crow, may be subject to less criticism for "going it alone" than women who are younger, earn less money, and have less education or social support.

A prevailing middle-class assumption about single mothers is that young women in the inner city become mothers to access welfare benefits. Kathryn Edin and Maria Kefalas (2005) spent five years doing in-depth research with 162 low-income single mothers to understand their attitudes about parenthood and marriage. They dispelled the myth that these women become mothers to cash in on welfare benefits and instead found that for these young women, having a baby is a symbol of belonging and being valued. While becoming a lawyer or a CEO may seem like a pipedream, being a good mother is an accessible role that can generate respect and admiration in the community.

Of the 11.2 million single-parent households in the United States, 2.6 million of them are headed by single men (Livingston 2013). Solo dads face dilemmas similar to those faced by single moms, but with the added suspicion and stigma surrounding society's notions of men who spend time with children. Even so, the number of single dads has increased almost tenfold since 1960, and this increase seems likely to continue.

Regardless of the circumstances of single parenting, raising children without the help of a partner is challenging and difficult. Financially, physically, and emotionally, single parents must perform a task that was traditionally shared by a community rather than an individual.

Blended Families

Most divorced people will eventually marry someone else, which means that four in ten Americans are members of stepfamilies or blended families (Pew Research Center 2011a). However, statistics about stepfamilies are inconsistent and often contradictory because quantifying and defining the intricate relationships involved in a stepfamily are difficult. The U.S. Census has not routinely accounted for them in its data gathering. There are no traditional norms or models for stepfamilies, and our firmly held notions of the "traditional" family lead many in stepfamilies to find the transition to a new family situation difficult. Stepfamilies face special challenges, for example, when there are children in different stages of the life cycle. The needs and concerns of teenagers may be vastly different from those of their infant half-sibling,

and it may take more work to adjust to the new living situation. With the added challenges of blending in-laws, finances, and households, remarriages are even more likely to end in divorce than first marriages. However, in successful remarriages, partners are usually older and have learned important lessons about compatibility and relationship maintenance from the failure of their first marriages.

Some partners in gay and lesbian couples have a heterosexual marriage (and divorce) in their past. While it is difficult to estimate, one study hypothesized that approximately 4 percent of heterosexual marriages have one gay or bisexual partner (Laumann et al. 1994). While not all these marriages end in divorce, when they do, the gay partner becomes free to form a new family with the partner of his or her choice, just as the heterosexual partner does. So while the majority of blended families are heterosexual, some will be "mixed-orientation" and include stepparents of more than one sexual orientation.

Childfree Living

Having children used to be seen as a mandate and being childless a tragedy—especially for women. We still cling to this imperative: 90 percent of adults surveyed in a 2013 poll either had children or wanted them (Reyes 2013). But because men and women (gay and straight, married and unmarried) now have more choice than ever about whether to have children, a growing number are choosing to live "childfree" rather than "childless." Childfree adults field all sorts of exasperating questions about their lives, from "Wait, don't you like kids?" to "Oh, that's too bad you can't get pregnant" to "Who is going to take care of you when you get old?" and the classic, "Well, that's just selfish." In fact, people who remain childfree may love kids, be quite fertile, be generous with others, and have a perfectly good plan in place for their retirement years; they just don't want to raise kids.

There are many reasons for this: children are expensive and exhausting, and raising them takes energy away from other things that individuals may value more, such as careers, avocations, and other relationships. But childfree people—especially women—are stigmatized for their choice and are often the object of pity, suspicion, and discrimination, according to Laura Scott (2009), primary researcher and author of the "Childless by Choice" project. Scott describes our society as "pronatalist," meaning that our cultural values support childbearing and child rearing as the normative and preferred practice, and those who choose to remain childfree must battle against the judgments others make about them based on their nonconformity.

Breaking Up

Although many people stay in bad marriages or other relationships, couples break up every day. In this section, we consider the changing patterns of breakups, divorce, and remarriage

If you've read this far in this chapter, you've probably already gotten the sociological message: family doesn't "just happen." Family is the product of interactional work. Jennifer Mitchell, an adoption social worker in Rockford, Illinois, does some of that work herself, along with her colleagues at Children's Home and Aid Society, an adoption and family welfare agency based in Chicago.

Mitchell came to her career in a slightly roundabout way. She majored in psychology and worked as an office manager for several years, but after a series of life changes, she found herself thinking about a career in social services and decided to return to school to complete a master's degree in counseling.

At Children's Home and Aid, Mitchell is one of several social workers who prepares prospective adoptive parents and helps them navigate the process of adding to their families through adoption (a different team of social workers at the agency counsels the birth parents, in order to avoid conflicts of interest). She screens prospective parents and takes them through the extensive state licensing procedures that will qualify them to adopt a child. Mitchell interviews people about their desire to be parents, their family life, and their hopes for the future. She visits their homes to make sure they provide a safe environment for a child. She collects all the information required by the state, including first aid and CPR certification, medical exams, letters of recommendation from friends and employers, and even veterinary clearances on the family pets!

Mitchell also leads training sessions where families learn about adoption and the important issues surrounding it—for example, how to talk about adoption with children and other family members, what to expect in cases of international or interracial adoption, or how to maintain an open relationship with an adopted child's birth family. And when a parent or parents bring their adopted child home for the first time, Mitchell monitors their first few months of family life, helping everyone adjust and making sure things are going well until all the legal procedures are completed.

Even after an adoption is legally finalized, Mitchell and her colleagues stay in the picture. The agency hosts parties for adoptive families so that kids and parents can meet and connect with one another. Mitchell and her colleagues also offer post-adoption counseling as a way to help adoptive families who are facing tough times. In some ways, this is what Mitchell likes most about her job—following the families she has helped construct, seeing how they develop, and keeping in touch with them as they make their futures together.

Mitchell has personal experiences that make her distinctively empathetic to the families she encounters in her line of work. She and her husband have been waiting for more than five years to adopt a baby from China. Because of changes in Chinese adoption laws and procedures, they do not know when—if ever—they will be matched with a Chinese child. In the meantime, they have become licensed foster parents and have welcomed two young brothers into their home. So Mitchell is now a foster mom. She gets the boys up in the morning, gets them fed and dressed and off to school, chauffeurs them to music lessons and sports practices, and makes sure they do their homework at night. She stays up with them when they're sick, takes them on fun vacations, and fills their stockings at Christmastime. She talks with them frankly about the situation they are in and what the chances are of returning to their family of origin. And if the court decides to make the boys available for adoption, Mitchell and her husband plan to become their legal parents. But if the court makes the opposite decision, the boys will go back to their biological family, and Mitchell and her husband will open their home to other foster children who need their support.

as they affect children and adults. We also look at the resulting social problems of custody, visitation, and child support.

For 2014, the U.S. Census Bureau reported that more than 127 million persons were married while about 25 million were divorced. Thus, in 2014 about 50 percent of the entire U.S. population were married while about 10 percent were divorced (U.S. Census Bureau 2014l). The percentage of married people who have divorced has greatly increased since 1950, but it is not accurate to say that approximately 50 percent of all marriages now end in divorce, although that myth persists (Miller 2014).

About 40 percent of those who divorce will eventually marry other people. Nearly a quarter (23 percent) of currently married adults have been married before. There is a gender gap in remarriage patterns, with 64 percent of previously married men having remarried compared to 52 percent of previously married women (Livingston 2014). Still, remarriage rates among younger Americans in the United States are actually lower now than they were before the 1960s, a fact attributable to the increase in cohabitation among unmarried couples. Census data reveal that about 6 percent of all households are occupied by unmarried heterosexual couples, which

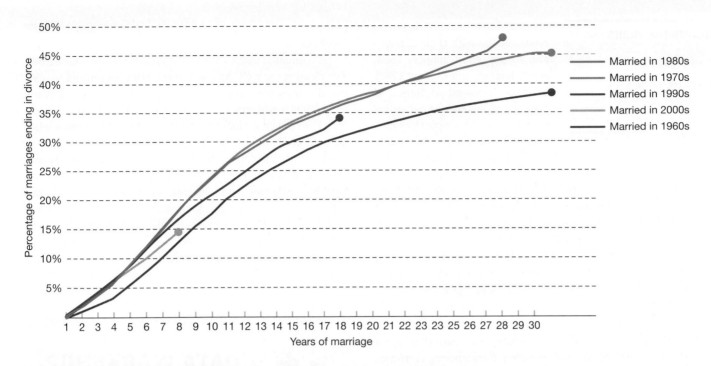

Figure 12.1   Share of Marriages Ending in Divorce by Decade of Marriage

SOURCE: Survey of Income and Program Participation

may reflect a certain caution about marriage as a result of high rates of divorce (U.S. Census Bureau 2014a).

In the early 1970s, the children of divorced parents were more than three times more likely to divorce than their peers from intact families. But by the mid-1990s, this figure had dropped to about one and a half times (Wolfinger 1999, 2000). According to Wolfinger (2003), the decline of intergenerational divorce and marriage rates probably has three sources. One is the growing acceptance of divorce. Children of divorced parents no longer suffer the social stigma that was once the by-product of divorce and are less likely to develop psychological problems as a result, which may have contributed to their divorces in the past. Second, the age of marriage has changed. Children of divorce are still more likely to marry as teenagers, but those not married by age twenty are more likely not to marry at all than their peers from intact families. Third, children of divorced parents are more likely to cohabitate with their partners and are less likely to marry them than children of nondivorced parents. Therefore, the decline in marriage rates among children of divorced parents can be explained by both increased rates of cohabitation and an increased propensity not to marry at all.

Legalization of same-sex marriage now presents the possibility of divorce for gay and lesbian couples as well. Since all U.S. states and territories recognize such marriages they should also allow for legal reciprocity when it comes to divorce. Divorcing isn't the only way to break up, of course. And since not all couples opt to marry, their breakups will not occur within the legal framework of divorce, either. Divorce laws can help streamline the process for those who

are married, while those who are not married must cobble together a package of separate legal contracts that meet their—and their children's—needs.

Custody, Visitation, and Child Support

Reviewing the legal policies that address the consequences of parental breakups for children, sociologists are concerned with whether custody, visitation, and child support effectively replace the resources, both emotional and financial, of an intact household. Do they help children?

Custody is the physical and legal responsibility for the everyday life and routines of children. In previous decades it was mothers who were disproportionately awarded sole custody of children. But more recently there has been a dramatic shift toward shared custody between both parents (Cancian and Meyer 1998; Cancian et al. 2014). By 2008, mother sole-custody had declined from a high of 80 percent to just 42 percent. This decline reflects an increase in shared custody from 5 percent to 27 percent of all cases. There has been little change in father sole-custody, which has remained at about 10 percent.

CUSTODY the physical and legal responsibility of caring for children; assigned by a court for divorced or unmarried parents

Courts award visitation to noncustodial parents to protect parent-child relationships. Generally, parents with regular visitation patterns are better able to meet the psychological and financial needs of their children. Fathers who visit regularly

INSTRUMENTAL TASKS the practical physical tasks necessary to maintain family life

EXPRESSIVE TASKS the emotional work necessary to support family members

are more likely to maintain strong relationships with their children and to pay child support (Seltzer, Schaeffer, and Charng 1989). Despite increased vigilance of courts and lawmakers regarding mandated child support policies, noncustodial parents often fail to make regular payments to custodial parents. Sociologists have found that many parents make informal arrangements, or decisions without the mediation of the legal system, about child support schedules soon after the divorce (Peters et al. 1993) and the stability of payments varies substantially, even among the most reliable payers (Meyer and Bartfeld 1998).

As children are more likely to live in poverty after their parents' divorce, child support policies are important. Women are more likely to suffer downward economic mobility after divorce, especially if they retain custody of their children. In 2011, the poverty rate for custodial-mother families was 32 percent, compared to 16 percent for custodial-father families (U.S. Census Bureau 2013c). Furstenberg, Hoffman, and Shrestha (1995) found that women experience on average a 25 percent decline in their economic well-being after a divorce. Accompanying this post-divorce decline in financial resources are often scholastic failure, disruptive conduct, and troubled relationships in children of divorced families (Keith and Finlay 1988; Morrison and Cherlin 1995). However, it is not clear whether these behavior problems are the effect of the divorce itself or of the problems that led up to the divorce. Jui-Chung Allen Li (2007), a researcher for the RAND Corporation, found that if the behavior of children is compared before and then after divorce, the divorce itself has very little impact on their grades or conduct.

The Work of Family

When we think of work, we usually think of activities done for a paycheck. But paid labor is not the only type of work that sociologists are interested in—especially in the study of family. Many types of work—both paid and unpaid—are necessary to keep a family operating: child care, housecleaning, car maintenance, cooking, bill paying, helping with homework, and doing laundry—the list seems endless, especially when you are the one doing the work!

These tasks can be instrumental or expressive. **Instrumental tasks** generally achieve a tangible goal (washing the dishes, fixing the gutters), whereas **expressive tasks** generally achieve emotional or relational goals (remembering relatives' birthdays, playing Chutes and Ladders with the kids). In a real-world family, however, much of the work has both instrumental and expressive elements. The expressive work of remembering and celebrating birthdays, for example, includes all sorts of instrumental tasks, such as buying presents, writing cards, and baking cakes (Di Leonardo 1987; Pleck 2000).

Instrumental tasks, such as cooking dinner, include expressive elements as well. As a social scientist committed to making the invisible labor of family visible, Marjorie DeVault (1991/1994) excavates all the knowledge, skills, and practices—both instrumental and expressive—we take for granted when we feed our families. Not only is the knowledge of cooking needed, but there must be appropriate shopping to keep a stocked kitchen; to make meals that account for family members' likes, dislikes, and allergies; and to create a varied and balanced menu. Producing meals that please, satisfy, and bring individuals together is just one of the ways that family is created and sustained through interactional work—both instrumental and expressive. We constitute family in and through meals and every other mundane activity of everyday life.

DATA WORKSHOP
Analyzing Everyday Life

Comparative Mealtime

Some of us carry a strong and positive image of our family gathered around the dining room table for dinner each evening. While we were growing up, dinner may have been the one time in the day when the whole family was together and shared food, stories, lessons, and news. For many of us, a great deal of socialization took place around the dinner table; we learned about manners ("Sit up straight," "Don't speak with your mouth full") as well as morality, politics, or anything else that seemed important to the adults raising us. Some of us, on the other hand, may have different memories of family mealtimes. Perhaps they were a time of tension and arguments, or perhaps the family rarely ate a meal together.

In this Data Workshop, you will be doing participant observation research and writing a short ethnography on mealtime activity. See Chapter 2 for a review of this research method. You will pick two different mealtime setting or situations to examine. You can choose from among a range of possibilities, including the following:

● Which meal you study—breakfast, lunch, or dinner

● Where the meal takes place—in your family home, at a friend's or a relative's house, at your own apartment

What's for Dinner? Compare these two family meals. What do our mealtime practices tell us about contemporary American families?

or dormitory dining hall, or at a workplace lunch room, picnic in the park, or restaurant

- Who is eating the meal—family members, roommates, friends, co-workers, or strangers

After you do the participant observation at the two mealtimes, write some field notes and answer the following questions in as much detail as you can. These field notes will serve as data for your analysis:

* What are the prevailing rules, rituals, norms, and values associated with the setting and situation? For example, does everyone sit down to eat at the same time? Do people leave after they finish even if others are still eating? Do you need to get in line to order or pay for food?

* What kinds of complementary roles are the various participants engaged in? Who cooks the food, sets the table, clears the table, does the dishes, and so forth? Or are you served in a cafeteria or restaurant?

* What other types of activities (besides eating) are taking place at mealtime? Are people watching TV, listening to music or a ballgame, reading the newspaper or texting?

* What social purposes do the setting or situation serve other than providing a mealtime environment for the participants? For example, what do the participants talk about? If children are involved, do they talk about school or their friends? Are family activities or problems discussed? What kinds of interactions do you see among co-workers or roommates?

Further analyze your field notes to identify patterns within each setting and meal. What are the similarities and differences between settings and meals? How do participants make these mealtimes meaningful as social events?

There are two options for completing this Data Workshop:

PREP-PAIR-SHARE Make the mealtime observations and prepare some written notes about your preliminary findings that you can refer to during class. Get together with one or two other students and discuss your research. Compare the analyses of the different meals observed by the group members. What are the similarities and differences in your findings? What patterns emerge from the data gathered by the entire group?

DO-IT-YOURSELF Complete the research process. Write a three- to four-page essay answering the questions provided and reflecting on your own experience in conducting this study. What do you think your observations tell us about contemporary Americans and the practices and functions of mealtimes? Don't forget to attach your field notes to your essay.

Gender, Sexuality, and Family Labor

Imagine working a labor-intensive forty to sixty hours waiting tables, making automobile parts, doing data entry, or teaching second graders. You arrive home feeling tired, hungry, and worn out, but you cannot sit down to relax. You still need to cook a meal, do some laundry and cleaning, and take care of your children or perhaps your elderly parents.

Who is more likely to come home to this scenario? Among heterosexual couples, women are more likely to have the dual workload of paid labor outside the home and unpaid labor inside the home. In this section, we will discuss the division of labor within the household.

Men and women have always performed different roles to ensure the survival of their families, but these roles were not considered unequal until after the Industrial Revolution. At that time, men began to leave their homes to earn wages working in factories. Women remained at home to take care of children and carry out other domestic responsibilities. As men's earned wages replaced subsistence farming—in which women had always participated—these wages became the primary mechanism for providing food, clothing, and shelter for families, thus giving men economic power over women.

Despite women's increasing participation in the paid workforce, they are still more likely to perform the bulk of household and caregiving labor. In a few cases, men share household chores (Coltrane 1997), but women bear the brunt of unpaid household labor. Arlie Hochschild and Anne Machung's 1989 study of working couples and parents found that women were indeed working two jobs: paid labor outside the home, or the first shift, and unpaid labor inside the home, or the **second shift**. Hochschild and Machung found that these women tried numerous strategies to achieve balance between work and home: hiring other women to clean their houses and care for their children; relying on friends or family members for help;

Supermom For many American women, "work" doesn't end when they leave the workplace. On returning home, many begin what Arlie Hochschild calls "the second shift," doing the unpaid work of running a household, including doing the laundry, feeding the children, and helping with homework.

refusing to do certain chores, especially those considered to be generally "men's work"; lowering their expectations for cleanliness or quality of child care; or reducing the number of hours they worked outside the home. But some women accept their dual workloads without any help to avoid conflicts with spouses and children. Hochschild and Machung called these women "Supermoms" but also found that these "Supermoms" often felt unhappy or emotionally numb.

Although Hochschild and Machung's observations were groundbreaking in their analysis of post-feminist families, their concept of the "Supermom" has been applicable to working-class mothers all along. The stay-at-home parent is possible only when one salary can support the entire family. Before college-educated women were encouraged to work in the paid labor force, working-class women were there out

SECOND SHIFT the unpaid housework and child care often expected of women after they their day's paid labor

of necessity. The strategies that middle-class women use to negotiate their second shift are available only to wealthier families. After all, a woman who cleans another family's house and takes care of their children rarely has the financial resources to hire someone to do the same for her. And so the second shift is present in working-class homes as well (Miller and Sassler 2012), with women rarely getting the privilege of "downtime" that men enjoy.

In same-sex couples, the household chores can't be unequally distributed by gender, but they aren't always divided equally, either. Mignon Moore (2011) found that, in lesbian families, the division of labor was a way of establishing power relationships within the family, rather than a way of enacting externally prescribed gender roles, as may seem to be the case in heterosexual relationships. In other words, the partner who does more household labor may be able to transform that role into more influence over domestic decision making in general, and decisions having to do with children in particular. This is itself a type of relational power and may be more valuable in such relationships than the power associated with higher income from paid labor.

And while there is very little sociological research on trans families, scholar Carla Pfeffer's (2012, 2014) studies of cisgender women in partnership with transgender men complicate things even further: should we frame the question of "who does what" along the lines of sex or gender at all? In these queer families, the designations of gay/straight, male/female, wife/husband, and mother/father are non-normative, making it problematic to ask if the women/wives/mothers who take on "second shift" work are doing so in fulfillment of traditionally female or feminine roles. How do we categorize the labor of a child's biological mother (childbearing, breastfeeding, and other child-care activities, especially in the early months) when the same person may also be the child's legal father? Perhaps it is time to reframe the work of family using categories other than sex and gender.

Family and the Life Course

As an agent of socialization and the most basic of primary groups, the family molds everyone—young children, teenagers, adults, and senior citizens—and its influences continue throughout the life course.

When we are children, our families provide us with our first lessons in how to be members of society. Children's experiences are shaped by family size, birth order, presence or absence of parents, socioeconomic status, and other sociological variables. Dalton Conley's 2004 work *The Pecking Order* maintains that inequality between siblings; things outside the family's control, such as the economy, war, illness, and death; and marital discord affect each child at different stages in his or her life, resulting in different experiences for each child. Conley argues that family proves not to be the consistent influence many people view it to be.

In addition, the presence of children shapes the lives of parents. Relationship satisfaction tends to decline when there are small children in the house, and heterosexual couples'

gendered division of labor becomes more traditional when children are born, even if it has been nontraditional up to that point. As children get older, they may exert other types of influence on their parents—for example, children can pressure their parents to quit smoking or eat healthier food. And of course, later in life, they may be called on to care for their elderly parents as well as their own offspring—a phenomenon known as "the sandwich generation" effect.

Aging in the Family

The American population is aging. The number of Americans sixty-five or older is growing twice as fast as the population as a whole (Werner 2011). This is because of the Baby Boom generation (the large number of Americans born in the post–World War II era) moving into middle age and beyond, concurrent with advances in medical technology. Average life expectancy in the United States was approximately 79 (with women living an average of five years longer than men) in 2013. More people are living longer, and that has an impact on families and society.

Planning for an aging population means taking into account both the basic and special needs of older individuals. Retirement income is an important part of this planning. Social Security benefits are the major source of income for about 65 percent of the elderly in the United States and the only source of income for 24 percent of America's retired population. Without other sources of income, retired citizens may find themselves with limited resources; in 2013, 9.5 percent of adults sixty-five and older lived below the poverty line (U.S. Census Bureau 2014g). Some seniors solve the problems by living with their adult children or with nonfamily members; even so, in 2013, 35 percent of women and 19 percent of men age sixty-five and older lived alone. The proportion of older adults living alone increases with age, with nearly half (45 percent) of women age seventy-five and older doing so in 2013 (Administration on Aging 2014). Like other traditional

The New Senior Citizen Americans are living longer and leading vibrant, active lives. Marie Wilcox-Little and Donald Goo, both age seventy-three, still enjoy swimming and surfing.

When people talk about the disappearance of the nuclear family, they are usually referring to the divorce rate, but, especially for the Baby Boom generation, families are changing in other ways as well. Traditionally, becoming middle-aged was associated with the "midlife crisis" but also with maturity, wisdom, and increased professional skills. While this might seem like a contradiction, changes in the nature of the family make these qualities seem more like a necessity! Increasing numbers of middle-aged people are becoming members of a "sandwich generation," adults who provide material and emotional support for both young children and older living parents (Lachman 2004, p. 322). This effect is magnified by the increasing number of so-called boomerang kids, who leave home at eighteen to attend college but often return home for at least a short period of time afterward.

Both of these dynamics are being driven less by choice than by demographic and economic necessity. In 1970, the average age at first marriage was less than twenty-one for women and a little over twenty-three for men. In 2014, the median age at first marriage for women was twenty-seven, and for men it was a little over twenty-nine (U.S. Census Bureau 2015h). As a result, people are having children later, increasing the chances that child-rearing and elder care will overlap. Advances in life expectancy also contribute to the sandwich effect, even as many of the medical advances that allow people to live longer also increase their need for material support.

While there have always been adults caring for their elderly parents, never before have there been this many elderly. According to the U.S. Census Bureau, the number of the "oldest old," those eighty-five and older, increased 30 percent between 2000 and 2010, while the total U.S. population grew by only 10 percent during that time (Werner 2011).

Meanwhile, between tuition increases, student loans, and the slow job market, students leaving college are more likely to need help from their parents than ever before. In 1980, less than 9 percent of all individuals between twenty-five and thirty-four lived with their parents. By 2011, this number had increased to almost 15 percent, still a small group but one that has increased significantly during the past three decades.

Members of the sandwich generation have found themselves with more responsibilities than ever before. Not only are their parents living longer, but medical costs associated with old age are growing rapidly, and often they have children, of all ages, still dependent on them as well. Never before has there been a substantial cohort of Americans so directly burdened with such a wide range of family responsibilities. However, in some ways, the more the sandwich generation adults and the boomerang kids change the family, the more they stay

functions of the family (such as educating children), care of the elderly is no longer a primary duty of family and has been taken over by other institutions: many senior citizens will spend time in a nursing home, being housed and cared for by people other than their family members. In 2012, approximately 1.5 million seniors ages sixty-five years and older, or about 3.6 percent, lived in institutional settings such as nursing homes. Another 2.7 percent lived in senior housing where various support services were provided to residents. These numbers increase dramatically with age; approximately 11 percent of people ages eighty-five and older lived in such institutional settings (U.S. Department of Health and Human Services 2012).

Coping with the transitions of retirement, loss of one's partner, declining health, and death are central tasks for seniors. However, as the average lifespan extends, the elderly are also taking on new roles in society. Many live healthy, vibrant, active lives and are engaged with their families and communities in ways that are productive for both the individual and the person's groups.

Trouble in Families

While families are often a place of comfort, support, and unconditional love, some are not a "haven in a heartless world" (Lasch 1977). The family may be where we are at the greatest risk—emotionally, socially, and physically. "People are more likely to be killed, physically assaulted, sexually victimized . . . in their own homes by other family members than anywhere else, or by anyone else, in our society" (Gelles 1995, p. 450).

Because family is the site of unequal power relations and intense feelings, and because of current social norms about the privacy of family life, the circumstances for trouble and violence are ripe. The concept of private nuclear families did not emerge in the United States until the early 1900s. In colonial times, child rearing was a collective effort in which community leaders and neighbors often overruled parental decisions about children. In the late 1800s, mothers looked to other mothers for advice about their children (Coontz 2000). Mothers' journals at the time show that the opinions of other women were often more important than the husband's in

the same, especially in the way that gender roles manifest themselves. Even among eighteen- to twenty-four-year-olds, boys are more likely to live at home than girls, and 60 percent of the boomerang kids between the ages of twenty-five and thirty-four are male. While men and women might be driven by the same financial troubles, moving back in with her parents has different consequences for a woman. She is likely to be asked to take on more domestic responsibilities, and typically she feels a greater loss of independence.

Gender functions in similar ways for the sandwich generation, as it is still mostly women who are called on to provide the emotional and instrumental support for elderly parents, even when those women also work. In fact, "working women who do take on caregiving tasks may reduce their work hours" (Velkoff and Lawson 1998, p. 2), finding themselves having to prioritize family over career in ways men often don't.

Despite the many costs associated with being a member of the sandwich generation, there is good news as well. Although there are challenges associated with "dual responsibilities," these are mostly experienced as "a 'squeeze' but not stress," and these relationships are also a source of happiness and well-being (Lachman 2004, p. 322). And while there is still a certain stigma associated with moving back in with your

The Sandwich Generation With four generations under one roof, the LaRock and Bruno families are an extreme example of the sandwich generation, where adults provide support for both young children and aging parents.

parents, the fact that so many are willing to do so suggests that today's boomerang kids may enjoy closer relationships with their parents than kids of previous generations did.

family decisions. Not until the 1900s did the isolated nuclear family become the ideal in the minds of Americans.

Domestic Abuse

Imagine that tomorrow's newspapers ran front-page headlines about a newly discovered disease epidemic that could potentially kill one-quarter of all American women. Between 1 million and 4 million women would be afflicted in the next year alone. What kind of public reaction would there be?

Let's reframe the scenario: in the United States, one out of every four women suffers physical violence at the hands of an intimate partner at some point in her adult life (National Coalition Against Domestic Violence 2007). In addition, millions of women suffer verbal, financial, and psychological abuse from those who are supposed to love them. Despite these statistics, such abuse is a silent epidemic, seldom reported.

Domestic abuse is an umbrella term for the behaviors abusers use to gain and maintain control over their victims. These behaviors fall into five main categories: physical (slapping, punching, kicking, choking, shoving, restraining), verbal (insults, taunts, threats, degrading statements), financial (insisting on complete control of all household finances, including making decisions about who will work and when), sexual (rape, molestation), and psychological or emotional abuse (mind games, threats, stalking, intimidation). Although not all abusers are physically violent toward their partners, any one type of abuse increases the likelihood of the others. In an abusive relationship, it is extremely rare to find only one form of abuse.

Rates of domestic abuse vary somewhat across racial, ethnic (Truman and Morgan 2014), and religious groups (National Resource Center on Domestic Violence 2007); LGBTQ partners experience up to twice as much relationship violence as heterosexual couples (Stiles-Shields and Carroll 2014). Women are certainly not the only group to suffer from domestic abuse, but statistically, they are

DOMESTIC ABUSE any physical, verbal, financial, sexual, or psychological behaviors abusers use to gain and maintain power over their victims

CYCLE OF VIOLENCE a common behavior pattern in abusive relationships; the cycle begins happily, then the relationship grows tense, and the tension explodes in abuse, followed by a period of contrition that allows the cycle to repeat

more likely than men to be victimized by an intimate partner: between 2003 and 2012, 76 percent of domestic violence was committed against women (Bureau of Justice Statistics 2014b). According to the U.S. Department of Justice, women between the ages of twenty and twenty-four are victims of abuse at the hands of an intimate partner more frequently than women in any other age group (National Coalition Against Domestic Violence 2007). Poor women are also more likely to be abused than women with higher incomes (Bachman and Saltzman 1995). Age and economic security, however, do not make someone immune to abuse.

Contrary to popular opinion, most abusive partners are not "out of control," nor do they have "anger management problems" in the traditional sense. They often seem charming and calm to co-workers, friends, and police officers; they deliberately decide to be violent with those least likely to report the crime and over whom they maintain the most control: their

family members. Domestic abuse results from the abuser's desire for power over the victim, and abusers often blame their victims: I wouldn't have beaten you if dinner had been on time, or if you hadn't been "flirting" with the sales associate at the mall. One abuser is reported to have said to police officers, "Yes, I hit her five or six times, but it was only to calm her down" ("Even in the Best of Homes" 2003).

A four-stage **cycle of violence** seems to occur in almost every abusive relationship. In the first stage, the abusive partner is charming, attentive, and thoughtful; disagreements are glossed over and the relationship looks stable and healthy. However, tension is building to the second stage, often described as "walking on eggshells." Here, both parties sense that something will happen no matter what the victim may do to try to avoid it. During the third stage, acute abuse and violence occur, lasting for seconds, hours, or even days. Whatever happens, the abuser will invariably blame the victim for the incident. The fourth stage, often referred to as "loving contrition," is the "honeymoon" phase and is one of the reasons victims remain in abusive relationships. After the violence, the abuser will apologize profusely and promise that it will never happen again. The abuser may buy the victim gifts, beg forgiveness, and talk about getting help or making a change. Most abusers, however, have no interest in changing because they don't want to give up their control over their victims. Soon the cycle starts again, with flowers and gifts giving way to tension, uneasiness, and another battering.

Victims of domestic abuse stay with their abusers for many reasons. After years of abuse, victims often believe what their abusers tell them: that they can't make it on their own and are somehow responsible for the abuse. If they have not been allowed to attend school or to work, they may not have employment skills. Often, children are involved, or abusers threaten to harm other family members. Many victims have been isolated from friends and family and are afraid to speak of the abuse to anyone, and they see no options but to remain where they are. Survivors who do manage to leave may find that their abusive partners present an even greater risk to their safety after they have exited the relationship (Dunn 2002).

Ray Rice Former Baltimore Ravens running back Ray Rice was caught on an Atlantic City surveillance camera as he coldcocked his then-fiancée, now wife and dragged her out of an elevator. This incident set in motion an investigation that effectively ended Rice's NFL career and shined a light on professional football as a game that involves violence both on and off the field.

DATA WORKSHOP
Analyzing Media and Pop Culture

Family Troubles in Film

Family relations have long been the basis of good comic, tragic, and dramatic films. This Data Workshop asks you to examine

Family Troubles? What do films like *The Kids Are All Right* and *Boyhood* tell us about contemporary American families?

family dynamics and, more specifically, family troubles, as depicted in a feature film. You will be using existing sources and doing both a content analysis and a historical comparative analysis of a film dealing with family troubles. Return to Chapter 2 for a review of this research method.

The following films depict a variety of family troubles: marital issues, divorce, domestic abuse, parental neglect, disabilities and illnesses, sex and dating, pregnancy, death, delinquency, and financial difficulties. Other movies could certainly be added to this list; ask your instructor if there is another you'd like to choose. Your movie should be available on DVD or online so that you can view (and review) it carefully. Please be aware of MPAA ratings and watch only those movies that are appropriate for your age and that you are comfortable viewing:

Affliction	*My Big Fat Greek Wedding*
American Beauty	*Ordinary People*
Amreeka	*Precious*
August: Osage County	*Rachel Getting Married*
Boyhood	*The Royal Tenenbaums*
The Descendants	*Saving Face*
The Ice Storm	*The Squid and the Whale*
In America	*Stepmom*
In the Bedroom	*Still Alice*
The Joy Luck Club	*Terms of Endearment*
The Kids Are All Right	*We Don't Live Here Anymore*
Kramer vs. Kramer	*What's Eating Gilbert Grape*
Mi Familia (My Family)	*You Can Count on Me*

Choose a movie that is primarily about contemporary family relations and problems, then read through the workshop prompts and keep them in mind while viewing. Watch the film closely and pay attention to the plotlines, scenes, characters, and dialogues in which family troubles are depicted. Take notes as you watch the movie; you may need to review certain segments several times to do a thorough content analysis. As part of the process, you will also be doing an Internet search to gather more data about

the family problems and their incidence in contemporary society. Be sure to note the source of your web references. Respond to the following points and questions:

* Give some background information on the film and why you chose it.

* Describe the family troubles that are the focus of the film. How are these problems manifested in the lives of the family members?

* How do the various characters deal with their problems? What solutions do they propose through their talk or actions? How effective are these solutions in addressing the family's troubles?

* Put the family's problems in a broader sociological context. In what ways are the individual troubles of family members linked to larger social patterns and problems?

* Gather some recent data from the U.S. Census Bureau, other government or private agencies, or various news sources. How widespread are these problems in the real world? How are they being discussed and dealt with at a public level?

* How accurately do you think the family's troubles, and their possible solutions, were depicted in the film? What kind of a role, if any, do you think the media can play in helping to improve family troubles and associated social problems?

There are two options for completing this Data Workshop:

PREP-PAIR-SHARE Complete the research activities and develop some preliminary analyses. Prepare some informal notes that you can refer to during in-class discussions. Pair up with one or more classmates and discuss your insights. Compare and contrast the analyses of the films observed by participants in your group.

The first successful progeny of in vitro fertilization, or IVF (referred to disparagingly as a "test-tube baby"), was born in 1978. Louise Brown Mullinder is now a parent herself, and millions of "test-tube babies" have been conceived, born, and raised all over the world. Assisted reproductive technology has come a long way since the experiment that resulted in Louise's birth. Now would-be parents have many options: fertility treatments, IVF, egg and sperm donations, and gestational surrogacy are all growing in popularity. And artificial wombs are being developed that would allow the entire gestation process to occur "in vitro"—no actual human pregnancy required (Mejia 2014). What do these developments mean for the future of the family?

Some of the benefits are already clear: people who were once unable to have biological children now can do so. Single people, LGBTQ people, infertile people, and postmenopausal women can access these ways of creating family—if they have the necessary financial resources. A round of IVF costs between $10,000 and $15,000, and a woman typically has to go through two to three rounds before getting pregnant, while expenses for surrogate birth can reach $100,000 or more.

Advances in technology have also made a variety of genetic screenings possible, allowing parents to determine whether an embryo carries certain diseases or disorders or if it provides the genetic match necessary to be a "savior sibling" for an older child in need of a transplant. Technologies like these make it possible to imagine a future of "designer" children, whose genetic characteristics, such as gender, intelligence, or disease susceptibility, can be manipulated by parents and doctors. The ethics of such a scenario are problematic to say the least.

At the same time that baby-making technologies depart for the future (while leaving cultural ethics struggling to catch up), there is a counter-movement to return to practices of the past when it comes to pregnancy and childbirth. A growing number of mothers-to-be are employing "doulas"—birth support professionals who help pregnant women through labor and delivery, providing assistance, encouragement, and care that medical staff and co-parents can't always provide. The rise in popularity of doulas is linked to women wanting to have a more pleasurable birth experience, along with growing criticism of hospital birth (Port 2014).

In the past, and in other cultures, women often labored and gave birth at home, surrounded by experienced and supportive female friends and family members. Hospital birthing practices have made that rarer now, especially in the United States. While most women still give birth in hospitals, attended by obstetrical staff, a growing minority (3 percent in 2006) seek the service of doulas (Declerq et al. 2007). And those who use doula services, within or outside of hospitals, are almost unanimously satisfied with them, giving doulas higher ratings as birth attendants than they give friends, family members, partners, doctors, or nurses. Until recently, the practices of doulas have been predominately passed down within family/communal traditions; now, more formal training is provided, with several organizations offering training and certification for doulas.

Despite the inevitable bureaucratization of even this traditional practice, the popularity of doulas indicates that the future of childbirth is not all about cutting-edge technology. Doulas take us "back to the future," with time-honored practices that women have used for centuries. And indeed, there is no reason why doulas can't coexist with assisted reproductive technologies. The past always has something to offer the future.

DO-IT-YOURSELF Complete the research activities described and develop some preliminary answers to the questions. Write a three- to four-page essay about the film's relevance. What do you think your observations tell us about contemporary American families and the ways in which family troubles are portrayed on film? Remember to include your notes and provide any references you used.

Child and Elder Abuse

Adult partners are not the only victims of domestic abuse. Children and the elderly also suffer at the hands of abusive family members—and can suffer in distinctive ways that are linked to their special status in the family. Child abuse and elder abuse are likely to be underreported, partly because of the relative powerlessness of the victims and the private settings of the abuse. Official statistics show that about 1 percent of children in the United States are abused in some way, though given underreporting the number is likely much higher

(U.S. Department of Health and Human Services 2015). About 5 percent of all seniors in the United States have been subjected to elder abuse in some form (Acierno et al. 2010). Both children and elders with chronic diseases or other sorts of impairments are at an increased risk of abuse.

In addition to physical violence and verbal, emotional, and sexual abuse, children may experience a distinctive type of abuse known as **neglect**—inadequate nutrition, insufficient clothing or shelter, and unhygienic or unsafe living conditions. Close to 80 percent of child abuse victims suffer from neglect (U.S. Department of Health and Human Services 2015). Because children depend on adults for their care and well-being, they suffer when those adults abandon or corrupt that responsibility. **Incest** is another form of child abuse that exploits the trust that children must place in their caregivers. Inappropriate sexual relationships between parents and children have devastating lifelong consequences for child victims, which may include self-destructive behavior, such as eating disorders and substance abuse, and the inability to form trusting relationships later in life. In addition, those who were physically or sexually abused as children have a much higher likelihood of becoming abusers themselves.

Elder abuse can also take distinctive forms. As well as physical, verbal, emotional, and sexual abuse, there is financial exploitation or theft; relatives or other caregivers may steal or misuse the elder's property or financial resources. Another form is neglect and abandonment. Some elders are dependent on others to care for them. Refusal to provide food, shelter, health care, or protection can be as devastating to an elder as it is to a child. Both elder and child abuse exploit the special powerlessness of victims and are difficult to monitor and control.

Postmodern Families: The New Normal

In 1960, over two-thirds of families consisted of a married couple with a male breadwinner, a stay-at-home mom, and their children. By 2012, less than one-quarter of families looked like this, and there was no single arrangement that could be used to describe the majority of families (Cohen 2014). Instead, we are looking at a growing diversity of family forms, including unmarried parents, blended families, multiracial families, LGBTQ families, and extended family households. This diversity is a result of a number of social changes over the past half-century, including technological innovations in household labor, improved birth control, greater employment opportunities and increasing educational attainment for women, rising divorce rates, increasing acceptance of mixed-race and LGBTQ persons and households, and changes in social welfare programs and laws. Families respond to these social-structural changes in ways that best fit and meet their needs. Indeed, diverse family forms are not especially new; they are merely new to mainstream working- and middle-class families. Minority families, those living in poverty, and gays and lesbians have always had to improvise to fit into a society that ignored or devalued their needs and activities (Stack 1974; Weston 1991; Edin and Lein 1997; Stacey 1998). Diverse, improvisational postmodern family forms will become more and more familiar to the rest of society as we all cope with the social and cultural changes of the twenty-first century.

NEGLECT a form of child abuse in which the caregiver fails to provide adequate nutrition, sufficient clothing or shelter, or hygienic and safe living conditions

INCEST sexual contact between family members; a form of child abuse when it occurs between a child and a caregiver

CLOSING COMMENTS

When sociologists study the dynamics of family, they must define the subject of their interest. What exactly is family? This process sometimes leads to definitions that lie outside the traditional notions of biological or legal relations that have historically defined family. Certainly, this is true if one looks outside the United States at the astonishing variety of customs and practices that define family around the world. Here, too, the nature of the nuclear family is changing, while new types of family groupings are becoming more commonplace. The emergence of these "brave new families" has led to a sea change in the study of families, with an increasing recognition of the diversity and plurality that characterize family arrangements.

Everything You Need to Know about Families

> **"** Sociology doesn't define a family by who its members are but by what they do, how they relate to one another, and what their relationship is to the larger society. **"**

THEORIES OF THE FAMILY

* **Structural functionalism:** the family is responsible for the reproduction of society as it produces and socializes children

* **Conflict theory:** conflict within the family is about the competition for scarce resources: time, energy, and leisure; exploitation occurs through a sexual rather than a class-based division of labor

* **Symbolic interactionism:** family is a social construction that is created, changed, and maintained through ongoing interaction

REVIEW

1. How does this chapter's definition of family differ from the one used by the U.S. Census Bureau? Make a list of everyone you consider a family member. Is there anyone on this list who wouldn't qualify according to the Census Bureau's definition?

2. Conflict theorists believe that strife within the family is fueled by competition for resources. What is the basis for inequality within the family? In families, who tends to receive fewer resources?

3. Arlie Hochschild and Anne Machung found that women who work outside the home often face a "second shift" of housework when they get home. How do men avoid doing their share of this work? Have you ever noticed someone—perhaps yourself—adopting these tactics?

Trends in American Families

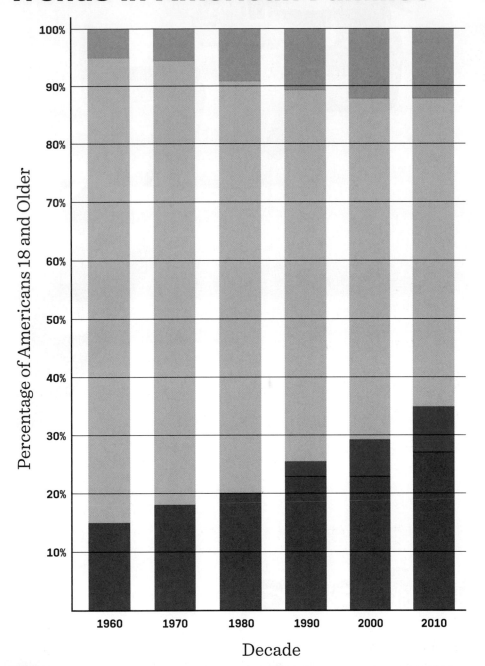

Percentage of Americans 18 and Older

100%
90%
80%
70%
60%
50%
40%
30%
20%
10%

1960   1970   1980   1990   2000   2010

Decade

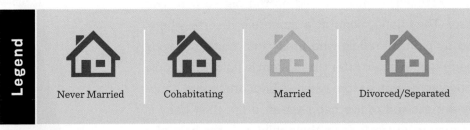

Legend

Never Married   Cohabitating   Married   Divorced/Separated

SOURCE: Pew Research Social and Demographic Trends 2010, "Interactive: The Changing American Family"

EXPLORE

Family Rules: What Is a Family?

When you think of a romantic couple, do you think of just two people involved? Yet other people are part of any romantic relationship, such as parents and friends but also society and the government, particularly if your relationship does not fall under the accepted norms. Visit the Everyday Sociology Blog to read a sociologist's explanation of different relationships.

http://wwnPag.es/trw412

CHAPTER 13

Leisure and Media

You're sitting in a darkened theater watching a movie unfold on the big screen. Two young lovers meet, woo, and marry. They honeymoon at a mountain resort—where, unfortunately, they are kidnapped by political rebels who break into song, swinging their rifles in unison as they dance in camouflage fatigues. After the ransom is paid, the couple return to the city, where they shop for housewares—at a store where clerks croon and shoppers dance in the aisles. But before they are allowed to live happily ever after, their baby is switched at birth with another infant, and they must track down their child with the help of a singing police detective/spiritual advisor. The film lasts more than three hours; during that time,

audience members (men in one section, women and children in another) come and go, fetching delicious snacks that extend far beyond prosaic popcorn and soda. They yell, groan, sing, talk back, and even throw things at the screen—but nobody shushes them. Where are you? You're in "Bollywood."

Unless you are South Asian, have traveled to India, or are a *very* dedicated film buff, you've probably never seen a Bollywood film. This term, an obvious takeoff on the American film capital, is used to describe a particular class of movies produced in Mumbai (or Bombay). The Indian film industry is the most prolific in the world, and the movies it produces are very different from those Americans are used to. A typical film usually includes romance, political intrigue, and dramatic events such as kidnappings, military battles, or natural disasters—and there is always lots of singing and dancing! In other words, Indian films are a mixture of what American audiences understand to be separate genres: romance, musical, action, thriller, and so on. As a result, Americans often react to Indian films as strange, exhausting, and disorganized, while Indians find American movies boring, unemotional, and too short (Srinivas 1998).

Some American audiences got their first taste of Bollywood from British director Danny Boyle's *Slumdog Millionaire*, a film that borrowed some of the same stylistic elements and won the Best Picture Academy Award in 2009. The film was a "sleeper hit" that gradually grew in popularity by good word of mouth, much of it about how different the movie looked and felt. Still, it's unlikely that the theater-going experience for U.S. audiences was anything close to what is typical in India. In Indian theaters, silence is not the norm; audience members respond to what's on-screen in ways that seem startling or even wrong to Americans. The only American film experience that resembles the Bollywood model is the midnight showings of *The Rocky Horror Picture Show*, where enthusiastic fans dress up, sing along, talk back, throw toast, and shoot squirt guns at the screen. In Bollywood, though, this type of behavior is the rule.

HOW TO READ THIS CHAPTER

In this chapter, we will look at leisure and some of the many things we do for fun. This does not mean that the chapter is any less important than others that cover more traditional ground. In fact, we can and should treat topics such as the media and entertainment, sports and recreation, tourism, and hobbies with the same analytic approaches we use to examine other core aspects of culture and society. The production and consumption of leisure activities may seem lightweight or trivial at first glance, but they are worthy of serious sociological consideration. As social institutions, the media and leisure industries play a key role in contemporary life. We will look at the structure and meaning of leisure, its impact on society, and its ubiquitous place in our everyday experiences. Paying attention to your own leisure activities and media usage will add to your understanding of the chapter.

A Sociology of Leisure

Leisure is time that can be spent doing whatever you want—or nothing at all. It can include any activity that is satisfying or amusing, experienced as refreshing for body and mind. This means that just about any activity could fall under this heading, depending on individual preference, and that people can spend their leisure time engaged in all sorts of activities. Leisure is broad enough, then, to encompass a wide variety of pastimes: playing volleyball, traveling to Italy, gardening, woodworking, doing needlepoint, gaming, listening to music, sleeping in, watching television, reading, shopping, writing poetry, hiking, building houses for Habitat for Humanity, baking cookies—the possibilities are endless. For some people, watching TV is a leisure activity. For others, leisure means such activities as skydiving or snowboarding. For many, it's both. It's important to note that what makes something a leisure activity is not its appearance on this or any other list, but rather the experience of the activity itself. Does it feel enjoyable, liberating, even transformative? Then we can call it leisure.

Leisure: More than Just the Opposite of Work

The study of leisure is somewhat new in sociology, but there are many reasons why it has become an important area of interest. The term "leisure" is primarily defined in contrast to paid labor or other obligatory activities, or as the opposite of work. Work has typically been understood as serious and consequential, while leisure activities are seen as minor or trivial. Leisure activities, though, absorb so much time, energy, and resources that they must represent "important developmental goals and meet other personal needs of both children and adults" (Kraus 1995). In many ways, it is leisure that provides the most "meaningful experiences" and allows people "opportunities to reveal their true selves" (Havitz and Dimanche 1999). This suggests that leisure is well worth studying. Indeed, leisure studies has become established as its own academic discipline within the social sciences. Alongside studies in communications and sociology, we can approach the topic of leisure in a variety of ways.

The idea of leisure itself is rather new historically. In the premodern world, the line between work and play was not nearly as clearly defined as it is today—in part because there was an awful lot of work to be done and there were fewer options for entertainment, especially among the working classes. Activities we now engage in almost exclusively as a form of **recreation** (like gardening, hunting and fishing, or knitting) were necessities in the past, and common pastimes like going to the movies and watching television didn't even exist. Even in the late nineteenth century, low wages and long hours meant that only the wealthy had the time and resources to pursue recreational activities with any consistency.

This situation began to change between 1890 and 1940, as the amount of time that the middle class could devote to leisure activities grew rapidly (Fischer 1994). The increase in leisure time was largely fueled by industrialization and technological progress that increased work productivity and spurred time-saving inventions for the home such as the washing machine, dishwasher, and vacuum cleaner. While contemporary Americans still work more hours than their counterparts in other developed nations, on an average day we manage to find about five hours of leisure time (U.S. Bureau of Labor Statistics 2014a). While this is true for the majority, not everyone has the same amount of time, money, or inclination to participate in leisure pursuits.

What we do with our leisure time is changing too. A little less than half of our leisure hours are devoted to recreation, whether it's some physical activity or playing inside. But the Information Age has ushered in technological innovations that have radically altered the nature and types of leisure activities we can enjoy. The average American spends more than half of his or her total leisure hours consuming media, from video games to social networking. Devices like smartphones, tablets, and laptops keep us plugged in virtually 24/7.

Many people think of their nonwork time as "free time" or leisure, using the terms interchangeably. But it's not always easy to determine whether an activity counts as leisure. Sometimes work and leisure seem to blend or overlap. And free time is not always the same thing as leisure time. Sociologist Chris Rojek (1985, 1995, 2000) warns us not to equate free time (or nonworking time) with

LEISURE a period of time that can be spent relaxing, engaging in recreation, or otherwise indulging in freely chosen activities

RECREATION any satisfying, amusing, and stimulating activity that is experienced as refreshing and renewing for body, mind, and spirit

CONSUMPTION the utilization of goods and services, either for personal use or in manufacturing

leisure time. He argues that leisure, by its very definition, constitutes some kind of choice about how to spend one's time. Let's look at a couple of examples.

In one scenario, Amber, Zack, and Juan—all taking the same sociology class—plan an evening study session at a local café. The café is bustling with other students studying too. Amber arrives late from her job as a sales clerk. Zack and Juan have already outlined a few chapters and drunk a few cups of coffee. The three chat for a while before continuing to study. Periodically, they check their cell phones and send text messages. At the end of the night, they plan to meet again the following day. When does work end and leisure begin? In this scenario, it is difficult to decide which is which. Meeting at a café to study seems more like a leisure activity than doing retail sales at a store. However, studying at a café seems more like work than merely meeting friends to chat.

In another scenario, Cheryl finishes work for the day, picks up her children from school, cooks her family an evening meal, helps her children with their schoolwork, and then puts them to bed. You could say that Cheryl leaves one workplace (her job) only to enter another (her home and family). When has she had any free time? Arguably, Cheryl continues to work after she leaves her job at 5:00 p.m. and thus has no free time. She, however, may think of spending time with her family as her free time. Or is free time when we have "nothing" to do? If so, what constitutes "nothing"? Because leisure is hard to define, it's also difficult to measure.

Rather than understanding leisure as the opposite of work, sociologists see the two as complementary activities within a capitalist economic system—two activities linked by **consumption** (Rojek 1985, 1995). Thus, we work for wages to consume a variety of goods and services, including leisure. As we consume more leisure, we must earn more wages to pay for it. We choose leisure time to supplement our working lives, and the connection between the two is more than merely oppositional.

Trends in Leisure

Many discussions of modern leisure-time activities emphasize three related trends that have changed the ways in which we engage in these activities. We now look at these developments in turn: the decline of public life, the formalization of recreation, and the commodification of leisure.

Sociologist Richard Sennett argues that modernity has seen the "fall of public man," as people increasingly seek refuge in "ties of family or intimate association" (Sennett 1977, p. 3). This decline in public life has affected leisure in far-reaching ways. After World War II, the mass migration to the suburbs and the introduction of television encouraged people to stay home and even usurped shared, public activities such as moviegoing (Fischer 1994). Television in particular has been called "the 800-pound gorilla of leisure time" (Putnam 1995). Despite the development of the Internet and its many options for online activities, TV watching remains an enduring and popular pastime. In 2013, the average American was still watching five hours of TV a day (Nielsen 2014).

One large-scale longitudinal study sponsored by the National Endowment for the Arts found that "Americans are increasingly less likely to go out for a dose of the arts, and more likely to stay home and enjoy performances in front of their home entertainment centers" (Yin 2003). The effect has been most obvious in music and theater, but even the visual arts are starting to see a change. People still visit museums and galleries, but a growing number are also looking at pictures online or in books and magazines.

If television began this process, then more recent developments have only intensified it. Digital entertainment across a variety of platforms has made the private home an even more attractive site for leisure. Critics fear that the Internet has further isolated individuals from the outside world and also

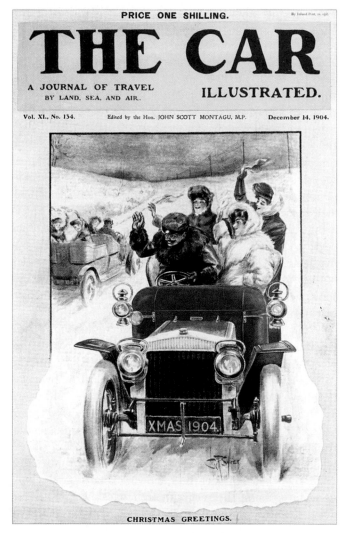

PRICE ONE SHILLING.

By Inland Post, 1s. 9½d.

THE CAR

A JOURNAL OF TRAVEL
BY LAND, SEA, AND AIR.

ILLUSTRATED.

Vol. XI., No. 134.　　Edited by the Hon. JOHN SCOTT MONTAGU, M.P.　　December 14, 1904.

XMAS 1904

CHRISTMAS GREETINGS.

Rise of the Leisure Class Around the turn of the twentieth century, industrial productivity and new technologies created new opportunities for leisure among the middle and upper classes. Note this early travel magazine.

ON THE JOB
Professional Musicians: Playing Is Work

Who wouldn't want to be a rock star? Lear-jetting from city to city, mobbed by adoring fans, staying in four-star hotel suites, partying backstage with celebrities, and getting paid tons of money to play—and the operative word is "play"—music. Such are the stereotypes of the professional musician's life. But a closer look at the real work they do reveals some underlying contradictions to the public images we see of their fame and success.

The casual observer is likely to underestimate what it takes to "make it" as a professional musician. Regardless of how talented, naturally gifted, or even lucky a musician might be, it's going to take a lot of hard work to succeed. We don't ordinarily appreciate all the seemingly endless hours musicians must devote to learning and perfecting their craft. In fact, it takes something like 10,000 hours to become an expert in any field, according to Malcolm Gladwell (2008), who studied "outliers" or exceptionally successful people. Gladwell claims that greatness takes an enormous amount of time, and that the "10,000 Hour Rule" applies to understanding how the Beatles honed their skills in the years prior to becoming famous. This dispels the notion that anybody can become an "overnight success" and upholds the truism that everybody must "pay their dues" in order to make it in the music business.

Of course, there are also many different versions of success as a professional musician, and some of them are a lot less glamorous than what we might imagine. Not every successful musician becomes rich and famous. Many work in relative obscurity as band members, back-up singers, session players, songwriters, or producers. Their careers can be tenuous, uneven, and short-lived. The recent films *20 Feet from Stardom* and *The Wrecking Crew* document the lives of such professionals, giving greater recognition to those who toil just outside the brightest spotlight. Still, most musicians love what they do and feel fortunate if they can make a living at it.

While professional musicians readily acknowledge the benefits inherent in their work, it doesn't mean they have nothing to complain about. True, they aren't doing strenuous manual labor and they aren't stuck in a cubicle from 9:00 to 5:00. But neither is what they do as fun and easy as it might appear. The work conditions can be difficult and the days long and grueling. Writing, recording, rehearsing, and touring require sustained concentration, teamwork, and stamina. The work is often characterized by drudgery and repetition rather than spontaneity and creativity. After years in the business, some musicians suffer from the same kind of disenchantment with their careers that workers in other fields experience, despite whatever notions of romance might have attracted them to the music business in the first place (Stein 1997).

The rewards of working in any glamorous profession, whether it's music, show business, or sports, probably seem well worth any of these difficulties. As social observers, however, we need to consider what goes on behind the scenes and remember that what looks like play to one person might feel a whole lot more like work to another.

20 Feet from Stardom Backup singers Jo Lawry, Judith Hill, and Lisa Fischer take the spotlight in the 2013 documentary.

from one another. Technology can divide us even when we're together. With everyone glued to small and big screens alike, are we losing our sense of civic and interpersonal engagement?

In a paradoxical twist, when we do come together to engage in shared leisure activities, they are more likely to be organized than spontaneous. Our entertainment and recreation are prepackaged and arranged for us. This development of "organization over spontaneity" is illustrated by the rise of Little League baseball as an organized alternative to impromptu after-school sandlot games (Fischer 1994). There is a great deal of debate as to whether this increased organization is good or bad. New technology has indirectly

assisted this process: smartphones, social media, radio, and TV advertising all make it easier to connect people for organized activities. Sites like Meetup.com are tools for further organization; someone can start a Meetup group around almost any shared interest.

Another development that is making an enormous impact on our lives is the massive increase in the **commodification** or commercialization of leisure activities. Where people formerly made their own fun, they now purchase it in the form of goods and services. In 2014,

COMMODIFICATION the process by which it becomes possible to buy and sell a particular good or service

Extreme Play Outdoor activities like scuba diving, sky diving, and snowboarding, which require participants to purchase a lot of gear, are changing the nature of play.

the average American spent over $2,500 on entertainment (U.S. Bureau of Labor Statistics 2015a). That is estimated to amount to almost $600 billion in 2016 (Snider 2012). Much of that is spent on media products (music, movies, video games, apps, books, magazines, newspapers, and so on), but it also includes spending on toys, hobbies, sporting equipment, and admissions fees to a variety of attractions.

Simple, inexpensive outdoor activities like hiking are still popular, but they increasingly compete with "technologically innovative forms of play such as scuba diving, parasailing, skydiving, and hang-gliding, snowmobiling, and other kinds of off-road travel [that] have opened up new environments for the play experience" (Kraus 1995). Even those activities that were once necessities, like hunting and fishing, now come with a dizzying array of commodities. Sport fishing relies on expensive boats, lures, rods, and sonar to help locate the fish. Hunting seems to demand special clothing, scent blockers, calls and decoys, infrared vision enhancement, and even special hearing aids that allow hunters to tune in to specific frequencies while stalking particular animals. Instead of visiting the local swimming hole, we pay to visit water parks. Instead of playing softball or soccer, we may simply watch sports on TV, played by professionals. In almost every case, our recreation is mediated by goods and services that we seem to "require" in order to have fun.

The ultimate example of the commercialization of leisure, however, is shopping: where the purchase of commodities becomes an end in itself. Recreational shopping is a recent historical development. Until the mid-twentieth century, people shopped mainly to acquire food, clothing, fuel, tools, and other essential goods. In addition, we have become aspirational shoppers; we shop to live out our fantasies and dreams, and the shopping experience itself delivers a "sensual and emotional high" (Zukin 2004, p. 220). Shopping is no longer just about "bread"—it has also become its own "circus." There are more than 100,000 malls and shopping centers nationwide to support our habit (U.S. Census Bureau 2012e).

In recent years, the shopping mall has undergone changes. The old-style enclosed shopping center has declined in popularity, and the country is littered with shuttered and empty malls. Some blame the mall's demise on the Internet and the ease and convenience of shopping online, but Americans still do most of their spending in brick-and-mortar stores. At the same time, new (or refurbished) malls are offering more than just a place to buy things. In order to attract and captivate shoppers, malls are becoming "lifestyle" centers for entertainment and social gathering (Nielsen 2013).

Leisure, money, and business intersect in other ways as well. Almost any kind of activity we enjoy must be supported in some way by others. From hiking in the local foothills (consider how the Parks and Recreation Department might be involved in maintaining trails) to eating an ice cream cone (consider the manufacturing, delivery, and service involved in getting the cone to your hand), many people work to make these activities possible. When you go to a professional baseball or basketball game, chances are that you're there to root for your favorite team, eat hot dogs and drink soda or beer, and generally have a good time with family or friends. Work is probably the last thing on your mind. But what about the people who help provide that experience for you—the parking attendants, ticket-takers, security officers, ushers, food and souvenir vendors, janitors, and maintenance workers? What about the team owners, talent scouts, agents, managers, coaches, trainers, and players themselves? If the game is covered by the media, then you can add announcers, reporters, sportscasters, photographers, camera crews, producers, editors, publishers, advertisers, and others. According to the U.S. Department of Labor more than 15 million people work in the leisure and hospitality sector of the economy. That includes jobs in the arts, entertainment, and recreation as well as the lodging and food services that often go along with them (U.S. Bureau of Labor Statistics 2015g).

Clearly, leisure is big business. Let's take the National Basketball Association (NBA) as an example. In 2015, the Los Angeles Lakers were the top-grossing team, worth an

Commercialization of Leisure Old-style shopping malls are being replaced with outdoor lifestyle centers like the Grove in Los Angeles.

estimated $2.6 billion (despite posting their worst season on record). The average NBA team is now valued at $1.1 billion (Badenhausen 2015). According to the Entertainment and Sports Programming Network (ESPN) the Chicago Bulls boasted the highest attendance of any team in 2014–2015 with more than 875,000 people attending forty-one home games, an average of about 21,000 spectators per game (ESPN 2015). Many more millions of fans tuned in to NBA games on radio and TV or watched online. Overall, the businesses that could be broadly classified as providing leisure or entertainment are easily worth trillions of dollars. As such, these industries account for a major part of the U.S. and global economies.

The Study of Media

Any study of leisure must necessarily consider media. As we have seen, people spend their leisure time engaged in a wide variety of activities. For many Americans, consuming media—reading the newspaper, watching TV, listening to the radio, or surfing the Internet—accounts for a large portion of this time. Clearly, the media have extensive reach. It is a major social institution and one with increasing power and importance in the digital age. At first glance, we might conclude that the media's purpose is simply to supply information, educate, or entertain. While this is not incorrect, it is a somewhat incomplete view of a complex and sophisticated social institution.

The Media and Democracy

One of the first things to remember about the media is their intimate relationship to a democratic system of government. The media have always been seen as both an instrument of the state and a tool for social change. Some of the original struggles during the fight for American independence were waged around these very issues. Early American leaders recognized the importance of news in educating and mobilizing the new citizenry. They were opposed to European governments' control over the media (which consisted at that time of books and newspapers) and sought instead to free the press so that it could be used as a voice of the people. That is precisely why the framers of the U.S. Constitution included guarantees to freedom of expression and freedom of the press in the First Amendment:

> Congress shall make no law respecting an establishment of religion, or prohibiting the free exercise thereof; or abridging the freedom of speech, or of the press; or the right of the people peaceably to assemble, and to petition the Government for a redress of grievances.

These are among our most precious and fiercely defended rights as Americans. The press was also intended to serve as a kind of "**Fourth Estate**." The press could act like a separate branch of the government, which could independently examine political leaders and give the people another means of checks and balances against the three branches (or "estates") of the government. It would ensure that no branch, whether the executive, legislative, or judicial, amassed too much power. Thus the media are a last defense of an open, democratic system. They play a critical role in uncovering and exposing all kinds of government malfeasance, corruption, and incompetence.

While the principle of a free press still stands today, it is worth considering just who is free to own what we currently refer to as "the press"; in other words, a media outlet. Who has access to the media, who controls media products, whose voice is reaching a mass audience, and what kind of message is being sent by these powerful instruments of "free speech"?

The Structure of Media Industries

Media companies are among the many big businesses that drive the U.S. economy, and their profits and losses are closely followed by investors in the stock market. Media products are among the country's biggest exports, fueling a worldwide demand for information and entertainment. The number of these companies seems to constantly expand, and there are almost too many publishing houses, production companies, TV networks, film studios, radio stations, record labels, and website and game developers to name. Then there are also the companies that make the hardware, software, and digital devices on which we consume it all. As the media industries grow, so does their power. Let's look at some interrelated trends in the structure of media industries.

CONGLOMERATION What is not readily evident from this seeming proliferation of media is that the businesses are often owned by the same large parent companies. The trend toward **conglomeration** began growing in the 1990s (McChesney 2000). Huge corporations were acquiring media companies as part of their larger holdings. This is why a company like Seagram's, which manufactures alcoholic beverages, bought (and later sold) Universal (then MCA), which produces film, television, and music. Or how General Electric, which makes everything from light bulbs to jet engines, came to own the NBC television network. Now Comcast owns both NBC and Universal. Buying successful media companies makes good sense as an economic investment, so it is not surprising that other corporations might want to share in the huge profits generated by the entertainment industry.

A typical media conglomerate might comprise many divisions: book and magazine publishing, radio and TV broadcasting,

FOURTH ESTATE the media are considered like a fourth branch of government (after the executive, legislative, and judiciary) and thus serve as another of the checks and balances on power

CONGLOMERATION the process by which a single corporation acquires ownership of a variety of otherwise unrelated businesses

SYNERGY a mutually beneficial interaction between parts of an organization that allows it to create something greater than the sum of its individual outputs

MERGER the legal combination of two companies, usually in order to maximize efficiency and profits by eliminating redundant infrastructure and personnel

a cable network, a movie studio and theaters, record labels, video game distribution, websites, a theme park, even a sports franchise. Also referred to as horizontal integration, this allows the company to take advantage of its own organizational structure and market its products across a wide range of media formats and outlets. Media companies favor products they can "cross-promote" along their various divisions, thus creating what is called **synergy**. For example, a company might produce a movie that is adapted from a book it published, distribute the film to theaters it owns, advertise and review it in company newspapers, magazines, and TV programs, put the soundtrack on its record label, create recognizable characters that appear in commercials or at its theme park, release the movie on its DVD label, and later broadcast it on the company's cable channel and television network.

The cornucopia of media choices is thus somewhat deceiving. Many brands and labels are all really just different company identities within a larger structure. There are actually very few "independent" media producers that can remain viable in such a marketplace. Often, once an independent becomes successful, it is quickly bought out by a larger conglomerate, which is searching for ways to increase revenues. Another trend consists of a **merger** between two or more companies to create an even bigger media giant. The model for this trend took place in 2000 with the merger between a new media company, AOL (America Online), and an older one, Time Warner. In 2014, Comcast made a bid to acquire Time Warner in a deal that would have merged the nation's two largest cable providers. Amid protests from consumers, lawmakers, and regulatory agencies, the deal was rescinded. But this is not expected to derail current trends; we are likely to see ever bigger and more powerful media conglomeration in the future (Brennan 2014).

DATA WORKSHOP
Analyzing Media and Pop Culture

Blockbuster Hits and the Business of Movies

The seventh installment in the *Star Wars* film series was released in December 2015. *Star Wars: The Force Awakens* is the first film

in what will be the third *Star Wars* trilogy. Yes, that means nine *Star Wars* movies released (or planned) so far. When the Walt Disney Co. bought Lucasfilm (the original home of *Star Wars*) for over $4 billion in 2012, the acquisition made big headlines in the business world. Just a few years earlier in 2009, Disney had pulled off another aggressive buyout of Marvel, the comic book and movie studio, for the same amount (Barnes 2009). Taken together, these two deals presented some of the most lucrative possibilities ever in terms of Disney's added ability for synergy, marketing, and future growth (Gabler 2012). Disney now owned some of the most recognizable and bankable brands in entertainment and was poised to translate them into greater successes and profits, a situation to which any media company would aspire.

Most people think of movies as primarily a form of entertainment. But in this Data Workshop we want you to consider them as a business. And the movie business is big business, especially when it comes to those mega blockbuster hits. Making movies for a mass audience is expensive (and risky), but it can also be highly profitable. The major studios that make these kinds of movies must come up with strategies to help maximize the potential for profits and minimize the potential risks of financing a costly "flop." How can media companies ensure that their biggest movies become their biggest hits? This is where their corporate practices and structures can benefit the bottom line.

Big media companies like Disney have an advantage when it comes to producing and distributing their products. When a parent company owns many other subsidiaries, it can market its properties across a variety of media outlets. In other words, such companies can benefit from cross-promotion. The greater the diversity and reach of a company's divisions, the more opportunities there are to create synergy. The most attractive properties are those that might start as a comic book but can then be turned into a movie and a video game, where the stars of the movie can be featured on TV talk shows or magazine covers and where fans will be able to follow additional story lines and interact on websites, through social media, or at fan conventions. Think of all the avenues for promotion that a media giant might own and exploit.

One common practice in filmmaking follows the adage that "nothing succeeds like success." Studio execs favor movie "franchises" from which many hits can be spawned. Think *James Bond*, *The Avengers*, *Mission Impossible*, *X-Men*, *Iron Man*, *Spider-Man*, *The Fast and the Furious*, *Transformers*, *Harry Potter*, *The Hunger Games*, and such. These films were the basis for producing many other, sometimes even more successful, films in the form of prequels, sequels, and spinoffs. A related approach is to do remakes by producing an updated version of an older film or show that was successful before, for instance, *Ocean's Eleven, 21 Jump Street,* or *Godzilla.*

Another strategy for increasing the odds of a hit, or at least diminishing the losses that might incur from a flop, is to partner with an outside company and engage in what is referred to as "co-promotion." In these relationships, the partner company invests in the film for some kind of consideration, primarily rights to promote its products in conjunction with the film. This takes several shapes. The partner can provide product placement within the film to more covertly "advertise" its particular brand (whether it's an automobile, cell phone, or soda) to audiences. Or the partner might be involved in merchandising tie-ins with the film, like when a fast-food chain offers customers a free toy or collector's cup with purchase. Many companies also create merchandise such as action figures, posters, T-shirts, or hats to further promote and profit from their films.

For this Data Workshop you will be asked to use existing sources to investigate the marketing and promotion for a recent blockbuster movie. Refer to Chapter 2 for a review of this research method. Choose a movie that exemplifies the strategies of hit making. It's not necessary that you see the film yourself (but you may) in order for you to analyze the corporate economics behind making it. There are a variety of sources and materials you can examine online. All the major studios create official websites for their movie releases. Or you can visit IMDb.com, the Internet Movie Database site that provides detailed information on every film made. Look for company credits like who produced and distributed the film and its soundtrack. Review the box office receipts, and note the film's costs and profits. Check out the studio's site for links to merchandise and related social media campaigns. Read some business news articles about the movie's success. There are likely to be other sites where you can find out more about how your blockbuster did business.

Once you have data, consider these questions:

* How many elements from the strategies described here can you find to help account for your film's success?

* Did the movie studio take advantage of all possible avenues to reap the greatest profits, or can you suggest other ways the studio could have improved or expanded its sales campaigns?

* How does the corporate business model shape the kind of movies that get made?

* What makes blockbusters popular with audiences, and why?

There are two options for completing this Data Workshop:

PREP-PAIR-SHARE Choose a blockbuster film to examine. Look at how the movie was marketed. Make notes about what you find to bring to class. Discuss with others in small groups, comparing the different films and their promotional campaigns.

DO-IT-YOURSELF Write a three- to four-page essay addressing the questions provided and the various ways that movie studios attempt to produce hits. Make reference to the data you collected about the marketing campaigns.

The Disney Empire Disney CEO Robert Iger (left) with *Star Wars* creator George Lucas in Walt Disney World. Through acquisitions of major companies like Lucasfilm and Marvel, Disney now occupies a more horizontally integrated position in the entertainment industry.

CONCENTRATION Mergers and acquisitions associated with conglomeration result in yet another major trend: **concentration**. The ownership of media companies of all kinds is now concentrated in the hands of fewer and fewer large conglomerates. Communication researchers who follow media ownership saw a consistent trend through the 1980s and 1990s characterized by mergers and buyouts and resulting in fewer but larger media companies in the 2000s (McChesney 1997, 2004; Bagdikian 2004). Researchers often refer to the big five or six global media conglomerates, down from more than twenty-five such companies just a decade or two ago, that now dominate the media industries (Klinenberg 2007; Shah 2007; FreePress.net 2011). The current list includes Comcast, Time Warner Inc., News Corporation, The Walt Disney Company, Viacom, and CBS, as shown in Table 13.1. While few in number, these media giants keep getting bigger. American companies comprise about 90 percent of all global media (Le 2014). That leaves only a small percentage of media companies truly independent from this corporate reality.

Two government agencies, the Federal Communications Commission (FCC) and the Securities and Exchange Commission (SEC), are charged with regulating the large conglomerates. The FCC has established some restrictions on media-outlet ownership by any single company in order to avoid a **monopoly** in any one market. Otherwise, one media giant might be able to own all the newspapers and TV and radio stations in a region, effectively stifling any competition and potentially providing a single voice for information where several voices serve a democracy better. And the SEC is involved in **antitrust legislation**, governing mergers between companies and further discouraging monopolies from forming. However, in recent years, increasing **deregulation**, the reduction or removal of government restrictions on the media industry, has allowed companies to gain control of ever-larger chunks of the media market.

These decisions are often fiercely debated by the U.S. Congress, media companies, and media watchdog groups. Social critics are concerned about increasing concentration and its possible consequences for a democratic society that values freedom of the press and a plurality of voices. "Net neutrality" has become an important frontier in the battle for control over the delivery of data over the Internet. Proponents want to ensure that Internet providers treat all data equally and that they don't discriminate among different companies, allowing some but not others faster or cheaper services. If the largest companies are allowed to control the dissemination of information, does that undermine the constitutional rights of average citizens to have their voices heard?

Even in today's heavily concentrated media market, there are still opportunities for alternative voices to be heard. This is thanks, in part, to a proliferation of digital technology. These alternative voices, though, are typically confined to small, marginal outlets. Still, almost anyone can now find a

CONCENTRATION the process by which the number of companies producing and distributing a particular commodity decreases, often through mergers and conglomeration

MONOPOLY a situation in which there is only one individual or organization, without competitors, providing a particular good or service

ANTITRUST LEGISLATION laws designed to maintain competition in the marketplace by prohibiting monopolies, price fixing, or other forms of collusion among businesses

DEREGULATION reduction or removal of government controls from an industry to allow for a free and efficient marketplace

Table 13.1 The Concentration of Media Outlets

Corporation	2014 Revenues (in billions)	Principal Holdings
Comcast	$66.8	NBC, Telemundo, MSNBC, Hulu, Bravo, USA Network
Walt Disney Company	$48.8	ABC, ESPN, A&E, Lifetime, Disney Channels, Walt Disney Studios, Pixar, Marvel Studios, Marvel Studios, Walt Disney Parks and Resorts
News Corporation	$33.7	FOX, 21st Century Fox, the Wall Street Journal, the New York Post, HarperCollins, MarketWatch.com
Time Warner Inc.	$27.4	HBO, CNN, DC Entertainment, Cartoon Network, TNT, TBS, CW (joint venture) Warner Brothers Pictures
CBS	$13.8	CBS, CW (joint venture) Showtime, Simon & Schuster
Viacom	$13.7	Paramount Pictures, Comedy Central, BET, MTV, VH1, Nickelodeon

SOURCE: Bloomberg 2015.

Net Neutrality In 2015, amid protests across the country, the FCC voted in favor of net neutrality—the principle that all Internet traffic be treated equally.

platform on which to express themselves. For instance, bloggers and podcasters are able to circumvent the constraints of commercial radio and print journalism to transmit their political opinions or musical sensibilities to an (admittedly small) audience online. Artists of all types can build their own websites to promote (and sometimes sell) their work. Websites like YouTube allow individuals to upload homemade videos to their own channels. Someone else may garner thousands, or tens of thousands, of followers on Twitter or Instagram. With the rapid development of faster, cheaper, and more user-friendly digital media, more people now have access to technologies that allow them to produce and distribute their own work in the global marketplace. It's worth asking, though, whose voices get heard in a saturated media landscape? Can an individual, or small enterprise, really hope to compete?

POWER SHIFTS The past decade has seen unprecedented change in the structure and organization of media industries. So called "new media" have exploded. Technology and communications companies have become key players in a marketplace once dominated by more traditional media leaders. We see many cases where new and old media firms combine forces to create the emerging giants of an evolving industry. These giants are increasingly structured around horizontal integration, a type of organization where the company can control almost every aspect of the production and distribution process and use its various subsidiaries and divisions to market products across many different platforms. The idea is always to reach a bigger share of audiences and consumers. Companies might also seek vertical integration, allowing them to effectively monopolize a particular industry. This

was the plan for the merger of the two cable industry giants, Comcast and Time Warner, and why so many objected to it.

New and converging media and communications technologies have revolutionized the way these industries work. Power has shifted from companies that produce products to companies that distribute them. What is becoming clear is that in a digital age, the companies that provide access to entertainment and media will be at least as important as the companies that actually make the entertainment. And many companies, such as Netflix, Hulu, and Amazon, will try to do both.

A look at Apple, and all the products that Apple has made ubiquitous, can help to illustrate these points. Apple used to make computers and still does, but they have expanded their products and furthered their reach. Along with iMacs, MacBooks, and Mac minis, there are iPods, iPads, iPhones, and the Apple Watch (no "i"). Of course, Apple also developed and owns a number of software programs that make the devices run, including the operating system (MacOS), streaming video player (QuickTime), and web browser (Safari). You can manage your Apple devices using iTunes, which is also a media library, music player, online radio station, and storefront. Remember that Apple devices are all designed to allow customers to buy other things as well—software, music, movies, books, apps, and games. If that weren't enough, Apple has made dozens of acquisitions in the past two years, including buying Beats Electronics for $2 billion in 2014. The company was founded by music moguls Dr. Dre and Jimmy Iovine; it originally made speakers and headphones and then added an online music streaming service. Buying up other companies and developing more products allows Apple to better compete with other media and tech companies. The goal, as always, is to increase their market share and profits.

Mobile Media The proliferation of smartphones like Apple's iPhone means we are seeing a shift in power toward telecommunications companies like AT&T and Verizon.

Another area of change involves the astronomical growth in mobile media. Seemingly everyone now carries a smartphone, and these devices are not only being used to make phone calls or text. We use them to do all sorts of things online—things that we used to do on a computer just a handful of years ago. This has translated into enormous economic power for the telecommunications industry and companies like Samsung that make the devices and wireless carriers like AT&T and Verizon. The other big winners are tech companies like Google and social media sites like Facebook and Snapchat. We're talking about a current consumer base of several billion users. As more people take their media on the go, these companies will be vying for consumers and looking to boost profits with ad revenues and sales. There will be more mergers, such as the 2015 deal between Verizon and AOL, as media giants adjust to and prosper from new technologies and new business trends. This increased consolidation is bound to affect users in numerous ways.

The Regulation of Media Content

Another area of intense debate about media industries revolves around the content they produce and government censorship. Some claim that media content, especially when it is violent or sexual in nature, has a negative effect on society and should therefore be restricted; others support a media free market or believe that the right to free speech or artistic freedom should in no way be infringed on. What role, if any, should the government play in negotiating these competing interests?

The FCC imposes regulations on what the media may produce, once again qualifying the notion of absolute freedom of expression. As you may be aware, certain types of speech are not protected under the Constitution. Material considered to be obscene, for example, is illegal. The criteria used to define obscenity are based on a momentous 1959 Supreme Court decision, *Roth v. United States*. According to the ruling, child pornography and other "material which deals with sex in a manner appealing to prurient interest" are considered obscene. However, the line between "indecent" material, which is restricted but not forbidden, and obscene material is sometimes hard to draw.

RATINGS AND WARNINGS Over the past several decades, various media industries have turned to self-regulation of the materials they produce, often in the face of threats of censorship and in an effort to avoid outside regulation by government agencies. These efforts first began in 1968 when the Motion Picture Association of America (MPAA) established the movie ratings with which you are likely familiar. Those ratings are G, PG, R, and more recently PG-13 and NC-17, the latter to distinguish material unfit for anyone under seventeen from adult or pornographic material carrying an X rating. Next was the music business in 1985, when the Recording Industry Association of America agreed to place warning stickers on certain albums containing songs about drugs, sex, violence, and other potentially objectionable subjects. These labels ("Parental Advisory: Explicit Lyrics") were the recording industry's response to pressure from U.S. Senate hearings and lobbying from the Parents' Music Resource Center, headed by Tipper Gore (former wife of then senator and future vice president Al Gore).

The 1990s ushered in self-regulation for other media industries eager to avoid government restrictions on their products. The Entertainment Software Rating Board established a rating system for video games in 1993 based on age appropriateness. In 1997, television programs began featuring a ratings system that not only suggests the appropriate age for viewers but also warns of violence (real-life or cartoon), sex (including dialogue with sexual innuendo), and offensive language. The "V-chip" was added to TV receivers to allow parents to block violent programs altogether. More means of controlling content appeared as digital media spread to new devices. In the 2000s, software programs were developed to limit access to certain types of websites. Parents could now choose to block or filter not only websites but also instant messaging, game apps, file transfers, and downloads. By the 2010s, parents had options to control mobile devices and even to do remote tracking of their children's activities.

These voluntary measures at regulating content, self-imposed by media industries, acknowledge the concern that some material is unsuitable, especially for children. Some studies of the effectiveness of these measures indicate that children are still being exposed to objectionable material and that parents may be misled if they believe ratings systems or blocking software are preventing their children from having access to those materials (Garry and Spurlin 2007; AV Comparatives 2014). With the massive proliferation of adult material that is available online, it has become increasingly difficult to police content and the possibility of exposure.

IN THE FUTURE
The Return of Free-Range Kids?

When Baby Boomers reminisce about their childhoods, their memories often include hours spent with friends riding bikes, playing in the street, walking to the park, tinkering in the backyard, and maybe riding the bus or the subway downtown for a movie or an ice cream cone. Kids were out exploring their immediate environment, whether it was urban, suburban, or rural. And they were usually doing so without much direct parental supervision. In other words, most of their leisure time was unstructured and unsupervised; they were on their own, and as long as they made it home in time for dinner, everything was cool. "Go out and play," said Mom, "and come back when the streetlights go on."

If you are in your twenties, you probably have a very different set of memories from your own childhood. You were probably driven to school (in an approved child safety seat) by a parent or other caregiver, then picked up and chauffeured to your after-school program, piano lesson, swim or soccer practice, Girl or Boy Scout meeting, or chess club, depending on what day of the week it was. Weekends were full of sports or robotics competitions or maybe a school play or musical recital. Chances are you were raised by what have come to be called "helicopter parents," or parents who hovered over you and made sure your calendar was filled with the kinds of organized activities they hoped would contribute to your future success in school and the workplace.

If your parents hovered, it was because they loved you and wanted the best for you. But children of helicopter parents may find it harder to seek and find independence as they move into adult life. So the latest crop of parents has begun rethinking child-rearing once again, and there is now a push to allow kids to enjoy more liberation and empowerment, even if that means some increase in risk. "Free-range parenting" is back in style.

New York journalist Lenore Skenazy (2008) became the accidental spokesperson for this movement when, in 2008, she wrote a column for the *New York Sun* about her nine-year-old son taking the subway home from a department store . . . alone. She had no idea how polarizing the column would be. People either praised her for encouraging her son's independence or threatened to turn her in to Child Protective Services! Skenazy's story took on a life of its own, and she made the rounds of talk shows and news interviews, eventually writing a book called *Free-Range Kids* (2009) with chapter headings like "Relax: Not Every Little Thing You Do Has That Much Impact on Your Child's Development," "Quit Trying to Control Everything. It Doesn't Work Anyway," and "Walking to School." Skenazy and her supporters argue that parents should be willing to loosen their grip on their kids' lives—let them explore on their own, make their own mistakes (and deal with the consequences), and essentially learn to fend for themselves.

This approach still creates controversy. In 2015, the Meitiv family of Montgomery County, Maryland, was twice reported to authorities for allowing their children, ten and six, to walk to and from a neighborhood park by themselves. Other free-range parents have faced similar interference. Despite the fact that their kids weren't lost, faced no particular danger, and weren't being abused or neglected, the parents were called to account for letting them walk around and play in their own familiar neighborhoods unsupervised.

Parents' fears of children being victimized, injured, kidnapped, or killed are something of a red herring. Statistics show that most of these hazards are at all-time lows and have been decreasing for decades. Of course, certain specific neighborhoods may not be conducive to unsupervised play, but most children in the United States live much safer lives than they did fifty years ago; bad things are more likely to befall children at the hands of their parents and caregivers than by strangers. But while crime is down, fear of crime is up, due in part to the amount of violence we can now watch on television (Jamieson and Romer 2014). This means that our perceptions of the dangers of simple, ordinary activities (like walking to the park) may be based in fictional rather than real-world experiences.

It's unclear how many parents are part of the free-range movement, but Skenazy's book was a bestseller and she now hosts a television show on the topic. Will the free-range movement grow? Will overprotective parents overcome their (possibly unfounded) fears and encourage their kids to become independent, responsible, and safe? Is free-range parenting old-fashioned—or is it the future of play?

Are the Kids All Right? Proponents of free-range parenting believe that free unsupervised play is critical for children's development into healthy, resilient adults.

Debates about the content and power of the media rage on. These issues are frequently in the spotlight, often in the wake of some high-profile or controversial event that exposes large audiences to something inappropriate that should have been censored. Consider Miley Cyrus's twerking at the Video Music Awards or when Kim Kardashian tried to break the Internet. These widely viewed incidents were met with a range of reactions from amusement to outrage. Such controversies highlight some of the conflicts between different types of culture, media, and audiences.

Culture and Consumption of Media

Conflicts about the appropriateness of this or that cultural product often hinge on perceived differences in the value of one kind of cultural consumption over another. For instance, is opera "better" for you, or for society, than heavy metal music? Does one elevate and the other debase? And if so, why, and who decides? Perhaps it's not even a question of either/or, but rather a matter of taste, time, and context.

High, Low, and Popular Culture

"Culture wars" about audiences and the appropriateness of material can be fought just about anywhere. In the summer of 1998, an exhibit opened at the Guggenheim Museum in New York City that was uniformly panned by the critics. The *New Republic* called the exhibit "a pop nostalgia orgy masquerading as a major artistic statement," and *Salon*'s art critic accused the Guggenheim of "wear[ing] its cultural pants around its ankles" and "sucking down to our lowest impulses." What were they so upset about? The exhibit was titled "The Art of the Motorcycle," and the critics were upset because motorcycles weren't, in their opinion, art. The public, on the other hand, loved it—the exhibit broke all previous museum attendance records. People who might never otherwise have set foot in the museum came to view this colorful collection of motorcycles dating back to 1868.

The motorcycles at the Guggenheim stirred up a longstanding debate over the very definitions of art and culture. The critics' objections were based on their perception that **popular culture**, or mass culture (motorcycles), had invaded a **high culture** venue (the Guggenheim Museum). In this case, popular culture was seen as unsavory and even dangerous—the implication being that pop culture is a mass phenomenon that somehow threatens the position of the elites by challenging their

Is This Art! The 1998 show "The Art of the Motorcycle" at the Guggenheim Museum in New York broke attendance records but attracted negative reviews from art critics for "sucking down to our lowest impulses."

preferences. As with so many sociological concepts, these terms come originally from the German; in this case, *kultur* (the culture of the elite classes) and *massenkultur* (the culture of the masses). But are these two categories really so separate?

First, there are multiple high cultures and multiple pop cultures, based on differences in taste and aesthetics. Also, each category has its own set of hierarchies. For example, rap and hip-hop music are definitely pop culture phenomena. Produced by mostly minority artists for whom "street credibility" is one of the most important qualifications, these musical forms have widespread popular appeal, especially among teenagers and young adults. But rap and hip-hop have their own elites, artists who are at the top of the charts and who have a great deal of influence within and outside their pop culture domain. Artists such as Kanye West, Pharrell Williams, Nicki Minaj, Beyoncé, and Jay-Z, the elites of the rap and hip-hop worlds, show that the distinction between mass and elite is a fuzzy one.

The boundaries between high culture and popular culture are often permeable, so the way we categorize any particular type of art or artist can change over time. We usually consider the works of Shakespeare as the pinnacle of high culture, but this was not always so; in previous eras, his plays were performed before commoners and aristocrats alike. The director Alfred Hitchcock is among the most revered filmmakers of all time, but he wasn't always held in such high esteem. Early on, critics dismissed his films as schlock; now they are considered pillars of the film canon. Even television is shedding its reputation as disposable fluff. Shows like *Mad Men* and *Game of Thrones* are the subject of serious literary criticism once reserved only for high art.

There is another way in which these kinds of distinctions are problematic. In the real world, most cultural products contain elements of both mass and high culture. Why do you think we call certain TV programs soap "operas"? The story lines and intense emotions of *The Young and the*

POPULAR CULTURE usually contrasted with the high culture of elite groups; forms of cultural expression usually associated with the masses, consumer goods, and commercial products

HIGH CULTURE those forms of cultural expression usually associated with the elite or dominant classes

High Art and Pop Art Are Not Mutually Exclusive Even though Andy Warhol's work is now exhibited in high-culture venues like esteemed modern art museums, he was perceived as a threat to the "real" art world when he began his work in the 1960s. At the bottom is Warhol's subversion of a high-art masterpiece, Leonardo da Vinci's *The Last Supper* (above).

Restless parallel and sometimes rival those of Puccini's *Madama Butterfly* and Wolfgang Amadeus Mozart's *Don Giovanni*. Led Zeppelin and Van Halen songs, when written out in standard musical notation, show a recognizable symphonic structure. Some of their compositions are as complex as those found in classical music. Rap and hip-hop overtly draw on other types of music in the practice of sampling, and Ludwig van Beethoven, Georges Bizet, and Béla Bartók have all been sampled by R&B artists. These examples, and many others, indicate that high and pop culture are not mutually exclusive and can coexist within the same product.

TASTES AND MEANING The distinctions between high and popular culture are based on the characteristics of their audiences. Differences of class, education, race, and even religion help create these categories. Sociologist Herbert Gans (1999) calls the groups of people who share similar artistic, recreational, and intellectual interests **taste publics**. Taste publics aren't necessarily organized groups, but they do inhabit the same aesthetic worlds, which Gans calls **taste cultures**; that is, people who share the same tastes will also usually move in the same cultural circles. For example, sociologist David Halle (1993) found that members of the upper class are more likely to have abstract paintings hanging in their homes, while members of the working class are more likely to display family photographs in their homes.

The music, movies, clothes, foods, art, books, magazines, cars, sports, and television

TASTE PUBLICS groups of people who share similar artistic, literary, media, recreational, and intellectual interests

TASTE CULTURES areas of culture that share similar aesthetics and standards of taste

programs you enjoy are influenced at least in part by your position in society. Unknowingly, you belong to a number of taste publics and inhabit a number of taste cultures, in that you share your interests with others who are similar to you demographically. What you think of as your own unique individual preferences are in some ways predetermined by your age, race, gender, class, level of education, and regional location.

Media Effects and Audiences

Media researchers have sought to understand whether popular culture can influence certain types of behavior (Gerbner and Gross 1976; Malamuth and Donnerstein 1984; Weinstein 1991, 2000; Anderson et al. 2010). Do TV crime shows increase our propensity to violence? Does pornography lead to the abuse of women? Does heavy metal music make teenagers suicidal? Such questions suggest that cultural products impose their intrinsic meanings on their audiences in a simplistic, stimulus-and-response fashion. But while it is true that media are potentially powerful transmitters of cultural values and norms, the process is neither immediate nor uncomplicated.

Sometimes dramatic current events like the 2012 mass shooting of audience members during a midnight showing of *The Dark Knight Rises* raise concerns about the relationship between media content and real life. The influence or effects of the media on society have been studied for many decades by scholars in a range of disciplines, including psychology, communications, and sociology. The theories they have generated run along a spectrum, from the media having great power and influence over audiences, to their having little or none, to audiences themselves being central in the creation of meaning. It is worth examining what each of these theories has to say about the effects of media on society and the individual and to consider the applicability of any theory to the postmodern, digital world in which we now live.

HYPODERMIC NEEDLE THEORY (MAGIC BULLET THEORY) a theory that explains the effects of media as if their contents simply entered directly into the consumer, who is powerless to resist their influence

Passive Audiences: The Hypodermic Needle (or Magic Bullet) Theory

In the early years of mass media, it was thought that audience members of all sorts (including readers) were passive recipients of content and that whatever meaning was in the "texts" they consumed was transmitted unaltered and absorbed straight into their consciousness. (The term "text" is a general one that can include sound and image as well as print.) This notion was contained in the model known as the **hypodermic needle theory** (or **magic bullet theory**). The assumption was that, like an injection, media content was shot directly into the audience members, who responded instantaneously to its stimulus (Lazarsfeld and Katz 1955). One of the key examples often cited to support this theory was the 1938 radio broadcast of H. G. Wells's short story "War of the Worlds" narrated by Orson Welles. The radio show used a mock news-bulletin format and was played uninterrupted by commercial breaks. Listeners who tuned in after the beginning of the show did not realize it was merely a dramatization of a Martian invasion. It was reported that audience members numbering in the millions actually believed the "news" was true and were so frightened as to have sparked widespread panic. Though this might seem rather exaggerated now, the theory still points to an important principle about the media's potential to directly influence behavior.

War of the Worlds A radio broadcast of H. G. Wells's short story "The War of the Worlds" caused widespread panic when listeners misinterpreted the mock news bulletin as an account of a real Martian invasion.

Active Audiences: Minimal Effects Theories

Media scholars quickly realized that the hypodermic needle theory was not accurate or applicable for the most part—that audience members were not as passive or easily persuaded as first believed and that the various forms of media themselves were not as all-powerful in their influence over individuals. A number of related theories were developed during the 1960s and '70s that proposed the media had limited or minimal effects.

Contemporary research on the effects of media has supported the idea of **active audiences**. The focus of research also shifted. Instead of asking, "What do media do to people?" scholars began to ask, "What do people do with media?" (Severin and Tankard 1997). The **uses and gratifications paradigm** contains several theories that emphasize a more actively engaged audience member (Katz 1959). Blumler and Katz (1974) highlighted five areas in which audiences sought gratification and fulfilled needs through their use of the media. First, audiences could achieve some sense of escape from reality; second, audiences could use media for social interaction, forming relationships to characters, or conversing with others about products and programs; third, they could gain some aspect of personal identity by incorporating elements found in the media into their everyday lives; fourth, the media could serve to inform and educate audiences; and fifth, audience members could consume media purely for the sake of entertainment.

Many media scholars have been interested in the persuasive powers of the media, whether used in advertising to get consumers to buy products or used in the political arena to sway public opinion or to garner votes. Two related theories suggest that the influence of the media is more limited than marketing executives or campaign managers might otherwise wish. **Reinforcement theory** argues that individuals tend to seek out and listen to only those messages that align with their existing attitudes and beliefs. Thus audience members typically tune out anything that might seem too challenging and instead prefer only those messages that support what they already believe (Klapper 1960; Atkin 1973, 1985).

The **agenda-setting theory** focuses on how the mass media can influence the public by the way stories are presented in the news (McCombs and Shaw 1972, 1977). Depending on which stories are chosen as newsworthy and how much time and space are devoted to their coverage, the public gets a sense of the value or importance of any given event. The media may not be able to tell audiences what to think, but they do set the agenda for what (stories) to think about. Finally, the **two-step flow model** of communication suggests that audiences get much of their information from "opinion leaders" who can convey and explain important news rather than from more direct or firsthand sources (Lazarsfeld and Katz 1955). Certainly someone like Oprah Winfrey exemplifies this; she is known for her widespread ability to influence and can introduce millions of her audience members to whatever is her latest concern.

Interpretive Strategies and Communities

Media research in the 1980s and '90s maintained its focus on active audiences. Theorists proposed that media consumers bring to the experience different **interpretive strategies**. This approach argues that different individuals, because of their different experiences, perspectives, and personalities, may respond to media content in unique and idiosyncratic ways. This means that whatever meanings may be inherent in texts, consumers may read them in the intended ways but can also modify and even invert the meanings of texts depending on their own backgrounds and purposes. Different interpretive strategies lead back to the idea of polysemy—that any given text may have multiple meanings.

Working within the cultural studies perspective, Stuart Hall's **encoding/decoding model** (1980, 1997) combines elements of the hypodermic needle/magic bullet and active audience theories. This model assumes on the one hand that specific ideological messages are loaded, or encoded, into cultural products and that they therefore have the potential to influence individuals, especially with regard to promoting the interests of capitalist elites. On the other hand, individuals may respond to messages embedded in the media in a variety of ways. In fact, when faced with ideologically encoded cultural products like movies or music, for example, we may decode them in novel ways. Further, we can engage in "cultural resistance" or choose "oppositional" or "against the grain" readings of products, subverting

ACTIVE AUDIENCES a term used to characterize audience members as active participants in "reading" or constructing the meaning of the media they consume

USES AND GRATIFICATIONS PARADIGM approaches to understanding media effects that focus on how the media fulfills individuals' psychological or social needs

REINFORCEMENT THEORY theory that suggests that audiences seek messages in the media that reinforce their existing attitudes and beliefs and are thus not influenced by challenging or contradictory information

AGENDA-SETTING THEORY theory that the media can set the public agenda by selecting certain news stories and excluding others, thus influencing what audiences think about

TWO-STEP FLOW MODEL theory on media effects that suggests audiences get information through opinion leaders who influence their attitudes and beliefs, rather than through direct, firsthand sources

INTERPRETIVE STRATEGIES the ideas and frameworks that audience members bring to bear on a particular media text to understand its meaning

ENCODING/DECODING MODEL a theory on media that combines models that privilege the media producer and models that view the audience as the primary source of meaning; this theory recognizes that media texts are created to deliver specific messages and that individuals actively interpret them

Do you know the rules for cricket, that complicated ball and bat sport so popular in India? What's up with the Canadians and their love of curling, you know, the game played on ice with the brooms? How about jai alai, what Spain proclaims is the world's fastest sport, the one with the three-walled court? Every country seems to have its favorite sport, but there is one that is most beloved the world over—football. No, not *that* football—the other one. What Americans call soccer but everyone else calls football is wildly popular internationally, but it is just beginning to take off among U.S. sports fans. American interest in soccer seems to spike every four years when the World Cup rolls around; otherwise, major league soccer is not even as popular as ice hockey and it still lags well behind the professional sports behemoths of football, baseball, and basketball.

The rest of the world, however, thinks Americans are crazy. In almost every other country around the world, football (soccer) is a major sport. There are local and national competitions between teams and international competition between national teams. Salaries for top players often surpass deals made with elite American athletes, with tens of millions of dollars going to heavyweights like Cristiano Ronaldo, Lionel Messi, and Zlatan Ibrahimovic. When British soccer superstar David Beckham signed a lucrative five-year deal in 2007 to play with the L.A. Galaxy, his celebrity status drew more attention to soccer in the United States. But he then moved on to play for teams in Italy and France, and is now retired.

While soccer has a lackluster fan base in the United States, the sport inspires intense devotion from fans across the globe. But sometimes that passion has a downside. More specifically, it's the rowdy and sometimes violent fans, often referred to as "hooligans," who have garnered attention from their association with soccer. The British, especially, are infamous for the mobs of "yobs" (slang for hooligans) who cause mayhem both in Great Britain and elsewhere in the soccer-playing world as they follow and fight over their teams. Violence typically breaks out between fans of rival teams. Brawls can quickly escalate into riots and stampedes, leading to widespread injury, death, and destruction of property. Soccer actually has a violent history: In the medieval period, entire towns would participate in soccer matches to resolve disputes, and kings and queens at times had the game banned because of violence. In those days, it was the players who had to be concerned for their safety; since the rise of contemporary hooliganism, it's now the spectators who need to be wary.

Hooliganism began in England in the 1960s and then quickly spread to many other European nations and beyond. Notorious gangs can be found in Turkey, Hungary, Russia, Peru, Argentina, Brazil, Egypt, Ghana, and elsewhere. While many soccer-playing countries, including Greece, Germany, Poland, and even Switzerland, have endured some form of hooliganism, England is still the site of the worst hooliganism (Buford 1993). The violence got so bad in the 1980s that hooliganism was referred to as "the English disease."

As the popularity of soccer increased over the next few decades, fatalities soared. Fortunately, there has been a marked reduction in the number of deadly incidents in recent years. This is due to a number of factors, including more self-regulation among fans, better stadium designs, more intervention by security personnel, and increased efforts on the part of police forces (Morris 2014). But these measures have not eliminated hooliganism, and every year people are injured and killed at soccer matches around the world.

Why does soccer spur brutality in some of its fans? There are a variety of theories. Some speculate that the fanaticism

TEXTUAL POACHING Henry Jenkins's term describing the ways that audience members manipulate an original cultural product to create a new one; a common way for fans to exert some control over the media they consume

their original or dominant meaning. For example, Madonna's classic video "Like a Virgin" can be read in a number of ways. It was widely seen by cultural critics as sexually exploitative and demeaning, while teen fans brought interpretive resistance to their understanding, subverting the meaning and embracing the video as empowering to them as young women. Such critical analysis can be applied to any number of contemporary music videos today.

Henry Jenkins (1992) extends the model to something he calls **textual poaching**, wherein audience members take the original product and manipulate it themselves—often to tell stories or express ideologies very different from the original. For example, fans of the TV show *Star Trek* have taken episodes of the program, deconstructed, and re-edited them to create new stories (called "K/S," or "Slash") in which Captain Kirk and Mr. Spock are not just best friends and co-workers but passionate gay lovers. This oppositional restructuring

A History of Violence
Russian fans riot during
a football match between
FK Austria Wien and
Zenit St. Petersburg.

of hooligans is only an excuse to be violent. Skinheads and other racists, for example, sometimes use soccer matches to broadcast their beliefs. Others assert that fandom can develop into a nationalistic fervor that increases the likelihood of violence. For example, for British fans who feel united against a foreign team while in a foreign country, it may be easy to feel both isolated and compelled to defend the honor of their team and country—especially when emotions are already heightened with the fury of athletic competition (King 1995). Some blame the countries themselves and point to their

underlying social, economic, and political tensions (Brimson 2010).

Fan violence at American sporting events is certainly not unheard of, but so far there's nothing on the scale of soccer hooliganism. Why is such extreme mob violence rare in the United States? Is it because U.S. teams are seldom involved in truly international competition? Or because there are so many different professional sports and teams to follow? As soccer—the real football—grows in popularity in the United States, will the violent history of the sport come with it too?

indicates that viewers can read different meanings into the text than were intended by the producers—indeed, can reproduce the text in order to make those meanings central. Jenkins's ideas have also been applied to new forms of digital media that provide fans with more control over content and more opportunities for engaging in what he calls participatory culture (Jenkins 2006). This happened in 2014 with Pharrell Williams's hit song "Happy." Williams gave permission to fans to create their own "cover" videos using his song. This resulted in nearly 2,000 different versions of the music video produced by fans in more than 150 different countries.

Responding to cultural texts is thus an exercise in the distribution of power. The more active the audience is in interpreting the text, the less control the producers have over the messages that are communicated. While you may not go so far as one of Jenkins's "textual poachers," neither are you a passive recipient of predigested pop-culture pabulum. Your consumption of media (film, television, music, books) and live performance (concerts, theater, sports) is active in the sense that you contribute your own interpretive resources—context, experience, and perspective. And to the extent that you share these experiences with others, you may find that

It is simply taken for granted that an American will know about a huge swarming throng of unmet figures through his [sic] consumption of the various media. (Caughey 1984, p. 32)

Who is this "huge, swarming throng"? Celebrities—people with whom few of us have actual face-to-face interactions but whom many of us feel we know, sometimes intimately. Celebrities can be important in the lives of ordinary people—as role models, objects of desire, or just friendly figures encountered daily on the TV or computer screen. And just because these relationships are one-sided doesn't mean that they aren't relationships.

Most of us put very little energy into developing these types of relationships. Frankly, we don't have to, as we are constantly bombarded with information about celebrities all the time. We can't help but acquire information about their professional and personal lives, even if it's just while standing in line at the supermarket (Ehrenreich 1990). But some fans deliberately pursue information about and contact with celebrities in more active ways. Maybe you read a magazine article or watched a TV show to learn more about your favorite athlete; maybe you bought a ticket to a performance with the hopes of seeing your favorite musician after the show. Maybe you serendipitously crossed paths with your favorite actor at the airport or in line at the post office. Encounters like these, while exciting, can also be expensive and unpredictable, and the contact between fan and celebrity is largely outside the fan's control (Ferris 2001, 2004; Ferris and Harris 2010).

Recently the Internet has made it easier for fans to engineer encounters with celebrities. Gawker, TMZ, Popsugar, and PerezHilton are a few of the websites that are making big business out of celebrity watching. They all carry the latest gossip and prized candid photos of stars that generate millions of web hits every month. Gawker, which is based in New York City, distinguished itself by publishing the "Stalker Map," visually pinpointing celebrities as soon as they were spotted. While this particular map is no longer available online, other maps and apps provide similar types of information (including UrbanSpoon's list of top restaurants and the celebrities who regularly dine in them). With more people using smartphones and other handheld devices with Internet access, news about celebrities travels fast, as do those wishing to pursue them. And sometimes, fan expectations and senses of entitlement to celebrity contact go dangerously awry.

Security experts usually try to keep the details under wraps, but it is safe to say that most public figures have a number of potentially dangerous fans whose activities are monitored by both public law enforcement and private security firms. Several celebrities have been killed (Beatle John Lennon, actress Rebecca Schaeffer, Tejano star Selena) or seriously wounded (actress Theresa Saldana) by obsessed fans. Others have endured repeated home break-ins (Sandra Bullock, Justin Timberlake, Mila Kunis, Madonna, and Brad Pitt), and many are plagued by "pop-up" visits from fans who

Table 13.2 Theory in Everyday Life

Perspective	Approach to Recreation and Leisure	Case Study: Spectator Sports in America
Structural Functionalism	Social institutions such as recreation and leisure provide for the needs of society and its members and help to maintain social cohesion and unity.	Participation in spectator sports helps to reaffirm social bonds; rooting for a team underscores the value of performance and competition.
Conflict Theory	Social institutions such as recreation and leisure reflect the existing power structures in society and thus create and maintain social inequalities.	Participation in spectator sports legitimizes conflict between groups in society and the belief in winners and losers.
Symbolic Interactionism	Social institutions such as recreation and leisure are produced when people act together; they play a meaningful role in the everyday lives of members.	Participation in spectator sports provides members with a sense of group affiliation and personal identification.

follow them surreptitiously and then reveal themselves in airports, restaurants, or public restrooms. Threatening letters are sometimes sent to the stars' management offices and even delivered to their home addresses. In order to protect Hollywood celebrities and other public figures from dangerous fans, the Los Angeles Police Department has created a division called the Threat Management Unit, and California further led the nation in passing anti-stalking laws in 1990 that have served as models for those in other states. Unfortunately, legislation doesn't deter all stalkers.

For some, celebrity stalking is a professional obligation. These people include members of the press, and especially the paparazzi—freelance photographers who pursue celebrities in order to get candid shots. Paparazzi may charter helicopters, hack through forests, or scale castle walls in daring stunts in order to capture images of celebrity dates, weddings, and newborn babies. Their intrusiveness can even provoke violence from celebrities, as witnessed when singer Britney Spears beat the car of a member of the paparazzi with the wooden handle of an umbrella, or when rapper Kanye West smashed the expensive camera equipment belonging to another. In some instances, it is actually the photographer who is assaulted, as in the case of one who took a punch in the jaw from actor Alec Baldwin.

While paparazzi can be annoying to celebrities, fans consume their products every day. When we read supermarket tabloids, watch TV entertainment news shows, or scan headlines on gossip blogs, we support the paparazzi's

Life in the Spotlight Brad Pitt and Angelina Jolie stop to take pictures with fans while they walk the red carpet at a movie premiere in Sydney, Australia.

activities—because they support ours. They feed our imaginations, provide us with information about celebrities, and help us envision the worlds of those who are part of our everyday lives but have no idea who we are.

Textual Poaching *Star Trek* fans manipulate old footage in order to create new stories that suggest a very different interpretation of Kirk and Spock's relationship than the one portrayed on the original show.

you are part of an **interpretive community**—a group of like-minded people who enjoy cultural products in the same way.

The concept of the interpretive community is usually attributed to literary theorist Stanley Fish (1980), who believed that although an author might have intended a certain meaning in a text, it is individual readers who inevitably interpret the text in their own ways, thus creating the potential for an almost infinite number of meanings of the same text. Sociologists use the term **polysemy** to describe how any cultural product is subject to multiple interpretations and hence has many

INTERPRETIVE COMMUNITY a group of people dedicated to the consumption and interpretation of a particular cultural product and who create a collective, social meaning for the product

POLYSEMY having many possible meanings or interpretations

possible meanings (Hall 1980; Fiske 1989). For instance, an animated show like *The Simpsons* or *Family Guy* can be enjoyed on a variety of levels, by children for its humor alone and by adults for its social commentary. Polysemy helps us understand how one person can absolutely love the same movie (or song, painting, cartoon, necklace, car, meal, or tattoo) that another person absolutely hates. When audiences are made up of people from different backgrounds, it is more likely that polysemy will come into play: that audience members will interpret the same texts in different ways. Meaning is not a given, nor is it entirely open—we make meaning individually and together, as audiences and consumers of culture.

The fact that we usually end up interpreting the same books in the same ways has to do with shared culture and frameworks that members of the same interpretive communities have in common. Janice Radway (1991), in her ethnography of romance-novel readers, argued that cultural context is the reason that readers share similar sets of reading strategies and interpretive codes. Whether visiting a museum exhibit, going to a concert, or watching a TV show, members of interpretive communities bring with them shared sensibilities about understanding cultural products through their own particular lenses.

Leisure and Relationships

As spectators, we have many choices for how to watch sports or other events. We can attend a live game if we can afford the tickets, or watch it played on TV or stream it online, or we can hear the play-by-play over radio or satellite. At the same time, we can participate through social media and weigh in on the action along with other commentators and fans. We can watch the game alone or with others, at home, in dorm lounges, or at a sports bar. We can also choose to record the game and watch it at a later time. With so many ways to follow our favorite teams and players, it's not surprising to find how important they are to our sense of self and belonging to a community.

Our recreational choices can lead us to form unique bonds with others. Some of those bonds take the form of **role model** relationships, in which more prominent members of a leisure subculture serve as examples for us to strive toward. It is a widely accepted practice to look up to, admire, and mold ourselves after exceptional people and celebrities of all types.

Let's look at the influence of sports figures. Athletes have always been role models, but they have never been as visible as they are now. Sports media is a constant, making it easier to follow our favorite players both on and off the court (or field). All that exposure can turn them into superstars, but it can also reveal their feet of clay. In the 1990s, for instance, kids chanted "I wanna be like Mike" to communicate their admiration for Chicago Bulls player Michael

ROLE MODEL an individual who serves as an example for others to strive toward and emulate

Jordan. Tiger Woods, who in 1997 became the youngest golfer and first person of color ever to win the Masters Tournament, generated the same type of hero worship among youngsters, who intoned "I am Tiger Woods" as they stepped up to the tee in record numbers.

Role models like Jordan and Woods may inspire us to excel in sports and in other areas as well, since both of them have excelled in business and in charity. But their personal failures (both men admitted to marital infidelity) make us wonder what kinds of role models they really are. Some would argue that sports figures are not appropriate role models: even though they must work hard in order to excel, they still possess unique skills and talents that the rest of us don't. In fact, another basketball player, Charles Barkley, who played with the Phoenix Suns at the time, famously asserted "I am not a role model," arguing that parents and teachers were more appropriate examples for children to follow. And interestingly, each of the above quotes ("I wanna be like Mike," "I am Tiger Woods," *and* "I am not a role model") was eventually

Deflategate 2015 In 2015 Tom Brady, quarterback for the New England Patriots, was accused of participating in a ball deflation scheme. Controversies such as this one beg the question of whether sports stars make good role models.

used in Nike commercials—all to inspire consumers to buy expensive sporting goods. In a 2010 Nike commercial, Cleveland Cavalier star LeBron James riffed on the "I am not a role model" theme by asking "What should I do?" of his audience. "Should I be who you want me to be?" or should he just be himself and not worry about what fans think of him? Can any celebrity afford to do that?

Aside from sports and entertainment role models, we also build relationships with people who share our interests—our soccer teammates, fellow collectors of *Star Wars* memorabilia, bluegrass aficionados, or backgammon players. These are important members of our social world.

Leisure and Community

Your friendship with the people you play pick-up basketball with every Thursday evening, the members of your gardening club, or the folks you watch *Game of Thrones* with is unlikely to be confined solely to a love of basketball, gardening, or television; your bonds probably extend into other areas of your lives as well. But it is your shared interests that have brought you together, and these activities speak to the heart of Émile Durkheim's pioneering sociological questions about community and social cohesion, first asked more than 100 years ago and still central today.

Some scholars argue that a critical problem has emerged in contemporary society that undermines social cohesion. They contend that group values in important social groups such as the family, the church, or a labor union have been eclipsed by a rhetoric that espouses radical individual rights first and foremost. For instance, dinner with the family might be passed up in favor of a mother's Pilates lesson or a brother's going to a friend's house to watch the fight on TV. Or the Catholic requirement to attend Mass each week might be fulfilled only on Christmas and Easter.

Sociologist Amitai Etzioni is the leading proponent of a movement that seeks to remedy this problem: **communitarianism** argues that individual rights do not cancel out collective responsibility. The movement is an attempt to rebuild a sense of group values that benefit all rather than merely the individual. Etzioni's version of communitarianism (1996) is specific in its proposals about how to balance individual rights with social responsibilities. But the question for us here is this: Are bonds based on shared leisure interests enough to constitute a sense of group responsibility compatible with communitarian aims? Or are basketball, gardening, television, and the like just too flimsy a basis for real group identity?

Robert Bellah, whose work has examined group values in the United States, supplies another critique, but also hints at a potential answer for us. He argues that bonds based on shared interests like those mentioned earlier don't create real community. Rather, such groups constitute **lifestyle enclaves**, which are different from real communities in that they are likely to remain private and segmented, focused on their own shared interests rather than involved in the larger group life (Bellah, Sullivan, and Tipton 1985). So you and your fellow ballplayers, knitters, or TV fans may find your connections to each other to be personally rewarding, but you aren't necessarily contributing to the common good. Or are you?

In Kerry Ferris's (2001) research on *Star Trek* and soap opera fan clubs, she found that while people in these clubs did initially bond solely because of their dedication to particular TV shows, these bonds developed over time in ways that Bellah might not have predicted. Eventually, the groups branched out from their narrow focus and began to pursue things like charitable fund-raising and community service projects that expanded the boundaries of their lifestyle enclave. One *Star Trek* fan club, for example, raised money to help an animal welfare organization that was sponsored by *Trek* actor William Shatner; while their contributions were guided by their specific interests (how many other people even know what Shatner's favorite charity is?), their community spirit was obvious. So perhaps a sense of shared mission within a small group of TV viewers or tulip enthusiasts is not incompatible with a larger sense of social responsibility after all. You can indulge your individual sense of play and work for the common good as well.

Collectors and Hobbyists

Sports are not the only recreational pursuits that draw people together. Many collectors' groups organize annual conventions so that members with shared interests can hobnob with one another for one intensive weekend (Rubel and Rosman 2001). Collectors of Dolly Parton memorabilia, for example, meet once a year in Pigeon Forge, Tennessee, to buy, sell, and trade Dolly-related items and share their love of the country music diva. Fans of a different kind of dolly, Barbie, also meet annually to connect with others who collect Barbie, her friends, and all their accessories. You'll find her on-again, off-again boyfriend Ken there as well, although he now has his own convention, or "Kenvention." And at yet another weekend convention, collectors gather together to "keep history alive" and honor real military heroes both past and present, by buying, selling, and trading twelve-inch action figures die-cast in the image of notable members of the armed forces.

But collectors and hobbyists are no longer limited to meeting face to face at an annual convention or weekend workshop. The Internet has helped spawn myriad virtual communities

COMMUNITARIANISM a political and moral philosophy focused on strengthening civil society and communal bonds

LIFESTYLE ENCLAVES groups of people drawn together by shared interests, especially those relating to hobbies, sports, and media

Creative Cosplay Events like Comic Con draw together fans of comic books, video games, anime, and sci-fi films. The Internet has made it easier for people with shared interests to find each other.

where enthusiasts can interact online. Do-it-yourselfers and garage woodworkers who might normally work alone have found compatriot crafters with whom they can converse. Connecting with others who share the same interests is facilitated by a plethora of websites and social media. Blogs, Facebook, YouTube, Instagram, Pinterest, eBay, and Etsy allow collectors and hobbyists to meet, organize activities, swap tips, show off their wares, and search for the perfect purchases. Such activities are not confined to only the most die-hard enthusiasts. Almost everyone who goes online has used the Internet to look for information about their hobbies (Fox and Griffith 2007). In some cases, like online gaming, the Internet is the sole source of the hobby.

Hangouts: The Third Place

Away from work or school, where else do you spend your time? Researcher Robert Putnam (2000) laments that, in the United States at least, you will probably be watching TV at home rather than gathering in a public place to socialize with others. But if you lived in France, you might head to the corner café; in Germany, the neighborhood *Bierstube*; in Greece, the local *taverna*. Establishments such as these bear the label **third place** (after home and work, which are first and second). They are informal public places where people come together regularly for conversation and

camaraderie. Sociologist Ray Oldenburg (1999, 2002) calls these "great good places" at the heart of community. He is among a growing number of critics who have begun to worry that there are few such places left in the United States—and that we might be suffering as a society because of it.

You know the place—the local diner with a counter that's always full of old men talking about fishing for bluegill, complaining about the cost of prescription medications, or bemoaning the irresponsibility of youth. You might have thought such talk trivial or silly, but the interactions and relationships that develop in third places are important far beyond any specific conversational content. Coffee-house, bar, or barbershop—third places are more than just hangouts. Oldenburg argues that they are core settings for informal but essential aspects of public and community life. They provide opportunities to connect with others in ways that relieve alienation and anomie, problems Durkheim attributed to modern society. And there are more generalized benefits to society as well—the feeling of public spirit generated in third places can strengthen **civil society**, increase political awareness and participation, and sustain democracy from the ground up. So that local hangout spot is more important than it appears to be. It helps maintain social cohesion and links the individual to the community.

In the years since Oldenburg coined the term, third places have not disappeared, but they have changed. Gone are the local bookstores where many once gathered. But new technology has also drawn people to new hot spots, as they huddle around free Wi-Fi wherever it may be. Some may bemoan that we have become a nation of isolated screen gazers, even when we're occupying the same space. But the Internet is also

THIRD PLACE any informal public place where people come together regularly for conversation and camaraderie when not at work or at home

CIVIL SOCIETY those organizations, institutions, and interactions outside government, family, and work that promote social bonds and the smooth functioning of society

Where's Your Third Place? Whether it's a coffeehouse, a barbershop, or a neighborhood pub, third places are informal public places where people come together regularly for conversation and camaraderie.

making it easier for people to find each other, and mobile apps like Meetup and Foursquare may actually support community building and bringing people back together.

DATA WORKSHOP
Analyzing Everyday Life

Now Go Hang Out

Third places are important to a sense of community and belonging. Are they at risk of disappearing, or are they still attracting people who want to hang out somewhere together? For this Data Workshop you will be doing a short ethnography of a third place. You'll investigate the social setting of a local hangout using participant observation. Refer to Chapter 2 for a review of this research method. You are encouraged to pick a place where you, or others you know, hang out for real, as this background knowledge can help with your analysis; in this case, you'll also be doing an autoethnography.

It doesn't matter which kind of hangout you choose; it could be a bar, restaurant, gym, park, student union, or bookstore. What's important is to make sure that it's a real hangout, someplace where people linger, that they return to regularly to socialize. Part of your work will be to determine just what constitutes a good hangout. So think a bit about your own habits and those of your friends, and choose what you think is a good hangout to study where you'll be both a participant and an observer.

Begin by spending about a half hour or more at the third place you've chosen to study. Even if you're already familiar with the setting, try to have a beginner's mind and take in as much detail about what's happening as possible. Be prepared to write some informal ethnographic field notes describing both the physical and social setting. Examine the items of material culture and the physical layout of the space. Watch the people and note how they interact around (and perhaps with) you, listen for snippets of conversation, and be aware of your own role as both a participant and observer.

Once you've completed your field notes, you're ready for some analysis. Consider these questions:

* What is the physical space like, and why is it conducive to people hanging out?

* What makes this place a good hangout for the people there?

* Can you distinguish who are the "regulars" and who are not? How do you tell a one-time visitor from a regular?

* How do people establish themselves as regulars?

* What kinds of interactions take place at the hangout? Are people congregated in pairs or small groups, or are they mostly alone?

* What kinds of activities are people engaged in at the hangout?

Finally, approach one or two people you think are regulars and ask them the following questions. Alternatively, if you're a regular, you can answer these questions yourself:

* What does the third place mean to the regulars who go there?

* How does the hangout function in the course of their everyday lives?

* In what respect is being a regular at the hangout a part of someone's identity?

IDIOCULTURE the customs, practices, and values expressed in a particular place by the people who interact there

---

In writing up your analysis, include some examples of the particular **idioculture** you find—the distinctive customs, values, and language expressed in the place and in the interactions of the people who hang out there.

There are two options for completing this Data Workshop:

PREP-PAIR-SHARE Visit a third place and prepare written field notes that you can refer to in class. Partner with one or two other students and discuss your findings. Listen for any differences or variations in each other's experiences and insights.

DO-IT-YOURSELF Conduct ethnographic research at a field site. Write a three- to four-page essay answering the questions provided. Use specific excerpts from your field notes to support your analysis and make sure to attach your field notes to your finished paper.

Travel and Tourism

While some people find respite in hangouts close to home, others relax and rejuvenate by seeing the world. The travel and tourism industries (which include airlines, hotels, car-rental agencies, restaurants, theme parks, resorts, and other attractions) are multibillion-dollar businesses and play an important part in the U.S. economy. And it's a sector that keeps growing. In 2014, the travel and tourism industries in the United States employed 5.5 million workers directly and helped support another 2.3 million jobs in related industries. Travel and tourism sales generated a total of $6.1 trillion (U.S. Department of Commerce 2015). The United States is the second-most popular destination (after France) for world travelers: more than 67 million, or 6.5 percent, of the world's 1.1 billion travelers came to the United States in 2013. International visitors spent over $222 billion on travel- and tourism-related goods and services. These dollar figures are important to the overall economy: travel and tourism accounts for about 26 percent of all U.S. service exports and nearly 8 percent of its total exports (U.S. Department of Commerce 2014).

The impact of tourism on a place is more than just economic. Tourism can have a profound effect on a culture as well. While we may travel to learn to appreciate different cultures, we may also exoticize or even mistreat other groups as we fit them into our own recreational needs, rather than learning about them on their own terms (Urry 1990, 1992, 2002). Travel and tourism shape not just our individual relations with others but also political relations between nations on a global scale.

Green Travel Finca Esperanza Verde Ecolodge in Nicaragua is part organic coffee farm, part eco-friendly tourist lodge.

One area of contention concerns the environmental impact of travel and tourism.

Ecotourism is characterized by the efforts of tourists and the travel industry to lessen the negative consequences of tourism on the environment as well as on local cultures. Ecotourism promotes a consciousness about environmentally and culturally sensitive travel options. Ecotourists are often from highly industrialized nations and are usually visiting less developed nations. But if they are truly aware of their potential to cause harm, shouldn't they avoid environmentally sensitive locations such as rain forests or the habitats of endangered species?

Sociologists who study ecotourism have mixed views about its effectiveness. Some argue that it is merely consumerism with a "green" wrapping, that the "eco" part of the label is a marketing technique to make tourists feel less guilty about traveling to places where they can't help but make a negative impact. Other sociologists argue that ecotourism, if effectively managed, *can* make positive contributions to both the environment and local communities (Bandy 1996; Wearing and Wearing 1999; Scheyvens 2000; Weinberg, Bellows, and Ekster 2002; Wood 2002). Tourists and travel companies must actively attempt to counterbalance their impact with sensitivity to the environment as well as to the values of local communities. The question remains whether ecotourism can live up to its claims and place environmental and cultural concerns before profits.

ECOTOURISM foreign travel with the goal of minimizing the environmental consequences of tourism as well as its possible negative effects on local cultures and economies, typically involving people from highly industrialized nations traveling to less developed countries

CLOSING COMMENTS

Who would have thought that the things you do for fun might actually be important? The many activities considered part of leisure—travel, entertainment, sports, hobbies—while prevalent features of our everyday lives, play an increasingly significant role in the shape of society. We hope we haven't spoiled their pleasure by asking you to examine their various structures and meanings. You can still enjoy your leisure activities even after you've learned to take a critical, sociological perspective on them!

Everything You Need to Know about Leisure and the Media

> "Leisure is time that can be spent doing whatever you want. A large portion of Americans' leisure time is spent consuming mass media."

THEORIES OF LEISURE AND THE MEDIA

* **Structural functionalism:** leisure activities and the media help maintain social cohesion through taste publics

* **Conflict theory:** leisure activities and the media reflect existing power inequalities, particularly in the commodification of leisure; the types of leisure and media we consume differ based on our social class

* **Symbolic interactionism:** people's everyday lives are greatly affected by shared leisure activities or the consumption of the same media

REVIEW

1. What does "commercialization of leisure" mean? Think of one of your favorite leisure activities and make a list of every aspect of this activity that costs money, either directly or indirectly.

2. Sociologists have long associated types of leisure activities with different social classes. Which leisure activities are associated with wealthy elites or with the working class? Which leisure activities, if any, have no class associations?

3. How powerful are the media in persuading us to buy certain products or hold particular beliefs? Discuss reinforcement theory, agenda setting, and/or the two-step flow model. Which of these theories best explains the influence of the media?

Leisure Time on an Average Day

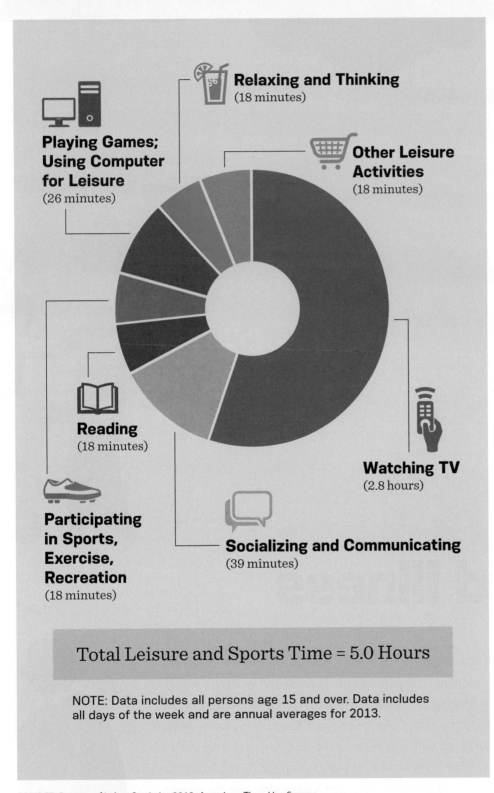

Relaxing and Thinking
(18 minutes)

Playing Games; Using Computer for Leisure
(26 minutes)

Other Leisure Activities
(18 minutes)

Reading
(18 minutes)

Watching TV
(2.8 hours)

Participating in Sports, Exercise, Recreation
(18 minutes)

Socializing and Communicating
(39 minutes)

Total Leisure and Sports Time = 5.0 Hours

NOTE: Data includes all persons age 15 and over. Data includes all days of the week and are annual averages for 2013.

SOURCE: Bureau of Labor Statistics 2013, American Time Use Survey.

EXPLORE

Consuming Elite Athleticism

Eugene, Oregon, is a major location for running and track and field, in part because of Bill Bowerman, the late coach for the University of Oregon and the co-founder of Nike. A running culture is prevalent in Eugene: the city celebrates its identity as TrackTown USA, formal activities like the Olympic trials are often held there, and many people wear Nike clothes and shoes. Nike had a significant presence at the 2012 Olympic trials, including shuttle buses with the Nike logo and a "Shoe Lab" showcasing the latest technology in running shoes. Visit the Everyday Sociology Blog to read more about a sociologist's analysis of how Nike successfully markets elite athleticism to consumers.

http:wwnPag.es/trw413

CHAPTER 14

Health and Illness

In the 1995 film *Leaving Las Vegas*, Nicolas Cage plays Ben, a down-and-out screenwriter who heads to Vegas intending to drink himself to death. His plan is delayed when he meets and befriends a local sex worker, Sera (played by Elisabeth Shue). Ben and Sera connect for a short while and come to an agreement: he won't ask her to quit her job, and she won't ask him to quit drinking. They provide each other with acceptance, companionship, and a temporary respite from their isolated lives. But not even their connection can stop Ben from fulfilling his self-destructive goal. He dies in Sera's arms, leaving Las Vegas the way he always planned. Cage won a Best Actor Oscar and Golden Globe Award for his performance (while

Shue received corresponding Best Actress nominations), and the film has taken its place among top Hollywood portrayals of the desperation and destruction of alcoholism.

But there's more to this story than the suicide of a fictional alcoholic in a seedy hotel. Las Vegas itself can be seen as another main character—a real American city with an unfortunate connection to self-destruction. According to sociologist Matt Wray and his colleagues (2008), merely being in Las Vegas, as either a resident or a tourist, increases one's suicide risk. Vegas residents' odds of suicide are 50 percent greater than those of people who live elsewhere, and visitors' risk of suicide doubles while there, compared with those who stay home or travel elsewhere. Indeed, if you are a resident of the city, getting out of town is good for you—leaving Las Vegas results in a reduction in suicide risk of more than 20 percent. Should Las Vegas, which consistently has the highest urban suicide rate in the nation, be nicknamed "Suicide City" rather than "Sin City"? What explains these disturbing statistics?

Wray and his colleagues (2008) offer three possible explanations: ecological, selection, and contagion theories of suicide. The ecological argument is place-based: there must be something about the city itself that makes people suicidal. For example, Vegas has long been one of the fastest-growing cities in the nation, although growth has slowed dramatically since the recession. This kind of rapid social change can lead to social isolation and dislocation and a weakening of community bonds (Trudeau 2008), all factors classically correlated with suicide by Émile Durkheim (1897/1951). Additionally, some research suggests that gambling and the large number of hotel rooms (where chances of rescuing someone midattempt are slim) make Vegas conducive to suicide (Phillips, Welty, and Smith 1997; Gemar, Zarkowski, and Avery 2008).

The selection argument is somewhat more psychological: Vegas residents and tourists might be disproportionately prone to impulsiveness or other risky behaviors (Wray et al. 2008) and indeed may be choosing Vegas as a site for making a new start or having a "last hurrah," a gamble that more frequently ends in their suicide because the city beckons people with these and other relevant personality traits, such as depression. The contagion argument combines ecological and selection concerns: the high suicide rate may inspire a kind of "copycat" effect (Cosgrove-Mather 2004), and through processes of social imitation the rate remains high.

So is it the place, the people, or a combination of the two that makes Las Vegas the suicide capital of the country? Wray and his colleagues cannot provide us with a definitive answer just yet. But their research recognizes what we will be exploring in this chapter: that although health, illness, and mortality are physiological phenomena, they are also unquestionably shaped by social factors.

HOW TO READ THIS CHAPTER

Health and illness are constants of human existence, a natural part of having a physical body that is subject to injury, disease, aging, and death. Health and illness are not just physical states—they also include aspects of our mental well-being and are influenced by shifting cultural beliefs about what is ideal and desirable. As a society, we have established the social institution of medicine to address the challenges of our physical existence. Sociologists ask you to consider how larger social forces help shape this institution and your own embodied experience of health or illness.

The Sociology of Medicine, Health, and Illness

Why is sociology interested in topics that might seem more at home in a medical school textbook? Well, for one thing, our bodies (where health and illness are ostensibly located) are social objects. Our physical selves have socially constructed meanings and are affected by social forces. This means that the very definition of health is social; our individual health is subject not just to cross-cultural or historically specific interpretive differences but also to different influences depending on where and when we live, as well as what statuses we hold in our society.

Let's look at a couple of examples where the nature of health is defined by its social rather than biological context. Think about what having a healthy body means in a developed country like the United States. We value slim, athletic builds and bodies with just the right amount of curves and consider people with these body types to be healthier than people with more fleshy builds. But in Dakar, Senegal, people tend to value body types that in the United States would be considered clinically overweight. Senegalese women in particular associate these body types with health (and by extension with wealth enough to eat well): slimmer women actually want to gain weight in order to attain the "desirable," "healthy" build (Holdsworth et al. 2004). Another example: In the United States, "healthy" teeth are not just free of cavities but also straight and white. So in addition to brushing teeth daily and visiting the dentist regularly, Americans spend big money on orthodontic and whitening procedures. Meanwhile, in many other parts of the world, irregularly shaped or unevenly colored teeth are not necessarily seen as "bad" or "unhealthy," and cosmetic dentistry is far less common. These examples indicate that our definitions of health (and beauty as a sign of health) are determined at least in part by our cultural context, and not always by a biological bottom line.

Another important aspect of health as a social phenomenon involves the spread of disease. Think about it: You've caught a good number of illnesses from other people. Someone behind you in the movie theater coughed, and you got a cold (if you were lucky) or tuberculosis (if you were unlucky). Someone flipping burgers at a fast-food restaurant forgot to wash her hands, and you got an upset stomach (if you were lucky) or hepatitis A (if you were unlucky). If you have young children in school or day care, you know that kids are like family disease vectors—they catch bugs from other kids, bring them home, and spread them around to family members.

Social milieu affects your risk of disease. Take, for example, the recent nationwide measles epidemic that began in California. Measles is a highly contagious disease that causes fever, a full-body rash, and sometimes other complications. Death is rare in developed countries like the United

 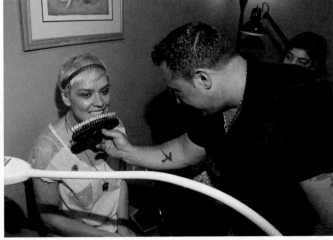

Health in a Cultural Context The Senegalese women live in a society that values fuller body types that might be classified as overweight in other cultures. The United States puts such a strong emphasis on straight, white teeth that many people spend thousands of dollars on cosmetic dental procedures.

Outbreak in California A large multi-state measles outbreak in 2015 prompted a nationwide debate over whether parents have the right to opt out of vaccinating their children for diseases like measles.

States, with widespread vaccination programs and high-quality health care, but fatality rates can be as high as 30 percent in places without such amenities, or in populations that cannot receive vaccines, such as infants under twelve months of age or people with compromised immune systems such as AIDS or chemotherapy patients. In early 2015, the Centers for Disease Control and Prevention (CDC) reported a measles outbreak that appears to have started at Disneyland. Multiple California cases eventually spread to almost two hundred cases in twenty-four states and the District of Columbia (CDC 2015). Most of the cases in the Disneyland outbreak were in unvaccinated people; about half were ineligible for vaccination because they were too young or had other illnesses, but the other half chose to go unvaccinated for other reasons, often related to fears of a link between the measles vaccination and autism. There is, it should be noted, no scientific evidence to support such a link.

A highly vaccinated community maintains what is called "herd immunity," a kind of group resistance that helps protect even the unvaccinated from contracting the disease (herd immunity for measles requires about a 95 percent vaccination rate). Those who voluntarily decline vaccinations, though, put both themselves and the rest of the "herd" at risk. The lower the vaccination rate of a community (residents of a town, for example, or students at a school, or visitors to a theme park), the lower the group's collective immunity and the more vulnerable to infection members become.

ACUTE DISEASES diseases that have a sudden onset, may be briefly incapacitating, and are either curable or fatal

CHRONIC DISEASES diseases that develop over a longer period of time and may not be detected until symptoms occur later in their progression

Our bodies are social objects, and our social experiences and social location shape our prospects for health and risks of disease. These are only some of the reasons that health and illness are social phenomena. As you read this chapter, you'll find that there are social, cultural, and subcultural factors affecting just about everything having to do with health and illness.

Defining Health and Illness

Terms such as "healthy" and "sick" may seem straight-forward, but their meanings are not absolute or universal. The World Health Organization (a division of the United Nations charged with overseeing global health issues) defines health as "a state of complete physical, mental, and social well-being and not merely the absence of disease or infirmity" (World Health Organization [WHO] 1946). Let's look further at how illnesses are defined and treated in the United States.

Types of Illnesses

Diseases and illnesses are commonly categorized as either acute or chronic. **Acute diseases** have a sudden onset, may be briefly incapacitating, and are either curable or fatal. These illnesses are often caused by an organism such as a germ, virus, or parasite that infects the body and disrupts the normal functioning of one or more areas. Many acute illnesses are contagious and can spread from one person to many people. The common cold, pneumonia, and measles could all be considered acute illnesses. **Chronic diseases**

Acute Diseases Patients in Sudan wait for treatment in the TB ward of a hospital. Diseases such as tuberculosis, diarrheal diseases, and malaria are the top causes of death in the developing world.

develop over a longer period of time and may not be detected until later in their progression. They can sometimes be related to environment, lifestyle, and personal choices. Many chronic diseases are manageable, but others progress and eventually become fatal. Cancer, cardiovascular disease, and some forms of diabetes can all be considered chronic diseases.

The kinds of diseases that affect us can vary over time and by place. For most of history, humans worried about becoming afflicted with acute diseases. Indeed, prior to 1900, the leading causes of death in the United States were influenza, pneumonia, tuberculosis, and gastroenteritis. Over the past century, drastic changes in medicine and public health have all but wiped out certain acute diseases (such as polio), while chronic ones (such as diabetes) have grown vastly in proportion (CDC 1998). Chronic diseases have become among the most important factors governing health and illness today. The top three causes of death in the United States are currently heart disease, cancer, and chronic respiratory illnesses like asthma and emphysema (Hoyert and Xu 2012). However, acute diseases continue to pose significant threats to people living in the developing world, where the top killers still include respiratory infections, diarrheal diseases, tuberculosis, and malaria (WHO 2008).

Approaches to Medical Treatment

The health-care system in the United States is characterized by three approaches: curative or crisis, preventive, and palliative. **Curative** or **crisis medicine** treats the disease once it has become apparent. Sometimes this works well, especially in the case of acute illnesses like food poisoning, or sports injuries like a torn ligament, that have no early treatment

option. But in the case of chronic illnesses, a delay in recognizing causes or symptoms before the disease advances may mean the difference between recovery and death. **Preventive medicine** aims to avoid or forestall the onset of disease by making lifestyle changes: regular exercise, proper diet and nutrition, smoking cessation, stress reduction, and other measures to maintain or improve one's health. Lifestyle changes are often the most effective and least costly ways to prevent a range of chronic conditions (McKinlay 1997). **Palliative care** focuses on symptom and pain relief and on providing a nurturing and supportive environment to those suffering from a serious illness or at the end of life, either in addition to or in place of fighting the illness or disease.

CURATIVE or **CRISIS MEDICINE** type of health care that treats the disease or condition once it has manifested

PREVENTIVE MEDICINE type of health care that aims to avoid or forestall the onset of disease by taking preventive measures, often including lifestyle changes

PALLIATIVE CARE type of health care that focuses on symptom and pain relief and providing a supportive environment for critically ill or dying patients

DATA WORKSHOP
Analyzing Everyday Life

Student Health Issues Survey

For many young people, moving away from home and going to college mark the beginning of their independent lives as adults. While there is much to celebrate at this milestone, it can also be a time full of new demands and challenges. Perhaps you or someone you know is dealing with homesickness, an abusive relationship, or stress and anxiety. As a college student, you can learn to become more responsible and disciplined, and more conscientious about taking care of yourself. But you can also be threatened by alcohol or substance abuse, eating disorders, or depression. The college years are an important phase of development and one in which many young people struggle to some degree with their newfound adult lives.

The American College Health Association (ACHA) is an organization that partners with colleges and universities to conduct large-scale surveys on the habits, behaviors, and perceptions affecting the health and well-being of their student populations. In 2014, the ACHA surveyed close to 80,000 students; the results are helping colleges and universities offer education and support services regarding a variety of issues (2014).

For this Data Workshop you will be conducting your own small-scale interview study on health and wellness issues. Refer to Chapter 2 for a review of this research method. You will be designing a questionnaire, conducting interviews, and then analyzing the responses you get.

Begin by thinking about whom you would like to interview and what kinds of questions you would like to ask them. Your respondents should all be college students; remember to ask for their consent to participate. You'll want to gather some basic demographic background from each respondent. Consider such variables as race and ethnicity, class, national background, gender, religion, and/or age of your sample. There are many possibilities for comparing and contrasting within or across categories. Because this is only a pilot study, the number of people you can interview will necessarily be small. You'll probably have to draw from what is referred to as a "convenience sample" of respondents, rather than using a more scientific random sample. How many people you include in your sample may also depend on how many questions you'd like to ask each respondent.

For this study you will be conducting one-on-one interviews. You will need to record your interviewees' answers, either by taking notes or by digital means. Your questionnaire is likely to have both closed- and open-ended questions. The kinds of questions you ask may also help to determine the number of questions to include. Closed-ended questions typically have yes or no answers, which can be quickly noted, but you can also ask your respondents to elaborate. Open-ended questions allow respondents to answer in a variety of ways. Before you begin designing your questionnaire, choose from the following list of topics:

anger	pregnancy
depression	relationships
drugs and alcohol	sexual assault
eating disorders	sexually transmitted diseases
exercise	sleep difficulties
financial issues	peer pressure
gambling	stress and anxiety
grades and studying	suicide
grief and loss	tobacco use
homesickness	violence

Questions about daily habits, relationships, and emotions can tell you something about an individual's mental and physical health. You might ask students about their lifestyles—what they eat, how much they sleep, whether they exercise, drink or smoke, or practice safe sex. Do they play a musical instrument, are they on a sports team, or do they belong to any campus clubs? You might ask about their physical health—how often they get sick, or what they do to stay healthy. Or you might ask about their mental health—whether they experience stress, depression, and/or anxiety, what causes them to feel it, and what they do to alleviate it. Some topics may be too sensitive or personal in nature, so use good judgment when approaching your subjects. Remember that you must respect the privacy and confidentiality of your respondents. Keep the questionnaires as clear and simple as possible. Once you've finalized the questions, you're ready to conduct the interviews.

After gathering data through interviews, you'll want to begin to analyze your findings. Sift through your notes or transcripts and compile the number of answers to various questions. See what kinds of patterns you can find—similarities, differences, comparisons, and contradictions. What do you think these data reveal about how your respondents cope with the health issues they encounter at school?

There are two options for completing this Data Workshop:

PREP-PAIR-SHARE Design a questionnaire and conduct interviews with a small sample from your population (perhaps three or four people). Look over their answers, make notes about any preliminary results, and bring them with you to class. Get together with one or two other students and discuss your findings. Look for similarities and differences in both your own findings and those of your discussion group members. See if you can

College Health A student at the University of Northern Iowa visits the school's student health clinic.

identify any patterns that emerge from the data gathered by the entire group.

DO-IT-YOURSELF Design a questionnaire and conduct interviews with a small group of respondents from your sample (perhaps six or seven people). Write a two- to three-page essay describing the interview process and analyzing your findings, attaching any notes or transcripts to your paper. How do your findings confirm or refute any hypotheses you might have had before beginning the study? What do your data suggest about the relationship between college life and student health?

Medicalization of Health and Illness

Since what constitutes illness can be socially constructed, it's interesting to look at how some problems that were once not considered medical conditions have been transformed into illnesses over time. This process is known as **medicalization**, and it has affected our perspective on a variety of behaviors and conditions. A half century ago, we thought of alcoholism and addiction as the result of weak will or bad character, but we now see them as diseases that respond to medical and therapeutic treatment. Kids who might have been written off as "unruly" or "incorrigible" in the 1950s are now diagnosed with attention-deficit/hyperactivity disorder, or ADHD, and given drugs to keep them calm and focused (Conrad 2006). Obesity, once seen as a failure of willpower, can now be treated with surgery and drugs.

Even birth and death have been medicalized. In the early years of the twentieth century, more than half of American women gave birth at home, attended only by family, friends, or midwives, without drugs or surgeries. By 1955, that number had declined steeply, to about 1 percent of American women (Cassidy 2006). While home births have increased in the past decade, they still account for less than 2 percent of births in the United States (CDC 2014e). We now see pregnancy as a "medical condition" for which a hospital birth—and, often, a doctor's intervention in the form of an episiotomy or caesarean section—is the "treatment." Death has undergone the same transformation: once a natural (though sad) part of family life, it is now something that we will go to great medical lengths to delay (though we can never stave it off forever). Death also used to occur at home, but today about 75 percent of patients die in other settings (CDC 2013b), despite the fact that studies show it is less stressful for terminally ill patients

to die at home (Searing 2010). For many people living great distances away from relatives, dying at home is no longer even an option.

Medicalization changes both the meaning of a condition and the meaning of the individual who suffers from it. In the case of birth and death, it turns a natural part of the human life cycle into something unfamiliar that we fear we can't handle on our own. We therefore turn to medical experts who may or may not intervene in ways that actually help and may in fact further traumatize patients and their families. In other cases, such as with conditions like addiction, obesity, or mental or emotional problems, medicalization takes the pressure off the person. The fact that they drink too much, eat too much, can't concentrate, or are sad all the time is no longer their fault as individuals—it is the fault of the disease. We would never advise someone to "just get over" pneumonia or a broken leg—and as the process of medicalization continues, we are less likely to think of addiction, obesity, and depression as conditions people should "just get over" on their own.

> **MEDICALIZATION** the process by which some behaviors or conditions that were once seen as personal problems are redefined as medical issues

The Social Construction of Mental Illness

Understanding that disease can be socially constructed allows us to see how its meanings can change over time. For example, take the social meaning of mental illness. Over the course of history and in different societies, theories of the causes of mental illness have varied widely. Each new theory led to a different type of treatment (and justification for that treatment), some of which seem shockingly inhuman to us now. For example, in fourteenth-century London, Bethlem Royal Hospital (which is still in operation today) became a kind of prison for those suffering from mental illnesses. Based on the theory that mental illness was a moral failing caused by demonic possession or individual weakness, the "treatment" for those who suffered was removal from society. Bethlem, or Bedlam as it came to be known, warehoused the mentally ill under the most horrifying of conditions, which included overcrowding, lack of food, water, and sanitation, whippings, and "exorcisms."

In Colonial America, the prevailing theory was that mental illness was caused by the astrological position of the moon at the time of the individual's birth; hence the term "lunatic." According to this theory, mental illness was located inside a lunatic's body, and the only possible cures involved treatments meant to release the illness, such as bleeding (which often killed the patients) and long-term induced vomiting (also potentially fatal). In the 1930s, the cause of mental illness was believed to be located in a particular portion of

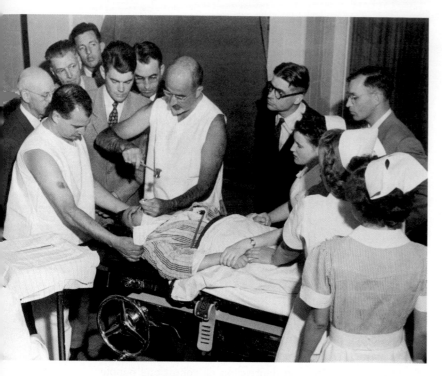

A Misguided Treatment Dr. Walter Freeman revolutionized the lobotomy procedure, which he performed with an ice pick–like instrument that severed nerve connections in the front part of the brain.

EPIDEMIOLOGY the study of disease patterns to understand the cause of illnesses, how they are spread, and what interventions to take

the brain, the removal of which would thus provide the cure. The lobotomy, in which a bit of the brain (or lobe) was surgically removed, often without anesthesia, seemed to work

nicely; patients became calm enough to leave the hospital and return home. We now know that lobotomies merely disconnected two critical parts of the brain from one another, leaving patients unable to feel emotions or act on the information provided to them by their senses.

These approaches to mental illness now seem ridiculous and cruel. We know that mental illness is not caused by demon possession, a weak will, or astrological accidents, and we know that beatings, exorcisms, and lobotomies cannot restore mental health. We are certain (aren't we?) that mental illness is caused by problems of brain chemistry and that proper treatment involves medications that restore that chemistry to its healthy balance. But given the history of changing meanings and treatments, we have to ask: What makes this theory any better than the others? How can we be sure that this time we've gotten it right? Isn't it possible that, a hundred years from now, we'll discover the "real" cause of mental illness and that drug treatments will seem as useless and inhuman as surgeries and bleedings do now?

Epidemiology and Patterns of Disease

As we have noted, sociologists are interested in the social aspect of disease patterns. The study of these patterns is known as **epidemiology**. Epidemiologists collect and analyze data in order to understand the causes of a particular illness, how it is communicated, the factors affecting its development and distribution in a population, where it is likely to spread, and what the most effective interventions might be. Over many centuries of human history, major

Table 14.1 Theory in Everyday Life: Explanations of Addiction

Perspective	Approach to Medicine and Health	Case Study: Drug and Alcohol Addiction
Structural Functionalism	Disease is a threat to social order, and sick people cannot fufill their roles and contribute to society; the health care system should return patients to health and normal functioning as members of society.	People who become addicted to drugs and alcohol may be responding to strains in the social system and their own lives; they may adapt by retreating or escaping through drugs and alcohol.
Conflict Theory	Health and the health care system are valuable resources that are unequally shared in society; conflict may arise among different groups seeking access to and control over these resources.	Those in power can define social policy and create laws regarding medicine and health care; people of lower social status are more likely to be scrutinized as problem drinkers or drug addicts and may be unduly punished.
Symbolic Interactionism	The meanings of health and illness are dependent on historical, cultural, and situational contexts. Stigma may be attached to certain disease states and to those who suffer from them.	People learn to use alcohol and drugs in social interaction and are influenced by peers and other groups; they may attach different meanings and values to substances and behaviors.

IN THE FUTURE
Solving the Mystery of Autism

Autism Spectrum Disorders (ASD), as defined by the American Psychiatric Association (2012), are a "range of complex developmental disorders that can cause problems with thinking, feeling, language and the ability to relate to others." These challenges can range from severe to very mild, and thus are categorized as a "spectrum." ASD symptoms generally become evident before the age of three and last throughout a person's life, though symptoms may improve over time with social skills training and behavioral therapy (Handleman and Harris 2000).

What causes ASD remains unclear, as no definite genetic link has been found. A widely accepted hypothesis is that ASD is multifactoral, meaning that both genetics and environment influence its prevalence (Hultman, Sparén, and Cnattingius 2002). A number of studies indicate that advanced maternal age (King et al. 2009), closely spaced pregnancies, birth weight, prematurity, birth order (Cheslack-Postava, Liu, and Bearman 2011), and exposure to toxins, viruses, or hormones (London and Etzel 2000) may be contributing factors in ASD.

While the causes for ASD are not totally understood, how we understand disabilities is socially constructed and thus has important ramifications for how a group of people are medically and socially treated. For example, Asperger's syndrome, one disorder in the ASD family, first appeared in the *Diagnostic and Statistical Manual of Mental Disorders* (DSM) in 1994 and was later removed in the fifth edition in 2013, to be folded back into ASD (*New York Times* 2012). These epidemiological changes are not simply a matter of categorization; diagnosis, treatment, and access to services often rest on the ability to identify and differentiate the disorders. Thus, how ASD and other disorders are understood can have far-reaching impacts. King and Bearman (2009) indicate that in the years when diagnostic criteria changed, the odds of a patient being diagnosed with ASD increased. Thus 26.4 percent of the increased California caseload of ASD diagnoses between 1992 and 2005 are a result of diagnostic changes.

Interactional as well as structural changes can further affect the diagnosis of disorder. For example, Liu, King, and Bearman (2010) show that independent of other factors, children living near another child diagnosed with autism are more likely to also be diagnosed with ASD. Evidence indicates that parents learn how to manage ASD primarily through interaction with other parents who have children with ASD. Thus, awareness of the characteristics and criteria of autism may lead parents to seek diagnosis for their own child.

Children with autism often have difficulty navigating social situations, as their language skills may be less developed, and behavior may be disruptive and occasionally violent. This behavior can be challenging for parents, who may experience stigma via hostile staring, avoidance, and rude comments from others and thus must engage in strategies to cope with stress. The most common and most effective strategies, are the use of service agencies and family support (Gray 1994, 2002). Until the mystery of autism is solved, early diagnosis and intervention is important, as is ongoing research to help provide support for those with ASD and their caregivers.

On the Spectrum These twin boys function on opposite ends of the autism spectrum. How is our understanding of ASD socially constructed?

illnesses such as cholera, typhus, yellow fever, and smallpox would sweep across vast stretches of the globe and decimate populations from practically every continent. More recently, such illnesses as tuberculosis, malaria, and measles continue to kill millions around the world. What future illnesses might threaten humanity next, and can we identify them before widespread devastation occurs? Epidemiologists combine data and methods from the biological and social sciences with a public health orientation to answer important questions about the origins and spread of disease.

Epidemiologists swing into action whenever a new disease emerges or an unexpected outbreak of a previously

EPIDEMIC occurs when a significantly higher number of cases of a particular disease occur during a particular time period than might otherwise be expected

PANDEMIC occurs when a significantly higher number of cases of a disease also spreads through an especially large geographical region spanning many countries or even continents

VECTOR ORGANISMS animals like mosquitoes, ticks, and birds that carry and spread pathogens (germs or other infectious agents) in a given area

eradicated disease resurfaces. For example, in the West African Ebola outbreak of 2014, epidemiological researchers established the connection between hundreds and then thousands of patients, analyzed the genetic makeup of the virus that infected them, and confirmed that they were suffering from a strain of Ebola that was evolving as it was being transmitted. As a result of this research, widespread public health awareness campaigns were put in place to educate people about the transmission, prevention, and treatment of the disease. In particular, traditional burial practices, including washing, touching, and kissing the body of the deceased, were targeted as the primary modes of transmission, since it was through these practices that the disease could devastate entire families and communities. Health-care workers were also at high risk due to their close contact with infected patients, and so Ebola prevention protocols were developed to help keep them safe. Despite these attempts at intervention, the disease spread quickly and eventually killed over 11,000 people, approximately 50 percent of those infected.

The Ebola epidemic spread to ten countries, but it never officially became what is known as a pandemic. What are the differences between the two terms? An **epidemic** occurs when a significantly higher number of cases of a particular disease occur during a particular time period than might otherwise be expected. The term **pandemic** is used when cases of the disease also cover an especially large geographical region (say, a continent or the entire globe). What constitutes an epidemic is usually determined by national public health organizations—in the United States, that would be the Centers for Disease Control and Prevention (CDC) in Atlanta (Koerner 2003). The World Health Organization (WHO) in Geneva, Switzerland, monitors and defines pandemics.

Epidemiologists are now identifying the role of global climate change in spreading some of the most important diseases afflicting the world, and they are tracking how this process occurs (Associated Press 2006). Because climate affects things like the availability of fresh water and "arable" (or farmable) land, it also affects where people live and their patterns of migration. As people leave places where climate change has made food, water, and other resources scarce, they crowd into other areas that may then experience overpopulation. When people live in very close quarters, the risks rise for malnutrition, water-borne illnesses such as cholera, and other infectious diseases to spread (Khasnis and Nettleman 2005).

Global climate change can also affect animal populations that spread diseases among humans. Even small increases in temperature can multiply the numbers of **vector organisms** that carry and spread pathogens (infectious agents) in a given area. Mosquitoes carrying malaria, for example, used to be limited to sub-Saharan Africa and other hot or tropical regions. But in Kenya, malaria has recently penetrated

A Modern-Day Epidemic A sign in Freetown, Sierra Leone, warns of the dangers of Ebola. The 2014 Ebola outbreak in West Africa has claimed more than 11,000 lives.

GLOBAL PERSPECTIVE
HIV and AIDS around the World

For a long time, the story of the human immunodeficiency virus (HIV) and the disease it causes, acquired immunodeficiency syndrome (AIDS), had a single narrative. Genetic analysis has led researchers to believe that the simian immunodeficiency virus (SIV) was present in primates in Africa for at least 32,000 years (Worobey et al. 2010). Researchers still disagree as to why, but at some point in the late nineteenth or early twentieth century, a strain of this virus mutated into a form that infected humans. Analysis of blood samples taken at different points in time suggests that HIV moved from the Congo to Haiti, and then migrated to the United States through Haitian immigrants. The disease continued its spread throughout the world.

At least 39 million people have died of HIV since the virus was identified in the early 1980s, and approximately 35 million people are currently infected with HIV/AIDS (WHO 2014). HIV/AIDS is now a pandemic—a global event made possible by the increasing connections that come with a global economy—but it has also become a series of epidemics. AIDS is always the same disease, but it is a very different epidemic depending on where it is.

Seeking Treatment Patients wait at the HIV/AIDS clinic in Arua Regional Hospital in northern Uganda, where Doctors Without Borders provides medical care and access to antiretroviral drugs.

One of the most important ways in which medical researchers study HIV/AIDS is by determining the ways in which it is transmitted and which parts of the population are most affected. In many places, HIV/AIDS is a concentrated epidemic, with the majority of cases transmitted by a particular method and concentrated in a particular subpopulation within a given country. In Central Europe and Central Asia, intravenous drug use is responsible for the majority of cases (O'Neill 2007). In Latin America, the routes by which HIV is transmitted are much more diverse, but same-sex male intercourse is a more common route to infection. In Southeast Asia, commercial sex workers make up a much larger percentage of the HIV-positive population. In sub-Saharan Africa, HIV/AIDS is a generalized epidemic, spread through the entire population, such that in some countries more than 30 percent of adults are infected.

Understanding the ways in which experiences with HIV differ globally is vital for those who seek to treat those who are infected and prevent future infections. For one thing, AIDS is distributed disproportionately: only about 4 percent of all cases are in the developed world—places like the United States, Western Europe, Japan, and other wealthy industrialized nations. This is important because in the developed world the vast majority of HIV/AIDS sufferers have access to antiretroviral drugs, which transform the disease into something much closer to a chronic condition and significantly improve the physical, emotional, and mental life of those who receive them. In the developing world, however, these drugs are prohibitively expensive for the vast majority of AIDS patients (Beard, Feeley, and Rosen 2009).

While research into new AIDS treatments continues, there is also a push toward prevention, both in terms of behavioral change and with the possibility of developing a vaccine. Human clinical trials of experimental vaccines are only in their earliest phases, so it will be years before we know which vaccine, if any, will protect people from acquiring HIV. And decades, perhaps, before a vaccine will be affordable for all.

mountainous regions that were once too chilly for mosquitoes to survive, and similar reports have come from parts of Europe and as far north as Moscow, Russia (Associated Press 2006; Bouzid et al. 2014). The United States is also at risk. Other illnesses such as Lyme disease (carried by ticks), yellow and dengue fevers and West Nile virus (carried by mosquitoes), avian influenza (carried by birds), and even plague (carried by fleas on rodents) may skyrocket as climate change drives these vector animals out of their customary territories and into new ecosystems (Dell'Amore 2008; Morin, Comrie, and Ernst 2013).

Foreseeing this serious threat to human health and the possibility of its resulting in greater epidemics in the future, networks of scientists have called for action by all nations to mandate caps on greenhouse gas emissions, as well as to begin preparing for what appear to be the unavoidable public health consequences of the global climate change that has already occurred.

Social Inequality, Health, and Illness

As we have seen in previous chapters, a person's socioeconomic status, race, and gender also shape their experiences of health and illness. Answers to such questions as "Who gets sick?" "What kinds of diseases do they get?" "Who gets treatment?" and "What kind of treatment do they get?" are all influenced by social hierarchies and structures of inequality. Since we gave you a fairly comprehensive picture of the relationships between different forms of inequality and different health outcomes in prior chapters, we'll just summarize some of the main findings first, and then go into more depth here about a specific problem that is linked to a variety of illnesses and is caused largely by social inequalities.

Intersections of Class, Race, and Gender

It's easy to see how one's social class might have an effect on one's health. People of higher socioeconomic status (SES) not only can afford more and better health care services (insurance plans, doctor visits, diagnostic tests and treatments, prescription medications) but also may have greater access to other resources (better nutrition, cleaner neighborhoods, more preventive practices like exercise) that positively influence their health. People of higher SES can expect to live longer lives, and they generally enjoy feeling more physical well-being than those in lower groups.

Being on the lower end of the social class ladder brings many problems that are the inverse of the advantages mentioned earlier. People with lower SES have substantially higher rates of various diseases along with higher death rates and shorter life expectancy (Lynch et al. 1998). They may have little regular access to health care providers, lack the ability to participate in preventive practices, or have trouble affording prescription medications and other recommended procedures (Lynch et al. 1997). The effects of poverty consistently correlate with higher incidences of depression and other mental health problems (Groh 2007).

Inequalities of race and gender are often connected to lower socioeconomic status. When we add race or gender to the health equation, we find significant differences between groups who are higher or lower in the social hierarchy. Many problems that affect people of lower SES are further exacerbated in minority

Socioeconomic Status and Health A man visits the Family Van in Boston, Massachusetts, to get his blood pressure checked. Many residents from low-income neighborhoods visit the Family Van, a nonprofit clinic, to get free health screenings they wouldn't normally have access to.

groups. African Americans have long been discriminated against and still suffer disproportionately from the stresses of poverty. They have higher rates of death and disease, and shorter life expectancy than whites. African Americans and Hispanics are less likely to be able to afford health insurance and, consequently, to engage in regular health practices (Centers for Disease Control 2011). Researchers have shown that minorities are more often exposed to unhealthful surroundings, whether in the workplace or in residential neighborhoods. For example, Emily Rosenbaum (2008) found that Hispanics and blacks in New York City tended to live in poorer quality housing in lower-income neighborhoods and to suffer much higher incidents of asthma than their Asian, white, and higher-SES counterparts.

Gender is another source of inequality that complicates the health picture for men and women. Health is one place where gender inequality tends to benefit women over men, as women are generally healthier and enjoy a longer life expectancy in spite of having a lower SES than men. Traditional male gender role expectations may result in men who work in more dangerous occupations and engage in more risky lifestyle behaviors (such as smoking, drinking, doing drugs, and driving fast). The more strongly men identify with the "macho" aspects of masculinity, the more likely they are to avoid preventive health care, regardless of their level of SES (Springer and Mouzon 2011). Men and women suffer some diseases, such as cancer and diabetes, in about equal numbers. However, men still have a higher incidence of heart disease and strokes, while women more often report that they suffer from mental health disorders like anxiety or depression (WomensHealth .gov 2010).

The Problem of Food Deserts

A **food desert** is a community in which the residents have little or no access to fresh, affordable, healthy foods. Most food deserts are located in densely populated urban areas that may have convenience stores and fast-food restaurants but no grocery stores or other outlet for fresh fruits, vegetables, meats, and other healthy foods. (Sparsely populated rural areas, where stores are far away and hard to access, can also be considered food deserts.) For example, more than 20 percent of Chicago's 3 million residents live in neighborhoods without supermarkets (Gray 2009), which means that they may have to shop at drug stores, liquor stores, or corner mini-marts for food items, or subsist on the chicken nuggets, burritos, or burgers and fries from the takeout chain on the corner. People who live in food deserts may have few meal choices that aren't highly processed and loaded with fat, sugar, and chemicals.

Food deserts are often in neighborhoods that are predominantly low-income or nonwhite in population. This means that the effects of food deserts are experienced disproportionately by the poor, African Americans, Hispanics, and other minority groups. The health effects of living in a food desert are significant: the risk of obesity, diabetes, and heart disease for African Americans increases by half, and for Hispanics by two-thirds (Powell et al. 2007; Whitacre et al. 2009). So, while any given individual may be at risk for obesity, diabetes, or heart disease, living in a food desert increases those risks.

Why do food deserts exist? They are not a new phenomenon. Grocery chains began leaving urban areas for the suburbs in the 1960s and 1970s as a result of perceived problems with security, profitability, real-estate costs, and parking (Ferguson and Abell 1998). In their place, bodegas, liquor stores, and fast-food chains popped up, leaving central urban populations with far fewer healthy food options. Some city and state governments are trying to entice supermarkets back to these neighborhoods with programs like tax incentives, grants, or loans for big food retailers and subsidies for farmers' markets. Similar programs are being proposed at the federal level (Haber 2010).

As we have seen, our individual health is shaped by our neighborhood context, which is itself shaped by race and class inequality, the actions of big corporations, and the responses of governmental bodies at all levels. This phenomenon is known as **deprivation amplification**, meaning that our individual disease risks (based on our heredity and physiology) may be amplified by social factors (Macintyre, MacDonald, and Ellaway 2008). The solutions to these health problems are not going to be found merely at the individual level—they must incorporate social action as well. Yes, you need to eat more healthily in order to control your diabetes . . . but you must be able to find healthy foods close by and at affordable prices in order to do so, and you are more likely to do that in some neighborhoods than in others, which you may be more likely to live in depending on your gender, race, and SES.

FOOD DESERT a community in which the residents have little or no access to fresh, affordable, healthy foods, usually located in densely populated, urban areas

DEPRIVATION AMPLIFICATION when our individual disease risks (based on our heredity and physiology) are amplified by social factors

Food Deserts The absence of grocery stores contributes to the lack of healthy food options available in urban and poor neighborhoods.

You've seen the ads in magazines, on television, and in subway stations: pictures of healthy-looking people enjoying life, along with the tagline, "Ask your doctor if [this medication] is right for you." It's called direct-to-consumer drug marketing. It was illegal in the United States until 1985 and was uncommon until the late 1990s. Now it is everywhere. Pharmaceutical companies can now appeal directly to potential patients, who then take their newfound knowledge into the exam room and suggest the drug to (or even demand it from) their doctors.

This is a reversal of the way the process originally worked, as only doctors used to have the specialized knowledge necessary to identify and prescribe drug treatments. Now patients are empowered with medical information—or is it that they are swayed by persuasive marketing campaigns? Most ordinary consumers don't have the ability to evaluate drugs based on their efficacy in clinical trials or their risk of possible side effects, so pharmaceutical advertisers often appeal instead to our desire for happy relationships at home, at work, and with friends. The images in the ads signal that these relationships will improve if we start a new drug regimen using their latest product.

Some of the most frequently advertised prescription-only drugs are those that treat erectile dysfunction, as well as those that treat depression and anxiety. Both of these classes of drugs are advertised directly to consumers as being the cure for troubles in their relationships. In the case of Cialis, Viagra, and Levitra, the goal is to make the male consumer ready to perform sexually at any time, and the ads show happy (hetero) relationships as the implied result of taking the drug. With drugs like Abilify or Cymbalta, the ads show depressed or anxious people (usually women) whose relationships with family, friends, co-workers, and even pets are no longer a source of pleasure for them. Then they take the drug and regain their ability to enjoy things like camping, board games, lunch dates with friends, and walks in the park. The appeal in both cases is to our desire to have enjoyable and fulfilling relationships with others, and we are advised that we can achieve these

relational goals by, quite literally, "swallowing" what the ads are selling.

Other direct-marketed drugs are also presented as being fixes for relationship issues. Aricept staves off dementia so that your beloved Alzheimer's patient can hold a coherent conversation with you for a few months longer; Crestor keeps your cholesterol down so that you can still play on your all-seniors softball team; Detrol calms your overactive bladder, allowing you to enjoy the annual employee BBQ without having to run to the bathroom every few minutes . . . and the list goes on. While technically about physical illnesses and treatments, many of these ads appeal to our longings for happy, healthy, pleasurable, and lasting relationships, all of which we hope can be achieved and maintained with help from the products of the pharmaceutical industry.

That's right: "Big Pharma" wants us to have sexy marriages, happy families, gratifying work lives, and enjoyable friendships. And it just so happens that their (often expensive) drugs can help us do so. Just ask your doctor!

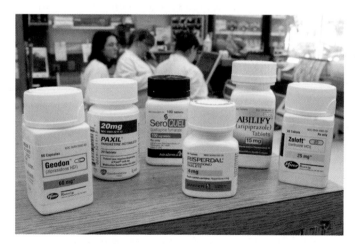

Brought to You by Big Pharma With direct-to-consumer marketing, pharmaceutical companies can advertise the benefits of new drugs directly to patients.

Medicine as a Social Institution

For proof that medicine is a social institution, take a look at the American Medical Association (AMA). The AMA is usually thought of as an organization that makes health recommendations on such topics as childhood obesity and cancer prevention to benefit the general public. But physicians and other medical professionals know the AMA as a trade union that creates the rules and regulations governing medical licensure. Almost all issues concerning medicine in both public health and professional regulation are governed by the AMA.

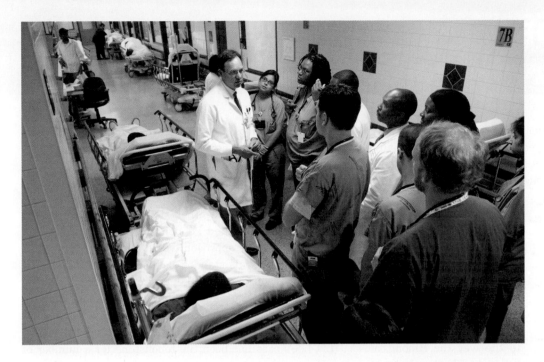

Medicine as a Social Institution Medical students shadow a doctor in an emergency room. The path to becoming a doctor is highly regimented, and only more rules and regulations apply once one becomes a doctor.

Milton Friedman (1994), the winner of the 1976 Nobel Prize in Economics and a vocal critic of the AMA, argued that the AMA limits admissions to medical schools and restricts medical licensing to advance the interests of physicians. He viewed the AMA as a monopolizing organization that reduced the quantity and quality of medical care by forcing the public to pay more for medical services because of the lack of qualified physicians.

For example, the AMA does not allow physicians who are trained in foreign countries to practice in the United States without passing the United States Medical Licensing Exam (USMLE). For many of these physicians, fulfilling the requirements of the USMLE is a lengthy and arduous process that often necessitates repeating medical residency before they are allowed to practice medicine—even though they were fully licensed and practicing physicians in their country of origin. The AMA and the American College of Obstetricians and Gynecologists also restrict such practices as home births. Even though trained midwives and doulas (who provide emotional support) can safely assist at home births, pregnant women have their options limited by the pressure that the AMA places on women to have labor and delivery at a hospital attended by physicians. As a result, these professionals are forced to operate on the margins of the industry, while physicians and hospitals are able to increase their profits from hospital births.

The AMA serves a number of purposes: it establishes and transmits the norms and values of medicine and medical knowledge; it regulates, licenses, and legitimizes the practitioners of medicine; and it polices various forms of encroachment on its own powers. In these ways, medicine itself can be seen as a social institution, with the AMA playing a primary role in creating and maintaining social order, legitimacy, and control.

Institutional Contexts

The institutional context can have a powerful effect on the interactions that occur within it. You might remember David Rosenhan's study "On Being Sane in Insane Places" (1973) from Chapter 6, in which "pseudo-patients" who were admitted to a mental hospital were unable to convince hospital staffers of their sanity. In this case, the place itself overrode the individuals' claims to normalcy: once they were defined by and situated within the institution, they could no longer exert any power over their own status, and every interaction they had served as "proof" of their presumed mental illness. Erving Goffman found something similar in his study of hospitalized mental patients, *Asylums* (1961): psychiatric patients frequently offered explanations for being there that highlighted their normalcy and attempted to reframe their selves as sane and healthy. They inevitably failed to change anyone's mind, however, since the power of their institutionally inflicted diagnoses was indisputable.

Sociologist Elaine Feder-Alford's (2006) ethnomethodological analysis of her own hospitalization (for streptococcal pneumonia) shows that these social processes are still at work in medical institutions. She describes being treated like a "piece of meat," an object, or an "incompetent child" by hospital staff during her illness. She felt dehumanized and powerless, as if they saw her as a diagnosis, rather than as a human being. Medical professionals plunged long syringes into her stomach without explaining why and accused her of

ON THE JOB
Cultural Competence in Health Professions

Lia Lee was a baby when her epileptic seizures began. In 1985, when she was three years old, she had an especially serious attack, and her parents, Hmong immigrants living in California's Central Valley, brought her to the Merced County Medical Center for treatment. What happened to Lia, her family, and her doctors during the next two years is the subject of journalist Anne Fadiman's 1998 book *The Spirit Catches You and You Fall Down*.

> **CULTURAL COMPETENCE**
> the concept of acknowledging and incorporating a patient's cultural background as part of the treatment process; the recognition that patients' beliefs shape their approach to health care

The book's title refers to the way the Hmong, a Southeast Asian ethnic group, view Lia's affliction. Indeed, their understanding of all health problems involves malevolent attempts by evil spirits, known as *dabs*, to meddle with human souls. The differences between Hmong understandings of epilepsy and its appropriate treatment and those of the Western medical establishment created the conflict in which Lia Lee was trapped.

The details of Lia's case are heart-wrenching: both her parents and her doctors tried their best to heal her. But because of cultural and language differences, they were unable to understand each other's perspective. They became suspicious and mistrustful of each other, which made collaboration even harder. The doctors firmly believed in Western biomedical approaches to epilepsy; they thought that if the Lees gave Lia the right medicines at the right times, she would be fine. Meanwhile, the Lees firmly believed that the *dab* had Lia's soul in its grip, and that traditional Hmong procedures (such as shamanic healing ceremonies) should be part of her treatment.

Both parties saw the other side's actions as counterproductive; they resisted cooperating because they each believed the other's approach would make Lia's condition worse. Caught in this standoff between Western medicine and Hmong tradition, Lia did get worse, eventually suffering "The Big One," a seizure that left her with severe and permanent brain damage. After decades spent in a vegetative state, tended lovingly by her family, Lia died in 2012.

Lia Lee's case has been the touchstone for a number of recent attempts to increase the cultural awareness of health care professionals, with the hopes of avoiding future cases like hers. This movement has coined the term **cultural competence** to describe the concept of acknowledging and incorporating a patient's cultural background as part of the treatment process. For example, the Association of American Medical Colleges (AAMC) is among the many organizations that have instituted cultural competence initiatives. The AAMC (2012) has produced a set of curriculum recommendations for medical schools and provides evaluation tools for assessing the impact of cultural competency initiatives once they are in place. The goal is to train new physicians to recognize the importance of cultural knowledge and beliefs—their patients'

---

being an alcoholic because she contracted a liver infection. The institution she inhabited as a patient defined her very differently than she defined herself, creating conflict at just the point in time when she was most ill, and hence least able to defend her definition of herself and the situation. As her condition improved, so did her ability to assert her humanity and negotiate for better treatment within the institutional setting. Her experience left her dismayed at the power of the hospital to reduce the patient to an object and led her to promote "proposals that acknowledge patients in a hospital setting as human beings with individual needs and feelings" (p. 618).

Doctor-Patient Relations

The institutional context of medicine shapes the interactions between individuals within it. But those interactions also contribute to the shape of the institution itself. Since the 1970s, ethnographers, conversation analysts, and other observational sociologists have studied interactions in health care settings. Studies of doctor-patient interactions have shown that while we may think that doctors automatically have more status (and hence more power) than patients, this actually has to be established in the interaction; it is not an inevitable feature of medical settings. The "smallest details of the way in which participants talk to one other can have sizable impacts on the eventual outcomes," and outcomes depend on who participates in the interaction (doctors, pharmacists, physical therapists, patients, parents, kids) and in what kind of setting the interaction takes place (office visits, phone consultations, surgical theaters) (Pilnick, Hindmarsh, and Teas Gill 2009, p. 11).

There are, however, both institutional and geographic influences on these kinds of interactions. Doctors in rural settings are more likely to spend time engaging in emotional

and their own—in health care encounters and to provide them with strategies for effective diagnosis, treatment, and interaction in cross-cultural encounters.

As part of the AAMC's plan, students are encouraged to examine their own cultural backgrounds, assumptions, and biases and to exercise nonjudgment when asking questions and listening to patients discuss their own health beliefs. They are trained to respect patients' diverse ideas about health and illness, to recognize when to use interpreters, and even to collaborate with traditional healers from their patients' cultures. They are also urged to appreciate the power imbalances between doctors and patients and to work to eliminate racism and stereotyping from health care practices.

Students often assume that they should major in a "hard" science such as biology if they want to go into a health profession. But given the rising importance of cultural competence in health professions, this may not be the ideal foundation. A student with a social science background, like sociology, may be even better prepared for working in the medical field than a biologist. An understanding of such issues as ethnocentrism, inequality, and the importance of culture in the lives of individuals means that students of sociology are already ahead of bio majors when it comes to issues of cultural competence in the practice of medicine. Indeed, for the fist time ever, the 2015 Medical College Admissions Test (MCAT) included questions in psychology and sociology.

Culture Clash Foua Yang holds a photo of her daughter Lia Lee, who fell into a vegetative state at the age of five after a catastrophic seizure. The heartbreaking case of this Hmong family and their experience with Western medicine inspired a movement to increase the cultural competence of health care professionals.

labor with their patients than doctors in urban settings, even when accounting for time spent per patient and number of patients seen per day. Doctors in rural settings are more likely to know their patients from their community and interact with them in less instrumental ways, which studies have demonstrated leads to improved patient outcomes (Desjarlais-deKlerk and Wallace 2013). It is through such subtle interactional processes that social institutions and the power of their participants are constituted, maintained, or changed.

Other findings are equally counterintuitive: while you might think that what constitutes good or bad medical news is pretty obvious (say, a benign tumor versus a malignant one), doctors and patients do not always agree on whether a particular diagnosis is pleasant or unpleasant, trivial or serious. Doctors' commentary during examinations, for example, is often an attempt to guide patients in their interpretation of the diagnostic findings. Patients do not always catch the doctor's drift and sometimes seem disappointed when the doctor informs them that there is nothing much wrong with them (Heritage and Stivers 1999; Maynard and Frankel 2006).

Additional research on medical interaction has moved beyond focusing merely on doctor-patient interaction, acknowledging that there are other important dyads (and triads and groups) in medical institutions that are worth examining. Interactions between patients and speech therapists, pharmacists, or dentists are structured differently and address different issues than those between patients and physicians. And interactions between health care practitioners (such as doctor-nurse, surgeon-anesthetist, or trainee-teacher), either within or outside of patients' presence, are equally important. So are interactions facilitated by medical technologies, such as ultrasound screenings, which place nurse practitioners into complex scenarios where their expertise is in tension with the technology's forced standardization (Pilnick, Hindmarsh, and Teas Gill 2009). One powerful analysis of an emergency-services call shows what happens "when words fail," as the dispatcher becomes irritated with the panic-stricken caller, and their clash about what constitutes an appropriate call for help results in the victim's death (Whalen, Zimmerman, and Whalen 1988). Studies such as this one indicate that rules, roles, and other elements of institutional order are emergent and situational. They are not necessarily written down somewhere for the rest of us to follow but instead are created and maintained (and sometimes distorted) in interaction.

The Sick Role

Of course, in addition to being shaped in interaction, rules and roles in medical institutions are influenced by external social structures as well. One example of this is the **sick role**. This concept, advanced by functionalist Talcott Parsons (1951), was a way of encapsulating the actions and attitudes that society expects from someone who is ill, as well as the actions and attitudes that a person might expect from other members of society. Being ill is, from a functionalist perspective, a form of deviance; it violates norms about health and productivity. So, as part of the sick role, a patient is exempted from his or her regular responsibilities (such as work, child care, or other, less tangible obligations) and is not held responsible for his or her illness. However, the patient also has a new set of duties, which include seeking medical help as part of an earnest effort to recuperate and get back to normal. If the sick person abides by these requirements, he or she will not be treated as deviant by society; but if the sick person languishes for too long, doesn't do much to improve his or her condition, or seems too interested in staying sick, that person is likely to experience negative sanctions from society.

As you might imagine, the concept of the sick role has changed over the many decades since Parsons first proposed it, in part because of advances in diagnostic technology. For example, with genetic testing, we can now identify people who are at risk of certain diseases before they ever become ill (indeed, not everyone who is at risk becomes ill). What does this new diagnostic label—"at risk"—mean for the performance of the sick role? Those people with genetic risk factors but no symptoms of disease exist in a liminal space between the healthy and the sick. They inhabit a "potential sick role," with a different set of expectations than in Parson's traditional model. One particularly interesting finding is that those who are in the lowest risk category sometimes try to get themselves recategorized as high risk. This may be because it is easier to determine the expectations for

SICK ROLE the actions and attitudes that society expects from someone who is ill

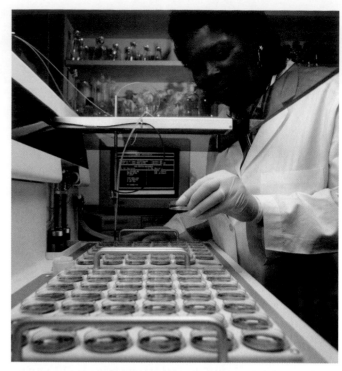

Sick Role and Genetic Risk How might people who have a genetic risk of certain diseases but who show no symptoms exist in a space between the healthy and the sick?

a high-risk patient (regular screenings, warning family members that they might be at risk, etc.) than for a low-risk patient. This suggests a more dynamic, nuanced definition of the "sick role" and provides for the possibility that the experience of health and illness is not as straightforward as Parsons originally hypothesized.

DATA WORKSHOP
Analyzing Media and Pop Culture

Medicine on Television

From *M*A*S*H* to *St. Elsewhere*, from *Dr. Kildare* to *Doogie Howser* and *House*, Americans have long been captivated by television shows about hospitals. Medical dramas and comedies have been some of the most critically acclaimed and highest-rated primetime television shows over the years. Many medical shows have multiple fan sites for discussing every detail of every episode. And because these shows are so prevalent and popular, they influence America's perception of different diseases and treatments, the roles of patients and medical staff, and the nature and function of the medical institution.

In conventional American television, the medical problems faced by the protagonists are easily solved. There is generally a patient or multiple patients with medical conditions that are triaged, diagnosed, treated, and healed within a single episode. Anyone who has dealt with a serious illness or accident knows that the reality of health care in the United States is a prolonged process that involves long waits, multiple visits to multiple doctors and different facilities for testing, and complicated interactions with insurance providers. The anger, sadness, and frustration of the patient's experience are generally glossed over in favor of the viewpoint of the medical professionals involved in the process.

For this Data Workshop, you will be using existing sources to do a content analysis comparing the world of TV with the real world. Refer back to Chapter 2 for a refresher on this research method. Select a scripted medical drama or comedy (not a reality or documentary show), using the following list as inspiration. You may choose a show that is currently being broadcast or one that is available online or on DVD:

Chicago Hope	*House, M.D.*
Chicago Med	*Nurse Jackie*
Children's Hospital	*Private Practice*
Code Black	*Rosewood*
Dr. Ken	*Royal Pains*
ER	*Scrubs*
Grey's Anatomy	*St. Elsewhere*

Select an episode or scene that deals with a specific disease or condition. Watch the episode closely and pay attention to the plotlines, scenes, characters, and dialogues in which the specific disease or medical condition is depicted. Take notes as you watch; you may have to review scenes several times before you can do a thorough content analysis.

Next, look up the epidemiology of that disease or condition. You may start with the Internet, but make sure you are consulting a medical journal site or an organization such as the Mayo Clinic or Centers for Disease Control and Prevention rather than Wikipedia or WebMD. For example, articles from the *New England Journal of Medicine*, the American Medical Association, or American Association of Family Physicians will yield more thorough and accurate data for the purposes of this exercise.

You may want to consider the following questions when looking at the disease's epidemiology:

* How common is the disease or condition?

* What are the causes of and contributing factors to the disease or condition?

* Does it affect different groups (for example, men and women, or patients of different races or ethnicities) in different ways?

* Which groups are more likely to contract the disease or condition? Why?

* Who is involved in the diagnosis and treatment of the disease or condition?

* How expensive, rare, dangerous, and/or available are the treatments, and are there any side effects?

* How rich, lucky, or well-insured would a patient have to be to undergo treatments?

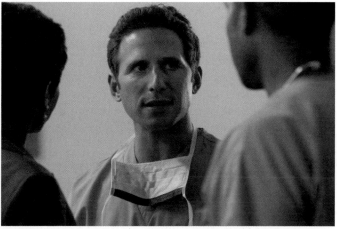

Medicine on Television *Nurse Jackie* and *Royal Pains* are both medical dramas that portray hospitals in ways that don't always resonate with real life.

Compare and contrast the show's treatment of the disease or condition to the statistics your research has revealed. How accurate was the portrayal? How does the show's treatment of illness reflect the average experience of an American patient with the same illness? And most important, what kinds of effects would any discrepancies have on audiences', patients', or even physicians' perceptions of the disease or condition and its treatment? How does this affect American viewers' understanding of the health care system?

There are two options for completing this Data Workshop:

PREP-PAIR-SHARE Conduct a content analysis of your chosen TV show and develop some preliminary answers to the questions posed. Prepare written notes that you can refer to during in-class discussions. Pair up with one or more classmates and discuss your findings in small groups. Compare and contrast the analyses of actual and fictional disease experiences as observed by participants in your group.

DO-IT-YOURSELF Complete your content analysis and develop some preliminary answers to the questions posed. Then write a three- to four-page essay discussing your answers and reflecting on your observations of the differences between fictional depictions of disease and treatment, and real-world data. What do you think your observations tell us about the contemporary U.S. health care system and the ways in which it is depicted on television?

Issues in Medicine and Health Care

The fields of medicine and health care have continued to evolve and advance, often affecting individual lives in profound ways and addressing some of the most pressing problems facing humanity. While much of the progress over the last decades has been tremendously positive, there are still unfulfilled promises and new questions to resolve. In this last section, we examine some of the current trends and future challenges in medicine and health care.

Health Care Reform in the United States

In 1974, when Richard Nixon gave his final State of the Union address before a joint session of Congress, he called for "a new system that makes high-quality health care available to every American in a dignified manner and at a price he can afford" (1974). Nixon, a Republican, had previously described comprehensive health care reform as the highest priority on his unfinished agenda for the United States (1972). It would remain a national priority that eluded many other politicians for many more decades until March 2010, when the Patient Protection and Affordable Care Act was signed into law. This legislation, commonly known as the ACA or "ObamaCare," finally brought something like universal health care coverage to all U.S. citizens. Yet the act was not met with universal approval. The bill simultaneously frustrated many longtime advocates of health care reform by not going far enough while infuriating others by going too far.

Almost as soon as the legislation was passed, opponents began organizing to repeal the law. Some believe that it will cost too much, raise taxes, hurt businesses, and lead to a government takeover of health care, among other complaints. Opponents have also challenged the constitutionality of the new law, taking their cause to state and federal courts. Health care reform is likely to remain a battleground, and new legislation may alter some aspects of the recent reforms. In the meantime, the ACA is being phased in slowly over ten years, with more and more Americans receiving health care coverage every year.

A major element of the bill took effect shortly after it was signed into law in 2010. Insurance companies must now allow children to remain on their parents' insurance plan through age twenty-six, rather than the previous limits of age twenty-one or after college graduation. Also, insurance companies can no longer deny coverage to anyone with preexisting conditions such as diabetes or epilepsy. Another major effect of the bill has been to close loopholes that once allowed insurance companies to deny or limit coverage to people who became ill. Insurers are no longer allowed to impose lifetime

Health Care Reform A volunteer helps people sign up for the Affordable Care Act, which, among other things, allows young adults to stay on their parents' plans until the age of twenty-six and prevents insurance companies from denying coverage to people with preexisting conditions such as diabetes.

spending caps—allotting a certain amount of money for a given patient over that patient's lifetime—a limit surpassed by many who have serious illnesses. Additionally, the new law bans **rescission**—canceling coverage only after a person gets sick. Women can no longer be charged more than men for their health insurance, Medicare recipients can get additional discounts on prescription drugs, and insurers cannot raise their rates more than 10 percent per year without justification.

Some of the ACA's extended coverage is achieved through insurance reforms, but one of the most important new provisions is the creation of both federal and state-run insurance exchange systems to cover the unemployed, self-employed, and anyone else without insurance. While mandates require more people to buy into coverage plans, there are some exceptions for the poor, and subsidies are offered for other low-income individuals and families to help in purchasing insurance. Companies that employ more than fifty people have to provide health insurance or suffer fines, but new small-business exchanges were created to help companies comply; there are also tax credits available to support small businesses in covering their employees. Indeed, the percentage of uninsured Americans has dropped from 18 percent in 2013 to just under 12 percent in 2014. At least 10 million people who once could not afford health coverage now can do so. And despite continued opposition from conservative politicians, in August 2015, 44 percent of all adults had a favorable opinion of the ACA, compared to 43 percent who had an unfavorable opinion (Kaiser Family Foundation 2015).

Until "ObamaCare," the United States was the last wealthy, industrialized nation in the world without some form of universal health coverage for its citizens. Although there may yet be challenges that change some aspects of the new law, the ACA undeniably constitutes a major change to the U.S. health care system.

Complementary and Alternative Medicine

In all likelihood, you or someone you know has participated in some form of alternative medicine. If you've ever tried deep breathing for relaxation, a nutritional supplement to gain or lose weight, or an herbal remedy for a cold, if you've gone to a chiropractor, had a massage, or taken a yoga class, then you've made use of alternative medicine. Complementary or alternative medicine (CAM) is a group of medical treatments, practices, and products that includes acupuncture, homeopathy, hypnosis, and meditation, as well as traditional healers like shamans and movement therapies like Pilates. **Complementary medicine** can be used in conjunction with conventional Western medicine, whereas **alternative medicine** is used instead of it. Some of these practices or products are ancient (such as acupuncture and herbs), while others are only new to the Western world—or arose in the past few decades (such as biofeedback, fasting, and "juice cleanses").

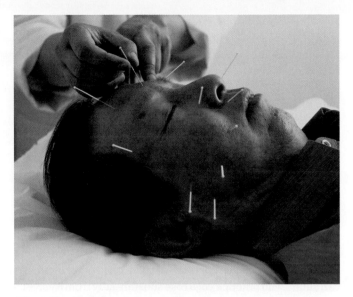

Alternative Medicine A man receives acupuncture treatment, an ancient medical practice that is sometimes used instead of conventional Western medicine.

Complementary and alternative medicine has generated both enthusiasts and critics. Some skeptics call this type of medicine "quackery," nothing more than modern-day "snake oil" that promotes false hopes to a vulnerable public. Others who may have found few satisfactory answers within the medical establishment become staunch believers in the benefits of various CAM treatments. Indeed, some CAM practices and practitioners are slowly gaining legitimacy (and popularity), and **integrative medicine** is a burgeoning part of the field that combines conventional medicine with particular CAM practices that have proven most safe and effective. Scientific studies of CAM practices lag behind those done on conventional medicine, and more evidence is needed about whether and how CAM practices work and on which patients with what conditions. It's possible that some forms of alternative medicine may one day prove better at treating some conditions than conventional medicine. But it is still rare for insurers to cover alternative medicine, so patients currently seeking those treatments typically have to pay out of pocket.

The increasing number of people who have turned to CAM practices is remarkable. In the United States in 2012, more than 33 percent of adults age eighteen and over and nearly

RESCISSION the practice by insurance companies of canceling coverage only after a person gets sick

COMPLEMENTARY MEDICINE a group of medical treatments, practices, and products that can be used in conjunction with conventional Western medicine

ALTERNATIVE MEDICINE a group of medical treatments, practices, and products that are used instead of conventional Western medicine

INTEGRATIVE MEDICINE the combination of conventional medicine with complementary practices and treatments that have proven to be safe and effective

12 percent of children had used one or more forms of CAM within the past year (Clarke et al. 2015). Celebrities and professional athletes often attribute successful recoveries from illnesses or injuries to CAM therapies. Both the New York Yankees and the San Francisco Giants employ a "staff acupuncturist" (Healthcare Medicine Institute 2010). Green Bay Packers quarterback Aaron Rodgers said in a 2015 interview that while he initially tried accupuncture at the urging of his girlfriend, actress Olivia Munn, he came to rely on it to help heal a serious calf injury later in the season (Dougherty 2015).

The largest category of CAM users is women with higher levels of education and income. Natural supplements (non-vitamin products such as fish oil/omega 3, glucosamine, echinacea, flaxseed, and ginseng), deep breathing, meditation, chiropractic, yoga, acupuncture, and massage are some of the most frequently used forms of CAM. The percentage of American adults who practice yoga rose substantially from 5 percent in 2002 to nearly 10 percent in 2012 (Clarke et al. 2015). Americans are most likely to seek these treatments for neck, back, joint, and headache pain but may also use them for anxiety, high cholesterol, head and chest colds, and insomnia. In 2007, American adults spent close to $34 billion on CAM treatments: two-thirds on self-care CAM products, classes, and materials; and one-third on visits to CAM practitioners. That amounts to just over 11 percent of the total out-of-pocket U.S. spending on all forms of health care (Nahin et al. 2009).

Medical Ethics

Medical science continues to progress at a rapid pace, bringing new discoveries and producing innovations that are bound to change human health in the future. We tend to think of these advancements as having a uniformly positive impact on society, but this is not always true. In many cases, new advancements bring new and sometimes troubling issues to the fore. **Bioethics** is the study of controversial moral or ethical issues related to scientific and medical advancements. Among hot topics are questions about extending life through artificial means, stem cell research, the use of animals in medical experiments, and even the idea of human cloning.

The Human Genome Project (HGP) is a scientific endeavor that seeks to identify and map the 20,000 to 25,000 genes that make up human DNA from both a physical and functional perspective. The project began in 1990, and the first version of the genome was completed in 2003, although research based on the project continues. Scientists hope that decoding DNA will help elucidate how the human body works, providing clues for how to treat and possibly prevent serious illnesses. One of the results of the HGP is the ability to identify predispositions to hereditary diseases such as certain types of cancer, cystic fibrosis, and liver disease through genetic testing. Results from the HGP may also provide the key to the management of diseases such as Alzheimer's.

The rapid advancement of medical technologies like the HGP also brings numerous ethical issues to the table. One of the more controversial aspects of these advances is genetic testing in utero and at birth. For example, pre-implantation genetic diagnosis allows doctors to test DNA samples from embryos that are grown in vitro. These tests can tell whether a baby will be born with certain disorders and allow for the selection of only certain embryos for implantation. Genetic testing in utero can inform parents of possible genetic mutations in the embryo, potentially allowing parents to choose whether to have a disabled child. There are ethical concerns about genetic testing becoming a modern-day form of **eugenics**, in which the human gene pool is "improved" through science.

In cases where genetic testing reveals future susceptibility to disease for otherwise healthy individuals, there are ethical issues about the use of the genetic profiles. Can a person be stigmatized because of his or her genetic profile? Will insurance companies be able to deny coverage or even treatment of illnesses that can now be revealed through in utero genetic testing? Will parents be encouraged to end pregnancies if the fetus's genetic profile reveals a torturous, expensive, or stigmatizing condition? Certainly, medical technology is advancing rapidly enough to cause a cultural lag or delay in the legal, ethical, and social issues surrounding its use.

End of Life

Another area in which ethics may lag behind science is end-of-life care. On the one hand, we now possess the technologies and treatments to prolong the lives of patients who in prior eras would have died much more rapidly than they now do from diseases such as ALS (Lou Gehrig's disease), Alzheimer's disease, cystic fibrosis, and certain cancers and from traumatic injuries. In addition, hospice and palliative care can now make terminally ill patients more comfortable and give them more time to prepare for the inevitable. On the other hand, this ability to prolong life can sometimes make it more difficult to distinguish between "living" and "dying" (such as cases of patients in persistent vegetative states), and hence to respond appropriately to those who are close to death (Kaufman 2005). The ability to rescue patients from the brink of death and to keep on life support those who would otherwise pass away raises the question: just because we can keep someone alive, does that mean that we should always do so?

Organizations such as the Hemlock Society and Final Exit promote the right of terminally ill patients to invoke medically assisted suicide and the ability to "die with dignity," or while they are still in control of their bodies and minds. But

BIOETHICS the study of controversial moral or ethical issues related to scientific and medical advancements

EUGENICS an attempt to selectively manipulate the gene pool in order to produce and "improve" human beings through medical science

Aid in Dying At the Capitol in Sacramento, Dan Diaz watches a video recording of his late wife, Brittany Maynard, who was diagnosed with terminal brain cancer at the age of twenty-nine. Maynard moved to Oregon from California in order to take advantage of Oregon's Death with Dignity Law, ending her life on November 1 with the help of doctors.

critics worry that this approach will encourage ending life for the "wrong" reasons, such as treatable depression or disability. This often leaves critically ill patients and their families wondering what to do and when to do it. How to approach death and dying has always challenged us as members of society; there is every indication that, even in our age of advanced medical technology, it will continue to do so.

Take the example of Brittany Maynard, who was diagnosed with terminal brain cancer at the age of twenty-nine and given six months to live. Like many who receive such a prognosis, Maynard and her husband, Dan Diaz, tried to make those six months count. They traveled, visited loved ones, and checked items off Maynard's "bucket list." But Maynard also decided that, when the time came, she wanted to have control over when and how she died. She knew that, as a resident of California, she would not be legally allowed to do this, so she and Dan packed up and moved to Oregon, where a "death with dignity" law allows doctors to prescribe medication that terminally ill patients can use to end their own lives when they see fit. Maynard did so on November 1, 2014, but not before becoming an activist for doctor-assisted suicide and voicing strong support for aid-in-dying legislation in a number of states, including California. However, as of August 2015, only four states—Oregon, Montana, Washington, and Vermont—allow physicians to prescribe certain patients life-ending medication.

CLOSING COMMENTS

Concerns about health and illness are a constant part of human existence. As individuals, we will each face the pleasures and frustrations of living in a physical body that is affected by our lifestyles and life chances. A sociological approach is especially helpful in allowing us to understand the links between social structures and processes and health outcomes. We recognize that health is not merely a biological state but rather another important area of human life affected by social institutions and social inequalities. Medicine and health care are rapidly advancing, and as a result, we may someday live longer and healthier lives, but we will always be shaped by the social contexts in which our lives take place. Science may soon discover new treatments for old diseases, but it is just as likely that we will have to continue dealing with current and as-yet-unknown challenges to our health in the future. It is certain that there will be cultural changes in our values and beliefs that bring about new understandings and practices regarding the relationship between society and the health of people and the planet.

Everything You Need to Know about Health and Illness

> " Health, illness, and mortality are physiological phenomena; they are also unquestionably shaped by social factors. "

THEORIES OF HEALTH AND ILLNESS

* **Structural functionalism:** disease is a threat to social order; therefore, the health-care system should return patients to health and normal functioning as members of society

* **Conflict theory:** health and the health-care system are valuable resources that are unequally shared in society

* **Symbolic interactionism:** the meaning of health and illness are dependent on historical, cultural, and situational contexts

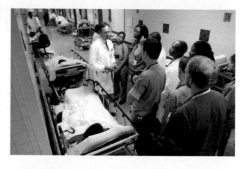

REVIEW

1. What do you think about the process by which such things as hyperactivity and obesity are now seen as medical conditions as opposed to behavioral problems? Can you think of other behaviors or conditions that are becoming "medicalized"? Should we consider video game or internet addiction as a medical condition?

2. Do you believe that the U.S. health-care reforms of 2010 will be successful in bringing comprehensive medical coverage to more Americans? Do you believe that health care is a basic right that should be provided to all citizens, or is it a privilege that individuals must earn? What are some of the benefits included in universal health-care systems in such countries as France, Canada, and Britain?

Female Life Expectancies in the Washington, DC, Area

National Average (2010): 80.8 Years

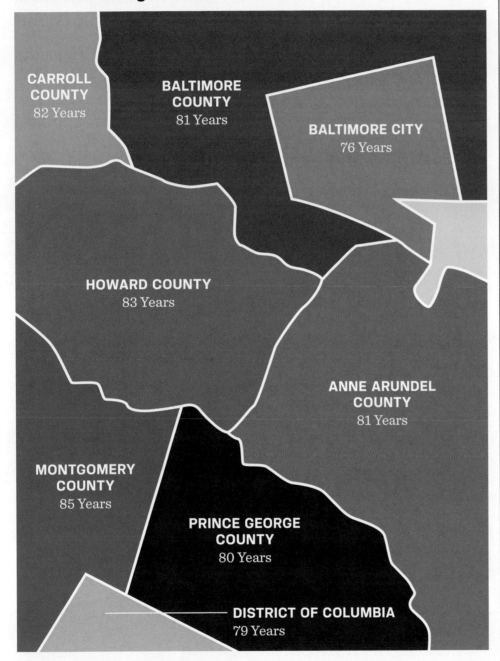

CARROLL COUNTY
82 Years

BALTIMORE COUNTY
81 Years

BALTIMORE CITY
76 Years

HOWARD COUNTY
83 Years

ANNE ARUNDEL COUNTY
81 Years

MONTGOMERY COUNTY
85 Years

PRINCE GEORGE COUNTY
80 Years

DISTRICT OF COLUMBIA
79 Years

Learn more about the health of your community at www.countyhealthrankings.org

SOURCE: Institute for Health Metrics and Evaluation 2013.

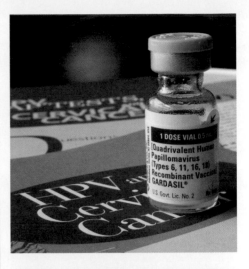

EXPLORE

Marketing Health

The HPV vaccine Gardasil has been highly controversial since it was first approved in 2006. It was originally approved for females and was marketed particularly toward 11- and 12-year-old girls. Later, Gardasil was approved for males, and now it is approved for females and males ages nine to twenty-six. The marketing message for Gardasil has changed throughout the years, from an anti-STD vaccine to an anti-cancer vaccine to an anti-STD vaccine again. Visit the Everyday Sociology Blog to read more about a sociologist's analysis of how social gender norms affected the marketing of this vaccine.

http://wwnPag.es/trw414

PART V
Envisioning the Future and Creating Social Change

Las Vegas—Sin City, Entertainment Capital of the World, home of glitz, glitter, and gambling; fantasy mecca, international tourist destination where fortunes and marriages are made and broken; populated by showgirls, gangsters, high-rollers, and Elvis impersonators. This is the "Hollywood Vegas" according to Mark Gottdiener, Claudia C. Collins, and David R. Dickens. Their book, *Las Vegas: The Social Production of an All-American City* (1999), chronicles the development of Las Vegas from its days as a pit stop for Spanish explorers in the early 1800s to the neon marvel it has become.

Gottdiener, Collins, and Dickens analyze the Hollywood Vegas, but they argue that there is another Las Vegas as well, where regular people live, work, and go to school, the supermarket, and the movies. What is the real Las Vegas like? It's big, it's growing fast, and its demographic, economic, and cultural trends represent the social changes taking place in many cities across the country—even those without pulsating neon or posh casinos.

In 2000, the Census confirmed that Las Vegas was the fastest-growing metropolitan area in the United States. Its population increased 83 percent during the 1990s and has continued to grow well into the twenty-first century, with the Clark County Metro Area (of which Las Vegas is a part) surpassing the 2 million mark in 2014. Las Vegas's population boom showed signs of slowing during the recession years and for some time after, but new Census data confirm continued growth in this once-again burgeoning urban locale (El Nasser 2010; U.S. Census Bureau 2015e).

People have flocked to Las Vegas because of its booming employment and housing market, and they have come from all over the country and around the world. Some of those newcomers to Las Vegas are former residents of California, seeking refuge from the state's high cost of living. Another segment of the Las Vegas population boom are senior citizens, who make up about 13 percent of the populace. Retirees are valued consumers who spend money on new homes and other items when they arrive in the city; however, as they age, they may create a strain on local health care resources. Another major population segment is Hispanic Americans, who make up more than 30 percent of Las Vegas's population. They are the fastest-growing ethnic group in southern Nevada, and they, too, are valued consumers, courted by advertisers in both English- and Spanish-language media. In addition, the area has a growing population of foreign-born immigrants, some of whom work at casinos, hotels, and resorts and whose labor supports the region's biggest industry, tourism.

In addition to these demographic trends, Las Vegas is also an economic trendsetter, for better or worse. Its employment rates were consistently high because of the large number of service jobs in the casino, resort, and tourist industries, but these jobs generally offer low pay and few benefits. There is also other work to do in Las Vegas. Major industries include construction and real estate sales (though these industries were hit hard by the recent recession), banking, and other financial services, often related to the casino industry (Gottdeiner et al. 1999). As the economy diversifies, the population grows—and as the population grows, more services and other work become necessary. Cards must be dealt, meals must be cooked, hotel rooms must be cleaned, children must be taught, cars must be repaired, and houses must be built, sold, and financed. However, if a population begins to decline, the market for all those goods and services diminishes, and jobs of all sorts become harder to find.

Las Vegas's housing boom began in the 1970s with the advent of master-planned communities. These residential developments, often built around golf courses, were move-in ready when the economy began growing and diversifying in the 1980s, and more middle-class families began moving into the city. Master-planned suburbs continue to sprout in and around Las Vegas, filling Clark County with people and all the things they use, including houses, schools, stores, roads, and cars. During the recent recession, this boom went bust. In 2014, Las Vegas held one of the highest real estate foreclosure rates in the country (Robison 2014). Whatever takes place in the larger U.S. real estate market happens even more spectacularly in Las Vegas.

Environmental issues are important to life in the real Las Vegas, which is located in a desert ecosystem where water is scarce and rainfall is infrequent. Hundreds of thousands of people live in this ecosystem, in sprawling suburban housing developments. Lawns, pools, and golf courses require billions of gallons of water that the immediate environment does not provide, yet growth continues. Las Vegas competes with several other arid states, including California, for water resources. Water from the Colorado River is pumped in at great expense from Lake Mead to fill pools and water lawns, as well as for household use. Lake Mead is also the destination for all of Las Vegas's outgoing effluent—treated sewage and runoff full of lawn chemicals. These environmental toxins cycle back into the drinking water consumed by the area's residents.

Water isn't the only environmental issue that Las Vegas faces. Atomic test sites from the 1950s and '60s, located in the Mojave Desert, were once in the middle of nowhere—but suburban sprawl continues to draw closer to these areas. The same is true of a number of desert chemical plants in areas that are also being encroached upon by residential development. Recently, environmental activists have successfully prohibited nuclear waste transport and dumping in the Las Vegas area.

A fluctuating population, an economy dominated by service-industry work, a natural environment strained to its limits by desert sprawl—this is the real Las Vegas. Add the glittery, neon-lit Hollywood fantasy town, and you have a vanguard city for the twenty-first century. Economic, environmental, and demographic trends that already appear in Las Vegas—including the booms and busts of the larger economy—will become increasingly visible in other U.S. cities.

Cultural and social changes occurring in Las Vegas may also be visible where you live—including the legalization of gambling. While Las Vegas was once the center of a gambling industry dominated by organized crime, legal casinos are now operated all over the country by groups of all sorts, including state governments and Native American tribes. Gambling boats float on many Midwestern lakes and rivers,

and resort casinos continue to spring up on Indian reservations in almost half the U.S. states.

Las Vegas is also the site of unusually powerful labor unions, which represent many of the service employees—cooks, waiters, musicians, hotel employees—whose work keeps the city running. At a time when union membership is down in the rest of the country, Las Vegas is a strong union city—ironically located in Nevada, a right-to-work state. Union laborers tend to have higher wages and more benefits than nonunion workers because of the power of collective bargaining. The resurgence of union membership in Las Vegas's service industries may inspire workers in other cities with service- and tourism-dominated economies.

Gottdiener and his coauthors argue that "in many ways Las Vegas represents, though often in exaggerated form, several important trends in contemporary American society as a whole" (p. xi). In Part V, we examine many of those trends from a sociological perspective as part of our focus on social change. In Chapter 15, we examine a variety of demographic and environmental trends, such as suburbanization, migration, and aging. And we consider processes of cultural and social change, such as activism by labor unions and environmentalists, in Chapter 16. As you read these chapters, think about your own city or town and the trends you have observed close to home. Also, think about the changes you would like to see in your surroundings; a sociological perspective can help you strategize to make those changes happen. In any case, keep an eye on Las Vegas for changes yet to come—because, as research demonstrates, what happens in Vegas doesn't necessarily stay in Vegas!

CHAPTER 15

Populations, Cities, and the Environment

Chris McCandless was the picture of success. The son of upper-middle-class professionals in Washington, D.C., he had just graduated from Emory University in Atlanta and was headed for law school. Nonetheless, he felt constrained and even betrayed by a society that perpetuated poverty and inequality and often seemed to care so little for its individual members. He wanted to experience the personal freedom of being untethered from obligations to family, school, and work—even though that meant letting go of the emotional and material security they provide.

In the summer of 1990, Chris headed for the wilderness, which he saw as pure and untainted while he viewed society as corrupt and damaged. Chris moved in and out of the social world during the next two years; he lived in the wilderness successfully for long stretches of time but always came back to civilization for supplies, to earn a little money, and to make some human connections. After spending months alone in the deserts of the Southwest, he arrived in Bullhead City, Arizona, and took a job at a McDonald's. He was leather-skinned and malnourished, had no money or belongings, and had lost his car in a flash flood—but he was still alive, and after a brief stint in what he considered the most sinister of all social institutions (the fast-food industry), he disappeared back into nature again, this time headed to the great unspoiled expanses of Alaska.

Chris did a lot of reading in preparation for his journey, and he seemed able to endure the physical and emotional hardships of being alone in the wilderness for months at a time. His journal entries reveal that he often felt exhilarated and truly believed that his was the superior way of life. But Chris's story did not end happily. Two years after he left his hometown of Atlanta, his body was found on the Alaskan tundra many miles outside Fairbanks by a group of moose hunters.

In his book *Into the Wild*, Jon Krakauer reconstructed Chris's journey through diaries and interviews. Krakauer determined that while living on the tundra for four months alone, Chris had inadvertently eaten something that may have poisoned him. Realizing how sick he was, he began to yearn for the saving presence of other humans—for both assistance and companionship. At the very end, Chris's journal entries reveal a desire to return to the social world and a recognition of the protection society offers from the rigors of nature. Chris did not get to reenter society with his newfound insight, but perhaps we can learn more about our own relationship to both the natural and the social worlds from his story.

HOW TO READ THIS CHAPTER

This chapter covers three big and deeply connected topics in sociology: population, urbanization, and the environment. To this point, we have focused mostly on society—on people and their effect on each other. But humans live in a natural as well as a social world, and their environment is another key factor in their lives. We are affected by and have a profound effect on the planet earth. The number of humans who live on the planet has nearly tripled since the middle of the last century, from 2.5 billion in 1950 to 7.3 billion in 2015. Population studies show that an ever-greater number of people are settling into large, sprawling cities—a trend called urbanization. Growing populations and increased urbanization create new demands and pressures on the global environment as more natural resources are consumed and more pollution and waste are produced. Remember that these huge global shifts are the result of the cumulative actions of many individuals over time.

Population

If we want to understand the relationship between the social world and the natural world, we must examine human population. The next sections look at how sociologists study population and its related issues. To paraphrase sociologist Samuel Preston, the study of population has something for everyone: the confrontations of nature and civilization; the dramas of sex and death, politics and war; and the tensions between self-interest and altruism.

Demography

Demography is the study of the size, composition, distribution, and changes in human population. Sociologists and others who study population are called demographers. Demography is essentially a macro-level, quantitative approach to society, but it is more than just simply counting heads. Population dynamics are influenced not only by biological factors such as births and deaths but also by sociological factors such as cultural values, religious beliefs, and political and economic systems. People are not just animals who reproduce by instinct; they are subject to structural constraints as well as individual agency, all of which affect their behavior and ultimately the world in which they live.

The U.S. government has long been interested in keeping track of those residing within its geographic boundaries. The U.S. Constitution mandates that a census be taken every ten years. The U.S. Census Bureau, a part of the Department of Commerce, regularly conducts these studies of the population, going back to the first such attempt in 1790. At the beginning of every new decade, census takers try to contact every person living in the country. Surveys, either short or long form, are sent to every household to gather a range of demographic information, from household size and age of family members to their gender, education level, income, and ethnic background. In the years between the decennial census, smaller-scale studies are continuously conducted by the Census Bureau. Other countries are less systematic at gathering data, so many statistics that refer to global population are necessarily based on scientific estimates.

Three basic demographic variables are crucial to understanding population dynamics. The first is **fertility rate**—the average number of births per 1,000 people in the total population. The total fertility rate is the average number of children a woman would be expected to have during her childbearing years. The fertility rate for 2013 in the United States was approximately 1.86 (U.S. Department of Health and Human Services 2015b). Fertility rates vary across the globe, with some of the highest rates in sub-Saharan Africa, with Niger at 6.9, and some of the lowest in Southeast Asia, with Singapore at 0.8 (Central Intelligence Agency 2014g).

The next demographic variable is **mortality rate** (or death rate)—the number of deaths that can be expected per 1,000 people per year. This statistic is usually modified by other factors, so the mortality rate within a particular country varies within age, sex, ethnic, and regional groups. A related concept is **infant mortality** rate, or the average number of deaths per 1,000 live births. The death rate for 2014 in the United States was approximately 8.2 and the infant mortality rate was approximately 6.2. Mortality and infant mortality rates vary across the globe, some of the highest being in African countries, with a death rate of 14.6 in Chad, for example, and an infant mortality rate of 90.3. Some of the lowest mortality rates are found in wealthier Middle Eastern countries such as Qatar with 1.5, and some of the lowest infant mortality rates are found in Asian countries such as Japan with 2.1 (Central Intelligence Agency 2014a).

Another related concept is **life expectancy**, or the average age to which a person can expect to live. Here, too, other factors are involved, so life expectancy of people within a particular country varies by sex, ethnicity, and social class. In general, life expectancy rose dramatically in the twentieth century. The life expectancy for a person born in the United States in 2014 is approximately 79.6 years of age; the

DEMOGRAPHY study of the size, composition, distribution, and changes in human population

FERTILITY RATE a measure of population growth through reproduction; often expressed as the number of births per 1,000 people in a particular population or the average number of children a woman would bear over a lifetime

MORTALITY RATE a measure of the decrease in population due to deaths; often expressed as the number of deaths per 1,000 people in a particular population

INFANT MORTALITY average number of infant deaths per 1,000 live births in a particular population

LIFE EXPECTANCY average age to which people in a particular population are expected to live

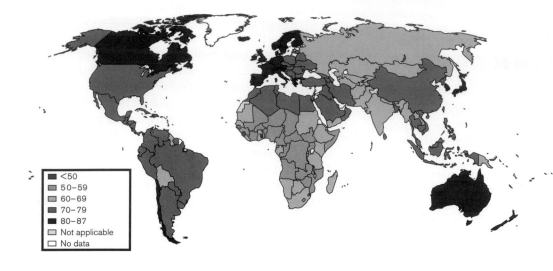

Figure 15.1 Global Life Expectancy at Birth, 2013

Legend:
- ■ <50
- 50–59
- 60–69
- 70–79
- ■ 80–87
- Not applicable
- No data

SOURCE: World Health Organization 2015.

average for men is 77.1, while for women it is nearly 82 (Central Intelligence Agency 2014c). As Figure 15.1 shows, life expectancy also varies greatly across the globe, with some of the highest averages in wealthier nations such as Monaco at almost 90, and some of the lowest in African countries such as Chad at approximately 49 years—in large part because of the AIDS epidemic (Central Intelligence Agency 2014c). **Life span**, or **longevity**, has also increased dramatically—again, depending on where you live. More people around the globe are living past 100 years of age. As of mid-2016, the oldest living person was Emma Movano, an Italian woman who was born on November 29, 1899; however, the world record for oldest person documented lived to age 122 (Mai-Duc 2015).

The last demographic variable that we will consider is **migration**—the movement of people from one geographic area to another for the purposes of resettling. Migrations have occurred throughout human history and have played an important part in populating the planet. As a demographic variable, migration neither adds to nor subtracts from the total number of people on the planet; it simply refers to their relocation from place to place. Related concepts are **immigration** and **emigration**. Immigrants are those people coming into a country or region to which they are not native. Emigrants are those departing from a country or region with the intention of settling permanently elsewhere. **Internal migration** refers to patterns within a country, where the movement is generally from rural to urban areas. The **net migration** for any country is the

LIFE SPAN or LONGEVITY the uppermost age to which a person can potentially live

MIGRATION movement of people from one geographic area to another for the purpose of resettling

IMMIGRATION entering one country from another to take up permanent residence

EMIGRATION leaving one country to live permanently in another

INTERNAL MIGRATION movement of a population within a country

NET MIGRATION net effect of immigration and emigration on a particular population; expressed as an increase or decrease

difference between the number of persons entering and leaving a country during the year. From 2013 to 2014, net migration in the United States was around 996,000 people. Similarly, the net migration rate in the United States was 2.45, which means that there was an increase of 2.45 persons for every 1,000 inhabitants in the United States. In general, worldwide migration patterns show that people are moving from least-industrialized to most-industrialized countries. There are often other economic or political reasons for migration, with refugees pouring in and out of some countries. Countries with the highest net migration rates include Lebanon and Qatar, while those with the lowest rates include Syria and Tonga (Central Intelligence Agency 2014d).

The study of population dynamics involves the interplay among the three sources of population change: fertility, mortality, and migration. These variables are used to construct current population models and future projections. We can apply demographic variables to the global population or to a population within a particular region or country.

If we focus on the United States, we can track several interesting population trends. The United States is currently the third most populous nation (after China and India), with more than 321 million people (U.S. Census Bureau 2015j). It is also one of the fastest-growing industrialized nations. According to the Census Bureau, the U.S. population is projected to grow by 98 million between 2014 and 2060—an average increase of 2.1 million people per year. The native population is projected to increase by 22 percent (62 million) while the foreign-born population is expected to grow by an astounding 85 percent (36 million) (U.S. Census Bureau 2015c). Colorado, Texas, Utah, and Florida are among the fastest-growing states. While the overall trend sees people moving to the "sunbelt" states in the South and West from "rustbelt" states in the North and East, there are notable exceptions: in recent years, North Dakota—fueled by an oil boom—has experienced the highest growth rates in the country. In contrast, Illinois, West Virginia, and Connecticut are experiencing the biggest declines in population (U.S. Census Bureau 2015i).

IN THE FUTURE
Living to 150

Author Sonia Arrison (2011) predicts that her own son, born in 2010, may very well live to be 150 years old. This preschooler and his generational cohort are poised to reap the benefits of health and technological advances that promise to extend their lifetimes far, far beyond those of their ancestors.

You are probably already familiar with some of the developments contributing to our increased life spans. Medical advances have conquered (or at least controlled) many of the diseases that once kept us from growing old, such as smallpox, measles, diphtheria, polio, and tuberculosis. Injuries that were once guaranteed to be fatal are now treatable and survivable through advanced surgical techniques. Public health measures have improved things like sanitation, food safety, water purity, and community education. New concerns with environmental degradation, pollution, pesticides, and chemicals are leading to less toxic exposure. Of course, all these things are more likely to be true in wealthier, developed regions such as the United States and Europe; life spans are still much shorter in areas where these advances are not widely available.

Even so, centenarians—people who live to be over 100 years of age—are getting more common worldwide. The United Nations estimated about 317,000 in 2012, with the United States, Japan, and China in the top three positions with approximately 50,000 centenarians each. And in the UK, one-third of all babies born in 2013 are expected to live to 100 (Christensen and Willingham 2014). Most current centenarians are women. And most current centenarians got old the old-fashioned way: clean living, healthy food, exercise, stress management, and good genes. Arrison's son and his friends may have the assistance of technological advances that sound like science fiction but are or will soon be reality.

Drugs to treat chronic illnesses such as diabetes, heart disease, and even inflammation may have the side effect of extending life spans (Duncan 2012). Stem cell research may allow for the regeneration of damaged cells, organs, and other body parts. Gene therapy may eradicate killers such as sickle cell disease, cystic fibrosis, various cancers, and other hereditary diseases (Glor 2012). Technology that replaces human body parts with machines and connects those machines directly to our brains may expand the number of "cyborgs" or partially bionic humans, in addition to expanding our definition of what constitutes "natural" life (Duncan 2012).

These possibilities sound fascinating, don't they? But they all focus solely on keeping individuals healthy and alive. What happens to society if people start living much longer, healthier lives? Arrison addresses some of these questions in her book.

For one thing, longer lives mean that we must reconsider the whole notion of retirement. Retiring at sixty-five seems ridiculous (not to mention boring!) if you'll be living another eighty years or so. The prospect arises, then, of people pursuing multiple careers (including the multiple educations necessary to prepare for them) in one lifetime. So, people may find themselves retiring two, three, or more times in their 100-plus years.

Our current notion of marriage as a "'til death do us part" contract also may deserve some revision if we're going to live to 150. Will we just marry later? Or will multiple marriages over the course of a lifetime become more common and acceptable? Will marriage contracts have to include "sunset clauses" or expiration dates, at which time we may renew them if we choose? Don't laugh—this has already been proposed by lawmakers in Mexico! And what about family planning? Will we push the boundaries of fertility as we push the boundaries of longevity? If so, will nuclear families be larger? Will extended family living become more common?

Finally, what will happen to our values, morals, and beliefs? So many of the social rules about things like marriage, family, and life in general are rooted in religion—how will religion itself respond if and when we find ourselves living longer and hence calling some of these rules into question? We already worry that attempts to extend life and stave off death amount to "playing God." If we live longer, will religions be forced to pay more attention to this life, and less to the afterlife?

All we can say in answer to these questions is, stick around and see for yourselves . . .

World's Oldest Woman Gertrude Weaver held the title of world's oldest woman before she passed away on April 6, 2015, at the age of 116.

Theories of Population Change

Concerns about population growth first emerged in the eighteenth century during the Industrial Revolution. Many demographic variables at that time contributed to rapid growth in the newly burgeoning urban areas of Europe. Mechanization, which increased agricultural production, and the introduction of a hearty new staple from South America—the potato—made available enough food for people to sustain themselves and support larger families. Other technological and scientific advances helped decrease infant mortality rates while increasing fertility and extending life expectancy. As a result, the first real population boom in human history occurred.

Thomas Malthus, a British clergy member turned political economist, was one of the first scholars to sound the alarm on overpopulation. Although he lived at a time when people believed in technology and progress, the promise of prosperity and abundance, and the perfectibility of human society, he himself was less than optimistic about the future. Based on his observation of the world around him, Malthus wrote a book in 1798 called *An Essay on the Principle of Population*, in which his basic premise, the **Malthusian theorem**, stated that the population would expand at a much faster rate than agriculture; inevitably at some future point, people would far outnumber the available land and food sources. If population increases surpass the ability of the earth to provide a basic level of subsistence, then massive suffering would follow. His theory has two simple principles: that population growth is exponential or geometric (1, 2, 4, 8, 16, 32 . . .) and that production is additive or arithmetic (1, 2, 3, 4, 5, 6 . . .).

According to his calculations, society was headed for disaster, or what is called the **Malthusian trap**. To avoid such a catastrophe, Malthus (1798/1997) made several rather radical policy recommendations. He may have been the first to propose that humans should collectively limit their propagation to save themselves and preserve their environments. He urged "moral restraint" in sexual reproduction to curtail overpopulation. If human beings were unable to restrain themselves (by postponing marriage or practicing abstinence), nature would exert "positive checks" on population growth through famine, war, and disease. Malthus also advocated state assistance to the lower classes so they could more readily achieve a middle-class lifestyle supported by decent wages and benefits and adopt the values associated with later marriage and smaller families (New School 2004).

Malthus's ideas were not always popular, though they were influential and widely read. Charles Darwin noted that Malthusian theory was an important influence on his own theory of evolution and natural selection. Malthus also influenced whole new generations of social thinkers, not just demographers but others as well, and their respective ideas on population growth.

More than 200 years later, some people, the **neo-Malthusians**, or New Malthusians, essentially still agree with him. Among the notable modern voices looking at the problem of overpopulation are William Catton (1980), Paul and Ann Ehrlich (1990), and Garrett Hardin (1993). They worry about the rapid pace of population growth and believe that Malthus's basic prediction could be true. In some respects, they claim, the problem has even gotten worse. There are a lot more people on the planet in the twenty-first century, so their continued reproduction expands even more quickly than in Malthus's time. And with continued technological advancements—such as wars that use "surgical strikes," modern standards of sanitation, and the eradication of many diseases—people are living much longer than before. When Malthus was alive, there were approximately 1 billion people on the planet; it was the first time in recorded history that the population reached that number. The time required for that number to double and for each additional billion to be added has continued to decrease (Figure 15.2). Today there are more than 7 billion people on the planet—and counting. The United Nations predicts that world population will surpass 9 billion by 2050 and continue to grow to more than 11 billion by the end of the century, ultimately stabilizing (United Nations Department of Economics and Social Affairs 2015).

The New Malthusians also point to several sociological factors that influence the reproductive lives of many and promote large families. Religion still plays a role in many societies, with the Old Testament commanding, "Go forth and multiply." The Catholic Church still forbids members to practice any birth control besides the rhythm method, even though 77 percent of American Catholics surveyed in a poll said the church should allow them to use some form of artificial contraception (Pew Research Center 2014f). In many poorer nations, more children mean more financial support for the family. They work various jobs in their youth to help sustain the household, and for parents, children may be the only source of support they have in old age. Some governments encourage the expansion of their population base and promote the addition of new citizens who can become taxpayers or soldiers. They may even provide incentives to parents, such as tax deductions for each child. Last, cultural influences, from "family values" to "machismo," sometimes confer more prestige on those with children; women gain status in the valued role of mother, while men gain status for their perceived virility.

MALTHUSIAN THEOREM the theory that exponential growth in population will outpace arithmetic growth in food production and other resources

MALTHUSIAN TRAP Malthus's prediction that a rapidly increasing population will overuse natural resources, leading inevitably to a public health disaster

NEO-MALTHUSIANS contemporary demographers who worry about the rapid pace of population growth and believe that Malthus's basic prediction could be true

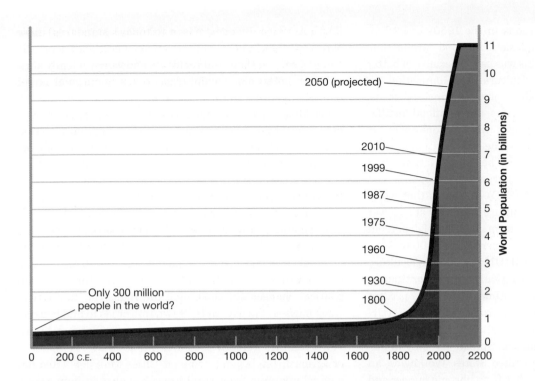

2050 (projected)

2010
1999
1987
1975
1960
1930
1800

Only 300 million
people in the world?

World Population (in billions)

Figure 15.2 World Population Growth over 2,000 Years

SOURCE: Population Reference Bureau 2010.

At the same time, contrary arguments are proposed by the **anti-Malthusians**. Economists such as Julian Simon (1996, 2000) and demographers such as William Peterson (2003) believe that Malthus reached faulty conclusions and that he couldn't have envisioned the many modern developments that would influence population dynamics. In fact, the anti-Malthusians are more concerned about the population shrinking and the possibility of a **demographic free fall**. Some countries, such as Japan, are already dealing with new problems caused by a rapidly shrinking population. The United States may soon face a similar dilemma as the birth rate falls below replacement levels (usually calculated as 2.1). Demographers don't anticipate a widespread free fall in population happening just yet, but they forecast a very different future when the pattern of **demographic transition**, now occurring in many industrialized nations, spreads to the rest of the developing world.

The Anti-Malthusians believe that when people have a better standard of living, they also prefer smaller families, as children become more of an economic liability than an asset. Better education and easier access to health care bring more reproductive choices such as methods of **family planning**. Governments in some countries are adopting policies that discourage large families. Further, the Anti-Malthusians claim that technological advancements have enabled humans to produce much larger quantities of food than ever before, thus providing for the nutritional needs of more of the world's population.

So who is right? Will the world population eventually stabilize, or will it continue to spiral out of control? We may not know the answer to those questions for many years, so in the meantime we continue to speculate. The populations of some countries continue to grow rapidly, while others remain stable or begin to decline. The **growth rate** is the number of births minus deaths plus net migration of a population, expressed as a percentage change from the beginning of the time period measured. This can be expressed as either positive growth or negative growth (shrinkage). Another related variable is **natural increase**. This gives some idea of a country's trajectory toward demographic transition but without taking migration into account. The growth rate for 2014 in the United States was approximately 0.8 percent. It was highest in countries such as Lebanon at 9.4 percent and Zimbabwe at 4.4 percent and lowest in Syria at –9.7 percent and the Cook Islands at –3 percent (Central Intelligence Agency 2014f).

What about the other elements in Malthus's theorem? Food production has grown remarkably since Malthus's time. In particular, the "Green Revolution" that began in Mexico in 1948 and spread to India and other less developed

ANTI-MALTHUSIANS contemporary demographers who believe Malthus's basic prediction was faulty and worry instead that worldwide population may shrink in the future

DEMOGRAPHIC FREE FALL rapid decrease in birth rates to below replacement levels; results in a shrinking population, mostly in industrialized nations

DEMOGRAPHIC TRANSITION a theory about change over time from high birth and death rates to low birth and death rates, resulting in a stabilized population

FAMILY PLANNING contraception, or any method of controlling family size and the birth of children

GROWTH RATE percentage change in population over time calculated by subtracting the number of deaths from the number of births, then adding the net migration; expressed as a fraction of the initial population

NATURAL INCREASE change in population size that results from births and deaths; linked to a country's progress toward demographic transition

RURAL relating to sparsely settled areas; in the United States, any county with a population density between 10 and 59.9 people per square mile

URBAN relating to cities; typically describes densely populated areas

URBANIZATION movement of increasing numbers of people from rural areas to cities

nations in the 1960s caused an explosion in food production. This was partly because of better agricultural mechanization as well as newly engineered seeds, pesticides, and artificial fertilizers. Was this a unique increase, or can it be expected again in the future? The United Nations Food and Agriculture Organization (UN FAO) estimates that world agriculture will grow at a slower pace, from an annual 2.2 percent over the past two decades to 1.3 percent from 2005 to 2030 and 0.8 percent from 2030 to 2050 (UN Food and Agriculture Organization 2012a). Growth in agriculture will continue to surpass world population growth, estimated to be 0.97 percent from 2006 to 2030 and 0.48 percent from 2030 to 2050 (UN Food and Agriculture Organization 2012b).

Nonetheless, hunger remains widespread, not only in foreign countries but also in the United States. Worldwide, an estimated 805 million people suffer from chronic hunger and malnutrition—a lack of adequate food plus other factors such as insufficient protein and nutrients, poor eating habits, and unsafe water and sanitation (UN Food and Agriculture Organization 2014). Nearly half (45 percent) of deaths in children are due to poor nutrition, with approximately 3.1 million children dying each year (United Nations World Food Programme 2014). In the United States, every day 14.3 percent of households—about 49 million people—experienced hunger or food insecurity in 2013, that is, the limited or uncertain ability to acquire adequate and safe foods (U.S. Department of Agriculture 2014).

Other factors must also be considered in projecting the future of the global population. Science constantly brings technological advancements that enhance health and prolong life, but new and deadly diseases such as AIDS claim an ever-greater death toll in nations too poor to afford the medicines to treat these diseases. As the world's current occupants, we have to live now with the consequences of our choices. Many policy and advocacy groups concerned with population issues have been established in the past few decades, including Zero Population Growth, World Overpopulation Awareness, the Population Institute, and the Population Reference Bureau. To find out more, visit their websites.

Cities

The dynamics of population growth (and sometimes shrinkage) throughout human history have been accompanied by the development of larger cities in which more people are now living. Cities, however, are not a modern development. They have been in existence for thousands of years. We find evidence of ancient cities in the Middle East, Africa, Asia, and South America. By comparison to today's standards, these early cities would be considered quite small. They generally had just several thousand residents and were typically agricultural centers along major trade routes. Some much larger cities, however, had hundreds of thousands of residents, such as the Mediterranean cities of Athens and Rome. One reason cities were able to thrive was advances in agriculture that allowed surpluses of food to be readily available to support a population that was not directly involved in its production. People were thus freed to engage in other activities necessary for the functioning of the city and its residents.

Cities were not the prevalent residential areas until well into the nineteenth and twentieth centuries. Until then, the vast majority of people worldwide lived in **rural** or country areas. The wide-scale development of cities, or **urban** areas, was made possible by the significant social, economic, and political changes accompanying the Industrial Revolution, when masses of people were drawn into cities to find housing and the manufacturing jobs they needed to earn a living. Fewer families were involved in farming, as large companies, or agribusiness, began to emerge. Cities were populated not only by migrants from rural areas but also by immigrants from other countries, seeking opportunity and a better way of life. Industrialization provided the jobs and the means of communication and transportation to build the burgeoning city infrastructure that could support growing numbers of residents. This process in which growing numbers of people move from rural to urban areas is called **urbanization**.

In the early 1800s, only about 3 percent of the world's population lived in urban areas and only one city had a population greater than 1 million people: Peking, China (now called Beijing). In the early 1900s, almost 14 percent of the world's population lived in urban areas, and a dozen or so cities around the world (including New York City, London, Paris, Moscow, and Tokyo) had 1 million or more residents. By the early 2000s, more than 50 percent of the world's population was living in urban areas, and we now have to count as large cities those with 10 million people or more; there were twenty-eight of these megacities in the world in 2014—home to 12 percent of all urban dwellers (UN Department of Social and Economic Affairs 2014).

A similar pattern can be seen in the United States. In the early 1800s, just 6 percent of the population lived in urban areas, whereas 94 percent lived in rural areas. In the early 1900s, the split was 40 percent urban and 60 percent rural. In 2014, 81 percent of the population was urban and 19 percent was rural. As of 2015, ten American cities had populations over 1 million; the largest, New York City, has a population of over 8 million (U.S. Census Bureau 2015j).

Features of Urbanization

The term "city" is currently used to refer to an urban settlement with a large population, usually at least 50,000 to

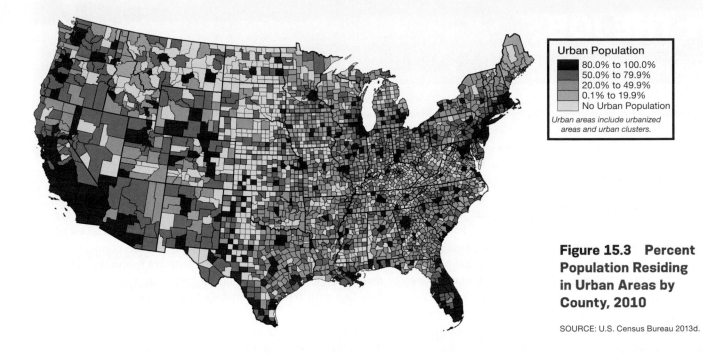

Figure 15.3   Percent Population Residing in Urban Areas by County, 2010

SOURCE: U.S. Census Bureau 2013d.

Urban Population
- 80.0% to 100.0%
- 50.0% to 79.9%
- 20.0% to 49.9%
- 0.1% to 19.9%
- No Urban Population

Urban areas include urbanized areas and urban clusters.

100,000 people. Although a few states, including Wyoming, West Virginia, Delaware, Maine, and Vermont, have no cities with populations of 100,000 people or more, California has seventy cities with more than 100,000 people, followed by Texas with thirty-six and Florida with twenty-one. Urban demographers use the word **metropolis** to refer to an urban area with an even larger population—usually at least 500,000 people—that typically serves as the economic, political, and cultural center for a region. The U.S. Census Bureau defines the term **Metropolitan Statistical Area (MSA)**, also called an **agglomeration**, as a metropolitan area that includes a major city of at least 50,000 inhabitants that is surrounded by an adjacent area that is socially and economically integrated with the city. In 2013, the United States (including Puerto Rico) contained 388 MSAs; more than fifty of these had populations of 1 million or more (Office of Management and Budget 2013). Many of the largest American cities, such as New York City, Los Angeles, Chicago, Houston, Philadelphia, Phoenix, and San Diego, have continued to grow rapidly in the past decade.

Largest of all is a **megalopolis**, also sometimes called a megacity—a group of densely populated metropolises (or agglomerations) that grow contiguous to each other and eventually combine to form a huge urban complex (Gottman 1961). One American megalopolis is referred to as "ChiPitts," or the Great Lakes Megalopolis, a group of metropolitan areas in the Midwest, extending from Pittsburgh to Chicago (and including Detroit, Cleveland, Columbus, Cincinnati, and Indianapolis), with a total population of almost 60 million. The ChiPitts metro areas are linked not only by geographic proximity but also by economics, transportation, and communications systems (Gottman and Harper 1990). Another megalopolis is "BosWash" or the Northeast

megalopolis, extending from Boston to Washington, D.C., and including twenty-two other metropolises such as New York City and Philadelphia. BosWash has a total population of almost 50 million, or approximately 17 percent of the entire U.S. population. Megalopolises are found worldwide, in countries including Brazil, Mexico, Indonesia, India, China, and Japan (Castells and Susser 2002). These are sometimes called megaregions or **global cities** to emphasize their position in an increasingly globalized world as centers of economic, political, and social power (Sassen 1991).

Cities are often characterized by **urban density**, measured by the total number of people per square mile. Some of the most densely populated cities in the United States include Guttenberg, New Jersey, with 58,821 residents per square mile; New York City with 27,016; San Francisco with 17,246; and San Juan, Puerto Rico, with 14,057 (U.S. Census Bureau 2010d). By contrast, rural areas are characterized by low density. Rural counties are those with populations of 10 to 59.9 people per square mile; frontier counties are those with 0.5 to 9.9 people;

METROPOLIS an urban area with a large population, usually 500,000 to 1 million people

METROPOLITAN STATISTICAL AREA (MSA) or **AGGLOMERATION** an area with at least one major city of 50,000 or more inhabitants that is surrounded by adjacent counties that are socially and economically integrated with the city core

MEGALOPOLIS a group of densely populated metropolises that grow dependent on each other and eventually combine to form a huge urban complex

GLOBAL CITIES a term for megacities that emphasizes their global impact as centers of economic, political, and social power

URBAN DENSITY concentration of people in a city, measured by the total number of people per square mile

ON THE JOB
Agriculture: From the Country to the City

John Peterson is not your average Midwestern farmer. First of all, he's an organic farmer: no pesticides or chemical fertilizers are allowed at Angelic Organics, a one-hundred-acre biodynamic farm located almost two hours west of Chicago. Angelic Organics is also one of the largest community supported agriculture (CSA) farms in the nation: the farm is supported in part by local shareholders, who buy a share of the farm and then receive a portion of its harvest, meaning that no supermarkets or cross-country truck travel stands between the shareholders and their weekly boxes of onions, kale, squash, tomatoes, peppers, basil, and rutabagas. John's unique and colorful story of saving his family's failing conventional farm by transforming it into a thriving organic CSA was featured in the critically acclaimed documentary *The Real Dirt on Farmer John*. Farmer John is an eccentric, biodynamic, community-supported vegetable and herb farmer in Caledonia, Illinois. And he's a man on a mission.

Understanding the need for education and outreach, Farmer John teamed up with Tom Spaulding and other Chicago-area shareholders to create a learning center at Angelic Organics. Angelic Organics Learning Center (AOLC) is dedicated to spreading the word about organic food production throughout the greater Chicago area. AOLC recognizes that while not everyone is destined to become a real rural farmer, even city dwellers can incorporate some of Farmer John's practices into their own backyard gardening endeavors and everyday household practices. Classes in soap making, chicken care, beekeeping, cheese making, and composting teach urban gardeners skills that help them save money, care for their families' health, and become more responsible stewards of their little patches of earth.

Angelic Organics Learning Center also sponsors an "urban initiative" that brings community gardening to the inner city. For example, their Roots and Wings program in Rockford, Illinois, involves local youth in growing organic produce in city plots. The kids also learn to cook, serve, and eat the fresh food they have produced themselves, and they sell their surplus at local farmers' markets so that their neighbors can enjoy the bounty as well. The youth participants don't just reap the benefits of learning about food and urban agriculture—they also become skilled at business, leadership, and problem solving. AOLC runs similar programs with city partners in the Chicago neighborhoods of Englewood and Little Village.

Urban farming like the type that Farmer John and the Angelic Organics Learning Center advocate and teach is becoming more popular in the United States. Gardeners lay sod on top of skyscrapers in New York City, Washington, D.C., Chicago, Detroit, and San Francisco, to grow vegetables and herbs for local chefs (Burros 2009). These rooftop gardens also provide insulation and drainage for the buildings and contribute to cooler cities (temperature-wise, that is). At ground level, community gardens provide space for apartment dwellers to grow their own healthy fruits and vegetables as well as save money and make connections with others by doing so. More chickens are becoming urban dwellers, too, as backyard coops spring up to provide city families with fresh eggs and early morning wake-up calls (Mann 2012).

There is probably an urban farm in your city or town. There may even be an urban farmer in your neighborhood. And anyone who recognizes the benefits—for individuals, society, and the environment—can try their hand at urban farming. All it takes is a little dirt.

Community Supported Agriculture A toddler picks flowers during a visit to Angelic Organics, a community supported farm in Caledonia, Illinois.

and remote counties are those with 0.04 people per square mile or fewer. Alaska is the most rural state in the United States, followed by Wyoming, Montana, North Dakota, and South Dakota.

Trends in Urbanization

Along with urbanization, an important countertrend surfaced in the years immediately following World War II. **Suburbanization** is the shift of large segments of population away from the urban core and toward the edges of cities, where larger expanses of land were available for housing developments that provided families with a chance to buy a home of their own and avoid the overcrowding of inner-city life. One of the first significant suburbs was called Levittown (based on the name of the builders), a community of 17,450 tract houses for 75,000 people built in Hempstead, New York, in the late 1940s. The simply designed homes were mass-produced and sold at prices affordable to returning veterans and the new growing middle class (Wattel 1958). In the 1950s, the second Levittown was built near Philadelphia, and in the 1960s a third in New Jersey. Herbert Gans's study *The Levittowners* (1967) found that homeownership gave suburbanites a sense of pride and more privacy and space, which they valued greatly.

Suburbanization also reflected a retreat from some of the problems associated with city living—crowding, noise, and crime. As more families were able to afford single-family homes, large yards with the proverbial white picket fence and a two-car garage became the literal image of the "American Dream" (Fava 1956; Kelly 1993). The decades-long shift of populations to the suburbs has accelerated and expanded throughout the nation, with more families moving farther and farther away into what's been called the "exurbs" (Frey 2003; Berube et al. 2006).

Suburban life has its own problems: long commutes, little contact between neighbors, and de facto racial segregation in housing and schools. Some observers have also criticized the monotonous uniformity of the new suburbs, claiming that they promote listless personalities, conformity, and escapism (Whyte 1956; Riesman 1957; Jackson 1985). Another problem related to suburbanization is **urban sprawl** (sometimes also called suburban sprawl). This phenomenon has to do with how cities and suburbs grow. It is often a derogatory term applied to the peripheral expansion of urban boundaries and is associated with irresponsible or poorly planned development. Critics say that such areas are often unsightly, characterized by a homogenous landscape of housing subdivisions, office parks, and corner strip-malls lacking character or green space (Kunstler 1993; Duany, Plater-Zyberk, and Speck 2001; Gutfreund 2004) and bringing problems of traffic, pollution, crowded schools, and high taxes.

While most suburbs remain "bedroom communities" or primarily residential, others have become **edge cities** with their own centers of employment and commerce (Garreau 1992). Edge cities are usually in close proximity to intersecting highways and urban areas. "Silicon Valley" is a

SUBURBANIZATION the shift of large segments of population away from the urban core and toward the edges of cities

URBAN SPRAWL a derogatory term for the expansion of urban or suburban boundaries, associated with irresponsible or poorly planned development

EDGE CITIES centers of employment and commerce that began as suburban commuter communities

Table 15.1   Theory in Everyday Life

Perspective	Approach to the Natural Environment	Case Study: Urban Sprawl
Structural Functionalism	The natural world exists in order to keep the social world running smoothly. The environment provides raw materials and space for development in order to meet society's needs.	As population increases, cities must grow in order to accommodate the growing population, so urban sprawl is functional for society.
Conflict Theory	Not all groups or individuals benefit equally from society's use of the natural environment.	Urban sprawl creates largely white, upper- and middle-class suburbs around cities whose residents are minorities, seniors, immigrants, working class, and/or poor. This means that suburban residents may have access to resources, like well-funded schools, that urban dwellers may not.
Symbolic Interactionism	The meanings assigned to the natural environment will determine how society sees and uses it.	Redefining open land as a scarce resource, and redefining urban areas as valuable spaces, may lead to the reduction of urban sprawl: open land could be conserved, while urban spaces could be rehabilitated and revitalized.

SMART GROWTH term for economic and urban planning policies that emphasize responsible development and renewal

WHITE FLIGHT movement of upper- and middle-class whites who could afford to leave the cities for the suburbs, especially in the 1950s and 1960s

URBAN RENEWAL efforts to rejuvenate decaying inner cities, including renovation, selective demolition, commercial development, and tax incentives

GENTRIFICATION transformation of the physical, social, economic, and cultural life of formerly working-class or poor inner-city neighborhoods into more affluent middle-class communities

RURAL REBOUND population increase in rural counties that adjoin urban centers or possess rich scenic or amenity values

prime example: the once-sleepy suburb of San Jose became a center of high-tech industry during the dot-com boom of the 1990s. Edge cities are one answer to the problems associated with suburbanization. **Smart growth** advocates are also promoting alternatives to suburban growth, emphasizing redevelopment of inner cities or older suburbs to create better communities. Elements of smart growth include town centers; transit- and pedestrian-friendly streets; a greater mix of housing, commercial, and retail properties; and the preservation of open space and other environmental amenities.

Many long-established cities suffered when populations began moving to the suburbs—including Detroit, Chicago, and Philadelphia in the North and East (the rustbelt) as well as New Orleans, St. Louis, and San Francisco in the South, Midwest, and West (U.S. Census Bureau 2005). Since the 1950s and '60s, people have left cities not only to find more space and bigger homes in the nearby suburbs but also to flee other problems endemic to the city. Largely, those escaping the cities were upper- and middle-class whites who could afford to leave—a trend often referred to as **white flight** (or sometimes "suburban flight"). Those remaining in cities were predominantly minorities, seniors, immigrants, working

class, or poor. White flight left urban areas abandoned by businesses and financial institutions, leading to broken-down and boarded-up shops and streets and creating ghettos that further exacerbated the problems associated with inner cities (Wilson 1996).

In the 1960s and '70s, to address the problem of decaying inner cities, local city governments and private investors took advantage of **urban renewal** efforts that included renovation, selective demolition, commercial development, and tax incentives aimed at revitalizing business districts and residential neighborhoods (Frieden and Sagalyn 1992). Urban renewal has been a limited success. While it did revitalize many areas, it often came at a high cost to existing communities. In many cases, it resulted in the destruction of vibrant, if rundown, neighborhoods (Mollenkopf 1983).

Urban renewal is linked to another trend that has also changed many formerly blighted cities: **gentrification**. This is the transformation of the physical, social, economic, and cultural life of formerly working-class or poor inner-city neighborhoods into more affluent middle-class communities as wealthier people return to the cities (Glass 1964). This trend, which took off in the 1990s, is evident in some of the nation's largest cities, such as Boston, New York, Philadelphia, Chicago, and San Francisco (Mele 2000). Various higher-income individuals, whether they were young professionals ("yuppies"), artists, or retirees, recognized the potential for rehabilitating downtown buildings (Castells 1984). They valued the variety and excitement of urban living more than the mini-malls of sleepy suburbia (Florida 2004). The term "gentrification" carries a distinct class connotation; while converting, renovating, remodeling, and constructing new buildings beautifies old city neighborhoods, it also increases property values and tends to displace poorer residents (Zukin 1987, 1989). Gentrification, then, does not eradicate the problems of poverty; it forces the poor to move elsewhere.

Real or Fake? People mingle outside Pastis restaurant in New York City's meatpacking district. Contrast this urban scene with Universal CityWalk in Los Angeles, which was designed to feel like an urban street.

Although urbanization (or suburbanization) is still the predominant demographic trend in the United States, an interesting reversal emerged in the 1990s, called the **rural rebound** (Johnson and Beale 1994; Johnson 1995, 1998). An increase in rural populations has resulted from a combination of fewer people leaving such areas and the in-migration of urban and suburban dwellers (Long and Nucci 1998). While most rural counties continue to decline, those near urban centers or with rich scenic or amenity values are generally experiencing an upsurge in population. Gains have been greatest in the Mountain West, the Upper Great Lakes, the Ozarks, parts of the South, and rural areas of the Northeast. Rural migrants include families with young children, small-scale farmers, retirees, blue-collar workers, single professionals, and disenchanted city dwellers all seeking a better way of life. They are willing to forsake the amenities of the city in exchange for a simpler, slower, more traditional rural lifestyle (Johnson 1999).

THE CASE OF SIMULATED CITIES Another example of our contemporary ambivalence about city life is simulated cities—social spaces engineered to maximize the benefits of city life without the risks. A prime example is Universal City-Walk, a collection of shops, restaurants, and movie theaters attached to the Universal Studios theme parks in Los Angeles, California; Orlando, Florida; and Osaka, Japan. CityWalk mimics an urban shopping street, with sidewalk café seating and strolling street performers. However, it has no connection to a real urban street. Both U.S. CityWalks are bordered on one side by the theme park and on the other by a vast expanse of parking lots and freeway traffic; the Japanese version is accessible by ferry and bullet train. The parking fees to visit this "street" range from $10 to $45, which makes CityWalk a semi-private attraction—distinctly unlike a real city street, which anyone can walk on without paying high fees for parking. The parking fees were instituted to minimize certain kinds of visitors found on real city streets, including homeless people and hustlers of various sorts.

The urban experience provided by CityWalk is sanitized, soothing, and a model of social control through architectural planning. As one critic noted, "They omitted . . . the handbill-passers, bag ladies, street vendors, and three-card monte—because part of CityWalk's attraction rests on the certainty that distractions will remain pleasing, never truly surprising, let alone shocking" (McNamara 1999). CityWalk doesn't reject the grit of urban life entirely: when laying the sidewalks, developers embedded fake trash in the concrete. CityWalk and other artificial urban environments such as Disney's Celebration, Florida, and *The Truman Show's* Seaside, Florida, reveal our desire to experience the positive aspects of urban life without having to endure the problems. But this kind of engineering tends to turn cities into theme parks, erasing what is authentically urban (Grazian 2008)—for better and for worse.

DATA WORKSHOP
Analyzing Media and Pop Culture

Imagining the Cities of Tomorrow

 People have always been interested in the future. Storytellers, inventors, scientists, politicians, and daydreamers have tried to imagine and, in some instances, create a vision of what will come.

Imagining the city of tomorrow is an almost constant theme in contemporary popular culture—books and comics, radio and TV, movies, and video games. Some of these represent a brighter vision of tomorrow, a **utopia** where humankind is finally freed from drudgery and disease, strife, and suffering. Some represent a darker vision of tomorrow, a **dystopia** where humankind is trapped in a ruthless, apocalyptic world of machines and nature gone mad.

UTOPIA literally "no place"; an ideal society in which all social ills have been overcome

DYSTOPIA opposite of a utopia; a world where social problems are magnified and the quality of life is extremely low

Although examples of the city of the future appear in many different media, this Data Workshop asks that you focus on film. You may have a favorite movie depicting the future, whether it's in the genre of science fiction, action adventure, thriller, horror, drama, or comedy. In deciding which movie to choose for your content analysis, consider whether the movie proposes a serious or realistic possibility of the future and avoid anything too far out in terms of monsters, aliens, or fantasy worlds.

The following is a partial list of movies that could satisfy the assignment. This list is not exhaustive, and you may prefer to use a film not in the list. (Please be aware of MPAA ratings for movies and select appropriate material for your age group.)

12 Monkeys	*Independence Day*
1984	*Left Behind*
A.I. (Artificial Intelligence)	*Mad Max*
Back to the Future	*The Matrix*
District 9	*Metropolis*
V for Vendetta	*Minority Report*
Her	*Chappie*
Divergent	*The Hunger Games*
Blade Runner	*Road Warrior*

City of the Future In the film *The Fifth Element*, flying cars buzz between ultra-tall skyscrapers. Could this version of the future realistically occur? Would you like to live in such a future?

Brazil
Children of Men
The Day after Tomorrow
Demolition Man
eXistenZ

Fahrenheit 451
The Fifth Element
Gattaca
Idiocracy

Slaughterhouse Five
Solaris
Strange Days
The Terminator
Terminator 2:
    Judgment Day
Total Recall
Tron
The Truman Show
Videodrome

For this Data Workshop, you will be using existing sources and doing a content analysis. Refer to Chapter 2 for a review of this research method. Now watch the movie while keeping in mind the concepts you have learned from this chapter, especially with regard to urbanization. Take notes about the settings and environments in the movie. Identify and capture key scenes or dialogue that address the city and city life in the film. In conducting your content analysis, consider some of the following questions.

* At what point in the future does the movie take place?

* What is the major theme of the movie? What is its overall message?

* Does the movie represent a utopian or dystopian vision of the future? Does it represent positive or negative changes to society?

* What sorts of futuristic elements are included in the movie, such as time travel, virtual reality, mind control, wars between humans and machines, apocalyptic destruction?

* How is the modern city or landscape of the future depicted? What are its structural features in both public and private realms?

* Compare the future with the present. How is the future the same or different? How is it better or worse?

* What are people like in the future? How are they affected by their environment? How does their environment affect their lives?

* Could this version of the future realistically occur? Would you like to live in such a future?

There are two options for completing this Data Workshop:

PREP-PAIR-SHARE Conduct your content analysis and develop some preliminary answers to the questions provided. Prepare some written notes that you can refer to during in-class discussions. Pair up with one or more classmates and discuss your findings in small groups. Compare and contrast the analyses of the films observed by participants in your group.

DO-IT-YOURSELF Complete the research activities described and develop some preliminary answers to the questions provided. Then write a three- to four-page essay discussing your answers and reflecting on your observations of the film. What do you think your observations tell us about our society's hopes and fears for the future of cities and city life?

Living in the City

Who lives in cities? What about city life continues to attract droves of people? Big cities offer residents bright lights, a fast pace, excitement, and opportunity. They differ from small rural towns and suburban neighborhoods, so a certain type of person is more likely to be found living there.

Louis Wirth, a member of the Chicago School of sociology, proposed "urbanism as a way of life" that affected the outlook, mentality, and lifestyle of those who lived in the city. He believed that cities provided personal freedom, relaxed moral restraints, relative anonymity, variety, and diversity. At the same time, there is a certain social cost involved. People tend to belong to more formal organizations with more

Cities are places where strangers come together. Before there were cities, there were also no strangers; those who were unknown were driven off, killed, or quickly assimilated into the clan, tribe, or group (Lofland 1973). With the advent of cities came the prospect of living life in close proximity to hundreds, thousands, or even millions of people we will never know and from whom we cannot be completely segregated. City life would seem to bring the prospect for all sorts of chaos and conflict—and yet every day, in contemporary cities, millions of people go about their business in relative harmony, brushing elbows with each other on the sidewalk or subway in encounters that are neither friendly nor unfriendly but merely orderly.

What are the interactional structures that order urban life? Public interactions with strangers can be treacherous, as we encounter people we do not know and whose reactions we cannot predict. For the most part, we are not talking about the danger of physical attack. More common than getting mugged is being "looked at funny," getting "goosed," or being the target of "wolf whistles." These are threats to self more than anything else—being treated as a nonperson, or as a piece of meat. How do we guard against these minor molestations when we walk down the street every day?

CIVIL INATTENTION an unspoken rule governing interactions in public places, whereby individuals briefly notice others before ignoring them

A specific way we deal with strangers in public is by practicing what Erving Goffman (1971) called **civil inattention**. This is a taken-for-granted rule of public place interaction, a basic public courtesy we extend to one another that helps guard against unpleasant interactions with strangers. About eight or ten feet away from each other, we tend to look at and then away from the person we are approaching—all in one sweep of our gaze. We have looked, but not too intently or for too long. This allows us to navigate through urban spaces without bumping into strangers and to avoid the kinds of interactions that might lead to trouble.

The practice of civil inattention is so commonplace that you may not realize you do it every day. Now, walk down the street and notice your own gazework and that of others—with full comprehension of how this simple act helps avoid conflict, enables smooth interactions between strangers, and basically makes city life possible.

What might move us to violate civil inattention—to interact with strangers in ways that might otherwise be forbidden? Anything, Goffman suggests, that makes us more "open." Open persons are those whose identities expose them to the overtures of others. Examples of open persons are police officers (and others in uniform), pregnant women, small children, the disabled, those with unusual physical characteristics such as height or hair color, same-sex couples . . . the list goes on and on. One type of open person you have probably encountered is a person walking a dog. Dogs serve as what Goffman called "bridging devices"—excuses for strangers to begin conversations that the rules of civil inattention would otherwise prevent. Dogs facilitate interactions in public places—indeed, dogs serve as (perhaps unwitting) team members in their masters' performances (Robins, Sanders, and Cahill 1991). They can be referred to by others as a kind of icebreaker as well (Wood et al. 2007). We've all found ourselves exclaiming, "Cute puppy!" or "Wow, that's a big dog" as we pass dogwalkers on the street, and sometimes those utterances develop into longer conversations.

And, of course, there's the classic notion of the dog as "chick magnet" or "dude magnet," helping its owner attract, converse with, and pick up women or men for romantic purposes. So perhaps we should give our pooches more credit for helping connect us with each other and make city life more humane.

Don't Talk to Strangers, Unless They're with a Dog Erving Goffman observed that dogs facilitate interactions among strangers by serving as bridging devices.

SOCIAL ATOMIZATION a social situation that emphasizes individualism over collective or group identities

URBANITES people who live in cities

ALIENATION decreasing importance of social ties and community and the corresponding increase in impersonal associations and instrumental logic

narrow goals and to engage less frequently in intimate interaction with one another. Wirth's (1938) analysis was in line with the belief that cities cause **social atomization**—that they are filled with free-floating individuals rather than members of a community. Another sociologist, Claude Fischer (1976), found that people create a sense of community by dividing the city into little worlds within which they feel familiar and involved. These groups allow for informal and close relationships, giving city dwellers more intimacy and a feeling of belonging.

In 1962, Herbert Gans published a major ethnographic study, *The Urban Villagers*, in which he identified distinct categories of **urbanites**, or people who live in urban areas. The first are called "cosmopolites"—students, intellectuals, artists, entertainers, and other professionals who are drawn to the city because of its cultural benefits and convenience to their lifestyles. The next group are the "singles," unmarried people seeking jobs, entertainment, and partners with whom to settle down. Singles may include cosmopolites as well. When singles do find a marriage partner or mate, they tend to move to the suburbs, often in preparation to start a family.

Another group of city dwellers are the "ethnic villagers," often recent immigrants to the area. They tend to settle near others with whom they share a common racial, ethnic, national, religious, or language background; these are often distant relatives or others with whom they have a connection. This is why many major cities still have Chinatowns, Little Italys, and other ethnic neighborhoods. Once here, immigrants form tightly knit ethnic enclaves that resemble the villages of their home countries. The last group of urban dwellers are the "deprived" and the "trapped." These are the people at the bottom of the social hierarchy—the poor, homeless, disabled, elderly, and mentally ill. Without resources and means of support, they cannot afford to leave the city, even if they could find jobs, services, or housing elsewhere; they are inescapably stuck where they are. This perpetuates a cycle of poverty and despair.

ALIENATION AND ALTRUISM: THE CASE OF NEW YORK CITY As products of the Industrial Revolution, cities are celebrated for providing unprecedented degrees of freedom for individuals. Life in rural agricultural communities was much more restrictive, with family and neighbors placing tight constraints on behavior. However, sociology has been suspicious of cities, seeing this very freedom as a source of **alienation**. Early sociologist Georg Simmel argued that while urban environments "allowed a much greater degree of individual liberty," they did so only "at the expense of treating others in objective and instrumental terms" and relating to others only through a "cold and heartless calculus" (Harvey 1990). In short, except for their chosen subcultures, city dwellers fail to develop community, feel little connection with neighbors, have relationships that are largely shallow and impersonal, and fail to care about each other (Simmel 1950).

The murder of Catherine "Kitty" Genovese in New York City has come to represent all such fears about modern urban life. Late on March 13, 1964, Genovese was returning home from her job as a bar manager when she was attacked by a man named Winston Moseley. He first attacked Genovese after she parked her car outside the Kew Gardens apartment building where she lived. She was stabbed several times before her attacker was frightened off when lights went on in nearby apartments. Badly wounded and bleeding, Genovese was later reported to have shouted, "Oh, my God, he stabbed me! Please help me! Please help me!" (Gansberg 1964). Somehow, she then made her way to the back of the building, apparently trying to get to the staircase that led to her apartment. However, her assailant returned and stabbed and beat her to death, before sexually assaulting her. The entire attack, although intermittent, was reported to have lasted nearly thirty minutes.

As horrible as this was, it wouldn't be remembered today if it were just a tragic murder. What has made this case memorable was the number of bystanders who must have heard the crime taking place but failed to take action. According to National Public Radio, some forty years after the crime took place:

> The police later established that thirty-eight people either saw Kitty Genovese stabbed and raped or heard her scream for her life, but no one called the police; no one rushed down to the street to try to scare off her attacker. Her death was a small story in the next day's newspapers, but two weeks later, the *New York Times* ran a story on how shocked the Queens police had been that so many people heard Kitty Genovese being murdered and didn't lift a finger to help her. The story set off a national soul-searching. How could so many Americans, even New Yorkers, it was sometimes added, have turned away from cries for help? The murder of Kitty Genovese became a kind of modern morality tale. Her death seemed to symbolize an age in which people counseled, "Don't get involved" and "Mind your own business" (Simon 2004).

A. M. Rosenthal, who was the editor of the *New York Times* in 1964, later wrote a book about the incident, which focused attention on the most disturbing aspect of the case: why didn't somebody help her? For many, this seemed to be the ultimate indictment of big cities in general, and New York City in particular, and much of the press coverage seemed to demonize the individuals involved. This original account of events has since been debunked in numerous articles and books (Cook 2015). It turns out that a man living nearby heard Genovese's screams and shouted at her attacker, scaring

Kitty Genovese The original account of the twenty-eight-year-old's murder outside her Queens apartment building claimed that there were thirty-eight witnesses—none of whom intervened.

him off temporarily. Another two people called the police while a fellow woman living in the building actually rushed down to help. Although we now know that some neighbors tried to intervene, it was not enough to change the outcome.

In the aftermath of the Genovese murder, John Darley and Bibb Latané (1968), who conducted several experiments on **altruism** and helping behaviors. These experiments were designed to test what came to be called the **bystander effect**, or the **diffusion of responsibility**. In one experiment, different-sized groups of test subjects heard what sounded like a woman having an accident in the next room. Darley and Latané found that the higher the number of bystanders present, the lower the chances that any of them would attempt to help. Basically, they theorized that the responsibility "diffused" throughout the crowd so that no one person felt responsible enough to do anything, most assuming that someone else would help. However, when groups were small, the chances that someone would do something increased greatly.

In a similar experiment, they placed different-sized groups of subjects in a room, under the pretense of taking a test, and gradually filled the room with smoke. Again, they found that the greater the number of subjects in a room, the lower the chances that anyone would mention the smoke. Here, along with the diffusion of responsibility, they argued that **pluralistic ignorance** was at work. When large groups of people encounter an ambiguous or unusual situation, they tend to look to each other for help in defining the situation. If no member of the group decides that it is an emergency, and therefore worthy of reacting, it is likely that all members will continue to ignore the situation.

On the twentieth anniversary of the Genovese murder, Fordham University held the "Catherine Genovese Memorial Conference on Bad Samaritanism," which attempted to shed some light on what sorts of situations would produce bystanders who would help. Although no single character trait correlated with being a Good Samaritan, researchers largely confirmed earlier findings—that bystanders in groups were tentative about helping, especially when they were unsure of the nature of the problem.

These conclusions can also help explain a time when New Yorkers did come to each other's aid out of a sense of belonging and **community**: in the wake of the September 11, 2001, attacks on the World Trade Center. In the hours and days after the attacks, Americans rushed to help however they could. "Tens of thousands of patriotic Americans rolled up their sleeves and gave blood," monetary donations poured in, and ordinary New Yorkers rushed to pitch in (Stapleton 2002). Some of the most heroic rescue efforts at the World Trade Center were made by ordinary people who rushed to help as soon as they heard. Two Port Authority police officers, Will Jimeno and John McLoughlin, were the last people to be found alive in the collapsed remains of the World Trade Center towers. They were discovered by Charles Sereika, a former paramedic, and David Karnes, an accountant from Connecticut who "had changed into his Marine camouflage outfit" and driven down to Manhattan as soon as he heard the news (Dwyer 2001). The movie *World Trade Center* (2006) by Oliver Stone depicts their story. And even if things have somewhat returned to normal (meaning people are less friendly now), almost everyone agrees that New Yorkers "were wonderful during the crisis, and we were tender to each other. . . . Volunteers streamed to the site" and "after only a few days there were so many, they were turned away by the hundreds. . . . Strangers spoke to each other in the street, in stores, and on the subway" (Hustvedt 2002).

So what made the difference in the two events? Many of those who heard Kitty Genovese being murdered believed that it was a bar fight or a lover's quarrel. Not knowing what was happening, they were unsure how to respond. With September 11, there was no ambiguity and many people understood where to go and how to help. In 1964, the "911" emergency system didn't exist, and many people were reluctant to get personally involved with the police. This largely supports the conclusions of sociologists like Lee Clarke (2001), who has studied how people respond to various kinds of disasters. His work shows

ALTRUISM unselfish concern for the well-being of others and helping behaviors performed without self-interested motivation

BYSTANDER EFFECT or **DIFFUSION OF RESPONSIBILITY** the social dynamic wherein the more people who are present in a moment of crisis, the less likely any one of them is to take action

PLURALISTIC IGNORANCE a process in which members of a group individually conclude that there is no need to take action because they see that other group members have not done so

COMMUNITY a group of people living in the same local area who share a sense of participation, belonging, and fellowship

that altruism, rather than panic, tends to prevail in disasters. Clarke posits that the rules for behavior in extreme situations are essentially the same as the rules of ordinary life—that when faced with danger, people help those next to them before helping themselves. This was the case in the destruction of the World Trade Center. People survived the disaster because they did not become hysterical but instead helped to facilitate a successful evacuation of the buildings (Clarke 2001).

There are many obvious reasons why the September 11 attacks would bring people together in ways that the attack on Kitty Genovese did not. September 11 was clearly and obviously a disaster; it was also an attack on the entire country, so loyalties were further cemented. Formal institutions were set up so people could easily volunteer and receive positive social sanctions in return. Kitty Genovese was just one young woman living in a building full of immigrants and elderly pensioners. However, whenever bystanders do jump in to help, it is in part because of the outrage her murder provoked. In the aftermath of the Kitty Genovese murder, the "911" emergency system was created, neighborhood watch groups were formed, Good Samaritan laws were passed to protect bystanders from liability in emergencies, and people started to get more involved. So, while alienation is part of life in cities, so is altruism. Both are part of our shared social worlds.

ENVIRONMENT in sociology, the natural world, the human-made environment, and the interaction between the two

BIOSPHERE the parts of the earth that can support life

The Environment

The final section of this chapter once again considers the connection between the social and the natural worlds. Human populations have grown tremendously, as have the cities in which most of them live. Now how do those people interact with the natural environment and what impact does the environment have on how they live? Whether we go camping, surfing, or just take a walk through Central Park, we all go to nature to escape, to recreate, to relax. It is ironic that we now seek out nature as a retreat from the demands of society, because society itself originated and evolved at least in part to protect us against the demands of nature.

The cooperation and interdependence that characterize most social groups allow individuals to withstand the risks of the natural environment. The products of culture—clothing, architecture, automobiles, and many others—contribute to our ability to live in what would otherwise be inhospitable surroundings. Without her insulated house and its furnace, her layers of clothing topped with a Gore-Tex parka, and her car with a remote starter and all-weather tires, Dr. Ferris would have a hard time surviving the harsh winters in northern Illinois. And all these survival tools are supplied because she is part of a society whose other members have created what she needs to be safe and warm in the elements. Society provides all of us with a buffer against nature; without it, we wouldn't last very long in the ocean, the snowdrifts, or the desert.

The environment is a somewhat recent area of interest among sociologists, coinciding with the general public's concern about environmental issues (Guber 2003). When sociologists use the term **environment**, it encompasses aspects of both the natural and the human-made environment and includes everything from the most micro level of organisms to the entire **biosphere**. Sociologists study the ways that societies are dependent on the natural world; how cultural values and beliefs shape views about and influence usage of the environment; the politics and economics of natural resources; and the social construction of conflicts, problems, and solutions that are a result of our relationship to the natural world.

The Social World and the Natural World Society affects nature even in the remotest places—including on the highest mountaintops and in outer space! Hikers leave garbage on Mount McKinley, and NASA illustrates the objects orbiting earth.

First, we will look at environmental problems as social problems. This discussion encompasses two big areas: problems of consumption and problems of waste. Sociologists, however, must look beyond descriptions of problems and attempt to apply analytic frameworks for understanding the social complexities underlying them.

Environmental Problems

Many students first become acquainted with the subject of the environment through the lens of social problems. Learning the "three Rs" in schools has now come to mean reduce, reuse, recycle. We need to help "save" the environment because it is under threat from consumption and waste.

PROBLEMS OF CONSUMPTION: RESOURCE DEPLE-TION The planet earth provides an abundance of natural resources, including air, water, land, wildlife, plants, and minerals. We have learned to exploit these resources not only for basic survival but also to build everything in material culture that is part of the modern world. Humans have long been presented with the challenge of managing their use of natural resources, but those challenges have changed in the postindustrial era.

Renewable resources are natural resources that can be regenerated; for instance, oxygen is replenished by plants and trees, water by evaporation and rain clouds, trees and plants by pollens and seeds, and animals by mating and reproduction. The wind blows and the sun shines in ample abundance. **Nonrenewable resources** are those that cannot be replaced (except through tens of thousands of years of geological processes); they include fossil fuels such as oil and minerals such as coal, copper, and iron. All natural resources are susceptible to overuse or overconsumption and eventually to depletion or even exhaustion. As a result of rising demands, we have already seen rising costs or outright shortages for such commodities as seafood, timber, and gasoline.

It may be hard to imagine that we'll ever run out of things like air and water, but even these are threatened. We may not be aware of the connection between the things we consume in our everyday life and their sources. We're removed from the fields and the mines, the oceans, and the mountains that are the origin of our goods. But we are already confronting real problems of resource depletion, and the course of such depletion may now be irreversible.

One of the world's most pressing problems is how to meet enormous and growing demands for energy. We need energy—gas, electric, or nuclear—to help power everything from cars and televisions to factories and airplanes. But these forms of energy are not inexhaustible. We have relied primarily on nonrenewable sources, such as coal and fossil fuels, to meet our needs. The current mix of fuel sources comes from 35 percent petroleum, 28 percent natural gas, 18 percent coal, 8.5 percent nuclear, and only about 10 percent renewable energy sources (U.S. Energy Information Administration 2015). Renewable sources such as wind and solar power are being developed, but they are not sufficient yet to provide the substantial quantities of energy we will need in the future.

Industrialized nations are the largest consumers of energy, using approximately 70 percent of the total energy produced in the world; of those nations, the United States uses over 18 percent, Russia uses more than 6 percent, and Germany less than 3 percent (U.S. Energy Information Administration 2013a). Developing nations that now use the remaining 30 percent are becoming more industrialized, and consequently their energy needs will also increase, thus closing the energy usage gap among nations during the next twenty-five years. In that same time, total worldwide energy consumption is projected to grow approximately 56 percent (U.S. Energy Information Administration 2013b). Oil is a finite resource, and at some point the supply will be exhausted. For many decades the United States has relied heavily on foreign oil imports. More recently there has been high demand for more domestic oil exploration and production. Hydraulic fracturing, or "fracking," involves drilling thousands of feet underground to extract natural gas stores from shale. Fracking has released vast new quantities of oil and natural gas in the United States, accounting for about half of domestic production (Prince and Tovar 2015). The practice is not without dangers and controversy. Our increasing demands for energy are likely to spur development of substitutes for oil.

Another critical area of consumption is the rain forests in South America, Central America, Australia, Africa, and Southeast Asia. Rain forests are ecosystems located in tropical and temperate regions that are home to diverse plant and animal life (as well as indigenous peoples). Although rain forests cover only about 6 percent of the earth's landmass,

RENEWABLE RESOURCES resources that replenish at a rate comparable to the rate at which they are consumed

NONRENEWABLE RESOURCES finite resources that can become exhausted; includes those that take so long to replenish as to be effectively finite

they contain close to 50 percent of all microorganisms and plant and animal species in the world (Mittermeier, Myers, and Mittermeier 2000). Previously unknown life forms are being discovered there every year, while thousands are being driven to extinction. Products derived from the rain forest include not only foods and woods but also pharmaceuticals: more than 7,000 medical compounds are derived from native plants. Rain forests also play a key role in global climate control, evaporation and rainfall, and clearing the air of carbon dioxide (Myers and Kent 2005).

In 1950, rain forests covered twice as much area as they do today, and they are disappearing at an alarming rate. Currently, there are approximately 3.5 billion acres of rain forest worldwide, down from more than 7 billion. More than 78 million acres of rain forest are lost every year—215,000 acres every day, or about 150 acres every minute! Destruction of the rain forests is of sociological import because it results

Threats to Biodiversity and the Climate Rain forests, which play a key role in regulating the global climate and are home to almost 50 percent of the world's plant and animal species, are being destroyed at a rate of millions of acres each year.

from collective human behavior. The immediate cause of this destruction is to accommodate the logging, mining, and ranching industries. Although these industries may benefit the peoples of those regions, they are primarily providing for the consumption demands of the more developed nations of the world (Myers and Kent 2004).

In addition to rain forests, worldwide **biodiversity** is in dangerous decline. According to the United Nations, humans pose a distinct threat to thousands of other species on the planet (UN Millennium Ecosystem Assessment 2005). The UN asserts that the natural rate of extinction has multiplied by as much as a thousand times within the past century. Perhaps hardest hit has been marine life, with a 90 percent decrease in the amount of fish in the world's fisheries. In addition, more than 22,000 species are threatened with extinction, including roughly 13 percent of birds, 25 percent of mammals, 41 percent of amphibians, and 34 percent of conifers (International Union for Conservation of Nature 2014). These mass die-offs are being driven by human activities, including the destruction of habitats, pollution, the introduction of nonnative species, and overuse. "We will need to make sure that we don't disrupt the biological web to the point where collapse of the whole system becomes irreversible," says researcher Anantha Duraiappah (Couvrette 2005).

BIODIVERSITY the variety of species of plants and animals existing at any given time

POLLUTION any environmental contaminant that harms living beings

ENVIRONMENTAL PROTECTION AGENCY (EPA) a U.S. government agency established in 1969 to protect public health and the environment through policies and enforcement

PROBLEMS OF WASTE: POLLUTION Problems of consumption are linked to problems of waste, often two sides of the same coin. Consider water and air. Water is another natural resource that can be overused; we understand what happens during a drought, or when lakes, rivers, or underground aquifers are drained and then go dry. But water can also be damaged by what we put into it. And while we don't normally think of consuming air, it is an essential natural resource, and we can damage its quality and change for the worse the very atmosphere of the planet. Let's look at these examples of **pollution**.

Water is indispensable for life. About 71 percent of the earth's surface is covered with water (U.S. Geological Survey 2014). Almost 97 percent of it is in oceans of saltwater, home to a vast array of sea creatures and plants. Only 1 percent of the total is freshwater, found in lakes, rivers, and underground aquifers; the other 2 percent is in polar ice caps and glaciers. This is a small percentage to meet human needs—from drinking water to water for agricultural and ranching purposes. The world's water supply, both in oceans and freshwater, has been under increased threat from pollution by industrial development and population growth—mostly by allowing contaminants to enter the oceans, lakes, and rivers or to seep into underground water supplies. The sources of this pollution are many: factories dumping chemical and solid wastes; agricultural run-off of manure, pesticides, and fertilizers; human sewage and urban run-off; and toxic chemicals falling from the skies in rain.

Access to freshwater is not equal throughout the world. Most Americans can take ample and safe drinking water for granted. Although the **Environmental Protection Agency (EPA)** claims that the United States has one of the safest supplies of drinking water, even here more than 10 percent of water systems in the nation don't meet EPA standards (Environmental Protection Agency 2008). In developing nations, infected water is a significant cause of disease and death. There is a definite link between water scarcity and poverty; in some African countries, around 38 percent of the population are without access to adequate water (UN-Water 2013).

The atmosphere is made up of thin layers of gases surrounding the planet and making life possible. It interacts with the land, oceans, and sun to produce the earth's climate and weather. The air that we breathe is ubiquitous, so we might

As the worldwide population continues to grow, water accessibility has become a central issue with a global context. With global population projected to grow approximately 2 to 3 billion people over the next forty years, the worldwide demand for food is consequently expected to skyrocket by 70 percent. While water is considered a "renewable resource," massive population growth matched with an ever-increasing demand for food has threatened the global water supply. Agriculture and food production make up the largest sources of freshwater consumption, with anywhere from 70 to 90 percent of global freshwater being used directly for food consumption (UN-Water 2013). With accessibility expected to decrease in many areas of the world, water has become a new battleground as many regions continue to struggle to secure clean water and maintain control of local water supplies.

At the forefront of the global water crisis are the nations of Africa, whose water supplies have been contentiously sought after by international corporations and wealthy investors alike (Bienkowski 2013). Unlike the national borders that divide countries, water is frequently a "transboundary" resource in that rivers can cross political boundaries (United Nations 2014b). Wealthy countries often exploit natural resources, such as water, from lesser-developed countries—often to the detriment of the local population. With around one-third of the world's transboundary water basins, Africa has become a hotspot for land grabs, or water grabs, by wealthy countries seeking more affordable access to supplies of water (GRAIN 2012). Despite the fact that Africa is one of the driest regions in the world, with more than 300 million people living in a water-scarce environment, wealthier countries also facing water scarcity—such as Saudi Arabia—have created incentives for corporations to capitalize on the continent's water supply and divest from using domestic water supplies (UN-Water 2013).

While Saudi Arabia has been able to save millions of gallons of water each year and avoid depleting its own natural water sources by tapping into Africa's water supply, Africa continues to face water scarcity alongside poverty and hunger. The Alwera River in Ethiopa provides water to thousands of people within the surrounding area and has recently become a site of water grabbing. Billionaire Mohammed al-Amoudi is one of the many wealthy Saudi investors who have established plantations in Africa with the intention to divest from nearby water sources (GRAIN 2012). Saudi companies have purchased millions of hectares of land in Africa to obtain access to water, including efforts to acquire the headwaters of the Nile River despite growing African unrest (Pierce 2012).

Take the case of Bolivia. In 2000, Bolivia's municipal water system was sold to a transnational consortium in exchange for debt relief, prompting the infamous Cochabamba Water War. Farmers, factory workers, students, and middle-class professionals all came together in opposition to water privatization, organizing strikes, road blockages, and protests and eventually forcing the return of the country's water supply to popular control. Despite this happy ending, Bolivia still struggles to control and monitor the activities of the country's 28,000 local water and sanitation providers, many of which are plagued by deteriorated systems and community conflicts (Achtenberg 2013).

Ultimately, the struggles for water across Africa, in Bolivia, and throughout the world signal larger issues around accessibility, rights, and control of natural and vital resources. In 2010, the United Nations created a resolution that officially recognized access to clean water as a human right; however, little has been resolved to combat water grabbing and privatization efforts within vulnerable developing countries (United Nations 2014a). While people in developing countries struggle to maintain control of their valuable water resources, threats of privatization and water grabbing have only escalated as the global population and demand for food production continue to increase.

Water Scarcity The UN estimates that 1.8 billion people will be living in areas with absolute water scarcity by 2050.

GREENHOUSE GASES any gases in the earth's atmosphere that allow sunlight to pass through but trap heat, thus affecting temperature

GREENHOUSE EFFECT the process in which increased production of greenhouse gases, especially those arising from human activity (e.g., carbon dioxide, nitrous oxide, and methane) cause changes to the earth's atmosphere

GLOBAL WARMING gradual increase in the earth's temperature, driven recently by an increase in greenhouse gases and other human activity

GLOBAL (or **SOLAR**) **DIMMING** a decline in the amount of light reaching the earth's surface because of increased air pollution, which reflects more light back into space

not even think of it as a natural resource. But the earth's atmosphere and its ability to sustain life are at risk from pollution. Not all threats come from humans; for instance, volcanoes or forest fires started by lightning can emit massive clouds of smoke, ash, and debris into the atmosphere. Human activity, however, accounts for a tremendous amount of air pollution, especially emissions from factories, power plants, and automobiles. The most common pollutants (carbon monoxide, lead, nitrogen dioxide, ozone, sulfur dioxide, and particulates such as soot, smoke, and dust) together are often referred to as **greenhouse gases**. These not only create ugly smog and haze but also are hazardous to the health of humans and other species.

The U.S. Congress passed the first Clean Air Act in 1963, which has been followed over the decades by numerous amendments and other legislation to help regulate industries involved in emissions. Regulations and technological advancements have helped reduce air pollution in the United States. Still, we have one of the highest per capita rates of any nation, emitting some 17.6 metric tons of greenhouse gases per person (World Bank 2015). It is estimated that more than 142 million people, or about 40 percent of the U.S. population, live in areas

reporting higher levels of ozone than are safe by national standards (NASA 2014). Pollution problems may be even greater in developing nations that are rapidly becoming industrialized.

Greenhouse gases are also contributing to a change in the makeup of the earth's atmosphere. Scientists call this the **greenhouse effect**. The earth's climate is regulated through a process in which some of the sun's heat and energy is retained within the atmosphere. Naturally occurring gases (such as water vapor or carbon dioxide) help trap some of the earth's outgoing heat, which in turn maintains a stable, livable climate. An increase in greenhouse gases from air pollution results in greater retention of heat within the earth's atmosphere, leading to **global warming**, an increase in the world's average temperature.

Scientists believe that in the past fifty to one hundred years, the average temperature of the earth has risen 1.4 degrees Fahrenheit. They predict that greenhouse gases will continue to increase the earth's temperature another 2 to 12 degrees by 2100 (Environmental Protection Agency 2014). A climate change of a few degrees can cause catastrophic consequences for the world and its inhabitants. Even slightly higher temperatures could melt polar ice caps and increase the sea level, shrink the landmasses of islands and continents, change global weather patterns, and alter ecosystems that support life on earth.

In addition to the greenhouse effect, pollutants in the air have caused **global dimming** (or **solar dimming**). This recently discovered phenomenon means that the earth is becoming darker than it used to be. Because of all the particles in the atmosphere, some natural and some from human activity, less light from the sun's rays reaches earth. Climate researchers estimate that the earth's surface is receiving 15 percent less sunlight than it did just fifty years ago

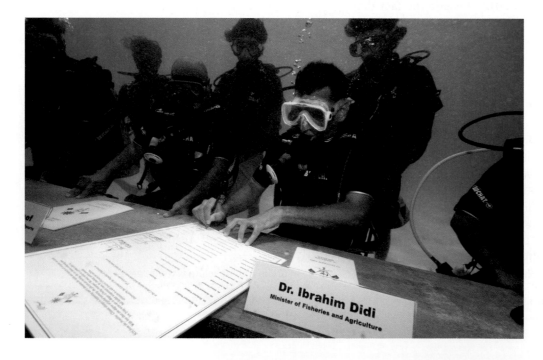

Climate Change Maldivian Minister of Fisheries and Agriculture Ibrahim Didi calls attention to the threat of global warming to low-lying countries by holding an underwater meeting to sign a document calling on all nations to cut down their carbon dioxide emissions.

(Boyd 2004). The sun has remained as bright as always, but the amount of energy or solar radiation that hits the earth has been decreasing by about 3 percent per decade. In some respects, global dimming is counteracting global warming, but that only means that global warming would be worse were it not for the pollutants that are blocking the sun.

Another pollution problem is garbage. U.S. waste production is twice that of any other nation. The average American generates about 4.4 pounds of trash per day—about 1,600 pounds per year (Environmental Protection Agency 2012). The country dumps about 251 million tons of garbage a year, and about 34.7 percent of it is recycled, leaving the rest for landfills and incinerators (Environmental Protection Agency 2012). Some of our trash even gets blasted into outer space (such as satellites and other objects that have become obsolete), where nearly 30,000 pieces of litter are orbiting the planet (BBC News 2013)! And have you ever thought about light pollution or noise pollution? Depending on your sensitivity to these, you may be dismayed not to see stars in the night sky because of so many street lights and neon signs, or be annoyed by the almost constant sound of traffic and other noise, both of which are part of life in big cities.

Environmental Sociology

To analyze problems of the environment, sociologists have developed **environmental sociology**, a distinct subfield of sociology that tackles environmental issues and examines the reciprocal interactions between the physical environment, social structure, and human behavior. Although this subfield is still developing, four major analytic frameworks within environmental sociology have emerged. These concern the political economy of the environment, attitudes about the environment, environmental movements (including environmental justice), and sustainable development.

THE POLITICAL ECONOMY OF THE ENVIRONMENT

The political economy of the environment is a core area of study within environmental sociology that takes a classical neo-Marxist and Weberian approach to understanding the environment (Schnaiberg 1975). Its focus is on how economic factors influence the way organizations (typically corporations) use the environment and how this use is often supported by political systems and policies.

Contemporary industrial societies have been built on the premise of progress—on conquering nature and using natural resources to fuel production and increase profits (Schnaiberg and Gould 1994). Government policies and economic systems have frequently supported this belief. While progress has usually meant great wealth for some and goods and services for many, it has come at a price: environmental degradation and the accompanying social problems.

Environmental sociologists refer to this process as the **treadmill of production** (Schnaiberg 1980). They assert that the drive for economic growth in capitalist societies persists, even at the expense of the environment and despite opposition from activists and other groups, because corporate expansion provides critical taxable wealth and the jobs essential to the economic life of a society. Although such development creates a multitude of problems, there are also serious consequences for attempts at regulating or limiting the production practices of these corporations (Schnaiberg 1975). Large corporations can typically defend themselves against calls for accountability for damages and exercise considerable influence through political lobbying and campaign contributions as well as appeals to change public opinion. Attacking the practices of these corporations can also be detrimental to the workers who need their jobs and to governments that depend on these industries for products critical to the nation's well-being and security (Schnaiberg and Gould 1994). Even though the treadmill of production is not an environmentally friendly process, numerous societies are invested in its continued existence, and we will likely see enduring conflict between the economy and the environment at the international, national, regional, and local levels.

ENVIRONMENTAL ATTITUDES Understanding societal attitudes about the environment is an essential part of environmental sociology. Early work in this area began with a group of Chicago School sociologists, including Robert Park (1961) and Amos Hawley (1950), who helped establish the field of human ecology. Extending on this in the 1970s, William Catton and Riley Dunlap (1978, 1980) developed the **new ecological paradigm**.

Historically, Westerners have had a particularly **anthropocentric**, or human-centered, relationship with the environment, perceiving nature as something to master. Nature is believed to be inexhaustible and hence can be used with impunity to serve humankind. Consumption is equated with success. This is consistent with the Judeo-Christian belief in man's dominion over the earth. Western culture thus perpetuates **human exceptionalism**, an attitude that humans are exempt from natural ecological limits (Dunlap and Catton 1994). Much of our progress through

ENVIRONMENTAL SOCIOLOGY the study of the interaction between society and the natural environment, including the social causes and consequences of environmental problems

TREADMILL OF PRODUCTION term describing the operation of modern economic systems that require constant growth, which causes increased exploitation of resources and environmental degradation

NEW ECOLOGICAL PARADIGM a way of understanding human life as just one part of an ecosystem that includes many species' interactions with the environment; suggests that there should be ecological limits on human activity

ANTHROPOCENTRIC literally "human centered"; the idea that needs and desires of human beings should take priority over concerns about other species or the natural environment

HUMAN EXCEPTIONALISM the attitude that humans are exempt from natural ecological limits

industrialization supports this notion that technology will allow us to overcome any environmental challenge. In contrast, the new ecological paradigm treats humans as part of the ecosystem or biosphere, one of many species that interact with the natural environment. Nature has limits that we must respect, and this may constrain economic development. The new ecological paradigm recognizes that human activity can have both intended and unintended consequences that shape social life and life on the planet.

Scientists as well as environmental advocates and policy makers are in disagreement about the future consequences of global climate change. Some argue that global warming is part of the natural progression of the earth. Others say it has been brought about primarily by human activity and that we are headed toward catastrophe. Still others argue that though global warming exists, it is not a cause for concern. How such problems as global warming are defined and understood depends on underlying values and beliefs. You might not consider global climate change so bad if you also thought that extinction of some plant and animal life was an acceptable part of the evolutionary process of natural selection. Or you might not be so concerned by such issues if you thought that clean air, fossil fuels, or other natural resources were commodities in a free market and that nations must compete for their availability and take responsibility for their consequences. Our definitions and interpretations of evidence regarding environmental problems are also filtered through our own cultural beliefs and values.

Research on environmental attitudes has had a marked influence on studies of environmental movements (Dunlap and Catton 1979; Buttel 1987). Environmental sociologists are interested in the processes that create attitude change and the relationship between attitudes and behavior. They want to understand why certain groups have become more "biocentric" (as opposed to anthropocentric), or more environmentally sensitive, and what inspires great numbers of people to participate in environmental movements.

DATA WORKSHOP
Analyzing Everyday Life

Student Attitudes on Environmentalism

"Sustainability," "environmentalism," and "being green" are all terms that refer to reducing human impact on the environment. Even though environmentally based social movements have become so mainstream that there is now an entire television channel, Planet Green, devoted to the topic, there are those who believe that environmentalists are alarmists who have invented issues like global warming, resource depletion, and growing landfills.

This Data Workshop asks you to examine the attitudes of your fellow college students in order to determine the extent of their environmental beliefs and behaviors. Do they believe that climate change has human causes? Do they recycle or conserve various resources, and, if so, how? Do they worry about things like their "carbon footprint"?

For this Data Workshop you will be creating a survey about environmental attitudes and actions, administering it to your fellow students, and analyzing the findings. Refer to Chapter 2 for a review of this research method. Because this is a preliminary or pilot study, your sample population will be small, between five and ten respondents. Make sure to collect some demographic data such as age, gender, class, race/ethnicity, GPA, and major so that you can determine whether there is any relationship between backgrounds and attitudes.

In constructing the survey, consider using a Likert scale (agree-disagree format) to collect data on attitudes, as doing so will help streamline your analysis. Survey respondents can select the degree to which they agree or disagree with statements. Use the following statements as a starting place:

* Eating facilities on campus should use environmentally friendly products.

* I use environmentally friendly products at home as much as I can.

* I feel motivated to recycle.

* I use the recycling bins on campus.

* There are enough recycling bins on campus.

* If I see a piece of trash on the ground when I am outside, I will pick it up and dispose of it properly.

* Global warming is a threat to our planet.

* Humans and industry have contributed to global warming.

* I make attempts to reduce my carbon footprint by driving less and conserving energy in my daily life.

* Sustainability is an important issue for the entire world.

* If we don't reduce, reuse, and recycle, our world will face serious consequences.

* Environmentalism is a worthwhile cause.

PREP-PAIR-SHARE Once you have administered the survey, analyze your findings. What kinds of patterns can you identify? Are college students concerned about the environment? Does this concern translate into action? How do your findings confirm or refute any hypotheses that you might have had before beginning this study? What do you think your data reveal overall? Note the similarities and differences in your findings and those of your group members. See if you can come up with a statement that identifies and incorporates the general patterns found in the data gathered by the entire group.

DO-IT-YOURSELF Compose and administer a survey to your sample population. Write a three- to four-page essay describing your research project and analyzing your findings. Attach your completed surveys and any notes to your paper.

THE ENVIRONMENTAL MOVEMENT People have long been concerned about the relationship between humans and nature and about the impact of society on the environment. When people organize around these concerns, their collective efforts can have profound effects. When sociologists study the **environmental movement**, topics of interest include the origins of the groups involved, their internal organization and social network formation, their political role, and their presence at local, regional, national, and international levels. In this section, we will trace the four major eras in the history of the environmental movement in the United States while discussing major flashpoints in its development.

Most social scientists and historians date the beginning of the American environmental movement to the writings of Henry David Thoreau in the mid-1800s, especially *Walden; or, Life in the Woods*, which concerns the rejection of urban materialism and the virtues of simple living (1854/1993). Thoreau has inspired many generations, and his central argument, about how humans affect the natural environment and thus must actively choose to preserve it, continues to be the backbone of environmental activism in the United States. While preservation or conservation remains a key focus, the environmental movement has become increasingly interested in how to respond to or prevent ecological disasters.

The late nineteenth and early twentieth centuries are often referred to as the **conservation era**; environmentalism in that time tended to reflect Thoreau's preservation argument. In this time, state and national parks, such as Yosemite (1864), Yellowstone (1872), and the Grand Canyon (1906), were established through legislative protection and funding. Congress approved the creation of the National Park Service in 1916 and continued to pass environmental laws to protect the wilderness and to regulate industries that impinged on it, such as mining and logging. Early environmental groups such as the Audubon Society (1886) and the Sierra Club (1892) that emphasized the conservation of wildlife and nature were also established around that time and are still in existence today.

From the mid-twentieth century on, environmentalism changed in response to several ecological disasters. For example, in 1948, in the town of Donora, Pennsylvania, twenty people died and more than 7,000 others were hospitalized when industrial waste that formed concentrated smog was released into the atmosphere and settled over the town, severely compromising the air quality for its residents. Congress responded to that ecological disaster (albeit late) by passing some of the first environmental legislation of the modern era, the Air Pollution Control Act of 1955.

The second era, the **modern environmental movement**, began in the 1960s in part as a response to Rachel Carson's landmark book *Silent Spring* (1962). Her book was an impassioned critique of the effects of pesticide use, specifically dichloro-diphenyl-trichloroethane, commonly known as DDT. The 1950s had witnessed an explosion of development in new chemicals such as fertilizers and pesticides, often hailed as revolutionary and miraculous in the practice of agriculture. But these same chemicals harmed or killed beneficial organisms and wildlife such as songbirds (hence the title of the book). There was even speculation that they could work their way up the food chain, becoming carcinogens in

ENVIRONMENTAL MOVEMENT a social movement organized around concerns about the relationship between humans and the environment

CONSERVATION ERA earliest stage of the environmental movement, which focused on the preservation of "wilderness" areas

MODERN ENVIRONMENTAL MOVEMENT beginning in the 1960s, the second major stage of the environmental movement; focused on the environmental consequences of new technologies, oil exploration, chemical production, and nuclear power plants

John Muir An early conservationist, Muir led the movement to establish national parks such as Yosemite.

**MAINSTREAM
ENVIRONMENTALISM**
beginning in the 1970s, the
third stage of the environmental
movement; characterized by
enhanced organization, improved
promotional campaigns and
political tactics, and an increased
reliance on economic and
scientific expertise

EARTH DAY an annual event
conceived of by environmental
activist and former senator
Gaylord Nelson to encourage
support for and increase
awareness of environmental
concerns; first celebrated on
March 22, 1970

humans. Although the companies manufacturing DDT and other chemicals vigorously fought such allegations, public outcry eventually led to government hearings and an EPA ban on DDT in the United States and other countries (Bailey 2002).

While there has been considerable debate about the validity of the science behind the DDT scare, it drew unprecedented public attention to environmental issues that had never been addressed before. As former vice president Al Gore explained in the introduction to the 1994 edition of the book, *Silent Spring* "brought environmental issues to the attention not just of industry and government; it brought them to the public, and put our democracy itself on the side of saving the Earth" (Carson 1994). As awareness about environmental issues grew, so did the amount of environmental legislation. As a result, environmentalism was able to find credibility in American society, and its practice has become an enduring force in public policy.

Unfortunately, many other ecological disasters occurred in the decades that followed. Some of the most notable were an oil spill in Santa Barbara in 1969 (Molotch 1970); the discovery of toxic waste in the Love Canal in 1978; the nuclear accident at Three Mile Island in 1979; the *Exxon Valdez* oil spill off the coast of Alaska in 1989; the discovery of a thirty-year oil spill at the Guadalupe Dunes in California in 1994 (Beamish 2002); and an even larger oil spill in the Gulf of Mexico in 2010. Each of these events elicited public outrage. Through a series of amendments and executive orders, the EPA was given broader powers that included the means to investigate ecological crises, organize cleanups, punish offenders, establish further regulations, and research environmentally friendly technologies.

The third era of the environmental movement, referred to as **mainstream environmentalism**, began in the 1970s. It emerged, in part, as a response to the Reagan administration's anti-environmental deregulation policies. National and international environmental organizations, such as the Sierra Club and Greenpeace as well as other watchdog groups, were becoming increasingly institutionalized. They began using well-crafted promotional campaigns and sophisticated political tactics to gain the attention of legislators and secure victories in their ongoing battles. Mainstream environmentalism evolved into a cluster of public interest groups, many of which had their own political action committees, or PACs, to lobby for positive legislative change. In addition to legal expertise, they developed economic and scientific expertise to support research, generate grants, and acquire land for preservation.

A link between the modern era and the mainstream era of environmentalism is **Earth Day**. The original event was conceived of by environmental activist and then-senator Gaylord Nelson as both a "teach-in" and a protest gathering to express concerns about environmental issues. On the first Earth Day—celebrated March 22, 1970—20 million people participated. Earth Day is still celebrated nationally and internationally. Typically, it includes a variety of

Nuclear Disaster Evacuees from Fukushima, Japan, receive radiation scans. This nuclear plant suffered severe damage from an earthquake-generated tsunami in 2011.

groups—environmentally friendly businesses, nonprofit organizations, local government agencies, and others—teaching people about ways to help the environment while celebrating their relationship to it.

A fourth era of the environmental movement, representing grassroots efforts, emerged in the 1980s amid criticism that although mainstream environmental organizations were serving important functions in the overall effort, they were too accommodating to industry and government (Gottlieb 1997). **Grassroots environmentalism** is distinguished from mainstream environmentalism by its belief in citizen participation in environmental decision making. Its focus is often regional or local, and it can include both urban and rural areas. Grassroots groups are often less formally organized than their mainstream counterparts, which, in some instances, frees members from ineffective bureaucratic structures as they fight for issues of great importance to them. Grassroots environmentalism draws on a variety of ideologies, including feminist, native, and spiritual ecologies, and cuts across ethnic, racial, and class lines.

NIMBY, which stands for "not in my back yard," was originally a derogatory term applied to those who complained about any kind of undesirable activity in their neighborhoods that would threaten their own health or local environment but were not concerned if it happened to people somewhere else. Now the term "NIMBY" has been appropriated by the environmental movement for the people "somewhere else" who are fighting against environmental degradation on their home turf, often without significant resources, to protect their families and surrounding communities. Sometimes it makes sense to wage battles at the local level where the problems are readily apparent and the approaches to solving them more tangible. And, of course, if people everywhere were willing to fight in this way, then anti-environmental corporations would have to change their practices or be forced out of all possible locations.

Another expression of grassroots environmentalism is the **Green Party**. Established in 1984, the basic Green Party platform of ten principles includes a commitment to environmentalism, social justice, decentralization, community-based economics, feminism, and diversity. The environmental goal is a sustainable world in which nature and human society coexist in harmony. The Green Party seeks to be an alternative voice in political and policy debates that often challenges the mainstream Republican and Democratic parties and rejects corporate backing. Members would like to see the political process returned to the people. Candidates from the Green Party have been elected to various political seats at the local and state levels, and Ralph Nader, a longtime consumer protection advocate, was its candidate in the presidential election of 2000, garnering enough votes to have perhaps changed the outcome of that election.

Ecoterrorism is an example of radical grassroots environmentalism. Ecoterrorists (or ecoextremists) use violent and often illegal methods to achieve their goals of protecting the environment. These groups operate underground, without centralized organization or known membership. Law enforcement officials call ecoterrorist tactics—including arson, explosives, vandalism, theft, sabotage, and harassment—"direct action" campaigns to disrupt or destroy businesses and organizations the groups believe are a threat to the environment. They have so far avoided targeting people, though there may be victims in the course of ecoterrorist operations. FBI counterterrorism agents told a Senate committee that radical environmental and animal rights activists represented the nation's top domestic terrorist threat (Heilprin 2005).

It is unclear how many ecoterrorist groups currently exist. One visible group called the Earth Liberation Front, or ELF, was founded in the United Kingdom in the early 1990s. Although it disavows any connection to illegal activity, ELF acknowledges that some individuals have used its name to claim responsibility for their violent actions. ELF says that those individuals have acted on their own without ELF's direction or endorsement. Targets are often chosen for their symbolic nature and have included logging operations, sport utility vehicle dealerships, recreational resorts, and new home and condominium developments.

The **environmental justice** (or "ecojustice") movement represents a significant branch of the environmental movement and is also an example of grassroots organization. It emerged as a response to environmental inequities, threats to public health, and the differential enforcement and treatment of certain communities with regard to ecological concerns. Despite significant improvements in environmental protections, millions of people in the United States live in communities threatened by ecological hazards. Those living in poverty, and other minority communities, are disproportionately at risk and bear a greater portion of the nation's environmental problems. The term **environmental racism** is applied when an environmental policy or practice negatively affects individuals, groups, or communities based on class, race, or ethnicity (Bullard 1993). Access to

GRASSROOTS ENVIRONMENTALISM
beginning in the 1980s, fourth stage of the environmental movement; distinguished by the diversity of its members and belief in citizen participation in environmental decision making

NIMBY short for "not in my back yard"; originally referred to protests aimed at shifting undesirable activities onto those with less power; now sometimes used without negative connotations to describe local environmental activists

GREEN PARTY
a U.S. political party established in 1984 to bring political attention to environmentalism, social justice, diversity, and related principles

ECOTERRORISM use of violence or criminal methods to protect the environment, often in high-profile, publicity-generating ways

ENVIRONMENTAL JUSTICE
a movement that aims to remedy environmental inequities such as threats to public health and the unequal treatment of certain communities with regard to ecological concerns

ENVIRONMENTAL RACISM
any environmental policy or practice that negatively affects individuals, groups, or communities because of their race or ethnicity

environmental equality, or living in a healthy environment, has been framed as a basic human right.

Research on environmental justice is one of the fastest-growing areas of scholarship within environmental sociology. Sociologist Robert Bullard is among the leading researchers in this area, linking social justice to environmental movements. His book *Dumping in Dixie: Race, Class, and Environmental Quality* (1990) examined the economic, social, and psychological effects associated with locating noxious facilities (such as landfills, hazardous-waste dumps, and lead smelters) within lower-income African American communities where they have been less likely to meet with significant opposition.

Blacks have historically been underrepresented in the environmental movement. Often, they were already engaged in other civil rights causes that seemed more pressing. They also lacked the experience and money to fight large corporations, and many had little hope of change, even though they strongly opposed environmental destruction, especially the

kinds found in their communities. However, some groups have been moved to action.

Bullard looked at five black communities in the South that challenged public policies and industrial practices threatening their neighborhoods. After years of environmental problems, these activists began to demand environmental justice and equal protection. They grew increasingly incensed at the industries and the government regulatory agencies that allowed those industries to violate codes and continue to wreak havoc on the environment. The industries, though heavy polluters, had often gained favor in the communities by promising a better tax base and much-needed jobs. Real environmental justice, however, would mean that communities could enjoy jobs and economic development without sacrificing their health and the environment. That is just what they achieved.

Work by Bullard and others in the field of environmental justice has had profound effects not only on academia but also on public policy, industry practices, and community organizations. Environmental justice groups are beginning to sway administrative decisions and have won several important court victories (Bullard and Wright 1990; Kaczor 1996; Bullard, Johnson, and Wright 1997). The EPA was even convinced to create an Office on Environmental Equity. There is still much work to be done in this area. Some of the most important battles in the environmental justice movement will be fought beyond U.S. borders, in other countries suffering from similar and even worse environmental problems.

SUSTAINABLE DEVELOPMENT The study of **sustainable development**, or sustainability, is among the most recent areas of environmental sociology, having emerged in the 1990s, and it continues to generate some controversy (McMichael 1996). The idea of sustainability was popularized in a United Nations World Commission on Environment and Development report titled "Our Common Future," often referred to as the Brundtland Report (1987). Sustainable development is a broad concept that tries to reconcile global economic development with environmental protection; it is based on the premise that the development aspirations of all countries cannot be met by following the path already taken by industrialized nations; the world's ecosystems cannot support it. Yet, since improving the conditions of the world's poor is an international goal, we must find ways to promote economic growth that both respect social justice and protect the environment, not only in the present but for future generations (Humphrey, Lewis, and Buttel 2002; Agyeman, Bullard, and Evans 2003).

One way to grasp the magnitude of supporting humans on the planet is the **ecological footprint**, an estimation of how much land and water area is required to produce all the goods we consume and to assimilate all the waste we generate. The current ecological footprint of the average American,

Not in My Back Yard In Manchester, a neighborhood on Houston's east side, children play in a playground that abuts an oil refinery.

approximately 30 acres, represents about three times his or her fair share of the earth's resources (Wackernagel and Rees 1996). Compare that to someone from the United Kingdom, whose ecological footprint is approximately 15 acres, or someone from Burundi with a little over 1 acre (People and the Planet 2002). Modern industrialized countries are appropriating the carrying capacity of "land vastly larger than the areas they physically occupy" (Rees and Wackernagel 1994). Projections are that we would need four additional planet earths to support the world's population if everyone else were to adopt the consumption habits of Americans. (You can measure your own ecological footprint by going to the Earth Day website.)

Working toward sustainable development is a challenge. We have to find ways to meet the needs of a growing world population—for food, shelter, health care, education, and employment—while ensuring we sustain nature and the environment, whether that is fresh water, clean air, wildlife, natural resources, or nontoxic communities. It is even more important to work toward sustainability as we become increasingly globalized and have to think about the rest of the world and far into the future (Holdren, Daily, and Ehrlich 1995).

Some solutions toward sustainable development are already being implemented. These include lifestyle modifications: engaging in voluntary simplicity, recycling, practicing vegetarianism and veganism, buying organic foods, and using goods or services from environmentally friendly and fair trade companies. Others are modifications to our infrastructure, such as green building, ecological design, xeriscape (water-conserving) gardening, and land conservation. Technological changes can be made in the way we use energy—from hybrid or biodiesel cars to solar power. Some state and local governments are enforcing stricter environmental standards and regulations than those imposed at the federal level. More than 700 U.S. mayors signed on to an urban anti–global warming agreement that some call the "municipal Kyoto" in reference to the Kyoto Protocol, an international treaty on global climate change that the United States has declined to ratify (Caplan 2005; Roosevelt 2007). All these efforts help move us toward sustainable development, but much more must be done if we are to create that vision for the future.

CLOSING COMMENTS

In this chapter, we have crossed a huge terrain—from population through urbanization to the environment. We hope that you can now see the connection among these three seemingly disparate areas of study. Human population has grown throughout history, particularly in the past 200 years. The rate at which the population increases is influenced by both biological and social factors. Where all these people live has also changed over time. As more of them locate in urban areas, cities play a key role in how we inhabit the world and what kind of world that becomes. The billions of people inhabiting the planet are part of an ecosystem, and they continue to have an impact on it. The natural environment both affects and is affected by human activity. So population, urbanization, and the environment are intimately related. There is a mutual effect and interdependence among them, where trends and changes in one reverberate through the others. As residents of planet earth, we all take part in the dynamic, both enjoying or suffering current realities and creating future ones.

Everything You Need to Know about Populations, Cities, and the Environment

THEORIES OF POPULATIONS, CITIES, AND THE ENVIRONMENT

* **Structural functionalism:** the natural world exists in order to keep the social world running smoothly

* **Conflict theory:** not all groups or individuals benefit equally from society's use of the natural environment

* **Symbolic interactionism:** the meanings assigned to the natural environment will determine how society uses it

REVIEW

1. How many children would you like to have? The demographic predictions of the neo-Malthusians and the anti-Malthusians disagree sharply. According to the anti-Malthusians, what changes in social structure might make people less interested in having lots of children?

2. This chapter described Americans as "pigs of the planet," in reference to the way we consume resources. Make a list of all the ways you use water other than for drinking. Do you believe that the planet can continue to support the kind of consumption in the American standard of living? What do you think will happen when growing populations in developing nations want to live like Americans?

3. Do you prefer to live in a dense urban area or a more lightly populated suburban one? What are the advantages and disadvantages of each? What sorts of social and/or environmental problems are created by the situation you prefer?

Estimated World Population

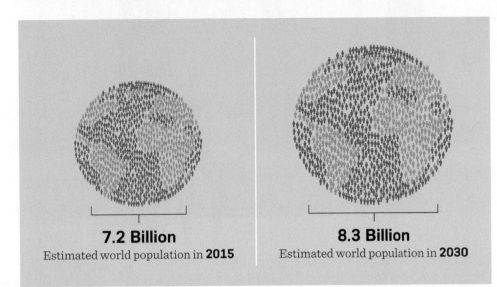

7.2 Billion
Estimated world population in **2015**

8.3 Billion
Estimated world population in **2030**

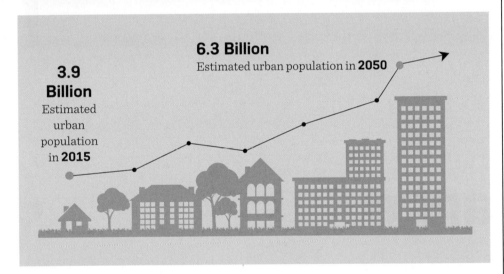

3.9 Billion
Estimated urban population in **2015**

6.3 Billion
Estimated urban population in **2050**

Every second, the urban population grows by **2 people.**

One in five city residents worldwide lives without access to improved sanitation facilities.

SOURCE: U.N. Population Division 2015, World Bank 2015, UN Water 2013.

EXPLORE

Social Movements and the Environment

Today it seems like environmental concerns are finally coming to a head: debates are roiling over climate change, overpopulation, the growing energy demands of China and India, and hydraulic fracturing. However, another big energy crisis occurred in 1973: OPEC embargoed oil to the United States. Individuals and businesses started practicing conservation . . . at least until the 1980s, when environmentalism seemed bad for business. Visit the Everyday Sociology blog to read more about environmentalism in the late twentieth century, and what issues are relevant for today.

http://wwnPag.es/trw415

CHAPTER 16

Social Change

f you haven't seen one already, ask your parents, older relatives, or maybe one of your professors to show you the scar from their smallpox vaccination. It's a dime-sized circle at the top of the left arm that was made with multiple pricks of a tiny fork-like needle that held one drop of vaccine. This little scar, now nearly invisible, shows that your parents and professors were protected from a disease that has killed billions of people and left billions more blind and disfigured, for which there is no effective treatment. Yet, if you check your own arm, it's doubtful you will see a similar scar. So in actuality, you are *not* protected from smallpox. Why not?

Smallpox is one of the diseases that has been effectively eliminated by the advances of medical technology. Scientific discoveries during the eighteenth and nineteenth centuries meant that by the middle of the twentieth century, a global campaign to stamp out the disease

was well under way. The last natural case of smallpox in the world occurred in Somalia in 1977, and a lab accident killed a British researcher in 1978. But since then, no one has contracted the disease. Smallpox vaccination ceased in the United States in 1972. The World Health Organization (WHO) declared smallpox officially eradicated in 1979, and vaccinations were discontinued worldwide by 1986.

Does the WHO declaration mean that the smallpox virus no longer exists? No. Two high-security research labs, one in the United States and one in Russia, hold samples of the virus, and another lab in the Netherlands houses the seed virus used to produce the vaccine. Why keep samples of a vanquished virus? If it ever reappears, if even the smallest amount somehow escapes laboratory quarantine, an epidemic is almost certain: smallpox is transmitted through face-to-face contact before individuals even know they are infected, and it can also be spread through building ventilation systems. It will thus be critical for us to have stores of the virus ready so that more vaccines can be made. The fact that large portions of the world's population—including you—are unprotected makes us vulnerable to the use of smallpox as a biological weapon. In the wake of the terrorist attacks of 9/11, U.S. health officials began considering reinstituting mass vaccination programs, although at this date, they have not yet done so.

The story of smallpox is a story of social change—change in the incidence, experience, and meaning of smallpox over time. The disease was a ubiquitous killer for thousands of years, up to the 1940s; in some cultures, families waited to name babies until after the infants had contracted and survived smallpox. It killed peasants and royalty alike, but through deliberate human effort a defense against the disease was eventually developed. Medicine, politics, culture, demography, individual and collective actions—smallpox was conquered through the synergy of all these elements. In the late 1700s, English physician Edward Jenner observed a pattern of smallpox immunity in milkmaids who had previously contracted the less virulent cowpox, and he developed the first vaccine.

Beginning in the 1950s, the WHO sought political and financial support for a worldwide vaccination campaign. Your grandparents obeyed the law and took your parents to be vaccinated when they were children. All these processes contributed to change in the meaning and incidence of smallpox. And the meaning could change yet again as a result of the actions of another group: bio-terrorists. So perhaps no disease can ever truly be eradicated. Ironically, it is our lingering fear of smallpox that prevents us from getting rid of it entirely.

HOW TO READ THIS CHAPTER

There are a couple of reasons why we are ending this book with a chapter on social change. The first is that, to paraphrase an old cliché, change is the only constant. It is happening everywhere, all the time, in myriad variations. One of your challenges after reading this chapter will be to identify some of these social changes and to understand their patterns, causes, and consequences.

The other reason is more personal: we hope that reading this chapter will motivate you to work for social change yourself. The study of sociology can sometimes be a bit disheartening, as we learn the many ways in which our lives are constrained by social forces and institutional structures. But this chapter helps us remember that C. Wright Mills's "intersection of biography and history" is a two-way street: while society shapes the individual, the individual can shape society. You have the power to bring about social change, especially when you work together with others who share your views, values, and visions for a better world. So we want you to read this chapter with optimism; by understanding the processes of social change, you will be better qualified to make it happen yourself.

What Is Social Change?

No doubt you've heard your parents, grandparents, or other older family members reflect on "the way things were" when they were children. Hard-to-imagine times such as those before indoor plumbing or television, or during the Great Depression or World War II, undeniably made older Americans' lives very different from your own. People born even one generation apart can have different overall life experiences as a result of ongoing processes of social change. Consider how different life was for your professors who grew up during the Cold War versus your own childhood experiences in the immediate aftermath of September 11, or how different you feel from your grandparents, who came of age without cell phones and the Internet. Our culture evolves over time, as do our social institutions—the family, work, religion, education, and political systems. Sociologists define the transformation of culture over time as **social change**.

It's easy to identify particular historical periods where major social transformation was unmistakable: the Renaissance, the French Revolution, the Civil War, the women's rights movement. But it's important to realize that social change is occurring at all times, not just at moments of obvious cultural or political upheaval. The rate at which it happens, however, varies over time, with some historical periods experiencing rapid social change and others experiencing more gradual change. For example, social scientists recognize several major "social revolutions"—periods of time during which large-scale

social change took place so rapidly that the whole of human society was dramatically redefined. The Agricultural Revolution made it possible for previously nomadic peoples to settle in one place, store surplus food for future use, and sustain larger populations with the products of their farms, herds, and flocks. The Industrial Revolution altered the way people worked, produced, and consumed goods and lived together in cities. And the Information Revolution (which is ongoing) has launched us into cyberspace thanks to digital technology and the Internet, and again society is being transformed because of it (Castells 2000; Rainee and Wellman 2012).

In addition to the pace, other elements of social change vary as well. Some changes are deliberate or intended, while others are unplanned or unintentional. For example, the invention of the automobile brought about intended changes—like the ability to travel greater distances more efficiently—yet it also brought about unforeseen events, such as the pollution of the atmosphere and the deaths of more than 30,000 people every year in car accidents. Some social changes are more controversial than others—the racial integration of public schools, for example, versus salsa's overtaking ketchup as America's top condiment—and some are more important than others. Most fashion trends have little lasting impact—remember the acid-washed jeans of the 1980s or grunge in the 1990s? Probably not. But some—like pants for women, miniskirts, and the bikini—have been extremely influential in their impact on gender roles in society.

So society is always changing, and the rates, intentionality, controversy, and importance of individual changes vary. But how does social change occur? One way is through a major physical event: tornadoes, hurricanes, earthquakes, tsunamis, and volcanic eruptions can radically alter the structures and cultures of the communities they strike. Demographic factors also come into play; for instance, as the Baby Boomers have aged, American society has had to build schools and colleges (in the 1950s and 1960s), suburbs (in the 1960s, '70s, and '80s), retirement facilities (in the 1990s and 2000s), and long-term care facilities and hospitals (in the 2010s) to accommodate this huge population bulge. Another source of social change lies in discoveries and innovations, such as fire and the wheel. Try to imagine what your life would be like if humans had not figured out how to generate light and heat by striking sparks into kindling.

SOCIAL CHANGE
the transformation of a culture over time

Social change is often the result of human action. Jonas Salk, for example, developed a cure for polio, and Helen Keller overcame her own physical limitations to advocate for the rights of the disabled. But our most important contributions to social change are made through the collective action of many: the civil rights movement, for example, fundamentally reshaped American society. For this reason, we will spend a good portion of this chapter examining collective behavior in its many variations.

What Are the Sources of Social Change? Disasters such as the wildfires that swept across Australia in 2009 can radically change the structures and cultures of the communities they destroy.

Collective Behavior

When we join a group, we don't disappear as individuals. But we do tend to act differently in groups than we might alone. **Collective behavior** occurs when individuals converge, thus creating a group or crowd, who join in some sort of shared action. Crowds may form for different reasons, and people may gather for different purposes, but there is a common pattern to their behavior. While crowds may seem disorderly from the outside, collective behavior theories suggest that such occurrences are often organized and do maintain a certain amount of order.

COLLECTIVE BEHAVIOR behavior that follows from the formation of a group or crowd of people who take action together toward a shared goal

CONTAGION THEORY one of the earliest theories of collective action; suggests that individuals who join a crowd can become "infected" by a mob mentality and lose the ability to reason

EMERGENT NORM THEORY a theory of collective behavior that assumes individual members of a crowd make their own decisions about behavior and that norms are created through others' acceptance or rejection of these behaviors

CROWD a temporary gathering of individuals, whether spontaneous or planned, who share a common focus

Gustave Le Bon (1896) was one of the first social theorists to focus on the phenomenon of crowd behavior and what he called the "popular mind." He coined the term **contagion theory**, which suggests that when people come together, they get swept up in a crowd, which develops a "mob mentality." Le Bon likened such groups to herds of animals, where individuality and rational thought disappear and the external stimulus of the collective action takes over. So, in the case of rampaging soccer hooligans, contagion theory would argue that these fans have given their rational thought over to a mob impulse and can no longer make independent decisions about their actions. But while the theory may seem useful when looking at cases like soccer hooliganism, it doesn't fully explain the wide range of collective behavior beyond the mindless mob.

A more recent idea gives us a better understanding. **Emergent norm theory** (Turner and Killian 1987) argues that collective behavior is not as uniform as Le Bon suggested, and that any number of factors can motivate people to participate in crowd activities. The underlying assumption here is that a group is guided by *norms* (shared cultural expectations for behavior) that emerge in response to a situation, and, as a result, the behavior of those in the crowd is structured to fit within the collective action. So while it may appear that a crowd is one large, indistinguishable mass, the individuals who make it up can have varying understandings of what their roles are within the crowd as well as the meaning of their actions.

Collective behavior generally takes three forms: crowd behavior, mass behavior, and social movements. While these three types are discussed separately here, they are not mutually exclusive. In the real world, they may overlap whenever collective behavior actually occurs.

Crowds

A **crowd** is formed when a large number of people come together, either on purpose or randomly. If you have ever strolled around a large city, you may have noticed a street performer (such as a mime, musician, or break dancer) trying to entertain passersby. In time, a crowd starts to develop. So despite the fact that those who stopped to watch had different reasons for walking down that street at that particular time, they have now become part of a crowd whose purpose is to be an audience for a street performer. As a crowd, they must adjust their behavior somewhat: perhaps they stop conversing or put away their cell phones so as not to disturb the performer or those around them, clapping at the end of the performance. Even with this conformity of behavior, however, the fact remains that the individual motivation for joining the onlookers may vary. One person may have stopped because he was struck by the performer's talent, another because her feet hurt from walking. At a certain point, others may pause simply because they see the existing crowd and are curious.

While the street performer type of crowd comes about in a somewhat random way and is most often benign and temporary, other types of crowds can form in a more deliberate manner and lead to more highly expressive and consequential action. Let's look at two recent examples with very different trajectories: a street party in Isla Vista, California, and a protest rally in Baltimore, Maryland.

"Floatopia" began as a social gathering for mostly college students attending the University of California, Santa Barbara, and quickly grew into a popular annual event. The idea was for partygoers to bring rafts and other floatation devices to adjacent beaches for a day (and night) of fun. By 2011 the event was attracting over 10,000 people (thanks to Facebook), a number that overwhelmed the scarce facilities, leaving behind a massive amount of trash and human waste sullying the shore. As university officials moved to close the beaches, the event relocated to Del Playa, the bluff-top street above the beach. "Deltopia," as the event was renamed, grew even bigger, and in 2014, it erupted in violence when partygoers clashed with police trying to control the scene. Fires broke out, cars were demolished, bottles and bricks became weapons. The ensuing melee led to dozens of injuries (both students and police), and over a hundred arrests (Duke 2014). Such collective action can be characterized as a **riot**: a group of people engaged in disorderly behavior directed toward other people and/or property that results in disturbing the peace.

On April 12, 2015, three white police officers in Baltimore pursued and apprehended twenty-five-year-old Freddie Gray after he reportedly made eye contact with the officers. Finding what they deemed an illegal switchblade knife clipped to Gray's pants, the officers proceeded to arrest Gray. Using her cell phone, a civilian onlooker captured the arrest on video, which showed officers dragging Gray, screaming in pain, into a police van. Upon arrival at the police station, Gray was already in a coma, having suffered a severe spinal injury. He died a week later in a local hospital. When news of Gray's death became public, Baltimore residents gathered to protest outside the police station. In the days that followed, the protests escalated; what was initially a demonstration against a specific case of alleged police brutality became an expression of frustration about the city's wider set of social problems, including poverty, racism, crime, and years of unaddressed complaints about law enforcement abuse of communities of color. Eventually a full-scale riot developed, with looters breaking windows and throwing rocks while police and National Guard advanced and a state of emergency was declared. The violence lasted for ten days, finally quieting after Gray's funeral was held and a curfew was put in place. Citizens awoke to relative quiet on April 29, and began the work of cleaning up their neighborhoods, while still expressing a desire to see justice done in Freddie Gray's case. Supporters in cities such as Chicago, New York, and Philadelphia also held anti-police-brutality demonstrations. On May 1, Gray's death was ruled a homicide, and charges were filed against the three arresting officers, as well as three more officers (all black) who participated in transporting Gray in the police van. Later, all were indicted by a grand jury.

The events in both Isla Vista and Baltimore demonstrate how collective behavior can develop into riots. Furthermore, they show how collective behavior can be both organized and chaotic, depending on the shared norms that emerge (McPhail 1991).

RIOT continuous disorderly behavior by a group of people that disturbs the peace and is directed toward other people and/or property

A Tale of Two Cities While the people involved gathered together for different reasons, the events in both Isla Vista, California, and Baltimore illustrate how collective behavior can evolve into riots.

Mass Behavior

Mass behavior occurs when large groups of people not necessarily in the same geographical location engage in similar behavior. Mass behavior can range from buying a certain type of sneakers or getting a tattoo to playing Candy Crush Saga on Facebook. Sociologists have focused on three areas of mass behavior in particular. Two areas, fads and fashions, should be familiar to you. The third too often goes unrecognized by those involved: social dilemmas.

FADS AND FASHIONS Fads are interests that are followed with great enthusiasm for a period of time. They can include products (such as electric cars or iPads), words or phrases ("selfie" or "sorry, not sorry"), clothing styles (aviator sunglasses or Ugg boots), activities (Zumba or vaping), or even pets (purse-sized toy dogs or anything mixed with a poodle, e.g., a Labradoodle). For fads to continue for any length of time, social networks are necessary to spread the enthusiasm (Aguirre, Quarantelli, and Mendoza 1988; Jones 2009). While fads tend not to result in lasting social change, they do follow certain social norms and can create a unified identity for those who practice them (Best 2006).

Dieting is a good example. Many Americans have followed such fad diets of the past as the all-grapefruit or the no-white-food diet; others have joined the low-carbohydrate fad of the Atkins and South Beach diets. During their heyday in the mid-2000s, the low-carbohydrate diets in particular had an impact on food industries, with grocery stores and fast-food chains trying to cater to the needs of their customers. Now, those same low-carb products take up less shelf space (if any), and it may be harder to find a "bunless" burger on the menu. Gluten-free diets seem to be the current reigning trend, with millions of consumers making gluten-free specialty products and menu items more and more popular. Whatever comes next, it is likely that in wealthy countries like the United States, diet fads are sure to continue.

Another type of mass behavior is **fashion**: a widespread style of behavior and appearance. Fashion can mark you as belonging to a certain group; military fatigues and school uniforms are two examples. Like fads, certain fashions (such as extremely baggy clothes for boys and leggings for girls) can enjoy huge popularity for a time. Celebrities can also drive fashion. A look back at two hit TV series is instructive. *Mad Men* (2007–2015) became popular not only for its great writing and acting but also for its celebration of 1950s and '60s fashion.

MASS BEHAVIOR large groups of people engaging in similar behaviors without necessarily being in the same place

FADS interests or practices followed enthusiastically for a relatively short period of time

FASHION the widespread custom or style of behavior and appearance at a particular time or in a particular place

SOCIAL DILEMMA a situation in which behavior that is rational for the individual can, when practiced by many people, lead to collective disaster

A Fashion Empire Taraji P. Henson's character Cookie, from the hit show *Empire*, is known for her glamourous high-fashion ensembles by top designers like Gucci, Alexander McQueen, and Balmain.

The men's dapper suits and the women's full skirts and cinched waists brought retro glamour back to the world of fashion. Similarly, *Gossip Girl* (2007–2012) was as closely watched for the designer clothing worn by its high school stars as for its shifting romantic relationships. January Jones and Blake Lively, the real-life stars of the two shows, are still closely followed in the tabloids and fashion magazines, where fans like to critique or emulate their styles, both onscreen and off.

Newer shows are sure to inspire similar trends. When the hip-hop drama *Empire* debuted in 2014, it became an overnight sensation, as much for its story lines as for its fashionable characters. And it's not just the women who flaunt the flashiest designer clothes, but the men in the series are equally noticeable for their style. You could say something similar about *Nashville*, the country-music series that began airing in 2012. The outfits worn by its country music stars (real and fictionalized) are showing up in magazines and on fashion blogs and Pinterest boards and are influencing styles far beyond Music Row.

SOCIAL DILEMMAS In the third category of mass behavior, called a **social dilemma**, behavior that is rational for an individual can lead to collective disaster. Let's take an example that's familiar to everyone: getting stuck in a traffic jam. You creep along slowly for what seems like forever and finally arrive at the source of the holdup. It's an accident, with two cars, a police cruiser, and an ambulance pulled over to the shoulder. But the accident isn't even on your side of the freeway, and there's nothing blocking your lanes of traffic. The holdup on your side is a result of everybody slowing down to get a good look. If they had just kept on driving at their normal speed there wouldn't be a traffic jam. So what do you do when you finally get up to the scene of the accident? You slow down and take a look too.

When many people make that same (seemingly) rational decision (to slow down for only a few seconds), the cumulative effect causes a kind of collective disaster (a traffic jam). As social beings, we deal with such situations almost daily, yet rarely do we see how best to handle them. According to many social thinkers, going all the way back to philosopher Thomas Hobbes (1588–1679), we live in a world governed by self-interest. How is our self-interest balanced with the interests of the collective? Social dilemmas help us understand this calculation.

There are two classes of social dilemmas. The first is known as a **tragedy of the commons**. In 1968, Garrett Hardin wrote an essay describing why this kind of dilemma emerges in society. He begins with the classic example of the "commons," which in the past served as a pasture shared by the whole community and on which anyone could graze their livestock. Because access to the commons was free and without restriction, each individual had an incentive to put as many head of livestock on the commons as possible, thereby increasing his own personal gain. But as everyone made that same decision, the commons inevitably became overgrazed. When a common resource is used beyond its carrying capacity, it eventually collapses, becoming totally incapable of supporting any life at all. This is the tragedy—when the commons is ruined. In a tragedy of the commons, the benefit is to the individual but the cost is shared by all.

The example of the commons applies to recent history as well. Our natural resources, such as water, air, fossil fuels, forests, plants, and animals, might all be considered similar to a commons. In the case of the U.S. fishing trade, especially, we have seen how, as Hardin put it, "freedom in a commons brings ruin to all" (1968). For example, Dr. Stein remembers living in Santa Barbara in the late 1970s, when local abalones were plentiful. Divers off the California coast and around the Channel Islands could make a good living harvesting these mollusks along rocky shorelines. Any good seafood restaurant regularly offered abalone steaks on its menu, and a casual beachgoer might find abalone shells strewn along the sand. By the 1990s, however, abalones had all but disappeared. As each diver reached the same conclusion—that catching as many abalones as possible would increase his own profits—and more divers moved into the same fishing territory, the abalones were no longer able to regenerate their stocks and were eventually depleted to near extinction.

A partial solution is now in place with the designation of the Channel Islands National Marine Sanctuary, a federally protected area where commercial fishing is prohibited. In a variety of similar cases, such as the lobster trappers off the New England coast, regulatory agencies have had to step in and place restrictions on the territories and amount of yields allowed. Otherwise, a tragedy of the commons is likely to ensue. We might also consider social, as well as natural, resources as similar to a commons. For example, when too many people crowd the freeways at rush hour or throw litter out the window of their cars, the result is the commons in ruin.

So what can we do to solve these problems? If we could somehow increase the number of abalones in the sea or the number of lanes on the freeway, that would help solve two of them, but only temporarily. At some point, use overwhelms

Tragedy of the Commons Abalone divers rest after making a climb up a cliff. Since the 1990s, abalones have all but disappeared from the central coast of California due to overfishing.

supply. To Hardin, social dilemmas are a "class of human problems which can be classified as having 'no technical solution'" (1968). What he means is that science or technology alone cannot solve the problems. The solutions must come from members of society: people will have to change their behavior.

The other class of social dilemmas is called a **public goods dilemma**, in which individuals must contribute to a collective resource they may not ever benefit from. Blood banks are a good example. Because human blood can't be stored for much longer than a month at a time, many people must volunteer to donate blood regularly in order to keep supplies steady. Blood donors can be viewed as helping to create what is referred to as a "public good," in this case a blood bank. What motivates these people, on average some 9.5 million a year, to contribute something vital to themselves for which they may never receive anything in return? Everyone is equally entitled to draw from the blood bank regardless of whether they have ever given blood. People who take advantage of a public good without having contributed to its creation are called "free riders." In a public goods dilemma, unlike a tragedy of the commons, the cost is to the individual but the benefit is shared by all.

So how do we get people to contribute to a public good if they are not required to? There are numerous examples of this social dilemma in everyday life, as you know if you've ever witnessed a membership drive on public radio or public television.

TRAGEDY OF THE COMMONS
a type of social dilemma in which many individuals' overexploitation of a public resource depletes or degrades that common resource

PUBLIC GOODS DILEMMA
a type of social dilemma in which individuals incur the cost to contribute to a collective resource, though they may never benefit from that resource

Table 16.1 Theory in Everyday Life

Perspective	Approach to Social Change	Case Study: The Environmental Movement
Structural Functionalism	Sometimes social change is necessary to maintain equilibrium and order in society.	Natural resources are necessary for the survival of society, so the growth of a social movement dedicated to the wise use and conservation of natural resources is functional for society.
Conflict Theory	Social change is the inevitable result of social inequality and conflict between groups over power and resources.	Environmental privileges (such as scenic natural vistas, clean water, and unpolluted air) are unequally distributed among groups in society. The environmental movement works to secure the rights of all citizens, rich and poor, to a clean, healthy, beautiful, and sustainable world.
Symbolic Interactionism	Social change involves changes in the meaning of things as well as changes in laws, culture, and social behavior.	The environmental movement works to safeguard animal species by having them declared "endangered" or "threatened." Redefining groups of animals in this way allows for their protection through endangered species laws rather than their decimation through hunting or habitat reduction.

These noncommercial networks must appeal to individuals to contribute money so that they can continue to produce and broadcast programs. But regardless of whether a person responds to the pledge drive, as free riders they can still tune into the station anytime at no cost. Public goods dilemmas are also a class of human problems for which there are no technical solutions. This is why the government requires us to make certain contributions, in the form of taxes, in order to create such public goods as roads, schools, and fire departments. But there are many other types of public goods, such as blood banks, that only individuals can create through their own voluntary contributions.

By examining social dilemmas, we are presented with a dramatic example of mass behavior. We begin to see how seemingly small individual acts add up and cumulatively shape society. So the next time you are faced with a problem like where to throw your litter or whether to give blood, ask yourself what kind of collective outcome you would like your behavior to contribute to.

Social Movements

If you're like most Americans, the term **social movement** is inextricably linked in your mind to thoughts of long-haired hippies, Volkswagen buses, and the antiwar protests of the 1960s. You may not think of the Nineteenth Amendment to the U.S. Constitution (giving women the right to vote), birth control, the AFL-CIO workers union, Pentecostalism, the Revolutionary War, or Nazism—and

SOCIAL MOVEMENT any social groups with leadership, organization, and an ideological commitment to promote or resist social change

yet all of these were, at the time of their inceptions, rightly termed "social movements."

So what precisely is a social movement? Does the term as accurately describe the efforts of liberals to elect a Democrat to Congress as it does the efforts of peace activists to end a war? The answer is no. According to Perry and Pugh (1978), "Social movements are collectives with a degree of leadership, organization, and ideological commitment to promote or resist change" (p. 221); Meyer (2000) adds that social movements "challenge cultural codes and transform the lives of their participants" (p. 39). A political campaign cannot usually be described as a social movement, because although it may be considered an organized collective with leadership and (sometimes) ideological commitment, and may indeed transform the lives of its participants, its purpose is not to fundamentally alter the status quo. Antiwar protesters, on the other hand, are usually trying not only to stop a specific violent conflict but also to change cultural support of war as an accepted means of solving disputes.

We can safely say that most of the institutions with which we are familiar began as social movements. How did they arise? Why do people join them? And how do today's radicals become tomorrow's establishment?

Several theories attempt to address these questions, but the assumptions behind them have evolved over time. For example, scholars working in the 1940s, '50s, and early '60s generally viewed social movements with suspicion—as "dysfunctional, irrational, and exceptionally dangerous" (Meyer 2000, p. 37). People who joined a movement were thought to be attracted not by its ideals but by the refuge it offered "from the anxieties, barrenness, and meaninglessness of an individual existence" (Zirakzadeh 1997, p. 9). This explanation, labeled by sociologists as **mass society theory**, was not so remarkable when you consider that researchers in those decades had witnessed the effects of Nazism, Fascism, Stalinism, and McCarthyism, all of which originated as social movements that eventually devastated millions of lives (Zirakzadeh 1997).

By the 1960s, however, a sea change had occurred, and a new generation of scholars researching the hows and whys of social movements were inclined to be more sympathetic. After all, the 1960s had seen the rise and relative success of the civil rights movement. While people of color may have been alienated from the larger white society, they were certainly not isolated "joiners" who took up with social movements simply to "satisfy some kind of psychological need" (Meyer 2000, p. 37). The civil rights movement and others were practical political responses to inequality and oppression and provided opportunities for the oppressed to "redistribute political and economic power democratically and fairly" (Zirakzadeh 1997, p. 15). This explanation is called **relative deprivation theory** because it focuses on the actions of deprived or oppressed groups who seek rights already enjoyed by others in society; they are deprived relative to other groups.

VOTING RIGHTS A look at the history of voting rights in the United States shows the power of relative deprivation theory to explain certain types of social movements. For more than a hundred years, women and persons of color lobbied hard for the right to vote. (We could also turn this claim on its head by saying that for more than a hundred years, many white men fought hard to exclude women and persons of color from voting.) Officially, African American males were granted the right to vote with the Fifteenth Amendment in 1870, but individual states effectively nullified this right by passing regulations requiring literacy tests, prohibitive poll taxes, and grandfather clauses (if your grandfather had voted, you could too) that specifically excluded them from voting. It wasn't until the 1965 Voting Rights Act was passed that all African American citizens (men *and* women) gained the ability to exercise their constitutionally protected right to vote.

The Voting Rights Act has achieved significant inroads in protecting African Americans' right to vote, in part by requiring certain states (Alabama, Arkansas, Arizona, Georgia, Louisiana, Mississippi, South Carolina, Texas, and Virginia) to seek federal approval to change voting laws. In fact, it has been so successful that the Supreme Court decided in June 2013 to remove that requirement. Not everyone has been in favor of that move: supporters of the Voting Rights Act argue that policies like redistricting, voter ID, proof of citizenship, and limited early voting discriminate against minority voters (Hurley 2013; Liptak 2013).

Women, meanwhile, won the right to vote in 1919 with passage of the Nineteenth Amendment. To reach this point, suffragists spent decades protesting male-only voting through parades, written propaganda, debates, sit-ins, and hunger strikes. The suffrage movement, however, was primarily a white women's battle. At a rally in 1851, Sojourner Truth gave a famous speech ("Ain't I a Woman?") highlighting the exclusion of women of color from the movement. These women would have to wait until the Voting Rights Act of 1965 before they could legally vote.

But neither the Voting Rights Act nor the Nineteenth Amendment secured voting rights for all Americans. To become a registered voter, you must be a U.S. citizen (either native born or naturalized), legally reside in the state in which you vote, and have an address of some kind. Most states do not allow ex-convicts, prisoners, or those designated mentally ill to vote. There are presently social movements under way to secure this right for some of these disenfranchised Americans, such as certain categories of prisoners and people with no stable addresses.

MOBILIZING RESOURCES The kind of society we live in has a lot to do with whether we are likely to join social movements, the tactics those movements will use, and whether the movements will succeed. For example, in a country like the United States, with strong free-speech protections, anyone wanting to support reproductive rights can publish books and articles, march in the streets (with some restrictions), promote their views on social media, or start a letter-writing campaign to pressure lawmakers. On the other hand, under a restrictive regime like that of the Taliban in Afghanistan, peaceful protest is not an option, and merely teaching a female to read has been

MASS SOCIETY THEORY a theory of social movements that assumes people join not because of the movement's ideals but to satisfy a psychological need to belong to something larger than themselves

RELATIVE DEPRIVATION THEORY a theory of social movements that focuses on the actions of oppressed groups who seek rights or opportunities already enjoyed by others in the society

Malala Yousafzai While boarding the bus to school, Pakistani teenager Malala Yousafzai was shot by Taliban gunmen. In 2014, she was awarded the Nobel Peace Prize for her efforts to promote the education of women and girls across the globe.

IN RELATIONSHIPS
#OccupyWallStreet and Hashtag Activism

How does an Estonian-Canadian filmmaker who runs a magazine in Vancouver, Canada, become inspired by social activism in Egypt to organize a protest in midtown Manhattan? It sounds like a riddle, but the answer is simple. He did it on Twitter.

Kalle Lasn is the founder and editor of the magazine *Adbusters*. Along with Micah White, a senior editor at the magazine, he had watched the Egyptian protests in Tahrir Square with interest, and concluded that "America needs its own Tahrir" (Schwartz 2011). After some brainstorming, the team at *Adbusters* sent out an e-mail to their mailing list calling for a protest in New York City. They created a poster, showing a ballerina atop the famous statue of a charging bull in Bowling Green Park near Wall Street, with a line of protesters wearing gas masks emerging behind it. To publicize the upcoming event, they started using the hashtag #occupy-wallstreet on Twitter. No one from the *Adbusters* team ever traveled to New York, or played any significant role in organizing the protest. Instead, people on the *Adbusters* mailing list used Twitter and Reddit to spread the word and raise awareness of the demonstration. On September 17, 2011, protesters marched on Wall Street, eventually gathering in Zuccotti Park after other places were blocked by police. At the end of the day, when most of the crowd dispersed, 300 people remained behind to camp in the park, "occupying" Wall Street.

Unlike traditional protest marches, this one didn't end. Many protesters returned, every day, and many continued to sleep in the park every night. On November 15, 2011, New York City police closed the park and arrested those who refused to leave, but by that time, other "Occupy" protests had sprung up all around the world and in hundreds of communities in the United States. Clearly this could not have happened had the message of Occupy Wall Street not struck a chord with people around the country, as many were deeply concerned with economic inequality, corporate corruption, and the role that money played in contemporary politics.

Shared concerns alone, however, cannot explain the incredibly rapid spread of the protests. What allowed the single protest to turn into a movement so quickly were social media: Listservs, Twitter, Facebook, and YouTube. These new media made it possible not just to organize the original protest but also for activists around the country to bring together grassroots communities and coordinate protests far beyond the confines of Zuccotti Park. Not only did social media help people connect and organize, but the steady stream of pictures, status updates, and videos of the protests helped "shape the narrative about the movement" and generate "online conversations" about the issues at hand (Lubin 2012, p. 187).

At the height of the Occupy Movement, there were hundreds of Facebook pages devoted to the protests, almost met with suspicion and hostility. In 2012, the Pakistani Taliban shot fourteen-year-old Malala Yousafzai in the head because she spoke out in favor of educating girls. She survived the attack, and was transferred to a British hospital for treatment. She has become an international symbol for women's rights and continues her activism—from afar; it is too dangerous for her to return to her home country, where she is still wanted by the Taliban (Walsh 2013). In 2014, Yousafzai was awarded the Nobel Peace Prize for her work; at just seventeen years of age, she is the youngest person to receive that distinction.

In addition to a tolerant society, social movements need a long list of practical and human resources, without which it would be impossible to accomplish their goals. This list includes volunteers, funding, office space, phone banks, computers, Internet access, copy machines, and pens and pencils—as well as the know-how to put these resources into action. Recruitment and fund-raising are critical to the success of a group. Funding may go to support staff or pay for overhead, but much of what is raised will be spent on producing and soliciting media coverage to get the message out. Social media have become an important resource both for fund-raising and spreading the word. Small start-ups can use "crowdfunding" sites like Indiegogo and Kickstarter to raise money to get their business off the ground. A nascent social movement can begin organizing online, raising money via crowdfunding to run its operations while simultaneously raising awareness and support through social networks.

Theorists who focus on how these practical constraints help or hinder social movements operate under the assumptions of **resource mobilization theory**. However interesting or important a type of social change may be, no progress will be made unless certain practical resources are available. So if we consider the plight of women in Taliban-ruled parts of Pakistan or Afghanistan, for instance, we realize that some of the most basic human activities, such as reading and meeting together freely, are actually social movement resources that not everyone can take for granted.

RESOURCE MOBILIZATION THEORY a theory of social movements that focuses on the practical constraints that help or hinder social movements' action

2 million YouTube videos were tagged "occupy" or "ows," and the official Twitter feed (@OccupyWallStNYC) had more than 137,000 followers (Preston 2011). Some observers view the protests as a failure, since they achieved no tangible political goals, but their supporters argue the movement had intentionally eschewed organizing around any one particular goal. *Adbusters* founder Kalle Lasn had initially hoped the protests would pick a single demand and that protesters would refuse

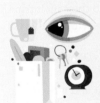

Social Media and Social Protest How different would Occupy Wall Street have been without social media sites like Twitter?

to leave until it was met. However, only days after the protests began, the protesters released a "Declaration of Occupation" that laid out a general critique rather than any particular demand: "We write so that all people who feel wronged by the corporate forces of the world can know that we are your allies. . . . No true democracy is attainable when the process is determined by economic power" (Schwartz 2011).

In many ways, this declaration reflected the organization and methods of the occupiers. They organized horizontally, without leaders or hierarchy, and attempted to work through consensus or supermajority rule. This organizational style reflected a movement that was resolutely grassroots. Social media helped bring together an unprecedented range of people from a wide variety of backgrounds and political orientations. One of the most celebrated moments in the occupation of Zuccotti Park came when union members affiliated with the AFL-CIO joined the protesters to help prevent police from clearing the park. As one commentator put it, "hard hats and hippies—together at last" (Wiener 2011). The OWS protests didn't achieve any specific political goal, but they did change the conversation about politics and economics in the United States, something that happened because the protests lived as much on Twitter as they did in the park. The Occupy Movement proved the efficacy of "hashtag activism"; social media had arrived as an invaluable resource in the process of social change.

DATA WORKSHOP
Analyzing Everyday Life

Activist Groups Get Organized

The day after Thanksgiving is also known as "Black Friday," the biggest shopping day of the year. On that day, which is thought of by many as the kickoff day to the holiday shopping season, retailers give incentives to customers by offering extended hours, tremendous discounts, and gifts. Customers sleep in parking lots waiting for the stores to open and are so eager to buy merchandise at discounted prices that injuries and even deaths have resulted. Every year seems

to bring another extreme case where someone is trampled to death by crowds rushing through the doors. In 2008, a stampede left one Walmart worker dead, while a shooting at Toys 'R' Us resulted in the deaths of two customers. In 2011, there were forty-six reported injuries but no deaths. In 2013, the hashtag #WalmartFights began trending, with Twitter users posting about incidents in numerous locations. The website Black Friday Death Count keeps a running tally; from 2006 to 2014 seven deaths and ninety-eight serious injuries were attributed to Black Friday.

In protest of the rampant consumerism of Black Friday, a group of social activists started "Buy Nothing Day." *Adbusters*, an anti-consumerist organization, promotes the event as "a day for society to examine the issue of overconsumption." The basic goal of Buy Nothing Day is to actually spend no money purchasing items on Black Friday in order to raise awareness of the dangers of consumerism and overconsumption. *Adbusters* also encourages other forms of awareness. Supporters have staged demonstrations in shopping malls where they brandish scissors and cut up credit cards while encouraging shoppers to liberate themselves from debt.

For some, the idea of Buy Nothing Day has grown into a Buy Nothing Year. The Compact is an anti-consumerist group whose members pledge to go a year without buying anything new. Members are only allowed to purchase new underwear, food, and health and safety items, such as brake fluid and toilet paper. Otherwise, they have to make do with the items they already have in their homes (come on: how many bottles of lotion or sunscreen are lurking in your bathroom cabinet right now?), buy from secondhand stores, trade for what they need, or make their own items. Other groups, like the Freegans, take a radical approach to consumerism and try to find everything for free. Web sites like Freegle and FreeCycle help in the cause.

Such groups have much in common: they wish to counteract the negative global environmental and socioeconomic effects of U.S. consumerist culture and to simplify their lives. While it might seem extreme to most Americans to go an entire year without buying new items, many people find multiple benefits to living simply, and, through their example, they are able to raise other people's consciousness about consumption, waste, and carbon footprints.

This Data Workshop asks you to analyze any activist group that is working for some kind of social change. You will be using existing sources to do a content analysis of various materials developed by the organization. Refer to the section in Chapter 2 for a review of this research method. In particular, you will be looking at how the group works to promote and advance its agenda. Examine the group's use of various forms of media—including websites and social media as well as the more traditional radio, television, newspapers, magazines, brochures, or direct mail. Gather data by bookmarking links, taking screenshots or photos, making printouts, or composing informal notes about what you find. Once you have enough data to analyze, follow these steps:

1. Describe the activist group you chose. Identify the group's commitment to a larger social movement or cause, and discuss its particular goals.
2. How is the group attempting to use resource mobilization for their cause? What are their strategies regarding these three important activities?

   a. recruiting members and organizing supporters
   b. raising funds
   c. transforming public opinion and/or achieving change

3. Describe the group's media campaign. What different forms of media do they use to convey their message? Which do you think is most successful? Least successful? Why?
4. In addition to the use of media, what other strategies does the group use to achieve its goals? For instance, does the group organize rallies or protests or participate in community events? (These activities may be connected to larger media strategies; for example, a film screening or protest march might be advertised to attract greater support, or be covered in the news.)
5. How effective is the group at convincing others to join the cause? What kind of reaction did they elicit from you? How might they improve their recruiting efforts?

There are two options for completing this Data Workshop:

PREP-PAIR-SHARE Collect your data and write some informal notes addressing the steps outlined earlier; bring these notes to class for reference. Partner with one or more students and present your findings. Compare your analyses and insights with others in your group.

DO-IT-YOURSELF Collect existing source data on your chosen activist group and follow the steps outlined earlier. Write a three- to four-page paper about the group's strategies, making specific reference to the materials it developed. Attach photos, screenshots, prints, links, or other relevant data to your paper.

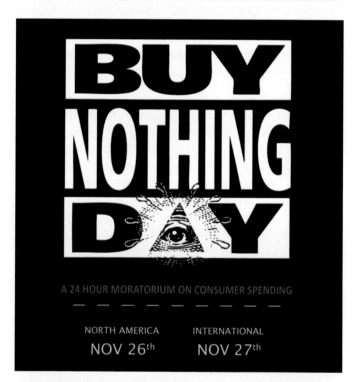

Anti-consumerism How do activist groups protest the excesses of consumerism?

STAGES IN A SOCIAL MOVEMENT Social movements begin with a few ideas and some people who believe in them. How do they reach the point of marching in the streets (or recruiting members online)? They develop in stages, and those stages were identified by Armand Mauss (1975). Mauss described the first one as the "incipient" stage, when the public takes notice of a situation and defines it as a problem (Perry and Pugh 1978). People do not start organizing because they are content; rather, they "see a discrepancy, either real or perceived, between what they are getting and what they believe they should be getting" and decide to take action (Perry and Pugh 1978, p. 237).

For example, in the late nineteenth and early twentieth centuries, many laborers were frustrated over their long working hours, low wages, lack of free weekends, and unsafe working conditions. In response, they began to organize—or, in Mauss's words, to "coalesce," which is the second stage—and their movement gained momentum. Laborers, long an exploited segment of the workforce, drew on both traditionally accepted means of dissent, such as pushing for legislation that would improve working conditions, and tactics that were (at the time) "at the edges of political legitimacy," such as striking (Meyer 2000, p. 40).

Today, working conditions have greatly improved for many (though by no means all) blue-collar workers, and unions, once considered marginal or radical, are now seen as part of the establishment. Mauss and others would argue that all successful social movements are eventually incorporated into institutions—that they become "bureaucratized" (stage three). Perry and Pugh assert that "in order to survive, social movements must adapt to their host society or succeed in changing it. When they are successful, they become social institutions in their own right" (1978, p. 265). To take another example, early American colonists rebelling against British rule were part of a social movement, but by the late 1700s, they had ceased to be radicals and had become part of the new nation's government.

A social movement's development can sometimes look a lot like failure; that is, one way or another, the movement will eventually "decline" (stage four). If it succeeds, it is incorporated into the dominant culture; if it fails, it ceases to exist as an active movement—but may have left an indelible mark on its host society nevertheless. Prohibitionists are an excellent case in point. Although those who wished to outlaw alcohol in the United States eventually failed, after the Eighteenth Amendment (Prohibition) was repealed in 1933 their efforts had a huge impact on American culture. There are still hundreds of "dry" municipalities (where alcohol is not sold) in the country, for example, and laws about what time of day (or night) you can purchase alcohol, as well as the legal age (now twenty-one in all states) for consumption.

WHO TAKES PART What kind of individual is most likely to respond to the recruitment efforts of a particular group? Certainly, more people are asked to join a social movement than ever actually end up participating. Studies done on student protesters in the 1960s showed that they "were more likely than their less active colleagues to be politically oriented, socially engaged, and psychologically well adapted" and that "participation in nonconventional politics tend[ed] to be an addition rather than an alternative to conventional means of participation" (Meyer 2000, pp. 37, 42). In other words, despite the assumptions of theorists working in the mid-twentieth century, activists are not disaffected loners but are instead highly engaged individuals seeking to address perceived injustices on several fronts.

Interestingly, the poorest and most oppressed people tend not to participate in social movements. For these individuals, the consequences of participation may be too high, and they may not have the resources necessary to join in (Perry and Pugh 1978; Zirakzadeh 1997). After all, if someone is working three jobs to support her family, it is unlikely that she has the time or energy to carry a sign in a street protest. There have been notable exceptions to this trend. In the American West during the 1960s and '70s, migrant farm workers organized successfully under the leadership of Cesar Chavez. In the 1980s and '90s, thousands of low-income janitors across the United States gained fairer wages and benefits by organizing unions as part of a Justice for Janitors campaign. And more recently, low-wage workers in New York City (in industries such as retail, fast-food, airport, and car washing) have continued to demand fair wages and the right to unionize (Lewis 2013; McGeehan 2015).

It is perhaps impossible to overstate the importance of social movements in any given society; life as we know it has been shaped by the rise and fall of all sorts of such movements. Imagine what the religious makeup of the world would be like if Martin Luther and his followers had not rebelled against the Catholic Church in the early sixteenth century, or what American culture would be like if Martin Luther King Jr. and the civil rights movement hadn't successfully organized. What would world politics have been like if the Nazis hadn't come to power in the 1930s or the Soviet Union hadn't broken up in 1991? The list is endless. Take a moment to consider a few ideas and movements that in today's culture seem radical. Regardless of whether those movements succeed in the traditional sense of the word, it is a pretty safe bet that they will help shape the world for generations to come. And while the progress made by any social movement tends to happen slowly, the possibility for change and a better society for those future generations is the driving force for those who participate.

Promoting and Resisting Change

Because society is constantly changing, new social movements are always on the horizon, and even long-standing ones change their goals, strategies, and organizational forms over

ON THE JOB
Helping Professions: Agents of Social Change

Does it sometimes seem as though there's no possible way you could ever make a contribution to changing the world? You're just one person, after all, and you may not be rich, famous, or all that influential. Right now, your primary concerns probably include graduating and perhaps getting your teaching credential (or social work certification or nursing license) so you can get a job! Also on the "to do" list: find a life partner, start a family, maybe buy a house. But don't think that focusing on your personal goals means that you're totally out of the social change loop. The way you live your life can make a difference all by itself.

Many sociology majors enter what are termed helping professions; these include nursing, counseling, and teaching and can also include careers in the social service, nonprofit, and law enforcement sectors. If you do go into this type of profession, you will find that every individual encounter you have with a client, student, patient, or offender will be an opportunity to make a tiny step toward social change.

As a first-grade teacher, for example, you will be able to introduce students to the joys of reading—a contribution to overcoming illiteracy, even if it involves only twenty kids. As a public health nurse, you urge patients with tuberculosis to finish their courses of antibiotics or you vaccinate children against polio, diphtheria, and measles—and in doing so, you protect the community's health as well as your patients'. When, as a social worker or psychologist, you lead a therapy group for husbands who batter their wives, you have the opportunity to help change the behavior of these men—and to protect their children from continuing a generational cycle of violence. When, as a police officer, you help run your neighborhood's antigang program, you give teenagers alternatives to violent crime, and their choices affect the entire community. When, as a lawyer, you donate your services to a legal clinic that helps undocumented workers gain residency, work permits, and citizenship, you contribute to solving the problems associated with illegal immigration and help change the demographic makeup of your city, state, and country. And even when you volunteer at the adult education center, teaching a computer-training class just once a week, you give your students the opportunity to add a new set of skills to their résumés, find new jobs, and reduce your county's unemployment figures, even if minutely.

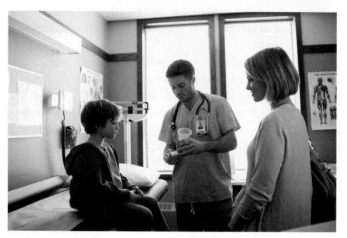

Helping Professions Teachers and nurses engage in small acts of social change in their everyday encounters with students and patients.

Your contributions to social change don't stop here—whom you marry, where you choose to live, and what you teach your children all contribute to the ever-present, ongoing processes of social change. So you don't have to sail away on Greenpeace's *Rainbow Warrior* or camp out in New York's Zuccotti Park to make a difference in the world—you can do so in your everyday life as a member of a helping profession, as a community volunteer, and as a parent.

time. For example, American feminism has taken multiple forms during the past 150 years. Contrast the focus in the early twentieth century on voting rights for women with the sixties era's broader concerns with equal opportunity and "liberation" from the constraints of sexism, and then with the crusade in the 1900s to include previously excluded groups like minority women; and finally with the greater emphasis in the 2000s on international women's rights. Feminism's self-definition, public profile, objectives, and tactics have changed in response to the movement's own successes and failures.

You may be involved yourself in social movements that didn't even exist in your grandparents' or parents' generation (or even ten years ago). Movements like Critical Mass (cyclists who ride through city streets in large groups each month to protest an automobile-centric society), Straight Edge (nonviolent, drug-free, politically aware, and sometimes even vegan punk rockers who reject promiscuous youth cultures), PETA (People for the Ethical Treatment of Animals, which campaigns against meat, leather and furs, animal experimentation, and other forms of cruelty) have taken shape in just the past few decades. You have different opportunities for **activism** because you live in a different world than your parents did—even if you're still in the same town.

Some emerging social movements are actually **regressive**, or reactionary; that is, they explicitly resist certain social changes, working to make sure things stay the same or even move backward to earlier forms of social order. For example, reactionary hate movements like the Council of Conservative Citizens, a white supremacist group based in Texas, want to stop the ethnic and religious integration of American society and create a homogeneous, all-white society. Dylann Roof—the perpetrator of a brutal attack on

a historic black church in Charleston, South Carolina, that claimed the lives of nine parishioners in June 2015—was reportedly inspired by the Council of Conservative Citizens. The American Border Patrol is a group of private citizens who patrol and surveil the U.S.-Mexico border in an attempt to deter and disrupt the passage of illegal immigrants; they are characterized as a hate group that blames immigrants for a slew of contemporary problems in the United States.

Other regressive movements aren't necessarily motivated by prejudice or hatred of diversity. The voluntary simplicity movement urges members to downsize in all areas of their lives—consumption, time at work, hours in front of the TV or computer screen, impact on the environment—in the belief that returning to a simpler approach to life will allow them more personal freedom and will benefit society in the long run by conserving resources and reducing stress. Similarly, the Slow Food movement was founded in 1989 as a radical response to the "McDonaldization" of world cuisines. It now focuses on fresh, local, traditional foods, prepared with care and served in an atmosphere of calm and hospitality—the polar opposite of overprocessed, reheated burgers and fries served in a paper bag and eaten in the car. Slow Food has even influenced the Chipotle restaurant chain, whose corporate philosophy—and menu—tries to align with the values of that movement.

The "rural rebound" that started in the 1990s, in which urban residents moved to non-metropolitan areas in unprecedented numbers, is a type of demographic change that seems,

ACTIVISM any activity intended to bring about social change

REGRESSIVE term describing resistance to particular social changes, efforts to maintain the status quo, or attempts to reestablish an earlier form of social order on its face, to represent a regressive, back-to-basics movement as well (Johnson 1999). But a rural rebound doesn't necessarily mean that people have returned to declining rural industries, such as farming or mining. The rebound occurred at least in part because of **progressive**, or forward-thinking, social changes—new technologies that made rural living less isolating and facilitated new ways of working. The Internet allows people to work from anywhere in the world, which means that high-powered stockbrokers don't need to live in Manhattan and work in a "pit" on Wall Street. They can move to Eagle County, Colorado, or Walworth County, Wisconsin, and enjoy cheaper real estate, less crime, and more natural beauty while still performing their jobs.

Emerging social movements, whether progressive, regressive, or some combination of both, will undoubtedly change the social landscape over time. If your activism is successful—and even if it isn't—then the social world will be a different place by the time your children are your age. What kinds of activism will they be able to engage in?

Technology and Social Change

As we have already seen, revolutionary social change is often the result of a technological development, whether that technological development is the plow, the assembly line, or the microchip. When new inventions spread from one society to another we call this process **cultural diffusion**. Social movements can also arise as a result of the diffusion of technological advancements: labor unions multiplied in the factories of the Industrial Revolution, and today the Internet can bring more people together to work for social change than ever before. As you might imagine, then, sociologists have generated theories that seek to explain the particular influence of technology in creating social change (Kurzweil 1990; Pool 1997). One common characteristic of these theories is an emphasis on **technological determinism**—the idea that technology plays a defining role in shaping society. As one of the earliest proponents of this approach, William Ogburn (1964) described the process of social change as beginning with invention or discovery and proceeding when the invention is spread from one group or society to another. In the remainder of the chapter, we look at the relationship between technology and social change.

PROGRESSIVE term describing efforts to promote forward-thinking social change

CULTURAL DIFFUSION the dissemination of beliefs and practices from one group to another

TECHNOLOGICAL DETERMINISM a theory of social change that assumes changes in technology drive changes in society, rather than vice versa

CULTURAL LAG the time between changes in material culture or technology and the resulting changes in the broader culture's relevant norms, values, meanings, and laws

Is Technology the Answer?

At the beginning of this chapter, we saw how the same medical breakthrough that vanquished smallpox has now made us vulnerable to an epidemic of this virus. It seems that no social change is without its unforeseen, unintentional outcomes, some of which are positive and some of which are not.

This is often especially noticeable in the case of technological advances. We may welcome the invention of a new vaccine, the World Wide Web, in vitro fertilization, or sport utility vehicles (SUVs) and notice only later that they bring unanticipated problems. For example, the web speeds up communication and gives us access to information, goods, services, and people we would never have been able to find otherwise. However, it has also created the opportunity for new kinds of problems: advertisers can now learn about your spending habits by infiltrating your PC with spyware; hackers use similar strategies to shut down entire networks with worms, bots, and viruses; states lose revenues to untaxed online purchases; and travel agencies struggle to stay in business as individuals use the Internet to make their own plane and hotel reservations, or bypass hotels altogether and use Airbnb to find lodging. Similarly, in vitro fertilization has opened up a Pandora's box of ethical and moral questions about intervening in the natural process of conception. And SUVs, besides guzzling gasoline (a nonrenewable resource), are more likely than other cars to kill or injure people when involved in an accident.

As a society, how do we respond to technological developments that seem to solve one set of problems (such as disease, infertility, communication, and transportation) while creating new ones? Often we must play "catch-up," scrambling to fix a problem once it manifests itself, rather than being able to plan ahead and prevent it in the first place. **Cultural lag** is the term sociologists use to describe this disconnect between a changing social condition and cultural adjustment to that change. Material culture (such as the technologies just discussed) often changes faster than nonmaterial culture (such as beliefs and laws), and we struggle to create new values and norms that correspond with new technologies.

DATA WORKSHOP

Analyzing Media and Pop Culture

The "Unplug" Experiment

Zen sociologist Bernard McGrane (1994; McGrane and Gunderson 2010) is noted for having designed a series of experiments that are widely used in teaching sociology

students. This includes the "Doing Nothing" Data Workshop featured in Chapter 1. The "Un-TV" experiment is another of his most popular, in which he asks students to "watch" TV without turning it on. While these experiments may appear simple at first, the ideas they highlight are very sophisticated. Students are required to use "beginner's mind" (setting aside all their prior judgments, opinions, and even experiences) to achieve an unusual level of consciousness about a particular aspect of their everyday lives.

This Data Workshop is inspired by the "Un-TV" experiment but lets you decide which form of media technology you'd like to unplug from. It should be something that regularly takes up your time and attention and that might actually be hard for you to give up. For most people, the most ubiquitous device in their world is a cell phone, but you could also choose a computer, music player, or a tablet, or some other media format you use a lot, like cable TV, radio, or video games. Think about how long you can go without using this technology or device on a typical day (or longer). If you're like many people, even a few hours away from your cell phone or computer screen might seem like a very long time.

How are you going to feel when you can't text message, watch videos on YouTube, post pictures on Instagram, or check your newsfeed on Facebook? We take these technologies for granted and cannot imagine our lives without them—but maybe life would be better! What are some of the benefits of unplugging? When we detach from our devices we also get to disconnect from the overstimulation that comes from living in a media-saturated world. Can just a few hours of being unplugged reduce anxiety, dependency, fatigue, and information overload? Or does unplugging make you feel even more stressed out? That's what this experiment is designed to reveal. A great part of the difficulty of this experiment is actually getting yourself to do it. But even more so, it can be a challenge to confront your own habits and dependencies on a deep level. The "Unplug" experiment asks you to do just that.

In this Data Workshop, you will be doing participant observation research while also preparing to write an autoethnography of your experience. Return to the section in Chapter 2 for a review of these research methods. You will be writing detailed field notes of what you observe during the experiment. Remember that you are attempting to use beginner's mind. Don't try to figure out what will happen before you begin. Just "see what you can see." The idea is for you to notice the way the technology permeates your everyday life and what happens when you try to resist using it. Follow the numbered prompts below.

1. Choose a media technology for the experiment. This should be something you use regularly but that you can safely turn off for a period of time. Why did you choose this technology, and how does it represent an interesting experiment?
2. Determine how long you will go without this technology; it could be for an hour, an afternoon, or three days, depending on how often you use it. What's important is to create an impact by turning it off. Is the time period you determined adequate in length to produce meaningful results?
3. Go about your daily business while you refrain from using your chosen technology during the designated period. Don't become distracted. Keep a part of your focus on what's happening with the experiment and check in on yourself frequently. Take field notes at points during the research process or immediately upon completing it.
4. What happens as the experiment unfolds? Are you having any difficulties? When and why? What are your thoughts, feelings, and sensations? How attentive are you to the details of your reactions?
5. What happens as time progresses? How is it different the further or closer you are to the end of the allotted time for the experiment? Are you relieved to turn on your device again? Or were there some unexpected benefits of turning it off? What do you see now about using the technology that you did not notice before? Does it feel any different to resume using the technology after having conducted the experiment?

There are two options for completing this Data Workshop:

PREP-PAIR-SHARE Complete your observations, and prepare some field notes about the experiment that you can refer to in class. Get together with one or more students. What devices or technologies did you unplug from? Who had more or less difficulty with the experiment? Compare your insights and experiences with each other.

DO-IT-YOURSELF Complete the experiment and discuss your results. Write a three- to four-page paper analyzing your experience and insights. Make sure to attach your field notes.

Technology in the Global Village

Over the years, social thinkers have expressed concerns about the effects of new technology. Some believed that electronic media would prove to be a dangerous, divisive, and degrading

While change may be inevitable, perhaps we can determine the direction, elements, and pace of that change. That is exactly what the current leaders of Bhutan are attempting to do. They provide an example of how to hold on to tradition, maintain a unique cultural identity, and exercise control over the pace of social change.

Bhutan is a tiny country of fewer than 1 million people, precariously perched at the "roof of the world" in the Himalayan Mountains. Despite its remote location between two of the world's most powerful and populous nations—China to the north and India to the south—Bhutan has remained a sovereign, independent nation throughout its history. In this ancient land, it seems almost as if time has stood still. It is only in the past few decades that Bhutan has emerged from its almost total isolation and taken some cautious steps into the postmodern era.

Bhutan is a predominantly Buddhist country that until recently had been ruled by a king who had four wives (who were all sisters!) along with a cadre of mostly Western-educated officials. In 2008, at the behest of its enlightened monarch, Bhutan held its first democratic elections. Despite that political change, it may still be the only country in the world where the government's number-one concern is something it calls "Gross National Happiness": a blend of economic development and cultural richness; food, clothing, and shelter; health care and education; spiritual values; and individual contentment.

The government hopes to achieve Gross National Happiness by carefully identifying and adopting what the West is doing right while also rejecting its cynicism and consumerism. For example, the Bhutanese do not allow exploitation of their natural resources. There is no lumber industry in their millions of acres of lush forests, which instead have been designated national parks. Although Mt. Everest is nearby in Nepal, mountain climbers are forbidden to ascend the peaks of Bhutan's mountains. The Bhutanese have, however, taken advantage of one natural resource originating in the snowcap—immense, fast-flowing rivers that generate hydroelectric power, which is then exported to neighboring countries. Tourism to Bhutan could also have become a lucrative trade. But here, too, the government has limited the number of visitors who can enter the country each year.

For the most part, Bhutan has managed to avoid being overwhelmed by the forces of globalization and cultural leveling. While some Bhutanese enjoy basic modern conveniences like cell phone service and wireless Internet, in the capital city of Thimphu there are still no chain stores—no Starbucks, Walmarts, or Burger Kings. Especially remarkable is that the Bhutanese have so far been able to defend themselves against what might be the most powerful global intruder of all—television. For many years Bhutan was the only country in the world to ban TV. It was not until 2006 that television service was widely available across the country. Even so, programming was strictly limited. Because networks like MTV and CNN were also sneaking in via satellite, the government created its own national television network, the Bhutan Broadcasting Service (BBS), to provide a counterbalance to Western programs (Schell 2002).

At first, the BBS produced only a daily half-hour newscast in both English and the native language of Dzongkha, but soon they added documentaries and entertainment shows. Most of the BBS's programming is geared toward the distinct tastes and interests of the Bhutanese audience, while still being aligned with the guiding principles of their country. The force in modern culture. Marshall McLuhan (1964), a Canadian communications researcher who also subscribed to the notion of technological determinism, expressed a degree of optimism that amounted to a utopian vision of what the various media could do for human society. McLuhan was particularly interested in television, which in the early 1960s was just then infiltrating households in North America. He imagined that television could re-create a sense of intimate community by linking people in disparate locations around the world through its broadcasts. Just as tribe members had once gathered to share stories around the light of a campfire, people would now sit in the glow of their TV screens, making television a kind of "virtual campfire" and those watching together members of a **virtual community**. McLuhan coined the term **global village** to capture that notion. He did not live to see the advent of the Internet a few decades later, but he certainly understood the potential for media to extend the human senses and join us to one another in unprecedented ways.

The intervening years have not totally confirmed McLuhan's utopian vision. New technologies have in fact had a

VIRTUAL COMMUNITY a community of people linked by their consumption of the same digital media

GLOBAL VILLAGE Marshall McLuhan's term describing the way that new communication technologies override barriers of space and time, joining together people all over the globe

Bhutanese broadcasters see audience members not as primarily consumers but as citizens in need of knowledge that can help them in their pursuit of Gross National Happiness.

Still, some worry about the homogenizing effects of television, especially for a new generation of children growing up with it. The arrival of the Internet has compounded such problems, and may be much harder to withstand. While the Bhutanese can now access BBS programming on YouTube, it is the plethora of media from outside their own borders that may pose the greatest threat to their way of life.

It is important not to romanticize life in Bhutan or even the pursuit of Gross National Happiness. Although the country is now a democracy, it still endures high rates of infant mortality, poverty, and illiteracy. Life expectancies are low, and women's opportunities are limited. Certain types of social change would seem to be necessary and inevitable. However, as they prepare for change, Bhutanese leaders remain idealistic about the ability of their traditional culture to resist Western values and to avoid the social problems that are so commonplace in the other parts of the world.

Gross National Happiness Global networks like MTV and CNN that cross borders via satellite concern Bhutanese leaders who see their children emulating foreign television programs. To counterbalance Western influence, the government created a national television network, the Bhutan Broadcasting Service (BBS).

profound impact on society, but in what ways and whether this impact has been positive or negative are still to be determined. What we do know is that media technology has become a global reality. Social scientists use the term **globalization** to refer to social structures and institutions such as politics and commerce that must now be conceived on a global rather than national scale. We can no longer remain isolated from social and political forces that reverberate around the world. There are now billions of people who have access to television and the Internet. More than 1 billion were estimated to have watched the first walk on the moon in 1969. Since then, other live events such as the funerals of Princess Diana in 1997 and Michael Jackson in 2009, as well as the catastrophic attacks of 9/11 in 2001 or the 2006 tsunami in Indonesia and 2011 nuclear disaster in Japan, have attracted even larger global audiences. These are among the most significant images burned into our collective minds. But would it be a surprise to know that some of the most watched broadcasts of all time are international sporting events like the FIFA World Cup, the Tour de France, and the Olympics? No, the SuperBowl does not top the list (Clark 2014).

While news and sports attract the largest audiences, entertainment media are not far behind. And it's television produced in the West that dominates the global market. The

GLOBALIZATION the increasing connections between economic, social, and political systems all over the globe

world's most valuable television networks, including CNN, MTV, Disney, FOX, and ESPN, all belong to U.S. media conglomerates. These networks produce programs that are aired to audiences in hundreds of other countries. For example, the largest television networks belong to MTV and CNN, which broadcast to 164 and 212 countries, respectively. In 2014, *NCIS (Naval Criminal Investigative Service)* was named the most popular dramatic television series in the world based on viewing surveys of sixty-five countries. The show, also the most popular drama in the United States, regularly garnered over 50 million viewers an episode. *Modern Family* was the number-one comedy in the world, and *The Bold and the Beautiful* topped the list of global soap operas for the ninth time (Kissel 2014). Very few other countries have the infrastructure or budgets to produce similar shows with the same technical quality. This makes it hard to compete with the most popular programs that set world tastes.

With this proliferation of Western media, we also find that the contents tend to reflect Western values. Communication researchers often talk about the "politics of information flow," and we can see that the message, or ideology, embedded in TV shows or films tends to flow from industrialized countries like the United States to the rest of the world (Schiller 1976, 1992, 1996; Tomlinson 1991). Americans brought up on the principle of a free press and living in a media-saturated society are not typically alarmed by the proliferation of our popular culture to other parts of the globe. In fact, we might assume that ours is the voice of freedom and democracy, a force for positive change in places marked by censorship and disinformation (Rothkop 1997). But others question this flood of ideas, especially ideas about individualism and consumerism, coming from the West.

And Western ideas can cross cultural boundaries all too easily: it is almost impossible to block the reception of satellite and Internet communications to audiences anywhere in the world. This sets up a new kind of tension in the struggle for power and influence. It is now possible for a country to be "occupied" by an invisible invader that arrives through the airwaves or by satellite and wireless networks. A country can be conquered by ideas rather than by force, a phenomenon known as **cultural imperialism**. Some consider the Western media's powerful influence as a kind of cultural domination. The result of this domination is often **cultural leveling**, a homogenizing process whereby societies lose their particular uniqueness as they all start to resemble one another.

As media technology makes possible a multiplicity of voices, Westerners have also been influenced by Eastern ideas (witness the popularity of yoga). Yet Western values continue to dominate and to shape the "village" that is the global village. They sometimes conflict with the values of other nations, some of which have tried to resist the Western media stranglehold and maintain their own distinctive cultural identity (see the case of Bhutan in this chapter's Global Perspective box). Challenges persist as to whether meaningful and egalitarian communication on a global level can really take place (Gozzi 1996; Fortner and Fackler 2011). Perhaps as technology advances, cultural distinctions can be maintained and divisions eliminated, thus approaching McLuhan's vision of a world united.

Living in a Postmodern World

Today, the Digital Age is but a few decades old, and already most of you probably cannot remember a time when you did not have a remote control, game controller, mouse, or cell phone in hand. And you cannot imagine living without them. It is safe to assume that we will see many more scientific and technological advancements in the near future. In particular, media technologies are likely to become cheaper, lighter and easier to use, faster, more flexible, interactive, and capable of carrying more information. Despite what some call the "digital divide" (the uneven distribution of technology among different groups of people), technologies will play an increasingly important role in almost every aspect of our lives, and technological literacy will be a necessary skill for anyone participating in contemporary society.

Is all progress good? Is every technological advance beneficial? These questions arise because our society is in the midst of a major transformation: we are moving from a modern

Cultural Diffusion *NCIS*, the most popular dramatic TV series in the world, acts as a medium for spreading American culture and ideas to other countries.

Have you ever wanted your own personal robot that could do your laundry or drive you safely home from a party? Well, you're about to get your wish. In fact, it's already here: meet the Internet of Things.

The Internet of Things (IoT) was a concept coined by British technology pioneer Kevin Ashton to describe a network of advanced connectivity between technological devices that allows for the transmission of data (Gabbai 2015). The Internet of Things describes a system in which devices, such as smartphones and computers, are able to "talk" to each other and exchange information from one device to another. It's been happening for about a decade but is just now gaining speed. There are already way more "things" connected to the Internet than there are people in the world. According to Cisco's Internet Business Solutions Group (IBSG), approximately 25 billion devices were connected to the Internet in 2015, and an estimated 50 billion will be connected by 2020 (Cisco 2011).

So how does it work? The IoT allows machine-to-machine, or M2M, communication, in which all devices utilize "smart" technology such as cloud computing and data-gathering sensors to usher in a new age of automation (Burrus 2014). You might already be enjoying some of the benefits. Cloud-based applications, such as Google Drive, Apple's iCloud, and Microsoft's One Drive, are making it possible for individuals to store, access, and send data from one electronic device to another, creating endless possibilities for the Internet of Things. So now your term paper is safe on the cloud, no excuses.

It's also driving the design of consumer goods and services. This sort of technology is being used in a variety of ways, from smart home thermostats that auto-adjust to the user's preferred temperature to smart washer and dryer machines that communicate with each other to transmit information regarding the wash load and appropriate dry cycle (Farrell 2014). The range and scope of the IoT are varied and virtually limitless as developers have found more and more ways to utilize smart technology that relies on inter-device communication. From self-driving cars that communicate with GPS systems for navigation and are equipped with external sensors to assess driving hazards and weather conditions, to "smart homes" that have all appliances, electronics, and technological devices synced with one another, the possibilities of the IoT are expansive (Gabbai 2015; Kastrenakes 2015).

In a 2014 study, researchers found an overall shift in consumer perception toward connected technology and an increased willingness to adopt IoT technology. While this technology is still relatively new (or unknown) to many consumers, 45 percent said they planned to purchase in-home connected technology within the next five years, with 92 percent planning to purchase a smart home product by 2019 (Acquity Group 2014). How long before your smartphone steers you toward a friend walking nearby (or away from an "ex"), or the office senses your car is nearby and turns on your workstation. If it's not happening already, it's coming soon.

The IoT has expanded beyond the realms of high-tech toys to include many more avenues for smart technology to address an ever-increasing host of problems within the modern world. For example, scientists have for years been warning us about the catastrophic consequences of the world's rapidly shrinking honeybee population on modern agriculture and food production. Because honeybees are responsible for the pollination of plants, their decline threatens to trigger a precipitous drop in food production at a time when the world's population is steadily growing. Recently, researchers have begun exploring how the IoT could be harnessed to help save the bees. IoT technology has been developed that utilizes data-transmitting sensors installed within beehives to regulate temperature and, in turn, help exterminate a species of mites that poses a serious threat to honeybee populations (Tynan 2015).

The development of smart technology to create more efficient and useful tools for consumers while also solving a range of modern problems in innovative ways has widened the scope of the IoT and changed the way in which people engage with technology in their everyday lives. By the time you read this, many more things will have been added to the Internet of Things, and the world will be a new place because of it.

---

society to a postmodern society. **Modernity** refers to the social conditions and attitudes characteristic of industrialized societies, which include the decline of traditional community, an increase in individual autonomy and diversity of beliefs, and a strong belief in the ability of science and technology to improve our quality of life (Berger 1977). In many ways, this last promise of modernity has in fact been fulfilled. Since the Industrial Revolution, rates of infant mortality have declined, life expectancies have increased, and a number of common diseases have been cured or controlled. However, along with these advances have come increases in income

MODERNITY a term that characterizes industrialized societies, including the decline of tradition, an increase in individualism, and a belief in progress, technology, and science

Wearable Technology Google Glass is a wearable computer that displays information and connects with the Internet— mostly by voice commands.

inequality, violent crime, and child poverty (Miringoff and Miringoff 1999). So while modern society has its benefits, there are also problems, which is where the postmodern critique begins.

Postmodernity refers to the social conditions and attitudes characteristic of postindustrialized societies, which include a focus on ideas and cultural debates rather than material things and a questioning of the achievements of science and technology. According to postmodern thought, the progress promised by modernity has failed to solve important social problems (such as income inequality), and modern institutions (families, schools, workplaces, governments) are implicated in this failure. Although change is forecast in all these areas, there is no agreed-upon blueprint for what that change might look like.

The Industrial Revolution transformed Western society from traditional to modern. The Information Revolution is transforming Western society from modern to postmodern. While we are not yet certain what this particular transformation will mean in our everyday lives, we can be sure that it will not be the final transformation our society will undergo. Society will continue to be shaped by technology, not only at the macro level of culture and social institutions but also at the micro level of groups and individuals. Technology will change what the world looks like as well as how we perceive it. It will greatly extend our abilities to obtain information and will influence the way we use it. We will become more comfortable with multitasking; navigating through nonlinear hyperspace; dealing with symbols, images, and sound as well as text; moving at a rapid pace; coping with a fractured sense of self; socializing online; experimenting with game strategies; and accepting the unpredictable.

Should we call such developments progress? What will we gain, and what do we stand to lose? Your parents and grandparents will not understand the postmodern, digital era in the same way that you do. So it is you who will be engineering the terms of the future. Perhaps now would be a good time to ask yourself what you can do as part of this new social revolution. Can you risk just sitting back and watching what will happen? Or are you willing to take what you have learned and go out and make a difference? We hope this chapter has inspired you to take an active role in creating whatever positive social change you envision.

CLOSING COMMENTS

Throughout this text, we have focused on the sociological features of everyday life, including the role of the media and popular culture in society. The media are often the place where new developments, trends, and social changes first become visible. And our everyday lives are the places where we experience both social constraints and social change at the most fundamental level. You now have the tools necessary to understand these phenomena, because you now possess the sociological perspective.

The sociological perspective sometimes highlights distressing facts—the persistence of poverty and prejudice, for example, or the realities of crime. But it allows for optimism as well. This is because the intersection of biography and history goes both ways: society shapes individual lives, but individuals influence their society as well. Any disconcerting realizations you may have had during the course of this semester should be tempered by your knowledge that change is possible, and that *you* are its primary source.

Ultimately, this should be the most relevant element of your education in sociology. Years from now, no one will care whether you remember the details of labeling theory or the difference between organic and mechanical solidarity. What will continue to matter is your sense of investment in your society—your commitment to your family, your workplace, your community, and your world. Your mindful involvement in all of these areas can make each of them better places— to raise children, to live, to work, to collaborate with others. Armed with the sociological perspective, you now have a new set of responsibilities: to investigate and participate in your social world, both locally and globally. We hope you do so with optimism and persistence, and in partnership with others.

Everything You Need to Know about Social Change

"" While society shapes the individual, the individual can shape society: you have the power to bring about social change.""

THEORIES OF SOCIAL CHANGE

* **Structural functionalism:** sometimes social change is necessary to maintain equilibrium and order in society

* **Conflict theory:** social change is the inevitable result of social inequality and conflict between groups over power and resources

* **Symbolic interactionism:** social change involves changes in the meanings of things as well as changes in laws, culture, and social behavior

REVIEW

1. People born even one generation apart can have quite different life experiences because of ongoing social and technological changes. List at least three technologies that did not exist when your parents were your age. What social changes have these technologies generated?

2. "Cultural lag" is the term sociologists use for the period of time when norms, values, and laws are not yet up to date with new technology because material culture changes faster than nonmaterial culture. Describe at least one change in material culture for which there is still some degree of cultural lag. What evidence suggests that we haven't developed adequate norms yet?

Changing Social Attitudes in the United States

Same-Sex Marriage (Percentage who Favor)

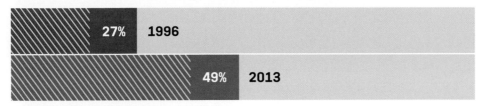

27% 1996

49% 2013

Legalized Marijuana (Percentage who Support)

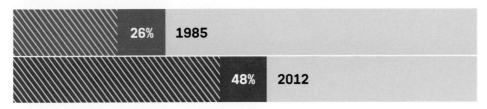

26% 1985

48% 2012

Black President (Percentage who Would Vote for)

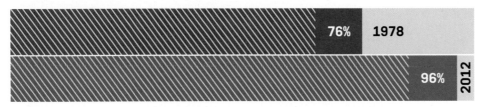

76% 1978

96% 2012

Interracial Marriage (Percentage who Approve)

4% 1958

86% 2011

Female President (Percentage who Would Vote for)

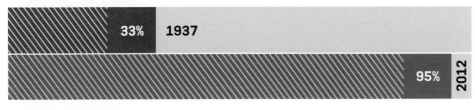

33% 1937

95% 2012

SOURCE: Parlapiano 2013.

EXPLORE

Life after Your Sociology Class

What happens when your sociology class ends? Visit the Everyday Sociology Blog for a sociology professor's suggestions on how to continue exploring the sociological imagination.

http://wwnPag.es/trw416

Glossary

absolute deprivation an objective measure of poverty, defined by the inability to meet minimal standards for food, shelter, clothing, or health care

access the process by which an ethnographer gains entry to a field setting

achieved status a status earned through individual effort or imposed by others

action research a type of research aimed at creating social change, in which the researcher works closely with members of a community who participate in the research process and collaborate toward the goal of social change

active audiences a term used to characterize audience members as active participants in "reading" or constructing the meaning of the media they consume

activism any activity intended to bring about social change

acute diseases diseases that have a sudden onset, may be briefly incapacitating, and are either curable or fatal

adoption the legal process of acquiring parental responsibilities for a child other than one's biological offspring

agency the ability of the individual to act freely and independently

agenda-setting theory theory that the media can set the public agenda by selecting certain news stories and excluding others, thus influencing what audiences think about

agents of socialization social groups, institutions, and individuals (especially the family, schools, peers, and the mass media) that provide structured situations in which socialization takes place

aggregates collections of people who share a physical location but do not have lasting social relations

Agricultural Revolution the social and economic changes, including population increases, that followed from the domestication of plants and animals and the gradually increasing efficiency of food production

alienation decreasing importance of social ties and community and the corresponding increase in impersonal associations and instrumental logic; also, according to Marx, the sense of dissatisfaction the modern worker feels as a result of producing goods that are owned and controlled by someone else

alternative medicine a group of medical treatments, practices, and products that are used instead of conventional Western medicine

altruism unselfish concern for the well-being of others and helping behaviors performed without self-interested motivation

anomie "normlessness"; term used to describe the alienation and loss of purpose that result from weaker social bonds and an increased pace of change

anthropocentric literally "human centered"; the idea that needs and desires of human beings should take priority over concerns about other species or the natural environment

anti-Malthusians contemporary demographers who believe Malthus's basic prediction was faulty and worry instead that worldwide population may shrink in the future

antimiscegenation the prohibition of interracial marriage, cohabitation, or sexual interaction

antithesis the opposition to the existing arrangements in a dialectical model

antitrust legislation laws designed to maintain competition in the marketplace by prohibiting monopolies, price fixing, or other forms of collusion among businesses

apartheid the system of segregation of racial and ethnic groups that was legal in South Africa between 1948 and 1991

applied research gathering knowledge that can be used to create social change

ascribed status a status that is inborn; usually difficult or impossible to change

asexuality the lack of sexual attraction of any kind; no interest in or desire for sex

assimilation a pattern of relations between ethnic or racial groups in which the minority group is absorbed into the mainstream or dominant group, making society more homogenous

authoritarianism system of government by and for a small number of elites that does not include representation of ordinary citizens

authority the legitimate right to wield power

autoethnography a form of participant observation where the feelings and actions of the researcher become a focal point of the ethnographic study

backstage the places in which we rehearse and prepare for our performances

basic research the search for knowledge without any agenda or practical goal in mind

beginner's mind approaching the world without preconceptions in order to see things in a new way

belief a proposition or idea held on the basis of faith

bias an opinion held by the researcher that might affect the research or analysis

binary a system of classification with only two distinct and opposite categories

biodiversity the variety of species of plants and animals existing at any given time

bioethics the study of controversial moral or ethical issues related to scientific and medical advancements

biosphere the parts of the earth that can support life

bisexuality sexual attraction toward members of both genders

blue collar a description characterizing skilled and semi-skilled workers who perform manual labor or work in service or clerical jobs

bourgeoisie owners; the class of modern capitalists who own the means of production and employ wage laborers

bureaucracies secondary groups designed to perform tasks efficiently, characterized by specialization, technical competence, hierarchy, written rules, impersonality, and formal written communication

bystander effect or **diffusion of responsibility** the social dynamic wherein the more people who are present in a moment of crisis, the less likely any one of them is to take action

capital punishment the death penalty

capitalism an economic system based on the laws of free market competition, privatization of the means of production, and production for profit

caste system a form of social stratification in which status is determined by one's family history and background and cannot be changed

category people who share one or more attributes but who lack a sense of common identity or belonging

causation a relationship between variables in which a change in one directly produces a change in the other

charismatic authority authority based in the perception of remarkable personal qualities in a leader

charter schools public schools run by private entities to give parents greater control over their children's education

Chicago School a type of sociology practiced at the University of Chicago in the 1920s and 1930s that centered on urban settings and field research methods

chronic diseases diseases that develop over a longer period of time and may not be detected until symptoms occur later in their progression

cisgender term used when gender identity and/or expression aligns with the sex assigned at birth

cisgenderism belief in the superiority of cisgender persons and identities

civil inattention an unspoken rule governing interactions in public places, whereby individuals briefly notice others before ignoring them

civil society those organizations, institutions, and interactions outside government, family, and work that promote social bonds and the smooth functioning of society

civil unions proposed as an alternative to gay marriage; a form of legally recognized commitment that provides gay couples some of the benefits and protections of marriage

class consciousness the recognition of social inequality on the part of the oppressed, leading to revolutionary action

closed-ended question a question asked of a respondent that imposes a limit on the possible responses

closed system a social system with very little opportunity to move from one class to another

code of ethics ethical guidelines for researchers to consult as they design a project

coercive power power that is backed by the threat of force

cohabitation living together as a romantic couple without being married

collective behavior behavior that follows from the formation of a group or crowd of people who take action together toward a shared goal

collective conscience the shared morals and beliefs that are common to a group and that foster social solidarity

collective effervescence an intense energy in shared events where people feel swept up in something larger than themselves

color-blind racism an ideology that removes race as an explanation for any form of unequal treatment

coming out to openly declare one's true identity to those who might not be aware of it; short for "coming out of the closet," a phrase used to describe how gays and lesbians have felt compelled to keep their sexual orientation secret

commodification the process by which it becomes possible to buy and sell a particular good or service

communism a system of government that eliminates private property; the most extreme form of socialism, because all citizens work for the government and there are no class distinctions

communitarianism a political and moral philosophy focused on strengthening civil society and communal bonds

community a group of people living in the same local area who share a sense of participation, belonging, and fellowship

community college two-year institution that provides students with general education and facilitates transfer to a four-year university

community supported agriculture (CSA) a model of food production and distribution in which small farmers recruit subscribers to purchase shares of the farm's harvest; subscribers or shareholders pay at the beginning of the year, and then receive regular deliveries of the farm's produce throughout the growing and harvest seasons

comparative historical research research that uses existing sources to study relationships among elements of society in various regions and time periods

complementary medicine a group of medical treatments, practices, and products that can be used in conjunction with conventional Western medicine

concentration the process by which the number of companies producing and distributing a particular commodity decreases, often through mergers and conglomeration

confidentiality the assurance that no one other than the researcher will know the identity of a respondent

conflict generated by the competition between different class groups for scarce resources and the source of all social change, according to Karl Marx

conflict theory a paradigm that sees social conflict as the basis of society and social change and that emphasizes a materialist view of society, a critical view of the status quo, and a dynamic model of historical change

conglomeration the process by which a single corporation acquires ownership of a variety of otherwise unrelated businesses

conservation era earliest stage of the environmental movement, which focused on the preservation of "wilderness" areas

constructionists those who believe that notions of gender are socially determined, such that a dichotomous system is just one possibility among many

consumption the utilization of goods and services, either for personal use or in manufacturing

contagion theory one of the earliest theories of collective action; suggests that individuals who join a crowd can become "infected" by a mob mentality and lose the ability to reason

content analysis a method in which researchers identify and study specific variables or themes that appear in a text, image, or media message

contingent workforce those who work in positions that are temporary or freelance or who work as independent contractors

control in an experiment, the process of regulating all factors except for the independent variable

control group the members of a test group who are allowed to continue without intervention so that they can be compared with the experimental group

conversation analysis a sociological approach that looks at how we create meaning in naturally occurring conversation, often by taping conversations and examining their transcripts

cooling the mark out behaviors that help others to save face or avoid embarrassment, often referred to as civility or tact

copresence face-to-face interaction or being in the presence of others

correlation a relationship between variables in which they change together, and may or may not be causal

counterculture a group within society that openly rejects or actively opposes society's values and norms

crime a violation of a norm that has been codified into law

criminal justice system a collection of social institutions, such as legislatures, police, courts, and prisons, that create and enforce laws

critical theory a contemporary form of conflict theory that criticizes many different systems and ideologies of domination and oppression

crowd a temporary gathering of people in a public place; members might interact but do not identify with each other and will not remain in contact

cultural appropriation the adoption of cultural elements belonging to an oppressed group by members of the dominant group, without permission and often for the dominant group's gain

cultural assimilation the process by which racial or ethnic groups are absorbed into the dominant group by adopting the dominant group's culture

cultural capital the tastes, habits, expectations, skills, knowledge, and other cultural assets that help us gain advantages in society

cultural competence the concept of acknowledging and incorporating a patient's cultural background as part of the treatment process; the recognition that patients' beliefs shape their approach to health care

cultural diffusion the dissemination of material and symbolic culture (tools and technology, beliefs and behavior) from one group to another

cultural imperialism the imposition of one culture's beliefs and practices on another culture through media and consumer products rather than by military force

cultural lag the time between changes in material culture or technology and the resulting changes in the broader culture's relevant norms, values, meanings, and laws

cultural leveling the process by which cultures that were once unique and distinct become increasingly similar

cultural relativism the principle of understanding other cultures on their own terms, rather than judging or evaluating according to one's own culture

culture the entire way of life of a group of people (including both material and symbolic elements) that acts as a lens through which one views the world and that is passed from one generation to the next

culture of poverty entrenched attitudes that can develop among poor communities and lead the poor to accept their fate rather than attempt to improve their lot

culture shock a sense of disorientation that occurs when entering a radically new social or cultural environment

culture wars clashes within mainstream society over the values and norms that should be upheld

curative or crisis medicine type of health care that treats the disease or condition once it has manifested

custody the physical and legal responsibility of caring for children; assigned by a court for divorced or unmarried parents

cyberbullying the use of electronic media (web pages, social networking sites, e-mail, Twitter, cell phones) to tease, harass, threaten, or humiliate someone

cycle of violence a common behavior pattern in abusive relationships; the cycle begins happily, then the relationship grows tense, and the tension explodes in abuse, followed by a period of contrition that allows the cycle to repeat

deception the extent to which the participants in a research project are unaware of the project or its goals

deconstruction a type of critical postmodern analysis that involves taking apart or disassembling old ways of thinking

definition of the situation an agreement with others about "what is going on" in a given circumstance; this consensus allows us to coordinate our actions with others and realize goals.

democracy a political system in which all citizens have the right to participate

demographic free fall rapid decrease in birth rates to below replacement levels; results in a shrinking population, mostly in industrialized nations

demographic transition a theory about change over time from high birth and death rates to low birth and death rates, resulting in a stabilized population

demography study of the size, composition, distribution, and changes in human population

dependent variable the factor that is changed (or not) by the independent variable

deprivation amplification when our individual disease risks (based on heredity and physiology) are amplified by social factors

deregulation reduction or removal of government controls from an industry to allow for a free and efficient marketplace

deterrence an approach to punishment that relies on the threat of harsh penalties to discourage people from committing crimes

deviance a behavior, trait, belief, or other characteristic that violates a norm and causes a negative reaction

deviance avowal process by which an individual self-identifies as deviant and initiates her own labeling process

dialectical model Karl Marx's model of historical change, whereby two extreme positions come into conflict and create some new outcome

differential association theory Edwin Sutherland's hypothesis that we learn to be deviant through our associations with deviant peers

digital divide the unequal access to computer and Internet technology, both globally and within the United States

discrimination unequal treatment of individuals based on their membership in a social group; usually motivated by prejudice

disenchantment the rationalization of modern society

disenfranchised stripped of voting rights, either temporarily or permanently

disenfranchisement the removal of the rights of citizenship through economic, political, or legal means

domestic abuse any physical, verbal, financial, sexual, or psychological behaviors abusers use to gain and maintain power over their victims

dominant culture the values, norms, and practices of the group within society that is most powerful (in terms of wealth, prestige, status, influence, etc.)

double-barreled questions questions that attempt to get at multiple issues at once, and so tend to receive incomplete or confusing answers

double-consciousness W.E.B. DuBois's term for the divided identity experienced by blacks in the United States

dramaturgy an approach pioneered by Erving Goffman in which social life is analyzed in terms of its similarities to theatrical performance

dual enrollment programs that allow high school students to simultaneously enroll in college classes, earning credit for both high school and college degrees

dual nature of the self the idea that we experience the self as both subject and object, the "I" and the "me"

dyad a two-person social group

dysfunction a disturbance to or undesirable consequence of some aspect of the social system

dystopia opposite of a utopia; a world where social problems are magnified and the quality of life is extremely low

early college high schools institutions in which students earn a high school diploma and two years of credit toward a bachelor's degree

Earth Day an annual event conceived of by environmental activist and former senator Gaylord Nelson to encourage support for and increase awareness of environmental concerns; first celebrated on March 22, 1970

ecological footprint an estimation of the land and water area required to produce all the goods an individual consumes and to assimilate all the wastes she generates

ecoterrorism use of violent or criminal methods to protect the environment, often in high-profile, publicity-generating ways

ecotourism foreign travel with the goal of minimizing the environmental consequences of tourism as well as its possible negative effects on local cultures and economies, typically involving people from highly industrialized nations traveling to less-developed countries

edge cities centers of employment and commerce that began as suburban commuter communities

education the process by which a society transmits its knowledge, values, and expectations to its members so they can function effectively

embodied identity those elements of identity that are generated through others' perceptions of our physical traits

embodied status a status generated by physical characteristics

emergent norm theory a theory of collective behavior that assumes individual members of a crowd make their own decisions about behavior and that norms are created through others' acceptance or rejection of these behaviors

emigration leaving one country to live permanently in another

emotion work (emotional labor) the process of evoking, suppressing, or otherwise managing feelings to create a publicly observable display of emotion

empirical based on scientific experimentation or observation

encoding/decoding model a theory on media that combines models that privilege the media producer and models that view the audience as the primary source of meaning; this theory recognizes that media texts are created to deliver specific messages and that individuals actively interpret them

endogamy marriage to someone within one's social group

environment in sociology, the natural world, the human-made environment, and the interaction between the two

environmental justice a movement that aims to remedy environmental inequities such as threats to public health and the unequal treatment of certain communities with regard to ecological concerns

environmental movement a social movement organized around concerns about the relationship between humans and the environment

Environmental Protection Agency (EPA) a U.S. government agency established in 1969 to protect public health and the environment through policies and enforcement

environmental racism any environmental policy or practice that negatively affects individuals, groups, or communities because of their race or ethnicity

environmental sociology the study of the interaction between society and the natural environment, including the social causes and consequences of environmental problems

epidemic occurs when a significantly higher number of cases of a particular disease occur during a particular time period than might otherwise be expected

epidemiology the study of disease patterns to understand the cause of illnesses, how they are spread, and what interventions to take

essentialists those who believe gender roles have a genetic or biological origin and therefore cannot be changed

ethnicity a socially defined category based on common language, religion, nationality, history, or another cultural factor

ethnocentrism the principle of using one's own culture as a means or standard by which to evaluate another group or individual, leading to the view that cultures other than one's own are abnormal or inferior

ethnography a naturalistic method based on studying people in their own environment in order to understand the meanings they attribute to their activities; also, the written work that results from the study

ethnomethodology the study of "folk methods" and background knowledge that sustains a shared sense of reality in everyday interactions

eugenics an attempt to selectively manipulate the gene pool in order to produce and "improve" human beings through medical science

Eurocentric the tendency to favor European or Western histories, cultures, and values over those of non-Western societies

evangelical a term describing conservative Christians who emphasize converting others to their faith

everyday class consciousness awareness of one's own social status and that of others

existing sources materials that have been produced for some other reason but that can be used as data for social research

exogamy marriage to someone from a different social group

experimental group the members of a test group who receive the experimental treatment

experiments formal tests of specific variables and effects, performed in a setting where all aspects of the situation can be controlled

expressions given expressions that are intentional and usually verbal, such as utterances

expressions given off observable expressions that can be either intended or unintended and are usually nonverbal

expressions of behavior small actions such as an eye roll or head nod that serve as an interactional tool to help project our definition of the situation to others

expressive leadership leadership concerned with maintaining emotional and relational harmony within the group

expressive role the position of the family member who provides emotional support and nurturing

expressive tasks the emotional work necessary to support family members

extended family a large group of relatives, usually including at least three generations living either in one household or in close proximity

extrinsic religiosity a person's public display of commitment to a religious faith

fads interests or practices followed enthusiastically for a relatively short period of time

false consciousness a denial of the truth on the part of the oppressed when they fail to recognize that the interests of the ruling class are embedded in the dominant ideology

family a social group whose members are bound by legal, biological, or emotional ties, or a combination of all three

family planning contraception, or any method of controlling family size and the birth of children

fashion the widespread custom or style of behavior and appearance at a particular time or in a particular place

feeling rules norms regarding the expression and display of emotions; expectations about the acceptable or desirable feelings in a given situation

feminism belief in the social, political, and economic equality of the sexes; also the social movements organized around that belief

feminist theory a theoretical approach that looks at gender inequities in society and the way that gender structures the social world

feminization of poverty the economic trend showing that women are more likely than men to live in poverty, caused in part by the gendered gap in wages, the higher proportion of single mothers compared to single fathers, and the increasing costs of child care

feral children in myths and rare real-world cases, children who have had little human contact and may have lived in social isolation from a young age

fertility rate a measure of population growth through reproduction; often expressed as the number of births per 1,000 people in a particular population or the average number of children a woman would bear over a lifetime

feudal system a system of social stratification based on a hereditary nobility who were responsible for and served by a lower stratum of forced laborers called serfs

fictive kin close relations with people considered "like family" but who are not related to us by blood or marriage

field notes detailed notes taken by an ethnographer describing her activities and interactions, which later become the basis of the analysis

first wave the earliest period of feminist activism, from the mid-nineteenth century until American women won the right to vote in 1920

527 committees organizations that have no official connection to a candidate but that raise and spend funds like a campaign does; named after the section of the tax code that authorizes their existence

focus group a process for interviewing a number of participants together, it also allows for interaction among group members

folkway a loosely enforced norm involving common customs, practices, or procedures that ensure smooth social interaction and acceptance

food desert a community in which the residents have little or no access to fresh, affordable, healthy foods, usually located in densely populated, urban areas

Fourth Estate the media, which are considered like a fourth branch of government (after the executive, legislative, and judiciary) and thus serve as another of the checks and balances on power

front in the dramaturgical perspective, the setting or scene of performances that helps establish the definition of the situation

frontstage the places in which we deliver our performances to an audience of others

fundamentalism the practice of emphasizing literal interpretation of texts and a "return" to a time of greater religious purity; represented by the most conservative group within any religion

game stage the third stage in Mead's theory of the development of self wherein children play organized games and take on the perspective of the generalized other

gender the physical, behavioral, and personality traits that a group considers normal for its male and female members

gender expression an individual's behavioral manifestations of gender

gender identity an individual's self-definition or sense of gender

gender nonconforming term used when gender identity and/or expression differs from societal expectations about gender roles

gender role socialization the lifelong process of learning to be masculine or feminine, primarily through agents of socialization

generalized other the perspectives and expectations of a network of others (or of society in general) that a child learns and then takes into account when shaping his or her own behavior

genocide the deliberate and systematic extermination of a racial, ethnic, national, or cultural group

gentrification transformation of the physical, social, economic, and cultural life of formerly working-class or poor inner-city neighborhoods into more affluent middle-class communities

gestures the ways in which people use their bodies to communicate without words; actions that have symbolic meaning

global (or **solar**) **dimming** a decline in the amount of light reaching the earth's surface because of increased air pollution, which reflects more light back into space

global cities a term for megacities that emphasizes their global impact as centers of economic, political, and social power

global village Marshall McLuhan's term describing the way that new communication technologies override barriers of space and time, joining together people all over the globe

global warming gradual increase in the earth's temperature, driven recently by an increase in greenhouse gases and other human activity

globalization the cultural and economic changes resulting from dramatically increased international trade and exchange in the late twentieth and early twenty-first centuries

government the formal, organized agency that exercises power and control in modern society, especially through the creation and enforcement of laws

grassroots environmentalism beginning in the 1980s, fourth stage of the environmental movement; distinguished by the diversity of its members and belief in citizen participation in environmental decision making

Green Party a U.S. political party established in 1984 to bring political attention to environmentalism, social justice, diversity, and related principles

greenhouse effect the process in which increased production of greenhouse gases, especially those arising from human activity (e.g., carbon dioxide, nitrous oxide, and methane) cause changes to the earth's atmosphere

greenhouse gases any gases in the earth's atmosphere that allow sunlight to pass through but trap heat, thus affecting temperature

grounded theory an inductive method of generating theory from data by creating categories in which to place data and then looking for relationships among categories

group a collection of people who share some attribute, identify with one another, and interact with each other

group cohesion the sense of solidarity or loyalty that individuals feel toward a group to which they belong

group dynamics the patterns of interaction between groups and individuals

groupthink in very cohesive groups, the tendency to enforce a high degree of conformity among members, creating a demand for unanimous agreement

growth rate percentage change in population over time figured by subtracting the number of deaths from the number of births, then adding the net migration; expressed as a fraction of the initial population

Hawthorne effect a specific example of reactivity, in which the desired effect is the result not of the independent variable but of the research itself

hegemony term developed by Antonio Gramsci to describe the cultural aspects of social control, whereby the ideas of the dominant group are accepted by all

heterogamy choosing romantic partners who are dissimilar in terms of class, race, education, religion, and other social group membership

heteronormativity the belief that heterosexuality is and should be the norm

heterosexism belief in the superiority of heterosexuality and heterosexuals

heterosexuality sexual attraction toward members of the other gender

hidden curriculum values or behaviors that students learn indirectly over the course of their schooling

high culture those forms of cultural expression usually associated with the elite or dominant classes

homeschooling the education of children by their parents, at home

homogamy the tendency to choose romantic partners who are similar to us in terms of class, race, religion, education, or other social group membership

homophobia fear of or discrimination toward gay, lesbian, and bisexual people

homosexuality sexual attraction toward members of one's own gender

honor killing the murder of a family member—usually female—who is believed to have brought dishonor to her family

horizontal social mobility the movement of individuals or groups within a particular social class, most often a result of changing occupations

human exceptionalism the attitude that humans are exempt from natural ecological limits

human sexual dimorphism the extent, much debated in recent years, to which inherent physical differences define the distinctions between the two sexes

hypergamy marrying "up" in the social class hierarchy

hypodermic needle theory (magic bullet theory) a theory that explains the effects of media as if their contents simply entered directly into the consumer, who is powerless to resist their influence

hypogamy marrying "down" in the social class hierarchy

hypothesis a theoretical statement explaining the relationship between two or more phenomena

id, **ego**, and **superego** according to Freud, the three interrelated parts that make up the mind: the id consists of basic inborn drives that are the source of instinctive psychic energy; the ego is the realistic aspect of the mind that balances the forces of the id and the superego; the superego has two components (the conscience and the ego-ideal) and represents the internalized demands of society

ideal culture the norms, values, and patterns of behavior that members of a society believe should be observed in principle

ideology a system of beliefs, attitudes, and values that directs a society and reproduces the status quo of the bourgeoisie

idioculture the customs, practices, and values expressed in a particular place by the people who interact there

immigration entering one country from another to take up permanent residence

impression management the effort to control the impressions we make on others so that they form a desired view of us and the situation; the use of self-presentation and performance tactics

incapacitation an approach to punishment that seeks to protect society from criminals by imprisoning or executing them

incest sexual contact between family members; a form of child abuse when it occurs between a child and a caregiver

Independent (or Third) Sector the part of the economy composed of nonprofit organizations; their workers are mission driven, rather than profit driven, and such organizations direct surplus funds to the causes they support

independent variable the factor that is predicted to cause change

individual discrimination discrimination carried out by one person against another

Industrial Revolution the rapid transformation of social life resulting from the technological and economic developments that began with the assembly line, steam power, and urbanization

infant mortality average number of infant deaths per 1,000 live births in a particular population

influential power power that is supported by persuasion

Information Revolution the recent social revolution made possible by the development of the microchip in the 1970s, which brought about vast improvements in the ability to manage information

information work work that involves the production, analysis, and distribution of information or knowledge; workers primarily think for a living

informed consent a safeguard through which the researcher makes sure that respondents are freely participating and understand the nature of the research

in-group a group that one identifies with and feels loyalty toward

in-group orientation among stigmatized individuals, the rejection of prevailing judgments or prejudice and the development of new standards that value their group identity

innovators individuals who accept society's approved goals but not society's approved means to achieve them

institutional discrimination discrimination carried out systematically by institutions (political, economic, educational, and others) that affect all members of a group who come into contact with it

institutional review board a group of scholars within a university who meet regularly to review and approve the research proposals of their colleagues and make recommendations for how to protect human subjects

instrumental leadership leadership that is task or goal oriented

instrumental role the position of the family member who provides material support; often an authority figure

instrumental tasks the practical physical tasks necessary to maintain family life

integrative medicine the combination of conventional medicine with complementary practices and treatments that have proven to be safe and effective

intentional community a group of people living together pursuing a common goal

intergenerational mobility movement between social classes that occurs from one generation to the next

internal colonialism the economic and political subjugation of the minority group by the dominant group within a nation

internal migration movement of a population within a country

interpretive community a group of people dedicated to the consumption and interpretation of a particular cultural product and who create a collective, social meaning for the product

interpretive strategies the ideas and frameworks that audience members bring to bear on a particular media text to understand its meaning

intersectionality a concept that identifies how different categories of inequality (race, class, gender, etc.) intersect to shape the lives of individuals and groups

intersex term used to describe a person whose chromosomes or sex characteristics are neither exclusively male nor exclusively female

intervening variable a third variable, sometimes overlooked, that explains the relationship between two other variables

interviews person-to-person conversations for the purpose of gathering information by means of questions posed to respondents

intragenerational mobility the movement between social classes that occurs during the course of an individual's lifetime

intrinsic religiosity a person's inner religious life or personal relationship to the divine

iron cage Max Weber's pessimistic description of modern life, in which we are caught in bureaucratic structures that control our lives through rigid rules and rationalization

just-world hypothesis argues that people have a deep need to see the world as orderly, predictable, and fair, which creates a tendency to view victims of social injustice as deserving of their fates

kin relatives or relations, usually those related by common descent

knowledge work work that primarily deals with information; producing value in the economy through ideas, judgments, analyses, designs, or innovations

labeling theory Howard Becker's idea that deviance is a consequence of external judgments, or labels, that modify the individual's self-concept and change the way others respond to the labeled person

language a system of communication using vocal sounds, gestures, or written symbols; the basis of symbolic culture and the primary means through which we communicate with one another and perpetuate our culture

latent functions the less obvious, perhaps unintended functions of a social structure

laws types of norms that are formally codified to provide an explicit statement about what is permissible or forbidden, legal or illegal in a given society

leading questions questions that predispose a respondent to answer in a certain way

legal-rational authority authority based in laws, rules, and procedures, not in the heredity or personality of any individual leader

leisure a period of time that can be spent relaxing, engaging in recreation, or otherwise indulging in freely chosen activities

LGBTQ lesbian, gay, bisexual, transgender, and queer (sometimes "A" is added to include "allies")

liberation theology a movement within the Catholic Church to understand Christianity from the perspective of the poor and oppressed, with a focus on fighting injustice

life expectancy average age to which people in a particular population are expected to live

life history an approach to interviewing that asks for a chronological account of the respondent's entire life, or some portion of it

life span or **longevity** the uppermost age to which a person can potentially live

lifestyle enclaves groups of people drawn together by shared interests, especially those relating to hobbies, sports, and media

Likert scale a way of formatting a survey questionnaire so that the respondent can choose an answer along a continuum

literature review a thorough search through previously published studies relevant to a particular topic

looking-glass self the notion that the self develops through our perception of others' evaluations and appraisals of us

lower-middle class see *working class*

macrosociology the level of analysis that studies large-scale social structures in order to determine how they affect the lives of groups and individuals

mainstream environmentalism beginning in the 1970s, the third stage of the environmental movement; characterized by enhanced organization, improved promotional campaigns and political tactics, and an increased reliance on economic and scientific expertise

Malthusian theorem the theory that exponential growth in population will outpace arithmetic growth in food production and other resources

Malthusian trap Malthus's prediction that a rapidly increasing population will overuse natural resources, leading inevitably to a public health disaster

manifest functions the obvious, intended functions of a social structure for the social system

marriage a formally recognized bond between two spouses, establishing contractual rights and obligations between them

mass behavior large groups of people engaging in similar behaviors without necessarily being in the same place

mass society theory a theory of social movements that assumes people join not because of the movements' ideals but to satisfy a psychological need to belong to something larger than themselves

master status a status that is always relevant and affects all other statuses we possess

material culture the objects associated with a cultural group, such as tools, machines, utensils, buildings, and artwork; any physical object to which we give social meaning

McDonaldization George Ritzer's term describing the spread of bureaucratic rationalization and the accompanying increases in efficiency and dehumanization

means of production anything that can create wealth: money, property, factories, and other types of businesses, and the infrastructure necessary to run them

mechanical solidarity the type of social bonds present in premodern, agrarian societies, in which shared traditions and beliefs created a sense of social cohesion

medicalization the process by which some behaviors or conditions that were once seen as personal problems are redefined as medical issues

megalopolis a group of densely populated metropolises that grow dependent on each other and eventually combine to form a huge urban complex

men's liberationism a movement that originated in the 1970s to discuss the challenges of masculinity

men's rights movement an offshoot of male liberationism whose members believe that feminism promotes discrimination against men

merger the legal combination of two companies, usually in order to maximize efficiency and profits by eliminating redundant infrastructure and personnel

meritocracy a system in which rewards are distributed based on merit

metropolis an urban area with a large population, usually 500,000 to 1 million people

Metropolitan Statistical Area (MSA) or **agglomeration** an area with at least one major city of 50,000 or more inhabitants that is surrounded by adjacent counties that are socially and economically integrated with the city core

microaggression everyday uses of ordinary language that may send denigrating messages to members of certain social groups

microsociology the level of analysis that studies face-to-face and small-group interactions in order to understand how they affect the larger patterns and structures of society

middle class social class composed primarily of white collar workers with a broad range of education and incomes; they constitute about 30 percent of the U.S. population

midrange theory an approach that integrates empiricism and grand theory

migration movement of people from one geographic area to another for the purpose of resettling

minority group social group that is systematically denied the same access to power and resources available to society's dominant groups though they are not necessarily fewer in number than the dominant groups

miscegenation romantic, sexual, or marital relationships between people of different races

modern environmental movement beginning in the 1960s, the second major stage of the environmental movement; focused on the environmental consequences of new technologies, oil exploration, chemical production, and nuclear power plants

modernism a paradigm that places trust in the power of science and technology to create progress, solve problems, and improve life

modernity a term that characterizes industrialized societies, including the decline of tradition, an increase in individualism, and a belief in progress, technology, and science

monarchy a government ruled by a king or queen, with succession of rulers kept within the family

monogamy the practice of marrying (or being in a relationship with) one person at a time

monopoly a situation in which there is only one individual or organization, without competitors, providing a particular good or service

monotheistic a term describing religions that worship a single divine figure

moral holiday a specified time period during which some norm violations are allowed

mores norms that carry great moral significance, are closely related to the core values of a cultural group, and often involve severe repercussions for violators

mortality rate a measure of the decrease in population due to deaths; often expressed as the number of deaths per 1,000 people in a particular population

multiculturalism a policy that values diverse racial, ethnic, national, and linguistic backgrounds and so encourages the retention of cultural differences within the larger society

natural increase change in population size that results from births and deaths; linked to a country's progress toward demographic transition

nature vs. nurture debate the ongoing discussion of the respective roles of genetics and socialization in determining individual behaviors and traits

negative questions survey questions that ask respondents what they don't think instead of what they do

neglect a form of child abuse in which the caregiver fails to provide adequate nutrition, sufficient clothing or shelter, or hygienic and safe living conditions

Neo-Malthusians contemporary demographers who worry about the rapid pace of population growth and believe that Malthus's basic prediction could be true

net migration net effect of immigration and emigration on a particular population; expressed as an increase or decrease

new ecological paradigm a way of understanding human life as just one part of an ecosystem that includes many species' interactions with the environment; suggests that there should be ecological limits on human activity

NIMBY short for "not in my back yard"; originally referred to protests aimed at shifting undesirable activities onto those with less power; now sometimes used without negative connotations to describe local environmental activists

nonrenewable resources finite resources that can become exhausted; includes those that take so long to replenish as to be effectively finite

norms rules or guidelines regarding what kinds of behavior are acceptable and appropriate within a particular culture; these typically emanate from the group's values

nuclear family a heterosexual couple with one or more children living in a single household

objectivity impartiality, the ability to allow the facts to speak for themselves

online education any educational course or program in which the teacher and the student meet via the Internet, rather than meeting physically in a classroom

open system a social system with ample opportunities to move from one class to another

open-ended question a question asked of a respondent that allows the answer to take whatever form the respondent chooses

operational definition a clear and precise definition of a variable that facilitates its measurement

opinion leaders high-profile individuals whose interpretation of events influences the public

organic solidarity the type of social bonds present in modern societies, based on difference, interdependence, and individual rights

out-groups groups toward which an individual feels opposition, rivalry, or hostility

outsiders according to Howard Becker, those labeled deviant and subsequently segregated from "normal" society

outsourcing "contracting out" or transferring to another country the labor that a company might otherwise have employed its own staff to perform; typically done for financial reasons

palliative care type of health care that focuses on symptom and pain relief and providing a supportive environment for critically ill or dying patients

pandemic occurs when a significantly higher number of cases of a disease also spreads through an especially large geographical region spanning many countries or even continents

paradigms a set of assumptions, theories, and perspectives that make up a way of understanding social reality

paradigm shift a major change in basic assumptions of a particular scientific discipline

participant observation a methodology associated with ethnography whereby the researcher both observes and becomes a member in a social setting

particular or significant other the perspectives and expectations of a particular role that a child learns and internalizes

passing presenting yourself as a member of a different group than the stigmatized group you belong to

patriarchy literally meaning "rule of the father"; a male-dominated society

personal front the performance tactics we use to present ourselves to others, including appearance, costume, and manner

pilot study a small-scale study carried out to test the feasibility of a larger one

play stage the second stage in Mead's theory of the development of self wherein children pretend to play the role of the particular or significant other

pluralism a cultural pattern of intergroup relations that encourages racial and ethnic variation and acceptance within a society

pluralist model a system of political power in which a wide variety of individuals and groups have equal access to resources and the mechanisms of power

pluralistic ignorance a process in which members of a group individually conclude that there is no need to take action because they see that other group members have not done so

political action committees (PACs) organizations that raise money to support the interests of a select group or organization

politics methods and tactics intended to influence government policy, policy-related attitudes, and activities

pollution any environmental contamination that harms living beings

polyamory a system of multiple-person partnership

polyandry a system of marriage that allows women to have multiple husbands

polygamy a system of marriage that allows people to have more than one spouse at a time

polygyny a system of marriage that allows men to have multiple wives

polysemy having many possible meanings or interpretations

popular culture usually contrasted with the high culture of elite groups; forms of cultural expression usually associated with the masses, consumer goods, and commercial products

population transfer the forcible removal of a group of people from the territory they have occupied

positive deviance actions considered deviant within a given context but are later reinterpreted as appropriate or even heroic

positivism the theory that sense perceptions are the only valid source of knowledge

postmodernism a paradigm that suggests that social reality is diverse, pluralistic, and constantly in flux

postmodernity a term that characterizes postindustrial societies, including a focus on the production and management of information and skepticism of science and technology

power the ability to control the actions of others

power elite a relatively small group of people in the top ranks of economic, political, and military institutions who make many of the important decisions in American society

pragmatism a perspective that assumes organisms (including humans) make practical adaptations to their environments; humans do this through cognition, interpretation, and interaction

praxis the application of theory to practical action in an effort to improve aspects of society

prejudice an idea about the characteristics of a group that is applied to all members of that group and is unlikely to change regardless of the evidence against it

preparatory stage the first stage in Mead's theory of the development of self wherein children mimic or imitate others

prestige the social honor people are given because of their membership in well-regarded social groups

preventive medicine type of health care that aims to avoid or forestall the onset of disease by taking preventive measures, often including lifestyle changes

primary deviance in labeling theory, the initial act or attitude that causes one to be labeled deviant

primary groups the people who are most important to one's sense of self; members' relationships are typically characterized by face-to-face interaction, high levels of cooperation, and intense feelings of belonging

privilege unearned advantage accorded to members of dominant social groups (males, whites, heterosexuals, the physically able, etc.)

probability sampling a procedure that results in a sample group that reflects the characteristics of members in the target population

profane the ordinary, mundane, or everyday

pro-feminist men's movement an offshoot of male liberationism whose members support feminism and believe that sexism harms both men and women

progressive term describing efforts to promote forward-thinking social change

proletariat workers; those who have no means of production of their own and so are reduced to selling their labor power in order to live

property crime crimes that do not involve violence, including burglary, larceny-theft, motor vehicle theft, and arson

propinquity the tendency to partner with people who live close by

psychosexual stages of development four distinct stages of the development of the self between birth and adulthood, according to Freud; personality quirks are a result of being fixated, or stuck, at any stage

public goods dilemma a type of social dilemma in which individuals incur the cost to contribute to a collective resource, though they may never benefit from that resource

qualitative research research that works with nonnumerical data such as texts, field notes, interview transcripts, photographs, and tape recordings; this type of research more often tries to understand how people make sense of their world

quantitative research research that translates the social world into numbers that can be treated mathematically; this type of research often tries to find cause-and-effect relationships

queer theory social theory about gender and sexual identity; emphasizes the importance of difference and rejects ideas of innate identities or restrictive categories

race a socially defined category based on real or perceived biological differences between groups of people

race consciousness an ideology that acknowledges race as a powerful social construct that shapes our individual and social experiences

racial assimilation the process by which racial minority groups are absorbed into the dominant group through intermarriage

racism a set of beliefs about the claimed superiority of one racial or ethnic group; used to justify inequality and often rooted in the assumption that differences among groups are genetic

rape culture a set of beliefs, norms, and values that normalizes sexual violence against women

rapport a positive relationship often characterized by mutual trust or sympathy

rationalization the application of economic logic to human activity; the use of formal rules and regulations in order to maximize efficiency without consideration of subjective or individual concerns

reactivity the tendency of people and events to react to the process of being studied

real culture the norms, values, and patterns of behavior that actually exist within a society (which may or may not correspond to the society's ideals)

rebels individuals who reject society's approved goals and means and instead create and work toward their own (sometimes revolutionary) goals using new means

recreation any satisfying, amusing, and stimulating activity that is experienced as refreshing and renewing for body, mind, and spirit

reference group a group that provides a standard of comparison against which we evaluate ourselves

reflexivity how the identity and activities of the researcher influence what is going on in the field setting

region the context in which the performance takes place, including location, décor, and props

regressive term describing resistance to particular social changes, efforts to maintain the status quo, or attempts to reestablish an earlier form of social order

rehabilitation an approach to punishment that attempts to reform criminals as part of their penalty

reinforcement theory theory suggesting that audiences seek messages in the media that reinforce their existing attitudes and beliefs and are thus not influenced by challenging or contradictory information

relative deprivation a relative measure of poverty based on the standard of living in a particular society

relative deprivation theory a theory of social movements that focuses on the actions of oppressed groups who seek rights or opportunities already enjoyed by others in the society

reliability the consistency of a question or measurement tool; the degree to which the same questions will produce similar answers

religion any institutionalized system of shared beliefs and rituals that identify a relationship between the sacred and the profane

religiosity the regular practice of religious beliefs, often measured in terms of frequency of attendance at worship services and the importance of religious beliefs to an individual

renewable resources resources that replenish at a rate comparable to the rate at which they are consumed

replicability research that can be repeated, and thus verified, by other researchers later

representative sample a sample taken so that findings from members of the sample group can be generalized to the larger population; also referred to as a stratified sample

representativeness the degree to which a particular studied group is similar to, or represents, any part of the larger society

rescission the practice by insurance companies of canceling coverage only after a person gets sick

residential segregation the geographical separation of the poor from the rest of an area's population

resistance strategies ways that workers express discontent with their working conditions and try to reclaim control of the conditions of their labor

resocialization the process of replacing previously learned norms and values with new ones as a part of a transition in life

resource mobilization theory a theory of social movements that focuses on the practical constraints that help or hinder social movements' action

respondent a participant in a study from whom the researcher seeks to gather information

response rate the number or percentage of surveys completed by respondents and returned to researchers

retreatists individuals who renounce society's approved goals and means entirely and live outside conventional norms altogether

retribution an approach to punishment that emphasizes retaliation or revenge for the crime as the appropriate goal

riot continuous disorderly behavior by a group of people that disturbs the peace and is directed toward other people and/or property

ritual a practice based on religious beliefs

ritualists individuals who have given up hope of achieving society's approved goals but still operate according to society's approved means

role the set of behaviors expected of someone because of his or her status

role conflict experienced when we occupy two or more roles with contradictory expectations

role exit the process of leaving a role that we will no longer occupy

role model an individual who serves as an example for others to strive toward and emulate

role strain experienced when there are contradictory expectations within one role

role-taking emotions emotions such as sympathy, embarrassment, or shame that require that we assume the perspective of another person or group and respond accordingly

rural relating to sparsely settled areas; in the United States, any county with a population density between 10 and 59.9 people per square mile

rural rebound population increase in rural counties that adjoin urban centers or possess rich scenic or amenity values

sacred the holy, divine, or supernatural

same-sex marriage federally recognized marriage between members of the same sex; made legal in the United States in 2015

sample the members of the target population who will actually be studied

sanctions positive or negative reactions to the ways that people follow or disobey norms, including rewards for conformity and punishments for violations

Sapir-Whorf hypothesis the idea that language structures thought and that ways of looking at the world are embedded in language

saturated self a postmodern idea that the self is now developed by multiple influences chosen from a wide range of media sources

school vouchers payments from the government to parents whose children attend failing public schools; the money helps parents pay private school tuition

scientific method a procedure for acquiring knowledge that emphasizes collecting concrete data through observation and experimentation

second shift the unpaid housework and child care often expected of women after they complete their day's paid labor

second wave the period of feminist activism during the 1960s and 1970s, often associated with the issues of women's equal access to employment and education

secondary deviance in labeling theory, the subsequent deviant identity or career that develops as a result of being labeled deviant

secondary groups groups that are larger and less intimate than primary groups; members' relationships are usually organized around a specific goal and are often temporary

secular nonreligious; a secular society separates church and state and does not endorse any religion

segregation the physical and legal separation of groups by race or ethnicity

self the individual's conscious, reflexive experience of a personal identity separate and distinct from others

self-fulfilling prophecy an inaccurate statement or belief that, by altering the situation, becomes accurate; a prediction that causes itself to come true

service work work that involves providing a service to businesses or individual clients, customers, or consumers rather than manufacturing goods

sex an individual's membership in one of two categories— male or female—based on biological factors

sexism the belief that one sex, usually male, is superior to the other

sexual orientation or **sexual identity** the inclination to feel sexual desire toward people of a particular gender or toward both genders

sexuality the character or quality of being sexual

sick role the actions and attitudes that society expects from someone who is ill

signs symbols that stand for or convey an idea

simple random sample a particular type of probability sample in which every member of the population has an equal chance of being selected

simplicity movement a loosely knit movement that opposes consumerism and encourages people to work less, earn less, and spend less, in accordance with nonmaterialistic values

simulacrum an image or media representation that does not reflect reality in any meaningful way but is treated as real

situational ethnicity an ethnic identity that can be either displayed or concealed depending on its usefulness in a given situation

slavery the most extreme form of social stratification, based on the legal ownership of people

smart growth term for economic and urban planning policies that emphasize responsible development and renewal

social atomization a social situation that emphasizes individualism over collective or group identities

social change the transformation of a culture over time

social class a system of stratification based on access to such resources as wealth, property, power, and prestige

social construction the process by which a concept or practice is created and maintained by participants who collectively agree that it exists

social control the formal and informal mechanisms used to elicit conformity to values and norms and thus promote social cohesion

social Darwinism the application of the theory of evolution and the notion of "survival of the fittest" to the study of society

social dilemma a situation in which behavior that is rational for the individual can, when practiced by many people, lead to collective disaster

social ecology the study of human populations and their impact on the natural world

social identity theory a theory of group formation and maintenance that stresses the need of individual members to feel a sense of belonging

social inequality the unequal distribution of wealth, power, or prestige among members of a society

social influence exerting group control over others' decisions

social institutions systems and structures within society that shape the activities of groups and individuals

social learning the process of learning behaviors and meanings through social interaction

social loafing the phenomenon in which as more individuals are added to a task, each individual contributes a little less; a source of inefficiency when working in teams

social mobility the movement of individuals or groups within the hierarchical system of social classes

social movement any social groups with leadership, organization, and an ideological commitment to promote or resist social change

social network the web of direct and indirect ties connecting an individual to other people who may also affect the individual

social reproduction the tendency of social classes to remain relatively stable as class status is passed down from one generation to the next

social sciences the disciplines that use the scientific method to examine the social world, in contrast to the natural sciences, which examine the physical world

social stratification the division of society into groups arranged in a social hierarchy

social ties connections between individuals

socialism an economic system based on the collective ownership of the means of production, collective distribution of goods and services, and government regulation of the economy

socialization the process of learning and internalizing the values, beliefs, and norms of our social group, by which we become functioning members of society

society a group of people who shape their lives in aggregated and patterned ways that distinguish their group from others

sociobiology a branch of science that uses biological and evolutionary explanations for social behavior

socioeconomic status (SES) a measure of an individual's place within a social class system; often used interchangeably with "class"

sociological imagination a quality of the mind that allows us to understand the relationship between our individual circumstances and larger social forces

sociological perspective a way of looking at the world through a sociological lens

sociology the systematic or scientific study of human society and social behavior, from large-scale institutions and mass culture to small groups and individual interactions

solidarity the degree of integration or unity within a particular society; the extent to which individuals feel connected to other members of their group

special interest groups organizations that raise and spend money to influence elected officials and/or public opinion

spurious correlation the appearance of causation produced by an intervening variable

status a position in a social hierarchy that carries a particular set of expectations

status inconsistency a situation in which an individual has differing levels of status in terms of wealth, power, prestige, or other elements of socioeconomic status

stereotype promise a kind of self-fulfilling prophecy in which positive stereotypes, such as the "model minority" label applied to Asian Americans, lead to positive performance outcomes for Asian Americans

stereotype threat a kind of self-fulfilling prophecy in which the fear of performing poorly—and confirming stereotypes about their social groups—causes students to perform poorly

stereotyping judging others based on preconceived generalizations about groups or categories of people

stigma Erving Goffman's term for any physical or social attribute that devalues a person or group's identity and that may exclude those who are devalued from normal social interaction

structural functionalism a paradigm based on the assumption that society is a unified whole that functions because of the contributions of its separate structures

structural mobility changes in the social status of large numbers of people as a result of structural changes in society

structure a social institution that is relatively stable over time and that meets the needs of society by performing functions necessary to maintain social order and stability

subculture a group within society that is differentiated by its distinctive values, norms, and lifestyle

suburbanization the shift of large segments of population away from the urban core and toward the edges of cities

suffrage movement the movement organized around gaining voting rights for women

surveys research method based on questionnaires that are administered to a sample of respondents selected from a target population

sustainable development economic development that aims to reconcile global economic growth with environmental protection

sweatshop a workplace where workers are subject to extreme exploitation, including below-standard wages, long hours, and poor working conditions that may pose health or safety hazards

symbolic culture the ideas associated with a cultural group, including ways of thinking (beliefs, values, and assumptions) and ways of behaving (norms, interactions, and communication)

symbolic ethnicity an ethnic identity that is only relevant on specific occasions and does not significantly affect everyday life

symbolic interactionism a paradigm that sees interaction and meaning as central to society and assumes that meanings are not inherent but are created through interaction

synergy a mutually beneficial interaction between parts of an organization that allows it to create something greater than the sum of its individual outputs

synthesis the new social system created out of the conflict between thesis and antithesis in a dialectical model

taboo a norm ingrained so deeply that even thinking about violating them evokes strong feelings of disgust, horror, or revulsion

target population the entire group about which a researcher would like to be able to generalize

taste cultures areas of culture that share similar aesthetics and standards of taste

taste publics groups of people who share similar artistic, literary, media, recreational, and intellectual interests

technological determinism a theory of social change that assumes changes in technology drive changes in society, rather than vice versa

technology material artifacts and the knowledge and techniques required to use them

telecommuting working from home while staying connected to the office through communications technology

tertiary deviance redefining the stigma associated with a deviant label as a positive phenomenon

textual poaching Henry Jenkins's term describing the ways that audience members manipulate an original cultural product to create a new one; a common way for fans to exert some control over the media they consume

theories abstract propositions that explain the social world and make predictions about the future

thesis the existing social arrangements in a dialectical model

thick description the presentation of detailed data on interactions and meaning within a cultural context, from the perspective of its members

third place any informal public place where people come together regularly for conversation and camaraderie when not at work or at home

third wave the most recent period of feminist activism, focusing on issues of diversity, globalization, and the variety of identities women can possess

Thomas theorem classic formulation of the way individuals determine reality, whereby "if people define situations as real, they are real in their consequences"

total institutions institutions in which individuals are cut off from the rest of society so that they can be controlled and regulated for the purpose of systematically stripping away previous roles and identities in order to create new ones

tracking the placement of students in educational "tracks," or programs of study (e.g., college prep, remedial), that determine the types of classes they take

traditional authority authority based in custom, birthright, or divine right

tragedy of the commons a type of social dilemma in which many individuals' overexploitation of a public resource depletes or degrades that common resource

transgender term used when gender identity and/or expression is different from the sex assigned at birth

transphobia fear of or discrimination toward transgender or other gender-nonconforming people

transsexuals individuals who identify with the other sex and have surgery to alter their own sex so it fits their self-image

treadmill of production term describing the operation of modern economic systems that require constant growth, which causes increased exploitation of resources and environmental degradation

triad a three-person social group

two-step flow model theory on media effects that suggests audiences get information through opinion leaders who influence their attitudes and beliefs, rather than through direct, firsthand sources

unchurched a term describing those who consider themselves spiritual but not religious and who often adopt aspects of various religious traditions

underclass the poorest group, comprising the homeless and chronically unemployed who may depend on public or private assistance; they constitute about 12 percent of the U.S. population

Uniform Crime Report (UCR) an official measure of crime in the United States, produced by the FBI's official tabulation of every crime reported by more than 18,000 law enforcement agencies

union an association of workers who bargain collectively for increased wages and benefits and better working conditions

unobtrusive measures research methods that rely on existing sources and where the researcher does not intrude upon or disturb the social setting or its subjects

unschooling a homeschooling alternative that rejects the standard curriculum in favor of student-driven types of learning

upper class an elite and largely self-sustaining group who possess most of the country's wealth; they constitute about 1 percent of the U.S. population

upper-middle class social class consisting of mostly highly educated professionals and managers who have considerable financial stability; they constitute about 14 percent of the U.S. population

urban relating to cities; typically describes densely populated areas

urban density concentration of people in a city, measured by the total number of people per square mile

urban renewal efforts to rejuvenate decaying inner cities, including renovation, selective demolition, commercial development, and tax incentives

urban sprawl a derogatory term for the expansion of urban or suburban boundaries, associated with irresponsible or poorly planned development

urbanites people who live in cities

urbanization movement of increasing numbers of people from rural areas to cities

uses and gratifications paradigm approaches to understanding media effects that focus on how the media fulfills individuals' psychological or social needs

utopia literally "no place"; an ideal society in which all social ills have been overcome

validity the accuracy of a question or measurement tool; the degree to which a researcher is measuring what he thinks he is measuring

value-free sociology an ideal whereby researchers identify facts without allowing their own personal beliefs or biases to interfere

values ideas about what is right or wrong, good or bad, desirable or worthy in a particular group; they express what the group cherishes and honors

variables two or more phenomena that a researcher believes are related; these will be examined in the experiment

vector organisms animals like mosquitoes, ticks, and birds that carry and spread pathogens (germs or other infectious agents) in a given area

verstehen "empathic understanding"; Weber's term to describe good social research, which tries to understand the meanings that individuals attach to various aspects of social reality

vertical social mobility the movement between different class statuses, often called either upward mobility or downward mobility

violent crime crimes in which violence is either the objective or the means to an end, including murder, rape, aggravated assault, and robbery

virtual communities social groups whose interactions are mediated through information technologies, particularly the Internet

wealth a measure of net worth that includes income, property, and other assets

weighting techniques for manipulating the sampling procedure so that the sample more closely resembles the larger population

white collar a description characterizing lower-level professional and management workers and some highly skilled laborers in technical jobs

white collar crime crime committed by a high-status individual in the course of his occupation

white flight movement of upper- and middle-class whites who could afford to leave the cities for the suburbs, especially in the 1950s and 1960s

working class or **lower-middle class** social class consisting of mostly blue collar or service industry workers who are less likely to have a college degree; they constitute about 30 percent of the U.S. population

working poor poorly educated manual and service workers who may work full-time but remain near or below the poverty line; they constitute about 13 percent of the U.S. population

References

Abel, Jaison R.; and Deitz, Richard. 2014. "Do the benefits of college still outweigh the costs?" *Current Issues in Economics and Finance: Federal Reserve Bank of New York*. http://www.newyorkfed.org/research/current_issues/ci20-3.pdf

Access Clark County. 2009. "Clark County/Las Vegas Valley average population and growth rates, 1990–2008." www.accessclarkcounty.com

Acedo, Mike. 2013. "10 pros and cons of a flipped classroom." *Teach-Thought*, October. http://www.teachthought.com/trends/10-pros-cons-flipped-classroom/

Achtenberg, Emily. 2013. "From water wars to water scarcity: Bolivia's cautionary tale." *North American Congress on Latina America*, June. https://nacla.org/blog/2013/6/5/water-wars-water-scarcity-bolivia's-cautionary-tale

Acierno, R.; Hernandez, M. A.; Amstadter, A. B.; Resnick, H. S.; Steve, K.; Muzzy, W.; et al. (2010). "Prevalence and correlates of emotional, physical, sexual, and financial abuse and potential neglect in the United States: The national elder mistreatment study." *American Journal of Public Health*, vol. 100, no. 2: 292–297.

ACLU. 2003. "Inadequate representation." American Civil Liberties Union online publication, October 8. www.aclu.org/capital/unequal/10390pub20031008.html

———. 2011. "Oppose Voter ID legislation—Fact sheet." July. https://www.aclu.org/voting-rights/oppose-voter-id-legislation-fact-sheet

Acquity Group. 2014. "The Internet of things: The future of consumer adoption." http://www.acquitygroup.com/docs/default-source/Whitepapers/acquitygroup-2014iotstudy.pdf?sfvrsn=0

Adler, Patricia A.; and Adler, Peter. 1991. *Backboards and Blackboards: College Athletes and Role Engulfment*. New York: Columbia University Press.

———. 2000. *Constructions of Deviance: Social Power, Context and Interaction*. Belmont, CA: Wadsworth.

Administration on Aging. 2012. "A profile of older Americans: 2012." http://www.aoa.gov/Aging_Statistics/Profile/2012/docs/2012profile.pdf

———. 2014. "A profile of older Americans: 2013." http://www.aoa.acl.gov/Aging_Statistics/Profile/2013/docs/2013_Profile.pdf

Adorno, T.; and Horkheimer, M. 1979. "The culture industry: Enlightenment as mass deception." In T. Adorno and M. Horkheimer, eds., *Dialectic of Enlightenment*. London: Verso.

Aguirre, Benigno; Quarantelli, Enrico; and Mendoza, Jorge L. 1988. "The collective behavior of fads: The characteristics, effects and career of streaking." *American Sociological Review*, vol. 53: 569–589.

Agyeman, Julian; Bullard, Robert D.; and Evans, Bob; eds. 2003. *Just Sustainabilities: Development in an Unequal World*. Cambridge, MA: MIT Press.

Ahmed, Farid. 2012. "At least 117 killed in fire at Bangladeshi clothing factory." CNN, November 25. www.cnn.com/2012/11/25/world/asia/bangladesh-factory-fire/index.html

Alatas, Syed Farid; and Sinha, Vineeta. 2001. "Teaching classical sociological theory in Singapore: The context of Eurocentrism." *Teaching Sociology*, vol. 29, no. 3: 316–331.

Alcoholics Anonymous. 2001 (orig. 1939). *Alcoholics Anonymous: The Story of How Many Thousands of Men and Women Have Recovered from Alcoholism*. 4th ed. New York: Alcoholics Anonymous World Service.

Alexander, Jeffrey. 1988. "Parsons' 'structure' in American sociology." *Sociological Theory*, vol. 6, no. 1: 96–102.

Alexander, Jeffrey; and Smelser, Neil. 1998. *Diversity and Its Discontents: Cultural Conflict and Common Ground in Contemporary American Society*. Princeton, NJ: Princeton University Press.

Allen, Drew; and Dadgar, Mina. 2012. "Does dual enrollment increase students' success in college? Evidence from a quasi-experimental analysis of dual enrollment in New York City." Wiley Periodicals, Inc. June. http://onlinelibrary.wiley.com/doi/10.1002/he.20010/abstract

Allen, I. Elaine; and Seaman, Jeff. 2013. "Changing course: Ten years of tracking online education in the United States." Wellesley MA: Babson College/Quahog Research Group. http://www.onlinelearningsurvey.com/reports/changingcourse.pdf

Allport, G.; and Ross, M. 1967. "Personal religious orientation and prejudice." *Journal of Personality and Social Psychology*, vol. 5, no. 4: 432–443.

Almaguer, Tomas. 2008. *Racial Fault Lines: The Historical Origins of White Supremacy in California*. Berkeley: University of California Press.

Altermatt, Ellen Rydell; and Pomerantz, Eva M. 2005. "The implications of having high-achieving versus low-achieving friends: A longitudinal analysis." *Social Development*, vol. 14, no. 1: 61–81.

American Association of Community Colleges. 2011. http://aacc.nche.edu/pages/default.aspx

———. 2015. "2015 Community college fact sheet." http://www.aacc.nche.edu/AboutCC/Pages/fastfactsfactsheet.aspx

American College Health Association. 2012. "American College Health Association–National College Health Assessment II: Reference group executive summary Spring 2012." Hanover, MD: American College Health Association. www.acha-ncha.org/docs

American Psychiatric Association (APA). 2012. "Autism spectrum disorders." www.psychiatry.org/mental-health/key-topics/autism

American Sociological Association (ASA). 2012. Sociology degrees awarded by degree level. www.asanet.org

Amott, Teresa; and Matthaei, Julie. 1996. *Race, Class, Gender, and Work: A Multicultural Ethnic History of Women in the United States*. 2nd ed. Boston: South End Press.

Ananat, Elizabeth Oltmans. 2005. "The wrong side of the tracks: Estimating the causal effects of racial segregation on city outcomes." Unpublished working paper. MIT Department of Economics.

Anderson, Craig A., et al. 2010. "Violent video game effects on aggression, empathy, and prosocial behavior in Eastern and

Western countries: A meta-analytic review." *Psychological Bulletin*, vol. 136, no. 2: 151–173.

Anderson, Doug. 2009. "The Changing face of unemployment." Nielsenwire. March 1. blog.nielsen.com/nielsenwire/consumer/the-changing-face-of-unemployment

Anderson, Elijah. 1990. *Streetwise: Race, Class and Change in an Urban Community*. Chicago: University of Chicago Press.

Anderson, Steven W.; Bechara, Antoine; Damasio, Hann; Tranel, Daniel; and Damasio, Antonio R. 1999. "Impairment of social and moral behavior related to early damage in human prefrontal cortex." *Nature Neuroscience*, vol. 2, no. 11: 1032–1037.

Anzaldúa, Gloria. 1987. *Borderlands/La Frontera: The New Mestiza*. San Francisco: Aunt Lute Books.

Arendt, Hannah. 1958. *The Origins of Totalitarianism*. London: Allen and Unwin Press.

Armitage, Angus. 1951. *The World of Copernicus*. New York: Mentor Books.

Armstrong, Elizabeth A.; Hamilton, Laura; and Sweeney, Brian. 2006. "Sexual assault on campus: A multilevel, integrative approach to party rape social problems," *Social Problems*. vol. 53, no. 4: 483–499.

Arnst, Catherine. 2010. "Tired of waiting for the doctor? Try one that gives same-day appointments." *Kaiser Health News–Boston Globe*, July 14. www.kaiserhealthnews.org/stories/2010/july/14/waiting-for-the-doctor.aspx?referrer=search

Arrison, Sonia. 2011. *One Hundred Plus: How the Coming Age of Longevity Will Change Everything, from Careers and Relationships to Family and Faith*. Boston: Basic Books.

Asch, S. 1958. "Effects of group pressure upon the modification and distortion of judgments." In E. E. Maccoby, T. M. Newcomb, and E. L. Hartley, eds., *Readings in Social Psychology*. New York: Holt, Rinehart, & Winston.

Associated Press. 2006. "Global warming causing disease to rise: Malaria, dengue fever increasing as temperature heats up, experts warn." November 14. www.msnbc.msn.com/id/15717706

———. 2013. "Bangladesh factory collapse blamed on swampy ground and heavy machinery." www.guardian.co.uk/world/2013/may/23/bangladesh-factory-collapse-rana-plaza

Association of American Medical Colleges. 2009. "Scientific foundations for future physicians." http://www.hhmi.org/grants/pdf/08-209_AAMC-HHMI_report.pdf

Association of Certified Fraud Examiners. 2012. *2012 Report to the Nations: Key Findings and Highlights*. www.acfe.com/rttn-highlights.aspx

Association of Statisticians of American Religious Bodies. 2012. "Second Largest Religious Tradition in Each State, 2010."

Astin, Alexander W.; Astin, Helen S.; and Lindholm, Jennifer A. 2010. "National study of spirituality in higher education: Students' search for meaning and purpose." *UCLA Higher Education Research Institute*. http://spirituality.ucla.edu/findings/

Atauhene, B (2011). "South Africa's Land Reform Crisis: Eliminating the Legacy of Apartheid". *Foreign Affairs* 90 (4): 121–129.

Atkin, C. 1973. "Instrumental utilities and information seeking." In P. Clark, ed., *New Models for Mass Communication Research*. Beverly Hills, CA: Sage.

———. 1985. "Informational utility and selective exposure." In D. Zillmann and J. Bryant, eds., *Selective Exposure to Communication*. Hillsdale, NJ: Erlbaum.

Attwood, F., ed. 2009. *Mainstreaming Sex: The Sexualization of Western Culture*. London and New York: I. B. Tauris.

———. 2011. "The paradigm shift: Pornography research, sexualization and extreme images." *Sociology Compass*, vol. 5, no. 1: 13–22.

AV Comparatives. 2014. "Parental control test & review 2014," September 14. http://www.av-comparatives.org/wp-content/uploads/2014/09/Parental_Control_Report_2014.pdf

Avishai, Orit. 2008. "Doing religion in a secular world: Women in conservative religions and the question of agency." *Gender and Society*, vol. 22, no. 4: 409–433.

Babbie, Earl. 2002. *The Basics of Social Research*. Belmont, CA: Wadsworth.

Babiak, T. 2004. "Everything goes at Burning Man: Counterculture fest is everything that North America isn't." *National Post*, September 6, p. B10.

Baca Zinn, Maxine; and Eitzen, D. Stanley. 2002. *Diversity in Families*. Boston: Allyn and Bacon.

Bachman, R.; and Saltzman, L. 1995. "Violence against women: Estimates from the redesigned survey." Bureau of Justice Statistics Special Report. www.ojp.usdoj.gov/bjs/pub/pdf/femvied.pdf

Badenhausen, Kurt. 2015. "Lakers top 2015 list of NBA's Most valuable teams: Average franchise is now worth record $1.1 billion." *Forbes*, February 2. http://www.forbes.com/sites/kurtbadenhausen/2015/01/21/average-nba-team-worth-record-1-1-billion-2/

Bagdikian, Ben H. 2004. *The New Media Monopoly*. Boston: Beacon Press.

Bailey, Holly. 2010. "ABC News/Yahoo! News Poll: People are losing faith in the American Dream." *Yahoo! News*, September 21. www.news.yahoo.com

Bailey, Martha J.; and Dynarski, Susan M. 2011. "Inequality in postsecondary attainment." In Greg Duncan and Richard Murnane, eds., *Whither Opportunity: Rising Inequality, Schools, and Children's Life Chances*, 117–132. New York: Russell Sage Foundation.

Bailey, Ronald. 2002. "*Silent Spring* at 40: Rachel Carson's classic is not aging well." *Reason Online Magazine*, June 12. http://reason.com/rb/rb061202.shtml

Baker, J. P.; and Crist, J. L. 1971. "Teacher expectancies: A review of the literature." In J. D. Elashoff and R. E. Snow, eds., *Pygmalion Reconsidered: A Case Study in Statistical Inference: Reconsideration of the Rosenthal-Jacobson Data on Teacher Expectancy*. Worthington, OH: Charles A. Jones.

Bales, Kevin. 2000. *Disposable People: New Slavery in the Global Economy*. Berkeley: University of California Press.

———; and Soodalter, Ron. 2009. *The Slave Next Door: Human Trafficking and Slavery in America Today*. Berkeley: University of California Press.

Balfanz, R.; Bridgeland, J. M.; Bruce, M.; and Fox, J. H. 2012. "Building a grad nation." www.americaspromise.org

Bandura, A. 1965. "Influence of models' reinforcement contingencies on the acquisition of imitative response." *Journal of Personality and Social Psychology*, vol. 1: 589–595.

Bandy, Joe. 1996. "Managing the other of nature: Sustainability, spectacle, and global regimes of capital in ecotourism." *Public Culture*, vol. 8, no. 3: 539–566.

Banfield, E. C. 1970. *The Unheavenly City*. Boston: Little, Brown and Co.

Banks, Ingrid. 2000. *Hair Matters: Beauty, Power, and Black Women's Consciousness*. New York: New York University Press.

Barner, Mark R. 1999. "Sex-role stereotyping in FCC-mandated children's educational television." *Journal of Broadcasting & Electronic Media*, vol. 43, no. 4: 551.

Barnes, Brooke. 2009. "Disney swoops into action buying Marvel for $4 billion." *New York Times*, August 31. www.nytimes.com

Barnes, P. M.; Bloom, B.; and Nahin, R. 2008. "Complementary and alternative medicine use among adults and children: United States, 2007." *National Health Statistics Reports*, no. 12 (December 10): 1–23.

Barnes, Robert. 2013. "At Supreme Court, victories for gay marriage." *Washington Post*, June 26. www.washingtonpost.com

Barounis, Cynthia. 2013. "Crippling heterosexuality, queering able-bodiedness: Murderball, Brokeback Mountain and the contested masculine body." In Lennard J. Davis, ed., *The Disability Studies Reader*. London: Routledge.

Bartels, Chuck. 2003. "Wal-Mart starting to look at all its 1.1 million U.S. workers." *Times-Picayune* (New Orleans, LA), October 25, "Money," p. 1.

Barry, Dave. 1987. *Dave Barry's Bad Habits: A 100% Fact-Free Book*. New York, NY: Holt, p. 203.

Bartkowski, John P.; and Read, Jen'nan Ghazal. 2003. "Veiled submission: Gender, power, and identity among evangelical and Muslim women in the United States." *Qualitative Sociology*, vol. 26: 71–92.

Batan, Clarence M. 2004. "Of strengths and tensions: A dialogue of ideas between the classics and Philippine sociology." *UNITAS*, vol. 77, no. 2: 163–186.

Baudrillard, Jean. 1994 (orig. 1981). *Simulacra and Simulation*. Trans. Sheila Glaser. Ann Arbor: University of Michigan Press.

Bauer, Martin W.; and Gaskell, George, eds. 2000. *Qualitative Researching with Text, Image and Sound*. London: Thousand Oaks, CA: Sage.

Baum, Sandry; Ma, Jennifer; and Payea, Kathleen. 2013. "Education Pays: The Benefits of Higher Education for Individuals and Society." https://trends.collegeboard.org/sites/default/files/education-pays-2013-full-report-022714.pdf

BBC News. 2013. "'Urgent need' to remove space debris," April 25. www.bbc.co.uk

Beamish, Thomas. 2002. *Silent Spill: The Organization of an Industrial Crisis*. Boston: MIT Press.

Beard, Jennifer; Feeley, Frank; and Rosen, Sydney. 2009. "Economic and quality of life outcomes of antiretroviral therapy for HIV/AIDS in developing countries: A systematic literature review." *AIDS Care*, vol. 21, no. 11: 1343–1356.

Becker, A.; Burwell, R.; Herzog, D.; Hamburg, P.; and Gilman, S. 2002. "Eating behaviours and attitudes following prolonged exposure to television among ethnic Fijian adolescent girls." *The British Journal of Psychiatry*, vol. 180: 509–514.

Becker, Howard S. 1963. *Outsiders: Studies in the Sociology of Deviance*. Chicago: University of Chicago Press.

———. 1986. *Doing Things Together: Selected Papers*. Evanston, IL: Northwestern University Press.

———; Greer, Blanche; Hughes, Everett C.; and Strauss, Anselm L. 1961. *Boys in White: Student Culture in Medical School*. Chicago: University of Chicago Press.

Beeghley, Leonard. 2008. *The Structure of Social Stratification in the United States*. Boston: Allyn and Bacon.

Bell, Daniel. 1976. *The Coming of Post-Industrial Society: A Venture in Social Forecasting*. New York: Basic Books.

Bellah, Robert; Sullivan, William; and Tipton, Steven. 1985. *Habits of the Heart: Individualism and Commitment in American Life*. Berkeley: University of California Press.

Bengali, Leila; and Daly, Mary C. 2014. "Is it still worth going to college?" *FRBSF Economic Letter*, May 5. http://www.frbsf.org/economic-research/publications/economic-letter/2014/may/is-college-worth-it-education-tuition-wages/

Berends, M. 1995. "Educational stratification and students' social bonding to school." *British Journal of Sociology of Education*, vol. 16, no. 3: 327–351.

———. 1977. *Facing Up to Modernity: Excursions in Society, Politics, and Religion*. New York: Basic Books.

———; and Luckmann, Thomas. 1966. *The Social Construction of Reality: A Treatise in the Sociology of Knowledge*. Garden City, NY: Doubleday.

Berger, Andrea; Turk-Bicakci, Lori; Garet, Michael; Knudson, Joel; and Hoshen, Gur. 2014. "Early college, continued success: Early college high school initiative impact study." *American Institutions for Research*, January 15. http://www.air.org/resource/early-college-continued-success-early-college-high-school-initiative-impact-study-2014

Berman, Mark. 2014. "Horror and few answers in small Florida town after man kills his daughter and six grandchildren." *Washington Post*, September 19.

Bernardes, Jon. 1985. "Do we really know what the family is?" In P. Close and R. Collins, eds., *Family and Economy in Modern Society*. New York: Macmillan.

Berube, A., Singer, A., Wilson, J.H. & Frey, W.H. 2006. "Finding exurbia: America's fast-growing communities at the metropolitan fringe." Washington, D.C.: The Brookings Institution.

Best, Joel. 2006. *Flavor of the Month: Why Smart People Fall for Fads*. Berkeley, CA: University of California Press.

Best, Samuel J., and Brian S. Krueger. 2004. *Internet Data Collection*. Sage University Paper Series no. 141. Thousand Oaks, CA: Sage.

Bienkowski, Brian. 2013. "Corporations grabbing land and water overseas." *Scientific American*, February. http://www.scientificamerican.com/article/corporations-grabbing-land-and-water-overseas/

Blank, Rolf K. 2011. "Closing the achievement gap for economically disadvantaged students?: Analyzing change since No Child Left Behind using state assessments and the national assessment of educational progress." Council of Chief State School Officers. http://files.eric.ed.gov/fulltext/ED518986.pdf

Blau, Judith R.; and Blau, Peter M. 1982. "The cost of inequality: Metropolitan structure and violent crime." *American Sociological Review*, vol. 47, no. 1: 114–129.

Blau, Melinda; and Fingerman, Karen. 2009. *Consequential Strangers: The Power of People Who Don't Seem To Matter . . . But Really Do*. New York: Norton.

Blaunstein, Albert; and Zangrando, Robert, eds. 1970. *Civil Rights and the Black American*. New York: Washington Square Press.

Bloom, Allan. 1987. *The Closing of the American Mind*. New York: Simon & Schuster.

Blumer, Herbert. 1969. *Symbolic Interactionism: Perspective and Method*. Berkeley: University of California Press.

Blumler, J. G.; and Katz, Elihu. 1974. *The Uses of Mass Communication: Current Perspectives on Gratifications Research*. Beverly Hills, CA: Sage.

Bly, Robert. 1990. *Iron John: A Book About Men*. Upper Saddle River, NJ: Addison-Wesley.

Bobo, Lawrence; Kluegel, James R.; and Smith, Ryan A. 1997. "Laissez-faire racism: The crystallization of a 'kindler, gentler' anti-black ideology." In Jack Martin, ed., *Racial Attitudes in the 1990s: Continuity and Change*. Westport, CT: Praeger.

Bobo, Lawrence; and Smith, Ryan A. 1998. "From Jim Crow racism to laissez-faire racism: The transformation of racial attitudes in America." In Wendy Katkin, Ned Landsman, and Andrea Tyree, eds., *Beyond Pluralism: Essays on the Conception of Groups and Group Identities in America*. Urbana: University of Illinois Press.

Boerma, Lindsay. 2014. "Midterm 2014 ad spending: How Karl Rove, NRA, and Koch Brothers fared." CBS News, November 6. cbsnews.com/news/midterm-2014-ad-spending-how-karl-rove-nra-koch-brothers-fared

Bogaert, Anthony F. 2004. "Asexuality: Prevalence and Associated factors in a national probability sample." *Journal of Sex*, vol. 41, no. 3: 279–287.

Bohner, Gerd; Siebler, Frank; and Schmelcher, Jurgen. 2006. "Social norms and the likelihood of raping: Perceived rape myth acceptance of others affects men's rape proclivity." *Personality and Social Psychology Bulletin*, vol. 32, no. 3: 286–297.

Bonacich, Edna. 1980. *The Economic Basis of Ethnic Solidarity: Small Business in the Japanese American Community.* Berkeley: University of California Press.

Bond, Rod; and Sussex, Peter B. 1996. "Culture and conformity: A meta-analysis of studies using Asch's (1952b, 1956) line judgment task." *Psychological Bulletin,* vol. 119, no. 1: 111–137.

Bonilla-Silva, Eduardo. 2013. *Racism Without Racists: Color-Blind Racism and the Persistence of Racial Inequality in America.* 4th ed. New York: Rowman & Littlefield.

Booth, A.; Shelley, G.; Mazur, A.; Tharp, G.; and Kittock, R. 1989. "Testosterone and winning and losing in human competition." *Hormones and Behavior,* vol. 23: 556–571.

Bordo, Susan. 1995. *Unbearable Weight: Feminism, Western Culture, and the Body.* Berkeley: University of California Press,

Borowitz, Andy. 2014. "Midterms prediction: Billionaires to retain control of government." *The New Yorker,* October 28. http://www.newyorker.com/humor/borowitz-report/midterms-prediction-billionaires-retain-control-government

Boudon, Raymond. 1991. "What middle-range theories are." *Contemporary Sociology,* vol. 20, no. 4: 519–522.

Bourassa, Loren; and Ashforth, Blake E. 1998. "You are about to party *Defiant* style: Socialization and identity aboard an Alaskan fishing boat." *Journal of Contemporary Ethnography,* vol. 27 (July): 171–196.

Bourdieu, Pierre. 1973. "Cultural reproduction and social reproduction." In Richard Brown, ed., *Knowledge, Education, and Social Change: Papers in the Sociology of Education.* London: Tavistock.

———. 1984. *Distinction: A Social Critique of the Judgement of Taste.* Cambridge, MA: Harvard University Press.

Bowles, Samuel; and Gintis, Herbert. 1977. *Schooling in Capitalist America: Educational Reform and the Contradictions of Economic Life.* New York: Basic Books.

boyd, danah. 2007. "Why youth (heart) social network sites: The role of networked publics in teenage social life." In David Buckingham, ed., *MacArthur Foundation Series on Digital Learning—Youth, Identity and Digital Media Volume.* Cambridge, MA: MIT Press.

———. 2011. "White flight in networked publics? How race and class shaped American teen engagement with MySpace and Facebook." In Lisa Nakamura and Peter A. Chow-White, eds., *Race After the Internet.* New York: Routledge.

———. 2014. *It's Complicated.* New Haven: Yale University Press.

Boyd, Robert. 2004. "World may be darkening as clouds, air pollution dim the sun's rays." Knight Ridder News Service, *Santa Barbara News-Press,* May 9.

Boyle, Brendan. 2009. "Income gap is growing: The rich are getting richer—and rich whites quicker than rich blacks." *South African Times,* October 8. www.timeslive.co.za/business/article143706.ece

Bozick, Robert; Alexander, Karl; and Entwisel, Doris, et al. 2010. "Framing the future: Revisiting the place of educational expectations in status attainment." *Social Forces,* vol. 88, no. 5: 2027–2052.

Bradley, Graham; and Wildman, Karen. 2002. "Psychosocial predictors of emerging adults' risk and reckless behaviors." *Journal of Youth and Adolescence,* vol. 31, no. 4: 253–265.

Brandon, Michael C. 1996. "From need to know to need to know." *Communication World,* vol. 13, no. 8 (October–November): 18.

Brennan, Morgan. 2014. "Huge media mergers are booming in 2014." *CNBC.com,* May 15. http://www.cnbc.com/id/101676246

Brief, Arthur P.; Buttram, Robert T.; Elliott, Jodi D.; Reizenstein, Robin M.; and McCline, Richard L. 1995. "Releasing the beast: A study of compliance with orders to use race as a selection criterion." *Journal of Social Issues,* vol. 51, no. 3: 177–193.

Brimson, Dougie. 2010. *March of the Hooligans: Soccer's Bloody Fraternity.* London: Virgin Books.

Brinkley-Rogers, Paul. 2002. "Pledge of allegiance reflects timeline of nation's history." *Columbus Dispatch,* June 28, p. 2A.

Brodkin, Karen. 1999. *How Jews Became White Folks and What That Says About Race in America.* New Brunswick, NJ: Rutgers University Press.

Brooks, Holifield E. 2014. "Understanding why Americans seem more religious than other Western powers." *Huffington Post,* February 15. https://www.opensecrets.org/lobby/top.php?showYear=a&indexType=s

Brooks, James F. 2002. *Confounding the Color Line: The Indian-Black Experience in North America.* Lincoln: University of Nebraska Press.

Browning, Lynnley. 2014. "Do team games for employees really improve productivity?" *Newsweek,* October 26.

Buford, Bill. 1993. *Among the Thugs.* New York: Vintage.

Bullard, Robert. 1990. *Dumping in Dixie: Race, Class and Environmental Quality.* Boulder, CO: Westview Press.

———. 1993. *Confronting Environmental Racism: Voices from the Grassroots.* Boston: South End Press.

———; Johnson, Glenn S.; and Wright, Beverly H. 1997. "Confronting environmental injustice: It's the right thing to do." *Race, Gender & Class,* vol. 5, no. 1: 63–79.

———; and Wright, Beverly H. 1990. "The quest for environmental equity: Mobilizing the African-American community for social change." *Society and Natural Resources,* vol. 3: 301–311.

Burger, Jerry M. 2009. "Replicating Milgram: Would people still obey today?" *American Psychologist,* vol. 64, no. 1: 1–11.

Burkhalter, Byron. 1999. "Reading race online." In Marc Smith and Peter Kollock, eds., *Communities in Cyberspace.* London: Routledge.

Burns, Crosby; and Krehely, Jeff. 2011. "Gay and transgender people face high rates of workplace discrimination and harassment." Center for American Progress, June 2. https://www.americanprogress.org/issues/lgbt/news/2011/06/02/9872/gay-and-transgender-people-face-high-rates-of-workplace-discrimination-and-harassment/

Burros, Marian. 2009. "Urban farming, a bit closer to the sun." *New York Times,* June 16.

Burrus, Daniel. 2014. "The Internet of Things is far bigger than anyone realizes." *Wired,* November. http://www.wired.com/2014/11/the-internet-of-things-bigger/

Burton, Neel. 2012. "Compared to men, women are twice as likely to develop depression." *Psychology Today,* May 17. http://archpsyc.jamanetwork.com/article.aspx?articleid=1733742

Butler, Judith. 1993. *Bodies That Matter: On the Discursive Limits of "Sex."* New York: Routledge.

———. 1999. *Gender Trouble.* New York: Routledge.

Buttel, Frederick H. 1987. "New directions in environmental sociology." *Annual Review of Sociology,* 13: 465–488.

Byrne, D. G. 1981. "Sex differences in the reporting of symptoms of depression in the general population." *British Journal of Clinical Psychology,* vol. 20: 83–92.

Cahill, Spencer. 1999. "Emotional capital and professional socialization: The case of mortuary science students (and me)." *Social Psychology Quarterly,* vol. 62 (June): 101–116.

Caincross, Francis. 1995. "The death of distance." Survey Telecommunications, *The Economist,* 30 (September): 5.

Califano, Joseph A., Jr. 1999. "What was really great about the Great Society." *Washington Monthly,* October.

California Community Colleges Chancellor's Office. 2015. "Key Facts About California Community Colleges," January. http://californiacommunitycolleges.cccco.edu/PolicyInAction/Key-Facts.aspx

Cancian, Maria; and Meyer, Daniel R. 1998. "Who gets custody?" *Demography,* vol. 35, no. 2: 147–157.

_____.; and Brown P. R.; and Cook S. T. 2014. "Who Gets Custody Now? Dramatic Changes in Children's Living Arrangements After Divorce." Demography. 51(4), 1381–1396.

Caplan, Jeremy. 2005. "How green is my town." U.S. Snapshot, _Time_, July 18.

Cappelli, Peter. 2015. _Will College Pay Off? A Guide to the Most Important Financial Decision You'll Ever Make._ New York: Public Affairs.

Carnevale, A.; Rose, S. J.; and Cheah, B. 2011. "The college payoff: Education, occupations, lifetime earnings." Georgetown University Center on Education and the Workforce, August 5. www.cew .georgetown.edu/collegepayoff.com

Carpenter, Sandra; and Meade-Pruitt, S. Maria. 2008. "Does the Twenty Statements Test elicit self-concept aspects that are most descriptive?" _World Cultures eJournal_, 16(1).

Carson, Rachel. 1962. _Silent Spring._ New York: Houghton Mifflin.

Cassel, Christine K.; and Demel, Beth. 2001. "Remembering death: Public policy in the USA." _Journal of the Royal Society of Medicine_, vol. 94, no. 9: 433–436.

Cassidy, Tina. 2006. _Birth._ New York: Atlantic Monthly Press.

Castells, Manuel. 1984. "Cultural identity, sexual liberation and urban structure: The gay community in San Francisco." In _The City and the Grassroots: A Cross-Cultural Theory of Urban Social Movements._ Berkeley: University of California Press.

_____. 2000. _The Rise of the Network Society_, vol. 1. 2nd ed. Malden, MA: Blackwell.

_____.; and Susser, Ida. 2002. _The Castells Reader on Cities and Social Theory._ Malden, MA: Blackwell.

Catalano, Shannan M. 2012. "Intimate Partner Violence, 1993–2010." DC: U.S. Department of Justice. NCJ #239203.

Catalyst. 2013. "Women on boards." May 31. http://catalyst.org /knowledge/women-boards

Catholics for a Free Choice. 2002. "Student Bodies: Reproductive Health Care at Catholic Universities." DC: _Catholics for a Free Choice._ http://www.catholicsforchoice.org/topics/healthcare /documents/2002studentbodies.pdf

Catton, William R., Jr. 1980. _Overshoot: The Ecological Basis of Revolutionary Change._ Urbana: University of Illinois Press.

_____.; and Dunlap, Riley E. 1978. "Environmental sociology: A new paradigm." _American Sociologist_, vol. 13: 41–49.

_____. 1980. "A new ecological paradigm for post-exuberant society." _American Behavioral Scientist_, vol. 24, no. 1: 15–47.

Caughey, John L. 1984. _Imaginary Social Worlds: A Cultural Approach._ Lincoln: University of Nebraska Press.

_____. 1999. "Imaginary social relationships." In Joseph Harris and Jay Rosen, eds., _Media Journal: Reading and Writing About Popular Culture._ Boston: Allyn and Bacon.

Center for Responsive Politics. 2013. "2012 Outside Spending, by Super PAC." www.opensecrets.org/outsidespending/summ.php? cycle=2012&chrt=V&type=S&ql3

Center for Responsive Politics. 2015. "Top Spenders." https://www .opensecrets.org/lobby/top.php?showYear=a&indexType=s

Centers for Disease Control. 1998. "Leading Cause of Death, 1900–1998." www.cdc.gov/nchs/data/dvs/lead1900_98.pdf

_____. 2011. "Health Disparities and Inequalities Report—United States, 2011." January 2011. www.cdc.gov/minorityhealth/reports /CHDIR11/ExecutiveSummary.pdf

_____. 2013a. "Health Behavior of Adults: United States, 2008–2010," http://www.cdc.gov/nchs/data/series/sr_10/sr10_257.pdf

_____. 2013b. "Health, United States, 2013." http://www.cdc.gov /nchs/data/hus/hus13.pdf#068

_____. 2014a. "Death in 5-year Age Groups, by Race and Sex: United States, 1999–2013," http://www.cdc.gov/nchs/nvss/mortality /lcwk1.htm

_____. 2014b. "Deaths: Final Data for 2013," Table 8: Life Expectancy at birth, by race, Hispanic origin, race for non-Hispanic population, and sex: United States, 1940, 1950, 1960, 1970, and 1975-2013." http://www.cdc.gov/nchs/data/nvsr/nvsr64/nvsr64_02.pdf

_____. 2014c. "Facts About Physical Activity." May 23. http://www .cdc.gov/physicalactivity

_____. 2014d. "Sexual Orientation and Health Among U.S. Adults: National Health Interview Survey, 2013." http://www.cdc.gov /nchs/data/nhsr/nhsr077.pdf

_____. 2014e. "Trends in Out-of-Hospital Births in the United States, 1990-2012." http://www.cdc.gov/nchs/data/databriefs/db144.htm

_____. 2015. "Measles Cases and Outbreaks." http://www.cdc.gov /measles/cases-outbreaks.html

Central Intelligence Agency. 2014a. "Country Comparison: Death Rate." https://www.cia.gov/library/publications/the-world-factbook /rankorder/2066rank.html

_____. 2014b. "Country Comparison: Infant Mortality Rate." https://www.cia.gov/library/publications/the-world-factbook /rankorder/2091rank.html

_____. 2014c. "Country Comparison: Life Expectancy at Birth." https://www.cia.gov/library/publications/the-world-factbook /rankorder/2102rank.html

_____. 2014d. "Country Comparison: Net Migration Rate." https://www.cia.gov/library/publications/the-world-factbook /rankorder/2112rank.html

_____. 2014e. "Country Comparison: Population." https://www.cia .gov/library/publications/the-world-factbook/rankorder /2119rank.html

_____. 2014f. "Country Comparison: Population Growth Rate." https://www.cia.gov/library/publications/the-world-factbook /rankorder/2002rank.html

_____. 2014g. "Country Comparison: Total Fertility Rate." https:// www.cia.gov/library/publications/the-world-factbook /rankorder/2127rank.html

_____. 2014h. "Deaths, percent of total deaths, and death rates for the 15 leading causes of death: United States and Each State, 1999–2013" http://www.cdc.gov/nchs/nvss/mortality/lcwk9.htm

_____. 2014i. "The World Factbook: Swaziland." https://www.cia .gov/library/publications/the-world-factbook/geos/wz.html

_____. 2015. Deaths: Final Data for 2013," Table 7. Life expectancy at selected ages, by race, Hispanic origin, race for non-Hispanic population, and sex: United States, 2013."

Champagne, Duane. 1994. _Native America: Portrait of the People._ Canton, MI: Visible Ink Press.

Charles, Camille Zubrinsky. 2001. "Processes of racial residential segregation." In Alice O'Connor, Chris Tilly, and Lawrence Bobo, eds., _Urban Inequality: Evidence from Four Cities._ New York: Russell Sage Foundation.

Chen, Katherine K. 2004. "The Burning Man organization grows up: Blending bureaucratic and alternative structures." Doctoral Dissertation. Harvard University.

Cherlin, Andrew J.; and Furstenberg, Frank F., Jr. 1994. "Stepfamilies in the United States: A reconsideration." _Annual Review of Sociology_, vol. 20: 359–381.

Cheslack-Postava, Keely; Liu, Kayuet; and Bearman, Peter S. 2011. "Closely spaced pregnancies are associated with increased odds of autism in California sibling births." _Pediatrics_, vol. 127, no. 2: 246–253.

Chesler, Phyllis. 2010. "Worldwide trends in honor killings." _Middle East Quarterly_, Spring. 3–11.

Chesley, Noelle. 2011. "Stay-at-home fathers and breadwinning mothers." _Gender & Society_, vol. 25, no. 5: 642–664.

Chetty, Raj, et. al. "Is the United States Still a Land of Opportunity? Recent Trends in Intergenerational Mobility" _National Bureau of_

Economic Research. January 2014. Accessed at: http://www.nber .org/papers/w19844

Chiles, Nick. "Huge Wage Gap Between Blacks and Whites Threatens to Tear South Africa Apart" *Atlanta Black Star*. September 4, 2012 Accessed at: http://atlantablackstar.com/2012/09/04/huge -wage-gap-between-blacks-and-whites-threatens-to-tear-south -africa-apart/

Chodorow, Nancy. 1978. *The Reproduction of Mothering: Psychoanalysis and the Sociology of Gender*. Berkeley: University of California Press.

———. 1994. *Femininities, Masculinities, Sexualities: Freud and Beyond*. Lexington: University Press of Kentucky.

Chordas, Lori. 2003. "Instant connection: Instant messaging is taking the business world by storm, and some insurers already are finding it improves productivity and reduces costs." *Best's Review*, vol. 104, no. 3 (July): 100.

Christakis, N. A. 1995. "The similarity and frequency of proposals to reform U.S. medical education: Constant concerns." *Journal of the American Medical Association*, vol. 274: 706.

———; and Fowler, James. 2009. *Connected: The Surprising Power of Our Social Networks and How They Shape Our Lives*. New York: Little, Brown and Company.

Christian Science Monitor. 2007. "Gender bias in college admissions." July 24. www.csmonitor.com/2007/0724/p08s01-comv.html

Christensen, Jen and Val Willingham. 2014. "Live to 100: Number of centenarians has doubled" CNN. June 4. http://www.cnn.com /2014/06/04/health/centenarian-death/

Cialdini, Robert B. 1998. *Influence: The Psychology of Persuasion*, rev. ed. Foxboro, Toronto Perennial Currents.

———; and Trost, M. R. 1998. "Social influence: Social norms, conformity, and compliance." In D. T. Gilbert, S. E. Fiske, and G. Lindzey, eds., *Handbook of Social Psychology*, vol. 2. 4th ed. Boston: McGraw-Hill.

Cicourel, Aaron V. 1972. "Basic and normative rules in the negotiation of status and role." In D. Sudnow, ed., *Studies in Social Interaction*. New York: Free Press.

Cisco. 2011. "The Internet of Things." http://share.cisco.com/internet -of-things.html

Clark, Meagan. 2014. "What is the world's most-watched TV program? Hint: It's not in the US." *International Business Times*, February 6. http://www.ibtimes.com/what-worlds-most-watched -tv-program-hint-its-not-us-1553678

Clarke, Lee. 2001. *Mission Improbable: Using Fantasy Documents to Tame Disaster*. Chicago: University of Chicago Press.

Clayman, Steven E. 2002. "Sequence and solidarity." *Advances in Group Processes*, vol. 19: 229–253.

Clinton, Catherine; and Gillespie, Michelle, eds. 1997. *The Devil's Lane: Sex and Race in the Early South*. New York: Oxford University Press.

CNN. 2005. "Poll: U.S. Catholics would support changes." April 3. www.edition.cnn.com/2005/US/04/03/pope.poll/

Coalition for the Homeless. 2015. "New York City Homelessness: A Fact Sheet," http://www.coalitionforthehomeless.org/wp-content /uploads/2015/01/NYC-Homelessness-Fact-Sheet-11-20145 .pdf

Cohen, Cathy J. 2005. "Punks, bulldaggers, and welfare queens: The radical potential of queer politics?" in E. Patrick Johnson and Mae G. Henderson, eds., *Black Queer Studies*. Durham, NC: Duke University Press.

Cohen, Lawrence J.; and DeBenedet, Anthony T. 2012. "Penn State cover-up: Groupthink in action: How do smart, principled men wind up defending a child abuser in their midst?" *Time*, July 17. http://ideas.time.com/2012/07/17/penn-state-cover-up-group -think-in-action/

Cohen, Philip. 2014. *The Family: Diversity, Inequality and Social Change*. New York: W. W. Norton & Company.

Cohen, S. P. 2001. *India: Emerging Power*. Washington, DC: Brookings Institution Press.

Coleman, James S. 1966. "Equality of Educational Opportunity (COLEMAN) Study (EEOS)," Ann Arbor, MI: Inter-university Consortium for Political and Social Research. http://doi .org/10.3886/ICPSR06389.v3.

Coleman, John R. 1983. "Diary of a homeless man." *New York Magazine*, February.

College Board. Annual Survey of Colleges. 2015a. "Average Published Undergraduate Charges by Sector, 2014–2015." http:// trends.collegeboard.org/college-pricing/figures-tables/average -published-undergraduate-charges-sector-2014-15

———. 2015b. "Trends in College Pricing: 2014." http://trends .collegeboard.org/sites/default/files/2014-trends-college -pricing-final-web.pdf

Collins, Patricia Hill. 2006. *From Black Power to Hip Hop: Racism, Nationalism, and Feminism*. Philadelphia: Temple University Press.

Collins, Randall. 1979. *The Credential Society: An Historical Sociology of Education and Stratification*. New York: Worthington Press.

Coltrane, Scott. 1997. *Family Man: Fatherhood, Housework and Gender Equity*. New York: Oxford University Press.

Common Core State Standards Initiative. 2015. "About the Standards." http://www.corestandards.org/about-the-standards/

Community Organizing and Family Issues (COFI). 2009. "Why isn't Johnny in preschool?" www.cofionline.org/files/earlylearningre port.pdf

Comte, Auguste. 1988 (orig. 1842). *Introduction to Positive Philosophy*. Frederick Ferré ed. and tr. Indianapolis, IN: Hackett.

Condon, Stephanie. 2011. "GOP rep. calls health reforms 'worst bill' ever, House votes to defund laws." *CBS News Political Hotsheet*. February 18. www.cbsnews.com/8301-503544_162-20033441-503544 .html

Conley, Dalton. 2000. *Honky*. Berkeley and Los Angeles: University of California Press.

———. 2002. *Wealth and Poverty in America: A Reader*. Malden, MA: Blackwell.

———. 2004. *The Pecking Order: Which Siblings Succeed and Why*. New York: Pantheon.

———. 2009. *Elsewhere, U.S.A.: How We Got from the Company Man, Family Dinners and the Affluent Society to the Home Office, Black-Berry Moms and Economic Anxiety*. New York: Pantheon.

Connell, R. W. 1995. *Masculinities*. Berkeley: University of California Press. *Contemporary Pediatrics*. vol. 17, no. 10: 12.

Conrad, Peter. 2006. *Identifying Hyperactive Children: The Medicalization of Deviant Behavior*. Burlington, VT: Ashgate.

Conti, Joseph. 2003. "Trade, power, and law: Dispute settlement in the World Trade Organization, 1995–2002." Unpublished Master's Thesis. University of California, Santa Barbara.

———. 2005. "Power through process: Determinants of dispute resolution outcomes in the World Trade Organization." Unpublished Dissertation. University of California, Santa Barbara, Department of Sociology.

Cook, Kevin. 2015. *Kitty Genovese: The Murder, the Bystanders, and the Crime that Changed America*. New York: W. W. Norton & Company.

Cook, Noble David. 1998. *Born to Die: Disease and New World Conquest, 1492–1650*. Cambridge, UK: Cambridge University Press.

Cook, Tim. 2015. "Pro discrimination 'religious freedom' laws are dangerous." *Washington Post*, March 29. http://www.washingtonpost .com/opinions/pro discrimination-religious-freedom-laws-are -dangerous-to-america/2015/03/29/bdb4ce9e-d66d 11e4-ba28 -f2a685dc7f89_story.html

Cooley, Charles Horton. 1909. *Social Organization: A Study of the Large Mind.* New York: Scribner.

Coontz, Stephanie. 2000. *The Way We Never Were: American Families and the Nostalgia Trap.* New York: Basic Books.

Cooper, David; and Essrow, Dan. 2013. "Low-wage workers are older than you think." *Economic Policy Institute,* August 28. http://www.epi.org/publication/wage-workers-older-88-percent-workers-benefit

Cooper, H. 2014. "Pentagon study finds 50% increase in reports of military sexual assaults." *New York Times,* May 1. http://www.nytimes.com/2014/05/02/us/military-sex-assault-report.html?_r=0

Corporation for National & Community Service. 2014. "Volunteering and Civic Life in America 2014." http://www.volunteeringinamerica.gov

Cosgrove-Mather, Bootie. 2004. "The suicide capital of America: They come to Las Vegas not to gamble but to kill themselves." *CBS News Healthwatch,* February 9. www.cbsnews.com/stories/2004/02/09/health/main599070.shtml

Cota, A. A.; Evans, C. R.; Dion, K. L.; Kilik, L. L.; and Longman, R. S. 1995. "The structure of group cohesion." *Personality and Social Psychology Bulletin,* vol. 21: 572–580.

Couvrette, Phil. 2005. "World's biodiversity declining at an alarming rate." Associated Press. May 20. www.enn.com/top_stories/article/1604

Credit.com. 2011. "Student Credit & Debt Statistics." www.credit.com/press/statistics/student-credit-and-debt-statistics.html

Crenshaw, Kimberle; Gotanda, Neil; Peller, Garry; and Thomas, Kendall, eds. 1996. *Critical Race Theory: The Key Writings That Formed the Movement.* New York: New Press.

Cunningham, M.; and Jones, J.W. 2010. "Attitude and behavior assessments versus personality tests for personnel selection: Impact on key business indicators." Human Capital Research Report. Chicago, IL: General Dynamics Information Technology.

Curtin, Sally C.; Ventura, Stephanie J.; and Martinez, Gladys M. 2014. "Recent declines in nonmarital childbearing in the United States." NCHS Data Brief, No. 162. August. http://www.cdc.gov/nchs/data/databriefs/db162.pdf

Cutter, Stephanie. 2015. "Behind Obama's social media rollout: Strategy, not spoilers." *The Wall Street Journal,* January 20. http://blogs.wsj.com/washwire/2015/01/20/behind-obamas-social-media-rollout-strategy-not-spoilers

Dahl, Robert A. 1961. *Who Governs?* New Haven, CT: Yale University Press.

Darley, John; and Latané, Bibb. 1968. "Bystander intervention in emergencies: Diffusion of responsibility." *Journal of Personality and Social Psychology,* vol. 8, 377–383. Davila, M. 1971. "Compadrazgo: Fictive kinship in Latin America." In N. Graburn, ed., *Readings in Kinship and Social Structure.* New York: Harper & Row.

Davis, Angela Y. 2001. "Outcast mothers and surrogates: Racism and reproductive politics." In Laurel Richardson, Verta Taylor, and Nancy Whittier, eds., *Feminist Frontiers IV.* Boston: McGraw-Hill.

Davis, Kingsley. 1940. "Extreme social isolation of a child." *American Journal of Sociology,* vol. 45 (January): 554–565.

———.; and Moore, Wilbert. 1945. "Some principles of stratification." *American Sociological Review,* vol. 10, no. 2: 242–249.

———. 1947. "Final note on a case of extreme isolation." *American Journal of Sociology,* vol. 52, no. 5: 432–437.

Davis, T. 1995. "The occupational mobility of Black males revisited—Does race matter?" *Social Science Journal,* vol. 32, no. 2: 121–135.

De Alth, Shelley. 2009. "ID at the polls: Assessing the impact of recent state voter ID laws on voter turnout." *Harvard Law and Policy Review,* vol. 3: 185–202.

Declercq E. R.; Sakala, C.; Corry, M. P.; and Applebaum, S. 2007. "Listening to mothers II: Report of the second national U.S. survey of women's childbearing experiences." *The Journal of Perinatal Education,* vol. 16: 9–14.

De Graaf, John; Waan, David; and Naylor, Thomas. 2002. *Affluenza: The All-Consuming Epidemic.* San Francisco: Berrett-Koehler.

Dell'Amore, Christine. 2008. "'Deadly dozen' diseases could stem from global warming." *National Geographic News,* October 7. www.news.nationalgeographic.com/news/2008/10/081007-climate-diseases.html

DeNavas-Walt, Carmen and Bernadette D. Proctor. 2014. "Income and Poverty in the United States: 2013: Current Population Reports." https://www.census.gov/content/dam/Census/library/publications/2014/demo/p60-249.pdf

DeParle, Jason. 2012. "Harder for Americans to Rise from lower rungs." *New York Times.* January 4. http://www.nytimes.com/2012/01/05/us/harder-for-americans-to-rise-from-lower-rungs.html?pagewanted=all

Desilver, Drew. 2013. "How many same-sex marriages in the U.S.? At least 71,165, probably more." June 26. http://www.pewresearch.org/fact-tank/2013/06/26/how-many-same-sex-marriages-in-the-u-s-at-least-71165-probably-more/

DeSilver, Drew. 2014a. "College enrollment among low-income students still trails richer groups" *Pew Research Center.* January 15. http://www.pewresearch.org/fact-tank/2014/01/15/college-enrollment-among-low-income-students-still-trails-richer-groups/

DeSilver, Drew. 2014b. "Voter turnout always drops off for midterm elections, but why?" http://www.pewresearch.org/fact-tank/2014/07/24/voter-turnout-always-drops-off-for-midterm-elections-but-why/

Desjarlais-deKlerk, Kristen; and Wallace, Jean E. 2013. "Instrumental and socioemotional communications in doctor-patient interactions in urban and rural clinics." *BMC Health Services Research,* vol. 13: 261.

DeVault, Marjorie. 1994 (orig. 1991). *Feeding the Family: The Social Organization of Caring as Gendered Work.* Chicago: University of Chicago Press.

Di Leonardo, Micaela. 1987. "The female world of cards and holidays: Women, families, and the work of kinship." *Signs,* vol. 12, no. 3: 340–350.

Dicken, Peter. 1998. *The Global Shift: Transforming the World Economy.* 3rd ed. New York: Guilford Press.

Dickson, Caitlyn. 2014. "Sovereign citizens are America's top cop-killers." *The Daily Beast,* November 25. http://www.thedailybeast.com/articles/2014/11/25/sovereign-citizens-are-america-s-top-cop-killers.html

Dickson, Kevin; and Lorenz, Alicia. 2009. "Psychological empowerment and job satisfaction of temporary and part-time nonstandard workers." Institute of Behavioral and Applied Management. www.ibam.com/pubs/jbam/articles/vol10/no2/JBAM_10_2_2.pdf

Doherty, Brian. 2000. "Burning Man grows up." *Reason,* vol. 31: 24–33. www.reason.com/0002/fe.bd.burning.shtml

———. 2004. *This Is Burning Man.* New York: Little, Brown and Company.

Domhoff, G. William. 1983. *Who Rules America Now? A View from the Eighties.* Englewood Cliffs, NJ: Prentice Hall.

———. 1987. *Power Elites and Organizations.* Newbury Park, CA: Sage.

———. 1990. *The Power Elite and the State: How Policy Is Made in America.* New York: de Gruyter.

_____. 2002. *Who Rules America Now? Power and Politics in the Year 2000*. 3rd ed. Mountain View, CA: Mayfield.

_____. 2013. *Who Rules America? The Triumph of the Corporate Rich*. New York: McGraw Hill.

Donnelly, Denise; and Finkelhor, David. 1993. "Who has joint custody? Class differences in the determination of custody arrangements." *Family Relations*, vol. 42, no. 1: 57–60.

Dougherty, P. 2015. "Despite skeptics, acupuncture finds favor with athletes." *Press-Gazette Media*, January 14. http://www.packersnews.com/story/sports/nfl/packers/2015/01/14/despite-skeptics-acupuncture-finds-favor-with-athletes/21782441/Packersnews.com

Drucker, Peter. 1959. *Landmarks of Tomorrow: A Report on the New "Post-Modern" World*. New York: Harper.

_____. 2003. *The Essential Drucker: The Best of Sixty Years of Peter Drucker's Writings on Management*. New York: Collins.

Duany, Andres; Plater-Zyberk, Elizabeth; and Speck, Jeff. 2001. *Suburban Nation: The Rise of Sprawl and the Decline of the American Dream*. New York: North Point Press.

DuBois, W. E. B. 1903. *The Souls of Black Folk*. Chicago: A.C. McClurg & Co.; [Cambridge]: University Press John Wilson and Son, Cambridge, U.S.A.

Duggan, Lisa. 2003. *The Twilight of Equality?: Neoliberalisam, Cultural Politics, and the Attack on Democracy*. Boston: Beacon Press.

Duke, Alan. 2014, "'Deltopia' party in California turns violent; dozens arrested." *CNN*, April 7. http://www.cnn.com/2014/04/06/us/california-street-party-melee/

Dunaway, Wilma. 2014. *Gendered Commodity Chains: Seeing Women's Work and Households in Global Production*. Stanford, CA: Stanford University Press.

Duncan, David Ewing. 2012. "How long do you want to live?" *New York Times Sunday Review*, August 25.

Duneier, Mitchell; and Carter, Ovie. 1999. *Sidewalk*. New York: Farrar, Straus and Giroux.

Dunlap, Riley, E.; and Catton, William, Jr. 1979. "Environmental sociology." *Annual Review of Sociology*, no. 5: 243–273.

Dunn, J. L. 2002. *Courting Disaster: Intimate Stalking, Culture, and Criminal Justice*. New Brunswick, NJ: Transaction Publishers.

Dupuis, Sherry L.; and Smale, Bryan J. A. 2000. "Bittersweet journeys: Meanings of leisure in the institution-based caregiving context." *Journal of Leisure Research*, vol. 32, no. 3: 303.

Durkheim, Emile. 1951 (orig. 1897). *Suicide: A Study in Sociology*. Trans. John A. Spaulding and George Simpson. Glencoe, IL: Free Press.

_____. 1984 (orig. 1893). *The Division of Labor in Society*. Trans. W. D. Halls. New York: Free Press.

_____. 1995 (orig. 1912). *The Elementary Forms of Religious Life*. Trans. Karen E. Fields. New York: Free Press.

Dutta, Soumitra; and Fraser, Mathew. 2008. "Barack Obama and the Facebook election." *U.S. News and World Report*, November 19. http://www.usnews.com/opinion/articles/2008/11/19/barack-obama-and-the-facebook-election

Dwyer, Jim. 2001. "A nation challenged." *New York Times*, November 6, p. A1.

Dye, Thomas R. 2002. *Who's Running America? The Bush Restoration*. 7th ed. Upper Saddle River, NJ: Prentice Hall.

Edgerton, Robert B. 1992. *Sick Societies: Challenging the Myth of Primitive Harmony*. New York: Free Press.

Edin, Kathryn. 2000. "Few good men." *American Prospect*, vol. 11, no. 4 (January 3).

_____; and Kefalas, Maria. 2005. *Promises I Can Keep: Why Poor Women Put Motherhood Before Marriage*. Berkeley: University of California Press.

_____; and Lein, Laura. 1997. *Making Ends Meet*. New York: Russell Sage Foundation.

Edwards-Levy, Ariel. 2012. "Students at Catholic colleges protest lack of access to birth control." *The Huffington Post*, February 9. http://www.huffingtonpost.com/2012/02/09/catholic-college-students-birth-control_n_1265771.html

Egelko, Bob. 2002. "Pledge of allegiance ruled unconstitutional; many say ruling by S. F. court hasn't a prayer after appeals." *San Francisco Chronicle*, June 27, p. A1.

Ehrenreich, Barbara. 1990. *The Worst Years of our Lives: Irreverent Notes from a Decade of Greed*. New York: Pantheon.

_____. 2001. *Nickel and Dimed: On (Not) Getting by in America*. New York: Metropolitan Books.

_____. 2004. "All together now." *New York Times*, July 15.

Ehrlich, Paul R.; and Ehrlich, Anne H. 1990. *The Population Explosion*. New York: Simon & Schuster.

Eisenstein, Zillah. 1979. "Capitalist patriarchy and the case for socialist feminism." *Monthly Review*, February.

El Nasser, Haye. 2010. "Downturn Douses Nevada's population Growth Streak." *USA Today*, November 8.

Ellis, Carolyn. 1995. "Emotional and ethical quagmires in returning to the field." *Journal of Contemporary Ethnography*, vol. 24: 68–96.

_____. 1997. "Evocative autoethnography: Writing emotionally about our lives." In W. G. Tierney and Y. S. Lincoln, eds., *Representation and the Text: Re-framing the Narrative Voice*. Albany, NY: SUNY Press.

_____. 2007. Telling secrets, revealing lives: Relational ethics in research with intimate others. *Qualitative Inquiry*, vol. 13, no. 3: 3–29.

Emerson, Robert. 2002. *Contemporary Field Research: Perspectives and Formulations*. 2nd ed. Long Grove, IL: Waveland Press.

England, Paula. 1992. *Comparable Worth: Theories and Evidence*. Edison, NJ: Aldine Transaction.

Entertainment and Sports Programming Network. 2015. "NBA Attendance Report—2015." http://espn.go.com/nba/attendance

Environmental Protection Agency. 2012. "Municipal Solid Waste." http://www.epa.gov/epawaste/nonhaz/municipal/

_____. 2014. "Climate Change Facts: Answers to Common Questions." http://www.epa.gov/climatechange/basics/facts.html

Epps, Edgar. 2001. "Race, class, and educational opportunity: Trends in the sociology of education." In Bruce R. Hare, ed., *Race Odyssey: African Americans and Sociology: A Critical Analysis*. Syracuse, NY: Syracuse University Press.

Eskridge, Larry. 2012. "How Many Evangelicals Are There?" The Institute for the Study of American Evangelicals. http://www.wheaton.edu/ISAE/Defining-Evangelicalism/How-Many-Are-There

Etzioni, Amitai. 1996. "The responsive community: A communitarian perspective." *American Sociological Review*, vol. 61, no. 1: 1–11.

Fabes, Richard A.; Martin, Carol Lynn; and Hanish, Laura D. 2003. "Young children's play qualities in same-, other-, and mixed-sex peer groups." *Child Development*, vol. 74, no. 3: 921.

Fadiman, Anne. 1998. *The Spirit Catches You and You Fall Down*. New York: Farrar, Straus and Giroux

Fairbanks, C. 1992. "Labels, literacy and enabled learning: Glenn's story." *Harvard Educational Review*, vol. 62, no. 4: 475–493.

Falconer, Renee C.; and Byrnes, Deborah A. 2003. "When good intentions are not enough: A response to increasing diversity in an early childhood setting." *Journal of Research in Childhood Education*, vol. 17, no. 2: 188.

Faludi, Susan. 1999. *Stiffed: The Betrayal of the American Man*. New York: William & Morrow.

Farghal, M.; and Shakir, A. 1994. "Kin terms and titles of address as relational social honorifics in Jordanian Arabic." *Anthropological Linguistics*, no. 36: 240–253.

Farrell, Mary. 2014. "Whirlpool's smart washer and dryer just got smarter." *Consumer Reports,* June. http://www.consumerreports.org/cro/news/2014/06/whirlpool-s-smart-washerand-dryer-just-got-smarter/index.htm

Farrell, Warren. 1975. *The Liberated Man*. New York: Bantam.

Fausto-Sterling, Anne. 2000. *Sexing the Body: Gender Politics and the Construction of Sexuality*. New York: Basic Books.

Fava, S. F. 1956. "Suburbanism as a way of life." *American Sociological Review*, vol. 21: 34–37.

Feder-Alford, Elaine. 2006. "Only a piece of meat: One patient's reflections on her eight-day hospital experience." *Qualitative Inquiry*, vol. 12, no. 3: 596–620.

Federal Bureau of Investigation. (FBI). 2014a. "Crime in the United States, 2013," Table 1: Crime in the United States By Volume and Rate per 100,000 Inhabitants, 1994–2013. http://www.fbi.gov/about-us/cjis/ucr/crime-in-the-u.s/2013/crime-in-the-u.s.-2013/violent-crime/violent-crime-topic-page/violentcrimemain_final

———. 2014b. "Crime in the United States: 2013." Expanded Homicide Data Table 1: Murder Victims by Age and Sex. http://www.fbi.gov/about-us/cjis/ucr/crime-in-the-u.s/2013/crime-in-the-u.s.-2013/offenses-known-to-law-enforcement/expanded-offense/expandedoffensemain_final

———.2014c. "Crime in the United States, 2013," Table 38: Arrests by Age, 2013. http://www.fbi.gov/about-us/cjis/ucr/crime-in-the-u.s/2013/crime-in-the-u.s.-2013/persons-arrested/persons-arrested

———. 2014d. "Crime in the United States," Table 33: Ten-Year Arrest Trends by Sex, 2004–2013. https://www.fbi.gov/about-us/cjis/ucr/crime-in-the-u.s/2013/crime-in-the-u.s.-2013/tables/table-33/table_33_ten_year_arrest_trends_by_sex_2013.xls

———. 2014e. Crime in the United States: 2013," Personas Arrested: Table 22: Arrests Trends by Sex, http://www.fbi.gov/about-us/cjis/ucr/crime-in-the-u.s/2013/crime-in-the-u.s.-2013/persons-arrested/persons-arrested

———. 2014f. "Expanded Homicide Data." https://www.fbi.gov/about-us/cjis/ucr/crime-in-the-u.s/2013/crime-in-the-u.s.-2013/offenses-known-to-law-enforcement/expanded-offense/expandedoffensemain_final

———. 2014g. "2013 Hate Crime Statistics, Incidents and Offenses" http://www.fbi.gov/about-us/cjis/ucr/hate-crime/2013/topic-pages/incidents-and-offenses/incidentsandoffenses_final.

Feingold, Alan. 1992. "Sex differences in variability in intellectual abilities: A new look at an old controversy." *Review of Educational Research*, vol. 62: 61–84.

Feingold, David. 2010. "Trafficking in numbers." In Peter Andreas and Kelly Greenhill, eds., *Sex, Drugs, and Body Counts*. Ithaca, NY: Cornell University Press.

Ferguson, Bruce; and Abell, Barbara. 1998. "The urban grocery store gap." *Commentary* (Winter): 6–14.

Ferris, Kerry. 2001. "Through a glass, darkly: The dynamics of fan-celebrity encounters." *Symbolic Interaction*, vol. 24, no. 1 (February): 25–47 . 2004. "Seeing and being seen: The moral order of celebrity sightings." *Journal of Contemporary Ethnography*, vol. 33, no. 3: 236–264.

———; and Harris, Scott R. 2010. *Stargazing: Celebrity, Fame and Social Interaction*. New York: Routledge

Fine, Gary Alan. 1993. "The sad demise, mysterious disappearance, and glorious triumph of symbolic interactionism." *Annual Review of Sociology*, vol. 19: 61–87.

———. 1996. *Kitchens: The Culture of Restaurant Work*. Berkeley: University of California Press.

———. 1998. *Morel Tales: The Culture of Mushrooming*. Cambridge, MA: Harvard University Press.

———. 2001. *Gifted Tongues: High School Debate and Adolescent Culture*. Princeton, NJ: Princeton University Press.

———. 2010. *Authors of the Storm: Meteorology and the Culture of Prediction*. Chicago, IL: Chicago Press.

Fischer, Claude S. 1976. *The Urban Experience*. New York: Harcourt Brace Jovanovich.

———. 1994. "Changes in leisure activities, 1890–1940." *Journal of Social History*, vol. 27, no. 3: 453.

———. 2011. *Still Connected*. New York: Russell Sage Foundation.

Fischer, Mary J.; and Kmec, Julie A. 2004. "Neighborhood socioeconomic conditions as moderators of family resource transmission: High school completion among at-risk youth." *Sociological Perspectives*, vol. 47, no. 4: 507–527.

Fish, Stanley. 1980. *Is There a Text in This Class? The Authority of Interpretive Communities*. Cambridge, MA: Harvard University Press.

Fishman, Pamela. 1978. "Interaction: The work women do." *Social Problems*, vol. 25: 433.

Fishman, Stephen. 2011. "Working as a Consultant or Independent Contractor." *Consultant and Independent Contractor Agreements*. Berkeley, CA: NOLO.

Fiske, Jonathan. 1989. *Understanding Popular Culture*. London: Unwin Hyman.

FitzGerald, Frances. 1980. *America Revised: History Schoolbooks in the Twentieth Century*. New York: Vintage Books.

Florida, Richard. 2002. *The Rise of the Creative Class: And How It Is Transforming Work, Leisure, Community and Everyday Life*. New York: Basic Books.

———. 2004. *Cities and the Creative Class*. New York: Routledge.

Forbes. 2014. "Forbes 400: The Richest People in America 2014." http://www.forbes.com/forbes-400/#tab:overall

———. 2015. "The World's Billionaires." http://www.forbes.com/billionaires/list/

Fortner, Robert S.; and Fackler, Mark P. 2011. *The Handbook of Global Communication and Media Ethics*. Hoboken, NJ: Wiley-Blackwell.

Fox, Greer Litton; and Kelly, Robert F. 1995. "Determinants of child custody arrangements at divorce." *Journal of Marriage and the Family*, vol. 57, no. 3: 693–708.

Fox, Renee. 1957. "Training for uncertainty." In Robert Merton, ed., *The Student Physician*. Cambridge, MA: Harvard University Press.

Fox, Susannah; and Griffith, Maggie. 2007. "Hobbyists online," Pew Research Center, September 19. http://www.pewinternet.org/2007/09/19/hobbyists-online

Frankovic, K. 2015. "Obama sees popularity gains on domestic issues only." YouGov.com, February 15. https://today.yougov.com/news/2015/02/17/obama-sees-popularity-gains-domestic-issues-only/?utm_content=bufferdf0f2&utm_medium=social&utm_source=twitter.com&utm_campaign=buffer

Frauenheim, Ed. 2012. "Outsourcing and the new global economy." *Workforce Management*, June 5. www.workforce.com/article/20120605/WORKFORCE90/120609985/vineet-nayar-interview-offshore-outsourcing-and-the-new-global-economy

Frayer, Lauren. 2012. "Pakistan's transgenders in a category of their own." National Public Radio, September 3. www.npr.org/2012/09/03/160496712/pakistans-transgenders-in-a-cate gory-of-their-own?sc=17&f=1001

Freud, Sigmund. 1955 (orig. 1900). *The Interpretation of Dreams*. London: Hogarth.

———. 1905. *Three Essays on the Theory of Sexuality*. New York: Avon Books.

_____. 2010 (orig. 1930). *Civilization and Its Discontents*. New York: W. W. Norton & Company.

Frey, William H. 2003. "The new migration equation." *Orlando Sentinel*, November 9.

Frey, W. H. 2014. *Diversity Explosion: How New Racial Demographics Are Remaking America*. Washington, DC: The Brookings Institute.

Freyre, Gilberto. 1970. *Order and Progress: Brazil from Monarchy to Republic*. Rod W. Horton, tr. New York: Alfred Knopf.

Friedan, Betty. 1963. *The Feminine Mystique*. New York: Norton.

Frieden, Bernard; and Sagalyn, Lynne B. 1992. *Downtown, Inc.: How America Rebuilds Cities*. Cambridge, MA: MIT Press.

Friedkin, Noah E. 2004. "Social cohesion." *Annual Review of Sociology*, vol. 30: 409–425.

_____; and Cook, Karen S. 1990. "Peer group influence." *Sociological Methods and Research*, vol. 19, no. 1: 122–143.

_____; and Granovetter, Mark, eds. 1998. *A Structural Theory of Social Influence*. Structural Analysis in the Social Sciences. Cambridge, UK: Cambridge University Press.

Friedman, Milton. 1994. "Medical licensure." *Freedom Daily*, January. www.fff.org/freedom/0194e.asp

Fuller, Robert C. 2002. *Spiritual but Not Religious: Understanding Unchurched America*. New York: Oxford University Press.

Furstenberg, Frank; Hoffman, Saul; and Shrestha, Laura. 1995. "The effect of divorce on intergenerational transfers: New evidence." *Demography*, vol. 32, no. 3: 319–333.

Fussell, Paul. 1983. *Class: A Guide Through the American Status System*. New York: Touchstone.

Gabbai, Arik. 2015. "Kevin Ashton describes the 'Internet of Things.'" *Smithsonian*, January. http://www.smithsonianmag.com/innovation/kevin-ashton-describes-the-internet-of-things-180953749/?no-ist

Gabler, Neil. 2012. "It's a brand-news day in Hollywood." *Los Angeles Times*, November 10. www.latimes.com/entertainment/movies/moviesnow/la-et-mn-ca-disney-lucasfilm-marvel-20121111,0,7695955.story

Gainous, Jason B.; and Wagner, Kevin M. 2011. *Rebooting American Politics: The Internet Revolution*. New York: Rowman and Littlefield.

Galbraith, Patrick W. 2012. *Otaku Spaces*. Seattle, WA: Chin Music Press.

Gallagher, Sally K. 2004. "The marginalization of evangelical feminism." *Sociology of Religion*, vol. 65, no. 3: 215–237.

Gallup. 2015. "Race Relations." http://www.gallup.com/poll/1687/race-relations.aspx

Gans, Herbert J. 1962. *The Urban Villagers*. New York: The Free Press of Glencoe, Inc., The Macmillan Company.

_____. 1967. *The Levittowners: Ways of Life and Politics in a New Suburban Community*. New York: Columbia University Press.

_____. 1971. "The uses of poverty: The poor pay all." *Social Policy*, July–August: 20–24.

_____. 1999. *Popular Culture and High Culture: An Analysis and Evaluation of Taste*. New York: Basic Books.

Gansberg, Martin. 1964. "37 who saw murder didn't call the police: Apathy at stabbing of Queens woman shocks inspector." *New York Times*, March 27.

Garber, Marjorie. 1997. *Vested Interests: Cross Dressing and Cultural Anxiety*. London: Routledge.

_____. 1998. *The Symptoms of Culture*. New York: Routledge.

Gardner, Phil. 2011. "The debate over unpaid college internships." Intern Bridge, Inc. http://citeseerx.ist.psu.edu/viewdoc/download?doi=10.1.1.372.1710&rep=rep1&type=pdf

Garfinkel, H. 1967/1984. *Studies in Ethnomethodology*. Cambridge: Polity Press.

Garr, Emily. 2008. "The unemployment trend by state." Economic Policy Institute Economic Snapshots. www.epi.org/content.cfm/webfeatures_snapshots_20080924

Garreau, Joel. 1992. *Edge City: Life on the New Frontier*. New York: Anchor Books.

Garry, Patrick M.; and Spurlin, Candice J. 2007. "The effectiveness of media rating systems in preventing children's exposure to violent and sexually explicit media content: An empirical study." *Oklahoma City University Law Review*, vol. 32, no. 2. http://ssrn.com/abstract=1139167

Garvin, Glenn. 2008. "Too pretty? That's when it got ugly." *The Miami Herald*, March 23.

Gates, Gary. 2012. "Gallup Special Report: The U.S. Adult LGBT Population." October. http://williamsinstitute.law.ucla.edu/research/census-lgbt-demographics-studies/gallup-special-report-18oct-2012/#sthash.61XZT5ub.dpuf

_____. 2014. "In US, LGBT More Likely Than Non-LGBT to Be Uninsured." August 26. http://www.gallup.com/poll/175445/lgbt-likely-non-lgbt-uninsured.aspx

Geertz, Clifford. 1973. "Deep play: Notes on the Balinese cockfight." In *The Interpretation of Cultures*. New York: Basic Books.

Gelles, Richard J. 1995. *Contemporary Families: A Sociological View*. Thousand Oaks, CA: Sage.

Gemar, K.; Zarkowski, P.; and Avery, D. 2008. "Hotel room suicide: Las Vegas and Clark County." *Social Psychiatry and Psychiatric Epidemiology*, 43:25–27.

Gerbner, George; and Gross, L. 1976. "Living with television: The Violence Profile." *Journal of Communication* (spring):173–199.

Gereffi, Gary; and Korzeniewicz, Miguel, eds. 1994. *Commodity Chains and Global Capitalism*. Westport, CT: Praeger.

Gergen, Kenneth. 1991. *The Saturated Self*. New York: Basic Books.

Gibson, Campbell; and Lennon, Emily. 2001. "Historical Census Statistics on the Foreign-Born Population of the United States: 1850–1990." U.S. Bureau of the Census, Population Division. www.census.gov/population/www/documentation/twps0029.html

Gibson, William. 2001. "Modern boys and mobile girls." *The Observer*. www.guardian.co.uk/books/2001/apr/01/science fictionfantasyandhorror.features

Gilbert, Dennis. 2014. *The American Class Structure in an Age of Growing Inequality*. Sage Publications. http://www.sagepub.com/upm-data/60307_Chapter_1.pdf

Gladwell, Malcolm. 2008. *Outliers: The Story of Success*. New York: Little, Brown and Company.

Glaser, Barney G; and Strauss, Anselm L. 1967. *The Discovery of Grounded Theory: Strategies for Qualitative Research*. Chicago, IL: Aldine Publishing Company.

Glaser, Jack; Dixit, Jay; and Green, Donald P. 2002. "Studying hate crime with the Internet: What makes racists advocate racial violence?" *Journal of Social Issues*, vol. 58, no. 1: 177–193.

Glaser, Mark. 2007. MediaShift. PBS. "Your guide to the digital divide." January 17. www.pbs.org/mediashift/2007/01/digging_deeperyour_guide_to_th.html

Glass, Ruth. 1964. "Aspects of change." In Centre for Urban Studies, ed., *London: Aspects of Change*. London: MacGibbon and Kee.

Gleick, P. H. 1998. "The world's water 1998–1999." Washington, DC: Island Press. www.worldwater.org/table7.html

Glor, Jeff. 2012. "Could babies born today live to 150?" CBS News, February 9. www.cbsnews.com/8301-505269_162-57373788/could-babies-born-today-live-to-150

Gould, Elise. "Why America's Workers Need Faster Wage Growth—And What We Can Do About It." Economic Policy Institute. August 27.

http://www.epi.org/publication/why-americas-workers-need-faster-wage-growth/

Goffman, Erving. 1956. *Presentation of Self in Everyday Life.* Garden City, NY: Anchor Books.

———. 1961. *Asylums: Essays on the Social Situation of Mental Patients and Other Inmates.* Garden City, NY: Anchor Books.

———. 1962. *Stigma: Notes on the Management of Spoiled Identity.* Upper Saddle River, NJ: Prentice Hall.

———. 1971. *Relations in Public: Microstudies of the Public Order.* New York: Basic Books.

Goldberg, Herb. 1976. *The Hazards of Being Male.* New York: Nash.

Gomez, Manuel. 2013. "Order in the desert: Law abiding behavior at Burning Man." *Journal of Dispute Resolution,* 349–374.

Goodacre, Daniel M. 1953. "Group characteristics of good and poor performing combat units." *Sociometry,* vol. 16, no. 2: 168–179.

Goode, Erich. 1997. *Deviant Behavior.* 5th ed. Upper Saddle River, NJ: Prentice Hall.

Goode, William J. 1982. *The Family.* Englewood Cliffs, NJ: Prentice Hall.

Goodman, Peter. 2010. "U.S. offers a hand to those on eviction's edge." *New York Times,* April 21. www.nytimes.com/2010/04/22/business/economy/22prevent.html

Goodstein, Laurie. 2004. "Personal and political, Bush's faith blurs lines." *New York Times,* October 26, p. A21.

Gottdiener, Mark; Collins, Claudia C.; and Dickens, David R. 1999. *Las Vegas: The Social Production of an All-American City.* Malden, MA: Blackwell.

Gottlieb, Robert. 1997. "Reconstructing Environmentalism: Complex Movements, Diverse Roots, in Out of the Woods: Essays in Environmental History." Char Miller & Hal Rothman eds., 145–47.

Gottman, Jean. 1961. *Megalopolis: The Urbanized Northeastern Seaboard of the United States.* New York: Twentieth Century Fund.

———; and Robert Harper. 1990. *Since Megalopolis: The Urban Writings of Jean Gottman.* Baltimore, MD: Johns Hopkins University Press.

Gottschalk, Simon. 1993. "Uncomfortably numb: Countercultural impulses in the postmodern era." *Symbolic Interaction,* vol. 16, no. 4: 357–378.

Goyette, Kimberly; and Xie, Yu. 1999. "Educational expectations of Asian-American youth: Determinants and ethnic differences." *Sociology of Education,* vol. 71: 24–38.

Gozzi, Raymond, Jr. 1996. "Will the media create a global village?" *ETC: A Review of General Semantics,* vol. 53: 65–68.

Graham, Lawrence Otis. 1996. *A Member of the Club: Reflections on Life in a Racially Polarized World.* New York: Harper Perennial.

GRAIN. 2012. "Squeezing Africa dry: behind every land grab is a water grab." June 11. http://www.grain.org/article/entries/4516-squeezing-africa-dry-behind-every-land-grab-is-a-water-grab

Graham, Lawrence Otis. 2014. "I taught my black kids that their elite upbringing would protect them from discrimination. I was wrong." Washington Post, November 6. http://www.washingtonpost.com/posteverything/wp/2014/11/06/i-taught-my-black-kids-that-their-elite-upbringing-would-protect-them-from-discrimination-i-was-wrong/

Grall, Timothy S. 2013. *Custodial Mothers and Fathers and Their Child Support: 2011.* U.S. Department of Commerce, Economics and Statistics Administration, U.S. Census Bureau. October. http://www.census.gov/prod/2013pubs/p60-246.pdf

Gramsci, Antonio. 1985. *Selections from Cultural Writings.* Cambridge, MA: Harvard University Press.

———. 1988. *An Antonio Gramsci Reader.* David Forgacs, ed. Boston: Schocken.

Grandey, A. 2003. "When 'the show must go on': Surface and deep acting as determinants of emotional exhaustion and peer-rated service delivery." *Academy of Management Journal,* vol. 46, no. 1: 86–96.

Granfield, Robert. 1992. *Making Elite Lawyers.* New York: Routledge.

Granovetter, Mark. 1973. "The strength of weak ties." *American Journal of Sociology,* vol. 78, no. 6: 1360–1380.

Gray, David E. 1994. "Coping with autism: Stresses and strategies." *Sociology of Health & Illness,* vol. 16, no. 3: 275–300.

———. 2002. "'Everybody just freezes. Everybody is just embarrassed': Felt and enacted stigma among parents of children with high functioning autism." *Sociology of Health & Illness,* vol. 24, no. 6: 734–749.

Gray, Steven. 2009. "Can America's urban food deserts bloom?" *Time,* May 26. www.time.com/time/nation/article/0,8599,1900947,00.html

Grazian, David. 2008. *On the Make: The Hustle of Urban Nightlife.* Chicago: University of Chicago Press.

Greenfeld, L., et al. 1998. "Violence by intimates: Analysis of data on crimes by current or former spouses, boyfriends, and girlfriends." *Bureau of Justice Statistics Factbook.* www.ojp.usdoj.gov/bjs/pub/pdf/vi.pdf

Greenhouse, Steven. 1999. "Activism surges at campuses nationwide, and labor is at issue." *New York Times,* March 29. www.sweatshopwatch.org/swatch/headlines/1999/nyt_mar.html

Groh, Carla J. 2007. "Poverty, Mental Health, and Women: Implications for Psychiatric Nurses in Primary Care Settings." *Journal of the American Psychiatric Nurses Association,* vol. 13, no. 5: 267–274.

Gross, Terry. 2010. "Jon Stewart: The most trusted name in fake news." National Public Radio. October 4. www.npr.org/templates/story/story.php?storyId=130321994

Guber, Deborah Lynn. 2003. *The Grassroots of a Green Revolution: Polling America on the Environment.* Cambridge, MA: MIT Press.

Gubrium, Jaber; and Buckholdt, D. R. 1982. "Fictive family: Everyday usage, analytic, and human service considerations." *American Anthropologist,* vol. 84, no. 4: 878.

Gustafson, Krystina. 2015. "Wal-Mart Pay Hike Starts Wage War." *NBC News.* February 25. http://www.nbcnews.com/business/economy/wal-mart-pay-hike-starts-wage-war-n312671

Gutfreund, Owen. 2004. *Twentieth Century Sprawl: Highways and the Reshaping of the American Landscape.* New York: Oxford University Press.

Haas, Jack; and Shaffir, William. 1977. "The professionalization of medical students: Development competence and a cloak of competence." *Symbolic Interaction,* vol. 1: 71–88.

———. 1982. "Taking on the role of doctor: A dramaturgical analysis of professionalization." *Symbolic Interaction,* vol. 5: 187–203.

Haber, Gary. 2010. "Bill tries to lure grocers to Maryland's poor areas." *Baltimore Business Journal,* March 26. http://baltimore.bizjournals.com/baltimore/stories/2010/03/29/story4.html

Habermas, Jürgen. 1984. *The Theory of Communicative Action, Vol. 1: Reason and the Rationalization of Society.* Thomas McCarthy, trans.. Boston: Beacon Press.

———. 1987. *The Theory of Communicative Action, Vol. 2: Lifeworld and System: A Critique of Functionalist Reason.* Thomas McCarthy, trans. Boston: Beacon Press.

Hall, Stuart. 1980. "Encoding/decoding." In S. Hall, D. Hobson, A. Lowe, and P. Willis, eds., *Culture, Media, Language.* London: Hutchinson.

———. 1997. *Representation: Cultural Representations and Signifying Practices.* London and Thousand Oaks, California: Sage in association with the Open University.

_____. 2006. "Constructing difference: Creating 'other' identities." In Paula Rothenberg, ed., *Beyond Borders: Thinking Critically About Global Issues*. New York: Worth Publishers.

Halle, David. 1993. *Inside Culture: Art and Class in the American Home*. Chicago, IL: University of Chicago Press.

Halloran, Liz. 2013. "After DOMA: What's Next for Gay Married Couples." NPR. June 26. www.npr.org/blogs/thetwo-way/2013/06/26/195881288/after-doma-whats-next-for-gay-married-couples

Hampton, Keith N.; Goulet, Lauren Sessions; Rainie, Lee; and Purcell, Kristen. 2011. "Social networking sites and our lives." Washington, DC: Pew Research Center's Internet and American Life Project, June 16. http://pewinternet.org/~/media//Files/Reports/2011/PIP%20-%20Social%20networking%20sites%20and%20our%20lives.pdf

Handleman, J. S.; and Harris, S., eds. 2000. *Preschool Education Programs for Children with Autism*, 2nd ed. Austin, TX: Pro-Ed.

Hao, Lingxin; and Cherlin, Andrew J. 2004. "Welfare reform and teenage pregnancy, childbirth, and school dropout." *Journal of Marriage and Family*, vol. 66: 179–194.

Hardin, Garrett. 1968. "The tragedy of the commons." *Science*, vol. 162: 1243–1248.

_____. 1993. *Living Within Limits*. New York: Oxford University Press.

Harnick, Chris. 2012. "Most-watched TV show in the world is 'CSI: Crime Scene Investigation.'" *Huffington Post*, June 6. www.huffingtonpost.com/2012/06/14/most-watched-tv-show-in-the-world-csi_n_1597968.html

Harvard Magazine. 2008. "Race in a genetic world." May–June: 62–65.

Harvey, David. 1990. *The Condition of Postmodernity: An Enquiry into the Origins of Cultural Change*. Cambridge, MA: Wiley-Blackwell.

Hatzenbuehler, M. L; Bellatorre, A.; Lee, Y.; Finch, B. K.; Muennig, P.; and Fiscella, K. 2014. "Structural stigma and all-cause mortality in sexual minority populations." *Social Science & Medicine, 103*, 33–41.

Havitz, Mark E.; and Dimanche, Frederic. 1999. "Leisure involvement revisited: Drive properties and paradoxes." *Journal of Leisure Research*, vol. 31, no. 2: 122.

Hawley, Amos H. 1950. *Human Ecology: A Theory of Community Structure*. New York: Ronald Press.

Hayase, Nozomi. 2010. "Otaku: A silent cultural revolution." Cultureunplugged.com. http://truthseekers.cultureunplugged.com/truth_seekers/2010/07/otaku-a-silent-cultural-revolution-.html

Hays, Sharon. 1996. *The Cultural Contradictions of Motherhood*. New Haven, CT: Yale University Press.

_____. 2003. *Flat Broke with Children: Women in the Age of Welfare Reform*. New York: Oxford University Press.

Healthcare Medicine Institute. 2010. "San Francisco Giants and New York Yankees Acupuncture." May 25. www.healthcmi.com/acupuncturist-news-online/260-sanfranciscogiantsnewyorkyankeesacupuncture

Heilprin, John. 2005. "FBI: Radical-activist groups are major threat." *Seattle Times*, May 19. http://seattletimes.nwsource.com/html/nationworld/2002280292_ecoterror19.html

Herek, G. M. 1990. "The context of anti-gay violence: Notes on cultural and psychological heterosexism." *Journal of Interpersonal Violence*, vol. 5: 316–333.

Heritage, J.; and Stivers, T. 1999. "Online commentary in acute medical visits: A method of shaping patient expectations." *Social Science and Medicine*, vol. 49, no. 11: 1501–1517.

Herrnstein, R.; and Murray, C. 1994. *The Bell Curve: Intelligence and Class Structure in American Life*. New York, NY: Free Press.

Hertz, Marci Feldman; and David-Ferdon, Corrine. 2009. "Electronic media and youth violence: A CDC issue brief for educators and caregivers." Atlanta, GA: Centers for Disease Control.

Hewitt, John. P. 2000. *Self and Society: A Symbolic Interactionist Social Psychology*. Boston: Allyn and Bacon.

Hill, Peter; and Wood, Ralph. 1999. *Measures of Religiosity*. Birmingham, AL: Religious Education Press.

Hochschild, Arlie Russel. 1975. "The sociology of feeling and emotion." In Marcia Millman and Rosabeth Moss Kanter, eds., *Another Voice*. Garden City, NJ: Doubleday.

_____. 1983. *The Managed Heart: The Commercialization of Human Feeling*. Berkeley: University of California Press.

_____; and Machung, Anne. 1989. *The Second Shift: Working Parents and the Revolution at Home*. New York: Viking.

Hochschild, Jennifer L. 1996. *Facing Up to the American Dream: Race, Class, and the Soul of the Nation*. Princeton, NJ: Princeton University Press.

Hodge, Robert; and Tripp, David. 1986. *Children and Television: A Semiotic Approach*. Cambridge, UK: Polity Press.

Hoffman, Matt; and Torres, Lisa. 2002. "It's not only 'who you know' that matters: Gender, personal contacts, and job lead quality." *Gender and Society*, vol. 16, no. 6: 793–813.

Holdren, John P.; Daily, Gretchen; and Ehrlich, Paul R. 1995. "The meaning of sustainability: Biogeophysical aspects." In M. Munasinghe and W. Shearer, eds., *Defining and Measuring Sustainability: The Biogeophysical Foundations*. Washington, DC: World Bank.

Holdsworth, M.; Gartner, A.; Landais, E.; Maire, B.; and Delpeuch, F. 2004.. "Perceptions of healthy and desirable body size in urban Senegalese women." *International Journal of Obesity and Related Metabolic Disorders*, vol. 28, no. 12: 1561–1568.

Holmes, Seth M. 2011. "Structural Vulnerability and hierarchies of ethnicity and citizenship on the farm, medical anthropology: Cross-cultural studies in health and illness." *Medical Anthropology*, vol. 30, no. 4: 425–449.

Holstein, James; and Gubrium, Jaber. 1995. "Deprivatization and the construction of domestic life." *Journal of Marriage and the Family*, vol. 57, no. 4: 894.

_____. 2000. *The Self We Live By: Narrative Identity in a Postmodern World*. New York: Oxford University Press.

Holstein, James; and Gubrium, Jaber. 1990. *What Is Family?* Mountain View, CA: Mayfield Publishing Company.

Homans, George. 1951. *The Human Group*. New York: Harcourt Brace Jovanovich.

hooks, bell. 1990. *Yearning: Race, Gender and Cultural Politics*. Boston: South End Press.

_____. 2003. *We Real Cool: Black Men and Masculinity*. London: Routledge.

Howard, Philip, et al. 2011. "Opening closed regimes: What was the role of social media during the Arab Spring?" Working paper no. 2011.1. *Project on Information Technology and Political Islam*. http://pitpi.org/wp-content/uploads/2013/02/2011_Howard-Duffy-Freelon-Hussain-Mari-Mazaid_pITPI.pdf

Hoyert, Donna; and Xu, Jiaquan. 2012. "Deaths: Preliminary data for 2011." *National Vital Statistics Reports*, vol. 61, no. 6. www.cdc.gov/nchs/data/nvsr/nvsr61/nvsr61_06.pdf

Hughes, Jonathon; and Cain, Louis. 1994. *American Economic History*. 4th ed. New York: HarperCollins College Publishers.

Hughes, Z. 2003. "Why some brothers only date whites and 'others.'" *Ebony*, vol. 58: 70–74.

Hull, Elizabeth. 2002. "Florida's former felons: You can't vote here." *Commonwealth*, vol. 129, no. 12: 16.

Hultman, Christina M.; Sparén, Pär; and Cnattingius, Sven. 2002. "Perinatal risk factors for infantile autism." *Epidemiology*, vol. 13, no. 4: 417–423.

Humphrey, Craig R.; Lewis, Tammy L.; and Buttel, Frederick H. 2002. *Environment, Energy, and Society: A New Synthesis.* Belmont, CA: Wadsworth.

Hunt, G.; and Satterlee, S. 1986. "Cohesion and division: Drinking in an English village." *Man* (New Series), vol. 21, no. 3: 521–537.

Hurley, Lawrence. 2013. "Supreme Court guts key part of landmark Voting Rights Act." Reuters. www.reuters.com/article/2013/06/25/us-usa-court-voting-idUSBRE95O0TU20130625

Hustvedt, Siri. 2002. "9/11 six months on." *The Observer*, March 10. Special Supplement, p. 6.

Ignatiev, Noel. 1996. *How the Irish Became White.* London: Routledge.

India Brand Equity Foundation. 2015. "IT & ITeS Industry in India." http://www.ibef.org/industry/information-technology-india.aspx

Institute for College Access and Success, The (TICAS). (2014). *Student Debt and the Class of 2013.* The Project on Student Debt. http://projectonstudentdebt.org/files/pub/classof2013.pdf

Insurance Institute for Highway Safety. 2014. "Teenagers. Fatality Facts." http://www.iihs.org/iihs/topics/t/teenagers/fatalityfacts/teenagers

International Union for Conservation of Nature. 2014. "Overview of The IUCN Red List." http://www.iucnredlist.org/about/overview

Isikoff, Michael. 2004. "The dots never existed." *Newsweek*, July 19.

Jackson, K. T. 1985. *Crabgrass Frontier: The Suburbanization of the United States.* New York: Oxford University Press.

Jackson, Phillip. 1968. *Life in Classrooms.* New York: Holt, Rinehart, and Winston.

Jackson-Jacobs, Curtis. 2004. "Taking a beating: The narrative gratifications of fighting as an underdog." In Hayward et al., eds., *Cultural Criminology Unleashed.* London: Glasshouse.

Jamieson, Patrick; and Romer, Don. 2014. "Violence in popular U.S. prime time TV dramas and the cultivation of fear: A time series analysis." *Media and Communication*, vol. 2, no. 2:31–41.

Janus, Irving L. 1971. "Groupthink." *Psychology Today*, November.

———. 1982. *Groupthink.* 2nd ed. Boston: Houghton-Mifflin.

Jenkins, Henry. 1992. *Textual Poachers: Television Fans and Participatory Culture.* London. Routledge.

Jenkins, Henry. 2006. *Fans, Bloggers, and Gamers: Exploring Participatory Culture.* New York: New York University Press.

Jin, Ge. 2006. "Chinese gold farmers." www.we-make-money-not-art.com/archives/2006/03/ge-jin-a-phd-st.php

Jobs for the Future. 2013. "Early College High Schools Get Results" http://www.jff.org/sites/default/files/ECHS_get_results_040113.pdf

Johnson, Cathryn. 1994. "Gender, legitimate authority, and leader-subordinate conversations." *American Sociological Review*, vol. 59, no. 1: 122–135.

Johnson, Kenneth M. 1995. "The rural rebound revisited." *American Demographics*, July.

———. 1998. "The revival of rural America." *Wilson Quarterly*, vol. 22, no. 2: 16–27.

———. 1999. "The rural rebound." *Population Reference Bureau Reports on America*, vol. 1, no. 3 (August).

———; and Beale, Calvin L. 1994. "The recent revival of widespread population growth in nonmetropolitan America." *Rural Sociology*, vol. 59, no. 4: 655–667.

Jones, Andrew R. 2009. *Fads, Fetishes, and Fun: A Sociological Analysis of Pop Culture.* San Diego, CA: Cognella.

Jones, Greg. 2012. "Good workers gone bad: How to spot employee theft." CNBC, February 12. www.cnbc.com/id/46556452/Good_Workers_Gone_Bad_How_to_Spot_Employee_Theft

Jones, N. 2012. *Between Good and Ghetto: African American Girls and Inner-City Violence.* New Brunswick, NJ: Rutgers University Press.

Jones, Robert P.; Cox, Daniel; and Banchoff, Thomas. 2012. *A Generation in Transition: Religion, Values, and Politics Among College-Age Millennials.* Washington, DC: Public Religion Research Institute, Georgetown University, 2012.

Jones, Steve. 1997. *Virtual Culture: Identity and Communication in Cybersociety.* Thousand Oaks, CA: Sage.

———; and Philip Howard, eds. 2003. *Society Online: The Internet in Context.* Thousand Oaks, CA: Sage.

Juergensmeyer, Mark. 2003. *Terror in the Mind of God: The Global Rise of Religious Violence.* Berkeley: University of California Press.

Kaczor, Bill. 1996. "Neighborhood blames years of woe on 'Mount Dioxin.'" *Charleston Gazette*, March 11.

Kalleberg, Arne L. 2009. "Precarious Work, Insecure Workers: Employment Relations in Transition." *American Sociological Review* 74(1):1–22.

Kang, Miliann. 2010. *The Managed Hand: Race, Gender, and the Body in Beauty Service Work.* Berkeley: University of California Press.

Karau, S. J.; and Williams, K. D. 1993. "Social loafing: A meta-analytic review and theoretical integration." *Journal of Personality and Social Psychology*, vol. 65: 681–706.

Kastrenakes, Jacob. 2015. "This is Samsung's grand vision for the Internet of Things." *The Verge*, January. http://www.theverge.com/2015/1/5/7497537/samsung-iot-internet-of-things-vision-presented-at-ces-2015-keynote

Katz, Elihu. 1959. "Mass communication research and the study of popular culture." *Studies in Public Communication*, Vol 2: 1–6 Retrieved from http://repository.upenn.edu/asc_papers/165; and Lazarsfeld, Paul F. 1955. *Personal Influence: The Part Played by People in the Flow of Mass Communications.* New York: Macmillan Free Press.

Katz, Jack. 1988. *Seductions of Crime: Moral and Sensual Attractions of Doing Evil.* New York: Basic Books.

———. 1997. "Ethnography's warrants." *Sociological Methods & Research*, vol. 25, no. 4: 391–423.

Katznelson, Ira. 2005. *When Affirmative Action Was White: An Untold History of Racial Inequality in Twentieth Century America.* New York: Norton.

Kaufman, Jason. 2008. Harvard University, Department of Sociology home page. www.wjh.harvard.edu/soc/faculty/kaufman/

Kaufman, Sharon. 2005. *. . . And a Time to Die: How American Hospitals Shape the End of Life.* New York: Scribner.

Kaley, Alexandra, Dobbin, Frank, and Erin Kelly. 2006. "Best Practices or Best Guesses? Assessing the Efficacy of Corporate Affirmative Action and Diversity Policies," *American Sociological Review* 2006, VOL. 71 (August: 589–617)

Keaton, Patrick. 2014. "Selected statistics from the public elementary and secondary education universe: School year 2012–13." National Center for Education Statistics, October 30. http://nces.ed.gov/pubs2013/2014098/findings.asp

Keith, Verna M.; and Finlay, Barbara. 1988. "The impact of parental divorce on children's educational attainment, marital timing, and likelihood of divorce." *Journal of Marriage and the Family*, vol. 50, no. 3: 797–809.

Kellner, Douglas. 2001. "Globalization, technopolitics and revolution." *Theoria*, no. 98: 14–34.

———. 2005. *Media Spectacle and the Crisis of Democracy: Terrorism, War and Election Battles.* Boulder, CO: Paradigm.

Kelly, Barbara. 1993. *Expanding the American Dream: Building and Rebuilding Levittown.* Albany: State University of New York Press.

Kelman, H. 1958. "Compliance, identification, and internalization: Three processes of attitude change." *Journal of Conflict Resolution*, vol. 1: 51–60.

Kena, G.; Aud, S.; Johnson, F.; Wang, X.; Zhang, J.; Rathbun, A.; and Kristapovich, P. 2014. *The Condition of Education 2014*. NCES 2014-083. National Center for Education Statistics.

Kennickell, Arthur B. 2009. "Ponds and Streams: Wealth and Income in the U.S., 1989 to 2007." Federal Reserve Board Working Paper, January 7. Figure A3a: 63.

Kephart, William. 2000. *Extraordinary Groups: An Examination of Unconventional Lifestyles*. New York: W. H. Freeman.

Kerbo, Harold R.; and Gonzalez, Juan J. 2003. "Class and nonvoting in comparative perspective: Possible causes and consequences in the United States." *Research in Political Sociology*, vol. 12: 175–196.

Kessler, R. C. 2003. "Epidemiology of women and depression." *Journal of Affective Disorders*, vol. 74, no. 1: 5–13.

Khasnis, Atul A.; and Nettleman, Mary D. 2005. "Global warming and infectious disease." *Archives of Medical Research*, vol. 36, no. 6: 689–696.

Kilbourne, Jean. 1999. *Killing Us Softly 3*. Dir. Sut Jhally. Center for Media Literacy.

Kimmel, Michael. 1987. *Changing Men: New Directions in Research on Men and Masculinity*. Thousand Oaks, CA: Sage.

King, A. 1995. "Outline of a practical theory of football violence." *Sociology*, vol. 24: 635–652.

King, Marissa D.; Fountain, Christine; Dakhlallah, Diana; and Bearman, Peter S. 2009. "Estimated autism risk and older reproductive age." *American Journal of Public Health*, vol. 99, no. 9: 1673–1679.

Kinsey, Alfred C.; Pomeroy, Wardell B.; and Martin, Clyde E. 1998 (orig. 1948). *Sexual Behavior in the Human Male*. Bloomington: Indiana University Press.

———; and Gebhard, Paul H. 1998 (orig. 1953). *Sexual Behavior in the Human Female*. Bloomington: Indiana University Press.

Kirkham, Chris. 2015. "U.S. is asked to forgive debt of Corinthian colleges students." *Los Angeles Times*, April 9. http://www.latimes.com/business/la-fi-corinthian-student-debt-20150410-story.html

Kirkham, Chris; and Tiffany Hsu. 2014. "LA Wage Hikes Spark Fierce Debate". *Los Angeles Times*. October 24, 2014. http://www.latimes.com/business/la-fi-minimum-wage-debates-20141025-story.html#page=1

Kissel, Rick. 2014. "NCIS has become world's most-watched TV drama." *Variety*, June 11. http://variety.com/2014/tv/news/ncis-most-popular-drama-in-worldwatched-tv-drama-1201218492/

Kitsuse, John I. 1980. "Coming out all over: Deviants and the politics of social problems." *Social Problems*, vol. 28: 1–13.

Kitzinger, C. 1987. *The Social Construction of Lesbianism*. London: Sage.

Klapper, J. 1960. *The Effects of Mass Communication*. New York: Free Press.

Klein, Naomi. 2000. *No Logo: Taking Aim at the Brand Bullies*. New York: Picador.

Kleinman, Sherryl. 1984. *Equals Before God: Seminarians as Humanistic Professionals*. Chicago: University of Chicago Press.

Klinenberg, Eric. 2002. *Heat Wave: A Social Autopsy of a Disaster in Chicago*. Chicago: University of Chicago Press.

———. 2007. "Breaking the news." *Mother Jones*, March/April. www.motherjones.com/news/feature/2007/03/breaking_the_news.html

———. 2012a. "Facebook isn't making us lonely." *Slate*, April 19. www.slate.com/articles/life/culturebox/2012/04/is_facebook_making_us_lonely_no_the_atlantic_cover_story_is_wrong_.single.html

———. 2012b. *Going Solo: The Extraordinary Rise of Living Alone*. New York: The Penguin Press.

Knewton, Inc. *The Flipped Classroom*. Digital image. http://www.knewton.com/flipped-classroom/

Kochhar, Rakesh. 2011. "Two years of economic recovery: Women lose jobs, men find them." Pew Social & Demographic Trends Report. Washington, DC: Pew Research Center.

Koerner, Brendan I. 2003. "Outbreaks vs. epidemics: Whether it's time to freak about the flu." *Slate*, December 19. www.slate.com/id/2092969

Kolbe, Richard H.; and Langefeld, Carl D. 1993. "Appraising gender role portrayals in TV commercials." *Sex Roles*, vol. 28, no. 7: 393–417.

Kosciw, Joseph G.; Greytak, Emily A.; Diaz, Elizabeth M.; and Bartkiewicz, Mark J. 2010. "The 2009 National School Climate Survey." www.glsen.org/cgibin/iowa/all/library/record/2624.html?state=research&type=research

Koseff, Alexei. 2014. "Jerry Brown approves community college bachelor's degrees." *Sacramento Bee*, September, 29. http://www.sacbee.com/news/politics-government/capitol-alert/article2615016.html

Kosmin, Barry A.; and Keysar, Ariela. 2013. "Religious, spiritual, and secular: The emergence of three distinct worldviews among American college students." Hartford, CT: Trinity College. http://www.trincoll.edu/Academics/centers/isssc/Documents/ARIS_2013_College%20Students_Sept_25_final_draft.pdf

Kosmin, Barry A.; Mayer, Egon; and Keysar, Ariela. 2001. "American Religious Identification Survey." The Graduate Center of the City University of New York. www.gc.cuny.edu/faculty/research_briefs/aris/aris_index.htm

Kotkin, Joel. 2012. "Generation screwed." *Newsweek*, July 23 and 30. www.thedailybeast.com/newsweek/2012/07/15/are-millennials-the-screwed-generation.html

Kozeny, Geoff. 1995. "Intentional communities: Lifestyle based on ideals." www.ic.org/pnp/cdir/1995/01kozeny.html

Kozol, J. 1991. *Savage Inequalities: Children in America's Schools*. New York: Crown Publishing.

Krakauer, Jon. 1997. *Into the Wild*. New York: Anchor Books.

Kramer, A. D. I.; Guillory, J. E.; and Hancock, J. T. 2014. "Experimental evidence of massive-scale emotional contagion through social networks," *Proceedings of the National Academy of Sciences of the United States*, vol. 111, no 24.

Krashen, S. D. 1996. *Under Attack: The Case against Bilingual Education*. Culver City, CA: Language Education Associates.

Kraus, Richard G. 1995. "Play's new identity: Big business." *Journal of Physical Education, Recreation & Dance*, vol. 66, no. 8: 36.

Kreider, Rose M.; and Fields, Jason M. 2001. "Number, timing, and duration of marriages and divorces: Fall 1996." *Current Population Reports*, P70-80. Washington, DC: U.S. Government Printing Office.

———. 2002. "Number, timing, and duration of marriages and divorces: 1996." *Current Population Reports*. Washington, DC: U.S. Government Printing Office.

Kristof, N.; and WuDunn, S. 2000. "Two cheers for sweatshops." *New York Times Magazine*, September 24. www.nytimes.com/library/magazine/home/20000924mag-sweatshops.html

Krivickas, Kristy; and Lofquist, Daphne. 2011. "Demographics of Same-Sex Couple Households with Children." www.census.gov/hhes/same sex/files/Krivickas-Lofquist%20PAA%202011.pdf

Krueger, Alan B. 2002. "The apple falls close to the tree, even in the land of opportunity." *New York Times*, November 14, p. C2.

———. 2012. "The Rise and Consequences of Inequality in the United States." Speech at the Center for American Progress, Washington D.C. on January 12, 2012.

Kuhn, Manfred; and McPartland, T. S. 1954. "An empirical investigation of self-attitude." *American Sociological Review*, vol. 19: 68–79.

Kuhn, Thomas S. 1970 (orig. 1962). *The Structure of Scientific Revolutions*. Chicago: University of Chicago Press.

Kunstler, J. H. 1993. *The Geography of Nowhere: The Rise and Decline of America's Man-Made Landscape*. New York: Simon & Schuster.

Kurtzleben, D. 2013. "Gay couples more educated, higher-income than heterosexual couples." *U.S. News and World Report*, March 1. http://www.usnews.com/news/articles/2013/03/01/gay-couples-more-educated-higher-income-than-heterosexual-couples

Kurzweil, Ray. 1990. *The Age of Intelligent Machines*. Cambridge, MA: MIT Press.

Lachman, Margie. 2004. "Development in midlife." *Annual Review of Psychology*, vol. 55: 305–31.

Lacy, Karyn R. 2007. *Blue Chip Black: Race, Class, and Status in the New Black Middle Class*. Berkeley: University of California Press.

LaMarre, Thomas. 2004. "An introduction to the otaku movement." *EnterText*, vol. 4, no. 1: 151–187.

Laing, Aislinn. 2012. "South Africa's whites still paid six times more than blacks." *The Telegraph*. October 30. http://www.telegraph.co.uk/news/worldnews/africaandindianocean/southafrica/9643548/South-Africas-whites-still-paid-six-times-more-than-blacks.html

Lane, J. Mark; and Tabak, Ronald J. 1991. "Judicial activism and legislative 'reform' of federal habeas corpus: A critical analysis of recent developments and current proposals." *Albany Law Review*, vol. 55, no. 1: 1–95.

Lareau, Annette. 2003. *Unequal Childhoods: Class, Race and Family Life*. Berkeley: University of California Press.

Larson, Doran. 2013. "Why Scandinavian prisons are superior." *The Atlantic*, September 24. http://www.theatlantic.com/international/archive/2013/09/why-scandinavian-prisons-are-superior/279949/

Larson, R. W.; and Richards, M. H. 1991. "Daily companionship in late childhood and early adolescence: Changing developmental contexts." *Child Development*, vol. 62: 284–300.

Lasch, Christopher. 1977. *Haven in a Heartless World: The Family Besieged*. New York: Basic Books.

Laumann, Edward O; Gagnon, John H.; Michael, Robert T.; and Michaels, Stuart. 1994. *The Social Organization of Sexuality*. Chicago: University of Chicago Press.

Lazarsfeld, Paul; and Katz, Elihu. 1955. *Personal Influence*. New York: Free Press.

Le Bon, Gustave. 1896. *The Crowd: A Study of the Popular Mind*. New York: Viking Press.

Leaper, Campbell; and Ayers, Melanie M. 2007. "A meta-analytic review of gender variations in adults' language use: Talkativeness, affiliative speech, and assertive speech." *Personality and Social Psychology Review*, Vol. 11: 328–363.Lederer, Edith. 2012. "U.N.: 4 million human trafficking victims." Associated Press, April 3. www.news.yahoo.com/un-2-4-million-human-trafficking-victims-004512192.html

Leidner, Robin. 1993. *Fast Food, Fast Talk*. Berkeley: University of California Press.

Lemert, Edwin M. 1951. *Social Pathology: A Systematic Approach to the Theory of Sociopathic Behavior*. New York: McGraw-Hill.

Lepowsky, Maria Alexandra. 1993. *Gender and Power from Fruit of the Motherland*. New York: Columbia University Press.

Lerner, Melvin. 1965. "Evaluation of performance as a function of performer's reward and attractiveness." *Journal of Personality and Social Psychology*, vol. 1, no. 4: 355–360.

———. 1980. *The Belief in a Just World: A Fundamental Delusion*. New York: Plenum Press.

Le, Vanna. 2014. "Global 2000: The world's largest media companies of 2014." *Forbes*, May 7. http://www.forbes.com/sites/vannale/2014/05/07/global-2000-the-worlds-largest-media-companies-of-2014/

Lee, Jennifer; and Bean, Frank D. 2012. *The Diversity Paradox: Immigration and the Color Line in Twenty-First Century America*. New York: Russell Sage Foundation.

Lee, Jennifer; and Zhou, Min. 2014. "The success frame and achievement paradox: The costs and consequences for Asian Americans." *Race and Social Problems*, vol. 6, no. 1: 38–55.

Levinson, David. 2002. *Encyclopedia of Crime and Punishment*. Thousand Oaks, CA: Sage.

Levi-Strauss, C. 1969 (orig. 1949). In R. Needham, ed., *The Elementary Structures of Kinship*. rev. ed. J. Bell and J. von Sturmer, trans.. Boston: Beacon Press.

Lewin, Tamar. 2012. "Harvard and M.I.T. team up to offer free online courses." *The New York Times*. May. http://www.nytimes.com/2012/05/03/education/harvard-and-mit-team-up-to-offer-free-online-courses.html?_r=0

Lewis, Christopher Alan; Shelvin, Mark; McGuckin, Conor; and Navratil, Marek. 2001. "The Santa Clara Strength of Religious Faith Questionnaire: Confirmatory factor analysis." *Pastoral Psychology*, vol. 49, no. 5. www.infm.ulst.ac.uk/~chris/64.pdf

Lewis, Jacqueline. 1998. "Learning to strip: The socialization experiences of exotic dancers." *Canadian Journal of Human Sexuality*, vol. 7: 1–16.

Lewis, Jason. 2013. "New report details plans for low-wage worker justice." *The Village Voice*, February 14. http://blogs.villagevoice.com/runninscared/2013/02/new_report_deta.php

Lewis, Oscar. 1959. *Five Families: Mexican Case Studies in the Culture of Poverty*. New York: Basic Books.

Li, J.; and Singelmann, J. 1998. "Gender differences in class mobility: A comparative study of the United States, Sweden, and West Germany." *Acta Sociologica*, vol. 41, no. 4: 315–333.

Li, Jui-Chung Allen. 2007. "The Impact of Divorce on Children's Behavior Problems." *A Briefing Paper Prepared for the Council on Contemporary Families*, July 21. https://contemporaryfamilies.org/impact-divorce-childrens-behavior-problems/

Liazos, Alexander. 1972. "The poverty of the sociology of deviance: Nuts, sluts and perverts." *Social Problems*, vol. 20: 103–120.

Lipka, Michael. 2013. "What surveys say about worship attendance—and why some stay home." September 13. http://www.pewresearch.org/fact-tank/2013/09/13/what-surveys-say-about-worship-attendance-and-why-some-stay-home/

Liptak, Adam. 2013. "Supreme Court invalidates key part of voting rights act." *New York Times*, June 25.

Liu, Ka-Yuet; King, Marissa; and Bearman, Peter S. 2010. "Social influence and the autism epidemic." *American Journal of Sociology*, vol. 115, no. 5: 1387–1434.

Livingston, Gretchen. 2013. "The rise of single fathers." July 2. http://www.pewsocialtrends.org/2013/07/02/the-rise-of-single-fathers/

Livingston, Gretchen. 2014. "Four-in-Ten Couples are Saying 'I Do,' Again," http://www.pewsocialtrends.org/2014/11/14/four-in-ten-couples-are-saying-i-do-again/.

Lofland, Lyn. 1973. *A World of Strangers: Order and Action in Urban Public Space*. New York: Basic Books.

London E.; and Etzel R. A. 2000. "The environment as an etiologic factor in autism: A new direction for research" *Environmental Health Perspectives*. 108 (suppl 3): 401–404.

Long, L.; and Nucci, A. 1998. "Accounting for two population turnarounds in nonmetropolitan America." *Research in Rural Sociology and Development*, no. 7: 47–70.

Lopez, Ricardo; White, Ronald D.; and Pfeifer, Stuart. 2012. "Deal brings end to L.A., Long Beach ports strike." *Los Angeles Times*,

December 5. www.latimes.com/business/la-fi-1205-ports-talks-20121205,0,7425017.story

Lortie, Dan. 1968. "Shared ordeal and induction to work." In Howard Becker, Blancher Greer, David Reisman, and Robert Weiss, eds., *Institutions and the Person*. Chicago: Aldine.

Loseke, Donileen; and Cahill, Spencer. 1986. "Actors in search of a character: Student social workers' quest for professional identity." *Symbolic Interaction*, vol. 9: 245–258.

Lubin, Judy. 2012. "The 'Occupy' movement: Emerging protest forms and contested urban spaces." *Berkeley Planning Journal*, vol. 25, no. 1, p. 184-197.

Lynch, J.W.; Kaplan, G.A.; and Shema, S.J. 1997. "Cumulative impact of sustained economic hardship on physical, cognitive, psychological, and social functioning." *New England Journal of Medicine*, vol. 337, no. 26: 1889–1895.

———. 1998. "Income inequality and mortality in metropolitan areas of the United States." *American Journal of Public Health*, vol. 88, no. 7: 1074–1080.

Lynd, Robert S.; and Lynd, Helen Merrell. 1937. *Middletown in Transition: A Study in Cultural Conflicts*. New York: Harcourt Brace.

———. 1959 (orig. 1929). *Middletown: A Study in Modern American Culture*. San Diego, CA: Harvest Books/Harcourt Brace.

Maccoby, E. E.; and Jacklin, C. N. 1987. "Sex segregation in childhood." In H. W. Reese, ed., *Advances in Child Development and Behavior*. Orlando, FL: Academic Press.

Macintyre, S.; MacDonald, L.; and Ellaway, A. 2008. "Do poorer people have poorer access to local resources and facilities? The distribution of local resources by area deprivation in Glasgow, Scotland." *Social Sciences & Medicine*, vol. 67, no. 6: 900–914.

MacKinnon, Catharine A. 2005. *Women's Lives, Men's Laws*. Cambridge, MA: Belknap Press.

Mahmood, Saba. 2004. *Politics of Piety: The Islamic Revival and the Feminist Subject*. Princeton, NJ: Princeton University Press.

Mai-Duc, Christine. 2015. "The world's new oldest person: Gertrude Weaver, 116, of Arkansas." *Los Angeles Times*, April 6. http://www.latimes.com/nation/nationnow/la-na-nn-arkansas-worlds-oldest-person-dies-20150406-story.html

Malamuth, Neil; and Donnerstein, Edward, eds. 1984. *Pornography and Sexual Aggression*. New York: Academic Press.

Malthus, Thomas. 1997 (orig. 1798). *An Essay on the Principle of Population, as it Affects the Future Improvement of Society with Remarks on the Speculations of Mr. Godwin, M. Condorcet, and Other Writers*. London: J. Johnson, St. Paul's Churchyard. www.ac.wwu.edu/~stephan/malthus/malthus.0.html

Manjoo, Farhad. 2013. "How Google became such a great place to work." *Slate Magazine*. January 21. http://www.slate.com/articles/technology/technology/2013/01/google_people_operations_the_secrets_of_the_world_s_most_scientific_human.html

Mann, Leslie. 2012. "Tips for raising backyard chickens to avoid getting egg on your face." *Chicago Tribune*, August 29. http://articles.chicagotribune.com/2012-08-29/health/ct-x-0829-backyard-chickens-salmonella-20120829_1_backyard-chickens-chicken-owners-raw-chicken

Mann, Susan A.; Grimes, Michael D.; Kemp, Alice Abel; and Jenkins, Pamela J. 1997. "Paradigm shifts in family sociology? Evidence from three decades of family textbooks." *Journal of Family Issues*, vol. 18, no. 3: 315.

Marche, Stephen. 2012. "Is Facebook making us lonely?" *The Atlantic*, May 2012. www.theatlantic.com/magazine/archive/2012/05/is-facebook-making-us-lonely/8930

Marcuse, Herbert. 1991 (orig. 1964). *One-Dimensional Man: Studies in the Ideology of Advanced Industrial Society*. Boston: Beacon Press.

Markon, Jerry. 2007. "Human trafficking evokes outrage, little evidence: U.S. estimates thousands of victims, but efforts to find them fall short." *Washington Post*, September 23.

Martin JA, Hamilton BE, Osterman MJK, et al. 2015. "Births: Final data for 2013." National vital statistics reports; vol. 64 no 1. Hyattsville, MD: National Center for Health Statistics.

Martin, Laura. 1986. "Eskimo words for snow: A case study in the genesis and decay of an anthropological example." *American Anthropologist*, vol. 88, no. 2: 418–423.

Martin, Lisa A.; Neighbors, Harold W.; and Griffith, Derek M. 2013. "The experience of symptoms of depression in men vs. women: Analysis of the National Comorbidity Survey Replication." *JAMA Psychiatry*, vol. 70, no. 10: 1100–1106.

Martineau, Harriet. 1837. *Society in America*. London: Saunders and Otley.

———. 1838. *Retrospect of Western Travel*. London: Saunders and Otley.

Marullo, Sam. 1999. "Sociology's essential role: Promoting critical analysis in service learning." In J. Ostrow, G. Hesser, and S. Enos, eds., *Cultivating the Sociological Imagination: Concepts and Models for Service Learning in Sociology*. Washington, DC: American Association for Higher Education.

Marx, Karl. 1982 (orig. 1848). *The Communist Manifesto*. New York: International.

———. 2001. *Selected Writings*. Ed. David McLellan. Oxford: Oxford University Press.

———. 2006 (orig. 1890). *Das Kapital*. Miami, FL: Synergy International of the Americas, Ltd.

Maslin Nir, Sarah. 2010. "Embracing A life of solitude." *New York Times*, April 14.

Massey, D. S.; and Denton N. A. 1993. *American Apartheid: Segregation and the Making of the Underclass*. Cambridge, MA: Harvard University Press.

Matsuda, Mari J.: Lawrence, C. R.; Delgado, Richard; and Crenshaw, Kimberle. 1993. *Words That Wound: Critical Race Theory, Assaultive Speech and the First Amendment*. Boulder, CO: Westview Press.

Matza, David. 1969. *Becoming Deviant*. Englewood Cliffs, NJ: Prentice Hall.

Mauss, Armand L. 1975. *Social Problems as Social Movements*. Philadelphia: J. B. Lippincott.

Maynard, D.W.; and Frankel, R.M. 2006. "On diagnostic rationality: Bad news, good news, and the symptom residue." In J. Heritage and D. Maynard, eds., *Communication in Medical Care: Interaction between Primary Care Physicians and Patients*. Cambridge: Cambridge University Press.

Mayo, Elton. 1949. *Hawthorne and the Western Electric Company, The Social Problems of an Industrial Civilisation*, New York, NY: Routledge.

Mazumder, Bhashkar. 2012. "Upward intergenerational economic mobility in the United States." PEW Charitable Trusts. http://www.pewtrusts.org/~/media/legacy/uploadedfiles/pcs_assets/2012/empreportsupward20intergen20mobility2008530pdf.pdf

McArdle, Megan. 2012. "Is college a lousy investment?" *Newsweek*, September 9.

McCaa, Robert. 1994. "Child marriage and complex families among the Nahuas of ancient Mexico." *Latin American Population History Bulletin*, 26: 2–11.

McCall, L. 2001. "Sources of racial wage inequality in metropolitan labor markets: Racial, ethnic, and gender differences." *American Sociological Review*, vol. 66, no. 4: 520–541.

McChesney, Robert. 1997. *Corporate Media and the Threat to Democracy*. Open Media Pamphlet Series. New York: Seven Stories Press.

_____. 2000. *Rich Media, Poor Democracy: Communication Politics in Dubious Times*. New York: New Press.

_____. 2004. *The Problem of the Media: U.S. Communication Politics in the Twenty-First Century*. New York: Monthly Review Press.

McCleary, Richard; and Tewksbury, Richard. 2010. "Female patrons of porn." *Deviant Behavior*, vol. 31, no. 2: 208–223.

McCombs, Maxwell; and Shaw, Donald. 1972. "The agenda-setting function of mass media." *Public Opinion Quarterly*, vol. 36, no.: 176–187.

_____. 1977. "The agenda-setting function of the press." In D. Shaw and M. McCombs, eds., *The Emergence of American Political Issues: The Agenda-Setting Function of the Press*. St. Paul, MN: West Publishing.

McCune, J. 2014. *Sexual Discretion: Black Masculinity and the Politics of Passing*. Chicago: University of Chicago Press.

McDonald, Michael. 2014. "National general election VEP turnout rates, 1789–Present." *United States Elections Project*. June. http://www.electproject.org/national-1789-present

McGhee, Paul E.; and Frueh, Terry. 1980. "Television viewing and the learning of sex-role stereotypes." *Sex Roles*, vol. 6, no. 2: 179.

McGheehan, Patrick. 2015. "Cuomo moves to raise wages for New York fast-food workers." *New York Times*, May 6. http://www.nytimes.com/2015/05/07/nyregion/cuomo-moves-to-raise-wages-for-new-york-fast-food-workers.html?_r=0

McGinn, Daniel. 2006. "Marriage by the numbers." *Newsweek*, June 5.

McGrane, Bernard. 1994. *The Un-TV and the 10 MPH Car: Experiments in Personal Freedom and Everyday Life*. New York: Small Press.

_____; and Gunderson, John. 2010. *Watching TV Is Not Required: Thinking About Media and Thinking About Thinking*. New York: Routledge.

McIntosh, Peggy. 1988. "White Privilege and Male Privilege: A Personal Account of Coming to See Correspondences Through Work in Women's Studies." Working Paper No. 189. *Center for Research on Women*. Wellsley College: Wellsey, MA.

McIntyre, Shelby; Moberg, Dennis J.; and Posner, Barry Z. 1980. "Preferential treatment in preselection decisions according to sex and race." *Academy of Management Journal*, vol. 23, no. 4: 738–749.

McKinlay, J.B. 1997. "A case for refocusing upstream: The political economy of health and illness." In P. Conrad, ed., *The Sociology of Health and Illness: Critical Perspectives*. New York: St. Martin's Press.

McLuhan, Marshall. 1964. *Understanding Media: The Extensions of Man*. New York: McGraw Hill.

McMichael, Philip. 1996. *Development and Social Change: A Global Perspective*. Thousand Oaks, CA: Pine Forge Press.

McNamara, Kevin. 1999. "CityWalk: Los(t) Angeles in the shape of a mall." In Ghent Urban Studies Team, ed., *The Urban Condition*. Rotterdam: 010 Publishers.

McNicol, Tony. 2006. "Meet the geek elite." *Wired Magazine*, vol. 14, no. 7. www.wired.com/wired/archive/14.07/posts.html?pg=5

McPhail, Clark. 1991. *The Myth of the Madding Crowd*. New York: de Gruyter.

Mead, George Herbert. 1934. *Mind, Self and Society*. Ed. Charles Morris. Chicago: University of Chicago Press.

Mechur Karp, M. 2012. "I don't know, I've never been to college!" Dual enrollment as a college readiness strategy." *New Directions for Higher Education*, 2012: 21–28.

Mehta, Stephanie. 2014X. "The Fortune Global 500, 2014," *Fortune*. http://fortune.com/global500/

Mejia, P. 2014. "Fetuses in artificial wombs: Medical marvel or misogynist malpractice?" *Newsweek*, August 6.

Mele, Christopher. 2000. *Selling the Lower East Side: Culture, Real Estate, and Resistance in New York City*. Minneapolis: University of Minnesota Press.

Melnick, Meredith. 2011. "Mixed race celebrities on race, in their own words." *Time*, February 15. www.healthland.time.com/2011/02/15/mixed-race-celebrities-in-their-own-words/

Menzel, Peter. 1995. *Material World: A Global Family Portrait*. Sierra Club Books.

Merton, Robert K. 1938. "Social Structure and Anomie." *American Sociological Review*, vol. 3, no. 5: 672–682.

_____. 1948. "The self-fulfilling prophecy." *Antioch Review*, vol. 8, no. 2: 193–210.

_____. 1968. *Social Theory and Social Structure*. 2nd rev. ed. New York: Free Press.

_____. 1996. *On Social Structure and Science*. Chicago: University of Chicago.

Messerschmidt, James W. 1993. *Masculinities and Crime: Critique and Reconceptualization of Theory*. Totowa, NJ: Rowman and Littlefield.

_____. 1998. "Men victimizing men: The case of lynching: 1865–1900." In Lee H. Bowker, ed., *Masculinities and Violence*. Thousand Oaks, CA: Sage.

Meyer, D. 2000. "Social movements: Creating communities of change." In R. Teske and M. Tetreault, eds., *Conscious Acts and the Politics of Social Change*. Columbia: University of South Carolina Press.

Meyer, Daniel R.; and Bartfeld, Judi. 1998. "Patterns of child support compliance in Wisconsin." *Journal of Marriage and the Family*, vol. 60, no. 2: 309–318.

Meyrowitz, Joshua. 1985. *No Sense of Place: The Impact of Electronic Media on Social Behavior*. New York: Oxford University Press.

Michael, Ali. 2015. "Sometimes I don't want to be white either." *Huffington Post*, June 16. http://www.huffingtonpost.com/ali-michael/i-sometimes-dont-want-to-be-white-either_b_7595852.html

Milgram, Stanley. 1963. "Behavioral Study of Obedience." *Journal of Abnormal Social Psychology*, vol. 67: 371–378.

_____. 1974. *Obedience to Authority: An Experimental View*. New York: Harper & Row.

Miller, Alice. 1990. *For Your Own Good: Hidden Cruelty in Child-Rearing and the Roots of Violence*. New York: Noonday Press.

Miller, Amanda Jayne; and Sassler, Sharon. 2012. "The Construction of Gender Among Working-Class Cohabiting Couples." *Qualitative Sociology*, vol. 35, no. 4: 427–446.

Miller, Claire Cain. 2012. "In Google's inner circle, a falling number of women." *The New York Times*, August 22.

Miller, Claire Cain. 2014. "The Divorce Surge Is Over, but the Myth Lives On." *New York Times*, December 2. http://www.nytimes.com/2014/12/02/upshot/the-divorce-surge-is-over-but-the-myth-lives-on.html?_r=0&abt=0002&abg=0

Miller, Laura. 1997. "Women in the military." *Social Psychology Quarterly*, vol. 60, no. 10: 32–51.

Mills, C. Wright. 1959. *The Sociological Imagination*. New York: Oxford University Press.

_____. 1970 (orig. 1956). *The Power Elite*. New York: Oxford University Press.

Miner, Horace. 1956. "Body ritual among the Nacirema." *American Anthropologist*, vol. 58, no. 3: 503–507.

Minton, Todd D. 2013. "Jail Inmates at Midyear 2012 - Statistical Tables," Bureau of Justice Statistics Table 2, p. 5. http://www.bjs.gov/content/pub/pdf/jim12st.pdf

Miringoff, Marc; and Miringoff, Marque-Luisa. 1999. *The Social Health of the Nation: How America Is Really Doing*. New York: Oxford University Press.

Mitchell, Katharyne. 1993. "Multiculturalism, or the united colors of capitalism?" *Antipode*, vol. 25, no. 4: 263–294.

Mitchell, Richard. 2001. *Dancing at Armageddon: Survivalism and Chaos in Modern Times*. Chicago: University of Chicago Press.

_____; and Charmaz, Kathy. 1996. "The myth of silent authorship: Self, substance and style in ethnographic writing." *Symbolic Interaction*, vol. 19, no. 4: 285–302.

Mittermeier, Russell A.; Myers, Norman; and Mittermeier, Cristina Goettsch. 2000. *Hotspots: Earth's Biologically Richest and Most Endangered Terrestrial Ecoregions*. Arlington, VA: Conservation International.

Mollenkopf, John. 1983. *The Contested City*. Princeton, NJ: Princeton University Press.

Molotch, Harvey. 1970. "Oil in Santa Barbara and power in America." *Sociological Inquiry*, vol. 40: 131–144.

Montagu, A. 1998. *Man's Most Dangerous Myth: The Fallacy of Race*. 6th ed. Thousand Oaks, CA: Altamira Press.

Moore, Andy. 2004. "No war for heavy metal!" *Vice*, December 1. https://www.vice.com/read/no-v11n1

Moore, Mignon R. 2011. *Invisible Families: Gay Identities, Relationships and Motherhood Among Black Women*. Berkeley: University of California Press.

Morgan, M.; and Signorielli, N. 1980. "The mainstreaming of America: Violence Profile No. 11." *Journal of Communication*, vol. 30: 10–29.

Morris, Bill. 2014. "What is it about soccer that brings out the hooligan in its fans?" *The Daily Beast*, June 25. http://www.thedailybeast.com/articles/2014/06/25/what-is-it-about-soccer-that-brings-out-the-hooligan-in-its-fans.html

Morrison, Donna Ruane; and Cherlin, Andrew J. 1995. "The divorce process and young children's well-being: A prospective analysis." *Journal of Marriage and the Family*, vol. 57, no. 3: 800–812.

Muhl, Charles J. 2002. "What is an employee? The answer depends on the federal law; in a legal context, the classification of a worker as either an employee or an independent contractor can have significant consequences." *Monthly Labor Review*, vol. 125, no. 1: 3–11.

Mullins, N. 1973. *Theories and Theory Groups in Contemporary American Sociology*. New York: Harper & Row.

Musgrove, Mike. 2009. "Twitter is a player in Iran's drama." *Washington Post*. June 17. http://articles.washingtonpost.com/2009-06-17/world/36805373_1_tweets-twitter-revolution-twitter-interface

Myers, Norman; and Kent, Jennifer. 2004. *The New Consumers: The Influence of Affluence on the Environment*. Washington, DC: Island Press.

_____, eds. 2005. *The New Atlas of Planet Management*. Berkeley: University of California Press.

Nahin, Richard, et al. 2009. "Costs of complementary and alternative medicine (CAM) and frequency of visits to CAM practitioners: United States, 2007." *National Health Statistics Reports*, July 30. www.cdc.gov/NCHS/data/nhsr/nhsr018.pdf

NASA. 2014. "New NASA images highlight U.S. air quality improvement." http://www.nasa.gov/content/goddard/new-nasa-images-highlight-us-air-quality-improvement/

National Association of Colleges and Employers. 2013a. "Class of 2013: Paid interns outpace unpaid peers in job offers, salaries." May 29. https://www.naceweb.org/s05292013/paid-unpaid-interns-job-offer.aspx

_____. 2013b. "Just 38 percent of unpaid internships were subject to FSLA guidelines." June 26. https://www.naceweb.org/s06262013/unpaid-internship-FLSA-guidelines.aspx

National Center for Education Statistics. 2012. The Higher Education General Information Survey (HEGIS) and the Integrated Postsecondary Education Data System (IPEDS). Washington, DC: Department of Education.

_____. 2015. *Fast Facts: Education Statistics*. http://nces.ed.gov/fastfacts/display.asp?id=372

National Center for Health Statistics. 2012. "Fertility of men and women aged 15–44 years in the United States: National Survey of Family Growth, 2006–2010." National Health Statistics Reports No. 51. April 12. www.cdc.gov/nchs/data/nhsr/nhsr051.pdf

National Center for the Study of Privatization in Education. 2015. "Charter schools." http://www.ncspe.org/publications_files/Charter%20Schools-FAQ.pdf

National Coalition Against Domestic Violence. 2007. "Domestic violence facts." www.NCADV.org

National Commission on Excellence in Education, The. 1983. *A Nation at Risk: The Imperative for Educational Reform*. Washington, DC: Government Printing Office.

National Domestic Violence Hotline. 2003. "What is domestic violence?" www.ndvh.org/dvInfo.html

National Employment Law Project (NELP). 2011. "Local Living Wage Laws and Coverage." http://www.nelp.org/index.php/site/issues/category/living_wage_laws/

National Institutes of Health. 2014. "SEER cancer statistics review, 1975–2011." http://seer.cancer.gov/archive/csr/1975_2011/

National Law Center on Homelessness and Poverty. 2015. "Homelessness in America: Overview of Data and Causes." http://www.nlchp.org/documents/Homeless_Stats_Fact_Sheet

National Opinion Research Center. 2015. "General Social Surveys, 1972-2014: Cumulative Codebook." http://publicdata.norc.org/GSS/DOCUMENTS/BOOK/GSS_Codebook.pdf

National Resource Center on Domestic Violence. 2007. "Religion and domestic violence." http://www.vawnet.org/Assoc_Files_VAWnet/NRC_ReligionOverview.pdf

Nattras, Nicoli; and Seekings, Jeremy. 2001. "Two nations? Race and economic inequality in South Africa today." *Daedalus*, vol. 139 (winter): 45–70.

NBC News Decision Desk. "Nearly 40 percent of voters say race relations have gotten worse." 2014. November 3. http://www.nbcnews.com/politics/elections/nearly-40-percent-voters-say-race-relations-have-gotten-worse-n241526

Neumark, David. 2004. "The Economic Effects of Mandated Wage Floors." *Public Policy Institute of California*. http://www.ppic.org/content/pubs/op/OP_204DNOP.pdf

New School. 2004. "Thomas Robert Malthus, 1766–1834." The History of Economic Thought. http://cepa.newschool.edu/het/profiles/malthus.htm

Newman, David M. 2000. *Sociology: Exploring the Architecture of Everyday Life*. 3rd ed. Thousand Oaks, CA: Pine Forge Press.

Newton, Michael. 2004. *Savage Girls and Wild Boys: A History of Feral Children*. New York: Picador.

Nielsen. 2013. "State of the media: U.S. Consumer usage report." January 7. www.nielsen.com/content/dam/corporate/us/en/reports-downloads/2013%20Reports/Nielsen-US-Consumer-Usage-Report-2012-FINAL.pdf

_____. 2014. "An era of growth: The cross-platform report." March 5. http://www.nielsen.com/content/corporate/us/en/reports/2014/an-era-of-growth-the-cross-platform-report.html

_____. 2015. "Brick by brick: The state of the shopping center." May 17. http://www.nielsen.com/us/en/insights/reports/2013/brick-by-brick—the-state-of-the-shopping-center.html

Nixon, Richard. 1974. "Address on the state of the union delivered before a joint session of the Congress," January 30. In J. T. Wooley and G. Peters, eds., *The American Presidency Project*. www.presidency.ucsb.edu/ws/index.php?pid=4327

Noah, Timothy. 2004. "Something nice about Bush." *Slate*, November 4. http://slate.msn.com/id/2109228/

Nogaki, Sylvia Weiland. 1993. "Judge oks Nordstrom lawsuit settlement." *Seattle Times*, April 13.

Nuwer, Hank. 1999. *Wrongs of Passage: Fraternities, Sororities, Hazing and Binge Drinking*. Bloomington: Indiana University Press.

——. 2004. *The Hazing Reader*. Bloomington: Indiana University Press.

——. 2014. "Hank Nuwer's List of Hazing Deaths." http://www.hanknuwer.com/hazingdeaths.html

O'Brien, Jodi; and Kollock, Peter. 1997. *The Production of Reality: Essays and Readings on Social Interaction*. Thousand Oaks, CA: Pine Forge Press.

Ochs, Elinor. 1986. "Introduction." In Bambi B. Schieffelin and Elinor Ochs, eds., *Language and Socialization Across Cultures*. New York: Cambridge University Press.

Office of Family Assistance. 2015. Administration for Children & Families. "TANF Caseload Data for 2014." February 5. http://www.acf.hhs.gov/programs/ofa/resource/caseload-data-2014

Office of Management and Budget. 2013. MB Bulletin 13-01. https://www.whitehouse.gov/sites/default/files/omb/bulletins/2013/b-13-01.pdf

Ogburn, William. 1964. *On Cultural and Social Change: Selected Papers*. Chicago: University of Chicago Press.

Oldenburg, Ray. 1999. *The Great Good Place: Cafes, Coffee Shops, Bookstores, Bars, Hair Salons, and Other Hangouts at the Heart of a Community*. Marlowe & Company.

——. 2002. *Celebrating the Third Place: Inspiring Stories about the "Great Good Places" at the Heart of Our Communities*. De Capo Press.

O'Leary, Michael Boyer. 2013. "Telecommuting can boost productivity and job performance." *U.S. News*. March 15. http://www.usnews.com/opinion/articles/2013/03/15/telecommuting-can-boost-productivity-and-job-performance

Omi, Michael; and Winant, Howard. 1994. *Racial Formation in the United States: From the 1960s to the 1990s*. 2nd ed. New York: Routledge.

O'Neill, J. 2007. "HIV/AIDS in the developing world: What can we do?" In R. Gallo, ed., *Retroviruses: Biology, Pathogenic Mechanisms and Treatment, The Biomedical & Life Sciences Collection*. London: Henry Stewart Talks.

O'Reilly, Brian. 1992. "Looking ahead: Jobs are fast moving abroad." *Fortune*, December 14, pp. 52–66.

Osborne, Lawrence. 2002. "Consuming rituals of the suburban tribe." *New York Times Magazine*, January 13.

Oswald, R. F.; Blume, l; and Marks, S. 2005. "Decentering heteronormativity: A model for Family studies." In V. L. Bengtson, A. C. Acock, K. R. Allen, P. Dilworth-Anderson, and D. M. Klein, eds., *Sourcebook of Family Theory and Research*. Thousand Oaks, CA: Sage.

Oswald, Ramona Faith; Kuvalanka, Katherine A.; Balter Blume, Libby; and Berkowitz, Dana. 2012. "Queering the family." In Sally A. Lloyd, April L. Few, and Katherine R. Allen, eds., *Handbook of Feminist Family Studies*. Thousand Oaks, CA: Sage.

Paasonen, S.; et al. 2007. "Pornification and the education of desire." In S. Paasonen et al., eds., *Pornification: Sex and Sexuality in Media Culture*. Oxford, England: Berg.

Page, Clarence. 2015. "Fake news never looked so good." *The Chicago Tribune*, February 13. http://www.chicagotribune.com/news/opinion/page/ct-brian-williams-jon-stewart-daily-show-perspec-0215-jm-20150213-column.html

Park, Robert Ezra. 1961. "Human ecology." Reprinted in G. A. Theodorson, ed., *Studies in Human Ecology*. New York: Row, Peterson & Company.

Parker, Lonnae O'Neal. 1998. "Brand identities." *Washington Post*, May 11.

Parlapiano, Alicia. 2013. "Movement on social issues." *New York Times*, March 25.

Parr, Chris. 2013. "Not staying the course." *Inside Higher Education*. https://www.insidehighered.com/news/2013/05/10/new-study-low-mooc-completion-rates

Parsons, Christi. 2015. "Obama plan for free community college: U.S. would pay 75%, states 25%." *Los Angeles Times*. January. http://www.latimes.com/nation/la-na-obama-community-college-20150108-story.html

Parsons, Talcott. 1951. *The Social System*. Glencoe, IL: The Free Press.

——. 1955. "The American family: Its relation to personality and social structure." In Talcott Parsons and R. Bales, eds., *Family Socialization and Interaction Process*. New York: Free Press.

——; and Bales, R.; eds. 1955. *Family, Socialization and Interaction Process*. New York: Free Press.

Pascoe, C. J. 2007. *Dude, you're a fag: masculinity and sexuality in high school*. Berkley: University of California Press, 5.

Patchin, Justin A.; and Hinduja, Sameer. 2014. "Lifetime cyberbullying victimization rates." Cyberbullying Research Center. http://cyberbullying.org/Cyberbullying-Identification-Prevention-Response.pdf

Patterson, Margot. 2004. "The rise of global fundamentalism." *National Catholic Reporter*, May 7.

PBS. 2001. "Frontline: Merchants of Cool." pbs.org/wgbh/pages/frontline/shows/cool/

Peavy, Linda; and Smith, Ursula. 1998. *Pioneer Women: The Lives of Women on the Frontier*. Norman: University of Oklahoma Press.

People and the Planet. 2002. "Two more Earths needed by 2050." www.peopleandplanet.net/doc.php?id+1685&section=17

Perlin, Ross. 2011. *Intern Nation: How to Earn Nothing and Learn Little in the Brave New Economy*. New York: Verso.

——. 2012. "Today's internships are a racket, not an opportunity." *The New York Times*, February 2. http://www.nytimes.com/roomfordebate/2012/02/04/do-unpaid-internships exploit-college-students/todays-internships-are-a-racket-not-an-opportunity

Perls, T. T.; and Fretts, R. 1998. "Why women live longer than men." *Scientific American Presents: Women's Health: A Lifelong Guide*, vol. 9, no. 4: 100–104.

Perrin, S.; and Spencer, C. P. 1980. "The Asch effect: A child of its time." *Bulletin of the British Psychological Society*, vol. 32: 405–406.

——. 1981. "Independence or conformity in the Asch experiment as a reflection of cultural and situational factors." *British Journal of Social Psychology*, vol. 20: 215–210.

Perry, J.; and Pugh, M. 1978. *Collective Behavior: Response to Social Stress*. St. Paul, MN: West Publishing Company.

Perry, Mark J. 2010. "The great mancession of 2008–2009." Paper presented at the Statement before the House Ways and Means Committee Subcommittee on Income Security and Family Support on Responsible Fatherhood Programs. American Enterprise Institute for Public Policy Research, June 17.

Peters, H. Elizabeth; Argys, Laura M.; Maccoby, Eleanor E.; and Mnookin, Robert H. 1993. "Enforcing divorce settlements: Evidence from child support compliance and award modifications." *Demography*, vol. 30, no. 4: 719–735.

Pettigrew, Thomas F., and Tropp, Linda R. 2011. *When Groups Meet: The Dynamics of Intergroup Contact*. East Sussex, UK: Psychology Press.

Pettijohn, Sarah L. 2014. "The Nonprofit sector in brief: Public charities, giving and volunteering, 2014." Urban Institute. October 27. http://www.urban.org/research/publication/nonprofit-sector-brief-public-charities-giving-and-volunteering-2014

Pettit, Becky; and Western, Bruce. 2004. "Mass imprisonment and the life course: Race and class inequality in U.S. incarceration." *American Sociological Review*, vol. 69: 151–169.

PEW Charitable Trusts. "Pursuing the American Dream: Economic mobility across generations." www.pewstates.org/uploadedFiles/PCS_Assets/2012/Pursuing_American_Dream.pdf

Pew Research Center for the People and the Press. 2012a. "Cable Leads the Pack as Campaign News Source." February 7. http://www.people-press.org/2012/02/07/cable-leads-the-pack-as-campaign-news-source/

Pew Research Center. 2008. U.S. Religious Landscape Survey. http://religions.pewforum.org

———. 2011a. "A Portrait of Stepfamilies." January 2011. http://www.pewsocialtrends.org/2011/01/13/a-portrait-of-stepfamilies/

———. 2011b. "Changes in religious affiliation in the United States." February 2011. www.pewforum.org/files/2009/04/fullreport.pdf

———. 2012a. "College graduation: Weighing the cost . . . and the payoff." May 17. http://www.pewresearch.org/2012/05/17/college-graduation-weighing-the-cost-and-the-payoff/

———. 2012b. "Little voter discomfort with Romney's Mormon religion." www.pewforum.org/2012/07/26/2012-romney-mormonism-obamas-religion/

———. 2012c. "'Nones' on the rise: One-in-five adults have no religious affiliation." www.pewforum.org/uploadedFiles/Topics/Religious_Affiliation/Unaffiliated/NonesOnTheRise-full.pdf

———. 2012d. "Pursuing the American Dream: Economic mobility across generations." www.pewstates.org/uploadedFiles/PCS_Assets/2012/Pursuing_American_Dream.pdf

———. 2012e. "Religion and the Unaffiliated." http://www.pewforum.org/2012/10/09/nones-on-the-rise-religion/#what-keeps-people-out-of-the-pews

———. 2012f "The rise of intermarriage." http://www.pewsocialtrends.org/2012/02/16/the-rise-of-intermarriage/

———. 2013. "The State of Digital Divides." http://www.pewinternet.org/2013/11/05/the-state-of-digital-divides-video-slides/

———. 2014a. "America's wealth gap between middle-income and upper-income families is widest ever." http://www.pewresearch.org/fact-tank/2014/12/17/wealth-gap-upper-middle-income/

———. 2014b. "Beyond Red vs. Blue: The Political Typology." http://www.people-press.org/2014/06/26/the-political-typology-beyond-red-vs-blue/

———. 2014c. "Global religious diversity." http://www.pewforum.org/2014/04/04/global-religious-diversity/

———. 2014d. "Internet User Demographics," http://www.pewinternet.org/data-trend/internet-use/latest-stats/

———. 2014e. "Millennnials in Adulthood. Chapter 3: Finances, Social Trends and Technology." http://www.pewsocialtrends.org/2014/03/07/chapter-3-finances-social-trends-and-technology/

———. 2014f. "U.S. Catholics View Pope Francis as a Change for the Better." March 6. http://www.pewforum.org/2014/03/06/catholics-view-pope-francis-as-a-change-for-the-better/

———. 2015a. "America's Changing Religious Landscape." http://www.pewforum.org/2015/05/12/americas-changing-religious-landscape/

———. 2015b. "Latest trends in religious restrictions and hostilities." http://www.pewforum.org/2015/02/26/religious-hostilities/

———.. 2015c. "Support for same-sex marriage at record high, but key segments remain opposed." http://www.people-press.org/2015/06/08/support-for-same-sex-marriage-at-record-high-but-key-segments-remain-opposed/

Pew Research Social and Demographic Trends. 2010. "Interactive: The changing American family. www.pewsocialtrends.org/2010/11/18/five-decades-of-marriage-trends/

Pfeffer, C. A. 2012. "Normative resistance and inventive pragmatism: Negotiating structure and agency in transgender families." *Gender & Society*, vol. 26, no. 4: 574–602.

———. 2014. "'I don't like passing as a straight woman': Queer negotiations of identity and social group membership." *American Journal of Sociology*, vol. 120, no.1: 1–44.

Phillips, D.P.; Welty, W. R.; and Smith, M. M. 1997. "Elevated suicide levels associated with legalized gambling." *Suicide Life Threat Behavior*, vol. 27. no. 4: 373–378.

Phillips. S. 2009. "Criminology: legal disparities in the capital of capital punishment." *Journal of Criminal Law & Criminology*, vol. 99, no. 3: 717.

Pierce, Fred. 2012. "Saudi Arabia takes a claim on the Nile." *National Geographic*, December. http://news.nationalgeographic.com/news/2012/12/121217-saudi-arabia-water-grabs ethiopia/

Pilnick, Alison; Hindmarsh, Jon; and Teas Gill, Virginia. 2009. "Beyond 'doctor and patient': developments in the study of healthcare interactions." *Sociology of Health & Illness*, vol. 31, no. 6: 787–802.

Pinker, Steven. 1995. *The Language Instinct: How the Mind Creates*. New York: Harper Perennial.

———. 2005. "Psychoanalysis Q-and-A: Steven Pinker." *The Harvard Crimson*, January 19. www.thecrimson.com/article/2005/1/19/psychoanalysis-q-and-a-steven-pinker-in-an/

Pinto, Barbara. 2005. "Small town USA may offer solution to outsourcing: Company redeploys workers to rural towns instead of sending jobs overseas." *ABC World News Tonight*, August 25.

Plante, Thomas G.; and Boccaccini, Marcus. 1997. "The Santa Clara Strength of Religious Faith Questionnaire." *Pastoral Psychology*, 45, 375–387.

Pleck, Elizabeth H. 2000. *Celebrating the Family: Ethnicity, Consumer Culture, and Family Ritual*. Cambridge. MA: Harvard University Press.

Plumer, Brad. 2013. "Poverty is growing twice as fast in the suburbs as in cities." *Washington Post*, May 23. www.washingtonpost.com/blogs/wonkblog/wp/2013/05/23/poverty-is-now-growing-twice-as-fast-in-the-suburbs-as-in-the-city/

Pollack, Andres. 1999. "Aerospace gets Japan's message: Without military largess, industry takes the lean path." *New York Times*, March 9, p. C1.

Pollner, Melvin; and Stein, Jill. 1996. "Narrative mapping of social worlds: The voice of experience in Alcoholics Anonymous." *Journal of Symbolic Interaction*, vol. 19, no. 3: 203–223.

———. 2001. "Doubled-over in laughter: Humor and the construction of selves in Alcoholics Anonymous." In Jaber Gubrium and James Holstein, eds., *Institutional Selves: Personal Troubles in Organizational Context*. New York: Oxford University Press.

Pool, Robert. 1997. *Beyond Engineering: How Society Shapes Technology*. Oxford, UK: Oxford University Press.

Port, Dina Roth. 2014. "Doulas: Not just for hippie moms." *Parents Magazine*. http://www.parents.com/pregnancy/giving-birth/doula/doulas-not-just-for-hippie-moms/

Poster, Mark. 2002. "Workers as cyborgs: Labor and networked computers." *Journal of Labor Research*, vol. 23, no. 3: 339.

Postman, Neil. 1987. *Amusing Ourselves to Death: Public Discourse in the Age of Show Business*. New York: Methuen.

Powell, Brian. 2003. Unpublished survey results. Bloomington: Indiana University, Department of Sociology, Center for Survey Research.

———; Bolzendahl, Catherine; Geist, Claudia; and Carr Stellman, Lala. 2010. *Counted Out: Same-Sex Relations and Americans' Definition of Family*. New York: Russell Sage Foundation.

Powell, L.M.; Slater, S.; Mirtcheva, D.; Bao, Y.; and Chaloupka, F. J. 2007. "Food store availability and neighborhood characteristics in the United States." *Preventive Medicine*, vol. 44, no. 3: 189–195.

Preston, Jennifer. 2011. "Protesters look for ways to feed the Web." *New York Times*, November 24.

Prince, Marcell and Carols Tovar. 2015. "How Much U.S. Oil and Gas Comes From Fracking?" *Wall Street Journal*. April 1. http://blogs.wsj.com/corporate-intelligence/2015/04/01/how-much-u-s-oil-and-gas-comes-from-fracking/

Project on Student Debt. 2014. "Student Debt and the Class of 2013." http://projectonstudentdebt.org/files/pub/classof2013.pdf

Pullum, Geoffrey K. 1991. *The Great Eskimo Vocabulary Hoax and Other Irreverent Essays on the Study of Language*. Chicago: University of Chicago Press.

Putnam, Robert D. 1995. "Tuning in, tuning out: The strange disappearance of social capital in America." *Political Science & Politics*, vol. 28, no. 4: 664.

———. 2000. *Bowling Alone: The Collapse and Revival of American Community*. New York: Simon & Schuster.

Rabin, Roni Caryn. 2008. "Severe heart attacks deadlier for women." *The New York Times*, December 8.

Rabow, Jerome; Stein, Jill; and Conley, Terri. 1999. "Teaching social justice and encountering society: The pink triangle experiment." *Youth and Society*, vol. 30, no. 4: 483–514.

Radway, A. Janice. 1991. *Reading the Romance: Women, Patriarchy, and Popular Literature*. Chapel Hill: University of North Carolina Press.

Rainee, L and Wellman, B. 2012. *Networked*. Cambridge, MA: MIT Press.

Rainer, Thom S. and Jess Rainer. 2011. *The Millennials: Connecting to America's Largest Generation*. B & H Books.

Rajaram, Shireen S. 2007. "An action research project: Community lead poisoning prevention." *Teaching Sociology*, vol. 35, no. 2: 138–150.

RAND Education. 2003. *Charter School Operation and Performance: Evidence from California*. Santa Monica, CA: The Rand Corporation. www.rand.org/pubs/monograph_reports/MR1700

Ray, Brian. 1997. "Strengths of their own—home schoolers across America: Academic achievement, family characteristics, and longitudinal traits." Salem, OR: National Home Education Research Institute.

———. 2008. "Research facts on homeschooling." National Home Education Research Institute. www.nheri.org/Research-Facts-on-Homeschooling.html

———. 2013. "Homeschooling associated with beneficial learner and societal outcomes but educators do not promote it." *Peabody Journal of Education: Issues of Leadership, Policy, and Organizations*, Vol. 88, No. 3.

Reece, M.; Herbenick, D.; Schick, V.; Sanders, S.; Dodge, B.; and Fortenberry, J. 2010. "Condom use rates in a national probability sample of males and females, ages 14 to 94 in the United States." *Journal of Sexual Medicine*, 7 (suppl. 5): 266–267.

Rees, W.; and Wackernagel, M. 1994. "Ecological footprints and appropriated carrying capacity: Measuring the natural capital requirements of the human economy." In A-M. Jansson, M. Hammer, C. Folke, and R. Costanza, eds., *Investing in Natural Capital: The Ecological Economics Approach to Sustainability*. Washington, DC: Island Press.

Reyes, Emily Alpert. 2013. "More married women in the U.S. aren't having children." *Los Angeles Times*, December 8, Section A.

Riel, M. 2010. "Understanding Action Research/" Center for Collaborative Action Research, Pepperdine University. http://cadres.pepperdine.edu/ccar/define.html

Riesman, D. 1957. "The suburban dislocation." *Annals of the American Academy of Political and Social Science*, vol. 314: 123.

Rios, Victor. 2009. "The consequence of the criminal justice pipeline on Black and Latino Masculinity." *The Annals of the American Academy of Political and Social Science*. May: 150–162.

Ritzer, George. 1996. *The McDonaldization of Society*. Thousand Oaks, CA: Pine Forge Press.

———. 2013. *The McDonaldization of Society: 20th Anniversary Edition*. Thousand Oaks, California: Sage.

Robins, Douglas; Sanders, Clinton; and Cahill, Spencer. 1991. "Dogs and their people: Pet-facilitated interaction in a public setting." *Journal of Contemporary Ethnography*, vol. 20, no. 1: 3–25.

Robison, Jennifer. 2014. "Nevada again posts one of higher foreclosure rates in U.S." *Las Vegas Journal-Review*, February 12.

Rojek, Chris. 1985. *Capitalism and Leisure Theory*. London: Tavistock.

———. 1995. *Decentering Leisure: Rethinking Leisure Theory*. London: Sage.

———. 1997. "Leisure theory: Retrospect and prospect." *Loisir et Société/Society and Leisure*, vol. 20, no. 2: 383–400.

———. 2000. "Leisure and the rich today: Veblen's thesis after a century." *Leisure Studies*, vol. 19, no. 1: 1–15.

Roosevelt, Margaret. 2007. "U.S. mayors find it's not easy to be green: Assessing progress is difficult for 728 cities in a Kyoto-like pact." Los Angeles Times. November 4. http://articles.latimes.com/2007/nov/04/nation/na-mayors4

Roscoe, W. 2000. "How to become a berdache: Toward a unified analysis of gender." In G. Herdt, ed., *Third Sex, Third Gender: Beyond Sexual Dimorphism in Culture and History*. New York: Zone Books.

Rosenbaum, Emily. 2008. "Racial/ethnic differences in asthma prevalence: The role of housing and neighborhood environments." *Journal of Health and Social Behavior*, vol. 49, no. 2: 131–145.

Rosenberg, Tina. 2013. "Turning education upside down." *New York Times*, October 9. http://opinionator.blogs.nytimes.com/2013/10/09/turning-education-upside-down/?_r=1

Rosenbloom, Stephanie. 2007. "On Facebook, scholars link up with data." *New York Times*, December 17. www.nytimes.com/2007/12/17/style/17facebook.html?ex=1355720400&en=33ca15953318a6f5&ei=5124&partner=permalink&exprod=permalink

Rosenfeld, Dana. 2003. *The Changing of the Guard: Lesbian and Gay Elders, Identity, and Social Change*. Philadelphia: Temple University Press.

Rosenhan, David. 1973. "On being sane in insane places." *Science*, vol. 179 (January): 250–258.

Rosenthal, A. M. 1964/2008. *Thirty-Eight Witnesses: The Kitty Genovese Case*. New York: Melville House.

Rosenthal, R.; and Jacobson, L. 1968. *Pygmalion in the Classroom: Teacher Expectation and Pupils' Intellectual Development*. New York: Rinehart and Winston.

Rosin, Hannah. 2012. *The End of Men: And the Rise of Women*. New York: Riverhead Books.

Ross, Andrew. 1997. "Introduction." In Andrew Ross, ed., *No Sweat: Fashion, Free Trade and the Rights of Garment Workers*. New York: Verso.

Rothblum, Esther. 1996. *Preventing Heterosexism and Homophobia*. Thousand Oaks, CA: Sage.

Rothkop, David. 1997. "In praise of cultural imperialism? Effects of globalization on culture." *Foreign Policy*, June 22.

Roy, D. F. 1959. "Banana time: Job satisfaction and informal interaction." *Human Organization*, 18: 158–168.

Rubel, Paula; and Rosman, Abraham. 2001. "The collecting passion in America." *Zeitschrift fur Ethnologie* (English), vol. 126, no. 2: 313–330.

Rubenstein, William B. 2001. "Do gay rights laws matter? An empirical assessment." *Southern California Law Review*, vol. 7565–120. www.law.ucla.edu/williamsinstitute/programs/dogayrightslawsmatter.pdf

Rubin, Adam. 2014. "Daniel Murphy: Right to take leave." April 4. http://espn.go.com/new-york/mlb/story/_/id/10721495/daniel-murphy-new-york-mets-deflects-criticism-taking-paternity-leave

Rubin, Zick; and Peplau, Letitia Anne. 1975. "Who believes in a just world?" *Journal of Social Issues*, vol. 31, no. 3: 65–89.

Rupp, Leila; and Taylor, Verta. 2003. *Drag Queens of the 801 Cabaret.* Chicago: University of Chicago Press.

Russakoff, Rich; and Goodman, Mary. 2011. "Employee theft: Are you blind to it?" *CBS Money Watch.* July 14. www.cbsnews.com/8301-505143_162-48640192/employee-theft-are-you-blind-to-it/

Ryan, Caitlin; Huebner, David; Diaz, Rafael; and Sanchez, Jorge. 2009. "Family rejection as a predictor of negative health outcomes in White and Latino lesbian, gay, and bisexual young adults." *Pediatrics*, vol. 123, no. 1: 346–352.

Ryan, George. 2003. "The death penalty: Arbitrary and capricious." http://www.salon.com/2003/01/14/ryan_4/

Rymer, Russ, 1994. *Genie: A Scientific Tragedy.* New York: HarperCollins.

Sadker, Myra; and Sadker, David. 1995. *Failing at Fairness: How Our Schools Cheat Girls.* New York: Scribner.

Sallie Mae. 2013. *How America Pays for College 2013.* https://salliemae.newshq.businesswire.com/sites/salliemae.newshq.businesswire.com/files/doc_library/file/Sallie_Mae_Report_-_How_America_Pays_for_College_Report_FINAL_0.pdf

Sampson, Robert J.; and Wilson, William Julius. 2005. "Toward a theory of race, crime and urban inequality." In Shaun L. Gabbidon and Helen Taylor Greene, eds., *Race, Crime and Justice: A Reader.* New York: Routledge.

Sapir, Edward. 1949. *Selected Writings in Language, Culture, and Personality.* Ed. David G. Mandelbaum. Berkeley: University of California Press.

Sassen, Saskia. 1991. *The Global City: New York, London, Tokyo.* Princeton, NJ: Princeton University Press.

Saul, Michael Howard. 2014. "New York City Street Homelessness Rises 6%," *The Wall Street Journal*, June 6. http://blogs.wsj.com/metropolis/2014/06/06/new-york-city-street-homelessness-rises-6/.

Sayer, Liana C.; and Mattingly, Maribeth. 2006. "Under pressure: Gender differences in the relationship between free time and feeling rushed." *Journal of Marriage and Family*, vol. 68, no. 1: 205–221.

Scarce, Rik. 2005. *Contempt of Court: A Scholar's Battle for Free Speech from Behind Bars.* Lanham, MD: Alta Mira Press.

Schegloff, Emanuel. 1986. "The routine as achievement." *Human Studies*, vol. 9, nos. 2–3: 111–151.

———. 1999. "What next? Language and social interaction study at the century's turn." *Research on Language and Social Interaction*, vol. 32, nos.1–2: 141–148.

Schein, Edgar H. 1997. *Organizational Culture and Leadership.* San Francisco: Jossey-Bass.

———. 2010. *Organizational Culture and Leadership.* 4th ed. Hoboken, NJ: Jossey-Bass.

Schell, Orville. 2002. "Gross national happiness." *Red Herring*, January 15. www.pbs.org/frontlineworld/stories/bhutan/gnh.html

Scheyvens, Regina. 2000. "Promoting women's empowerment through involvement in ecotourism: Experiences from the Third World." *Journal of Sustainable Tourism*, vol. 8, no. 3: 232–249.

Schiller, Herbert I. 1976. *Communication and Cultural Domination.* White Plains, NY: International Arts and Sciences Press.

———. 1992. *Mass Communications and American Empire.* 2nd ed. Boulder, CO: Westview Press.

———. 1995. "The global information highway: Project for an ungovernable world." In J. Brook and I. A. Boal, eds., *Resisting the Virtual Life: The Culture and Politics of Information.* San Francisco: City Lights Books.

———. 1996. *Information Inequality.* New York: Routledge.

———; Schlenker, Jennifer A.; Caron, Sandra L.; and Halteman, William A. 1998. "A feminist analysis of *Seventeen* magazine: Content analysis from 1945 to 1995." *Sex Roles: A Journal of Research*, vol. 38, no. 1–2: 135.

Schlegel, H. 2014. "The Future of Money." The Institute of Customer Experience, September 8. http://www.slideshare.net/UXTrendspotting/reputation-currencies

Schlosser, Eric. 2002. *Fast Food Nation: The Dark Side of the All-American Meal.* New York: Perennial.

Schnaiberg, Allan. 1975. "Social synthesis of the societal-environmental dialectic: The role of distributional impacts." *Social Science Quarterly*, vol. 56: 5–20.

———. 1980. *The Environment: From Surplus to Scarcity.* New York: Oxford University Press.

———; and Gould, Kenneth Alan. 1994. *Environment and Society: The Enduring Conflict.* New York: St. Martin's Press.

Schofield, Jack. 2004. "Social network software; software to help you network." *Computer Weekly*, March 16, p. 32.

Schor, Juliet B. 1999. *The Overspent American: Why We Want What We Don't Need.* New York: HarperCollins.

Schudson, Michael. 2003. *The Sociology of News.* New York: Norton.

Schutz, Alfred P. 1962. "The stranger: An essay in social psychology." In A. Brodersen, ed, *Collected Papers II: Studies in Social Theory.* Dordrecht, The Netherlands: Martinus Nijhoff.

Schwartz, Mattathias. 2011. "Pre-occupied: The origins and future of Occupy Wall Street." *The New Yorker*, November 28. www.newyorker.com/reporting/2011/11/28/111128fa_fact_schwartz#ixzz2LdswEsh1

Schwellenbach, Nick. 2008. "Finance: A good time to be a white-collar criminal?" Center for Public Integrity, December 18. www.publicintegrity.org/blog/entry/1096

Schwimmer, B. 2001. "Figure 43. Hawaiian kin terms (actual usage)." www.umanitoba.ca/faculties/arts/anthropology/tutor/image_list/43.html

Scott, Laura S. 2009. *Two Is Enough: A Couple's Guide to Living Childless by Choice.* Berkeley: Seal Press.

Scott, Robert E.; and Kimball, Will. 2014. "China trade, outsourcing and jobs." *Economic Policy Institute,* December 11. http://www.epi.org/publication/china-trade-outsourcing-and-jobs/

Scutt, J. A. 1983. *Even in the Best of Homes.* Ringwood, Victoria: Penguin Books.

Searing, Linda. 2010. "Study: Dying at home may be less traumatic for patients as well as caregivers." *Washington Post*, September 27. www.washingtonpost.com/wp-dyn/content/article/2010/09/27/AR2010092705374.html

Sears, Brad; and Badgett, M.V. Lee. 2008. "The Impact of Extending Marriage to Same-Sex Couples on the California Budget." The Williams Institute. UCLA School of Law. www.law.ucla.edu/williamsinstitute/publications/EconImpactCAMarriage.pdf

Sedgwick, Eve Kosofsky. 1993. *Tendencies.* Durham, NC: Duke University Press.

Seekings, Jeremy; and Nattras, Nicoli. 2005. *Class, Race and Inequality in South Africa.* New Haven, CT: Yale University Press.

Segal, Lynne. 1990. *Slow Motion: Changing Masculinities, Changing Men.* New Brunswick, NJ: Rutgers University Press.

Seidman, Steven. 2003. *The Social Construction of Sexuality*. New York: Norton.

Seltzer, Judith A.; Schaeffer, Nora Cate; and Charng, Hong-Wen. 1989. "Family ties after divorce: The relationship between visiting and paying child support." *Journal of Marriage and the Family*, vol. 51, no. 4: 1013–1031.

Sennett, Richard. 1977. *The Fall of Public Man*. New York: Norton.

Severin, W. J.; and Tankard, J. W. 1997. *Communication Theories: Origins, Methods, and Uses in the Mass Media*. 4th ed. New York: Longman.

Sexton, Lori; Jenness, Valerie; and Sumner, Jennifer. 2009. "Where the margins meet: A demographic assessment of transgender inmates in men's prisons." Ucicorrections/seweb/uci.edu

Shah, Anup. 2007. "Media conglomerates, mergers, concentration of ownership." *Global Issues*, April 29. www.globalissues.org/article /159/media-conglomerates-mergers-concentration-of-ownership

Shanahan, M. J.; Bauldry, S.; and Freeman, J. 2010. "Beyond Mendel's ghost." *Contexts*, vol. 9: 34–39.

Sharp, Shane. 2010. "How does prayer help manage emotions?" *Social Psychology Quarterly*, vol. 73: 417–437.

Sherman, Aloc. 2012. "SNAP (food stamps) and earned income tax credit had big antipoverty impact in 2011." Center on Budget and Policy Priorities. September 12. www.offthechartsblog.org /snap-food-stamps-and-earned-income-tax-credit-had-big -antipoverty-impact-in-2011

Shiach, Morag. 1999. *Feminism and Cultural Studies*. New York: Oxford University Press.

Shierholz, Heidi , Natalie Sabadish, and Nicholas Finio. 2013. "The Class of 2013: Young graduates still face dim job prospects." April 10. *Economic Policy Institute*.

Shover, Neal; and Wright, John Paul. 2001. *Crimes of Privilege: Readings in White-Collar Crime*. New York: Oxford University Press.

Sifry, Micah L. 2014. "Facebook wants you to vote on Tuesday. Here's how it messed with your feed in 2012." *Mother Jones*, October 31. http://www.motherjones.com/politics/2014/10/can -voting-facebook-button-improve-voter-turnout

Simmel, Georg. 1950. *The Sociology of George Simmel*. Ed. Kurt Wolff. New York: Free Press.

Simon, Julian. 1996. *The Ultimate Resource 2*. Princeton, NJ: Princeton University Press

———. 2000. *The Great Breakthrough and Its Cause*. Ann Arbor: University of Michigan Press.

Simon, Scott. 2004. "Friend of Kitty Genovese discusses her memories of Kitty and her murder." "Weekend Edition Saturday," National Public Radio, March 13.

Singh, Gopal K.; and Siahpush, Mohammad. 2006. "Widening socioeconomic inequalities in U.S. life expectancy, 1980–2000." *International Journal of Epidemiology*, May 9. http://ije.oxfordjournals .org/cgi/reprint/dyl083v1.pdf

Skarzynska, Krystyna. 2004. "Politicians in television: The big five in impression formation." *Journal of Political Marketing*, vol. 3, no. 2: 31–45.

Skenazy, Lenore. 2008. "Why I let my 9-year-old ride the subway alone." *New York Sun*, April 1. http://www.nysun.com/news/why -i-let-my-9-year-old-ride-subway-alone

———. 2009. *Free Range Kids*. San Francisco: Jossey-Bass.

Slack, Kristin; et al. 2006. "Family economic well-being following the 1996 welfare reform: Trend data from five non-experimental panel studies." *Children and Youth Services Review*, vol. 29, no. 6: 698–720.

Smelser, Neil. 1985. "Evaluating the model of structural differentiation in relation to educational change in the nineteenth century." In Jeffrey C. Alexander, ed., *Neofunctionalism*. Beverly Hills, CA: Sage.

Smith, Aaron. 2014. "Cell phones, social media and Campaign 2014." Pew Research Center, November 3. http://www.pewinternet .org/2014/11/03/cell-phones-social-media-and-campaign-2014/

Smith, Dorothy. 1999. "Schooling for inequality." *Signs: Journal for Women in Culture and Society*, vol. 5, no. 4: 1147–1151.

Smith, Herbert L. 1990. "Specification problems in experimental and nonexperimental social research." *Sociological Methodology*, vol. 20: 59–91.

Smith, Kara. 2005. "Gender talk: A case study in prenatal socialization." *Women and Languages*, March 22.

Smith, Marc; and Kollock, Peter. 1998. *Communities in Cyberspace*. London: Routledge.

Snider, Mike. 2012. "Net connections, movies and music are worthy expenditures despite downturn." *USA Today*, June 11. http://usatoday30.usatoday.com/tech/news/story/2012-06-12 /entertainment-spending/55530446/1

Snider, Susanna. 2014. "Three must-know facts about for-profit colleges, student debt." *U.S. News and World Report,* October. http:// www.usnews.com/education/best-colleges/paying-for-college /articles/2014/10/01/3-facts-for-students-to-know-about-for -profit-colleges-and-student-debt

Sociological Initiatives Foundation. 2010. "Chicago mothers receive Chall Award." February 18. www.sifoundation.org/2010 /02/chicago-mothers-recieve-chall-award/#more-35

Sonner, Scott. 2002. "Burning Man gives fodder for questing sociologists." Associated Press, August 28. www.religionnewsblog .com/641-Scientists_find_Burning_Man_a_research_bonanza .html

Southern Poverty Law Center. 2014. *The Year in Hate and Extremism,* no. 153. http://www.splcenter.org/get-informed/intelligence -report/browse-all-issues/2014/spring/The-Year-in-Hate -and-Extremism

Sparks, Sarah D. 2013. "Poor children are now a majority in 17 states' public schools." *Education Week*, October. http://www.edweek .org/ew/articles/2013/10/23/09poverty.h33.html

Sparks, Sarah D.; and Adams, Caralee J. 2013. "High school poverty levels tied to college-going." *Education Week*. October. http:// www.edweek.org/ew/articles/2013/10/23/09college.h33.html

Spector, Robert; and McCarthy, Patrick D. 1996. *The Nordstrom Way: The Inside Story of America's #1 Customer Service Company*. Hoboken, NJ: John Wiley & Sons.

Spencer, Herbert. 1862. *First Principles*. London: Williams and Norgate.

———. 1873. *The Study of Sociology*. London: King.

———. 1897. *The Principles of Sociology*. 3 vols. New York: Appleton.

Spencer, S. J.; Steele, C. M.; and Quinn, D. M. 1999. "Stereotype threat and women's math performance." *Journal of Experimental Social Psychology*, vol. 35: 4–28.

Springer, Kristen W.; and Mouzon, Dawne. 2011. "Masculinity and health care seeking among older men: implications for men in different social classes." *Journal of Health and Social Behavior*. vol. 52, no. 2: 212–227.

Srinivas, Lakshmi. 1998. "Active viewing: An ethnography of the Indian film audience." *Visual Anthropology*, vol. 11, no. 4: 323–353.

———. 1998. "Gay and lesbian families: Queer like us." In Mary Ann Mason, Arlene Skolnick, and Stephen D. Sugarman, eds., *All Our Families: New Policies for a New Century*. New York: Oxford University Press.

Stack, Carol. 1974. *All Our Kin*. New York: Harper & Row.

Stannard, David E. 1993. *American Holocaust: The Conquest of the New World*. New York: Oxford University Press.

Stanton, M. E. 1995. "Patterns of kinship and residence." In B. Ingoldsby and S. Smith, eds., *Families in Multicultural Perspective*. New York: Guilford Press.

Stapleton, Christine. 2002. "Donated blood sold off overseas after 9/11." *Atlanta Journal-Constitution*, September 8, p. 19A.

Steele, Claude M. 1997. "A threat in the air: How stereotypes shape intellectual identity and performance." *American Psychologist*, vol. 52, no. 6: 613–629.

Stein, Jill. 1997. "Rock musician careers: The culture of the long-term professional." Unpublished doctoral dissertation. University of California, Los Angeles.

Steiner, I. D. 1972. *Group Process and Productivity*. New York: Academic Press.

Steinfatt, T. M.; Baker, S.; and Beesey, A. 2002. *Measuring the Number of Trafficked Women in Cambodia: 2002*. Part I of a series. Manoa: University of Hawaii, Globalization Research Center.

Stetser, Marie. 2014. "Public high school four-year on-time graduation rates and event dropout rates: School years 2010–11 and 2011–12." U.S. Department of Education, National Center for Education Statistics, April. http://nces.ed.gov/pubs2014/2014391/findings.asp

Stiglitz, Joseph. 2011. "Of the 1%, by the 1%, for the 1%." *Vanity Fair*, May. www.vanityfair.com/society/features/2011/05/top-one-percent-201105

Stiles-Shields, Colleen; and Carroll, Richard A. 2014. "Same-sex domestic violence: Prevalence, unique aspects, and clinical implications." *Journal of Sex & Marital Therapy*, October 10. http://www.tandfonline.com/doi/abs/10.1080/0092623X.2014.958792

Stimson, Ida H. 1967. "Patterns of socialization into professions: The case of student nurses." *Sociological Inquiry*, vol. 37: 47–54.

Stroebaek, Pernille S. 2013. "Let's have a cup of coffee! Coffee and coping communities at work." *Symbolic Interaction*, vol. 36, no. 4: 381–397.

Sudnow, David. 1972. "Temporal parameters of interpersonal observation." In D. Sudnow, ed., *Studies in Social Interaction*. New York: Free Press.

Sue, D. W. 2010. *Microaggressions in Everyday Life: Race, Gender, and Sexual Orientation*. Hoboken, NJ: John Wiley & Sons.

Sue, Valerie M., and Lois A. Ritter. 2007. *Conducting Online Surveys*. Thousand Oaks, CA: Sage.

Sumner, William Graham. 1906. *Folkways: A Study of the Sociological Importance of Usages, Manners, Customs, Mores, and Morals*. Boston: Ginn and Co.

Sutherland, Edwin. 1939. *Principles of Criminology*. 3rd ed. Philadelphia: J. B. Lipincott.

———; Cressey, Donald R.; and Luckenbill, David F. 1992. *Principles of Criminology*. 11th ed. Dix Hills, NY: General Hall.

Tapscott, Don. 1997. *Growing Up Digital: The Rise of the Net Generation*. New York: McGraw-Hill.

Tassi, Paul. 2014. "'World of warcraft' still a $1B powerhouse even as subscription MMOs decline." *Forbes*, July 19. http://www.forbes.com/sites/insertcoin/2014/07/19/world-of-warcraft-still-a-1b-powerhouse-even-as-subscription-mmos-decline/

Telles, Edward. 2004. *Race in Another America: The Significance of Color in Brazil*. Princeton, NJ: Princeton University Press.

Thomas, William I; and Thomas, Dorothy. 1928. *The Child in America: Behavior Problems and Programs*. New York, NY: Knopf.

Thompson, Derek. 2012. "The power of a college degree: 2 awesome clip-and-save graphs." *The Atlantic*, September 14. http://m.theatlantic.com/business/archive/2012/09/the-power-of-a-college-degree-2-awesome-clip-and-save-graphs/262423

Thompson, John B. 2012. "The media and politics." In *The Wiley-Blackwell Companion to Political Sociology*. Chichester, West Sussex, UK: Wiley-Blackwell.Thoreau, Henry David. 1854/1993. *Walden; or, a Life in the Woods*. Ticknor and Fields (1854); Everyman's Library (1993).

Thorne, Barrie. 1992. "Feminism and the family: Two decades of thought." In Barrie Thorne and Marilyn Yalom, eds., *Rethinking the Family: Some Feminist Questions*. Boston: Northeastern University Press.

———. 1993. *Gender Play: Girls and Boys in School*. New Brunswick, NJ: Rutgers University Press.

Thornton, Stephen J. 2003. "Silence on gays and lesbians in social studies curriculum." *Social Education*, vol. 67, no. 4: 226.

Thye, Shane R.; and Lawler, Edward J., eds. 2002. *Advances in Group Processes: Group Cohesion, Trust and Solidarity*, vol. 19. Oxford, UK: Elsevier Science.

Tibbals, Chauntelle Anne. 2010. "From The Devil in Miss Jones to DMJ6—Power, inequality, and consistency in the content of us adult films." *Sexualities*, vol. 13, no. 5: 625–644.

———. 2012. "'Anything that forces itself into my vagina is by definition raping me . . .'—Adult performers and occupational safety and health." *Stanford Law and Policy Review*, vol. 23, no. 1: 231–251.

———. 2013. "Sex work, office work—Women working behind the scenes in the U.S. Adult film industry." *Gender, Work & Organization*, vol. 20, no. 1: 20–35.

———. 2015. *A Sociologist Explores Sex, Society, and Adult Entertainment*. Austin, TX: Greenleaf Book Group.

Tomlinson, John. 1991. *Cultural Imperialism*. Baltimore, MD: John Hopkins University Press.

Toossi, Mitra. 2006. "A new look at long-term labor force projections to 2050." *Monthly Labor Review* (November): 19–39.

Trexler, R. C. 2002. "Making the American berdache: Choice or constraint." *Journal of Social History*, vol. 35: 613–636.

Trudeau, Michelle. 2008. "Las Vegas: The suicide capital of America." NPR, December 10. www.npr.org/templates/story/story.php?storyId=98042717

Truman J, Morgan R. 2014. "Special report. Nonfatal domestic violence, 2003–2012." Bureau of Justice Statistics. www.bjs.gov/index.cfm?ty=pbdetail&iid=4984

Tugend, A. 2014. "It's clearly defined, but telecommuting is fast on the rise." *The New York Times*, March 7. http://www.nytimes.com/2014/03/08/your-money/when-working-in-your-pajamas-is-more-productive.html?_r=0

Turkle, Sherry. 1997. *Life on the Screen: Identity in the Age of the Internet*. New York: Touchstone Books.

———. 2005. *The Second Self: Computers and the Human Spirit* Cambridge, MA: MIT Press.

———. 2011. *Alone Together*. New York: Basic Books.

Turner, Ralph. 1972. "Deviance avowal as neutralization of commitment." *Social Problems*, vol. 19, no. 3: 308–321.

———. 1976. "The real self: From institution to impulse." *American Journal of Sociology*, vol. 81: 989–1016.

———. 1978. "The role and the person." *American Journal of Sociology*, vol. 84, no. 1: 1–3.

———; and Killian, Lewis M. 1987. *Collective Behavior*. 3rd ed. Englewood Cliffs, NJ: Prentice Hall.

Twine, France Winddance. 2011a. *Outsourcing the Womb: Race, Class and Gestational Surrogacy in a Global Market*. Florence, KY: Routledge.

———. 2011b. *A White Side of Black Britain: Interracial Intimacy and Racial Literacy*. Durham, NC: Duke University Press.

Tynan, Dan 2015. "How the Internet of Things could save the bees." *Yahoo!*, April 22. https://www.yahoo.com/tech/how-the-internet-of-things-could-save-the-bees-117114866924.html

Uggen, Christopher; Shannon, Sarah; and Manza, Jeff. 2012. "State-level estimates of felon disenfranchisement in the United States, 2010." The Sentencing Project, July. http://sentencingproject.org

/doc/publications/fd_State_Level_Estimates_of_Felon_Disen_2010.pdf

Ulbrich, Chris. 2004. "Blogs pump bucks into campaigns." *Wired*, February 18.

United Nations. 2006. "World population prospects, 2006 revision." www.un.org/esa/population/publications/wpp2006/WPP2006_Highlights_rev.pdf

United Nations. 2014a. "The human right to water and sanitation." May. http://www.un.org/waterforlifedecade/human_right_to_water.shtml

United Nations. 2014b. "Transboundary waters." http://www.un.org/waterforlifedecade/transboundary_waters.shtml

United Nations Conference on Trade and Development. 2014. "World Investment Report 2014: Annex Tables." http://unctad.org/en/pages/DIAE/World%20Investment%20Report/Annex Tables.aspx

United Nations Department of Economic and Social Affairs (UN DESA). 2014. "World Urbanization Prospects: 2014 Revision," http://esa.un.org/unpd/wup/Highlights/WUP2014-Highlights.pdf

———. 2015. "World Population Prospects: The 2015 Revision." http://esa.un.org/unpd/wpp/Publications/Files/Key_Findings_WPP_2015.pdf

United Nations Food and Agriculture Organization. 2012a. "Annual Crop Production Growth, Table 4.3." Shttp://www.fao.org/docrep/016/ap106e/ap106e.pdf

———. 2012b. "Demographics." http://www.fao.org/docrep/016/ap106e/ap106e.pdf

———. 2012c. "Part 3: Feeding the World." Statistical Yearbook 2012: World Food and Agriculture. www.fao.org/docrep/015/i2490e/i2490e03a.pdf

———. 2014. "The State of Food Insecurity in the World 2014." http://www.fao.org/publications/sofi/en/

United Nations Millennium Ecosystem Assessment. 2005. *Ecosystems and Human Well-Being: the Biodiversity Synthesis Report*. New York: United Nations Environment Program.

United Nations News Centre. 2011. "Global population to pass 10 billion by 2100, UN projections indicate." May 3. www.un.org/apps/news/story.asp?NewsID=38253

United Nations World Commission on Environment and Development. 1987. *Our Common Future*. Oxford, UK: Oxford University Press.

United Nations World Food Programme. 2014. "Hunger Statistics." http://www.wfp.org/hunger/stats

UNICEF. 2010. "Humanitarian Action Report 2010: Eastern and Southern Africa, feature story for Burundi." www.unicef.org/har2010/index_burundi_feature.html

UN Water. 2013a. "Facts and Figures." http://www.unwater.org/water-cooperation-2013/water cooperation/facts-and-figures/en/

———. 2013b. "Statistics: Graphs & Maps." www.unwater.org/statistics_urb.html

———. 2013c. "World Water Day 2013: International Year of Water Cooperation." http://www.unwater.org/water-cooperation-2013/water-cooperation/facts-and figures/en/

United States Geological Survey. 2014. "How much water is there on, in, and above the Earth?" https://water.usgs.gov/edu/earthhowmuch.html

Urry, John. 1990. *The Tourist Gaze*. London: Sage.

———. 1992. "The tourist gaze and the 'environment.'" *Theory, Culture & Society*, vol. 9, no. 3: 1–26.

———. 2002. *The Tourist Gaze*. 2nd ed. London: Sage.

U.S. Bureau of Justice Statistics. 2014a. "Correctional populations in the United States, 2013." December. http://www.bjs.gov/content/pub/pdf/cpus13.pdf

———. 2014b. "Domestic Violence Accounted for About a Fifth of all Violent Victimizations Between 2003 and 2012." http://www.bjs.gov/content/pub/press/ndv0312pr.cfm

———. 2014c. "Prisoners in 2013." http://www.bjs.gov/content/pub/pdf/p13.pdf

U.S. Bureau of Labor Statistics. 2011b. "Household data annual averages." www.bls.gov/cps/cpsaat18.pdf

———. 2012a. "Employment outlook: 2010–2020 industry employment and output projections to 2020." www.bls.gov/opub/mlr/2012/01/art4full.pdf

———. 2012b. "Unemployment rates for states." www.bls.gov/web/laus/laumstrk.htm

———. 2013. "Employed persons detailed by occupation, sex, race and Hispanic or Latino ethnicity." www.bls.gov/cps/cpsaat11.pdf

———. 2014a. "American Time Use Surveys—2013 Results." http://www.bls.gov/news.release/atus.nr0.htm

———. 2014b. "Earnings and unemployment rates by educational attainment." March. Current Population Survey, U.S. Department of Labor. http://www.bls.gov/emp/ep_chart_001.htm

———. 2014b. "Employed persons by detailed occupation, sex, race, and Hispanic or Latino ethnicity," http://www.bls.gov/cps/cpsaat11.pdf

———. 2014c. "Highlights of women's earnings in 2013." http://www.bls.gov/opub/reports/cps/highlights-of-womens-earnings-in-2013.pdf

———. 2014d. "Women in the labor force: A databook," http://www.bls.gov/cps/wlf-databook-2013.pdf

———. 2015a. "Consumer expenditures midyear update—July 2013 through June 2014 average." http://www.bls.gov/news.release/cesmy.nr0.htm

———. 2015b. "Economic news release: Table A-14. Unemployed persons by industry and class of worker, not seasonally adjusted." March 2. http://www.bls.gov/news.release/empsit.t14.htm

———. 2015c. "Employed persons by detailed occupation, sex, race, and Hispanic or Latino ethnicity," http://www.bls.gov/cps/cpsaat11.htm

———. 2015d. "Employment status of the civilian noninstitutional population 16 years and over by sex, 1973 to date." http://www.bls.gov/cps/cpsaat02.htm

———. 2015e. "Industries at a glance." http://www.bls.gov/iag/tgs/iag_index_naics.htm

———. 2015f. "Union Members Summary." http://www.bls.gov/news.release/union2.nr0.htm

———. 2015g. "Industries at a glance: Hospitality and leisure." http://www.bls.gov/iag/tgs/iag70.htm

———. 2015h. "Volunteering in the United States, 2014." http://www.bls.gov/news.release/volun.nr0.htm

———. 2015i. "Work stoppages summary." February. http://www.bls.gov/news.release/wkstp.nr0.htm

U.S. Census Bureau. 1994. "Table 1. Race of wife by race of husband: 1960, 1970, 1980, 1991, and 1992." https://www.census.gov/population/socdemo/race/interractab1.txt

———. 2003. "Married couple and unmarried partner households: 2000." Census 2000 Special Report. February. www.census.gov/prod/2003pubs/censr-5.pdf

———. 2005. "Interim projections: Ranking of census 2000 and projected 2030 state population and change: 2000 to 2030." April. www.census.gov/Press-Release/www/2005/stateproj7.xls

———. 2011. "Population distribution and change: 2000 to 2010." www.census.gov/prod/cen2010/briefs/c2010br-01.pdf

———. 2012a. "Home-based workers in the United States: 2012." www.census.gov/hhes/commuting/files/2010/P70-132.pdf

———. 2012b. "Labor force, employment, and earnings." www.census.gov/prod/2011pubs/12statab/labor.pdf

_____. 2012c. "Most children younger than age 1 are minorities." www.census.gov/newsroom/releases/archives/population/cb12-90.html

_____. 2012d. "Reasons For Not voting, by selected characteristics: November 2012." Table 10. https://www.census.gov/hhes/www/socdemo/voting/publications/p20/2012/tables.html

_____. 2012e. "Shopping centers—number and gross leasable area: 1990–2010." www.census.gov/compendia/statab/2012/tables/12s1061.pdf

_____. 2012f. "Table UC3. Opposite sex unmarried couples by presence of biological children under 18, and age, earnings, education, and race and Hispanic origin of both partners: 2012." www.census.gov/hhes/families/files/cps2012/tabUC3-all.xls

_____. 2012g. "The Two or More Races Population: 2010." http://www.census.gov/prod/cen2010/briefs/c2010br-13.pdf

_____. 2012h. "Voting and registration in the election of November 2012." www.census.gov/hhes/www/socdemo/voting/publications/p20/2012/tables.htm

_____. 2013a. "Age and sex composition in the United States: 2012," Table 1: Population by Age and Sex, 2012. http://www.census.gov/population/age/data/2012comp.html

_____. 2013b. "Custodial Mothers and Fathers and Their Child Support: 2011." https://www.census.gov/prod/2013pubs/p60-246.pdf

_____. 2013c. "Same-sex couples fact sheet." http://www.census.gov/hhes/samesex/files/SScplfactsheet_final.pdf

_____. 2013d. "Percent Population Residing in Urban Areas by County: 2010." http://www2.census.gov/geo/pdfs/maps-data/maps/thematic/2010ua/UA2010_Urban_Pop_Map.pdf

_____. 2014a. "America's Family and Living Arrangements: 2014: Adults" Table A1 http://www.census.gov/hhes/families/data/cps2014A.html

_____. 2014b. "Annual Estimates of the Resident Population by Sex, Race, and Hispanic Origin for the United States, States, and Counties: April 1, 2010 to July 1, 2013," http://factfinder.census.gov/faces/tableservices/jsf/pages/productview.xhtml?src=bkmk

_____. 2014c. "Annual high school dropout rates by sex, race, grade, and Hispanic Origin: October 1967 to 2013" Table A-4. https://www.census.gov/hhes/school/data/cps/historical/index.html

_____. 2014d. "College enrollment declines for second year in a row." September. http://www.census.gov/newsroom/press-releases/2014/cb14-177.html

_____. 2014e. "Educational attainment in the United States: 2014." http://www.census.gov/hhes/socdemo/education/data/cps/2014/tables.html

_____. 2014f. "Health Coverage in the United States: 2013." https://www.census.gov/content/dam/Census/library/publications/2014/demo/p60-250.pdf

_____. 2014g. "Income and poverty in the United States: 2013," http://www.census.gov/content/dam/Census/library/publications/2014/demo/p60-249.pdf

_____. 2014h. "The population 14 to 24 years old by high school graduate status, college enrollment, attainment, sex, race, and Hispanic origin: October 1967 to 2013." Table A-5a. https://www.census.gov/hhes/school/data/cps/historical/index.html

_____. 2014i. "Population Estimates: National Characteristics 2013." https://www.census.gov/popest/data/national/asrh/2013/

_____. 2014j. "Table A1. marital status of people 15 years and over, by age, sex, personal earnings, race, and Hispanic origin: 2014." http://www.census.gov/hhes/families/data/cps2014A.html

_____. 2014k. "Table H3. Households by Race and Hispanic Origin of Household Reference Person and Detailed Type: 2014." http://www.census.gov/hhes/families/data/cps2014H.html

_____. 2014l. "Table UC1. Opposite Sex Unmarried Couples By Labor Force Status Of Both Partners: 2014." http://www.census.gov/hhes/families/data/cps2014UC.html

_____. 2015a "Educational attainment in the United States, 2014," Table 2, Educational Attainment of the Population 25 Years and Over, by Selected Characteristics: 2014. https://www.census.gov/hhes/socdemo/education/data/cps/2014/tables.html

_____. 2015b. "Estimates of the Components of Resident Population Change: April 1, 2010 to July 1, 2014." 2014 Population Estimates. http://factfinder.census.gov/faces/tableservices/jsf/pages/productview.xhtml?pid=PEP_2014_PEPTCOMP&prodType=table

_____. 2015c. "Projections of the Size and Composition of the U.S. Population: 2014 to 2060." https://www.census.gov/content/dam/Census/library/publications/2015/demo/p25-1143.pdf

_____. 2015d. "Facts for Features: Irish-American Heritage Month (March) and St. Patrick's Day (March 17): 2015"http://www.census.gov/newsroom/facts-for-features/2015/cb15-ff04.html

_____. 2015e. "State and Country Quick Facts: California." http://quickfacts.census.gov/qfd/states/06000.html

_____. 2015f. "State & County QuickFacts. Clark County, NV." August 5. http://quickfacts.census.gov/qfd/states/32/32003.html

_____. 2015g. "Table MS 1: Marital Status of the population 15 years old and over, by sex, race and Hispanic origin: 1950 to present", http://www.census.gov/hhes/families/data/marital.html

_____. 2015h. "Table MS-2: Estimated median age at first marriage, by sex: 1890 to the Present." http://www.census.gov/hhes/families/data/marital.html

_____. 2015i. "Ten U.S. Cities Now Have 1 Million People or More; California and Texas Each Have Three of These Places." May 21. http://www.census.gov/newsroom/press-releases/2015/cb15-89.html

_____. 2015j. "U.S. and World Population Clock." Aug. 8. http://www.census.gov/popclock/

U.S. Department of Agriculture. 2014. "Household food security in the United States in 2013." http://www.ers.usda.gov/topics/food-nutrition-assistance/food-security-in-the-us/key-statistics-graphics.aspx#insecure

_____. 2015. "Supplemental Nutrition Assistance Program (SNAP)". March 6. http://www.fns.usda.gov/snap/supplemental-nutrition-assistance-program-snap

U.S. Department of Commerce. 2012. "Summary estimates for multinational companies: Employment, sales, and capital expenditures for 2010." www.bea.gov/news releases/international/mnc/mncnewsrelease.htm

_____. 2014. "U.S. travel and tourism industry sets new export record in 2013." February 28. http://www.commerce.gov/news/press-releases/2014/02/us-travel-and-tourism-industry-sets-new-export-record-2013

_____. 2015. "Travel and tourism spending accelerated in the fourth quarter of 2014." March 18. https://www.bea.gov/newsreleases/industry/tourism/tournewsrelease.htm

U.S. Department of Defense. 2014. *Report to the President of the United States on Sexual Assault Prevention and Response.* http://www.sapr.mil/public/docs/reports/FY14_POTUS/FY14_DoD_Report_to_POTUS_Full_Report.pdf

U.S. Department of Education, National Center for Education Statistics. 2013. "Number and percentage distribution of all children ages 5–17 who were homeschooled and homeschooling rate, by selected characteristics: 2011–12." http://nces.ed.gov/pubs2013/2013028/tables/table_07.asp

_____. 2014a. "Charter school enrollment." April. http://nces.ed.gov/programs/coe/indicator_cgb.asp

_____. 2014b. "Educational attainment." http://nces.ed.gov/fastfacts /display.asp?id=27

U.S. Department of Health and Human Services. 2015a. "Child maltreatment 2013." http://www.acf.hhs.gov/sites/default/files/cb /cm2013.pdf

_____. 2015b. "Births final data for 2013." *National Vital Statistics Reports*. Vol 64, No. 1. http://www.cdc.gov/nchs/data/nvsr /nvsr64/nvsr64_01.pdf

U.S. Department of Labor. 2012. "Extensive violations of federal, state laws found among garment contractors at Los Angeles Garment District location." http://www.dol.gov/opa/media/press /whd/WHD20122378.htm

U.S. Energy Information Administration. 2013a. "Countries overview." http://www.eia.gov/countries/index.cfm?topL=conFjsdlkjfk

_____. 2013b. "World energy use to rise by 56 percent, driven by growth in the developing world." http://www.eia.gov/pressroom /releases/press395.cfm

_____. 2015. "Primary Energy Consumption by Source." http://www .eia.gov/totalenergy/data/monthly/pdf/sec1_7.pdf

U.S. Government Printing Office. 2011. "Budget of the U.S. government." www.gpo.gov/fdsys/pkg/BUDGET-2011-BUD/pdf/BUDGET -2011-BUD.pdf

U.S. Sentencing Commission. 2010. "Preliminary Crack Cocaine Retroactivity Data Report." http://www.ussc.gov/sites/default/files /pdf/research-and-publications/federal-sentencing-statistics /fsa-amendment/2013-07_USSC_Prelim_Crack_Retro_Data _Report_FSA.pdf

Useem, E. L. 1990. "You're good but you're not good enough: Tracking students out of advanced mathematics." *American Educator*, vol. 14, no. 3, 24–46.

Usher, Alexandra; and Kober, Nancy. 2011. "Keeping informed about school vouchers: A review of major developments and research." *Center on Education Policy*, July. http://www.cep-dc.org /displayDocument.cfm?DocumentID=369#sthash.WDWRI2p8 .dpuf

Valkyrie, Zek Cypress. 2011. "Cybersexuality in MMORPGs: Virtual sexual revolution untapped." *Men and Masculinities*, vol. 14, no. 1: 76–96.

Vandewalker, Ian; and Perty, Eric. 2015. "Election spending 2014: Outside spending in Senate races since 'Citizens United.'" *Brennan Center for Justice at New York University School of Law*. January. http://www.brennancenter.org/publication/election-spending -2014-outside-spending-senate-races-citizens-united

Van Cleve, Thomas Curtis. 1972. *The Emperor Frederick of Hohenstaufen, Immutator Mundi*. Oxford, UK: Clarendon Press.

van den Berghe, P. L. 1979. *Human Family Systems: An Evolutionary View*. New York: Elsevier/North-Holland.

Van Goozen, S.; Frijda, N.; and Van DePoll, N. 1994. "Anger and aggression in women: Influence of sports choice and testosterone administration." *Aggressive Behavior*, vol. 20: 213–222.

Vankin, Deborah. 2010. "Blue says MOCA's removal of his mural amounts to censorship." *Los Angeles Times*, December 15. www .latimes.com/entertainment/news/la-et-moca-mural-20101215, 0,6698582.story

Vaughan, Diane. 1996. *The Challenger Launch Decisions: Risky Technology, Culture and Deviance at NASA*. Chicago: University of Chicago Press.

Veblen, Thorstein. 2004 (orig. 1921). *Engineers and the Price System*. Whitefish, MT: Kessinger Publishing.

Vedantam, Shankar. 2010. "Why do Americans claim to be more religious than they are?" *Slate*, December 22. www.slate.com/id /2278923

Veiga, Alex. 2014. "US credit card late payments down in 2Q." *The Associated Press*. August 26. http://bigstory.ap.org/article /us-credit-card-late-payments-down-2q

Velkoff, Victoria; and Lawson, Valerie. 1998. "Caregiving." *Gender and Aging*, December: 1–7.

Vincent, Danny. 2011. "China used prisoners in lucrative Internet gaming work." *The Guardian*, May 25. www.guardian.co.uk /world/2011/may/25/china-prisoners-internet-gaming-scam

Waber, B. et al. 2010. "Productivity through coffee breaks: Changing social networks by changing break structure." *Massachusetts Institute of Technology*. January.

Wackernagel, Mathis; and Rees, William. 1996. *Our Ecological Footprint: Reducing Human Impact on the Earth*. Philadelphia: New Society.

Waldron, T.; Roberts, B.; and Reamer, A. 2004. "Working hard, falling short: America's working families and the pursuit of economic security." A national report by the Working Poor Families Project. Baltimore, MD: Annie E. Casey Foundation.

Walk Free Foundation. 2014. "The Global Slavery Index: 2014." http://www.globalslaveryindex.org/download/

Walker, Samuel. 1997. *Popular Justice: A History of American Criminal Justice*. New York: Oxford University Press.

Walker, Susan C. 2004. "U.S. consumer credit card debt may crash economy." FoxNews.com, December 31.

Walsh, Declan. 2013. "Girl shot by Pakistani Taliban is discharged from hospital." *New York Times*, January 4. www.nytimes.com/2013 /01/05/world/asia/malala-yousafzai-shot-by-pakistani -taliban-is-discharged-from-hospital.html

Waskul, D. D.; ed. 2004. *Net.SeXXX: Readings on Sex, Pornography, and the Internet*. New York: Peter Lang.

Watanabe, Teresa. 2008. "Home of the freed." *Los Angeles Times*, August 14. www.articles.latimes.com/2008/aug/14/local/me -thai14

Waters, Mary. 1990. *Ethnic Options: Choosing Identities in America*. Berkeley: University of California Press.

Wattel, Harold. 1958. "Levittown: A suburban community." In William M. Dobriner, ed., *The Suburban Community*. New York: Putnam.

Watts, Duncan. 2003. *Six Degrees: The Science of a Connected Age*. New York: Norton.

Wearing, Stephen; and Wearing, Michael. 1999. "Decommodifying ecotourism: Rethinking global-local interactions with host communities." *Loisir et Société/Society and Leisure*, vol. 22, no. 1: 39–70.

Weber, Max. 1930 (orig. 1904). *The Protestant Ethic and the Spirit of Capitalism*. Trans. Talcott Parsons. New York: Scribner's.

_____. 1946 (orig. 1925). "Science as a vocation." In Hans Gerth and C. Wright Mills, ed. and trans., *From Max Weber: Essays in Sociology*. New York: Oxford University Press.

_____. 1962 (orig. 1913). *Basic Concepts of Sociology*. Westport, CT: Greenwood Publishing.

_____. 1968 (orig. 1921). *Economy and Society*. Ed. and trans. Guenther Roth and Claus Wittich. New York: Bedminster Press.

Weinberg, Adam; Bellows, Story; and Ekster, Dara. 2002. "Sustaining ecotourism: Insights and implications from two successful case studies." *Society and Natural Resources*, vol. 15, no. 4: 371–380.

Weinstein, Deena. 1991. *Heavy Metal: A Cultural Sociology*. New York: Macmillan/Lexington.

_____. 2000. *Heavy Metal: The Music and Its Culture*. New York: DaCapo.

Weinstein, Harvey. 2003. "Controversial ruling on pledge reaffirmed." *Los Angeles Times*, Metro Desk, March 1, 1:1.

Weise, Elizabeth; and Woodyard, Chris. 2015. "Deal reached in West Coast dockworkers dispute." *USA Today*, February. http://www.usatoday.com/story/news/2015/02/20/west-coast-ports dispute-union-labor-secretary-tom-perez/23744299/

Weissbourd, Richard. 1994. "Divided families, whole children." *American Prospect*, vol. 18 (summer): 66–72.

Wellman, Barry. 2004. "Connecting community: On- and off-line." *Contexts* vol. 3, no. 4: 22–28.

Werner, Carrie A. 2011. "The older population: 2010." U.S. Census Briefs.https://www.census.gov/prod/cen2010/briefs/c2010br-09.pdfWessel, David. 2011. "Big U.S. firms shift hiring abroad." *Wall Street Journal*, April 19.

Weston, Kath. 1991. *Families We Choose*. New York: Columbia University Press.

Whalen, J.; Zimmerman, D.; and Whalen, M. 1988. "When words fail: a single case analysis." *Social Problems*, vol. 35, no. 4: 335–362.

Wharton, Amy S.; and Blair-Loy, Mary. 2002. "Employees' use of work–family policies and the workplace social context." *Social Forces*, vol. 80, no. 3: 813–845.

Whitacre, Paula Tarnapol; Tsai, Peggy, and Mulligan, Janet. 2009. *The Public Health Effects of Food Deserts: Workshop Summary*. Washington, DC: The National Academies Press.

White, Glen. 1989. "Groupthink reconsidered." *Academy of Management Review*, vol. 14: 40–56.

Whorf, Benjamin. 1956. *Language, Thought and Reality: Selected Writings of Benjamin Lee Whorf*. Ed. John B. Carroll. Cambridge, MA: MIT Press.

Whyte, W. H. 1956. *The Organization Man*. New York: Simon & Schuster.

Wicks-Lim, Jeannette; and Thompson, Jeffrey. 2010. "Combining minimum wage and earned income tax credit policies to guarantee a decent living standard to all U.S. workers." Political Economy Research Institute. October 18. www.peri.umass.edu/236/hash/9b8a787cfa16226190e4f96e582348cd/publication/428

Wiener, Jon. 2011. "Hard hats and hippies, together at last: The action at Occupy Wall Street." *The Nation*, October 14. www.thenation.com/blog/163983/hard-hats-and-hippies-together-last-action-occupy-wall-street#sthash.bRyK8MEO

Wilkinson, Richard G. 2005. *The Impact of Inequality*. New York: The New Press.

Williams, Christine L. 1995. *Still a Man's World: Men Who Do Women's Work*. Berkeley: University of California Press.

Williams, Linda. 2004. "Porn studies: Proliferating pornographies on/scene: An introduction." In Linda Williams, ed., *Porn Studies*. Durham, NC: Duke University Press.

Williams, Patricia J. 1997. "Of race and risk." *The Nation*, December 29: 10.

Williams, Robin. 1965. *American Society: A Sociological Interpretation*. 2nd ed. New York: Knopf.

Wilson, Edward O. 1975/2000. *Sociobiology: The New Synthesis*. Cambridge, MA: The Belknap Press of Harvard University Press.

———. 1978. *On Human Nature*. Cambridge, MA: Harvard University Press.

Wilson, William Julius. 1980. *The Declining Significance of Race*. Chicago: University of Chicago Press.

———. 1996. *When Work Disappears: The World of the New Urban Poor*. New York: Knopf.

———. 2009. *More Than Just Race: Being Black and Poor in the Inner City*. New York: Norton.

Wirth, Louis. 1938. "Urbanism as a way of life." *American Journal of Sociology*, vol. 44: 3–24.

———. 1945. "The problem of minority groups." In Ralph Litton, ed., *The Science of Man in the World Crisis*. New York: Columbia University Press.

Wiseman, Rosalind. 2002. *Queen Bees and Wannabes*. New York: Three Rivers Press.

Wisenberg Brin, Dinah. 2013. "Telecommuting likely to grow despite high-profile defections." *Society for Human Resource Management*. July 24. http://www.shrm.org/hrdisciplines/technology/articles/pages/telecommuting-likely-to-grow-bans.aspx

Wolf, Rosalie S. 2000. "The nature and scope of elder abuse." *Generations*, vol. 24 (summer): 6–12.

———. 2004. "Changes in household wealth in the 1980s and 1990s in the U.S." Working paper no. 407. Levy Economics Institute of Bard College.

Wolfinger, Nicholas H. 1999. "Trends in the intergenerational transmission of divorce." *Demography*, vol. 36, no. 3: 415–420.

———. 2000. "Beyond the intergenerational transmission of divorce: Do people replicate the patterns of marital instability they grew up with?" *Journal of Family Issues*, vol. 21: 1061–1086.

———. 2003. "Parental divorce and offspring marriage: Early or late?" *Social Forces*, vol. 82, no. 1: 337–353.

Wolfson, Andrew. 2005. "A hoax most cruel." *Courier-Journal*. Louisville, KY. October 9. www.courier-journal.com/apps/pbcs.dll/article?AID=/20051009/NEWS01/510090392

WomensHealth.gov. 2010. The National Women's Health Information Center. U.S. Department of Health and Human Services. www.womenshealth.gov/faq/alpha-index.cfm

Wood, Lisa J.; Giles-Corti, Billie; Bulsara, Max K.; and Bosch, Darcy. 2007. "More than a furry companion: The ripple effect of companion animals on neighborhood interactions and sense of community." *Society and Animals*, vol. 15: 43–56.

Wood, Megan Epler. 2002. *Ecotourism: Principles, Practices and Policies for Sustainability*. Burlington, VT: International Ecotourism Society.

World Bank. 2014. "World development indicators: Structure of output 2014." Table 4.2 http://wdi.worldbank.org/table/4.2

———. 2015. "CO2 emissions (metric tons per capita)." http://data.worldbank.org/indicator/EN.ATM.CO2E.PC

World Health Organization (WHO). 1946. "Constitution of the World Health Organization." July 26. www.who.int/governance/eb/constitution/en/

———. 2008. "The 10 leading causes of death by broad income group (2004)." Fact sheet no. 310, October. www.who.int/mediacentre/factsheets/fs310/en/index.html

———. 2014. "Global health observatory data." www.who.int/gho/hiv/en.

———. 2015. "World Health Statistics: Life expectancy at birth, 2013." http://gamapserver.who.int/gho/interactive_charts/mbd/life_expectancy/atlas.html

Worobey, Michael, et al. 2010. "Island biogeography reveals the deep history of SIV." *Science*, vol. 329, no. 5998: 1487.

Wray, M.; Miller, M.; Gurvey, J.; Carroll, J.; and Kawachi, I. 2008. "Leaving Las Vegas: Exposure to Las Vegas and risk of suicide." *Social Science and Medicine*, vol. 67, no. 11: 1882–1888.

Wray, Matt. "Review of *On the Edge of Utopia: Performance & Ritual at Burning Man*, by Rachel Bowditch." *Modern Drama*, vol. 54: 564–567.

Wright, Erik Olin. 1997. *Class Counts: Comparative Studies in Class Analysis*. Cambridge, UK: Cambridge University Press.

Wright, Erik Olin; Costello, Cynthia; Hachen, David; and Spragues, Joey. 1982. "The American class structure." *American Sociological Review*, vol. 47, no. 6: 709–726.

Yin, Sandra. 2003. "The art of staying at home." *American Demographics*, vol. 25, no. 9 (November 1).

Yuan, Jada. 2007. "The White-Castle ceiling." *New York Magazine*, March 4.

Zellner, William W. 1995. *Countercultures: A Sociological Analysis.* New York: St. Martin's Press.

Zemke, Ron; and Schaaf, Dick. 1990. *The Service Edge: 101 Companies That Profit from Customer Care.* New York: Plume.

Zerubavel, Eviatar. 2003. *Time Maps: Collective Memory and the Social Shape of the Past.* Chicago: University of Chicago Press.

Zheng, Yangpeng. 2012. "Economic downturn benefits China's service outsourcing." *China Daily.* September 25. www.chinadaily .com.cn/china/2012-09/25/content_15782738.htm

Zimbardo, Philip G. 1971. "The power and pathology of imprisonment." *Congressional Record.* (Serial No. 15, October 25, 1971). Hearings before Subcommittee No. 3, of the Committee on the Judiciary, House of Representatives, 92nd Congress, First Session on Corrections, Part II, Prisons, Prison Reform and Prisoner's Rights: California. Washington, DC: U.S. Government Printing Office.

Zirakzadeh, C. 1997. *Social Movements in Politics: A Comparative Study.* London: Longman.

Zukin, S. 1987. "Gentrification: Culture and capital in the urban core." *American Review of Sociology,* vol. 13: 139–147.

_____. 1989. *Loft Living: Culture and Capital in Urban Change.* New Brunswick, NJ: Rutgers University Press.

_____. 2004. *Point of Purchase: How Shopping Changed American Culture.* London: Routledge.

Zurcher, Louis. 1977. *The Mutable Self.* Beverly Hills, CA: Sage.

Zweigenhaft, R. L.; and Domhoff, G. W. 2014. *The New CEOs: Women, African American, Latino, and Asian American Leaders of Fortune 500 Companies.* New York: Rowman and Littlefield.

Credits

Text

Figure 7.2: From "College Enrollment among Low-Income Students Still Trails Richer Groups." Pew Research Center, Washington, DC. January 2014. Reprinted with permission from The Pew Research Center.

Figure 8.2: From "A Post-Racial Society or a Diversity Paradox?" by Jennifer Lee. Reprinted with permission of the Russell Sage Foundation via the Copyright Clearance Center.

Chapter 8, p. 232: Excerpt from "One Today A Poem for Barack Obama's Presidential Inauguration, January 21, 2013" by Richard Blanco, Copyright © 2013. Reprinted by permission of the University of Pittsburgh Press.

Figure 10.2: "Second Largest Religious Tradition in Each State, 2010," from the 2010 U.S. Religion Census, sponsored by the Association of Statisticians of American Religious Bodies. Reprinted with permission.

Table 10.2: "Top 10 Spenders on Lobbying, 1998–2014," from the Center for Responsive Politics, OpenSecrets.org. Reprinted with permission.

Table 10.3: From "Cable Leads the Pack as Campaign News Source." Pew Research Center for the People & the Press. February 7, 2012. Reprinted with permission from The Pew Research Center for People & the Press.

Photo

Part Opener 1: p. 4 (center) Victor Rios; **p. 4 (left)** Pepper Schwartz; **p. 4 (right)** August Jennewein/USML

Chapter 1: p. 11 James Leynse/Corbis; **p. 12** Jeff Kravitz/FilmMagic/Getty Images; **p. 13** Fritz Goro/The LIFE Picture Collection/Getty Images; **p. 14 (left)** Bettmann/Corbis; **p. 14 (right)** Kris Connor/Getty Images; **p. 14 (center)** Olivier Douliery/UPI/Landov; **p. 16 (left)** © McPHOTOs/ageFotostock; **p. 16 (right)** Demitrius Balevski/AP Photo; **p. 17** Joe Raedle/Getty Images; **p. 18 (top)** Mark Scheuern/Alamy; **p. 18 (bottom left)** Bettmann/Corbis; **p. 18 (bottom right)** Hulton-Deutsch Collection/Corbis; **p. 20** Herbert Spencer (1820–1903) (print)/London Library, St James's Square, London, UK/Bridgeman Images; **p. 21** Bettmann/Corbis; **p. 22 (left)** American Sociological Association; **p. 22 (right)** American Sociological Association; **p. 23** Bettmann/Corbis; **p. 25 (top)** AP Photo; **p. 25 (bottom)** Librado Romero/The New York Times/Redux; **p. 26** Hulton Archive/Getty Images; **p. 27** The Granger Collection, NY; **p. 28** Trip/Alamy; **p. 29 (left)** Courtesy of University Archives, University of Missouri at Columbia; **p. 29 (right)** Library of Congress; **p. 30 (left)** Library of Congress; **p. 30 (right)** University of Pennsylvania Archives; **p. 32** Camera Press/Caroline Eluyemi/Redux; **p. 33 (left)** Steve Pyke/Getty Images; **p. 33 (center)** Bettmann/Corbis; **p. 33 (right)** Steve Pyke/Getty Images; **p. 37** Alex Segre/Alamy

Chapter 2: p. 41 Roel Burgler/Hollandse Hoogte/Redux; **p. 42** Bandura, Ross and Ross, from "Social Learning of Aggression through Imitation of Film-Mediated Aggressive Models," Journal of Abnormal and Social Psychology 66 (1963), 3–11; **p. 44** John Dominis/The LIFE Picture Collection/Getty Images; **p. 46** Dale Atkins/AP Photo; **p. 48** Brooke Fasini/Corbis; **p. 51** Antonio Perez/Chicago Tribune/MCT/Newscom; **p. 54** Bettmann/Corbis; **p. 56 (left)** Michael Dunning/Getty Images; **p. 56 (right)** Michael Dunning/Getty Images; **p. 57** Christin Gilbert/agefotostock; **p. 59** Chiaki Tskumo/AP Photo; **p. 60** Bettmann/Corbis; **p. 61** © Universal Images Group (Lake County Discovery Museum)/Alamy; **p. 62** Corbis; **p. 64 (left)** John Dominis/The LIFE Picture Collection/Getty Images; **p. 64 (right)** Christin Gilbert/agefotostock; **p. 65** Roel Burgler/Hollandse Hoogte/Redux

Part Opener 2: p. 68 Courtesy Verta Taylor and Leila Rupp; **p. 69 (top)** Courtesy Verta Taylor and Leila Rupp; **p. 69 (bottom)** Courtesy Verta Taylor and Leila Rupp

Chapter 3: p. 74 Laura Doss/Corbis; **p. 75** © Androniki Christodoulou; **p. 76** Carl & Ann Purcell/Corbis; **p. 77 (top left)** William West/AFP/Getty Images; **p. 77 (top center)** Elaine Thompson/AP Photo; **p. 77 (top right)** Pascal Guyot/AFP/Getty Images; **p. 77 (bottom left)** AarStudio/Getty Images; **p. 77 (bottom right)** Carl De Souza/AFP/Getty Images; **p. 78** Paramount Pictures/Courtesy of the Everett Collection; **p. 80 (left)** Alex Brandon/AP Photo; **p. 80 (right)** Eric Grigorian/Polaris; **p. 81 (top)** Robert Nickelsberg/Getty Images; **p. 81 (middle)** Bikas Das/AP Photo; **p. 81 (bottom)** Mike Derer/AP Photo; **p. 83 (left)** Martin H. Simon/© ABC/Getty Images; **p. 83 (right)** Dana Edelson/NBC/NBCU Photo Bank via Getty Images; **p. 84** Ted S. Warren/AP Photo; **p. 85 (bottom)** Alex Segre/Alamy; **p. 87** David Paul Morris/Bloomberg via Getty Images; **p. 88** Hiroshi Otabe/AP Photo; **p. 89** John Moore/Getty Images; **p. 90** Ali Haider/epa european pressphoto agency b.v./Alamy; **p. 92 (left)** Carl De Souza/AFP/Getty Images; **p. 92 (right)** Alex Segre/Alamy; **p. 93** NBC/Photofest

Chapter 4: p. 99 Carol and Mike Werner/Science Source; **p. 100** © Walt Disney Pictures/Courtesy Everett Collection; **p. 101** Smithsonian American Art Museum, Washington, DC/Art Resource, NY. © 2009 The Jacob and Gwendolyn Lawrence Foundation, Seattle/Artists Rights Society (ARS), New York; **p. 103** Blend Images/Alamy; **p. 105 (left)** Alberto E. Rodriguez/Getty Images for AFI; **p. 105 (right)** HBO/Photos 12/Alamy; **p. 107** 20th Century Fox/Photofest; **p. 109** Richard Milnes/Splash News/Corbis; **p. 111 (left)** Randy Stotler/AP Photo; **p. 111 (right)** Yun Jai-hyoung/AP Photo; **p. 112** Jill Brady/Portland Press Herald via Getty Images; **p. 114** Kris Connor/New York Daily News; **p. 115 (top)** Ross Setford/NZPA/AP Photo; **p. 115 (middle)** Alan Chin; **p. 115 (bottom)** Madison J. Gray/AP Photo; **p. 116** Dario Pignatelli/Bloomberg via Getty Images; **p. 117** Paul Sakuma/AP Photo; **p. 118 (right)** Paul Sakuma/AP Photo; **p. 118 (left)** 20th Century Fox/Photofest; **p. 119** Apatow Productions/The Kobal Collection/Art Resource

Chapter 5: p. 124 Haraz N. Ghanbari/AP Photo; **p. 126** Simon Dawson/Bloomberg via Getty Images; **p. 127 (left)** Bettmann/Corbis; **p. 127 (right)** redsnapper/Alamy; **p. 131** Bloomberg/Getty Images; **p. 133 (top)** Jan Greune/LOOK-foto/Getty Images; **p. 133 (bottom)** © Steve Skjold/Alamy; **p. 137 (top)** Courtesy of Alexandra Milgram; **p. 137 (bottom)** PGZimbardo Inc.; **p. 138** Christian Petersen/Getty Images; **p. 139** Bryn Lennon/Getty Images; **p. 141** Peter Mckenzie/Maxppp/Landov; **p. 142** © 2006 Scott Adams, Inc. Dist. By UFS, Inc.; **p. 143** Andy Rain/epa/Corbis; **p. 144** BLM Photo/Alamy; **p. 145** Maddie Meyer/FIFA via Getty Images; **p. 146** © 2006 Scott Adams, Inc. Dist. By UFS, Inc.; **p. 147** Jan Greune/LOOK-foto/Getty Images

Index

Note: Page numbers in **boldface** refer to definitions of key words.

comparative historical research, **54**
comparative mealtime, 360–61
complementary medicine, **423**
complementary or alternative
      medicine (CAM), 423, 424
compliance, 134, 135
Comte, Auguste, 18, 21, 28, 60
concentration (in business), **382**–84
Condé Nast, 342
Confederate flag removal,
      Charleston, S.C., 231
confidentiality, **61**
conflict
    intergroup, based on race/
      ethnicity, 233–34, 236–37
      assimilation, 236
      internal colonialism and
        segregation, 236
      pluralism, 236–37
      population transfer, 234, 236
conflict theory, **23**–26, 35, 36, 172
    addiction in, 410
    advantages and critiques of, 26
    approach to culture and religion,
      90
    deviance in, 155–56, 158
    in education study, 294–95
    family in, 353, 354, 370
    founder and key contributions to,
      23–24
    gender inequality in, 254, 255, 268
    groups in, 144
    medicine and health in, 426
    natural environment in, 443, 462
    offshoots of, 24–26
    original principles of, 24
    race and ethnicity in, 224, 238
    recreation and leisure in, 392, 400
    religion in, 302–3
    social change in, 472, 488
    social class in, 187–88, 210
    social inequality in, 194
    social institutions in, 279, 312
    structural functionalism *vs.*, 23
    work and the economy in, 340, 346
conformity, 134
conformity experiments
    Asch experiment, 135
    Milgram experiment, 135, 137
    Milgram revisited, 138
    Stanford Prison Experiment,
      137–38
conglomeration, **379**–80

Conley, Dalton, 34, 203, 363
connection, in social networks, 125
conscious, in psychoanalytic theory,
    100
"consequential strangers," 124
conservation era, **457**
constitutional monarchs, 278
constraints, bureaucratic, 243–45
constructionists, **246**
consumerism, 208
consumption, **376**
Contador, Alberto, 139
contagion, in social networks, 125
contagion theory, **468**
    of suicide, 404
content analysis, **54**
Conti, Joseph, 124, 125
contingent workforce, **343**–44
contraception, university culture
    and, 84
contract company workers, 343
control group, **55**
conversation analysis, **31**
Cook, Tim, 333
Cook Islands, 439
Cooley, Charles Horton, 102, 104, 123
"cool hunters," 59
cooling the mark out, **105**
Copernicus, Nicolaus, 43
copresence, **114**
Corinthian Colleges, 301
corporal punishment, 152
corporate America, 332–33
corporate social responsibility
    (CSR), 332–33
"corporate welfare," 323
corporations
    best and worst, 332–33
    employee theft in, 168
    outsourcing by, 338–40
    transnational, 334
    and treadmill of production, 455
    and union activity, 329
correlation, **42**
cosmopolites, 448
Couchsurfing.com, 87
Council of Conservative Citizens,
    479
Counted Out (Powell), 350
counterculture, **83**
Coursera, 301
courtship, Internet and, 355
covert research, 46

Cox, LaVerne, 250
craft unions, 331
"creative class," 197
Credential Society, The (Collins),
    295, 330
credit card debt, 208
crime, **166**–71, 167
    categories of, 166
    in cities, 167
    and curfews, 155
    demographics of, 167–69
    deterrence and punishment,
      169–71
    imprisonment for, 170
    and social class, 197–98
criminal justice
    and gender, 262–64
    and race/ethnicity, 231
    and socioeconomic status, 197–98
criminal justice system, **169**
crisis medicine, **407**
Critical Mass, 479
critical theory, **25**
"crossing over," 120
Crow, Sheryl, 357
crowd, **123, 468**
crowd behavior, 468–69
crowdfunding, 474
cults, 111
cultural appropriation, **222**–23
cultural assimilation, **236**
cultural capital, **191**
cultural change, 86, 88, 90
cultural competence, **418**–19
cultural diffusion, **88, 480**
cultural imperialism, 88, **90,** 222,
    484
cultural lag, **480**
cultural leveling, **88, 484**
cultural relativism, 74, **74,** 76
culture, 70–93, **73**
    American, 91
    change in, 86, 88
    countercultures, 83
    culture wars, 85
    defining, 73, 92
    deviance across, 151–52
    dominant, 82–83
    ethnocentrism and cultural
      relativism, 73–74, 75
    ideal *vs.* real, 85
    material, 76, 92
    media consumption and, 386–88

culture (*continued*)

    multiculturalism, 82

    norms, 79–80

    in religious services, 81–82

    sanctions, 80, 92

    studying, 73

    subcultures, 83

    symbolic, 77–79

    tourism and, 398

    university, 84

    values, 79, 92

culture of poverty, **203**

culture shock, **11,** 13

culture wars, **85,** 386

Cuomo, Andrew, 192

Cuomo, Mario, 192

curative medicine, **407**

custody, 256, **359**–60

cyberbullying, 163, **165**

cybersex, 164

cycle of violence, **366**

Cyrus, Miley, 85

D

Daily Show, The, 286, 287

Daly, Mary, 330

Dancing at Armageddon (Mithcell), 46

Dancing with the Stars, 58

Danger Mouse, 34

Daniels, Deborah, 124

Daniels family, 124

Darfur, 234

Dark Knight, The, 154, 155

Dark Knight Rises, The, 388

Darley, John, 449

Darwin, Charles, 20, 438

Das Kapital (Marx), 24

Data Workshops

    analyzing everyday life

        AA members' personal stories, 161

        activist groups and social change, 475–76

        clothing in global commodity chain, 337

        comparative mealtime, 360–61

        doing nothing, 10–11

        doing symbolic ethnicity, 218–19

        everyday class consciousness, 194–95

        impression management, 106–7

        measures of religiosity, 307–8

        observing hangouts, 397–98

        second shift, 260–61

        seeing culture in religious services, 81–82

        student attitudes on environmentalism, 456–57

        student health issues, 407–9

        Twenty Statements Test, 130–33

        watching people talk, 47

    analyzing mass media and popular culture

        advertising and the American Dream, 208–9

        celebrity gossip, 31–32

        cities of tomorrow, 445–46

        culture in popular magazines and web sites, 85–86

        family troubles in film, 366–67

        gender and rules of beauty, 251–52

        groups in the digital age, 127–28

        how the image shapes the need, 85–86

        media usage patterns, 53

        medicine on television, 420–22

        move megahits and flops, 380–81

        norm breaking on television, 165–66

        racial identity, 232–33

        real and fake news, 286–88

        television as agent of socialization, 109–10

        televisions' portrayal of working life, 321–22

        "unplug" experiment, 480–81

dating, 226–27, 355

da Vinci, Leonardo, 387

Davis, Angely Y., 228

Davis, Kingsley, 189

DDT, 457, 458

death penalty, 171, 198

death(s)

    beliefs about, 115

    end-of-life care, 424–25

    medicalization of, 409

    mortality rates, 435

    in United States, 407

deception, **61**

deconstruction, **33**

deep integration, 333, 334

definition of the situation, **104**

de Man, Henri, 327

democracy, **278**–79, 379

demographers, 435

demographic free fall, **439**

demographic transition, **439**

demography, **435**

dengue fevers, 413

dependent variable, **55**

depression, and gender, 256

deprivation amplification, 415

deregulation, **382**

Derrida, Jacques, 33

Descartes, René, 100

"designer" children, 368

desocialization, 111

deterrence, **169**

DeVault, Marjorie, 360

deviance, 148–73, **151**

    across cultures, 151–52

    background factors in, 151

    body modification, 152

    changing definitions of, 164

    choosing, 159

    crime, 166–71

    cyberbullying, 163, 165

    defining, 151

    and emotional attraction of doing bad deeds, 163

    in-group orientation and, 160

    outsiders, 160

    passing, 159

    and pornography industry, 164

    positive, 171

    stigma and, 159–60

    studying, 163

    theories of, 154–59

        conflict theory, 156–57

        functionalism, 154–55, 172

        symbolic interactionism, 156–59

deviance avowal, **160,** 161

DeVry University, 300

Dewey, John, 28

diabetes, 407, 415

Diagnostic and Statistical Manual of Mental Disorders (DSM), 411

dialectical model, **24**

Diana, Princess, 483

diarrheal diseases, 407

Diaz, Dan, 425

Dickens, David R., 430

dictatorship, 277–78

Didi, Ibrahim, 454

education (*continued*)
spending on, 208, 300–301, 330
trends in, 294–95
worth of college degrees, 292, 330
see also schools
edX, 301
ego, **101**
Egypt, 89
Ehrenreich, Barbara, 325, 326
Ehrlich, Ann, 438
Ehrlich, Paul, 438
Eichmann, Adolf, 135
801 Cabaret, 68–69
Eighteenth Amendment, 477
Eisenhower, David, 192
Eisenhower, Dwight D., 276, 311
Eisenstein, Zillah, 254
elder abuse, 369
"electronic aggression," 165
*Elementary Forms of Religious Life,
The* (Durkheim), 21
Ellen, 250
Elliot, Jane, 230
Ellis, Carolyn, 63
embodied identity, **226**
embodied status, **113**
Emergency Economic Stabilization
Act of 2008, 323
emergent norm theory, **468**
emigration, **436**
emojis, 77
emotions
attraction of doing bad deeds, 163
cross-cultural responses to grief,
115
and personality, 114
social construction of, 114
emotion work (emotional labor),
114
by flight attendants, 114
on the job, 116
emphysema, 407
Empire, 470
empirical, **21**
employee theft, 168
Employment Non-Discrimination
Act (ENDA), 259
encoding/decoding model, **389**
endangered species, 452
end-of-life care, 424–25
End of Men, The (Rosin), 263
endogamy, 220, **354**
energy consumption, 451

E! News, 32
Engels, Friedrich, 23, 24, 254
Enlightenment, 291
Enron, 198
Entertainment Software Rating
Board, 384
entertainment spending, 378
Entertainment Tonight, 32
entitlements, 201, 323
environment, **450**–61
demographics and, 462
environmental sociology, 455–61
of Las Vegas, 430–31
pollution, 452, 454–55
resource depletion, 451–52
social ecology, 451
social movements and, 463
as social problem, 451–55
studying, 456–57
water crisis, 453
environmental justice, **459,** 460
environmental movement, **457**–60
Environmental Protection Agency
(EPA), **452,** 458, 460
environmental racism, **459**
environmental sociology, **455**–61
epidemic, **412**–13
epidemiology, **410**–14
ESPN, 379, 484
*Essay on the Principle of Population,
An* (Malthus), 438
essentialists, **245**
ethics
in action research, 51
bioethics, 424
in Nuremberg Code, 62
in research, 61–63
Ethiopia, 453
ethnic cleansing, 234
ethnicity, **216**
defining, 216, 218
intergroup conflict or cooperation,
233–37
and life chances, 228–29,
231–32
situational, 218
symbolic, 218
see also individual ethnic groups
ethnic villagers, 448
ethnocentrism, **74**
ethnography, 31, **44**–47, 59, 65
ethnomethodology, **31**
Etsy, 396

Etzioni, Amitai, 395
Eugene, Oregon, running culture in,
401
eugenics, **424**
Eurocentric, **28**
Europe
conflict theory in, 25
HIV/AIDS in, 413
monarchies in, 278
structural functionalism in, 20
*see also specific regions and
countries*
evangelical, **306**
Evans, Spencer, 152
everyday class consciousness, **192,**
194–95
evolution, 20, 438
existing sources, **53**–55, 65
exogamy, **354**
exotic dancers, 341
experiential learning, 342
experimental group, **55**
experiments, **55,** 65
expressions given, **104**
expressions given off, **104**
expressions of behavior, **104**
expressive leadership, **140**
expressive role, **253,** 254
expressive tasks, **360**
extended family, **351**
extrinsic religiosity, **304**
exurbs, 443
ExxonMobil, 334
Exxon Valdez oil spill, 458

F
Facebook, 57, 96, 117, 127, 130, 131,
188, 384
collectors and hobbyists, 396
group ties on, 126
and Occupy Movement, 474
politics and, 288, 289
pros and cons of posting on,
130–31
relationship data from, 57
and social change, 89
Facetime, 114
face time, in defense of, 347
Fadiman, Anne, 418
fads, **470**
Fair Labor Association, 336
false consciousness, **24,** 206
Family Guy, 394

government, **277**–79
  criminal justice system, 169
  groupthink in, 134
Graham, Billy, 309–11
Graham, Lawrence Otis, 221
Granite Mountain Hotshots
    (Arizona), 138
Granovetter, Mark, 125
Gran Torino, 220–21
grassroots environmentalism, **459**
Gray, Freddie, 469
Gray Album (Danger Mouse), 34
Great Britain, 278, 390–91
Great Depression, 17, 199, 201, 202,
    320, 467
Great Lakes Megalopolis (ChiPitts),
    441
Great Recession of 2008, 199, 289,
    332
  and "mancession," 262–63
  personal *vs.* public issues in, 17
  unemployment rates during,
    320–21
Great Society program, 201
greenhouse effect, **454**
greenhouse gases, **454**
Green Party, **459**
Greenpeace, 458
Green Revolution, 439–40
Greenwich Village, New York,
    176–77
Greenwood family, 235
Grey's Anatomy, 91
grief, cross-cultural responses to, 115
gross domestic product (GDP), 334
Gross National Happiness (Bhutan),
    482–83
grounded theory, **46**
group cohesion, **133**–34
group dynamics, **128**
group(s), **123**
  and anomie, 125
  bureaucracies, 141–45
  conformity experiments, 135,
    137–38
  dyads, 129, 146
  group cohesion, 133–34
  group dynamics, 128
  honor killings, 136
  in- and out-groups, 129, 146
  intergroup conflict or cooperation,
    based on race/ethnicity,
    233–34, 236–37

leadership qualities, 140–41
  primary, 123, 124, 146
  reference, 129–30, 146
  secondary, 123, 124, 146
  social influence in, 134–35, 137–38
  social networks, 124–25
  teamwork, 138–40
  triads, 129, 146
  virtual, 125–26
groupthink, **134**
growth rate, **439**
Gubrium, Jay, 353
Gugghenheim Museum, 386
Guo, Guang, 99

H
Hague, The, 278
Hale, Matt, 81
Hall, Stuart, 225, 389
Halle, David, 387
Hancock, Harvey, 281
hangouts, 396–97
Hannity, Sean, 285
"Happy" (Williams), 391
Hardin, Garrett, 438, 471
Harris-Perry, Melissa, 285
Harvest Cathedral Chapel (Macon,
    Georgia), 310
hate crimes, 231, 263, 267
Hawaii, 352
Hawley, Amos, 455
Hawthorne effect, **61**
Hays, Sharon, 34
hazing, 120, 122
Head Start, 201
health
  in cultural context, 405
  definitions of, 406–7
  and gender, 256–57
  and illness
    definitions of, 406–7
    epidemiology of, 410–14
    medicalization of, 409–10
    medical treatment approaches,
      407
    mental illness, 409–10
    spread of disease, 405
    types of illnesses, 406–7
  inequalities in
    food deserts, 415
    intersections of class, race, and
      gender, 414
  issues in, 422–25

and race/ethnicity, 228–29
  smallpox, 411, 464, 466
  and socioeconomic status, 195
  sociology of, 405–6
health care (medicine)
  approaches to, 407
  cultural competence in, 418–19
  and extended life spans, 414, 437
  issues in, 422–25
  medicalization of illness, 409–10
  as social institution, 416–20
  on television, 420–22
  treatment approaches, 407
Hearst, William Randolph, 150
Heat Wave (Klinenberg), 272, 273
Heavy Metal in Baghdad, 72
heavy metal music, 71–72, 388
Heckman, James, 330
hegemony, **82**
"helicopter parents," 385
Hell's Kitchen, 8
helping professions, 478
Hemlock Society, 424
hemp, 150
herd immunity, 406
heritage tourism, 217
Herrnstein, Richard, 98
heterogamy, **192**
heteronormativity, **247,** 249
heterosexism, **252**
heterosexuality, **246,** 253
hidden curriculum, **108, 292**–93
high culture, **386**–87
hijras, 244–45
Hill, Judith, 377
Hilton, Paris, 189
Hinduism, 183
hip-hop, 34, 386, 387
Hirosue, Ryoko, 182
Hispanic/Latino Americans
  birth rates for, 228
  and criminal justice, 231
  and "culture of poverty" theory,
    203
  education level of, 229
  family status of, 228
  health inequalities for, 414
  health insurance for, 228–29
  high school graduation rate for,
    292
  Internet use by, 205
  and interracial dating/marriage,
    228

meanings (*continued*)
    shared, 390–91
    in symbolic interactionism, 30
means of production, **23**
measles, 411
measles epidemic, 405–6
mechanical solidarity, **21**
media
    as agent of socialization, 108–9,
        118
    and commercialization of leisure,
        377–78
    concentration of power in, 382–84
    conglomeration of, 379–80
    and cultural imperialism, 90–91
    cultural wars in, 386
    and decline in public life, 376–77
    and democracy, 379
    diffusion of content from Western
        culture, 88, 90
    as Fourth Estate, 283–84
    gender role socialization by,
        249–51
    global diffusion of, 482–84
    in the Information Age, 86
    moral and political values
        exported by, 90–91
    new voices in, 383
    and political process, 285
    "pornification" of, 164
    regulation of content, 384, 386
    self-regulation and censorship in,
        384
    and spectatorship, 378–79
    see also mass media and popular
        culture; television
media industries, structure of,
    379–80, 382–84
Medicaid, 201, 323
Medical College Admissions Test
    (MCAT), 419
medicalization, **409**
medical marijuana, 150
medical technology, 424
Medicare, 323, 423
medicine. *see* healthcare (medicine)
Meetup app, 397
Meetup.com, 377
megacities, 441
megalopolis, **441**
Meier, Megan, 163, 165
Meier, Tina, 165
men

domestic abuse and, 365–66
    heart problems in, 256
    life expectancy, 256
men's liberation, **266**
men's movements, 266
men's rights movement, **266**
mental illness, 409–10, 417
merger, **380**
meritocracy, **207**
Merrill Lynch, 332
Merton, Robert, 22, 34, 129, 154, 158,
    167, 169
Messerschmidt, James, 169
Messi, Lionel, 390
metropolis, **441**
Metropolitan Statistical Area (MSA),
    441
Mexican Americans, 218
Mexico, 441
Meyerowitz, Josh, 106, 116
microaggression, **253**
microsociological theory, 27–31
microsociology, **14**–16
    of education, 302
    of politics, 290
    of religion, 311
Microsoft, 188, 320, 326, 328, 338,
    343
MidAmerica Bank, 204
middle class, **186,** 197, 221, 318
Middle East, 305, 440
"Middletown" studies, 61, 63
midrange theory, **34,** 36
migration, **436**
Milgram, Stanley, 135, 137, 138
Milgram experiment, 135, 137
military, 111
    Don't Ask Don't Tell in, 261
    resocialization in, 111
    sexual assault in, 261–62
    women in, 261
militia movement, 83
Millennial generation, 208, 227, 304
Miller, Alice, 54
Miller, Jody, 4–5
Miller, Laura, 261, 262
Million Dollar Listing, 8
Million Pound March, 160
Mills, C. Wright, 13, 17, 281, 467
Milošević, Slobodan, 234
Minaj, Nicki, 386
mind, self, and society (theory),
    102–3

Miner, Horace, 73, 74
Ming Dynasty, 278
minimal effects theories, 389
minimum wage, 347
minimum wage workers, 202
minority group(s), 219–**20**
    food deserts for, 415
    majority-minority generation, 235
    see also ethnicity; race
miscegenation, **226**
Mitchell, Jennifer, 358
Mitchell, Richard, 46
Miyazaki, Hayao, 88
mobile media, astronomical growth
    in, 384
modern environmental movement,
    457
Modern Family, 54, 110, 484
modernism, **33**
modernity, **485**
Modi, Kalpen, 14, 15
Moldova, 89
monarchy, **278**
monogamy, **355**
monopoly, **382**
monotheistic, **303**
monotheistic religions, 303
Montgomery bus boycott, 171
Moon, Sun Myung, 111
"Moonies," 111
Moore, Mignon, 362
Moore, Wilbert, 189
Moore's Law, 319–20
moral holiday, **80**
moral reasoning, 97
mores, **79**
Morgan Stanley, 332
Mormons, 236
mortality rate, **435**
Moseley, Winston, 448
motherhood
    cultural definitions of, 352
    single mothers, 45, 46
Mothers of East Los Angeles, 204
Mother Teresa, 187
Motion Picture Association of
    America (MPAA), 384
Motor-Voter Act of 2000, 280
Mott, Lucretia, 265
movies
    cities of tomorrow in, 446
    ratings system, 384
    see also media; *specific movies*

Mozart, Wolfgang Amadeus, 387
Mt. McKinley, garbage left on, 450
MTV, 85, 482, 483, 484
MTV Video Music Awards, 85
Muir, John, 457
Mulberry Street, New York, 216
Mullinder, Louise Brown, 368
multiculturalism, **82,** 236, 237
multiplayer online role-playing
  games (MMOR-PGs),
  338–39
multiracial individuals, 212, 214
Munn, Olivia, 212, 424
Murderball, 162
Murguia, Janet, 232
Murphy, Daniel, 113, 114
Murphy, Tori, 113, 114
Murray, Charles, 98
Museum of Contemporary Art
  (MOCA), 289
music
  content warnings for, 384
  of dominant culture, 82–83
  heavy metal, 71–72
  hip-hop, 34
  popular and high cultures in, 386
musicians, professional, 377
Muslim holidays, 309
Muslims, 305
My Lai, South Vietnam, 171

N
"Nacerima," 74
Nader, Ralph, 459
NAFTA. *see* North American Free
  Trade Agreement (NAFTA)
Namgay family, 180, 181
Nashville, 470
National Association for the
  Advancement of Colored
  People (NAACP), 29, 30, 280
National Association of Colleges and
  Employers, 342
National Association of the Deaf
  (NAD), 160
National Association to Advance Fat
  Acceptance (NAAFA), 160
National Basketball Association
  (NBA), 32, 378–79
National Commission on Excellence
  in Education, 296
National Education Association, 283
National Football League, 283

National Law Center on
  Homelessness and Poverty,
  205
National Marriage Project, 50, 52
National Organization for Women
  (NOW), 265
National Park Service, 457
National Rifle Association (NRA),
  283
National School Climate Survey, 257
National Survey of Sexual Health and
  Behavior, 246
Nation at Risk, A, 296
Native Americans, 224, 233
  assimilation of, 236
  banishment as punishment for,
  151
  berdaches, 244, 245
  genocide, 234
  as minority group, 219
  population transfer, 234, 236
  pre-colonial societies of, 317
  school dropout rate for, 299
  voting rights of, 279
Natoma family, 180, 181
natural increase, **439**
natural selection, 438
nature *vs.* nurture debate, 97–98
Nazi war criminals, 62
NBC, 379
NBC Universal, 342
NCIS, 484
negative questions, 50, **51**
negative sanctions, 80
neglect, **369**
Nelson, Gaylord, 458
neofunctionalism (new
  functionalism), 22
neo-Malthusians, **438**
neo-Marxism, 25
Netflix, 383
net migration, 436
net neutrality, 382, 383
New Deal, 201, 202
Newdow, Michael, 276
new ecological paradigm, **455**
New England Patriots, 394
new media, 383–84
News Corporation, 382
Newsweek magazine, 55
New York City
  Genovese murder in, 448–49, 450
  homelessness in, 205–6

Lower East Side, 216
Occupy Movement in, 474–75
population of, 440
population trends in, 441
protests in, 289
September 11 in, 449–50
New York Public Library, 16
Nibali, Vincenzo, 139
niche interests, globalization of, 75
Nickel and Dimed (Ehrenreich),
  325–26
Niger, 435
*Nightly Show with Larry Wilmore,
  The,* 286, 287
Nike, 333, 336, 337, 395, 401
NIMBY, **459**
Nineteenth Amendment, 473
Nissan Motors, 59
Nixon, Julie, 192
Nixon, Richard M., 281, 285, 422
No Child Left Behind (NCLB), 296
nongender, 245
nonmaterial culture, 77
nonprofit organizations, 344
nonrenewable resources, **451**
Nordstrom, 116
norm(s), **79**–80, 92, 468
  breaching, on television, 93,
  165–66
  and deviance, 151
  group *vs.* individual, 138–40
North American Free Trade
  Agreement (NAFTA), 333,
  334
North Korea, 278
Norwegian Correctional Service, 170
NOW PAC, 282
nuclear family, **351,** 364, 437
Nuremberg Code, 62
nurture, nature *vs.,* 97–98

O
Obama, Barack, 148, 150, 222, 232,
  235, 261, 267, 272, 279, 280,
  283, 289, 296, 299, 300, 309
Obama, Michelle Robinson, 14, 15,
  280
ObamaCare, 422–23
Obergefell v. Hodges, 267
obesity, 409
  food deserts and, 415
  income and, 211
objectivity, **60**

race (*continued*)
and social stratification in Brazil, 188–89
theoretical approaches to, 223–27, 238
race consciousness, **222**
race relations
biases in research on, 59
since Obama's election, 222
Race to the Top, 296
racial assimilation, **236**
"racial democracy," 188
Racial Fault Lines (Almaguer), 224
Racial Formation in the United States (Omi and Winant), 225
racial identity, 226–27, 232–33
racism, **220**
entertainment and, 239
environmental, 459
forms of, 220–23
and objectivity in research, 60
Radway, Janice, 394
rain forest depletion, 451–52
Ramsey, Gordon, 8
rap, 386, 387
rape, 263
rape culture, **248**
rapport, **45**
Raseboya, Violet, 242
rationalization, **26, 142**
reactivity, **61**
Reagan, Ronald, 14, 140, 281, 285
real culture, **85**
Real Dirt on Farmer John, The (documentary), 442
real estate foreclosures, in Las Vegas, 430
"reality television," 8
Real World, The (MTV), 8
rebels, **154**
Recording Industry Association of America, 384
recreation, **375**
red, meaning in different cultures, 93
Reddit, 474
"redlining," 204
Reefer Madness, 148
reference group, **129–30,** 146
reflexivity, **46**
region (social setting), **105**
regressive, **479**
regressive movements, 479, 480
rehabilitation, **169**

reinforcement theory, **389**
relationships
breakups, 357–59
direct-to-consumer drug marketing, 416
doctor-patient, 418–20
dog training by prisoners, 112
effect of group size on, 129
family living arrangements, 364–65
fan-celebrity relations, 392–93
forming, 356
with God, 310–11
institutional values and college life, 84
interracial romance, dating, and marriage, 226–27
leisure and, 394–95
masculinity and disability in murderball, 162
and Occupy Movement, 474–75
in primary and secondary groups, 123–24
rape culture and campus social life, 248
SES and mate selection, 192–93
social networking sites, 57, 130–31
sports role models, 394–95
talking by men *vs.* women in, 15–16
trends in, 356–57
urban encounters with strangers, 447
value of break time, 327
relative deprivation, **199**
relative deprivation theory, **473**
reliability, **52**
religion(s), **302**–11
fundamentalism, 304, 306–7
Marx on, 24
micro- and macrosociology of, 311
and religiosity, 307–8, 310
and secular society, 308–9
as source of solidarity, 21
theoretical approaches to, 302–4
unchurched spirituality, 307
in the United States, 304
and the White House, 310
religiosity, **304,** 307–8, 310
Religious Freedom Restoration Act, 333
religious services, seeing culture in, 81–82

religious violence, 305
remarriage, 358
renewable resources, **451,** 453
replicability, 46, **47**
representativeness, 46, **47**
representative sample, **52**
rescission, **423**
research, 41–65
action, 50–51
choosing methods for, 43–44
covert, 46
ethics of, 61–63
ethnographic, 44–47, 65
experimental, 55–57, 65
interviews, 48–49, 65
issues with, 57–63
nonacademic uses of, 58
objectivity in, 60–61
overt, 46
overview of methods, 41–43
qualitative, 41
quantitative, 41
reactivity in, 61
scientific method, 41–43
surveys, 49–52, 65
using existing sources, 53–55, 65
values in, 58–60
residential segregation, **204**
resistance strategies, **328,** 329, 331–32
resocialization, **111,** 112
resource mobilization theory, **474**
resources
as commons, 471
depletion of, 451–52
mobilizing, 473–74
respiratory infections, 407
respondents, **48**
response rate, **52**
retirement, 363, 430, 437
retreatists, **154**
retribution, **169**
Retrospect of Western Travel (Martineau), 20
Rhetoric (Aristotle), 134
Rice, Ray, 366
"right-to-work" laws, 331
Rios, Victor, 4–5, 169
riot, **469**
ritualists (in structural strain theory), **154**
ritual(s), **302**
Ritzer, George, 27, 37, 142

spurious correlation, **42**

Stack, Carol, 353

Stanford Prison Experiment, 137–38

Stanton, Elizabeth Cady, 265

Star Trek, 235, 390, 393, 395

Star Wars, 380, 381

status, **111**

status inconsistency, **187**

Steele, Claude, 158

Stein, Jill, 161

Steiner, Ivan, 138

stepfamilies, 357

Stephanopoulos, George, 83

stepparents, 357

stereotype promise, **159**

stereotypes, 267

stereotype threat, **158**–59

stereotyping, **113**

    based on status, 193

    gender, 247

    in the media, 249–50

    of racial/ethnic groups, 227

    sexual, 249–50, 254

Sterling, Donals, 32

Stewart, Jon, 286, 287

stigma

    and depression, 256

    and deviance, **159**

    for female athletes, 242

Stone, Oliver, 449

Stonewall riots (New York City), 266

Stowe, Harriet Beecher, 227

Straight Edge, 479

stratification

    around the world, 188–89

    by caste, 183–84

    by sexual orientation, 267

    by slavery, 182–83

    by social class, 184

    and social mobility, 198–99

    of workforce, 320–21

Streetwise (Anderson), 158

"Strength of Weak Ties, The"
        (Granovetter), 125

strikes, 331, 332

structural functionalism, **20**–23, 35,
      36

    addiction in, 410

    advantages and critiques of, 22–23

    approach to culture and religion,
        90

    conflict theory *vs.,* 23

    deviance in, 154–55, 158, 172

    in education study, 295–96

    family in, 352–53, 354, 370

    founder and key contributions of,
        20–21

    gender inequality in, 253–54, 255,
        268

    groups in, 144

    medicine and health in, 426

    natural environment in, 443, 462

    offshoots of, 22

    original principles in, 21–22

    race and ethnicity in, 223–24, 238

    recreation and leisure in, 392, 400

    religion in, 302

    social change in, 472, 488

    social class in, 189–91, 210

    social inequality in, 194

    social institutions in, 279, 312

    structural strain theory, 154–55

    work and the economy in, 340, 346

structural mobility, 198, **199**

structural strain theory, 154–55, 158,
    172

structure(s), **22**

student health issues, 407–9

student loan debt, 208, 300–301, 330

Study of Sociology, The (Spencer), 20

subculture(s), **83**

    as deviant groups, 160

    heavy metal, 71, 72

    of Key West, 68

suburbanization, 431, **443,** 444

suburban sprawl, 443

Sudnow, David, 191

suffrage movement, **265,** 473

suicide

    Durkheim's view of, 21

    in Las Vegas, 404

    LGBTQ youth and, 257

    medically-assisted, 424, 425

    and undermining of social
        institutions, 352

Suicide (Durkheim), 21, 352

Sullivan, Andrew, 285

Summers, Larry, 98

Sumner, William Graham, 59

superego, **101**

Supermom, 362

Super PACs, 283

Supplemental Nutrition Assistance
        Program (SNAP), 323

Suri lip modifications, 152–53

surrogate baby boom, 340

surveys, 48, **49**–52, 65

survivalist groups, 46

"survival of the fittest," 20

sustainable development, **460**–61

Sutherland, Edwin, 156, 168

Swaziland, 199

sweatshops, **334,** 336, 338–39

Sweden, 189, 278, 323

Swift, Taylor, 12

symbolic culture, **77**–79

symbolic ethnicity, **218**

symbolic interactionism, **27**–31, 35,
      36

    addiction in, 410

    advantages and critiques of, 31

    approach to culture and religion
        in, 90

    deviance in, 156–59, 158

    differential association theory,
        158–59

    education study, 293–94

    family in, 353, 354, 370

    founder and key contributions in,
        27–30

    gender inequality and, 254–55

    groups in, 144

    labeling theory, 156–57

    medicine and health in, 426

    natural environment in, 443, 462

    offshoots of, 30–31

    original principles of, 30

    race and ethnicity in, 224, 238

    recreation and leisure in, 392, 400

    religion in, 303–4

    social change in, 472, 488

    social class in, 191–93, 210

    social inequality in, 194

    social institutions in, 279, 312

    society in, 37

    work and the economy in, 340, 346

synergy, **380**

synthesis, **24**

Syria, 89, 305, 436, 439

T

T. J. Maxx, 202

taboo(s), **80**

Taft-Hartley Act of 1947, 331

Taibbi, Matt, 285

Takei, George, 333

Taliban, 278, 474–74

talking, gender difference in, 12

Tambor, Jeffrey, 250

target population, **48**
Tarzan of the Apes, 100
taste cultures, **387**
taste publics, **387**
Taylor, Charles, 278
Taylor, Verta, 68, 69, 163
teachers
    and gender role socialization,
        247–49
    role of, 108
teamwork, 138–40
Tea Party, 85
technological change, 89
    and alienation in knowledge or
        information work, 326
    and leisure activities, 276–77
    postindustrial knowledge work,
        326, 328
    social problem created by, 480
    for sustainability, 460–61
technological determinism, **480**
technology, 86, **88**
    digital age, 319, 484
    digital divide, 205
    Digital Revolution, 126, 319
    in the global village, 481–84
    and Information Revolution,
        319–21
    Internet of Things, 485
    and leisure, 377
    medical, 424
    and social change, 480
    wearable, 486
    see also specific technologies
Teen Mom, 165
telecommuting, **326**
television
    as agent of socialization, 109–10
    breaching age norms on, 93
    culture wars on, 83
    gays and lesbians represented on,
        250
    global diffusion of, 483–84
    in Information Age, 86
    leisure trends and, 376
    LGBTQ persons on, 250
    medicine on, 420–22
    norm breaking on, 165–66
    political debates on, 285
    portrayal of working life on,
        321–22
    ratings system for, 384
    real and fake news on, 286–88

reality shows on, 8
    soap operas on, 386
    "unplug" experiment, 480–81
    violence on, 42
    see also media; *specific shows*
Temporary Assistance for Needy
        Families (TANF), 197, 201,
        323
temporary workers, 343
Terror in the Mind of God
        (Juergensmeyer), 305
tertiary deviance, 158
testosterone, 97
Texas
    antisodomy laws in, 155
    cities in, 441
    as "majority-minority" state, 235
    population trends in, 436
    racial groups in, 219
Texas Christian University, 84
textual poaching, **390**–91, 393
Thailand, 178, 180, 181, 258, 278
theory(-ies), **18**
    Eurocentric, 28
    macrosociological, 20–23
    microsociological, 27–31
    new approaches, 33–35
    see also specific theories and topics
Theron, Charlize, 357
thesis, **24**
thick description, **45,** 47
Thiel, Peter, 330
third-gender individuals, 244–45
third place, **396**–97
Third Sector, **344**–45
third wave (women's movement), 265
*This Week with George
        Stephanopoulos,* 83
Thomas, W. I., **103,** 158
Thomas theorem, **103**
Thompson, Hugh, 171
Thoreau, Henry David, 457
Thoroddsen family, 180, 181
Three Mile Island nuclear accident,
        458
Tibbals, Chauntelle, 164
Tibet, 355
Timberlake, Justin, 392
Time Warner, 380, 382, 383
TMZ, 31, 32, 392
Tonga, 436
Torres, Lisa, 125
total institutions, **111**

totalitarianism, 278
Tour de France, 139, 483
tourism, 398–99
toxic waste, 458
Toyota, 143
tracking, **292**
traditional authority, **140**
tragedy of the commons, **471**
Trail of Tears, 234
traits, deviant, 151
transgender, **244**–45, 254, 255
transgender individuals, 263, 267
transnational corporations (TNCs),
        334
Transparent, 250
transphobia, **252,** 267
transportation, spending on, 201
transsexuals, 250
travel and tourism, 398–99
treadmill of production, **455**
TrekDating.com, 193
triad, **129,** 146
trigender, 245
"trolls," 165
Truth, Sojourner, 473
tuberculosis, 407, 411
Tudors of England, 278
Tunisia, 89
Turkle, Sherry, 116, 117, 126
Turner, Ralph, 113, 131, 133, 138, 160
Tuskegee Syphilis Study, 62
20 Feet from Stardom, 377
Twenty Statements Test (TST),
        130–33
Twine, France Winddance, 231, 232,
        340
Twitter, 57, 89, 96, 117, 127, 130, 288,
        383, 474, 475
Two and a Half Men, 54
Two Broke Girls, 54
two-step flow model, **389**
typhus, 411
Typographical Union, 331

U
Uber, 87
Udacity, 301
Uganda, 413
Unbearable Weight (Bordo), 17
unchurched, **306**
unchurched spirituality, **307**
Uncle Tom's Cabin (Stowe), 227
unconscious, 100